THE LE
ENVIRONM
OF BUSIN

FOURTH EDI

THE LEGAL ENVIRONMENT OF BUSINESS

FOURTH EDITION

ROGER E. MEINERS, Ph.D., J.D.
Clemson University

AL H. RINGLEB, Ph.D., J.D.
Clemson University

FRANCES L. EDWARDS, J.D.
Clemson University

West Publishing Company
St. Paul   New York   Los Angeles   San Francisco

Artwork Alice Thiede
Composition Carlisle Communications, Ltd.
Copyeditor Rosalie Maggio

Library of Congress Cataloging-in-Publication Data

Meiners, Roger E.
    The legal environment of business / Roger E. Meiners, Al H.
  Ringleb, Frances Edwards. — 4th ed.
      p. cm.
    Includes index.
    ISBN 0–314–79787–4
    1. Industrial laws and legislation—United States. 2. Commercial
  law—United States. I. Ringleb, Al H. II. Edwards, Frances L.
  III. Title.
  KF1600.M43   1990
  346.73′065 — dc20
  [347.30665]
                                90–47936
                                  CIP

To the next generation: Callie O'Keefe, Jayme Keegan, William Evert, and Alix Joseph.

Contents in Brief

Contents

Table of Cases

Principal cases are in bold type. Nonprincipal cases are in roman type. References are to pages.

Preface

The classroom course on the legal environment of business has continued to change, develop, and mature. Originally intended to provide business students with an overview of regulatory law, the course now also encompasses important elements of business ethics, business legal strategy, international legal environment, and corporate social responsibility. Following the insightful suggestions of our reviewers and adopters, this textbook presents these important topics to the student in several unique ways. In addition, several chapters have been significantly expanded and updated in response to important changes in the legal environment since the last edition of *The Legal Environment of Business*.

NEW CHAPTERS AND EXPANDED COVERAGE

Since the publication of the third edition, the activities of Congress, the Supreme Court, regulatory agencies, and state governing bodies have had a significant impact on the legal environment of business. Virtually all subject areas making up the legal environment of business have been affected. In many areas changes in the text could be made by updating the material and adding new cases. However, in several important areas the changes and modifications to the legal environment required that chapters be significantly revised and expanded.

Chapter 6: Business Ethics and Corporate Social Responsibility

In recognition of the growing importance of ethics to the business community, the authors sought the expertise of a recognized business ethicist, Dr. Charles E. Harris of Texas A&M University. Dr. Harris not only helped us provide a comprehensive overview of business ethics for Chapter 6, but he also suggested several conceptual tools to use in evaluating the kinds of ethical problems often confronting today's managers and business professionals.

Chapters 12 and 13: Antitrust Law

The antitrust environment has changed dramatically over the past decade. Several important recent Supreme Court cases have clarified legal issues that had created some uncertainty in the legal environment. These chapters were also reorganized and the material presented in a sequence that is easier for students to follow.

Chapters 14 and 15: Labor and Employment Law

Chapters 14 and 15 were substantially revised and expanded to include new and important information on the growing use of employee manuals and on employer responses to drug abuse concerns in the workplace. The chapters were also revised to include the Supreme Court's recent affirmative action decisions and the important Americans with Disabilities Act of 1990.

Chapter 17: Environmental Law

Chapter 17 has been amended to include important 1990 amendments to the Clean Air Act. The passage of the new standards is a clear manifestation of the growing importance of environmental law to the business community and the legal environment.

Chapter 21: International Legal Environment

The world economy has seen dramatic changes recently that could not have been anticipated just a few years ago. The opening of Eastern Europe and the Soviet Union has brought enormous economic opportunities to the western business community along with sudden changes in the international legal environment. Chapter 21 has been expanded to include a discussion of these important changes in the international legal environment.

In addition, several adopters suggested that the order of the chapters be changed. Because they felt the material on contracts provided a more natural lead-in to the agency and business organizations chapters, the chapter on contracts was moved to just before the chapters on agency and business organizations. The adopters also requested that the chapter on environmental law be placed before the chapters on federal consumer protection as a way of emphasizing its increased importance to the business community and the legal environment of business.

NEW AND UPDATED TABLES AND EXHIBITS

The majority of our adopters indicated that the increased use of tables and exhibits in the third edition greatly enhanced the readability of the text. The tables and exhibits also improved students' perceptions of the relevance and applicability of the laws and regulations being discussed. In addition to updating the material in those tables and exhibits, several new tables and exhibits were added to this edition to further enhance student comprehension. For example, tabular summaries of important and leading research on business ethics were added to Chapter 6. Surveys by leading research organizations were added to Chapter 21 to provide students with a comprehensive overview of the likely future direction of the rapidly expanding international legal environment. As in previous editions of the textbook, emphasis has been placed on providing students with important information and statistics clearly demonstrating how the laws and regulations discussed are impacting managers and the business community.

NEW ISSUES ARTICLES

A feature that has been used uniquely by this text since the first edition are the Issue articles. In this edition, nearly all the readings are new. To improve the applicability and timeliness of the articles, most of the new articles were chosen from such leading business publications as the *Wall Street Journal*, *Forbes*, *Fortune*, and *Business Week*. Some of the topics discussed include indoor air pollution, price fixing in Japan, the ethics of the Arab boycott, and the rights of workers to privacy in the workplace. Each Issue article is accompanied by several Issue questions to facilitate and enhance class discussions.

INTERNATIONAL PERSPECTIVES

Over the past decade, the differences between international and domestic business practices have diminished significantly. In fact, there are relatively few truly domestic industries remaining in the United States. To compete more effectively, virtually all companies are undertaking extensive efforts to globalize their operations. Managers must now be much more cognizant of the laws and legal cultures of those countries with which they do business to be successful in the long term.

In recognition of these important changes, each chapter now contains a section entitled International Perspectives. These sections provide insights into the legal traditions, customs, and institutions of several important countries. Particular attention is given to those aspects of the international legal environment that differ from U.S. laws and regulations. The topics discussed include joint venture agreements in the Soviet Union, the French court system, administrative law in Japan, pollution control in Europe, and the problems faced by American franchises operating in Europe.

SUPPLEMENTAL MATERIAL

Teaching the legal environment of business requires an in-depth presentation of legal, social, and ethical materials on a variety of subjects. The time required both to teach and to learn these important subjects can be extensive and taxing. To ease these time pressures, several supplements have been developed to assist both the student and the instructor.

An Accompanying Study Guide

Professor June A. Horrigan of California State University-Sacramento has been responsible for the Student Study Guide to accompany *The Legal Environment of Business* since the second edition. With the help of Lynda S. Hamilton of Georgia Southern University, the Guide to accompany the fourth edition has been revised to include the considerable new material introduced in the fourth edition. Our adopters have found the Guide to be an effective learning device when used in the classroom or by students studying the material individually or in groups.

An Expanded Instructor's Manual and Testbank

The Instructor's Manual to accompany the fourth edition has been expanded. The Manual contains answers to each chapter's case questions, Issues questions, and Review and Discussion Questions. The answers have been expanded to provide instructors with additional information to better facilitate classroom discussions.

The testbank has been greatly revised and expanded to include more than 2,000 multiple choice and true and false questions, each referenced to the main text page. The multiple choice library has been expanded to include fact-situation questions to test the students' analytical as well as recall abilities.

The testbank is available to adopters in computerized form. Called WestTest, the software allows instructors to create new tests, modify existing tests, change and add questions to the testbank, and print the tests in a variety of formats. The WestTest software developed for *The Legal Environment of Business* is available for use on both IBM-PCs or compatibles and Apple systems.

Student Software

West Publishing Company has developed a unique software for students using *The Legal Environment of Business*. Called Legal Clerk—A Software Package for Research and Learning, the software allows students to retrieve specific cases found in the textbook for the purpose of studying the case more extensively. Legal Clerk is a user-friendly, interactive software package that strengthens the student's understanding of the legal environment while simultaneously introducing the student to computer-assisted legal research. Clerk cases are identified in the textbook by the presence of the following logo:

Transparency Masters

To assist the instructor in presenting various tabular and graphic material in the textbook, the supplemental materials include a set of transparency masters.

ACKNOWLEDGMENTS

The authors would like to thank the faculty from around the country who reviewed the manuscript while it was being prepared. Much of the credit for making the text more teachable belongs to them. These generous individuals include: Arnold Celnicker, Ohio State University; John Houlihan, University of

Southern Maine; Jack E. Karns, East Carolina University; Nancy Kratzke, Memphis State University; John M. Norwood, University of Arkansas; Michael Pustay, Texas A&M University; Burke T. Ward, Villanova University; and Mark Wilkening, Blinn College.

The authors extend a special thanks to Dr. Charles E. Harris of Texas A&M University, for his contribution to Chapter 6, "Business Ethics and Corporate Social Responsibility," and for his suggestions on ethics material presented in the book.

The authors, too, extend thanks to the professionals in business, law, and government who assisted us in making this textbook as up to date and accurate as possible. In particular, Mr. Franco Gori provided a number of suggestions on the international legal environment, and the expertise of Ms. Nicole House helped improve the consumer law and credit protection chapters.

Finally, we thank the editors and staff of West Publishing Company. In particular, we thank the sales representatives who continually give us valuable information on the day-to-day perceptions of the textbook—information provided by the instructors and students who are using it. We thank Mr. Thomas Hilt whose patience and determination got us through the production process on schedule. Most important, we offer a very special thanks to our Developmental Editor, Ms. Esther Craig, who always makes even the darkest days seem much brighter.

We welcome and encourage comments from the users of this textbook—both students and instructors. By incorporating those comments and suggestions we can make this text an even better one in the future.

Roger E. Meiners
Al H. Ringleb
Frances L. Edwards

Part One   Law and the Judicial Process

The legal environment of business has expanded enormously over the past two decades. Congress enacted major legislation allowing for the government regulation of the environment, consumer credit, product safety, worker safety, consumer protection, energy, and employment. More than twenty new administrative agencies were created to implement and enforce those laws, substantially increasing the size of government and government's role in the legal environment of business. An acute awareness of the legal environment and its requirements has become critical to the business firm.

The legal environment, however, has become more than just a set of laws with which a business must comply. The past two decades have also witnessed the use of the legal environment as an integral element in the strategic management process of most businesses. Strategic management is concerned with making decisions about a business's future direction and implementing those decisions. Continental Airlines, for example, made strategic use of the legal environment to break costly union contracts. Other companies and individuals have made strategic use of the legal environment to dump expensive supply contracts, avoid hostile takeovers, limit the company's liabilities arising from the use and production of hazardous substances, avoid taxes, avoid liability for managerial decisions that severely impacted workers or consumers, and protect future earnings. The use of the legal environment in this fashion has generated serious ethical and public policy debates.

The subject matter of this book is both timely and timeless. It is timely because the legal environment of business is always in a state of flux. Legal and regulatory issues are frequently debated in the business community, among academics, and in the political arena. Changes in the law directly determine boundaries on our market system and our personal lives. The subject matter is timeless because many elements of our legal system have been in existence in one form or another for several centuries. Because many aspects of the law will remain stable for decades, the coverage in this and other books will hold for many years. On the other hand, several new and important issues undoubtedly will come up in the legal environment of business that will deeply affect us all as we enter the 1990s.

Part I of this book provides an overview of the essential elements of the law and the legal system. Chapter 1 gives an overview of the functions, sources, and classifications of law and defines the legal environment of business, the differences in legal environments among businesses, and the important legal environments within a business.

Chapter 2 explains the American court system's structure, role, and relationship to the legal environment of business. Chapter 3 considers the growing importance of business litigation and examines the litigatory process as a method for resolving business disputes. It also discusses the important and growing role played by alternative dispute resolution processes— arbitration and negotiation—in resolving business disputes.

Chapter 4 reviews the U.S. Constitution with a focus on the constitutional issues most affecting business. Chapter 5 discusses the interrelationship between business and the administrative agencies of the federal government. The chapter concentrates on the role government agencies play in the regulation of business behavior. Chapter 6 ends Part I of the book with a discussion of business political activity, business ethics, and social responsibility and how they affect the legal environment of business.

Subsequent sections of the book study the more substantive areas of law that make up the legal environment of business. Part II discusses those important areas of the common law affecting the legal environment, including contract law, torts, products liability, the law of agency, and business organizations.

Part III considers the public law most affecting the legal environment of business. It begins with a discussion of the notion of market failure, the principal justification proffered for the enactment and enforcement of the laws presented in Part III. The major areas of the public law discussed include antitrust, labor relations law, securities regulation, consumer protection, and environmental law.

The final part, Part IV, discusses the international legal environment of business. As our international trade deficit grew to more than $130 billion in 1990, trade reform continued to be an important regulatory issue. The possibility looms that significant government energy will be directed toward enhancing our international competitiveness with the goal of reducing the deficit. In that very few businesses are truly domestic anymore, changes in the international legal environment of business can now have profound impacts on the domestic legal environment. The legal environment has clearly grown well beyond the bounds of this country and its laws.

1 Introduction to the Legal Environment of Business

THIS study of the legal environment of business begins with an overview of the general nature of law and the legal system. Made up of law from several different sources, the legal environment of business has been strongly influenced by the needs and demands of the business community, consumers, and government. It is not surprising, then, that the laws that make up the legal environment reflect many different perspectives, viewpoints, and legal philosophies. This chapter provides a general understanding of the fundamental objectives of law, the creation of law, the functions of law in an orderly society, the classifications of law, and the important major sources of law. It then defines the legal environment of business.

The chapter goes on to illustrate that the legal environment is not identical for every business. The legal environment of any particular business may differ depending upon the industry in which it operates; its size, location, and business organization; and the markets it serves or relies upon for inputs. Furthermore, the important elements of the legal environment of business may differ from department to department within the same business. The marketing department, for example, will emphasize those aspects of the legal environment that are important and necessary in fulfilling its responsibilities. In contrast, other departments may have entirely different legal needs, obligations, and responsibilities.

The chapter closes with the Issue Article. The Issue Articles throughout the text are intended to provide the student with important insights into the materials discussed in the chapter. Written by leading legal and business scholars, these articles reflect important policy, political, social, or legal points of view. The Issue Article in this chapter is excerpted from an article written by the legal scholar Professor Jerry Frug. It philosophically discusses the topic of whether judges should be influenced by political and social factors in reaching their decisions.

INTRODUCTION TO LAW

In the study of the legal environment of business, *law* refers to a general code of conduct that defines the behavioral boundaries for all business activity. A more precise definition of law, however, is somewhat elusive. For a variety of reasons, law is necessarily an abstract term. Consider, for example, the following definitions offered by leading legal authorities. *Black's Law Dictionary*, regarded by attorneys as the most authoritative general legal dictionary in the profession, defines law as follows:

1. Law, in its generic sense, is a body of rules of action or conduct prescribed by controlling authority, and having binding legal force.
2. That which must be obeyed and followed by [members of a society] subject to sanctions or legal consequences is a law.

Writing just before the turn of the century, the legal scholar Justice Oliver Wendell Holmes offered the following famous definition of law:

Law is a statement of the circumstances, in which the public force is brought to bear . . . through the courts.

In his famous book, *Growth of Law*, the jurist Benjamin Nathan Cardozo defined law as follows:

A principle or rule of conduct so established as to justify a prediction with reasonable certainty that it will be enforced by the courts if its authority is challenged.

Writing from an entirely different perspective, the anthropologist Bronislaw Kasper Malinowski, in his classic study of primitive law, defined law in this way:

[T]he specific result of the configuration of obligations, which makes it impossible for [any society member] to shirk his responsibility without suffering for it in the future.

From these definitions it is evident that law may be viewed as a collection of rules or principles intended to prescribe and control human behavior. Through their enforcement, those rules or principles are intended to provide a measure of predictability and uniformity to the boundaries of acceptable conduct within a society. It is also evident that this collection of rules or principles will necessarily encompass and reflect both the *formal rules* of the society as established by the governing authority and the *informal* or *implicit rules* of a society as dictated by the society's history, values, customs, traditions, commercial aspirations, and ethics.

IMPORTANT FUNCTIONS OF LAW
AND THE LEGAL SYSTEM

Law and the legal system serve several important functions in an orderly society. Several of the most important functions are considered in this section, including influencing the behavior of the members of a society, resolving the society's disputes, maintaining the important values of the society, and providing a conduit for social changes deemed important.

Assuring Social Control by Influencing Behavior

It is important for the law and the legal system to define acceptable human behavior and to provide a means to control unacceptable behavior. Law and the legal system must function to instruct the various members of the society on what to do and what not to do in a variety of circumstances. The law thus imposes a necessary structure on society by limiting those activities determined to be detrimental to the public interest and encouraging those activities determined to be beneficial. Within the legal environment of business, the law will work to prohibit business transactions and practices that are viewed as being dishonest or otherwise outside the ethical and social confines of the society. At the same time, the law works to encourage those transactions and practices that further society's prosperity goals.

The legal system must be backed up, however, by some measure of "force" to effectively encourage or discourage certain activities. Managers and other members of a society will quickly readjust their behavior when they learn that a law is being inadequately enforced by the governing authority. The behavior of society in such circumstances will differ little from society's behavior if there were no law governing the matter.

This force requirement may involve fines, imprisonment, or other sanctions imposed by the appropriate governing authority. A business that has been found to have polluted a river, for example, may be fined by the federal government to compel that business to comply with laws prohibiting such pollution. The force may also involve a social stigma that effectively isolates the wrongdoer from social interactions. A business that gains a reputation for unreasonably overworking and underpaying its salaried employees, for example, will eventually find it difficult to hire new workers. The force in this situation is the costs associated with the social stigma of being considered a difficult company to work for. Although no formal law specifically directs this aspect of the business's operations, society demands that businesses conform to certain norms of behavior. Deviations from those generally accepted norms will often result in reactions by society members to discipline the business. Society may demand, for example, that the business pay higher wages as a consequence of its unreasonable behavior. The business can then elect to either pay the higher wage demanded or alter its unreasonable behavior to conform to the norms of society.

In either case, the force employed is intended to provide incentives for the wrongdoer to conform to the norms of acceptable behavior as dictated by society. A business will monitor its conduct, as it can ill afford to damage its reputation or goodwill any more than it can afford to pay large fines.

Conflict Resolution

The next important function of the law is the resolution of society's disputes. Disagreements are inevitable in a technological society made up of individuals with differing viewpoints, material desires, and social preferences. To ensure order, the law and the legal system must provide a formal means through which to resolve conflicts and disputes. According to Karl N. Llewellyn, a legal theorist:

> What, then, is this law business about? It is about the fact that our society is honeycombed with disputes. Disputes actual and potential, disputes to

be settled and disputes to be prevented; both appealing to law, both making up the business of law. . . . This doing of something about disputes, this doing of it reasonably, is the business of law.

Society's formal mechanism for the resolution of disputes will involve both an institution and procedures for resolving *private disputes* between society members and *public disputes* arising between a society member and the governing authority. Within our society, that institution is the court system, and the formalized procedures are the codes of civil and criminal procedure. This court system forms the *structure* of our legal system. Within that structure, society enjoys an objective, unbiased mechanism for resolving disputes, and order within the society is maintained.

In the absence of a formal mechanism, society members would be compelled to provide their own means of resolving disputes and conflicts. If that were the case, an important function of the conflict resolution process would be foregone. In resolving disputes, the court system establishes substantive rules of conduct to be followed by others who may become involved in similar disputes in the future. These rules of conduct form an important body of law called the *common law,* a part of the legal environment of business to be studied in subsequent chapters. The common law and other rules of behavior form the *substance* of law and the legal environment of business.

Social Maintenance

The norms of a society are shaped and molded by society's values, commercial aspirations, customs, and traditions. It is not surprising, then, that the laws of society work to preserve those norms. In this way, law plays a crucial role in maintaining the social environment of society. The values of honesty and integrity are reflected, for example, by the legality and enforceability of agreements; a genuine respect for the property of others is reflected in laws protecting private property rights; and society's measure of acceptable behavior is reflected in laws requiring wrongdoers to compensate parties they injure.

The effectiveness of the social maintenance function of law and the legal system is strongly influenced by the *legal culture* of the society. The legal culture is defined by the attitudes of society members toward law and the legal system. The legal culture of the society determines whether law will be enforced, obeyed, avoided, or abused.

Social Change

Law and the legal system provide an effective means through which the governing authority can bring about important changes in "acceptable" behavior. Behavior in a past period may not serve society well in future periods if new circumstances make certain activities less beneficial or acceptable. One can only envision, for example, the extensive changes brought about in the legal environment of business with the advent of the automobile, telecommunications, and the computer.

As dictated by the maturation of society and the development of technologies that affect it, laws that serve to alter, promote, or discourage specific business behaviors and activities can be enacted and enforced. To alter behavior, for example, laws can be enacted to prohibit racial discrimination in business decisions to hire, promote, or discharge a worker. In the past, racial discrimination may have been an accepted—or at least a tolerated—norm of business behavior for which no sanctions were imposed. Such behavior, however, is no longer considered acceptable to society.

Laws can also be enacted to promote a particular business activity by providing tax incentives or *property rights.* The production of domestic crude oil and other strategic minerals, for example, can be encouraged by a law allowing the government to lease (or sell) government lands to entrepreneurs. Through a lease, the entrepreneur gains a valuable property right to explore, produce, and sell any minerals on that land. Without the property right, an entrepreneur would not have the incentive to undertake that economic activity.

A business activity can be discouraged by the threat of a sanction. Laws can be enacted and enforced that impose substantial penalties when a business is found to have unreasonably polluted the environment. Without the threat of a sanction, businesses may be tempted to act in ways that may be detrimental to other society members.

ORIGIN OF LAW IN THE UNITED STATES: THE COMMON LAW

The original source of law in this country is judge-made or common law—that law that is made and applied by judges as they resolve disputes between private parties. Under the common law, the judge's resolution of any particular dispute will generally be consistent with the pattern of previous judicial decisions in the resolution of similar disputes.

The origin of the common law in this country dates to the colonial period. Law and a legal system were needed to maintain social order and to encourage commerce. To those ends, the colonists adopted and implemented the law and legal system of England, the legal tradition with which they were most familiar. The principal feature of the English law and legal system was its reliance on this judge-made or common law.

Common Law

The origin of our law and legal system can be more easily understood by considering the origin, workings, and functions of English common law. In 1066, the Normans conquered England. William the Conqueror and his successors began the task of unifying the country under their rule. An important element in that unification process was the establishment of King's Courts, called *Curia Regis.* Those courts were to develop and then apply a common or uniform set of rules for the entire country. The set of rules that developed marked the beginning of English *common law.*

The decisions in more important cases were gathered periodically. and recorded in books. To settle disputes that were similar to past disputes, judges used cases recorded in those books as the basis for their decisions. A prior decided case that is similar in legal principle or in facts to a case under consideration is referred to as *precedent.* To settle new or unique disputes, judges created new laws. Those new laws, however, were based on the general principles suggested by the recorded cases.

Doctrine of Stare Decisis

The practice of deciding new cases by referencing former decisions is the foundation of the English and American judicial processes. The use of precedent in deciding present cases forms a doctrine called *stare decisis,* meaning literally "to stand on decided cases." Under this doctrine, judges are encouraged to stand by precedents. According to Judge Posner:

> Judge-made rules are the outcome of the practice of decision according to precedent (stare decisis). When a case is decided, the decision is thereafter a precedent, i.e., a reason for deciding a similar case the same way. While a single precedent is a fragile thing . . . an accumulation of precedents dealing with the same question will create a rule of law having virtually the force of an explicit statutory rule.

The doctrine of stare decisis promotes several useful functions in our legal system. First, there is more uniformity in the decisions of the courts and more certainty in the enforcement practices of the judicial system. As a rule is applied in more and more disputes involving the same (or similar) fact pattern, businesses and their attorneys will be increasingly confident that the rule will be followed in the resolution of future disputes. As a consequence, businesses will be encouraged to expand and foster economic activity in that area. Second, clarity and consistency in the legal system enhances the ability of businesses to plan and execute business transactions. Under the doctrine of stare decisis, businesses have reasonable expectations about the future enforcement of their agreements and the legal standards that will be applied.

One of the major advantages of dispute resolution through the common law is the law's ability to change with the times. As changes in technology or the social consciousness of a society occur, the common law can evolve and provide new rules that better fit the new environment. Although most cases are decided on the basis of stare decisis, judges are not restrained from changing legal principles if conditions warrant the change. If a judge feels that conditions have changed, the decision may be made to modify or reverse existing legal principles. If that decision is appealed to a higher court for review, the higher court will agree or disagree with the change depending upon how persuasively the trial judge has formulated supporting arguments.

In the past decade, for example, the business world has experienced rapid change and development in the manner and methods in which its members communicate with one another. While simple telephone systems were adequate in the past, the businesses of the 1990s need sophisticated telecommunications systems connected by complex networks to be competitive. Modems connect computers to distant computers to allow instantaneous transfers of information and statistics; facsimile machines rapidly transmit copies of documents around the world. These communications devices have made it easier to authenticate documents. While business travel is easier than ever before, communications technology has made personal contact with distant clients less necessary—dramatically reducing the costs of doing business.

Prior to these developments, the legal system required parties to a transaction to sign agreements in person to authenticate the signatures and avoid the potential for fraud. As commerce advanced, typewritten signatures were allowed, followed shortly thereafter by telegraphed communications. In the following case, the court responds to recent developments in electronic mail to further adapt the law to changing business technologies.

Hessenthaler v. Farzin
Superior Court of Pennsylvania
564 A. 2d 990
(1989)

Case Background. *Farzin (the defendant) hired a real estate agent to help sell a parcel of commercial property. Farzin indicated to the agent that she would accept an offer of $520,000. Pursuant to those instructions, the agent met with Hessenthaler (the plaintiff) and drafted a sales agreement exactly as Farzin had instructed the agent to draft it. Hessenthaler signed the agreement as prepared by Farzin's agent. The agent told Farzin that if she wanted to accept the offer of November 17 she had to send him a telegram confirming the acceptance. On November 19 Farzin sent the agent a mailgram confirming acceptance. The agent mailed the agreement of November 17 to Farzin for her signature. Farzin then attempted to add an additional term to the agreement. Hessenthaler sued for specific performance of the November 17 agreement.*

Following a hearing, the trial court found that a binding contract had been created by the mailgram, and directed Farzin to perform her obligations under the agreement and convey the property to Hessenthaler. Farzin appealed.

Case Decision. Judge Hoffman delivered the opinion of the court.

* * *

The first question we must decide is whether or not the mailgram Farzin sent to [the agent] constitutes a "signed" writing as contemplated by the Statute of Frauds. The Statute requires that agreements for the sale of land be signed and in writing. Neither our research nor that of the parties has revealed any . . . cases that address the issue of whether or not a mailgram can be sufficient to satisfy the Statute. Although the issue is one of first impression . . . , these types of questions are likely to arise with greater frequency in the future, as businesses and individuals increasingly rely on similar methods of negotiation such as electronic mail, telexes and facsimile machines in conducting their business affairs.

* * *

The purpose of the Statute is to prevent the possibility of enforcing unfounded, fraudulent claims by requiring that contracts pertaining to interests in real estate be supported by written evidence signed by the party creating the interest.

* * *

Turning to the specific question before us, we should emphasize that there is no requirement in the Statute or the [case] law that a signature be in any particular form . . . [T]he proper, realistic approach in these cases is to look to the reliability of the memorandum, rather than to insist on a formal signature [as has commonly been required in the past].

Applying these principles to the case at bar, it is clear that the mailgram sent by appellants constitutes a signed writing. The mailgram states, in its entirety:

> We, Dr. Mehdi and Marie Farzin, accept the offer of $520,000 for our property at 6175 and 6185 Hocker Drive, Harrisburg, Pennsylvania.

The detail contained in this mailgram is such that there can be little question of its reliability. Appellants were careful to begin the mailgram by identifying themselves. They then made certain that their intention would be properly understood by declaring their acceptance, and identifying both the property and the consideration involved. In light of the primary declaration of identity, combined with the inclusion of the precise terms of the agreement, we are satisfied that the mailgram sufficiently reveals the defendant's intention to adopt the writing as their own, and thus is sufficient to constitute a "signed" writing for purposes of the Statute.

* * *

Case Holding. *The decision of the lower court is affirmed. Since the reliability of the mailgram could not be questioned, the defendant's claims that there was no memorandum sufficient to satisfy the Statute of Frauds is meritless. Under the law of contracts, a communication that sufficiently reveals a party's intention that the communication is to be considered as a writing will satisfy the Statute of Frauds.*

Case Questions

1. What factors forced the court to adopt the more flexible rule that if the "writing" is reliable it is sufficient to satisfy the Statute of Frauds?
2. Suppose technology advances to the point where computers are able to accurately identify an individual by his or her voice print. Can you make an argument that a business contract formed completely over the telephone with a voice "signature" confirmed by computer will be a sufficient "writing" to satisfy the Statute of Frauds?

SOURCES OF LAW MORE RECENT IN ORIGIN

In addition to the judge-made common law, there are several other important sources of law of more recent origin. Most fundamental of these sources are the state and federal constitutions, through which other important sources of law are created. The U.S. Constitution, for example, creates the executive, legislative, and judicial branches of government—each of which has the ability to make law. In addition, Congress—the legislative branch of government—has used its constitutionally granted powers to create what is often referred to as the fourth branch of government—the administrative agencies, a source of law of increasing importance to business.

Constitutions

A *constitution* is the fundamental law of a nation that establishes both the powers of the government and the limits of that power. The U.S. Constitution allocates the powers of government between the states on the one hand and the federal government on the other. Those powers not explicitly granted to the federal government are retained by the state governments and allocated by their individual constitutions.

The U.S. Constitution
The U.S. Constitution, having recently celebrated its two-hundredth birthday, is by far the oldest written constitution still in force anywhere in the world. The Constitution sets forth the general organization, powers, and limits of the federal government. Specifically, the Constitution creates the legislative, executive, and judicial branches of the U.S. government:

THE LEGISLATIVE BRANCH
Article I, Section 1

All legislative Powers herein granted shall be vested in a Congress of the United States, which shall consist of a Senate and House of Representatives.

THE EXECUTIVE BRANCH
Article II, Section 1

The executive Power shall be vested in a President of the United States of America.

THE JUDICIAL BRANCH
Article III, Section 1

The judicial Power of the United States, shall be vested in one supreme Court, and in such inferior Courts as the Congress may from time to time ordain and establish.

This division in governmental power as established by the Constitution is referred to as the doctrine of *separation of powers*. This separation of powers is broadly, yet clearly, defined and arose out of a fear by the founders of this country that too much power might become concentrated in one governmental branch. The doctrine provides that each of the three branches of government has a separate function to perform that can be checked by the other two branches. The government structure that has developed from these constitutional provisions is illustrated in Figure 1–1.

The U.S. Constitution clearly establishes itself as the supreme law of this country. According to Article VI:

> This Constitution, and the Laws of the United States which shall be made in Pursuance thereof; and all Treaties made, or which shall be made, under the Authority of the United States, shall be the supreme Law of the Land; and the Judges in every State shall be bound thereby, any Thing in the Constitution or Laws of any State to the Contrary notwithstanding.

Thus, a state or federal law found to be in violation of the U.S. Constitution will be declared unconstitutional and will not be enforced.

The Constitution also establishes the supremacy of federal law. In those areas where the Constitution grants powers to the federal government and elects to exercise those powers, state law is superseded. States may not, therefore, work to reduce or alter the intended effects of a federal law unless Congress has specifically allowed for the states to do so. In that regard, consider the following grant of power provided to the states in the Clean Air Act:

> [N]othing in this [act] shall preclude or deny any state . . . the right to adopt or enforce . . . any limitations respecting emissions of air pollutants . . . except that . . . such state . . . may not adopt or enforce any emission standard or limitation which is less stringent than the standard . . . under [this act].

State Constitutions

All powers not granted to the federal government are retained by the state governments. According to the Tenth Amendment to the Constitution:

Figure 1–1 The Government of the United States

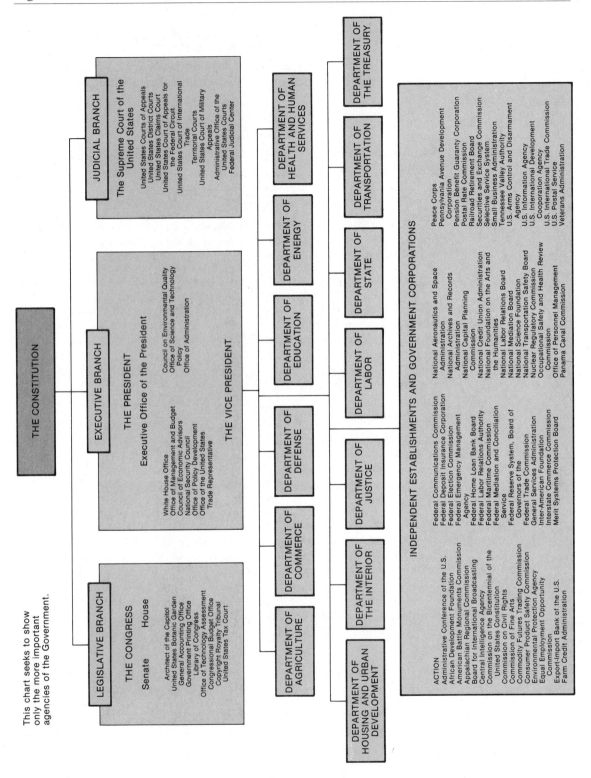

This chart seeks to show only the more important agencies of the Government.

The powers not delegated to the United States by the Constitution . . . are reserved to the states respectively. . . .

The powers and structures of all fifty state governments are based on written constitutions. Like the federal government, the state governments are divided into legislative, judicial, and executive branches. The constitutions specify how state officials shall be chosen and removed, how laws are passed, how the court system shall be run, and how finances and revenues will be paid and collected. Like their federal counterpart, each state constitution is the highest form of law in that state.

Legislatures

The Congress and the various state legislative bodies are an important source of law called *statutory law*. Statutory law comprises much of the law that most significantly affects business behavior. The most important constraint on this body of law is that it cannot violate the U.S. Constitution or the relevant state constitutions.

United States Congress

Article I, Section 1, of the U.S. Constitution provides that all power to make laws for the federal government shall be given to Congress. It further provides that Congress shall be a bicameral legislature consisting of a Senate and a House of Representatives. The specific powers delegated to the Congress affecting business are presented in Exhibit 1–1 and discussed in Chapter 4.

The process of enacting a law through the federal legislative process is illustrated in Figure 1–2. Of the 20,000 pieces of legislation that are proposed in each session of Congress, only about 175 ever reach the House and Senate floors for debate. A significant portion of those laws will, however, have an impact on the legal environment of business.

Exhibit 1–1   Powers Delegated to Congress by the Constitution Most Affecting Business

1. To lay and collect taxes, duties, imports, and excises for the purpose of paying the debts and providing for the common defense and general welfare of the United States.
2. To borrow money.
3. To regulate foreign and interstate commerce.
4. To formulate rules for bankruptcies and naturalization.
5. To coin money and set standards of weights and measures.
6. To punish counterfeiting.
7. To establish post offices and post roads.
8. To grant copyrights and patents.
9. To set up federal courts below the Supreme Court.
10. To punish piracy and offenses against the law of nations.
11. To declare war.
12. To raise and support armies.
13. To provide and maintain a navy.
14. To call out the national militia.
15. To regulate, arm, and discipline the militia.
16. To make all laws necessary and proper for carrying out the foregoing powers.

Figure 1–2 Legislative Process

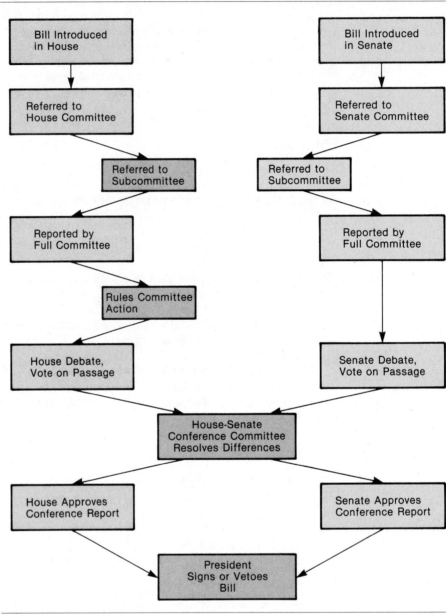

State Legislatures

Each state has a lawmaking body similar to Congress in its functions and procedures. With the exception of Nebraska, all states have a bicameral legislature containing a House of Representatives (sometimes called a House of Delegates or Assembly) and a Senate. The actual lawmaking process in state legislatures is nearly identical to the procedure followed by the Congress as illustrated in Figure 1–2. Note, however, that in some states voters may propose or even draft legislation. In recent years, state statutory law has become an important source of regulatory law affecting the legal environment of business.

Administrative Agencies

An administrative agency is created when either the legislative or executive branch of the government delegates some of its authority to an appropriate group. Through Congress (or the state legislature), that delegation usually takes the form of an enactment of a law that specifies the duties and responsibilities of the agency. Consider the following delegation of authority by Congress under the Clean Water Act:

> . . . [T]he Administrator of the Environmental Protection Agency . . . shall administer this [act]. . . . The Administrator is authorized to prescribe such regulations as are necessary to carry out his functions under this [act].

With congressional delegation, administrative agencies are able to exercise broad legislative, judicial, and executive powers. In enacting regulations to implement the act delegating authority to it, an agency uses its legislative powers. In supervising compliance with those regulations, an agency uses its executive powers. Finally, in the adjudication of violations of those regulations, administrative agencies use their judicial powers. The regulations, agency opinions, and agency orders flowing from administrative agencies are perhaps the most important source of law affecting the legal environment of business. The practices and procedures of administrative agencies are discussed in Chapter 5.

The Judiciary

As previously discussed, judge-made common law is a major source of law affecting the legal environment of business. In addition to contributing to common law, the judiciary serves to interpret (where unclear and ambiguous) and enforce laws enacted by legislative bodies. The judiciary also reviews actions taken by the executive branch.

The legal environment of business, however, is significantly impacted by the judicial review of the actions and activities of the administrative agencies. According to Professors Robinson and Gellhorn:

> The function of judicial review is to assure that the administrator's action is authorized (within his delegated authority) and not an abuse of discretion (an unreasonable choice not supported by available evidence). It assures that, when challenged, the administrative action has not encroached excessively on private rights. . . . [J]udicial review tests whether the agency (a) has exceeded its constitutional or statutory authority, (b) has properly interpreted the applicable law, (c) has conducted a fair proceeding, and (d) has not acted capriciously and unreasonably.

Thus, in combination with the statute enacted by Congress, the agency's interpretation of the statute and the court's review of the agency's interpretation all form the law on the subject in question.

The Environmental Protection Agency, for example, may interpret the Clean Air Act as requiring the installation of air scrubbers on all steel mills. It will then promulgate a regulation specifying that requirement. ABX, a large steel company, may challenge the agency's interpretation of the act by seeking judicial review. The court, in reviewing the agency's interpretation, will examine the act and consider the agency's interpretation before reaching a decision. The court's decision then becomes a precedent on that particular aspect of the act. This particular function of the judiciary is a major source of law affecting the legal environment of business.

The Executive

In addition to approving (or disapproving) bills passed by Congress, the President is a major source of law affecting the legal environment of business. Although the lawmaking authority of the President is limited by the Constitution, the President can create law by issuing *executive orders*. Although the power to issue an executive order usually results from a congressional delegation of that power, the power in some cases may be justified on constitutional grounds.

The President can also indirectly influence the degree to which administrative agencies undertake their duties and responsibilities. A probusiness administration, for example, may pursue environmental, antitrust, or international trade issues much less ardently than another, less business oriented administration. Thus, business may face a seemingly hostile legal environment under one administration and a much more permissive one under another.

INTERNATIONAL PERSPECTIVES: SOURCES OF LAW IN JAPAN

INTERNATIONAL

PERSPECTIVES

There is an overwhelming variety of legal systems throughout the world. Every country has its own basic system, and no two systems are exactly the same. Fortunately, these seemingly diverse legal systems can be placed into workable groups or "families" based on similarities in structure, substance, and culture. The legal system of the United States and most other English-speaking countries, for example, belongs to the family of legal systems based on the common law, the system discussed earlier in this chapter. A second family would include the legal systems of the Far East, Israel, and the Islamic countries.

The largest family, however, would include those countries that follow a *civil law approach*. The countries in this group would include the countries of Western Europe (France, Germany, Italy, and Spain) and Eastern Europe (Poland, Hungary, and Russia). Through past colonization efforts of these countries, civil law was taken to Latin America, French-speaking Canada, Africa, and parts of the Middle East.

An important member of the civil-law family is the country of Japan. Japan adopted much of the German civil law legal system in the late 1800s to make itself more attractive to western businesses and traders. Like its civil-law counterparts throughout the world, Japan's basic source of law is its codes. In contrast to common-law systems where the basic laws are developed over time by judges, the codes of the civil-law countries are enacted by the government—in Japan, the Diet or national parliament. These codes attempt to arrange whole categories of law in an orderly, comprehensive, and logical way. In Japan, the basic codes consist of the Civil Code, the Commercial Code, the Penal Code, and the Procedural Codes such as the Code of Criminal Procedure and the Code of Civil Procedure. In contrast to the common law of the United States where judges have developed the rules for unlawful intentional and negligent acts, Article 709 of the Japanese Civil Code provides:

> A person who violates intentionally or negligently the right of another is bound to make compensation for damages (for injuries to the person, his liberty, or reputation as well as his property) arising therefrom.

More detailed statutes support each of these basic codes.

The Japanese courts apply these codes very strictly. The application of a particular code provision to a dispute is influenced by past applications, particularly those of the highest courts in the country. Because the Japanese rely heavily on informal means of dispute resolution—negotiation, mediation, and conciliation—many parts of the codes have not been the subject of litigation. In those situations, the Japanese lawyer relies largely on interpretations of the codes by academic legal scholars. In those situations in which no specific code provision is applicable to a dispute that has arisen, the court may look to customs, traditions, and equity in reaching a decision, or it may apply a code provision intended to be applicable to another type of dispute. Through this process—and coupled with the enactment of new code provisions by the Diet—Japan's civil-law legal system is able to adjust to societal and technological changes. This process is very similar to the process used in other civil-law countries.

CLASSIFICATIONS OF LAW

Law can be grouped or classified in several ways. As the previous section has illustrated, law could be classified according to its source. That is, law could be classified according to whether it originated with a constitution, a legislative body, the judiciary, or the executive branch of government. It could be further classified according to whether the source was a state body—a state constitution, court, legislature, or governor—or a federal body—the federal Constitution, courts, Congress, or the President. The more common classification systems, however, classify law on the basis of whether it is public or private, civil or criminal, or procedural or substantive. It is important to note that these classifications are not mutually exclusive. A particular law, for example, could be public, criminal, and procedural.

Public or Private Law

Some examples of public and private law are provided in Table 1–1. *Public law* is concerned with the legal relationship between society members—businesses as well as individuals—and its governing authority. Public law includes the

Table 1–1 Examples of Public and Private Law

Public Law	Private Law
Administrative law	Agency law
Antitrust	Contract law
Appellate procedure	Corporation law
Civil procedure	Partnership law
Constitutional law	Personal property
Criminal law	Real property
Criminal procedure	Torts
Environmental law	
Evidence	
Labor law	
Securities regulation	

statutory laws enacted and enforced by Congress and the state legislatures. It serves principally to influence the behavior of society members and to provide a conduit for social change. In this way, public law plays an important regulatory role in a society.

Private law sets forth rules governing the legal relationships among society members. It serves principally to resolve disputes among society members and to provide a means through which the important values, customs, and traditions of the society can influence law. Private law includes the common or judge-made law and is enforced primarily through the state court system.

Civil or Criminal Law

The appropriate legislative body generally decides if a law is to be civil, criminal, or both. Unless a law is specifically designated by statute as being criminal, it is considered civil law. Examples of civil and criminal law are provided in Table 1–2.

Civil law is concerned with the rights and duties that exist among individual society members or between individual society members and the governing authority in noncriminal matters. A society member found liable for a *civil wrong* may be required to pay money damages to the injured party or to do or refrain from doing a specific act or both. In finding the wrongdoer liable, the jury (or the judge in a nonjury trial) must find that the *preponderance* (majority) of the evidence favored the injured party.

Criminal law concerns legal wrongs, or crimes, committed against all of society. As determined by the appropriate federal or state statute or local *ordinance,* a crime is classified as treason, a felony, or a misdemeanor. The crime of treason, established by the U.S. Constitution, is committed by an individual who levies war against the United States or adheres to or gives aid or comfort to its enemies.

The objective of criminal law is to punish the wrongdoer for violating the rules of society. Although the victim may have been killed, injured, or otherwise wronged because of the criminal act of the wrongdoer, criminal law

Table 1–2   Examples of Civil and Criminal Law

Civil Law	Criminal Law
Contract Law	**Misdemeanor Offenses**
Business formation	Assault and battery (simple)
Insurance	Disturbing the peace
Real estate	Larceny (petit)
Sales	Prostitution
Services	Public intoxication
	Trespass
Tort Law	**Felony Offenses**
Assault and battery	Arson
Defamation	Bribery
Fraud	Burglary
Invasion of privacy	Homicide
Negligence	Larceny (grand)
Strict liability	Manslaughter
Trespass	Robbery

is not designed to provide restitution for the victim of the crime. Individual restitution is a matter for civil law.

An individual found guilty of a criminal offense is usually fined, imprisoned, or both. In finding an individual guilty of a crime, the jury (or the judge in a nonjury trial) must find that the evidence presented at the trial demonstrated *beyond a reasonable doubt* that the individual committed the crime. The severity of punishment depends upon whether the offense was a felony or a misdemeanor. Generally only those offenses punishable by death or by imprisonment for more than a year are classified as felonies. Misdemeanors are less serious crimes, punishable by a fine and/or imprisonment for less than a year.

One category of criminal law currently receiving considerable attention is white-collar crime. This category includes crimes committed by business or by persons who manage the business. The traditional white-collar crimes include embezzlement and larceny, both of which involve taking the property of a business. A rapidly growing area of white-collar crime is computer crime. The computer provides white-collar criminals with access to important and valuable business assets in the form of information that can be appropriated and sold by the computer criminal.

Substantive or Procedural Law

Substantive law includes common law and statutory law that define and establish legal rights and regulate behavior. *Procedural law* determines how substantive law will be enforced through the courts. A criminal law case, for example, must follow criminal procedural law. The appropriate appellate procedure must be followed when a lower-court decision is appealed to a higher court for review. Similarly, the appropriate procedures must be followed by agencies enforcing administrative laws and regulations. Examples of substantive and procedural laws are provided in Table 1–3.

Table 1–3 Examples of Substantive and Procedural Law

Substantive Law	Procedural Law
Administrative law	Administrative procedure
Agency law	Appellate procedure
Antitrust law	Civil procedure
Constitutional law	Criminal procedure
Contract law	
Corporation law	
Criminal law	
Environmental law	
Labor law	
Personal property law	
Real property law	
Securities regulation	
Tort law	

WHAT IS THE LEGAL ENVIRONMENT OF BUSINESS?

Scholars can only speculate as to how the legal environment of business initially developed. Conceivably, in the early days of civilization, people discovered they could share in the fruits of the labor of others as long as they were willing to give up part of the fruits of their own labor. That is, commercial activity centered around the ability of the parties to engage in *barter*. In a primitive economic society, legal mechanisms were necessarily simple, based largely on the customs and traditions of the area.

As business transactions became more complex—particularly as sales agreements called for longer term relationships than those present in barter economies—mechanisms became increasingly more important. To encourage businesses to undertake more complex transactions, some form of contract law, private property rights, and a formal dispute resolution system in which to enforce those rights and contracts had to be established. With the expectation that their rights would be adequately enforced and protected, businesses would then have the confidence to undertake more complex commercial activity.

Through the Industrial Revolution, workers combined with machines to make products. This allowed for increased specialization of labor and had the effect of distancing workers from consumers. As a consequence, consumers pressed for additional legal safeguards to increase their confidence in business transactions.

As transportation and communication technologies expanded the size of trading areas, legal mechanisms to facilitate transactions necessarily became even more complex. As markets and businesses grew beyond state lines, state governments, bar associations, and the business community sought to make the commercial laws more uniform from state to state to encourage interstate commerce. In addition, Congress enacted laws to protect workers in the factories, laws to prevent businesses from engaging in uncompetitive activities, and laws to protect investors who put their capital into businesses, as well as other laws, all of which, together with the common law, became the legal environment of business.

Defining the Legal Environment of Business

The legal environment of business can be defined, then, as that collection of laws that influence the behavior and conduct of commercial activity. The collection of laws within the legal environment of business encompasses all of the legal rights, duties, and responsibilities associated with any commercial activity. The legal environment of business dictates the appropriate code of conduct within which all businesses must operate. The legal environment impacts business decisions and constrains selection of alternative courses of action. It establishes the legal boundaries of all interrelationships between a business and its governing authority, competitors, consumers, investors, employees, and the community. The legal environment of business will even dictate the process through which a prospective business must go to be recognized as a business.

Businesses must operate within the code of conduct established by the legal environment of business, or *sanctions* may be imposed. Those sanctions may include liability for damages if the conduct involves a wrongful act (is tortious) or a breach of contract. The sanctions may involve fines or imprisonment if the business's conduct is declared to be a crime. Furthermore, sanctions may be used either to prevent the business from undertaking certain activities or, conversely, to assure that the business undertakes certain activities. As illustrated in Table 1-4, severe penalties can be imposed on managers who violate federal statutes.

The managers of any business—sole proprietorships, partnerships, corporations, or multinationals—will be expected to be fully aware of their legal environment. As the following case illustrates, ignorance of a law will not excuse a business from sanctions in the event of a violation of the law or other wrongdoing.

Table 1-4 Criminal Liability Penalties for Managers in Violation of Selected Federal Statutes

Federal Statute	Maximum Criminal Penalty
Food, Drug, and Cosmetic Act	$250,000 fine or imprisonment for up to ten years or both
Foreign Corrupt Practices Act	$100,000 fine or imprisonment for up to five years or both
Occupational Safety and Health Act	$10,000 fine or imprisonment for up to six months or both
Resource Conservation and Recovery Act	$250,000 fine or imprisonment for up to fifteen years or both
Securities Act of 1933	$10,000 fine or imprisonment for up to five years or both
Sherman and Clayton Antitrust Acts	$100,000 fine or imprisonment for up to three years or both

Barcellona v. Tiffany English Pub
United States Court of Appeals, Fifth Circuit
597 F.2d 464 (1979)

Case Background. *The former waiters of Tiffany English Pub, Inc., a restaurant doing business under the name TGI Friday's, brought suit against the restaurant under the* Fair Labor Standards Act. *The waiters attacked the restaurant's policy of using their tips to satisfy its obligation to pay a minimum wage. The restaurant contended that the tips were withheld pursuant to a valid agreement with the waiters that considered tips to be the property of the restaurant and were to be used towards the satisfaction of the minimum wage requirement.*

The district court, however, found no such agreement and held that the evidence showed a flagrant violation of the Fair Labor Standards Act. *The statute allows an employee to sue for back wages, attorney's fees, and liquidated damages in the event of a minimum wage violation. The liquidated damages may be equal in amount to the unpaid wages recovered. The district court found the restaurant liable for $34,141.50 in actual damages and awarded $17,000 in attorney's fees. The court refused to allow liquidated damages, however, on the grounds that "there was nothing defiant intended by the [restaurant]. . . . It simply did not know and did not understand exactly what it was to do with respect to these records on these waiters." Note that the statute does allow the court to deny liquidated damages if an employer proves he or she acted in good faith and had a reasonable basis for believing he or she was not in violation of the statute.*

Case Decision. Circuit Judge Tuttle delivered the opinion of the court.

* * *

We understand the language of . . . the Act to impose upon the employer who would escape the payment of liquidated damages a plain and substantial burden of persuading the court by proof that his failure to obey the statute was both in good faith and predicated upon such reasonable grounds that it would be unfair to impose upon him more than a compensatory verdict. . . . On the present record, the restaurant never seemed to attempt to meet the burden. The only indication we can glean from the record concerning Friday's good faith and the reasonableness of its belief in the legalities of its actions is the restaurant's contention that the owners were merely a couple of farmers, acting for the first time as employers, with blind faith in their franchisor. Perhaps this argument was the basis for the district court's decision to deny liquidated damages due to nondefiant ignorance. This is curious because the court's conclusory justification for its denial of liquidated damages is so totally inconsistent with its earlier finding of a willful and flagrant violation of the FLSA.

In addition to our concern over the inconsistency between the finding of a flagrant violation and yet a later denial of liquidated damages based on nondefiant ignorance, we also doubt the validity of ignorance as a defense to liability for liquidated damages. . . . We do not believe an employer may rely on ignorance alone as *reasonable* grounds for believing that its actions were not in violation of the Act. . . . Further, we feel that good faith requires some duty to investigate potential liability under the FLSA. . . . Even inexperienced businessmen cannot claim good faith when they blindly operate a business without making any investigation as to their responsibilities under the labor laws. Apathetic ignorance is never the basis of a reasonable belief.

* * *

Case Holding. *The court affirmed the lower court's decision on the restaurant's liability. It also affirmed the lower court's actual damage and attorney's fees awards. It reversed the lower court's decision not to award liquidated damages, finding that* *ignorance of the law is not evidence that an employer was acting in good faith under the Fair Labor Standards Act.*

Case Questions

1. Should ignorance of the legal environment of business be a defense to a business executive involved in wrongdoing?

2. Would an excessively large penalty in those instances where the executive actually was innocently ignorant discourage entrepreneurial behavior?

3. Does this case illustrate any benefits associated with "preventive lawyering"?

Consideration of the Law's Impact

The study of the legal environment also requires consideration of the impact of law, particularly those laws enacted by legislative bodies. A law enacted with good intentions may have important negative unintended effects on innocent parties. Studies have shown, for example, that in those states where seat belt laws have been enacted, the number of pedestrians killed by automobiles has increased. Those studies have concluded that drivers feel safer with seat belts and therefore drive less carefully. Clearly, that result was not contemplated by the legislative bodies that enacted seat belt laws.

A law may be enacted for the express purpose of helping a particular disadvantaged group but may actually end up hurting it. Minimum wage laws were originally enacted with the intent to enhance the quality of life of unskilled workers by increasing their incomes. Numerous studies have shown, however, that minimum wage laws actually have generated increases in unemployment in unskilled workers, the very group the law was intended to benefit.

Impact of Government Objectives

An understanding of the legal environment requires an awareness of the economic, social, and political objectives of society and the governing authority. Social change, for example, may be imposed through laws directing businesses to hire minorities, reduce pollution, or improve the safety of their products. Businesses can be encouraged to participate in the achievement of social and community objectives by being granted *tax incentives* (such as being allowed tax deductions for charitable contributions) or *subsidies* (as in the form of direct payments to businesses from the government for the employment of handicapped workers).

The governing authority's political and social goals and objectives can be furthered through laws containing no intended behavioral impacts on business. Nevertheless, the law may indirectly force the business to alter its business patterns or practices. Income taxes may be imposed on business, for example, for the purpose of increasing government revenues to reduce spending deficits. A law may be enacted to encourage the use of a particular technology. In the international sector, a law may be enacted to discourage or prohibit businesses from buying from or selling to foreign traders whose governments are out of favor with the U.S. government.

Consideration of Ethical Customs

The legal environment of business reaches beyond the formal collection of law and regulations imposed by the governing authority. It also encompasses society's informal rules of conduct and behavior as dictated by its social customs, values, morals, and traditions. With regard to business practices and the importance of these informal rules to the legal environment of business, Nobel laureate Milton Friedman has said:

> [It is the responsibility of managers] to make as much money as possible while conforming to the basic rules of the society, both those embodied in law and those embodied in ethical custom.

The ethical custom to which Friedman refers is the set of informal rules of the society. Those rules involve characteristics of trust, honesty, and integrity, all of which are important and fundamental elements of the legal environment of business within a society. The interaction of the legal environment of business with ethical customs is discussed more fully in Chapter 6.

CHARACTERISTICS BRINGING ABOUT DIFFERING LEGAL ENVIRONMENTS AMONG BUSINESSES

Before moving to the discussion in subsequent chapters of specific laws that make up the legal environment of business, it is helpful to consider some of the general characteristics of a business that might influence the business's specific legal environment. As mentioned previously, the more important characteristics that will influence a business's legal environment include the type of industry the business is in, the kind of business organization it has selected, the size of the business, its location, the markets in which the business's products are sold, and the markets it relies upon for its raw materials.

Industry

The legal environment of business differs significantly from one industry to another. Some industries, such as public utilities, are subject to heavy regulation by the governing authority. Generally granted the sole right to operate in certain geographic areas by the governing authority, these regulated industries are accustomed to extensive government regulation. According to Professor F. M. Scherer:

> ... For industries that are regarded as public utilities, control by a regulatory authority often extends not only to prices, but also to entry [into] and exit [from the industry], service standards, financial structure, accounting methods, and a host of other elements.

Although the legal environment of the public utility industry will clearly differ from the legal environments of other industries, those other industries are not free from government regulation. The government may still impose regulations to control the product quality, disclosure of information, degree of pollution, labor-management relations, and workplace safety standards of those industries. As a consequence, the legal environments of business may also differ between industries. If one is more heavily unionized, it requires greater concerns about labor law; if one pollutes more than most, it requires greater emphasis on environmental law; or if one engages in more credit relations with the public, it requires greater awareness of the laws governing creditor/debtor relationships. In addition, an industry that operates extensively in international markets will require a greater knowledge of international law than an industry that operates primarily in the domestic market.

Business Organization

The form of business organization a business selects can have a profound consequence on the business's legal environment. Of the several forms of business organizations available, the most prominent are sole proprietorships, partnerships, limited partnerships, and corporations. Among these organizations, the form selected can influence the business's marginal income tax rate, the owner's liability for the expenses of the business, the lifespan of the business, and the degree of managerial control enjoyed by its owners. In addition, the choice of business organization can influence the regulatory requirements with which the business must comply. If the business elects to be a publicly held corporation, for example, it will necessarily have to comply with the reporting requirements imposed by the Securities and Exchange Commission. Those reporting requirements are generally not imposed on either sole proprietorships or partnerships. Finally, the business may be formed for charitable purposes, in which case it may elect nonprofit status. Nonprofit organizations are treated differently by the Internal Revenue Service and other governmental agencies. Business organizations and their differences and similarities are discussed in more detail in Chapter 11.

Size of the Business

The size of a business can have a significant impact on the business's legal environment. As Table 1–5 illustrates, the vast majority of businesses are small, having fewer than fifty employees. The smallest category—those busi-

Table 1–5   Distribution of Businesses in United States by Employment Size Class

Size Category by Number of Employees	Percent of All Businesses
1 to 9 employees	50.7
10 to 49 employees	29.6
50 to 99 employees	8.7
100 to 249 employees	6.7
250 to 499 employees	2.6
500 to 999 employees	1.1
1,000 employees or more	0.6

Source: U.S. Dept. of Commerce, Bureau of Census, *Survey of Manufacturers.*

nesses with fewer than ten employees—comprises more than fifty percent of all businesses in the United States. These smaller businesses tend to be involved in the production of one product, contracting for the majority of their supplies and other necessary inputs from other businesses. In contrast to larger businesses, which may have production facilities throughout the world, smaller firms tend to concentrate on local markets. As a consequence, their legal and regulatory obligations and responsibilities are considerably fewer in number than those of larger businesses.

Although larger businesses engage themselves in more business transactions, they also find themselves involved in much more complex legal and regulatory matters. Antitrust laws, for example, generally apply only to larger businesses, although small businesses are not exempt. Labor relations law tends to be a much greater concern for larger rather than smaller businesses because larger businesses are more likely to be unionized than are smaller businesses. Since larger businesses are usually publicly held corporations that require access to stock markets as a source of their capital, they are much more concerned about securities regulations than are smaller businesses. A reflection of both the increased number of business transactions and their legal and regulatory complexity is found in the fact that each of the fifty largest corporate legal departments have nearly ten times more *attorneys* than smaller businesses have *employees*. Exxon and AT&T, for example, each employ more than 400 in-house attorneys.

Many federal laws regulating business activities specify the minimum size of business subject to the law. The Civil Rights Act of 1964, for example, specifies that for purposes of employment discrimination the law applies only to those businesses with fifteen or more employees. Most *businesses* have fewer than fifteen employees and are not immediately affected by that law. Most *employees*, however, are covered by the law, since the majority work for larger businesses.

Business Location

Laws on various subjects differ dramatically from state to state and therefore vary considerably in their impact on business. Some states apply particular legal rules more rigidly than other states and have regulatory requirements that go beyond federal standards. The legal environment in a state where certain rules are less rigidly applied may be more attractive to some businesses because the cost of doing business there will be lower.

In products liability cases, for example, some states apply a negligence standard in some instances, which places a duty of care on both the business and the consumers of its products to avoid accidents. Other states apply a strict liability standard, which places that responsibility almost entirely on the business. The costs of doing business in a negligence state will likely be less, since the amount of company resources spent on product testing, the size of adverse legal judgments, and liability insurance premiums will all likely be less.

Similar differences in the statutory laws enacted by state legislatures can influence the legal environment of business. Many corporations, for example, find Delaware an attractive state in which to incorporate because of the state's liberal incorporation statute and the expertise of its judiciary in handling complex corporate legal matters. A business incorporated in Kansas may therefore have a somewhat less desirable legal environment with respect to business organization law than a business incorporated in Delaware. A business can significantly influence its legal environment by carefully selecting the state in which it intends to operate.

Markets the Business Serves

A business's legal environment also will be affected by both the markets it serves and the markets it relies upon for its inputs. The legal environments of two businesses will differ as those markets differ. A business that primarily sells locally, for example, has a different legal environment than a firm that sells its product abroad. A business operating in international markets must be concerned about the laws and regulations of the foreign countries in which it operates as well as the laws and regulations of the United States and the individual states in which it does business.

LEGAL ENVIRONMENT WITHIN A BUSINESS

Besides varying among businesses, the legal environment can vary significantly from department to department within a business. The larger an organization becomes, the more specialized each department's legal environment will become. As illustrated in Figure 1–3, a business may consist of

Figure 1–3   Overview of a Business's Legal Environment

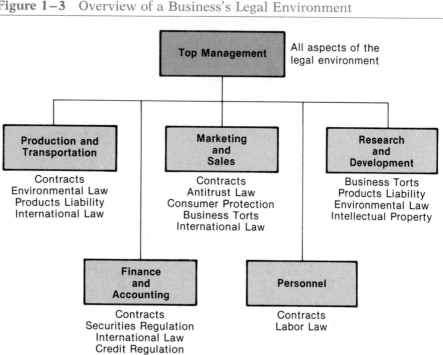

departments in charge of production and transportation, finance and account-ing, marketing and sales, personnel, and research and development. While the legal environment of each department overlaps that of other departments to a degree, there are legal considerations unique to each department. A manager in personnel for example, will have different concerns than a manager in marketing. Both must be concerned, however, with meeting the requirements of and any changes in their legal environment that might affect their performance and that of the business.

SUMMARY

Law is a collection of principles and rules whose purpose it is to establish, guide, and alter the behavior of society members. This collection of rules encompasses and reflects both the formal rules of the society as established by the governing authority and the society's informal rules as dictated by its customs, traditions, commercial aspirations, and social ethics.

The law and the legal system serve several important functions in an orderly society. It is important for the law to define acceptable behavior. In effectively serving this important function, the law and the legal system must be backed up by some measure of force—such as through the imposition and enforcement of fines or imprisonment. Those society members found to be in violation of a social ethic will be forced to endure some social stigma that effectively isolates them from social interactions. To ensure order, the law and the legal system must provide a formal means through which to resolve disputes. The law must function to maintain the important values of the society. Finally, law and the legal system function to provide a means through which important changes in social consciousness can result.

Judge-made or common law is the original source of law in this country. Derived from English common law, our common law system encourages judges to use prior decisions—called precedents—for guidance in deciding new disputes. This use of precedent is the basis of the doctrine of stare decisis. Judges are not restrained from changing legal principles, however, if social or business conditions warrant the change.

Other sources of law more recent in origin in this country include the constitutions, legislatures, judiciary, executive branches, and administrative agencies. The constitutions—that of the United States and those of the individual states—are the most basic source of law. They set forth the general organization, powers, and limits of their respective governments. The legisla-tive, judicial, and executive branches of government are created through the constitutions. In addition, Congress has used its congressional powers to create what is referred to as the fourth branch of government—the adminis-trative agencies. The state constitutions have provided for the development of a similar governmental structure in each of the states. All are important sources of law.

Law can be classified on the basis of whether it is public or private, civil or criminal, or substantive or procedural. Public law includes laws enacted by Congress and enforced by the federal government. Antitrust, securities regu-lation, and the environmental laws are examples of public law. Private law includes most of the common law. The law of torts, contracts, and products liability are examples of private law. Another way of classifying law is by whether it is substantive or procedural. Substantive law defines and establishes legal rights and duties. Procedural law sets forth the rules to be followed by courts in enforcing the rights and duties created by substantive law. The study of the legal environment of business emphasizes the study of the laws affecting business. Understanding how business is affected by regulatory laws is an important function for the business executive.

The legal environment may vary between businesses because of differences in the industry in which a business operates, the form of business organization selected, the size and location of the business, and the markets it serves or relies upon for inputs. A business operating in international markets must also be concerned with the laws of the countries in which it operates.

The managers of the major departments making up the business—the departments of personnel, research and development, marketing, finance, and production—must be most knowledgeable about the regulations that affect the performance of their individual departments. Top management, on the other hand, must be knowledgeable about all elements of the business's legal environment.

ISSUE

Do Social and Political Factors Influence Judges?

The role of judges in the common-law process is a controversial subject in legal circles. When a judge's decision adversely affects one group relative to another, it is common to hear cries of judicial activism—the judge is making a personal decision on what the law should be rather than following past precedent and applying the law as it is. This reading discusses the role judges play in making law in the context of several important legal issues—abortion, discrimination, and employment-at-will—and considers several factors influencing their decision-making process.

Why Courts Are Always Making Law
Jerry Frug*

Most judges do not like to admit that they make social and political choices. It's time to get the truth out in the open.

* * *

These days conservatives often criticize judges for trying to make law rather than simply apply it. [Some legal scholars argue] that it's [not] possible simply to apply the law. They insist that whenever judges make legal decisions they choose among alternative possible results. Making such a choice requires courts to select among different sets of values and ways to organize society.

Fortune, Copyright 1989, The Time, Inc. Magazine Company. All Rights Reserved.

—continued

—continuing

In some contexts, the political nature of judicial decision-making is obvious to everyone. The debate over the constitutional status of abortion, for example, is plainly connected with the current political struggle between those who support the right to life and those who are pro-choice. In deciding the constitutional issue, the Supreme Court cannot avoid choosing one of these positions over the other.

Another example is the current controversy over the definition of racial discrimination in the job market. Employment discrimination can be defined narrowly to prohibit only employer action that is intentionally motivated by racial bias, but it also can be defined broadly to prohibit any systematic exclusion of blacks or other minorities from parts of the job market, whether or not the exclusion is intentional. The choice between these positions is a political one, and any choice the courts make involves judicial activism. Either judicial result would be an intervention in social life.

What is not so obvious is that even an interpretation of the rules of contract and property law involves a choice. With corporate legal expenses mounting and litigation a national pastime, understanding what this means for the world of everyday business has significance far beyond the classroom.

Consider in some depth, for example, the legal issues raised by employment-at-will contracts. Most American workers—including many executives—have employment contracts that don't specify how long their jobs will last or the reasons for which they might be fired. The extent of their job security depends on how these contracts are interpreted.

Many nonlawyers expect the law to have a ready answer to this kind of issue. They think that law is a cut-and-dried body of rules that lawyers either know or can easily look up. Many people seem to think, for example, that because employees can quit their jobs at any time, they can also be fired at any time for any reason.

Lawyers these days, in fact, rarely offer such a definitive description of the law. The difficulty in specifying the precise legal status of employees-at-will illustrates why. Over the past 25 years, courts have carved a number of exceptions into the freewheeling notion that employees can be fired for any reason. Employers have been held liable, for example, for attempting to fire employees who refused to perjure themselves before a legislative hearing, who blew the whistle about illegal conduct by their employers, and who filed workers' compensation claims. One way to sum up these recent cases is to say that employees can now recover damages from their employer if they are fired for reasons that undermine an important public policy.

But what counts as such a public policy? One court has decided that it does not violate an important public policy to fire an employee for reporting to company (rather than public) officials that his supervisor is taking bribes. Another court has decided that it does not violate an important public policy to fire an employee who refused to reduce staffing in a hospital's intensive care unit on the grounds that it would endanger patients' lives. On the other hand, a third court has decided that firing an employee for refusing to date her foreman did violate "the best interest of the economic system or the public good." No wonder there's confusion about the law.

For decades legal scholars have devoted a vast amount of energy trying to make sense of conflicting decisions such as these. Over the past ten years, an increasing number of them have argued that the conflicts can best be understood in [moral and] political terms. [T]hey contend that the decisions conflict with one another because they are based on different, and controversial, moral and political ideals. Lawyers cannot give a simple answer to a question ... because the legal system, like our society at large, cannot

—continued

–continuing

reconcile the contradictory instincts people feel when they confront social problems.Rather than deciding which of these conflicting instincts to honor, the law embraces them all.

Looking at the employment-at-will issue in this way points up something important about the judicial activism many conservatives find so abhorrent. The courts' acceptance for many years of the extensive employer power over employees reflected the conventional conservative idea that employers are entitled to run their business as they see fit. The more recent decisions limiting employers' power, by contrast, have been justified by conventional liberal arguments emphasizing the unfairness of arbitrary employer power over employees and the inefficiencies that result when people work under the threat of losing their jobs without adequate justification. Conservatives often treat these recent decisions as classic instances of liberal judges making law rather than following it.

But the conservative interpretation of employment-at-will itself became part of the law only through judicial activism. The conservative version of employment-at-will was first articulated by courts only in the late 19th century, and it replaced an earlier rule providing that employment contracts that were silent as to the length of the term of employment were presumed to last for a year. Modern courts have changed existing law no more than did the 19th-century courts in their own time.

Some legal experts are currently seeking to create an even more extensive limitation on employer power. They have suggested, for example, that in the absence of an agreement to the contrary, all employees are entitled to at least some defensible explanation before they can be dismissed from their jobs. Others have argued that employees ought at least to have adequate notice before they can be fired. One way to implement this requirement would be to reintroduce the presumption that employ-

ment contracts are meant to last for a year. It is important to recognize that both these interpretations of employment-at-will are as legally defensible today as the earlier positions were when adopted.

There is, in short, no neutral basis on which to choose the proper legal interpretation of employment-at-will. Each interpretation represents a [moral and political] choice about the proper nature of the employment relationship in the United States. None can be justified by reference to statute. Congress or state legislatures could decide the issue, but they haven't. Yet choosing among these different positions is of great significance to the American work force.

* * *

Judges go to great lengths to deny, even to themselves, the extent to which they make law rather than simply apply it. They consider employer power over employees not a matter of choice but a natural and necessary implication of modern workplace organization. They discount the influence of their moral and political views on their decisions by treating their own understanding of the employment relationship as common sense. They think of themselves as constrained by their professional role and by their understanding of legal precedent. For reasons such as these, they are very unlikely to experience their decision-making as a personal decision. The choices involved in selecting legal rules, in other words, are largely made unselfconsciously.

* * *

Questions

1. Is it possible for judges to ignore their personal values in reaching a decision that may have significant effects on society? Should they?

2. What factors might lead one judge to rule that a person cannot be fired because he told the Internal Revenue Service that his employer was filing an inaccurate return, and

–continued

–continuing

another judge to rule that a person can be fired for telling the owner of the business (and not the appropriate government body) that his supervisor was paying bribes to foreign buyers?

3. Should judges or the Congress make legal decisions on social issues such as abortion? Which body would probably make that decision in Japan?

REVIEW AND DISCUSSION QUESTIONS

1. Define the following terms:
   law
   informal rules or principles
   substantive law
   common law
   stare decisis
   constitution
   executive order

2. Compare and contrast the following:
   a. Civil law and criminal law
   b. Felony and misdemeanor
   c. Substantive law and procedural law
   d. Judge-made law and law enacted by a legislature
   e. Social maintenance and conflict resolution functions of law
   f. Formal rules and ethical custom

3. What is white-collar crime? Which of the following are typically white-collar crimes?
   a. Gambling
   b. Traffic offenses
   c. Embezzlement
   d. Littering
   e. Forgery

4. What is the difference between a *preponderance of the evidence* and *beyond a reasonable doubt?*

5. How might the legal environment of business differ between Baskin–Robbins Ice Cream and General Motors? How might it be the same?

Case Questions

6. Consider the following fact situation:
   [T]he crew of an English yacht . . . were cast away in a storm on the high seas . . . and were compelled to put into an open boat belonging to the said yacht. That in this boat they had no supply of water and no supply of food. . . . That on the eighteenth day . . . they . . . suggested that one should be sacrificed to save the rest. . . . That next day . . . they . . . went to the boy

. . . put a knife into his throat and killed him then and there; that the three men fed upon the body . . . of the boy for four days; that on the fourth day after the act had been committed the boat was picked up by a passing vessel, and [they] were rescued, still alive. . . . That they were carried to the port of Falmouth, and committed for trial . . . That if the men had not fed upon the body of the boy they would probably not have survived to be so picked up and rescued, but would within the four days have died of famine. That the boy, being in a much weaker condition, was likely to have died before them. . . . The real question in this case [is] whether killing under the conditions set forth . . . be or be not murder. [*Regina v. Dudley and Stephens*, 14 Queens Bench Division 273 (1884)]

In deciding this case, what factors should the judge take into account?

7. Consider the following fact situation:

In the late 1940s, a chemist for the Allied Chemical Co. invented a compound commonly known as Kepone, used in the manufacture of various insecticides and pesticides.

Virtually all Kepone produced in the United States was exported because the Food and Drug Administration prohibited its use on food crops in the United States in the early 1960s. For several years, several independent companies produced most of the Kepone requirements for Allied. However, in 1966, Allied decided to produce Kepone in its "semi-works" facility at Hopewell, Virginia. Production commenced in that year and continued until 1974.

For reasons that are in dispute, Allied decided to terminate its production of Kepone and "go outside" for its Kepone. On November 30, 1973, Allied executed an agreement with Life Science Products Company (LSP) for the production of Kepone. Under the agreement, Allied agreed to provide LSP with the necessary raw materials that LSP would process and convert into Kepone. Allied agreed to receive the finished product in drums supplied by Allied at LSP's plant. Title to all raw materials and to the Kepone produced by LSP remained at all times with Allied.

The only shareholders of LSP were plaintiffs William P. Moore and Virgil Hundtofte. Prior to his retirement, Moore worked as an inorganic chemist for Allied for twenty-seven years. Hundtofte worked for Allied from 1965 to 1973; for three years, he was plant manager at Allied's Hopewell plant.

Shortly thereafter, workers in LSP began to show signs of serious illness. Medical evidence later established that exposure to Kepone was the cause. The workers then brought suit against LSP, but the company had no assets. Allied was found to be not liable for the injuries, because it was only contracting with LSP for the production of Kepone.

a. What are the principal differences in the legal environment of business between the two companies? Did Allied make strategic use of those differences?

b. Were the societal functions of the law and the legal system served by the decision in this case? Was the judge bound by past precedent?

c. If Allied knew of the dangers associated with Kepone, was it ethical for it to encourage Moore and Hundtofte to undertake this activity?

8. In 1986, Japan experienced 1.7 major crimes per 100,000 persons. The U.S. experienced 7.2 major crimes per 100,000 persons. Without any more information than that contained in the chapter, on what basis could you explain that difference in crime rates?

Policy Questions

9. Does the common law produce "better" law than that which would exist if only the Congress or the state legislatures were allowed to enact law?

10. It is not uncommon for a pro-business presidential administration to cut the enforcement budgets of those regulatory agencies to which it is opposed on ideological grounds. With its enforcement efforts thereby reduced, the laws and regulations of that agency are rendered much less effective.
    a. How might a business benefit from a reduction in the budget of an agency that regulates its activities?
    b. What function of the law and the legal system is the administration working on to reduce the impact of regulation on the business community?
    c. Why would the administration reduce the budget of an administrative agency rather than enact new laws reducing the impact of current regulation?

11. The chapter discusses the functions of the law and the legal system. Are there any serious dysfunctional aspects of law in society? In responding, consider the following circumstances:
    a. An energy crisis.
    b. An individual caught stealing because of hunger (rather than, say, for profit).
    c. The regulation of price fixing through an agreement among small manufacturers.

Ethics Questions

12. Should judges consider the social consequences of their decisions? Suppose the case involves an individual who has committed a hideous crime and the judge is being asked to release him or her on a technicality?

13. Suppose you are the president of a corporation that is planning to build a large production facility. Suppose the product you are going to produce will cause serious injury if not constructed properly. The decision as to where to build the plant has come down to two states. One state's laws, however, are much more favorable to the business. Specifically, the state's laws impose a much lower product testing standard on business than does the other state. Your business, as a consequence, will need to spend far less money testing the product. If the company meets that standard, the state's courts will find it not liable for injuries to consumers due to defective products. You know, however, that if you test at that level, many more people will be injured than if you tested at the level required in the other state. Which state will you select and why?

14. You are the president of a large airline. Competition has increased dramatically, forcing you to consider a variety of cost-cutting alternatives. One such alternative is to declare bankruptcy. Although the company is not in serious financial condition, you know that the court will invalidate your union labor contract. The company could then hire workers at much lower wages and save a considerable amount of money. Should you make strategic use of the law and the legal system in this fashion? Is this within the societal functions discussed in the chapter?

2 Business and the Court System

T HIS chapter provides a general overview of the American court system and discusses how an injured party can gain access to the relief the system can provide. Through normal operations and activities, every business faces the potential for a dispute with its competitors, its suppliers, its customers and the general public. Of those disputes that do arise, the vast majority will be amicably resolved by the parties with no disruption in business relationships or activities. A significant portion of the remainder, however, will require resolution through the court system.

The chapter begins by defining the litigation process, describing the procedural rules that govern it, and considering the important functions it provides society. In discussing the means through which aggrieved parties gain access to the court system, the important procedural requirement of jurisdiction is examined. Within a jurisdictional framework of analysis, the chapter then examines the two interrelated systems making up our American court system: the federal court system and the basic system of courts that exist in each of the fifty states and major territories.

The chapter then provides general background information and insights into the dispute resolution process. It discusses the important role played by judicial officials, the remedies available through litigation, and some important considerations to be undertaken by a business before selecting a court or a court system. The Issue Article at the end of the chapter discusses an issue of growing interest to both businesses and the judicial community: Are plaintiff attorneys unduly influencing judges and ignoring professional ethics?

THE LITIGATORY PROCESS

Civil litigation involves the use of the law and the legal process to resolve disputes among individuals, businesses, and governments. It is a formal process, involving a mechanism provided by the government to allow for a means of impartial dispute resolution. Litigation is intended to provide a means of resolving disputes without the need to resort to acts of violence, coercion, or economic duress.

Rules of Civil Procedure

Virtually from the moment the *plaintiff*—the injured party bringing the action—decides to initiate it, a lawsuit is governed by a detailed set of procedural rules intended to define the issues of law and of fact forming the dispute with the intent to assist in the dispute's resolution. The rules are also intended to control the manner in which the parties to the dispute—the plaintiff and the *defendant* (the party who allegedly injured the plaintiff)—present evidence and arguments in support of their respective positions.

Although the states are free to develop their own procedural rules, most have adopted the *Federal Rules of Civil Procedure*, developed by an advisory committee appointed by the U.S. Supreme Court. The Federal Rules govern all procedural aspects of the litigation process, including the pleadings, discovery, trial procedures, and all relevant motions. It is the avowed purpose of the Federal Rules of Civil Procedure to facilitate the litigatory process:

> These rules . . . shall be construed to secure the just, speedy, and inexpensive determination of every action.

Note that these rules govern only civil litigation; slightly different procedures for resolving disputes are used in criminal and administrative litigation.

The Federal Rules of Civil Procedure are contained in the United States Code, Title 28. In addition to establishing trial procedural rules, Title 28 establishes the organization of the federal courts, judicial officials and agencies, and the important rules governing jurisdiction and venue. This chapter concentrates on jurisdiction, venue, judicial officials, and the organization of the American court system. Chapter 3 examines basic trial procedures and processes as they are dictated by the Federal Rules.

Functions of Litigation

The civil litigation process has three principal functions through which it serves society. First, civil litigation is designed to bring a peaceful resolution to disputes between society members. No orderly society could exist without a formal dispute resolution process. Second, the legal process not only decides who is right and wrong but also provides a mechanism for enforcing its decisions. Those legal mechanisms ensure that corrective measures will be undertaken to remedy wrongs. Finally, the courts not only apply the law of the society but also develop it. As a consequence of our rapidly changing society, the courts are a constant source of important new law reflective of those changes.

THE CONCEPT OF JURISDICTION

The literal meaning of the term *jurisdiction* is the power to speak of the law. A court's jurisdiction defines the limits within which it may declare, expound, administer, or apply the law. The basic limitations imposed upon a court by a constitution and the statutes that created it establish its subject-matter and territorial jurisdictions.

It is the initial responsibility of the plaintiff to decide in which court the dispute is to be resolved. While there are a number of courts from which to choose, the plaintiff's choices will be limited to those courts having appropriate jurisdiction. In bringing the lawsuit, the plaintiff must select a court that has both of the following:

1. Jurisdiction over the subject matter of the dispute.
2. Jurisdiction over either the person of the defendant or the property of the defendant.

If a court should grant relief in a particular situation and it is later determined that jurisdiction was lacking, the judgment of that court will be declared null and void upon appeal. Without appropriate jurisdiction, then, a court cannot exercise its authority. The various types of jurisdiction to be discussed in this chapter are listed and defined in Table 2–1.

SUBJECT-MATTER JURISDICTION

Subject-matter jurisdiction is a constitutional or statutory limitation on the types of disputes a court can resolve. Subject-matter limitations imposed on a court may encompass minimum requirements on the amount in controversy and restrictions on the type of disputes the court can hear. A state statute, for

Table 2–1   An Overview of the Concept of Jurisdiction

Type of Jurisdiction	Definition
Original jurisdiction	Power to take cognizance of a lawsuit at its beginning, try it and pass judgment upon the law and facts.
Appellate jurisdiction	Power to revise or correct the proceedings in a cause already instituted and acted upon by an inferior court.
General jurisdiction	Power to hear all controversies that may be brought before a court.
Jurisdiction over the subject matter	Power to validly affect the thing or issue in dispute.
Jurisdiction over the person	Power to lawfully bind a party to a dispute.
Concurrent jurisdiction	Situation where at least two different courts are each empowered to deal with the subject matter at issue in the dispute.
Exclusive jurisdiction	Power over particular subject matter is provided by statute to a specific court or court system to the exclusion of all others.
Limited or special jurisdiction	Power to hear particular causes, or power that can be exercised only under the limitations and circumstances prescribed by a statute.

example, may restrict the disputes its district courts can hear to civil disputes where the *amount in controversy* is $2,000 or more.

General Organization of the American Court System

The state and federal court systems both have lower courts of *original jurisdiction*, where disputes are initially brought and tried, and courts of *appellate jurisdiction*, where the decisions of a lower court can be taken for review. The courts of original jurisdiction are trial courts in both systems. Generally, one judge will preside over the proceeding. The courts' principal function is to determine the true facts in the dispute and to apply the appropriate law to those facts in rendering a decision. The jury has the responsibility for determining the facts in a dispute; if a jury is not requested, that responsibility is placed on the judge.

Appellate courts are concerned with errors in the application of the law and in the procedural rules applied during the trial court proceeding. Normally three-judge panels review decisions at the intermediate appellate court level, while panels of seven or more are typical in the highest appellate courts. Courts with appellate jurisdiction, in contrast to courts with original jurisdiction, are generally more centrally located, often residing in the region's most populous city. The structure of the American court system is illustrated in Figure 2–1.

Subject-Matter Jurisdiction and the State Court Systems

Although the names and organization differ somewhat from state to state, the state court systems are quite similar in general framework and jurisdictional authorities. Like the federal system, the state court system is basically a three-level court system. In addition, the state court system has several important local courts of special or limited jurisdiction.

State Courts of Original Jurisdiction

Each state court system will have courts of *original jurisdiction*, or trial courts, where disputes are initially brought and tried. These courts usually consist of one set of courts of *general jurisdiction* and several courts of *limited* or *special jurisdiction*. The courts of general jurisdiction have authority to decide almost any kind of dispute and are able to grant virtually every type of relief. In many states the amount in controversy, however, must generally exceed a specific amount, typically two to five thousand dollars.

The state courts of general jurisdiction are usually organized into districts, often comprising several counties. These district courts are called different names in different states, although their jurisdictional limitations are very similar. In the state of Washington, for example, the courts of general jurisdiction are called the Superior Courts. The same courts in Pennsylvania are called the Court of Common Pleas, and in Oregon, the Circuit Courts.

The state courts of limited or special jurisdiction include municipal courts, justice of the peace courts, and other more specialized tribunals (such as probate courts, which handle only those matters related to wills and trusts). The jurisdiction of the municipal courts is similar to that of the district courts except the claims they hear are generally of less economic importance—that is, the plaintiff's claims are often less than the minimum amount in contro-

Figure 2–1   The American Court System

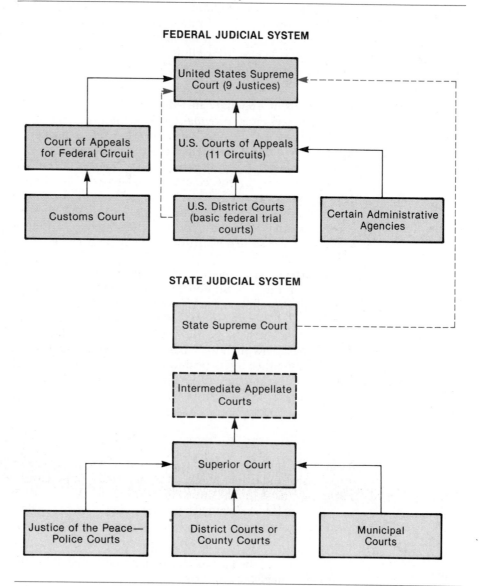

FEDERAL JUDICIAL SYSTEM

STATE JUDICIAL SYSTEM

versy necessary to fall within the jurisdiction of the district court. Litigants who are unsatisfied with the decision of the municipal court can appeal to the district court within the area. On appeal, the parties will get a whole new trial or, in legal terminology, a *trial de novo*.

In addition, many states allow for local *small claims courts*. These courts have very limited jurisdiction, with restrictions imposed on both the subject matter they can hear and the amount in controversy. In Texas, for example, the amount in controversy must not exceed $1,500, and the subject matter is limited to debts and contract disputes. Small claims courts are particularly advantageous for small debts in that the procedure requirements are much less formal and legal representation is not necessary and usually not permitted. In addition, small claims courts are a much more expedient forum than the district courts, with disputes generally being heard within a month or two after their filing date. Although the majority of business disputes involve amounts in excess of that allowed in small claims courts, businesses do use them in attempts to collect smaller unpaid accounts.

State Courts of Appellate Jurisdiction
Every judicial system provides for the review of trial court decisions by a court with *appellate jurisdiction.* Generally a party has the right to appeal any judgment to at least one higher court. When the system contains two levels of appellate courts, appeal usually lies as a matter of right to the first level and at the discretion of the court at the second. The higher appellate court's discretion is generally exercised to review only those cases having legal issues of broad importance to the state and its legal environment. The most common issues reaching the highest court in the state typically involve the validity of a state law, the state constitution, or a federal law as it is affected by a state law.

A party seeking further review from the highest state court may seek review from the U.S. Supreme Court. However, in those cases involving only matters of state law, the state courts are supreme and no appeal to the U.S. Supreme Court is permitted. On the other hand, the U.S. Supreme Court is required to hear the appeal in those cases where the state's highest court has held a federal law invalid or has upheld a state law that has been challenged as violating either a federal law or the Constitution. In other cases, the U.S. Supreme Court may grant the appeal at its discretion. Such review, however, is rarely granted.

Subject-Matter Jurisdiction of the Federal Courts

As dictated by Article III of the Constitution, the federal courts have limited jurisdiction and are empowered to hear only those cases within the judicial power of the United States. According to Article III, Section 2, of the Constitution, federal courts have the judicial power to hear cases involving a *federal question:*

> The judicial Power shall extend to all Cases ... arising under this Constitution, the Laws of the United States, and Treaties made, or which shall be made, under their Authority. ...

They may also hear cases based on the relationship of the parties involved:

> [The judicial Power shall extend] to all Cases affecting Ambassadors, other public Ministers and Consuls ... to Controversies between two or more States;—between a State and Citizens of another State;—between Citizens of different States ... and between a State, or the Citizens thereof, and foreign States, Citizens or Subjects.

Of those cases or controversies where federal jurisdiction is based on the parties involved, most of the litigation is generated by cases in which the United States is a party to the suit or by cases involving citizens of different states. The original purpose for allowing federal jurisdiction when a legal dispute arises between citizens of different states—commonly referred to as federal *diversity-of-citizenship* jurisdiction—was to provide a neutral forum for handling such disputes. It was (and is) generally believed that state courts might be biased in favor of their own citizens and against "strangers" from other states. In addition to showing that the parties are from different states, to establish federal jurisdiction the plaintiff must also show that the claim against the defendant—that is, the *amount in controversy*—is more than $50,000.

Federal Court System

The federal court system was created pursuant to the declaration in Article III of the U.S. Constitution:

> The judicial Power of the United States, shall be vested in one supreme Court and in such inferior Courts [Courts subordinate to the Supreme Court] as the Congress may from time to time ordain and establish.

After a long period of adjustment, the federal court system developed into a three-level system. It currently consists of the U.S. district courts, the U.S. courts of appeals, and the U.S. Supreme Court. Each court has its own distinct role in the process of dispute resolution.

Federal District Courts

The U.S. district courts are the courts of original jurisdiction in the federal system. Most federal question cases originate in these courts. The geographical boundaries of a district court's jurisdiction will not extend across state lines. Thus, each state has at least one federal district court, and the more populated states are divided into two, three, or—as in California, New York, and Texas—four districts. In addition, there are federal district courts in the District of Columbia, Puerto Rico, Guam, and the Virgin Islands.

As a matter of general practice, a single judge will preside over a case heard by the district court. There are, however, situations dictated by statute that require a three-judge panel. As the trial court of the federal system, the U.S. district courts are the only courts in the system that use juries.

Federal Appellate Courts

Federal district court decisions are reviewable in the U.S. courts of appeals. Established in 1891, the U.S. courts of appeals are the intermediate-level appellate courts in the federal system. There are twelve courts of appeals, one for each of the eleven circuits into which the United States is divided and one for the District of Columbia. The division of the states into circuits and the location of the U.S. courts of appeals are presented in Figure 2–2.

As an appellate court, the U.S. courts of appeals can exercise only appellate jurisdiction. With one exception, if either party to the litigation is not satisfied with a federal district court's decision, it has the *right* to appeal to the court of appeals for the circuit in which that district court is located. The Fourth Circuit U.S. Court of Appeals in Richmond, Virginia, for example, will hear appeals only from the federal district courts in the states of Maryland, North Carolina, South Carolina, Virginia, and West Virginia. The

Figure 2–2   The Thirteen Federal Judicial Circuits

one exception is the U.S. government, which does not have the right to appeal a decision involving a criminal dispute.

The U.S. courts of appeals assign three-judge panels to review decisions of the district courts within their circuits. They also review orders of federal administrative agencies when a party believes he has been adversely affected by an action of a regulatory agency. As a practical matter, because it is so difficult to obtain review by the U.S. Supreme Court, the decision of the court of appeals represents the court of final review for most litigants.

Specialized Federal Courts

Although the U.S. Supreme Court, courts of appeals, and district courts are the most visible federal courts, there are a few courts with limited or special jurisdiction of importance within the federal court system. These courts differ from other federal courts in that their jurisdictions are defined in terms of subject matter rather than by geography.

The most prominent of these courts is the Court of Appeals for the Federal Circuit, which was created in 1982. Although its territorial jurisdiction is nationwide, its subject-matter jurisdiction is limited to appeals from the U.S. district courts in patent, trademark, and copyright cases and in cases where the United States is a defendant; appeals from the U.S. Claims Court and U.S.

Court of International Trade; and the review of administrative rulings of the U.S. Patent and Trademark Office. The court sits principally in Washington, D.C., but it may sit anywhere a court of appeals sits. Like the U.S. courts of appeals, cases before the Court of Appeals for the Federal Circuit are presided over by three-judge panels.

Other special jurisdiction courts within the federal system include the U.S. Claims Court, the Temporary Emergency Courts of Appeals, the U.S. Court of International Trade, and the U.S. Court of Military Appeals. Each of these courts has broad territorial jurisdiction but limited or special subject-matter jurisdiction. The Tax Court, despite its name, is an executive agency that reviews decisions of the Internal Revenue Service. Although there have been efforts to include it in the federal judicial system, it is a part of the executive branch of government.

U.S. Supreme Court

The U.S. Supreme Court is the highest court in both the federal system and the country. Created by the Constitution, the U.S. Supreme Court is primarily an appellate review court. Cases reaching this court are generally heard by nine justices, one of whom is the Chief Justice. The term of the Court begins, by law, on the first Monday in October and continues as long as the business of the Court requires. The Court sits in Washington, D.C.

In the exercise of its appellate jurisdiction, the Supreme Court may review appeals from the U.S. district courts, the U.S. courts of appeals, and the highest courts of the states. In rare instances, such as in the case of a dispute between two state governments, the U.S. Supreme Court has *original and exclusive jurisdiction*. Although the Congress may change the court's appellate jurisdiction, it cannot change the Court's original jurisdiction as conferred upon it by the Constitution.

The growing size of the Supreme Court's case load has been a major concern of Congress and the legal community for several decades. During its first century of existence, the Supreme Court decided all cases appealed to it over which it had jurisdiction. When the case load first became too burden-some in the late 1800s, Congress created the U.S. Courts of Appeals. At the same time, Congress gave the Court discretionary review authority over cases in a few specific areas. The vast majority of cases, however, were still able to appeal to the Supreme Court for review as "a matter of right."

Writ of Certiorari. Parties seeking review in those areas where the court had discretion were required to petition the Court for a *writ of certiorari*. In a procedure still used today, the judges review the petition and if fewer than four judges are interested in a full consideration of the matter, *certiorari* is denied. The substantive basis for the denial will be either that the Court agrees with the lower court's decision or that the federal question presented is not substantial enough to warrant the Court's review. With the denial of *certiorari*, the lower court's decision becomes final. If *certiorari* is granted, the Supreme Court issues the writ directing the lower court to send up for review its record in the case. Although it receives thousands of such petitions each term, the Court accepts only a few hundred. The majority of those petitions granted generally involve an issue of constitutional importance, or a conflict between the decisions of two or more U.S. courts of appeals.

Supreme Court Case Selections Act. Despite these early improvements, the Court's case load continued to grow. Congress responded on several occasions by reducing the types of cases subject to a right of appeal. Finally, with the enactment of the Supreme Court Selections Act of 1988, Congress eliminated the last major categories of cases subject to a right of appeal by the Supreme Court. With the exception of certain federal laws authorizing the convening of three-judge panels at the federal district court level (for example, certain cases under the Civil Rights, Voting Rights, and Presidential Election Campaign Fund Acts), all appeals to the Supreme Court are now at the Court's discretion.

Congress and the Supreme Court. There is no formal judicial review of Supreme Court decisions. In some instances, however, the U.S. Supreme Court decision does not end the controversy. Decisions that turn on statutory interpretation, for example, may be *reversed* or *modified* by Congress. Congress may enact legislation specifically intended to invalidate a decision of the Court. In this way, the Congress has the ability to informally review the decisions of the U.S. Supreme Court. In *National Labor Relations Board* v. *Bildisco & Bildisco* (1984), for example, the Supreme Court interpreted the Bankruptcy Act to allow a business filing for Chapter 11 reorganization to cancel the collective bargaining agreement with the union representing its employees. Dissatisfied with the Court's decision, Congress amended the Bankruptcy Act to prohibit the cancellation of collective bargaining agreements in that manner.

TERRITORIAL JURISDICTION

Once the plaintiff has established that the court of her preference has subject-matter jurisdiction, the plaintiff must meet the territorial jurisdiction requirements of that court. A court's jurisdictional authority is generally limited to the territorial boundaries of the state in which it resides. Territorial jurisdiction usually does not become an issue unless the defendant is not a permanent resident of the state in which the plaintiff wishes to bring the action. In such a case, the plaintiff must determine how to bring the defendant—or her property—before the court. Jurisdiction over the person of the defendant—or over property in which she has an interest—is required before the court can enter a personal judgment against a defendant.

Jurisdiction Over the Person

The court's power over the person of the defendant is referred to as *in personam jurisdiction*, which is usually established by serving the defendant with a *summons*—a notice of the lawsuit. After having selected the court, the plaintiff must officially notify the defendant of the action against her by *service of process*, consisting of this summons. The summons will direct the defendant to appear before the court and defend herself against the plaintiff's allegations. If the defendant fails to appear, the court will order that a *default judgment* be entered against her. An example of a summons is presented in Exhibit 2–1.

Exhibit 2–1   A Typical Summons

UNITED STATES DISTRICT COURT
FOR THE
SOUTHERN DISTRICT OF NEW YORK

Civil Action, File Number **80151**

Franco Gori
Plaintiff

vs.   SUMMONS

Tom Eyestone
Defendant

To the above-named Defendant:

You are hereby summoned and required to serve upon *Ronald Johnson,* plaintiff's attorney, whose address is 5450 *Trump Tower New York, New York,* and answer to the complaint which is herewith served upon you, within 20 days after service of this summons upon you, exclusive of the day of service. If you fail to do so, judgment by default will be taken against you for the relief demanded in the complaint.

Frank Hough
Clerk of Court

[Seal of the U.S. District Court]

Dated: 2/5/91

Service of process is traditionally achieved by *personal service.* The summons is physically delivered to the defendant (or left at the defendant's home with a responsible adult) by either the plaintiff, the plaintiff's attorney, a private process server, or a public official such as a sheriff or a U.S. marshal. If the defendant cannot be located, courts will allow the limited use of *substituted service*, such as publication of the pending lawsuit in a newspaper for a certain period of time. The U.S. Supreme Court, however, has repeatedly emphasized that substituted service must be of a kind reasonably calculated to alert the defendant of the action against her.

Jurisdiction Over Out-of-State Defendants

The most obvious method for obtaining in personam jurisdiction over nonresident defendants is to serve them with process while they are within the state. The nonresident defendant need only be passing through the state to be legally served with a summons. The defendant does not have to have intended to enter the state. A business executive, for example, could be on an airplane with no intent of landing in the state. In the event that foul weather or mechanical difficulties forces the plane to land in that state, the individual could be served with summons when departing the plane. Note that although nonresident defendants need not have the intent to return to the state when process is served, they cannot be tricked into coming into the area for the purpose of being served.

It is much more difficult to obtain jurisdiction over nonresident defendants when they have no need or intent to return to the state. The difficulties of obtaining in personam jurisdiction over a nonresident business have been compounded by the fact that a substantial amount of business can be transacted solely by mail or telephone communications across state lines. A business, then, would have no need to have a physical presence in that state.

While it would seem as though the business can avoid lawsuits under such circumstances, there are still several means by which the court can still exert its jurisdiction. If the defendant has committed a wrong within the court's territorial boundaries (such as being involved in an automobile accident) or has done business within the state, the court can exercise jurisdiction under the authority of the state's *long-arm statute*. A long-arm statute is a state law that permits the state's courts to reach beyond the state's boundaries and obtain jurisdiction over nonresident defendants. Long-arm statutes have been subject to considerable scrutiny regarding constitutional due process requirements by the U.S. Supreme Court. An example of a constitutional long-arm statute is provided in Exhibit 2–2.

Jurisdiction Over Out-of-State Corporate Defendants

The long-established differential treatment of corporations in the law of jurisdiction is the result of the hostility that developed towards corporations in their early history. As a consequence, several requirements are imposed upon them that could not be imposed on individuals. As a general rule, a court can exercise jurisdiction over a corporation in any of three situations:

1. The court is located in the state in which the corporation was incorporated.
2. The court is located in the state where the corporation has its headquarters or its main plant.
3. The court is located in a state in which the corporation is doing business.

Exhibit 2–2   Long-Arm Statute: Revised Statutes of Missouri

Sec. 506.500 Actions in which out-of-state service is authorized—jurisdiction of Missouri Courts is applicable, when:

1. Any person or firm, whether or not a citizen or resident to this state, or any corporations, who in person or through an agent does any of the acts enumerated in this section, thereby submits such person, firm, or corporation, and, if an individual, (his/her) personal representative, to the jurisdiction of the courts of this state as to any cause of action arising from the doing of any such acts:

   (1) The transaction of any business within this state;

   (2) The making of any contract within this state;

   (3) The commission of a tortious act within this state;

   (4) The ownership, use, or possession of any real estate situated in this state;

* * *

[2]. Only cases of action arising from acts enumerated in this section may be asserted against a defendant in an action in which jurisdiction over him is based upon this section.

The first situation is the consequence of the corporation being created by the state as an "artificial person." One of the requirements in obtaining a corporate charter from a state is the designation of a registered office within the state. This office is analogous to an individual's residence and is a place where the corporation can always be served in the state.

In the second situation, the corporation is arguably a resident of the state. As a consequence of the corporation's being physically located there, the plaintiff can serve the corporation with process without resorting to any extraordinary measures. Like an individual's residence, the plant or corporate headquarters is effectively the domicile of the corporation within the state.

The third requirement—doing business in the state—has been subjected to close constitutional scrutiny by the U.S. Supreme Court. In attempting to reach out-of-state corporate defendants, states have relied heavily upon long-arm statutes. As Exhibit 2–2 demonstrates, those statutes often list "doing business" within the state as a basis for jurisdiction. According to the Court in *International Shoe Company* v. *Washington* (1945), the state's long-arm statutes must identify certain minimum contacts between the corporation and the state where the suit is being filed in order to qualify as doing business. The case that follows illustrates the extent of constitutional limitations placed on modern long-arm statutes in their efforts to establish jurisdiction over out-of-state corporations.

World-Wide Volkswagen Corp. v. Woodson

United States Supreme Court
444 U.S. 286, 100 S.Ct. 559 (1980)

Case Background. *The Robinsons purchased a new Audi from Seaway Volkswagen, Inc., in New York in 1976. The following year the Robinsons, who had resided in New York, left for a new home in Arizona. As they passed through Oklahoma, the Audi was struck in the rear by another car causing a fire which severely burned Mrs. Robinson. The Robinsons subsequently brought a products liability action in the District Court for Creek County, Oklahoma. The Honorable Judge Charles S. Woodson was the presiding judge.*

The Robinsons claimed their injuries were the result of a defective design in the Audi's fuel system. They named as defendants Audi, Audi's importer Volkswagen of America, its regional distributor World-Wide Volkswagen Corp., and Seaway. World-Wide is incorporated in New York. It distributes vehicles, parts, and accessories, under contract with Volkswagen, to retailers in New York, New Jersey, and Connecticut. Seaway is one of its customers. World-Wide does no business in Oklahoma.

World-Wide made a special appearance to contest the court's exercise of jurisdiction over it. The court rejected World-Wide's claim. World-Wide appealed to the Supreme Court of Oklahoma to restrain the judge from exercising in personam jurisdiction over it. World-Wide again asserted that it did not have minimum contacts with the State of Oklahoma. The Supreme Court disagreed, holding that personal jurisdiction was authorized by the Oklahoma's long-arm statute. World-Wide appealed to the U.S. Supreme Court.

Case Decision. Justice White delivered the opinion of the Court.

* * *

As has long been settled, . . . a state court may exercise personal jurisdiction over a nonresident defendant only so long as there exist "minimum contacts" between the defendant and the forum State. The concept of minimum contacts, in turn, can be seen to perform two related, but distinguishable, functions. It protects the defendant against the burdens of litigating in a distant or inconvenient forum. And it acts to ensure that the States through their courts, do not reach out beyond the limits imposed on them by their status as coequal sovereigns in a federal system.

The protection against inconvenient litigation is typically described in terms of "reasonableness" or "fairness." We have said that the defendant's contacts with the forum State must be such that maintenance of the suit "does not offend 'traditional notions of fair play and substantial justice.' " *International Shoe Co.* v. *Washington*. . . . The relationship between the defendant and the forum must be such that it is "reasonable . . . to require the corporation to defend the particular suit which is brought there." . . . Implicit in this emphasis on reasonableness is the understanding that the burden on the defendant, while always a primary concern, will in an appropriate case be considered in light of other relevant factors, including the forum State's interest in adjudicating the dispute; . . . the plaintiff's interest in obtaining convenient and effective relief, . . . at least when that interest is not adequately protected by the plaintiff's power to choose the forum; . . . the interstate judicial system's interest in obtaining the most efficient resolution of controversies; and the shared interest of the several States in furthering fundamental substantive social policies. . . .

The limits imposed on state jurisdiction . . . have been substantially relaxed over the years. As we noted in *McGee v. International Life Ins. Co.*, . . . this trend is largely attributable to a fundamental transformation in the American economy:

> Today many commercial transactions touch two or more States and may involve parties separated by the full continent. With this increasing nationalization of

commerce has come a great increase in the amount of business conducted by mail across state lines. At the same time modern transportation and communication have made it much less burdensome for a party sued to defend himself in a State where he engages in economic activity.

The historical developments noted in *McGee*, of course, have only accelerated in the generation since that case was decided.

Nevertheless, we have never accepted the proposition that state lines are irrelevant for jurisdictional purposes. . . . [We have] stressed that the Due Process Clause ensures not only fairness, but also the "orderly administration of the laws."

* * *

Thus, the Due Process Clause "does not contemplate that a state may make binding a judgment *in personam* against an individual or corporate defendant with which the state has no contacts, ties, or relations." *International Shoe Co. v. Washington*. . . . Even if the defendant would suffer minimal or no inconvenience from being forced to litigate before the tribunals of another State; even if the forum State has a strong interest in applying its law to the controversy; even if the forum State is the most convenient location for litigation, the Due Process Clause . . . may sometimes act to divest the State of its power to render a valid judgment. . . .

Applying these principles to the case at hand, we find in the record before us a total absence of those affiliating circumstances that are a necessary predicate to any exercise of state-court jurisdiction. Petitioners carry on no activity whatsoever in Oklahoma. They close no sales and perform no services there. They avail themselves of none of the privileges and benefits of Oklahoma law. They solicit no business there either through salespersons or through advertising reasonably calculated to reach the State. Nor does the record show that they regularly sell cars at wholesale or retail to Oklahoma customers or residents or that they indirectly, through others, serve or seek to serve the Oklahoma market. In short, respondents seek to base jurisdiction on one, isolated occurrence and whatever inferences can be drawn therefrom: the fortuitous circumstance that a single Audi automobile, sold in New York to New York residents, happened to suffer an accident while passing through Oklahoma.

It is argued, however, that because an automobile is mobile by its very design and purpose it was "foreseeable" that the Robinsons' Audi would cause injury in Oklahoma. Yet "foreseeability" alone has never been a sufficient benchmark for personal jurisdiction.

* * *

If foreseeability were the criterion, a local California tire retailer could be forced to defend in Pennsylvania when a blowout occurs there . . . a Wisconsin seller of a defective automobile jack could be haled before a distant court for damage caused in New Jersey . . . or a Florida soft-drink concessionaire could be summoned to Alaska to account for injuries happening there. . . .

This is not to say, of course, that foreseeability is wholly irrelevant. But the foreseeability that is critical to due process analysis is not the mere likelihood that a product will find its way into the forum State. Rather, it is that the defendant's conduct and connection with the forum State are such that he should reasonably anticipate being haled into court there. . . . The Due Process Clause, by ensuring the "orderly administration of the laws," gives a degree of predictability to the legal system that allows potential defendants to structure their primary conduct with some minimum assurance as to where that conduct will and will not render them liable to suit.

When a corporation "purposefully avails itself of the privilege of conducting activities within the forum State," . . . it has clear notice that it is subject to suit there, and can act to alleviate the risk of burdensome litigation by procuring insurance, passing the expected costs on to customers, or, if the risks are too great, severing its connection with the State. Hence if the sale of a product of a manufacturer or distributor such as Audi or Volkswagen is not simply an isolated occurrence, but arises from the efforts of the manufacturer or distributor to serve directly or indirectly, the market for its product in other States, it is not unreasonable to subject it to suit in one of those States if its allegedly defective merchandise has there been the source of injury to its owner or to others. The forum State does not exceed its powers under the Due Process Clause if it asserts personal jurisdiction over a corporation that delivers its products into the stream of commerce with the expectation that they will be purchased by consumers in the forum State. . . .

But there is no such or similar basis for Oklahoma jurisdiction over World-Wide. . . . World-Wide's market . . . is limited to dealers in New York, New Jersey, and Connecticut. There is no evidence of record that any automobiles distributed by World-Wide are sold to retail customers outside this tristate area. It is foreseeable that the purchasers of automobiles sold by World-Wide . . . may take them to Oklahoma. But the mere "unilateral activity of those who claim some relationship with a nonresident defendant cannot satisfy the requirement of contact with the forum State."

* * *

Case Holding. *Since World-Wide has no contacts, ties, or relations with the state of Oklahoma, the judgment of the Supreme Court of Oklahoma is reversed.*

Case Questions
1. What contacts did World-Wide have with the state of Oklahoma? What would have established minimum contacts on the part of World-Wide?
2. Why is the Court so concerned about determining whether or not minimum contacts were established?
3. World-Wide is virtually judgment-proof as a consequence of this decision. On similar reasoning, Audi is as well. If the vehicle is truly defective, should the liabilities associated with it be the responsibility of the retailer? Who is better equipped to test for defects? Even if the manufacturer is not directly responsible, are there other important ways it will suffer economically? Will it be sufficient to induce Audi to make changes?

Jurisdiction Based Upon Power Over Property

In those instances where the court is unable to obtain jurisdiction over the person of the defendant, it has limited authority to establish jurisdiction based on the existence of the defendant's property within the state's territorial boundaries. Jurisdiction is established by moving directly against the defendant's property, either *in rem* or *quasi in rem*.

Jurisdiction *in Rem*
In those disputes where property is the matter in controversy, a court in the area in which the property is situated will have jurisdiction to resolve all claims against that property. In these situations, the court is said to have *in rem jurisdiction*. The basis of *in rem* jurisdiction is the presence of the subject property within the territorial jurisdiction of the forum state—the state in which the lawsuit has been initiated. Because of the state's exclusive control

over property within its boundaries, any judgment entered in such action would "bind the world."

Property in an *in rem* proceeding can include tangible property—real estate and personal property—and intangible property—bank accounts and stocks. To satisfy the minimum contacts standard, however, the courts cannot properly exercise jurisdiction over property that has been forcibly and temporarily removed from another state in which it is usually kept.

Quasi in Rem Jurisdiction

Quasi in rem jurisdiction is exercised when the defendant's property within the state is attached (or seized) to secure payment for an unrelated matter. For example, Dr. Roth may owe Jefferson AutoBody for painting her automobile. Unable to collect for that service from Roth, AutoBody decides to bring suit against her. AutoBody, however, is unable to serve Dr. Roth personally with process to establish personal jurisdiction because Dr. Roth is a resident of another state. AutoBody then discovers that Dr. Roth has real estate within the territorial jurisdiction of the court. To gain jurisdiction, AutoBody attaches the property of Dr. Roth for the purpose of satisfying the debt. The basis of the court's jurisdiction is the existence of the property owned by the defendant in the state. In such a situation, the court is said to have *quasi in rem jurisdiction*, and the decision it renders will bind the parties. As in an *in rem* proceeding, the property involved can be either tangible or intangible.

In most states, *quasi in rem* jurisdiction is granted by statute. Usually the statutes permit plaintiffs to reach any assets located in the state. Under the U.S. Supreme Court's ruling in *Shaffer v. Heitner* (1977), however, the assets must satisfy the minimum contacts standard. There must be a reasonable connection between the assets being attached and the state in which they are attached. Thus, assets that are merely moving through the state would not meet the minimum contacts standard and could not be attached in a *quasi in rem* proceeding.

Notification Limitations

In using the defendant's property as a basis for jurisdiction, notice must be given in a manner that actually notifies either the defendant or someone who can adequately represent the defendant. In the past, constructive notice—such as by publication in a newspaper for a specified time period—had been sufficient. In light of the rapid growth in interstate commerce and migration in the past several decades, constructive notice alone has been held to be unconstitutional by the U.S. Supreme Court. Many states have subsequently enacted statutes providing for mail or personal service in cases where jurisdiction is to be based on the property of the defendant.

INTERNATIONAL PERSPECTIVES: INTERNATIONAL SERVICE OF PROCESS

INTERNATIONAL

PERSPECTIVES

The world business community's efforts to internationalize markets has prompted a significant growth in world economic activity, particularly over the past decade. Consumers in the United States, as in most other industrialized economies, now enjoy a selection of products from around the world in virtually every major product field. The increased use of foreign products has also resulted in an increase in products liability actions against foreign manufacturers. In bringing a products liability action against a foreign manufacturer, the first major task confronting the plaintiff's attorney is service of process.

In the interest of creating an "appropriate means to ensure that judicial documents to be served abroad shall be brought to the notice of the addressee in sufficient time," the 1965 Hague Convention sets out specific procedures to be followed. Articles 2 through 6 provide for service through a central authority in each country. Article 8 allows service by way of diplomatic channels. Article 19 allows service by any method of service permitted by the internal law of the country in which service is to be made. Article 21 allows each country to ratify the provisions subject to their particular conditions or objections.

An important issue that has arisen in U.S. courts is whether service of process on international companies may be effected by direct mail. In *Bankston* v. *Toyota Motor Corporation*, the 8th Circuit Court of Appeals held that sending a summons and complaint by registered mail to a defendant in a foreign country is not a method of service of process permitted by the Hague Convention. The court ruled that while the mail system could be used for sending subsequent documents, service on the Japanese defendant must be effected through a central authority with a translation of the documents in Japanese. The practical effect of the court's decision was that the plaintiff had to incur an additional $800 to $1,000 in expenses to serve the Japanese company with process.

VENUE

Not every court that has jurisdiction over the subject matter and the person of the defendant will hear a case. It is also necessary that the lawsuit be brought in a court having proper *venue*. Thus, although every court in the plaintiff's state could assert personal jurisdiction over the defendant if he is within the state's boundaries, state statutes on the basis of fairness typically provide that the lawsuit be brought in a court whose district includes the county in which either the plaintiff or the defendant resides. Similarly, although the defendant might be found in a number of states, he can be sued in a federal court only in a district in which either the defendant or the plaintiff resides or where the dispute arose. Once this additional fairness requirement is met, the court selected will have jurisdiction and venue.

APPLYING THE APPROPRIATE SUBSTANTIVE LAW IN FEDERAL COURT

In civil disputes involving citizens of the same state, the court system to be chosen and the proper body of law to be applied in resolving the dispute is clear. The citizens go to the state court system with proper jurisdiction and venue, and the state common and statutory law are applied. If the dispute involves citizens from more than one state, however, the parties may be confronted with a choice of bringing the suit in a state or a federal court.

Concurrent Jurisdiction and The Concept of Removal

In many instances, a dispute will meet all the jurisdictional requirements of both the state and the federal court systems. The concept of having jurisdiction in both forums for the resolution of a dispute is called *concurrent jurisdiction*. In such situations, the plaintiff may choose either forum.

Removal Jurisdiction

Where there is concurrent jurisdiction, the defendant may choose to litigate in the federal system even if the plaintiff has elected to bring the action in a state court. The federal court's jurisdiction in the event the defendant does choose the federal system is called *removal jurisdiction*. However, an action may be removed by the defendant after it has begun in the state court only if it could have originally been brought in the federal court by the plaintiff. Removal jurisdiction affords the defendant the same option that a plaintiff has in selecting between state and federal forums.

Note also that the federal court may refrain from exercising its removal jurisdiction under the *Abstention Doctrine*. Under the Doctrine, the court may assert that an issue in the case revolves around a question of state law that is uncertain. The court will generally assert that the state court should resolve that question and then either remand the entire case to the state court, or retain jurisdiction but wait until the state court has decided just that particular question.

Shopping for a Court

When concurrent jurisdiction does exist, the plaintiff and his attorney will carefully assess the probabilities of being successful in either a federal or a state court before choosing a court in which to bring the action. If the plaintiff finds that the state court is a considerably more attractive alternative, it may be very tempting to name a state resident as a defendant for the purpose of destroying the federal court's diversity of citizenship jurisdiction. If the plaintiff is successful in convincing the court that the resident defendant is a *real and substantial party* to the action, the case cannot be removed to the federal court—the defendant will not be able to establish diversity of citizenship.

The following removal case received considerable media attention. In an effort to maintain the action in state court, Pete Rose named the Cincinnati Reds and Major League baseball as resident defendants in his complaint. Commissioner Giamatti sought to remove the case to federal court on the basis of diversity of citizenship. In determining whether removal was proper, the federal court carefully examined the resident defendants' interests in the action.

Peter E. Rose v. A. Bartlett Giamatti

U.S. District Court
S.D. Ohio, E.D.
721 F.Supp. 906
(1989)

Case Background. *Plaintiff Peter Edward Rose was the manager of the Cincinnati Reds baseball team. In February 1989, Commissioner of Baseball A. Bartlett Giamatti initiated an investigation regarding allegations that Rose wagered on major league baseball games. Shortly thereafter, Commissioner Giamatti scheduled a hearing concerning the allegations.*

In an effort to prevent Giamatti from conducting the hearing, Rose filed an action in the Court of Common Pleas of Hamilton County, Ohio, seeking a temporary restraining order and preliminary injunction against the pending disciplinary proceedings. Named as defendants in that action were Giamatti, Major League Baseball, and the Cincinnati Reds. The crux of the complaint was Rose's contention that he was being denied the right to a fair hearing on the gambling allegations by Giamatti who he viewed as a biased decision-maker.

Giamatti then filed a notice of removal of the action from the state court to the Federal District Court for the Southern District of Ohio, Western Division at Cincinnati, contending that the federal court had diversity jurisdiction over the action.

Rose responded by filing a motion to remand the action to the Court of Common Pleas of Hamilton County, Ohio, asserting that there was a lack of complete diversity of citizenship between himself and the defendants. According to the motions filed, the plaintiff Rose was a citizen of the State of Ohio, defendant Giamatti was a citizen of the State of New York, defendant Cincinnati Reds was a citizen of the State of Ohio, and defendant Major League Baseball was comprised of the two major professional baseball leagues and their constituent twenty-six major league baseball clubs, at least one of which, the Cincinnati Reds, was a citizen of the State of Ohio.

Case Decision. Judge Holschuh delivered the opinion of the court.

* * *

It is fundamental law that a plaintiff cannot confer jurisdiction upon the federal court, nor prevent a defendant from removing a case to the federal court on diversity grounds, by plaintiff's own determination as to who are proper plaintiffs and defendants to the action. . . . In considering whether diversity of citizenship exists . . . , certain doctrines are well established.

First, a plaintiff cannot defeat a defendant's right of removal on the basis of diversity of citizenship by the "fraudulent joinder" of a non-diverse defendant against whom the plaintiff has no real cause of action. . . . The joinder of a resident defendant against whom no cause of action is stated is a patent sham, and though a cause of action be stated, the joinder is similarly fraudulent if in fact no cause of action exists.

* * *

Second, it is also a long-established doctrine that a federal court, in its determination of whether there is diversity of citizenship between the parties, must disregard nominal or formal parties to the action and determine jurisdiction based only upon the citizenship of the real parties to the controversy. . . . A real party in interest defendant is one who, by the substantive law, has the duty sought to be enforced or enjoined. In contrast to a "real party in interest," a formal or nominal party is one who, in a genuine legal sense, has no interest in the result of the suit.

The Court turns, then, to the realities of the record in this case to determine the real parties to this controversy.

1. Defendant Giamatti It is apparent from the complaint that the actual controversy in this case is between Rose and Commissioner Giamatti. The complaint is replete with allegations of wrongdoing on the part of Giamatti. For example, Rose asserts that Giamatti and investigators hired by him attempted to bolster the credibility of witnesses against Rose, prejudged the truthfulness of certain testimony given as a part of the investigation, acted unreasonably in demanding information from Rose, improperly threatened him with refusing to cooperate in the investigation, requested that Rose step aside as the Reds' Field Manager without revealing to him the evidence which has been compiled concerning his alleged gambling activities, and otherwise acted improperly in violation of Giamatti's alleged duty to provide Rose with a fair and impartial hearing with respect to the allegations against him. The ultimate purpose of the action is to prevent Giamatti from conducting any hearing because of his alleged improper conduct and bias against Rose.

* * *

2. The Cincinnati Reds   Just as it is clear that the crux of the present controversy is between Rose and Giamatti, it is equally clear that, in reality, there is no controversy between Rose and the Cincinnati Reds.

* * *

It is undeniable that the Cincinnati Reds has, as a practical matter, an interest in the outcome of these proceedings, but not in the legal sense that requires its joinder as a defendant in this action. Rose's complaint specifically alleges that there has been no wrongdoing on the part of the Cincinnati Reds, and the Reds specifically states that it will comply with the terms and conditions of its contract with Rose; there is no real controversy between these parties. The Court concludes that, for the purpose of determining diversity of citizenship, the defendant Cincinnati Reds was, in a legal sense, fraudulently joined as a defendant and that it is, at best, a nominal party in this action. Consequently, the citizenship of the Cincinnati Reds as a defendant may be disregarded for the purpose of determining whether there is complete diversity of citizenship among the parties to this action. In addition to being sued individually as a defendant, the Cincinnati Reds, for the purpose of this analysis of diversity of citizenship, is also a member of Major League Baseball, and the Court turns next to the consideration of that named defendant.

3. Major League Baseball   If Major League Baseball were a typical unincorporated association, its jurisdictional status would be more easily determined. The reality, however, is that Major League Baseball is a unique organization.

* * *

The Commissioner's jurisdiction under the Major League Agreement to investigate violations of Major League Rules, or any activity he believes is "not in the best interests" of baseball, is exclusive. The major leagues and the twenty-six major league clubs have absolutely no control over such an investigation or the manner in which the Commissioner conducts it. Rose does not challenge any provision of the Major League Agreement or the Major League Rules, including the rule prohibiting wagering on major league baseball games, nor does he challenge the Commissioner's authority to promulgate his own rules of procedure dealing with investigations of suspected violations of the Major League Rules. What Rose challenges is Commissioner Giamatti's conduct in the investigation and disciplinary proceedings in his particular case. In short, Rose's controversy is not with Major League Baseball, but is with the office of the Commissioner of Baseball for the Commissioner's alleged failure to follow his own procedural rules in conducting the investigation of Rose's alleged gambling activities. Clearly, complete relief can be afforded with regard to the primary relief sought in the complaint— preventing Commissioner Giamatti from conducting a disciplinary hearing— without the need for any order against Major League Baseball or its constituent major league professional baseball clubs.

* * *

Case Holding.   *The action was properly removable to federal court from the Court of Common Pleas of Hamilton County, Ohio. Plaintiff Rose's motion to remand was denied. The controversy in this case is between plaintiff Rose and defendant Giamatti. The Cincinnati Reds and Major League Baseball, are, at best, nominal parties in this controversy, and, consequently, their citizenship may be disregarded for diversity purposes.*

Case Questions.

1. Why did Rose name Major League Baseball and the Cincinnati Reds as defendants in this action?
2. Why would Rose want this case decided in state court rather than in federal court? Weren't both courts located in the city of Cincinnati?

The Erie Doctrine

If a federal court is chosen, the central question becomes, Which body of substantive law does the court apply to resolve the dispute—federal law or the law of the state?

In its decision in *Swift* v. *Tyson* (1842), the U.S. Supreme Court held that federal courts need apply only the statutory law of the state; the federal courts were free to follow their own common law. As a consequence, a state court and a federal court could reach different conclusions in resolving the same dispute.

In the landmark case *Erie* v. *Tompkins*, the Supreme Court overturned *Swift* v. *Tyson* and held that except in matters governed by the federal Constitution or by acts of Congress, the law to be applied in federal courts is the law of the state. This means that federal judges must apply both a state's common law as well as its statutory law when they decide diversity-of-citizenship cases. An individual bringing a lawsuit in a federal court can expect that the appropriate law of the state will be applied in determining the rights and liabilities of the parties to the dispute, although the federal court will follow federal procedural law.

Erie Railroad Co. v. Tompkins
United States Supreme Court
304 U.S. 64, 58 S.Ct. 817(1938)

Case Background. *Tompkins was injured on "a dark night" by a passing freight train owned by Erie Railroad Company. Tompkins was injured by something protruding from the train as he stood next to the tracks. He claimed the accident occurred through negligence in the operation or maintenance of the train. Tompkins was a citizen of Pennsylvania, and Erie was a company incorporated in New York. Tompkins brought suit in the federal district court for southern New York.*

Erie argued that the court, in deciding the case, should apply the law of Pennsylvania. Under Pennsylvania common law, Tompkins would be a trespasser and Erie would therefore not be liable for his injuries. Tompkins argued that because no statute existed on the subject in Pennsylvania, federal common law should apply. Under federal common law, that had evolved since Swift, Erie would be liable for Tompkins's injuries.

The trial court agreed with Tompkins, and the jury awarded him thirty thousand dollars. The decision was affirmed by the circuit court of appeals. Erie sought review of the case by the U.S. Supreme Court, which granted certiorari. The issue before the Court is whether or not the federal court was free to disregard Pennsylvania law.

Case Decision. Mr. Justice Brandeis delivered the opinion of the Court.
The question for decision is whether the oft-challenged doctrine of Swift v. Tyson shall now be disapproved.

* * *

First. *Swift* v. *Tyson*, held that federal courts exercising jurisdiction on the ground of diversity of citizenship need not, in matters of general jurisprudence, apply the unwritten law [the common law or the "general law"] of the State as declared by its highest court; that they are free to exercise an independent judgment as to what the common law of the State is—or should be. . . .

* * *

Second. Experience in applying the doctrine of *Swift* v. *Tyson*, had revealed its defects, political and social; and the benefits expected to flow from the rule did not accrue. Persistence of state courts in their own opinions on questions of common law prevented uniformity; and the impossibility of discovering a satisfactory line of demarcation between the province of general law and that of local law developed a new well of uncertainties.

On the other hand, the mischievous results of the doctrine had become apparent. Diversity of citizenship jurisdiction was conferred in order to prevent apprehended discrimination in state courts against those not citizens of the State. *Swift* v. *Tyson* introduced grave discrimination by non-citizens against citizens. It made rights enjoyed under the unwritten "general law" vary according to whether enforcement was sought in the state or in the federal court; and the privilege of selecting the court in which the right should be determined was conferred upon the non-citizen. Thus, the doctrine rendered impossible equal protection of the law. In attempting to promote uniformity of law throughout the United States, the doctrine had prevented uniformity in the administration of the law of the State.

* * *

The injustice and confusion incident to the doctrine of *Swift* v. *Tyson* have been repeatedly urged as reasons for abolishing or limiting diversity of citizenship jurisdiction. . . .

Third. Except in matters governed by the Federal Constitution or by Acts of Congress, the law to be applied in any case is the law of the State. And whether the law of the State shall be declared by its Legislature in a statute or by its highest court in a decision is not a matter of federal concern. There is no federal general common law. Congress has no power to declare substantive rules of common law applicable in a State whether they be local in their nature or "general," be they commercial law or a part of the law of torts. And no clause in the Constitution purports to confer such a power upon the federal courts.

* * *

We . . . declare that in applying the doctrine this Court and the lower courts have invaded rights which in our opinion are reserved by the Constitution to the several States.

Fourth. The defendant contended that by the common law of Pennsylvania as declared by its highest court in *Falchetti* v. *Pennsylvania R. Co.*, the only duty owed to the plaintiff was to refrain from wilful or wanton injury. The plaintiff denied that such is the Pennsylvania law. In support of their respective contentions the parties discussed and cited many decisions of the Supreme Court of the State. The Circuit Court of Appeals ruled that the question of liability is one of general law; and on that ground declined to decide the issue of state law. As we hold this was error, the judgment is reversed and the case remanded to it for further proceedings in conformity with our opinion.

Reversed.

Case Holding. *The decisions of the trial court and the circuit court of appeals were reversed. Pennsylvania common law should be applied. The concept of federal common law in diversity-of-citizenship cases was dismissed. Tompkins was a trespasser, and Erie was not liable for his injuries.*

Case Questions

1. Why had the decision in *Swift* v. *Tyson* prevented uniformity in the administration of the law of the state?
2. Which law—*Swift* v. *Tyson* or *Erie* v. *Tompkins*—is more beneficial to the plaintiff?
3. After *Erie,* which court's procedural law must be applied in a diversity-of-citizenship case?

APPLYING THE APPROPRIATE SUBSTANTIVE LAW IN STATE COURT

When a dispute is brought in a state court involving incidents that have taken place in more than one state or entirely in a different state, a conflict-of-law problem may arise. The state court will have to determine if its own substantive law or the substantive law of another state is to apply. To aid courts in such situations, the states have developed *conflict-of-law* rules. Some general conflict-of-law rules most affecting businesses are presented in Table 2–2.

Conflict-of-Law

The conflict-of-law rules vary according to the nature of the dispute. In contracts cases, for example, the general rule is that the law of the state in which the contract was made determines the interpretation of the contract. In tort cases, for several decades the traditional rule was that the substantive law of the place where the tort occurred is to apply. Many states, however, have reconsidered the traditional tort rule, replacing it with a policy-based approach to the conflict-of-law question. Under the policy-based approach, the courts apply the law of the state having the most significant relationship to the dispute.

Table 2–2 Conflict of Law Principles Most Frequently Affecting Business

Substantive Law Issue	State Whose Law Is to Apply
1. Contract disagreement	State in which contract was formed or State in which contract was to be performed or State most significantly in contact with the contract or State designated in the contract
2. Liability issues arising from injury	State in which injury occurred or State having most significant relationship to the case
3. Workers' compensation	State of employment or State in which injury occurred

As a consequence, the state in which the tort occurred will not necessarily be the controlling state law.

In the following case, the Connecticut Supreme Court battled the decision to reject the traditional tort rule and replace it with a policy-based rule. The case provides valuable insights into both the conflict-of-law question and the process courts go through in changing established precedent.

O'Connor v. O'Connor

**Supreme Court of Connecticut
201 Conn. 632,
519 A.2d 13 (1986)**

Case Background. *Roseann O'Connor, the plaintiff was injured in a one-car automobile accident. The accident occurred in Quebec, Canada. At the time of the accident, Brian O'Connor, the defendant, was the driver and Roseann, his wife, was the sole passenger. Both parties are residents of the state of Connecticut. To obtain an insurance payment, Roseann brought an action in Connecticut against Brian alleging she had suffered serious and permanent injuries as a consequence of his negligent operation of the automobile. Roseann's action was brought under the laws of Connecticut. Brian moved to strike the complaint on the grounds that the applicable law was the law of Quebec. The law of Quebec does not allow private suits for damages.*

The trial court granted the motion to strike on the grounds that Connecticut conflict-of-law rules provide that in accident cases the state or province in which the accident occurred is the applicable law. On appeal, the Connecticut Appellate Court agreed, considering itself bound by Connecticut's past adherence to the location of the accident rule (lex loci delicti). Roseann appealed to the Connecticut Supreme Court urging it to reconsider the lex loci rule.

Case Decision. Chief Justice Peters delivered the opinion of the Court.

* * *

I

This court has traditionally adhered to the doctrine that the substantive rights and obligations arising out of a tort controversy are determined by the law of the place of injury, or lex loci delicti.

* * *

II

We have consistently held that "a court should not overrule its earlier decisions unless the most cogent reasons and inescapable logic requires it." We have also recognized, however, that "(p)rinciples of law which serve one generation well may, by reason of changing conditions, deserve a later one," and that "(e)xperience can and often does demonstrate that a rule, once believed sound, needs modification to serve justice better." . . . Accordingly, we now undertake to analyze the policies and principles underlying the doctrine of lex loci delicti, as a preliminary step to determining whether "cogent reasons and inescapable logic" demand that we abandon the doctrine under the circumstances of the present case.

* * *

[W]e now consider the principal reasons advanced for [the] retention [of the] lex loci delicti rule[.] These are: (1) the desirability of allowing the legislature to alter established choice of law doctrines; (2) stare decisis; (3) the certainty and predictability of result afforded by a categorical choice of law rule and the concomitant ease of applying such a rule; and (4) the prevention of parochial applications of forum law in controversies involving foreign jurisdictions. . . .

Because choice of law is a matter of "broad public policy," the defendant argues that it is the province of the legislature, and not the courts, to make doctrinal changes in established law. . . . We disagree. The lex loci doctrine is the creation of jurists and scholars, not legislators. . . . The legislature of course retains plenary authority, subject to constitutional mandates, to formulate statutory choice of law rules. Until the legislature chooses to act, however, this court has an independent responsibility to modernize rules of law that have traditionally reposed with the judiciary. . . .

Regarding stare decisis, the second argument in favor of retaining lex loci, we have already noted that, while courts should not overrule established precedent except in compelling circumstances, the force of precedent will not hinder our rejection of a rule whose application no longer serves the ends of justice. The arguments for adherence to precedent are least compelling . . . when in its origin it was the product of institutions or conditions which have gained a new significance or development with the progress of the years."

* * *

The third argument in favor of retention of the doctrine of lex loci is that it imparts certainty, predictability, and ease of application to choice of law rules. We do not underestimate these characteristics. "Simplicity in law is a virtue. Judicial efficiency often depends upon it." The virtue of simplicity must, however, be balanced against the vice of arbitrary and inflexible application of a rigid rule. "Ease of determining applicable law and uniformity of rules of decision . . . must be subordinated to the objective of proper choice of law in conflict cases, i.e., to determine the law that most appropriately applies to the issue involved. . . ." In the present case, application of the lex loci delicti doctrine makes determination of the governing law turn upon a purely fortuitous circumstance: the geographical location of the parties' automobile at the time the accident occurred. Choice of law must not be rendered a matter of happenstance, in which the respective interests of the parties and the concerned jurisdictions receive only coincidental consideration.

We note, furthermore, that lex loci's arguable advantages of uniformity and predictability have been undermined by its widespread rejection by courts and scholars. . . .

* * *

We now consider the fourth principal argument in favor of retention of lex loci, that application of the doctrine prevents forum courts from exercising parochial favoritism. Without lex loci, there is a risk that the forum will not take seriously the foreign jurisdiction's legitimate interest in the controversy. How seriously this risk is viewed depends upon an assessment of the available alternatives. . . . Existing case law in other jurisdictions demonstrates that conflicts principles need not depend solely upon lex loci to assure proper deference to the legitimate claims of foreign law. . . .

We are, therefore, persuaded that the time has come for the law in this state to abandon categorical allegiance to the doctrine of lex loci delicti in tort actions. Lex loci has lost its theoretical underpinnings. Its formerly broad base of support has suffered erosion. . . . A majority of the courts that have abandoned lex loci have adopted the principles of the Restatement Second as representing the most comprehensive and equitably balanced approach to conflict of laws. It is therefore our conclusion that we too should incorporate the guidelines of the Restatement as the governing principles for those cases in which application of the doctrine of lex loci would produce an arbitrary, irrational result.

III

We turn now to an examination of the relevant provisions of the Restatement Second of Conflict of Laws in the context of the dispute presently before us. . . .

[T]he Restatement Second provides that "[t]he rights and liabilities of the parties with respect to an issue are determined by the local law of the state which has the most significant relationship to the occurrence and the parties. . . .

Contacts to be taken into account . . . to determine the law applicable to an issue include: (a) the place where the injury occurred, (b) the place where the conduct causing the injury occurred, (c) the domicile, residence, nationality, place of incorporation and place of business of the parties, and (d) the place where the relationship, if any, between the parties is centered. These contacts are to be evaluated according to their relative importance with respect to the particular issue."

In the circumstances of the present case, because the plaintiff was injured in Quebec and the tortious conduct occurred there, (a) and (b) weigh in favor of applying Quebec law. Because both parties are Connecticut domiciliaries and their relationship is centered here, (c) and (d) indicate that Connecticut law should be applied. To resolve this potential standoff, we need to recall that it is the significance, and not the number, of contacts that determines the outcome of the choice of law inquiry under the Restatement approach. . . .

In order to apply the guidelines to the circumstances of the present case, we must, therefore, turn our attention once more to the particular issue whose disparate resolution by two relevant jurisdictions gives rise to the conflict of laws. Specifically, we must analyze the respective policies and interests of Quebec, the place of injury, and Connecticut, the forum state, with respect to the issue of whether the plaintiff should be allowed to recover damages from the defendant in a private cause of action premised on the defendant's negligent operation of an automobile.

We first consider the policies and interests of Quebec in this regard. Quebec, as the place of injury, has an obvious interest in applying its standards of conduct to govern the liability, both civil and criminal, of persons who use its highways.

In the present case, however, the relevant Quebec law expresses no interest in regulating the conduct of the defendant, but rather limits the liability exposure to which his conduct subjects him. . . . They are concerned not with how people should behave but with how survivors should be compensated.

The policies behind Quebec's no-fault rule would not be substantially furthered by application of Quebec law in the circumstances of the present case.

* * *

The foregoing analysis leads us to conclude that Quebec's status as the place of injury is not a significant contact for purposes of our choice of law inquiry in this case. Accordingly, since Quebec has no other contacts with this litigation, we hold that Quebec has no interest in applying its no-fault act to bar the plaintiff's action.

* * *

Connecticut has a significant interest in this litigation because both the plaintiff and the defendant are, and were at the time of the accident, Connecticut domiciliaries. Consequently, to the extent that they might have anticipated being involved in an automobile accident, they could reasonably have expected to be subject to the provisions of Connecticut's no-fault act. More importantly, however, Connecticut has a strong interest in assuring that the plaintiff may avail herself of the full scope of remedies for tortious conduct that Connecticut law affords. . . .

Case Holding. *The court reversed the judgment of the appellate court, upholding the trial court's granting of the motion to strike the plaintiff's complaint. It directed that the case be remanded to the trial court for further proceedings consistent with this opinion, which changed the state's rule on conflict-of-laws.*

Case Questions

1. What are the principal differences between lex loci and the policy analysis approach forwarded by the court?
2. What important factors did the court consider in overruling the long-standing precedent in the case?
3. Has this trend in the law reduced the level of certainty available on this important issue?

JUDICIAL OFFICIALS AND THEIR SELECTION

Judges in the United States in the overwhelming majority of cases are attorneys by professional training. It is their responsibility to interpret the rules that govern the legal proceedings over which they preside. The overall performance of our legal system depends to a great extent upon the character and competence of our judges.

Functions of the Judge in the Legal Process

In serving as the principal link between law and society, the judge provides several important functions. Most obviously, the judge renders decisions to resolve disputes between society members. In undertaking this function, the judge must apply the law evenly and consistently and not be swayed by public opinion (although, as in *O'Connor,* they are often affected by public policy concerns). Acting in the role of a legal administrator, a judge facilitates the efforts of the disputing parties to abstract the full benefits from our adversarial system of justice. In providing this function, the judge will not interfere unreasonably in the legal proceeding.

The judge also serves to uphold the dignity of the law and the legal system. It is the judge's responsibility to uphold the legal system's reputation for honesty and impartiality. Also, the judge must serve to maintain and enhance the legal culture of the society by maintaining respect for the law and the legal system.

Federal Judicial Officials

Federal judges are nominated by the President and confirmed by a majority vote in the U.S. Senate. Guaranteed by the Constitution the right to serve "during good behavior," federal judges enjoy a secure lifetime position. Constitutionally, only impeachment by Congress for treason, bribery, or other high crimes and misdemeanors can remove a federal judge from office. Specifically, a judge must first be impeached by the House of Representatives, and brought to trial before and convicted by a two-thirds majority of the Senate. In practice, this legislative impeachment process has proven to be both intricate and time-consuming.

Prior to 1986, only ten federal judges had ever been impeached by the House of Representatives, and only four were convicted and removed from office by the Senate. Since then, three judges have been removed from office through this process. Among other offenses, the judges were alleged to have committed perjury, tax evasion, bribery, conspiracy, racketeering, and obstruction of justice. Not surprisingly, the sudden increase in the number of removals, the length of time required to complete the formal procedure for removing judges, and the fact that the judges were able to continue to draw their salaries until finally removed from office by the Senate have created considerable controversy within the judicial community.

In part, the uninterrupted salaries enjoyed by the impeached judges were the consequence of concerns specifically addressed by the writers of the Constitution. While Congress may change the structure of the federal court system, it may not reduce a judge's salary or term of office once an appointment has been made. The writers of the Constitution gave federal judges job security because they wanted to guarantee that judges would be independent, nonpartisan, and free from the pressure of politics. In reaching decisions, judges must be independent decision–makers protected from the political process in the event of a controversial dispute.

State Judicial Officials

Judges at the state level are chosen by a variety of methods. They are elected, appointed, or chosen by a method that mixes the election and appointment processes. In several of the states with the mixed system, the state bar association has a committee to recommend qualified attorneys for the bench. The governor then appoints a judge from its list. The judge selected then serves until the next election, at which time the public is asked to vote *for* or *against* him. This system for selecting judges is referred to as the *Missouri System*.

In contrast to the position enjoyed by federal judges, most state judges serve for a fixed term regardless of whether they are appointed or elected. Those terms range from one year for judges in several midwestern states to a fourteen-year term for judges in New York. Although Massachusetts and New Hampshire appoint judges to serve until they reach age seventy, only Rhode Island provides a lifetime term of office.

Some observers claim that appointed judges are of higher quality than elected judges. On the other hand, others claim that elected judges work harder than appointed judges. No clear evidence exists, however, that convincingly demonstrates that one approach is more effective than another. Table 2–3 shows the selection process employed for judges to the highest court in each of the states.

Judicial Immunity

Under the established common law *doctrine of judicial immunity,* a judge is absolutely immune from suit for damages for judicial acts taken within or even in excess of his or her jurisdiction. This immunity applies even when the judge acts maliciously. There are several justifications for the doctrine. It is generally asserted that in the absence of the doctrine, judges would face undue influence on their judicial decisions. As a consequence, judges would lose their ability to be independent decision makers. In addition, it is asserted that judicial immunity protects judges from the burden of defending retaliatory suits by unsuccessful litigants. By protecting judges from such suits, the doctrine of judicial immunity serves to bring disputes and the litigation process to a close.

Table 2–3   Selection of State Supreme Court Judges

Selection Process	Number	States
Appointment Systems		
Merit selection by committee	20	Alaska, Arizona, Colorado, Delaware, Florida, Hawaii, Indiana, Iowa, Kansas, Maryland, Massachusetts, Missouri, Nebraska, New York, Oklahoma, South Dakota, Texas, Utah, Vermont, Wyoming
Government appointment	8	California, Connecticut, Maine, New Hampshire, New Jersey, Rhode Island, South Carolina, Virginia
Election Systems		
Nonpartisan election	13	Georgia, Idaho, Kentucky, Louisiana, Michigan, Minnesota, Montana, Nevada, North Dakota, Ohio, Oregon, Washington, Wisconsin
Partisan election	9	Alabama, Arkansas, Illinois, Mississippi, New Mexico, North Carolina, Pennsylvania, Tennessee, West Virginia

Source: American Judicature Society, Chicago, IL 60606.

Limitations on the Doctrine

The U.S. Supreme Court issued a novel opinion in 1984 involving the doctrine of judicial immunity. In *Pulliam* v. *Allen,* the Court held 5–4 that there is no absolute judicial immunity for state judges who commit judicial errors. *Pulliam* was the first U.S. Supreme Court case to reject absolute judicial immunity by holding a judge accountable at civil law for her conduct. The case demonstrates that although judges are immune from suits for damages, they may be sued for equitable relief and held personally liable for money judgments in the form of court costs and attorney's fees. After the *Pulliam* decision, the American Bar Association (ABA) developed an insurance plan for judges to defray liability costs. For those judges participating, the premium is nearly $1,000 a year. In addition, several states and the District of Columbia have developed master policies to provide insurance coverage for their judges.

Several prominent legal scholars argue that the loss of absolute judicial immunity constitutes a loss of judicial independence. They argue that a judge could conceivably structure his or her ruling to avoid being sued—possibly to the detriment of one of the parties to the action. In response to these and other concerns, the ABA is working with Congress to enact legislation that would restore absolute judicial immunity.

REMEDIES AVAILABLE IN CIVIL LITIGATION

Most civil disputes are settled outside the court system. The expense of a lawsuit, the delay before judicial relief can be obtained, and concerns about how the dispute will be resolved by the court encourage litigants to settle before trial. If the dispute does go to trial, however, the individuals involved are seeking resolution of the dispute in the form of a specific remedy provided by the court. Within the American court system, the remedies awarded by courts in civil disputes are classified as either *equitable remedies* or *monetary damages*. The remedies available in civil litigation are summarized in Figure 2–3.

Monetary Damages

A monetary damage remedy is provided when the court finds that some specific legal right has been violated and has resulted in an injury. The monetary damage awards most frequently imposed by the courts include compensatory, punitive, and nominal damages. More recently, as disputes have become more and more complex and the expertise for assessing damages has improved and become more reliable, the courts have developed important novel approaches to providing adequate compensation to injured parties.

Compensatory Damages

The intent of *compensatory damages* is to provide the injured parties with sufficient compensation to restore them to the economic position they were in before the injury. It is the most common form of monetary damages. Compensatory damages may be awarded for loss of time and money, pain and suffering, injury to reputation, and mental anguish. Suppose Album Shipping contracts to sell tomato paste to Camerican International for $2,000. In the event that Album does not deliver, and Camerican must buy it from another source for $2,500, Camerican is entitled to $500 in compensatory damages from Album. It has suffered a net loss of $500 in the purchase.

Punitive Damages

In those situations in which the wrongdoer's actions were particularly reprehensible, or in situations in which the defendant's conduct was willful or malicious, the court may award the injured party *punitive* or *exemplary damages* in addition to compensatory damages. The court's intent in awarding punitive damages is to punish the wrongdoer and discourage others from similar conduct in the future. Punitive damages have become a major concern for businesses. Punitive damages in product liability cases, for example, were upheld on appeal just three times in the first 200 years of U.S. history; they now have become commonplace.

Nominal Damages

In the event the plaintiff is found to have suffered a technical injury but has not suffered actual damages to his person or property (or the damages are considered trivial by the court), the court may award *nominal damages*. The amount of recovery to the injured party will often be as little as one dollar plus court costs. Note, however, that while the damages imposed may be trivial, the court costs can still be very significant.

In a case brought by the now-defunct United States Football League (USFL) against the National Football League (NFL), a federal court found that the NFL had violated antitrust laws. The court found the damages suffered by the USFL as a consequence were trivial and awarded the USFL one dollar in nominal damages. The NFL owner's relief with the decision was shortlived,

Figure 2–3   Equitable Remedies and Monetary Damages

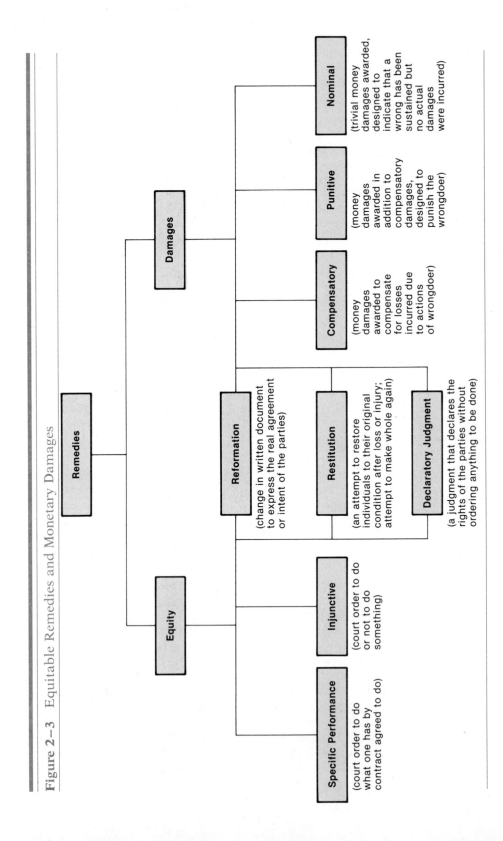

however, as the judge awarded attorneys' fees and court costs to the USFL in excess of $6 million. Furthermore, the court was able to establish a precedent that technical injuries such as those caused by the NFL's activities will be recognized at law, thereby upholding the importance of government regulations and other legal obligations.

Novel Remedies

The courts are creating several new categories of monetary damages in particular situations. Under contract law, for example, some courts have moved to impose so-called *expectancy damages* rather than compensatory damages. Expectancy damages are awarded to an injured party when the losses—including lost profit—can be estimated with certainty. The injured party is placed in the economic position she would have enjoyed had the contract been fully performed. Other monetary damage remedies available under contract law are discussed in Chapter 9.

The most novel remedy under tort law has been the use of the so-called market-share liability. Under this remedy, the parties have been injured by a dangerous product that was manufactured by several companies. However, the parties are unable to determine the specific manufacturer's product that caused their injury. Under this remedy, the court will impose monetary damages on all the manufacturers based on each company's share of the market for the product. The smaller companies will pay less, and the larger companies will pay more.

Equitable Remedies

Equitable remedies are not necessarily based on any clearly established legal right. The dispute generally involves some question of morality, justice, or conscience, where monetary damages either will not provide the injured party with adequate relief, or simply cannot be determined. Equitable remedies have a unique and interesting origin; they are one of the curious features of our legal history.

Chapter 1 discussed the English origin of our common law—the King's Courts called *Curia Regis*. Medieval England developed another, almost entirely different system of courts, with its own procedures and rules. Called the Chancery Courts, the rules and procedures made up the system called *equity.* Developed by the Chancellor—one of the king's highest officers, a clergyman, and possessing a fuller understanding of church or canon law and not the common law—these courts were able to provide relief not available in the common-law courts. For example, only the Chancery Courts could order a defendant to stop doing a specified activity that was injuring the plaintiff. On the other hand, only the common-law courts could award monetary damages.

While each system of courts was, by itself, somewhat inadequate, together they were very effective. In the United States, these two court systems coexisted until the nineteenth century when most jurisdictions reformed their procedures and merged law and equity into one system. Only the state of Delaware now maintains any kind of formal distinction. Still, many traces of past law and equity procedures remain. In most jurisdictions, for example, a jury may not be used to determine questions of equity.

In resolving disputes in equity, courts are allowed to be much more creative in granting relief than in disputes calling for monetary judgments. Generally speaking, the courts can order specific performance or impose an injunction.

Specific Performance

In equity, the courts can order *specific performance* as a remedy and require the offending party to do what she had originally promised to do. This remedy is frequently applied under the law of contracts in those circumstances where monetary damages would not adequately compensate the wronged party or where the subject matter is unique. If the owner of a particular tract of land enters into a contract for the sale of that land, and then later changes her mind, the courts will often order the owner to perform as promised. This is particularly the case when the subject matter is land or rare properties, such as art, antiques, or even baseball cards, because such items are considered unique and irreplaceable.

Injunction

An *injunction* is a court order directing a person to do something, not to do something, or to stop doing something. Injunctions may be temporary or permanent. In ordering a temporary injunction, the court imposes conditions on the activities of the alleged wrongdoer until the rights of the parties have been determined, or the wrongdoer has made changes or alterations in the activity to make them less offensive. In ordering a permanent injunction, the rights of the parties have generally been determined and the court has found that the activities of the wrongdoer are incompatible with the rights of the injured party, and that they can not be corrected or modified to satisfy the court.

Suppose that Amacher decides to store low-level radioactive wastes on his farm. His neighbor may ask the court for a temporary injunction stopping Amacher from undertaking the activity until the potential or actual harmful effects on the neighborhood can be determined. If the activity is determined by the court to be harmful, the court may then issue a permanent injunction ordering Amacher to stop the storage operation and move it elsewhere.

SUMMARY

In civil litigation, individuals, businesses, and governments use the law and the legal process to resolve disputes. Litigation provides a means of resolving those disputes without resorting to force. Most courts follow the Federal Rules of Civil Procedure in governing the important procedural aspects of the litigation process.

The constitution or statutes creating a court establish the court's territorial and subject-matter jurisdictions. A court's subject-matter jurisdiction limits the types of disputes a court can resolve. Typical subject-matter constraints include minimum requirements on the amount in controversy in the dispute and restrictions on the type of dispute the court can resolve.

The American court system consists of a system of federal courts and the court systems of each of the fifty states. The subject-matter jurisdiction of a court varies according to both its relative position within the court system and the court system it is in. The courts of original jurisdiction in both the federal and state court systems are trial courts. They have the authority to hear virtually any kind of dispute and provide any kind of relief. The courts with appellate jurisdiction have the power to review cases decided at the lower courts. They are concerned with whether any errors of law had been made during the trial. The highest level of appellate court has the discretion to review the majority of cases appealed to it.

The federal courts have limited subject-matter jurisdiction relative to state courts. The federal courts are limited by the U.S. Constitution to cases involving a federal question or diversity of citizenship where the amount in controversy exceeds $50,000. State courts can try virtually any kind of dispute.

In addition to jurisdiction over the subject matter, the court must also have jurisdiction over the parties to the dispute. Jurisdiction over the defendant is usually obtained through personal service of process. For out-of-state defendants, however, the court may need to exercise jurisdiction under the authority of the state's long-arm statute.

Jurisdiction over out-of-state corporate defendants is generally obtained through the long-arm statute's requirement of doing business within the state. The state's long-arm statute, however, must identify certain minimum contacts between the corporation and the state to qualify as doing business.

In those situations where the court is unable to establish jurisdiction over the person of the defendant, it can obtain jurisdiction over property within the state owned by the defendant. If the property is the object of the suit, the court can establish in rem jurisdiction and resolve the case. Quasi in rem jurisdiction will supply the appropriate authority for the court to attach property within the state to secure payment for an unrelated matter.

The federal courts in their diversity-of-citizenship cases must apply the appropriate state common and statutory law. For cases brought in a state court and where the incident in question took place in another state, the court must look to the forum state's conflict-of-law rule to determine which state's substantive law is to apply.

In the United States, nearly all judges are attorneys by professional training. It is their responsibility to uphold the legal system's reputation for honesty and impartiality. Federal judges are nominated by the President and confirmed by the Senate. They have lifetime employment once appointed. State judges are variously appointed and elected.

Within the American court system the remedies awarded by the courts in resolving civil disputes include monetary damages and equitable relief. Monetary damages include compensatory, punitive, and nominal damages. Equitable remedies include specific performance and injunction.

ISSUE

Are Plaintiff Attorneys Unduly Influencing Judges and Ignoring Professional Ethics?

Over the past decade, businesses and consumers have become increasingly concerned about our court system and the judicial process. The costs of litigating, lengthy delays, enormous judgments, and wealthy lawyers all received considerable media attention. Critics and scholars have at one time or another blamed insurance companies, judges, lawyers, Congress, and juries. In this article, the authors raise significant concerns about the role plaintiff attorneys are playing in this process. The authors inquire into the legitimacy of the relationships between plaintiff attorneys and both judges and legislators. The authors also question the professional ethics of some of the attorneys.

The Plaintiff Attorneys' Great Honey Rush
Peter Brimelow and Leslie Spencer*

We are freedom fighters. We all consider ourselves social engineers. . . . We are crusaders of good. None of us do it for the money, what we are paid is coincidental.
                     Mr. Ned Good, plaintiff attorney
                         * * *

Roll over, Wall Street. Meet the real champions of the great American greed game: the plaintiff attorneys who specialize in suing.

Top money maker in 1988, according to *Forbes'* list was Houston's Joe Jamail. He made most of his $450 million . . . by inducing Texas courts to accept the . . . theory that Pennzoil had a binding contract to buy Getty Oil even though there was nothing on paper. His victim, Texaco, the country's third-largest oil company, was forced into bankruptcy. . . .

Jamail is merely the most spectacular example to date of a powerful emerging trend. The 62 other plaintiff attorneys on *Forbes'* list all made above $2 million in both 1987 and 1988. And *Forbes* has identified at

least 15 more $2-million-a-year-plus suspects, with another 50 in the $1-million-to-$2-million range. . . . Law Professor Lester Brickman estimates that [plaintiff attorneys' annual] total income from contingent fees—their share of the settlement, apart from their expenses—"exceeds $10 billion." And their boodle is growing rapidly. The top moneymakers on *Forbes'* list typically said that they've been hitting the big numbers only for the last decade. . . .

Why has a single, relatively obscure corner of U.S. legal practice created so many million-dollar incomes? . . . How has this happened?

The essential mechanism is simple. Two distinctively American phenomena have interacted: the contingent fee system and the "liability crisis," the explosion of litigation and awards that has occurred during the past 30 years in the previously sleepy area of tort law—the law of accidents and personal-injury. Both have been historically unknown in other common-law jurisdictions, such as

---

*Forbes, October 16, 1989. Reprinted with permission.

—continued

–continuing

Britain. And plaintiff attorneys there are a lot poorer.

A startlingly large part of the recent massive damage awards goes to the lawyers. Plaintiff attorneys commonly insist on a contingency fee of 33% to 40%. Plus they get expenses—whatever has been spent to litigate the case . . . . [T]he Rand Corp.'s Institute for Civil Justice has estimated that in the asbestos claims settled in the early 1980s, plaintiff attorneys' fees and expenses amounted to some 70 cents for every dollar that the injured parties received.

And by one estimate the asbestos industry's liability may be anywhere from $7.6 billion to $87 billion.

Why has this happened?

The lid was knocked off the honey pot in the last 30 years by judges arbitrarily deciding to rewrite the law.

* * *

A man is injured after he deliberately throws himself in front of a New York subway train. He sues the city, alleging the driver should have stopped faster, and wins $650,000.

Another example: Spanish-speaking farmhands in Texas accidentally kill a prize bull with pesticide because they couldn't read the warning label. Their employer sues the manufacturer and is awarded $8.5 million, including $7 million of punitive damages. . . .

But these judicial atrocities are just the culmination of a step-by-step process that began in theoretical arguments among legal intellectuals in law schools and on the bench some 30 years ago—a classic demonstration that ideas do have consequences. *Forbes* columnist Peter W. Huber, author of *Liability: The Legal Revolution and its Consequences* (Basic Books) and himself a lawyer and engineer, calls the men who started the process—including William Prosser of Hastings College, John Wade of Vanderbilt University Law School, Roger Traynor of the California Supreme Court—"the Founders." Judges under their influence overthrew the

common law of tort as it had developed over six centuries. The chaos that has replaced it has been highly profitable to the plaintiff bar.

For example, before the 1960s, damages could generally be collected only under a number of fixed conditions—if the defendant was actually at fault, if the plaintiff had not contributed to the accident, if the plaintiff had not voluntarily assumed obvious risk and so on. . . . But gradually, judges undermined these conditions. Defendants, particularly if they are perceived to have "deep pockets," have begun to find they run the risk of losing lawsuits even if their involvement is minimal. . . .

"In a nutshell, the law now says 'Be careless, get paid,'" summarizes Victor E. Schwartz, a partner with Washington, D.C.'s Crowell & Moring and a tort reform lobbyist.

Similarly, judges have allowed a proliferation of ever-more-ingenious damage claims. Formerly, damages were primarily a question of compensating the plaintiff for out-of-pocket costs, like medical expenses. Now nonmeasurable damage claims like "pain and suffering," "loss of consortium" (a spouse's company) and "mental anguish" have burgeoned. And "punitive" damages in product liability cases, upheld only three times in the first 200 years of U.S. history, have become an epidemic. Even compliance with federal regulatory standards does not protect defendants against them.

"Since the 1960s, courts have become more political," says Schwartz. "Also, there is a feeling on the part of judges that the U.S. is behind in not having a comprehensive social welfare system. Tort law has become a system of social insurance."

* * *

A more complex factor: the disintegration of the traditional code of legal ethics . . . . Manhattan Institute Senior Fellow Walter Olson argues that the "legal revolution" has also seen the effective erosion of

–continued

–continuing

long-standing rules against barratry (inciting clients to litigate). "The old rules told lawyers to sit around passively and wait for business," says Olson. "The new rules encourage them to recruit clients, stoke their grievances and run the suit for maximum dollar output."

The traditional code was enforced partly by statute and judicial rulings, but also by consensus within the profession. Now, however, many plaintiff attorneys are openly hostile to its restraints .... John O'Quinn ... justified his hiring nonlawyers to solicit clients on the grounds that this "case running" should be legalized in Texas. An attempt to disbar him failed.

But the plaintiff attorneys' most important leverage on the honey pot is provided by their interlocking relationship with two key groups: judges and politicians.

The fellow-feeling between lawyers and judges is one of the more obvious facts of life. So obvious that some years ago a judge admitted frankly in an opinion that invalidating contingent fees was "an unpleasant task for courts, especially this one, for it has practiced law for so long ... before coming to the bench and recognizes the difficulties of maintaining a law office. . . ."

* * *

In some states, and at the federal level, judges are appointed. But the American Bar Association rating system, which has become a crucial test for judicial nominees, is weighted toward trial experience—even for appellate courts, although they focus exclusively on points of law. This obviously favors both the plaintiff and defense bars over corporate lawyers and legal academics.

Where judges are elected, the role of the plaintiff attorneys has become notorious: campaign contributions. In Texas, the fundraising drive supported by Joe Jamail . . . was so successful that, according to one Texas attorney, " . . . the plaintiff bar owned and controlled the Texas Supreme Court." . . .

It is another obvious fact of life that many politicians are lawyers. Sixty out of 100 U.S. senators and 186 out of 435 House members have law degrees. At least 48 senators and 161 House members have been practicing lawyers, including majorities on both Senate and House Judiciary Committees. . . .

[Association of Trial Lawyers of America (ATLA)] has given money to 1,485 Congressional Democrats and 656 Republicans since 1977. In 1987–88, it disbursed $3.9 million. And this doesn't include plaintiff attorneys' individual contributions.

"They're a highly focused lobby," says tort reform lobbyist Victor Schwartz ruefully. "They've *never* lost on an issue before Congress."

* * *

The legislative influence of trial lawyers may extend far beyond such obvious causes as blocking tort reform and attempts to cap damages and restrict contingent fees. Some observers suspect it in the chronic vagueness of many recent statutes, whose meaning must be fought out in litigation. Two other legislative habits that make life nicer for plaintiff attorneys, particularly in the environmental, civil rights and regulatory areas: provision for paying fees of attorneys suing the government—not merely if they win but sometimes even if they just raise a "novel legal argument"—and the provision for private causes of action, so that private individuals can sue to ensure compliance with the law.

* * *

Plaintiff attorneys unquestionably believe their own rhetoric. At least ATLA's Civil Justice Foundation thinks so. Its fundraising leaflet at the convention began: "As a trial lawyer, you profit from your work in many ways—the sweet success of righting an egregious wrong, the triumph of empowering the powerless, the certain knowledge of your role in penalizing wrongdoers."

All this and $10 billion, too.

* * *

–continued

—continuing

Questions

1. According to the authors, how have judges contributed to the rapid increase in both the size of court judgments and the wealth of lawyers representing plaintiffs in those court cases?

2. How are judges being influenced by plaintiff attorneys?

3. How might lawyers influence legislation to their benefit? Do they have an advantage relative to other special-interest groups?

REVIEW AND DISCUSSION QUESTIONS

1. Define the following terms:
   plaintiff
   defendant
   jurisdiction
   general jurisdiction
   limited jurisdiction
   appellate jurisdiction
   trial de novo
   diversity of citizenship
   writ of certiorari
   in personam jurisdiction
   summons
   substituted service
   service of process
   in rem jurisdiction
   quasi in rem jurisdiction
   conflict-of-law
   venue
   damages
   compensatory damages
   punitive damages
   nominal damages
   equity
   specific performance
   injunction

2. Compare and contrast the following:
   a. Service of process and substituted process
   b. Appellate jurisdiction and original jurisdiction
   c. Federal question jurisdiction and diversity-of-citizenship jurisdiction
   d. Jurisdiction over the person and jurisdiction over property

Case Questions

3. According to the court in *Smith* v. *Gibson* (1987):
   > The general rule is, that every country has jurisdiction over all persons found within its territorial limits. . . . It is not a debatable

question, that such actions may be maintained in any jurisdiction in which the defendant may be found, and is legally served with process. However transiently the defendant may have been in the State, the summons having been legally served upon him, the jurisdiction of the person was complete, in the absence of a fraudulent inducement to come.

Suppose John Adams, president of Mieller Company, is served with process in an airplane while the plane is flying over a state with this territorial concept of jurisdiction. Is the service of process valid? Would the altitude of the airplane at the time of the service affect your answer?

4. BurgerQueen is a Florida corporation whose principal office is in Miami. It conducts most of its restaurant business through a franchise operation. Those who franchise with the company—the franchisees—are licensed to use BurgerQueen's trademark for a period of twenty years. BurgerQueen then leases the franchisee a standardized restaurant facility. The contract between BurgerQueen and its franchisees provides that the franchise relationship is established in Miami and is governed by Florida law. It requires that all monthly payments be made to the Miami headquarters. The Miami office sets policy and works directly with the franchisee to resolve major difficulties. District offices, however, monitor the day-to-day functions. Those district offices are located throughout the country.

Jim Skivington, a Michigan resident, entered into a twenty-year franchise to operate a restaurant in Michigan. After several good months, the restaurant fell on hard times. Skivington eventually fell behind in his monthly payments. Despite negotiations with the Michigan district office and with the Miami headquarters, the franchise was terminated and Skivington was ordered to vacate the premises. He refused. BurgerQueen then brought suit in Federal District Court in Florida. Skivington claimed because he was a Michigan resident and because the dispute did not arise under Florida law, the District Court lacked jurisdiction over him. BurgerQueen argued that Florida's long-arm statute provided the court with jurisdiction. Assuming the long-arm statute reads like the Missouri statute in Exhibit 2–2, how would this jurisdictional issue likely be resolved?

5. Big Fruit Pie (Pie) and Berry Wholesale Company (Wholesale) were Missouri corporations doing business in Missouri. Pie and Wholesale had been contracting with each other for the sale and purchase of strawberries for years. Wholesale acquired its strawberries for Pie through Strawberry Brokers, Inc. (Broker). Broker, in turn, contacted Consolidated Growers (Grower), a California company. Broker and Grower exchanged documents. The documents were the same—listing Grower as the seller and Wholesale as the buyer—except that Broker's contract contained a price protection clause and Grower's contract did not. The provision would protect Pie in the event of a drop in the market price for strawberries.

Broker notified Wholesale that Grower was not honoring the clause. Nevertheless, Grower shipped nine truckloads to Pie over a three-month period. The market price for strawberries then fell below the contract price. Broker and Grower had several discussions about the price, but Grower refused to sell to Pie at a lower price. That position was unacceptable to Wholesale, who by contract was to protect Pie from market price declines. When Grower and Wholesale were unable to come to an agreement, Wholesale obtained strawberries from a different source. Wholesale and Pie then sued Grower in the federal district court in Missouri for interfering in their contractual relationship. They named Broker as the agent for Grower. Does the court have jurisdiction? [*Institution Food Marketing Assoc., Ltd.* v. *Golden State Strawberries, Inc.*, 747 F.2d 448 (8th Cir. 1984)]

6. Mr. White, a resident of Kansas, owes Mr. Black, a resident of Texas, for services rendered. Mr. White took his summer vacation in Missouri, where he was served with process by Mr. Smithson, a Missouri resident. Mr. Black owed Mr. Smithson a debt in Missouri, but Mr. Smithson had been unable to establish personal jurisdiction over him. Thus, with Mr. Black's property in the state in the form of Mr. White, Mr. Smithson attached that property for the purpose of establishing jurisdiction and satisfying the debt. Will the court have jurisdiction in this case? [*Harris* v. *Black*, 1965; overruled by *Shaffer* v. *Heitner*, 1977] Why didn't Mr. Smithson use Missouri's long-arm statute?

7. Suppose that John Nordin and Jack Emerson are in a dispute that involves the interpretation of a federal statute. They have elected to bring the dispute to the state district court for resolution. Which substantive and procedural law will that court apply?

8. Rose Hauptli and Donna Morgan are both residents and prominent business-women in the state of Kansas. They have been involved in a dispute for several months. Hauptli has filed a lawsuit in the state district court, and the action has just commenced. Morgan, being from a more liberal part of the state, would like to get the case removed to the federal court system. Can this action be removed?

9. Colemill Enterprises, a South Carolina company, purchased an airplane from Southeastern Flight Services, a Georgia company. The purchase price included a maintenance package that required Southeastern to keep the airplane in top operating condition. Shortly after the purchase, and while carrying Colemill's top executive, the airplane crashed and all passengers and crew were killed. There was evidence that the aircraft was defectively manufactured and improperly maintained. The airplane was manufactured in Michigan and maintained in Georgia; the crash occurred in South Carolina. In a subsequent wrongful death action brought in Georgia, which state's law will apply? [*Risdon Enterprises, Inc.* v. *Colemill Enterprises, Inc.*, 172 Ga.App. 902, 324 S.E.2d 738 (1984)]

10. Cote, who lives in Wisconsin, brought a diversity suit against Wadel, a lawyer in Michigan, in the federal district court in Wisconsin. The suit charged that Wadel committed malpractice in representing Cote in a matter in Michigan. The federal district court dismissed the suit for lack of personal jurisdiction over Wadel (the incident took place in Michigan and Wadel did not have sufficient contacts with the state of Wisconsin) and turned down Cote's plea to transfer the case to a federal district court in Michigan rather than dismiss it. Cote cannot file a new suit because the statute of limitations had run out. She appealed, arguing that either there was personal jurisdiction over Wadel or, if not, the district judge should have transferred rather than dismissed the suit. How will the appellate court rule? Is it appropriate for a district court to dismiss rather than transfer a case for lack of personal jurisdiction? If it is, would that be too severe a penalty on Cote for filing the case in the wrong court? Could Cote's attorney have avoided this situation entirely? [*Cote* v. *Wadel*, 796 F.2d 981 (1986)]

Policy Questions

11. Are the jurisdictional limitations on the courts intended to benefit either the plaintiff or the defendant? Can you determine any detrimental impacts if they were eliminated?

12. Why are there appellate courts? Should judicial officers be required to take a competency examination before "taking the bench"? Should they be appointed or elected? Should they serve a lifetime term or some fixed number of years like most elected officials?

13. What incentives do judges have to follow precedent?

Ethics Question

14. Tom Eyestone, a California resident, was invited to Utah by the West States Refining Company to negotiate a dispute. When discussions proved fruitless, West had process served on Eyestone before he could leave the state. Should the service be allowed to stand? Is this a sound business decision?

15. A federal judge was recently accused of using his office to do favors for felons. The judge allegedly approached fellow judges in an attempt to try and influence the outcomes of cases, helped his former secretary remain a fugitive from the law, tipped off a defendant about wiretaps, and told a witness to lie to a grand jury. Should this judge continue to receive his pay while these issues are resolved by the courts? Suppose he is convicted. Should he continue to receive his pay while in prison? Should he be allowed to return to the bench after serving his term?

3 Business and the Resolution of Disputes

T HIS chapter discusses the basic formal procedures for the resolution of disputes. We begin with a discussion of the adversarial nature of our judicial system and the requirements it brings to bear on the parties to any lawsuit. We also discuss the fact that most business lawsuits differ dramatically from nonbusiness lawsuits, particularly in their complexity, their evidentiary requirements, and the average size of damages awarded.

The basic procedures and processes involved in litigating a dispute are then considered. We discuss the important stages in the litigation process including the pleadings, discovery, trial, and appellate stages. Finally, alternative methods of dispute resolution, including arbitration, conciliation, and mediation, are examined. The growing delays and rapidly rising costs associated with the litigation process are making such alternatives increasingly more attractive to businesses. The chapter closes with the Issue Article, which discusses an issue of growing importance to business litigants as disputes become more complex and the time it takes to resolve them increases: Should We Consider the Use of Professional Juries?

THE NATURE OF OUR ADVERSARY SYSTEM

A distinctive element of our judicial system is that it is an *adversary system of justice*. It requires each of the opposing parties to contest the position of the other before a court in a true case or controversy and not in a hypothetical question or inquiry. It means that the responsibility for bringing a lawsuit, shaping its issues, and presenting convincing evidence rests almost entirely upon the parties to the dispute. The adversary system reflects the American belief that truth is best discovered through the presentation of competing ideas.

In resolving disputes, the courts take almost no active role in establishing the facts. They will not undertake their own investigation of the parties, the basis of the dispute, or the issues. Rather, the function of the court is to apply the relevant rules of law to the true facts of the dispute with the intent to bring the dispute to a peaceful resolution. Under this system of justice, then, a business (which is a legal entity) considering a lawsuit must intelligently weigh several important factors before bringing the lawsuit.

Is the Disagreement One for Which the Law Furnishes Relief?

The business obviously feels aggrieved or it would not be considering a lawsuit. However, the business must determine whether the grievance is one for which the law provides some form of relief. There are a substantial number of "injuries" a business may sustain but for which the law simply will not or cannot provide a remedy.

The business may be so injured, for example, when the marketing department works for weeks to persuade a major account to buy its product, only to see the sale go to a competitor. Similarly, the finance department goes to great effort and expense in attempting to hire an outstanding MBA graduate, only to see her accept a job with another company. If, as in these situations, the grievance is not redressable by a court of law, a lawsuit would be a fruitless and wasteful undertaking.

What Is the Probability of Winning the Lawsuit?

Even in the event the business decides that its grievance can be redressed by the courts, it must consider the probability of winning the lawsuit. In making this estimation, the business must consider several important factors. It must consider whether it can find and bring the defendant into court. It must ask whether it can produce the necessary witnesses and documents that will prove its case.

It must consider whether the *finder of fact*—the *jury* or, if there is no jury, the *judge*—will believe the evidence presented. The business must also surmise whether the defendant will be able to justify its conduct or prove the existence of a *defense*—a legal excuse—to its conduct. Finally, the business must consider whether its attorney's estimation that the law governing the dispute is in its favor will turn out to be correct.

Would the Relief Provided Make the Lawsuit Worthwhile?

Perhaps most important of all, the business must consider whether the relief the court may provide is worth the time, effort, and monetary expense. In making this determination, the business must weigh those costs against its alternatives to suit: settlement, arbitration, self-help, or simply letting matters rest. To the extent the court's award is to be limited to monetary damages, the business must also consider whether the defendant will even be able to pay. On the other hand, the defendant may be able to pay but may make the court's award difficult and expensive to collect. Further, in the event it is able to collect, the business must be concerned about whether anything will remain after paying attorney's fees, court costs, and other litigation expenses.

The business must also consider the risks to its operations not directly connected to the lawsuit. The business must take into account the likely impact on its reputation and its goodwill as a consequence of bringing the action. In some circumstances, the business may decide to ignore the injury because a lawsuit would open up its operations to close scrutiny by the public. The necessary evidence at the trial, for example, may require the disclosure of a company trade secret. The business may decide that in such circumstances close scrutiny is not in its long-run interest.

BUSINESS AS A DEFENDANT

The questions and concerns confronting a business as defendant are not dramatically different from those confronting a business considering a lawsuit. The business will request that its legal counsel determine the suit's likelihood of success and estimate the costs, both of defending the company against the lawsuit and of a judgment against the company. After accounting for its available insurance coverage, the business will then begin to establish its response to the lawsuit. Throughout this process, the business will consider several other important questions.

How Will Litigation Affect the Company's Goodwill?

In reaching a decision regarding the suit, the business must be concerned about the impact the lawsuit will have on the company's reputation and goodwill. Under some circumstances, the impact will be such that it will be in the company's interest to avoid litigation. The costs of litigation and the likely negative impact on consumers can make alternatives to litigation a viable and important option to the company.

Under other circumstances, however, the lawsuit may seriously threaten the company's survival. Thus, the company may have no creditable option other than litigation. The cigarette industry, for example, has taken a very proactive posture with regard to lawsuits in which the plaintiff alleges that smoking cigarettes led to the death of a family member or serious incapacity in the plaintiff. The industry litigates each such lawsuit vigorously. It recognizes that even a single judicial decision imposing liability upon it on the basis of a causal link between lung disease and smoking will likely invite more lawsuits, reduce sales, and encourage government regulation.

How Important Is the Underlying Relationship?

The business must also consider the importance of the relationship between the company and the plaintiff. If the plaintiff has a business relationship with the company—for example, is a supplier or wholesale customer—management may decide that continuation of that relationship is more important than prevailing in a court of law. The business may then find it in its interest to pursue a settlement, despite the fact that it believes it would prevail if the dispute went to court.

When natural gas and other energy prices fell sharply in the early 1980s, for example, Natural Gas Pipeline Company of America found that it was unable to fulfill contractual commitments to natural gas producers. Several hundred producers eventually filed suit against Natural Gas Pipeline and other pipeline companies alleging breach of contract. Management believed it could demonstrate through litigation that provisions in many of the contracts were against public policy. Rather than litigate, however, Natural Gas Pipeline worked diligently to renegotiate those contracts to preserve the valuable underlying business relationships. Had they pursued resolution through litigation, it would have taken years to reestablish the trust and confidence needed to form the basis for long-term, profitable business relationships with the producers.

Is Settlement a Viable Alternative?

Management may consider settlement a viable response if it determines that the costs of a settlement are likely to be less than the costs of litigation and of any judgments likely to be imposed on the company by the court. In estimating the costs of litigating the dispute, the company will consider more than just the direct costs of litigation (attorney's fees, expert witness fees, and court costs). Management will also consider costs associated with lost productivity as its executives prepare for the trial, the likely damage to the company's goodwill, and the costs (if any) of having the company's operations held up to close pubic scrutiny.

Are We Encouraging Spurious Lawsuits?

Businesses will also be cognizant of so-called "nuisance actions." In a nuisance action, the plaintiff files a claim that is essentially baseless in hopes of gaining a settlement payment from the company. The company, for example, may desire to settle rather than incur either unwanted media attention or the costs of litigation. Depending on the nature of the claim, it has been estimated that it costs major corporations $10,000 to $50,000 to defend against a single nuisance action.

A company's plan to avoid publicity or the costs of litigation provides plaintiffs with incentives to bring spurious lawsuits. Such plaintiffs bank on the hope that the company will consider paying a settlement of some amount less than the expected cost of litigation. To discourage nuisance actions, many companies have implemented a policy to litigate all such actions with the intent of sending a signal to would-be plaintiffs that they should not sue unless they are serious.

Is the Lawsuit an Integral Part of the Company's Strategic Plan?

Several of the questions a business will typically ask itself when faced with a lawsuit will be irrelevant if the lawsuit itself is part of management's strategic plan. Suppose, for example, that Richland Foods had entered into a long-term contract with Scharmato Vegetables for the purchase of tomato paste. As the world price of tomato paste declined, Richland decided that the terms of the contract were no longer acceptable and could significantly impair the company's viability. Despite efforts by Richland, Scharmato refused to renegotiate the contract. Richland then decided to breach the contract. The company waited until the harvest season when supplies were abundant, then informed Scharmato that it was not accepting any further shipments of tomato paste. Scharmato sued Richland for breach of contract (to the relief of Richland management). Richland had decided that a breach of contract suit was likely to be more cost effective strategically than purchasing tomato paste under the terms of the contract. While such a practice raises difficult ethical questions, it is nonetheless a fairly common practice within the business community.

How Much Are Legal Services

To determine the average fees for a variety of services, the National Resource Center for Consumers of Legal Services surveyed more than 800 law firms. The survey found that lawyers' rates and other legal fees for business varied widely among firms. Hourly rates depended significantly on the size of the firm and its location. As illustrated in Figure 3–1, lawyers in areas with fewer than 100,000 people charged an average hourly fee of $83. Law firms in cities of more than one million people averaged $103 per hour. Considering that a simple contract dispute that goes to court could involve 120 lawyer hours or more as well as expert testimony, the costs to the business—including lost productivity— could exceed $30,000. More complex cases easily exceed $1 million.

The survey found less variation in the contingent fees charged by plaintiff lawyers. Under a *contingent fee* arrangement, the lawyer receives nothing if the client loses. If, however, the client is successful—either by settlement or through litigation—the lawyer receives a predetermined percentage of the

Figure 3–1   Average Hourly Fees Charged by Lawyers, 1988

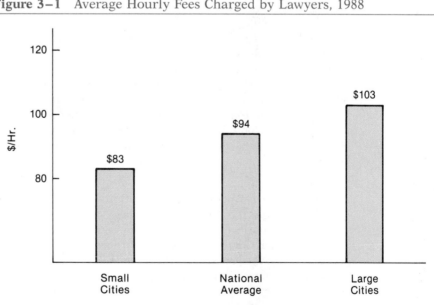

Source: National Resource Center for Consumers of Legal Services

recovery. According to the survey, the average contingent fee in personal injury cases was 30 percent of the recovery. Thus, if the lawyer is able to negotiate a settlement of $500,000 in a case in which the client was injured by the alleged negligent acts of a business's employee, the lawyer will receive $150,000 of the recovery. In most cases, the lawyer will also receive reimbursement for the costs of lawsuit.

RESOLVING DISPUTES THROUGH THE COURTS

After considering the alternatives and their costs, the business may decide that it is in its interest to bring a lawsuit. With regard to the basic trial procedures to be employed, lawsuits involving a business will not differ significantly from lawsuits involving nonbusiness parties. With rare exception, all parties must follow the procedural rules of the court system in which the dispute is to be resolved.

Although there are no significant procedural differences between business and nonbusiness trials, there are fundamental substantive differences. Those substantive differences are important because they may affect both the decision to engage in a lawsuit and the tactics and strategies the business may employ in that lawsuit. Several of the more important substantive differences between business and nonbusiness cases are that the typical business case is more complex, it generally involves a more extensive need for documents and exhibits as evidence, it relies more heavily on expert testimony, it is much longer in duration, and, if the business loses, the damage award will be significantly larger.

Complexity of Litigation

The legal issues in a business dispute are typically more complex than in a nonbusiness dispute. Business activities that allegedly violate federal regulatory law, particularly the antitrust laws, can involve intricate fact situations that can take several months to unwind. In a recent antitrust case, for example, the presiding judge required both sides to write out in detail what they intended to prove. Even after three refinements, the response was nearly 5,000 pages long. Given that degree of complexity, it is not uncommon for several teams of attorneys to be involved in preparing and presenting the case.

Greater Use of Documents and Exhibits
In resolving a more complex business dispute, thousands of documents and exhibits could be presented at the trial. More important, the documents involved may be part of a series of related documents, thereby adding to the complexity of the case. The documents, for example, may be part of a series of related papers, correspondence, internal memos, an exchange of letters that allegedly make up a contract, or annual reports. The judge and the jury will have an enormous task in such a case just to assimilate and understand the documents and exhibits.

Heavier Reliance on Expert Testimony

The testimony of the expert witnesses often is an important part of the successful business lawsuit. Even a relatively simple business dispute can require expert testimony at the trial on fundamental economic and finance issues. In environmental pollution cases, for example, the presentation of the issues may require testimony from a variety of experts, including scientists, medical doctors, engineers, and economists. In more complex cases and where there is more at stake, the expert testimony can involve intricate econometric and other statistical models presented by experts in the field. The cost of that testimony can represent a sizable portion of the total costs of the lawsuit. For example, it was estimated that the bill for expert testimony alone exceeded $2 million in litigation against the Hunt brothers of Texas who were accused of rigging silver pieces.

Longer Trials

Because of the complexity of the issues involved, the average business lawsuit is considerably longer than a nonbusiness lawsuit. While the more simple business lawsuit trial may last three days or less, a more complex case may take a year or more to complete. Each party could call scores of witnesses and enter thousands of documents and exhibits into evidence. In addition, it is not uncommon for several years to pass before the dispute even reaches the trial stage. The AT&T antitrust case, for example, was filed in 1974 but did not reach the courts until the 1980s. Legal fees in that case exceeded $100 million.

Larger Damage Awards Imposed on Businesses

In litigatory matters where the remedy being sought is monetary damages, businesses—and particularly large businesses—are often viewed as "deep pockets." That is, the jury will often award a larger damage award to a party injured by a business than to a party injured in the same way by another individual. The business is viewed by the jury as having more than enough resources—either in the form of insurance or profits—to compensate injured victims. A recent jury study found that injured plaintiffs who sue businesses receive awards that are 400 percent greater, on the average, than awards to plaintiffs with similar injuries who sue individuals.

The Growing Significance of Business Litigation

Over the past thirty years, the United States has experienced an explosion in business litigation. Since 1960, the number of disputes brought to the court system has increased by more than 300 percent. As Table 3–1 shows, more than 100,000 business-related lawsuits—more than 400 suits every working day—were filed in the federal district court alone in 1988. In nearly 40,000 of those disputes, the interpretation, implementation, or application of a federal regulatory law was at the heart of the dispute.

The Growing Size of Judgments Against Businesses

Not only has the number of lawsuits increased, so has the size of judgments. According to Jury Verdict Research, from the 1970s to the 1980s jury awards in products liability cases nearly tripled, to an average over $1 million. As Figure 3–2 indicates, both the size of awards and the fees paid to attorneys and

---

Table 3–1　Business Litigation, U.S. District Courts 1988

Nature of Dispute	Number of Cases
Contracts	44,135
Real property	12,209
Products liability	16,166
Asbestos	10,715
Bankruptcy	5,558
Environmental matters	889
Commerce (ICC)	1,694
Patent, copyright, trademark	6,059
Labor laws	12,688
Employment discrimination	8,563
Securities and commodities	2,638
Total business cases	**121,314**

Source: *1989 Annual Report of the Director,* Administration Office of the U.S. Courts.

---

expert witnesses have continued to increase at a very rapid rate. Fees paid to attorneys and expert witnesses have increased most dramatically, advancing by more than 400 percent since 1979.

Examples of Large Judgment Litigation

Among noteworthy cases, $100 million was recently awarded to the family of a chemical worker who died of leukemia as a result of workplace exposure to the chemical benzene. In 1984, a Texas jury returned a $10.3 billion verdict against Texaco. The jury found that Texaco had interfered with Pennzoil's attempted merger with Getty Oil Company. In 1987, to avoid posting a bond in its appeal of the judgment, the company filed for bankruptcy. Texaco became the largest company in U.S. history to file for bankruptcy. The companies eventually settled the case for $3 billion.

Texaco was not the only major blue chip company to be adversely affected by legal proceedings. In 1986, the A. H. Robbins Company filed for bankruptcy to forestall the some 6,000 legal liabilities associated with its manufacture of the Dalkon Shield, a contraceptive device. The company was required to establish a $2 billion plus fund to compensate victims.

In August 1982, the Manville Corporation filed for bankruptcy. The firm saw bankruptcy as an effective means for dealing with a rapidly growing number of lawsuits filed by individuals claiming health damages from Manville-made asbestos. At the time of the filing, Manville had more than 16,000 lawsuits filed against it with about 500 additional suits expected each month thereafter. The liabilities from those lawsuits were expected to exceed Manville's net worth by more than $3 billion. Manville's reorganization plan called for the company to establish the Manville Asbestos Injury Trust and Settlement Vehicle and to fund it with $75 million plus up to 20 percent of its profits each year for more than twenty-five years.

Legislative Limits to Litigation

Concern about rising litigation costs and court delays has led the Senate Judiciary Committee to consider several important changes. A thirty-six-member task force comprised of plaintiff's and defense attorneys, corporate

Figure 3–2   Growth in Litigation Costs, 1979 to 1988

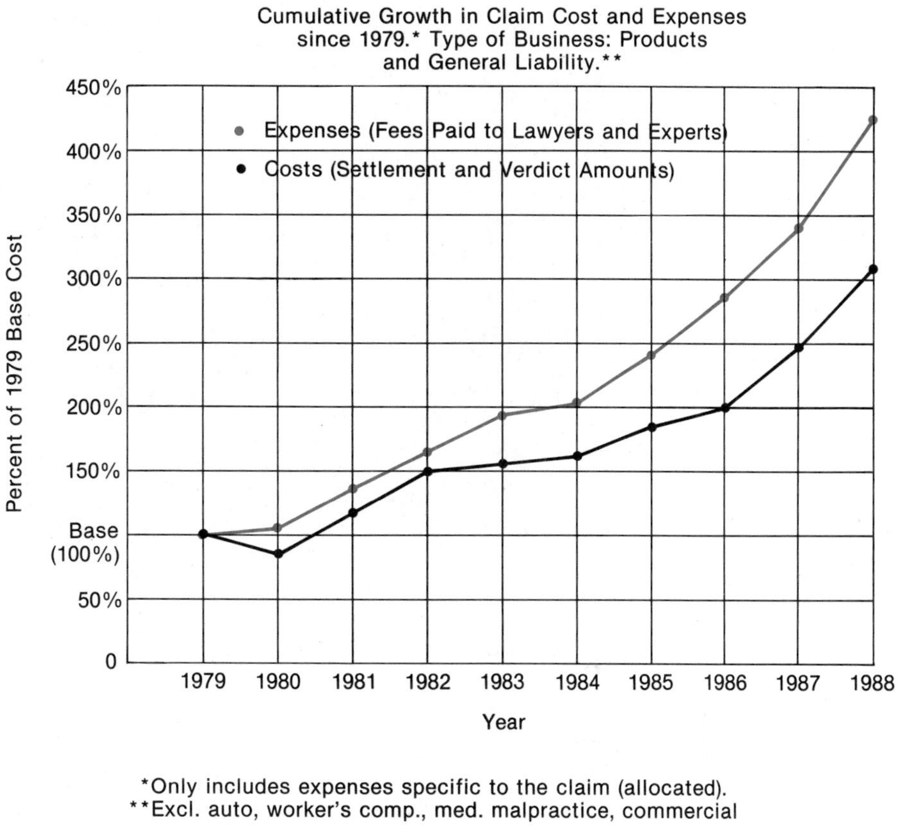

Cumulative Growth in Claim Cost and Expenses
since 1979.* Type of Business: Products
and General Liability.**

* Expenses (Fees Paid to Lawyers and Experts)
* Costs (Settlement and Verdict Amounts)

*Only includes expenses specific to the claim (allocated).
**Excl. auto, worker's comp., med. malpractice, commercial

Source: A. M. Best Aggregates & Averages Insurance Industry.

general counsel, insurance representatives, civil-rights and consumer advocates, former judges, and law professors is currently examining the problem. The task force is expected to recommend a greater reliance on alternative dispute resolution processes (discussed later in this chapter) as a means to reduce both litigation costs and delays.

BASIC TRIAL PROCEDURES

As discussed in the opening section, the American legal system follows the adversary system of justice. That is, the responsibility for bringing a lawsuit, shaping its issues, and presenting convincing evidence rests upon the parties to the dispute. This section discusses the major procedural rules governing the civil litigation process. A summary of a typical lawsuit is presented in Figure 3–3.

For the litigatory process to begin, the plaintiff must first determine in which court to bring the action. That is, the plaintiff selects a court that has

Figure 3–3 Example of a Typical Lawsuit

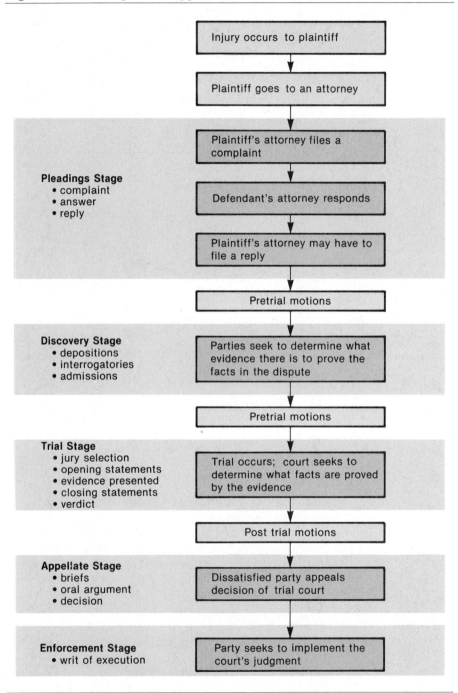

Injury occurs to plaintiff

Plaintiff goes to an attorney

Pleadings Stage
- complaint
- answer
- reply

Plaintiff's attorney files a complaint

Defendant's attorney responds

Plaintiff's attorney may have to file a reply

Pretrial motions

Discovery Stage
- depositions
- interrogatories
- admissions

Parties seek to determine what evidence there is to prove the facts in the dispute

Pretrial motions

Trial Stage
- jury selection
- opening statements
- evidence presented
- closing statements
- verdict

Trial occurs; court seeks to determine what facts are proved by the evidence

Post trial motions

Appellate Stage
- briefs
- oral argument
- decision

Dissatisfied party appeals decision of trial court

Enforcement Stage
- writ of execution

Party seeks to implement the court's judgment

both subject-matter jurisdiction and jurisdiction over the parties to the dispute. The plaintiff gives notice to the defendant by *service of process*, typically consisting of a summons, an example of which was presented in Exhibit 2–1.

Pleadings Stage

With the summons, the plaintiff serves the defendant with the first of the pleadings, commonly called the *complaint*. The complaint is a written state-ment that sets forth the plaintiff's claim against the defendant. Specifically, the complaint contains (1) a statement alleging the facts necessary for the court to take jurisdiction, (2) a short statement of the facts necessary to show that the plaintiff is entitled to a remedy, and (3) a statement of the remedy the plaintiff is seeking. A typical complaint is presented in Exhibit 3–1.

Note that state civil procedure rules vary greatly in the detail required in the pleadings. Some state court systems require a detailed and precise statement, while others consider little more than a simple assertion to be sufficient.

Responses to the Complaint

Following the service of the plaintiff's complaint, the defendant must file a responsive pleading. Depending on the circumstances, the defendant may file a motion to dismiss or an answer with or without an affirmative defense or a counterclaim. In those situations in which the defendant files a counterclaim, the plaintiff may be required to file a reply.

Motion to Dismiss

The defendant may respond by challenging the plaintiff's complaint by filing a *motion to dismiss*. This motion may challenge the court's jurisdiction over either the subject matter of the dispute or the defendant's person, the venue, or the sufficiency of the service of process. The defendant may also file a *motion to dismiss for failure to state a claim or cause of action* or a *demurrer*. (Note that the rules of civil procedure in some states do not use the term *demurrer*; they use only the term *motion to dismiss*.)

The motion to dismiss for failure to state a claim is an allegation on the part of the defendant that even if the facts were true, the injury claimed by plaintiff is an injury for which the law furnishes no remedy. In addition, the defendant may file this motion if he believes that the plaintiff has failed to include in the pleadings an important part of the case. The extent to which motions to dismiss will be granted on the basis of the facts and allegations asserted in the plaintiff's complaint will vary directly with the degree of detail required in the pleadings.

Answer

If the defendant's motion to dismiss is denied or if the defendant decides not to make one, the defendant must then file an *answer* with the court. In this pleading, the defendant must admit or deny the allegations made by the plaintiff in the complaint. If the defendant admits all the allegations in the plaintiff's complaint, or fails to deny the claims, a judgment will be entered

Exhibit 3–1   Example of a Typical Complaint

**UNITED STATES DISTRICT COURT
FOR THE
SOUTHERN DISTRICT OF NEW YORK**

Civil No. 2–80151

Rene Hofman
Plaintiff

vs.   COMPLAINT

Tom Eyestone Company,
Defendant

Comes now the plaintiff and for his cause of action against the defendant alleges and states as follows:

1. The plaintiff is a citizen of the state of New York and defendant is a corporation incorporated under the laws of the state of Delaware having its principal place of business in the state of Massachusetts. There is diversity-of-citizenship between parties.

2. The amount-in-controversy, exclusive of interest and costs, exceeds the sum of ten thousand dollars.

3. On January 10, 1990, in a public highway called Pleasant Street in Newburyport, Massachusetts, defendant's agent, John Kluttz, negligently drove a motor vehicle against plaintiff who was then crossing said highway.

4. As a result, plaintiff was thrown down and had his leg broken and was otherwise injured, was prevented from transacting his business, suffered great pain of body and mind, and incurred expenses for medical attention and hospitalization.

5. The costs plaintiff incurred included: $20,000 in medical care and $5,000 in lost business.

WHEREFORE plaintiff demands judgment against defendant in the sum of $25,000 and costs.

by
Ronald Johnson
Attorney for Plaintiff
5450 Trump Tower
New York, New York

Dated: 2/5/91

for the plaintiff. If the defendant denies the allegations, the dispute will be set for trial.

Counterclaim

The defendant can deny the allegations and assert his claim against the plaintiff. Called a *counterclaim,* this is particularly relevant when the defendant's claim arises out of the same occurrence that the defendant is being sued for by the plaintiff. The counterclaim is in essence a complaint by the defendant, and the plaintiff will have to respond to it just as the defendant had to respond to the original complaint.

Affirmative Defenses

In answering the complaint, the defendant may admit to the plaintiff's allegations but may assert additional facts that will result in the action's being dismissed. Called an *affirmative defense,* the defendant admits that he injured the plaintiff, but that the additional facts he asserts constitute a defense to the plaintiff's complaint. The defendant could admit to being negligent in a car accident involving the plaintiff, for example, but could also admit that the claim is now barred by the statute of limitations.

Reply

In the majority of court systems, the close of the pleadings stage ends after the answer. In many systems, any new matters raised by the defendant's answer are automatically taken as denied by the plaintiff. In those situations when the defendant does file a counterclaim, the plaintiff may answer it with an additional pleading called a *reply,* which is in essence an answer to the counterclaim.

The complaint, answer, and, if present, the counterclaim and reply form the *pleadings.* The purpose of the pleadings is to notify each of the parties of the claims, defenses, and counterclaims of parties' adversaries. The pleadings focus the issues, thereby removing the element of surprise from the resolution of the dispute. By so doing, it is argued that the pleadings allow the advocates in this adversarial system of justice to prepare their arguments better, thus assuring that a truer decision will be reached.

Motion for Judgment on the Pleading

After the pleadings are completed, either party may file a *motion for judgment on the pleadings.* This motion is essentially the same as a motion to dismiss, but it occurs after the pleadings have been completed. Like the motion to dismiss, the probability of its being granted varies directly with the substance of the argument and the degree of detail required in the pleadings. Essentially the plaintiff claims that the defendant has no defense, so the judge should rule immediately for the plaintiff; or the defendant claims that the plaintiff failed to state a case, so the case should be dismissed.

Discovery Stage: Obtaining Information Before Trial

After the pleadings, the litigation enters the discovery stage. During this stage, the parties are allowed to use a variety of procedural devices to obtain information and gather evidence about the dispute. Information can be obtained from the opposing parties or from the witnesses they intend to rely upon to support their position. The process of obtaining information is known as *discovery.*

The Federal Rules of Civil Procedure and the similar procedural codes in the states set down the guidelines and the boundaries for the discovery process.

Purpose of Discovery

Discovery serves several important functions in the litigation process. In this country's early legal history, disputes moved from the pleadings stage directly to the trial stage. As a consequence, the parties had little information about the specific evidence upon which the other party was going to base its arguments. Understandably, the evidence presented often caught the opposing party completely by surprise. The discovery process was developed to prevent surprises by giving the parties access to information that would otherwise remain hidden.

Discovery functions to preserve evidence of those witnesses who might not be available at the time of the trial. It also serves to preserve the testimony of those witnesses whose memories may fade with the passage of time or who may later attempt to change their testimony.

By allowing both parties the legal opportunity to become knowledgeable of the facts, the discovery process also serves to encourage pretrial settlements. Often, after a determination of the facts, one party will conclude that the opponent's case is too strong to challenge and will offer to settle the dispute out of court, as happens in most cases. If settlement efforts are unsuccessful, the discovery process will have functioned to narrow and more closely specify the issues of the dispute so the trial can focus on the important questions in the case.

Tools of the Discovery Process

The discovery rules offer several methods of obtaining information from an opposing party or witnesses. Discovery rules allow access to the testimonies of those parties and to relevant documents, records, and virtually any other type of evidence relevant to the resolution of the dispute. The specific tools of discovery include depositions, written interrogatories, orders for production of documents, requests for admissions, and orders for a mental or physical examination.

Depositions and Interrogatories. The principal discovery tool is the *deposition* — the sworn testimony of a witness recorded by a court official. In this procedure, the person whose deposition is to be taken is questioned by attorneys from both sides. The questions and the answers are taken down, sworn to, signed, and transcribed.

The deposition is useful in finding information that is relevant to the resolution of the dispute, including the unearthing of important leads to other witnesses or documents. It is also useful during the trial to impeach a witness who attempts to change his or her story at the trial. Finally, the deposition of a witness who is unavailable at the time of the trial may, in some circumstances, be used in place of live testimony. Note that depositions may also be taken from written questions prepared in advance by both parties to the dispute.

A discovery tool particularly adapted to probing the content of an opponent's case is *written interrogatories* — written questions submitted by the opposing party. The party receiving the interrogatories must prepare written answers with the aid of an attorney and then sign them under oath. The principal difference between written interrogatories and depositions with written questions is that the interrogatories may be addressed only to a party to the suit and not to other witnesses. Although the interrogatories will lack the spontaneity of a deposition, they will require the party to provide information from her records and files—the kind of information not carried in one's head. Note that the court will not compel a party to furnish answers to written interrogatories that are determined to be unduly burdensome, particularly where alternate and less burdensome means for obtaining the same information are available.

Orders for the Production of Documents. An order for the production of documents allows a party to gain access to information in the sole possession of the other party. The kinds of information that are often the subject of such an order are medical bills, business records, letters, and repair bills. The party seeking the information usually has the right to gain access for the purposes of inspection, examination, and reproduction. Similarly, if the nature of the dispute so dictates, an order can be obtained to provide entry upon land to inspect the premises.

Requests for Admissions. Either party can serve the other party with a written request for an admission of the truth in matters relating to the dispute. Requests for admissions are to be used not to cover the entire case and every item of information but rather to force admissions of facts about which there are no real disputes between the parties. Their purpose is to eliminate the need to establish at the trial those facts about which there is no real controversy.

After a party has admitted the truthfulness of a fact related to the dispute, the parties are relieved of the burden of proving the fact and trial time is reduced. The court may, under certain circumstances, allow the admissions to be withdrawn or amended. As a general rule, a party is not required to admit or deny facts not within her knowledge.

Mental and Physical Examinations. In those disputes where the physical or mental condition of a party is an issue in the dispute, the court may be asked to order that party to submit to an examination. Because of concerns for that party's rights to privacy, the party requesting the order must show a greater need for the information than in requests for other forms of discovery. Generally, the party requesting the order specifies the exact type of mental or physical examination desired, the time, the place, and the specialists who are to do the examinations. If the court makes the order, the party can then obtain the needed information.

Sanctions for Failing to Respond to a Discovery Request. Under the Federal Rules of Civil Procedure and the procedural codes of most states, the court has broad powers to impose sanctions against a party who fails to comply with discovery requirements. If a party fails to comply with the requirements of a deposition, written interrogatories, or a request, the court may issue an order directing the party to comply. If the party does not comply with the order, the court may find the party in *contempt of court* (resulting in imprisonment or fines) and require him or her to pay the expenses incurred by the other party as a consequence. The purpose of these sanctions is to effectuate the discovery process.

Discovery: Impacts on Business
Despite its value to the litigation process, discovery can impose significant costs on businesses, managers, and executives. Businesses can be forced to endure the expense and the disruption of their administrative and executive

staff while the various officers and employees answer questions and produce documents. In one regulatory dispute between Ford Motor Company and the Federal Trade Commission, for example, it cost Ford nearly $4 million to copy and produce required documents.

Of all discovery tools, depositions are often the major source of expense for a business involved in litigation. The burdens imposed by depositions are particularly heavy when administrative and executive personnel have to take time away from more productive undertakings to prepare for and provide a deposition. In disputes involving technical matters or significant detail, the deposition of the manager with the responsibility for the project or with the most knowledge regarding the matter may take two weeks or more.

Further, in many disputes it is not uncommon for the chief executive officer of the corporation to be issued a subpoena requesting that he appear to make a deposition. In most cases, the information being sought is in the hands of subordinates. While the court will attempt to protect executives if the purpose in seeking the deposition is largely to harass, the deposition is difficult to avoid simply because the presence of the chief executive is requested. In some cases the courts will examine the circumstances and recommend an alternative discovery tool.

Plaintiffs seeking damages for injuries from an alleged defective design in a Dodge van, for example, sought the deposition of Lee Iacocca, chairman of Chrysler Corporation. The court held that the although "[Iacocca's] prestigious position is an unimpressive paper barrier shielding him from the judicial process, . . . he is a singularly unique and important individual who can be easily subjected to harassment and abuse. . . . Therefore, . . . an orderly discovery process will be best served by resorting to interrogatories at this time. . . ." In the following case, the court is confronted with a similar request for a deposition of executives, but the issue in the case more fully encompasses the executive and administrative staff.

Travelers Rental Co., Inc., d/b/a Dollar Rent a Car v. Ford Motor Company, Hertz Rental Car, Avis Rental Car

United States District Court, D. Massachusetts
116 F.R.D. 140, 7 Fed.R.Serv.3d 1349 (1987)

Case Background. *Travelers (the plaintiff), doing business as Dollar Rent a Car, alleged in its complaint that Ford Motor Company (the defendant) had violated antitrust laws in a program it had developed with Hertz and Avis. Under the program, Ford had agreed with Hertz and Avis, but not with Dollar, that they would receive a certain price when they disposed of certain vehicles after use in their car-rental businesses. Travelers contended that the practice had the effect of fixing prices, thereby giving Hertz and Avis an unfair competitive advantage. To establish its claim, Travelers sought to take the depositions of four high-level executives at Ford, including the president and executive vice-president. Ford refused to produce the four executives, stating that Travelers was demanding the depositions "solely for the purposes of harassment and oppression, and not because the additional depositions are reasonably calculated to lead to the discovery of admissible evidence." Travelers asserted that there was an important connection between the executives and the evidence and the issues in the case. The district court was asked to determine whether Travelers had the right to take the depositions.*

Case Decision. Judge Collings delivered the opinion of the court.

* * *

On the record before the Court in this case, the cases cited support Travelers' contention that the depositions should be allowed to go forward. Ford, however, asks the Court to invoke its power under the [Federal Rules of Civil Procedure] which reads, in pertinent part, as follows:

> The frequency or extent of use of discovery methods . . . shall be limited by the court if it determines that:
>
> (i) the discovery sought is unreasonably cumulative or duplicative, or is obtainable from some other source that is more convenient, less burdensome, or less expensive;

* * *

I agree with Ford that the discovery is somewhat duplicative and cumulative but because of the nature of the inquiry at issue, I do not believe that the discovery is unreasonably so. It is to be recalled that one of the reasons Travelers wants these depositions is to explore Ford's motive and intent in instituting and administering the plan, and each of the four officials whose depositions are sought was a participant in those endeavors. Lower-level executives may have greater knowledge of the manner in which the plan was implemented or administered. The lower-level executives may even have their own views as to why the plan was implemented or administered in a particular way. But those with greater authority may have the last word on why Ford formulated and/or administered the plan in the manner which the lower-level executives described it as being formulated and/or administered. And as the ultimate authority, their views as to why may be of far greater probative value on the issue of intent and motive than the views of the lower-level executives.

In short, this is a very different case from the situation where the issue is the design of a particular transmission used in a Ford automobile and where there was no evidence that the higher-level executives had any role in deciding what the design was to be. In such a situation, the depositions of higher-level executives probably would be prohibited on the basis of the [Federal Rules of Civil Procedure]. If, however, there was evidence that the choice as to which design of a transmission system was to be placed in a particular model automobile was made by higher level executives, the depositions would probably be permitted.

* * *

Case Holding. *The motion to compel production of the four Ford executives for deposition by Travelers was allowed. When the motives behind a corporate action are at issue, an opposing party usually has to depose those officers and employees who approved the particular action.*

Case Questions
1. Why would Ford want to keep the executives from giving depositions in the case? Why were their depositions needed?
2. Generally speaking, in what kinds of situations would the depositions of lower-level employees be sufficient? In what kinds of situations would the depositions of higher-level executives be necessary?

Pretrial Stage

Either party or the court may request a *pretrial conference*. Usually the conference involves the attorneys and the judge, but it may also involve the parties themselves. The pretrial conference is intended to be a forum for simplifying the issues making up the dispute and to plan the course of the trial. To ensure a meaningful trial, the judge may find it necessary to request that the parties seek additional admissions of facts or documents or limit the number of witnesses. In some court systems, the pretrial conference is viewed as a forum for obtaining settlements or otherwise disposing of the case without a trial.

Summary Judgment

If through discovery it is determined that there are no disagreements about the facts to a dispute, either party may move for *summary judgment*. Because there are no facts in dispute, the judge will be asked simply to apply the law to those facts and resolve the dispute. In reaching a decision, the judge will be free to consider evidence not contained in the pleadings. Generally that evidence—often a sworn statement or affidavit concerning some aspect of the facts in the dispute—will be provided by the party moving for summary judgment.

To be successful, the evidence provided must demonstrate that a crucial issue in the case would be resolved in favor of that party if the dispute went to trial. Unless the other party can refute the evidence, the judge will grant summary judgment. The judge's ruling will have the same legal effect in resolving the dispute as a decision of the trial court. Motions for summary judgment may be made before or during the trial, but they will be granted only if there are no disagreements about the facts to a dispute.

Trial Stage

After the completion of discovery, and if it has not been resolved by dismissal, summary judgment, or settlement, the dispute must be set for *trial*. In many court systems, the trial calendar has become quite long, with delays up to three years before a civil dispute is called to trial.

The Jury

The Seventh Amendment of the U.S. Constitution as well as most state constitutions provides for the right to have the true facts in a common law dispute determined by a *jury*. In the federal court system, the right is guaranteed if the amount in controversy exceeds $20. Most state court systems have similar guarantees, although the minimum amount in controversy may be higher. The state of Iowa, for example, requires that the amount in controversy equal or exceed $1,000. Aside from cases not meeting the amount-in-controversy requirement, there is no right to a jury trial in cases in which the plaintiff requests an equitable remedy, not monetary damages, nor is there a right to a jury trial in civil cases involving statutory enforcement, as will be discussed in Chapter 4.

Decision to Use a Jury. The right to a jury trial does not have to be exercised. If a jury has not been requested, the judge will both determine the true facts in the dispute and apply the law to resolve it. Several important considerations enter into the decision whether or not to request a jury trial, including the judge's perceived temperament, the complexity of the evidence, and the degree to which the emotions of the jury are likely to affect the judgment. The Issue Article at the end of this chapter suggests a need for professional juries in those disputes in which the facts are complex and require several weeks and even months to present to a jury.

Selection of the Jury. The jury selection process formally begins when the clerk of the court sends a notice to individuals selected from a pool of community members requesting that those individuals appear for jury duty. Under federal jury selection statutes, the procedures used in selecting this pool of citizens must obtain a cross-section of the community population. From this jury pool, the court will select the jury that will hear the case.

The screening process used in selecting the jury members is called *voir dire*. Depending upon the court, either the judge or the attorneys will conduct voir dire. The purpose of this screening process is to determine if a prospective juror is likely to be so biased or prejudiced that she could not reach an objective decision based on the evidence presented. If such a determination is made and the judge agrees, the attorney may *challenge for cause*, and that person will be disqualified. Attorneys are also allowed a limited number of preemptory challenges that allow an attorney to reject a prospective juror without stating a reason why. Juries have typically involved a panel of twelve persons. However, in some states panels of fewer than twelve—frequently six—are used.

The Trial

Although the court has discretion to determine the order of the trial, it usually does not deviate much from the order of the jury and nonjury trials summarized in Table 3–2. Although jury and nonjury trials are generally handled in much the same way, they can have a number of important procedural differences. The judge, for example, will often dispense with the attorney's opening statements and closing arguments. Also, the instructions to the jury

---

Table 3–2   Summaries of Typical Jury and Nonjury Trials

Jury Trial	Nonjury Trial
1. The selection of a jury	1. Plaintiff's presentation of direct evidence
2. Plaintiff's opening statement	2. Defendant's presentation of direct evidence
3. Defendant's opening statement	3. Plaintiff's presentation of rebuttal evidence
4. Plaintiff's presentation of direct evidence	4. Defendant's presentation of rebuttal evidence
5. Defendant's presentation of direct evidence	5. Judge's deliberation and verdict
6. Plaintiff's presentation of rebuttal evidence	
7. Defendant's presentation of rebuttal evidence	
8. Opening final argument by the plaintiff	
9. Defendant's final argument	
10. Closing final argument by the plaintiff	
11. Instructions to the jury	
12. Jury deliberation and verdict	

will quite obviously not be needed. With those differences in mind, the following discussion details the various steps involved in a typical jury trial.

Opening Statements. After the jurors have been sworn in, both attorneys are allowed to make *opening statements*. In those statements, the attorneys will tell the jury what the crucial facts to the dispute are and how they will prove that those facts support their contentions and allegations. In the interest of time, opening statements are generally limited to twenty minutes, with the plaintiff's attorney giving the first statement.

Presentation of Direct Testimony. Following the opening statement, the plaintiff's attorney will call witnesses. The plaintiff goes first, having the burden of proving that the claims are correct. Each witness is first questioned by the plaintiff's attorney; this is called *direct examination*. The defendant's attorney then examines that witness on *cross-examination*. Cross-examination may be followed by *re-direct examination* on the part of the plaintiff's attorney and then by *re-cross examination* on the part of the defendant's attorney. The judge will serve to control the length and the course of these latter examinations.

After having called and examined all witnesses, the plaintiff will *rest*. The defendant's attorney may then ask for a *directed verdict* on the grounds that the plaintiff has not presented sufficient evidence to support the claims—has not met the burden of proof. As the following case illustrates, the plaintiff must structure the evidence so as to demonstrate to the court that the defendant's actions were the cause of the injuries.

May v. Hall County Livestock Improvement Association
Supreme Court of Nebraska
216 Neb. 476, 344 N.W.2d 629 (1984)

Case Background. *May, the plaintiff, had slipped and fallen at a racetrack owned by Hall County, the defendant. May brought an action against Hall County for the injuries she incurred in that fall. At the close of the plaintiff's case, the trial court sustained the defendant's motion for a directed verdict. The court asserted that although the evidence the plaintiff had presented established her injuries, it did not provide a factual basis for finding the defendant responsible. The plaintiff appealed, contending that the evidence presented by her was sufficient to sustain a jury verdict against the defendant.*

Case Decision. District Judge Cambridge delivered the opinion of the court.
* * *
As we must, we assume the truth of the material and relevant evidence presented by the plaintiff, find every controverted fact in her favor, and give her the benefit of every reasonable inference deducible from the evidence.

On April 12, 1977, the plaintiff attended the horseraces at Fonner Park Racetrack, Grand Island, Nebraska. The defendant owned and operated the park. The plaintiff, in addition to paying the general charge for admission into the grandstand, paid for admittance into a reserved area thereof, enclosed by metal railings, where there were tables and chairs from which the races could be observed. The area had a cement floor. Food, soft drinks, and beer, purchased either at concession stands located in the area or from waitresses who served the tables, were consumed in the area. The plaintiff sat at one of those tables, and on various trips from and to the table [said] she saw "slippery places" and liquid on the cement in the areas around her table but not near her table; she never looked under her own table before the accident to see if there was any liquid under the table or around her chair. The plaintiff stood up most, if not all, of the sixth race, and when she saw that the horse she had bet was going to win, she started to take steps to go, and her left foot slipped; she tried to break her fall by catching the leg of the table with her right foot, but did not succeed. After regaining consciousness the plaintiff recalled that the bottom or lower part of her right pantleg was wet. According to the food concession manager, who arrived on the scene while the plaintiff was still lying on the floor and who remained there until the plaintiff had left, there were no spills, liquids, or debris of any kind on the floor where the plaintiff had fallen, and the floor was dry; and when spills did occur, there was a procedure for cleaning them up. As a result of the fall, the plaintiff sustained head injuries and a broken right hip with complications in the healing of that fracture.

The defendant [is] not an insurer of the safety of business invitees on its premises. It is well-established law in this state that a possessor of premises is under a duty to use reasonable care to make his premises safe for a business visitor or to give him adequate warning to enable him to avoid harm when certain conditions are true. . . .

The plaintiff contends in her brief to this court that something wet on the floor caused her to slip and fall, but the bill of exceptions in this case simply does not support that claim. It is apparent from the foregoing recital of facts that the plaintiff failed to produce any evidence which could have reasonably satisfied the jury that the physical harm suffered by the plaintiff was caused by a condition or activity on the defendant's premises. Giving full weight to all of the plaintiff's evidence and all inferences reasonably deducible therefrom, it can be concluded that such conditions and activities did in fact exist on the defendant's premises at the time in question, but there is literally no evidence in the record establishing that any one of them was the proximate cause or a proximately contributing cause of the plaintiff's slip and fall and the physical harm which resulted therefrom.

* * *

Case Holding. *The lower court's decision to dismiss the case was affirmed. Where the facts presented to sustain an issue are such that but one conclusion can be drawn when related to the applicable law, it is the duty of the court to decide the question as a matter of law and not submit it to a jury.*

Case Questions

1. What are the requirements placed on the court in sustaining a directed verdict?
2. What basic element of the plaintiff's case was missing in her presentation of the evidence?
3. Would this case have made it to trial if the plaintiff had been required to more completely detail her legal arguments at the pleading stage?

If the motion for a directed verdict is denied, the defendant's attorney may either rest and rely on the jury agreeing with her or present her own case. If the attorney presents her own arguments, which is most frequently the situation, the witnesses will be exposed to the same process of direct and cross-examination as the plaintiff's witnesses.

Presentation of Rebuttal Testimony.   When the defendant rests, the plaintiff may present additional evidence to rebut the evidence presented by the defendant in *rebuttal*. The defendant's attorney, in turn, can meet that evidence in a *rejoinder*. This procedure will continue until both sides rest. Note, however, that the judge will maintain considerable control over the length and tenor of these latter proceedings.

Presentation of Evidence. In presenting the evidence, the parties are restricted only by the rules of law regarding the presentation of evidence and due process. The judge functions as a referee, keeping the parties within those rules. The most influential source of evidence rules is the Federal Rules of Evidence.

Witnesses are allowed to testify only as to matters of fact. They are to present *relevant and material information* to the court on what they saw, heard (unless it is hearsay, as explained below), smelled, touched, or felt. Witnesses may also identify pictures, documents, or other physical exhibits important to the resolution of the dispute. If a witness is asked a question that has no bearing on the facts germane to the resolution of the dispute, the opposing attorney may object on the basis that the answer would be "irrelevant." The court will likely sustain the objection, and disallow the question.

Hearsay. Several restrictions are imposed on the type of information witnesses may provide. Unless a witness is an *expert*, for example, he cannot state an opinion or draw a conclusion on particular matters beyond his physical senses or common knowledge. Witnesses are not allowed to testify to *hearsay*— what someone has told them not in the presence of the parties to the actions. The prohibition against hearsay evidence exists because there is no opportunity to cross-examine the person who made the statement. As a consequence, the evidence is deemed unreliable.

Suppose that McNeil has been accused of stealing property from his employer. Laren may testify that he saw McNeil take the property (direct evidence), but not that he heard from a third person that McNeil had taken property from the company (hearsay). Laren may testify, however, that he heard McNeil tell a third party that he was stealing from his employer.

Restrictions on Testimony. Several restrictions are imposed on the kinds of questions an attorney may ask a witness. An attorney, for example, may not ask *leading* questions of her *own* witnesses. A leading question is one that suggests the answer desired by the attorney. In addition, the attorney cannot ask a witness to reveal the substance of communications deemed to be *privileged matter*. An attorney cannot, for example, inquire into the private communications between a doctor and a patient or an attorney and a client. The law places a high value on the sanctity of such relationships.

Motion for a Directed Verdict. After both parties have rested, either party may move for a directed verdict. As it did previously, this motion asks the judge to rule that the evidence presented is not sufficient to support the claims alleged by the opposing party. If the motion for a directed verdict is denied by the judge, the case goes to the jury.

Closing Arguments. Before the case goes to the jury, the attorneys each present a *closing argument*. Here, the attorneys will try to organize the evidence for the jury in a concise manner, thereby fashioning an argument most favorable to their case. Normally, the plaintiff has the discretion to present closing arguments both before and after the defendant. As in the opening statement, the judge will limit the amount of time available to the attorneys for their closing arguments. It is improper for an attorney to discuss in the closing argument a matter that was excluded from the trial by the judge or that was not discussed at the trial.

Verdict Format. To be assured that the jury performs only its principal function of determining the true facts in the dispute, the attorneys may request one of the several different types of verdict formats. As summarized in Table 3–3, there are three basic formats. The most frequently employed format is the *general verdict*. Under the general verdict format, the judge instructs the jury on the law, and the jury applies the law to the facts as it determines them to be. The jury thus determines who prevails and what relief is to be granted. The general verdict allows the court the least amount of control over the jury.

The *general verdict with interrogatories* is similar to the general verdict except that the jury is also required to answer specific questions— interrogatories—provided by the judge. The interrogatories are intended to provide a means to check the consistency between the jury's fact determination and the verdict.

The *special verdict* requires only that the jury determine the facts; the judge then applies the law to those facts. The jury is not instructed on the legal implications of the facts before its deliberations. The special verdict is designed to make the process more scientific by preventing the jury from being able to ignore the facts as it reaches its decision. The special verdict has been criticized, however, because it slows jury deliberations and makes the process much more difficult. In the remainder of our discussion on trial procedures, we will assume that the court is applying the general verdict format.

Instructions to the Jury. Before the jury retires to deliberate and reach a verdict, the judge will give the jury *instructions* or *charges*. In the instructions, the judge will detail the applicable law, summarize the facts and issues of the

Table 3–3 Summary of the Types of Jury Verdicts in a Civil Case

Type of Verdict	Description
General verdict	Permits the jury to determine the facts and apply the law as charged. Jury determines who prevails and the damages to be awarded.
General verdict with interrogatories	Combines the form of the general verdict with several key questions designed to test the jury's understanding of the issues in the dispute. In the event of an inconsistency between the verdict and the answers, the answers control.
Special verdict	All of the factual issues are submitted to the jury as questions without instructions as to their legal effect. The judge then applies the law to the jury's answers and determines who prevails.

dispute, provide a general discussion on determining the credibility of witnesses, and state which of the parties has the *burden of persuasion* on each issue of fact.

Ordinarily in a civil trial, the burden of persuasion requires that the responsible party prove its contentions by a *preponderance of the evidence.* That is, if jurors are unable to resolve an issue in their mind, they should find against the party who has the burden of persuasion for that issue.

After the instructions have been given, the jurors are placed in the custody of the *bailiff* or similar court official who oversees them during their deliberations. It is that court official's responsibility to see that the jurors remain together and have contact with no one else unless the contact is directed by the court.

The jury will then deliberate to reach an agreement among themselves and find either for the plaintiff or the defendant. In some cases, however, juries are simply unable to reach a unanimous decision. If such is the case, the jury is said to be *hung,* and a new trial before a different jury is necessary. The jury is then discharged and a *mistrial* declared.

Because of the cost and delay associated with a new trial, courts are reluctant to discharge a jury without having reached a decision. Although many jurisdictions still require a unanimous jury decision, some reduce the number of jury deadlocks by allowing verdicts in civil disputes to be based on less than unanimity. In Minnesota, for example, a less-than-unanimous verdict is permitted but only after the jury has deliberated for a specified period of time.

After the jury has reached a verdict, the verdict is read in open court by the foreman of the jury in some court systems and by the judge or the clerk of the court in others. The judgment is then entered on the basis of the jury's verdict.

Motions After the Verdict. After the verdict has been presented, the parties are given the opportunity to challenge it through certain *post-trial motions.* If the challenging party—the party who has lost the decision—had previously moved for a directed verdict, it can now move for a *judgment notwithstanding the verdict* or *judgment n.o.v.* This motion raises the same question as the motion for a directed verdict. The party moving for the judgment n.o.v. is stating that even if the evidence is viewed in the light most favorable to the other party, a reasonable jury would not have found for that party. That is, as a matter of law, the jury's verdict is not supportable by the evidence presented at the trial. If the judge agrees, the jury's verdict will be reversed.

The losing party can also move for a new trial. There are several important grounds for this motion, including assertions that the judge erred in admitting certain evidence; the judge's instructions to the jury were inappropriate; there was misconduct on the part of the attorneys, parties, or the jurors; or the monetary damages awarded were either excessive or inadequate. In any case, the party requesting the motion is asking the court to set aside the adverse verdict and judgment and to hold a new trial. A new trial may also be granted if new and crucial evidence, a clerical mistake, or fraud is discovered subsequent to the trial, but the granting of a new trial under these circumstances is a very rare occurrence. The following case considers the important issue of jury misconduct.

Caterpillar Tractor Company v. Hulvey

Supreme Court of Virginia
233 Va. 77, 353 S.E.2d 747 (1987)

Case Background. *Hulvey was a forklift operator. He brought a products liability action against Caterpillar, the forklift manufacturer, for injuries sustained while operating the forklift. Three trials were held. In the first trial, the jury was hung. In the second trial, the jury found for the defendant. That verdict, however, was set aside for alleged jury misconduct and a new trial was ordered. In the third trial, the jury found for the plaintiff and awarded him $250,000. The defendant appealed the trial court's action in setting aside the second verdict for jury misconduct.*

Case Decision. Judge Compton delivered the opinion of the court.

* * *

The second trial concluded on Friday, February 25, 1983, after the jury had deliberated "four or five" hours. Within the next several days, juror Joy Ann Reges contacted plaintiff's trial attorney. Subsequently, plaintiff's counsel arranged for a hearing upon a motion to set aside the verdict based on juror misconduct and sent letters to four jurors "inviting" them to attend the hearing. Two jurors, Reges and Patricia O. Most, appeared voluntarily and testified at a hearing held about a month after the trial. A second hearing on the motion to set aside was held four days later. John F. Olmstead, the juror accused of misconduct, testified at the second hearing.

Olmstead was president of a corporation and an attorney at law. He was licensed to practice in the District of Columbia but not in the Commonwealth of Virginia. The jury list showed his occupation only as "corporate executive." The fact that he was an attorney did not become known to the trial participants until after the jury had been sworn and the trial progressed.

At the hearing, jurors Reges and Most testified that the trial judge admonished the jurors as the case commenced not to discuss the case among themselves until the issues finally had been submitted to them for decision and to consider only information properly received in evidence. Reges stated that, during a recess on the second day of the trial, Olmstead "at one point opened his briefcase and said . . . in passing, 'What do you think of this?' and read us something about people who sue for injuries." The juror testified, "What I recall is, he was reading [and] said that people who sue for injuries were people who didn't like to work. . . . I remember it was derogatory toward people who sue for injuries." When asked the type of publication from which Olmstead was reading, Reges stated, "I remember him saying it was an insurance weekly. It looked like an insurance newsletter." The juror assumed Olmstead was "an insurance salesman" but, she said, "He told us he was a lawyer."

Testifying about this incident, the juror Most stated [that] . . . Olmstead read the article, "a paragraph or two," in the presence of all the jurors and returned the publication to his briefcase. Most stated that she thought "it" was "derogatory because we hadn't come to the conclusion that (the plaintiff) was trying to take the company. . . ."

During the hearing, juror Reges described other incidents involving Olmstead. At one point during a recess, she stated, there were a "lot of comments" among the jurors about the case and Mr. Olmstead said this is just a lot of garbage and he seemed to not like being here because it took a lot of his time." She testified, "One of the jurors . . . said it looked like somebody was going to fatten his pocketbook, and that pretty much started the conversation." According to Reges, Olmstead said "that the lawyers are taking a long time. But then we began to talk about the fact of the injury." She testified, "It was discussed by several of the jurors whether (the plaintiff) really was in any pain" and that Olmstead and another juror discussed the fact [that] the plaintiff "could sit there in the chair for a long time" while the jurors found it difficult to sit in the uncomfortable chairs. Reges further testified that, during this general discussion, "Mr. Olmstead and another juror talked about the fact that people were suing corporations these days because they thought they could get a lot of money off of them." Also, Reges testified that, early in the trial, Olmstead "emphatically" said the trial judge was wrong in one of his rulings.

Describing the effect of Olmstead's conduct, Reges stated she "would never serve on another jury with a lawyer or with Mr. Olmstead again." She said she felt that Olmstead's legal training "gave him an advantage" and that during deliberations "he seemed to be so right. . . ." Responding to a question from the trial judge, Reges stated that her decision in the case was influenced adversely by the conduct she had described.

Also describing the effect of Olmstead's conduct, Most stated that the foreman of the jury was "laid back a little bit" and that Olmstead "sort of took over." Most said that Olmstead "had a firm opinion" and that because he was "a corporate lawyer," she "was a little intimidated." According to Most, "it just seemed like (Olmstead) was taking over the discussions too much. . . ."

Both Reges and Most testified, however, that during the four to five hour period of deliberation everyone on the jury fully discussed the issues, expressed opinions, and "spoke what they wanted to say." In addition, Most testified that Olmstead waited until the other six jurors had given their final views on the case before he expressed his opinions on the decision to be reached.

Testifying during the second day of the post-trial hearings, Olmstead admitted reading to the jury from a publication carried in his briefcase. Olmstead recalled that the incidents occurred during final deliberations on the case, when one of the jurors asked why no information on insurance had been presented. According to Olmstead, he responded that the subject of insurance intentionally was kept from the jury because, he said, it would "taint" the jurors' views. At that time, Olmstead stated, he took the opportunity to read from "Board Room Reports," a business magazine he had possessed but discarded before the hearing, that reported "negligence suits are up substantially due to the recession." Olmstead testified he followed that comment with the statement, "isn't that ironic they're saying it's on the rise and look what kind of case we have." According to Olmstead, there was no further discussion among the jurors on the subject.

Olmstead testified that his "garbage" comment made in the jurors' presence was directed toward both counsel in the case who, in his opinion, were spending an undue amount of trial time qualifying expert witnesses by delving into every detail of the expert's professional background. Olmstead stated that the "whole jury was disgusted" about the length of time counsel were taking with the expert witnesses.

The trial court sustained the plaintiff's motion to set aside the verdict [based on jury misconduct]. . . .

* * *

In most cases, misconduct outside the jury room has prejudicially affected the jury's deliberation of the case by injecting facts connected with the case which had not been admitted in evidence. For example, the rule has been applied . . . to unauthorized private conversations between jurors and third persons.

In the present case, the trial court focused upon the publication read by Olmstead and upon his "garbage" comment as the bases for setting aside the verdict. That alleged misconduct, however, occurred within the confines of the jury room and did not involve procurement outside the jury room of specific facts about the case which later were injected into the deliberations.

The extraneous news from the publication about the proliferation of damage suits against corporations was nothing more than a reference to information which every individual acquires in his or her everyday experiences. One is naive who labors under the impression that jurors of today are not aware of the proliferation of lawsuits generally and damage suits against corporations specifically. As the evidence demonstrates, many of the jurors, not just Olmstead, discussed whether "somebody was going to fatten his pocketbook" and generally talked about insurance coverage. While such topics are irrelevant to the legal issues in a damage suit, we are convinced that the evil which would result from overturning verdicts based on post-trial disclosure of every irrelevant comment or discussion which occurred during jury deliberations would be more detrimental to the administration of justice than the harm which may possibly result from permitting robust, wide-ranging discussions in the jury room to proceed in an unrestrained manner. Indeed, the evidence here fails to show that the information contained in the publication alone caused any juror to vote for a defendant's verdict. Rather, Olmstead's entire "conduct" swayed [just] two jurors.

* * *

The "garbage" comment, directed to dilatory trial tactics of counsel, and other statements by Olmstead, such as his disagreement with a ruling of the trial judge, were nothing more than the expressions of an opinionated, forceful juror.

* * *

Case Holding. *The judgment appealed from rendered in favor of the plaintiff on the third verdict was reversed. The verdict returned in the second trial was reinstated, and judgment was entered on that verdict in favor of the defendant.*

Case Questions

1. What is the rationale for not allowing the jury to discuss the case as it develops?
2. Should juries be allowed to consult materials not presented as evidence at the trial?
3. What impact did the fact that Olmstead was an attorney have on the jury? Is it good practice to include such a person on the jury?

Appellate Stage

The litigation may enter the appellate stage if one of the litigants believes that an *error of law* was made during the trial. Litigants generally cannot, however, appeal the factual determinations made at the trial. Common grounds for appeal include errors made by the trial court judge in admitting evidence that should have been excluded, refusals to admit evidence that should have been heard, improper instructions given to the jury, and the granting or denying of motions to dismiss the case. A principal function served by the appellate courts is to ensure the fairness of a trial, that is, to ensure that the trial court judge correctly applied the law.

Arguments before Appeals Courts

The parties present their arguments to the appellate court through written *briefs* and *oral arguments*. These arguments are restricted to discussions of law, not the facts in the case. Although the number varies from court system to court system, there will always be more than one judge hearing an appeal. In reviewing the trial court's decision, the appellate court has the authority to review any ruling of law by the trial judge. It has the power to *affirm, reverse,* or *modify* the judgment of the trial court.

Decisions by Appeals Courts

If the appellate court *reverses* the decision of the trial court, it may either order that that judgment be entered or *remand* the case to the trial court for a new trial. The appellate court may also remand the case to the trial court for other proceedings consistent with its opinion.

The appellate court decision will be accompanied by a written *opinion* that represents the views of the majority of the court. *Concurring opinions*— opinions by judges who agree with the decision of the majority but for different reasons—and *dissenting opinions*—opinions written by judges who disagree with the decision of the majority—may also be filed. Those written opinions are intended to set forth the rationale for the judges' decisions and to furnish guidance for the resolution of similar future disputes to attorneys, judges, and the public.

Enforcement Stage

After a dispute has been tried at the trial level, if no appeal is taken or if no further appeal is available, the *judgment* becomes final. The same dispute cannot be considered again in this or any other forum. It is *res judicata*— literally, a thing decided. Note that *res judicata* applies only to civil actions brought for monetary damages and not disputes where something other than monetary damages was sought.

The judgment may be in the form of a monetary award to the plaintiff, a declaration of the rights between the parties, or an order requiring or prohibiting some activity on the part of the defendant. In cases where the defendant prevails, the judgment generally will not involve an award but rather will state that the defendant is not responsible for the plaintiff's injuries.

In the case where the plaintiff recovers a monetary damage award, it is the plaintiff's responsibility to collect from the defendant. In the event the defendant does not pay, the plaintiff can seek a *writ of execution* that commands an official such as the sheriff to seize the property of the defendant and, if necessary, to sell the property to satisfy the judgment. A defendant refusing to obey a judgment that requires or prohibits some specific activity may be found in *contempt of court* and fined or imprisoned.

INTERNATIONAL PERSPECTIVES: TRIAL PROCEDURES

INTERNATIONAL

PERSPECTIVES

Depending upon the culture of a particular society, the rules governing trial procedures can differ dramatically from country to country. The Italian rules of procedure, for example, collapse the pleading, discovery, and pretrial conference stages of U.S. civil procedure into the initial "pleadings" stage. While this can substantially reduce litigation expenses, it also can impose burdens in complicated and detailed business cases. In contrast to civil cases in the United States, juries are not used in France, Germany, Italy, and most other civil law countries, or in the common law countries of England and Canada.

In several civil law countries, witnesses do not appear in open court. Rather, their testimonies are given to an investigation judge who then presents their testimony in summary form to the judges charged with resolving the dispute. In contrast to the United States, where the emphasis is on monetary damages and other forms of substituted redress to injured parties, the primary objective in the Italian system is to rehabilitate the person and return him to a productive life as quickly as possible. Thus, while our courts are clogged with automobile cases, a very small percentage of such cases end up in Italian court.

DISPUTE RESOLUTION ALTERNATIVES TO THE COURT SYSTEM

The business litigation explosion in the United States coupled with the high costs and delay associated with the litigatory process has prompted an increased reliance on *alternative dispute resolution* (ADR) processes. While many of the ADR processes have been legally recognized for decades, recent dissatisfaction with juries as triers of fact in business litigation has led to dramatic changes in the business community's sentiments toward these processes. This frustration with the litigatory process was well stated by former Chief Justice of the Supreme Court Warren Burger:

> We, as lawyers, know that litigation is not only stressful and frustrating but expensive and frequently unrewarding for litigants. . . . Commercial litigation takes business executives and their staffs away from the creative paths of the development and production [of goods and services] and often inflicts more wear and tear on them than the most difficult business problems.

Alternatives to the court system are employed largely because they provide an impartial, low-cost, expeditious method for resolving disputes. In their absence, many of those disputes would be resolved with resort to the court system where the adversarial nature of the proceedings could irreparably damage the underlying business relationship.

As a rule, the choice of an alternative to the court system in resolving disputes must be mutually agreed upon by the parties before a dispute occurs. Often parties will include a clause in the contract calling for the parties to submit to a particular alternative method of dispute resolution should a dispute arise. The most common ADR processes include arbitration, minitrials, and negotiations. As Figure 3–4 illustrates, negotiation offers the parties the most control over the process and the outcome. Virtually all ADR processes, however, provide the parties with more control than litigation.

Arbitration

Arbitration is the most widely recognized and accepted ADR process. It is a legal process in which two or more persons agree to allow an impartial person (or panel) to resolve their disputes. The impartial person, called the *arbiter*, is often an expert in the field who understands the technical nuances of the dispute. Business litigants frequently find the opinion of such a third party

Figure 3–4 Relative Comparison of Disputant Control Under Various ADR Processes

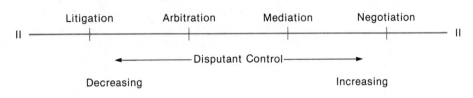

Source: Adapted from Larry Ray, "Emerging Options in Dispute Resolution," *ABA Journal,* June 1989, pp. 66–68.

invaluable in deciding how best to settle complicated disputes. The decision of the arbiter may be legally binding and can be appealed to the courts only under specific and limited circumstances. As Figure 3–5 illustrates, there has been a steady increase in the number of commercial disputes going to arbitration. Disputes over construction, securities, computer software, labor, and insurance make up the bulk of commercial cases.

Punitive Damages
An arbitration decision can provide virtually all of the same forms of relief that are available through the courts. Punitive damage awards, however, have traditionally not been allowed in arbitration proceedings. Punitive damages

Figure 3–5 Growth in Commercial Cases Going to Arbitration

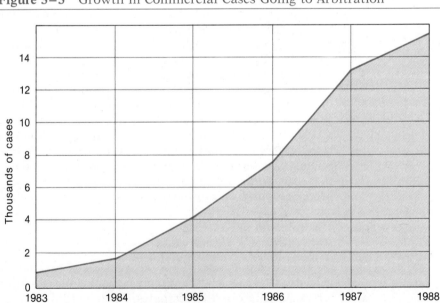

have been considered a public remedy, dispensable only by the courts. The courts have reasoned that since arbitration is a private process, the award of punitive damages would be against public policy. Several courts, however, have recently reconsidered the traditional rule. The *Willoughby Roofing* decision was the first arbitration case concerning the award of punitive damages to be reviewed in a federal court.

Willoughby Roofing & Supply Co., Inc. v. Kajima International, Inc.

U.S. District Court, N.D. Alabama
598 F.Supp. 353 (1984)

Case Background. *Willoughby Roofing, the plaintiff, subcontracted to install a roof on a building for Kajima, the defendant. Kajima was the general contractor on the construction project. Following its acceptance of Willoughby's bid, Kajima altered the plans so much that it substantially raised the costs to Willoughby. Willoughby sought to renegotiate the contract price. Despite the fact that Willoughby had gone to considerable expense in preparing for the work prescribed in the original contract, Kajima cancelled the contract and hired another subcontractor. Willoughby initiated a lawsuit against Kajima. Before the trial, Kajima filed a motion for a stay of the proceeding pending the outcome of the required arbitration hearing. This motion was based on the following arbitration clause in the contract between the parties:*

> All claims, disputes, and other matters in question arising out of, or relating to, this Agreement or a Work Assignment or the breach thereof, except with respect to matters for which the Architect's decision shall be final and binding as provided in this Agreement, shall be resolved by arbitration in accordance with the Construction Industry Arbitration Rules of the American Arbitration Association unless the parties mutually agree otherwise. This agreement to arbitrate shall be specifically enforceable under the prevailing arbitration law. The award rendered by the arbitrators shall be final, and judgment may be entered upon it in accordance with applicable law in any court having jurisdiction thereof.

An arbitration panel was selected, and Willoughby's claims were presented to it. Finding those claims to be with merit, the panel awarded Willoughby $49,091.25 in compensatory damages and $108,908.75 in punitive damages. Kajima took this decision to federal court, arguing that the award of punitive damages is against public policy and should not be included in the award.

Case Decision.   Senior District Judge Lynne delivered the opinion of the court.

* * *

In resolving questions pertaining to the arbitrator's authority, courts must broadly construe the agreement and resolve all doubts in favor of the arbitrator's authority. . . . This is particularly true with respect to the remedial authority of arbitrators, for it is essential that arbitrators have a great deal of flexibility in fashioning remedies if the national policy favoring the settlement of disputes by arbitration is to have any real substance.

* * *

It is true, as Kajima points out, that certain state courts have held that under the law of those states arbitrators cannot award punitive damages even if the parties authorize them to do so.

* * *

The Supreme Court has emphasized that the arbitration process can be a viable method of dispute resolution only if "it serves as a vehicle for handling any and all disputes that arise under the agreement," . . . and only if the arbitrators are given a great deal of flexibility in the fashioning of appropriate remedies. . . . The remedy of punitive damages is one to which a plaintiff is traditionally entitled . . . "when the fraud is malicious, oppressive or gross and the misrepresentation is made with knowledge of its falsity and with the purpose of injuring him." . . . That is precisely what the arbitrators found in this case. Where the arbitrators are concededly vested with the authority to hear and resolve the plaintiff's claim of fraud, it would be anomalous indeed to deny them remedial power commensurate with that authority. . . . To deny arbitrators the full range of remedial tools generally available under the law would be to hamstring arbitrators and to lessen the value and efficiency of arbitration as an alternative method of dispute resolution. . . . This would not sit well with the strong federal policy favoring arbitration.

The defendant insists, however, that because an award of punitive damages serves not only to punish the present wrongdoer for willful or wanton misconduct, but also to deter others in society at large, the power to award them should not be wielded by anyone other than a judge or jury. The defendant raises the spectre of overly partial arbiters manipulated by the party in a superior bargaining position, who may award punitive damages out of bias and prejudice. That spectre has more bark than bite, however, for the Arbitration Act expressly provides for the vacation of an arbitral award where the award was "procured by corruption, fraud or undue means," . . . or where there was "evident partiality or corruption in the arbitrators." . . . The mere possibility of bias or corruption no more justifies a wholesale withdrawal of the authority of arbitrators to make an award of punitive damages than it would a wholesale withdrawal of their authority to resolve disputes at all.

* * *

There is no reason to believe that the [Arbitration] Act's mandate of enforceability did not extend to agreements to arbitrate issues of punitive damages. Nor is there reason to believe that the purposes of punitive awards—punishment of the present wrongdoer and deterrence of others who might otherwise engage in similar conduct—will not be furthered by arbitral awards every bit as much as by formal judicial awards. Indeed, an arbitrator steeped in the practice of a given trade is often better equipped than a judge not only to decide what behavior so transgresses the limits of acceptable commercial practice in that trade as to warrant a punitive award, but also to determine the amount of punitive damages needed to (1) adequately deter others in the trade from engaging in similar misconduct, and (2) punish the particular defendant in accordance with the magnitude of his misdeed.

* * *

It may be, as the defendant belatedly claims, that the informalities and lack of judicial review attendant to arbitration render that method of dispute resolution less desirable than a full judicial trial when it comes to the airing of claims for punitive damages. But having chosen arbitration as the method of resolution of "all claims, disputes *and other matters* . . . arising out of or relating to" its agreement with Willoughby Roofing, and having vested the arbitrators with authority to grant "any remedy or relief which is just and equitable," it may fairly be said that Kajima got what it bargained for.

* * *

Case Holding. *The motion to vacate or modify the arbitrator's award was denied. The court entered judgment for plaintiff in accordance with the arbitral award. If parties to an arbitration agreement desire to exclude the issue of punitive damages from the consideration of an arbitrator and reserve it for judicial hearing, they are free to specify that in their contract. Otherwise, the strong federal policies favoring arbitrability of issues and remedial flexibility of arbitrators will govern.*

Case Questions

1. What are the court's basic arguments for the award of punitive damages in an arbitration decision?
2. What are the public policy arguments against the award of punitive damage awards in arbitration?
3. Will the potential for a sizable award of punitive damages discourage the use of arbitration?

Expanding the Use of Arbitration

As the use of arbitration has increased over the past decade, the courts have expanded the areas in which it may be applied. Citing with approval the Federal Arbitration Act's stated public policy of favoring arbitration, the Supreme Court held in *Shearson/American Express v. McMahon* (1987) that agreements between brokerage houses and their customers requiring that disputes go to arbitration are binding. As a consequence of the Court's holding, securities brokers are expected to see a dramatic decline in the number of lawsuits they must face.

RICO and Arbitration

The *McMahon* case has been cited as providing arbitrators with greatly expanded authority to impose judgment under federal law. For example, Kerr-McGee Refining Company was recently awarded damages by an arbiter under the federal Racketeer Influenced and Corrupt Practices Act (RICO). Enacted in 1970 as a weapon against organized crime, RICO has been used successfully against such legitimate businesses as General Motors, Merrill Lynch, and Prudential Insurance Company. RICO provides for civil and criminal penalties for a "pattern" of unlawful activity such as fraud, extortion, interstate transportation of stolen property, interference with interstate commerce by violence or by threats of violence, and other similar acts.

A tanker company from whom Kerr-McGee had chartered a tanker had illegally taken a substantial quantity of the oil from Kerr-McGee by diverting it into a secret tank in the tanker. By establishing that the tanker company had diverted oil on other voyages, the pattern of unlawful activity required by RICO was proven. Because civil damages are tripled under RICO, the panel's award was also tripled. The decision clearly indicates that arbitration should not be taken lightly by the business community in civil disputes involving violations of federal law.

Court-Annexed Arbitration

A few court systems are requiring arbitration as a pretrial requirement. Called *court-annexed arbitration*, these programs have been limited to disputes in which the amount in controversy is relatively small. Eligible cases are referred to mandatory pretrial arbitration which is typically conducted by a practicing attorney, a retired judge, or, in some court systems, a panel of three attorneys. The procedure employed usually consists of a quasi-judicial hearing leading to a resolution of the dispute. Court-annexed arbitration has many of the characteristics of a trial, most notably the application of rules of law by neutral decision makers.

Either party may elect to reject the decision and insist on a trial before a judge or a jury. In some programs, if the party who rejected the decision fails to improve its position at trial, it will be ordered to pay at least the arbitration costs. Relatively few cases submitted to the process, however, have then later proceeded to trial.

Surveys of both attorneys and their parties whose disputes have been submitted to this ADR process have reported a high level of satisfaction. Courts using this process have also experienced significant reductions in both case backlogs and case processing time. In Pittsburgh, for example, this ADR process ends nearly three quarters of all disputes referred to it. In addition, the average delay before a hearing is only three months, in contrast to the eighteen-month delay before a trial.

Minitrials

As the name implies, *minitrials* are abbreviated, nonbinding hearings on disputed matters. The hearings are held before an expert who is jointly selected by the parties. The expert is expected to render a confidential opinion on the strengths and weaknesses of each party's case. That opinion, then, is used to assist in settlement negotiation. The procedures to be used in the hearing are themselves negotiable and informal.

The minitrial concept was developed by practicing attorneys who wanted to reduce the delay and costs of resolving disputes between corporations. The procedure has been successful in dealing with a variety of intellectual property, product liability, and breach of contract disputes.

Summary Trials

A *summary trial* is the jury equivalent of a minitrial. It generally takes place after discovery has been completed and shortly before trial. The summary trial begins with the selection of jurors. Each side is then given a short period of time to summarize its case. Presentations are limited to evidence admissible at trial, and based on depositions, discovered documents, expert reports, and other discovery material. At the conclusion of these presentations, the judge gives the jury abbreviated instructions on the law. The jury then reaches an advisory decision. After the proceeding, a judicial officer generally meets with the parties to discuss the decision and encourage settlement. The United States District Court for the Northern District of Ohio reports that of the 153 cases assigned to summary jury trial, 148 settled prior to trial.

The trial judge may not compel the parties to engage in a summary trial, despite its cost and flexibility advantages. In *Strandell v. Jackson County, Illinois*, the Seventh Circuit Court of Appeals held that the Federal Rules of Civil Procedure do not authorize mandatory summary jury trials. The court stated that the Federal Rules do allow the trial judge to "explor(e) the use of procedures other than litigation to resolve the dispute," including "urging the litigants to employ adjudicatory techniques outside the courthouse." The court, however, concluded that:

> A crowded docket does not permit the court to *avoid* the adjudication of cases properly within its congressionally mandated jurisdiction.

Negotiation

In the ADR process of *negotiation,* the parties choose to work out their differences among themselves rather than through either arbitration or litigation. The process of negotiation can take on many different forms and approaches.

The best-known and most widely used negotiation technique is *mediation,* which involves the use of a neutral outsider who helps the parties in reaching a permanent resolution to their dispute. Collective bargaining in labor-management relations has contributed to the bulk of the experience in mediation techniques and has led to the creation of the American Arbitration Association and the Federal Mediation and Conciliation Service.

Mediators essentially manage the negotiation process, arranging for scheduling, setting the agenda of events, and maintaining the records of the dispute. They also facilitate communications outside the meetings by holding confidential talks with the individual parties and suggesting areas where they may be unreasonable. In some circumstances, the mediator may offer creative suggestions, remind the parties of the costs if they fail to reach an agreement, and recommend the terms of an agreement.

ADR Processes and Federal Government Agencies

In addition to making inroads into private dispute resolution practices, ADR processes are becoming widely used by government agencies. Many of the Environmental Protection Agency's environmental disputes, for example, are now settled by negotiation and mediation instead of litigation. Other agencies using ADR processes include the Merit Systems Protection Board, Commodities Futures Trading Board, Federal Aviation Administration, Federal Energy Regulatory Commission, Federal Trade Commission, and the Occupational Health and Safety Administration. Industry has generally been favorable to the use of ADR processes because they avoid the bad publicity often associated with a government lawsuit.

Advantages of ADR Processes to Businesses

The use of ADR processes by the business community has increased dramatically in the past fifteen years. Businesses have used these processes to resolve both large and small disputes between themselves, their consumers, and the government. In 1980, for example, General Motors and the Council of Better Business Bureaus initiated a Mediation/Arbitration Program to successfully resolve manufacturing and dealership complaints. The company has subsequently written this program into their new car warranties.

Several important motivating factors contribute to this increase in the use of ADR processes by the business community. Some of the more important factors include the following:

1. The avoidance of high cost litigation.
2. The fear that litigation will result in an outcome far more adverse than reasonably anticipated.
3. The need to return employees involved in the litigation to more productive activities.
4. The desire to maintain the business relationship.

Limitations on Arbitration and Other ADR Processes

In strictly private disputes, ADR processes often work well, effectively reducing delays and the great expense associated with litigation in resolving disputes. Tens of thousands of cases are resolved each year by labor and commercial arbitration. ADR processes, however, are not allowed to be employed in the resolution of disputes involving certain important public rights and duties.

Private antitrust violations, for example, cannot be resolved by ADR processes. It has been asserted by the courts:

> Because of the paramount importance of antitrust policy to national economic policy, even private antitrust disputes are not purely private but are semipublic in nature. The precedents that are established in the resolution of even private antitrust cases are important in establishing acceptable conduct in this important area. If these disputes are resolved by ADR processes, important precedents are lost.

Similarly, claims brought under other public laws have been held to be foreclosed from using ADR processes. Despite increased use and availability of ADR processes as applied to disputes involving federal law, certain claims under the Securities Acts and the Bankruptcy Code have been found to be of such public importance that ADR processes could not be applied.

SUMMARY

The American legal system follows the adversary system of justice. The responsibility for bringing and presenting a lawsuit rests upon the litigants. The system reflects the belief that truth is best discovered through the presentation of competing ideas.

Several important considerations, including the probability of winning and the likelihood of collecting a judgment, are fundamental to the decision to bring a lawsuit. The typical business lawsuit is more complex, utilizes more documents and evidence, relies more heavily on expert testimony, and results in larger damage awards. The volume of business litigation has increased dramatically since 1960. Judgments for a million dollars are not uncommon, with several large companies forced to file for bankruptcy.

The typical litigation process involves pleadings, discovery, a pretrial conference, the trial, and the judgment and enforcement. If either party is dissatisfied with the decision of the trial court, it can appeal to an appellate court. Once a dispute becomes final, the same dispute cannot be considered again in that or any other forum.

The high costs and delay associated with the litigation process has increased interest among businesses in alternative dispute resolution processes, the most common of which are arbitration, minitrials, and negotiation. These processes cannot, however, be employed in the resolution of important public rights and duties.

Should We Consider the Use of Professional Juries?

Business litigation is becoming more and more complex. The evidence presented often involves testimony from a variety of disciplines including finance, engineering, medicine, and economics. Trials can go on for months and even years. In determining the true facts in such situations, the American legal system has long relied on juries. Increasingly, however, legislators and scholars are concluding that a jury trial where the jury is made up of laypeople is not appropriate for settling all disputes. In his article, Sartwelle suggests using professional juries. Sartwelle is a Houston attorney with twenty years' experience defending civil personal-injury cases. He represented the Autumn Hills Nursing Home in a seven-month trial, which ended in a hung jury.

The Case for Professional Juries
T. Sartwelle*

They endured for almost seven months. Coming and going when told. Eating when allowed. Working at their regular jobs or businesses one day a week, if at all. In between the coming and going, they were compelled to sit and listen hour after hour. They were told to remember what they heard but were barred from taking notes. They were expected to understand the subject matter they heard but none had any knowledge or expertise remotely related to it. They were prohibited from asking questions. Above all they were to ignore the emotion in an emotionally charged atmosphere.

Who were those people? Why did they all but give up their jobs and businesses, their personal lives? Why did they consent to listen without taking notes, learn without asking questions?

Strangely, none volunteered. All were compelled. They had no choice to serve or not serve. They were jurors in the American criminal justice system.

The trial was unusual only because of its length. The jurors' burdens were typical of

complex criminal and civil jury trials anywhere in the United States, only magnified by the excruciating length of the case being tried: five individuals and a corporation charged with murder by neglect of 56 old, infirmed residents of a Texas City nursing home, Autumn Hills. As in any trial, the jury had to choose between diametrically opposing views: the state, contending that the "victims" died from neglect, abuse and bed sores: the defense, contending that the residents died of natural but complicated disease processes common to aged, infirmed people no longer able to care for themselves or be cared for by family at home. Ultimately, they were unable to unanimously decide.

The medical testimony representing these two contentions, which the jurors were supposed to comprehend and remember, represented a cornucopia of internal diseases: Alzheimer's disease, cancer of all varieties, Parkinson's Syndrome, peripheral vascular disease, heart diseases of all kinds, neurological diseases, arterial disease,

*Reprinted with the permission of the *Houston Chronicle*, January 18, 1986, Section 6 p. 1.

–continued

—continuing

chronic obstructive pulmonary disease, kidney, liver, gallbladder disease, urological problems including incontinence of bowel and bladder and, one process common to almost all, decubitus ulcers or bed sores. They heard more than 80 witnesses, most experts in some area of medicine or nursing. They were expected to understand these complex, complicated medical and nursing principles and determine the validity of the opposing contentions even though the experts they heard could not agree on the simplest matters.

At the same time, they could not ask questions to clarify testimony they did not understand or fully appreciate. Instead, witnesses were questioned by lawyers who did not know when jurors wanted or needed clarification. Extraordinary amounts of time were spent repetitiously questioning witnesses about basic scientific principles in order to lay a foundation for the jury's understanding of the complex medical testimony. As odd as it may seem, the jurors were not allowed the luxury given to any student expected to learn a complex subject—lecture notes.

Above all else, this jury, without training or practice, was supposed to shut out all the emotional aspects involved in the subject matter of nursing homes and old people. Practically speaking, we know that any juror growing up in our complex society is a product of his/her individual and peculiar biases, prejudices and sympathies. An individual's ability to exclude emotion from influencing a verdict depends upon that person's degree of sophistication as it relates to the facts of any individual case. There is simply no way to measure the influence these extraneous factors may have on a particular juror's verdict, and no way to avoid verdicts totally or partially rendered on these elements rather than the evidence. Why else would trial lawyers try so hard to appeal to emotions?

Despite these drawbacks, we continue to use ordinary citizens to solve our modern society's complexities. Lay juries cost litigants time as well as enormous sums of money because these ordinary citizens mustbe educated in the factual intricacies of a particular dispute. In the end, this cost in time and money is paid by every member of society in the form of taxes to support the court system, higher prices for goods and services, and sky-rocketing premiums for liability insurance. The present-day insurance/tort reform crisis is the reaction to the enormous costs of the present-day jury system.

Is this cost worth the end result which proponents of the jury system call justice? Why is a lay jury better able to arbitrate a complex medical malpractice dispute or a product liability action than would be individuals with special expertise in medicine or product design?

If we each devised a system to arbitrate a dispute between a patient claiming injury from surgery and a doctor claiming that the injury was an inherent risk of surgery, the last solution any of us would propose is selecting 12 people off the street, having no medical knowledge, and allowing them to decide whether a physician properly conducted surgery.

Why then does the jury system persist in American society?

The answer is because the trial system is nurtured by judges and lawyers who have a historical and self-taught myopic view of a system that is, in reality, an archaic ritual. Our present-day dispute-resolution system of lay jurors is far too cumbersome, unwieldy, costly and time-consuming to accomplish what, in a simpler age, was an obtainable goal of justice for all.

Our jury system originated in ancient times when ordinary citizens required protection from a king and a system of government intent on complete domination. This revolutionary idea worked well in this country during its development into an international power primarily because the issues presented to juries were basic to all citizens. Today, however, we use lay people to solve

—continued

–continuing

technical, complex, complicated issues gen-rated by the most advanced, sophisticated society in the world's long history.

Is there another way? Are the lay citizens of this country the only alternative this society has for solving our disputes? Is the legal system as we now know it, with its technical rules of law, evidence and procedure, the only alternative to resolve disputes? Surely, there must be a more time- and cost-effective system.

What would replace jurors? How would legal disputes be resolved? Numerous alternatives are available. Professional jurors, people with expertise in the particular factual dispute on trial might be one way: Engineers for engineering disputes, doctors and nurses for medical problems, architects, accountants, businessmen and every other kind of specialist involved in our complex economy. Such a system would also help reduce lawyers' emotional appeals to sympathy which dominate our present jury system. Trained professionals would be better able to ignore the emotion used to influence verdicts and concentrate solely on facts. Disputes could then be resolved without lawyers' theatrics and emotional appeals to prejudice.

Would we need 123 experts like we now need 12 lay jurors? No, there is absolutely no magic in the number 12. One would do, or, if the society can absorb the cost, use three— majority rules. We could even call the professional jurors "judges." They could be fact judges. Present-day legally trained lawyer-judges (remember every judge was once a lawyer) could then apply whatever principles of law were applicable to the facts found by the fact judge. This concept could be expensive because professional fact judges would require salaries commensurate with their degree of expertise.

In the long run, however, it would be less expensive than the cost of present-day lay jurors who must be laboriously educated in the fashion endured by the 12 brave souls who endured the Autumn Hills trial. Would lay jurors become extinct? Maybe not. They could still be used to resolve simpler problems such as criminal cases or simple civil disputes. In any event, it is clear that changes must be made.

The Ancient Mariner once lamented that he could find no water to drink despite being afloat in an endless ocean. So it is with the American jury system, afloat in a sea of historical platitudes associated with days and issues long past. It is this albatross of anachronism that must be reckoned with before the jury system as we know it today can be modernized to effectively and efficiently deal with the complex issues generated by our society.

Questions

1. What are the basic arguments provided by the author against juries made up of lay people?

2. According to the author, how would professional juries resolve the difficulties posed by juries made up of lay people?

REVIEW AND DISCUSSION QUESTIONS

1. Define the following terms:
   complaint
   motion
   answer
   counterclaim
   affirmative defense
   pleadings

deposition
interrogatory
voir dire
directed verdict
summary judgment
hearsay
judgment n.o.v.
remand
dissenting opinion
arbitration
summary trial

2. Compare and contrast the following concepts:
   a. Motion to dismiss and a motion for directed verdict
   b. Deposition and written interrogatories
   c. Voir dire and challenge for cause
   d. Special verdict and general verdict
   e. Direct examination and cross-examination
   f. Briefs and oral argument

3. Describe the decision-making process a business goes through in determining whether to undertake a lawsuit.

4. How do lawsuits involving a business differ from lawsuits involving individuals?

5. What are the advantages to a business provided by alternative dispute resolution (ADR) processes?

6. Why are ADR processes prohibited from deciding issues on significant public rights and duties?

Case Questions

7. Larry Folsom, an independent truck driver, was unloading potatoes at A & P's warehouse. During the unloading process, he was injured. Folsom brought an action against A & P, alleging it was their negligence that brought about his injuries. At the close of a two and one-half day trial, the jury deliberated just thirty-five minutes and found for A & P. Folsom alleges jury misconduct and moved for a new trial. What result? [*Folsom v. Great Atlantic & Pacific Tea Company*, 521 A.2d 678 (Me.1987)]

8. In resolving an appeal from a district court, the appellate court had the following to say:

   > The appellant has based his appeal on the instructions provided by the judge to the jury. While his assertion has merit, we need not consider it today. The information provided by appellants' witnesses on the issue were clearly ignored by the jury. Thus, we reverse the lower court's finding and remand the case for further proceedings not inconsistent with our ruling.

   The appellee to this proceeding has appealed to the supreme court of the state. What will be the result?

9. Broadway Realty sold Hembree a house. The purchase contract between the parties provided as follows: "Any controversy or claim arising out of or relating to this contract, or the breach thereof, shall be settled by arbitration in the city of contract origin, in accordance with the rules of the American

Arbitration Association." After the sale, Hembree found that the home had a defective roof. He sought arbitration, and his claim came before an arbitrator. The arbitrator ultimately found for Hembree on the theory of implied warranty and awarded him damages. In applying the theory, however, the arbitrator made an error in the application of the law. Since Broadway was the developer and not the builder, it could not be liable to Hembree on an implied warranty theory. On that basis, Broadway appealed the arbitrator's decision to the state court system. How will the state court rule? [*Hembree v. Broadway Realty and Trust Company,* 151 Ariz. 418, 728 P.2d 288 (1986)]

Policy Questions

10. As the text discusses, the parties to a dispute often reach a settlement before trial. As a rule, settlement is encouraged as an effort to save the parties and the state the costs of the litigation. In such cases, it is not uncommon for the parties to agree to keep the terms of the settlement secret—often referred to as protective orders. Is it in the interest of the general public that settlements be kept secret? Suppose the protective order was imposed to keep confidential a business trade secret? The size of the settlement? The fact that the product is inherently dangerous?

11. A party who deliberately disobeys a court order requiring compliance with a discovery request can be held in contempt of court and hence fined or imprisoned *except* in those cases where the party has refused to submit to a physical examination. Why?

12. Legal proceedings in the federal court system are heavily subsidized by the government, particularly when the case involves a jury. During the fiscal year 1982, for example, the estimated cost to the federal government for a tort suit filed in a United States District Court was $1,740. In similar tort cases tried before juries, the average cost was $15,028. Given that the federal government receives only $60 per case in filing fees, is this subsidy too great?

13. Much has been made of the apparent explosion in litigation in this country over the past twenty-five years. Indeed, former Chief Justice of the Supreme Court Warren Burger has asserted, "Mass neurosis . . . leads people to think courts were created to solve the problems of society." The assertion is that changes in social norms have somehow caused us to become oriented toward resolving even trivial disputes through the court systems. Could any of the following events also help explain the growth in litigation over the past twenty-five years?
    a. A concurrent growth in the number of laws.
    b. An enormous increase in the number of attorneys.
    c. The legalization of advertising by lawyers.
    d. The invalidation of minimum fee schedules.
    e. The enactment of regulatory statutes that authorize the award of attorney's fees to victorious plaintiffs.
    f. The liberalization of the Federal Rules of Civil Procedure, changes in the bankruptcy code, the creation of no-fault automobile accident compensation, and other such regulatory alterations undertaken by the legal profession in recent years.
    g. The active participation by the courts in major social issues such as capital punishment, prison conditions, and abortion.

14. A person may legally be his or her own attorney in almost any legal matter. In what circumstances and for what reasons would it be unwise for a person to act as his or her own attorney?

15. Proponents of the adversary system believe that allowing the parties to the dispute to make competing arguments of fact and law gives the judge and jury the best opportunity to reach an accurate decision. Critics contend that it encourages the parties to employ incomplete, distorted, and sometimes false statements in order to win. Do attorneys have the responsibility to undertake such activities in the interest of the clients? What would motivate an attorney to distort the truth?

Ethics Questions

16. As the text discussed, businesses are considered by juries to be deep pockets. Suppose a business found itself in the following circumstances:

> A large energy company comprises an exploration division, a development division, a transportation division, and a marketing division. The transportation division purchased natural gas from the company's own development division, but the majority of the company's purchases were from smaller producers. The contracts called for the transportation division to take and pay for gas, regardless of whether it had sold it. Energy prices dropped dramatically, and the transportation division found that for every ten units of natural gas it was forced to take and pay for, it could sell only one unit. At some point, the transportation division will not be able to continue this uneconomic practice caused by its contracts. The producers will sue the company, which has sufficient assets to pay the judgments. Or, the company could protect its assets by selling the transportation division. The new owner could then threaten to put the transportation company—which has far fewer assets than the whole company—into bankruptcy if the producers do not renegotiate the contracts.

What do you suggest?

17. In giving instructions to the jury, should judges be allowed to comment on the evidence presented at the trial? Consider the following charge provided to the jury:

> . . . I am going to tell you what I think of the defendant's testimony. You may have noticed, Mr. Foreman and ladies and gentlemen, that he wiped his hands during his testimony. It is rather a curious thing, but that is almost always an indication of lying. Why it should be so we don't know, but that is a fact. I think that every single word that man said, except when he agreed with the government's testimony, was a lie.

18. According to Professors Rosenberg, Smit, and Korn:

> If it were possible for the parties to a lawsuit—and if they could be motivated—to state the facts underlying their controversy fully and accurately at the outset in the pleadings, there would be no need for trials. . . .

Why do litigants "exaggerate" or omit the facts in the pleadings? What do they stand to gain by postponing the inevitable?

4 Business and the Constitution

G EORGE Washington presided over a convention in Philadelphia from May to September 1787 at which the Constitution of the United States was drafted. Having been ratified by nine of the thirteen original states, the Constitution became effective in March 1789. It is composed of the preamble and seven articles. The preamble reads:

> We the people of the United States, in order to form a more perfect Union, establish justice, insure domestic tranquility, provide for the common defense, promote the general welfare, and secure the blessings of liberty to ourselves and our posterity, do ordain and establish this Constitution for the United States of America.

The Articles, which are divided into sections, provide for the following:

I. Composition and powers of Congress
II. Selection and powers of the president
III. Creation and powers of the federal judiciary
IV. Role of the states in the federal system
V. Methods of amending the Constitution
VI. Declaring the Constitution to be supreme law of the land
VII. Method for ratifying the Constitution

The process of amending the Constitution began almost immediately. In 1791 the first ten amendments (the Bill of Rights) were ratified by the states after having been approved by the First Session of Congress. The Twenty-sixth Amendment, lowering the voting age to eighteen, was ratified in 1971. Numerous other amendments have been proposed, but many, such as the Equal Rights Amendment, have failed. A proposed amendment must pass three-fourths of the state legislatures within a time period specified by

Congress, which must pass amendments by a two-thirds vote in the Senate and House. The Constitution is reprinted in Appendix B of the book.

Except for a few rights that are clearly expressed, most of the Constitution is written in general terms or in terms that can be interpreted in different ways. Justice Story noted this in 1816 in *Martin v. Hunter's Lessee:*

> The constitution unavoidably deals in general language. It did not suit the purposes of the people, in framing this great charter of our liberties, to provide for minute specifications of its powers, or to declare the means by which those powers should be carried into execution. It was foreseen that this would be a perilous and difficult, if not an impracticable, task. The instrument was not intended to provide merely for the exigencies of a few years, but was to endure through a long lapse of ages, the events of which were locked up in the inscrutable purposes of Providence. It could not be foreseen what new changes and modifications of power might be indispensable to effectuate the general objects of the charter; and restrictions and specifications which, at the present, might seem salutary, might, in the end, prove the overthrow of the system itself. Hence its powers are expressed in general terms, leaving to the legislature, from time to time, to adopt its own means to effectuate legitimate objects, and to mold and model the exercise of its powers, as its own wisdom and the public interest should require.

This chapter concentrates on constitutional law that affects business. All citizens are affected by all parts of the Constitution. Court rulings about the rights of individuals when they are accused of crimes draw the most popular attention. The Constitution provides safeguards against overzealous law enforcement agencies, primarily through the Bill of Rights. Supreme Court interpretation of the rights of persons accused of crimes and Court interpretation of other constitutionally protected rights changes as the attitude of society changes. The Court has reversed itself on major constitutional issues over the years, reading the same words in an opposite manner. While some would say that this means that the Court is political, others say that it simply reflects changes in technology, social values, economic conditions, and political realities.

CONSTITUTIONAL BASIS OF REGULATION

The Constitution has significant effects on the operations of business. While all parts of the Constitution have application to business as well as to individuals, certain provisions have had a much more substantial impact on the business community.

The Commerce Clause

"The Congress shall have Power . . . To regulate Commerce with foreign Nations, and among the several States, and with the Indian Tribes;" states Article I, Section 8, of the United States Constitution. Known as the *commerce clause*, these few words have been interpreted to give Congress the power to enact most of the federal regulation of business discussed in this text. In fact, the clause might be reduced to "Regulate Commerce . . . among the several

States" to show the essential basis of federal regulation. Many other important parts of the Constitution affect business, but the commerce clause is without a doubt the single most important provision.

Defining "Commerce" Among the Several States

Although most federal regulation of business has evolved in the twentieth century, Congress has had broad regulatory powers since the early days of the Republic. In 1824, Chief Justice Marshall established some of the basic guidelines of the commerce clause in *Gibbons* v. *Ogden*. He held that commerce among the states means *interstate commerce*, that is, "commerce which concerns more States than one." This distinction between interstate and intrastate commerce has remained central to constitutional limits on federal regulatory actions, since commerce was broadly defined to include all commercial dealings.

Further, Justice Marshall held, "What is this power? It is the power to regulate; that is, to prescribe the rule by which commerce is to be governed. This power, like all others vested in Congress, is complete in itself, may be exercised to its utmost extent, and acknowledges no limitations other than are prescribed in the Constitution." Exclusive power over regulation of foreign commerce also resides with Congress.

The Necessary and Proper Clause

The Constitution specifies a long list of congressional powers (including collecting taxes, regulating interstate commerce, providing for national defense). At the end of the list, clause 18 of Article I, Section 8, gives Congress power "to make all Laws which shall be necessary and proper for carrying into Execution the foregoing Powers, and all other Powers vested by this Constitution in the Government of the United States, or in any Department or Officer thereof." This provision is known as the *necessary and proper clause*.

The necessary and proper clause, along with the commerce clause, has been held to provide justification for broad congressional control of commerce. Often the distinction between the clauses is difficult to find in the interpretations by the Supreme Court. Essentially, the necessary and proper clause gives Congress power to deal with matters beyond the list of specified federal concerns as long as control of those matters will help Congress be more effective in executing control over specified concerns. For example, the Supreme Court has held that a federal statute limiting tort liabilities arising out of nuclear accidents was necessary and proper to achieving an objective of encouraging the development of privately operated nuclear power plants.

Limits on Congressional Powers to Regulate Commerce

Some limits are placed on congressional power to regulate commerce. Intrastate commerce may be subject to federal governance only to assist in the regulation of interstate commerce. Obviously, it is very difficult to know where to draw the line. The Supreme Court does not set a firm rule, recognizing that as business and society change, so will the need or desire for certain regulatory actions. Congressional power is flexible. The Supreme Court has said that it is not possible to have a mechanical definition of when a federal law may affect intrastate commerce. Rather, congressional control applies when the *intrastate commerce* being regulated "have such a close and substantial relation to interstate commerce that their control is essential or appropriate to protect that commerce from burdens and obstructions."

Interstate Commerce Broadly Defined

Just because the effect of a business on interstate commerce is small does not mean that a business will be exempt from federal regulation. For example, in the 1942 Supreme Court case *Wickard* v. *Filburn*, federal controls on the production of wheat were held to apply to a small farm in Ohio that produced only 239 bushels of wheat for consumption on the farm. The Court reasoned that Congress intended to regulate the wheat industry. To control wheat prices effectively, there could not be an exemption for small intrastate producers. Although one farmer would not make a difference, all the small farmers added together would have a substantial impact on the wheat market.

"Local" Business Rarely Exempt

In another case, *Perez* v. *United States* (1971), the Supreme Court upheld congressional regulation of credit markets including federal regulation of local loan sharking activities. The Court held that even though the activity may be local, in sum it may be substantial, and the funds behind local loan sharks are often interstate in origin, since they may come from organized crime, which is a national concern.

In the *Katzenbach* v. *McClung* decision, the Court used the commerce clause to extend nondiscrimination requirements of the 1964 Civil Rights Act to local operations.

Katzenbach v. McClung
United States Supreme Court
379 U.S. 294,
85 S.Ct. 377
(1964)

Case Background. *Ollie's Barbecue was a family-owned restaurant in Birmingham, Alabama. It had 220 seats for white customers. Although most of the employees were black, black customers were allowed to buy food only at a take-out window. The Department of Justice (Attorney General Katzenbach) sued the restaurant for violating Section 201 of Title II of the 1964 Civil Rights Act, which prohibits racial segregation in places of public accommodation. This includes restaurants that offer "to serve interstate travelers or [if] a substantial portion of the food which it serves ... has moved in interstate commerce." Ollie's (McClung) contended that its customers were local, not in interstate travel, so it should be exempt from the law. The government noted that $70,000 of the $150,000 worth of food Ollie's bought the year before had moved in interstate commerce, which was enough to make the business interstate. The district court agreed with the government; McClung appealed to the Supreme Court.*

Case Decision. Justice Clark delivered the opinion of the court.

* * *

... [T]here was an impressive array of testimony that discrimination in restaurants had a direct and highly restrictive effect upon interstate travel by Negroes. This resulted, it was said, because discrimination practices prevent Negroes from buying prepared food served on the premises while on a trip, except in isolated and unkempt restaurants and under most unsatisfactory and often unpleasant conditions. This obviously discourages travel and obstructs interstate commerce for one can hardly travel without eating. Likewise, it was said, that discrimination deterred professional, as well as skilled, people from moving into areas where such practices occurred and thereby caused industry to be reluctant to establish there. . . .

We believe that this testimony afforded ample basis for the conclusion that established restaurants in such areas sold less interstate goods because of the discrimination, that interstate travel was obstructed directly by it, that business in general suffered and that many new businesses refrained from establishing there as a result of it.

* * *

. . . Much is said about a restaurant business being local but "even if appellee's activity be local and though it may not be regarded as commerce, it may still, whatever its nature, be reached by Congress if it exerts a substantial economic effect on interstate commerce." *Wickard v. Filburn.*

This Court has held time and again that this power extends to activities of retail establishments, including restaurants, which directly or indirectly burden or obstruct interstate commerce.

* * *

Congress has determined for itself that refusals of service to Negroes have imposed burdens both upon the interstate flow of food and upon the movement of products generally. Of course, the mere fact that Congress has said when particular activity shall be deemed to affect commerce does not preclude further examination by this Court. But where we find that the legislators, in light of the facts and testimony before them, have a rational basis for finding a chosen regulatory scheme necessary to the protection of commerce, our investigation is at an end. The only remaining question—one answered in the affirmative by the court below—is whether the particular restaurant either serves or offers to serve interstate travelers or serves food a substantial portion of which has moved in interstate commerce.

* * *

Confronted as we are with the facts laid before Congress, we must conclude that it had a rational basis for finding that racial discrimination in restaurants had a direct and adverse effect on the free flow of interstate commerce. Insofar as the section of the Civil Rights Act here relevant is concerned, Congress prohibited discrimination only in those establishments having a close tie to interstate commerce, i.e., those, like McClung's, serving food that has come from out of the State. We think in so doing that Congress acted well within its power to protect and foster commerce in extending the coverage of Title II only to those restaurants offering to serve interstate travelers or serving food, a substantial portion of which has moved in interstate commerce.

The absence of direct evidence connecting discriminatory restaurant service with the flow of interstate food, a factor on which the appellees place much reliance, is not, given the evidence as to the effect of such practices on other aspects of commerce, a crucial matter.

The power of Congress in this field is broad and sweeping: where it keeps within its sphere and violates no express constitutional limitation it has been the rule of this Court, going back almost to the founding days of the Republic, not to interfere. The Civil Rights Act of 1964, as here applied, we find to be plainly appropriate in the resolution of what the Congress found to be a national commercial problem of the first magnitude. We find in it no violation of any express limitations of the Constitution and we therefore declare it valid.

* * *

Case Holding. *The Supreme Court upheld the constitutionality of the Civil Rights Act of 1964 as it applied to public accommodations. The Court noted that Congress found a rational basis to support this regulation under the necessary and proper clause. It was irrelevant that the amount of commerce involved in this particular case was trivial; Congress has the power to regulate it.*

Case Questions

1. Do you think the court might have found differently if the restaurant could have shown that ninety-nine percent of its food was from sources within the state?

2. Suppose evidence was presented that when restaurants were required by law to integrate, they often closed their doors and refused to do any more business. Does this go against the argument that the law enhances interstate commerce?

Federal/State Regulatory Relations

The legal environment is made up of a vast array of state and federal laws and regulations. As Figure 4–1 illustrates, the responsibility for regulating a particular business activity may be the sole responsibility of a state governing body, the sole responsibility of a federal governing body, or, in some instances, the shared responsibility of the state and federal governments. Federal environmental regulation, for example, requires the federal government to set national pollution control standards. Given the federal standards, state

Figure 4–1   Relationship Between State and Federal Regulatory Environments

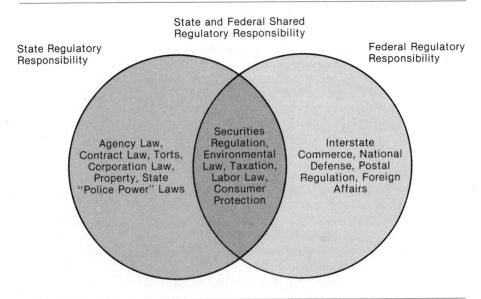

environmental regulations may provide the actual requirements to be met by plants within a state's jurisdiction.

On occasion, a state may legislate on the same subject matter as does Congress. The question then arises whether or not state law can exist along with federal law. Federal regulation takes precedence over state regulation that directly contradicts or reduces the standards imposed by federal law. In addition, states may not enact laws that create an unreasonable burden on interstate commerce. In some areas, such as postal authority, Congress is said to have preempted the power of the states to regulate at all. States may not pass laws in these areas even if the laws do not contradict federal laws.

When State and Federal Laws Conflict

The limits on state regulatory activities have given the Supreme Court problems for years. Like many constitutional areas, the court's interpretation has changed over the years. As federal regulation of business became more common in this century, the Court had to give more weight to congressional action or make it ineffective because of conflicting state rules.

It is clear that if Congress passes a regulation that is constitutional, the states may not pass regulations that would impede the effect of the federal rule. In many areas, the states are free to add rules of their own that strengthen the impact of the federal rule, so long as they do not conflict with the intent of the law and do not impede interstate commerce. For example, states may pass air pollution regulations to apply to their industries that are stricter than the federal air pollution rules. However, unless specifically allowed by Congress, states may not pass rules less strict than the federal rule.

When State Law Impedes Interstate Commerce

In 1945, the Supreme Court, in *Southern Pacific Co.* v. *Arizona,* had to consider Arizona regulations that for "safety considerations" required trains to be shorter in Arizona than in other states. Although the Arizona law was not intended to conflict with the federal rules about train length, the effect of the Arizona safety requirement was to impede interstate commerce. At the Arizona border, trains had to be shortened.

The Supreme Court struck down the Arizona law. Chief Justice Stone said, "The decisive question is whether in the circumstances the total effect of the law as a safety measure in reducing accidents and casualties is so slight or problematical as not to outweigh the national interest in keeping interstate commerce free from interferences which seriously impede it. . . ." He noted further, "The matters for ultimate determination here are the nature and extent of the burden which the state regulation of interstate trains, adopted as a safety measure, imposes on interstate commerce, and whether the relative weights of the state and national interests involved are such as to make inapplicable the rule, generally observed, that the free flow of interstate commerce . . . [is] safeguarded by the commerce clause from state interference."

There are numerous Supreme Court cases in this area, so the exact boundaries of the constitutional rules are constantly being probed. For example, in 1988, three Supreme Court cases examined federal and state regulatory relations:

● In *Schneidewind* v. *ANR Pipeline Co.,* the Court held that the federal Natural Gas Act prevented the state of Michigan from regulating the issuance of new securities by natural gas companies in interstate commerce. Since state control over the securities could affect the financing of the gas companies, it could influence their ability to do interstate business, which means that the Michigan statute could conflict with the commerce clause.

- In *New York City* v. *Federal Communications Commission*, the right of the Federal Communications Commission (FCC) to preempt existing state and local regulations of cable television was upheld. Since Congress gave the FCC board regulatory powers, the commission's action in this respect was reasonable since Congress did not prevent it from controlling this area and because it acted to prevent conflicting state standards.

- In *Mississippi Power & Light Co.* v. *Mississippi*, the Federal Energy Regulatory Commission (FERC) assigned costs to various utilities of a nuclear power plant that the utilities were sharing. The Court held that the costs set by the FERC preempted those that state utility regulators attempted to fix.

Even when there are federal regulations, the states may not necessarily imitate those regulations, if that will inhibit interstate commerce. Consider the following situation. Since the 1920s, Congress stipulated that timber removed from federal lands in Alaska may not be exported from Alaska or shipped to other states unless processed in Alaska. This meant that unprocessed logs could not be shipped out of Alaska; they had to be cut into boards first. The state of Alaska imitated the federal rule in 1980, requiring that timber cut on state lands be processed within the state before shipment out of state.

The Supreme Court struck down the state requirement in a 1984 case, *South-Central Timber Development, Inc.* v. *Wunnicke*. "Although the Commerce Clause is by its text an affirmative grant of power to Congress to regulate interstate and foreign commerce, the Clause has long been recognized as a self-executing limitation on the power of the States to enact laws imposing substantial burdens on such commerce." That is, although Congress could impose such a requirement on its timber, the state could not do so, too, unless authorized to do so by Congress. "In light of the substantial attention given by Congress to the subject of export restrictions on unprocessed timber, it would be peculiarly inappropriate to permit state regulation of the subject."

The Contract Clause

Article I, Section 10, clause 1, of the Constitution appears to be quite simple: "No State shall . . . pass any . . . Law impairing the Obligation of Contracts. . . ." Generally, in applying the *contract clause*, the Court has attempted to accommodate both the legitimate interests of the contracting parties and the need of the state to pass rules in the public interest.

One important decision is *United States Trust Co. of New York* v. *New Jersey* (1977). The Port Authority of New York and New Jersey was established in 1921 to improve transportation facilities connected with the port of New York. Bonds were sold to private investors to finance construction. To enhance the marketability of its bonds, in 1962 the Port Authority placed a ceiling on the amount of mass transit deficits it could finance at any time. This decision was backed by statutes passed by New York and New Jersey. In 1974, the mass transit system was in financial trouble. To provide an increase in funding for the system, the states repealed the 1962 debt limits. Because of the increased uncertainty of the financial viability of the system, the value of bonds sold before 1974 dropped. The bondholders sued the states, claiming that the repeal of the 1962 bond agreement was a violation of the contract clause of the Constitution.

The Supreme Court agreed with the bondholders. The repeal of the 1962 statute broke a contractual obligation. The Court noted that in some cases contractual obligations could be impaired by the states. "The Contract Clause does not require a State to adhere to a contract that surrenders an essential attribute of its sovereignty." That is, a state legislature cannot bargain away state police powers and other essential powers. A contract may be broken by the states if it is reasonable and necessary to serve an important public purpose. In this case, since the states knew of the impending mass transit problems, they had time to act responsibly without impairing the rights of existing bondholders.

The Taxing Power

Congress is given the power to "lay and collect Taxes, Duties, Imposts and Excises" by Article I, Section 8, clause 1, of the Constitution. Although this text does not investigate federal taxation (since that is a complex topic requiring specialized courses), it should be remembered that taxation can be a potent tool of regulation. Taxes can be used for more than simply raising revenue. They can be used to deter and to punish certain behavior. For example, a tax may be tied to a requirement to keep detailed records about goods subject to the tax. In this manner, goods such as explosives, firearms, drugs, and liquors may be kept under federal supervision.

Federal Taxation

The Supreme Court rarely questions federal taxing schemes. In 1937, the Court noted in *Sonzinsky* v. *U.S.*, "Inquiry into the hidden motives which may move Congress to exercise a power constitutionally conferred upon it is beyond the competency of courts. . . . We are not free to speculate as to the motives which moved Congress to impose it, or as to the extent to which it may operate to restrict the activities taxed. As it is not attended by offensive regulation, and since it operates as a tax, it is within the taxing power."

The Court has upheld taxes on illegal gambling and narcotics. This enhances the ability of the government to prosecute those involved in illegal activities. If the income from such activities is reported, the government has evidence of illegal dealings. If the income is not reported, and money is found, then the tax laws have been violated. As the Court held in *U.S.* v. *Kahriger*, "It is axiomatic that the power of Congress to tax is extensive and sometimes falls with crushing effect on businesses deemed unessential or inimical to the public welfare, or where, as in dealings with narcotics, the collection of the tax also is difficult."

State Taxing Schemes

Although the power of Congress to tax is nearly unlimited, the states may not interfere with interstate commerce through their taxing schemes. Further, since the Constitution gives Congress the power to regulate international trade, as it does interstate commerce, the states may not interfere with international commerce.

The Supreme Court emphasized that point in the 1979 case *Japan Line, Ltd.* v. *County of Los Angeles.* Several California cities and counties imposed a property tax on cargo-shipping containers owned by Japanese companies. The containers were used only in international commerce on Japanese ships. The California taxes were levied on the containers in the state during loading and unloading. The Supreme Court held the tax to be unconstitutional. The commerce clause reserves to Congress the power over foreign commerce. Foreign commerce may not be subject to state taxes, or the states could effectively regulate foreign trade. Only the federal government may speak on foreign trade and tax matters.

State Taxes Not Allowed to Impede Interstate Commerce. Since most commerce is interstate, what can the states tax? The intent of the Constitution is to protect interstate commerce from impediments established by state taxes. As the Court noted in the 1959 case *Northwestern States Portland Cement Co.* v. *Minnesota:* "... a State 'cannot impose taxes upon persons passing through the state or coming into it merely for a temporary purpose.' ... Moreover, it is beyond dispute that a State may not lay a tax on the 'privilege' of engaging in interstate commerce. ... Nor may a State impose a tax which discriminates against interstate commerce either by providing a direct commercial advantage to local business ... or by subjecting interstate commerce to the burden of 'multiple taxation.' ... Such impositions have been stricken because the States, under the Commerce Clause, are not allowed 'one single tax-dollar worth of direct interference with the free flow of commerce.' "

Consider the following cases in which the Supreme Court reviewed state taxing schemes to decide if they interfered with interstate commerce:

- The state of Hawaii imposed a tax on all alcoholic beverages except for a local product. The Court struck this down in 1984, holding that the tax imposed on alcoholic products had to be the same regardless of origin.

- Pennsylvania imposed an annual tax on out-of-state trucks that carried goods through the state. The tax was not imposed on trucks registered in Pennsylvania because those trucks paid an annual registration fee. The Court struck this down in 1987 as a violation of the commerce clause because it imposed a heavier tax burden on out-of-state businesses engaged in interstate commerce in Pennsylvania than it did on Pennsylvania businesses engaged in interstate commerce.

- Michigan's state income tax exempted from taxation the retirement benefits paid to Michigan government employees. The state taxed all other employee retirement benefits, such as retired federal government employees' benefits. The Supreme Court struck this down in 1989 as discriminatory. State income taxes must apply to all government retirement benefits equally.

● Illinois imposes a 5-percent tax on all long-distance calls to or from the state. If a taxpayer can show that another state has billed the call, the Illinois tax will be refunded. This tax was held by the Supreme Court not to violate the commerce clause in *Goldberg* v. *Sweet* (1989) because it satisfies a four-part test:

1. the tax applies to an activity having a substantial nexus within the state;
2. the tax is fairly apportioned;
3. the tax does not discriminate against interstate commerce, compared to intrastate commerce; and
4. the tax is fairly related to services that the state provides to the benefit of taxpayers.

Apportioning State Tax Burden. The Supreme Court has held that the income of businesses may be taxed by the states—so long as the proceeds are fairly apportioned among the states—using formulas that account for the intrastate share of interstate commerce. A tax on income "from interstate commerce, as distinguished from a tax on the privilege of engaging in interstate commerce, does not conflict with the Commerce Clause. . . ."

The apportionment issue generates substantial litigation because there are many difficult issues. Firms often have manufacturing and distribution systems that involve activities in numerous states. It is nearly impossible to know how to assign the various costs to the different portions of an operation—different accounting techniques will produce different legitimate results. A state may tax the portion of a business that occurs within its borders. The federal courts are concerned not with the level of taxation, but with whether the intent or effect of a tax is to impose greater burdens on transactions that cross state lines than on those that occur entirely within a state.

BUSINESS AND FREE SPEECH

The First Amendment prohibits congressional encroachment on *freedom of speech:* "Congress shall make no law . . . abridging the freedom of speech. . . ." Since this right is not absolute—it will not protect someone who falsely shouts "fire" in a theatre and causes panic—the Supreme Court has had to define what type of speech may be regulated.

People have debated whether commercial speech, advertisements, and political statements by corporations, such as statements about public issues, deserve the same freedoms as political speech by private citizens. Political speech is generally provided First Amendment protection. While it is clear that citizens have very broad rights of free speech, some people contend that commercial speech, since it is for profit, does not deserve the same protections as political speech. Others say it does deserve the same freedoms.

The Constitution did not distinguish between the two kinds of speech; and in both cases, the parties, private or public, are usually trying to convince some group of people about something—to buy soap, to buy a political program, or to buy a politician. The Supreme Court has helped resolve the issue in several important cases that have tended to extend First Amendment protection to commercial speech.

Political Statements by Corporations

First National Bank of Boston v. *Bellotti* (1978) provided the Supreme Court the opportunity to address the issue of *political speech* by corporations and First Amendment freedoms. A Massachusetts criminal statute prohibited corporations from making contributions or expenditures "for the purpose of . . . influencing or affecting the vote on any question submitted to the voters, other than one materially affecting any of the property, business or assets of the corporation." The First National Bank of Boston and other firms wished to make contributions to help defeat a referendum proposition to amend the Massachusetts Constitution to allow the legislature to impose a graduated personal income tax. The United States Supreme Court struck down the statute: "The speech proposed by appellants is at the heart of the First Amendment's protection. The freedom of speech . . . guaranteed by the Constitution embraces at the least the liberty to discuss publicly and truthfully all matters of public concern without previous restraint or fear of subsequent punishment. . . ."

The Court could "find no support in the First or Fourteenth Amendments . . . for the proposition that speech that otherwise would be within the protection of the First Amendment loses that protection simply because its source is a corporation that cannot prove, to the satisfaction of a court, a material effect on its business or property . . . it amounts to an impermissible legislative prohibition of speech based on the identity of the interests that spokesmen may represent in public debate over controversial issues. . . ." The Court reemphasized the right of free speech regarding political issues on the part of business in the *Consolidated Edison Co.* v. *Public Service Commission* decision.

Consolidated Edison Company v. Public Service Commission of New York
United States Supreme Court
447 U.S. 530,
100 S.Ct. 2326
(1980)

Case Background. *The Consolidated Edison Company of New York, the appellant in this case, placed written material titled "Independence Is Still a Goal, and Nuclear Power Is Needed to Win the Battle" in its January 1976 billing envelope. The bill insert stated Consolidated Edison's views on nuclear power. Soon after that the Public Service Commission of New York prohibited Consolidated Edison from using bill inserts to discuss its opinions on controversial issues of public policy. The commission concluded that utility customers who receive bills containing inserts are a captive audience who should not be subjected to the utility's views. The commission did not bar topics that are noncontroversial.*

The New York Court of Appeals upheld the commission's prohibition on political issue inserts. Consolidated Edison appealed to the U.S. Supreme Court. The issue in the case is whether the First Amendment of the Constitution, as incorporated by the Fourteenth Amendment, is violated by an order of the Public Service Commission that prohibits the inclusion in monthly electric bills of inserts discussing controversial issues of public policy.

Case Decision. Justice Powell delivered the opinion of the Court.

* * *

The Commission's ban on bill inserts is not, of course, invalid merely because it imposes a limitation upon speech. We must consider whether the State can demonstrate that its regulation is constitutionally permissible. The Commission's arguments require us to consider three theories that might justify the state action.

We must determine whether the prohibition is (1) a reasonable time, place, or manner restriction, (2) a permissible subject-matter regulation, or (3) a narrowly tailored means of serving a compelling state interest.

This Court has recognized the validity of reasonable time, place, or manner regulations that serve a significant governmental interest and leave ample alternative channels for communication. . . .

A restriction that regulates only the time, place or manner of speech may be imposed so long as it's reasonable. But when regulation is based on the content of speech, governmental action must be scrutinized more carefully to ensure that communication has not been prohibited "merely because public officials disapprove the speaker's views."

* * *

The Commission does not pretend that its action is unrelated to the content or subject matter of bill inserts. Indeed, it has undertaken to suppress certain bill inserts precisely because they address controversial issues of public policy. The Commission allows inserts that present information to consumers on certain subjects, such as energy conservation measures, but it forbids the use of inserts that discuss public controversies. The Commission, with commendable candor, justifies its ban on the ground that consumers will benefit from receiving "useful" information, but not from the prohibited information. The Commission's own rationale demonstrates that its action cannot be upheld as a content-neutral time, place, or manner regulation.

The Commission next argues that its order is acceptable because it applies to all discussion of nuclear power, whether pro or con, in bill inserts. The prohibition, the Commission contends, is related to subject matter rather than to the views of a particular speaker. Because the regulation does not favor either side of a political controversy, the Commission asserts that it does not unconstitutionally suppress freedom of speech.

The First Amendment's hostility to content-based regulation extends not only to restrictions on particular viewpoints, but also to prohibition of public discussion of an entire topic. . . .

To allow a government the choice of permissible subjects for public debate would be to allow that government control over the search for political truth.

* * *

Where a government restricts the speech of a private person, the state action may be sustained only if the government can show that the regulation is a precisely drawn means of serving a compelling state interest.

* * *

The State Court of Appeals largely based its approval of the prohibition upon its conclusion that the bill inserts intruded upon individual privacy. The court stated that the Commission could act to protect the privacy of the utility's customers because they have no choice whether to receive the insert and the views expressed in the insert may inflame their sensibilities. But the Court of Appeals erred in its assessment of the seriousness of the intrusion.

* * *

Where a single speaker communicates to many listeners, the First Amendment does not permit the government to prohibit speech as intrusive unless the "captive" audience cannot avoid objectionable speech.

Passengers on public transportation or residents of a neighborhood disturbed by the raucous broadcasts from a passing soundtruck may well be unable to escape an unwanted message. But customers who encounter an objectionable billing insert may "effectively avoid further bombardment of their sensibilities simply by averting their eyes." The customer of Consolidated Edison may escape exposure to objectionable material simply by transferring the bill insert from envelope to wastebasket.

* * *

Case Holding. *The Supreme Court reversed the high court of New York, holding that the regulation suppressing bill inserts that discuss controversial public issues directly infringes on the freedom of speech protected by the First and Fourteenth Amendments.*

Case Questions

1. Do you think a distinction should be drawn between political speech paid for by private persons and that paid for by customers who may not want the speech? That is, the political inserts in this case were paid for by the customers of Con Ed who obtain their electricity from that company.

2. Would you distinguish between speech that addresses issues and corporate political speech that endorses particular candidates for office or attacks others?

The Supreme Court reaffirmed in a 1987 case, *Board of Airport Commissioners of Los Angeles* v. *Jews for Jesus*, that blanket restrictions on speech in commercial establishments will not be allowed by the First Amendment. The Court held that the airport authority could not impose an outright ban on all political and other controversial speech in the Los Angeles International Airport. However, the Court indicated, as in *Consolidated Edison*, that some restrictions may be allowed but will be reviewed for their reasonableness.

An example of such a restriction comes from a controversial 1990 decision, *Austin* v. *Michigan Chamber of Commerce*, which is discussed in the *Issue* at the end of the chapter. In that case, the Supreme Court allows states to prohibit the use of general corporate money for supporting or opposing political candidates. The compelling government interest that allows this regulation is the desire to eliminate distortions caused by corporate spending for this purpose out of general corporate funds, as opposed to corporate spending for this purpose that comes from corporate money that has been set aside for specific political purposes.

Commercial Speech

Drawing the line between *commercial speech,* such as advertising a product for sale, and political speech by a corporation is difficult. In many cases, the intent is the same: to increase the expected profits of the business over time. In one case, it is done by trying to convince people to buy a product. In another case, it is done by trying to influence governmental policy in a way that will favor the business or to reduce prospects of passage of a law that would hurt the business. The Supreme Court has recognized that free speech applies to both commercial speech and political speech by business.

In 1980, in *Central Hudson Gas & Electric Corp.* v. *Public Service Comm. of N.Y.,* the Court addressed the issue of controls on commercial speech and established a four-part test that must be met to justify restrictions on commercial speech.

Central Hudson Gas & Electric Corporation v. Public Service Commission of New York

United States Supreme Court
447 U.S. 557,
100 S.Ct. 2343
(1980)

Case Background. *The winter of 1973–74 was a difficult one for this country because of the Organization of Petroleum Exporting Countries (OPEC) embargo, shortages of natural gas, and public perceptions about rapidly declining energy supplies. The Public Service Commission of New York ordered electric utilities in New York State to cease all advertising that "promot[es] the use of electricity." The order was based on the commission's finding that the utility system in New York State did not have sufficient capacity to continue furnishing all customer demands for the 1973–74 winter. The commission declared all promotional advertising contrary to the national policy of conserving energy. It offered to review any proposed advertising that would encourage energy conservation. The high court of New York State upheld the constitutionality of the regulation. The utility company appealed to the Supreme Court.*

Case Decision. Justice Powell delivered the opinion of the Court.

* * *

The Commission's order restricts only commercial speech, that is, expression related solely to the economic interests of the speaker and its audience. . . . The First Amendment, as applied to the States through the Fourteenth Amendment, protects commercial speech from unwarranted government regulation. Commercial expression not only serves the economic interest of the speaker, but also assists consumers . . . in the fullest possible dissemination of information. In applying the First Amendment to this area, we have rejected the "highly paternalistic" view that government has complete power to suppress or regulate commercial speech. "[P]eople will perceive their own best interests if only they are well enough informed and . . . the best means to that end is to open the channels of communication, rather than to close them. . . ." Even when advertising communicates only an incomplete version of the relevant facts, the First Amendment presumes that some accurate information is better than no information at all.

Nevertheless, our decisions have recognized "the 'common-sense' distinction between speech proposing a commercial transaction, which occurs in an area traditionally subject to government regulation and other varieties of speech." . . . The Constitution therefore accords a lesser protection to commercial speech than to other constitutionally guaranteed expression. The protection available for particular commercial expression turns on the nature both of the expression and of the governmental interests served by its regulation.

The First Amendment's concern for commercial speech is based on the informational function of advertising. Consequently, there can be no constitutional objection to the suppression of commercial messages that do not accurately inform the public about lawful activity. The government may ban forms of communication more likely to deceive the public than to inform it, or commercial speech related to illegal activity.

If the communication is neither misleading nor related to unlawful activity, the government's power is more circumscribed.

* * *

In commercial speech cases . . . a four-part analysis has developed. At the outset, we must determine whether the expression is protected by the First Amendment. For commercial speech to come within that provision, it at least must concern lawful activity and not be misleading. Next, we ask whether the asserted governmental interest is substantial. If both inquiries yield positive answers, we must determine whether the regulation directly advances the governmental interest asserted, and whether it is not more extensive than is necessary to serve that interest.

We now apply this four-step analysis for commercial speech to the Commission's arguments in support of its ban on promotional advertising.

The Commission does not claim that the expression at issue either is inaccurate or relates to unlawful activity. Yet the New York Court of Appeals questioned whether Central Hudson's advertising is protected commercial speech. Because appellant holds a monopoly over the sale of electricity in its service area, the state court suggested that the Commission's order restricts no commercial speech of any worth. The court stated that advertising in a "noncompetitive market" could not improve the decisionmaking of consumers. The court saw no constitutional problem with barring commercial speech that it viewed as conveying little useful information.

This reasoning falls short of establishing that appellant's advertising is not commercial speech protected by the First Amendment.

* * *

Even in monopoly markets, the suppression of advertising reduces the information available for consumer decisions and thereby defeats the purpose of the First Amendment. The New York court's argument appears to assume that the providers of a monopoly service or product are willing to pay for wholly ineffective advertising. Most businesses—even regulated monopolies—are unlikely to underwrite promotional advertising that is of no interest or use to consumers. Indeed, a monopoly enterprise legitimately may wish to inform the public that it has developed new services or terms of doing business. A consumer may need information to aid his decision whether or not to use the monopoly service at all, or how much of the service he should purchase. In the absence of factors that would distort the decision to advertise, we may assume that the willingness of a business to promote its products reflects a belief that consumers are interested in the advertising. Since no such extraordinary conditions have been identified in this case, appellant's monopoly position does not alter the First Amendment's protection for its commercial speech.

The Commission offers two state interests as justifications for the ban on promotional advertising. The first concerns energy conservation. Any increase in demand for electricity—during peak or off-peak periods—means greater consumption of energy. The Commission argues, and the New York court agreed, that the State's interest in conserving energy is sufficient to support suppression of advertising designed to increase consumption of electricity. In view of our country's dependence on energy resources beyond our control, no one can doubt the importance of energy conservation. Plainly, therefore, the state interest asserted is substantial.

* * *

We come finally to the critical inquiry in this case: whether the Commission's complete suppression of speech ordinarily protected by the First Amendment is no more extensive than necessary to further the State's interest in energy conservation. The Commission's order reaches all promotional advertising, regardless of the impact of the touted service on overall energy use. But the energy conservation rationale, as important as it is, cannot justify suppressing information about electric devices or services that would cause no net increase in total energy use. In addition, no showing has been made that a more limited restriction on the content of promotional advertising would not serve adequately the State's interests.

* * *

To the extent that the Commission's order suppresses speech that in no way impairs the State's interest in energy conservation, the Commission's order violates the First and Fourteenth Amendments and must be invalidated.

* * *

Case Holding. *The Supreme Court reversed the decision of the New York Court of Appeals in holding the ban on all electricity advertising to be unconstitutional under the First Amendment. Non-misleading advertising of legal products may be regulated only if the regulation advances a substantial government interest, and the regulation is not more extensive than what is needed to advance the public interest.*

Case Questions

1. Since the court found that the state had a substantial interest in the subject in question (electricity and its conservation), why did it still find the ad restrictions to be unconstitutional? What part of the four-part test was not met?

2. Suppose the commission had ordered that only advertising designed to promote energy conservation was allowed. Would that have met the Supreme Court test?

The Court further discussed the regulation of commercial speech in the 1989 case, *Board of Trustees of the State University of New York* v. *Fox.* The standard for judging commercial speech regulation is one that is "not necessarily perfect but reasonable," and one "narrowly tailored to achieve the desired objective." The basis of the regulation must be a substantial state interest in controlling an undesirable activity, balanced against the cost imposed by the restrictions. When the regulations are challenged, the state bears the burden of justifying the restriction on commercial speech.

Speech and Competition

Part of the push for fewer restrictions on commercial speech came as a part of the enforcement of the antitrust laws. In some cases, restrictions were put on commercial speech to limit competition. Such restrictions have not been viewed favorably in recent years.

In 1975, in *Bigelow* v. *Virginia,* the Supreme Court reversed a conviction of a Virginia newspaper editor who published ads about the availability of low-cost abortions in New York City. A Virginia law prohibited publications from encouraging abortions. The Court held that speech that is related to products or services has value in the marketplace of ideas.

The following year, in *Virginia State Board of Pharmacy* v. *Virginia Citizens Consumer Council,* the Court struck down a Virginia law prohibiting the advertising of prices of prescription drugs. Justice Blackmun held, "It is clear . . . that speech does not lose its First Amendment protection because money is spent . . . as in a paid advertisement. . . ." The Board of Pharmacy argued that the restrictions on advertising were needed to protect the public from their own ignorance about drugs. The Court responded, "There is, of course, an alternative to this highly paternalistic approach (of prohibiting advertising of drug prices). That alternative is to assume that this information is not in itself harmful, that people will perceive their own best interests if only they are well enough informed, and that the best means to that end is to open the channels of communication rather than to close them."

The Supreme Court has ruled in several cases that First Amendment rights may be violated by restrictions on advertising for professional services, such as by lawyers or doctors. The Court addressed the issue in the 1989 case *Shapero* v. *Kentucky Bar Association*, when it held that the Bar Association violated the First Amendment by prohibiting lawyers from soliciting business by sending truthful letters to prospective clients known to face particular legal problems. If an attorney engages in misleading or deceptive solicitation practices, the attorney may be punished by the Bar for doing do, but the Bar may not act as a censor on commercial speech.

Freedom to Criticize

Freedom of speech can mean that a business will find itself criticized in a commercial setting. The Supreme Court upheld this right in the 1984 decision *Bose Corp.* v. *Consumers Union*. Consumers Union published a report in *Consumer Reports* that was critical of the quality of a particular loudspeaker made by Bose. Bose sued, claiming product disparagement.

The Supreme Court held that there must be actual malice for a public figure, such as a corporation selling products, to recover damages for a defamatory falsehood. Since actual malice was not shown in this case, the suit was dismissed. Speaking for the majority, Justice Stevens said: "The First Amendment presupposes that the freedom to speak one's mind is not only an aspect of individual liberty—and thus a good unto itself—but also is essential to the common quest for truth and the vitality of society as a whole. Under our Constitution 'there is no such thing as a false idea. However pernicious an opinion may seem, we depend for its correction not on the conscience of judges and juries but on the competition of other ideas.' " Nevertheless, libelous speech is limited by the First Amendment, but the standard is strong in the case of most commercial speech.

The right to criticize is not the right to make false statements that injure another. As the Court noted in the 1990 case, *Milkovich v. Lorain Journal Co.*, a business such as a newspaper is not protected by the First Amendment when it makes false statements that defame someone. If a reasonable person can conclude that there is injury to reputation, it does not matter if the false information is stated as an opinion rather than as fact.

UNREASONABLE SEARCH AND SEIZURE

The Fourth Amendment reads: "The right of the people to be secure in their persons, houses, papers, and effects, against unreasonable searches and seizures, shall not be violated, and no Warrants shall issue, but upon probable cause. . . ." Most cases arising under this Amendment are criminal and concern the proper method of search and seizure of suspected criminals and evidence. However, there has been a recent increase in the number of cases brought under the Fourth Amendment in response to the methods used by regulatory agencies executing their functions. In Fourth Amendment cases asking the question of whether or not proper search and seizure procedures were used, the Supreme Court consistently refers to a 1968 decision, *Katz* v. *United States*, that said that in such cases the premier issue is whether a person has a constitutionally protected reasonable expectation of privacy. Essentially, closed places, such as homes and businesses, are not subject to random police searches.

Limitations on Searches of Businesses

If a government inspector shows up at a business and asks to inspect the premises or search company records for some purpose related to the law's being enforced by the inspector's agency, does the business have to allow admission? Not without a warrant, the Supreme Court held in *Marshall* v. *Barlow's, Inc.* (1978). In that case, an inspector for the Occupational Safety and Health Administration (OSHA) arrived at Barlow's plant in Pocatello, Idaho, and asked to search the work areas. Barlow asked the inspector if he had a warrant. Since he did not, Barlow refused admission to the plant. OSHA asked the Court to require businesses to admit inspectors to conduct warrant-less searches. The Court refused, saying that warrantless searches are generally unreasonable, and that this rule applies to commercial premises as well as homes. The government argued that if inspectors had to obtain warrants, businesses would have time to hide safety and health defects on work sites. The Court responded: "We are unconvinced . . . that requiring warrants to inspect will impose serious burdens on the inspection system or the courts, will prevent inspections necessary to enforce the statute, or will make them less effective. In the first place the great majority of businessmen can be expected in normal course to consent to inspection without warrant; the Secretary (of Labor) has not brought to this Court's attention any widespread pattern of refusal. . . ." As the Court predicted, in fact, most businesses do allow warrant-less searches; the requirement to obtain a warrant when demanded has not become burdensome or retarded law enforcement.

Restrictions on the Use of Evidence Collected

When evidence is collected by an inspector, with or without a warrant, the evidence is to be used for the purposes intended. The government cannot abuse the evidence by passing it around to various federal agencies for their inspection or releasing it to the public. Protections of the constitutional rights of business have remained similar to those of individuals in this regard.

Evidence gathered by enforcement officials in a manner that violates Fourth Amendment rights regarding search and seizure may not be used in prosecution under the exclusionary rule. However, recent decisions have indicated that the Court may be expanding the ability of enforcement officials to seize and use evidence under specific regulatory statutes.

Illinois v. Krull
United States Supreme Court
480 U.S. 340,
107 S.Ct. 1160
(1987)

Case Background. *An Illinois statute required licensed motor vehicle parts sellers to permit state officials to inspect certain records, such as vehicle purchase information and identification numbers, and required parts sellers to allow officials to examine their place of business on demand to determine the accuracy of such records. Krull and his associates ran an auto junkyard. Police entered the yard and determined that three cars were stolen and a fourth had its identification number removed.*

Krull was arrested and charged with various criminal violations. By the time the case got to trial, the warrantless search part of the statute had been stricken as unconstitutional. The trial court suppressed the evidence seized from the junkyard because it violated the Fourth Amendment by allowing police unbridled discretion in warrantless searches. The Illinois Supreme Court affirmed the decision of the trial court not allowing the evidence. The case was appealed to the Supreme Court to see if the evidence were admissible because the police acted in good faith under a statute that was on the books at the time of the action.

Case Decision. Justice Blackmun delivered the opinion of the Court.

* * *

When evidence is obtained in violation of the Fourth Amendment, the judicially developed exclusionary rule usually precludes its use in a criminal proceeding against the victim of the illegal search and seizure. . . . The Court has stressed that the "prime purpose" of the exclusionary rule "is to deter future unlawful police conduct and thereby effectuate the guarantee of the Fourth Amendment against unreasonable searches and seizures."

* * *

The application of the exclusionary rule to suppress evidence obtained by an officer acting in objectively reasonable reliance on a statute would have as little deterrent effect on the officer's actions as would the exclusion of evidence when an officer acts in objectively reasonable reliance on a warrant. Unless a statute is clearly unconstitutional, an officer cannot be expected to question the judgment of the legislature that passed the law. If the statute is subsequently declared unconstitutional, excluding evidence obtained pursuant to it prior to such a judicial declaration will not deter future Fourth Amendment violations by an officer who has simply fulfilled his responsibility to enforce the statute as written.

* * *

There is no evidence suggesting that Congress or state legislatures have enacted a significant number of statutes permitting warrantless administrative searches violative of the Fourth Amendment. Legislatures generally have confined their efforts to authorizing administrative searches of specific categories of businesses that require regulation, and the resulting statutes usually have been held to be constitutional. . . . Thus, we are given no basis for believing that legislators are inclined to subvert their oaths and the Fourth Amendment and that "lawlessness among these actors requires application of the extreme sanction of exclusion."

* * *

Applying the principle enunciated in this case, we necessarily conclude that Detective McNally's reliance on the Illinois statute was objectively reasonable. On several occasions, this Court has upheld legislative schemes that authorized warrantless administrative searches of heavily regulated industries. . . . It has recognized that an inspection program may be a necessary component of regulation in certain industries, and has acknowledged that unannounced, warrantless inspections may be necessary "if the law is to be properly enforced and inspection made effective."

* * *

Case Holding. *The Supreme Court reversed the decision of the Illinois Supreme Court by holding that the evidence gathered under the statute that violated warrantless search requirements could be used as evidence at trial, because the evidence was collected in good faith by the police before it was held to be improper.*

Case Questions

1. Four justices dissented, saying that since the statute under which the evidence was gathered was unconstitutional with respect to the powers it gave police to gather evidence, the evidence should be stricken. Do you agree?

2. The majority notes that there was no evidence that the legislature intended to violate Fourth Amendment rights by the statute in question. Should such a good-faith determination matter in terms of the impact of the statute on constitutional rights?

A similar case was decided during the same 1987 Supreme Court term. In that case (*New York* v. *Burger,* which had a fact pattern almost identical to that of *Krull*), the Court upheld a New York statute allowing warrantless searches of junkyards. The searches were upheld because they are needed to inspect closely regulated businesses, such as auto junkyards. The regulations were valid because of the substantial interest the state has to reduce auto theft. The statute met the time, place, and scope requirements that must exist to impose restraints on inspecting officers' discretion. If, during a legitimate warrantless search of the business under the conditions established by the statute, evidence of other crimes is discovered, such evidence is legal.

INTERNATIONAL PERSPECTIVES: CONSTITUTIONAL LAW IN FOREIGN JURISDICTIONS

INTERNATIONAL

PERSPECTIVES

The United Kingdom, unlike the United States and most other nations, does not have a written constitution, yet it has a body of constitutional law. The courts there recognize three kinds of rules: statutory law, case law, and custom or constitutional convention. Statutory law, which comes from Parliament, is potentially unlimited in scope.

The courts may not strike down statutes because of constitutional restrictions, as may U.S. courts. There is no official separation of powers; the courts in the U.K. cannot use constitutional custom to overrule parliamentary law. By custom, the current monarch (Queen Elizabeth) cannot veto laws, but prior monarchs did have such authority.

The United Kingdom is clearly a democratic nation with a high regard for civil liberties. While that nation works well without a formal constitution, it was that lack of fixed constitutional standards that convinced the founders of the United States that a written constitution was desirable. In the United Kingdom, constitutional customs change over time, just as the U.S. Supreme Court infers different standards at different times from the Constitution, often reflecting changes in social values and economic realities.

It should be remembered that U.S. constitutional rights do not protect American citizens if they are subject to legal action in another nation.

Similarly, U.S. constitutional rights do not always extend to non-citizens not in the U.S. The Supreme Court, in *U.S.* v. *Verdugo-Urquidez* (1990), held that the Fourth Amendment does not apply to the search and seizure by U.S. agents of property located outside the U.S. that is owned by a non-U.S. citizen. The Amendment protects people in the United States against arbitrary action by the government; it does not restrain the federal government's actions against aliens outside American territory.

SELF–INCRIMINATION

The Fifth Amendment protects individuals against *self-incrimination:* "No person shall be . . . compelled in any criminal case to be a witness against himself." This constitutional protection applies to persons, not to corporations. Although corporate executives cannot be made to testify against themselves, business records that might incriminate the corporation (and executives) must be produced, since such records are not protected by the Fifth Amendment.

Businesses have contested fines imposed by an agency resulting from mandatory self-reporting of information. Their argument is that the reporting of self-incriminating evidence violates the Fifth Amendment's assurance that no persons shall be compelled in any criminal case to testify against themselves. Self-incrimination in criminal cases cannot be required, but many regulatory statutes impose civil penalties, which do not receive the same level of constitutional protection.

The Supreme Court discussed an interesting twist on self-incrimination in a 1988 case, *John Doe* v. *U.S.*, where Doe was the target of a federal investigation into suspected illegal manipulation of oil cargo and failure to report income from the deal. He refused to answer questions about the existence or location of foreign bank accounts he owned. The Court held that he could be required to sign a form authorizing the foreign bank to release his records to the U.S. government, even though the records could be incriminating. He has the right to refuse to testify about the records, but cannot refuse to cooperate in producing testimony.

JUST COMPENSATION

The Fifth Amendment states, ". . . nor shall private property be taken for public use, without just compensation." Termed the *just compensation or takings clause*, its traditional primary use was to require governments to pay for property the government required someone to sell because public officials determined that the property should be used for some specific purpose, such as for the construction of a highway or military base.

The Supreme Court appears to have broadened the application of the just compensation clause by two 1987 decisions. Before these decisions, the clause had not changed much in interpretation for many years. Local governments, where most land use requirements are determined, had broad powers to change zoning and land use requirements without paying compensation, even though the value of the land might be affected by the change in land use rules. This power has been restricted by the *First English* decision.

First English Evangelical Lutheran Church of Glendale v. Los Angeles County

Supreme Court of the United States
482 U.S. 304,
107 S.Ct. 2378
(1987)

Case Background. *The First English Evangelical Luther Church purchased twenty-one acres in 1957 in a canyon in a forest area. It built and operated a campground as a retreat center and a recreational area for disabled children. In 1977, a forest fire upstream of the camp destroyed a watershed area and created a flood hazard, which was recognized in 1978 when a rain storm caused a flood that destroyed the buildings. Soon after, the county adopted an interim ordinance prohibiting any building in the area. The ordinance was justified as needed for public health and safety. The church sued the county to challenge the ordinance. The church sought to recover damages for loss of use of the land due to the building restriction. The trial court ruled against the church, as did the Court of Appeals of California. The church appealed to the Supreme Court.*

Case Decision. Chief Justice Rehnquist delivered the opinion of the Court.

* * *

Consideration of the compensation question must begin with direct reference to the language of the Fifth Amendment, which provides in relevant part that "private property [shall not] be taken for public use, without just compensation." As its language indicates, and as the Court has frequently noted, this provision does not prohibit the taking of private property, but instead places a condition on the exercise of that power. This basic understanding of the Amendment makes clear that it is designed not to limit the governmental interference with property rights *per se*, but rather to secure *compensation* in the event of otherwise proper interference amounting to a taking. Thus, government action that works a taking of property rights necessarily implicates the "constitutional obligation to pay just compensation."

* * *

These cases reflect the fact that "temporary" takings which, as here, deny a landowner all use of his property, are not different in kind from permanent takings, for which the Constitution clearly requires compensation. It is axiomatic that the Fifth Amendment's just compensation provision is "designed to bar Government from forcing some people alone to bear public burdens which, in all fairness and justice, should be borne by the public as a whole."

In the present case the interim ordinance was adopted by the county of Los Angeles in January 1979, and became effective immediately. The church filed suit within a month after the effective date of the ordinance and yet when the Supreme Court of California denied a hearing in the case on October 17, 1985, the merits of the church's claim had yet to be determined. The United States has been required to pay compensation for leasehold interests of shorter duration than this. The value of a leasehold interest in property for a period of years may be substantial, and the burden on the property owner in extinguishing such an interest for a period of years may be great indeed. Where this burden results from governmental action that amounted to a taking, the Just Compensation Clause of the Fifth Amendment requires that the government pay the landowner for the value of the use of the land during this period. . . . Invalidation of the ordinance or its successor ordinance after this period of time, though converting the taking into a "temporary" one, is not a sufficient remedy to meet the demands of the Just Compensation Clause.

* * *

We merely hold that where the government's activities have already worked a taking of all use of property, no subsequent action by the government can relieve it of the duty to provide compensation for the period during which the taking was effective. . . . We realize that even our present holding will undoubtedly lessen to some extent the freedom and flexibility of land-use planners and governing bodies of municipal corporations when enacting land-use regulations. But such consequences necessarily flow from any decision upholding a claim of constitutional right; many of the provisions of the Constitution are designed to limit the flexibility and freedom of governmental authorities and the Just Compensation Clause of the Fifth Amendment is one of them. As Justice Holmes aptly noted more than 50 years ago, "a strong public desire to improve the public condition is not enough to warrant achieving the desire by a shorter cut than the constitutional way of paying for the change."

* * *

Case Holding. *Reversing the decision of the California Court of Appeals, the Supreme Court ordered the trial court to make a determination of the compensation due the church for the temporary taking of its property.*

Case Questions

1. This case involved a taking that lasted over five years. What if it had been a one-month or a six-month delay?
2. The dissenters in this case argued that since public health and safety outweigh private concerns, the public power as used in this case should not be restricted. Do you agree?

The 1987 Supreme Court decision, *Nollan* v. *California Coastal Commission,* also addressed compensation in land-use rules. The Nollan family wished to tear down their house and build a larger one on their beach property in Ventura, California. The California Coastal Commission told the Nollans that their permit would be granted only if they agreed to allow the public an easement (access) to pass across their beach. The historic high tide line determines the lot's oceanside boundary. The Coastal Commission wanted the public to have the right to walk across what had been the Nollans' back yard—above the high tide line—along the beach. This was a common requirement that had been imposed for several years whenever private property owners requested a building permit.

The Supreme Court reversed the decision of the California Court of Appeals by holding that the takings clause of the Fifth Amendment had been violated. The state could not tie a rebuilding permit to an easement that it would have to pay for if it simply imposed the easement. "California is free to advance its 'comprehensive program,' if it wishes [of increased beach access] by using its power of eminent domain for this 'public purpose,' but if it wants an easement across the Nollans' property, it must pay for it."

RIGHT TO TRIAL

The Sixth Amendment addresses the right of persons to trial by jury in criminal cases. The Seventh Amendment provides for the right to jury trial in common-law cases. Although the law is well established about the constitutional right to jury trial in criminal cases and common-law cases, what about cases in which a business is charged with a violation of a statute that regulates the business? If the charge is criminal, the right to request a jury trial remains. What if the charge is only civil? The Supreme Court has addressed that question several times, most recently in *Tull* v. *U.S.*

Tull, a real-estate developer, was charged by the federal government with violating the Clean Water Act. The Act authorizes injunctive relief against violators (such as a court order to stop work on the land) and subjects violators to a civil penalty not to exceed $10,000 per day. The government sued Tull for violations of the Clean Water Act with respect to damage to wetlands. The government sought an injunction to force Tull to stop work and asked for $23 million in civil penalties. Tull requested a jury trial, which was denied by the federal district court. At the bench trial, Tull admitted not having the required permits and dumping fill dirt where the government claimed. He did claim, however, that because the land in question was not wetland covered by the statute, he was not liable. The district court held that the lands were wetlands and ordered Tull to restore the lands to their original condition and to pay several hundred thousand dollars in civil penalties.

On appeal, the Supreme Court ruled that Tull was due a jury trial under the Seventh Amendment with respect to the issue of whether or not he was liable because the lands were wetlands. If the only question was that of imposing civil penalties, no right to jury trial existed. Since civil penalties are imposed by statute, there is no constitutional right to trial on such matters. There is a right to jury trial on the question of the liability of the defendant only when there is the "substance of the common-law right of trial by jury." That is, when the legal issue involved is close to that of a common-law right, jury trial rights exist. If the legal issue is one of statutory law only, there is no right to jury trial to determine liability.

EXCESSIVE FINES

The Eighth Amendment is most famous for its restriction on "cruel and unusual punishments," but it also holds that "no excessive fines" may be imposed. Since large jury awards have become more common in the last two decades, as we will see in the chapters on torts and products liability, defendants have looked to see if the Eighth Amendment offers protection against huge awards.

A jury awarded the plaintiff in a tort suit $51,146 in compensatory damages and $6 million in punitive damages. The defendant appealed to the Supreme Court, claiming the punitive damages violated the Eighth Amendment. In 1989, in *Browning-Ferris Industries* v. *Kelco Disposal*, the Court held that the excessive fines clause does not apply to punitive damage awards in cases between private parties. Reaching back as far as the Magna Carta, the

Court found that the purpose of the Eighth Amendment was to restrict the potential for governmental abuse of "prosecutorial" power by the imposition of excessive fines.

DUE PROCESS

The Fourteenth Amendment holds, in part, "No state shall . . . deprive any person of life, liberty, or property, without due process of law; nor deny to any person within its jurisdiction the equal protection of the laws." This amendment, called the *due process clause,* has been a powerful device for extending federal constitutional guarantees to the states and preventing states from passing laws that diminish any federal constitutional protections. Such protections hold for businesses. An example of this arose in a case concerning the burden of a foreign producer to respond to a legal claim.

Asahi Metal Industry Co. v. Superior Court of California
Supreme Court of the United States
480 U.S. 102,
107 S.Ct. 1026
(1987)

Case Background. *Asahi, a Japanese company, did worldwide business, but only a trivial amount in California. It sold component parts to a Taiwanese manufacturer (Cheng Shin) who sold its finished products in California. Cheng Shin was sued in California in a products liability suit. It settled the case, but sued Asahi in California for indemnity for its losses. Asahi argued that California courts could not exercise jurisdiction over Asahi and force it to appear in court in this matter. The California Supreme Court held that because some of Asahi's parts ended up in a product in commerce in California, Asahi was subject to jurisdiction under California's long-arm statute. Asahi appealed to the Supreme Court.*

Case Decision. Justice O'Connor delivered the opinion of the Court.

* * *

The placement of a product into the stream of commerce, without more, is not an act of the defendant purposefully directed toward the forum State. Additional conduct of the defendant may indicate an intent or purpose to serve the market in the forum State, for example, designing the product for the market in the forum State, advertising in the forum State, establishing channels for providing regular advice to customers in the forum State, or marketing the product through a distributor who has agreed to serve as the sales agent in the forum State. But a defendant's awareness that the stream of commerce may or will sweep the product into the forum State does not convert the mere act of placing the product into the stream into an act purposefully directed toward the forum State. . . . There is no evidence that Asahi designed its product in anticipation of sales in California. . . . On the basis of these facts, the exertion of personal jurisdiction over Asahi by the Superior Court of California" exceeds the limits of Due Process.

The strictures of the Due Process Clause forbid a state court from exercising personal jurisdiction over Asahi under circumstances that would offend "traditional notions of fair play and substantial justice." . . . A court must consider the burden on the defendant, the interests of the forum state, and the plaintiff's interest in obtaining relief. It must also weigh in its determination "the interstate judicial system's interest in obtaining the most efficient resolution of controversies; and the shared interest of the several States in furthering fundamental substantive social policies."

A consideration of these factors in the present case clearly reveals the unreasonableness of the assertion of jurisdiction over Asahi, even apart from the question of the placement of goods in the stream of commerce.

Certainly the burden on the defendant in this case is severe. Asahi has been commanded by the Supreme Court of California not only to traverse the distance between Asahi's headquarters in Japan and the Superior Court of California in and for the County of Solano, but also to submit its dispute with Cheng Shin to a foreign nation's judicial system. The unique burdens placed upon one who must defend oneself in a foreign legal system should have significant weight in assessing the reasonableness of stretching the long arm of personal jurisdiction over national borders.

When minimum contacts have been established, often the interests of the plaintiff and the forum in the exercise of jurisdiction will justify even the serious burdens placed on the alien defendant. In the present case, however, the interests of the plaintiff and the forum in California's assertion of jurisdiction over Asahi are slight. All that remains is a claim for indemnification asserted by Cheng Shin, a Taiwanese corporation, against Asahi. The transaction on which the indemnification claim is based took place in Taiwan; Asahi's components were shipped from Japan to Taiwan. Cheng Shin has not demonstrated that it is more convenient for it to litigate its indemnification claim against Asahi in California rather than in Taiwan or Japan.

* * *

Considering the international context, the heavy burden on the alien defendant, and the slight interests of the plaintiff and the forum State, the exercise of personal jurisdiction by a California court over Asahi in this instance would be unreasonable and unfair.

* * *

Case Holding. *The Supreme Court reversed the California Supreme Court and ordered the case against Asahi to be dismissed because the courts of California do not have jurisdiction over Asahi under the due process protection offered any defendant by the Fourteenth Amendment. Before a court can claim jurisdiction over a business, there must be evidence of a certain level of business contacts in the area of the court's authority.*

Case Questions

1. The California high court argued that jurisdiction was just, because any firm that places goods into commerce knowing that such goods will end up in California or any other jurisdiction should know that the consumers of those products are due the same protection they receive from producers of any other products. To not allow jurisdiction over Asahi would be to encourage firms to evade potential legal liability by hiding in foreign places, which may lead to more injuries to consumers. Does this seem correct?

2. Should foreign producers be treated any differently than domestic producers located in other states?

Due process, on one hand, concerns the fairness of law enforcement procedures, as in the *Asahi* case. The substance of due process, however, concerns the content of legislation. All laws must be constitutional so as not to violate the due process clause. If a law restricts a fundamental constitutional right, there must be a compelling interest for it. As we have seen already, when it comes to the regulation of business, most regulations will meet constitutionality tests.

The fact that due process rights are not as strong in business matters as in the personal sphere can be seen in the 1988 Supreme Court case *Federal Deposit Insurance Corp.* v. *Mallen*. Under a federal statute, the Federal Deposit Insurance Corp. (FDIC) suspended Mallen from his job as president of a bank when he was indicted for conspiracy to commit mail fraud. The law allowed such suspensions to protect public confidence in banks. Mallen claimed that his due process rights meant that he should have been allowed a hearing by the FDIC before his suspension, that he should have been allowed a hearing immediately after the suspension, and that he should have been allowed to give oral testimony at a hearing.

The Court held that he had no such rights. The Court stated that the FDIC, acting under the statute, behaved properly and did not have to allow a hearing before the suspension, did not have to accept any oral testimony if written testimony was sufficient, and had to have a hearing only within the ninety days set by the statute. Clearly, fewer substantive guarantees exist under the Constitution for businesses and individuals in a business capacity than for individuals in a private capacity.

EQUAL PROTECTION

The Fourteenth Amendment, as noted above, says that "No state shall . . . deny . . . the equal protection of the laws." This *equal protection clause* is often closely tied to the due process clause. The equal protection clause arose in two recent cases involving business and state governments.

In 1988, in *Pennell* v. *City of San Jose*, the Supreme Court upheld the San Jose rent control ordinance. That ordinance limited rent increases to a maximum of 8 percent per year, unless the tenant objected, in which case there was a hearing to determine if a rent increase was justified. The Court held this did not violate the taking clause or the due process clause. The rent controls also did not violate the equal protection clause because they met the test of being "rationally related to a legitimate state interest." The controls exist to protect the interests of tenants, which is a legitimate concern of the state, so they may stand.

In the 1989 case *Allegheny Pittsburgh Coal Co.* v. *County Commission of Webster County*, the Supreme Court struck down certain features of the West Virginia property tax system as violating the equal protection clause. West Virginia counties would assess real property taxes on the basis of recent purchase price, but would make only minor modifications to assessments of properties not recently transferred. The result was that there arose, over time, a great disparity in assessed values of comparable properties. For taxpayers to be treated so differently was held to violate the equal protection clause of the Fourteenth Amendment.

SUMMARY

The Constitution is a dynamic document that changes over time. While its words remain the same, they are interpreted to say different things at different times. With respect to business, some constitutional provisions have been clear for years: the federal government is supreme in matters of interstate commerce, the states may not pass laws that conflict with the intent of federal laws that are the supreme law of the land, and Congress has the power to tax business.

In other matters, especially the Supreme Court's reading of the Bill of Rights as it applies to business, significant changes have been made in recent years. Commercial speech has been granted many of the safeguards about public and private matters that speech by individuals has long been accorded. The right of governmental inspectors to search a business without a warrant has been restricted.

While according business more rights in certain areas, the Supreme Court has also made it clear that business has responsibilities to society. These responsibilities are often decided by Congress through regulatory agencies. While the Court may limit certain actions of such agencies, in general it has allowed Congress to regulate many aspects of business constitutionally.

ISSUE

Should Political Speech by Business Be Limited?

As noted in the chapter, the Supreme Court issued a controversial decision in 1990 in Austin v. Michigan Chamber of Commerce, *where it limited the right of private organizations to spend money in support of or in opposition to political candidates. This decision was opposed by private groups, from far-left political activists to staid corporate conservatives. Should corporate monies be regulated by the politicians that private organizations may wish to campaign against? A journalist expresses the fear that the Supreme Court may be repressing free speech.*

If Corporations Are Silenced In Political Debate, Who's Next?
Michael Gartner*

...[L]et me tell you what the Supreme Court was up to last week.

It was up to no good.

The court said, in effect, that political debate can become one-sided and that states can censor it. It said corporations, be they

Reprinted with permission from *The Wall Street Journal,* © 1990 Dow Jones & Company, Inc. All Rights Resered. Gartner is president of NBC News in New York.

–continued

—continuing

for-profit or not-for-profit, can be barred from telling you what they think about a candidate, and it will take no great leap to expand that thinking to include causes and issues.

The court said, in the words of dissenting Justice Antonin Scalia, that "too much speech is an evil" that states can stamp out.

As the comedians say, I am not making this up.

Here are the facts:

In 1976, the state of Michigan passed a campaign-finance law that said, among other things, that a corporation can't use its general treasury funds to make so-called independent expenditures in a political campaign. That means the corporation can't, for instance, take out an ad or send out a brochure endorsing or opposing this or that candidate.

In 1985, the Michigan Chamber of Commerce decided that a man named Richard Bandstra was the best candidate in a special election in Grand Rapids to fill a seat in the state house of representatives. The chamber proposed taking out an advertisement talking about the need for Michigan to change its workers'-compensation law and to lower its personal income-tax rate. In that ad it proposed saying, "The State Chamber is committed to job development in Michigan. We believe Richard Bandstra shares that commitment."

But the chamber, reading the 1976 law, decided maybe its ad was illegal. So it sought to find out. A federal district judge said yes, indeed, the ad was barred by the statute. The Sixth Circuit Court of Appeals reversed, saying the statute violated the First Amendment. Then, last week, the Supreme Court, in a 6–3 vote, reversed again, upholding the statute and ignoring the Constitution.

The opinion was written by Justice Thurgood Marshall, one of the court's liberals, and was joined by Justice William J. Brennan, the man liberals always look to to defend their rights to speak or write orgather or pray. They were joined by the court's moderates and Chief Justice William Rehnquist, a man always ready to rein in the

First Amendment. Opposing the decision—and thus favoring full rights of free speech—were Justices Scalia and Anthony Kennedy and Sandra Day O'Connor.

Opposing, too, in friend-of-the-court briefs were such disparate groups as the American Civil Liberties Union, the American Medical Association, the National Association of Realtors, Greenpeace Action, the Fund for the Feminist Majority and the American Insurance Association. Clearly, a lot of people were worried. And their worries turned out to be well-founded.

Justice Marshall, in the opinion, said it was OK to squelch speech because there was "a compelling state interest"—preventing corruption or the appearance of corruption in the political arena by reducing the threat that huge corporate treasuries will be used to influence unfairly election outcomes.

This is absurd—and dangerous.

It's absurd because this is America, and America isn't supposed to stifle the speech of man or corporation. (The fact that corporations amass large treasuries does not justify the suppression of political speech, Justice Scalia wrote, "unless one thinks it would be lawful to prohibit men and women whose net worth is above a certain figure from endorsing political candidates.")

It's absurd because money—from political action committees and others—already plays a huge role in American elections. It's absurd because censorship is a far greater political sin than is overspending or even buying an election.

It's dangerous because it sets a new course, a course in which a government can censor speech that simply has the potential for causing harm, not speech (like Justice Holmes's example of shouting fire in a crowded theater) that actually causes harm.

"Today's reversal of field will require adjustment of a fairly large number of significant First Amendment holdings," Justice Scalia said in a dissent that he actually

—continued

–continuing

read from the bench because he felt so strongly about the issue.

"Presumably the State may now convict individuals for selling books found to have a potentially harmful influence on minors . . ., ban indecent telephone communications that have the potential of reaching minors . . ., restrict the press from publishing information that has the potential of jeopardizing a criminal defendant's right to a fair trial . . . and compel an applicant for bar membership to reveal her political beliefs and affiliations to eliminate the potential for subversive activity."

Perhaps the bill has a noble objective, Mr. Scalia wrote. "But government abridgement of liberty is always undertaken with the very best of announced objectives (dictators promise to bring order, not tyranny), and often with the very best of genuinely intended objectives (zealous policemen conduct unlawful searches in order to put dangerous felons behind bars).

"The premise of our Bill of Rights, however, is that there are some things—even some seemingly desirable things—that government cannot be trusted to do. The very first of these is establishing the restrictions upon speech that will assure 'fair' political debate."

The theory behind the ruling is that corporations are owned by their stockholders and those people might not want the corporation to spend its money for political purposes.

If that's the case, then it seems logical to rule, too, that no executive—whose pay comes from general corporate funds—can speak out in political debate. And no stockholder can use his dividends for political purposes. That, of course, is absurd, as absurd as last week's ruling.

In a separate dissent, Justice Kennedy wrote: "With the imprimatur of this Court, it is now a felony in Michigan for the Sierra Club, or the American Civil Liberties Union, or the Michigan State Chamber of Commerce, to advise the public how a candidate voted on issues of urgent concern to their members. In both practice and theory, the prohibition aims at the heart of political debate."

Twenty states have laws similar to Michigan's. So, in about half this nation, we now have what Justice Kennedy calls "the rawest form of censorship: the state censors what a particular segment of the political community might say with regard to candidates who stand for election."

Any kind of censorship is dreadful. But censorship of political talk is the worst of all. And that's what we have in the United States.

Questions

1. Does Gartner overstate the effect of the ruling? Is there not an easy way around this or will it lead to real restrictions on the ability of groups from Greenpeace to the American Insurance Institute to spend funds endorsing candidates?

2. Would our political system be improved if private organizations were prevented from addressing political issues

REVIEW AND DISCUSSION QUESTIONS

1. Define the following terms:
   commerce clause
   interstate commerce
   necessary and proper clause
   contract clause
   political speech

commercial speech
self-incrimination
just compensation clause
due process clause

2. Taken together, do the commerce clause and necessary and proper clause, as read by the Supreme Court, restrict the ability of Congress to regulate business?

3. Suppose Congress imposes a water pollution restriction. Can a state set its own limits on water pollution that are higher or lower than the federal limits?

4. Goods are produced in New Mexico. Some are shipped to Louisiana by truck for further processing. Can the state of Texas place a tax on those goods as they are shipped across the state that is the same as the tax they impose on such goods that are produced in Texas for shipment within and outside Texas?

5. Congress requires, via the Internal Revenue Service, that you report to the IRS any income from illegal activities, such as drug dealing. If you report the income, you reveal your illegal activities. If you do not report the income and the dealing is discovered, you can be charged with income tax evasion. Does this violate the Fifth Amendment? If not, why not?

Case Questions

6. An employee hears a news report that terrorists were suspected of trying to set off a bomb to kill the President. The employee says to other employees: "I hope they kill that no-good jerk." The employer fires the employee for the statement. Is the statement protected by the First Amendment? What if the employee made the statement in public, such as by a letter to the editor of the newspaper?

7. Taylor sold live minnows as fishing bait in Maine. He imported some minnows from another state in violation of Maine law. He was then indicted under a federal law that makes it illegal to move fish in interstate commerce in violation of state law. Taylor claimed that the indictment should be dismissed because the Maine statute unconstitutionally burdened interstate commerce. Maine argued that it needed the statute to protect the state's fisheries from diseases and undesired varieties of fish. The U.S. Court of Appeals sided with Taylor, and the state of Maine appealed to the Supreme Court. Do the indictment and the statute stand? [*Maine v. Taylor*, 477 U.S. 131, 106 S.Ct. 2440 (1986)]

8. The city of San Diego passed an ordinance regulating outdoor advertising. Signs were allowed on the property where the advertised goods and services were located, but off-property fixed-structure signs (billboards) for commercial and noncommercial advertisements were prohibited, except for temporary political campaign signs. The Supreme Court of California held the ordinance did not violate the First Amendment and was a proper use of the city's police power. The sign companies took the case to the U.S. Supreme Court. What was the result? [*Metromedia, Inc. v. City of San Diego*, 453 U.S. 490, 101 S.Ct. 2882 (1981)]

9. Hospitals are regulated by statute in each state. The state sends inspectors to hospitals to check on such areas as sanitation and proper procedure and to assure that only qualified personnel are performing certain functions. A state inspector enters a hospital without being recognized or volunteering the

purpose of the visit. While looking around, the inspector discovers some prescription medicines on a nurse's desk without any evidence that there is a prescription. He asks the nurse if the pills belong to her; she says yes. The inspector then identifies himself and asks the nurse to produce a prescription, which she cannot do. The inspector files charges against the nurse, who will say only that a doctor gave her the pills but not which doctor. Is the evidence gathered in this case good evidence, or will it be tossed out?

Policy Questions

10. Some intrastate business is not regulated by Congress. Would it be more desirable to have all regulations apply equally to all businesses? That is, is it desirable that some firms be subject to certain regulations that are not imposed on small intrastate firms? Is there any restriction on Congress specifying that various regulations will, in fact, be imposed on all firms in commerce?

11. Would a constitutional restriction on political speech that is sponsored by commercial interests produce a less biased, more fair system of political decision making?

Ethics Questions

12. Since it is now legal for physicians and other professionals to engage in a certain amount of commercial advertising, a physician puts an ad in the newspaper telling people that the flu season could be bad this year and that the flu kills hundreds of people every year (which is true). She urges people to come to her office to get a flu shot to protect themselves. Is this ethical? The medical associations used to hold such ads unethical.

13. A firm subject to OSHA inspections requires an OSHA inspector, who shows up unexpectedly one day, to get a warrant before engaging in the search. The firm owner knows that the inspector is a genuine inspector and that there is no question that the warrant to search will be issued. However, requiring the inspector to get the warrant takes half a day of the inspector's time (which is paid for by taxpayers). Is it ethical to bar such inspections?

5 Government Agencies and the Administrative Process

THE powers and procedures of federal administrative agencies are discussed in this chapter. Although only a little more than a century old, administrative agencies have had a significant impact on the legal environment of business. More than fifty federal agencies share the responsibility for regulating virtually all business activity from the transportation of raw materials to the quality of final products.

The chapter begins with a discussion of the nature of administrative agencies and the administrative process. The history of administrative agencies and the impact that social and economic conditions have had on their creation and development are also examined. Next, we consider the powers delegated to the administrative agencies by Congress, including their legislative, investigative, adjudicatory, and enforcement powers. The discussion then turns to the concept of judicial review—the power of the judicial branch of government to review an agency's actions or decisions. Finally, the chapter closes with a discussion of the limits placed on the power and authorities of administrative agencies by Congress.

The chapter closes with the Issue Article entitled "Did Deregulation Destroy the Savings and Loan Industry?" Deregulated in the early 80s, several hundred savings and loan institutions have failed with huge loan losses due to years of high inflation, poor management, and lax government supervision. It is estimated that the federal government's bailout of those savings and loans will cost taxpayers more than $325 billion.

ADMINISTRATIVE AGENCIES AND ADMINISTRATIVE LAW

Administrative agencies have become an indispensable component of modern government. In a relatively short period of time, agencies have become the primary tool through which local, state, and federal governments perform virtually all of their regulatory functions. In the words of Supreme Court Justice Jackson:

> The rise of administration bodies probably has been the most significant legal trend of the last century and perhaps more values today are affected by their decisions than by those of all the courts. . . . They also have . . . important consequences on personal rights. They have become a veritable fourth branch of the government, which has deranged all our three-branch legal theories. . . .

Creating an Administrative Agency

An *administrative agency* can be defined as an authority of the government—other than a legislature or a court—created to administer a particular legislative enactment. To administer that legislation, an agency will generally be provided with the authority to perform some functions of the three constitutional branches of government: legislative, judicial, and executive. The agency's authority will generally be provided by Congress in the legislation that created the agency.

Delegation of Authority

In the process of creating an administrative agency, Congress gives the agency power and authority through a *legislative delegation*. Among the powers generally delegated to the agency by Congress is the authorization to perform its specific regulatory purpose, formulate appropriate public policy, and perform certain fundamental activities in implementing that policy. A statute delegating those powers to the agency is called an *enabling statute*.

In the development of administrative agencies, some legal scholars argued that creation of agencies was a constitutional violation of the *doctrine of nondelegability of powers*. The doctrine holds that a power delegated to one branch of government may not be redelegated to another. Legal scholars contended that since the U.S. Constitution delegated all legislative powers to Congress, Congress could not redelegate those powers to an agency.

The doctrine has not proven to be an obstacle to the creation of agencies by Congress. In fact, questions of delegation are now rarely raised when agency authority is challenged. Congress has often been able to delegate its lawmaking power with minimal guidance to the administrative agency on how the power is to be used. General guidelines or standards, for example, that require an agency to regulate "in the public interest" or "in the public convenience" are sufficient.

Purpose for Creation of an Agency

Administrative agencies are generally created by Congress when a problem is perceived as requiring a considerable degree of expertise, flexibility, and continuous supervision in working toward solutions. In the late 1960s, for example, Congress and the general public became very concerned about air pollution. Congress could have enacted a law requiring that air pollution from factories be reduced or eliminated. Congress as an institution, however, has neither the time nor the expertise to determine how such a law might be applied to numerous industries and thousands of individual factories emitting substances that cause air pollution. Moreover, Congress recognized that it lacked the ability to adequately enforce compliance with any limitation on air pollution it might have imposed on business. Instead, Congress enacted the Clean Air Act, delegating the responsibility for its implementation to the Environmental Protection Agency, and providing the agency with legislative, investigative, adjudicatory, and enforcement powers to accomplish the task. According to Professor James M. Landis:

> [T]he administrative process springs from the inadequacy of a simple tripartite form of government to deal with modern problems. It represents a striving to adapt governmental technique, that still divides under three rubrics [legislative, judicial, and executive], to modern needs and, at the same time, to preserve those elements of responsibility and those conditions of balance that have distinguished American government.

Administrative agencies offer several advantages over Congress and the courts in the management of complex and technical regulatory problems. Because agencies are specialized bodies charged with the responsibility for regulating one specific area of public policy, they can consider technical details more effectively than can Congress. In comparison to the judicial system, agencies are able to bring claims more quickly, enjoy greater flexibility and informality in their procedures, and acquire a technical expertise in intricate regulatory matters. In addition, agencies have the ability to monitor a regulated industry on a continuous basis, while courts generally function to monitor business behavior only after a dispute or a violation has arisen.

Administrative Law

Administrative law consists of those legal rules that define the authority and structure of administrative agencies, specify an agency's procedural formalities, and define the roles of the courts and other governmental bodies in their relationships with agencies. The primary sources of administrative law include:

1. The enabling statutes of the administrative agencies.
2. The Administrative Procedures Act.
3. Court decisions that review the validity of agency actions or decisions.

In addition, Congress has enacted several statutes that have had significant procedural impacts on administrative agencies, including the Freedom of Information Act and Government in the Sunshine Act. Those acts created new opportunities for public participation, and clearance requirements for agencies to follow and for litigants to invoke against the agencies.

The most fundamental administrative law is the Administrative Procedures Act (APA). Enacted by Congress in 1946, the APA was intended to define and systematize the basic procedural rules and formalities for all federal agencies. An agency is required to abide by APA requirements unless Congress has passed a law specifically imposing different or additional requirements on that agency. The major provisions of the APA are summarized in Table 5–1.

Table 5–1   Summary of the Major Provisions of the Administrative Procedures Act

Section	United States Code	Summary of Provision
2	5 U.S.C. § 551	Provides definitions establishing the Act's terms and coverage.
3	5 U.S.C. § 552	Sets forth requirements for the publication of certain rules and regulations in the Federal Register; requires agencies to make other documents available to the public upon request.
4–8	5 U.S.C. §§ 553–558	Establishes the basic procedural rules applicable to agency actions, including the procedures in rule-making, adjudication, and procedures for review of agency decisions by the agency.
10	5 U.S.C. §§ 701–706	Establishes the availability, form, and scope of judicial review of agency decisions.

DEVELOPMENT OF REGULATORY AGENCIES

State governments first developed agencies to impose rate regulation on railroads, grain elevators, and other natural monopolies. The state regulatory requirements on railroads helped spur the creation of the first federal regulatory agency, the Interstate Commerce Commission (ICC). In 1887, Congress established the ICC to regulate railroad rates and routes "in the public interest," a function it still performs.

A number of federal administrative agencies were developed in the years following the creation of the ICC. For example, the Food and Drug Administration, responsible for monitoring food and drug safety, was created in 1907. The Federal Trade Commission, whose function is to enforce the antitrust laws and prevent unfair and deceptive trade practices, was established in 1914. As Figure 5–1 illustrates, however, the first big expansion in administrative agencies came during the New Deal era of the 1930s.

New Deal Agencies

The New Deal era changed the face of government and bureaucracy and, in so doing, gave impetus to the development of modern administrative law. During the New Deal era, regulation was imposed on business in response to concerns generated by the collapse of the stock market and the Great Depression that followed. The Great Depression was viewed as demonstrating that unregulated markets could not be trusted to serve the social and economic welfare of the nation. In response, Congress created several administrative agencies substantially extending federal economic regulation over private activities.

Most significant of the New Deal agencies are the Securities and Exchange Commission (SEC), the Civil Aeronautics Board (CAB), and the Federal

Figure 5–1   Growth and Development of Federal Administrative Agencies

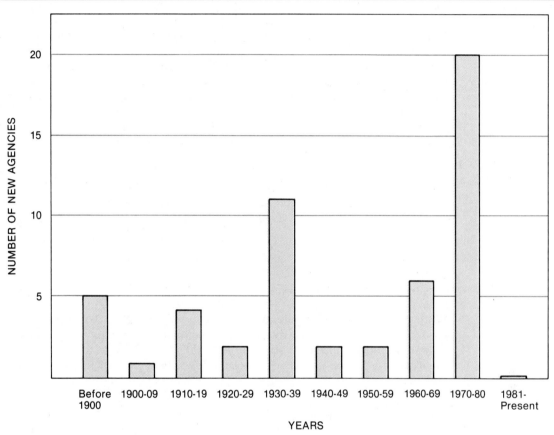

Source: Data from *U.S. Government Manual* and Herman E. Knooss, *American Economic Development* (Englewood Cliffs, N.J.: Prentice-Hall, 1966)

Communications Commission (FCC). Other agencies formed by Congress during the New Deal era regulate various aspects of banking, labor relations, energy, and agriculture. Of all the agencies developed during the New Deal era, the CAB incurred the greatest pressures for regulatory reform. The Airline Deregulation Act of 1978 phased out many of the federal regulations imposed on the airline industry by the CAB, which ceased to exist in 1985.

Social Reform and the Agencies of the '60s and '70s

Agencies created in the 1960s and 1970s are generally not oriented toward a specific industry as they were previously. During those years, the regulatory focus shifted from direct control of industry to include social reform goals and objectives. The increased emphasis on social reform led to the creation of such agencies as the Environmental Protection Agency (EPA), whose function is "to assure protection of the environment by a systematic abatement and control of pollution"; the Occupational Safety and Health Administration (OSHA), whose function is to "insure just and equitable enforcement of . . . occupational health and safety standards"; the Equal Employment Opportunity Commission (EEOC), whose function is to "end discrimination based on race, color, religion, sex, or national origin in hiring, promoting, firing, wages, testing, training, apprenticeship, and all other conditions of employment"; and the Consumer Product Safety Commission (CPSC), which works to set mandatory product safety standards "to reduce the risk of injury to consumers from consumer products." In part, these agencies are a response to repeated calls by special interest groups for increased federal controls in the areas of the environment, health, and safety.

Since the creation of the Interstate Commerce Commission one hundred years ago, administrative agencies have grown to become a dominant part of the federal government. Today there are fifty-seven independent establishments and government corporations along with fourteen cabinet-level departments—all with significant regulatory responsibilities. Those agencies issue about 50,000 pages of regulations per year. Exhibit 5–1 provides a selected list of administrative agencies that perform a broad range of regulatory tasks.

AGENCY STRUCTURE

While administrative agencies are similar in terms of their delegated investigatory, adjudicatory, legislative, and enforcement powers, they vary considerably in both organizational structure and their attachments to other government bodies. It is on the basis of those differences that agencies are generally classified.

Exhibit 5–1   Selected Federal Administrative Agencies

Direct and Indirect Regulators of Business

Civil Aeronautics Board (1938)	Federal Energy Regulatory Commission (1977)
Commission on Civil Rights (1957)	Federal Maritime Commission (1961)
Consumer Product Safety Commission (1972)	Federal Reserve System (1913)
Council of Consumer Affairs (1971)	Federal Trade Commission (1914)
Council of Environmental Quality (1970)	Food and Drug Administration (1907)
Department of Agriculture (1862)	Interstate Commerce Commission (1887)
Department of Commerce (1913)	National Labor Relations Board (1935)
Department of Energy (1977)	National Railroad Passenger Corporation (Amtrak) (1970)
Department of Health and Human Services (1980)	Nuclear Regulatory Commission (1975)
Department of Housing and Urban Development (1965)	Occupational Safety and Health Review Commission (1970)
Department of the Interior (1849)	Office of Federal Contract Compliance Programs (1965)
Department of Labor (1913)	Regulatory Analysis Review Group (1978)
Department of Transportation (1966)	Regulatory Council (1978)
Department of the Treasury (1789)	Securities and Exchange Commission (1934)
Environmental Protection Agency (1970)	Small Business Administration (1953)
Equal Employment Opportunity Commission (1965)	Tennessee Valley Authority (1933)
Federal Communications Commission (1934)	United States Postal Service (1971)
Federal Deposit Insurance Corporation (1933)	United States Tariff Commission (1916)

Organizational Structure

Administrative agencies may be separated on the basis of general differences in organizational structure into either agencies and departments or commissions and boards. The principal differences lie in the manner in which upper management is organized. In terms of the application of administrative law, however, there are few functional differences between the two administrative structures.

Consider, for example, the internal organizational structure of the Federal Trade Commission (FTC) presented in Figure 5–2. As illustrated by the FTC, commissions and boards are generally managed or headed by a group of *commissioners*. Although the FTC is headed by five commissioners, one of whom is designated by the President as the chair, depending on the agency, there may be as many as eleven commissioners. The commissioners are appointed by the President, with the consent of the Senate, to five-year terms.

To contrast the structure of the commissions, agencies and departments are headed by a single person called the *administrator* or, as in most cabinet-level departments, the *secretary*. The administrator (secretary) is

Figure 5–2   Organizational Structure of the Federal Trade Commission

FEDERAL TRADE COMMISSION

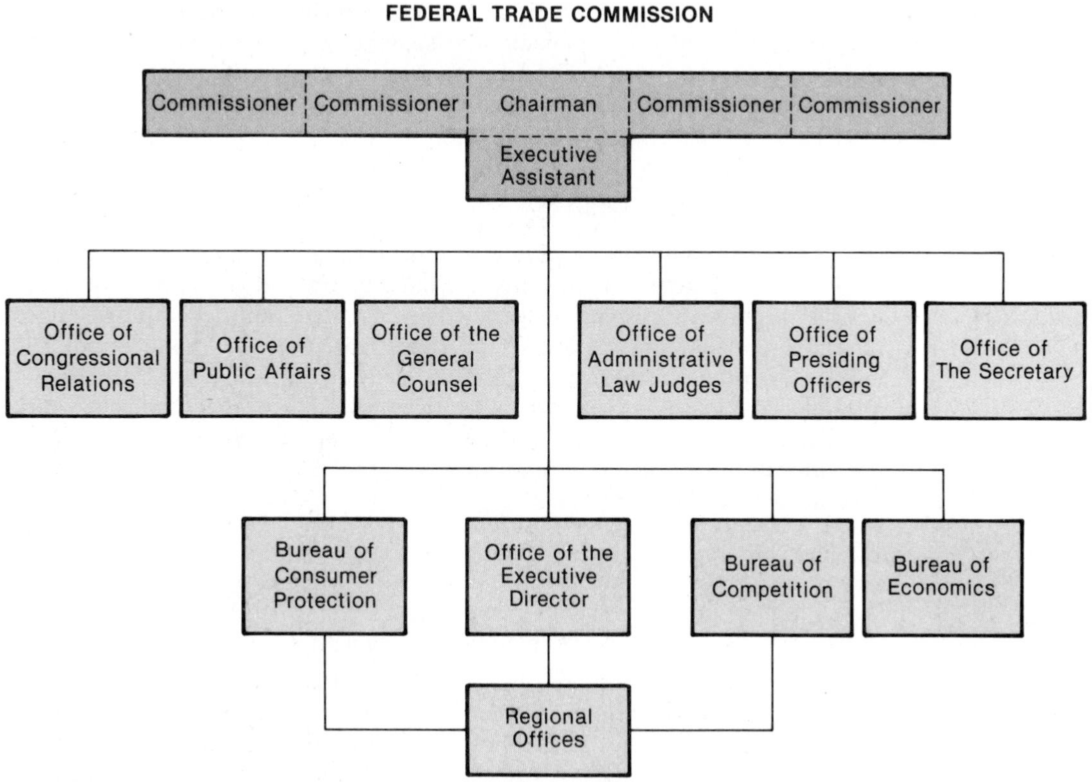

Source: *United States Government Manual.*

appointed by the President—with the consent of the Senate—to serve as the principal authority of the agency (department). Other important agencies include the Food and Drug Administration, the Department of Labor, and the Department of Energy.

Government Attachment

In addition to being classified on the basis of their organizational structure, federal agencies can be classified on the basis of whether the agency is attached to a branch of government. Specifically, executive (or dependent) agencies are a part of the executive branch of government, while the independent agencies are not.

Administrative agencies designated as either commissions or boards are generally *independent agencies*. Although commissioners are appointed by the President, they do not serve at the President's discretion and can generally be removed only for cause, usually inefficiency, neglect of duty, or malfeasance in office. As a consequence of this independence, however, there is often a statutory restriction that a commission's membership can be made up only of a bare majority from the same political party. Thus, only three commissioners of the SEC may be members of the same political party.

Administrative agencies designated as agencies or departments are generally *executive agencies*. In contrast to the commissioners in independent agencies, the person of highest authority in an executive agency is directly accountable to the President and may be removed by the President for job performance deemed unsatisfactory. Also, when a presidential administration changes, a person who headed up an executive agency under the previous administration will generally be replaced.

Agency Staffing Needs

Administrative agencies employ staff officers to assist in carrying out agency work. Staff members are usually technically trained in matters of specific interest to the administrative agency. The EPA, for example, employs environmental engineers and scientists to investigate and to monitor pollution, lawyers to process lawsuits involving agency regulation enforcement, and administrative law judges to preside over formal adjudicatory proceedings. Finally, agencies will employ a supporting staff of secretaries, clerks, and accountants. Administrative agencies vary in size from a few hundred to several thousand employees.

REGULATORY POWERS OF ADMINISTRATIVE AGENCIES

Congress creates and confers significant regulatory powers upon an administrative agency to promulgate legislative rules consistent with the agency's statutory responsibilities. An agency is also invested with power to investigate violations of its rules and regulations and to prosecute violators. Although these specific powers and their application differ from agency to agency, it is

Table 5–2   Administrative Agencies: Summary of Regulatory Powers

Regulatory Power	Definition	Comparison to the Judiciary, Congress, and the Executive Branch
Legislative or rulemaking power	The ability to develop administrative rules for the implementation of the agency's regulatory policies	In formulating rules, agencies can employ experts to consider technical detail more effectively than Congress.
Investigative power	The ability to obtain the necessary information to ensure that the statute and the agency's rules are being observed	In contrast to the judicial system, agencies are able to monitor a regulated industry on a continuous basis—whether or not there has been a violation or a dispute.
Adjudicatory power	The ability to resolve disputes and violations through a judicial-type proceeding	In contrast to the judicial system, agencies are able to bring actions more quickly, and enjoy greater flexibility and informality in their procedures.
Enforcement power	The ability to impose various sanctions for the purpose of encouraging compliance with the regulatory law, with the rules developed and implemented by the agency, and with an agency's adjudicatory outcomes	In contrast to the judiciary and the executive branch, agencies enjoy greater flexibility in imposing sanctions, including fines, prohibitions, restrictions on licenses and permits, and the threat of public exposure.

possible to generalize to a typical administrative agency. A summary of agency regulatory powers is provided in Table 5–2.

Rulemaking Authority

To implement the statutory responsibilities delegated to them by Congress, most agencies have the authority to engage in *rulemaking*. Through its rulemaking procedures, the agency seeks formally to develop administrative rules and to articulate its regulatory policy. Agency rulemaking has been called "the most distinctive administrative process" and "one of the greatest inventions of modern government."

A precise definition of an administrative rule resulting from an agency rulemaking is, however, somewhat elusive. Compounding the difficulty of defining such a rule is the fact that agencies maintain their own distinctive terminologies. The Treasury Department, for example, calls its rules "decisions"; other agencies refer to their rules as standards, guidelines, and opinions. The Administrative Procedures Act defines a rule as follows:

> The whole or part of an agency statement of general or particular applicability and future effect designed to implement, interpret, or prescribe law or policy describing the organization, procedure, or practice requirements of an agency.

As an aid to a more precise definition, administrative rules are classified as being either substantive (legislative), interpretative, or procedural.

Substantive or Legislative Rules

Substantive rules are, in effect, administrative "statutes" with the same force and effect of law as statutes enacted by Congress. In issuing a substantive rule, the agency exercises the lawmaking power delegated to it by Congress. Before issuing such a rule, the agency is generally required by the Administrative Procedures Act to provide public notice and the opportunity for interested parties to comment. In some circumstances, a legislative rule may be required to be on the record. The agency is then required to conduct a formal trial-like hearing as a forum for interested parties to present evidence and arguments for or against the proposed rule. The procedural requirements and basic agency rulemaking processes are discussed in more detail in the next major section.

Interpretative Rules

Interpretative rules are statements issued by an agency to provide both its staff and the public with guidance regarding the interpretation of a particular statute or regulation within the scope of its regulatory responsibility. That is, interpretative rules are statements as to what an agency thinks a statute or regulation means. Interpretative rules range from informal *general policy statements* to authoritative rulings that are binding on the agency.

In contrast to legislative rules, interpretative rules are exempt from the notice and comment requirements of the Administrative Procedures Act. As a consequence, an agency is able to issue interpretative rules without soliciting input from those parties that will be affected by the rule. However, adversely affected parties frequently challenge an agency's interpretative rule by contending that it is really a legislative rule. If the challenge is successful, the agency will be required to provide public notice and interested parties with the opportunity to comment. Thus, from a procedural standpoint, the ability of an agency to distinguish between the two types of rules is important. The *Jerri's Ceramic Arts* case discusses the distinction between legislative and interpretative rules in that regard.

Jerri's Ceramic Arts, Inc. v. Consumer Product Safety Commission

United States Court of Appeals, Fourth Circuit
874 F.2d 205 (1989)

Case Background. *Jerri's Ceramic Arts challenged a "Statement of Interpretation" issued by the Consumer Product Safety Commission. The "interpretation" at issue was published in 1988 and effects a change in the Commission's enforcement policy of the "Small Parts Rule." The Small Parts Rule allows the Commission to ban small toys and other children's items that present potential health hazards by choking, aspiration, or ingestion. Issued in 1980, the original regulation provided that "Any components or pieces (excluding paper, fabric, yarn, fuzz, elastic and string) that become detached from the article during testing, and which then fit entirely within a testing cylinder one and one-quarter inches in diameter, and one inch to two and one-quarter inches deep do not comply with the test." Previously, the Commission had banned only hard components, generally plastic, that were sufficiently small to fit into the cylinder. Through its "Statement of Interpretation" the Commission sought to modify its previous position by stating that "paper, fabric, yarn, fuzz, elastic, string" and other soft components would also be banned. The Commission asserted that the earlier exclusion was intended to apply only to "pieces" and not to "components." This decision was appealed to the Court of Appeals.*

Case Decision.   Judge Chapman delivered the opinion of the court.

* * *

[T]he Commission's characterization of its statement as an exposition of its policy or interpretation of the standard does not preclude our finding that it is something more. Such a distinction between "interpretative" rules and "something more," i.e., "substantive" or "legislative" rules, is not always easily made. Nonetheless, courts are in general agreement that interpretative rules simply state what the administrative agency thinks the statute means, and only "remind" affected parties of existing duties. In contrast, a substantive or legislative rule, pursuant to properly delegated authority, has the force of law, and creates new law or imposes new rights or duties. The distinction between interpretative and legislative rules is significant because the Administrative Procedures Act exempts "interpretative rules, general statements of policy, or rules of agency organization, procedure (and) practice" from the process of notice and comment. Legislative rules which fail to satisfy such procedural [notice and comment] requirements must be set aside.

In deciding whether the [Commission's "Statement of Interpretation"] is an interpretative rule, this court should consider the Commission's intent in authoring it, as ascertained by an examination of the provision's language, its context, and any available extrinsic evidence. Here, the language of the statement and related comments establishes that more is involved than mere "interpretation," because the proposed statement has the clear intent of eliminating a former exemption and of providing the Commission with power to enforce violations of a new rule. For example, the statement gives the Commission authority to impose the full range of civil and criminal penalties provided by Congress. The Commission specifically maintained that in "any enforcement action" based on the new interpretation, "affected parties who disagree with the action will have a full opportunity in a federal district court and/or administrative proceeding to challenge the Commission's interpretation." This is conclusive evidence that the agency believes its statement imposes new duties that have the force of law and that it can proceed to enforce those duties. ... For these reasons, the Commission's contention that the rule does not "command performance" is simply incredible.

* * *

The broader context of the statement also confirms that the Commission's act is an attempt at legislative rulemaking. The fact that the statement altered a long-standing position cannot readily be discounted. If "interpretation" is a process of "reminding" one of existing duties, a decision to modify former duties demands close scrutiny by a reviewing court. Certainly this does not mean that an agency may never consider its interpretation of a regulation. But it must do so with regard to the effects of such a decision, and the greater such effects, the less likely the change can be considered merely interpretative. Here, the new rule directly impacts on an enormous range of children's products industries, including toys, apparel, furniture and furnishings, the latter of which, because of the fabric exemption, were formerly excluded from the rule. As a result, the statement would, for the first time, have the effect of bringing within the sweep of the regulation entirely new classes of business.

Because the tests distinguishing legislative and interpretative rulemaking are largely concerned with intent and effect, we believe that the above facts establish that the Commission has made a legislative rule and called it an interpretation. Congress has made it clear that the promulgation of such legislative rules must be preceded by the procedural notice and comment requirements elaborated in [the Administrative Procedures Act]. Because the

Commission has not complied with such requirements, the "interpretation" by the Commission must be set aside.

* * *

Case Holding. *The Commission's "Statement of Interpretation" is a substantive or legislative rule and not an interpretative rule as the Commission asserts. As a legislative rule, it must meet the procedural requirements of the Administrative Procedures Act. Since it has not met those requirements, the Commission's rule must be set aside.*

Case Questions

1. On what basis did the court characterize the Commission's rule as a legislative rule?
2. Why would the Commission elect to represent its rule as an interpretative rather than as a legislative rule?
3. Why are the toy manufacturers concerned about the designation of the rule as an interpretative rather than as a legislative rule?

Procedural Rules

Procedural rules identify an agency's organization, describe its method of operation, and detail the agency's internal practices. The power to promulgate such rules is generally authorized by the agency's enabling statute. Once procedural rules are issued, the agency is bound by them. A challenge to an agency decision will usually be upheld if the challenging party can demonstrate that the agency did not comply with its own procedural rules in reaching its decision.

Investigative Powers

Without information, administrative agencies could not adequately perform their regulatory responsibilities. Whatever the administrative action, its effectiveness is determined by the information the agency has or can obtain. The agency's authority to investigate possible violations of its rules and regulations is one of the functions that distinguishes agencies from courts.

The majority of agency information is obtained through staff analysis and the agency's accumulated records. In some cases, information is obtained from private sources willing to divulge what they know. When these information sources prove inadequate, however, an agency may rely on its statutory authority to seek further information. Because the need for information varies widely both within and among agencies, Congress has traditionally conferred broad and expansive investigative power upon agencies. Those powers are constrained principally by the limitations imposed by the Constitution, particularly the Fourth Amendment. Notwithstanding constitutional constraints, if an agency is persistent and careful, very little information in the possession of a business is beyond its reach.

Agencies with appropriate statutory authority usually take one of three approaches in obtaining needed information:

1. The regulated business is required to do self-reporting on a regular basis.
2. Direct observation is made through physical inspections to determine if a particular business is in compliance.
3. Agency subpoena power is used, requiring the business to produce documents from its files.

Requiring Businesses to Monitor and Self–Report

Given the complexity of regulatory matters and the large number of activities that come under supervision, agencies increasingly require businesses to monitor themselves. Generally an agency will require a business to report certain information to it either at fixed time intervals or upon the occurrence of an event (often a violation) deemed important by the agency. The Clean Air Act, for example, provides that a business may be required to monitor its air pollution emissions and report the data to the Environmental Protection Agency:

> The Administrator may require any person who owns or operates any emission source . . . to (A) establish and maintain such records, (B) make such reports, (C) install, use, and maintain such monitoring equipment or methods, (D) sample such emissions, and (E) provide such other information as the Administrator may reasonably require. . . .

Businesses have incentives to comply with self-reporting requirements, because failure to report or reporting false information can lead to fines and other more severe sanctions. On the other hand, accurate reporting of information can also lead to fines and agency sanctions if, for example, that information indicates that the business has violated agency regulations.

Businesses have contested fines resulting from the mandatory self-reporting of data, arguing that reporting of self-incriminating evidence violates the Fifth Amendment. The Supreme Court has ruled, however, that the self-incrimination privilege of the Fifth Amendment applies only to individuals and does not protect corporations.

Direct Observation by Agency

Agencies also acquire information through direct observation of the business and its activities. Techniques frequently employed include, for example, on-the-spot worksite safety inspections conducted by OSHA inspectors or the detection of excessive air pollution emissions from a smokestack by the EPA.

As was discussed in the last chapter, the Supreme Court has held that agencies are required to obtain warrants for routine inspections. There are, however, several exceptions to the warrant requirement. Employers are free to consent to routine agency inspections, in which case no warrant is required. In addition, no warrant is required if an agency's evidence is obtained from an "open field" observation. That is, a warrant is not required if the evidence is gathered by the inspector from observations in areas to which the public has access. In the *Dow* case, the Court considers whether the taking of photographs from the airplane above a factory falls within the open-field exception.

**Dow
Chemical
Company v.
United States**
**United States
Supreme Court**
476 U.S. 227, 106
S.Ct. 1819 (1986)

Case Background. *Dow Chemical Company brought an action for declaratory and injunctive relief against aerial surveillance and photography of its industrial complex by the Environmental Protection Agency (EPA). The EPA had requested an on-site inspection of the plant, but the request had been denied. Instead of seeking an administrative search warrant, EPA employed a commercial aerial photographer, who took photographs of the facility using a precision aerial mapping camera. The photographs were taken from various altitudes, all of which were within lawful navigable airspace.*

Dow Chemical brought suit in federal district court, alleging that EPA's action violated the Fourth Amendment to the Constitution. The district court granted summary judgment for Dow Chemical, but the court of appeals reversed. Dow Chemical appealed to the U.S. Supreme Court.

Case Decision. Chief Justice Burger delivered the opinion of the Court.

* * *

The photographs at issue in this case are essentially like those commonly used in map-making. Any person with an airplane and aerial camera could readily duplicate them. Dow claims EPA's use of aerial photography was a "search" of an area . . . and that it had a reasonable expectation of privacy from such photography protected by the Fourth Amendment.

Congress has vested in EPA certain investigatory and enforcement authority. . . . When Congress invests an agency with enforcement and investigatory authority, it is not necessary to identify explicitly each and every technique that may be used in the course of executing the statutory mission.

* * *

Regulatory or enforcement authority generally carries with it all the modes of inquiry and investigation traditionally employed or useful to execute the authority granted. Environmental standards such as clean air and clean water cannot be enforced only in libraries and laboratories, helpful as those institutions may be.

* * *

Dow's inner manufacturing areas are elaborately secured to ensure they are not open or exposed to the public from the ground. Any actual physical entry by EPA into any enclosed area would raise significantly different questions, because "(t)he businessman, like the occupant of a residence, has a constitutional right to go about his business free from unreasonable official entries upon his private commercial property." The narrow issue raised by Dow's claim of search and seizure, however, concerns aerial observation of a 2,000–acre outdoor manufacturing facility without physical entry.

We pointed out in *Donovan* v. *Dewey* (1981), that the Government has "greater latitude to conduct warrantless inspections of commercial property" because "the expectation of privacy that the owner of commercial property enjoys in such property differs significantly from the sanctity accorded an individual's home." We emphasized that unlike a homeowner's interest in his dwelling, "(t)he interest of the owner of commercial property is not one in being free from any inspections." And with regard to regulatory inspections, we have held that "(w)hat is observable by the public is observable without a warrant, by the Government inspector as well." *Marshall* v. *Barlow's, Inc.* (1978) . . . Here, EPA was not employing some unique sensory device that, for example, could penetrate the walls of buildings and record conversations in Dow's plants, offices or laboratories, but rather a conventional, albeit precise, commercial camera commonly used in map-making. . . .

It may well be, as the Government concedes, that surveillance of private property by using highly sophisticated surveillance equipment not generally available to the public, such as satellite technology, might be constitutionally proscribed absent a warrant. But the photographs here are not so revealing of intimate details as to raise constitutional concerns. Although they undoubtedly give EPA more detailed information than naked-eye views, they remain limited to an outline of the facility's buildings and equipment. The mere fact that human vision is enhanced somewhat, at least to the degree here, does not give rise to constitutional problems. An electronic device to penetrate walls or windows so as to hear and record confidential discussions of chemical formulae or other trade secrets would raise very different and far more serious questions.

* * *

Case Holding. *The Court concluded that the open areas of an industrial plant complex with numerous plant structures spread over an area of 2,000 acres are open to the view and observation of persons in aircraft lawfully in the public airspace immediately or sufficiently near the area for the reach of cameras. The decision of the court of appeals was affirmed.*

Case Questions

1. What was the Court's rationale for finding this search to be a constitutional search?
2. If the Court had decided differently, how could the EPA have obtained the same information?
3. Are there disadvantages associated with using administrative search warrants that are so serious that it forces agencies to undertake alternative activity such as aerial photography without notifying the other party?

Agency Subpoena Power

An agency may also attempt to obtain information by issuing a subpoena if the power to do so has been provided by Congress. Recall that a *subpoena* is a legal instrument that directs the recipient to appear at a specified time and place either to testify or to produce documents. The Clean Air Act provides a typical example of explicit congressional authorization of the power to issue subpoenas and the normal procedure used to enforce them:

> [F]or purposes of obtaining information . . . the Administrator may issue subpoenas for the attendance and testimony of witnesses and the production of relevant papers, books, and documents, and he may administer oaths. . . . In case of . . . refusal to obey a subpoena served upon any person . . . , the district court for any district in which such person is found or resides or transacts business . . . shall have jurisdiction to issue an order requiring such person to appear and give testimony before the Administrator . . . and any failure to obey such an order may be punished by such court as a contempt thereof.

Unless the request for information by the agency is vague, or if the burden imposed on the business clearly outweighs the possible benefits to the agency, the business is required to comply with the subpoena. Even trade secrets and other confidential information cannot necessarily be kept from agency scrutiny. If a business asserts that the information requested by the subpoena deserves confidential treatment, the agency will allow the information to be presented secretly to it by the business.

The Administrative Procedures Act deals only generally with agency subpoena powers and procedures. The APA provides that a subpoena may be issued only in the situations authorized by law. In addition, the APA provides that a person compelled to appear before an agency in response to a subpoena has the right to be accompanied, represented, and advised by counsel.

Adjudicatory Power

Administrative agencies have the power not only to investigate but also to adjudicate rule violations. In this sense, the agency is empowered to act much like a court of law. The administrative agency counterpart to a judicial trial is called an *adjudication*. The procedural requirements of the adjudicatory process are discussed in the next section.

The constitutionality of agency adjudicatory power has been justified by the Supreme Court on the grounds that Congress has delegated authority to agencies to adjudicate cases involving public rights. *Public rights* have been defined by the Court as those rights that arise between the government and others, as contrasted with private rights, which involve the liability of one individual to another under the law. The Court has also determined that private rights created by Congress may also be adjudicated by an administrative agency.

Enforcement Power

To assure that its regulatory mandate is met, Congress generally provides an agency with a broad array of enforcement tools intended to be used to encourage voluntary compliance with the regulatory law, the rules developed and implemented by an agency, and an agency's adjudicatory outcomes directed at individual violators. The EPA, for example, can ensure compliance with air pollution control requirements by seeking judicially imposed civil and criminal penalties and injunctions. In the Clean Air Act, for example, Congress provided that

> The Administrator shall commence a civil action for a permanent or temporary injunction, or to assess and recover a civil penalty of not more than $25,000 per day of violation, or both, whenever [the owner or operator of a major stationary source] . . . violates or fails to comply with any order. . . .

In addition to suing in federal court for civil and criminal penalties, agencies are generally given authority to impose several other types of sanctions. To illustrate the sanctions available to an agency, consider the terms offered by the APA in its definition of *sanction:*

(a) Prohibition, requirement, limitation, or other condition affecting the freedom of a person;

(b) Withholding of relief;

(c) Imposition of a penalty or fine;

(d) Destruction, taking, seizing, or withholding of property;

(e) Assessment of damages, reimbursement, restitution, compensation, costs, charges, or fees;

(f) Requirement, revocation, or suspension of a license; or,

(g) Taking other compulsory or restrictive action.

Although an agency could seek to impose any of the preceding sanctions, enforcement methods vary from agency to agency. Some agencies, for example, have found that the mere threat of public exposure of a violation is sufficient to bring about compliance.

ADMINISTRATIVE PROCEDURES

Administrative law concerns itself primarily with the procedural requirements imposed upon agencies by the Administrative Procedures Act. The APA, however, imposes procedural requirements only when the agency is engaged in formal procedures such as rulemaking or determining the application of its rules to a particular situation through an adjudication. For the vast majority of agency informal decisions, the APA provides little procedural guidance. This section discusses the basic agency formal and informal procedures and the constraints imposed on those procedures.

Informal Agency Procedures

As agency regulatory activities have expanded, the administrative process has tended to rely increasingly on *informal procedures*. Because of their nature, informal procedures lie outside the procedural controls provided by the APA, thereby allowing considerable agency discretion in forcing compliance. Since informal procedures generally require less time and are less costly than formal procedures in bringing about industry compliance—primarily because few procedural controls are applied—agencies prefer to employ them.

Nature of an Informal Procedure

Informal agency procedures take the form of tests and inspections, day-to-day supervision, the processing of applications and permits, settlements and negotiations, and the exchange of interpretative advice in the form of advisory opinions and declaratory orders. Some agency observers also consider publicity or the threat of it as an additional (and very potent) informal procedure through which an agency can coerce industry compliance with its rules and regulations.

In many cases, the agency's response is based on an inspector's on-the-spot analysis. For example, an OSHA inspector may, upon finding that a manufacturing process places a worker's health in peril, order immediate changes or, in the extreme, order the business to cease production until the changes are made. In other situations, the mere existence of the agency in its supervisory and enforcement capacities may "coerce" the desired industry behavior. When the Food and Drug Administration (FDA) finds botulism in canned foods, for example, the manufacturer will "voluntarily" withdraw the product from the shelves and destroy it in response to a tacit threat of prosecution by the FDA.

Both situations are examples of agency informal procedures enforcing compliance with the agency's rules and regulations.

Review of Agency Decision in an Informal Procedure

A business dissatisfied with an agency action involving an informal procedure may seek review through the same process available for appeals from formal procedures. The decision is reviewed by the agency; if dissatisfied with the agency's final decision, parties may seek review by the appropriate federal court. In reviewing agency informal procedures, the courts are generally most concerned with whether the particular agency procedure was fair and the decision was consistent with the legislative intent of Congress. The procedural requirements and the limitations of judicial review are discussed in the next section.

Formal Agency Procedures

The two basic *formal procedures* used by most federal regulatory agencies are investigatory and adjudicatory hearings. The manner in which the hearings are generally defined and conducted is dictated by the APA. In some instances, however, an agency's enabling statute may require procedures that differ somewhat from those prescribed by the APA.

Adjudicatory Hearings

Under the APA, an *adjudicatory hearing* is a formal process involving the agency and an individual or a small group of individuals. The procedures required by the APA for an adjudicatory hearing are similar to those followed in a court trial, although the agency has some discretion to act much less formally. In contrast to the industry-wide breadth of coverage of a rule promulgated by an agency, the decision reached at the close of an adjudicatory hearing is generally applicable only to the party involved in the hearing.

As Figure 5–3 illustrates, an adjudicatory hearing is typically initiated by the filing of a complaint by the agency (or by a citizen, the U.S. Attorney General, or an injured party) against a business whose behavior is in question. The business is then required to respond to the complaint. In some cases, the agency will do research, collect information relevant to the complainant's charges, and reach a decision as to whether a hearing is warranted. If it is determined that a hearing is warranted, an administrative law judge from the agency will be selected to preside over the hearing. The administrative law judge differs from a judge in a trial court in that the administrative law judge is a Civil Service employee of the agency conducting the hearing. The agency is represented by its counsel, who presents the agency's evidence in support of the complaint; the business then presents its evidence. Witnesses may be cross-examined and objections raised just as in a trial court.

The adjudicatory hearing must conform to the procedural due process guarantees provided by the Constitution. However, although the litigants in an agency adjudicatory hearing are entitled to rights similar to those available at a trial court, they are not entitled to a jury trial. In the *Atlas Roofing* case, the Supreme Court discusses the applicability of the Seventh Amendment's guarantee of the right to a jury trial to an agency adjudicatory hearing.

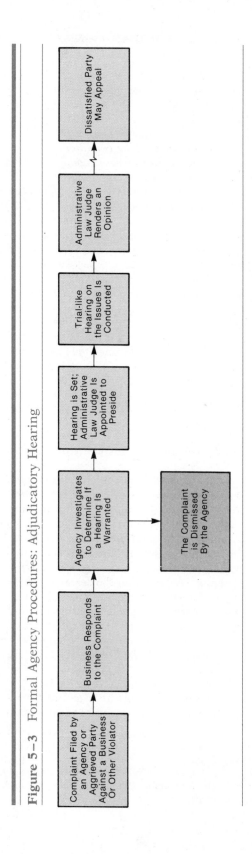

Figure 5–3   Formal Agency Procedures: Adjudicatory Hearing

Atlas Roofing Company, Inc. v. Occupational Safety and Health Review Commission

Supreme Court of the United States
430 U.S. 442, 97 S.Ct. 1261 (1977)

Case Background. *In response to growing workplace safety concerns, Congress enacted the Occupational Safety and Health Act in 1970 (OSHA). Two new remedies were provided by the Act that permitted the federal government, proceeding before an administrative agency, to (1) obtain abatement orders requiring employers to correct unsafe working conditions, and (2) impose civil penalties on any employer maintaining any unsafe working condition.*

If an employer wishes to contest the penalty or the abatement order, an evidentiary hearing is held before an administrative law judge of the Occupational Safety and Health Review Commission. The judge is empowered to affirm, modify, or vacate the abatement order or penalty assessed. The judge's decision is subject to review by the full commission. If review is granted, the commission's subsequent order directing abatement and the payment of any assessed penalty becomes final unless the employer petitions the appropriate court of appeals for judicial review. If review by the court of appeals is granted, the Act specifies that "the findings of the Commission with respect to questions of fact, if supported by substantial evidence, shall be conclusive." If the employer fails to pay the assessed penalty, the Secretary of the Commission may commence a collection action in a federal district court. In that proceeding, neither the fact of the violation nor the propriety of the penalty assessed may be retried.

Atlas Roofing was issued an abatement order and a penalty for safety violations. It appealed the case through the review procedures outlined above and challenged the constitutionality of the Act's enforcement proceedings. It argued that the proceedings failed to provide a jury trial, a violation of the Seventh Amendment. The court of appeals confirmed the commission's finding and stated that jury trials are not required in agency hearings. The Supreme Court granted certiorari to consider the question.

Case Decision. Mr. Justice White delivered the opinion of the Court.

* * *

The Seventh Amendment provides that "(i)n Suits at common law, where the value in controversy shall exceed twenty dollars, the right of trial by jury shall be preserved. . . ." The phrase "Suits at common law" has been construed to refer to cases tried . . . in courts of law in which jury trial was customary as distinguished from courts of equity or admiralty in which jury trial was not. [Atlas Roofing] claims that a suit in a federal court by the Government for civil penalties for violation of a statute is a suit for a money judgment which is classically a suit at common law; and that the defendant therefore has a Seventh Amendment right to a jury determination of all issues of fact is such a case. [Atlas Roofing] then claims that to permit Congress to assign the function of adjudicating the Government's rights to civil penalties for violation of the statute to a different forum, an administrative agency in which no jury is available, would be to permit Congress to deprive a defendant of his Seventh Amendment jury right.

* * *

In *NLRB v. Jones & Laughlin Steel Corp.* (1937), the Court squarely addressed the Seventh Amendment issue involved when Congress commits the factfinding function under a new statute to an administrative tribunal. . . . The Court stated:

> The instant case is not a suit at common law or in the nature of such a suit. The proceeding is one unknown to the common law. It is a statutory proceeding. Reinstatement of the employee and payment for time lost are requirements (administratively) imposed for violation of the statute and are remedies appropriate to its enforcement. The contention under the Seventh Amendment is without merit.

In sum, . . . when Congress creates new statutory "public rights," it may assign their adjudication to an administrative agency with which a jury trial would be incompatible, without violating the Seventh Amendment's injunction that jury trial is to be "preserved" in "suits at common law." Congress is not required by the Seventh Amendment to choke the already crowded federal courts with new types of litigation or prevented from committing some new types of litigation to administrative agencies with special competence in the relevant field. This is the case even if the Seventh Amendment would have required a jury where the adjudication of those rights is assigned instead to a federal court of law instead of an administrative agency.

* * *

Case Holding. *The Seventh Amendment's right to a jury trial is no bar to the creation of new public rights—rights created by statutes within the power of Congress to enact—or their enforcement outside the regular courts of law. Agency adjudicatory hearings are not unconstitutional because jury trials are not provided. The decision of the court of appeals was affirmed.*

Case Questions

1. On the basis of the Court's decision, can you make the argument that administrative agencies play a role similar to that played by the alternative dispute resolution methods discussed in Chapter 3?
2. Why would a violator seek a jury trial in its dispute with an agency?
3. The Court refers to the creation of public rights in its opinion. What are public rights? On the basis of this opinion, could you argue that public rights are subject to different protections under the law than are private rights?

Shortly after the hearing ends, the administrative law judge renders a decision, usually in the form of a written opinion. If the business does not object to the decision, the agency normally adopts the decision. If the business is dissatisfied with the administrative law judge's decision, the commissioners or agency administrator will review the decision in the manner of an appellate court. If the business is dissatisfied after this final agency review, it may then proceed to the federal court system for further review.

Investigatory Hearings: Rulemaking Under the APA

An agency's legislative or rulemaking function under the APA takes place in investigatory hearings. Under the APA, an investigatory hearing deals with the formulation of a regulatory policy that the agency will apply in the future to all parties engaged in the regulated activity. The agency's principal goal in an investigatory hearing is to gather information about the feasibility and desirability of a proposed rule or regulatory policy.

To allow an agency to exercise its rulemaking authority, the APA provides for both informal and formal rulemaking procedures. A comparison of the two rulemaking procedures is provided in Figure 5–4. Regardless of which procedure is to be used, the agency will initially propose a specific rule or regulation. The APA requires official notice of that proposed rule in the *Federal Register*. The notice will generally appear as a "Notice of Proposed Rulemaking" by the agency and will contain information on the nature (formal or

Figure 5-4   Formal Agency Procedures: Formal vs. Informal Rulemaking

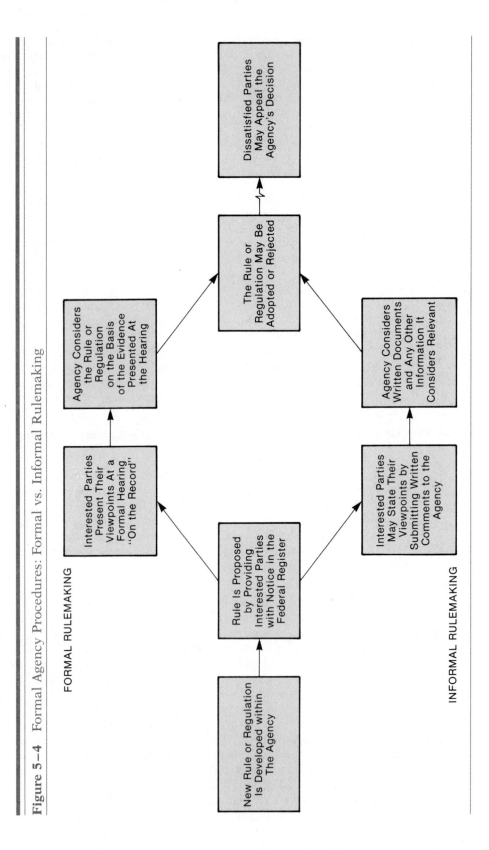

informal) of the rulemaking and the time frame within which interested parties must respond. If a formal hearing is to be held, the notice will provide information about the time and place of the hearing. The notice will also contain a discussion of the proposed rule or regulation and the authority under which it is being proposed.

Informal Rulemaking. If the rulemaking is informal, the APA provides that interested parties may submit written comments to the agency stating their position on the proposed rule. Oral testimony and cross-examination of witnesses, however, are generally not permitted in an informal rulemaking. In addition, in reaching its decision as to whether the rule or regulation should be enacted, the agency is free to consider other sources of information beyond the written comments submitted by interested parties.

Formal Rulemaking. Under some statutes, rules are required to be made *on the record* after any interested parties have had an opportunity for an agency hearing. In such situations, the agency is required to undertake a formal, trial-like investigatory hearing. Interested parties may introduce exhibits and call witnesses, who are then subject to both examination and cross-examination.

Only a small number of federal statutes, however, provide for rulemaking proceedings "on the record." Although there is reason to believe that formal rulemaking may provide interested parties with a greater opportunity to be heard, the costs associated with formal rulemaking—particularly with regard to the time required to formulate and implement policy—can be considerably greater than under informal rulemaking.

As with other agency decisions, dissatisfied parties may seek review of rules promulgated through either formal or informal rulemaking. Dissatisfied parties first must appeal to the agency and then, after exhausting agency procedures, they may seek review with the appropriate federal court.

INTERNATIONAL PERSPECTIVES: ADMINISTRATIVE AGENCIES IN JAPAN

INTERNATIONAL

PERSPECTIVES

Along with differences in the law and legal structures among the developed countries, there are important differences in administrative agencies and administrative law. Those differences can significantly impact the legal environment of business for firms interested in operating in that country. For example, one of the most interesting and worrisome areas of Japanese law and legal culture for the American corporate practitioner is the formal body of administrative "law" known as "administrative guidance" (*gyosei shido*). While this term eludes precise definition, it generally includes all the different means the ministries and agencies of the Japanese government can use to exert formal and informal regulatory authority over businesses in Japan. An administrative agency, for example, may issue guidance by direction (*shiji*), request (*yobo*), warning (*keikoku*), encouragement (*kansho*), or suggestion (*kankoku*).

The power basis of administrative guidance is normally government power over foreign trade, foreign exchange, or loanable funds, but the subject of such guidance might extend far beyond these fields. In theory, businesses are not forced to comply with such administrative guidance. A business that ignores a government suggestion, however, might find that its quota of imported raw materials has been reduced, that it cannot get the necessary legal permission for foreign exchange remittances needed in its business, that it is being denied long-term government financing for future expansions, or that some other governmental sanction is imposed unrelated to that area in which the original guidance was given. The Foreign Exchange Control and Foreign Investment Acts, for example, require that any agreement or contract involving expenditures abroad must be approved before its execution by the Foreign Investment Council. A business that has not complied with an agency's request that a pollution control device be installed might find that a contract requiring remittance abroad has not been approved.

While this type of government influence assumes business cooperation on a voluntary basis, it clearly draws its authority from the ability of agencies to punish noncompliance by a business in a variety of ways. It should be noted, however, that businesses that work within this system are able both to gain considerable support from the government and to influence regulatory policies. The Japanese judiciary has taken a hands-off policy toward administrative guidance. As long as the agency action is within its discretion, the action will not be reviewed unfavorably even if it is abusive. This gives Japanese administrative agencies considerably broader power than their U.S. counterparts.

JUDICIAL REVIEW: JUDICIAL CONSTRAINTS ON AGENCY POWERS

The APA sets forth procedural requirements for a party seeking a court review of an agency decision. If those requirements are met, the party may challenge the decision with an appeal to the appropriate federal court of appeals. That appeal is referred to as *judicial review*, considered by most administrative law scholars to be a powerful and effective external check on administrative agency power. Its very existence ensures that agencies are careful to follow required procedures, prepared to justify their actions, and respectful of the constitutional and legal rights of individuals.

Procedural Requirements: The Right to Judicial Review

Several threshold *procedural requirements* must be overcome by a party challenging an agency decision through judicial review, the most prominent of which are jurisdiction, reviewability, standing, ripeness, and exhaustion. In each case, if a party challenging an agency decision is unable to meet the requirement, it will be denied judicial review. These procedural requirements are summarized in Table 5–3.

Jurisdiction
Most modern regulatory statutes provide explicitly for judicial review of specified agency actions in specified courts. Most commonly, specific statutory provisions provide that a party can petition a particular court of appeals for review. The Clean Air Act, for example, provides that

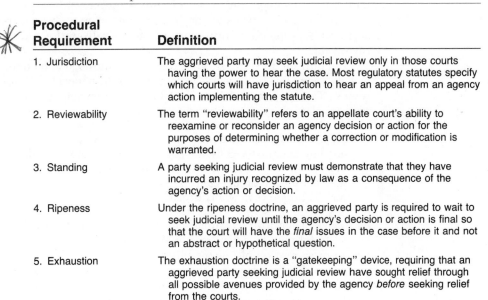

Table 5–3   Judicial Review of Agency Actions: Summary of Procedural
Requirements

Procedural Requirement	Definition
1. Jurisdiction	The aggrieved party may seek judicial review only in those courts having the power to hear the case. Most regulatory statutes specify which courts will have jurisdiction to hear an appeal from an agency action implementing the statute.
2. Reviewability	The term "reviewability" refers to an appellate court's ability to reexamine or reconsider an agency decision or action for the purposes of determining whether a correction or modification is warranted.
3. Standing	A party seeking judicial review must demonstrate that they have incurred an injury recognized by law as a consequence of the agency's action or decision.
4. Ripeness	Under the ripeness doctrine, an aggrieved party is required to wait to seek judicial review until the agency's decision or action is final so that the court will have the *final* issues in the case before it and not an abstract or hypothetical question.
5. Exhaustion	The exhaustion doctrine is a "gatekeeping" device, requiring that an aggrieved party seeking judicial review have sought relief through all possible avenues provided by the agency *before* seeking relief from the courts.

A petition for review of an action of the Administrator in promulgating any national ambient air quality standard . . . or any other nationally applicable regulation . . . may be filed only in the United States Court of Appeals for the District of Columbia. A petition for review of the Administrator's actions in approving or promulgating any . . . regulation . . . or any other final action . . . which is locally or regionally applicable may be filed only in the United States Court of Appeals for the appropriate circuit. . . . Any petition for review . . . shall be filed within sixty days from the date of notice of such promulgation . . . or action.

If no specific statutory review provision is provided by the agency's statutory authority, the party may seek judicial review under more general statutory authority, which has been granted to federal district courts.

Reviewability

Statutes conferring jurisdiction to review agency actions and decisions are often drafted broadly. As a consequence, virtually every decision made by an agency according to its delegated authority is susceptible to judicial review. There are, however, some instances where Congress has prohibited judicial review. Two such instances (or exceptions) are provided by Section 701 of the APA:

(a) This chapter [on judicial review] applies, according to the provisions thereof, except to the extent that—
(1) Statutes preclude judicial review; or
(2) Agency action is committed to agency discretion by law.

The exception from judicial review for actions "committed to agency discretion" is based on functional concerns. Some agency actions and decisions have a compelling need for speed, flexibility, or secrecy that is inconsistent with the open processes of judicial review. If a court finds that a compelling reason exists for denying review, it may decide that the agency's action or decision is committed to the agency's discretion and is, therefore, not reviewable.

In addition, in some statutes delegating authority to an agency, Congress has elected to provide specific exceptions to the general availability of judicial review. The Secretary of Veteran Affairs, for example, has the final authority over the determination of benefits due veterans:

> [T]he decisions of the administrator on any question of law or fact under any law administered by the [Department of Veterans Affairs] providing benefits for veterans and their dependents or survivors shall be final and no other official or any court of the United States shall have the power or jurisdiction to review any decision.

As long as such a preclusion of judicial review is constitutional, courts are bound to follow those congressional directives. As a rule, however, there is a strong presumption of reviewability.

A typical statutory preclusion is a *time limit* imposed on parties who intend to seek review of an administrative decision. Once an agency has reached its decision and has issued an order, parties adversely affected have a specified time period in which to file for review—usually thirty days. The intent of Congress in providing such a preclusion is to bring agency proceedings to a timely close, thereby enhancing the efficiency of the regulatory process.

Standing

A party seeking a court challenge to an agency decision or action must have *standing* to seek judicial review. American administrative law has traditionally restricted the right of judicial review to those parties who can show an injury recognized by law as being entitled to protection. A party who is unable to demonstrate such an injury is prohibited from obtaining judicial review and is said to lack standing.

The standing requirement is rooted in Section 2 of Article III of the U.S. Constitution, which limits the judicial power to *actual cases or controversies*. Federal courts cannot hear complaints from parties who have no stake in a real dispute or who raise only hypothetical questions. The APA affords standing for a "person suffering legal wrong because of agency action or adversely affected or aggrieved by agency action within the meaning of a relevant statute."

The test for standing is whether the agency decision or action challenged has caused the party seeking review *injury in fact*, economic or otherwise, and whether the interest sought to be protected falls within the *zone of interests* to be governed by the statute in question. The *Tax Analysts and Advocates* v. *Blumenthal* case illustrates the application and importance of standing in challenging agency decisions.

Tax Analysts and Advocates v. Blumenthal
District of Columbia Court of Appeals
566 F.2d 130
(1977)

Case Background. *Tax Analysts and Advocates (TAA), a nonprofit corporation organized to promote tax reform, and Thomas Field, a businessman, filed suit in district court seeking a declaratory judgment that certain rulings of the Internal Revenue Service allowing tax credits to companies—both foreign and domestic—for tax payments made to foreign nations in connection with oil extraction are contrary to the Internal Revenue Code and therefore are unlawful. The parties claimed to have standing to sue as federal taxpayers. Field argued that he had standing as a competitor in his capacity as the owner of a currently producing domestic oil well not eligible for the tax credit.*

The district court dismissed the action on the grounds that appellants lacked standing. The appellants appealed the decision to the D.C. Circuit Court of Appeals.

Case Decision.   Judge Wilkey filed the opinion of the court.

* * *

The standing doctrine has two sources: the case or controversy requirement of Article III of the Constitution, and judicially imposed rules of self-restraint known as "prudential limitations." In the context of this case, we have occasion to apply both the constitutional and prudential dimensions of the standing doctrine. . . . The Article III constitutional requirement is one of injury in fact, economic and otherwise. . . . If a court finds that there is no injury in fact, no other inquiry is relevant to a consideration of standing. . . .

Prudential limitations, on the other hand, are not constitutional requirements; these limitations are developed and imposed by the Supreme Court in its supervisory capacity over the federal judiciary. . . . The first of these limitations to be enunciated, and the one which will be the focus of our concern is the so-called "zone test:" "whether the interest sought to be protected by the complainant is arguably within the zone of interests to be protected or regulated by the statute or constitutional guarantee in question." . . .

1. Injury in Fact. We conclude that Field has suffered injury in fact in his capacity as a competitor. Although [his] economic injury is relatively small in magnitude, this does not negate our finding of injury in fact. Field has alleged "a distinct and palpable injury to himself" which meets the requirements of Article III of the Constitution; given that the constitutional hurdle has been surmounted, we must now proceed to examine [Field's] claim in light of the zone test.

2. Zone of Interests. . . . The relevant zone test inquiry with respect to Field's standing as a competitor is: did Congress arguably legislate with respect to competition in the [Federal Tax] Code so as to protect the competitive interests of domestic oil producers [like Field]?

We answer the posed query in the negative for the following reasons. The purpose of the tax credit provision of the Code is to prevent the double taxation of any United States companies operating abroad. . . . The tax credit envisioned . . . is also available to U.S. companies operating outside the [oil industry], with the same purpose of avoiding the double taxation of United States taxpayers, whether such companies have domestic competition or not. Given this purpose, it is obvious that the protective intent of the statutory section extends to all those U.S. companies doing business abroad and paying foreign income taxes.

In addition it cannot be said that parties in the position of Field are arguably intended to be regulated by the provision granting tax credits; that is, Field cannot be said to fall within the regulatory field of concern without stretching the concept of regulation to implausible limits. Therefore, we conclude that the interests being asserted by Field as a competitor are not the interests arguably intended to be protected by the tax credit provision of which is the statutory basis for the challenge in this case.

* * *

Case Holding. *The decision of the district court was affirmed. The test for standing is a two-part test. First, there must be injury in fact. Second, the interest sought to be protected must be within the zone of interests to be protected by the statute in question. Field's interest as competitor falls outside the zone of interest, and therefore he lacks standing.*

Case Questions
1. Why was Field's interest outside the zone of interests?
2. Distinguish between the injury and zone of interests requirements.
3. Is the fact that no party can be found who has standing to challenge an agency's decision a shortcoming in the court's ability to check agency powers through judicial review?

Ripeness and Exhaustion
Several procedural requirements govern the appropriate time in which a party can obtain judicial review of an agency action or decision. The most significant of these requirements are the doctrines of ripeness and exhaustion. The *ripeness doctrine* is concerned with whether the agency decision is final enough to warrant judicial review. According to the Supreme Court in *Abbott Labs* v. *Gardner* (1967), the doctrine is designed to

> . . . [prevent courts] through avoidance of premature adjudication, from entangling themselves in abstract disagreements over administrative policies, and also to protect the agencies from judicial interference until an administrative decision has been formalized and its effects felt in a concrete way by the challenging parties.

The *exhaustion doctrine* requires a party to complete relevant agency appellate procedures before turning to a court for review. That is, aggrieved parties may not resort to the courts for assistance until they have exhausted all internal agency review procedures. Until an action is considered final by the agency, the possibility remains open that the agency will change its mind. Given that possibility, courts are reluctant to assert their jurisdiction until a party has exhausted all agency review procedures.

Scope of Judicial Review

After all procedural requirements have been met, the court of appeals is then able to review the agency's decision or action. The court's *scope of review* determines how far it can go in examining the agency's action or decision. Generally speaking, the court's scope of review will depend upon whether the issue before it involves a question of procedure, statutory interpretation, or substantive law. Each imposes different scope requirements on the reviewing court.

Review of Agency's Substantive Determinations

The court's review of an agency's substantive determinations and formulations is generally provided the lowest scope of judicial review. As a rule, the courts are willing to yield to the agency's judgment in technical and scientific matters. The courts will generally not find that an agency's actions or decisions are *arbitrary, capricious, or an abuse of discretion* if the following are true:

1. The agency has sufficiently explained the facts and its policy concerns.
2. Those facts have some basis in the agency's record.
3. On the basis of those facts and legislative concerns, a reasonable person could reach the same judgments the agency has reached.

Review of Agency's Statutory Interpretation

The court's review of an agency's statutory interpretation is generally afforded a middle intensity scope of review. In contrast to the technical judgments required of the agency in implementing a statute, the courts have primary responsibility for the interpretation of the reach and meaning of statutes enacted by Congress. Although the courts will consider the interpretation of a statute by the agency responsible for its implementation, they will reject that interpretation if it does not comport with interpretations dictated by established principles of statutory construction. Consider, for example, the *National Recycling Coalition* case concerning the judicial review of an agency's statutory interpretation.

National Recycling Coalition, Inc. v. Reilly
U.S. Court of Appeals, District of Columbia Circuit
884 F.2d 1431 (1989)

Case Background. *The National Recycling Coalition challenged the Environmental Protection Agency's (EPA's) interpretation of a provision of the Resource Conservation and Recovery Act (RCRA). The provision at issue required administrative agencies to purchase products containing recycled materials whenever possible except products found to be "only available at an unreasonable price." In its interpretation of the phrase "unreasonable price," the EPA stated in its final rule that agencies must purchase recycled products (1) when they are the low-bid item, and (2) in tie-breaking situations where products made of recycled and virgin materials are offered at the same price. The EPA interpreted the provision as not requiring agencies to pay a premium in order to purchase recycled products.*

National Recycling challenged EPA's interpretation of the phrase "unreasonable price," arguing that the phrase should be interpreted as requiring agencies to purchase recycled products even if they are more expensive. They asserted that EPA's interpretation contravened the intent of RCRA. RCRA provided the court of appeals with jurisdiction to hear the challenge.

Case Decision. Circuit Judge Buckley presented the opinion of the court.

* * *

Our review will be guided by the [Supreme Court's] test established in *Chevron U.S.A. Inc.* v. *NRDC, Inc.* (1984). First, if Congress has clearly expressed its intent on the precise question involved, a reviewing court will enforce it. In ascertaining a statute's plain meaning, we must look to the particular statutory language at issue, as well as the language and design of the statute as a whole. Second, if the statute is silent or ambiguous with respect to the specific issue addressed by the agency's regulation, the question becomes whether the agency regulation is a *permissible* construction of the statute. If the agency regulation is not in conflict with the plain language of the statute, a reviewing court must give deference to the agency's interpretation of the statute.

In making this determination, we first focus on the language of the Act, which relieves a procuring agency of the obligation to purchase recycled items if it determines that they "are only available at an unreasonable price." As the word "unreasonable" is inherently subjective, the language of the Act provides little guidance as to Congress's specific intent.

National Recycling nevertheless challenges EPA's interpretation as contrary to the plain meaning of the Act. They maintain that a "reasonable price" means one that is "not excessive or extreme; fair; moderate," citing a dictionary definition to support their position that a reasonable price need not be the lowest price. National Recycling then argues that if the ordinary meaning of this language is read in light of the Act's purpose of encouraging recycling, it must be construed to permit the purchase of the statutorily preferred recycled products at prices higher than the lowest at which goods made from virgin materials are offered. . . . National Recycling further contends that EPA's interpretation renders the Act meaningless because in all but the rare tie-breaking case, procuring agencies would only be required to buy recycled products when offered at the lowest bid, which is the normal requirement under the current rules governing federal purchases.

We reject this argument. National Recycling contends that the statutory objective of encouraging recycling can only be fulfilled if agencies are permitted to pay something over the minimum bid for products made of virgin materials. This reasoning, however, rests on the unsupported assumption that price was the critical obstacle to the marketing of recycled products prior to the Act's passage. If this were true, the inference that Congress contemplated the preferential prices might be compelling. Counsel for both National Recycling and the EPA agreed at oral argument, however, that nothing in the record suggests that products containing reclaimed materials are more expensive than those made from virgin materials. . . .

While there is no evidence that Congress viewed price as the inhibiting factor in the use of reclaimed materials, the Act's provisions suggest that Congress relied on factors other than price to achieve its policy goals. The Act requires the EPA to identify acceptable recycled alternatives to products made of virgin materials and to develop specifications for their purchase, and it establishes a major market for such goods by mobilizing the purchasing power of the federal government. These requirements are entirely compatible with a strategy that depends on a heightened awareness of the need to utilize recycled materials, the dissemination of information through the EPA guidelines, and on an assured market to encourage the development, production, and sale of recycled goods at competitive prices.

* * *

Wald, Chief Judge, dissenting:

* * *

I respectfully dissent from the majority's opinion. . . .

Congress passed RCRA to address the serious waste management problems facing this nation. One goal of the Act was to encourage recovery, rather than disposal, of discarded materials. Congress decided to use the power of federal procurement dollars as a means to further this goal: it directed that federal agencies purchase items with the "highest percentage of recovered materials practicable, consistent with maintaining a satisfactory level of competition," although not when such items "are only available at an unreasonable price."

How did Congress envision that the RCRA would lead to an increase in federal purchasing of recycled goods? There are two possible answers. One is that Congress thought the increased purchase of such goods to be a worthy social objective, for which the United States ought to be willing to pay something. Congress, according to this view, therefore created an exception to the usual rule that requires federal procurement agencies to purchase goods at the lowest bid price, and authorized such agencies to pay some extra amount for goods made of recovered materials. . . . The other possibility is that, although Congress wanted to increase federal purchasing of goods made of recovered materials, it did not want federal agencies ever to pay anything extra for such goods.

The error of the majority opinion lies in its conclusion that because the Act uses an imprecise term—"unreasonable"—to describe the limits on the price that a federal agency can pay for recycled goods, it does not instruct us as to which of the two strategies just described Congress meant to adopt. But in fact, the language and structure of the Act strongly suggest that, although Congress certainly desired to pursue the "awareness" strategy, it also intended to authorize federal agencies to pay some extra amount for the purchase of recycled goods. The EPA's role in the statutory scheme is to aid agencies in determining what this extra amount should be; it does not have the authority to make the policy decision, already made by Congress, as to which strategy should be used to increase federal purchases of recycled goods.

* * *

Case Holding. *The court found that EPA acted within its authority in interpreting the "unreasonable price" exception to purchasing recycled products to mean that agencies were not required to purchase recycled products if they were more expensive than alternatives made from virgin material. The EPA's interpretation of the Act was permissible.*

Case Questions

1. In what way did EPA's interpretation of the Act change the existing rules governing agency purchases of supplies and other products?
2. How would National Recycling have changed the existing agency procurement rules?
3. How would the implementation of the dissenting opinion differ from the majority opinion?

Review of Agency's Procedural Requirements

The court's review of the agency's procedural requirements is provided the most intense scope of review. The court is responsible for ensuring that the agency has not acted unfairly or in disregard of statutorily prescribed procedures. The courts have been regarded historically as the authority in procedural fair play. According to the court in *Weyerhaeuser v. Costle* (1978):

> [W]e are willing to entrust the agency with wide ranging regulatory discretion, and even, to a lesser extent, with an interpretive discretion vis-à-vis its statutory mandate, so long as we are assured that its promulgation process as a whole and in each of its major aspects provides

a degree of public awareness, understanding, and participation commensurate with the complexity and intrusiveness of the resulting regulations.

CONGRESSIONAL RESTRICTIONS ON AGENCY POWER

In addition to the checks imposed on agency power by the judicial system through judicial review, there are also several ways in which agency powers are checked by Congress. Just as it is able to delegate powers to an agency, Congress may also revoke those powers. In most instances, however, the interests of Congress are usually served by providing checks on agency behavior and performance. This section discusses measures that Congress has made use of or considered in undertaking those checks.

Direct Congressional Checks on Agency Power

Public awareness and concern about the costs and effectiveness of regulation have prompted various responses from Congress intended to improve its control over agency activities. The most immediate control mechanism enjoyed by Congress is the ability to influence agency activity through the budget process. In addition, in attempting to increase congressional control over the regulatory process, members of Congress have proposed bills calling for, among other things, *sunset provisions*, *legislative vetoes*, and a mandatory *cost-benefit analysis*.

Agency Appropriations

Administrative agencies are dependent on public funding to support their programs. Each year, administrative agencies are required to submit their budget requests for review first by the President and then by Congress. The President or Congress can work to cut the agency's budget if either is opposed to the activities of an agency. Budget cuts, which can be directed at specific agency activities, serve to reduce the overall effectiveness and regulatory impact of an agency. Furthermore, Congress can mandate in the budget that an agency address a specific issue. Thus, control of an agency's budget gives both Congress and the President leverage to influence the implementation and enforcement of agency regulatory policy.

Statutory Reporting Requirements

Congress often requires agencies to periodically report their progress on certain programs or activities. The reporting requirements vary from annual reports on specific programs to reports more frequently submitted on a broader scope of agency activities. Consider, for example, the reporting requirements imposed by Congress on the Environmental Protection Agency through the Clean Air Act:

> [N]ot later than January 10 of each calendar year . . . , the Administrator shall report to the Congress on measures taken toward implementing the purpose and intent of this [Act] including, but not limited to, (1) the progress and problems associated with control of automotive exhaust emissions and the research efforts related thereto; (2) the development of air quality criteria and recommended emission control requirements; [and] (3) the status of enforcement actions taken pursuant to this [Act]. . . .

Sunset Laws

To increase its control over administrative agencies, Congress has considered including mandatory sunset provisions in all federal regulatory laws. A sunset provision would require Congress to periodically review an agency's regulations, programs, or general usefulness. If it is determined that the agency is no longer needed, it is abolished, that is, the sun is allowed to set upon it. Theoretically, sunset provisions would require Congress to be more active and involved in evaluating agency activities and agencies to be more responsive to Congress. While not common at the federal level, some states have routine sunset review of all agencies.

Legislative Veto

Through a legislative veto provision in a regulatory statute, Congress gives itself veto power over any individual regulation promulgated by an agency when Congress finds that regulation objectionable. The legislative veto is intended to increase congressional control over the regulatory process. There are two variants of the legislative veto: the two-house veto, under which both houses of Congress must veto a regulation; and the one-house veto, under which only one house need veto the regulation. The Supreme Court, however, found the one-house legislative veto to be unconstitutional in *Chadha* v. *Immigration and Naturalization Service* (1983). Congress is currently considering alternatives that could meet the requirements established by the Court.

Mandatory Cost–Benefit Analysis

A mandatory cost–benefit analysis would require an administrative agency to undertake a cost-benefit analysis of all regulations it promulgates. When the costs exceed the benefits derived from a regulation, the regulation would be eliminated or scaled down. The aim of mandatory cost–benefit analysis is to make the government's decision-making process more cost-effective. According to the Supreme Court in *American Textile Manufacturers Institute* v. *Donovan* (1981), a cost–benefit requirement must necessarily be expressly provided in the enabling statute. In the absence of an explicit requirement, an agency is not required to undertake a cost-benefit analysis of the regulations it promulgates.

Indirect Congressional Checks on Agency Power

In recent years, Congress has enacted several acts that have had the effect of indirectly curtailing the power and authority of administrative agencies. Through those acts, which include the Freedom of Information Act, the Privacy Act, and the Government in the Sunshine Act, Congress effectively made it easier for parties external to an agency to obtain information in the possession of the agency.

Freedom of Information Act

The Freedom of Information Act (FOIA) was enacted in 1966 and amended in 1974. FOIA makes most documents submitted to or held by federal agencies available to the general public. Unless the document falls within one of the specifically exempted categories, it must be released upon a request for a copy by a citizen. Exempted categories include, for example, trade secrets and documents that would, if disclosed, constitute an unwarranted invasion of personal privacy. The issue of whether certain information in the possession of an agency could be exempted from FOIA's requirements is the subject of the *Critical Mass* case.

Critical Mass Energy Project v. Nuclear Regulatory Commission

U.S. District Court, District of Columbia
731 F.Supp. 554 (1990)

Case Background. *The Critical Mass Energy Project (Critical Mass), a nonprofit organization, brought suit under the Freedom of Information Act (FOIA) against the Nuclear Regulatory Commission (NRC). In the suit, Critical Mass sought copies of various reports prepared by a utility industry consortium called the Institute of Nuclear Power Operations (INPO). INPO voluntarily submitted the reports to the NRC upon the express condition that the NRC not make them public without INPO's consent. In this case, INPO would not consent to Critical Mass's request to view the reports. The court of appeals had remanded the case to the district court for the determination of whether the reports were entitled to an exemption from FOIA disclosure requirements. The reports provided the NRC with INPO's investigations of safety-related events or experiences at its members' nuclear power plants. The NRC argued that disclosure without the consent of INPO would jeopardize its relationship with INPO and result in the loss of a source of information that would be difficult and expensive to replace. As a consequence, the NRC's regulatory efficiency and effectiveness would be diminished.*

Case Decision. Judge Jackson delivered the opinion of the court.

* * *

The determination mandated by the court of appeals requires this court to balance the individual litigant's (i.e., the requester's) need for information against the government's need to obtain the information in the future, and the extent to which the government's ability to obtain the information would be impaired against the public interest in disclosure. It also necessitates a prediction of sorts as to the nature of the INPO/NRC relationship without the protection of a FOIA exemption for INPO reports in NRC's possession.

[If our] decision renders the INPO reports disclosable under FOIA, . . . one certain consequence will be the cessation of [INPO's] practice of sharing them with NRC voluntarily. Thenceforth NRC would have to resort to compulsion to get the reports, and, INPO declares, it would resist vigorously (and it represents that its individual members will resist as well).

NRC and INPO are nevertheless fully in accord in one respect: the limited confidentiality the INPO reports presently enjoy, i.e., their general unavailability to the public at large, is indispensable to the quality of the information they contain. A host of [personnel] from both NRC and INPO (all of whom are highly qualified nuclear professionals possessing both years of relevant experience and the responsibility of currently relevant office) ardently attest to the importance of [the reports not being disclosed] as assuring maximum candor on the part of INPO's sources for the substance of its reports.

The Court also perceives the position taken by NRC in this dispute as being more than perfunctory lip service to its commitment to INPO not to divulge the reports. From the NRC declarations alone it is apparent that NRC is convinced that it will experience a genuine loss of valuable regulatory intelligence, one way or another, if the INPO reporting process is made subject to general public scrutiny. NRC believes that it is now deriving from the INPO reports, and contemporaneously with the industry itself, the most insightful thinking of the best informed people within the industry on matters of safety, a commodity otherwise unavailable to it.

For its part Critical Mass suggests no particularized need of its own for the reports. It is thus remitted to the general public interest in disclosure for disclosure's sake to support its request. To be sure, the public has an interest of significantly greater moment than idle curiosity in information bearing upon the safety of nuclear power plants. But so does NRC, and so do INPO and its members, and of a much more immediate and direct nature, in addition to their share of the general public interest.

Critical Mass also offers no affirmative evidence of its own to contradict NRC's [personnel] as to the importance of the information to the NRC, as to the extent to which NRC's ability to obtain it might be impaired were the INPO reports to be made public, or as to whether the NRC would be otherwise diminished in efficiency or effectiveness thereby. Critical Mass's case consists entirely of common sense inferences it asks the court to draw from seeming concessions made by NRC to several of its discovery initiatives. The gist of those inferences is that the assertions of the NRC and INPO [personnel] are not to be credited, or at least not taken at face value.

For example, Critical Mass argues, INPO members are already required to submit "event reports" to NRC which are routinely made available to the public, although often containing revelations of human error, yet are conceded by the NRC to be truthful as far as they go. Moreover, Critical Mass suggests, candor on the part of sources interviewed by INPO is more likely to be inhibited by fear of summary discipline or reprisal by an employer (or NRC) than by apprehension of eventual public exposure for confessions of job-related mistakes. Yet nothing about the current reporting process protects an INPO source's anonymity from any of the multiple intra-industry recipients of the reports, including the source's own employer. Finally, Critical Mass observes, NRC wields the whip hand: not only does it have subpoena and near-plenary regulatory powers should it choose to use them to get the INPO reports, NRC can also effectively hold the licenses of INPO members hostage until it gets what it wants from anyone in the industry.

The court finds the effect of the NRC's multiple declarations and affidavits, in the aggregate, to exceed the sum of their parts, and to carry the NRC's burden of establishing entitlement to the exemption they claim for the INPO reports. Taken together they evince . . . a relationship between NRC and INPO which the Court foresees as being damaged were the INPO reports in NRC's possession to be subject to FOIA disclosure. Whether or not the reporting process would truly experience a loss of candor—an issue neither more declarations nor a parade of witnesses could definitively resolve in advance of the event—both NRC and INPO share the conviction that it would. The consequence would be that the information now freely shared by INPO with NRC would be withheld until it was demanded under some form of compulsion. The demand would have to be enforced, which would likely precipitate both acrimony and some form of litigation with attendant expense and delay.

NRC and INPO would then no longer be collaborators in a quest for optimum industry safety, putting aside their other regulatory differences. If not outright antagonists, they would at best be wary allies, working independently of one another, duplicating one another's efforts, and mistrustful of one another's initiatives or overtures. That deterioration of the relationship, in this court's opinion, represents a sufficient showing that NRC's efficiency and effectiveness would be impaired were it not permitted to honor its commitment to INPO to keep the INPO reports in confidence.

* * *

Case Holding. *The disclosure of the reports under a Freedom of Information Act request would damage the underlying relationship and, as a consequence, significantly reduce the agency's regulatory effectiveness and efficiency. The reports, therefore, are entitled to an exemption from the disclosure requirements of the Act.*

Case Questions

1. Suppose the nondisclosure of the information had placed members of the general public at some risk. Would the case have been decided differently?
2. What was the court's principal argument for denying Critical Mass's request? Would disclosure reduce the willingness of the personnel supplying the information to participate with INPO?
3. As both the court and Critical Mass are aware, the NRC has subpoena power. Why wouldn't the agency's investigatory powers provide it with means for securing the reports even if INPO refused to provide them voluntarily?

Privacy Act

The Privacy Act, enacted by Congress in 1974, is intended to give citizens more control over what information is collected about them and how that information is used. It requires that unless an exception applies, notice and prior consent are required before an agency can disclose information that particularly concerns and identifies an individual. Individuals are given rights of access to agency records and rights to request amendments to correct inaccuracies. The Act provides that individuals can enforce their rights under it in the federal district courts.

Government in the Sunshine Act

In 1976, Congress enacted the Federal Sunshine Act. In combination with the Federal Advisory Committee Act of 1972, the Sunshine Act limits secret meetings by agencies. Its purpose is to enhance citizen access to government operations.

Under the Sunshine Act, the public is entitled to at least one week's notice of the time, place, and subject matter of any agency meeting, notice of whether the meeting is to be open or closed to the public, and notice of the name and phone number of the official designated by the agency to respond to requests for information about the meeting.

The Sunshine Act lists numerous situations in which a meeting may be properly closed. An open meeting is not required, for example, when the meeting is likely to concern disclosure of matters authorized by executive order to be kept secret in the interest of national defense or foreign policy or disclosure of certain trade secrets and commercial or financial information. Agency day-to-day activities are not subject to the Act's requirements.

Federal courts are given authority to enforce the provisions of the Sunshine Act. They may not, however, invalidate an agency action taken at a meeting in violation of the Sunshine Act merely because of such violation; some other basis for overturning an agency action must be established. The court may grant an injunction against future violations of the Sunshine Act or order an agency to make transcripts or recordings of the meeting available to the public.

SUMMARY

Administrative agencies have become an important part of modern U.S. government. They are created by Congress and granted legislative, adjudicatory, investigative, and enforcement powers. Congress has created an administrative agency when confronted with problems requiring expertise, flexibility, and supervision. Agencies are classified as being dependent (a part of the executive branch of government) or independent.

Administrative law consists of legal rules defining the authority and structure of administrative agencies, specifying procedural requirements, and defining the roles of government bodies (particularly the courts) in their relationship with agencies. The most fundamental administrative law is the Administrative Procedures Act (APA).

Administrative agencies were first used by state governments to regulate private economic activities in the latter half of the nineteenth century. The first federal agency was the Interstate Commerce Commission, established by Congress in 1887. The most significant growth periods in the history of administrative agencies took place during the New Deal era of the 1930s and the social reform era of the 1960s and 1970s.

Agencies perform their regulatory responsibilities through the use of either formal or informal procedures. Informal procedures, which consist of tests and inspections, are not subject to the procedural requirements of the APA. Formal procedures, which include adjudicatory and investigative hearings, must meet the APA's procedural requirements.

The judicial system imposes a valuable check on agency powers through judicial review of agency decisions. Congress imposes checks on agency power through the budget process and legislative enactments providing parties with greater access to agencies and agency records.

ISSUE

Did Deregulation Destroy the Savings and Loans?

The savings and loan (S&L) industry grew from a group of small, mutually owned institutions into the prime supplier of mortgage money for American home buyers. In the 1930s, federal legislation was enacted to protect the S&Ls from competition, and to provide them with several advantages in the market for home mortgages. With the creation of the Federal Savings and Loan Insurance Corporation (FSLIC), the industry was designed to be failure-proof. The FSLIC provided depositors with government insurance up to $100,000 per account in the event of an S&L failure. For fifty years, S&Ls were restricted to making relatively low-risk loans to consumers for the purchase of homes.

In the early 1980s, the S&L industry was deregulated. Several years of high rates of inflation had done considerable damage to the financial

—continuing

health of the industry. Deregulation suddenly gave S&Ls the opportunity to increase earnings by making new kinds of loans and investments. Given federal guarantees in case of failure, and freedom from much government supervision, it was not surprising that S&L managers made billions of dollars in loans in areas where they had little experience. Many of those loans went sour and hundreds of S&Ls failed. The government's bailout of the S&L industry could cost taxpayers from $325 billion to $500 billion— about $1,500 per American citizen. Many questions are now being raised about the quality of regulation that did exist. The following article describes the collapse of one S&L.

Boom to Bust In Arkansas

John M. Berry,
Washington Post Staff Writer*

LITTLE ROCK, Ark.—By the fall of 1983, Howard J. Wiechern Jr. had put it all together. With the help and encouragement of federal regulators, Wiechern had turned a small, stodgy savings and loan association in Pine Bluff, Ark., into the state's largest thrift institution. Southern Building and Loan had grown into FirstSouth FSB and its stock was snapped up by investors eager to share in its future.

Four years later, FirstSouth is gone. Last December federal authorities closed it down because it was running out of cash. At the end, FirstSouth was still holding loans and other assets supposedly worth $1.7 billion. But it was so short of cash that it had sold its furniture and many of its branches and was leasing them back. The once-sought stock was worthless.

Officials involved in sorting out what is left of FirstSouth say it probably will take seven to 10 years to sell off its assets and pay whatever money is left to a multitude of creditors, many of whom may get only a few cents on the dollar. Depositors have been protected by the Federal Savings and Loan Insurance Corp., but the FSLIC now has to salvage what it can from FirstSouth's bad loans and bankrupt investments.

The loan losses at FirstSouth are so large that its failure is likely to be the most costly savings and loan collapse in history, costing FSLIC several hundred million dollars, said an official at the Federal Home Loan Bank Board, the federal agency that regulates savings and loan associations.

When the bank board ordered First-South closed, more than $500 million worth of loans were in default and others have gone bad since. More than $600 million in loans to stockholders was discovered, though not all of them were in default or illegal. . . .

FirstSouth failed not just because of the plunge in oil prices that depressed the Sun Belt real estate markets in which it made many loans, but also because of stunningly sloppy business practices, reckless real estate speculation and massive insider loans, many of them illegal. . . .

Summing up charges against FirstSouth executives, the FSLIC lawsuit said the defendants "recklessly and negligently allowed FirstSouth to become a source of funds for favored real estate speculators and developers who gambled FirstSouth's resources away at little risk to themselves and at great cost to FirstSouth."

---

*Reprinted with permission from the August 30, 1987 *Washington Post.*

—continued

—continuing

Though federal officials are now aggressively cleaning up after FirstSouth's fall, they not only consented to, but encouraged its rise and failed to monitor its explosive growth.

Despite danger signals flashed by earlier audits, FirstSouth was not examined by federal regulators between December 1982, and February 1985, Home Loan Bank Board officials admit. . . . During the critical 26 months when examiners weren't watching, FirstSouth grew from a $500 million institution to one with assets of $1.3 billion. Eventually it had more than $1.8 billion in assets on its books, though their true value was hundreds of millions less than that.

Howard Wiechern's strategy for growth was to deemphasize long-term home mortgages—the safe, stodgy mission for which federally insured savings and loans were created. The Wiechern method—as it came to be called in Arkansas—did not demand waiting to earn interest over the life of a 20-year loan, it paid off immediately. FirstSouth concentrated on generating big up-front fees by making so-called acquisition, development and construction loans. Though enabling FirstSouth to pocket the equivalent of points on a home mortgage, development lending proved to be a disaster.

Since it was paying high interest rates to its depositors to attract funds from around the country, FirstSouth also charged its borrowers high rates—which meant it attracted borrowers who had been turned down by lenders charging lower rates.

Among those eager to borrow at FirstSouth's high rates were several of the S&L's major shareholders, who borrowed millions to finance real estate speculation, much of it in the Dallas area.

Some of the insider loans were so large they violated the legal limits on loans to a single or related group of borrowers, the bank board charged. Hundreds of millions of dollars worth of insider loans were in default when the institution failed. FirstSouth's biggest stockholders became its biggest debtors.

Meanwhile, FirstSouth's approach to making loans to those who didn't have inside connections was just as loose. In one instance FirstSouth agreed to give a $20 million mortgage on a Palm Springs, Calif., condominium called Sundance, owned by Clint Murchison, the well-known Texas oil man and then owner of the Dallas Cowboys. It was the largest single loan the institution had made up to that time and Murchison personally guaranteed it.

Murchison's name was apparently all FirstSouth needed to know. Before making the loan, no one at FirstSouth checked with Seafirst Bank of Seattle, which held a smaller existing mortgage on the property. If FirstSouth loan officers had asked, they would have discovered the original loan was already in default and the bank was pressing to have it paid off immediately.

No one at FirstSouth asked why none of the 60 condo units had been sold during the 10 months since several Dallas Cowboys and cheerleaders presided over the grand opening. Nor did anyone inquire into the unaudited financial statements provided by Murchison, or question the strength of Murchison's personal guarantee. Before he sold his beloved football team and went bankrupt, Murchison had given hundreds of millions of dollars worth of such guarantees, which proved worthless when Sundance failed.

And while no one at FirstSouth was looking too deeply into the loans being made, no one at the Federal Home Loan Bank Board was paying much attention to FirstSouth.

* * *

FSLIC, as receiver for FirstSouth, recently filed a suit in federal district court here seeking $150 million in damages from Wiechern, FirstSouth Chairman Del L. Brannon and several outside directors. A similar claim was filed earlier in a bankruptcy proceeding involving Roderick D. Reed, presi-

—continued

–continuing

dent of FirstSouth and Wiechern's right hand man.

The suit charged that the FirstSouth officials "made staggering sums of money available to certain favored borrowers on terms and conditions in flagrant disregard of prudent lending practices and with serious adverse effects on FirstSouth's financial condition." It also charged that:

• "A substantial amount of FirstSouth's resources [were] devoted to speculation in high-risk real estate transactions in which loans were made without proper underwriting procedures;

• "Favored borrowers were not required to put any equity into the properties or projects on which they received loans;

• "Loan payments were taken from the loan proceeds themselves or from refinancings;

• "The security pledged for the loans was frequently insufficient to cover potential losses upon default."

Wiechern, Brannon and the six outside directors named in the suit all filed responses denying any wrongdoing in managing FirstSouth's affairs. Reed has also denied any wrongdoing. Wiechern, Reed and Cox all declined comment on FirstSouth or failed to return phone calls.

* * *

At the time Wiechern took control, First-South, like its counterparts across the nation, was being squeezed between a portfolio of single-family home mortgages yielding low, fixed returns and tight money markets in which interest rates were soaring to the highest levels since the Civil War. . . .

Partly in response to this squeeze, federal legislation was passed in 1980 to begin eliminating virtually all restrictions on the interest rates financial institutions could pay on deposits other than regular checking accounts. The same legislation and another law passed in 1982 also opened up new lines of businesses to S&Ls and broadened the variety of loans they could make.

With deregulation of the industry under way, Wiechern moved aggressively to change FirstSouth's way of doing business. According to FirstSouth's descriptions of its business activities, it began in 1981 to concentrate on making land acquisition, development and construction loans from Florida to California.

These so-called ADC loans were "short-term, with adjustable, market-sensitive interest rates and included origination fees in excess of those which could be obtained on single-family loans," explained a FirstSouth press release. "The origination of these commercial real estate loans produced sufficiently high fee income and interest income to return the association to profitability" after 1981.

The prospectus offering to sell First-South shares to the public in November 1983 described the new loans this way: "The ADC loans are typically made in amounts covering full cost of construction or development of the product, including the full cost of acquiring the underlying property, if applicable, and loan fees, interest and other carrying costs during the construction term."

In other words, the developers did not necessarily have to put up any money at all—no down payment, no fees, nothing. The so-called "interest reserve" meant that no payments would be required for many months. Instead, FirstSouth agreed to take the interest out of the loan itself and to collect its upfront fees from the money it loaned the borrower.

This meant the borrower could speculate with FirstSouth's money—money the S&L had gotten from depositors by paying high rates insured by the federal government. It meant FirstSouth could record the up-front fees as profit, even though it was simply taking back money it has just loaned. With no payments due soon, any danger of default on a bad loan was delayed. And when loans did come due, it turned out, FirstSouth

–continued

–continuing

often was happy to refinance the loan, collect new fees up front and postpone again the inevitable failures.

In addition to the up-front fees, the prospectus explained to investors, FirstSouth was also entitled to receive a "profit participation" in any gain when the property was sold.

FirstSouth not only kept a piece of the action for itself, it sold pieces of the loans to other financial institutions, so they too could share in the profits. . . . FirstSouth received fees for collecting payments and keeping an eye on the deals and was supposed to keep at least 10 percent of each loan, so that it had its own money at stake.

* * *

Why take the risk of making loans in far away places? Gerry E. Powell, a FirstSouth board member who is president of Ben Pearson Manufacturing Co. Inc., of Pine Bluff, a well-known maker of archery products, provided one answer in a deposition taken in a suit filed by a number of financial institutions that had bought participations in the Sundance loan in Palm Springs.

Branching out from Arkansas mortgages to Dallas development loans was "more or less as a directive from the chief of the Federal Home Loan Bank. If we couldn't make a profit, we would not exist if we hadn't gone into that business. And I think you are going to find some of the participants [the suing institutions] in the same situation."

"Was FirstSouth in a loss situation in 1980–81," asked Allan Gates, the Little Rock attorney questioning Powell.

"We sure weren't making any money of consequence," said Powell. "We had loans on the books of 7 or 8 percent, you know, and we were paying 12 and 14 percent for the money, or more. So, there was a dead-end there."

Dallas Federal Home Loan Bank President Roy Green offered a variant of this view in testimony this spring before a House Banking subcommittee, "In a sense," he said, "we had a problem with an industry that was locked into single-family home portfo-

lios" that did not pay enough interest to cover an institution's cost of funds, much less other operating expenses.

Noting the laws that began deregulating savings and loans, Green continued, "Both the 1980 and 1982 legislation were necessary landmark initiatives which have provided us with both benefits and challenges."

"The legislation deregulating portfolios in order to combat interest-rate-spread problems also placed new responsibilities on the thrift industry and the regulators. We believe the industry and the regulators have in large measure responded promptly and appropriately."

"However, the new deregulated environment was vulnerable to abuse by some individuals," Green declared. "The excessive growth that these so-called entrepreneurs directed FSLIC-insured institutions to pursue for quick profits has resulted in asset portfolios that fall far short of industry standards for long-term value and sound underwriting."

Or as he also put it, more simply: "Some individuals reached too far."

* * *

Today, FSLIC receivers are trying to sort out the pieces of the FirstSouth wreckage. About $200 million worth of assets have been sold. Many others have been foreclosed. . . .

Each day the legal fees and other costs mount, eating away at the value of the FirstSouth remains and increasing the losses to the FSLIC insurance fund and other creditors.

But if the losses are mounting for the federal government, the bank board and FSLIC can only blame themselves—because above all else, FirstSouth is a monument to regulatory failure.

Roy Green, of the Dallas Home Loan Bank—the region's regulator of S&L's—acknowledged as much in that congressional hearing this year.

The Dallas district, like most others around the country, he said, did not have

–continued

–continuing

enough bank examiners and those they did have generally were poorly paid and not very good.

"Because of salaries and regulations, we were not able to attract staff and expertise," Green said. . . .

Like so many of the savings and loan associations around the nation that decided to grow fast, FirstSouth had relied on the twin attractions of high interest rates and federal insurance up to $100,000 per account to attract deposits. A major share of the deposits were in $100,000 jumbo certificates of deposit.

As the FirstSouth news got worse and worse, depositors began pulling out their money when their CDs matured.

Last November, virtually none of the CDs were renewed, recalled a bank board spokesman. If that happened again in December, as appeared likely, FirstSouth would run out of cash and have no way to borrow any. Thus the Bank Board decided the only course was to close it.

* * *

Only a few FirstSouth depositors lost any money in the failure—those with more than $100,000 in their accounts. Only $14.4 million turned out to be uninsured, most of that interest on Jumbo CDs, Bank Board officials said.

* * *

Questions

1. How might have the collapse of this and other S&Ls been avoided? In what way was deregulation a cause for the collapse of the S&L?

2. Did the investors in the S&L really take any risks given that the government insured deposits to $100,000?

3. Obviously, some of the financial difficulties facing the S&Ls was caused by poor management. Would consumers have taken a more diligent look at management if their deposits had not been insured by the government?

REVIEW AND DISCUSSION QUESTIONS

1. Define the following terms and concepts:
   enabling legislation
   delegation of powers
   rulemaking
   substantive rules
   interpretative rules
   sanctions

2. Compare and contrast the following concepts:
   a. Investigatory hearing and an adjudicatory hearing
   b. Agency order and agency regulation
   c. Independent and executive agencies
   d. Informal and formal agency procedures

3. What are the advantages of informal agency procedures over formal procedures?

4. What advantages does an agency have over the judicial system in monitoring business behavior?

5. Many of the regulatory agencies established before the 1960s were oriented to regulating a specific industry—air travel, trucking, railroads, securities, com-

munications, and shipping. Many of the regulatory agencies established in the 1960s and 1970s apply to business in general—the environment, employee relations, worker safety, and product quality. Why would there be such a shift in emphasis from single-industry orientation to general business? What factors might have caused a change like this?

6. Congress often gives the regulatory agencies it creates very broad mandates. Congress may say something to the effect of "go regulate the environment in the public interest." The agencies then devise regulations to execute the intent of Congress. Should Congress be more specific when chartering agencies (that is, be more restrictive in setting agency mandates)?

Case Questions

7. Dewey owned a mine in Wisconsin. He refused to allow agents of the Department of Labor to inspect the mine without a search warrant. The Department of Labor wanted to determine whether twenty-five violations discovered in a previous search had been corrected. The Federal Mine Safety and Health Act authorizes a specific number of warrantless inspections, but it does not dictate the procedures that inspectors must follow. Will the warrantless search violate Mr. Dewey's Fourth Amendment right to privacy?

8. Suppose the Federal Trade Commission has decided to act to eliminate vacation scams—telephone calls by high-pressure salespeople who are selling virtually worthless vacations. Discuss how they could attack this problem through a rulemaking strategy. Conversely, discuss how they could attack the problem by adopting an adjudicatory strategy. Are there any major differences in the two strategies? Should the choice between the two strategies be left entirely up to the commissioners?

Policy Questions

9. It is frequently asserted that the ineptitude of agency bureaucrats is the primary factor behind the inability of agencies to effectuate public interest goals. This inability, it is asserted, could be overcome by hiring better people. The fact that some agency personnel are paid less than their private-sector counterparts is often cited as evidence in support of this allegation. As a student, can you think of a compelling reason why a capable individual might seek a position with an agency at lower pay for a limited time period? Are there other plausible arguments to counter the assertions outlined?

10. Are the regulatory reform measures—cost-benefit analysis, sunset laws, and legislative vetoes—good ideas, or are they likely to cause more problems than they solve? Do they allow private interests to have more say in the continued existence of regulations?

Ethics Questions

11. The vast majority of regulatory matters are settled informally. Only a very small number of disputes results in litigation. When a company is engaged in a dispute with a federal agency it knows that if it does not reach a settlement there can be costly litigation. From the perspective of the government agency, the litigation is costless—the taxpayers foot the bill. The government representatives know that the threat of costly litigation enhances their chance of extracting a settlement from the company. Should the government use this

leverage to extract more in a settlement than it knows it would be likely to get in a court-resolved dispute?

12. Suppose you are working for an agency that has you collecting information about a business to determine whether the business has violated the agency's rules or regulations. In the process, you discover how the company develops and markets its products. If you were to use that information, you are convinced you could make a lot of money. Should agency employees use such information for personal gain?

13. Suppose you are the administrator of the Environmental Protection Agency. It has been reported to you that a small plant in a small midwestern town is in violation of the environmental laws. If you impose the laws' requirements, the plant will not be able to afford pollution control devices and will be forced to shut down. The plant, however, is a major source of employment for the small town, and its closure would impose severe economic hardships. Do you close down the plant by imposing pollution control as required by the law?

14. The Environmental Protection Agency requires your company to self-report pollution discharges on a day-to-day basis. It is your job to make those reports. It has become apparent to you and your superior that those reports could be easily fudged in the event the company exceeded its designated limits. Suppose that any such excessive discharge would cost the company $25,000 for each day its limit is exceeded. On one particular morning your superior negligently failed to start the pollution control device and the designated amount of pollution was exceeded. Your superior has strongly implied that if you do not fudge the figures, you may not be employed at the end of the day because of the costs that will be imposed on the business by the EPA. Should you report the correct figures to the EPA? Would your answer be different if you knew whether the excessive pollution caused serious damage or no damage at all?

6 Business Ethics and Corporate Social Responsibility

This chapter surveys some of the moral problems that are raised by the new level of ethical awareness. It begins by considering the nature of ethics and some conceptual tools that may be useful in thinking about moral problems. Within this discussion, the text comments on ethical problems that often arise in the conduct of business, such as the morality of preferential hiring, proper treatment of employees, obligations with respect to the environment, the ethics of advertising, and moral obligations in international business.

The chapter then examines the ethical responsibilities of corporations and their managements. It considers whether corporations should be morally responsible or whether moral responsibility should be attributed only to the management of the corporation. Finally, the growing emphasis on corporate social responsibility and the tools being used to influence corporations are discussed.

The public image of business executives in America has been slipping since the 1960s. According to a Harris poll conducted in 1966, 55 percent of the American people had a "great deal of confidence" in American business executives. By 1986, however, that percentage had dropped to just 16 percent. More recent polls by both Harris and Gallup continue to indicate that confidence in American business leaders remains low—especially with regard to honesty and ethical standards.

One possible explanation of this is that the ethical standards of American business have plummeted and that business is indeed operating at a lower level of personal and corporate ethics. Stories of insider trading, product-content deceptions, bribery, industrial pollution, and other kinds of individual and corporate misconduct could be seen as confirmation of this interpretation. It is more likely, however, that at least some of the decline in the image of business is due to the increased concern with ethical issues on the part of the American public generally. Morally speaking, the public simply expects more from business now than it did in the past.

PERSONAL AND CORPORATE ETHICS: SURVEYS AND PERCEPTIONS

In response to its declining public image, corporations have developed and written codes of ethics. Despite these and other efforts, however, there is growing concern that today's business climate—as reflected in the *corporate culture*—may be at least partially to blame. In a recent article in the *Wall Street Journal* that examined corporate goals and ethics, the author found:

> [A] fresh look at data culled from 10 academic studies suggests that [corporate codes of ethics] merely pay lip service to a larger—and clearly unmet—problem: a business climate that condones malfeasance. Indeed, the studies indicate that even the most upright people are apt to become dishonest and unmindful of their civic responsibilities when placed in a typical corporate environment.

Several studies have found that the recent development of corporate codes of ethics by the business community has done little to improve corporate culture. In fact, Professor William Frederick found that corporations with codes of ethics were cited for legal infractions by federal regulatory agencies more frequently than corporations without codes. In those corporations making a special effort to improve corporate ethics by placing more individuals with a socially conscious perspective on their boards of directors, relatively little change in the corporate culture was found.

Table 6–1 presents the results of a codes of ethics survey of 202 *Fortune 500* companies. As the table illustrates, the provisions most commonly included emphasized improving the "bottom line"—customer/supplier relations, relations with the government, and conflicts of interest. Surprisingly, more than 75 percent of the codes of ethics surveyed failed to mention product quality, product safety, and environmental concerns.

Does the pressure for employees to conform to corporate organizational standards come at the expense of their personal principles? Table 6–2 presents the results of a survey of 220 managers. Not surprisingly, the managers listed self-respect as the most important personal value and honesty as the most

---

Table 6–1   A Survey of Company Codes of Ethics

Provisions Included in 75 Percent of Codes	Frequency	Provisions Excluded in 75 Percent of Codes	Frequency
Relations with government	86.6%	Personal characteristics	93.6%
Customer/supplier relations	86.1	Product safety	91.0
Political contributions	84.7	Environmental affairs	87.1
Conflicts of interest	75.3	Product quality	78.7
Honest records	75.3	Civic affairs	75.2

Source: Marilynn Cash Mathews, Washington State University, *Wall Street Journal*, October 9, 1987, p. 2.

Table 6–2   Survey of Managers' Personal Values and Characteristics

Personal Values		Personal Attributes	
Ranked Highest	**Ranked Lowest**	**Ranked Highest**	**Ranked Lowest**
Self-respect	Pleasure seeking	Honesty	Obedience
Family security	World of beauty	Responsibility	Cleanliness
Freedom	Salvation	Capability	Cheerfulness
Accomplishment	Social recognition	Ambition	Politeness
Happiness	Equality	Independence	Helpfulness

Source: William Frederick and James Webber, University of Pittsburgh, *Wall Street Journal,* October 9, 1987, p. 2.

important personal attribute. Yet when these same employees are asked to write company codes of ethics, company honesty and integrity fail to make even the top five among corporate values and attributes. Furthermore, a congressional subcommittee has estimated that one out of three corporate employees is hired with educational or career credentials that have been altered—and thus falsified—in some way. What motivates people with strong personal beliefs in the importance of honesty and integrity to disregard those values and attributes once they enter the workplace? Has it become more important to do whatever is necessary to beat the competition—even if it means being dishonest?

A recent *U.S. News*-CNN poll found that the majority of Americans believe that dishonesty is significantly greater than it was just ten years ago. To some extent, the public's outrage is understandable—in the most recent presidential election they were inundated with negative, misleading advertising; Wall Street insider trading scandals have become almost commonplace; corporate chief executive officers of large corporations have been found to have "cooked the books" at the expense of shareholders (see the Issue article at the end of the chapter); and scientists have been found to have falsified data and then published the results in leading journals. This growing belief by Americans that dishonesty has increased is reflected in their perceptions about activities in the workplace. The survey results presented in Table 6–3 show that 70 percent of the public believes that many or most of their co-workers steal office supplies from their employer. Nearly 60 percent believe that most or many of their fellow workers pad their expense accounts, thus increasing their incomes at the expense of the employer.

Many companies are now hiring ethics specialists in an effort to improve their business practices and, thus, the perceptions about them held by the general public. Managers are increasingly being provided with incentives to be more concerned about ethics and to comply with company codes of conduct. To better screen its employees, companies are administering lie-detector and drug tests, and devoting more resources to checking out perspective employees. Still, many executives believe that the answer lies in educating and informing business students on basic ethical concepts and issues.

Table 6-3   Survey of Employers Regarding the Perceived Activities
of Co-Workers

	Most	Many	Not Many	Very Few
Employees take office supplies or small tools home	35%	34%	18%	12%
Business people who pad expense accounts	28%	32%	21%	10%
Labor leaders who use union funds for personal expenses	18%	29%	28%	14%
Employees take time off pretending to be ill	17%	32%	33%	15%
Job applicants exaggerate their past achievements	17%	27%	31%	17%

Adapted from *U.S. News & World Report*, Feb. 23, 1987; a *U.S. News*—CNN poll by Roper Organization.

ETHICS AND MORALS: DEFINITIONS, THEORIES, AND APPLICATIONS

In debating standards of behavior, a distinction is sometimes made between morals and ethics. The term *morals* is taken to refer to generally accepted standards of right and wrong in a society. The term *ethics* is taken to refer to more general and abstract concepts that might be encountered in business and professional codes of ethics or in the study of the standards of right and wrong in philosophy and theology. For the purposes of the discussion here, however, the terms morals and ethics are generally interchangeable.

A clear and concise definition of the concepts of and the relationship between morals and ethics can be somewhat elusive. To better clarify the relationship, contrast these concepts with two other subjects with which they are likely to be confused: etiquette and the law.

Ethics and Etiquette Compared

Moral and ethical statements must not be confused with statements about etiquette or good manners. The fact that both kinds of statements can use terms such as *should* or *ought* makes this confusion tempting. A person may say, "You should not slurp your soup," or "You ought to introduce yourself when you enter a home for a party." While these statements prescribe conduct just as ethical statements do, they should be considered part of good taste, not moral or ethical behavior.

Moral and ethical statements differ from the directives of etiquette in at least two important ways. Moral and ethical statements are generally thought to have greater importance than etiquette statements. Most of us would take a violation of a rule such as "You should not lie to your father" as much more serious than a violation of a rule such as "You should compliment your host after a good dinner." In addition, moral and ethical rules cannot be established or changed by decisions of authoritative bodies or by majority vote. However, the rules prescribing the placement of knives, forks, and spoons on a table can be changed.

Ethics and the Law Compared

Moral and ethical statements should not be confused with rules of law. The fact that an action is legally permissible does not establish that it is morally and ethically permissible. Suppose management discovers that its company is emitting a toxic pollutant into the atmosphere that is not currently regulated by the Environmental Protection Agency (EPA). Suppose further that the company's internal studies show that the pollutant causes respiratory problems and may also cause other, more serious health problems. Should management voluntarily decide to stop emitting the pollutant? Should it wait until the EPA makes the emission illegal? Whatever your view on this matter, it is clear that the mere fact that emitting the toxic pollutant is legally permissible does not also mean it is morally and ethically permissible for management to do so.

Just as legality does not imply morality, illegality does not imply immorality. The fact that an action is illegal does not necessarily mean that it is immoral or unethical. Most people would admit that the moral status of the civil rights activities of the 1960s is not settled merely by the fact that some of those activities were illegal. In his *Letter from Birmingham Jail*, Martin Luther King, Jr., said, "I can urge [people] to disobey segregation ordinances, for the [ordinances] are morally wrong."

Questions about legality and morality are not necessarily the same. In the following case, the court faces this very issue. The plaintiff asserts that if the defendant had acted, a life would have been saved. Although the defendant's refusal to act may have been unethical or immoral, the court is asked to decide whether it was illegal.

Soldano v. O'Daniels

California Court of Appeal
141 Cal.App.3d 443, 190 Cal.Rptr. 310 (1983)

Case Background. *In August of 1977, a man named Villanueva entered Happy Jack's Saloon, pulled a gun, and threatened to kill Soldano. A patron of Happy Jack's quickly crossed the street to a bar called the Circle Inn, told the bartender (the defendant) about the incident going on at Happy Jack's, and requested the bartender to either call the police or allow the patron to make the call. The bartender refused. Soldano was subsequently fatally shot by Villanueva. Soldano's child (the plaintiff) brought a wrongful death action against the bartender.*

On the grounds that an individual cannot be liable for nonactions, the trial court granted the bartender/defendant's motion for summary judgment and dismissed the plaintiff's action. The plaintiff appealed to the Court of Appeal, arguing that the case should have been allowed to go to trial.

Case Decision. Associate Justice Andreen delivered the opinion of the court.

* * *

Does a business establishment incur liability for wrongful death if it denies use of its telephone to a good samaritan who explains an emergency situation occurring without and wishes to call the police?

* * *

There is a distinction, well rooted in the common law, between action and nonaction. It has found its way into the prestigious Restatement Second of Torts (hereafter cited as "Restatement"), which provides in section 314:

> The fact that the actor realizes or should realize that action on his part is necessary for another's aid or protection does not of itself impose upon him a duty to take such action.

The distinction between . . . active misconduct [causing] injury and failure to act to prevent [injury] not brought on by the defendant, is founded on "that attitude of extreme individualism so typical of anglo-saxon legal thought."

Defendant argues that the request that its employee call the police is a request that it do something. He points to the *established rule* that one who has not created a peril ordinarily does not have a duty to take affirmative action to assist an imperiled person. It is urged that the alternative request of the patron from Happy Jack's Saloon that he be allowed to use defendant's telephone so that he personally could make the call is again a request that the defendant do something—assist another to give aid. Defendant points out that the Restatement sections which impose liability for negligent interference with a third person giving aid to another do not impose the additional duty to aid the good samaritan.

The refusal of the law to recognize the moral obligation of one to aid another when he is in peril and when such aid may be given without danger and at little cost in effort has been roundly criticized. Prosser describes the case law sanctioning such inaction as a "refus(al) to recognize the moral obligation of common decency and common humanity" and characterizes some of these decisions as "shocking in the extreme. . . . Such decisions are revolting to any moral sense. They have been denounced with vigor by legal writers." A similar rule has been termed "morally questionable" by our Supreme Court. . . . It is time to re-examine the common law rule of nonliability for [nonaction] in the special circumstances of the instant case.

* * *

The Supreme Court has identified certain factors to be considered in determining whether a duty is owed to third persons. These factors include: "the foreseeability of harm to the plaintiff, the degree of certainty that the plaintiff suffered injury, the closeness of the connection between the defendant's conduct and the injury suffered, the moral blame attached to the defendant's conduct, the policy of preventing future harm, the extent of the burden to the defendant and consequences to the community of imposing a duty to exercise care with resulting liability for breach, and the availability, cost, and prevalence of insurance for the risk involved."

We examine those factors in reference to this case. (1) The harm to the decedent was abundantly foreseeable; it was imminent. The employee was expressly told that a man had been threatened. The employee was a bartender. As such he knew it is foreseeable that some people who drink alcohol in the milieu of a bar setting are prone to violence. (2) The certainty of decedent's injury is undisputed. (3) There is arguably a close connection between the employee's conduct and the injury: the patron wanted to use the phone to summon the police to intervene. The employee's refusal to allow the use of the phone prevented this anticipated intervention. If permitted to go to trial, the plaintiff may be able to show that the probable response time of the police would have been shorter than the time between the prohibited telephone call and the fatal shot. (4) The employee's conduct displayed a disregard for human life that can be characterized as morally wrong (The moral right of plaintiff's decedent to have the defendant's bartender permit the telephone call is so apparent that legal philosophers treat such rights as given and requiring no supporting argument. The concept flows from the principle that each member of a community has a right to have each other member treat him with the minimal respect due a fellow human being): he was callously indifferent to the possibility that Darrell Soldano would die as the result of his refusal to allow a person to use the telephone. Under the circumstances before us the bartender's burden was minimal and exposed him to no risk: all he had to do was allow the use of the telephone. It would have cost him or his employer nothing. It could have saved a life. (5) Finding a duty in these circumstances would promote a policy of preventing future harm. A citizen would not be required to summon the police but would be required, in circumstances such as those before us, not to impede another who has chosen to summon aid. (6) We have no information on the question of the availability, cost, and prevalence of insurance for the risk, but note that the liability which is sought to be imposed here is that of employee negligence, which is covered by many insurance policies. (7) The extent of the burden on the defendant was minimal, as noted.

* * *

The words of the Supreme Court on the role of the courts in a common law system are well suited to our obligation here:

> The inherent capacity of the common law for growth and change is its most significant feature. Its development has been determined by the social needs of the community which it serves. It is constantly expanding and developing in keeping with advancing civilization and the new conditions and progress of society, and adapting itself to the gradual change of trade, commerce, arts, inventions, and the needs of the country. . . .

In short, as the United States Supreme Court has aptly said, "This flexibility and capacity for growth and adaptation is the peculiar boast and excellence of the common law."

* * *

The possible imposition of liability on the defendant in this case is not a global change in the law. It is but a slight departure from the "morally questionable" rule of nonliability for inaction absent a special relationship. It is one of the predicted "inroads upon the older rule."

* * *

Case Holding. *The court of appeal reversed the trial court, and concluded there were issues that should allow the case to go to trial.*

Case Questions
1. Under the "established rule," was the bartender obligated to provide assistance? Is the established rule overly broad? Why or why not?
2. What factors motivated the court to modify the established rule in this case?

Conceptual Tools for Moral Thinking

A major source of confusion in thinking about ethics is the failure to distinguish the three basic kinds of issues that can be in dispute in a so-called moral disagreement. Distinguishing these disagreements is crucial because they are resolved in very different ways. The three kinds of disagreements can be illustrated using the Foreign Corrupt Practices Act as an example.

Congress passed the Foreign Corrupt Practices Act (FCPA) in 1977. The statute makes it unlawful to "corruptly" pay, or authorize to pay, money, gifts, or anything of value to any official of a foreign government, candidate for office in a foreign government, foreign political party, or official in a foreign political party. The Act was passed after it was discovered that nearly 400 American companies had paid approximately $300 million to foreign officials for business favors over a five-year period. Lockheed Aircraft Corporation, for example, had paid $22 million to foreign politicians to ensure that it would receive aircraft contracts. In the same period, Gulf Oil Corporation had secretly paid $4 million to foreign politicians to protect its oil interests.

Suppose that two people disagree over whether the FCPA is *morally and ethically justifiable*. While their disagreement could be over genuine moral principles, it could also be over the facts or conceptual issues.

Disagreements over the Facts

One major source of disagreement in determining whether a law or practice is morally and ethically justifiable is simply the facts. If two people disagree about the facts in a given case, they will probably disagree about what ought to be done—even if they agree on the conceptual issues and moral principles. Many international managers have argued, for example, that the FCPA causes U.S. firms to lose out in competition with foreign firms legally permitted to pay foreign officials. The determination of the factual basis for this assertion is a critical and decisive factor in the debate. If it is true, the welfare of many American workers would be adversely affected. Thus, disagreement over the moral and ethical justifiability of the FCPA could be traced to this factual disagreement rather than to a disagreement over moral principles.

Factual disagreements can sometimes be settled by making the proper observations. Here, the Ford Administration investigated the nature of payments to foreign officials and found that many payments were being made by American firms to gain a competitive advantage over other American firms, not just foreign firms. Ethics debates over the FCPA were then forced to center on other sources of disagreements. However, factual disagreements may also involve predictions or forecasts of future events or empirical observations that are not so easily substantiated or verified. Such disagreements can be very difficult to resolve.

Disagreements Over Conceptual Issues

A second source of disagreement can be over conceptual issues—the proper definition and scope of the concepts that are crucial to the issue in question. The FCPA, for example, explicitly permits payments made in response to *extortion demands*. A payment to an official to keep an oil rig from being blown up is permitted by the FCPA because it is in response to extortion. On the other hand, although no definition of "extortion" is given in the law, the term has been interpreted narrowly by the courts to rule out "economic extortion." If foreign officials instruct a company that its product will not be considered by their government unless a "side payment" is made—economic extortion—the payment would be illegal under the FCPA. It would be considered a bribe rather than an extortion payment.

Some critics of the FCPA have argued, however, that such actions should be classified as a type of extortion—a type, furthermore, that should be permitted under the FCPA. Philosopher Thomas Carson argues that

> [bribery should be defined as] a payment of money (or something of value) to a person in exchange for his giving [the paying party] special consideration that is incompatible with the duties of his office, position, or role.

While he was not able to offer a complete definition of extortion, Carson believes that

> extortion [is anything] that involves threatening someone with harm (that the person is neither morally nor legally entitled to inflict) unless that someone gives the person benefits to which he is neither morally nor legally entitled.

Suppose the foreign official in the example above makes similar demands from all suppliers and then makes an impartial selection. Carson would argue that a company's payment under these circumstances would be an extortion payment rather than the payment of a bribe. Carson reaches this conclusion because the payment is for something to which the company is legally entitled. In addition, it is made for the purpose of avoiding threatened harm, namely a refusal to consider the company's product. By comparing the court's narrow interpretation with Carson's broad definition, it is clear that the manner in which the terms *bribery* and *extortion* are defined can be decisive in determining the moral and ethical acceptability of the FCPA.

An illuminating example of the key role played by conceptual issues is provided by the abortion debate. Since most people consider it immoral to kill another individual, the debate over abortion hinges on whether a fetus is an individual. If one group reaches the conclusion that the fetus is an individual, it will maintain that abortion is immoral. On the other hand, if the fetus is not considered an individual, abortion will be considered to be as moral as the removal of an appendix. The determination of whether the fetus is in fact an individual is not a simple one. The abortion debate thus remains the classical conceptual controversy. In the *Webster* case, the Supreme Court is asked to make a decision on abortion. The Court termed the abortion issue "the most politically divisive domestic legal issue of our time."

Webster v. Reproductive Health Services

United States Supreme Court
109 S.Ct. 3040
(1989)

Case Background. *The state of Missouri enacted a statute concerning abortions and unborn children. The statute's preamble states that "(t)he life of each human being begins at conception" and that "unborn children have protectable interests in life, health, and well-being." Among other things, the statute prohibits using public facilities or employees to perform or assist in abortions unless the abortion is necessary to save the mother's life, and requires that, prior to performing an abortion on any woman whom a physician has reason to believe is twenty or more weeks pregnant, the physician must ascertain whether the fetus is* viable *by performing "such medical examinations and tests as are necessary to make a finding of the gestational age, weight, and lung maturity of the unborn child." The Act then mandates that state laws be interpreted to provide unborn children with "all the rights,* *privileges, and immunities available to other persons, citizens, and residents of this state," subject to the Constitution and the U.S. Supreme Court's precedents.*

Two nonprofit corporations and five state health professionals brought a class action suit against William L. Webster, the Attorney General for the state of Missouri, challenging the constitutionality of the Missouri statute. The U.S. District Court ruled that several provisions of the statute were unconstitutional and issued an injunction against their enforcement. The Court of Appeals affirmed, holding that the statute's statement that life begins at conception was not permissible. The court ruled that states do not have the right to legislatively adopt a theory as to the time life begins to justify the regulation of abortion. The Court of Appeals relied on Roe v. Wade, *a 1973 Supreme Court decision giving the constitutional right to women to have abortions in all but the third trimester. Webster and the state of Missouri appealed to the U.S. Supreme Court.*

Case Decision.   Chief Justice Rehnquist announced the judgment of the Court and delivered the majority opinion.

* * *

The viability-testing provision of the Act is concerned with promoting the State's interest in human life rather than in maternal health. [The Act] creates what is essentially a presumption of viability at 20 weeks, which the physician must rebut with tests indicating that the fetus is not viable prior to performing an abortion. . . . It also directs the physician's determination as to viability by specifying consideration, if feasible, of gestational age, fetal weight, and lung capacity. The District Court found that "the medical evidence is uncontradicted that a 20-week fetus is not viable," and that "23½ to 24 weeks' gestation [or at the beginning of the third trimester] is the earliest point in pregnancy where a reasonable possibility of viability exists."

In *Roe v. Wade*, the Court recognized that the State has "important and legitimate" interests in protecting maternal health and in the potentiality of human life. During the second trimester, the State "may, if it chooses, regulate the abortion procedure in ways that are reasonably related to maternal health." After viability, when the State's interest in potential human life was held to become compelling, the State "may, if it chooses, regulate, and even outlaw, abortion except where it is necessary, in appropriate medical judgment, for the preservation of the life or health of the mother."

. . . [T]he Court [has] held that . . . "the determination of whether a particular fetus is viable is, and must be, a matter for the judgment of the responsible attending physician." [N]either the legislature nor the courts may proclaim one of the elements entering into the ascertainment of viability—be it weeks of gestation or fetal weight or any other single factor—as the determinant of when the State has a compelling interest in the life or health of the fetus. To the extent that [the Act] regulates the method for determining viability, it undoubtedly does superimpose state regulation on the medical determination of whether a particular fetus is viable.

* * *

Stare decisis is a cornerstone of our legal system, but it has less power in constitutional cases, where, save for constitutional amendments, this Court is the only body able to make needed changes. We have not refrained from reconsideration of a prior construction of the Constitution that has proved "unsound in principle and unworkable in practice." We think the *Roe* trimester framework falls into that category.

In the first place, . . . the key elements of the *Roe* framework—trimesters and viability—are not found in the text of the Constitution or in any place else one would expect to find a constitutional principle. Since the bounds of the inquiry [in considering the legality of an abortion] are essentially indeterminate, the result has been a web of legal rules that have become increasingly intricate, resembling a code of regulations rather than a body of constitutional doctrine. As Justice White has put it, the trimester framework has left this Court to serve as the country's "ex officio medical board with powers to approve or disapprove medical and operative practices and standards throughout the United States."

In the second place, we do not see why the State's interest in protecting potential human life should come into existence only at the point of viability, and that there should therefore be a rigid line allowing state regulation after viability but prohibiting it before viability. . . . "(T)he State's interest, if compelling after viability, is equally compelling before viability."

The tests that [the Act] requires the physician to perform are designed to determine viability. The State here has chosen viability as the point at which its interest in potential human life must be safeguarded. It is true that the tests in question increase the expense of abortion, and regulate the discretion of the physician in determining the viability of the fetus. . . . But we are satisfied that the requirement of these tests permissibly furthers the State's interest in protecting potential human life, and we therefore believe [the Act] to be constitutional.

* * *

Justice Blackmun, with whom Justice Brennan and Justice Marshall join, concurring in part and dissenting in part.

* * *

In the majority's view, the viability-testing provision imposes a burden on second-trimester abortions as a way of furthering the State's interest in protecting the potential life of the fetus. Since under the *Roe* framework, the State may not fully regulate abortion in the interest of potential life (as opposed to maternal health) until the third trimester, the majority finds it necessary, in order to save the Missouri testing provision, to throw out *Roe*'s trimester framework. In flat contradiction to *Roe*, the majority concludes that the State's interest in potential life is compelling before viability, and upholds the testing provision because it "permissibly furthers" that state interest.

* * *

With respect to the *Roe* framework, the general constitutional principle, indeed the fundamental constitutional right, for which it was developed is the right to privacy, a species of "liberty" protected by the Due Process Clause, which under our past decisions safeguards the right of women to exercise some control over their own role in procreation. . . . [F]ew decisions are "more basic to individual dignity and autonomy" or more appropriate to that "certain private sphere of individual liberty" that the Constitution reserves from the intrusive reach of government than the right to make the uniquely personal, intimate, and self-defining decision whether to end a pregnancy. It is this general principle, the "moral fact that a person belongs to himself and not others nor to society as a whole," that is found in the Constitution.

The trimester framework simply defines and limits that right to privacy in the abortion context to accommodate, not destroy, a State's legitimate interest in protecting the health of pregnant women and in preserving potential human life.

* * *

[T]he majority asserts that the trimester framework cannot stand because the State's interest in potential life is compelling throughout pregnancy, not merely after viability. . . . In answering the majority's claim that the State's interest in the fetus is uniform and compelling throughout pregnancy, I cannot improve upon what Justice Stevens has written:

I should think it obvious that the State's interest in the protection of an embryo—
even if that interest is defined as "protecting those who will be citizens" ...—
increases progressively and dramatically as the organism's capacity to feel pain, to
experience pleasure, to survive, and to react to its surroundings increases day by
day. The development of a fetus—and pregnancy itself—are not static conditions,
and the assertion that the government's interest is static simply ignores this reality.
... (U)nless the religious view that a fetus is a "person" is adopted ... there is a
fundamental and well-recognized difference between a fetus and a human being;
indeed, if there is not such a difference, the permissibility of terminating the life of
a fetus could scarcely be left to the will of the state legislatures. And if distinctions
may be drawn between a fetus and a human being in terms of the state interest in
their protection—even though the fetus represents one of "those who will be
citizens"—it seems to me quite odd to argue that distinctions may not also be
drawn between the state interest in protecting the freshly fertilized egg and the
state interest in protecting the 9-month-gestated, fully sentient fetus on the eve of
birth. Recognition of this distinction is supported not only by logic, by also by
history and by our shared experiences.

* * *

Case Holding. *The Court reversed the lower court's ruling and held that the Missouri
statute does not create constitutional violations.* Roe v. Wade *and other precedents do
not imply a limitation on a state's authority to legislate value judgments favoring
childbirth over abortion. The statute's preamble embodies a viewpoint about life that
is not a regulation, but rather is just such a value judgment. (The Court further stated
that the Constitution does not impose a duty on the state to subsidize or fund
childbirth or abortions. The use of public funds is a decision made by the democratic
process and the Constitution does not forbid such processes.)*

Case Questions

1. How does the majority's viewpoint differ from the dissent's viewpoint on the
    importance of the viability of the fetus?
2. Shortly after the Supreme Court's ruling, a *USA Today* poll found that 50
    percent of the public opposed the Court's decision, 40 percent supported it, and
    10 percent were undecided. Nearly 40 percent of the respondents stated that
    they would vote for candidates solely on the basis of their abortion stand.
    Should candidates' credentials to hold public office be dictated solely by their
    stand on abortion? Should a prospective employee's position on abortion be a
    criterion in a hiring decision?

Conceptual disagreements can be settled by agreeing on the proper
definition and scope of a concept. It is important to understand, however, that
good supporting arguments can often be made for differing definitions. Many
so-called "moral" disagreements are actually disagreements over definitions.
Two individuals, for example, might agree that suicide is immoral. They may
disagree, however, over whether asking someone to "pull the plug" on a
life-support system is a genuine case of suicide.

Disagreements Over Genuine Moral Principles

Finally, some moral disagreements involve genuine debates over moral principles. Should payments of extortion, as Carson defines the term, be allowed?
In the example above, Carson would argue that payments by the company to

the foreign official would not break the moral rule prohibiting attempts to gain an unfair advantage over competitors. He would rationalize that those competitors are also willing to make the same payments themselves. In addition, by placing its product in competition with other products, the company gives the official a wider array of products from which to choose. Assuming quality and price are important, a wider selection and an increased level of competition may provide benefits to the official's government. On the other hand, the company would be contributing to a practice that probably corrupts foreign officials and may increase the cost of doing business. This in turn raises the further moral question of how much one company is morally required to sacrifice to eliminate a fundamentally unsound practice when other competing companies may not be willing to make the same sacrifice.

Moral disagreements are generally settled by appealing to moral principles. Two individuals can agree about the relevant facts and conceptual issues and still disagree over moral principles. Is bribery immoral? Is suicide immoral? These are genuine moral disagreements and must be settled by appealing to moral principles. How these moral principles are determined is discussed in the following section.

Moral Theories

The previous section raised questions about fairness, the value of allowing a foreign official to purchase the best product at the lowest price, the obligation not to contribute to the corruption of others, the obligation to refuse to participate in an undesirable practice when others will not refuse, and the morality of abortion and suicide. The evaluation of these arguments could be overwhelming due to conflicting moral claims that can be offered in support of one view over another. Moral philosophers, however, have found that most moral claims fall into two broad categories or moral theories. These two moral theories are termed *utilitarianism* and *ethics of respect for persons.* Before discussing those theories, it will be beneficial to examine the concept of a moral theory more closely.

The Nature of a Moral Theory
A *moral theory* is a system of moral principles that can be divided into three parts. First, there is a *moral standard,* a criterion or test of what is right or wrong. It has the general form:

Those actions are right that possess characteristic X.

Thus, those and only those actions are right that possess some characteristic X. An example of a moral standard would be, "Those actions are right that produce the greatest total amount of happiness."

Second, there are *moral principles* that serve to categorize different types of actions as right or wrong. Moral principles have the following form:

Those actions of type Y are right (or wrong).

Such actions are right because they conform to the moral standard by possessing characteristic X or wrong because they fail to conform. An example of a moral principle would be, "Discrimination is wrong." Here, the general practice of discrimination would be wrong because it fails to promote happiness.

Third, there are *moral judgments* that are statements about the rightness or wrongness of particular actions. Moral judgments have the following form:

This action is right (or wrong).

The action is right because it is of type Y or wrong because it is not of type Y. Type Y actions must possess characteristic X. An example would be, "ABC Widget Company was wrong when it practiced discrimination in refusing to employ John Roe." Here, the action of ABC Widget is declared wrong because it is an instance of discrimination, and discrimination does not promote happiness.

Utilitarianism

The moral standard of utilitarianism is: "Those actions are right that produce the greatest total amount of happiness." Utilitarianism has great intuitive appeal to many people because human happiness seems to be the most reasonable candidate for the ultimate purpose of morality. There is, however, a problem with defining the term *happiness*.

What comprises happiness for one individual may not comprise happiness for another. If utilitarianism requires that society arrange its actions to produce the greatest overall happiness, does it mean that society must define happiness as it is generally understood? May society then impose this definition on those society members who do not agree with it?

Suppose the generally accepted definition within the society is that happiness is the greatest amount of physical pleasure. Some society members, however, may not be as interested in pleasure as they are in wealth or power. Does society as a whole then have a right to select one definition of happiness over another by majority vote?

Preference Utilitarianism. In responding to this problem, utilitarians have proposed *preference utilitarianism*. Under preference utilitarianism, those conditions are promoted that allow each individual within the society to pursue happiness as he or she defines it. Individuals may use their own preferences as a guide. One individual does not decide whether another individual should prefer the happiness produced by physical pleasure over the happiness produced by money or power. Rather, each individual tries to promote those general conditions in society that allow most individuals to realize their preferences, whatever they may be.

Necessary Conditions for the Implementation of Utilitarianism. It seems reasonable to assume that at least two conditions must be met if individuals are to pursue their preferences: freedom and well-being. *Freedom* involves an individual's ability to make unforced choices in following his or her preferences. It refers primarily to an individual's freedom from interference by others in making decisions. *Well-being* refers to the conditions necessary to make effective use of this freedom. Individuals who are poor, sick, and uneducated will not be able to effectively realize their freedom—even if no one else is actively trying to inhibit them. Well-being, therefore, includes a minimal amount of wealth, physical health, and education necessary to allow individuals to pursue their own preferences.

Applying the Utilitarian Theory. A utilitarian analysis consists of three steps. First, the analyst must determine the audience of the action or policy—those people whose freedom or well-being would be affected. Second, the positive and negative effects imposed on members of the audience by alternative courses of action need to be determined. Third, the analyst must decide which course of action produces the greatest overall utility.

Shortcomings in Utilitarianism. The moral ideal of the utilitarian is to promote a society in which as many people as possible can pursue their own preferences. In undertaking their affairs in this fashion, society members achieve their own versions of happiness. It is an appealing ideal, but it has two major drawbacks in its application.

First, its implementation requires extensive knowledge of facts, especially the probable future negative and positive consequences of actions. An individual has to know which actions and policies will produce the greatest total amount of freedom and well-being. This knowledge may sometimes be difficult to obtain. Are freedom and well-being promoted more by policies that impose strict controls on pollution that are expensive to implement and reduce U.S. international competitiveness? Or are they promoted more by policies that allow greater pollution but promote international competitiveness? In resolving this dilemma, the analyst must balance considerations of health against considerations of employment and affluence in a "utilitarian calculus" that is difficult to perform. While knowledge from the physical and social sciences is often invaluable in determining which policies produce the most utility, often the analyst simply has to make an educated guess.

The second problem with utilitarianism is that it can lead to injustice for certain individuals. Suppose the management of a company is considering closing a plant in an economically depressed region. The closing may make good sense from an economic—and a utilitarian—standpoint. The plant is so inefficient that its production is simply not competitive in the marketplace. Shifting the production to more modern plants would result in more efficient production, better prices for consumers, and greater returns for the company's shareholders. Although the closing will produce a real hardship on workers in the depressed region, preference utilitarianism dictates that the plant should be closed: the workers' preference-satisfaction is outweighed by the preference-satisfaction of those who will benefit from the closing. It is primarily this injustice problem that has led some philosophers to advocate the second moral theory, ethics of respect for persons.

The Ethics of Respect for Persons

The second major moral theory, *ethic of respect for persons* or RP morality, attempts to resolve the utilitarian problem of injustice. The moral standard of RP morality can be stated as follows: "Those actions are right that equally respect each human person as a moral agent." A *moral agent* is an individual capable of both formulating and pursuing actions and being responsible for those actions. Thus, moral agents must be distinguished from things, such as a knives or automobiles, that can only fulfill actions imposed externally.

The Golden Rule. This emphasis on respect for each individual, as contrasted with concern for the greatest overall utility, is expressed in the Golden Rule:

"Do unto others as you would have them do unto you." This moral maxim is found in one form or another in most major religious traditions. It forces members of society to consider other members by imaginatively placing themselves in the position of other members who could be affected by their actions.

The Golden Rule is an excellent rule of thumb in many practical moral deliberations. However, it can lead to seemingly perverse results in some applications. In the business world, for example, it can be too narrow and restrictive. Suppose that a manager must terminate an employee. While the manager might not want to be dismissed herself, this does not imply that her dismissal of the employee is morally unjustified.

On the other hand, there are applications of the rule in the business world where it may be too permissive. Suppose that an extroverted and rather insensitive manager treats his employees in a way they consider to be too rough and abusive. Suppose further that he would be perfectly happy to be treated in the same way by his superiors. Although he may be fulfilling the requirements of the Golden Rule, the moral justifiability of his actions could still be questioned.

Doctrine of Rights. Clearly, a more precise and objective guideline for respecting the moral agency of individuals is needed other than the Golden Rule. Several moral philosophers have concluded that a *doctrine of rights* answers this need. A *right* may be defined as an entitlement to act or to have another individual act in a certain way. Rights serve as a protective barrier, shielding individuals from the unjustified infringements of others. Not surprisingly, these rights are essentially the rights to freedom and well-being, the same rights prized under utilitarianism.

In RP morality, however, these basic rights may not be sacrificed for the greater overall utility. More specifically, one individual's (or group's) rights may be overridden to protect another individual's (or group's) rights that are considered to be more *basic*, but those rights to be overridden cannot be sacrificed merely to provide greater freedom or well-being for the other individual (or group).

Hierarchy of Rights. If an individual's rights may be overridden only to protect a more fundamental or basic right of another individual, those rights that are most fundamental must be known. This requirement calls for a *hierarchy of rights*. Philosopher Alan Gewirth has proposed a three-tiered hierarchy of rights. The first tier includes the most basic rights, the essential preconditions of action: life, physical integrity, and mental health. The second tier includes rights to maintaining the level of purpose fulfillment an individual has already achieved. This tier includes the right not to be deceived or cheated, to have one's possessions stolen, to be defamed, or to suffer broken promises. The third tier includes those rights necessary to increase one's level of purpose fulfillment. It includes the right to such things as property, self-respect, and nondiscrimination.

According to this hierarchy, the government could tax some individuals, and thus partially infringe upon their right to own property, for the purpose of providing a survival income to other individuals who cannot provide for themselves. The government could not, however, enslave some individuals to be the servants of others, even if the total utility of the society were thereby promoted. The basic rights of those individuals enslaved would be sacrificed in the process.

Applying RP Morality Theory. To apply RP morality, the audience of the action or policy must be determined. The audience whose rights are affected would ordinarily be the same as the audience under the utilitarian analysis. The analyst must evaluate the seriousness of the rights infringements each action will impose. Then, the alternative course of action that produces the least serious rights infringement must be chosen.

Rights infringements can be measured in three dimensions. First, some rights are more basic than others. A right to life, for example, is more basic than the right to property. Second, an action that abrogates a right altogether is more serious than one that merely limits it. Taking away all of an individual's property, for example, is a more serious rights infringement than taking away only some of it. Third, there is a difference between an actual and a merely potential rights infringement. An action that actually produces a disease, for example, is a more serious rights infringement than one that merely increases the risk of having it.

Shortcomings in RP Morality. There are two principal difficulties with RP morality. First, it is sometimes difficult to apply. In some cases, any alternative open to one individual involves interference with another individual's rights claim. In an affirmative action case, for example, management may hire a minority and violate the rights claim of a nonminority who may be more qualified. Alternatively, management could hire a nonminority and violate the rights claim of a minority who may claim an entitlement to compensation for past discrimination. Since both rights claims cannot be honored, management must determine which rights claim is most deserving. In looking for guidance, management will find that Gewirth's hierarchy of rights is difficult to apply or simply not applicable in such cases.

A second problem with RP morality is that the moral judgments implied by it sometimes appear implausible because they conflict so strongly with overall welfare or utility. Suppose that due to a company's severe financial problems, its management is considering instituting an early-retirement program. The program will effectively end the working careers of many older employees. It is, however, necessary for the firm's economic survival. While the program will promote more overall utility, it does involve an injustice to a few—an injustice given considerable importance under the RP morality theory. In this instance, utilitarianism seems to be a better guide to action than RP morality. In the *Bodnar* case, management is attempting to implement such an early-retirement program.

Bodnar v. Snypol, Inc.
United States Court of Appeals, Fifth Circuit
843 F.2d 190
(1988)

Case Background. *Three employees of Synpol, Inc. sued the company for age discrimination. Because of a serious decline in the market for its products, Synpol began a program to cut operating costs. Part of the program involved the implementation of a Special Early Retirement Incentive Program (SERIP). Under the SERIP, salaried non-essential employees who had reached age fifty-five and had been with the company for ten years were eligible for early retirement.*

Twenty-eight employees were offered early retirement under the SERIP. They were given fifteen days to reject or accept the company's offer. Twenty-one employees accepted the plan. The three employees who brought this suit were among the seven employees who rejected the program and remained with the company.

The employees asserted they were constructively discharged through the threats of the defendant/company urging early retirement. They stated the company told them that if they did not take part in the SERIP, they might be released later without severance pay or benefits. Further, the presentation of the SERIP program was allegedly made in a "threatening" manner. The U.S. District Court granted the defendant/company's motion for a summary judgment. The plaintiff/employees appealed.

Case Decision. Judge Jones delivered the opinion of the court.

* * *

[The] evidence [of the three employees] focuses on certain facts that are claimed to raise a jury issue concerning constructive discharge. First, they assert that the eligible employees were told that if they did not participate in the SERIP and their job was eliminated, they would not receive any severance pay or benefits. The employees did not "volunteer" to participate in early retirement but were "chosen" by the employer. They were told there would be a reduction in the work force. They were not given information concerning who, or how many, employees had been offered or had accepted the retirement plan. They were instructed not to discuss the SERIP offer with anyone else. Requests for additional time to consider the plan beyond the 15-day period were denied. Finally, presentations concerning early retirement under the SERIP were made to the employees in an allegedly "threatening" manner.

* * *

In general, an employer's adoption of an early retirement plan does not create a prima facie case of age discrimination under the ADEA. We need not recite the manifold reasons that justify such plans and render them, in many situations, the fairest alternative available to a company. But, from the employee's perspective, as Judge Easterbrook explained in Henn:

> Provided the employee may decline the (early retirement) offer and keep working under lawful conditions, the offer makes him better off. He has an additional option, one that may be . . . worth a great deal of money. He may retire, receive the value of the package, and either take a new job (increasing his income) or enjoy new leisure. He also may elect to keep working and forfeit the package. This may put him to a hard choice; he may think the offer too good to refuse; but it is not Don Corleone "make him an offer he can't refuse." "Your money or your life?" calls for a choice, but each option makes the recipient of the offer worse off. When one option makes the recipient better off, and the other is the status quo, then the offer is beneficial. That the benefits may overwhelm the recipient and dictate the choice can not be dispositive.

The picture becomes more complicated, however, when the offer of early retirement irrevocably changes the employee's status quo. In the *Downey* case, for example, the employee was apparently singled out, told his company had nothing for him to do and that he was in danger of being discharged and losing retirement benefits. We held that the threat of being discharged with a loss of benefits created a sufficient contested issue of material fact to make summary judgment on the employee's age discrimination claim improper. *Downey* does set an outer bound on permissible employer activity. An employer's "offer" of early retirement may create a prima facie case of age discrimination by constructive discharge if it sufficiently alters the status quo that each choice facing the employee makes him worse off. Of course, no individual employee or employee group may claim constructive discharge where all employees are subject to the same working conditions.

Judged by the foregoing standards, there are two complicating features in Synpol's SERIP plan. First, it was not offered to all employees at or near retirement age but only to non-essential employees. Unlike the [three employees], we do not find this feature consistent with a Downey-like possibility that they were discriminatorily "singled out." Although [the three employees] allege that they were "singled out," their summary judgment evidence does not refute or undermine in any way Synpol's failure to extend SERIP to otherwise eligible non-essential managerial employees. Surely an employer faced with the need to cut its workforce in order to survive may not be required to cut off its ability to survive as well in order to escape ADEA liability for an early retirement bonus program.

[The three employees'] second significant area of objection to SERIP is that they were not really offered a "voluntary" opportunity for an early retirement bonus. Coercion allegedly resulted from (1) the short time afforded appellants for considering their options, (2) the supervisors' "threat" that if not enough employees accepted early retirement and the offeree's job was eliminated he would not receive any severance pay or non-pension benefits and (3) the tone and manner of those who explained the plan. None of these factors, taken individually or cumulatively, constitutes objective evidence that working conditions had become so intolerable as to force [the three employees'] resignation. The fifteen-day time period, although not generous, is a far cry from a twenty-four-hour take-it-or-leave-it proposal. . . . Employee Bodnar, for instance, had ample time to and did consult with a lawyer and examine his options. We would be inclined to scrutinize closely any plan that was offered to employees on a shorter schedule, but one must concurrently recognize that a struggling business often has to take rapid and decisive action to stem losses.

That risk inhered in eligible employees' failure to accept the SERIP bonus offer, the risk that their jobs might be eliminated because of economic pressure on the company, is likewise insufficient to suggest age discrimination. . . . [The three employees'] risk, if they stayed on, would be shared by all remaining employees of Synpol. It is thus fair to say that the SERIP afforded [the three employees] a means to mitigate that risk which was not available to other employees.

* * *

Case Holding. *The lower court's decision in favor of the defendant/company was affirmed. The fact that an employer has an early retirement program does not necessarily violate the Age Discrimination in Employment Act.*

Case Questions

1. Would this case have been brought if the company's personnel managers had handled the situation with greater concern for employee reactions?

2. Suppose Synpol had given employees just twenty-four hours to make a decision. Would the result in this case have been different?

3. What responsibilities and obligations do companies have to employees who are about to retire? Does it make a difference if the retirement is voluntary or involuntary?

4. Will a company's actions in handling involuntary retirements affect the morale of remaining employees?

A Manager's Ethics Analysis

With most complex moral problems, it is usually helpful to apply both moral theories together. In resolving some problems, the utilitarian and RP morality analyses will agree and the ethical conclusion will be clear. When the two analyses disagree, as in the case of the early retirement program, management must balance the severity of rights violations against the severity of the threat to overall utility. There is, however, no general formula for establishing such a balance. Clearly, a manager's own ethical sensitivities and commitments will play a critical role in resolving this dilemma.

THE NOTION OF CORPORATE SOCIAL RESPONSIBILITY

In 1978, the U.S. Supreme Court was asked to rule on whether businesses in Massachusetts could spend money to express opposition to the enactment of a state personal income tax. The Supreme Judicial Court of Massachusetts had said that any such expenditure of corporate funds was illegal. The U.S. Supreme Court, in a 5–4 decision (*First National Bank of Boston* v. *Bellotti*), reversed the Massachusetts decision. The Court in effect said that corporations could participate in the political process in much the same way as individuals do. Although the Supreme Court established corporate rights and responsibilities under the law, the question still remains as to what rights and responsibilities corporations should have in those actions not required by law.

Should corporations be confined to making a profit for their stockholders, or should they enter into the political arena, contribute to charities, and help revitalize inner cities? Should they install expensive antipollution devices that are not required by law? Should ethical considerations ever restrain their efforts to expand into new markets, increase sales, and earn profits? With sales of cigarettes declining in this country, should tobacco companies mount an intensive advertising campaign to sell cigarettes in third-world countries, even though the health hazards of smoking are well known?

Corporate Social Responsibility: Conceptual Issues

The debate over corporate social responsibility involves a major conceptual issue. Are corporations the kinds of entities that can be praised or blamed for their actions in a way that is roughly analogous to the way individuals are praised or blamed? Corporations exhibit many types of "behavior" that resemble those of people: they pay taxes, enter into legal arrangements, exercise certain rights of freedom of speech, and own property. On the other hand, unlike individuals, they are strictly liable for the injuries caused by their products, do not have the right to vote or the obligation to register for the draft, and have an indefinite life. So while corporations are not full-fledged persons, are they moral agents in the sense of being entities that can be held morally accountable for their actions?

Corporate Social Responsibility and Organizational Goals

One leading philosopher, John Ladd, answers that question in the negative: corporations are not moral agents that can be held morally accountable for their actions. Following the views of organizational theorist Herbert Simon,

Ladd holds that corporations are controlled by their structures, so they can act only in accordance with a means-end formula. That is, they can act only in accordance with specified organizational goals. In the case of business corporations, those goals will include the company's survival, autonomy, and growth.

According to Ladd, an organization is "rational" when it employs effective means to achieve its goals. Moral precepts are relevant only insofar as they relate directly to the organization's goals. Thus, if the public finds a television commercial sponsored by a corporation morally offensive, the corporation might well decide to eliminate the commercial. The reason, however, would be that the commercial might result in a boycott of the corporation's products and a reduction in profits—not that the corporation subscribes to moral ideals.

Ladd's conclusion is that organizations with "formal structures" (such as corporations) cannot have moral obligations and hence "cannot have moral responsibilities in the sense of having obligations towards those affected by their actions or subject to their actions. . . . Organizations have tremendous power, but no responsibilities." Thus, Ladd finds that society cannot afford to have such organizations acting like amoral machines, controlled only by considerations of self-preservation and profit. Since corporations cannot govern themselves by moral principles, they must be controlled by government. The state must see to it, presumably by extensive regulation, that corporations do not act in a way that is detrimental to society.

Moral Principles as Corporate Goals

Many writers, however, do not accept the view that corporate organizational structure precludes the possibility of moral responsibility. Ladd has not established by any convincing argument that moral principles cannot be corporate goals. Why cannot the goal of acting ethically be included in corporate objectives, along with those of self-preservation and profit? In fact, many corporate policy statements include moral objectives. It is possible to hold that these statements are mere window dressing and do not express operating policy. It is not evident, however, that this is always the case. At any rate, the presence of such statements strongly suggests that corporations can be morally responsible.

The philosopher Kenneth Goodpaster provides positive support for the view that it makes sense to attribute moral responsibility to corporations. Goodpaster isolates four elements of moral responsibility (perception, moral reasoning, coordination, and implementation) and finds close analogies to each of them in corporate life.

Perception
All rational decision-making must begin with a moral agent's perception of his or her environment. Corporations exhibit this characteristic when they gather information before making a decision. As indicated earlier, there is no reason why a corporation cannot take into account the moral as well as the economic and legal dimensions of a decision. For example, it can take into account the effects of plant closings and the discharge of pollution on the community.

Moral Reasoning
A moral agent must be able to move from premises to conclusions about what ought to be done. Similarly, a corporation can certainly weigh alternative

decisions with attention to such considerations as possible injustice to employees or the community.

Coordination

A moral agent must be able to integrate the moral evaluation with various nonmoral considerations, such as self-interest, the law, economics, and politics. A corporation can engage in similar deliberations. Goodpaster believes that this is where considerable moral failure occurs in corporate life. Corporations often trade off moral for nonmoral considerations and end up in undesirable moral compromises. Sound business practices, for example, necessitate the use of a cost-benefit analysis—either explicitly or implicitly. In the vast majority of cases, the analysis involves some assessment of the number and costs of injuries to users. Knives, power tools, lawnmowers, airplanes, fishing tackle, guns, electrical appliances, and many other products all have the potential to inflict great bodily harm on their users. Since such products often cannot be made both perfectly safe and affordable to consumers, management will compare the costs of injuries—both the costs of compensating injured parties and the costs associated with repairing the company's reputation if the calculation proves grossly inaccurate—with the costs of making the products safer. Profits are thus traded off against injuries. Within this quasi-objective approach to decision-making, management must resolve the ethical and moral dilemma of what cost is to be placed on human life and human suffering in assessing the amount of safety to be provided. As the *Grimshaw* case illustrates, the management of Ford Motor Company traded off safety for the cost imperatives imposed by fuel-efficient imports and tough domestic competition in its inexpensive Pinto.

Grimshaw v. Ford Motor Company
California Court of Appeals, Fourth District, Division 2
119 Cal.App.3d 757, 174 Cal.Rptr. 348 (1981)

Case Background. *The plaintiffs, thirteen-year-old Richard Grimshaw and the heirs of Mrs. Lilly Gray, brought a products liability action against Ford Motor Company. The Grays had purchased an automobile manufactured by Ford Motor Company, a Ford Pinto hatchback. The auto stalled unexpectedly on a freeway, was struck in the rear by another auto, and the interior burst into flames. Mrs. Gray, the driver, died as a result of burns from the accident. Grimshaw, a passenger in the Grays' car, suffered permanent and disfiguring burns over his entire body, including his face. At the time of the accident, the Grays' Pinto was six months old and had been driven approximately 3,000 miles.*

It was alleged that the management of Ford had engaged in a cost-benefit analysis prior to marketing the Pinto. Management had balanced the costs of redesigning the fuel tank against the possible liability to the company if the design remained unchanged. Management decided that the cost of the change in design would far exceed the liability costs resulting from accidents. On that basis, the Pinto was marketed without incorporating safety features that the plaintiffs alleged could have prevented their injuries.

The jury awarded $2,516,000 compensatory and $125 million in punitive damages to Grimshaw, and $559,680 in compensatory damages to the Grays. (The Grays did not seek punitive damages in their complaint, and were not allowed to amend it by the trial court.) Although the punitive damages were reduced significantly from that awarded by the jury, Ford appealed, arguing that the punitive damages awarded were still excessive.

Case Decision.   Judge Tamura delivered the opinion of the court.

* * *

Ordinarily marketing surveys and preliminary engineering studies precede the styling of a new automobile line. Pinto, however, was a rush project, so that styling preceded engineering and dictated engineering design to a greater degree than usual. Among the engineering decisions dictated by styling was the placement of the fuel tank. It was then the preferred practice in Europe and Japan to locate the gas tank over the rear axle in subcompacts because a small vehicle has less "crush space" between the rear axle and the bumper than larger cars. The Pinto's styling, however, required the tank to be placed behind the rear axle leaving only 9 or 10 inches of "crush space," far less than in any other American automobile or overseas subcompact. In addition, the Pinto was designed so that its bumper was little more than a chrome strip, less substantial than the bumper of any other American car produced. The Pinto's rear structure also lacked reinforcing members . . . [making] the Pinto less crush resistant than other vehicles. Finally, the differential housing selected for the Pinto had an exposed flange and a line of exposed bolt heads. These protrusions were sufficient to puncture a gas tank driven forward against the differential upon rear impact.

* * *

During the development of the Pinto, prototypes were built and tested. . . . These prototypes as well as two production Pintos were crash tested by Ford to determine, among other things, the integrity of the fuel system in rear-end accidents. . . . The crash tests revealed that the Pinto's fuel system as designed could not meet the federal 20 or 30-mile-per-hour [fixed barrier impact without significant fuel spillage requirements]. . . . A production Pinto crash tested at 21-miles-per-hour into a fixed barrier caused the fuel neck to be torn from the gas tank and the tank to be punctured by a bolt head on the differential housing. In at least one test, spilled fuel entered the driver's compartment. . . . Vehicles with fuel tanks installed above rather than behind the rear axle passed the fuel system integrity test at 31-miles-per-hour fixed barrier.

* * *

When a prototype failed the fuel system integrity test, the standard of care for engineers in the industry was to redesign and retest it. The vulnerability of the production Pinto's fuel tank at speeds of 20 and 30-miles-per-hour fixed barrier tests could have been remedied by inexpensive "fixes," but Ford produced and sold the Pinto to the public without doing anything to remedy the defects. Design changes [could have been implemented] that would have enhanced the integrity of the fuel tank system at relatively little cost per car. . . . Equipping the car with a reinforced rear structure, smooth axle, improved bumper and additional crush space at a total cost of $15.30 would have made the fuel tank safe in a 34 to 38-mile-per-hour rear end collision.

* * *

Harley Copp, a former Ford engineer and executive in charge of the crash testing program, testified that the highest level of Ford's management made the decision to go forward with the production of the Pinto, knowing that the gas tank was vulnerable to puncture and rupture at low rear impact speeds creating a significant risk of death or injury from fire and knowing that "fixes" were feasible at nominal cost. He testified that management's decision was based on the cost savings which would inure from omitting or delaying the "fixes."

* * *

Through the results of the crash tests Ford knew that the Pinto's fuel tank and rear structure would expose consumers to serious injury or death in a 20 to 30 mile-per-hour collision. There was evidence that Ford could have corrected the hazardous design defects at minimal cost but decided to defer correction of the shortcomings by engaging in a cost-benefit analysis balancing human lives and limbs against corporate profits. Ford's institutional mentality was shown to be one of callous indifference to public safety. There was substantial evidence that Ford's conduct constituted "conscious disregard" of the probability of injury to members of the consuming public.

* * *

There is substantial evidence that management was aware of the crash tests showing the vulnerability of the Pinto's fuel tank to rupture at low speed rear impacts with consequent significant risk of injury or death of the occupants by fire. There was testimony from several sources that the test results were forwarded up the chain of command. . . . While much of the evidence was necessarily circumstantial, there was substantial evidence from which the jury could reasonably find that Ford's management decided to proceed with the production of the Pinto with knowledge of test results revealing design defects which rendered the fuel tank extremely vulnerable on rear impact at low speeds and endangered the safety and lives of the occupants. Such conduct constitutes corporate malice.

* * *

Case Holding. *The court of appeals affirmed the trial court's ruling, finding, among other things, that the trial court's assessment of punitive damages was proper and not excessive.*

Case Questions

1. What was the court's principal objection to Ford's decision-making process?
2. Has the court found all managerial trade-offs between safety and profits to constitute "corporate malice"? If not, when does corporate malice begin? Would it differ by industry?
3. Suppose that the Pinto could be redesigned to safely withstand a 60-mph rear-end impact but the redesign would dramatically increase its price. Thus, the auto would became safer for those who could afford it, but deprive others who could not afford the auto of its useful benefits. Would those consumers who are deprived be willing to pay a lower price by receiving less safety equipment and accepting more of the risk of accidents? Should they be allowed to do so?

Implementation

A moral agent must be able to carry out a strategic decision in the "real world" by understanding the environment, implementing the strategy, and guiding it toward realization. A corporation must be able to implement its decisions in a similar way.

Since the decision-making process used by corporations is strongly analogous to that of morally responsible agents, Goodpaster concludes that there is nothing logically absurd about holding corporations morally responsible. The question that now arises is: what should corporate moral responsibilities include?

The Scope of Corporate Responsibility: the Narrow View

There are two views of the scope of corporate responsibility. The first view is called the *narrow* or the *agents-of-capital view.* According to Nobel Laureate Milton Friedman, perhaps the best-known advocate of the narrow view, the social responsibility of a business executive (and hence of a corporation) is "to make as much money as possible while conforming to the basic rules of the society, both those embodied in law and those embodied in ethical custom." Although Friedman never explains what he means by "ethical custom," it is safe to say that he intends it to be understood in a highly restricted sense.

The Corporation's Self-Interest Motivation

In examining Friedman's viewpoint, "negative" and "positive" moral obligations must be distinguished. *Negative moral obligations* include obligations *not* to undertake actions that might be grossly offensive to the general public. Examples would include engaging in deception or committing fraud. Because its public image would be harmed, a corporation clearly would have self-interested motivations for not engaging in such grossly offensive activities. *Positive moral obligations* include the kinds of "social obligations" that the broad view of social responsibility espouses—proactive considerations for the quality of life and the integrity of the environment, among other things. Friedman seems to understand adherence to social custom in terms of negative moral obligations. Thus, a corporation should not reduce pollution below the level required by law merely to improve the environment or hire the hard-core unemployed merely to reduce poverty.

Friedman does believe that under certain circumstances, it may be in the corporation's self-interest to do things that have the appearance of altruism. A corporation might institute day-care centers to improve the morale of employees or to attract a higher-quality work force. It might improve safety in a factory beyond that required by law for similar reasons. Friedman asserts, however, that management should never do these things for any other motive than to promote the economic self-interest of stockholders.

RP Morality and Utilitarian Justifications

Friedman provides both RP morality and utilitarian justifications for his position. From an RP standpoint, Friedman argues that business executives are agents of their principals, the stockholders. Since the corporate goal is to increase profits, a management decision to spend stockholders' money for purposes other than meeting that goal will not likely meet with their approval. If management so designates funds for such other purposes, it is infringing on the rights of stockholders. If individual stockholders want to promote a social cause, they can make contributions out of the profits they receive from the corporation. In this way, they will be able to more effectively honor their own moral agency without infringing on the rights of other stockholders. Those other stockholders either may not want to contribute to social causes or may want to contribute in a different way.

Friedman also gives some utilitarian justifications for his view of corporate social responsibility. First, Friedman points out that corporate managers are not trained in social policy. They are not necessarily the best equipped people, either by training or inclination, to deal with pollution, urban decay, and other social problems. Second, the general social well-being can be more effectively pursued if business is allowed to do what it does best—provide goods and services and make a profit for its stockholders. Friedman's second argument is a version of the so-called invisible hand argument. Adam Smith, an eighteenth-century Scottish economist, maintained that when people are left to pursue their own economic self-interest, they produce more good for society than when they are motivated by avowedly altruistic concerns. According to Smith:

> It is not from the benevolence of the butcher, the brewer, or the baker that we expect our dinner, but from their regard for their own interests. Following their own interests, it is as if they were lead by an invisible hand to produce greater overall utility.

The Scope of Corporate Responsibility: the Broad View

In contrast to Friedman, Melvin Anshen maintains that there has always been a kind of "social contract" between business and society. This "contract" represents an implicit understanding of the proper goals and responsibilities of business. In the nineteenth century, the major social goal was rapid economic growth. Accordingly, the function of business was to promote that growth in an atmosphere of unfettered competition and minimal government regulation. Today, our society has concerns beyond economic growth, particularly regarding the quality of life and the integrity of the environment. Anshen asserts that the social contract between business and society has changed and the narrow view of corporate responsibility is no longer appropriate.

Keith Davis, a professor of business administration, agrees. "One basic proposition," he says, "is that social responsibility arises from social power." The immense economic and political power of corporations means that the actions of corporations vitally "affect the interests of others." In a speech to the Harvard Business School in 1969, Henry Ford II stated a similar idea:

> The terms of the contract between industry and society are changing. . . . Now we are being asked to serve a wider range of human values and to accept an obligation to members of the public with whom we have no commercial transactions.

The RP Perspective

How can the seemingly contradictory claims of Friedman and Anshen be justified? The RP argument given by Friedman was based on the property rights of stockholders. The rebuttal is based on the observation that rights can conflict. While it is true that stockholders have rights to have their corporations promote their economic well-being, it is also true that this can interfere with the rights of others. According to advocates of the broad view of corporate social responsibility, Friedman's position does not balance rights infringements in the proper way. When a firm continues to sell tires that are a safety hazard, its pursuit of its own right to make a profit constitutes a violation or potential violation of a more basic right, namely consumer rights to health and safety.

Not all the corporate policies advocated by proponents of the broad view, however, can be justified on the basis that corporations are infringing the rights of individuals. It is reasonably clear that when a corporation emits a pollutant that causes serious health risks, it is infringing on community members' rights to life and health. However, it is considerably less clear how a corporation's failure to introduce a program to employ the hard-core unemployed is an infringement on anyone's rights. Whether corporations have such obligations is much more controversial.

The basis of such "positive" obligations, if they exist, is found in an equal respect for the rights of persons. If individuals in society are obligated to respect equally the rights of both themselves and others, it might seem that the individuals should consent to have their less basic rights infringed to protect the more basic rights of others. It would seem that others should agree to do the same. An example of this notion can be found in the *Soldano* case presented earlier in this chapter. Most of us would say that the defendant in the case had an obligation to assist the plaintiff at least to the extent of calling the police. His obligation grows out of the fact that he could have saved a life with relatively little risk to himself. Similarly, perhaps corporations should be morally obligated to assist the hard-core unemployed—if they can do so with relatively little infringement on their own general well-being.

But even on an individual level, the extent of such positive obligations to "rescue" others is controversial. Would the bartender in the *Soldano* case have been obligated to run out in the street and attempt to restrain the attacker physically? Similarly, would corporations be obligated to help the unemployed if it seriously endangered their own efficiency or profit-making potential?

The Utilitarian Perspective

Under a utilitarian argument against the broad view of social responsibility, Friedman asserted that managers were unqualified to wage war against social evils, such as inflation and unemployment. In some instances, however, managers do possess expertise that can be useful in solving larger social problems. Therefore, the utilitarian case for corporate obligations to help solve such problems as unemployment may be somewhat stronger than the RP case. But again, this would depend on the extent to which business efficiency and profitability would be diminished.

Another aspect of the utilitarian argument seemingly against the broad view was a version of Adam Smith's "invisible hand" argument. According to Smith, corporations can contribute more to the public good if left to do what they do best, namely make a profit within the bounds of the law and the most basic moral guidelines prohibiting fraud and deception. A counter to this argument has been called the "invisible foot" argument. According to this argument, corporations, while unquestionably able to contribute to the public good, also can cause a great deal of public harm if they operate only under the restraints suggested by Friedman. While being helped by the invisible hand, society can also be kicked by the invisible foot. Critics of Friedman cite a number of examples.

First, the free market, if left to itself, allows business to pass off some of the costs of its more detrimental activities to the general public. These costs (called "externalities" by economists) are especially evident in the area of pollution and other environmental concerns. Environmental degradation can have profoundly negative consequences for the well-being of our own and future generations. A counterargument is that managers are themselves consumers of the environment and the extent to which they may be willing to degrade it to improve stockholders' well-being will be limited.

Second, it is argued that the general quality of life for both employees and the larger community can be seriously eroded if the narrow view is embraced. For example, operating under the narrow view of corporate responsibility, a corporation will improve working conditions for its employees only when it is in the corporation's self-interest to do so. It will be concerned with such issues as product safety and advertising to children only when the law requires it or when competitive conditions force it to do so. However, management will go to great lengths to maintain the company image. A reputation for shoddy work, difficult working conditions, and poor product safety will quickly lead to lower profits and then losses. Managers will have a difficult time finding employment after leaving a company in that condition.

Third, if the narrow view is widely accepted by corporations, society will increasingly expect the law to force corporations to adhere to the very policies that the narrow view abhors. There are, however, limits to relying on the law to enforce a wider view of corporate responsibility. For one thing, laws often do not apply to novel or unusual circumstances. Also, laws tend to be enacted only after disasters or other dramatic events have pointed out the need for them. Finally, once in place, laws may not change with the times and can quickly become clumsy and inefficient.

Making Corporations More Morally Responsive

The debate about the extent of corporate responsibility is still open. Regardless of the outcome of the debate, however, American business is being asked to be more active in carrying out in its social responsibilities and to be more assertive in seeking changes in the political and social environments. Shareholders are seeking to prompt more activity from corporations through stockholder resolutions and other devices. "Public interest" representatives are being placed on corporate boards of directors to review management decisions. Codes of conduct and corporate policy statements are being developed and promoted to clarify what is ethical activity within the corporation.

It is generally agreed that improving corporate social responsibility ultimately depends, however, upon changing something much more nebulous. This factor usually goes under the title of "corporate culture," and it refers to the values and attitudes that pervade the corporate workplace. It is further agreed that corporate culture is set by top management. Thus, the support of top management and boards of directors for corporate social responsibility is crucial. Encouraging students who will be the future managers and board members to think clearly about ethical issues is one way to ensure this support.

SUMMARY

Over the past two decades, the public image of business and business executives has been declining. In addition, the general public believes that dishonesty in general is greater than it was just ten years ago. In an effort to overcome these image problems, the business community is encouraging companies to write codes of ethics, screen its prospective employees, and teach business ethics and principles.

The terms *ethics* and *morals* are generally interchangeable. These terms, however, should not be confused with statements about etiquette or good manners or with rules of law.

A major source of confusion in discussing and evaluating ethics is the failure to distinguish three basic kinds of issues: disagreement over the facts, disagreements over conceptual issues, and disagreements over genuine moral principles. Moral disagreements are generally settled by appealing to moral principles.

According to moral philosophers, moral claims fall within two moral theories: utilitarianism and ethics of respect for persons (or RP morality). The moral standard of utilitarianism is: Those actions are right that produce the most happiness. The application of utilitarianism by individuals requires two conditions: freedom and well-being. In applying the theory, the analyst must first determine the audience of the action. Then the analyst must determine the positive and negative effects imposed on members by the action and its alternatives. Finally the analyst must decide which course of action produces the most happiness or utility. The utilitarianism theory is criticized because it requires extensive information and can lead to injustice for certain individuals.

The RP morality theory can be stated as: Those actions are right that equally respect each human person as a moral agent. The golden rule has been characterized as representative of RP morality. However, because the golden rule may be too permissive in its application in the business world, moral philosophers have developed a doctrine of rights. Under this approach, an individual's rights may be overridden only to protect a more fundamental or basic right of another individual. In defining basic rights, a hierarchy of rights has been proposed by moral philosophers. At the top of the hierarchy is life, while at the third tier are such rights as the right to property and self-respect. In applying the theory, the analyst must determine the audience, the policy alternatives, and which course of action produces the least serious rights infringements. The principal shortcomings of the theory are that it is difficult to apply and that its outcomes can appear to be implausible because they conflict with overall welfare.

The responsibilities of corporations beyond that required by the law and the profit motivations of their shareholders have been heavily debated. Some scholars assert that corporations are not moral agents, and thus cannot have moral responsibilities. Others assert that corporate life has all the elements of moral responsibility and therefore corporations should be considered as moral agents.

The two competing theories of social responsibility include the agents-of-capital view and the social contract view. The agents-of-capital view asserts that the corporation has the responsibility to make as much money as possible while conforming to the basic rules of society. Under the social contract theory, philosophers assert that our society has moved beyond an emphasis on economic growth so that corporations should now focus more on quality of life and environmental concerns.

Does Corporate Culture Make People Dishonest or Do Dishonest People Make Corporate Culture?

There is growing concern about the interplay between the demands of corporate life and the people who work in corporations. With the majority of surveys indicating a divergence in personal morals and beliefs and the activities of corporations, the simplest explanation is that people with high moral standards and integrity are adversely affected by a corporate culture and its demands to "win at any cost." But how can a corporation comprised of employees with high moral standards and integrity breed such a culture independent of those employee beliefs? Do the personal rewards for profits, rising stock prices, increasing market shares, and other corporate financial "wins" push morals and integrity aside?

The following article relates how the desire for success drove the chief executive officer of a large company to "cook" the company's books. As you read the article, consider the factors that may have motivated this executive to react to adversity the way he did.

How Don Sheelen Made a Mess That Regina Couldn't Clean Up

John A. Byrne*

The letter G has broken apart in the huge sign atop the Regina Co. corporate headquarters in Rahway, N.J. A tattered flag flaps above the squat concrete building on the street named for the vacuum-cleaner company.

Within a month, the few remaining employees at the huge complex that once employed hundreds will bolt the door on another symbol of failure in American business. This was not, however, a company whose fatal flaw was an inability to compete. This was a company whose entrepreneurial CEO turned out to be a con man.

Donald D. Sheelen had taken over the single-product company in 1984 at the age of 38 and, everyone thought, transformed it into a marketing powerhouse, with a host of new products. By 1988, he had more than tripled reported sales in a string of four years of record profits and sales. He talked about setting off "consumer hot buttons" and of achieving his "dream of entrepreneurship." What he didn't say was that he cooked the books, plunging Regina into a morass of lawsuits and, finally, bankruptcy. Sheelen, who pleaded guilty to fraud, is serving time in a work-release correction center.

What happened to the company is a tale of the '80s, the story of an overzealous MBA entrepreneur, cheerleading Wall Street analysts, and independent auditors who failed to uncover a less-than-subtle fraud. "The story of Don Sheelen," his lawyers contend with hyperbole, "is similar to the great fictional Shakespearean and Greek tragedies."

*Reprinted from the February 12, 1990 *Business Week* by special permission. © 1990 McGraw-Hill, Inc.

–continued

—continuing

Sheelen, who declines comment, seemed more suited to the role of Shakespeare's conniving Iago than the tragic hero Othello.

It depends on whose story you believe. His wife, Louise, a former Franciscan nun, described him in a presentencing appeal to the judge as a "good, honest, sincere, andloving" man. She related how he helped his eldest son set up a business selling flowers on Mother's Day at the local supermarket.

Sheelen's business colleagues saw a different side of him. They saw him as a tough, aggressive boss. Some associates found him so abrasive that even when he was a marketing vice-president, they discouraged him from making calls for fear he would offend customers. And once Sheelen became CEO, he committed fraud rather than accept failure.

Son of a Gulf Oil Co. salesman, Sheelen was born into a middle-class family in Middletown, N.Y. The boy with rugged good looks was an overachiever from the start, playing varsity football and basketball in high school and emerging as a Big Man On Campus at the University of Dayton. He was senior-class president and graduated with a business degree in 1968. Armed with an MBA from Syracuse University, he joined Bache & Co. as a stockbroker in 1970. Three years later, he landed an accounting job with Johnson & Johnson, ending up at a small subsidiary called Jelco, which made catheters and syringes. In 1980, he joined Regina, where he became head of marketing. The company, founded in Rahway in 1892 as a maker of music boxes, virtually owned the market for electric brooms, but growth was slowing.

What his colleagues quickly noticed about Sheelen was his ambition. He put in long hours, and he talked about the success of others in his family, particularly his sister, a real estate broker. "He was envious that his sister had done so well," recalls Ronald Nolan, then vice president of sales. "And he said he didn't feel like being last in the foot race with them."

They noticed something else: Sheelen's drive to succeed alienated people. Turnover in his department was high. "When you reported to him, you faced a good grilling," says John Borowiec, a former sales manager. "He would just intimidate people."

Still, Sheelen brought good ideas with him. He moved Regina, then owned by conglomerate General Signal Corp., into higher-margin accessories, such as vacuum bags. He also promoted a new product, a carpet shampooer. He climbed the ladder, becoming CEO in 1984, the same year he led Regina in a $31.4 million leveraged buyout. Sheelen anted up $750,000 for nearly a 54% stake in the company. Little more than 17 months later, he brought Regina public.

The shareholders who attended his first annual meeting in 1986 at The Landmark Inn in Woodbridge, N.J., were treated to their first glimpse of his showmanship. A woman clad in a bathing suit sat in a see-through bathtub to demonstrate one of his newest products, the Homespa. It used the exhaust side of a vacuum motor to blow bubbles in water and create, for less than $100, the effect of a whirlpool. He also launched the Housekeeper, his bid to compete in the upright vacuum-clearner market. Huge ad spending helped 1987 sales surge 68%, to $128 million. Earnings grew 74%, to $7.1 million.

Wall Street, eager to feed investors' frenzy for hot growth companies, began to take notice. "If you listened to Don and looked at the company's numbers, it was a very sexy story," says James M. Meyer of Janney Montgomery. His firm jumped on the bandwagon, and so did many other brokerage houses, including Shearson Lehman Hutton Inc. Shearson promoted Regina on its emerging growth-stock list, informing investors on June 16, 1988, that the company's stock could appreciate by 50% in the next year. Meyer was one of the first to remove

—continued

—continuing

Regina from his "aggressive buy" list, but Shearson, which declined comment, didn't advise investors to retreat until the stock began dropping like a stone.

Analysts liked Sheelen's combative, no-frills approach to business. A tall, stocky man with dark, curly hair, he showed up at analysts' meetings in rumpled suits with his shirttails untucked. He was going to "bomb" industry leader Hoover Co. And at the entrance to his office, Sheelen placed a Hoover doormat on the orange shag carpet so that people could "walk over" his rival. Once inside, analysts couldn't help but notice the mousetrap with cheese under the radiator.

Yet, nothing fired Sheelen's emotions like the company's stock price. Even a temporary flutter would cause him to rush to the phone to drum up support. "He would pick up the phone himself and say, 'Why don't you write something to get the stock up?' " says Meyer.

No wonder. By July, 1988, it had soared to a peak of $27.50 from the equivalent of $5.25 a share when the company went public in 1985—making Sheelen's stake worth more than $99 million. His 1988 compensation, amounting to $577,500 in salary and bonus, enabled him to live in a spacious 12-room house on 1.8 acres on Sycamore Lane in tony Rumson, N.J.

Trouble was brewing, though. Sheelen's secretary tried out one of the first Housekeeper vacuums and quickly reported to Sheelen that when she lifted the vacuum, its handle fell off and the belt often slipped off the motor. "There were so many things wrong with it," recalls Barbara Drozdowski, "but he didn't want to hear it. He said, 'Well, we'll fix it on the next go-round, but we've got to get it out of here.' "

So anxious was he to ramp up the company's revenues that he skipped proper testing, says David A. Jones, who has headed Regina since its purchase by Electrolux Corp. in June. Product returns swamped the company, beginning as early as the spring of 1987. An internal memo showed that cus-

tomers returned more than 40,000 Housekeeper vacuums in the quarter ended on Sept. 30, a daunting 16% of sales.

Sheelen became desperate. In December, 1987, he ordered his chief financial officer, Vincent P. Golden, not to record the company's returned products. Golden, who declined to be interviewed for this story, initially protested but obliged by having his staff alter Regina's computer systems. He went along, his lawyer would later say, "to protect his job." The returns, meanwhile, kept piling up. The problem became so severe that Sheelen leased a building to store the defective products.

Even as brokers advised their clients to buy Regina stock in mid-1988, Sheelen was making his deceit more elaborate. As detailed in stipulations entered as part of their guilty pleas, Sheelen told Golden to come up with sales of about $180 million and per-share earnings of $1.20. The solution: By booking a sale when Regina received an order, rather than when it shipped the goods, Golden put $6 million worth of extra sales into Regina's fourth quarter. By understating expenses, he squeezed $3 million in profits from the income statement. Golden then rigged the computer systems to generate about 200 fake invoices worth $5.4 million on the last three business days of the fiscal year ended on June 30.

These machinations enabled Sheelen to fool Wall Street one last time. On Sept. 15, Sheelen and his secretary met the analysts in New York. He was buoyant, showing the superiority of a Housekeeper over a Hoover by sprinkling corn flakes on the carpet and vacuuming them up. The impressed analysts didn't know that the Regina model was rigged by engineers to have greater suction and could not be purchased in stores, says Drozdowski.

If Sheelen worried that he would be discovered, he didn't show it. At board meetings, he played the cool, confident CEO, recalls Malcolm L. Sherman, former head of

—continued

—continuing

Zayre Stores Inc., who joined Regina's board earlier in 1988. But the board sessions were largely consumed by product and marketing plans.

"At the first board meeting, the fact that I didn't get any numbers didn't bother me," says Sherman. "By the third meeting, I was extremely concerned. 'If we don't start seeing something specific, this isn't the right board for me,' I told him. He said, 'Don't worry. From here on, you'll get numbers.' "

Sherman did not realize how shocking those numbers would be. On Sept. 20, Sheelen called his two outside directors separately to read a press release saying that Regina would post substantially lower sales and a loss for the September quarter because of a slowdown in orders and product returns. Sheelen assigned most of the blame to a computer snafu. "He seemed very upset, extremely upset," remembers board director Richard Skelly. "He started to cry."

The news sent Regina's stock tumbling. On Sept. 21, a Wednesday, shares fell from 17 to 7⅛. Shearson finally yanked the stock from its growth list. Sheelen closeted himself in his office, refusing to take all but a few of the 100 calls being logged in daily from angry investors and analysts.

Over the weekend, according to his lawyers, Sheelen confessed to his wife and then to his priest. On Monday, he resigned. A week later, Sheelen would make a full confession to the U.S. attorney in Newark and he eventually would plead guilty to one count of mail and securities fraud.

Sheelen is now serving a one-year sentence in the Goodwill Industries Community Correction Center in St. Petersburg, Fla. It is not a hard life. There are no bars on the windows nor locks on the doors. With its brightly painted beds and lockers, the building has the feel of a college dorm. Sheelen, his lawyer says, leaves the center every weekday to work at an undisclosed business. Sheelen also was fined $25,000. (Golden's sentence and fine were exactly half of Sheelen's.) The court ultimately refunded the fine from Sheelen's Regina stock that had been turned over to the court as restitution to the shareholders in April. The stock is now virtually worthless.

Sheelen hasn't given up hope of resuming his business career. Prior to his sentencing, he asked Sherman then interim chairman if he could return to Regina. "When his attorney asked me what I thought," says Sherman, "I said, 'You could tell him it's a straight no. Or you could say to him, Are you f--- crazy? Pick whichever one you want.' "

Questions

1. What factors motivated this executive to alter the company books?

2. How did his family and those outside his work view his personal values and attributes? How did his fellow executives view him? Was he adversely affected by the corporate culture of the company?

REVIEW AND DISCUSSION QUESTIONS

1. Define the following terms:
   ethics
   morals
   moral agent
   moral principles
   corporate social responsibility
   agents of capital view of corporate social responsibility

2. Compare and contrast the following terms and phrases:
   a. Ethics and etiquette
   b. Ethics and the law
   c. Moral theory and moral judgment
   d. Utilitarianism and RP morality
   e. Freedom and well-being
   f. The Golden Rule and a moral standard
   g. Negative moral obligation and positive moral obligation

3. Suppose upper management decides to adopt a corporate ethics code. The company is a manufacturer, distributor, and wholesaler of consumer products—primarily consumer pain medicines, cold remedies, and other similar nonprescription medicines. Who are the company's constituents? Which of those constituencies should the company ethics code address? To what punishments, if any, should employees be subjected if they violate the code?

4. The engineers at your company estimate that by making certain quality improvements in the production process, the risk of death from using your product will drop from one in two million to one in four million per year. Given the current use rate of the product, one death occurs every other year and costs the firm an average of $1 million in settlement. The quality improvements would cost $30 million to make—less than the value of the expected settlement savings. What do you do?

Case Questions

5. The evidence is continuing to mount implicating smoking as a serious health hazard. Consumer groups are forcefully asserting that tobacco manufacturers and growers are well aware of the health hazards associated with smoking but are failing to adequately inform consumers. Should cigarette manufacturers be liable for the serious illnesses and untimely deaths caused by their products—even though they posted a warning on the package and consumers voluntarily assumed the health risks by smoking? [*Cipollone* v. *Liggett Group, Inc.*, 644 F. Supp. 283 (D.N.J. 1986)]

6. Through the mid-1980s, Corona, a Mexican beer, became very popular in the United States. Several domestic beers were seriously hurt by Corona's sudden success. In 1988, Corona experienced a surprising slump in sales. Through the diligence of the company's management, the decline was eventually attributed to rumors about the quality of Corona—particularly, that it had traces of urine in it. The company traced the rumors to several southwestern domestic beer distributors. How should the domestic brewers who supply those distributors react to such practices? If one brewery responds by severing its relationship with the offending distributor, will the other breweries likely follow suit and sever their relationships? Should they?

Policy Questions

7. The United States has stringent restrictions on toxic substance disposal compared to many poor countries that have no regulations regarding such matters. Firms can move operations to such countries, not spend millions on expensive pollution controls required in the United States, and so produce the product for less. Should we effectively extend our pollution laws to other countries by not allowing the import of products made in countries or at plants that do not meet American pollution standards? If we do that, it will

retard the development of poor countries, which may gladly trade some pollution for higher incomes. Should that make a difference?

8. The local opera company visits your company's headquarters. It asks for a donation of $10,000, claiming that without such corporate support the opera will close. What factors do you consider in making a recommendation to your company about such a donation?

9. Migrant farm workers are at about the bottom of our employment force and quality of life standards. They work very hard, do not make much money, and live with their families in what are often miserable conditions. You run a large vegetable farm operation that hires migrant workers an average of four weeks per year. You pay the going wage rate for the workers, who rent dumps to live in while they work in your area before moving north. Do you have an ethical responsibility to pay more than the market wage so these workers could live in better conditions? Do you have a responsibility to provide housing to the workers you employ? If you pay above-market rates, your neighbor farmers will be mad at you and point out that—as you know—most of the farm operations run on thin margins as it is, so that much higher wages could drive you all out of business. Assuming these to be facts, what responsibilities do you think you have? Closing the Mexican border will reduce the number of migrant workers, which will drive up the wage rate. The migrant workers in the United States will be better off, but those who used to cross from Mexico will be worse off. Is it ethical to close the border?

10. The ABC Company has been supplying widgets to your XYZ Company for many years. The widgets are needed in the production of gidgets. ABC has always been a fair company to deal with. When problems have arisen, ABC has usually resolved them to your satisfaction. Now the LMN firm from Singapore has approached you, saying it will provide widgets to you for 10 percent less than you were paying ABC. ABC tells you there is no way it can cut its prices and if you cut it off, it will have to pare back production so that fifty people will be fired. Should you stick with ABC to protect American jobs? What other considerations may be involved?

11. In the mid-1970s, the Justice Department began a probe into allegations of price fixing in the folding-carton industry. The Justice Department was having difficulty establishing its case when it discovered two boxes of personal notes in the home of a retired Weyerhaeuser Company executive. In the notes, the Justice Department found details of years of illegal price-fixing agreements with officials from other companies. The material helped lead to the price-fixing convictions of twenty-three companies.

    The case made it clear that in the event of a lawsuit, nearly any corporate document can be obtained and used by the opposing party. Companies are now shredding company documents to avoid future liabilities arising from such lawsuits. Is it ethical to shred documents if the purpose is to avoid potential liability for wrongdoing?

12. According to the *Wall Street Journal* (May 2, 1990), "Seven insiders at T. Rowe Price Associates, Inc. sold 80,765 shares of the mutual fund between March 6 and 13." The price of the stock then fell 16 percent "chiefly on the company's March 30 announcement" of bad financial developments. Assuming this sale did not violate the federal restrictions on insider trading of securities, is it unethical for corporate insiders to sell stocks to avoid losses they know will be forthcoming when bad news becomes public?

Part Two

Business and the Common Law

Inherent in the common law is a dynamic principle which allows it to grow and to tailor itself to meet changing needs within the doctrine of stare decisis, which, if correctly understood, was not static and did not forever prevent the courts from reversing themselves or from applying principles of common law to new situations as the need arose. If this were not so, we must succumb to a rule of law that a judge should let others "long dead and unaware of the problems of the age in which he lives, do his thinking for him."

Justice William O. Douglas

Long before the state and federal government began regulating business through the enactment of regulatory statutes, the common law was the dominant legal force affecting business behavior and conduct. As technology and business practices have advanced over the years, the common law has changed, often in subtle ways, to adapt to those changes. Many statutes and regulatory laws passed in modern times to standardize or to regulate business practices were strongly influenced by common law principles.

This part of the book on the regulation of business and the common law begins in Chapters 7 and 9 with a discussion of the laws forming the fundamental basis for the common law as applied to business—the laws of contract and torts. Products liability law, discussed in Chapter 8, has been an area vital to business and consumers in recent years. Chapter 8 illustrates the effect of tort and contract law on business in a particular context and illustrates how the common law can change, adapt, and be influenced by society. Chapter 10 discusses the common law principles of agency. The law of agency, like the law of contracts, is basic to almost every other area of the law affecting the legal environment of business. Part II closes with Chapter 11, which provides an introduction to the basic forms of business organizations available in the United States.

233

7 Torts and the Protection of Intellectual Property

THIS chapter discusses the law of torts and how it affects the business community. It begins with a general discussion that defines the term tort, describes the various avenues through which a business may find itself involved in a tort action, and considers the costs of tort litigation. Torts classified as intentional torts are discussed, including wrongs generally designated as either intentional interference with personal rights or intentional interference with property rights. That discussion is followed by an examination of the unintentional tort of negligence, including the elements to a negligence action and the important defenses available to such an action. Strict liability in tort, often defined as liability without fault, is then discussed.

The final section of the chapter considers those torts classified as business torts, which emphasize the harms or injuries a business can inflict on another business. Here we emphasize interference with contractual relations, interference with business relations, infringement of tradename, trademark, patent, and copyright, and the appropriation of trade secrets.

The chapter closes with the Issue article: "Are We Trading Off Privacy for Worker Performance?" The authors of the article examine new methods of workplace surveillance used by employers for the purpose of enhancing worker productivity and performance including tapping telephones, monitoring workers on their computers, and even using special chairs to measure wiggling on the assumption that wigglers are not workers. The authors argue that without the permission of the workers, several of these practices may constitute an invasion of privacy.

DEFINITION AND PURPOSES OF TORT LAW

Although there are many definitions of the word *tort*, a completely satisfactory definition is somewhat elusive. The word is derived from the Latin *tortus* (twisted) and means "wrong" in French. Although the word faded from the general vocabulary in the nineteenth century, it remained in the law and has gradually acquired a technical meaning. Today a *tort* is broadly defined as a civil wrong, other than a breach of contract, for which the law provides a remedy.

Purposes of Tort Law

Many accidents and injuries occur each year that result in personal injury and property damage. To constitute a legal action in tort, however, the injury an individual or business has sustained must be the *consequence* of the wrong-doing of another. In a tort action, the injured individual or business sues the party allegedly responsible for that injury.

In contrast to the criminal law, the purpose of the law of torts is not to punish the wrongdoer. Rather, the main purposes of tort law are to provide compensation for wrongful injuries and to place the burden of compensation on the wrongdoer who, in justice, ought to bear it. In the words of the Alaska Supreme Court, "an injured party is entitled to be placed as nearly as possible in the position he would have occupied had it not been for the defendant's tort." In addition, it is hoped that payment or fear of payment of compensation for tortious conduct will deter future dangerous or injurious behavior by individuals and businesses.

Business and the Law of Torts

Broadly speaking, a business can become involved in a tort action in one of three ways: (1) an individual is harmed or injured by the actions of the business or its employees, (2) an individual is harmed or injured by a product manufactured or distributed by the business, or (3) a business is harmed or injured by the wrongful actions of another business or individual.

While employees of the business may be harmed or injured in the course of their employment, those injuries are generally covered by state workers' compensation laws and are rarely the subject of a tort action. State workers' compensation laws are specifically designed to protect workers and their families from the risks of injury, disease, and death in the workplace. Tort actions for injuries caused by the products manufactured or distributed by the business involve the law of products liability, discussed in detail in Chapter 8. The law applicable to the other ways in which a business may become involved in a tort action—where the actions of its employees injure another individual or when the business harms or injures another business—is the principal subject of this chapter.

Costs of Tort Litigation

In 1985, more than one million lawsuits involving a tort claim were initiated in our nation's court systems. Those lawsuits imposed costs of more than $27 billion dollars on the society in the form of litigants' time, attorneys' fees, court costs, and the compensation of injured parties. As Figure 7–1 illustrates, injured party compensation—the principal purpose of tort law—accounted for less than half the total cost.

The rising costs associated with tort litigation have prompted concern about the ability of our court system to effectively and efficiently compensate injured parties. That concern has been manifested in efforts by businesses,

Figure 7-1   The Costs of Tort Litigation, 1985

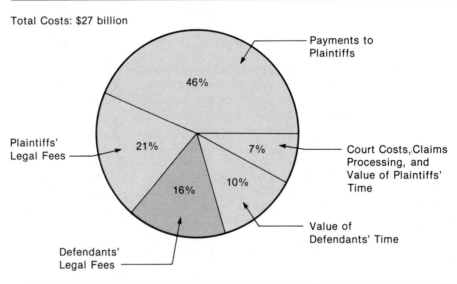

Total Costs: $27 billion

Source: Institute for Civil Justice, Rand Corporation, 1987.

insurance companies, trial attorneys, and the general public to reform tort law. Although Florida's tort reform legislation was recently held to be unconstitutional, it is clear that continuing efforts toward tort reform will be an important topic in the legal environment of business. As evidence of its growing importance, note that nearly forty states have enacted legislation to limit the size of tort judgments, despite the fact that the constitutionality of tort reform legislation remains in question. Still, as Table 7-1 illustrates, the size of the judgments in tort actions can be very large.

Few commentators are concerned about awards for *economic injuries*—loss of wages, ability to earn an income, or medical expenses. However, of increasing concern if the level of compensation being provided by juries for *noneconomic injuries*—primarily pain and suffering. The noneconomic injury category of compensation is encouraging creativity in tort damage theory. In addition to pain and suffering, for example, the category now includes compensation for such mental injuries as the "loss of enjoyment of the pursuits and pleasures of life." A Georgia court recently awarded $250,000 in specific compensation for "loss of the pleasures of life," in addition to nearly $1.5 million for economic injuries. Courts in Connecticut, Mississippi, New Mexico, and New York now allow specific recovery for loss of the pleasures of life in wrongful death and personal injury cases.

GENERAL CLASSIFICATION OF TORTS

Torts are traditionally classified on the basis of how the harm or injury was inflicted: intentionally, negligently, or without fault (strict liability). In the study of the legal environment of business, however, emphasis is placed on

Table 7–1   Largest Jury Verdicts Won by Individuals in 1989

AMOUNT	CAUSE	PLAINTIFF(S)	DEFENDANT(S)	COURT
$76,000,000	Injury from asbestos exposure as a result of factory and shipyard work	Michael Coyne and A. McCoubrey Jr. ($76 million each)	Celotex Corp.	Baltimore Circuit Court
$58,000,000	Loss of both legs after falling onto subway tracks in front of oncoming train	Sam Young Chung	New York City Transit Authority	Kings County Supreme Court, N.Y.
$54,000,000	Brain damage due to medical malpractice during routine x-ray testing	Maichi Nguyen (an infant)	County of Los Angeles	Los Angeles County Superior Court
$44,000,000	Deaths of plaintiff's husband and daughters when car exploded in a collision	Nike Adegbite	Toyota Motor Sales USA Inc.	Harris County (Texas) District Court
$31,000,000	Wrongful firing of an acountant who refused to sign what he believed were fraudulent tax returns	Roger Sims	Kaneb Services Inc.	Harris County (Texas) District Court
$30,000,000	Playground injury in which 7-year-old boy became quadriplegic	Eric Abreu	City of New York	New York County Supreme Court

Source: Lawyers Alert.

those laws most affecting business. Thus, a fourth classification may be included, called *business torts*, which emphasize the harms or injuries a business may inflict on other businesses.

INTENTIONAL TORTS

In the law, there is a tendency to attach greater blame to intentional misconduct than to lesser degrees of fault. In such circumstances, the law will impose a greater degree of responsibility upon a defendant. The rules are much more liberally applied, imposing liability on a broader range of the defendant's activities, requiring less certainty in the proof presented by the plaintiff as a basis upon which to find the defendant liable, and allowing compensation for a wider range of injuries and damages. The defendant's interests are accorded considerably less weight than are the plaintiff's claims to protection. Thus, to establish a case, the plaintiff need prove only that the defendant intentionally invaded a protected interest. *Intentional torts* are classified generally on the basis of those interests the law seeks to protect: intentional interference with personal rights and intentional interference with property rights.

Establishing Intent

Intentional torts are based on *willful misconduct* or an intentional wrong. To establish liability for an intentional tort, the injured party needs to prove only that the wrongdoer intentionally invaded a protected interest. The requirement of *intent* for tort liability is not concerned with malicious intent to do serious harm to another. Rather, there must be an intent to invade the rights or interests of another in a way that the law does not permit. Even in those instances where the wrongdoer meant to do a beneficial act for a party and that party is injured in the process, the required intent would be present for purposes of tort liability.

Interference with Personal Rights

A business will ordinarily find itself involved in a lawsuit for an intentional tort involving *interference with personal rights* through the wrongful actions of an employee. As discussed in Chapter 10, a business is liable under the *law of agency* for the torts of its workers, if the tort results from an activity carried out within the scope of the worker's employment. Intentional torts involving interference with personal rights include assault, battery, false imprisonment, defamation, intentional infliction of emotional distress, invasion of privacy, and malicious prosecution.

Assault and Battery

Assault is intentional conduct directed at a person by an individual who places that person in apprehension of immediate bodily harm or offensive contact. Actual contact with the body, however, is not necessary. For example, pointing a gun or swinging a club at another can constitute an assault. The requirement of apprehension is satisfied if a reasonable person under the same or similar circumstances would have had apprehension of immediate bodily harm or offensive contact. An essential element of this tort is that the individual in danger of harm or injury must have knowledge of the danger and be apprehensive of its imminent threat. If an individual points a gun at another while the other person is sleeping, for example, there is no assault.

Battery is an unlawful touching, a direct and intentional physical contact without consent. The contact is not limited to an actual touching of another. Rather, the contact may be made with anything that is attached to or identified with the wrongdoer. Contact through the use of a cane or a gun, for example, may constitute the required unlawful touching. Even if the touching does not cause actual physical harm, it is unlawful if it would offend a reasonable person's sense of dignity.

Although assault and battery are often associated with one another, the offenses are separate and distinct. The difference between the basic requirements of apprehension of an offensive physical contact for an assault and of actual physical contact for a battery is the principal distinction between the two torts. In addition, the two torts are separable in that one may exist without the other. An individual may strike another who is asleep, for example, thus committing battery but not assault. On the other hand, an individual may shoot at another and miss, thereby creating an assault but no battery. The *Hill* case is a classic case involving an employee of Western Union Telegraph who was accused of assaulting a customer.

Western Union Telegraph Co. v. Hill

Supreme Court of Alabama
25 Ala.App. 540, 150 So. 709 (1933)

Case Background. *Sapp, the defendant, was the agent and manager of a telegraph office belonging to the defendant, Western Union Telegraph Company. Mrs. Hill, the plaintiff, owned an electric clock whose repair was under contract with Western Union. If the clock needed repair, the plaintiff was to report that to Sapp. One evening, Mrs. Hill went to the Western Union office where Sapp worked to report that the clock needed repair. She found Sapp behind the counter, "still slightly feeling the effects of whiskey." When Mrs. Hill told Sapp that she needed her clock repaired, Sapp stated, "If you will come back here and let me love and pet you, I will fix your clock," at the same time reaching toward her across the counter.*

Sapp did not touch the plaintiff, and evidence proved that even if he had wanted to, he could not have reached across the counter because the counter was as high as his shoulders, making it impossible to reach Mrs. Hill.

Hill filed damages for assault against the Western Union Telegraph Company and was awarded damages. The defendant appealed.

Case Decision. Judge Samford delivered the opinion of the court.

* * *

The first question that addresses itself to us is, was there such an assault as will justify an action for damages?

* * *

. . . [A]n assault does not necessarily require a battery to complete it. What it does take to constitute an assault is an unlawful attempt to commit a battery, incomplete by reason of some intervening cause; or, to state it differently, to constitute an actionable assault there must be an intentional, unlawful, offer to touch the person of another in a rude or angry manner under such circumstances as to create in the mind of the party alleging the assault a well-founded fear of an imminent battery, coupled with the apparent present ability to effectuate the attempt, if not prevented.

* * *

The . . . evidence offered by plaintiff tend[s] to prove an assault . . . [A]side from the positive denial by Sapp of any effort to touch Mrs. Hill, the physical surroundings as evidenced by the photographs of the locus tend to rebut any evidence going to prove that Sapp could have touched plaintiff across the counter even if he had reached his hand in her direction unless she was leaning against the counter or Sapp should have stood upon something so as to elevate him and allow him to reach beyond the counter. However, there is testimony tending to prove that, notwithstanding the width of the counter and the height of Sapp, Sapp could have reached from six to eighteen inches beyond the desk in an effort to place his hand on Mrs. Hill. The evidence as a whole presents a question for the jury. This was the view taken by the trial judge and in the several rulings bearing on this question there is no error.

* * *

Case Holding. *There was no error by the trial judge in his application of the law to the alleged assault. The jury could find that there was an assault given the facts of the case.*

Case Questions

1. The evidence appears to support Mr. Sapp's physical inability to reach Mrs. Hill from behind the counter. However, the court still found evidence of an

assault. On what basis did the court make its determination on the assault charge?

2. Could you alter the facts in the case so that there would be no assault? For example, suppose in its concern for the cash handled by the business, Western Union required Mr. Sapp to be enclosed in a locked wire cage.

There are situations in which assault and battery are legally permitted. The law recognizes that an individual allegedly committing these torts may have a *defense* —a legally recognized justification for the defendant's actions —that relieves her of liability. Two of the most common defenses to assault and battery—and most other intentional torts—are consent and privilege.

Consent occurs when the injured party gives permission to the wrongdoer to interfere with a personal right. The consent may be either expressed or implied by words or conduct. An example of consent in a battery case includes the voluntary participation in a contact sport such as boxing or football.

A *privilege* involves a right to an immunity from liability. An individual may, for example, have a privilege to use force or the threat of force for self-defense or to evict another lawfully from her property. The force used, however, must be reasonable under the circumstances. Consider, for example, the force used to protect property in the following case.

Katko v. Briney
Supreme Court of Iowa
183 N.W.2d 657 (1971)

Case Background. *Marvin Katko, the plaintiff, and his companion, Marvin McDonough, hunted in an area in which there were a number of uninhabited homes. One such home belonged to the defendants, Edward and Bertha Briney. For about ten years, the Brineys had suffered losses of household items from this house. Break-ins occurred with some regularity. To prevent such intrusions, the Brineys had posted No Trespassing signs and had boarded up the windows and doors of the house, but to no avail. Finally, the defendants set up a "shotgun trap" in the north bedroom of the house, securing the shotgun to an old bed with the barrel of the gun pointing at the bedroom door. The shotgun's trigger was wired so that the gun would fire when the door was opened. No sign of the trap gun could be seen by a trespasser, and there was no warning of its presence posted. Upon Mrs. Briney's suggestion, Mr. Briney lowered the gun so that trespasser would be hit in the legs rather than the stomach.*

Before the date of the accident, Katko and McDonough had found on the premises several fruit jars and old bottles, which they took to add to their antique collection. On the day of the accident, they entered the house to gather more collectibles. McDonough went into the kitchen of the house, and Katko went into the north bedroom. As Katko entered, the shotgun went off, seriously wounding him in the right leg above the ankle. The injuries resulted in a forty-day hospital stay, approximately a year with the leg in a cast, pain and suffering, permanent deformity, and a shortening of the leg, plus medical costs.

Katko brought an action for damages against the defendants. The district court held for the plaintiff for both actual and punitive damages, and the defendant appealed.

Case Decision. Chief Justice Moore delivered the opinion of the court.

* * *

The primary issue presented here is whether an owner may protect personal property in an unoccupied boarded-up farm house against trespassers and thieves by a spring gun capable of inflicting death or serious injury.

We are not here concerned with a man's right to protect his home and members of his family. Defendants' home was several miles from the scene of the incident to which we refer. . . .

* * *

Plaintiff testified he knew he had no right to break and enter the house with intent to steal bottles and fruit jars therefrom. He further testified he had entered a plea of guilty to larceny in the nighttime of property of less than $20 value from a private building. He stated he had been fined $50 and costs and paroled during good behavior from a 60-day jail sentence.

* * *

The main thrust of defendants' defense in the trial court and on this appeal is that "the law permits use of a spring gun in a dwelling or warehouse for the purpose of preventing the unlawful entry of a burglar or thief."

* * *

The overwhelming weight of authority, both textbook and case law, supports the trial court's statement of the applicable principles of law.

". . . the law has always placed a higher value upon human safety than upon mere rights in property. [I]t is the accepted rule that there is no privilege to use any force calculated to cause death or serious bodily injury to repel the threat to land or chattels, unless there is also such a threat to the defendant's personal safety as to justify a self-defense. . . . [S]pring guns and other man-killing devices are not justifiable against a mere trespasser, or even a petty thief. They are privileged only against those upon whom the landowner, if he were present in person would be free to inflict injury of the same kind."

* * *

"The possessor of land may not arrange his premises intentionally so as to cause death or serious bodily harm to a trespasser. The possessor may of course take some steps to repel a trespass. If he is present he may use force to do so, but only that amount which is reasonable necessary to effect the repulse. Moreover if the trespass threatens harm to property only—even a theft of property—the possessor would not be privileged to use deadly force, he may not arrange his premises so that such force will be inflicted by mechanical means. If he does, he will be liable even to a thief who is injured by such device."

* * *

Case Holding. *The defendant acted with reckless disregard in setting the shotgun trap. The trial court's decision was affirmed. Defendant was not privileged to use the force employed here, and therefore was responsible for the battery.*

Case Questions

1. The defendants here were attempting to protect their property, which had been subject to several break-ins and thefts in the past. Is this decision fair? Would it make a difference if we told you the defendants had to sell 270 acres of farmland to pay the judgment?

2. Should a distinction be made in the law for those parties who are injured trespassing with criminal intent versus those without criminal intent?

False Imprisonment

The tort of *false imprisonment* (or false arrest) is the intentional detention of an individual within boundaries if that individual knows about the detention or is harmed by it. The required detention need not, however, be physical; verbal restraints, such as threats, may also be the basis of a successful action for false imprisonment. As with assault and battery, a wrongdoer who is able to prove the consent of the injured party or privileged action may be relieved of liability.

Until recently, a business commonly found itself involved in a false imprisonment suit with the detention of a suspected shoplifter. If the suspected shoplifter were found innocent, it was not uncommon for the individual to initiate a legal action against the business for false imprisonment. Despite the fact that shoplifters were costing stores millions of dollars each year, such legal actions deterred stores in their attempts to apprehend shoplifters. As a consequence, most states passed antishoplifting statutes, which generally provide businesses with a defense to a charge of false imprisonment for detaining a shoplifter. The merchant must, however, have a *reasonable basis* for the detention. Such a statute is the subject of the *Jacques* case.

Jacques v. Sears, Roebuck & Co.
Court of Appeals of New York
30 N.Y.2d 466, 334 N.Y.S.2d 632, 285 N.E.2d 871 (1972)

Case Background. *Section 218 of the General Business Law of New York gives retail merchants a defense in action for false arrest and imprisonment for its detention of a suspected shoplifter. The statute provides that if the suspected shoplifter were detained for a reasonable time and if there were reasonable grounds for detaining the shopper, the merchant has a complete defense to a charge of false imprisonment.*

On May 7, 1966, plaintiff Jacques entered a Sears, Roebuck store to purchase business supplies. He picked up nineteen reflectorized letters and numbers worth ten cents apiece and put them in his pants pocket. He then selected a mailbox and had two extra keys made for it. He paid for the mailbox and keys but left the store without paying for the letters, which were still in his pocket. A Sears security officer had observed plaintiff put the letters in his pocket and leave the store without paying. The security guard stopped him, told him he was under arrest, and took him back to the security office. Sears' security officers called the police, who arrived about twenty minutes after the detention began. With the security officers accompanying them, the police took plaintiff to police headquarters, booked him for larceny, and released him on bail. Later, the charge of larceny was dismissed because of lack of proof of intent.

In a subsequent action for false imprisonment, the jury found that plaintiff was detained for a reasonable time at Sears, Roebuck & Co., and that there were reasonable grounds to detain him. The plaintiff appealed, asserting that since he was not convicted of larceny, section 218 does not provide Sears with immunity from civil liability.

Case Decision. Judge Breitel delivered the opinion of the court.

* * *

The legislative history [of Section 218 of the General Business Law] indicates a purpose to protect merchants from false arrest suits even where the criminal actions are eventually dismissed. The governor's memorandum stated in part: "The sponsors of this measure urge that it will reduce such costs by helping to overcome the extreme reluctance with which merchants now attempt to interfere with or apprehend shoplifters. This reluctance is apparently caused by the vulnerability of merchants to suits for false arrest in the event of dismissal of the criminal case against a shoplifter."

Antishoplifting statutes in other states with provisions similar to section 218 have been interpreted to provide merchants with immunity from civil liability for false arrest where there were reasonable grounds for the arrest, but no criminal conviction resulted.

In this case, there was overwhelming evidence supporting the finding of reasonable detention, from the initial arrest to the arrival of the police.

* * *

It makes no difference that, subjectively, plaintiff may not have had the requisite intent to commit a crime. Thus, it is assumed, as he described it, that the letters were put in his pocket to facilitate carrying other bulky items . . . and that leaving the store without paying for them was done inadvertently. He had much more than enough cash on his person to make the small purchase. The point is that even he thought he had committed a crime, and the objective facts established as much.

* * *

Case Holding. *Where merchandise is taken from a store without payment, the store detective is not required to probe further the nature of the intent before making an arrest. Under the circumstances, the plaintiff Jacques was detained for a reasonable time and the store detective had a reasonable basis for such detention. The trial court's decision was affirmed.*

Case Questions

1. In the absence of the statute, what course of action can Sears take to protect itself from shoplifting?
2. Is this result too harsh? Does the law lack the ability to adequately distinguish between those with intent and those without?

Infliction of Emotional Distress

One of the newest torts at common law is the tort of *infliction of emotional distress*. The tort of mental distress involves intentional conduct by an individual that is so reckless or outrageous it creates severe mental or emotional distress in another. This cause of action will protect an individual from conduct that goes beyond the bounds of decency, but not from mere bad manners or rough language. Some courts at first were reluctant to find a tort without some accompanying physical injury. Most courts, however, have moved away from this requirement as methods of measuring psychological harm have developed. In addition, several courts have provided third parties with compensation based on emotional distress. A Louisiana court, for example, recently provided compensation for emotional distress to a wife who found that her comatose husband had suffered rat bites due to the negligence of the hospital in which he was being treated.

Businesspeople most often involved in emotional-distress suits are bill collectors, landlords, and insurance adjusters. Debt collection is a particularly common area if the debt collector is "overenthusiastic" in collection efforts. Badgering, late-night phone calls, profanity, threats, and name calling lay the groundwork for a potential emotional-distress suit.

In the *Floyd* v. *Eastern Airlines,* Inc. case, the court is asked to consider the application of the intentional infliction of emotional distress doctrine in a case in which a passenger airplane nearly crashed, allegedly due to the negligence of the airline. The case is interesting in that it illustrates not only the growing applications of the emotional distress tort, but also the increasing importance of international legal issues within the business community. In reaching its decision, the court was forced to consider and compare the official French wording of a treaty with its unofficial English-language counterpart.

Floyd v. Eastern Airlines
United States Court of Appeals, Eleventh Circuit
872 F.2d 1462
(1989)

Case Background. *Eastern Airlines Flight 855 left Miami en route to Nassau, the Bahamas. During the flight, one of the airplanes's three engines lost oil pressure. The crew shut down the ailing engine and headed back to Miami. Shortly thereafter, the second and third engines failed. Without power, the plane began losing altitude, and the crew told the passengers that they would have to ditch the plane in the Atlantic Ocean. Fortunately, the crew managed to restart the engine that had initially failed and to land the plane safely at Miami International Airport.*

The passengers on the flight brought suit, alleging that Eastern's maintenance personnel responsible for Flight 855 had failed to install the required oil seals or "O-rings" necessary to prevent oil leaks, that Eastern's records revealed that its aircraft had experienced a dozen prior engine failures stemming from the absence of O-rings, and that Eastern knowingly failed to institute appropriate procedures to correct the problem. The plaintiffs had suffered no physical injuries but rather sought damages for intentional infliction of emotional distress.

The governing federal law examined by the trial court was the Warsaw Convention. The Convention is an international treaty to which the United States is a party. Most of the major countries of the world adhere to the Warsaw Convention, including the Bahamas, the intended destination of Flight 855. The Convention established a presumption under Article 17 that air carriers are liable for injuries sustained by passengers as a result of the carrier's negligent conduct. The district court ruled, however, that Article 17 does not allow recovery for mental or emotional injuries and granted judgment on the pleadings in favor of Eastern. The court held that the plaintiffs had failed to state a claim upon which relief could be granted under the Convention. The plaintiffs appealed.

Case Decision. Judge Anderson delivered the opinion of the court.

* * *

The Warsaw Convention is a self-executing treaty which requires no implementing legislation by the [countries who are parties to the it]. Therefore, we must look to the terms of the Warsaw Convention itself to determine whether Eastern can be held liable to the plaintiffs for their alleged emotional injuries . . . [although] unaccompanied by physical injury.

In assessing the validity of their claim, we are required to determine the French legal meaning of the Convention's terms. The French text of the Warsaw Convention is the only official text and the one officially adopted and ratified by the U.S. Senate. . . .

The original French text of Article 17 reads as follows:

Le transporteur est responsable du dommage survenu en cas de mort, de blessure, ou de toute autre lésion corporelle subie par un voyageur lorsque l'accident qui a causé le dommage s'est produit à bord de l'aéronef au cours de toutes opérations d'embarquement et de débarquement.

The unofficial United States translation of Article 17 is as follows:

> The carrier shall be liable for damage sustained in the event of the death or wounding of a passenger or any other bodily injury suffered by a passenger, if the accident which caused the damage so sustained took place on board the aircraft or in the course of any of the operations of embarking or disembarking.

The incident here clearly occurred on board the aircraft. The district court held that the loss of power and preparation for ditching on Flight 855 was an "accident" for Article 17 purposes, and Eastern has not contested that ruling. The crucial issue, then, is whether the phrase *lésion corporelle* [—translated as "bodily injury"—] encompasses purely emotional distress. . . .

While the use of the word *corporelle* would, if read literally, appear to imply that recovery for *dommage mentale* is unavailable, we are persuaded that this literal reading is unwarranted. The literal translation of *lésion corporelle* does not fully capture its French legal meaning. While 'bodily injury' is undoubtedly a grammatically correct translation of *lésion corporelle*, it may rightly be argued that the meaning of that expression in French law and its equivalents in other civil laws are more correctly rendered by the expression 'personal injury' [which would include mental injuries].

* * *

. . . There is no counterpart in French law to our common law doctrine which distinguishes between physical injury (compensable), and purely mental or emotional injury unaccompanied by physical injury (not compensable). To the contrary, French law permits recovery for any damage whether material or moral. This includes damages such as medical expenses, funeral expenses, lost earnings, and pain and suffering. It also includes recovery for mental suffering unaccompanied by physical injury.

* * *

Case Decision. Based upon its interpretation of the French legal meaning of the text, the concurrent and subsequent legislative history, and the case law, the court concluded that the Convention provides recovery for purely emotional injuries unaccompanied by physical injury. The trial court's decision was reversed.

Case Questions

1. According to the court, what is the common-law doctrine regarding recovery for mental injuries unaccompanied by physical injury?
2. Why was the court required to consider the French translation in determining whether the Warsaw Convention provided recovery for mental injuries?

Invasion of Privacy

The tort of *invasion of privacy* is a fairly recent development in tort law and is not yet fully defined by the courts. The concept behind the tort is an individual's right to solitude and to be free from unwarranted public exposure. The tort of invasion of privacy may be committed in any of four ways:

1. The appropriation of an individual's name or picture without permission (a practice in which advertisers and marketing companies have found themselves liable).

2. The intrusion into one's solitude (illegal wiretapping, illegal searches of one's residence, and harassment through unwanted and continual telephoning).

3. The placing of an individual in a false light (for example, the publication of a story representing that an individual has certain ideas and beliefs when, in fact, he or she does not).

4. The public exposure of facts that are private in nature (such as the public disclosure of one's nonpayment of debts).

Although this is a relatively new area of the law, courts have not been reluctant to give relief to individuals who make successful claims. In fact, some states have passed statutes to recognize a right to privacy. In either case, the right to privacy is largely waived when an individual becomes a public figure, such as an entertainer, a politician, or a sports personality. In addition, the publication of information about an individual taken from public files and records does not constitute an invasion of privacy. The Issue article at the end of the chapter examines several privacy issues growing out of employer workplace surveillance activities.

Malicious Prosecution

The tort of *malicious prosecution* or wrongful use of legal proceedings consists of bringing an unsuccessful, unwarranted legal proceeding against another with malice that results in harm or injury. According to most courts, the same principle governs whether the malicious prosecution involved bringing a criminal complaint or filing and maintaining a civil suit. The plaintiff must show that the wrongdoer lacked probable cause and initiated the suit for an improper purpose and that the malicious prosecution was resolved in his or her favor.

Defamation

The tort of *defamation* is an intentional false communication that injures an individual's reputation or good name. If the defamatory communication was spoken, *slander* is the tort. If the communication was in the form of a printing, a writing, a picture, or a radio or television broadcast, the tort is *libel*. The elements of both torts involve:

1. The making of a false or defamatory statement about another individual.

2. The publication or communication of that statement in some manner to a third person.

3. Harm caused to the individual about whom the statement was made.

Some statements are considered *defamation per se*. That is, they are presumed by law to be harmful to the individual to whom they were directed and therefore require no proof of harm or injury. Statements, for example, that an individual has committed a serious crime, has had an unsavory communicable disease, or has been improper in carrying out business activities are statements considered dafamatory per se.

Defenses to Defamation Action. Truth and privilege are defenses to an action for the tort of defamation. If the statement that caused harm to an individual's reputation is in fact the truth, some states hold that truth is a complete defense regardless of the purpose or intent in publishing the statement. The defense of *truth* is a common defense to a defamation suit.

Depending on the circumstances, there are three privileges—absolute, conditional, and constitutional—that may be used as a defense to a defamation action. *Absolute privilege* is an immunity applied in those situations where public policy favors complete freedom of speech. For example, state legislators in legislative or committee sessions, participants in judicial proceedings, and state and federal government executives in the discharge of their duties have absolute immunity from liability that could result from their statements. A *conditional privilege* exempts a wrongdoer from liability only when the defamatory statement was published in good faith and with proper motives. Individuals have a conditional privilege, for example, to publish defamatory matter to protect their own legitimate interests or to reasonably defend their reputation against the defamation of another.

As discussed in Chapter 4, the First Amendment to the Constitution guarantees freedom of speech and freedom of press. This *constitutional privilege* protects members of the press who publish "opinion" material about public officials, public figures, or persons of legitimate public interest. However, this privilege is lost if, as the Supreme Court has noted, the statement is "provable as false." In addition, members of Congress are protected from tort liability for defamatory statements by the speech or debate clause of the Constitution (Article I, Section 6). The constitutional privilege for members of Congress does not, however, extend beyond the legislative forum.

Business Communications and Defamation. Letters or other communications between businesses regarding the work performance of past employees have become a major source of defamation suits. Accounting for nearly one-third of defamation suits, the typical case involves an individual who has been fired by one company and is seeking employment with another. The letter or other communication describing the work performance of the individual becomes the focus for why the individual failed to get hired. The individual then brings an action against the former employer alleging defamation. As the *Buck* case illustrates, in the event the individual proves his or her case, the jury awards can be substantial. However, even if the court agrees with the defendant, it has been estimated that it costs between $150,000 and $200,000 to defend against a defamation suit. As a consequence, several major companies have made it company policy not to provide information—good or bad—on past or current employees.

Frank B. Hall & Co., Inc. v. Buck
Court of Appeals of Texas Fourteenth District
678 S.W.2d 612 (1984)

Case Background. *Buck, the plaintiff, was an established insurance salesman. He was hired by Frank B. Hall & Company, the defendant, in 1976. In terms of commissions generated, Buck was one of the five best salespeople in the country for the company for whom he was working when Hall & Company hired him. During the next several months, Buck generated substantial commission income for Hall & Company and succeeded in bringing several major accounts to the firm. At a meeting in 1977, Lester Eckert, Hall & Company's office manager, abruptly fired Buck.*

Buck sought employment at several other insurance firms, but his efforts were fruitless. Buck then hired an investigator, Lloyd Barber, in an attempt to discover why Hall & Company had fired him. On the basis of statements made by Eckert and others to Lloyd Barber and to Charles Burton, Buck sued Hall & Company for defamation of *character. The jury found for Buck and awarded $1.9 million in damages, plus interest, attorney's fees, and court costs. Hall & Company appealed.*

Case Decision. Justice Junell delivered the opinion of the court.

* * *

Eckert, Hall & Company's office manager, had told Barber that Buck was horrible in a business sense, irrational, ruthless, and disliked by office personnel. He described Buck as a "classical sociopath," who would verbally abuse and embarrass Hall employees. Eckert said Buck had stolen files and records from [his previous company]. He called Buck "a zero," "a Jekyll and Hyde person" who was "lacking . . . in scruples." . . . Charles Burton, then president of another large insurance brokerage firm . . . testified that Buck had contacted him in the summer of 1977 to discuss employment possibilities with [his company]. When asked why he was no longer with Hall & Company, Buck told Burton that he "really (didn't) know." Because he was seriously interested in hiring Buck, Burton telephoned Eckert to find out the circumstances surrounding Buck's termination. Eckert told Burton, "Larry didn't reach his production goals." Burton, who was very familiar with Buck's exceptional record as a good producer in the insurance business, was surprised at Eckert's response. When pressed for more information, Eckert declined to comment, stating, "I can't go into it." Burton then asked if Eckert would rehire Buck, to which Eckert answered, "No."

Hall & Company urges the evidence is legally and factually insufficient to prove the statements were made and published, that the statements were invited as a matter of law, and that there is no evidence to support the jury's finding that the statement was calculated to convey that Buck was terminated for serious misconduct. The record before us belies these contentions.

Burton testified that Eckert made the statements and that because of Eckert's comments, he was not willing to extend an offer of employment to Buck. He stated, "When I talked to Mr. Eckert at Frank B. Hall agency, he led me to believe that there was something that he was unable to discuss with me" and "(t)here was something that he was unwilling to tell me about that I had to know."

Hall argues . . . there is no evidence that Burton attached any defamatory significance to Eckert's statements. We find the evidence sufficient to show that Burton reasonably understood them in a defamatory sense.

* * *

Case Holding. *When an ambiguity exists, a fact issue is presented. The court, by submission of proper fact issues, should let the jury render its verdict on whether the statements were fairly susceptible to the construction placed thereon by the plaintiff. Here, the jury found (1) Eckert made a statement calculated to convey that Buck had been terminated because of serious misconduct; (2) the statement was slanderous or libelous; (3) the statement was made with malice; (4) the statement was published; and (5) damage directly resulted from the statement. The jury also found the statements were not substantially true. The jury thus determined that these statements, which were capable of a defamatory meaning, were understood as such by Burton. The judgment of the trial court was affirmed.*

Case Questions

1. What evidentiary requirements do fired employees need to meet in establishing defamation of character?
2. How could Hall have avoided liability for defamation in this case?

Interference with Property Rights

Some wrongs do not harm individuals themselves but rather do harm or injury to their property rights or property interests. Property refers to both *real property*—land and anything attached to it—and *personal property*—an individual's possessions other than an interest in land. While a business most often finds itself involved in a tort action for the intentional interference with personal rights through its employees, both the business and its employees become involved in tort actions for interference with property rights. The tort actions that may be initiated when an individual or a business has intentionally violated the property rights of another include trespass to land, nuisance, trespass to personal property, and conversion.

Trespass to Land

The modern meaning of the tort of *trespass to land* is an unauthorized intrusion by an individual or a thing on land belonging to another. If the intruder intended to be on another's property, it is irrelevant that the intruder believed he owned the land or had permission to enter upon it. In addition, it is not necessary for the property owner to demonstrate actual injury to the property. For example, shooting across another's property with a gun may create a cause of action for the tort of trespass to land despite the fact that there is no actual damage to the property. Further, the intruder may be liable for trespass even if the entry was made for or resulted in an improvement to another's land. If, however, an individual enters the property of another to protect the property from damage or to assist someone on the property who is in danger, that is a defense against the tort of trespass to land.

The original concept of possession of land included dominion over a space "from the center of the earth to the heavens." A trespass could be committed on, beneath, or above the surface of the land. That rule is much more relaxed today. The temporary intrusion by aircraft into a property owner's airspace, for example, does not create an action in trespass so long as the aircraft are flying at reasonable altitudes.

Nuisance (Private and Public)

The common law of torts recognizes two kinds of nuisance: a private nuisance and a public nuisance. A *private nuisance* is an activity that substantially and unreasonably interferes with the use and enjoyment of the land or an interest in the land of another. The interference may be physical, such as vibration, the destruction of crops, or the throwing of objects upon the land. Or the interference may cause discomfort or poor health from water pollution, odors, smoke, excessive noise, dust, or noxious fumes. Under some circumstances, a nuisance may extend to offensive conditions on adjoining land that impair the occupants' mental tranquillity through the fear those conditions impart or simply through their offensive nature. Individuals may find, for example, that the transformation of the house next door into a house used by drug dealers is upsetting to their mental tranquillity.

In recent years, common-law nuisance actions have been useful vehicles for challenging environmental damage. In fact, nuisance actions have challenged virtually every major industrial activity that causes some form of pollution. Chapter 17 discusses in detail the importance of common-law nuisance actions on the early development of federal environmental law.

A *public nuisance* is an unreasonable interference with a right held in common by the general public. Generally, a public nuisance involves interference with the public health and welfare. For example, a hog pen located within the city limits, illegal liquor and gambling establishments, bad odors and smells, and the obstruction of a highway would be grounds for a public nuisance action.

Whether the action creates a private or a public nuisance depends upon who is affected by it. The pollution of a river by an isolated plant, for example, is a private nuisance if it interferes only with the rights of landowners living next to the plant. The suit will be brought privately by those landowners against the owners of the plant. If the pollution adversely affects the public water supply, however, it is also a public nuisance. In such circumstances, the legal representative of the community will bring the action for the people against the owners of the plant.

In addition to the common law, every state has a sizable number of statutes that define a wide variety of activities as being public nuisances. For example, certain manufacturing plants, buildings where narcotics are sold, and unhealthy multiple-family dwellings have been declared by statute to be public nuisances. In the *City of Virginia Beach* v. *Murphy* case, the court is asked to consider the constitutionality of such a statute. In its analysis, the court is required to distinguish between a public and a private nuisance.

City of Virginia Beach v. Murphy

Supreme Court of Virginia

389 S.E.2d 462 (1990)

Case Background. *Maureen Murphy (the defendant) was prosecuted for violating a Virginia Beach City noise ordinance because she permitted loud music to emanate from her restaurant located in the City of Virginia Beach (the plaintiff). The noise ordinance provided:*

(a) It shall be unlawful for any person to create, or allow to be created any unreasonably loud, disturbing and unnecessary noise in the city or any noise of such character, intensity and duration as to be detrimental to the life or health of any person or persons or to unreasonably disturb or annoy the quiet, comfort or repose of any person or persons. The following acts, among others, are declared to be loud, disturbing and unnecessary noise in violation of this section, but such enumeration shall not be deemed to be exclusive:

(1) The playing of any television set, radio, tape player, phonograph or any musical instrument in such a manner or with such volume as to annoy or disturb the quiet, comfort or repose of any person or persons.

At the conclusion of the city's case in a non-jury trial, the trial court found that noise ordinance to unconstitutional because the city "may not under its general police power undertake to make conduct which affects only one person a public nuisance." The city appealed to the state supreme court.

Case Decision. Judge Whiting delivered the opinion of the court.

* * *

If an ordinance makes criminal that conduct which is a public nuisance, it is a presumptively valid exercise of the locality's police power. On the other hand, if the prohibited conduct is merely a private nuisance, it cannot be made criminal because a municipality has no authority under its police power to punish conduct which is a private nuisance. Thus, this decision turns on whether the forbidden conduct can be classified as a public nuisance or only a private nuisance.

In an earlier previous case, we described the difference between the two concepts as follows:

> Nuisances are of two kinds—public or common nuisances, which affect people generally, and private nuisances which may be defined as anything done to the hurt of the lands . . . of another.

We have described a private nuisance as "an activity which unreasonably interferes with the use and enjoyment of another's property." In other words, a private nuisance is one which implicates or interferes with a right or interest that is unique to an individual, such as an interest in land. . . .

In a case involving a noisy business, Judge Cardozo pointed out that a public nuisance may arise in two situations:

> Public is the nuisance whereby a public right or privilege common to every person in the community is interrupted or interfered with, as by the obstruction of a public way. Public also is the nuisance committed in such place and in such manner that the aggregation of private injuries becomes so great and extensive as to constitute a public annoyance and inconvenience, and a wrong against the community, which may be properly the subject of a public prosecution.

Thus, the distinction between a public and a private nuisance does not depend solely upon the number of people who are actually affected, as the trial court held. As one jurisdiction has noted:

> If the annoyance is one that is common to the public generally, then it is a public nuisance. . . . The test is not the number of persons annoyed, but the possibility of annoyance to the public by the invasion of its rights. A public nuisance is one that injures the citizens generally who may be so circumstanced as to come within its influence.

The right not to be subjected to "unreasonably loud, disturbing and unnecessary noise," as provided in the Virginia Beach ordinance, is "common to all members of the general public," and not particular to individuals in the enjoyment of their property. In that sense, this ordinance would differ from [similar ordinances previously found to be unconstitutional such as those] attempting to control door-to-door solicitation and thus affecting only the individual property rights of householders.

* * *

Case Holding. *The decision of the trial court was reversed. The trial court erroneously concluded that the activity proscribed in the ordinance could only be a private nuisance. Therefore, the trial court erred in declaring the ordinance facially unconstitutional on that ground.*

Case Questions

1. From the court's viewpoint, how would an ordinance making unreasonable noise a criminal act differ from an ordinance making door-to-door solicitation without a permit a criminal act?
2. What was the nature of the activity undertaken by Murphy that caused the court to view it as a public rather than as a private nuisance?

Trespass to Personal Property

The intentional and wrongful interference with possession of personal property of another without consent is a *trespass to personal property*. An important element in this tort is that an individual has interfered with the right of the owner to exclusive possession and enjoyment of his or her personal property. Liability is usually limited to instances where the trespasser dispossesses the other of the property, damages the property, or deprives the owner of the use of the property for a substantial time. However, if the interference with the personal property of another is warranted, there is a complete defense to the trespass. Many states have statutes, for example, allowing innkeepers to retain the personal property of guests who have not paid their lodging bills.

Conversion

The tort of *conversion* is an intentional and unlawful control or appropriation of the personal property of another. In contrast to trespass to personal property, conversion requires that the control or appropriation so seriously interferes with the owner's right of control that it justifies payment for the property. Several factors are considered in determining whether the interference is serious to warrant a finding of conversion: the extent of dominion or control, the duration of the interference, the damage to the property, and the inconvenience and expense to the owner. As with trespass to land, mistake does not constitute a defense to conversion.

Generally, one who wrongfully acquires possession of another's personal property—as by theft, duress, or fraud—is said to have committed the tort of conversion. In most court systems, a bona fide purchaser (a good-faith purchaser who believes the seller had a right to sell the property) is liable for conversion if the property was purchased from a thief but is not liable if the property was purchased from one who acquired the property through duress or fraud. Suppose, for example, that Mobley buys a cement mixer from RMC, Inc., a masonry contractor. If Mobley believes that RMC is the owner of the mixer and has the right to sell it, Mobley is a bona fide purchaser. Later, if it is determined that RMC has committed the tort of conversion, having stolen the cement mixer from Baumer Distributing Company, Mobley has committed conversion. If RMC had wrongly obtained possession of the cement mixer from Baumer through fraud or duress, however, RMC would be liable in conversion, but Mobley, the bona fide purchaser, would not.

INTERNATIONAL PERSPECTIVES: LIBEL IN FOREIGN COURTS

INTERNATIONAL

PERSPECTIVES

In contrast to the United States, many foreign countries do not provide constitutional freedom of speech and press quarantees to the news media. The news media in the United States can communicate defamatory material about public officials and figures or individuals of legitimate public interest as long as the material is provided without actual malice. In the United Kingdom, for example, the news media is not provided with this extensive privilege. Plaintiffs need show only that the alleged defamatory statement was communicated in the United Kingdom, and that their reputation as previously held by the people of the country was damaged. To avoid liability, a defendant in the United Kingdom must then demonstrate either that the statements made were in fact true, or that they had been made in either a court of law or Parliament.

As a consequence of this important difference in the law of defamation, a growing number of U.S. communications and publishing companies are finding themselves in foreign courts defending against defamation suits.

Although the broadcasts and publications in question may have originated in the United States, and may even have been rebroadcast or distributed in the foreign country without the consent of the U.S. company, the responsible company will not be relieved of liability on that basis alone. In addition, the fact that the U.S. government may have printed a document containing the alleged defamatory material will not relieve the company of liability.

The need to defend against libel actions in foreign jurisdictions, however, is not the aspect of this problem that has U.S companies concerned. Rather their primary concern is with the growing number of libel suits being filed by individuals who are admittedly filing them outside the United States to take advantage of the more favorable laws. The majority of such cases would not likely prevail in U.S. courts. At present, *Time* magazine, NBC, and Dow Jones are facing serious libel actions in foreign jurisdictions. In each case, the plaintiff has selected the foreign court knowing that they would not prevail in the U.S. courts.

NEGLIGENCE

The tort of negligence protects individuals from harm from others' unintentional but careless conduct. As a general rule, all individuals are under a duty to conduct themselves in all their activities so as to not create an unreasonable risk of harm or injury to others. Individuals who do not exercise due care in their conduct will be liable for negligence if the following elements can be shown by the injured party:

1. The wrongdoer owed a duty to the injured party (often known as the duty of ordinary care).

2. The duty of care owed to the injured party was breached through some act or omission on the part of the wrongdoer (often this breach itself is termed *negligence*).

3. There is a causal connection between the wrongdoer's negligent conduct and the resulting harm to the injured party.

4. The injured party suffered actual harm or damage recognized as actionable by law as a result of the negligent conduct.

Broadly defined, then, *negligence* is conduct—an act or omission—by an individual that results in harm to another to whom the individual owes a duty of care. In contrast to an intentional tort, the injurious consequences of an individual's conduct are neither intended nor desired by the individual. If the individual's conduct creates an unreasonable risk of harm to others, such conduct may be termed negligent even though there was no intent by the individual to harm another. Thus, the individual who intentionally runs over another while driving a car, has committed the intentional tort of battery. However, an individual who unintentionally runs over another while driving unreasonably has committed the tort of negligence.

The Reasonable Person Test

In determining whether an individual's conduct is negligent, the law generally applies an objective standard of reasonableness. The standard is usually stated as *ordinary care* or *due care,* as measured against the conduct of a hypothetical person—the *reasonable person*. While in most jurisdictions the reasonable person standard has been developed by the courts, in some states the reasonable person standard is established by legislation.

The reasonable person represents a standard of how typical persons in the community *ought* to behave. If the individual is a skilled professional, such as a doctor, attorney, or business executive, the standard is that of a reasonably skilled, competent, and experienced person who is a qualified member of the group authorized to engage in that profession. In determining whether an individual's conduct was negligent, the question is, What would a reasonable person have done under the same or similar circumstances? If the individual's conduct was not that of a reasonable person in the eyes of the jury or the judge, the individual has failed the reasonableness test and has acted in a negligent manner.

It should be noted that this reasonableness standard or the reasonable person standard is a theoretical concept created in law. It describes an individual who acts in a reasonable manner under the given circumstances. The standard, however, is not always easy to live up to. Although the law does not require perfection, errors in judgment must be reasonable or excusable under the circumstances or negligence will be found.

Causation

The most basic element of the tort of negligence is a *causal connection* between the act or omission of an individual and another's injury. For an individual to have caused an injury to another and be held negligent, that individual's acts must have been the cause in fact and the proximate cause of the other's injury.

Cause in Fact

Cause in fact is established by evidence showing that an individual's conduct is the cause of an event because the event would not have occurred without it. Courts express this in the form of a rule commonly referred to as the *but for* or *sine qua non* rule. That is, the individual's injury would not have occurred *but for* the conduct of the wrongdoer. A hotel's failure to install a proper fire escape, for example, is not the cause in fact for the death of an individual who suffocated in bed from the smoke. The individual would have died regardless of whether the hotel had properly installed a fire escape.

Proximate Cause

The injured party must prove that the individual's act or omission was not only the cause in fact of the injury but also the proximate cause of the injury. *Proximate cause* is a judicially imposed limitation on an individual's liability for the consequences of his or her negligence: The individual's liability is limited to consequences that bear some reasonable relationship to the negligent conduct. Consequences that are too remote or too far removed from the negligent conduct will not result in liability.

Underlying this notion is the idea that the individual's act may set off a chain of events and injuries that were not *foreseeable*. The principal cause in fact of the Great Chicago Fire, for example, may have been Mrs. O'Leary's negligent conduct, but no court would hold her liable for the full consequences of her conduct. The *Palsgraf* case is considered a landmark decision for its discussion and application of the concept of proximate cause. The majority of courts have taken the view of proximate cause stated in this case.

Palsgraf v. Long Island Railroad Company

Court of Appeals of New York
248 N.Y. 339, 162 N.E. 99 (1928)

Case Background.   *The plaintiff, Helen Palsgraf, was waiting on a platform to catch a train to Rockaway Beach. As she stood there, another train stopped at the station. As the other train began leaving the station, two men ran to catch it. One man was able to get aboard without a problem, but the other man, who was carrying a package, jumped on the car but appeared to fall from the train. One of the guards on the train was holding the door open for the man. He reached forward to help the falling man, while another guard, who was standing on the platform, pushed the teetering man from behind. As the man regained his balance, the package he was holding fell from his arms onto the rails. The package contained fireworks, and when the package fell, the fireworks exploded. The shock from the explosion caused some scales that were located on the other end of the platform to fall, striking the plaintiff.*

The plaintiff sued the railroad company for the negligence of its employees during this event. The jury found in favor of the plaintiff, and the appellate division affirmed the jury's decision. The defendant appealed to the Court of Appeals of New York.

Case Decision.   Judge C.J. Cardozo delivered the opinion of the court.

* * *

Negligence is not actionable unless it involves the invasion of a legally protected interest, the violation of a right. "Proof of negligence in the air, so to speak, will not do." "Negligence is the absence of care, according to the circumstances." The plaintiff, as she stood upon the platform of the station, might claim to be protected against intentional invasion of her bodily security. Such invasion is not charged. She might claim to be protected against unintentional invasion by conduct involving in the thought of reasonable men an unreasonable hazard that such invasion would ensue. . . . If no hazard was apparent to the eye of ordinary vigilance, an act innocent and harmless, at least to outward seeming, with reference to her, did not take to itself the quality of a tort because it happened to be a wrong, though apparently not one involving the risk of bodily insecurity, with reference to someone else. "In every instance, before negligence can be predicated of a given act, back of the act must be sought and found a duty to the individual complaining, the observance of which would have averted or avoided the injury. The ideas of negligence and duty are strictly correlative." . . .

A different conclusion will involve us . . . in a maze of contradictions. A guard stumbles over a package which has been left upon a platform. It seems to be a bundle of newspapers. It turns out to be a can of dynamite. To the eye of ordinary vigilance, the bundle is abandoned waste, which may be kicked or trod on with impunity. Is a passenger at the other end of the platform protected by the law against the unsuspected hazard concealed beneath the waste? If not, is the result to be any different, so far as the distant passenger is concerned, when the guard stumbles over a valise which a truckman or a porter has left upon the walk? The passenger far away, if the victim of a wrong at all, has a cause of action, not derivative, but original and primary. His claim to be protected against invasion of his bodily security is neither greater nor less because the act resulting in the invasion is a wrong to another far removed. In this case, the rights that are said to have been violated, the interests said to have been invaded, are not even of the same order. The man was not injured in his person nor even put in danger. The purpose of the act, as well as its effect, was to make his person safe. If there was a wrong to him at all, which may very well be doubted, it was a wrong to a property, . . . which threatened injury to nothing else, there has passed, we are told, to the plaintiff by derivation or succession a right of action for the invasion of an interest of another order, the right to bodily security. The diversity of interests emphasizes the futility of the effort to build the plaintiff's right upon the basis of a wrong to someone else. The gain is one of emphasis, for a like result would follow if the interests were the same. Even then, the orbit of the danger as disclosed to the eye of reasonable vigilance would be the orbit of the duty. One who jostles one's neighbor in a crowd does not invade the rights of others standing at the outer fringe when the unintended contact casts a bomb upon the ground. The wrongdoer as to them is the man who carries the bomb, not the one who explodes it without suspicion of the danger. Life will have to be made over, and human nature transformed, before prevision so extravagant can be accepted as the norm of conduct, the customary standard to which behavior must conform.

The argument for the plaintiff is built upon the shifting meanings of such words as "wrong" and "wrongful" and shares their instability. What the plaintiff must show is a "wrong" to herself; i.e., a violation of her own right, and not merely a wrong to someone else, nor conduct "wrongful" because unsocial, but not "a wrong" to any one. . . .

The range of reasonable apprehension is at times a question for the court, and at times, if varying inferences are possible, a question for the jury. Here, by concession, there was nothing in the situation to suggest to the most cautious mind that the parcel wrapped in newspaper would spread wreckage through the station. If the guard had thrown it down knowingly and willfully, he would not have threatened the plaintiff's safety, so far as appearances could warn him. His conduct would not have involved, even then, an unreasonable probability of invasion of her bodily security. Liability can be no greater where the act is inadvertent.

Negligence, like risk, is thus a term of relation. Negligence in the abstract, apart from things related, is surely not a tort, if indeed it is understandable at all. Negligence is not a tort unless it results in the commission of a wrong, and the commission of a wrong imports the violation of a right, in this case, we are told, the right to be protected against interference with one's bodily security. But bodily security is protected, not against all forms of interference or aggression, but only against some. One who seeks redress at law does not make out a cause of action by showing without more that there has been damage to his person. If the harm was not willful, he must show that the act as to him had possibilities of danger so many and apparent as to entitle him to be protected against the doing of it though the harm was unintended.

* * *

Case Holding. *The judgments of the appellate division and of the trial term were reversed. The railroad was not negligent because the injury was not foreseeable.*

Case Questions

1. If the guard had purposefully and with intent caused the fireworks to be discharged, would this case have ended differently?

2. For the plaintiff to recover, what is the court requiring that she demonstrate?

3. Why did the plaintiff sue the railroad company? Could she have made a better case against the owner of the fireworks?

Intervening Conduct

One important problem with determining proximate cause is the difficulties posed by *intervening conduct*. If the causal connection between an individual's act and the resulting harm to another is broken by an intervening act or event, such an act or event is called a *superseding cause*. Most likely, liability will still rest with the wrongdoer if the intervening act was foreseeable or was a direct result of the wrongdoer's negligent or careless conduct. However, if the causal relationship between the defendant's act and resulting harm is in fact *broken* by the intervening act (the intervening act was unforeseeable under the circumstances), the defendant will likely not be liable in negligence. Suppose, for example, that LMN, Inc. negligently leaves a ditch intended for a utility hookup uncovered and the ditch crosses a public sidewalk. If Washburn intentionally shoves Daft into the ditch, LMN is not liable to Daft for its negligence. Washburn's conduct is a superseding cause that relieves LMN of liability.

Defenses to a Negligence Action

Although an injured party has established all the required elements of negligence, the party may nevertheless be denied compensation if the wrong-doer establishes a *valid defense*. As a general rule, any defense to an intentional tort is also available in a negligence action. In addition, several other defenses are available to defendants in negligence actions, including assumption of risk, contributory negligence, and comparative negligence.

Assumption of Risk

An injured party who has voluntarily assumed the risk of harm arising from the negligent or reckless conduct of another will generally not recover compensation for such harm. Such a voluntary decision by the injured party is called *assumption of risk* and creates a defense for the wrongdoer. The basic requirements of this defense are that the injured party knew or should have known of the risk and that he voluntarily assumed that risk. Thus, athletic participants, such as football players, are said to assume the risk of some injuries on the field. Similarly, spectators at sporting events such as baseball games assume the risk for injuries that result from the usual playing of the game and the reaction of the crowd.

Assumption of risk is an affirmative defense. It must be specifically raised by the defendant to take advantage of it. When established, assumption of risk usually bars the plaintiff from any recovery—even if the defendant was negligent.

Contributory Negligence

We have established that an individual who does not use reasonable care in the exercise of a duty to another will be liable for the injuries that result. In some situations, however, both parties will have acted in an unreasonable manner. If the wrongdoer in a negligence action can prove that the plaintiff failed to exercise due care for their own protection, in some courts the negligence of the injured party will create a *complete defense*, called *contributory negligence*. Under this defense, the injured party's conduct is found to fall below a standard reasonable for their own protection, and as a consequence, the injured party has legally contributed to the wrongdoer's negligence in bringing about the harmed caused. In effect, the injured party's own negligence has become the superseding cause of the injury. For example, in a negligence suit in which the injured party is claiming damages for injuries resulting from an automobile accident, if it can be demonstrated that the injured party was a contributing cause of the accident—she had been drinking—the wrongdoer has a complete defense to the negligence suit.

The most commonly accepted modification of the strict rule of contributory negligence is the *last clear chance doctrine*, which allows an injured party to recover from a wrongdoer, despite the injured party's contributory negligence, if the wrongdoer was the last actor under the circumstances able to avoid the injury. Suppose that a worker for DEF, Inc. was digging a ditch across a public sidewalk but had negligently failed to post warning signs. Katz, who was driving her moped along the sidewalk, saw the ditch in sufficient time to stop. However, Katz negligently pulled on the accelerator rather than the brake and ran into the ditch, injuring the worker. Because Katz had the last clear chance to stop her moped before going into the ditch, the worker's contributory negligence is excused.

Comparative Negligence

Because of the harshness of the contributory negligence and assumption of risk doctrines in creating a complete bar to recovery, an increasing number of states are substituting the doctrine of *comparative negligence*. Under comparative negligence, damages are reduced by the percentage of the injuries caused by the plaintiff's own negligence. Suppose that Eyestone runs over Glenn with his automobile. As a consequence, Glenn sustains $10,000 in injuries and sues Eyestone. If the court determines that Eyestone's negligence contributed 80 percent to Glenn's injuries and that Glenn's negligence contributed 20 percent, the court would award Glenn $8,000. Note, however, that many courts allow no recovery under comparative negligence when the injured party's degree of negligence is equal to or greater than that of the wrongdoer, that is 50 percent or more.

In the *Brooks* case, the court is asked to review a jury's determination of comparative fault. The case provides valuable insight into the factors to be considered in determining the relative faults of the parties.

**Brooks v.
City of Baton
Rouge**
**Court of Appeal of
Louisiana, First
Circuit**
558 So.2d 1177
(1990)

Case Background. *Mrs. Brooks (the plaintiff) was operating her automobile in a southerly direction on O'Neal Lane in Baton Rouge. At the same time, Mrs. Ferrara was operating her automobile in a northerly direction on O'Neal Lane. For some unknown reason the right wheels of the Brooks vehicle drifted off the roadway for approximately six inches before Mrs. Brooks instinctively oversteered her automobile to get it back onto the roadway. In the attempt to return the vehicle to the highway, Mrs. Brooks lost control, crossed the center line of the highway, and was broadsided by the Ferrara vehicle. Mrs. Brooks died as a result of this accident.*

O'Neal Lane had been recently repaved and was freshly striped. Though the paving job was contracted out on a public contract, the shoulder work was done by city employees. In constructing the shoulder at the site of the accident, a size No. 57 limestone aggregate was used. The experts agreed that a size No. 610 was the better aggregate for shoulder surfacing because of the compaction ability. On that basis, Mrs.

Brooks' estate sued the City of Baton Rouge (the defendant) for negligence in the construction of the shoulder of the highway.

Applying the comparative negligence doctrine, the trial court found Mrs. Brooks 15 percent at fault and the defendant 85 percent at fault for their respective contributions to the accident. The defendant appealed this division of fault, asserting that the negligence of Mrs. Brooks accounted for more than 15 percent of the causation of the accident.

Case Decision. Judge Lottinger delivered the opinion of the court.

* * *

[The state's] Supreme Court has indicated which factors should be considered in order to apportion fault under a system of comparative fault:

> In determining the percentages of fault, the trier of fact shall consider both the nature of the conduct of each party at fault and the extent of the causal relation between the conduct and the damages claimed. In assessing the nature of the conduct of the parties various factors may influence the degree of fault assigned, including: (1) whether the conduct resulted from inadvertence of involved an awareness of the danger, (2) how great a risk was created by the conduct, (3) the significance of what was sought by the conduct, (4) the capacities of the extenuating circumstances which might require the actor to proceed in haste without proper thought. And of course, as evidenced by concepts such as last clear chance, the relationship between the fault/negligent conduct and the harm to the plaintiff are considerations in determining the relative fault of the parties.

Mrs. Brooks committed two acts of negligence: her inattention which caused her to leave the roadway, and her improper attempt to regain the paved portion of the highway before reducing speed. She should have perceived the great risk of attempting to reenter the roadway at speed. There was no need for her to proceed in such a hasty fashion. The roadway was straight and there were no obstructions in Mrs. Brooks' path which required her to return immediately to the paved portion of the roadway. The accident occurred during the day, and thus visibility was not limited as it might have been at night. There was no evidence of any emergency situation requiring her to proceed with haste and without proper thought. She traveled the road daily and therefore was very familiar with the road. The only factor tending to lessen her percentage of fault is the fact that her conduct was described as inadvertent or instinctive.

On the other hand, the City/Parish constructed the shoulder with a No. 57 limestone aggregate rather than the normally used No. 610 resulting in a less stable shoulder. This shoulder contained a two and one half to three and one half inch drop which the trial court concluded was defective. The No. 57 limestone aggregate was used for approximately 40 feet along the shoulder.

Plaintiff argues that in *LeBlanc* v. *State* (1982), when faced with a similar instinctive reaction, the court said:

> the natural instinct of an ordinary driver, without prior warning or specific training, is to attempt to regain immediate entry onto the highway, thereby creating a risk of loss of control. Because a substantial percentage, if not a majority, of ordinary drivers encountering an unexpected four to six inch descent upon inadvertently deviating slightly from the roadway would react instinctively as Mrs. LeBlanc did, the legal duty of the Department to maintain safe highway shoulders is imposed to protect against this risk.

However, we note that in *Pitre* v. *Aetna Insurance Company* (1984), though the driver traveled 300 feet on the shoulder of the road before striking a bridge quadrail, the [state] Supreme Court said:

> Prudent behavior for a motorist who inadvertently drives off the paved roadway onto the shoulder is first to reduce speed and then to attempt a gradual reentry after he has regained control of the vehicle.

Plaintiffs would suggest that *Pitre* is distinguishable because the driver traveled on the shoulder for some distance before striking the quardrail. But, the Supreme Court said that the first thing an inadvertent driver who goes off the paved roadway is to do is reduce speed, not instinctively jerk the steering wheel to bring the vehicle back on the highway.

* * *

Case Holding. *Under the facts and circumstances of this case, the court concluded that the trial court was erroneous in finding that Mrs. Brooks was only 15 percent at fault. The trial court should have allocated to Mrs. Brooks 50 percent of the fault.*

Case Questions

1. If the jury had determined that the plaintiff's injuries had been $100,000, what was her total recovery after this appeal? What would it have been if the state recognized only contributory negligence? If the state did not recognize either contributory or comparative negligence?

2. What factors most influenced the court that the plaintiff was more at fault than the trial court had determined?

STRICT LIABILITY IN TORT

Strict liability is often defined as liability without fault. That is, there is no need to prove negligence or intent. In contrast to negligence, then, liability under the doctrine of *strict liability in tort* will be established if the following elements can be shown by the injured party:

1. There is a causal connection between the wrongdoer's conduct and the resulting harm to the injured party.

2. The injured party suffered actual harm or damage recognized as actionable by law as a result of the wrongdoer's conduct.

Abnormally Dangerous Activities

Although the use of strict liability has been expanded recently, the concept is not a new one. In an early English case, *Rylands* v. *Fletcher* (1868), the defendants were found liable for damages when water from their property broke through an abandoned coal shaft and flooded the plaintiff's active mine. At the time, the case did not fit into any of the conventional tort liability theories, since the defendant was free of negligence and did not know of the abandoned coal shaft (so there was no intentional tort). The court therefore introduced the concept of strict liability, emphasizing the abnormal or nonnatural character of the activity that caused the harm.

Today courts draw on *Rylands* and other cases and impose strict liability for harms resulting from the undertaking of extraordinarily and exceptionally dangerous or inappropriate activities. Activities such as blasting with dynamite, storing or using dangerous substances, or keeping dangerous animals have all been held to be sufficiently dangerous to justify strict liability. Thus, if Randy's Construction Company is using dynamite to blast a path for a new roadway and a bystander is injured, Randy's is strictly liable for those injuries regardless of whether it was negligent. More recently, the tort of strict liability for abnormally dangerous activities has been applied in "toxic tort" cases, those cases involving individuals injured by exposure to toxic or hazardous substances.

Products Liability

In most courts, a manufacturer is strictly liable for harm caused by its defective products. Although the manufacturer may not have been negligent or have intended to cause harm, the law nonetheless will find legal fault with the manufacturer for the production of a product that was unreasonably dangerous to the consumer and resulted in harm. Under this doctrine, the injured party must show the following:

1. The product was defective.
2. The defect created an unreasonably dangerous product.
3. The defect was the proximate cause of injury.

The rationale given for imposing strict liability on manufacturers of defective products is that negligence is often too difficult to prove, strict liability provides manufacturers with needed safety incentives, and the manufacturer rather than the consumer is in a better position to bear accident costs. A detailed discussion of strict liability in relation to product safety is discussed in Chapter Eight.

BUSINESS TORTS

Our society is based on general principles of competition and free enterprise. Its strength lies in the ability of individuals to maximize the value of their assets in the market by being able to compete in the most efficient manner. The policy of the common law has always been in favor of this notion of free competition.

Some overzealous competitors may act to the detriment of society and the market system. The concept of fair competition under the law restrains businesspeople from intentionally or carelessly injuring others involved in business. This area of the law is concerned with business torts—those torts unique to business forums. A *business tort* is defined as the wrongful interference with the business rights of another. The business tort theories discussed below include disparagement; intentional interference with contractual relations of another; interference with a business relationship; infringement of trademarks, trade names, patents, and copyrights; and theft of trade secrets.

Disparagement

Disparagement is defined as a false communication that creates injury to people in their business profession or trade. In contrast to defamation, the false and damaging statement applies to the injured party's business rather than to his or her personal reputation or character. Sometimes called trade disparagement, this tort arises when an untrue statement is published regarding the business and the statement plays a substantial part in inducing others not to deal with that business.

The disparaging statement can take many forms, including statements about a business's goods, credit, honesty, or efficiency. The disparaging statement, for example, may falsely point out that a firm's beer and liquor is watered down or that its gasoline has low octane. It may also refer to the principal asset of the business, such as a disparaging statement about a hotel or a restaurant.

In most circumstances, the business must prove it has suffered a specific monetary loss. That loss may be from a single transaction or from a general decline in customers. Like defamation, this tort is subject to the defenses of truth and privilege.

Interference with Contractual Relations

One of the more common business torts is *intentional interference with contractual relations of another*. The basis of the claim is that the injured business's contractual relations were wrongfully interfered with by another business or by someone with whom the business has done business. The elements of this tort are (1) the existence of a contractual relationship between the injured business and another party, (2) that was known to the wrongdoer, who (3) intentionally interfered with that relationship.

The fact that the wrongdoer benefited by the breaking of the contractual relationship is not enough to create a cause of action. Rather, the injured business or person must prove that the breach of the contractual relationship was induced by the actions of the wrongdoer. The use of force or coercion is actionable, for example, when it brings about an interference with a contractual relationship. In addition, persuasion exerted upon a business to induce a breach or a refusal to deal with the business unless it is willing to avoid a contractual obligation is actionable when engaged in by a competitor. The most common case, however, involves an employee-employer relationship. In that regard, consider the following case.

James S. Kemper & Company v. Cox & Associates

Supreme Court of Alabama

434 So.2d 1380 (1983)

Case Background. *Kemper, the plaintiff, is an insurance brokerage company. The company has only one office in Alabama and employed Earl Tillery in that office beginning in 1963. Tillery was Kemper's only salesman in Alabama until his resignation in 1981. He then went to work for Cox & Associates.*

In 1963 and in 1976, Tillery entered into employment contracts with Kemper. The 1976 contract included a covenant not to compete. Although Tillery had informed Cox of the covenant, Cox authorized and paid for a trip by Tillery through Alabama to call on Kemper clients for purposes of soliciting business for Cox. It was established that Cox encouraged Tillery to exploit his longstanding relations with Kemper's customers and prospective customers in order to secure their business.

Kemper brought an action against Tillery and Cox seeking injunctive relief and damages for interference with contractual relations. The trial court granted partial injunctive relief but denied damages. The defendant appealed.

Case Decision. Justice Adams delivered the opinion of the court.

* * *

Defendant Cox submits that under the law of Alabama, there is no action for interference with a contract in the absence of fraud, force of some form, or coercion. . . .

As Justice Jones indicated in Homa-Goff Interiors, Inc. v. Cowden, "generally Alabama does not recognize a cause of action for . . . interference with a contract." He went on to note, however, two important exceptions to the rule: "The first involves employer-employee relationships; and the second occurs when a party to a lease has been induced, by fraud or coercion, to breach his contract." It must be noted carefully that the requirement of fraud or coercion applies only to the second of the two exceptions. . . .

To be actionable, interference with the employer-employee relationship must be an affirmative, intentional, knowing, malicious, unjustified or unlawful interference with the contractual rights.

In the present case, there is no doubt that Cox knew of Tillery's covenant not to compete and intended that Tillery should breach it. Indeed, Cox authorized and financed a trip by Tillery to call on Kemper's customers and prospects in order to solicit their business for Cox. It is clear that the results of this solicitation, and other similar exploitation of Tillery's long-standing relations with Kemper's customers and prospects, were the losses for which Kemper has sought damages. It is only appropriate that Kemper should be awarded compensatory damages for the losses it has incurred as a result of Cox's tortious interference with Tillery's employment contract.

* * *

Case Holding. *The court held there was interference with contractual relations, and the trial court's decision to deny damages was reversed with instructions to the trial court to grant damages to the plaintiff.*

Case Questions

1. Which activity or event by Cox established the tort in this case?
2. In the absence of the tort for interference with contract relations, how would employers maintain their customer ties when employees left for jobs with other firms?

Interference with a Business Relationship

Similar to the tort of interference with contractual rights is the tort of *interference with a business relationship*. While businesses devise countless schemes to attract customers, it is a tort when a business attempts to improve its place in the market by interfering with another's business in an unreasonable and improper manner. An employee of Steve's Clothiers, for example, cannot be positioned at the entrance of Lakeside Sportswear for the purpose of diverting customers to Steve's. Most courts define such conduct as *predatory behavior.* If this type of business activity were permitted, Steve's could reap the benefits of Lakeside's advertising. If the behavior of the defendant is, however, merely competitive and not predatory in nature—for example, the defendant is so effective in advertising and marketing that customers are drawn from the allegedly injured business—the courts will not find the defendant liable. In fact, as the following case illustrates, some activity is, in the spirit of free competition, considered privileged.

Miller Chemical Company v. Tams

Supreme Court of Nebraska

211 Neb. 837, 320 N.W.2d 759 (1982)

Case Background. *Miller, the plaintiff, distributed agricultural chemicals and animal feed additives for livestock and crops. In February 1979, Tom Henderson, a Miller salesman in the company's southeast Iowa district, went to work for Lane Agri Supply in the same district. Miller feared it would lose sales in the area, so it sent out a letter offering 5 percent discounts for large orders. About one week after the letter was sent out, Miller learned that some of its customers outside the district had also received copies of the letter. Several of those customers inquired about the discount. As a consequence of having to extend the discounts, Miller lost nearly $9,000. It was later learned that Robert Tams, a former Miller employee who was now in competition with Miller, had received the letter, made copies of it, and distributed it to between ten and fifteen customers of Miller outside the southeastern Iowa district. Miller brought an action for interference with a business relation against Tams. The trial court found no interference. The plaintiff appealed.*

Case Decision. Justice White delivered the opinion of the court.

* * *

The essential elements of tortious interference with business relationships are: (1) The existence of a valid business relationship or expectancy; (2) Knowledge by the interferer of the relationship or expectancy; (3) An intentional act of interference on the part of the interferer; (4) Proof that the interference caused the harm sustained; and (5) Damage to the party whose relationship or expectancy was disrupted.

* * *

The evidence shows that Robert Tams was a competitor of Miller. During the trial Tams testified that he had received anonymously in the mail a copy of the discount letter Miller had sent to its customers in the southeast Iowa trade area. Tams stated that prior to receiving the letter he had been contacted by several Miller customers inquiring whether he had any CTC or OTC (an agricultural chemical fertilizer). At that time CTC and OTC were in short supply in the southeast Nebraska area. After receiving Miller's letter, Tams stated that he sent copies to those Miller customers in the southeast Nebraska trade area that had inquired about the short supply of CTC and OTC so that they would know why it was in such short supply. Tams circled the following portion of the letter: "All of you are probably aware of the critical short supply of chlortetracycline and oxytetracycline. EFFECTIVE IMMEDIATELY ALL Miller Chemical production of our label CTC 50, CTC 10, Oxy 10 will be TOTALLY available to customers in the previously mentioned Iowa counties and Missouri . . . AND THE 5% DISCOUNT APPLIES. However, the same stipulation on our ability to ship as of 5:00 P.M. March 7, 1979 as indicated above holds true here too. WE WILL attempt to divert our total production of CTC and Oxy to you for an UNLIMITED time (hopefully through March 30th)."

The Restatement of Torts recognizes the privilege of a competitor and provides: "(1) One is privileged purposely to cause a third person not to enter into or continue a business relation with a competitor of the actor if (a) the relation concerns a matter involved in the competition between the actor and the competitor, and (b) the actor does not employ improper means, and (c) the actor does not intend thereby to create or continue an illegal restraint of competition, and (d) the actor's purpose is at least in part to advance his interest in his competition with the other."

The Comment on subsection (1) states in part at 72: "One's privilege to engage in business and to compete with others . . . implies a privilege to induce third persons to do their business with him rather than with his competitors. In order not to hamper competition unduly, the rules . . . entitles one not only to seek to divert custom(ers) from his competitors generally but also from a particular competitor. And he may seek to do so directly by express inducement, as well as indirectly by attractive offers of his own goods or services."

Tams' actions fall within the area of privilege. The fact that he sent the letter out only to those Miller customers who contacted him about the short supply of CTC and OTC supports this position. This also indicates that his contact was not directed solely to spite or ill will. The fact that hate or desire for revenge was part of the reason is insufficient to make interference improper if the conduct is directed at least in part to advancement of his own competitive interest and social benefits arising therefrom.

* * *

Case Holding. *The judgment of the trial court was affirmed. The court concluded that the action was justified and was competitive in nature. The business relationship between Miller and its customers was strictly an "at will" relationship. There was no evidence of any contract in the record. Further, there was no evidence that any customers had ceased doing business with Miller. Miller was forced to allow the discount in the Southeast Nebraska trade area because of the competitive pressure put on it by Tams.*

Case Questions

1. Which elements of interference with business relations were lacking in this case?

2. In the absence of the privilege provided by tort law in these circumstances, could companies have advertisements that compare products?

Infringement of Trademarks, Trade Names, Patents, and Copyrights

In discussing intentional torts involving interference with property rights, recall that property is divided into real property and personal property. Trademarks, trade names, patents, and copyrights represent an important category of personal property called *intangible personal property*. Intangible personal property has no real physical existence but represents a set of legal rights and duties that are of considerable commercial value.

Intangible property is a valuable asset. Trademarks and trade names are developed to sustain demand for a firm's products. Patents and copyrights usually reflect how a firm produces its supply of products. Because intangible property is much more difficult to protect against appropriation and use by others, the law has developed to establish private property rights and to provide a cause of action against those who wrongfully and improperly infringe on those rights. *Infringement* of trademark, trade name, patent, or copyright occurs when another business or person uses one of those property interests in violation of the owner's rights. The use of a trademark or trade name of another, the use of any or all of the patent contrary to the holder of the patent, or the copying of a substantial part of copyrighted material constitutes an infringement of those protected interests. Ill intent against the holder of the original trademark, trade name, patent, or copyright is not a requirement in an infringement case. If an individual or business infringes on those rights, the owner is entitled to injunctive relief and damages.

Protection of Trademarks and Trade Names

A *trademark* is a design, logo, distinctive mark, picture, or word that a manufacturer stamps, prints, or otherwise affixes to its goods so they can be readily identified in the marketplace. Under federal law, a trademark can be registered by its owner or user if it is distinctive and unique. As long as the owner continues to use it, the exclusive use of the trademark can be perpetual.

A *trade name*, like a trademark, serves to identify the product of a particular manufacturer. Unlike a trademark, which is entitled to protection immediately upon its adoption and use, the designation of a term as a trade name must be earned through actual use over a considerable period of time. The courts will require that through its use the term has lost its primary meaning and acquired an important secondary meaning. As the *Coca-Cola* case illustrates, Coke has become a trade name for Coca-Cola. The court also discusses that its protection is not available if the trade name would perpetrate a fraud on the public.

Coca-Cola Co. v. Koke Co. of America

United States Supreme Court
254 U.S. 143, 41 S.Ct. 113, (1920)

Case Background.   *Koke Company, the defendant in this case, was imitating the soft drink Coca-Cola under the name "Koke." The plaintiff, Coca-Cola Company, sought to prevent Koke Company from infringing on its trademark, Coca-Cola. Koke Company contended that the Coca-Cola trademark was a fraudulent representation and that Coca-Cola was therefore not entitled to any relief from the courts. The district court issued a decree for Coca-Cola Company, and the court of appeals reversed. The plaintiff appealed to the Supreme Court.*

Case Decision.   Justice Holmes delivered the opinion of the Court.

* * *

[A] man is not to be protected in the use of a device the very purpose and effect of which is to swindle the public. But the defects of a plaintiff do not offer a very broad ground for allowing another to swindle him. The defense relied on here should be scrutinized with a critical eye. The main point is this: Before 1900 the beginning of the good will was more or less helped by the presence of cocaine, a drug that, like alcohol or caffeine or opium, may be described as a deadly poison or as a valuable item of the pharmacopoeia according to the rhetorical purposes in view. The amount seems to have been very small, but it may have been enough to begin a bad habit and after the Food and Drug Act, if not earlier, long before this suit was brought, it was eliminated from the plaintiff's compound. Coca leaves still are used to be sure, but after they have been subjected to a drastic process that removes from them every characteristic substance except a little tannin and still less chlorophyl. The cola nut, at best, on its side furnishes but a small portion of the caffeine, which now is the only element that has appreciable effect. That comes mainly from other sources. It is argued that the continued use of the name imports a representation that has ceased to be true and that the representation is reinforced by a picture of coca leaves and cola nuts upon the label and by advertisements, which however were many years before this suit was brought, that the drink is an "ideal nerve tonic and stimulant," etc., and that thus the very thing sought to be protected is used as a fraud.

The argument does not satisfy us. We are dealing here with a popular drink not with a medicine, and although what has been said might suggest that its attraction lay in producing the expectation of a toxic effect the facts point to a different conclusion. Since 1900 the sales have increased at a very great rate corresponding to a like increase in advertising. The name now characterizes a beverage to be had at almost any soda fountain. It means a single thing coming from a single source, and well known to the community. It hardly would be too much to say that the drink characterizes the name as much as the name the drink. In other words "Coca-Cola" probably means to most persons the plaintiff's familiar product to be had everywhere rather than a compound of particular substances. Although the fact did not appear . . ., we see no reason to doubt that, as we have said, it has acquired a secondary meaning in which perhaps the product is more emphasized than the producer but to which the producer is entitled. The coca leaves and whatever of cola nut is employed may be used to justify the continuance of the name or they may affect the flavor as the plaintiff contends, but before this suit was brought the plaintiff had advertised to the public that it must not expect and would not find cocaine, and had eliminated everything tending to suggest cocaine effects except the name and the picture of the leaves and nuts, which probably conveyed little or nothing to most who saw it. It appears to us that it would be going too far to deny the plaintiff relief against a palpable fraud because possibly here and there an ignorant person might call for the drink with the hope for incipient cocaine intoxication. The plaintiff's position must be judged by the facts as they were when the suit was begun, not by the facts of a different condition and an earlier time.

* * *

Case Holding. *The appellate court's decision denying trademark protection to Coca Cola Company for "Coca-Cola" was reversed.*

Case Questions

1. Why is it important for companies to protect trademarks?
2. Clearly the "Coke" and "Coca-Cola" names have been protected by Coca-Cola Company. Why not the term cola?
3. In the absence of property right protection for trademarks, how would a company distinguish its product?

Although the common law protects the use of trademarks, the principle protection for trademarks is the Lanham Act of 1946. To acquire the protection of the Act, the company must register the trademark on the Principal Register. Only a trademark in current use in interstate commerce may be registered. The trademark is required to be nondescriptive and uniquely distinctive. If the trademark simply describes the product or its uses, it generally cannot be registered. A hamburger shop, for example, could not trademark the name "Big Burger." The owner of the trademark has the responsibility to prevent the trademark's unauthorized use in order to maintain the trademark.

Protection of Patents

A *patent* is a grant from the government conveying and securing for an investor the exclusive right to make, use, and sell an invention for seventeen years. To be patentable, the invention, design, or process must be genuine, useful, novel, and not obvious in light of presently known technology. The owner of the patent may also profit by licensing others to use the invention on a royalty basis.

A major advantage of patent protection is that it is stronger than a copyright: It covers the idea and not merely the expression of the idea. Patent law also provides up to treble damages—and, in some circumstances, attorneys' fees—in the event of infringement. Despite these strengths, however, there are several drawbacks to patent protection. The application process is technical, expensive, and very time consuming. Usually it takes two to three years to find out if a patent will be granted. By the time the application is approved, changes in the industry may have preempted the need for patent protection on the claimant's invention. Furthermore, the public disclosure requirements may jeopardize trade secret protection. For these reasons, most commentators state that a combination of copyright and trade secrecy will continue to be the preferred protection for many businesses.

Protection of Copyrights

A *copyright* provides the copyright holder with the exclusive right to print, reprint, publish, copy, and sell books, periodicals, newspapers, dramatic and musical compositions, letters, works of art, photographs, pictorial illustrations, and motion pictures for the period of the author's life plus fifty years. The Copyright Act of 1976 governs the rights of the holder of such copyright interests. Federal protection begins automatically with the author's creation of a work and will run for the author's lifetime plus fifty years.

The law provides for the limited use of the copyrighted material for purposes of research, comment, news reporting, and teaching without permission if the use is reasonable and not harmful to the copyright owner (referred to as "fair use"). The *Sony* case considers whether videotaping television programs for home use violates the copyright laws.

Sony Corp. of America v. Universal City Studios

U.S. Supreme Court

464 U.S. 417, 104 S.Ct. 774, (1984)

Case Background. *Universal City Studios, the plaintiff, owns the copyrights on several television programs that are aired on television. Sony, the defendant, makes videotape recorders (VCRs) that allow its customers to record Universal's programs at home. Universal has asserted that such recordings are an infringement of its copyright and that Sony is liable because it sold the machines. The federal district court denied relief, finding that home use for noncommercial purposes was not a copyright infringement. The court of appeals reversed the decision. The defendant appealed to the Supreme Court.*

Case Decision. J. Stevens delivered the opinion of the court.

* * *

[U]nauthorized uses of a copyrighted work are not necessarily infringing. An unlicensed use of the copyright is not an infringement unless it conflicts with one of the specific exclusive rights conferred by the copyright statute. Moreover, the definition of exclusive rights in the Act is prefaced by the words "subject to sections 107 through 118." Those sections describe a variety of uses of copyrighted material that "are not infringements of copyright." The most pertinent in this case is section 107, the legislative endorsement of the doctrine of "fair use."

That section identifies various factors that enable a Court to apply an "equitable rule of reason" analysis to particular claims of infringement. Although not conclusive, the first factor requires that "the commercial or nonprofit character of an activity" be weighed in any fair use decision. If the Betamax were used to make copies for a commercial or profit-making purpose, such use would presumptively be unfair. The contrary presumption is appropriate here, however, because the District Court's findings plainly establish that time-shifting for private home use must be characterized as a noncommercial, nonprofit activity. Moreover, when one considers the nature of a televised copyrighted audiovisual work, and that timeshifting merely enables a viewer to see such a work which he had been invited to witness in its entirety free of charge, the fact that the entire work is reproduced, does not have its ordinary effect of militating against a finding of fair use.

This is not, however, the end of the inquiry because Congress has also directed us to consider "the effect of the use upon the potential market for or value of the copyrighted work." The purpose of the copyright is to create incentives for creative effort. Even copying for noncommercial purposes may impair the copyright holder's ability to obtain the rewards that Congress intended him to have. But a use that has no demonstrable effect upon the potential market for, or the value of, the copyrighted work need not be prohibited in order to protect the author's incentive to create. The prohibition of such noncommercial uses would merely inhibit access to ideas without any countervailing benefit.

Thus, although every commercial use of copyrighted material is presumptively an unfair exploitation of the monopoly privilege that belongs to the owner of the copyright, noncommercial uses are a different matter. A challenge to a noncommercial use of a copyrighted work requires proof either that the particular use is harmful, or that if it should become widespread, it would adversely affect the potential market for the copyrighted work. Actual present harm need not be shown; such a requirement would leave the copyright holder with no defense against predictable damage. Nor is it necessary to show with certainty that future harm will result. What is necessary is a showing by a preponderance of the evidence that some meaningful likelihood of future harm exists. If the intended use is for commercial gain, that likelihood may be presumed. But if it is for a noncommercial purpose, the likelihood must be demonstrated.

There was no need for the District Court to say much about past harm: "Plaintiffs have admitted that no actual harm to their copyrights has occurred to date."

* * *

Case Holding. *The court agreed with the district court's decision that time shifting of videotaped programs for home viewing is fair use. The court of appeals' decision was reversed.*

Case Questions

1. What is the plaintiff required to show to establish copyright infringement?
2. Was the court's decision in any way influenced by the fact that many thousands of these machines had already been sold?
3. If Universal's position had been upheld, how would it have affected the VCR market?

The procedure for obtaining copyright protection is relatively simple. As dictated by the Copyright Act, it requires the following steps. The first step involves giving notice that a copyright has been published. A developer must place a notice containing the symbol "©" or "Copyright," the year of the first publication of the work, and the name of the copyright owner in a conspicuous place.

The next step involves filing a registration form with the copyright office. Registration is not necessary to obtain statutory protection under the Act, but it is a prerequisite to filing suit alleging copyright infringement. It is necessary to register within three months of publication to obtain statutory damages, court costs, and attorneys' fees in an infringement case. Therefore, most attorneys recommend paying the ten-dollar registration fee at the outset rather than risk losing these remedies in the event of litigation.

Protection of Trade Secrets

Some formulas, processes, and other forms of information that are not patented or may not be patentable are nevertheless protected by law against appropriation by a competitor. Called *trade secrets*, they consist of any formula, process, or methods used in the production of a business's goods, or any information, such as customer lists, that provides the business with an opportunity to obtain an advantage over its competition. The word *secret* connotes both that such information is not known by the competition and that if the competition were to obtain it, the business would lose its advantage. If the trade secret is appropriated by another business either through the abuse of confidence of an employee or through predatory means such as trespass, electronic surveillance, or bribery, the courts will provide relief to the injured business by way of injunction and damages.

Generally, businesses with trade secrets protect themselves by having employees agree in their employment contracts never to divulge those secrets. Still, the classic example of a theft of a trade secret involves an employee who steals a secret and then uses it in direct competition with the former employer or sells it to a competitor for personal gain. The general requirement, however, is that the stolen information be confidential. As the following case illustrates, if the employee draws on general knowledge gained in the course of employment, the courts will not find liability under this tort if he later uses that general knowledge for personal gain.

Templeton v. Creative Loafing Tampa, Inc.
District Court of Appeal of Florida, Second District.
552 So.2d 288 (1989)

Case Background. *For eight years, Templeton was an employee of Steppin' Out-Suncoast Edition, Inc. (Steppin' Out), the owner of a publication known as* Music, *which was distributed to local restaurants, nightclubs, and music and record stores in the Tampa Bay area. The magazine was free for the taking at the establishments that carried copies of it, and the company derived its revenues solely from its advertisers, most of whom were local merchants. Templeton worked in both the editorial and advertising departments of* Music *and was the principal contact for the magazine's advertising clients. During his employment, Templeton developed a list of potential advertisers, including actual advertisers in* Music *and a larger number of merchants who fit into the class likely to advertise in the publication but who had not chosen to* *do so. The list contained the names, addresses, and contact persons of the various merchants. Templeton also kept a distribution list, which contained information regarding the order of delivery and the number of magazines to be dropped off at each location.*

Steppin' Out was purchased by Creative Loafing, which began to publish a magazine in the Tampa Bay area. Approximately two weeks after the sale, Templeton resigned and started a competing magazine called Music Pulse. *Most of the 80 to 100 advertisers in* Music Pulse *were the same merchants who had advertised in* Music, *and* Music Pulse *was distributed to many of the same establishments to which* Music *had been distributed.*

Creative Loafing sued Templeton, seeking damages and injunctive relief against Templeton for the use of Creative Loafing's trade secrets, consisting of the allegedly confidential information contained in the advertiser and distribution lists. After evidentiary hearings, the trial court granted Creative Loafing's motion for temporary injunction, finding that Creative Loafing had suffered irreparable harm as a result of Templeton's use of its trade secrets. The trial court enjoined Templeton from using the lists and from soliciting or contacting any advertisers on the advertiser list or delivering to anyone on the distribution list. Templeton appealed.

Case Decision. Judge Ryder delivered the opinion of the court.

* * *

In our view, the lists in question do not qualify as trade secrets entitled to injunctive protection. There is no evidence that they are the product of any great expense or effort, that they are distillations of larger lists, or that they include information not available from public sources.

In fact, the information on the lists is easy to obtain merely by looking at the advertisements in past issues of *Music,* in addition to many other sources, such as the weekend sections of local newspapers and the yellow pages. Templeton testified that this was the method he used to compile his own advertiser and distribution lists in a very short period of time. We do not doubt that Templeton was able to construct his own lists without reference to the lists he kept at *Music,* because there was no great secret as to the identity of likely advertisers and distributors, all of whom are members of a readily ascertainable class.

The only arguably secret information on the advertiser list was the contact person information. However, the testimony shows that Templeton knows all of these persons on a first name basis as a result of his experience working for *Music* and that he did not need a secret list to enable him to ascertain their identity. Templeton cannot be precluded from utilizing contacts and expertise gained during his former employment or even customer lists he himself developed. As for the distribution information concerning the delivery route and the number of copies to be dropped off at each location, no great amount of expertise or even common sense is needed to fathom this data, which in any event does not appear to be overly crucial. Even if completely lacking in expertise and common sense, one could nevertheless obtain the distribution information merely by following Creative Loafing's delivery truck.

Creative Loafing cites cases in which courts have held that a secret customer list or other trade secret is entitled to injunctive protection. These cases, however, are inapposite because the lists in those cases were not available from public sources, were distillations of larger lists, and great effort and expense went into their preparation.

There is no other basis upon which the trial court could have imposed its injunction against Templeton. There was no convenant not to compete between Templeton and either Creative Loafing or its predecessor. Templeton was not an owner of the selling corporation, Steppin' Out, so as to possibly entitle Creative

Loafing to injunctive relief for impairment of good will. There is no evidence Templeton engaged in disloyal acts in anticipation of future competition.

* * *

Case Holding. *Since the lists were available from public sources, were not distillations of larger lists, were not expensive to prepare, and the evidence did not demonstrate that the information on the lists was confidential or was a business or trade secret, the court reversed the trial court's decision.*

Case Questions
1. What difference, if any, would it have made to the outcome of the case if Templeton had been an owner of Steppin' Out?
2. Would the new owner have been protected if Templeton had signed an employment agreement restricting the use of the list?

SUMMARY

A tort is broadly defined to be a civil wrong, other than a breach of contract, for which the law provides a remedy. While there are many accidents and injuries each year, the requirement that an individual's harm or injury be a consequence of the wrongdoing of another is basic to any legal action in tort. The main goals of tort law are to compensate the individual or business injured as a result of another's conduct and to place the burden of compensation on those who ought to bear it. The payment or fear of compensation by a wrongdoer provides incentives that influence future behavior.

A business will find itself involved in a tort action in one of three ways: (1) an individual is harmed or injured by the actions of the business or its employees, (2) an individual is harmed or injured by a product manufactured or distributed by the business, or (3) another business is harmed or injured by the wrongful actions of the business.

As discussed here, there are four basic categories of torts: intentional torts, negligence, strict liability, and business torts. The intentional tort category includes intentional interference with personal rights (such as assault, battery, false imprisonment, defamation, infliction of emotional distress, invasion of the rights of privacy, and malicious prosecution) and intentional interference with property rights (such as trespass, conversion, and nuisance). The tort of negligence involves unintentional but careless conduct that harms others. Strict liability in tort provides that individuals undertaking dangerous activities will be liable without fault for the harm they cause to others.

A business tort is the wrongful interference with the business rights of another. Business torts include disparagement; interference with contractual relations of another; interference with a business relationship; theft of trade secrets; and infringement of trademarks, trade names, patents, and copyrights.

Are We Trading Off Privacy for Worker Performance?

Most employees have little difficulty understanding the need for an employer to supervise worker performance. Such devices as time-clocks and periodic performance assessments, while not necessarily a source of workplace enjoyment, are generally tolerated as part of the employee-employer relationship. For the most part, workers do not view such intrusions as invasions of their privacy. However, recent enhancements in electronics and communications have made it more difficult for workers to protect their privacy from intrusions by employers. In the following article, the authors examine a variety of methods used by employers to both predict and monitor worker performance. The authors assert that several employer techniques may invade worker rights to privacy.

Is Your Boss Spying on You?
Jeffrey Rothfeder, Michele Galen, and Lisa Driscoll*

"True or false:

- *I am very strongly attracted to members of my own sex.*
- *I believe in the second coming of Christ.*
- *I have no difficulty starting or holding my urine."*

It isn't information that most people volunteer. But applicants for security guard at Minneapolis-based Target Stores must answer those and 701 similar questions. Last April, Sibi Soroka passed the test and snagged a job. Afterward, though, he felt "humiliated" and "embarassed" at having to reveal "my innermost beliefs and feelings." So in a class action filed last September, he has accused Target of illegal prying.

That dispute over workplace privacy highlights what will be "the hottest employment-law topic of the 1990s," predicts Eric H. Joss, a corporate lawyer in Santa Monica, Calif. More than employees imagine, federal and state laws always have given private employers wide latitude for

prying. Bosses could rifle through desks or listen in on calls, though they may not have done so often.

But now, new snooping technology is leading to more frequent and foolproof spying. Employers are bugging and taping workers, monitoring them at their computers, even using special chairs to measure wiggling (wigglers aren't working). "The electronic sweatshop is here," says Sanford Sherizen, president of Data Security Systems Inc. in Natick, Mass., a computer-security consultant. And getting new attention. Last year, Congress outlawed the use of lie detectors at work. This year, it may go further.

No one knows exactly how much workplace spying goes on. But it's spreading, says William P. Callahan, president of United Intelligence Inc. in New York, which does everything from installing bugs to tailing workers. Some examples: General Electric Co. says it uses tiny, fish-eye lenses installed behind pinholes in walls and ceilings to watch employees suspected of crimes. Du Pont Co. says it uses hidden, long-distance

*Reprinted from the January 15, 1990 *Business Week* by special permission. © 1990 McGraw-Hill, Inc.

—continued

–continuing

cameras to monitor its loading docks around the clock. At airlines such as Delta, computers track who writes the most reservations. And Management Recruiters Inc. in Chicago says its bosses surreptitiously watch computerized schedules to see who interviews the most job candidates.

There are lots of good reasons for checking up on workers. Court cases have led to the so-called negligent hiring theory, which holds a boss liable for a worker's crimes or negligence on the job if the employer fails to screen for personality quirks or past misdeeds. "If *Encyclopaedia Britannica* sends a convicted rapist door-to-door, the company will pay mightily in court if something goes wrong," says Lawrence Z. Lorber, attorney for the American Society for Personnel Administration.

Another goal is preventing theft. Holy Cross Hospital in Silver Spring, Md., says it was trying to track disappearing narcotics in 1987 when nurses discovered by chance that the silver box with red lights hanging on their locker-room wall was a camera. Trouble was, the images it captured were broadcast over the hospital's closed-circuit TV network. Holy Cross said only the security chief should have seen them, which upset the nurses even more, since that person was a man.

Monitoring can create friction even when employees know about it. Safeway Stores Inc. in Oakland, Calif., has dashboard computers on its 782 trucks. The boxes record driving speed, oil pressure, engine RPMs, idling time, and when and how long a truck is stopped. If anything is abnormal, the driver is questioned. Safeway says this helps hold down maintenance and fuel costs; monitored drivers are more careful, knowing that the data can help build a disciplinary case. George Sveum, secretary of Teamsters Local 350 in Martinez, Calif., says Safeway tries to suspend or discharge up to 20 drivers a year using the computer data—prompting grievance filings. "If a trucker is just two minutes late, he can be brought up on charges," says Sveum.

Electronic snooping can get employers in trouble if it isn't done right. In an internal investigation last year, a high-tech company found that an executive had a checkered past and was sharing confidential marketing plans with competitors. With the manager nearing dismissal, his attorney, August Bequai, says he "did a reverse investigation to find out how they discovered the truth about my client." Bequai found that the company—he won't name it—had improperly gotten copies of the executive's credit reports, used a law-enforcement source to look at confidential arrest records, and may have tapped the executive's office phone without a warrant or his permission. Bequai got the company to let his client resign— with a settlement in the high six figures.

For the most part, a company must be sloppy to get cornered. Federal and state laws let employers intercept phone and electronic communications with a court order or the consent of at least one party to the call. They also permit monitoring of business-related conversations. In 1987, some 14,000 employers eavesdropped on the telephone conversations of close to 1.5 million workers—most of whom had no idea they were being monitored, says Representative Don Edwards (D-Calif.).

Employees can sue for invasion of privacy. But to win damages, judges have said, workers must prove that their "reasonable expectations of privacy" outweigh the company's reasons for spying. Employers can get around even this rule by informing workers of surveillance policies. Some have applicants sign privacy waivers as a condition for hiring.

And despite their loss last year on polygraphs, employers usually have fended off attempts to stiffen the rules on privacy. In 1987, the telemarketing industry helped kill a bill that would have required an audible beep when employers eavesdrop on worker phone calls. A year earlier, American Telephone & Telegraph Co. says, it helped repeal

–continued

—continuing

a similar law in West Virginia by threatening to locate a proposed credit management center elsewhere.

Still, privacy advocates have gotten new life from a recent police scandal. Last November, a special governor's committee in Connecticut found that for 15 years the state police had illegally bugged incoming and outgoing calls at its barracks—including privileged discussions between defendants and lawyers. Within weeks, unauthorized phone taping also was uncovered at police departments in Rhode Island, West Virginia, and Utah.

Now, two proposed federal laws, once considered dead, may have a better chance. Last June, Representative Ronald V. Dellums (D-Calif.) introduced a bill that would ban phone bugging without a warrant, unless all parties to the call consent. The Dellums bill also would require that voice-activated tape recorders be equipped with beep tones. The other bill, introduce by Representative William L. Clay (D-Mo.), goes further. Employers would have to notify workers with a visual or aural signal when they're being monitored with computers, cameras, or taping machines. It also would give employees access to records collected on them electronically—and bar job-performance decisions based solely on such

data. While chances of passage this year seem slim, growing public awareness of abuses "is strengthening the drive for remedial legislation," says Janlori Goldman, the American Civil Liberties Union's privacy expert.

Such measures wouldn't be foolproof. Polygraphs have been replaced with so-called honesty tests, such as the one at Target. A Target spokesperson says the test is required only for security guards, about 1,200 of its 85,000 employees, and helps assess suitability for "high stress" positions. Now, the Congressional Office of Technology Assessment is studying whether such tests can predict behavior relevant to job performance. Its findings are expected in February.

Privacy advocates aren't looking for a ban on surveillance, just better controls. But even that isn't likely soon. So workers may just have to live with the idea that bosses can learn more about them than they would tell their best friends.

Questions
1. Should employees be informed of their employer's surveillance policies?
2. Would an employer's efforts to reduce employee theft constitute invasion of pri vacy?

REVIEW AND DISCUSSION QUESTIONS

1. Define the following terms and expressions:
    tort
    false imprisonment
    emotional distress
    invasion of privacy
    defamation
    defense
    trespass
    conversion
    nuisance
    disparagement
    infringement
    trade secret

2. Compare and contrast the following concepts:
   a. Intentional tort and negligence
   b. Negligence and strict liability in tort
   c. Assault and battery
   d. Public nuisance and private nuisance

3. What is the purpose of tort law?

4. Are most accidents and injuries covered by tort law?

Case Questions

5. Mr. C. owns a hamburger stand that nets $50,000 a year. Mr. B's hamburger stand nets only $40,000 a year. Therefore, Mr. B. embarks on a campaign to discredit Mr. C.'s business. Mr. B. places signs around Mr. C.'s hamburger stand that says, "Mr. C.'s uses soybean meal in its burgers," and places an employee at Mr. C.'s entrance who encourages Mr. C.'s customers to go to Mr. B.'s for "real burgers." What torts can Mr. C. claim against Mr. B.? What difference does it make if the claim being made about soybean meal is true or not?

6. Mr. Rouse went to Russell-Vaughn Ford, Inc. to discuss trading his Falcon automobile in on a new Ford. A salesman asked Mr. Rouse for the keys to his Falcon. After negotiating with the salesman, Mr. Rouse decided not to buy the new Ford. Mr. Rouse then asked for the return of the keys to the Falcon. The salesman said that he did not know where the keys were. After a time, Mr. Rouse called the police. Shortly after the arrival of the policeman, the salesman returned the keys with the statement that Mr. Rouse was a crybaby and that he just wanted to see him cry a while. Did the salesman commit the tort of conversion? Of the keys? The car? [Russell-Vaughn Ford v. Rouse, 206 So.2d 371 (1968)]

7. The Coxes have noticed that their water is tasting like bug spray. An investigation shows that the source of their water supply is being heavily polluted by the ABC Chemical Company. Under what tort theory might the Coxes sue ABC?

8. Fisher was invited by Ampex Corporation and Defense Electronics to a one-day meeting on telemetry equipment at the Carousel. The invitation included a luncheon. The guests were asked to reply by telephone whether they could attend the luncheon, and Fisher called in his acceptance. After the morning session, the group of twenty-five or thirty guests adjourned to the Brass Ring Club for lunch. The luncheon was buffet style, and Fisher stood in line with the others. As Fisher was about to be served, he was approached by Flynn, who snatched the plate from Fisher's hand and shouted that he, a Negro, could not be served in the club. Fisher was not actually touched and did not suffer fear or apprehension of physical injury, but he did testify that he was highly embarrassed and hurt by Flynn's conduct in the presence of his associates. Has Flynn committed a tort? [Fisher v. Carrousel Motor Hotel, 424 S.W.2d 627 (1967)]

9. Fran Gabas owns a condo at Winding Lake II. Shortly after moving in, she began to experience difficulties with cold, dampness, and mildew on various interior walls. The builder's efforts to remedy the situation proved fruitless. Gabas and other occupants then stationed themselves in front of the sales office to the condo complex and proceeded to walk about carrying signs and speaking to passersby. One sign read: "Open House, See Mildew, Feel Dampness, No Extra Charge." Several prospective buyers departed from the project without visiting the sales office. No new units were sold during the time in which the occupants walked about. The company brought an action against Gabas and the other occupants who participated. What will be the action alleged, and what will be the result? [Zimmerman v. D.C.A. at Welleby (1987)]

10. For a variety of reasons, Pennzoil decided to acquire Getty Oil Company. After considerable negotiations, Pennzoil and Getty reached an agreement that was subject to approval by the Getty shareholders. Before the agreement could be signed, however, Texaco offered Getty a higher price and obtained Getty shareholder approval. Pennzoil protested and then sued Texaco. Has Texaco committed a tort? [Texaco v. Pennzoil, 729 S.W. 2nd 768 (1987)]

11. Jerry Katz was a politician. To persuade the major local newspaper to support him, Katz stated he would not raise taxes if elected. The paper supported Katz, who ultimately won the election. At his first board meeting, Katz moved to raise taxes. His actions prompted an editorial that began "Jerry Katz is a liar. He has lied to us in the past, and he will lie to us in the future." Katz brought an action against the newspaper. What will that action be, and what will be the likely result? [*Costello* v. *Capital Cities Communications* (1987)]

12. Boeing Company employed a subcontractor to make a special aircraft window. The window was uniquely described in great detail. Later, because the subcontractor failed to make timely delivery of the windows, Boeing decided not to renew the contract. The subcontractor, however, continued to make the windows for other manufacturers. Boeing then brought suit against the subcontractor. What will that action be, and what will be the likely result? [*Boeing Company* v. *Sierracin Corp.* (1987)]

Policy Questions

13. It is argued that the tort of strict liability provides businesses with incentives to make products safer. Some argue that the defense of contributory negligence is needed when strict liability is applied to provide users with similar incentives to protect themselves. Why? Would there be any greater motivation to users than the fear of personal injury? A recent study has found that since federal regulation has required the addition of seat belts, stronger bumpers, and padded dashes, the automobile accident rate has increased. Are the findings of that study consistent with your answer above?

Ethics Question

14. You run a supermarket. An employee mopped one of the aisles in the store and placed signs at the ends of the aisles to warn people not to use the aisle until the floor dried. One customer walked around the sign, slipped, fell, and suffered serious injuries. Her lawyer comes to you with the following story. He says that he is going to sue the store for negligence that led to her injuries. However, he says that he doubts that he can win, because case law in the state makes it clear that the sign is considered a reasonable warning so that contributory negligence by the customer would eliminate liability of the store. This means that she will get nothing. The worst part is that she has no insurance, has incurred large hospital bills, cannot work for several months, and has no source of support. He makes the following deal. He will forgo any fee for the case and will sue only for an amount equal to the costs incurred and the wages lost if you will agree to testify that there was no sign in place to warn that the floor was wet. The payment will be made by the insurance company. This will not affect your position with the company and you will save attorneys' fees. Should you make such a deal? What if you knew that the law in most states would provide an award because their law held that warning signs were not sufficient and a complete physical barrier had to be in place?

8 Common Law Consumer Protection: Products Liability

THE legal rights of consumers who are injured as the result of some defect in the construction, design, or labeling of a product is the topic of this chapter. Over the past fifty years, the common-law treatment of consumer product safety has changed dramatically from liability rules that strongly favored the manufacturer to rules that now favor the consumer. With consumer products causing or contributing to thousands of injuries and deaths every year, and with the legal expenses associated with those injuries and deaths increasing rapidly, products liability law has become an important component of the legal environment of business.

The chapter begins with a discussion of early common-law liability rules as applied to unsafe products. Initially, in an effort to stimulate the industrialization of the U.S. economy, the courts favored the manufacturer by placing the burden for product-related injuries on consumers, users, and bystanders. As society evolved to an industrialized, mass-production economy with a strong consumer orientation, the courts relaxed the early products liability rules. The chapter traces that evolution in liability rules, discussing both the procedures and rationale for the courts' application of negligence standards in the early twentieth century and then the application of strict liability doctrines in the 1960s.

Since producer liability grew out of contract law before it moved into tort law, liability was tied to contract notions such as implied or express warranty. While those concepts still exist, most products liability suits are now tried on the basis of strict liability, which holds producers responsible for damages caused by defects in products. Few defenses are allowed in such cases.

In recent years, liability suits based on the ideas of defects in the way a product is designed, failure to warn consumers sufficiently of the dangers associated with products, and latent hazards in products that were often not known when they were first marketed have caused an increase in litigation.

Business interests have responded by going to the federal and state legislatures seeking statutory relief from a legal standard they claim is reducing the competitiveness of American industry.

THE NEGLIGENCE STANDARD

In the nineteenth century, the courts adopted the rule that a manufacturer was not liable for injuries caused by defects in its products unless the manufacturer had a contractual relationship with the person injured by the product. That is, the manufacturer was not liable for product-related injuries unless the injured party had privity of contract with the manufacturer. The term *privity of contract* refers to the relationship that exists between two contracting parties. It was essential to the maintenance of a legal action involving a contract that privity existed between the plaintiff and defendant. Since consumers rarely purchased directly from—and thus were not in privity with—manufacturers, producers were effectively isolated from liability for product-related injuries.

Privity and Negligence

Although the privity requirement in early products liability law had its origin in the common law of contracts, it also prevented injured parties from recovering under the traditional tort theory of negligence. Recall from the discussion in Chapter 7, that to be successful in a negligence action the injured party has to demonstrate, among other things, that the defendant owed a legal duty. In a product-related injury case, the injured party would contend that the manufacturer has a duty to provide reasonably safe products.

When applied to a negligence action, the privity requirement between the consumer and the manufacturer directly affected the existence of that legal duty. If no privity was found to exist, the courts held that no legal duty existed between the manufacturer and the consumer. Thus, the manufacturer could not be found negligent in the construction or design of its product in cases brought by an injured consumer who lacked privity.

Rule of Caveat Emptor
Parties who were injured by a defective product, and did not have privity of contract with the manufacturer, were forced to operate under the rule of *caveat emptor*, which means "let the buyer beware." According to the Supreme Court, the rule of caveat emptor "requires that the buyer examine, judge, and test [the product] for himself." Thus, consumers without privity took the risk that a product was of adequate quality and condition to meet their needs. In the event the product did not meet safety expectations and an injury resulted, the financial burdens caused by that injury were the responsibility of the consumer.

Demise of the Privity Rule
In justifying the application of the privity rule, the courts reasoned that it would place too heavy a burden on manufacturers to hold them responsible to thousands of consumers located all over, and whose identity they did not know. The rule raised concerns, however, because it often left injured consum-

ers without redress. In response to the harsh result a rigid application of the rule would frequently impose, the courts began to recognize several exceptions so that consumers could be provided with redress in many more cases. Finally in 1916, in the famous case of *MacPherson* v. *Buick Motor Company*, New York's high court struck down the privity rule and its various exceptions, and held manufacturers liable for negligence for product-related injuries.

MacPherson v. Buick Motor Company

Court of Appeals of New York
217 N.Y. 382,
111 N.E. 1050
(1916)

Case Background. *Buick Motor Company produced cars and sold them to retail dealers. MacPherson bought a new Buick from a dealer in New York. The wheels on MacPherson's Buick were made by another company for Buick. Not long after MacPherson bought the car, one of the wheels suddenly collapsed, causing an accident that injured MacPherson.*

MacPherson's suit against Buick traditionally would have been barred because of lack of privity. Buick sold the car to the dealer, who in turn sold it to MacPherson. The dealer had privity with MacPherson but was not responsible for the defect. The trial court and the appellate division ruled for MacPherson, finding Buick liable in tort for injuries caused by the defect. Buick appealed to the highest court in New York.

Case Decision. Justice Cardozo delivered the opinion of the court.

* * *

One of the wheels was made of defective wood, and its spokes crumbled into fragments. The wheel was not made by Buick; it was bought from another manufacturer. There is evidence, however, that its defects could have been discovered by reasonable inspection, and that inspection was omitted. There is no claim that Buick knew of the defect and willfully concealed it. . . . The charge is one, not of fraud, but of negligence. The question to be determined is whether Buick owed a duty of care and vigilance to anyone but the immediate purchaser.

* * *

If the nature of a thing is such that it is reasonably certain to place life and limb in peril when negligently made, it is then a thing of danger. Its nature gives warning of the consequences to be expected. If to the element of danger there is added knowledge that the thing will be used by persons other than the purchaser, and used without new tests, then, irrespective of contract, the manufacturer of this thing of danger is under a duty to make it carefully. That is as far as we are required to go for the decision of this case. There must be knowledge of a danger, not merely possible, but probable. It is possible to use almost anything in a way that will make it dangerous if defective. That is not enough to charge the manufacturer with a duty independent of his contract. Whether a given thing is dangerous may be sometimes a question for the court and sometimes a question for the jury. There must also be knowledge that in the usual course of events the danger will be shared by others than the buyer. Such knowledge may often be inferred from the nature of the transaction. But it is possible that even the knowledge of the danger and of the use will not always be enough. The proximity or remoteness of the relation is a factor to be considered. We are dealing now with the liability of the manufacturer of the finished product, who puts it on the market to be used without inspection by his customers. If he is negligent, where danger is to be foreseen, a liability will follow.

* * *

We think Buick was not absolved from a duty of inspection because it bought the wheels from a reputable manufacturer. It was not merely a dealer in automobiles. It was responsible for the finished product. It was not at liberty to put the finished product on the market without subjecting the component parts to ordinary and simple tests. Under the charge of the trial judge nothing more was required of it. The obligation to inspect must vary with the nature of the thing to be inspected. The more probable the danger the greater the need of caution.

* * *

Case Holding. *The court of appeals affirmed the lower court, allowing MacPherson to sue Buick under the newly established rule of liability in tort for negligence.*

Case Questions

1. Buick argued that it should not be liable because it did not make the wheels—some other company did. Why not make the injured party sue the producer of the defective part?

2. Buick argued that this was the only wheel out of 60,000 sold that had been shown defective. Should 1/60,000 be sufficient to establish negligence?

Negligence in Tort

By eliminating the requirement of a contractual relationship between the manufacturer and the consumer, manufacturers are held to assume a responsibility for product safety to consumers by fact of a sale. Manufacturers must, therefore, produce products using proper care to eliminate foreseeable harm, or they risk being found negligent if a consumer is injured by a defective product. The rule originating with *MacPherson*, and eventually adopted by the courts in every state, provided that:

> The manufacturer of a product is liable in the production and sale of a product for negligence, if the product may reasonably be expected to inflict harm on the user if the product is defective.

The Negligence Standard

When liability is based on negligence, a manufacturer is required to exercise *reasonable care*, under the circumstances, in the production of its product. As the court determines them, the circumstances are influenced by the probability of a defect, magnitude of the possible harm, cost of effective inspection, and customs of the business. Liability may be imposed on the manufacturer for negligence in the preparation of the product: for failing to inspect or test the materials, for below normal quality workmanship, or for failing to discover possible defects. Defects and dangers must be revealed, even if the manufacturer becomes aware of them only after the sale of the product to the consumer. Reasonable care must also be taken by the manufacturer in presenting the product to the public—through advertisements or other promotions—to avoid misrepresentation. If a causal connection can be established between the failure of the manufacturer to exercise reasonable care in any of these areas and an injury suffered by a consumer, liability for damages will be imposed on the manufacturer by the court.

Current Applications of Negligence

For nearly fifty years after *MacPherson*, negligence was the universal law of products liability. Beginning in the early 1960s, however, the courts began to apply a strict liability doctrine to manufactured products and that doctrine has gradually become the common method for holding manufacturers liable for product-related injuries. Despite the current predominance of strict liability, there are still several types of product-related injuries that are brought under a theory of negligence.

One important area in which the theory of negligence is applied by the courts is where the crashworthiness of an automobile is called into question. Of particular concern are those instances in which the occupants of an automobile suffer injuries by coming into contact with various automobile parts after a crash. That is, car producers are not responsible for driver carelessness that produces an accident, but are held to a negligence standard for the injuries suffered by car occupants when their bodies are thrown around inside the car due to the crash. To avoid being held negligent in the design and construction of their products, automobile manufacturers must design automobiles to prevent *foreseeable dangers* to occupants in the event of a crash. *Mickle* v. *Blackmon* concerns the application of negligence in cases involving injuries to the occupants of an automobile involved in a crash.

Mickle v. Blackmon

Supreme Court of South Carolina
252 S.C. 202,
166 S.E.2d 173
(1969)

Case Background. *In 1962, seventeen-year-old Janet Mickle was a passenger in a 1949 Ford that was involved in a collision with a car driven by Larry Blackmon. Mickle was thrown against the gearshift lever on the steering column. The knob on the lever shattered, and she was impaled on the lever, suffered spinal damage, and was left paralyzed. She sued Blackmon for causing the accident and Ford for producing a defective gearshift knob that would shatter in such an accident.*

The jury awarded Mickle $312,000. The state appellate court upheld the award, but only against Blackmon. The verdict against Ford was set aside. Since Blackmon could not pay the judgment, Mickle appealed the verdict with respect to Ford.

Case Decision. Judge Brailsford delivered the opinion of the court.

* * *

There is scant authority on the specific issue which Ford tenders, i.e., whether the manufacturer of an automobile owes a duty in the design and composition of his product to avoid creating unreasonable risks of injury to passengers in a collision of the automobile with another object. Stated differently, does the manufacturer owe a duty of care to reasonably minimize the risk of death or serious injury to collision victims who, quite predictably, will upon impact be forcefully thrown against the interior of the car or outside of it?

Whether Ford owed such a duty is a question of the law. If not, Mickle has no case against Ford. If so, whether Ford breached this duty to Mickle's injury is a question of fact, unless, of course, the evidence is susceptible of only one reasonable inference.

It is a matter of common knowledge that a high incidence of injury-producing motor vehicle collisions is a dread concomitant of travel upon our streets and highways, and that a significant proportion of all automobiles produced are involved in such smashups at some time during their use. Thus, an automobile manufacturer knows with certainty that many users of his product will be involved in collisions, and that the incidence and extent of injury to them will frequently be determined by the placement, design and construction of such interior components as shafts, levers, knobs, handles and others. By ordinary negligence standards, a known risk of harm raises a duty of commensurate care. We perceive no reason in logic or law why an automobile manufacturer should be exempt from this duty.

* * *

Having resolved the legal question of Ford's duty to exercise care in plaintiff's favor, we now examine the sufficiency of the evidence to support the jury's factual finding that there was a breach of that duty. Of course, the evidence and all inferences to be drawn therefrom must be viewed in the light most favorable to plaintiff. . . .

It is implicit in the verdict that the gearshift lever presented an unreasonable risk of injury if not adequately guarded. At the time of Mickle's injury the knob on the car continued to serve its functional purpose as a handhold, but it had become useless as a protective guard. It is inferable that the condition of the knob did not arise from ordinary wear and tear, but from an inherent weakness in the material of which Ford was aware when the selection was made. In the light of the insidious effect on this material of exposure to sunlight in the normal use of an automobile, it could reasonably be concluded that Ford should have foreseen that many thousands of the one million vehicles produced by it in 1949 would, in the course of time, be operated millions of miles with gearshift lever balls which, while yet serving adequately as handholds, would furnish no protection to an occupant who might be thrown against the gearshift lever. The jury could reasonably conclude that Ford's conduct, in manufacturing a needed safety device of a material which could not tolerate a frequently encountered aspect of the environment in which it would be employed, exposed many users of its product to unreasonably great risk of harm.

* * *

Case Holding.   *The Supreme Court of South Carolina reversed the decision of the trial judge to set aside the verdict against Ford. The high court held that Ford was liable for injuries suffered by Mickle because the jury could find construction of the gear knob to be negligent.*

Case Questions

1. Blackmon caused the accident, not Ford, so why should Ford be held responsible for damages? (Actually Blackmon was held responsible, too, but he did not have $312,000 to pay Mickle.)

2. Would it be a good defense for Ford to note that in 1949, when the car was made, plastics were not of the higher quality they had reached by 1962, so that it is not surprising the knob shattered on impact after thirteen years of use in the car?

Negligence in the crashworthiness of automobiles is a major source of litigation. Most recently, there has been considerable litigation regarding the crashworthiness of rear-seat seatbelts. As of 1990, about 1,000 lawsuits per year were being filed against automakers on the theory of liability for injuries made worse in accidents because backseat occupants had only been provided lap-belts instead of lap-and-shoulder belts. Lap-belts were standard backseat equipment before the government made three-point belts mandatory in December 1989. Because juries have found that the serious injuries suffered could have been reduced had lap-and-shoulder belts been provided, damage awards up to $6 million per accident have been imposed on automakers.

A negligence standard has also been imposed in those instances where a manufacturer has failed to warn of dangers involved in the use of its product. Manufacturers are required to warn users of any *foreseeable dangers* that could arise in the use, handling, or storage of a product. The fact that a manufacturer has not considered a possible danger associated with the product will not relieve it of liability for failure to warn of such danger. If that dangerous event should arise, cause an injury to a consumer, and be determined to have been a foreseeable event, the courts will hold the manufacturer liable for the injury. Note, however, that failure-to-warn cases are increasingly subject to a rule of strict liability. Failure-to-warn cases and recent applications of strict liability are discussed in detail in the next section.

STRICT LIABILITY

Through the 1950s and early 1960s, there was increasing frustration with the rule of negligence in tort as it was applied in product-related injury cases. In particular, consumers were concerned with the difficulties in establishing that a manufacturer had not exercised reasonable care in the production of its product. The strict liability doctrine, however, requires manufacturers to pay compensation to consumers injured by defective products even though the manufacturer exercised all reasonable care. Thus, under a rule of *strict liability*, the injured party is not required to attack the conduct of the manufacturer, but rather is required to attack the product. To be successful, an injured party must show the following:

1. The product was defective.
2. The defect created an unreasonably dangerous product.
3. The defect was the proximate cause of injury.

Through the late 1950s and early 1960s, a variety of policy justifications advocating the imposition of strict liability in product-related injuries were presented to the courts. According to Professor Keeton, the justifications that proved convincing to the state courts, as they moved to adopt strict liability, included the following:

1. The costs of damaging events due to defectively dangerous products can best be borne by the enterprises who make and sell these products. Those . . . in the manufacturing enterprises have the capacity to distribute the losses of the few among the many who purchase the products. . . . The manufacturer can shift the costs of accidents to purchasers . . . by charging higher prices for . . . the products.
2. The cause of accident prevention can be promoted by the adoption of strict liability and elimination of the necessity for proving fault on the part of the manufacturer.
3. [E]ven if fault . . . were regarded as the primary justification for the imposition of liability on a manufacturer . . . , it is often present but

difficult to prove, and ... in the sale of a defective product should no longer be required.

Strict Liability Under Contract Law

Strict liability was first applied to product-related injuries through a warranty theory under contract law. Later, the adoption of strict liability in tort by the American Law Institute brought about a modification of the authoritative *Second Restatement of Torts* and spurred the adoption of strict liability in tort in product-related injury cases throughout the country.

Strict liability under contract law is based on the relationship between the injured party and the manufacturer because of the existence of a warranty. The concept of *warranty* is based upon the manufacturer's assurance to the consumer that the product will meet certain quality and performance standards.

A warranty may be either express or implied. An *implied warranty* is one that the law derives by implication or inference from the nature of the transaction between the parties. A manufacturer can create an *express warranty* by either oral or written representations about the quality, condition, description, or performance of the product. Strict liability under contract for product-related injuries can be based on either an express or an implied warranty.

Strict Liability Based on Implied Warranty

The first major application of the doctrine of strict liability was in the area of food and drink. In a 1913 case from Washington State, *Mazetti* v. *Armour*, the court disregarded the privity of contract requirement and held that a manufacturer of food implies the food's safety for human consumption through the act of selling it to the general public. There is an *implied warranty of safety* governing the quality of food and drink products. A consumer injury caused by a defective food or drink product constitutes a breach of that warranty, and the manufacturer is strictly liable for the injury. By the mid-1950s, the majority of courts were imposing strict liability based on an implied warranty of safety in defective food and drink cases.

In 1960, the Supreme Court of New Jersey extended an implied warranty of safety to a vast array of consumer products. In the case *Henningsen* v. *Bloomfield Motors, Inc.*, the New Jersey court held both the manufacturer of an automobile and the dealer who sold it strictly liable to the purchaser's wife (who was driving the car when the accident occurred) for her injuries on the basis of an implied warranty of safety. This was the first major decision to expand the implied warranty theory beyond its application in food and drink cases.

The *Henningsen* case had a dramatic impact on the liability rules to be applied to product injury cases. According to Professor Keeton:

> What followed [the *Henningsen* case] was the most rapid and altogether spectacular overturn of an established rule in the entire history of the law of torts. There was a deluge of cases in other jurisdictions following the lead of New Jersey, and finding an implied warranty of safety as to a wide assortment of products [e.g., tires, airplane, power golf cart, water heater, and an insecticide]. It [was] clear that the "citadel of privity" [had] fallen.

In addition to the implied warranties of safety under the common law, the Uniform Commercial Code (UCC) creates statutory implied warranties governing product quality and performance. Under Section 2–314, the UCC provides that if the seller of a product is a merchant under the Code—defined as an individual who deals in those kinds of products he or she has sold to the consumer—the products are statutorily warranted as *merchantable*. A product is considered merchantable if it is fit for the purpose for which it is being sold. In addition, Section 2–315 of the UCC provides that in those instances in which the seller knows the purpose to which the buyer intends to put the product, and the buyer relies on the seller's expertise to supply a suitable product, there is an implied warranty that the goods will be fit for that particular purpose.

Strict Liability Based on Express Warranty

Strict liability under contract law is also applied in cases in which a manufacturer makes an *express representation* about its product to consumers. A manufacturer, for example, could place an advertisement in a newspaper that promotes certain quality or performance characteristics about its product. To the extent the representation becomes a part of the basis for the bargain between the manufacturer and a consumer, the manufacturer is held to have a duty of performance as to that representation.

Strict liability based on express warranty does not require that injured consumers have purchased the product directly from the manufacturer from who they are seeking compensation. As the court's decision in *Baxter* v. *Ford Motor Company* illustrates, the courts often disregard privity of contract as a prerequisite to recovery where the consumer has purchased the product from someone other than the manufacturer. Injured consumers are not required to prove fault because the courts obligate the manufacturer to guarantee the truthfulness of its representations.

Baxter v. Ford Motor Company
Supreme Court of Washington
168 Wash. 456,
12 P.2d 409
(1932)

Case Background. *Baxter purchased a new Model A Ford sedan from a Washington State Ford dealer in May 1930. Printed material from Ford, distributed by the dealer, stated that the windshield in the car was "Triple Shatter-Proof Glass." This innovation was advertised by Ford as a safety feature, because the windshield "will not fly or shatter under the hardest impact . . . it eliminates the dangers of flying glass." In October 1930, Baxter was driving the car through Snoqualmie Pass. A pebble from a passing car hit the windshield, causing a small piece of glass to fly into Baxter's left eye, leaving it permanently damaged.*

Baxter sued Ford because the windshield was not shatter-proof glass. The trial court did not allow the advertising by Ford to be admitted in evidence and entered judgment for Ford. Baxter appealed.

Case Decision. Justice Herman delivered the opinion of the court.

* * *

Ford Motor Company contends that there can be no implied or express warranty without privity of contract, and warranties as to personal property do not attach themselves to, and run with, the article sold.

* * *

In the case at bar the automobile was represented by the manufacturer as having a windshield of nonshatterable glass "so made that it will not fly or shatter under the hardest impact." An ordinary person would be unable to discover by the usual and customary examination of the automobile whether glass which would not fly or shatter was used in the windshield. In that respect the purchaser was in a position similar to that of the consumer of a wrongly labeled drug, who has bought the same from a retailer, and who has relied upon the manufacturer's representation that the label correctly set forth the contents of the container. For many years it has been held that, under such circumstances, the manufacturer is liable to the consumer, even though the consumer purchased from a third person the commodity causing the damage. . . . The rule in such cases does not rest upon contractual obligations, but rather on the principle that the original act of delivering an article is wrong, when, because of the lack of those qualities which the manufacturer represented it as having, the absence of which could not be readily detected by the consumer, the article is not safe for the purposes for which the consumer would ordinarily use it.

* * *

Since the rule of caveat emptor was first formulated, vast changes have taken place in the economic structures of the English speaking peoples. Methods of doing business have undergone a great transition. Radio, billboards, and the products of the printing press have become the means of creating a large part of the demand that causes goods to depart from factories to the ultimate consumer. It would be unjust to recognize a rule that would permit manufacturers of goods to create a demand for their products by representing that they possess qualities which they, in fact, do not possess, and then, because there is no privity of contract existing between the consumer and the manufacturer, deny the consumer the right to recover if damages result from the absence of those qualities, when such absence is not readily noticeable.

* * *

The nature of nonshatterable glass is such that the falsity of the representations with reference to the glass would not be readily detected by a person of ordinary experience and reasonable prudence. Baxter, under the circumstances shown in this case, had the right to rely upon the representations made by Ford Motor Company relative to qualities possessed by its products, even though there was no privity of contract between Baxter and Ford Motor Company.

* * *

Case Holding. *The Supreme Court of Washington reversed the lower court. The catalogues and printed matter furnished by Ford Motor Company for distribution and assistance in sales were improperly excluded from evidence, because they set forth representations by the manufacturer that the windshield of the car that Baxter bought contained Triplex nonshatterable glass that would not shatter.*

Case Questions

1. Ford claims there was no contractual right upon which Baxter could base his claim, because the purchase documents said nothing about shatterproof glass. Does that argument have merit? Do you think Baxter would have bought the car anyway if he had known that it did not have shatterproof glass?

2. Suppose a passenger riding in Baxter's car was the one injured by the flying glass. Would the passenger have had a claim against Ford on the basis of express warranty in contract?

Strict liability based on express warranty was the basis for a $400,000 judgment awarded to the spouse of a deceased cigarette smoker in *Cipollone* v. *Liggett Group, Inc.* (1986). The jury found that the cigarette manufacturer had run advertisements during the 1940s and 1950s in which it represented its tobacco products as being "good for you." It was during that time period that the deceased had become addicted to cigarettes. Since 1966, however, health warning labels have been placed on cigarette packages. Thus, it is unlikely that strict liability based on express warranty would extend to smokers claiming adverse health effects who became addicted to cigarettes since the introduction of those health warnings.

As in the case of implied warranties, the UCC also creates express warranties. Section 2–313 provides that if the seller makes promises or statements about the product that become part of the basis of the bargain for sale between the seller and buyer an express warranty is created by those promises or statements. As under the common law, the UCC provides that the seller need not use the words "warranty" or "guarantee" for an express warranty to be created.

Strict Liability in Tort

In their efforts to impose strict liability under contract law, the courts were often faced with the difficulty of determining what constituted a warranty. In addition, the courts were frequently stymied by the express limits on liability manufacturers wrote in their warranties. In response to these and other difficulties, the courts supplemented strict liability under contract law with a rule of *strict liability in tort*. The Supreme Court of California was the first court to impose a strict liability in tort rule in a product injury case with its 1963 decision in *Greenman* v. *Yuma Power Products*.

Greenman v. Yuba Power Products, Inc.

Supreme Court of California
59 Cal.2d 57,
27 Cal.Rptr. 697,
377 P.2d 897
(1963)

Case Background. *Greenman's wife bought him a Shopsmith—a power tool that could be used as a saw, drill, and wood lathe—for Christmas in 1955. Greenman had studied material about the product and had requested his wife to buy it. Two years later, Greenman was using the machine as a lathe. After working on the same piece of wood several times without incident, the wood suddenly flew out of the machine and struck Greenman on the forehead, inflicting serious injuries.*

Greenman sued the manufacturer, Shopsmith, and the retail dealer, Yuma Power, alleging breaches of warranties and negligence. The verdict in Greenman's favor was appealed to the Supreme Court of California.

Case Decision. Justice Traynor delivered the opinion of the court.

* * *

A manufacturer is strictly liable in tort when an article he places on the market, knowing that it is to be used without inspection for defects, proves to have a defect that causes injury to a human being. Recognized first in the case of unwholesome food products, such liability has now been extended to a variety of other products that create as great or greater hazards if defective.

* * *

We need not recanvass the reasons for imposing strict liability on the manufacturer. . . . The purpose of such liability is to insure that the costs of injuries resulting from defective products are borne by the manufacturers that put such products on the market rather than by the injured persons who are powerless to protect themselves. Sales warranties serve this purpose fitfully at best. In the present case, for example, Greenman was able to plead and prove an express warranty only because he read and relied on the representations of the Shop-smith's ruggedness contained in the manufacturer's brochure. Implicit in the machine's presence on the market, however, was a representation that it would safely do the jobs for which it was built. Under these circumstances, it should not be controlling whether Greenman selected the machine because of the statements in the brochure, or because of the machine's own appearance of excellence that belied the defect lurking beneath the surface, or because he merely assumed that it would safely do the jobs it was built to do. It should not be controlling whether the details of the sales from manufacturer to retailer and from retailer to Greenman's wife were such that one or more of the implied warranties of the sales act arose. The remedies of injured consumers ought not to be made to depend upon the intricacies of the law of sales. To establish the manufacturer's liability it was sufficient that Greenman proved that he was injured while using the Shopsmith in a way it was intended to be used as a result of a defect in design and manufacture of which Greenman was not aware that made the Shopsmith unsafe for its intended use.

* * *

Case Holding. *The Supreme Court of California upheld the verdict in favor of Greenman and established the rule of strict liability in tort for manufacturers of products sold to consumers. During the following decade all other state courts adopted this general rule.*

Case Questions

1. Why did the court move to strict liability in tort rather than do like the New Jersey court had done a few years previously and hold that strict liability could be imposed on the basis of implied warranty in contract?
2. Would strict liability be imposed on the manufacturer if a friend of Greenman's had come over to use the machine and was hurt while using it?

In 1964, the principal author of the *Second Restatement of Torts*, the American Law Institute (ALI), adopted a strict liability in tort rule in product-related injury cases similar to that imposed in *Greenman*. The decision in *Greenman* coupled with the adoption by the ALI in the *Restatement* quickly brought about a country-wide acceptance of the strict liability in tort rule. The *Restatement's* strict liability in tort rule is found in Section 402A:

> Sec. 402A (1) One who sells any product in a defective condition unreasonably dangerous to the user or consumer or to his property is subject to liability for physical harm thereby caused to the ultimate user or consumer, or to his property, if
>
> > (a) the seller is engaged in the business of selling such a product, and
> > (b) it is expected to and does reach the user of consumer without substantial change in the condition in which it is sold.

(2) The rule stated in Subsection (1) applies although
(a) the seller has exercised all possible care in the preparation and
sale of his product, and
(b) the user or consumer has not bought the product from or entered
into any contractual relation with the seller.

Extensions of Strict Liability

The *Greenman* decision illustrates the application of the strict liability in tort
doctrine to a case in which a defective product has caused an injury to a
consumer. This application of the doctrine is relatively simple and uncontroversial. Since the *Greenman* decision, however, the application of the doctrine
has been extended to more controversial product injury cases. Those extensions include cases in which (1) the manufacturer has failed to warn the
consumer of known hazards in certain uses of the product, (2) the product is
poorly designed (as opposed to simply being defectively manufactured), and
(3) the product produces latent injuries (injuries that occur years after the
consumer has used the product).

Failure to Warn

Even before the widespread adoption of strict liability, the manufacturer's
failure to warn consumers of dangers involved in the use of a product or to
instruct consumers about proper procedures in using a product was actionable under the rule of negligence. Manufacturers have to think of possible
dangers in the use, storage, and handling of their products. For example,
although household cleansers are dangerous and not intended for consumption, manufacturers know that parents often leave such products in places
where children might get at them. Thus, it may be negligent not to warn
people of such dangers and to take steps to reduce possible tragedies, such as
by using containers that are not attractive to children, using hard-to-remove
caps, and putting danger labels or symbols on the containers.

How far will the failure-to-warn application of strict liability in tort
extend? While the limits of the application are still being defined by the courts,
several recent cases provide insights:

- A Pennsylvania court found that a gun manufacturer that had failed to
  warn users of possible damage to their hearing from long-term exposure to
  gun fire was strictly liable for such injuries.

- A Texas court found a liquor manufacturer liable for failing to warn
  consumers about the adverse health effects associated with drinking its
  products. In the case, an eighteen-year-old first-year college student died
  after consuming a large quantity of tequila.

- The Supreme Court of Alaska upheld a verdict against a diet food producer
  who failed to provide adequate warnings about using the adult diet food
  as baby food. Because the food was safe for dieting adults but not for
  infants, the company should have stated so on its product rather than
  assume that adults would have enough sense not to use the product as
  baby food.

- The highest court of New York held the producer of a commercial pizza
  dough roller machine liable for injuries suffered by a worker who stuck his

hands in the machine while it was on as he tried to clean it. Although the machine had a safety switch that was supposed to be used in such cases, the worker had turned off the safety switch so that he could stick his hands in the machine. The manufacturer failed to warn when it did not clearly explain the dangers of turning off the safety switch.

- The Eleventh Circuit Court of Appeals held that the warnings printed on a bottle of Campho-Phenique, an external medicine, stating "Keep out of reach of children," "For external use," and "in case of ingestion—seek medical help and call poison center" were not strong enough to explain the dangers. A four-year-old child drank the medicine and suffered severe injuries. The suit proceeded on the basis of failure to warn.

Design Defects

In contrast to defective product cases, *design defect* cases are not concerned with a particular unit of a product that has been poorly manufactured, sold to a consumer, and then caused injury. A design defect case, for example, would not involve a determination of whether the manufacturer was liable for injuries caused by a defectively manufactured toaster. Rather, a design defect case focuses on the determination of whether a particular injury to users could have been prevented by a differently designed product. The inquiry is relevant even if the product itself is not defectively manufactured. In that regard, consider the following design defect cases:

- In a Washington State case a worker received a $750,000 judgment for the loss of a leg. The accident occurred at work. Co-workers had removed a metal plate from the top of the machine. When they finished repairing the machine, the workers failed to put the metal plate back on and covered the machine with cardboard. The plaintiff later walked on what he thought was the metal plate, as was customary, and fell into the machine. The court held that it was a design defect to allow the machine to be able to run when the metal plate was removed.

- A restaurant employee was seriously burned when he tried to retrieve something that fell out of his shirt pocket and into a commercial French fryer machine. The D.C. Circuit Court of Appeals held that a jury could find a safer alternative design of the machine was possible, in which case it could impose liability.

- A child pushed the emergency stop button on an escalator, causing a person to fall and be injured. The Seventh Circuit Court of Appeals ruled it was a design defect to both make the button red, because that color is attractive to children, and place the button so that it was accessible to children.

- In an Eleventh Circuit Court of Appeals case, the plaintiff was injured when he took his riding mower up a hill that was too steep, the mower rolled over, and he was cut by the whirring blades. The court held that there was technology in existence at the time the mower was built that would have caused the mower to automatically shut off when the mower was lifted off the ground or when the rider let go of the controls. Because such technology was not included in the product's design, the manufacturer was strictly liable for the plaintiff's injuries.

Unknown Hazards

The largest dollar volume and number of products liability cases are now based on *unknown hazards*—dangers that were not known, or not fully appreciated, at the time the product was manufactured. Since the hazard associated with the product may not be learned for years, neither the producer nor the consumer may be able to do anything to prevent injury.

Billions of dollars have been awarded in thousands of suits involving the health effects of asbestos, injuries caused by IUDs, and damage caused by the side effects of drugs that did not appear for years. For example, A.H. Robins marketed the Dalkon Shield contraceptive device in the early 1970s. It caused injuries ranging from spontaneous abortions to sterility in thousands of women. The result was bankruptcy in 1985 and a $2.23 billion settlement fund that began operation in 1990.

The most notable area of activity has involved asbestos, which has resulted in billions of dollars being awarded by all asbestos makers to tens of thousands of plaintiffs. In 1988, two-thirds of all products liability suits filed in federal court were asbestos related. Manville, the largest supplier of asbestos, filed for bankruptcy when it faced $2 billion in claims but had only $1 billion net worth. In such cases, the companies have continued to operate under bankruptcy supervision with most claims being pooled and then paid out of a fund generated by company earnings. The *Borel* case was one of the most important in opening the way for the asbestos litigation.

Borel v. Fibreboard Paper Products Corp.
United States Court of Appeals, Fifth Circuit
493 F.2d 1076 (1973)

Case Background. *Clarence Borel, an industrial insulation worker, was exposed to asbestos from 1936 through 1969 as he worked at various jobs in Texas. In 1964, an x-ray showed his lungs to be cloudy, and his doctor advised him to avoid asbestos dust as much as possible. In 1969, a lung biopsy revealed pulmonary asbestosis. The following year, Borel had a lung removed because of mesothelioma, a lung cancer caused by asbestosis. Shortly thereafter, Borel died.*

His heirs continued the litigation he had begun against eleven manufacturers of asbestos insulation materials he had used over the years. Four manufacturers settled out of court, and one was dismissed at trial, leaving six manufacturers, including Fibreboard and Manville. The jury found the defendants liable under strict liability. The asbestos producers appealed the judgment of the district court.

Case Decision. Justice Wisdom delivered the opinion of the court.

* * *

The evidence . . . indicated . . . that during Borel's working career no manufacturer ever warned contractors of insulation workers, including Borel, of the dangers associated with inhaling asbestos dust. . . . Furthermore, no manufacturer ever tested the effect of their products on the workers using them or attempted to discover whether the exposure of insulation workers to asbestos dust exceeded the suggested threshold limits.

* * *

Under Texas law, a manufacturer of a defective product may be liable to a user or consumer in either warranty or tort. With respect to personal injuries caused by a defective product, the Texas Supreme Court has adopted the theory of strict liability in tort as expressed in section 402A of the Restatement (Second) of Torts (1964). . . .

Under the Restatement, liability may not be imposed merely because a product involves some risk of harm or is not entirely safe for all uses. Products liability does not mean that a seller is an insurer for all harm resulting from the use of his product. Rather, a product is "defective" under the Restatement only if it is "unreasonably dangerous" to the ultimate user or consumer. The requirement that the defect render the product "unreasonably dangerous" reflects a realization that many products have both utility and danger. The determination that a product is unreasonably dangerous, or not reasonably safe, means that, on balance, the utility of the product does not outweigh the magnitude of the danger.

* * *

As Borel has argued, insulation materials containing asbestos may be viewed as "unavoidably unsafe products."

* * *

As a practical matter, the decision to market such a product requires a balancing of the product's utility against its known or foreseeable danger. . . . [E]ven when such balancing leads to the conclusion that marketing is justified, the seller still has a responsibility to inform the user or consumer of the risk of harm. The failure to give adequate warnings in these circumstances renders the product unreasonably dangerous. . . .

* * *

Furthermore, in cases such as the instant case, the manufacturer is held to the knowledge and skill of an expert. This is relevant in determining (1) whether the manufacturer knew or should have known the danger, and (2) whether the manufacturer was negligent in failing to communicate this superior knowledge to the user or consumer of its product. . . . The manufacturer's status as expert means that at a minimum he must keep abreast of scientific knowledge, discoveries, and advances and is presumed to know what is imparted thereby. But even more importantly, a manufacturer has a duty to test and inspect his product. The extent of research and experiment must be commensurate with the dangers involved. A product must not be made available to the public without disclosure of those dangers that the application of reasonable foresight would reveal. Nor may a manufacturer rely unquestioningly on others to sound the hue and cry concerning a danger in its product. Rather, each manufacturer must bear the burden of showing that its own conduct was proportionate to the scope of its duty.

* * *

We agree with the Restatement: a seller may be liable to the *ultimate* consumer or user for failure to give adequate warnings. The seller's warning must be reasonably calculated to reach such persons and the presence of an intermediate party will not by itself relieve the seller of this duty.

* * *

Case Holding. *The court of appeals upheld the verdict in favor of Borel by holding the asbestos manufacturers strictly liable in tort for Borel's injuries.*

Case Questions

1. The levels of asbestos that Borel was exposed to were usually within "safe" levels established by government studies. Should adherence to such studies and, in some cases, regulations relieve a manufacturer of liability?

2. Borel was a worker exposed to asbestos on the job. Should liability be imposed on employers who expose employees to dangerous products or on the producers of the products?

The *Borel* decision has been surpassed in stringency in subsequent decisions that apply what some observers contend is a standard of *absolute* liability, that is, there is no defense available for manufacturers if injury can be shown. For example, in a 1983 federal district court case in Texas, *Carter* v. *Manville*, the court held "that the stipulation that defendant, held to the knowledge and skill of an expert, could not reasonably have known of or foreseen the dangers involved in using its products does not defeat plaintiff's claim that defendant's products were defective and unreasonably dangerous, and is in fact irrelevant to that claim." In that case a worker had been exposed to asbestos from 1942 to 1946. He died of lung cancer decades later. The court held that under strict liability it does not matter what the producer knew at the time the products were placed in commerce (during the 1940s) but rather what we know today about the dangers of the products, because the product was inherently defective.

The *Collins* v. *Eli Lilly* case is another example of liability being imposed for injuries from an unknown hazard. Manufacturers argue against such liability, saying that they should not be responsible for damages which, at the time the product was made and sold, they could not have known were going to occur. In many states, the courts have ruled that strict liability does apply. Real injuries have occurred, those courts argue, and it makes more sense to impose the costs on the manufacturers than on the consumers who suffered the injuries.

Collins v. Eli Lilly Co.
Wisconsin Supreme Court
116 Wis.2d 166,
342 N.W.2d 37
(1984)

Case Background. *Therese Collins was born in 1958. Her mother took DES (diethylstilbestrol) during pregnancy, as prescribed, to prevent miscarriage. DES was banned in 1971 when its cancer risks became known. Collins had radical cancer surgery in 1975. Like at least 1,000 other cancer victims, she attributed the cancer to the DES taken by her mother and sued a dozen drug companies that had produced DES. Under tort law as it existed, Collins would be unlikely to recover damages because of the lack of ability to prove which specific drug company produced the pills her mother consumed. The Supreme Court of Wisconsin had to decide how to handle this kind of case.*

Case Decision. Justice Callow delivered the opinion of the court.

* * *

We are faced with a choice of either fashioning a method of recovery for the DES case which will deviate from traditional notions of tort law, or permitting possibly negligent defendants to escape liability to an innocent, injured plaintiff. In the interests of justice and fundamental fairness, we choose to follow the former alternative.

* * *

We recognize that DES cases pose difficult problems. The entirely innocent plaintiffs may have been severely harmed by a drug they had no control over, and they may never know or be able to prove with certainty which drug company produced or marketed the DES taken by their mothers. The defendants are faced with possible liability for DES which they may not have produced or marketed. We conclude, however, that as between the plaintiff, who probably is not at fault, and the defendants, who may have provided the product which caused the injury, the interests of justice and fundamental fairness demand that the latter should bear the cost of injury. Accordingly, we have formulated a method of recovery for plaintiffs in DES cases in Wisconsin. We note that this method of recovery could apply in situations which are factually similar to the DES cases.

Although the defendants in this case may not have acted in concert under the concert of action theory, all participated in either gaining approval of DES for use in pregnancy or in producing or marketing DES in subsequent years. Each defendant contributed to the *risk* of injury to the public and, consequently, the risk of injury to individual plaintiffs such as Therese Collins. Thus each defendant shares, in some measure, a degree of culpability in producing or marketing what the FDA, many scientists, and medical researchers ultimately concluded was a drug with possibly harmful side effects. Moreover, as between the injured plaintiff and the possibly responsible drug company, the drug company is in a better position to absorb the cost of the injury. The drug company can either insure itself against liability, absorb the damage award, or pass the cost along to the consuming public as a cost of doing business. We conclude that it is better to have drug companies or consumers share the cost of the injury than to place the burden solely on the innocent plaintiff. Finally, the cost of damages awards will act as an incentive for drug companies to test adequately the drugs they place on the market for general medical use. This incentive is especially important in the case of mass-marketed drugs because consumers and their physicians in most instances rely upon advice given by supplier and the scientific community and, consequently, are virtually helpless to protect themselves from serious injuries caused by deleterious drugs.

* * *

Thus, the plaintiff need commence suit against only one defendant and allege the following elements: that the plaintiff's mother took DES; that DES caused the plaintiff's subsequent injuries; that the defendant produced or marketed the type of DES taken by the plaintiff's mother; and that the defendant's conduct in producing or marketing the DES constituted a breach of a legally recognized duty to the plaintiff. In the situation where the plaintiff cannot allege and prove what type of DES the mother took, as to the third element the plaintiff need only allege and prove that the defendant drug company produced or marketed the drug DES for use in preventing miscarriages during pregnancy.

* * *

Case Holding. *The Supreme Court held that Collins could sue any or all of the manufacturers of the drug in question, even though she did not know which particular company made the pills that directly caused her injuries.*

Case Questions

1. Why would Collins be allowed to sue for something that occurred thirty years before?

2. Compare this ruling to that of the Supreme Court of California, which held that the major drug companies would pay the damages on a proportionate share according to their share of the drug market in question. Are these different in impact?

Market Share Liability

An intriguing development in products liability arose in a 1980 California appeals court case, *Sindell* v. *Abbott Laboratories*. It pioneered the notion of *market liability*, or *market share liability*. This application of strict liability has arisen in response to a number of suits filed involving the daughters of women who had taken DES (diethylstilbestrol) during pregnancy. DES is responsible for cancer and other cellular abnormalities in the reproductive systems of (now adult) daughters of women who took DES before it was banned. Because DES was produced by numerous companies and was ingested twenty or more years ago, plaintiffs could not identify the manufacturer of the drug taken by their mothers. The California court allowed plaintiffs to sue all drug manufacturers who marketed DES and said that those manufacturers would share liability according to their share of the market for the drug.

Rules similar to that adopted in the *Sindell* decision have appeared in a few other states. In a 1984 case, *Abel* v. *Eli Lilly*, the Supreme Court of Michigan adopted a "DES-modified alternative liability" that allows plaintiffs to sue any or all manufacturers of the drug in question at the time it was taken by the plaintiffs' mothers.

The Wisconsin Supreme Court addressed the same question in *Collins* v. *Eli Lilly*. It rejected the market share liability approach but held that plaintiff(s) could sue any or all manufacturers and that the manufacturers could bring in other manufacturers as defendants so they would all share the liability. This is the more traditional *joint and several liability* rule, which has been abolished in some states, that allows any defendant to be held responsible for all damages.

Defenses

The application of strict liability holds manufacturers to a high standard of product safety. Strict liability, however, does not mean absolute liability. Manufacturers may escape liability if the consumer has undertaken some activity that increases the risk of injury. Most courts recognize product abuse, assumption of the risk, and contributory negligence as defenses in product-related injury cases. Defenses to tort actions were discussed more generally in Chapter 7.

Product Abuse

If it can be shown that the product was abused, was combined with another product to make it dangerous, was used in some unforeseen and unusual manner, or was mishandled, the negligence of the consumer may preclude recovery for damages. If proper warnings and instructions concerning the use of the product (especially in a situation where the consumer could be expected to heed the warnings) are ignored by the consumer and lead to injury, it is possible that liability will not be imposed on the manufacturer.

In one case the court barred recovery by plaintiffs who were injured when the blowout of a fairly new tire was shown to be caused by plaintiff overinflating the tires. The court noted, "To hold otherwise would be to convert a strict liability cause of action into one of absolute liability." In another case, drunkenness by a consumer was held to have led to *product misuse* that resulted in injury.

Assumption of Risk

There are two primary types of products of concern here: (1) medicinal drugs that have unavoidable, known side effects and (2) goods, such as cigarettes and alcohol, that inflict undesirable side effects. In the first case, most courts have held that because drugs are unavoidably dangerous, strict liability is not to be imposed on producers for the side effects. Producers have a duty to warn consumers of dangers (through the pamphlets that accompany most drugs), but unless a safer alternative is available, drug makers are not liable for unfortunate side effects.

In the second case, one must ask whether a cigarette manufacturer should be held liable if a person smokes cigarettes for forty years and contracts lung cancer. Similarly, if one drinks large quantities of alcoholic beverages for years and contracts cirrhosis of the liver, should the liquor industry be liable? In general, the courts have said no; the persons consuming the cigarettes and alcohol know of the risks involved and will bear the costs. It is not hard to imagine what the impact would be on the liquor and cigarette industries if they were held liable for health problems reasonably believed to be associated with a person's use of their products.

Contributory Negligence

Some states allow the defense of *contributory negligence*. If the manufacturer can prove that the injured party failed to exercise due care for his or her own protection in the use, handling, or storage of the product, that failure will create a complete defense. Generally this must involve the user of the product having voluntarily assumed the risk to use a product known to be defective or to use the product in a situation involving unreasonable danger.

Most jurisdictions have adopted some form of *comparative fault*, where the finder of fact determines if the plaintiff shares in the blame. In some states, even if the plaintiff is mostly at fault, the defendant may be held responsible for all damages. In other states, the plaintiff and defendant share the damages on a percentage of fault basis (see the discussion of comparative negligence in Chapter 7).

INTERNATIONAL PERSPECTIVES:
PRODUCTS LIABILITY IN EUROPE

INTERNATIONAL

PERSPECTIVES

Products liability law is more developed in the United States than in other western countries. While many western countries are undertaking efforts to evaluate and change their product liability law, most currently apply some form of a negligence standard. The differences between the United States and other western countries in the application of traditional negligence law in product-injury cases is best illustrated by litigation in Britain involving the severely deformed children of women who took the drug thalidomide. That litigation spanned two decades and resulted in relatively modest recoveries for plaintiffs with very severe deformities. In this country, the theory of recovery would have been strict liability in tort and the recovery would very likely have been substantial.

Several countries, however, are moving toward legal standards that make it easier for plaintiffs to recover in product-injury cases. West Germany, for example, statutorily imposes strict liability on drug manufacturers. In addition, it has made recovery easier under its negligent standard for other product-related injuries by requiring the manufacturer to disprove a presumption of fault once the plaintiff has demonstrated a defect. France has developed a theory of products liability not based on fault, but it is being applied only in certain courts.

These countries also have several procedural rules that inhibit plaintiffs' ability to recover. For example, plaintiffs face prohibitions on discovery, punitive damages, and the use of juries. The biggest difference between these countries and the United States, however, may be that contingency fees (see Chapter 3) are generally not available in them. Injured parties must be prepared to manage the full financial burden of bringing the lawsuit, including the defense costs, if they lose. These procedural restrictions greatly reduce the number of products liability suits in Europe and the United Kingdom, compared to the United States.

PRODUCT LIABILITY REFORM

In his 1990 State of the Union address, President Bush stated that "it is time to act on product liability reform." Like the Reagan administration, the Bush administration wants a federal products liability law that would set statutory limits on the kinds of actions that consumers could bring under products liability laws. The concept of a federal products liability law, however, is not without controversy.

A Liability Crisis?

At the center of the controversy is the debate over the existence of a liability crisis. In arguing that a crisis exists, business and insurance interests point to the growing size and numbers of damage awards being provided to injured parties in products liability cases. They cite evidence that U.S. manufacturers are responding to the crisis in ways that may adversely affect the competitiveness of the U.S. economy. For example, a recent survey attempting to gauge manufacturer response to the crisis found that:

- Forty-seven percent had withdrawn products from the market.
- Thirty-nine percent had decided against introducing new products.
- Twenty-five percent had discontinued new product research.

In addition, those advocating the existence of a liability crisis note that liability insurance costs fifteen to twenty times more in the U.S. than it does in Canada, Europe, and Japan. In those countries, liability and procedural rules limit the number and size of awards. Also, there are more stringent controls placed upon the legal community. As a consequence of these and other differences, a department store chain found that it had to pay about $6,000 in liability insurance for each of its stores in Canada. The liability insurance for its U.S. based stores exceeded $250,000.

The legal community, and particularly plaintiff attorneys, oppose limitations on product liability actions. They assert that the liability crisis is overblown and due largely to mass litigation over injuries from asbestos, DES,

Dalcon Shields, and other similar products. In such cases, large awards are justified because the injured party may require constant and expensive medical care over an extended period of time. In addition, they point to the fact that less than one in one-hundred of all manufacturers will ever face a products liability action in a court of law. Relatively few manufacturers will face such an action, they assert, because strict liability as applied in product injury cases has served the public well by providing incentives for manufacturers to increase the safety of consumer products.

Federal Statutory Provisions Sought By Business

Business and insurance interests have been lobbying Congress for several years seeking statutory relief from what they see as a liability crisis. In large measure, the efforts are intended to bring about uniformity in differing state liability rules. In the various federal proposals presented to Congress, the following attributes are most desired:

- Uniform time deadlines after product manufacture for bringing injury lawsuits caused by the product (Some products liability actions have been brought more than 20 years after the product was last manufactured).

- A "state-of-the-art" defense requiring that the technology in existence at the time the product was marketed be the standard used at trial—and not the current technology.

- Limits on punitive damages and make them more difficult to obtain.

- Limits on joint and several liability so that one defendant cannot be required to provide compensation for all injuries when it may be responsible for only a fraction of those injuries.

State Statutory Changes

In response to the inability of Congress to enact product liability reform legislation, the business and insurance communities have been working with state legislatures to bring about some measure of reform. Many states have adopted statutes to limit product liability actions. For example, statutes have imposed ten-year time limits on product liability actions, abolished design defect cause of actions, and limited the application of strict liability.

The most controversial of the state statutes, however, are those placing "caps" or limits on either punitive damage awards or the fees plaintiff attorneys may receive. The courts have not reacted favorably to such legislative enactments, often finding them in violation of constitutional rights. For example, the Georgia Tort Reform Act provides:

> (1) . . . Only one award of punitive damages may be recovered in a court of this state from a defendant for any act or omission if the cause of action arises from product liability, regardless of the number of causes of action which may arise from such act or omission. (2) Seventy-five percent of any amounts awarded under this subsection as punitive damages, less a proportionate part of the costs of litigation . . . shall be paid into the treasury of this state. . . .

Upon its initial examination (as has happened in many states), the statute was held to be unconstitutional. Thus, although states can legislate reforms in product liability law, they must be cautious in adopting statutes that cap or limit damage awards or attorney's fees.

SUMMARY

Product liability is an important part of the legal environment of business based mostly on common law developments in the laws of torts and contracts. Although the common law usually changes very slowly, an example of relatively rapid change was seen in the shift from caveat emptor to strict liability in a matter of decades.

The rule of negligence dominated the first half of this century. It requires producers to take the care of a reasonable and prudent person when making consumer products. While suits may still be brought on that rule, as is the case in the crashworthiness of automobiles, most product liability cases are now based on the rule of strict liability. During the 1960s, the rule of strict liability in tort emerged from cases of implied warranty and express warranty to become the general rule. The rule of strict liability in tort holds that the producer is responsible for damages inflicted on consumers and their property due to a defect in a product.

Strict liability in tort cases often arises because a manufacturer has failed to warn consumers of dangers involved in using a product. If consumers are properly notified of certain dangers, the manufacturer may escape liability due to the user's contributory negligence.

Manufacturers are required to know all relevant information about their products and must take steps to change the design of their product once new information about dangers becomes known or must warn consumers of the new dangers. Ignorance about new developments is not a defense for manufacturers.

The makers of defective products that inflict injuries may not be able to escape liability simply because the injured party cannot identify the specific producer of the product that caused the injury. Under various theories of market share liability, all manufacturers of a generic product may be held responsible for damages.

A primary defense for manufacturers in product liability cases is to show produce misuse or abuse by the consumer. The likelihood of this being so is increased if the consumer has been informed, or had the opportunity to be informed, about the proper use of the product. Similarly, contributory negligence by a consumer can relieve part or all of the liability of a manufacturer, because the jury finds that the consumer failed to use ordinary sense. Finally, for some products that are unavoidably dangerous, such as some medicinal drugs and goods like alcohol and tobacco, the consumer may be held to assume the known risks associated with the product.

Can a Company's Reputation be Injured by a Rumored Product Defect?

While the size of judgments awarded by juries in products liability cases has increased dramatically over the past decade, the dollar value of those judgments may be small when compared to the damage product liability actions inflict on a company's reputation. A small number of injuries— real or rumored—can cause consumers to perceive a company's products as defective and dangerous. Unless the company takes assertive action to protect its reputation, the damage can be difficult and expensive to repair.

In the following article, the author considers the manner in which Volkswagen of America managed a "sudden acceleration" problem in its Audi 5000 models. The author asserts sales declined partly due to the fact that the company never acknowledged that the problem was a defective design in pedal placement. The company's inability to manage the negative publicity regarding its product also encouraged juries to find it liable for injuries—despite the fact that a government agency study found no defects in the automobile. The article illustrates the importance of understanding all aspects of the legal environment—its formal and informal rules.

Audi Runaway Problem: Responsibility v. Public Relations

James Hely*

Last summer, in full-page ads in newspapers around the country, Volkswagen of America claimed its Audi had been vindicated of its unintended-acceleration problems. The ads read, in part:

CASE
CLOSED

Is there anyone who has not heard the rumors of "sudden acceleration" and Audi? We doubt it.

What you may not know, however, is that the final chapter has just been written.

Because on July 11, 1989, the National Highway Traffic Safety Administration officially completed its investigation and closed the file.

* * *

Their conclusion? No mechanical or electrical defect which would cause "sudden acceleration."

Their explanation? Pedal misapplication.

* * *

While there can be no happy ending to such a sad episode, the faith of our loyal owners and dealers has been justified.

Audi has been vindicated. Case closed.

*James Hely, an attorney, works with Jac B. Weiseman, P.A. The firm has offices in Westfield, Mountainside, and Newark, New Jersey. Reprinted with permission of *Trial* (December 1989). Copyright the Association of Trial Lawyers of America.

–continued

–continuing

Curiously, the same week the advertisement ran, Volkswagen was forced to pay punitive damages to a family struck by an Audi 5000 in 1983. The U.S. Supreme Court had refused to block a 1988 jury award in the case. That jury not only found the Audi 5000 defective, but also cited Volkswagen's handling of the unintended-acceleration problem as "outrageous" and "egregious." Both the determination of the defect and the finding of punitive damages were upheld through the New Jersey appellate courts.

Why would the courts permit the punishment of Volkswagen if the Audi 5000 had been vindicated by the National Highway Traffic Safety Administration (NHTSA)? What is supposedly wrong with the Audi 5000? Just what is "pedal misapplication"?

A look at the Audi 5000 since its introduction in 1978 provides some answers to these quetions. The record gives an intriguing view of a corporation's response to a crisis and the persistent use of public relations techniques for damage control.

Unintended Acceleration

The fundamental question is, If the reason Audi 5000s were suddenly accelerating was simply because of pedal misapplication, wouldn't the rate of unintended acceleration for the car be similar to the rates for other vehicles? At the outset, then, it is critical to know the comparative rates of unintended-acceleration accidents.

Comparative rates cannot be found in the Audi public relations literature. Arguably, negative publicity about the Audi 5000 and unintended acceleration in recent years may have led to an inflated number of claims. Therefore, any objective comparisons can only be made using statistics gathered before the problem first received significant press attention in 1986.

From 1978 through 1986, NHTSA studied sudden acceleration on millions of General Motors models, analyzing accident data for Buick, Cadillac, Chevrolet, Oldsmobile, and Pontiac models. The study found that the average sudden-acceleration accident rate for all the GM models was just under 3 accidents for every 100,000 vehicles. There was some range in these rates among the various models. For example, Chevrolets averaged 2.38 accidents per 100,000 vehicles; Cadillacs, 9.29 accidents per 100,000 vehicles; and Oldsmobiles, 3.59 accidents per 100,000 vehicles.

NHTSA concluded that drivers who unknowingly applied the accelerator pedal instead of the brake caused this rate of unintended-acceleration accidents. NHTSA found no other defect to explain the phenomenon.

The actual rate of unintended-acceleration accidents for the Audi 5000 is revealed in an internal Volkswagen memorandum dated November 14, 1983. That memo uses statistics gathered long before the Audi 5000 received any publicity, positive or negative, regarding unintended acceleration.

By November 1983, in 101,526 Audi 5000 cars on the road, there had been 404 unintended-acceleration accidents— 397 accidents per 100,000 cars. With GM vehicles as a benchmark, averaging 3 accidents per 100,000 cars, the Audi 5000 was 132 times more likely to have an unintended-acceleration accident.

Volkswagen has admitted, under oath, that the Audi 5000 is 50 to 100 times more likely to have an unintended-acceleration incident than its other models, such as the Quantum and the Audi 4000.

What is different about the Audi 5000? The answer is something Volkswagen has been aware of for a long time: the design of its pedal cluster or—more specifically—how the gas and brake pedals are arranged and how drivers use them.

NHTSA's July 1989 report on the Audi 5000 and unwanted acceleration does not vindicate Audi. To the contrary, in fact, the report goes into great detail regarding the pedal-cluster problem, and it recounts no fewer than three full-scale recalls of the cars to reduce unintended acceleration.

–continued

–continuing

As long ago as 1979, an internal Volkswagen memo on an Audi 5000 sudden-acceleration incident stated, "We suspect that the customer operated the accelerator at the same time when applying the brakes, and thus the vehicle may have moved." This is the earliest documented proof of Volkswagen's knowledge of the pedal-cluster-design problem.

By September 1981, Volkswagen had received 91 reports of unintended acceleration for the Audi 5000. NHTSA had also received reports about the phenomenon and requested a meeting with Volkswagen. At the January 26, 1982, meeting, Volkswagen conceded there was an abnormally small gap between the accelerator and brake pedals that makes inadvertent driver application of both pedals possible. In a February 1982 internal Volkswagen survey of brake-gas pedal clearance, the Audi 5000 compared unfavorably with other Volkswagen models.

Blaming the Driver

In April 1982, Volkswagen told NHTSA it would recall all Audi 5000 cars to make a slight adjustment to the bottom of the accelerator pedal to help avoid accidental sticking of accelerators to misplaced floor mats (called the FN recall campaign). Volkswagen, however, said the fundamental problem of driver interaction with the pedal cluster was the driver's fault.

Volkswagen wrote to NHTSA:

> Some reports indicate that possibly the gas pedal was actuated inadvertently instead of or together with the brake pedal, resulting in unanticipated vehicle acceleration. Causes are operator-related and could be attributed to unfamiliarity with vehicle, slippery footwear, etc. However, there is no indication that the actual configuration of the pedal cluster was a contributing factor.

In short, Volkswagen chose to blame the cluster problem on the driver.

Also, in 1982, Volkswagen appointed a troubleshooter, Dan Anderson, to inspect Audi 5000s reportedly involved in unintended-acceleration incidents. Anderson's inspections repeatedly found nothing wrong with the engine.

Anderson concluded that when drivers intended to brake, they stepped on the brake and simultaneously hit the accelerator due to the pedal-cluster design. The car would still accelerate under this circumstance. . . .

As the first recall, the FN campaign, began, Volkswagen recognized that the adjustment it had made to the underside of the accelerator pedal to prevent its sticking to the floor mat had no effect on the incident rate of unintended acceleration. Thus, by mid-1982, Volkswagen knew driver interaction with the Audi 5000 pedal cluster was the principal culprit. By explaining that phenomenon as "driver error," it would not have to recall the car again and acknowledge its responsibility for an inherent design problem difficult to eliminate.

Incredibly, during this period Anderson told drivers that they might want to consider braking with their left foot and accelerating with their right foot, contradicting what they had learned in driver education classes. . . .

Sales of the Audi 5000 had nearly doubled from 1982 to 1983, a period when there was little or no negative publicity about the unintended-acceleration problem. A frank explanation of Volkswagen policy was given by the former head of Audi of America, Peter Fisher, who was also vice president of Volkswagen of America.

When asked at a deposition if he had ever wondered why there was a pedal misapplication presumably in the Audi 5000 and not in other Audi or Volkswagen models, Fisher said,

> Yes, I—I definitely wondered about that. I also asked some other people about it, and—but we never came up with a good solution . . . We looked at our customer profiles, and we were discussing even the fact that maybe we were, just from strictly a marketing point of view, too

–continued

—continuing

former domestic owners . . . I recall we were above 60 percent conquest sales for the 5000, from General Motors and Ford owners. Maybe that had something to do with it. But we did not come up with a definitive answer.

Between September 1981 and August 1983, complaints to Volkswagen of unintended acceleration averaged 10.25 per month. At the time there were about 100,000 Audi 5000s with automatic transmissions on the road.

Unintended-acceleration incidents often resulted in harm. People were getting injured and killed. Property was getting damaged.

By August 1983, NHTSA had looked into the design of the Audi 5000 pedal cluster. NHTSA had tested the Audi 5000 and the phenomenon of drivers hitting both the accelerator and the brake. The agency found that only in the Audi 5000 would the brakes fail to fully override the engine power if the driver stepped on both pedals.

In light of this testing, NHTSA, in a letter to Volkswagen on August 14, 1988, criticized its failure to make pedal-cluster adjustments. NHTSA reminded the company that in 1982, it had acknowledged the problem of the narrow gap between the gas and brake pedals. Yet there had been no attempt to remedy it.

It was this failure and the attempt to blame drivers that led the jury in New Jersey, which permits punitive damages where the conduct of the corporation or individual is "especially egregious," to award punitive damages. To award these damages, a jury must find there was a deliberate act or omission with knowledge of a high degree of probability of harm and a reckless indifference to the consequences. Volkswagen's deliberate failure to address the pedal-cluster problem, knowing that unintended-acceleration accidents would continue to occur as a result, met that standard.

After receiving the NHTSA letter, Volkswagen wrote back that it would recall all the cars to adjust the pedal cluster. Volkswa-

gen tried to modify it by padding the brake pedal, changing the height between the two pedals.

But the modification did not change the horizontal gap distance between the brake and the gas pedal. A major modification would require an expensive, perhaps impossible, redesign to cars already on the road.

The fall 1983 recall to change the pedal-height differential affected the number of unintended-acceleration complaints for 1978–1983 models. There were no complaints for six months on vehicles that had the pedal adjustment. During the three years after the recall, according to Volkswagen records, the pedal-height modification reduced but did not eliminate the complaints of unintended acceleration.

Beginning with the 1984 Audi 5000 models, the Audi underwent some major design changes, though the basic design of the pedal cluster did not change. The idle stabilizer was redesigned, but later analysis revealed that unexpectedly high engine-idle surges from the stabilizer could surprise drivers. Given the Audi 5000 cluster design, the unintended-acceleration problem was exacerbated by the idle-stabilizer flaw. The high idle itself could not cause the car to surge out of control.

Starting in 1986, negative publicity about the Audi 5000 and unintended acceleration began to surface. Audi's rates of unintended-acceleration complaints continued to be far out of proportion to the rates of other vehicles. The complaint rate for the 1984 and 1985 models was about 600 complaints per 100,000 cars.

In March 1986, the New York Attorney General and some consumer groups called a press conference to demand a full investigation of the phenomenon. When media attention grew, independent engineers and NHTSA began to look at the problem, offering a number of explanations in addition to the pedal-cluster problem for the runaway incidents. But none of those causes can ex

—continued

–continuing

plain the incidents for all the models from 1978 through 1986. Outside of the pedal-cluster design, there is no one gremlin inside the engine causing the incidents, concluded engineers both inside and outside NHTSA.

How did Volkswagen and the media deal with the issue? Volkswagen tried to attribute the incidents to "driver error," and float the notion that all manufacturers were having this problem. In a November 1986 TV interview, a Volkswagen spokesman said, "We're not saying we can't find anything wrong with the car. There isn't anything wrong with the car."

By 1987, Volkswagen had instituted two more recalls. One changed a valve on the idle stabilizer to prevent a surprising high idle that might trigger a driver to press the gas in the tricky pedal cluster.

In the final recall, the automatic shift lock was installed. This device, which is connected to the gear shift, prevents the gear from being shifted out of park to forward or reverse unless the driver's foot is on the brake. Most of the unintended-acceleration incidents occurred when the car was in park and then was shifted into gear.

So far, there have been four recalls. The data suggest that all the recalls have reduced the number of unintended-acceleration accidents. The government records show that the Audi 5000, which never had the automatic shift locks installed, have accident rates 2.8 times the rate for cars that do have the locks. But the record of unintended acceleration, even after the installation of the shift locks,

remains far out of line. In 1988 alone, on just the Audi 5000 cars that had the shift lock installed, the unintended-acceleration rate was 35 accidents per 100,000 vehicles. That's more than 10 times the General Motors benchmark rate.

What has been NHTSA's determination as to why pedal misapplication in the Audi 5000 is far out of the normal range? According to its report, "The frequency of such pedal misapplications (in the Audi) appears to have been increased by the location and possibly the feel of the control pedals and by problems involving unexpectedly fast engine-idle speed which could startle drivers at inopportune times."

Audi is correct when it refers in its recent advertisement to this "sad episode." But the sadness is not over a company that was wrongfully blamed. The sad fact is the company's persistent failure to accept responsibility for the design of its cars.

Questions

1. If a federal agency, like the National Highway Traffic Safety Administration, investigates a problem and rules that it has been solved, that there is no problem, or that a recall for repairs is sufficient to fix the problem, should manufacturer tort liability be relieved?

2. Should juries have the right to impose punitive damages if they think the conduct of the defendant is "especially egregious" or should only normal compensatory damages be allowed?

REVIEW AND DISCUSSION QUESTIONS

1. Define the following terms:
   caveat emptor
   privity of contract
   negligence
   foreseeable dangers
   strict liability
   express warranty

implied warranty
design defect
failure to warn
unknown hazard
market share liability
contributory negligence
assumption of risk

2. Compare the standards of care a producer must take under the rule of negligence compared to under the rule of strict liability. Can you think of a stricter standard of care to hold producers to?

3. Distinguish the logic between *express* and *implied* in the cases of express warranty and implied warranty.

4. Refer to § 402A of the *Second Restatement of Torts:* What does "the seller is engaged in the business of selling such a product" mean? Who is excluded by this? What does "it is expected to and does reach the user or consumer without substantial change in the condition in which it is sold" mean? What situations does this cover? What is the difference between the idea that the rule applies although "the seller has exercised all possible care in the preparation and sale of his product" and the rule of negligence? What is covered by the provision "the user or consumer has not bought the product from or entered into any contractual relation with the seller"?

5. Should contributory negligence on the part of the consumer bar recovery? What factors might limit a bar to recovery?

Case Questions

6. Lawnmowers are now made with handles that automatically shut off the machine if you let go of them. They are required by a federal regulation. Suppose a mower is produced on which the automatic shutoff does not work. That is, the mower runs until the user turns it off, since the automatic shutoff feature is not connected. The consumer knows of the defect but ignores it because the automatic shutoff is a nuisance; the consumer is glad it came with the defect. When using the mower, the consumer sticks his hand in the grass chute to loosen a chunk of grass and gets his fingers cut off. He sues the mower manufacturer for producing a defective product that caused an injury. Will the consumer win the case? What factors will make a difference?

7. Many crimes involve the use of cheap handguns. Producers and sellers of such handguns know that some percent of these guns will be used in crimes by the purchaser of the gun or by a criminal who steals the gun. Could the producers and retailers of such handguns be held liable for the injuries suffered by victims of crimes committed using such handguns where the victim is shot? That is, should such a producer be held strictly liable or negligent for selling a "defective" product, in that one of its known end uses is crime?

8. A national company sells pesticides nationwide that are usually used for agricultural purposes. All bags of the pesticides are clearly labeled with respect to ingredients, proper usage, and dangers. Some farm workers speak only Spanish, and some cannot read at all. Does the producer have a legal responsibility for such users of the product? If so, how can the matter be handled?

9. A rainstorm blew water into a grocery store every time the door was opened by a customer going in or out, and customers tracked water into the store. The manager had an employee frequently mop up the water around the door.

Nevertheless, a women entering the store slipped in the water on the floor inside the door, fell, and was injured. No sign had been posted to warn customers of the water. Was the store liable for her injuries? [*H.E. Butt Grocery Company* v. *Hawkins*, 594 S.W.2d 187 (Tex. Cir. Appl. 1980)]

10. The owner of a home located next to a gasoline station determined that gasoline was seeping into his well from a gasoline storage tank. The storage tank was replaced, but the water was still not fit for consumption. The gasoline station owner argued that he was not negligent. The homeowner argued that the gasoline station owner should be liable in strict liability for damages. What was the result? [*Yommer* v. *McKenzie*, 255 Md. 220, 257 A.2d 138 (1969)]

Policy Questions

11. In recent years, drug companies have been held liable for side effects of drugs that are widely distributed for public health reasons. That is, our population receives shots for polio, whooping cough, and other diseases that used to kill thousands of people each year. However, some people who receive the shots will either die from them or suffer permanent injuries. The shots they receive are not defective, and it is not possible to predict who will suffer such horrible consequences. Should drug companies and doctors be required to tell all potential shot users—including parents of children who get shots—about the risk involved and let them decide if they want the shots or not? If everyone else gets the shots, the person who does not is probably safe from the disease because no one else will carry it. Some people know this, so they avoid the shots and let everyone else provide the public health benefit by getting the shots. Should public policy considerations take precedent over personal wishes? That is, should we all be forced to get the shots, or do we let everyone choose, even though that increases the risk of disease for many more people? Given that some people will be injured or killed by the shots, what should the policy be—nothing (tough luck), the producer of the shots pays the victims, or the government has a special fund for such things?

12. In an Illinois case (*Dunham*), a farmer was blinded in one eye when a chip flew off a hammer he was using to pound on a farm implement. Assuming that this happened because the hammer was made of a softer metal than the farm implement, should the hammer maker be liable? There are different grades of hammers—cheaper hammers made of softer metal and more expensive hammers made of good-quality tempered steel. It can be argued that the cheaper hammers are good enough for ordinary household use—pounding a few nails a year—but not for farm use. Should the farmer have known to buy a high-quality hammer? Will the result of the case be that only high-quality hammers will be sold so that many consumers will be forced to buy a more expensive product than they need?

Ethics Questions

13. You are an executive with a drug company. It has recently been selling a highly effective, FDA-approved, prescription drug that greatly reduces the pain of migraine headaches. This patented drug is earning a high rate of return for your company and is expected to do so for several years. One of the research scientists comes to you and reports that she thinks that the drug may have long-term effects that lead to brain tumors. She says that tests on rats and mice are not conclusive and probably will not be. There will have to be long, expensive tests run on other animals to determine if this is the case, but she

believes that the results are likely to be bad. She claims that a small percentage of the users will develop tumors after about twenty years. Since no one else is likely to run the tests needed to determine if this is possibly true, if you do nothing there may be no consequences for twenty years. Since it may not be true, there may never be any consequences. You know that twenty years from now you will no longer be where you are and, in any event, cannot be held liable for what happens. You can do nothing, order more rat and mice tests, or order expensive testing of other animals. You know that if word gets out sales may be likely to drop and your job security may be threatened. What should you do? Suppose you think tests should be started, but your superiors say no. What should you do?

14. Your company makes Happy Pressure Popcorn Popper, a popper that explodes the corn kernels under heat and pressure very quickly. It is a quality product that sells well. You earn a normal profit rate from the sale of the product. After a while, it is clear that about one in 500,000 units is defective. It blows up. Some accidents have caused only minor damage because no one was standing near, but two people have been hurt badly. Reviewing production procedures in all respects, no one can figure out why there is this defect that shows up so rarely. You estimate that at present prices, sales, and profits, the liability imposed in strict liability suits will cost you 25 percent of your profits. This is less than your production people tell you it will cost to revamp the whole production process to try to increase safety. They think it will enhance safety but cannot guarantee that it will. If you revamp production and all injuries are prevented, it will cost you 50 percent of profits. If you revamp production and the injury rate does not decline, it will put you out of business. What do you do?

9 Business Transactions: The Law of Contracts

B USINESS transactions and the law of contracts are examined in this chapter. It begins by considering the fundamental concept of freedom of contract and some of the limitations and restrictions contract law places on that freedom. A further discussion is provided on the principal sources of contract law, including common-law judicial opinions, the *Restatement of Contracts, 2d*, and the Uniform Commercial Code. Next, we examine the definition of contract and various classifications of contracts.

The chapter then develops the basic elements of a contract, including the agreement, consideration, legal capacity, lawful subject matter, and genuine consent. It discusses the various ways in which a contract can be discharged and the remedies available to the parties in the event of a breach.

The chapter closes with the Issues article, "Negotiating Contracts with the Japanese." International business and the international legal environment have become very important to U.S. businesses in the past decade. To assist in gaining an understanding of international business and business practices, the article discusses some of the potential cultural pitfalls in contracting with a Japanese company.

THE NOTION OF FREEDOM OF CONTRACT

The *law of contracts* affects practically every aspect of domestic and international trade. It establishes the legal rules governing agreements between businesses and their employees, customers, and suppliers. In day-to-day commercial activity, businesses enter into a multitude of contractual relationships. From selling a Coke to creating a purchase contract for the procurement of a large quantity of goods, a business day is filled with contracts and contracting.

Basic to the law of contracts is the underlying principle that every business has the freedom to enter into and create nearly any contract it desires. Business can bind suppliers to exacting specifications on their input requirements, customers to specific purchase agreements and payment terms, and employees to designated salaries and responsibilities, all with intent to facilitate commerce.

Business and economic historians have called *freedom of contract* the fundamental and indispensable requisite of progress. This freedom is not, however, without restrictions and limitations imposed by contract law. For example, prohibitions are placed on contracts for criminal purposes, contracts among businesses designed to restrain trade, and contracts that do not comply with regulatory restrictions. Contracts for these purposes will not be judged valid or enforceable by the courts. A business's freedom to enter into employment contracts, for example, is restricted by a wide range of federal and state laws concerning wages, hours, working conditions, and required social insurance programs. These and other restrictions on a business's freedom of contract are implemented by the government and the courts to achieve public policy goals and objectives.

PRINCIPLE SOURCES OF CONTRACT LAW

Contract law is primarily state common law embodied in judicial opinions. One of the most fundamental of common laws, contract law has developed through centuries of judicial opinions that have resolved virtually every kind of contract dispute. The *Restatement of Contracts*, now in its second edition, is an authoritative document that provides an orderly presentation and summary of the common law of contract.

Common-law principles of contract, however, are significantly influenced by many legislative enactments. Of particular importance are Articles 2 and 9 of the *Uniform Commercial Code* (UCC), a statute adopted in similar form in all states except Louisiana. Article 2 of the UCC applies to sales of goods, while Article 9 deals, in part, with the assignment (transfer) of some contractual rights. The UCC was designed to bring the field of commercial law (legal dealings between businesses) in line with contemporary business practice, and to promote uniformity of the laws relating to commercial transactions among the states. It does not apply to employment contracts, service contracts, insurance contracts, contracts involving real property (land and anything attached to it), and contracts for the sale of intangibles, such as patents and copyrights, all of which are governed by general contract law and various statutes.

DEFINITION AND CLASSIFICATIONS OF CONTRACTS

Before discussing contracts, we will define a contract and discuss the important classifications of contracts. A contract is one of the most basic tools used by a business in both its domestic and international commercial activities. Its fundamental purpose is to facilitate voluntary, mutually beneficial exchanges and to allocate risk among contracting parties in exchanges where time is an important factor. Contract law serves a valuable social function by providing a legal environment conducive to such exchanges.

Definitions of a Contract

Sir William Blackstone, a famous English jurist, defined a *contract* simply as "an agreement, upon sufficient consideration, to do or not to do a particular thing." Modern definitions center on a *promise*—the element common to all contracts. Section I of the *Restatement of Contracts 2d* defines a contract as "a promise or a set of promises for the breach of which the law gives a remedy, or the performance of which the law in some way recognizes as a duty." The *Restatement 2d* then defines a promise as: "a manifestation of the intention [of a party] to act or refrain from acting in a specified manner."

A contract, then, is the legal relationship that consists of the rights and duties of the contracting parties growing out of promises. Contract law governs the enforceability of that legal relationship.

Not all promises, however, are enforceable contracts. A promise may be either binding (contractual) or nonbinding (noncontractual). For a promise to be binding, and thus enforceable, it must meet all the essential requirements of a contract. If a party fails to properly perform a nonbinding promise—that is, if the party is in breach of the promise—contract law will not provide a remedy. This concept is important because it emphasizes the necessity of meeting the requirements of a contract when the parties want their exchange of promises to be binding. It is equally important, however, when the parties do not want it to be binding. In the words of Professor Felix Cohen:

> Contract law is commonly supposed to enforce promises. Why should promises be enforced? The simplest answer is that ... promises are sacred ..., that there is something inherently despicable about not keeping a promise, and that a properly organized society should not tolerate this. ...
>
> There can be no doubt that from an empirical or historical point of view, the ability to rely on the promises of others adds to the confidence necessary for social intercourse and enterprise. But as an absolute proposition this is untenable. ...
>
> Many business transactions, such as those on a stock or commodity exchange, could not be carried on unless we could rely on a mere verbal agreement or hasty memorandum. But other transactions, like those on real estate, are more complicated and would become too risky if we were bound by every chance promise that escapes us. ... The issue obviously depends upon such factors as the relative simplicity of a given transaction, the speed with which it must be concluded, and the availability of necessary information [Harvard Law Review, Vol. 46, pp. 571–574 (1933)].

Classifications of Contracts

Contracts can be classified in a variety of ways, ranging from their method of formation to their legal effect. The standard classifications are express and implied contracts; bilateral and unilateral contracts; executory and executed contracts; valid, void, voidable, and unenforceable contracts; and quasi-contracts. Note, however, that these classifications are not mutually exclusive. For example, a bilateral contract can also be an express, executory, and valid contract.

Express and Implied Contracts

An *express contract* is a contract created by a direct statement by the parties of a promise or promises to each other. Nothing is left to implication. The statement may be either oral or in writing. If Ms. A offers to sell her car for four hundred dollars to Mr. B, who tells her that he will buy it for that price, an express contract has been created orally for selling the automobile for four hundred dollars. If Ms. A makes the same offer in a letter and Mr. B accepts by letter, an express contract has been created in writing.

In an *implied contract,* the parties do not state directly the promise or promises to one another, but rather the promises are inferred from the behavior of the parties or the circumstances. Words, conduct, gestures, and the like will reasonably imply the existence of certain kinds of contracts. Suppose a woman enters a service station, for example, and tells the attendant that she wants her car's engine oil changed but says nothing about the price. A court will infer from the conduct of the parties that they have bargained for the oil change and that the customer has promised to pay the standard fee for the service.

Both express and implied contracts are genuine contracts and are equally enforceable at law. Express and implied contracts differ primarily in the manner in which the assent of the parties is manifested.

Bilateral and Unilateral Contracts

Every contract has an offeror and an offeree. The person making the offer is called the *offeror,* and the person to whom the offer is made is called the *offeree.* A contract is formed only when the offer is accepted by the offeree. The offeree may accept the offer by a promise to perform now or in the future. If the offeree accepts the offer through an exchange of a mutual promise, a *bilateral contract* is formed. If the offeree accepts the offer through the exchange of performance for the offeror's promise, a *unilateral contract* is formed. Figure 9–1 compares unilateral and bilateral contracts.

Although most contracts are bilateral in nature, there are situations in which unilateral contracts are a standard business practice. In contracts for the sale of real estate, for example, the seller of property often promises to pay a real estate agent a commission upon the sale of the property. The agent cannot accept this promise by merely promising to sell the property. The contract is unilateral, because the real estate agent accepts the seller's promise to pay a commission only by selling the property. The sale of the property is the performance required in this unilateral contract. There is no obligation to pay the agent if the property is not sold.

An important distinction between unilateral and bilateral contracts is in the timing of the acceptance and the ability of the offeror to revoke an offer. A bilateral contract is formed by an exchange of promises to perform. Once that exchange of promises has occurred, the offeror cannot then revoke the offer. In contrast, revocation of the offer by the offeror in a unilateral contract technically can take place anytime before performance has actually been rendered. Since a mere promise to perform by the offeree is not enough to create a unilateral contract, the offeror may revoke the offer up until the time the contract is formed by performance. Many states do hold, however, that once the required performance begins, a unilateral contract is created and the offer is no longer revocable.

The importance of the distinction between a bilateral and a unilateral contract has been diminished by a number of authorities, including the UCC

Figure 9–1   Comparing Unilateral and Bilateral Contracts

Bilateral Contract

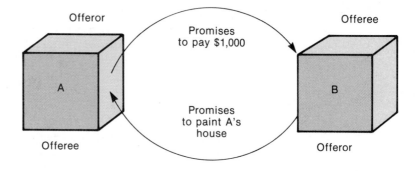

Unilateral Contract

and the *Restatement of Contracts 2d.* In fact, the UCC and the *Restatement* avoid the use of "bilateral" and "unilateral." The abandonment of the use of the terminology is part of an attempt by the legal and business communities to soften the harsh legal consequences that can flow from a literal application of unilateral and bilateral contract definitions.

Executory and Executed Contracts

Some contracts are classified on the basis of when they are performed. *Executory contracts* are contracts that have not been fully performed by either party, while *executed contracts* are those that have been fully performed by both parties. Contracts fully performed by one party but not by the other are partially executed, or partially performed. The difference is important because the remedies available depend on whether the party has performed fully or partially under the terms of the contract.

Valid, Void, Voidable, and Unenforceable Contracts

A *valid contract* is one in which all the elements of a contract are present. Such contracts are enforceable at law. A *void contract* is one that does not exist at law, such as a contract whose subject matter is illegal or a contract made by an individual without capacity to make a contract.

Voidable contracts are valid contracts, but one of the parties to the contract has the right to avoid legal obligation without incurring liability. For this reason, the contract is not void but rather is voidable, or capable of becoming void at one party's option. A contract entered into by an individual of less than the legal age (a minor), for example, is a voidable contract. The contract is valid but may become void at the minor's request.

Unenforceable contracts are contracts that once were valid but, because of a subsequent illegality, will not be enforced by the courts. The passing of a statute that makes previously valid contracts illegal creates an unenforceable contract.

Quasi-contracts

A *quasi-contract* is not a true contract. This term is used by the courts to impose obligations on one party to a dispute when to do otherwise would create an injustice to the other party. Suppose, for example that Glaze's son, without Glaze's permission, asks Pokorny Construction Company to build an addition onto a warehouse owned by Glaze. Glaze watches the warehouse being built. When the warehouse is built, Glaze refuses to pay, saying there was no contract between him and Pokorny. The court would require Glaze to pay under quasi-contract, because Glaze was unjustly enriched by the construction of the addition to the warehouse.

The courts created the concept of quasi-contract to give relief to innocent parties even though no "true" contract exists. In the words of the New York Supreme Court in *Bradken* v. *Leverton* (1970):

> Quasi contracts are not contracts at all. . . . The contract is a mere fiction, a form imposed in order to adapt the case to a given remedy. . . . Briefly stated, a quasi-contractual obligation is one imposed by law where there has been no agreement or expression of assent, by word or act, on the part of either party involved. The law creates it, regardless of the intention of the parties, to assure a just and equitable result.

ELEMENTS OF A CONTRACT

A contract is one of the basic tools used by business in both domestic and international commercial activity. An understanding of its elements provides businesses with reasonable assurance that its bargained-for exchanges will be enforceable. This section develops and discusses the basic elements necessary for a bargain between two or more parties to be a valid contract. Most business contracts consist of standardized forms containing basic elements that rarely change. Those elements include agreement, consideration, legal capacity of the parties to contract, lawful subject matter, and genuine consent to the contract. In addition, compliance with the Statute of Frauds may be necessary. To be a valid contract, an agreement must comply with the principles these basic elements represent.

The Agreement

In contract law, an *agreement* means there is a mutual understanding between the parties as to the substance of the contract. This agreement between the parties is reached through a process of *offer* and *acceptance*. Table 9–1

Table 9–1   Summary of the Legal Effect of Offer and Acceptance Communications

Communications	Time Effective	Legal Effect
By offeror:		
1. Offer	When received by offeree	Creates in offeree the power to form a contract
2. Revocation	When received by offeree	Terminates offeree's power to form a contract
By offeree:		
1. Rejection	When received by offeror	Terminates the offer
2. Counteroffer	When received by offeror	Terminates the offer
3. Acceptance	When sent by offeree	Forms a contract*

*A contract will also require consideration, legal capacity, lawful subject matter, genuine consent, and, in some cases, compliance with the Statute of Frauds.

provides a summary of offer and acceptance communications and their legal effect.

The Offer

An *offer* is a promise to do or refrain from doing some specified thing. The party making an offer to another party to enter into an agreement is called the *offeror*. The *offeree* is the party to whom the offer is made. To be an effective offer, three requirements must be met: clear manifestation of intent, definite terms and conditions, and communication of the offer.

Manifestation of Intent.   In making the proposition, the offeror must have the intent to be bound to the contract, and that intent must be clearly manifested. *Preliminary negotiations* are not viewed as an offer but rather as invitations to negotiate or to make an offer. Many advertisements, an auctioneer's invitation for a bid at an auction, and dickering are examples of preliminary negotiations where there is *intent* to negotiate but not to create a firm offer.

An individual's intent is always tested by an objective standard. The court decides from the evidence whether a reasonable person familiar with the business being transacted would be justified in believing an offer had been made. If, under the circumstances, the court decides intent was lacking, a contract could not be formed.

Definite Terms and Conditions.   Although every detail of the offer does not need to be present or completely unambiguous, the terms of the offer must be sufficiently detailed so that each party's promises are reasonably certain. An offer that has *ambiguous* or *missing* terms cannot serve as the basis for a contract. Sometimes the court will supply the missing terms if they are minor or immaterial, so that the offer (and subsequently the contract) will not fail for *indefiniteness*.

In a business transaction, the terms of the trade generally used by the industry supply the missing terms. Under the UCC, if the parties clearly intended to make a contract, an offer or a contract for the sale of goods does not fail for indefiniteness of terms even though one or more terms are left open. UCC Section 2–305, for example, provides that if no price is stated or if the price is left open to be agreed upon later, the price will be a reasonable price at the time of delivery. Similar provisions provide for the time and place of delivery and the terms of payment.

Communication of the Offer. An appropriate acceptance requires prior *knowledge of the offer* by the offeree. The case of a person who captures a fugitive and then learns of a reward is a good example of an offer failing for lack of communication. Because the communication of the offer occurred after the act of acceptance (capturing the fugitive), a proper acceptance did not take place. It is impossible to form a contract by accepting an unknown offer.

Terminating the Offer

Termination of the offer can occur either through the action of the parties or by the operation of law. The parties can *terminate* the offer by withdrawing it (by the offeror) or rejecting it (by the offeree) or through lapse of time (by the inaction of the offeree). Termination of the offer by operation of law may occur through intervening illegality, destruction of the subject matter of the offer, or death or insanity of the offeror or the offeree.

Note that the UCC provides that certain *firm offers*—those in writing specifying that the offer will remain open for a given time period—cannot be revoked until that stated time period expires. The UCC's firm offer is similar to option contract under the common law. An *option contract* requires the offeror to hold open an offer for a specified time.

Termination by the Parties. The offeror can terminate the offer by withdrawing it before it has been accepted by the offeree. The withdrawal of the offer by the offeror is termed a *revocation*. To be effective, the revocation must be communicated to the offeree. Generally, the offeror may revoke the offer anytime before acceptance. If the offer states that it must be accepted within a designated period, the expiration of that time period terminates the offer.

After the offer has been made by the offeror, the offeree has the power to create a contract by accepting the offer or to terminate the offer by rejecting it. One important form of rejection is a *counteroffer*—a proposal by the offeree to change the terms of the original offer. By indicating an unwillingness to agree to the original terms of the offer, the counteroffer operates as a rejection. For example, if Warisch (the *offeror*) offers to buy Kohl's (the *offeree*) automobile for five hundred dollars, and Kohl says that he will sell the automobile for six hundred dollars, a counteroffer has been made. The original offer made by Warisch is terminated by the counteroffer. The offeree now has to wait for the offeror's acceptance or rejection of the counteroffer to determine whether a contract is formed. Suppose Warisch rejects the counteroffer and Kohl says, "Oh, all right. I will sell the automobile for the five hundred dollars you originally offered me." Warisch is now the offeree and may accept or reject Kohl's offer to sell for five hundred dollars. As a consequence of the counteroffer, he is not bound by his original offer to buy.

Finally, the offer may terminate through *lapse of time*. If the offer does not state a specific period for acceptance, the passage of a reasonable length of time after the offer has been made will work to terminate it. What is considered reasonable will be determined by the court on a case-by-case basis. An offer to buy stock in a company at a specified price will terminate through lapse of time much more quickly than, for example, an offer for the capture of criminals.

Termination by the Operation of Law. Termination of the offer by operation of law through *intervening illegality* occurs when a court decision or legislative enactment makes an offer illegal after it has been made. Although intervening illegality will terminate an offer, the same rule does not necessarily apply to a contract. Although a newly enacted regulatory statute may not terminate a contract already formed, the contract may be unenforceable.

The offer will also terminate by law if the subject matter of the offer is destroyed. The subject matter, however, must be destroyed before the offer is accepted. If Mrs. Cook offers to sell Miss Washburn an automobile, for example, and then is involved in an accident in that automobile, the courts will hold that the offer terminated when the accident occurred.

The *death or insanity of the offeror or the offeree* will terminate the offer by operation of law. Upon the death or insanity of the offeror, the offer (and any other outstanding offers) is terminated because the offeror no longer has capacity to enter into a contract. The death of the offeree terminates the offer because an offer can be accepted only by the person to whom it is made. Upon insanity, the offeree no longer has legal capacity to enter into a contract and thus cannot accept an offer.

The Acceptance

In contract law, the term *acceptance* is defined as the offeree's expression of assent or agreement to the exact terms of the offer. To be effective, an acceptance must be unconditional, unequivocal, and legally communicated. A purported acceptance that lacks one or more of these elements will generally not bring about a binding contract between the parties.

Must Be Unconditional. The offeree must accept the offer as presented by offeror. In effect, the acceptance must be the *mirror image* of the offer. The common-law rule is that a purported acceptance that adds conditions to the original offer is a counteroffer. By changing the terms of the offer, the offeree rejects the offer.

This rule is often rigidly applied and can be detrimental to businesses that rely on *printed-form contracts*. If the offeror-business sends its printed form contract through the mail as an offer, and the offeree-business sends back a signed copy of its own printed form contract as its acceptance, the courts may rule that a counteroffer, not a contract, has been made.

The UCC, however, alleviates this *battle of forms* problem when the Code applies. The UCC focuses on the intent of the parties in determining whether a contract has been formed. According to Section 2–207 of the Code:

> (1) A definite and reasonable expression of acceptance or a written confirmation which is sent within a reasonable time operates as an acceptance even though it states terms additional to or different from those offered or agreed upon, unless acceptance is expressly made conditional on assent to the additional or different terms.

> (2) The additional terms are to be construed as proposals for addition to the contract. Between merchants such terms become part of the contract unless:

(a) the offer expressly limits acceptance to the terms of the offer;

(b) they materially alter it; or

(c) notification of objection to them has already been given or is given within a reasonable time after notice of them is received.

(3) Conduct by both parties which recognizes the existence of a contract is sufficient to establish a contract for sale although the writings of the parties do not otherwise establish a contract. In such case the terms of the particular contract consist of those terms on which the writings of the parties agree, together with any supplementary terms incorporated under any other provisions of this Act.

Must Be Unequivocal. Acceptance must be unequivocal or definite. If, for example, an offeree receives an offer to buy some merchandise for $10,000 and responds to the offer with "I see" or "What a good idea," the expressions fail the unequivocal test and there is no acceptance.

While the words "I accept" would be clear indication of an offeree's acceptance, any words or conduct expressing the offeree's intent to accept the offer is an effective acceptance. When negotiations are taking place, however, much is expressed both in words and conduct that is neither a complete rejection nor an easily defined acceptance. In such circumstances, the courts will look at the offeree's expressions to determine whether a reasonable person would consider them as an acceptance of the offer.

As a general rule, silence is not considered acceptance for the simple reason that it is not unequivocal; it could mean either yes or no to the offeree. However, the past business dealings of the offeror and the offeree may create a pattern of silence as acceptance by the offeree.

Must Be Legally Communicated. The final requirement of acceptance is that it must be legally communicated to the offeror or the offeror's agent. Three factors are important in meeting this requirement: the method of acceptance, the timeliness of acceptance, and, in the case of unilateral contracts, performance as acceptance.

The general rule in communicating an acceptance is that any reasonable method will be adequate. Problems arise when the offeror authorizes one mode of communicating the acceptance but the offeree uses another. If, for example, the offeror requires that acceptance be made by telegram, a response by letter will not create an acceptance. If no method of acceptance is specified, the offeree may use any reasonable means to communicate acceptance. The safest approach is to use the method used by the offeror in communicating the offer.

The timeliness of the acceptance is important, especially when the distance between the parties creates the potential for long passages of time between the offer and the acceptance. To deal with this time problem, the courts created the general rule that if the method of acceptance is reasonable under the circumstances, the acceptance is effective when it is sent.

In some cases the offeror tried to revoke the offer before receiving the offeree's acceptance. This led to the *mailbox rule*, which states that acceptance is effective when it is mailed and revocation is effective when it is received by the offeree. For example, the offeror sends the offer July 1, and the offer is received by the offeree on July 3. The offeror then sends a revocation of the offer on July 2, and the revocation is received by the offeree on July 4. If the offeree had sent an acceptance to the offeror on July 3, and the acceptance had reached the offeror on July 5, would there be a valid acceptance?

Applying the mailbox rule, the answer is yes, since the acceptance is effective upon being sent or dispatched by the offeree (July 3), while the revocation is effective upon receipt (July 4). Thus, the acceptance is created by the offeree before the revocation by the offeror, and a valid contract is formed. The following case provides an interesting example of the application of the mailbox rule.

Cushing v. Thomson

Court of Appeals of New Hampshire
118 N.H. 292, 386 A.2d 805 (1978)

Case Background. *Cushing and four other members of an antinuclear protest group called the Portsmouth Clamshell Alliance brought this suit against Governor Thomson and Blatsos, adjutant general, both of the state of New Hampshire. The Alliance sought specific performance of a contract allegedly entered into by the parties for use of the New Hampshire National Guard Armory in Portsmouth. The trial court ruled that a binding contract existed. The defendant, Thomson, appealed.*

Case Decision. Per curiam.

* * *

On or about March 30, 1978, the adjutant general's office received an application from plaintiff Cushing for the use of the Portsmouth armory to hold a dance on the evening of April 29, 1978. On March 31 the adjutant general mailed a signed contract offer agreeing to rent the armory to the Portsmouth Clamshell Alliance for the evening of April 29. The agreement required acceptance by the renter affixing his signature to the accompanying copy of the agreement and returning the same to the adjutant general within five days after its receipt. On Monday, April 3, plaintiff Cushing received the contract offer and signed it on behalf of the Portsmouth Clamshell Alliance. At 6:30 on the evening of Tuesday, April 4, Mr. Cushing received a telephone call from the adjutant general advising him that the Governor had ordered withdrawal of the rental offer, and accordingly the offer was being withdrawn. During that conversation Mr. Cushing stated that he had already signed the contract. A written confirmation of the withdrawal was sent by the adjutant general to the plaintiffs on April 5. On April 6 defendants received by mail the signed contract dated April 3, postmarked April 5.

The first issue presented is whether the trial erred in determining that a binding contract existed. Neither party challenges the applicable law. "To establish a contract of this character . . . there must be . . . an offer and an acceptance thereof in accordance with its terms. . . . [W]hen the parties to such a contract are at a distance from one another, and the offer is sent by mail, . . . the reply accepting the offer may be sent through the same medium . . . and the contract will be complete when the acceptance is mailed, . . . properly addressed to the party making the offer, and beyond the acceptor's control." Withdrawal of the offer is ineffectual once the offer has been accepted by posting in the mail.

* * *

Plaintiffs introduced the sworn affidavit of Mr. Cushing in which he stated that on April 3, he executed the contract and placed it in the outbox for mailing. Moreover plaintiffs' counsel represented to the court that it was customary office practice for outgoing letters to be picked up from the outbox daily and put in the U.S. mail. . . . Thus the representation that it was customary office procedure for the letters to be sent out the same day that they are placed in the office outbox, together with the affidavit, supported the implied finding that the completed contract was mailed before the attempted revocation. . . .

Case Holding. *The trial court's decision that a binding contract existed was affirmed. An acceptance of a contract is effective when it is mailed.*

Case Questions

1. Why was the telephone call from the adjutant general on April 4 not an effective revocation of the offer?
2. How could the adjutant general have obtained an effective revocation in this case?

Special considerations govern the acceptance of unilateral contracts. A unilateral contract is a contract in which a promise is made in exchange for a performance. Thus, a unilateral contract offer is accepted by *performance*. There is no requirement that the offeree give the offeror notification of the performance unless either the offer specifically requires notification or the offeror could not otherwise be reasonably expected to know of the offeree's performance. Courts usually require that the performance be completed for the acceptance to take place. Depending on the circumstances, if performance has started the offeror may lose the right to revoke the offer. Even if performance is only partial, courts usually allow recovery of the value of the work performed by the offeree in reliance on the offer under quasi-contract.

Consideration

For a promise or agreement to be binding, the requirement of legally sufficient consideration must be satisfied. *Consideration* is defined as something of value or something bargained for in exchange for a promise. It is the element of a contract that keeps it from being gratuitous.

Legal Detriments and Benefits

If consideration is absent, neither party can enforce the promise or agreement. The traditional rule is that an exchange will constitute consideration if it creates a legal detriment to the *promisee* (the party to whom a promise is made) *or* a legal benefit to the *promisor* (the party making a promise). A *legal detriment* is defined as an act, or a promise to act, or the refraining of an action in a way that one is not legally obligated to do. A *legal benefit* to the promisor exists when the promisor acquires some legal right through the promisee's act, promise to act, or refraining to do some act.

Even though consideration requires either a legal detriment to the promisee or a legal benefit to the promisor, in actuality, both concepts often occur at the same time. If Ms. Leasure buys a watch from Mr. Glasgow for one hundred dollars, for example, Ms. Leasure suffers a legal detriment (gives up the right to keep the one hundred dollars) in exchange for a benefit (the watch), and Mr. Glasgow also suffers a legal detriment (gives up the watch) in exchange for a benefit (the one hundred dollars). As the *Hamer* v. *Sidway* case illustrates, many courts use this *detriment-benefit test* to determine whether there is consideration for a contract.

Hamer v. Sidway
Court of Appeals of New York Second Division
124 N.Y. 538,
27 N.E. 256
(1891)

Case Background. *William E. Story, Sr., was the uncle of William E. Story, II. At a celebration at which various family members and guests were present, William E. Story, Sr., promised his nephew, that he would pay him $5,000 if he would refrain from "drinking, using tobacco, swearing, and playing cards or billiards for money" until he was twenty-one years of age. Upon turning twenty-one, the nephew wrote to the uncle, informing him that he had performed his part of the agreement and wished to be awarded the $5,000. The uncle wrote a letter to the nephew stating, "Your letter . . . came to hand all right, saying that you had lived up the promise made to me several years ago. I have no doubt but you have, for which you shall have five thousand dollars, as I promised you."*

Two years later the uncle died, without having paid the nephew the $5,000. During that time, Hamer had acquired the nephew's interest in the $5,000 (plus interest) through a series of assignments. Hamer then brought suit against Sidway, the executor of Story, Sr.'s, estate, for the payment of the money owed to the nephew under the contract with the uncle. The executor refused to pay five thousand dollars, stating that there had been no consideration on the part of the nephew for receipt of the money. The court reviewed the agreement, discussing the element of consideration as a part of the contract.

Case Decision. Judge Parker delivered the opinion of the court.

* * *

The question [before us] . . . is whether by virtue of a contract, William E. Story became indebted to his nephew, William E. Story, II, on his twenty-first birthday in the sum of $5,000.

* * *

Sidway contends that the contract was without consideration to support it, and therefore invalid. He asserts that the nephew, by refraining from the use of liquor and tobacco, was not harmed, but benefited; that that which he did was best for him to do, independently of his uncle's promise,—and insists that it follows that, unless the promisor was benefited, the contract was without consideration,—a contention which if well founded, would seem to leave open for controversy in many cases whether that which the promisee did or omitted to do was in fact of such benefit to him as to leave no consideration to support the enforcement of the promisor's agreement. Such a rule could not be tolerated, and is without foundation in the law. [We have] defined "consideration" as follows: "A valuable consideration, in the sense of the law, may consist either in some right, interest, profit, or benefit accruing to the one party, or some forbearance, detriment, loss, or responsibility given, suffered, or undertaken by the other."

Courts will not ask whether the thing which forms the consideration does in fact benefit the promisee or a third party, or is of any substantial value to any one. It is enough that something is promised, done, forborne, or suffered by the party to whom the promise is made as consideration for the promise made to them. In general a waiver of any legal right at the request of another party is a sufficient consideration for a promise. Any damage, or suspension or forbearance of a right will be sufficient to sustain a promise. Pollock in his work on Contracts . . . says:

" 'Consideration' means not so much that one party is profiting as that the other abandons some legal right in the present, or limits his legal freedom of action in the future, as an inducement for the promise of the first.'

Now, applying this rule to the facts before us, the (nephew) used tobacco, occasionally drank liquor, and he had a legal right to do so. That right he abandoned for a period of years upon the strength of the promise of (his uncle) that for such forbearance he would give him $5,000. We need not speculate on the effort which may have been required to give up the use of those stimulants. It is sufficient that he restricted his lawful freedom of the action within certain prescribed limits upon the faith of his uncle's agreement, and now, having fully performed the conditions imposed, it is of no moment whether such performance actually proved a benefit to (the uncle), and the court will not inquire into it; but, were it a proper subject of inquiry, we see nothing in this record that would permit a determination that the uncle was not benefited in a legal sense.

* * *

Case Holding. *By refraining from drinking, using tobacco, swearing, and playing cards or billiards for money, the nephew had provided sufficient consideration to establish a contract with his uncle. Hamer, having been assigned the rights to the contract by the nephew, was entitled to collect $5,000 from Sidway, the executor of the uncle's estate.*

Case Questions

1. What was the consideration in this case?
2. Was it important that the activities the nephew refrained from did not harm but benefited him?
3. What detriment did the nephew incur?

Adequacy of Consideration

For the most part, courts do not wish to inquire into the *adequacy of consideration* given in a contract. In a business transaction, this places the bargaining responsibility on the parties to the contract. Even if one party bargains poorly and the values of the items to be exchanged are unequal, the courts will generally not interfere. A majority of the courts will support contracts that are bargained for even if the consideration is one dollar or some other trivial sum.

Past Consideration

Consideration is essentially a bargained-for exchange. Thus, if a promise is given today in exchange for some past occurrence, the element of exchange is absent. Referred to as *past consideration*, an agreement based on such a promise is unenforceable for *lack of consideration*. Suppose, for example, that Ellen Eyestone names her consulting company after her favorite business professor. Years later, after the company has become very successful and gained considerable notoriety, the professor tells Eyestone, "In consideration of the fact that you named your company after me, I promise to pay you $5,000." The promise in unenforceable because the detriment—the naming of the company—could not induce the promise because the company has already been named. In addition, the promised $5,000 did not induce Eyestone to so name the company because the offer was not known to her at the time she named the company. Thus, unbargained-for events that have already taken place are not consideration—despite their unfortunate designation as past consideration.

Preexisting Duty

Consideration is a present detriment to the promisee or a present benefit to the promisor. An obligation that existed before the present agreement (*preexisting duty*) does not constitute consideration. The reasoning behind this requirement is that the promisee has not incurred a detriment if there were already a prior obligation to perform it; without a detriment, there can be no consideration. For example, Mississippi River Pipeline Company promised to deliver natural gas to Duke Power Company for $0.10 per unit of gas. Duke Power was buying the natural gas from a Texas producer and Mississippi River was performing the delivery service. Thereafter, Mississippi River decided the price was not sufficient and increased it to $0.15. Duke Power agreed to pay the higher price. After delivery of the gas, Duke Power paid $0.10 per unit, claiming that the promise to pay the additional $0.05 was unsupported by new consideration. Under these circumstances, Duke Power would ordinarily prevail. Only if the parties had modified the existing contract—say by increasing the quantity of gas being bought and sold—would there be new consideration.

Most jurisdictions provide an exception to the preexisting duty rule when the parties modify their contract without consideration after unforeseen difficulties occur in the performance of that contract. Under such circumstances, the courts will uphold the modification despite the fact that it violates the preexisting duty rule. In addition, if the parties had rescinded their original contract and entered into a new contract, the preexisting duty rule would not be violated. At the time of the new agreement, there is no preexisting duty on the part of either party because their duties were discharged by the agreement to rescind the original contract. In comparison to common exceptions to the preexisting duty rule, the UCC goes much further by providing under § 2–209(1) that "an agreement modifying a contract within this Article (on the sale of goods) needs no consideration to be binding."

Settlement of Business Debts

Sometimes in business relationships debts become due that the debtor cannot or will not pay. In such situations, it is often efficient for the debtor and the creditor to enter into a *settlement agreement*, whereby the creditor releases the debtor from the full obligation of the debt in return for some partial payment. At law, such a settlement agreement is called an *accord and satisfaction*.

The *accord* occurs when one of the parties agrees to perform by making the partial payment. The *satisfaction* occurs when the accord has been fully executed. If the creditor wishes later to claim the remainder of the amount owed by the debtor, the ability to do so is dependent on whether the debt is defined as a liquidated debt or an unliquidated debt.

Liquidated Debt. A *liquidated debt* exists when there is no dispute about the amount owed. Agreements to pay an amount less than the original debt usually do not preclude later claims by the creditor for the remainder owed. The rationale is that the debtor has promised to pay a particular amount when the original contract with the creditor was created. Therefore, the new settlement agreement is likely to fail for lack of new consideration.

Unliquidated Debt. An *unliquidated debt* exists when there is a genuine dispute between the parties as to the amount owed by the debtor. The general rule is that settlement agreements for unliquidated debts are usually binding and the creditor may not later claim the remainder of the original amount owed. The rationale is that the debtor and creditor have given new consideration in the creation of the settlement agreement—the debtor has promised to pay an amount that she otherwise did not feel she had the responsibility to pay (thereby giving up a legal right), and the creditor has promised not to sue the debtor for the prior amount believed to be owed (giving up the legal right to enforce the claim in court).

Enforceable Promises Without Consideration

Circumstances exist where consideration for a promise is not required by the courts for the promise to be enforceable. *Promissory estoppel,* also known as *detrimental reliance,* is a doctrine used by the courts to bind a promisor to promises for which a reasonable person would expect to induce action or forbearance on the part of the promisee and in fact does induce such action or forbearance. If, for example, Falconi promises to give $10,000 to a church building fund and construction proceeds based on that promise, she is bound to the promise. The rationale for the doctrine is that it will avoid an injustice due to the promisee's reliance on the promisor's promise. As in the *Red Owl* decision, the doctrine is being applied in a growing number of business situations.

Hoffman v. Red Owl Stores, Inc.

Supreme Court of Wisconsin
26 Wis.2d 683,
133 N.W.2d 267
(1965)

Case Background. *Hoffman, an owner of a bakery, wanted to own a grocery store. In 1959, he contacted Red Owl, which operated a chain of supermarkets and sold franchises to some individuals. Several conversations between Hoffman and Red Owl took place, leading to the idea that they might establish a Red Owl franchise store in Wautoma, Wisconsin. In September 1960, Lukowitz continued negotiations on behalf of Red Owl. It was discussed that Hoffman would need $18,000 capital to invest in the business. Upon the advice of Lukowitz, to get more experience Hoffman leased a building, bought inventory and fixtures, and began operating a small grocery store in Wautoma.*

After three months, Lukowitz advised Hoffman to sell the store, which was making a profit, assuring Hoffman that Red Owl would find a larger store for him. Hoffman sold the fixtures and inventory in June 1961. Before Hoffman sold the store, he told Red Owl that he had $18,000 for the start-up costs of the Red Owl franchise. Red Owl selected a site, and at Red Owl's suggestion, Hoffman obtained an option through a $1,000 down payment. Upon the assurances of the representative of Red Owl that the business was ready to begin, Hoffman sold the bakery for $10,000, incurring a $2,000 loss.

In November, Lukowitz and Hoffman met to discuss Hoffman's financial standing. A document titled "Proposed Financing for an Agency Store" stated that Hoffman was to contribute $24,100 instead of the original $18,000. Through a series of loans, Hoffman came up with the required money. A week later, Hoffman was told that if he *could get another $2,000, the deal would be made for $26,000. Hoffman objected to this new requirement and other demands by Red Owl, and negotiations ended.*

Hoffman sued Red Owl for breach of contract. Red Owl defended that no contract had been completed due to a lack of consideration, since there was no franchise agreement and no formal financing plan that had been agreed upon by the parties. Hoffman contended that Red Owl was liable under the theory of promissory estoppel. The trial court held for Hoffman, stating that an "injustice would result if plaintiffs were not granted damages." The defendants appealed.

Case Decision. Chief Justice Currie delivered the opinion of the court.

* * *

Many courts of other jurisdictions have seen fit over the years to adopt the principle of promissory estoppel, and the tendency in that direction continues. . . . [T]he development of the law of promissory estoppel "is an attempt by the courts to keep remedies abreast of increased moral consciousness of honesty and fair representations in all business dealings."

* * *

The record here discloses a number of promises and assurances given to Hoffman by Lukowitz in behalf of Red Owl upon which plaintiffs relied and acted upon to their detriment.

Foremost were the promises that for the sum of $18,000 Red Owl would establish Hoffman in a store. After Hoffman had sold his grocery store and paid the $1,000 [down payment] on the Chilton lot, the $18,000 figure was changed to $24,100. Then in November, 1961, Hoffman was assured that if the $24,100 figure were increased by $2,000 the deal would go through. Hoffman was induced to sell his grocery store fixtures and inventory in June, 1961, on the promise that he would be in his new store by fall. In November, plaintiffs sold their bakery building on the urging of defendants and on the assurance that this was the last step necessary to have the deal with Red Owl go through.

We determine that there was ample evidence to sustain the answers of the jury . . . with respect to the promissory representations made by Red Owl, Hoffman's reliance thereon in the exercise of ordinary care, and his fulfillment of the conditions required of him by the terms of the negotiations . . . with Red Owl.

* * *

Case Holding. *The court held for Hoffman, stating that "injustice would result . . . if Hoffman was not granted some relief because of the failure of Red Owl to keep their promises which induced Hoffman to act to his detriment." The trial court's decision was affirmed.*

Case Questions

1. How could Red Owl have avoided the outcome in this case?
2. How could Hoffman have protected himself against being placed in this position?

A number of other situations exist where the courts, due to public policy concerns, will not require consideration for a promise to be enforceable. They include a debtor's promise to pay a lender a past debt even though the statute of limitations has run out and the creditor is barred from recovering the debt

Table 9–2 A Summary of Contractual Capacity

Incapacity	Degree of Incapacity	Legal Effect on Contract
Minor	Partial capacity	Voidable
Intoxicated person	Partial capacity	Voidable
Mentally insane		
Adjudicated	No capacity	Void
Insane in fact	Partial capacity	Voidable

and, to a very limited extent, a promise by a bankrupt debtor to pay a debt later even though the bankruptcy proceeding extinguished the debt.

Capacity to Contract

One of the essential elements of a contract is the *contractual capacity*, or legal capacity, to create a contract. The term *capacity* refers to a party's ability to perform legally valid acts, acquire legal rights, and incur legal liabilities. Generally, minors, intoxicated persons, and the insane lack capacity to contract. A party claiming incapacity has the burden of proving it.

Most individuals have complete capacity to contract. If an individual, such as an insane person, has no capacity to contract, the contract entered into is void. If an individual, such as a minor or an intoxicated person, has *partial capacity*, the contract is enforceable unless the individual exercises his or her right to disaffirm the contract. Contracts created by those with partial capacity are said to be voidable. A summary of the legal effects on contracts resulting from less than complete capacity is presented in Table 9–2.

Minors

A *minor* is a person under the legal age of majority. Although many states have reduced the age of majority by statute (most provide majority status at eighteen), the common-law age of majority traditionally has been twenty-one. At common law, the general rule is that a minor may enter into contracts, but those contracts are voidable at the option of the minor. This *right to disaffirm* contracts stems from the traditions of the English courts wishing to protect the young from the results "of their own folly." As the *Robertson v. King* case illustrates, a contract is voidable at the minor's option unless the other party can demonstrate that the good or service is a *necessary*—a physical necessity.

Robertson v. King

Supreme Court of Arkansas
225 Ark. 276, 280 S.W.2d 402 (1955)

Case Background. *Robertson entered into a sales agreement with King and Julian, doing business as Julian Pontiac Company, for the purchase of a pickup truck. Robertson was seventeen years old on the day of the purchase. The purchase price was $1,743.85, and Robertson was given $723.85 in trade for his old car.*

Robertson had trouble with the truck's wiring and returned the truck several times for repairs. About two months after Robertson purchased it, the truck caught fire and *was destroyed. The automobile dealer's insurance company refused to pay when it found out Robertson was only seventeen years of age. Robertson sought to rescind the contract on the basis that he was a minor and to recover $776.51 from the automobile dealer ($723.85 trade-in plus one monthly payment of $52.66). The trial court ruled in favor of the automobile dealer, and Robertson appealed.*

Case Decision. Judge J. Robinson delivered the opinion of the court.

* * *

Julian Pontiac contends that the minor [Robertson] is bound by the contract because the automobile was a necessary. The record does not contain any substantial evidence to support this contention. The only evidence on this issue is that the boy quit school in 1951 and has been earning his own living since that time, and that he has been working for a construction company and traveling around the country to different jobs with his father in his father's truck. The boy lives at home with his parents and there is no showing whatever that he needed the truck in connection with any work he was doing. One of the witnesses for Julian Pontiac testified that the boy stated he wanted to use the truck in a farming operation. The record contains no evidence that he was engaged in farming at any time. . . . The law is settled in this State that a minor may rescind a contract to purchase where the property involved is not a necessary.

Julian Pontiac has disposed of the car they received in the trade, and cannot restore it to the minor. In a situation of this kind, the weight of authority is that the actual value of the property given as part of the purchase price by the minor is the correct measure of damages.

* * *

In the case at bar, although the minor was allowed over $700 on his car in the trade, there is evidence to the effect that it was actually worth about $350. Although there is conflict among the authorities . . . we believe the better rule holds that the value of an article given in trade by a minor as a part of the purchase price is the reasonable market value of the article at the time of the purchase, and that neither party is bound by the value fixed in the purchase agreement.

* * *

Case Holding. *The lower court's decision for the automobile dealers was reversed. Robertson, a minor, could rescind a contract to purchase where the property was not a necessary.*

Case Questions

1. As the court alludes to, contractual incapacity does excuse minors from the purchase of necessaries. What do you suppose necessaries are, and why are minors bound to contracts involving them?
2. According to the court, what damages will Robertson be entitled to receive?

There are some contracts, however, that minors may not disaffirm. Enlistment contracts and marriage contracts are classic examples of *nonvoidable contracts.* Further, some states do not allow minors to disaffirm contracts for insurance, educational loans, medical care loans, bank account agreements, and transfers of stock.

After a minor reaches the age of majority, most states provide that the individual may *ratify* contracts made while a minor through a showing of intent to be bound. Ratification may be either expressed through words or a writing or implied by the individual's conduct.

Insane and Intoxicated Persons

If an individual is *intoxicated* at the time a contract is made, most courts hold that the contract is voidable. The test is whether the individual was too intoxicated to understand the nature of the agreement. When the intoxicated person becomes sober, he or she may then disaffirm the contract.

Contract law classifies insane persons as either adjudicated insane or insane in fact. A person is *adjudicated insane* if a court rules that the person is not competent to carry on contractual activities. A contract entered into by a person who is adjudicated insane is void. A person not adjudicated insane but who nonetheless lacks the capacity to enter into a contract is *insane in fact*. A person who is insane in fact has the right to disaffirm a contract. The right to disaffirm or to ratify a contract arises after an insane person is restored to competency or after a guardian is appointed to act in their behalf. A guardian may disaffirm or ratify an existing contract and may enter into a new contract on behalf of the insane person. A few states do not allow disaffirmance of a contract made by an insane person if the contract is just and reasonable.

Legality

For a contract to be valid, its subject matter must be *lawful*. The contract will be illegal and unenforceable if its subject matter violates a state or federal statutory law or the common law or is contrary to public policy. Commentators often insist on using the term *illegal bargain* or *illegal agreement* rather than illegal contract, because the word *contract* by definition refers to a legal and enforceable agreement.

Contracts Contrary to Public Policy

Some contracts are unenforceable because their subject matter is *contrary to public policy*. In some situations, a contract will not violate any particular statute or law. However, its effect is said to have a negative impact on public welfare. Some of the types of contracts that courts have frequently held to be illegal on the ground that they are contrary to public policy are exculpatory agreements, unconscionable contracts, contracts with public servants, and contracts in restraint of trade.

Exculpatory Agreements. An *exculpatory agreement* releases one party from the consequences brought about by wrongful acts or negligence. An example of an exculpatory agreement is an employment contract with a clause stating that employees will not hold the employer liable for any harm to them caused by the employer while on the job. Such exculpatory clauses are frequently objected to on the grounds that they tend to induce a lack of care on the part of the employer by reducing the employer's concerns about being sued for negligent acts. Such clauses are generally held to be contrary to public policy and not enforceable.

Although limited either by statute or by the common law in several jurisdictions, exculpatory clauses are generally permitted in certain commercial leases. Under such leases, the landlord is protected from both personal and property damage, and may even provide that the tenant will reimburse the landlord for any legal expense in the event that a third party sues to recover for injuries sustained on the property.

Unconscionable Contracts. Usually the courts will not concern themselves with the fairness of the bargain struck by the parties. If a contract, however, is grossly unfair or oppressive to an innocent party, the courts, in equity, will not enforce it. Such contracts are called *unconscionable contracts;* they occur when one of the parties, being in a strong bargaining position, takes advantage of the other party and convinces them to enter into a contract contrary to their well-being. Such agreements are generally held to violate public policy and are not enforceable.

The UCC denies or limits the enforceability of an unconscionable contract for the sale of goods in the interest of fairness and decency and to correct the harshness in contracts resulting from unequal bargaining positions of the parties. As the *Jones* v. *Star Credit Corp.* case illustrates, unconscionable contracts most frequently arise in retail sales to individuals. In such circumstances, it is not unusual for the individual to have neither read nor understood the provisions of the contract.

Jones v. Star Credit Corp.

Supreme Court of New York
59 Misc. 2d 189,
298 N.Y.S.2d 264
(1969)

Case Background. *Clifton and Clara Jones, the plaintiffs, were welfare recipients. They agreed to purchase a home freezer unit for $900 from a door-to-door salesman representing Your Shop at Home Services, Inc. With credit charges, credit life insurance, credit property insurance, and sales tax, the purchase price totaled $1,439.69. At the time of this suit, the Jones had paid $619.88 toward the purchase. Evidence presented at the trial established that the freezer had a maximum retail value of $300.*

Case Decision. Justice Sol M. Wachtler delivered the opinion of the court.

* * *

The question is whether this transaction and the resulting contract could be considered unconscionable within the meaning of the Uniform Commercial Code which provides in part:

(1) If the court as a matter of law finds the contract or any clause of the contract to have been unconscionable at the time it was made the court may refuse to enforce the contract, or it may enforce the remainder of the contract without the unconscionable clause, or it may so limit the application of any unconscionable clause as to avoid any unconscionable result.

(2) When it is claimed or appears to the court that the contract or any clause thereof may be unconscionable the parties shall be afforded a reasonable opportunity to present evidence as to its commercial setting, purpose and effect to aid the court in making the determination.

* * *

On the one hand it is necessary to recognize the importance of preserving the integrity of agreements and the fundamental right of parties to deal, trade, bargain, and contract. On the other hand there is the concern for the uneducated and often illiterate individual who is the victim of gross inequality of bargaining power, usually the poorest members of the community. Concern for the protection of these consumers against overreaching by the small but hardy breed of merchants who would prey on them is not novel. The dangers of inequality of bargaining power were vaguely recognized in the early English common law when Lord Hardwicke wrote of a fraud, which "may be apparent from the intrinsic nature and subject of the bargain itself; such as no man in his senses and not under delusion would make." [T]he United States Supreme Court [has] characterized these as 'cases in which one party took advantage of the other's ignorance of arithmetic to impose upon him, and the fraud was apparent from the face of the contracts.'

The law is beginning to fight back against those who once took advantage of the poor and illiterate without risk of either exposure or interference. From the common law doctrine of intrinsic fraud we have, over the years, developed common and statutory law which tells not only the buyer but also the seller to beware. This body of laws recognizes the importance of a free enterprise system but at the same time will provide the legal armor to protect and safeguard the prospective victim from the harshness of an unconscionable contract.

The Uniform Commercial Code enacts the moral sense of the community into the law of commercial transactions. It authorizes the court to find, as a matter of law, that a contract or a clause of a contract was "unconscionable at the time it was made", and upon so finding the court may refuse to enforce the contract, excise the objectionable clause or limit the application of the clause to avoid an unconscionable result. "The principle", states the Official Comment to this section, "is one of the prevention of oppression and unfair surprise." It permits a court to accomplish directly what heretofore was often accomplished by construction of language, manipulations of fluid rules of contract law and determinations based upon a presumed public policy.

* * *

Fraud, in the instant case, is not present; nor is it necessary under the statute. The question which presents itself is whether or not, under the circumstances of this case, the sale of a freezer unit having a retail value of $300 for $900 ($1,439.69 including credit charges and $18 sales tax) is unconscionable as a matter of law. . . .

Concededly, deciding the issue is substantially easier than explaining it. No doubt, the mathematical disparity between $300, which presumably includes a reasonable profit margin, and $900, which is exorbitant on its face, carries the greatest weight. Credit charges alone exceed by more than $100 the retail value of the freezer. These alone may be insufficient to sustain the decision. Yet, a caveat is warranted lest we reduced the import of [the UCC] solely to a mathematical ratio formula. It may, at times, be that; yet it may also be much more. The very limited financial resources of the purchaser, known to the sellers at the time of the sale, is entitled to weight in the balance. Indeed, the value disparity itself leads inevitably to the felt conclusion that knowing advantage was taken of the plaintiffs. In addition, the meaningfulness of choice essential to the making of a contract, can be negated by a gross inequality of bargaining power.

There is no question about the necessity and even the desirability of installment sales and the extension of credit. Indeed, there are many, including welfare recipients, who would be deprived of even the most basic conveniences without the use of these devices. Similarly, the retail merchant selling on installment or extending credit is expected to establish a pricing factor which will afford a degree of protection commensurate with the risk of selling to those who might be default prone. However, neither of these accepted premises can clothe the sale of this freezer with respectability.

* * *

Case Holding. *The contract is unconscionable under the UCC. The plaintiffs had already paid more than $600 toward the purchase of the $300 freezer unit. In accordance with the statute, the contract was reformed and amended by changing the payments owed to equal the amount already paid by the plaintiffs.*

Case Questions

1. What was unconscionable in this case? Is that something for which the law should apply a remedy?
2. Will this decision be expected to impact the way in which Your Shop at Home Services, Inc. does business in the future?
3. Suppose that an installment purchase was the only avenue available for the plaintiffs for the purchase of a freezer. Would they have elected this same route to its purchase? What if the plaintiff had been middle class rather than poor?

Contracts with Public Servants. A contract whose purpose is to influence a public servant to deviate from the duty the public servant owes to the general public is contrary to public policy and illegal. For example, if a lobbyist contracts to pay a legislator if a bill is passed or not passed, the contract would be unenforceable. However, note that a lobbying contract under which a person is hired to influence a legislator's vote or decision is not illegal unless it also includes direct payments to legislators for their votes on certain issues.

Contracts in Restraint of Trade. Contracts that restrain trade or unreasonably restrict competition are considered contrary to public policy and are not enforced by the courts. Part of the common law on this subject became the basis for the federal antitrust laws, especially the Sherman and Clayton Acts. Antitrust laws are discussed in detail in Part III of this text.

Even if a contract does not violate a federal or state statute, however, it still may be an unenforceable restraint of trade. A *covenant not to compete*, for example, may constitute a restraint of trade if it does not meet certain guidelines. A covenant not to compete typically arises in contracts for the sale of a business and for employment. The seller (or employee) agrees not to compete with the buyer (or employer). If the covenant is ancillary to the contract, limited by time, and limited by territory, it will be enforceable. The *Shah* case discusses a covenant not to compete in an agreement for the sale of a business.

Fogle v. Shah
Court of Appeals of Indiana, Fourth District
539 N.E.2d 500
(1989)

Case Background. *Fogle and Associates (F&A) was a pension consulting firm owned and operated by John and Karen Fogle. John held 80 percent of its stock. Shah, after meeting the Fogles, began negotiations to purchase F&A with the intention of merging F&A with his company. During these negotiations, Shah agreed to pay the Fogles a total of $1,000,000 — $850,000 for John's stock and $150,000 for the following covenant not to compete:*

> For a period of three (3) years from the date of closing, neither Seller (John Fogle) nor (Karen) Fogle shall, directly or indirectly, engage in any activities within the States of Indiana, Michigan, Ohio, Illinois, Kentucky, Missouri, Louisiana, Oklahoma, Wisconsin, Tennessee, Pennsylvania or West Virginia either as an owner, shareholder, director, officer, employee or in any other capacity, on behalf of himself or herself or any third party, which are competitive with respect to the services provided by the Seller prior to closing.

Shah also agreed that John and Karen would become employees of EBC, the new pension consulting firm Shah was creating by the merger. However, a year later Karen was terminated for insubordination and John resigned. They then formed another pension consulting business, Actuaries and Benefit Consultants, Inc. (ABC). The Fogles began competing with Shah by contacting former clients.

The Fogles filed a complaint alleging Shah materially breached the stock purchase agreement. Shah answered and filed a counterclaim for injunctive relief. After trial on the merits, the court granted a permanent injunction against the Fogles, finding the covenant not to compete reasonable. The Fogles appealed.

Case Decision. Judge Conover delivered the opinion of the court.

* * *

Covenants not to compete in employment contracts are in restraint of trade and not favored by the law. . . . On the other hand, covenants involved in the sale of a business are not as ill-favored at law. . . . The reasons for this distinction were well-stated by [the Massachusetts courts]:

> In the [sale of a business] there is more likely to be equal bargaining power between the parties; the proceeds of the sale generally enable the seller to support himself temporarily without the immediate practical need to enter into competition with his former business; and a seller is usually paid a premium for agreeing not to compete with the buyer. Where the sale of the business includes goodwill, a broad noncompetition agreement may be necessary to assure that the buyer receives that which he purchased. . . .
>
> On the other hand, an ordinary employee typically has only his own labor or skills to sell and often is not in a position to bargain with his employer. Postemployment restraints in such cases must be scrutinized carefully to see that they go no further than necessary to protect an employer's legitimate interests, such as trade secrets or confidential customer information.

Employer-employee covenants not to compete are reviewed with stricter scrutiny than covenants not to compete ancillary to the sale of a business. The territorial extent of a covenant not to compete ancillary to the sale of a business will be found reasonable with much greater readiness than the same provision would as part of a restrictive covenant ancillary to a contract of employment.

* * *

A three-pronged test is applied in determining whether covenants not to compete ancillary to the sale of a business are overly broad. The elements of the test are: (a) whether the covenant is broader than necessary for the protection of the covenantee (here, Shah) in some legitimate interest, (b) the effect of the covenant upon the covenantor (the Fogles), and (c) the effect of the covenant upon the public interest. Of primary importance is the question of whether the covenant not to compete is reasonable as to the covenantee, and whether it is reasonable as to time, space and the activity restricted.

* * *

There are several factors considered in determining whether the protection afforded a covenantee in a territorial restraint covenant ancillary to the sale of a business is reasonable under the circumstances. The most important of these factors is the type or nature of the business purchased. . . . A covenant not to compete ancillary to the sale of a service-oriented business normally will be localized because services generally are performed within a small geographic area. However, there will be cases such as this one where the territory covered reasonably may extend over several states because of the business's nature.

* * *

The uncontroverted evidence established that the pension consulting business is dependent upon familiarity with clients or client sources. Customers have repeated and multiple consulting needs. Prompt service, integrity, and loyalty are of great importance to customers. They tend to rely on key personnel who have demonstrated these qualities in the past. The record here establishes John and Karen had a successful rapport with their clients. The clients kept returning and referred their friends. As a result, F&A grew into a business which had gross billings of $1,040,000 from September 1985 to August 1986. If the Fogles were allowed to solicit their former pension consulting customers again, the goodwill Shah purchased would be destroyed. . . .

The second element regards the effect of the covenant upon the covenantor (the Fogles). While the influence of this factor on the enforceability of employer-employee restraints is great, its importance in the sale or transfer of property is rather negligible.

As stated by a leading authority:

> Generally speaking, an employee entering into a covenant not to compete receives little or no monetary compensation directly traceable to the covenant, as distinguished from the compensation for his work during his employment. The seller of a business on the other hand, in determining the sale price of the business, definitely puts a separate value on its goodwill, which is brought into existence or greatly enhanced by the agreement not to compete with the purchaser in a stated area. Having thus been specifically recompensed for his promise not to compete, the seller, whose bargaining power is usually not substantially inferior to that of the purchaser, has little appeal to the courts in a claim that the covenant is unduly harsh and oppressive as to the territory covered thereby. The courts have a natural reluctance to come to the aid of a person who has voluntarily entered into an agreement not to compete, accepted the—frequently very considerable—consideration for his promise and afterward wants to be absolved of his part of the bargain.

The covenant is thus reasonable as to the Fogles.

The third element, reasonableness as to the general public, is also met in this case because any restraint on trade will be minimal at best. Shah testified there are twelve pension consulting firms in Indianapolis alone. Thus, the general public will not likely be harmed here by a restraint of trade. . . . The time restraint is not injurious to the general public since there is an abundance of pension consulting businesses.

* * *

Case Holding. *The decision of the lower court was affirmed. In this sale of a business, both the twelve-state geographical restriction contained in the agreement and the three-year time limitation that precluded seller from doing business with purchaser's customers were reasonable.*

Case Questions

1. According to the court, what are the important differences between a covenant not to compete in an employee-employer agreement and one in an agreement for the sale of a business.

2. What is "goodwill" and what function does it play in the evaluation of a covenant not to compete in an agreement for the sale of a business?

Effect of Illegal Agreements

Generally the courts will not enforce *illegal agreements*. The courts will leave parties as they found them and will not allow the parties to recover damages for breach or for services already rendered. Under some circumstances, however, the courts will enforce obligations even though the agreement is basically illegal. When one of the parties is innocent of wrongdoing, for example, the courts will ordinarily grant relief to the innocent party and refuse any relief to the guilty party. Or, if the contract can be separated into an illegal portion and a legal portion, some courts will enforce the promises in the legal portion.

Reality and Genuineness of Consent

The concept of freedom of contract has as its basis the right of individuals to enter into the bargains of their choice. The courts will assume that if an individual has entered into a contract, there was a desire to do so. Under some circumstances, however, an individual may enter into an agreement without full knowledge of the consequences. Without full knowledge, there is no *reality of consent* or *genuineness of assent* by the parties, and the contract is void or voidable depending upon the circumstances. It is often said that there must be a meeting of the minds for there to be consent to the contract. As illustrated by the *Sherwood* case, if the parties enter into a contract by *mutual mistake*, the contract may be voidable. If an individual consents to a contract due to *fraud, deceit, duress,* or *undue influence*, that individual has the right to disaffirm the contract.

Sherwood v. Walker
Supreme Court of Michigan
66 Mich. 568,
33 N.W. 919
(1887)

Case Background. *Sherwood, the plaintiff, and Walker, the defendant, entered into a contract for the sale of a cow for $80. In reaching the agreement, both parties believed that the cow was barren—incapable of producing offspring. Before the cow was to be delivered, however, Walker discovered that the cow was pregnant. Thus, the cow would be worth considerably more than the $80 contract price. Walker refused to deliver the cow asserting that the contract was for a barren cow and not one for one capable of producing offspring. Sherwood sued to enforce the contract and the lower courts ruled in his favor. Walker appealed to the Supreme Court of Michigan.*

Case Decision. Judge Morse delivered the opinion of the court.

* * *

[I]t must be considered as well settled that a party who has given an apparent consent to a contract of sale may refuse to execute it, or he may avoid it after it has been completed, if the assent was founded, or the contract made, upon the mistake of a material fact, such as the subject-matter of the sale, the price, or some collateral fact materially inducing the agreement; and this can be done when the mistake is mutual.

If there is a difference or misapprehension as to the substance of the thing bargained for; if the thing actually delivered or received is different in substance from the thing bargained for, and intended to be sold, then there is no contract; but if it be only a difference in some quality or accident, even though the mistake may have been the actuating motive to the purchaser or seller, or both of them, the contract remains binding. "The difficulty in every case is to determine whether the mistake or misapprehension is as to the substance of the whole contract, going, as it were, to the root of the matter, or only to some point, even though a material point, an error as to which does not affect the substance of the whole consideration." It has been held, in accordance with the principles above stated, that where a horse is bought under the belief that he is sound, and both vendor and vendee honestly believe him to be sound, the purchaser must stand by this bargain, and pay the full price, unless there was a warranty.

It seems to me, however, in the case made by the record, that the mistake or misapprehension of the parties went to the whole substance of the agreement. If the cow was a breeder she was worth at least $750; if barren, she was worth not over $80. The parties would not have made the contract of sale except upon the understanding and belief that she was incapable of breeding, and of no use as a cow. It is true she is now the identical animal that they thought her to be when the contract was made; there is no mistake as to the identity of the creature. Yet the mistake was not of the mere quality of the animal, but went to the very nature of the thing. A barren cow is substantially a different creature than a breeding one. There is as much difference between them for all purposes of use as there is between an ox and a cow that is capable of breeding and giving milk. If the mutual mistake had simply related to the fact whether she was with calf or not for one season, then it might have been a good sale, but the mistake affected the character of the animal for all time, and for its present and ultimate use. She was not in fact the animal, or the kind of animal, the defendants intended to sell or the plaintiff to buy. She was not a barren cow, and, if this fact had been known, there would have been no contract. The mistake affected the substance of the whole consideration, and it must be considered that there was no contract to sell or sale of the cow as she actually was. The thing sold and bought had in fact no existence. She was sold as a beef creature would be sold; she is in fact a breeding cow, and a valuable one.

* * *

Case Holding. *The judgments of the lower courts were reversed. Because of mutual mistake, the contract was void.*

Case Questions
1. Was there a meeting of the minds in this case?
2. Do the parties to a contract have a responsibility to fully assess themselves of the risk before entering the agreement? Did the parties do that in this case?

In some circumstances, reality or genuineness of consent is governed by statute. Typical statutes deal with high-pressure selling techniques by door-to-door salespeople. These "home solicitation" statutes allow contracts to be rescinded if undue influence or duress can be proved to be the basis for the innocent party's consent to enter into the contract. Under federal law, the Federal Trade Commission's cooling-off rule allows purchasers of door-to-door sales with a value over twenty-five dollars to rescind the contract if the rescission is done in writing within three business days.

Contracts in Writing and the Statute of Frauds

In contract law, the general rule is that an express or implied contract, written or oral, is enforceable. Some contracts, however, must be in writing and signed to be enforceable. Such contracts are subject to the requirements of the *Statute of Frauds.*

The Statute of Frauds evolved from a 1677 English statute called "An Act for the Prevention of Frauds and Perjuries." The purpose of the act was to prevent individuals from committing fraud by claiming that a contract was in existence when in fact it was not. To prevent this fraud, the statute required that for certain contractual transactions to be enforceable, they must be in writing and be signed by the person to be bound.

Virtually every state has a statute similar to the English act. Most states have six types of contracts that are covered by the Statute of Frauds and that must therefore be in writing:

1. Contracts for the sale of land and real property.
2. Contracts that cannot be performed within one year.
3. Promises to pay the debt of another.
4. Promises by an administrator to personally pay the debts of the estate.
5. Promises made in consideration of marriage.
6. Contracts for the sale of goods under the UCC.

Sufficiency of the Writing

For a writing to be *sufficient* under the Statute of Frauds, it must set out all the material terms in writing and must be signed by the party against whom its enforcement is being sought. Courts usually require it to contain the names of the parties and an outline of the consideration tendered by the parties, the subject matter of the contract, and other terms material to the agreement. However, confirmations, invoices, telegrams, sales orders, and even checks may sometimes satisfy the sufficiency of the writing requirement.

The UCC requires that for the sale of goods in the amount of five hundred dollars or more a written memorandum be executed. That writing is not insufficient because it omits or incorrectly states a term agreed upon by the parties.

Parol Evidence Rule

A contract is often preceded by lengthy preliminary negotiations. The parties may exchange letters, memorandums, and other similar communications before signing the actual contract. Occasionally, the parties will omit from the final contract subject matter agreed upon in those preliminary negotiations. In a subsequent lawsuit over the contract, information on that preliminary agreement will not be admitted into evidence by the court. It will be excluded on the basis of the parol evidence rule.

The *parol evidence rule* prohibits the introduction of oral evidence into a lawsuit where the evidence to be presented is contrary to the terms of a written contract. Oral evidence cannot contradict, change, or add terms to a written contract. Oral or parol evidence may, however, be introduced when the written contract is incomplete or ambiguous, when it will prove fraud, mistake, or misrepresentation, or when the parol evidence will explain the written instrument through previous trade usage or course of dealing. The parol evidence rule has been made a part of the law of sales under the UCC.

INTERNATIONAL PERSPECTIVES: COMPARATIVE CONTRACT ISSUES

INTERNATIONAL

PERSPECTIVES

When seeking international business opportunities, contract law issues often surprise Americans and their lawyers. Some civil law countries like Mexico, France, and Italy, for example, require that an offer remain open for a statutory period of time—unless a different period is stipulated in the offer. In Mexico, this statutory period is three days plus mail turnaround time. In accepting an offer, the mailbox rules can differ significantly from the U.S. rules. Most civil law countries put the time of acceptance not when the offer is placed in the control of the post office as in the United States, but rather when it is actually received by the offeror.

These and other comparative law problems can be reduced partially by contractual incorporation of the *United Nations Convention on the International Sale of Goods*. The Sales Convention represents the consequences of lengthy negotiations by sixty-two countries. Since the civil law countries are in the majority among the world's legal systems, it is not surprising that the Convention incorporates a large number of civil law concepts. Thus, it can be a potential trap for the unwary American. The Sales Convention does not, for example, contain a Statute of Frauds, thereby allowing enforcement of both oral and written contracts (the offeror can, however, require that the agreement be in writing). Most interesting to American lawyers is the fact that it imposes no consideration requirement as an element for the creation of a contract. Clearly, the business lawyer will want to be very careful in drafting international business contracts to avoid confusion and potentially serious legal consequences.

DISCHARGE OF CONTRACTS

Eventually contracts must come to an end. When the obligations of a contract are satisfied, the contract is terminated or *discharged*. Just as there are laws to govern the creation of contracts, so are there laws to govern and define the termination or discharge of contracts. The various ways in which a contract can be discharged and the legal effects of a discharge on the parties are summarized in Figure 9–2.

Discharge by Performance

Most contracts are terminated by the *complete performance* of the parties' obligations under the contract. A promisor is obligated to perform as promised. Sometimes, however, parties do not perform their obligations. The nonperformance of the obligations promised in a contract is called a *breach of contract*. If performance is clearly inferior to the requirements of the contract, there is a *material breach*. The party wronged by the breach has a cause of action against the breaching party for any damages and is discharged from the performance promised under the contract. If, however, the breaching party has deviated from the contract only slightly and not in bad faith, there has been *substantial performance* of the contract. In such cases, the courts will usually provide the breaching party with payment for services performed, less any damages resulting from the deviation from complete performance.

Figure 9–2   Summary of Discharge of a Contract and Its Effect on
                 the Parties

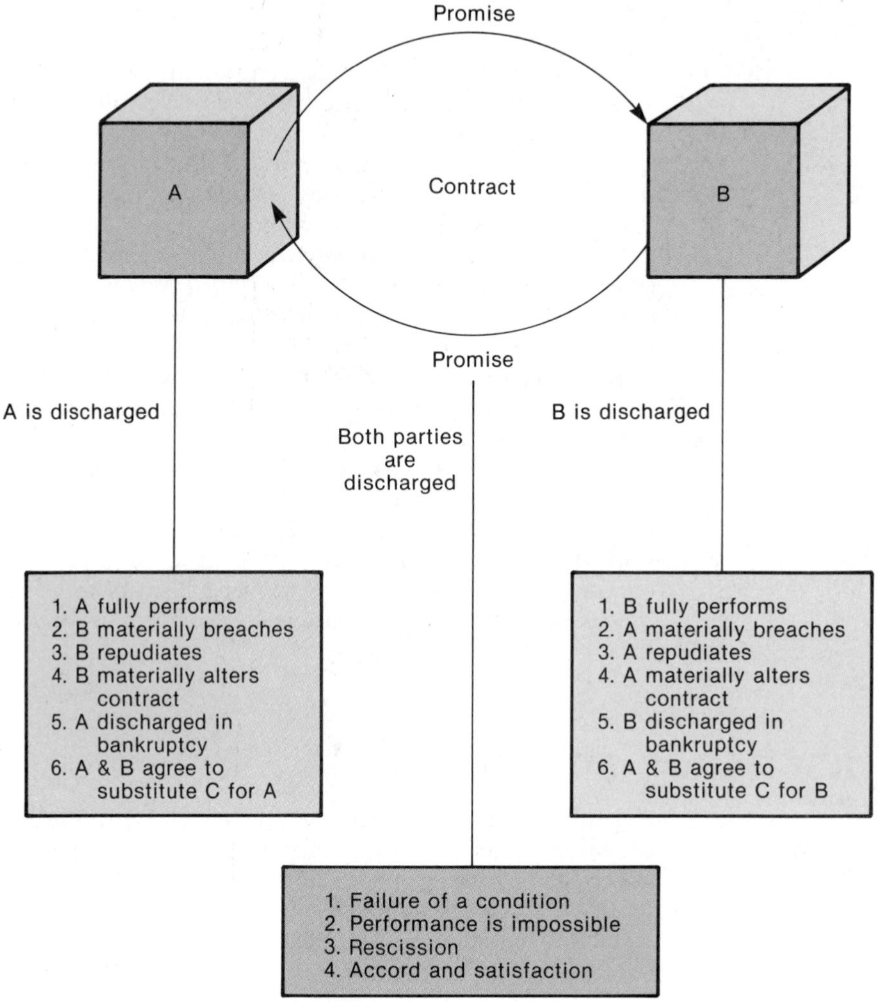

Promise

Contract

Promise

A

B

A is discharged

Both parties
are
discharged

B is discharged

1. A fully performs
2. B materially breaches
3. B repudiates
4. B materially alters
   contract
5. A discharged in
   bankruptcy
6. A & B agree to
   substitute C for A

1. B fully performs
2. A materially breaches
3. A repudiates
4. A materially alters
   contract
5. B discharged in
   bankruptcy
6. A & B agree to
   substitute C for B

1. Failure of a condition
2. Performance is impossible
3. Rescission
4. Accord and satisfaction

Anticipatory Breach

Before the performance of the contract is to take place, an *anticipatory breach*
or *repudiation* occurs if one party expresses inability or lack of desire to
perform the contract. The doctrine of anticipatory breach discharges the
duties of the nonbreaching party under the contract and allows the nonbreaching party to sue for damages incurred from the repudiation. However,
until the nonbreaching party treats the expression not to perform as a
repudiation, the breaching party may retract the repudiation, and the duties
of the contract will be reinstated.

Discharge by Condition

A party's duty to perform under a contract is not always certain. Sometimes the duty of the party is conditioned on the occurrence or nonoccurrence of some event. The condition is often stated expressly in the contract. The contract might state, for example, that the party will perform as promised if the price of a product rises above three dollars or as soon as a warehouse is built. Contract law defines three kinds of conditions: *conditions precedent*, where some stated event must take place before the promises of the parties become operative; *conditions subsequent*, where some event will expressly terminate the duties of the parties to the contract; and *conditions concurrent*, where performance of the promise of the parties to the contract occur at the same time.

Failure of a Condition Precedent

Contracts may be discharged by the *failure of a condition precedent*. For example, if the businesses along a street agree, "If the city paves the street in front of our shops by March 19, 1994, we agree to plant trees between the sidewalk and the street in front of our shops by May 1, 1994," they have created a contract based on a condition precedent. The city must pave the street by March 19 before the businesses must begin performance—planting the trees. If the city does not pave the street, the contract among the businesses will be discharged by failure of the condition precedent.

Express Condition Subsequent

Contracts may also be discharged by an *express condition subsequent*. For example, contracts between U.S. and German firms in 1939 stated: "In case of declared war between our nations, this contract will become null and void." The outbreak of war between U.S. and Germany in 1941 (the express condition subsequent) terminated the obligations of the parties.

Condition Concurrent

Duties under a contract that occur simultaneously are termed *concurrent conditions*. A sales contract for a house between a buyer and a seller is a good example of the performance of concurrent conditions. If either party does not perform, the other party's duty does not arise.

Discharge by Impossibility

The doctrine of *discharge by legal impossibility* is used to discharge the obligations of the parties to a contract when some event occurs that makes performance impossible by one or both parties. In determining whether the parties to a contract are discharged from their duties, the courts distinguish between objective impossibility (or true impossibility) and subjective impossibility. *Objective impossibility* occurs when a party to a contract dies or is incapacitated, a law is passed making performance of the contract illegal, there is complete destruction of the subject matter of the contract, or the performance contemplated by the contract turns out to be massively more expensive or difficult than anticipated. Objective impossibility discharges the obligations of the parties to the contract.

In contrast to occurrences that bring about a finding of objective impossibility by the courts are occurrences such as strikes by workers, shortages in raw materials or other supplies, and an anticipated loss of profits in the performance of the contract. The courts will find that such occurrences bring about *subjective impossibility* and do not discharge the obligations of the parties under the contract. The rationale behind this seemingly rigid rule is that unless otherwise specified in the contract, the businessperson assumes the risk of certain occurrences and the business should adjust privately to those occurrences without intervention by the courts. The *Busse* case applies the concept of subjective impossibility.

F. J. Busse, Inc. v. Department of General Services

Commonwealth Court of Pennsylvania
47 Pa.Cmwlth. 539, 408 A.2d 578 (1979)

Case Background. *Busse and the General State Authority (GSA) entered into a contract for the construction by Busse of a fountain at Point State Park in Pittsburgh, Pennsylvania, where the Allegheny and Monongahela Rivers join to form the Ohio River; a place where flooding frequently occurred. Busse began construction; just as the grading and excavation work was almost completed, Hurricane Agnes struck, depositing silt and mud on the construction site. For Busse to complete construction under the contract, the mud had to be removed.*

Busse delivered to GSA a change order for over $85,000, the cost of the additional work to remove the mud. Although GSA granted an extension on the time required for Busse to perform under the contract, it did not accept the change order. GSA alleged that the risk of loss from the damage rendered by Hurricane Agnes was on Busse. Busse completed construction and then filed a complaint against GSA with the Board of Arbitration of Claims. Busse asserted that it was impossible to perform the contract as originally written because of the unexpected consequences of Hurricane Agnes. The board denied Busse's claim for contract damages for the cost to remove the mud. Busse appealed.

Case Decision. Judge MacPhail delivered the opinion of the court.

* * *

We think that the GSA has succinctly stated the narrow issue to be decided by this Court—who must bear the loss from a destruction of part of the unfinished work which the contractor had contracted to do where the destruction is caused by an act of God through no fault of either contracting parties?

* * *

Our law is to the effect that where one of two innocent persons must sustain a loss, the law will place that burden on the party that has agreed to sustain it. In their carefully researched briefs, both counsel have referred us to cases where the courts have come down on both sides of the question now before us, but in nearly all of those cases, the decision reached depended on which party the terms of the contract imposed the risk of loss. In the instant case the Board found that the contract placed the risk of flooding on Busse by virtue of the language found in [certain] subparagraphs of the contract.

* * *

Even in the absence of contractual language imposing the risk on Busse, our law is that a contractor is presumed to have assumed the risk of unforeseen contingencies arising during the course of the work unless performance is rendered impossible by an act of God. There is no dispute that a hurricane is an act of God, but the flooding did not make performance of the contract impossible as that term has been construed under the law. Legal impossibility means not only strict impossibility, but impracticability because of extreme and unreasonable difficulty, expense, injury or loss involved. Here, flood damage did not make the performance impracticable, even though it did make it more expensive.

* * *

Case Holding. *The Board of Arbitration of Claims decision to deny Busse's claim of impossibility was affirmed. Legal impossibility means not only strict impossibility, but impracticability. The flood damage did not make performance impracticable.*

Case Questions

1. Under what circumstances would the court have found for Busse?
2. Are there ways in which Busse could have protected himself?

Discharge by Operations of Law

The occurrence of certain legal events will sometimes serve to terminate the obligations of the parties to a contract. This termination is called *discharge by operation of law*. The material alteration of the contract by one of the parties, for example, will serve to discharge the innocent party's duties under the contract. When a contract has been breached, the running of the statute of limitations will discharge the obligations of the parties if the aggrieved party fails to bring a suit within a specified time. Also, a bankruptcy proceeding will often culminate in the discharge of contractual obligations of the bankrupt party.

Discharge by Agreement of the Parties

Just as parties have the freedom to contract, they also have the freedom to agree to modify or to terminate their obligations under the contracts. Discharge by agreement between the parties may take various forms. Among the most important are rescission, novation, and accord and satisfaction.

Rescission

A *rescission* occurs when both parties agree that their contractual relationship should be terminated without performance. A rescission discharges completely the obligations of both parties under the contract. Note, however, that if one of the parties has partially performed, a mere agreement to terminate the contract will not be sufficient. The agreement will not form a contract to rescind because it will lack consideration.

Novation

In a *novation* the parties agree to discharge one party from the contract and create a new contract with another party who is to become responsible for the discharged party's performance. If, for example, A and B have a contract and A, B, and C all agree that C will perform B's obligations under that contract, the new agreement will be called a novation. The effect of the agreement is to release B from the original contract and replace B with C.

Accord and Satisfaction

Another way parties may agree to discharge their duties to one another under a contract is through *accord and satisfaction.* An *accord* is an agreement by the parties to give and accept some performance different from that originally bargained for. *Satisfaction* is the actual performance of substituted obligation. Discharge of the original obligation occurs when the performance of the substituted obligation takes place.

REMEDIES

In the large majority of the thousands of business contracts written every day, the parties perform their contractual obligations as required. Interestingly, of the contracts in which one of the parties does not perform appropriately, relatively few are then resolved in a court of law. Professor Friedman found an explanation for this phenomenon in a study by Macaulay:

> Macaulay explored the behavior of businessmen in Wisconsin. He found that may of them tended to avoid or sidestep formal contract law and contract doctrine. They especially shied away from suing each other, even when they had a "good case" according to law. The reason was not at all mysterious. Businessmen depended upon each other; they lived and worked in networks of continuing relationships. A manufacturer might buy paper clips, pens, and office supplies from the same dealer, year in and year out. Suing at the drop of a hat, or arguing excessively, or sticking up for abstract "rights," was disruptive; it tended to rip apart these valuable relationships. Also, there were norms, practices, and conceptions of honor and fairness that businessmen customarily followed. These were more subtle, more complicated, than the formal norms of the lawyers. (Friedman, *American Law*, pg. 143)

Still, thousands of contract disputes are resolved through the court system every year. In the resolution of such disputes, there is a basic premise in contract law that after a breach, innocent parties should be placed in the same economic position they would have been had the contract been fully performed. Under normal business circumstances, a monetary judgment for damages will place the injured party in such a position. If, however, the circumstances are such that the legal remedy of monetary damages is inadequate, the court may grant the injured party an appropriate equitable remedy. The types of remedies available to the parties are presented in Table 9–3.

Table 9–3 Contract Remedies

Monetary Damages	Equitable Remedies
Compensatory damages	Specific performance
Expectancy damages	Injunction
Liquidated damages	
Nominal damages	
Punitive damages	
Special damages	

Monetary Damages

The remedy usually granted for breach of contract is the legal remedy of monetary damages. The innocent party seeks a money judgment for the thing contracted for, for lost profit, and for any other special damages incurred. A variety of damage awards is available to the courts, including compensatory, expectancy, liquidated, nominal, punitive, and special damages.

Compensatory Damages

The rationale behind *compensatory damages* is to provide innocent parties with the sum of money necessary to restore them to the position they were in before entering into the contract. Suppose, for example, Takenaka contracts to buy lumber from a lumber company for $1,000. Based on that contract, Takenaka creates another contract to sell the lumber for $1,200. If the lumber company breaches the contract (fails to deliver the lumber) and Takenaka must pay $1,300 for the lumber elsewhere, Takenaka has a net loss of $100 for complying with the contract to sell the lumber for $1,200. In such a case, Takenaka could sue for compensatory damages of $100. The right to recover compensatory damages for breach of contract is always available to the injured party.

Expectancy Damages

Many courts provide an expectancy damage award to innocent parties to allow them to recover the expectation interest in the contract. *Expectancy damages* may be given instead of compensatory damages when the loss from the breach can be estimated with a fair degree of certainty. In the example just given, Takenaka expected to pay $1,000 but had to pay $1,300 for the lumber. The expectancy damages are $300. Expectancy damages are intended to place individuals in the same economic position they would have been in had contracts been performed as promised.

Liquidated Damages

Liquidated damages are damages specified in the contract to be paid in the event of breach by either party. They serve as a deterrent to both parties from taking actions that will result in a breach of contract. Liquidated damages will not be allowed if the court finds they are so excessive that in actuality they impose a penalty. The court will then provide the innocent party with an amount more in line with the costs actually incurred due to the other party's failure to perform the contract in part or in whole.

Nominal Damages

When a plaintiff has suffered a technical injury in contract law but has not suffered an actual loss, the courts will sometimes award *nominal damages*. The amount of recovery to the injured party will often be as little as a dollar plus the court costs. These awards are important because courts are able to establish a precedent that effectively states that even technical wrongs will be recognized at law, thereby upholding the importance of contractual obligations.

Punitive Damages

Punitive or *exemplary damages* are usually awarded when the wrongdoer's conduct has been willful or malicious. They punish the wrongdoer by allowing the plaintiff to receive relief beyond compensatory or expectancy damages.

Punitive damages are intended to discourage the wrongdoer and others from similar conduct in the future. Although imposed with more frequency in recent years, punitive damages have not traditionally been awarded in contract actions.

Special Damages

Special damages are damages not contemplated by the parties at the time of the making of the contract. Generally, special damages are not recoverable by the innocent party if they do not flow directly and immediately from the breach of a contract and if the consequential damages are not reasonably foreseeable. In one of the most famous contract cases—*Hadley* v. *Baxendale,* an 1854 English case—the court established the general rule that damages should not be speculative; they should naturally and obviously flow from the breach and be foreseeable.

If there are factors that may create nonobvious or special damages and those factors were foreseeable to the parties at the time the contract was entered into, the court will grant relief. If, for example, a wholesale seller of food states that a product is wholesome when in fact it is not, and if the restaurant serves the product and its customers become ill, the seller will be liable for the medical and hospital expenses of the restaurant's customers. Those special damages may be far in excess of the price of the product. Under the UCC, special damages are designated as consequential damages and are recoverable.

Mitigation of Damages

When a breach of contract does occur, the injured party is required to undertake reasonable efforts to *mitigate* or lessen the losses that may be sustained. The injured party may not recover for losses that could have been avoided without undue risk, burden, or humiliation. In the *Copenhaver* case, the plaintiff avoided the loss but attempted to recover damages as though he had not.

Copenhaver v. Berryman

Texas Court of Civil Appeals
602 S.W.2d 540 (1980)

Case Background. *Copenhaver, the plaintiff, was the owner of a laundry business. Berryman, the defendant, owned a large apartment complex. Copenhaver contracted with Berryman to allow Copenhaver to own and operate the laundry facilities within the apartment complex. With forty-seven months remaining on a five-year contract, Berryman terminated the contract. Within six months, Copenhaver had put the equipment into use in other locations.*

Copenhaver filed suit, claiming he was entitled to conduct the laundry service for the entire length of the contract. If he had been allowed to do so, he would have earned a net profit of $13,886.58. The trial court awarded Copenhaver $3,525.84. Copenhaver appealed the decision.

Case Decision. C. J. Ney delivered the opinion of the court.

* * *

While the defendant is liable for the loss sustained by the party injured by the breach, the party so injured must exercise, as a general rule, reasonable efforts in an attempt to minimize his damages. As stated by our Supreme Court:

> Where a party is entitled to the benefits of a contract and can save himself from the damages resulting from its breach at a trifling expense or with reasonable exertions, it is his duty to incur such expense and make such exertions.

Although the injured party has a duty to minimize his loss, the burden of proof as to the extent to which the damages were or could have been mitigated lies with the party who has breached the contract.

* * *

We are of the opinion that there is evidence in the record to support the finding of fact that the plaintiffs suffered no damage from September 10 to the date of trial. After September 10, all of the equipment was in use in other locations. There is also some evidence . . . that plaintiffs were generating at least as much income, if not more, from the operation of the machines in question after September 10.

* * *

Plaintiffs, however, apparently contend the case before us is different because of the nature of their over-all business. In effect, plaintiffs contend the proof established, as a matter of law, that they were capable of performing a number of concurrent laundry facility contracts which performance is limited solely by the availability of facilities for the placement of such equipment. Implicit in this contention is the assumption that, when defendants breached the contract in question, the expansion of plaintiffs' business was thereby limited because they were forced to place the equipment in question into a location they would have acquired anyway.

The testimony concerning the plaintiff's over-all business is vague, speculative, and conclusory. The only evidence we can find to substantiate this contention is some general testimony to the effect that plaintiffs acquired some 14 to 15 new locations after the breach. Plaintiffs admitted they did not even know where the machines in question were ultimately placed. Nor, did the plaintiffs introduce evidence from which it could be reasonably concluded that they would have expanded to each new location even had defendants not breached the contract in question and that defendants' breach somehow limited their expansion.

* * *

Case Holding. *The lower court's decision was affirmed. The injured party has a duty to minimize losses resulting from the other party's breach.*

Case Questions
1. How did the plaintiff mitigate the losses stemming from the defendant's breach in this case?
2. Suppose the plaintiff had not been able to move the machines into other locations. How would he have then mitigated the losses?
3. What is the purpose of this mitigation of losses rule?

If a buyer does not receive goods ordered under contract, the buyer is required to make reasonable efforts to secure substitutes. Suppose Ganguet is a manufacturer of a product that requires a plastic resin. If his supplier does not deliver, Ganguet is required to mitigate the damages by attempting to secure a substitute resin from another supplier. The damages are then the difference in price between the substitute and the resin of the supplier with whom he had the contract.

Equitable Remedies

If money damages are inadequate to redress the injury caused by the breach of contract, *equitable remedies* such as specific performance or an injunction are available. These remedies are not available to injured parties as a matter of right but rather are available at the discretion of the courts. They will generally not be granted where an adequate damage remedy exists or where enforcement would be onerous.

Specific Performance

In some circumstances, a plaintiff in a contract action may be entitled to specific performance. *Specific performance* is an order by the court requiring the party who created the wrong to perform the obligations contracted for. The remedy is frequently granted for breach of a contract in those circumstances where the payment of money damages is inadequate. Contracts for the sale of a particular piece of property or for the performance of a personal service are the types of contract where specific performance may be granted by the courts.

Injunction

As with the remedy of specific performance, the remedy of injunction is allowed by the courts in circumstances where the payment of damages does not suffice or offer a satisfactory substitute for the performance promised. An *injunction* is an order by the court that requires one of the parties to do or to refrain from doing certain acts. Suppose a partnership agreement had a clause stating that a partner who quits could not compete against the partnership for three years. If a partner quits the partnership to start a new competing firm, the payment of damages may be an inadequate remedy for the partnership. The court, through the granting of an injunction, may order that individual to stop operating the new business.

SUMMARY

The law of contracts is one of the most important laws making up the legal environment of business. Basic to the law of contracts is the underlying notion of freedom to contract. This freedom is not without restrictions, however. State and federal laws restrict a business's freedom of contract in many cases to achieve important public policy goals. A business may not, for example, enter into a contract designed to restrain trade.

A contract is a promise or set of promises that creates an agreement between parties. It creates legal rights and duties enforceable at law. At common law, contracts have certain elements in common. There must be agreement (in which there is offer and acceptance) between the parties to the contract; each of the parties to the contract must give consideration; both of the parties must possess contractual capacity; the subject matter of the contract must be legal; and the consent of parties to the contract must be genuine. Some types of contract must be in writing to fulfill requirements of the Statute of Frauds. The standard classifications of contracts are express and implied contracts; unilateral and bilateral contracts; executory and executed contracts; valid, void, voidable, and unenforceable contracts; and quasi-contracts.

Just as contracts can be created, so may they be discharged. They can be discharged in a number of ways: by performance, through a breach by one or both of the parties, by failure of a condition precedent or the occurrence of an express condition subsequent, by impossibility of performance, by operation of law, or through mutual agreement of the parties.

If one of the parties breaches the contract, the innocent party may look to the court for relief. In those circumstances where money damages will compensate the innocent party, the court may award compensatory, expectancy, liquidated, nominal, punitive, or special damages. When money damages will not adequately compensate the innocent party, the court may grant specific performance or an injunction.

ISSUE

Is Contracting Different With a Japanese Company?

International business relationships are becoming more important as U.S. firms enter world markets. However, U.S. firms are finding that business is often conducted differently in foreign countries and that business practices common in the United States are often not productive in international business transactions. Using Japan as an example, the following article provides some insights into the difficulties the American businessperson may encounter in doing business in a foreign country.

Negotiating Contracts With the Japanese
by Elliot Hahn*

From the bestseller book lists to television, art, and magazines—indeed, to literally every imaginable fount of information—Japan today looms large in the American consciousness. Of course, the greatest impact on Americans has been Japan's tremendous economic success. Yet, for all of the material written about Japan's economic success, very few words of practical advice have been offered to Americans on the topic of doing business with the Japanese. This essay will discuss the non-legal points that an American lawyer should remember when . . . negotiating a contract with a Japanese businessman or representing a Japanese client. . . . [T]he American lawyer must be cognizant of the personal views of the Japanese businessman. . . .

*Copyright 1982, *Case Western Reserve Journal of International Law*, 14:377–85. Reprinted with permission.

—continued

—continuing

The American lawyer who either conducts negotiations with the Japanese or who represents Japanese clients will have many problems if . . . Western values and ideas [are brought] into the negotiations. Although on the surface Japan is a Westernized nation, it is a country whose people have maintained the traditional beliefs that have marked their country for centuries. There are striking differences between the attitudes and behavior of American and Japanese businessmen. The lawyer negotiating in Japan should be aware of and respect these fundamental differences. The attorney should ensure that consideration is given to the laws of the two countries throughout the negotiation, drafting, execution, and performance of the contract. However, the American negotiator may easily displease or anger the Japanese negotiator by transgressing on a strongly held Japanese value through his ignorance or lack of attentiveness. Such a transgression could jeopardize the business relationship of the parties. To avoid committing this fundamental mistake, the American lawyer should take time to . . . [learn] the cultural, sociological, economic, and political beliefs of the Japanese.

* * *

The key factor that should be kept in mind by every American lawyer involved in negotiations with the Japanese is the Japanese attitude toward contracts. To Americans, the word "contract" means a legal agreement defining the rights and responsibilities of the parties. The Japanese, on the other hand, envision a business transaction as an ongoing, harmonious relationship between the participants. Once the contract is executed, the Japanese believe that the parties have impliedly agreed that any problem that might arise between them will be resolved in an atmosphere characterized by congeniality and trust. One author has expressed the view that the Japanese do not really negotiate contracts, but rather relationships. What the Japanese traditionally strive to achieve, even in a business relationship, is the spirit of what the Japanese call

"wa," or harmony. Consequently, during initial negotiations, the Japanese will often seek to probe the attitudes and ideas of the Western participant to ensure that he also desires a long-term business relationship characterized by friendship and trust. This negotiation process may take a longer period of time than do negotiations between two American[s]. . . . Rather than becoming impatient or resenting the delay involved, the American attorney should facilitate this process by being frank about . . . client's long-term interests and goals. . . .

In order to get to know their American business partner personally and to develop a relationship characterized by friendship and trust, the Japanese . . . devote a great deal of time to socializing with their prospective partners. . . .

A second reason why the Japanese often spend more time on contract negotiations than do Americans is a consequence of the method by which contracts are approved in a Japanese corporation. This process, called "ringi-sho" in Japanese, depends on the achievement of a consensus among the officers within the Japanese corporation. Reaching this consensus takes a considerable amount of time.

* * *

The American attorney who is negotiating a contract in Japan . . . should never show indignation or anger towards the Japanese. To lose one's temper is disruptive to the harmonious relationship ("wa") that the Japanese seek to establish. Neither the American lawyer nor the American businessman should ever flatly reject ideas proffered by the Japanese; such an event would cause the Japanese to lose face. . . .

Another important point is that the American must not give any indications that he expects the negotiations to be completed within a stated deadline. The Japanese are notorious for delaying serious negotiations until the deadline draws near and then, knowing that the prospects for career ad-

—continued

—continuing

vancement may hinge on whether the American . . . brings home a signed contract, attaining significant concessions that would not have been agreed to earlier.

Great care should be exercised by the American . . . in making initial contact with a Japanese businessman. This point is especially true for potential exporters of goods to Japan. Japanese companies frequently do not respond to initial correspondence in the same way American companies do. For example, Japanese companies sometimes do not answer written inquiries concerning possible business dealings. The reason for this is that Japanese companies usually prefer initial discussion of these matters in person so that they can decide whether they wish to do business with the exporter. Thus, a more effective method of contact for the American . . . may be to follow contact by letter with personal contact. Failure by the Japanese to respond quickly to an inquiry by letter should not be deemed to indicate a lack of interest on their part. This is especially true when contacting a small Japanese company, which may not be accustomed to being contacted in English by foreign companies. . . .

In Japan, personal introductions often play a crucial role in ensuring that initial meetings proceed smoothly. If at all possible, the American custom of telephoning governmental or business officials directly to set up an appointment should be avoided. Instead, a longstanding acquaintance of the official should arrange an introduction.

* * *

Before arriving in Japan, the American . . . should take steps to procure items . . . not [often used] in negotiations with Westerners but that are indispensable when doing business with the Japanese. One is the "meishi," or business card. The card serves several functions. It informs each party of the other's position in a Japanese society that is still highly stratified. In addition, the card prevents the embarrassment that may occur when one party forgets the name of another, and it provides a record of the name, position, and company affiliation of each person

one meets. The American . . . going to Japan should ensure not only that his meishi is properly written in Japanese, but also . . . keep a file of these calling cards when . . . in Japan. . . .

Unless fluent in the nuances of Japanese, the American should conduct . . . negotiations in English. Obviously, though, the American should be certain that the opposing Japanese party understands exactly what he is saying. Although English is a compulsory subject in Japanese schools, most Japanese read and write the language far better than they speak it. . . . If the Japanese party is not fluent in English, an interpreter should be used. Similarly, if a contract is prepared, either the English or Japanese version should be mutually stipulated to be the authoritative one.

* * *

If the negotiations are conducted in English without the presence of an interpreter, the American should keep in mind that a constant Japanese response of "yes" to an American's business proposal does not necessarily signify . . . agreement. . . . Rather, it may be a reflection of the differences between the English and Japanese languages. In Japanese, use of the word for "yes," "hai," does not mean that the listener agrees with the other person's assertions. Instead, "hai" may be used simply to indicate an understanding of what has been said. Many Japanese will use the English word "yes" in the same way that "hai" is used.

The desire of the Japanese to preserve the appearance of harmony may also lead them to use "yes" as a device to avoid outright rejection of the point being discussed. To overcome this reluctance, it is often advisable for the American to suggest at the beginning of negotiations that, although he too desires to establish a harmonious relationship, the best way to prevent misunderstandings may be for each party to state frankly their ideas and reactions to the oth-

—continued

—continuing

er's ideas with each party taking no offence at the candor. . . .

In conclusion, let me emphasize how important it is for the American involved in contract negotiations with the Japanese to remember that no matter how "Westernized" the Japanese may appear on the surface, they have far different beliefs, customs, modes of behavior, and values than do Americans. The American must be sensitive to these differences, and respect them. . . . Only in this way [might there be] a contractual relationship that will subsequently benefit both sides.

Questions

1. How do Japanese attitudes toward contract differ from American attitudes?

2. What are the key differences between American and Japanese negotiation techniques?

3. Why is it good business practice to understand a foreigner's values and ideas before negotiating contracts with him or her?

REVIEW AND DISCUSSION QUESTIONS

1. Define the following terms and expressions:
   offer
   acceptance
   consideration
   breach of contract
   promissory estoppel
   legal capacity
   unconscionable contract
   mutual mistake
   parol evidence rule
   discharge
   impossibility
   damages

2. Compare and contrast the following concepts.
   a. Binding and nonbinding promises
   b. Bilateral and unilateral contracts
   c. Contracts and quasi-contracts
   d. Offer and acceptance and offer and counteroffer
   e. Monetary damages and equitable relief
   f. Adjudicated insane and insane in fact

3. What is the concept of freedom to contract? How does it affect the law of contracts?

4. Mr. Jones walks into a grocery store, puts fifty cents down on the counter, and says, "A Coke please." Under contract law, what has just occurred? If the grocery store owner hands him a Coke and takes the fifty cents, what type of contract has been agreed upon?

5. What are the differences between valid, void, voidable, and unenforceable contracts?

6. What is the purpose of the Statute of Frauds in modern contract law? Do the areas covered by the statute need the protection afforded them?

Case Questions

7. Mr. Burt executed a pledge for $50,000 in 1968. The pledge was delivered to St. Joseph's Hospital. It provided, "In consideration of and to induce the subscription of others, I promise to pay to St. Joseph's Hospital the sum of $50,000 in five installments." Mr. Burt made two installment payments of $10,000 each before his death. The hospital filed a claim for the unpaid balance against his estate. Is this a contract for which the estate is now liable? [*Mount Sinai Hospital* v. *Jordan*, 290 So.2d 484 (Fla.1974)]

8. Rose, a minor, purchased a new car from Sheehan Buick for $5,000. Rose later elected to disaffirm the purchase and notified Sheehan of her decision. She also requested a full refund of the purchase price. Sheehan refused, and Rose brought an action to invalidate the contract and to seek a refund of the purchase price. What will be the likely result? [*Rose* v. *Sheehan Buick, Inc.*, 204 So.2d 903 (Fla.App.1967)]

9. Monica wishes to rent a hall for her class reunion dance. She writes to the owner of the hall asking for the rental price. The owner replies, "Agreed that you may have the hall for the class reunion dance May twenty-nine. Price is $100." Monica sends a reply, "Look forward to the 29th. $100 is acceptable price." Upon inquiring, the owner learns that other halls are renting for $150. He writes to Monica, "Original price is off. Will rent hall for $200." His note reaches Monica the day after her last letter was sent. Was there an offer, acceptance, revocation, or counteroffer?

10. Louise and Mary were partaking of too much wine when Louise said to Mary, "You have been such a dear friend this year. Please accept my car in payment for your friendship." Coming to her senses the next day, Louise decides not to turn over her car to Mary. Have Louise and Mary entered into a contractual relationship?

11. On November 1, 1990, Arwood Stowe and Company, wine importers and distributors, mailed to Ira's, a retail wine franchise, a letter stating that Stowe would sell to Ira's two hundred cases of 1966 Château Lafite-Rothschild at $1,000 a case and that "the offer would remain open for thirty days." On November 15, 1990, Stowe received a notice informing him that 1966 Lafite was increasing dramatically in price. Stowe decided to withdraw its offer to Ira's and so notified Ira's. Ira's decided to ignore Stowe's letter of revocation and mailed a letter on November 29, 1990, which Stowe received on December 3, 1990. Ira's has demanded delivery of the 1966 Lafite. Is there a contract?

12. BZB Corporation agreed to sell property to C & S Corporation for a new development project. Five days before the actual sales date, BZB backed out of the contract. As a result, C & S lost $170,000 in related building contracts. Is there a breach? If it is a breach, what remedies are available to C & S? What if BZB were malicious in its breach?

13. Ben, Harry, and Cary go into partnership together to do tree surgery in Miami. As a part of their partnership, each agrees that if any of them leave the partnership, the leaving partner will not perform any tree surgery in the United States for twenty years. Cary leaves the partnership, and one year later performs tree surgery in Milwaukee. Ben and Harry sue Cary for breach of the partnership covenant not to compete. What are their chances of a successful suit against Cary?

14. XYZ Corporation contracted with Smith Company to build a twenty-story building within a twelve-month period. Due to labor strikes, heavy weather, and increased costs of building materials, XYZ is unable to perform within the

specified period of time. Are XYZ's duties discharged under the impossibility doctrine? Why or why not?

Policy Questions

15. Why might the legal environment encourage breach of contract as an inexpensive process to mitigate social losses associated with economic mistakes?

16. How does contract law facilitate mutually beneficial exchange, and why is that important? Are there alternative systems of exchange?

17. What function does contract law play in the allocation of risk between the parties to a contract?

Ethics Questions

18. Michele works long and hard to develop the perfect recipe for chocolate-covered ants. After perfecting the method, she has it patented but fails to sell much of her product. Web buys the patent rights from Michele for $100. The next year there is a craze for chocolate-covered ants. Web makes a fortune, Michele gets nothing. The contract between the two was legal in every respect. Should Web give Michele some portion of the profits? Suppose, instead, that Michele had promised to supply Web all the boxes of chocolate-covered ants that he wanted for one dollar a box for a five-year period. Because of the subsequent craze for chocolate-covered ants, Web can sell the boxes for ten dollars each. Should he share the unexpected profits with Michele? Suppose the price of chocolate and ants rose so that Michele lost one cent on each box supplied to Web but Web continued to make high profits, should Web be forced to rewrite the terms of the deal? Should he, as an ethical businessman, voluntarily do so?

19. Three armed men robbed the First State Bank of Kentucky of over $30,000. The Kentucky Bankers Association provided and advertised a reward of $500 for the arrest and conviction of the bank robbers. The robbers were later captured and convicted. The arresting officers and the employees of the bank who provided important information leading to the arrest have all claimed the reward. Is there a contract between these parties and the Bankers Association? [*Denney* v. *Reppert*, 432 S.W.2d 647 (Ky.1968)]

10 Business and the Law of Agency

THIS chapter reviews the important common-law concept of agency. Since most business transactions or contracts can be performed by an agent, it is common practice to make extensive use of agency relationships. The agency relationship is a basic arrangement in most commercial activity in industrialized nations.

The chapter begins with a discussion of the nature of the agency relationship, how it is created, and the legal constraints imposed on its formation and functions. The agency relationship is then compared and contrasted with other legal relationships that are similar to it, including the relationships of master-servant and employer-independent contractor. Next, the chapter discusses the agent's authority to act for the principal and how that affects the principal's liability for the contracts and torts of the agent. The chapter concludes with a discussion of the means through which an agency relationship can be terminated.

According to the traditional common law of agency, a principal is ordinarily not liable for the crimes of agents if the principal did not direct the agent to commit the criminal act. A recent series of cases have held, however, that companies have a duty to check the criminal records of their prospective employees. Several courts have awarded compensation to injured parties from companies found to have violated that duty. The Issue article focuses on whether companies should have such a duty and when it should be imposed.

THE AGENCY RELATIONSHIP

According to *Black's Law Dictionary*, an *agency relationship* involves the following:

> An employment [of an agent] for the purpose of representation in establishing relations between a principal and third parties.

An agency relationship is created, then, whenever an individual or company—the *agent*—agrees to act on behalf of and for, and to be subject to the control of another individual or company—the *principal*. Through this legal relationship, the agent becomes a business representative of the principal. Agents may negotiate the terms of and legally bind principals to contracts with third parties as long as they are acting within the scope of the authority granted by their principals. In dealing with third parties—normally the customers or suppliers of the principal—the agent acts for and in the same name and place of the principal. The typical agency relationship is compared with the typical two-party business transaction in Figure 10-1.

By using agents, the principal is able to conduct business affairs in different locations at the same time. In fact, since a principal can appoint an

Figure 10–1   A Contract and an Agency Relationship

(a) Typical two-party Contract.

(b) Typical contract with agency relationship.

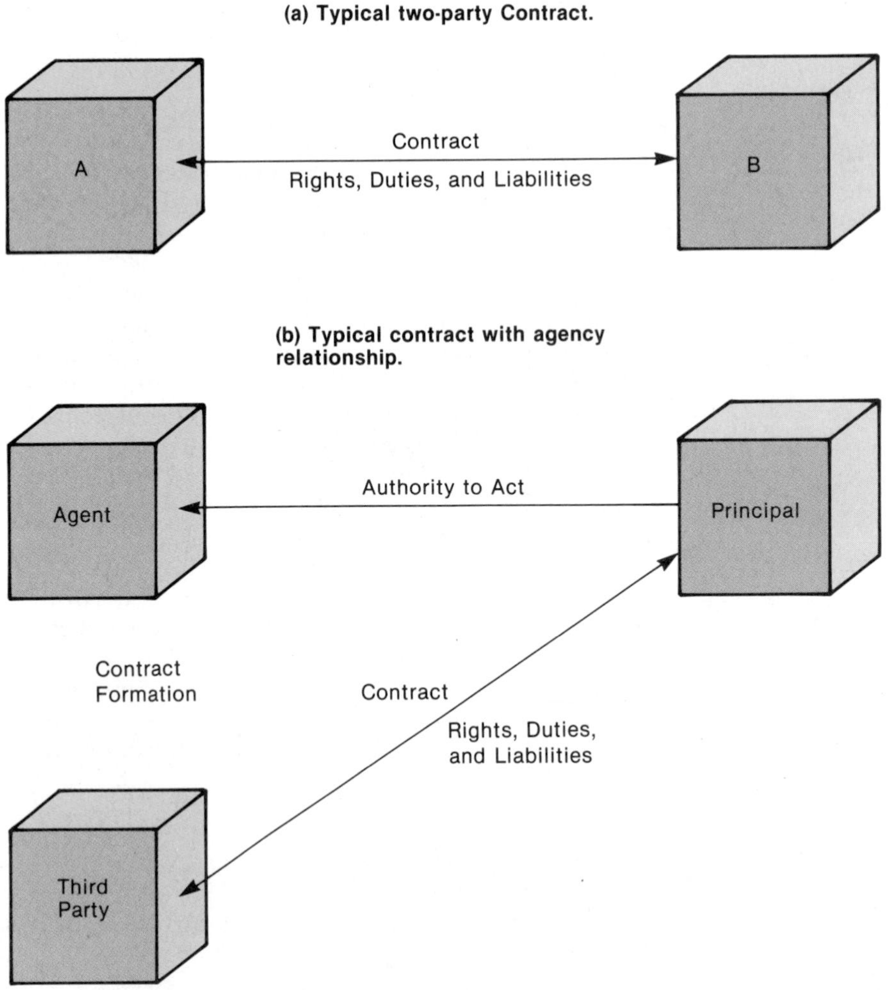

agent to conduct almost any business transaction, the principal's fundamental purpose for developing agency relationships is to expand business operations and opportunities. Charles Gabus Ford, for example, employs several sales agents so it can show and sell cars to several customers at one time. The benefits of the sales volume that Charles Gabus Ford and its customers enjoy as a consequence would not be possible without the ability to enter into legally recognized agency relationships.

Similarly, the board of directors of a corporation enter into agency relationships with individuals who, as officers of the corporation, will be charged with the authority to manage the corporation. The managers represent the directors or principals, and have the authority to bind the principals to contracts. Clearly, the agency relationship and the law that creates and enforces it are essential to the existence and operation of the corporate form of business organization.

Creating an Agency Relationship

There is no particular formal procedure through which an agency relationship is established. There must, however, be some affirmative indication to enter into an agency relationship by the parties: The principal must manifest a desire for the agent to act on behalf of the principal, and the agent must consent to do so. Most agency relationships are consensual, but they can be based on a formal, written contract. Within this framework, then, an agency relationship can be established in four ways:

1.   Through an agreement of the parties.
2.   Through ratification of the agent's activities by the principal.
3.   Through the application of the doctrine of estoppel.
4.   Through the operation of law.

Agency by Agreement of the Parties

An agency relationship is usually formed through the voluntary consent and agreement of the parties. The principal and agent may wish to establish their relationship through an oral or written contract, but a contract is generally not necessary or required. However, in several instances a written contract will be required by law. For example, where the agency relationship is to be longer than one year or is for the sale of land, many states require that the contract establishing the agency be in writing. Note, however, that most agency relationships are established by consensual agreements that do not qualify as contracts. The fundamental basis of the relationship is that the agent acts for the benefit of the principal and is subject to the principal's control.

A legal document intended for the purpose of expressly establishing an agency relationship is the *power of attorney*. As illustrated in Exhibit 10-1, a power of attorney is a written document authorizing an individual or a company to act as an agent for a principal. The power of attorney can be broad and general, or it can provide the agent with very limited authority to act on behalf of the principal for a specific transaction. Note that the term *power of attorney* serves only to describe the document itself and does not imply that the agent (who may be referred to as an attorney-in-fact) is actually an attorney.

Exhibit 10–1 General Power of Attorney

POWER OF ATTORNEY

KNOW ALL MEN BY THESE PRESENTS: That I, _____, of _____, have made, constituted and appointed, and by these presents do hereby make, constitute and appoint _____, of _____, my true and lawful attorney for me and in my name, place and stead and for my use and benefit:

(a) To ask, demand, sue for, collect, recover and receive all such sums of money, debts, dues, accounts, legacies, bequests, interests, dividends, annuities and demands whatsoever as are now or shall hereafter become due, owing, payable or belonging to me, and have, use and take all lawful ways and means in my name or otherwise for the recovery thereof, by actions at law or in equity, attachments, or otherwise, and to compromise and agree for the same, and acquittances, releases and other sufficient discharges for the same for me, and in my name to make, seal and deliver;

(b) To bargain, contract, agree for, purchase, receive and take lands, tenements and hereditaments and accept the seisin and possession of all lands and all deeds and other assurances in the law therefore;

(c) To lease, let, demise, bargain, sell, remise, release, convey, mortgage and hypothecate my lands or interests in lands, tenements and hereditaments, upon such terms and conditions, and under such covenants as he shall think fit;

(d) To vote at all meetings of any corporation or corporations and otherwise to act as my representative in respect of any shares now held or which may hereafter be acquired by me therein and for that purpose to sign and execute any proxies or other instruments in my name and on my behalf;

(e) To make deposits and withdrawals and otherwise engage in all banking transactions at any and all banking institution or institutions;

(f) To have access to such safety deposit box as may be leased by me;

(g) To borrow money on the security of the same or surrender the same and receive the surrender value thereof;

(h) To bargain and agree for, buy, sell, mortgage and hypothecate and in any and every way and manner deal in and with goods, wares and merchandise, shares of stock, bonds, choses in action, and other property, in possession or in action, and to make, do and transact all and every kind of business of what nature and kind soever; also for me and in my name and as my act and deed to sign, seal, execute, deliver and acknowledge such deeds, releases of dower, leases and assignments of leases, covenants, indentures, agreements, mortgages, hypothecations, bottomries, charter parties, bills of lading, bills, bonds, checks, notes, receipts, evidences of debt, releases and satisfaction of mortgages, judgments, and other debts, proofs of claims in receiverships and estates and such other instruments in writing of whatever kind or nature as may be necessary or proper in the premises.

GIVING AND GRANTING unto my said attorney, and his substitute or substitutes, full power and authority to do and perform all and every act and thing whatsoever requisite and necessary to be done in and about the premises, as fully to all intents and purposes as I might or could do if personally present, hereby ratifying and confirming all that my said attorney, or his substitute or substitutes, shall lawfully do or cause to be done in the premises.

In WITNESS whereof, I have hereunto set my hand this _____day of _____, 19 ___.

_____   _____

State of South Carolina \
County of _____ }

On _____, before me, the undersigned, a Notary Public in and for said State personally appeared _____

known to me to be the person _____ whose name _____ subscribed to the within instrument and acknowledged that _____ executed the same.

(Seal) _____
                 Notary Public in and for said State

Witness my hand and official seal.

Agency Through Ratification by the Principal

On occasion, someone who is not an agent, or is an agent acting beyond actual authority, will enter into a contract with a third party on behalf of another individual (the alleged principal). Although under no legal obligation to be bound to such a contract, a person can accept responsibility as principal through the legal process of *ratification*. A ratification constitutes an affirmation by the principal of the unauthorized agreement. It binds the principal the same as if the agent had originally been provided the proper authority to enter into such an agreement.

As in the creation of an agency relationship, the ratification may occur expressly or by implication. An *express ratification* involves the principal's affirmative indication (to either the individual or the third party) to be bound to the otherwise unauthorized agreement. *Implied ratification* takes place when principals behave as if they have the intention of ratifying the unauthorized agreement. In most cases, an implied ratification occurs when the principal in some way accepts the benefits of the agreement. As the *Watson* v. *Schmidt* case illustrates, ratification can also be implied if the principal merely fails to object to the unauthorized activities of the agent.

Watson v. Schmidt

Louisiana Supreme Court
173 La. 92,
136 So. 99
(1931)

Case Background. *On October 6th, Watson, the plaintiff and principal, wired her agent, Holman, informing him that because she needed some money he should sell a horse named Easter for $300. On October 16th, Holman wired the plaintiff to inform her: "We are lucky. Sold Kadiak for $2,000." On December 26th, the plaintiff brought an action contending that her agent was without authority to sell the more valuable horse named Kadiak. The lower court found for the plaintiff, and the defendant appealed.*

Case Decision.   J. Land delivered the opinion of the court.

* * *

Plaintiff admits that she received the telegram [of October 16th from her agent] the next day after it was sent, and that she actually knew of the sale at that time.

At no time, prior to the institution of this suit on December 26th . . . did plaintiff notify defendant that Holman was without authority to sell the horse, Kadiak; nor did plaintiff at any time before this suit tender to defendant the amount of the purchase price received by her, and demand the return to her of the horse.

* * *

Kadiak ran but once from August 30 . . . until October 15 . . ., the date of the sale by Holman to Schmidt, but, after the sale, he ran at the Jefferson Parish Fair in November and December, at least six times and won four races. During all of this time the horse was in the possession of the defendant. Under the above state of facts, it is clear that plaintiff has ratified the sale, for it is well settled that silence of a principal, after knowledge of an unauthorized or illegal act of his agent, is equivalent in law to an acquiescence in and ratification of the act or conduct of the agent.

It is also hornbook law that the owner who receives in whole or part the proceeds of a sale, made without his authority, ratifies it and cannot disturb the purchaser.

* * *

Case Holding. *The lower court's decision was reversed. A principal who accepts in silence the benefits of a sale, made by an agent who has acted without authority, ratifies that sale.*

Case Questions

1. What factors swayed the court's decision to find that the principal had ratified the agent's sale of the horse?

2. What do you suppose may have caused the principal in this case to want the horse returned? Can you formulate a public policy argument for why silence would constitute a ratification in such a case?

Whether express or implied, there are limits on what can constitute a ratification. Principals must have contractual capacity and can ratify only those agreements about which they have knowledge of all the material facts. Further, an agreement can be ratified only if the agent purported to act on behalf of the principal. The principal must ratify the agreement as a whole and must do so before the third party involved withdraws. Finally, if the original agreement between the agent and the third party was required by law to be in writing, any ratification must also be in writing.

Agency by Estoppel

In some cases, a principal's conduct appears consistent with the existence of an agency relationship. The principal's words or actions may lead a person to reasonably believe that he has the authority to act as an agent on her behalf. When the agent then enters into a contract with a third party for the principal, the principal is bound to the contract, and will be *estopped* to deny the existence of the agent's authority.

Thus, if Nicki, the manager of a car dealership, allows Russ to assume the duties of a salesperson, without actually authorizing him to do so, Russ may reasonably infer, from Nicki's conduct, the authority to act as a salesperson. Russ may enter into sales contracts with third parties, who can reasonably assume that Russ is an agent, and Nicki will be estopped from denying the existence of the agent's authority. Note, however, that the conduct of the agent does not create *agency by estoppel;* rather, it is the conduct of the principal that establishes the agency.

Agency Through Operation of Law

On the basis of concerns for public policy and the general welfare, courts will impose an agency relationship in the absence of a formal agreement under certain circumstances. Termed an *agency of necessity,* this agency relationship is created and enforced most frequently by the courts to mitigate difficulties arising from strained family relationships. A minor, for example, may purchase "necessaries" and charge them to a parent(s)' account when they do not provide them.

An agency relationship may also be created by law in certain emergencies. If an emergency arises that requires the agent to act outside delegated authority, and the agent is unable to communicate the urgency of the situation to the principal, the agent may act to avoid a substantial loss on the part of the principal. The agent, although acting beyond authority as specified by the principal, is essentially provided the authority to do so in emergencies by operation of law.

Classification of Agents

An agent's *authority* can be defined as the power to change the principal's legal status. That is, whenever the agent exercises that authority, say, by making a contract with a third party, new legal rights and duties are created for the principal. The principal can control changes in legal status through an ability to establish the extent and the scope of the agent's authority to act on the principal's behalf.

Agents may be generally classified on the basis of the authority they are provided. The general classifications of agents include general, universal, and special agents. In addition, three special agency relationships are also considered: agency coupled with an interest, gratuitous agents, and subagents.

General Agents

By authorizing an individual to execute all transactions connected with a particular business or trade, the principal designates a *general agent*. For example, the principal designates a general agent when appointing a manager to execute all business transactions to operate a hotel. In some situations, the principal may designate a general agent to execute all business transactions in a particular geographical area.

Universal Agents

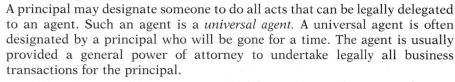

A principal may designate someone to do all acts that can be legally delegated to an agent. Such an agent is a *universal agent*. A universal agent is often designated by a principal who will be gone for a time. The agent is usually provided a general power of attorney to undertake legally all business transactions for the principal.

Special Agents

In certain situations, the principal provides an agent with authority to execute a specific transaction or to do some act. Termed a *special agent*, the agent has authority to represent the principal only on the specified transaction or activity. A common example of a special agent is an agent designated to buy or sell a piece of real estate.

Agency Coupled with an Interest

When an agent has paid for the right to exercise authority for a business, there is considered to be an *agency coupled with an interest*. Suppose, for example, a bank gives a loan to a company that gives the bank the authority to collect monthly rent payments due to the borrower and to apply the proceeds to the loan repayment. The bank becomes the company's agent to collect the rent payments, with an interest in applying those payments to the repayment of the loan.

Gratuitous Agent

The agent is not required to receive compensation in an agency relationship. One who volunteers services without an agreement or an expectation of compensation is termed a *gratuitous agent*. Like other agency relationships, a gratuitous agency is also consensual in nature: One party must volunteer to assist the other, and the other party must consent to being so assisted. On that basis, the principal and agent share duties and responsibilities to each other and to third parties much the same as if the agent were being paid. To illustrate, suppose that in the construction of a store, Catlin agrees to help Ira by driving to a wholesaler to purchase necessary supplies. If Catlin has an accident, or enters into a contract with the third-party wholesaler, Ira is liable as Catlin's principal despite the fact that Catlin acted gratuitously.

Subagents

In some instances, a principal may find it advantageous to authorize an agent to delegate authority. The individuals appointed by the agent are referred to as *subagents*. Subagents are generally intended to assist the agent in the performance of duties. Their acts bind the principal just as if they had been undertaken by the agent. Since subagents are agents of both the principal and agent, they owe fiduciary duties to both. Note, however, that subagents do not have authority to bind the principal without the principal's express consent—despite any actions by the agent to the contrary.

Constraints on the Agency Relationships

Generally, whatever business activity an individual may legally accomplish in person may also be conducted through an agent. As a rule, however, an agency relationship may be void or voidable if either the principal lacks contractual capacity, or the purpose of the agency relationship is illegal or unlawful.

Contractual Incapacity of the Principal

Contractual incapacity of the principal may render any agreements between the principal and the agent, or those involving the agent and third parties, either void or voidable depending upon the nature of the incapacity. The incapacity of a principal would affect the validity of any contract made by an agent on the principal's behalf because the contract is treated as being between the principal and the third party, with the agent acting as a go-between. If the principal lacks capacity as a minor, for example, any contracts made by an agent would be voidable at the option of the principal.

In negotiating and establishing contractual relations with third parties on behalf of a principal, the agent is not a party to the contract at all. Rather, as long as the agent is acting within the scope of employment, the agent derives the authority to enter contracts from the principal. Thus, it is immaterial whether the agent has the legal capacity to enter a contract. An agent may be a minor or be otherwise legally incompetent and still create contracts for the principal. The primary requirement imposed on the agent is to be able to perform the required function the agency relationship establishes.

Agency for Unlawful or Nondelegable Purposes

An agency relationship can be created to perform any legal activity. An agency relationship created to conduct an illegal or criminal activity is contrary to public policy and will not be enforceable. Similarly, certain activities cannot be delegated to an agent for their completion. An agent cannot be used by the principal, for example, to vote, to make a will, or to testify in court. Also, if the principal's vocation is very personal in nature—for example, the principal is an artist—the principal cannot appoint an agent to undertake work the principal has been personally commissioned to do.

AGENCY RELATIONSHIPS DISTINGUISHED FROM OTHER RELATIONSHIPS

The agency relationship creates certain rights and duties generally not present in other legal relationships. As a consequence, it is important to distinguish the agency relationship from other relationships. Two important legal relationships that are similar to the agency relationships are the *master-servant* (or employment) and *employer-independent contractor* relationships. As Table 10-1 illustrates, while both of these share similarities with an agency relationship, each differs in important ways. The distinction is important because the employer may be liable for the torts committed by an agent or an employee, but not for those of an independent contractor. In addition, neither servants nor independent contractors generally represent their employers in contractual dealings.

Master-Servant Relationship

The terms master and servant are used today to describe an employment relationship whereby the *servant* (the employee) is employed by a *master* (the employer) to perform some physical labor or service. If a bookstore owner employs a worker to take new books from crates and place them on shelves, their relationship is that of master and servant. The chief difference between an agent and a servant is that the servant often is not employed to represent a principal in business dealings. That is, the servant generally does not have authority to act on behalf of the master in contractual matters involving third parties. In addition, agents are usually allowed more personal discretion in deciding how a certain objective will be accomplished, whereas a servant is subject to the closer control of the master. The master is, however, liable for the torts of the servant if the tort is committed within the scope of the servant's employment.

Employer-Independent Contractor Relationship

The employer-independent contractor relationship differs from both the agency and the master-servant relationships in several important ways. In this regard, consider the definition of an *independent contractor* as defined by the *Restatement (2d) Agency*:

Table 10–1 Distinguishing Legal Relationships

Types of Relationships	Characteristics
Principal-Agent	Agent acts on behalf of or for the principal, with a degree of personal discretion.
Master-Servant	The servant is an employee whose conduct is controlled by the employer. A servant can also be an agent.
Employer-Independent contractor	An independent contractor is not an employee, and the employer has no control over the details of the independent contractor's performance. The contractor is not usually an agent.

An independent contractor is a person who contracts with another to do something for him but who is not controlled by the other nor subject to the other's right to control with respect to his physical conduct in the performance of the undertaking.

As this definition implies, the independent contractor is distinguishable from an agent or a servant on the basis of the extent of control that the employer retains over the performance of the work. The greater the degree of control that the employee retains, the greater the likelihood that the relationship will be characterized as that of an independent contractor. As a rule, the employer is not liable for the torts of an independent contractor, and an independent contractor cannot enter into business relationships on behalf of the employer.

Determining Liability

In determining tort or contract liability, courts must frequently decide whether a particular individual has acted as an agent or as an independent contractor. There are, however, no hard and fast rules by which courts make this determination. Even the label that the parties place on the relationship does not, by itself, decide the issue. While it will certainly take the parties' label into account, the court will consider various aspects of the relationship. Factors that would lead a court to find an independent contractor relationship generally include the following:

1. The employee has the right to control the progress of the work (except as to final results) and without direct supervision.
2. The employee furnishes the tools, materials, and supplies to perform the job.
3. The employee is employed only for the time necessary to complete the job.
4. The employee is paid by the job.
5. The employee is engaged in a business distinct from that of the employer.

Although all these factors may be considered by the court, the single most important factor is the degree of control the employer retains over the job. The greater that degree of control, the more likely the employee will be characterized as an agent or as a servant rather than as an independent contractor. Consider the importance of this distinction with regard to the employer's tort liability in the *Amear* case.

Amear v. Hall

Court of Appeals of Georgia
164 Ga.App. 163, 296 S.E.2d 611 (1982)

Case Background. *Hall, the defendant, hired Davey and Amear, the plaintiff, to do landscaping and other work around his residence. There was no written contract. Hall would tell Davey what needed to be done, and Davey would give Hall an estimate. Hall would accept the estimate, and Davey, Amear, and other employees of Davey's would do the work. Hall would then be billed. The evidence established that Davey and Amear controlled their hours and methods of work.*

Hall employed Davey to construct a greenhouse in a space formed by beams connecting the carport and the house. The beams were decorative and nonfunctional. Hall did not instruct Davey and Amear on how to complete the work, nor was he present when the work was done. Amear walked on the beams so he could nail rafters to them. The nails used to hold the beam to the carport and the house pulled free under his weight, and Amear fell to the ground, severely injuring himself.

Amear asserted that a master-servant relationship existed. Hall asserted that the relationship was one of employer-independent contractor. The lower court found for Hall, and the plaintiff appealed.

Case Decision. Chief Justice Quillian delivered the opinion of the court.

* * *

The test to be applied in determining whether the relationship of the parties under a contract for the performance of labor is that of master and servant, or employer and independent contractor, lies in whether the contract gives, or the employer assumes, the right to control the time, manner and method of executing the work, as distinguished from the right merely to require certain definite results in conformity to the contract. . . . Where one is employed generally to perform certain services for another, and there is no specific contract to do a certain piece of work according to specification for a stipulated sum, it is inferable that the employer has retained the right to control the manner, method and means of the performance of the contract, and that the employee is not an independent contractor. The test is not whether the employer did in fact control and direct the employee in the work but it is whether the employer had that right under the employment contract . . . .

* * *

An individual contractor is expected to determine for himself whether his place of employment is safe or unsafe, and ordinarily may not recover against the owner for injuries sustained in the performance of the contract . . . . Unless the owner and an injured employee have a relationship of master-servant, the employer is generally not responsible for injuries occasioned by the method by which work is done by the employee . . . . It is also the general rule that the employer is under no duty to take affirmative steps to guard or protect the [individual] contractor's employees against the consequences of the contractor's negligence or to provide for their safety.

* * *

Case Holding. *A worker who controls the hours and method of work is an independent contractor and is responsible for work-related injuries. Because Amear was an independent contractor, Hall was not liable for injuries. The lower court's decision was affirmed.*

Case Questions

1. What could the plaintiffs have done that would have influenced the court to rule differently?

2. Why should independent contractors be treated differently than employees with regard to their work-related injuries? Will those differences be reflected in the cost the employer must bear in hiring employees as opposed to independent contractors?

Agents as Independent Contractors or Servants

It is important to note that master-servant and employer-independent contractor relationships may also involve an agency relationship. That is, in some circumstances these relationships may be commingled. Suppose that Wiggins

Soft Drink Distributor employs Held as a traveling salesperson and Buchannan as a delivery person. Held is both a servant of the company and, to the extent she has authority to negotiate and write sales contracts, an agent. Buchannan, on the other hand, has only a master-servant relationship, since he is unable to represent the company in its contractual activities.

DUTIES OF THE AGENCY PARTIES

Once they have created an agency relationship, the parties share specific duties that govern their conduct and behavior toward each other. Each party, for example, is required to act in good faith toward the other and to share relevant information having an important bearing on their relationship. In addition, as Figure 10-2 summarizes, there are duties each party specifically owes the other.

Principal's Duties to an Agent

The law of agency places primary emphasis on the duties the agent owes to the principal. This emphasis is understandable, since the acts central to the agency relationship are to be performed by the agent. Nevertheless, the principal does owe the agent certain duties. Unless the parties have agreed otherwise, the principal is required to do the following:

1. Cooperate with the agent in the performance of the agency.
2. Compensate the agent for services rendered.
3. Reimburse the agent for any reasonable expense.
4. Indemnify the agent, under certain circumstances, for liabilities incurred in completing the purpose of the agency.

Figure 10–2 Overview of the Agency Relationship

Principal's Duties to the Agent
1. Cooperate
2. Compensate
3. Reimburse
4. Indemnify

Agent

Agency Relationship

Principal

Agent's Duties to the Principal
1. Loyalty
2. Obedience and performance
3. Reasonable care
4. Accounting
5. Notification

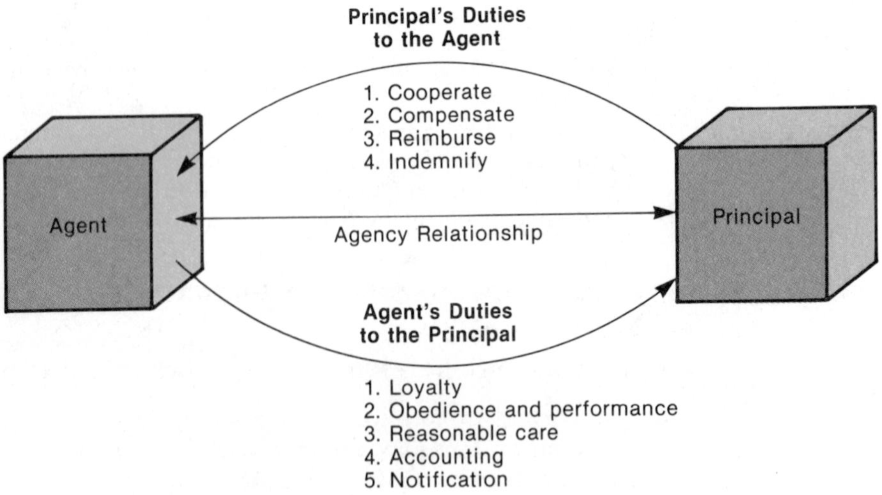

Duty to Cooperate With the Agent

The principal is under a *duty to cooperate* with the agent by performing responsibilities defined in the contract or agreement forming the agency relationship. This duty generally includes the responsibility to compensate the agent, to not wrongfully terminate the agency relationship, and, in some circumstances, to furnish the agent with a means of employment or opportunity to work. In this regard, the principal is responsible for providing a safe working environment and warning the agent of any unreasonable risk associated with the purpose of the agency. In addition, the principal must not furnish goods of inferior quality to the agent if the agency agreement calls for the sale of goods of a specific quality.

Duty to Compensate the Agent

Unless the agent has agreed to serve gratuitously, the principal is under a *duty to compensate* the agent. If the agency relationship does not specify a definite amount or rate of compensation, the principal is under a duty to pay for the reasonable value of the services provided by the agent. Often in such circumstances, the agent is paid the "customary" rate of compensation for the services rendered. The principal is also required to maintain an accounting of the compensation owed to the agent.

Duty to Reimburse the Agent's Reasonable Expenses

A principal is under a duty to pay the reasonable expenses incurred by an agent carrying out responsibilities of the agency relationship. The principal would be expected, for example, to pay reasonable travel and lodging expenses of the agent carrying out the purposes of the agency relationship. In addition, the principal is under a *duty to reimburse* any authorized payments the agent makes to third parties on behalf of the principal.

The agent cannot, however, recover expenses incurred as a consequence of misconduct or negligence. If, for example, the agent sells property to the wrong person, the agent cannot recover from the principal the expenses associated with correcting the error.

Duty to Indemnify the Agent for Losses

The principal is under a *duty to indemnify* — to pay for damages or, in effect, to insure—the agent for losses suffered while undertaking authorized transactions on the principal's behalf. Suppose that the principal has goods that belong to someone else, and as part of an agency agreement, directs the agent to sell them. If the agent sells those goods believing they are the property of the principal, and is later sued by the legal owner, the principal has a duty to indemnify the agent for any losses incurred in the lawsuit, including attorney's fees. If, however, the agent knows that the goods belong to another, the principal is not subject to a duty to indemnify the agent for losses from subsequent lawsuits.

Agent's Duties to the Principal

The agent's duties to the principal arise from the fact that the agent is a *fiduciary* of the principal. That is, the agent occupies a position of trust and confidence with regard to the principal. In addition to whatever responsibilities the principal and agent may agree upon within the agency relationship, the law imposes certain duties upon an agent, known as fiduciary duties. Those duties include:

1. Loyalty.
2. Obedience and Performance.
3. Reasonable care.
4. Accounting.
5. Notification.

Duty of Loyalty

Because an agent has a fiduciary relationship with the principal, she is required to meet a higher standard of conduct than is ordinarily imposed upon parties to business dealings. This is often stated as a *duty of loyalty*. It requires the agent to place the principal's interests before the agent's personal interests or those of any third party. Thus, it would be a violation of this duty if the agent also represented another individual or company whose interests were in conflict with those of the principal.

Suppose that a sales agent represented an electronics manufacturer and the agent's primary responsibility under the agency relationship was to locate potential customers for that manufacturer's products and to attempt to arrange sales. If the agent also represented a competing manufacturer, there would be a violation of the duty of loyalty to the original manufacturer. Of course, the agent could legally represent both manufacturers with their consent.

It would also be a violation of the duty of loyalty if the agent were involved in self-dealing. That is, the agent must avoid acting on her own behalf while simultaneously acting for the principal. Self-dealing would occur, for example, if an agent whose job it was to buy particular goods for the principal bought them from herself. If the agent has engaged in self-dealing, the principal is entitled to void or rescind the transaction.

An agent's duty of loyalty also requires that the agent maintain as confidential all information and knowledge acquired through the agency relationship. If, for example, a real estate agent representing a homeowner trying to sell a house finds out in confidence that the owner would be willing to accept $10,000 less than the asking price, it would be a violation of the duty of loyalty to give that information to potential buyers. That duty continues even after any contract between the agent and the homeowner expired. Note, however, that an agent may use skills acquired in past agency relationships as long as the confidential rights of the principal are not violated. The real estate agent, although constrained in the use of information regarding the asking price, would not be so constrained from using any sales techniques developed in attempting to sell the property.

Duty of Obedience and Performance

An agent is under a duty to follow all instructions provided by the principal as closely as possible. The agent violates this *duty of obedience and performance* and is liable to the principal whenever he deviates from the principal's instructions. However, an agent has no obligation to engage in illegal activity on behalf of a principal that would lead to personal liability. Nor is it a breach of this duty if the agent refuses to engage in behavior that would be considered unethical. For example, a sales clerk in a sporting goods store who refuses to inform customers (as instructed by the principal) that sleeping bags are filled with goose down, when in fact they are filled with a less expensive mixture, would not be in violation of this duty.

In an emergency it may be necessary for the agent to act contrary to instructions to protect the principal's interest. Suppose that Klein appoints Martinez as her agent for the purpose of selling her sports car. Suppose further that Klein gives Martinez the keys to the car with strict instructions not to drive the car without her permission. If an emergency arose, such as a hailstorm that would damage the car, and he could not communicate with Klein, Martinez would not be in violation of his duty of obedience and performance if he drove the car to a safe place.

If a principal's instructions are not clear, it is the duty of the agent to obtain clarification. The agent can fulfill the duty of obedience and duty to perform one's tasks, however, by acting in good faith and in a manner that is reasonable under the circumstances.

Duty of Reasonable Care

An agent is required to exercise *reasonable care* and skill in the performance of duties. Unless the agent has claimed to be an expert in the particular subject matter of the agency relationship, or to possess a special skill as in the case of an attorney or a broker, the duty is to carry out responsibilities with the degree of care that a reasonable person would exercise under the circumstances.

For example, an accountant employed as an agent to prepare an income tax return who failed to take advantage of a legal tax deduction would violate this duty of reasonable care. Similarly, if a client (the principal) employed an attorney (the agent) to pursue a personal injury claim resulting from an automobile accident, and the attorney carelessly failed to file the suit within the time allowed by the applicable statute of limitations, the attorney would be in violation of the duty to use reasonable care in the performance of his agency.

Duty to Account

By virtue of the existence of the agency relationship, an agent acquires a *duty to account* for the funds and property of the principal that have been entrusted to or come into possession of the agent. This does not imply that an agent must be a bookkeeper or accountant, but rather that the agent must keep a record of all money or property received in the course of the agency, whether from the principal or from third parties. The agent must be able to show where money or property went. An agent must also avoid mingling personal funds with funds belonging to the principal. If funds are mingled without the principal's express permission, a violation of the duty to account has occurred whether or not the principal is actually harmed in any way. A real estate broker, for example, who has received an earnest money deposit from a buyer of a property would be required to place the deposit in a separate bank account maintained for that purpose, not in a personal bank account.

The agent's duty to account extends to any personal profits the agent makes through any breach of a duty. If, for example, an agent were charged with the responsibility to purchase products for the principal and received a kickback from a seller, there would be a duty to account to the principal for that kickback. As the *Tarnowski* case illustrates, the principal would be entitled to recover the kickback from the agent.

Tarnowski v. Resop

Minnesota Supreme Court
236 Minn. 33, 51 N.W.2d 801 (1952)

Case Background. *Tarnowski, the plaintiff, hired Resop, the defendant, as his agent to investigate and negotiate the purchase of a jukebox route. Relying on the advice of Resop, Tarnowski purchased such a business from a third party. Later, Tarnowski discovered that Resop's representation of the business was false. Tarnowski then demanded his money back and, when the sellers refused, he successfully brought suit against them.*

Tarnowski then brought this action against Resop, alleging that he had collected a "secret commission" from the sellers for consummating the sale. Tarnowski sought to recover that commission. The lower court found for Tarnowski, and Resop appealed. Resop argued that because Tarnowski collected from the sellers he was not also entitled to collect from him.

Case Decision. Justice Knutson delivered the opinion of the court.

* * *

. . . [T]he principle that all profits made by an agent in the course of an agency belong to the principal, whether they are the fruits of performance or the violation of an agent's duty, is firmly established and universally recognized.

It matters not that the principal has suffered no damage or even that the transaction has been profitable to him.

The rule and the basis therefor [have been well stated by this court]: "Actual injury is not the principle the law proceeds on, in holding such transactions void. Fidelity in the agent is what is aimed at, and, as a means of securing it, the law will not permit him to place himself in a position in which he may be tempted by his own private interests to disregard those of his principal . . . ."

The right to recover profits made by the agent in the course of the agency is not affected by the fact that the principal, upon discovering a fraud, has rescinded the contract and recovered that with which he parted. [The] Restatement, Agency, . . . reads: "If an agent has violated a duty . . . to the principal so that the principal is entitled to profits which the agent has thereby made, the fact that the principal has brought an action against a third person and has been made whole by such action does not prevent the principal from recovering from the agent the profits which the agent has made. Thus, if the other contracting party has given a bribe to the agent to make a contract with him on behalf of the principal, the principal can rescind the transaction, recovering from the other party anything received by him, or he can maintain an action for damages against him; in either event the principal may recover from the agent the amount of the bribe."

It follows that, insofar as the secret commission of $2,000 received by the agent is concerned, Tarnowski had an absolute right thereto, irrespective of any recovery resulting from the action against the sellers for rescission.

* * *

Case Holding. *The lower court's decision in favor of the principal-plaintiff was affirmed. The principal is entitled to recover from the agent any and all profits associated with contracts the agent enters into on the principal's behalf, regardless of whether the principal has also recovered from other parties involved in the transaction.*

Case Questions

1. If the principal had been fully compensated as a consequence of his legal action against the sellers, will this court also let him recover the commission from the agent?

2. What if the principal would have made a profit as a consequence of collecting from the agent?

3. What social function does this rule of law serve?

Duty to Notify

Finally, the agent is under a duty to keep the principal informed of all facts and occurrences relevant to the agency purpose. Suppose that Clayton employs Amacher as her agent to sell 500 acres of farmland at a given price per acre. Suppose further that Amacher finds that in the next several months the farmland will likely dramatically increase in value due to a major new highway planned to be constructed nearby. Amacher is under a duty to inform Clayton of this information so that Clayton can decide if she still wishes Amacher to proceed according to her original instructions.

AGENT'S AUTHORITY TO ACT FOR THE PRINCIPAL

The agent's ability to transact business on behalf of and for the principal depends, in large part, upon the scope of authority given to the agent by the principal. The scope of an agent's authority is determined from the oral or written expressions of the principal, the principal's conduct, or the customs of trade or business for which the agent is employed. An agent can possess two general classifications of authority: *actual authority* and *apparent authority*. Although each arises in a different fashion, both may be present at the same time.

Actual Authority

Actual authority is sometimes referred to as real authority because it is authority given by the principal to the agent. Actual authority can be further divided into express and implied authority. In either case, actual authority confers upon an agent the power and the right to change the principal's legal status.

Express Authority

Express authority consists of instructions given by the principal to an agent, either orally or in writing. If, for example, the owner of an automobile franchise told sales personnel to give a 10 percent discount on all sales of compact cars, the sales personnel would have express authority to do so. Similarly, if the owner of an apartment complex hired a leasing agent and told the agent to rent apartments at a certain price, the agent would have express authority to rent the apartments as instructed.

Implied Authority

In many cases, when an agent receives express authority to accomplish some task, there is also some *implied authority*. Implied authority consists of the power to do whatever is reasonable and customary to carry out the agency purpose. If a landowner authorizes a real estate agent to find a buyer for some acreage, the landowner need not describe to the agent each and every step that could be taken to try to locate a buyer. Thus, even though the parties never explicitly discussed the matter, the agent would have the implied authority to post a "For Sale" sign on the property, advertise the offer for sale in a newspaper, and take prospective purchasers onto the property to inspect it unless instructed to the contrary by the principal.

Apparent Authority

On occasion, principals can be bound by unauthorized actions of agents if the agent appears to have authority to act. Unlike actual authority, which is given by the principal to the agent, *apparent authority* or authority by estoppel results from a third party's reasonable perceptions from the principal's behavior. That is, apparent authority arises when the principal creates an appearance of authority in an agent that leads a third party to conclude reasonably that the agent has authority to perform certain acts for the principal. Note, however, that apparent authority cannot be created by the agent, but can exist only when the principal acts so as to lead a reasonably prudent third person to believe that the agent has certain authority.

Apparent authority commonly arises when a principal hires a business manager as an agent. As a rule, the general authority to manage a business confers upon the agent the implied authority to undertake activities that are customary in that business. Suppose that Whitney hired Taylor as a business manager of his sporting goods store. Taylor would have the authority to make relevant contracts, procure supplies, interact with employees, sell goods, and collect payments. Suppose further that Whitney provided Taylor with business cards that identified her as the business manager and introduced her to all his suppliers in that capacity. However, Whitney specifically instructed Taylor not to purchase any tennis rackets, because he wished to choose them himself. Clearly, Taylor would have no actual authority to purchase tennis rackets, but under the circumstances, third parties would be justified in presuming that Taylor has such authority. If Taylor bought tennis rackets despite Whitney's instructions, he would be bound by Taylor's action unless he had informed third parties to the contrary.

LIABILITY FOR CONTRACTS

A fundamental purpose of an agency relationship is to provide the principal with a legal means to expand business opportunities and activities. That is accomplished by authorizing agents to enter into contracts on behalf of the principal. The principal is thus able to do business in several places simultaneously. In large part, the rights and liabilities of the principal and agent are determined by whether the principal is disclosed, partially disclosed, or undisclosed, and by whether the agent acted with or without authority.

Liabilities of Disclosed and Partially Disclosed Principals

According to the *Restatement (2d) Agency*, a *disclosed principal* is a principal whose identity is known by the third party at the time a contract is entered into with the agent. In contrast, although a *partially disclosed principal's* identity is unknown to the third party, the third party does know that the agent is acting for a principal at the time the contract is made.

Agents With Actual Authority

As illustrated in Figure 10–3(a), a disclosed or partially disclosed principal is liable to a third party for a contract made by the agent if the agent has actual authority to so act on behalf of the principal. If the principal is disclosed to the third party, the agent has no contractual liability for the nonperformance of the principal or the third party. If the principal is just partially disclosed, however, most states hold that both the agent and the principal are parties to the contract, and the third party can hold either liable for contractual nonperformance.

Suppose that Cook instructs Chan, his agent, to purchase a vehicle for his use. Suppose further that Chan enters into a contract for such a vehicle with a third party who is aware that Chan is acting in an agency capacity. Cook is bound by the contract and must honor it. The third-party seller of the vehicle is entitled to sue either Cook or Chan if Cook fails to perform according to the agreement made on his behalf by Chan.

Agents With Apparent Authority

As illustrated in Figure 10–3(b), the principal is contractually liable to a third party if the third party enters into a contract presented by an agent with the apparent authority to act for the principal. Under such circumstances, however, and in contrast to agents with actual authority, the agent has violated her duty of obedience to the principal. As a consequence, the agent will be required to indemnify (or reimburse) the principal for any losses she incurs in fulfilling that contract. The agent's responsibility to indemnify the principal grows out of the fact that in acting on the basis of apparent rather than actual authority, she has exceeded her authority.

To illustrate, suppose in the preceding example that Cook did not provide Chan with express authority to purchase a vehicle. Suppose further that Cook's conduct in the past has led third parties to believe that Chan has such authority. If Chan enters into a contract for a vehicle, the principal is bound by it, but Chan must indemnify Cook for losses incurred as a consequence.

Liabilities of Undisclosed Principals

An *undisclosed principal* is a principal whose identity is unknown by the third party. The third party also must have no knowledge that the agent is acting on behalf of another when the contract is made. Thus, the third party is unaware of both the identity of the principal and the existence of the agency relationship. In this situation, and as the *Rosen* case illustrates, unless the agent reveals the agency or the identity of the principal, the agent is liable to the third party for the principal's nonperformance of the contract.

Figure 10–3 Contract Liabilities if Principal Is Disclosed or Partially Disclosed

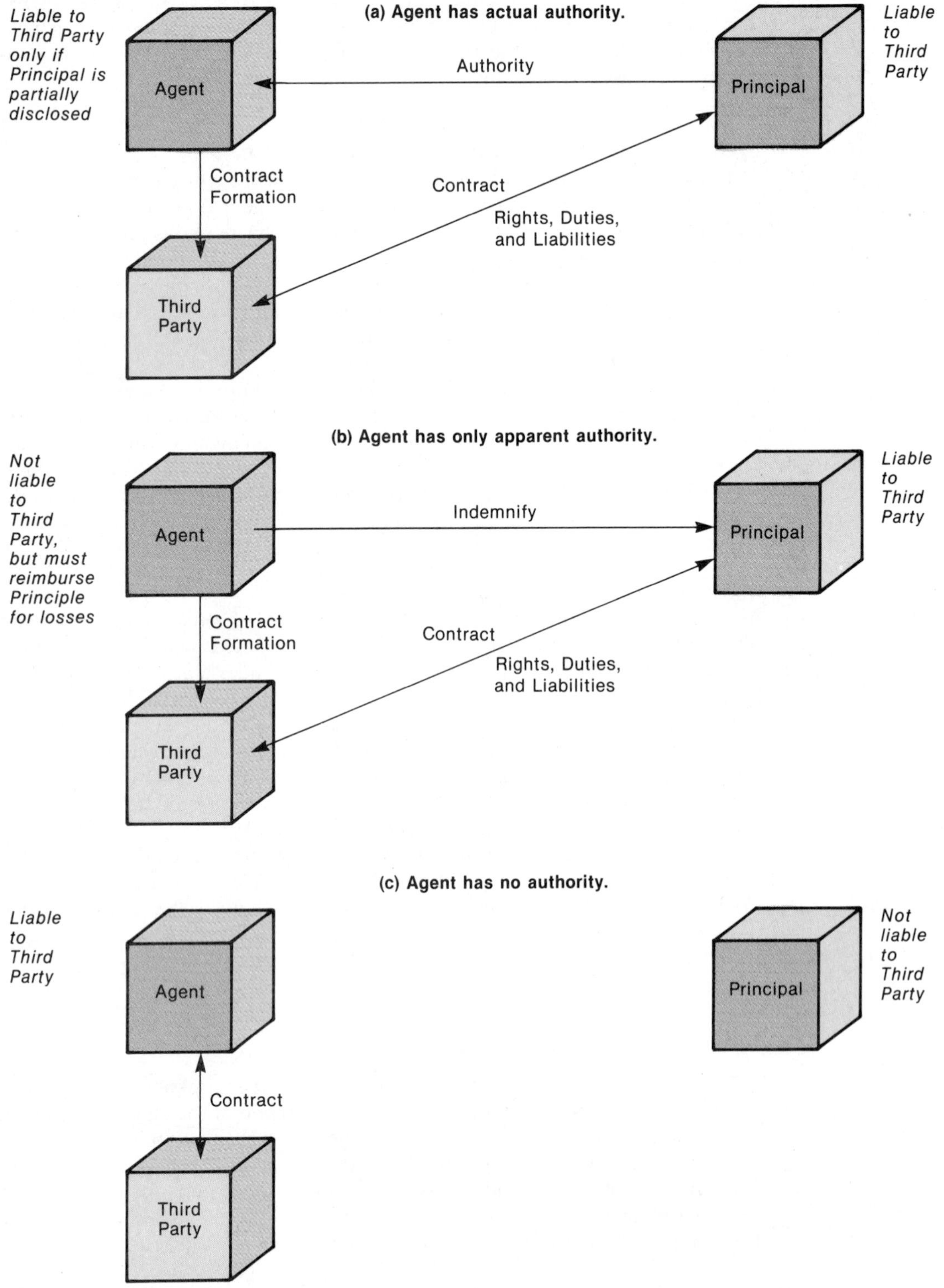

(a) Agent has actual authority.

Liable to Third Party only if Principal is partially disclosed

Agent

Liable to Third Party

Principal

Authority

Contract Formation

Contract

Rights, Duties, and Liabilities

Third Party

(b) Agent has only apparent authority.

Not liable to Third Party, but must reimburse Principle for losses

Agent

Liable to Third Party

Principal

Indemnify

Contract Formation

Contract

Rights, Duties, and Liabilities

Third Party

(c) Agent has no authority.

Liable to Third Party

Agent

Not liable to Third Party

Principal

Contract

Third Party

**Rosen v.
DePorter-
Butterworth
Tours, Inc.**

**Appellate Court of
Illinois**
62 Ill.App.3d 762,
19 Ill.Dec. 743,
379 N.E.2d 407
(1978)

Case Background. *Rosen, the plaintiff, bought an African safari tour from DePorter-Butterworth Tours, Inc., the defendant. DePorter-Butterworth did not disclose that it was an agent for the safari's sponsor, World Trek. Thus, World Trek was an undisclosed principal.*

Rosen informed DePorter-Butterworth that he was leaving two months early and would be taking a casual trip through Europe before joining the safari tour group in Cairo. At the urging of DePorter-Butterworth, Rosen agreed to contact the American Express office in Athens periodically in case it became necessary for DePorter-Butterworth to make any changes in the safari's itinerary. DePorter-Butterworth, however, failed to contact Rosen through the American Express office as agreed when a change in the itinerary had to be made. As a consequence, Rosen missed the tour and was stranded in Cairo for a week.

Rosen brought an action to recover amounts paid to DePorter-Butterworth for the tour. DePorter-Butterworth responded that it was not liable to Rosen because it was merely an agent for World Trek. The lower court found for Rosen, and DePorter-Butterworth appealed.

Case Decision. Presiding Justice Barry delivered the opinion of the court.

* * *

The . . . issue presented for review is whether the trial court erred in finding Deporter-Butterworth liable to Rosen for the price of the tour. Inherent in a decision of this issue is a determination of the relationship between Rosen and Deporter-Butterworth and Deporter-Butterworth and the tour sponsor, World Trek . . . . [I]n the normal situation between a travel bureau and its traveler client a special agency relationship arises for the limited object of the one business transaction between the two parties. It is clear in the present case that Rosen employed the Deporter-Butterworth travel bureau as his special agent for the limited purpose of arranging the African Safari Tour sponsored by World Trek.

Although the sponsor of the tour, World Trek, as advertised in the brochure, was not a party to this lawsuit, their relationship to Deporter-Butterworth is an important factor in deciding liability. The record contains a letter from Deporter-Butterworth to World Trek as plaintiff's Exhibit no. 4, which admits to Deporter-Butterworth's selling of World Trek's tour to Rosen and hints of a principal-agent relationship between World Trek and Deporter-Butterworth. The evidence also disclosed that Deporter-Butterworth received a 10% Commission from World Trek for selling its tour. The legal principle that an agent is liable as a principal [to] a third party in the case of an undisclosed agency relationship is well established and needs no citation for authority. In the instant case Rosen was aware that World Trek was sponsoring the tour but was without knowledge as to whether Deporter-Butterworth was truly representing him as his special agent for arranging the tour or whether Deporter-Butterworth was acting as an agent for World Trek in selling its tour to Rosen.

The traditional relationship between a travel bureau, such as Deporter-Butterworth, and the tour sponsors of the various tours sold has been categorized as one of agent and principal particularly in the field of tort liability of the travel bureau for injuries that occur to the traveler . . . . No sound reason exists for not finding the same principal-agent relationship between a tour sponsor and a travel bureau in the case of alleged liability for breach of an agreement involving the ultimate sale of the tour to an ordinary member of the traveling public, such as Rosen.

. . . [I]f an agent does not disclose the existence of an agency relationship and the identity of his principal, he binds himself to the third party with whom he acts as if he, himself, were the principal . . . . The fact that Rosen knew that World Trek and not Deporter-Butterworth was the tour sponsor does not satisfy the necessary disclosure to prevent Deporter-Butterworth from becoming liable as principal.

* * *

Case Holding. *The judgment of the lower court was affirmed. In the event of a breach of contract, the agent is liable to third parties if the existence of an agency relationship or the identity of the principal has not been revealed.*

Case Questions

1. What did Rosen know and not know about World Trek and Deporter-Butterworth that was important here?
2. Why was Deporter-Butterworth held liable in this case? How could Deporter-Butterworth have avoided the lawsuit?
3. Is World Trek responsible for any of the difficulties Rosen encountered here?

As Figure 10-4 illustrates, if the agent had actual authority, the undisclosed principal is bound to the contract just as if the identity had been disclosed at the time the contract was made. In fact, the principal may hold the third party to the contract except in the following cases:

1. The undisclosed principal is expressly excluded as a party to the contract between the agent and the third party.
2. The contract is a negotiable instrument. According to the UCC, if the identity of the principal or existence of the agency relationship is not shown in the instrument, only the agent is liable.
3. The agent's performance is personal to the contract.

In the event the agent is found liable to the third party and is forced to pay—say, in the event the principal has failed to perform and the third party has elected to sue the agent—the agent is entitled to be indemnified by the principal. However, the agent must have been operating within the scope of his authority. If the agent has acted outside his authority or has no authority, the undisclosed principal is under no legal obligation to accept responsibility for the agent's actions.

LIABILITY FOR TORTS OF THE AGENT

In addition to creating contractual liability on behalf of a principal, an agent can create tort liability. As Figure 10–5 illustrates, the principal can be liable for the torts of an agent if the agent's tort was authorized by the principal, or was unauthorized, but occurred within the scope of the agent's employment. In the event the agent commits an unauthorized tort outside the scope of employment, the agent is liable to the third party for damages incurred.

Figure 10-4   Contract Liabilities if Principal Is Undisclosed

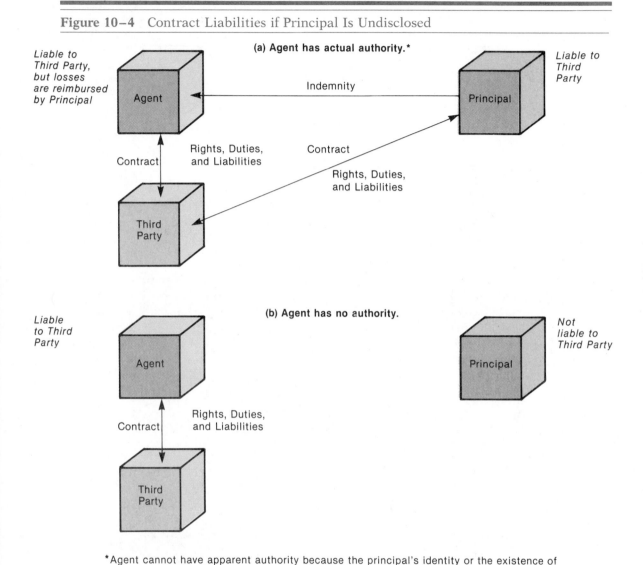

(a) Agent has actual authority.*

Liable to Third Party, but losses are reimbursed by Principal

Agent

Indemnity

Principal

Liable to Third Party

Contract

Rights, Duties, and Liabilities

Contract

Rights, Duties, and Liabilities

Third Party

(b) Agent has no authority.

Liable to Third Party

Agent

Principal

Not liable to Third Party

Contract

Rights, Duties, and Liabilities

Third Party

*Agent cannot have apparent authority because the principal's identity or the existence of an agency relationship was not revealed.

Principal's Liability

As the Issue article at the end of the chapter illustrates, the tortious activities undertaken by agents to which the principal's liability may extend has become a controversial issue. Imposing liability on the principal for the tortious acts the principal has ordered the agent to undertake—under the doctrine of vicarious liability—is relatively uncontroversial. However, the extent to which the agent's tortious activities are undertaken within the scope of employment and thus would be the responsibility of the principal—under the concept of respondeat superior—has generated considerable controversy as the courts have struggled to define "scope of employment."

Figure 10–5   Tort Liability Under an Agency Relationship

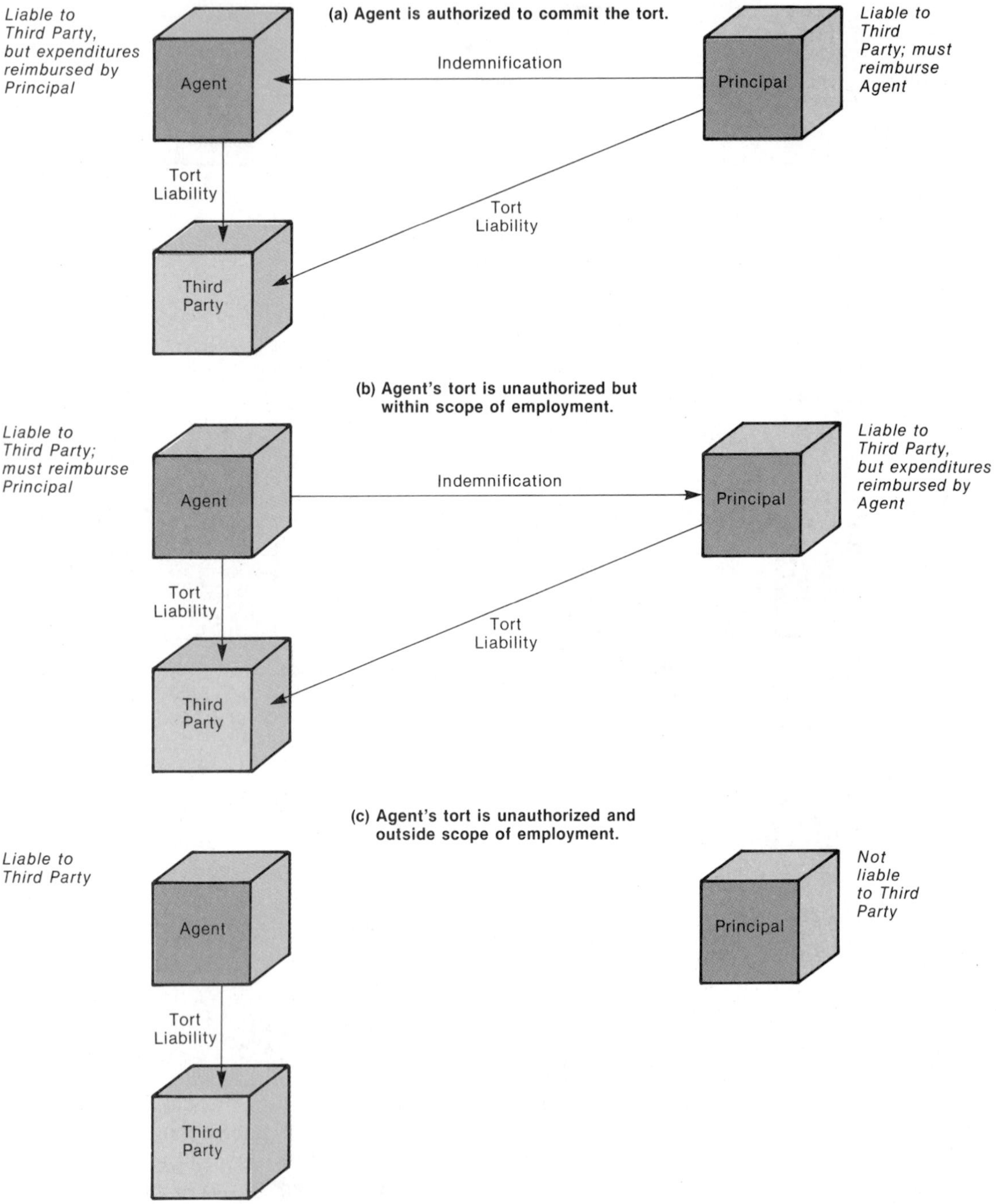

Liable to Third Party, but expenditures reimbursed by Principal

(a) Agent is authorized to commit the tort.

Agent

Indemnification

Principal

Liable to Third Party; must reimburse Agent

Tort Liability

Tort Liability

Third Party

(b) Agent's tort is unauthorized but within scope of employment.

Liable to Third Party; must reimburse Principal

Agent

Indemnification

Principal

Liable to Third Party, but expenditures reimbursed by Agent

Tort Liability

Tort Liability

Third Party

(c) Agent's tort is unauthorized and outside scope of employment.

Liable to Third Party

Agent

Principal

Not liable to Third Party

Tort Liability

Third Party

Vicarious Liability

A principal who directs an agent to commit a tort will be liable for any resulting damage. Liability imposed on someone other than the individual who has committed the tort is known as *vicarious liability*. Suppose that Mike is the owner of an appliance store. Suppose further that Mike purchased some cheap "knock-off" toasters from China that are labeled as a quality American brand name. Susan, a salesperson, does not know that they are not authentic. Acting on Mike's instructions, Susan sells a toaster to a customer who is later severely injured by the toaster. Since Susan has acted according to her principal's instructions, the principal is vicariously liable to the customer. Should the customer sue Susan, she is entitled to be indemnified by her principal.

Respondeat Superior

A principal is likely to be liable for the unauthorized intentional or negligent torts of an agent, if the agent was acting within the scope of employment. The rule of law imposing vicarious liability upon an innocent principal for the torts of an agent acting within the scope of employment is known as *respondeat superior*. This doctrine has been justified on the grounds that the principal-business is in a better position to protect the public from such torts (through careful selection of agents) and to compensate those injured (through its ability to acquire insurance).

An important question in such cases is whether the agent was acting within the course and scope of employment at the time the tort occurred. Courts may consider many factors in determining whether an act was within the course and scope of employment. Some of the most important factors are:

1. Whether the act was of the same general nature of those authorized by the principal.
2. Whether the agent was authorized to be in the location at the time the act occurred.
3. Whether the agent was serving (or attempting to serve) the principal's interests at the time of the tort.

As Figure 10-5 illustrates, in contrast to authorized torts, the agent is required to indemnify the principal for amounts the principal has to pay to the wronged party as a consequence of the agent's unauthorized torts. In the majority of cases, however, the agent is unable to reimburse the principal who must then bear the brunt of the liability.

The Agent's Liability

As a rule, the principal is not liable for the torts of an agent when the tort is both unauthorized and outside the scope of employment. In such cases, the agent alone is liable to the wronged party. More difficult to decide, however, are those cases in which the agent was not clearly doing her job at the time of the tort, but may have been engaged in an authorized action.

Such cases frequently involve agents entrusted with vehicles who use those vehicles for unauthorized purposes. If Burns, a salesperson for Reno's Wholesale Pizza, negligently injures a pedestrian while driving a company car between sales calls, she is clearly acting within the course and scope of her employment. Her principal would be liable for the pedestrian's injuries. If Burns has the accident while on her way to visit a friend, the principal may or may not be liable depending on the extent to which Burns has deviated from the principal's business. The exact point at which the principal gains or loses liability varies among jurisdictions. Traditionally, if an agent departs from her employment to the point of abandonment, the agent is no longer within the course and scope of her employment.

INTERNATIONAL PERSPECTIVES: AGENT UNDER A CIVIL LAW SYSTEM

INTERNATIONAL

PERSPECTIVES

In agency relationships, civil law countries are generally much more explicit in defining the legal relationships between the principal, the agent, and third parties. For example, suppose P (the principal) contracts with A (the agent) to represent him in the purchase of household goods from T (any other third party). Under German law, if the contract between P and A is later determined to be invalid (say, because A was a minor), P is liable to T because A still has *actual authority* to buy the goods for P. The agent's *power* to perform under German law is independent of the validity of the contract between the agent and the principal.

Thus, under certain circumstances the civil and common law systems would reach opposite results. Under the common law, the courts could find P liable to T on the basis of the doctrine of apparent authority if the contract between A and P were found to be invalid. If P has not created the appearance of authority in A to T, however, P would not be liable to T. In contrast, it is not important under German civil law that the doctrine of apparent authority apply. That is, it is immaterial under German civil law that P either informed T of A's authority or created the appearance of authority in A. Despite the invalidity of the contract between A and P, A still has *actual authority* to contract for P with T under German civil law.

TERMINATION OF AN AGENCY RELATIONSHIP

The agency relationship is largely consensual in nature. Thus, when the principal withdraws or when the consent otherwise ceases to exist, the agency relationship is *terminated*. Once an agency relationship is terminated, the agent's actual authority to act for the principal ceases. However, it may be necessary to give notice of the termination to third parties to end the agent's apparent authority. While many different events can terminate agencies, they are usually grouped into two categories: termination by act or agreement of the parties and termination by operation of law.

Termination by Act or Agreement

Most commonly the agency relationship is terminated by mutual agreement of the parties, by one of the parties, through lapse of time, or by fulfillment of the agency's purpose.

Mutual Agreement

The agency relationship is most frequently established through an agreement between the principal and the agent. Thereafter, the parties may, at their discretion, mutually amend the agreement to call for its termination or to extend it beyond its original time period.

By One of the Parties
Similarly, the agency relationship can be ended unilaterally upon reasonable notice by either the agent or principal. A unilateral termination is effective even though it is in breach of a contract between the parties. The breaching party may, however, be liable for contract damages.

Lapse of Time
In establishing the agency relationship, the principal and agent may agree that the agency will continue for a specific time period. If the agreed-upon time lapses, the agency terminates. Occasionally, the parties will enter into an agency agreement with no time specified for its termination. Such an agency relationship will normally continue until terminated by one or both of the parties. If the agent is not actively engaged in the agency purpose, the agency will terminate after a reasonable time, the length of which would depend upon the purpose of the agency relationship.

Suppose that Gooden authorizes Mattingly to sell his homemade chocolate-rum-raisin cake to restaurants. Suppose that Mattingly works diligently at her task for several months and then abandons her sales efforts. At some reasonable time, her authority will lapse, and the agency relationship will terminate.

Fulfillment of the Agency Purpose
If the purpose of the agency relationship is achieved, the agency will terminate. Clearly, there is no reason for it to continue. If Gary hires Jeff to sell his car for him, the agency would terminate upon completion of the sale.

Termination by Operation of Law

A variety of occurrences will automatically terminate an agent's ability to act on behalf of the principal. Termed *termination by operation of law,* an agency relationship is terminated without any required action on the part of the principal or the agent. For example, if either the principal or the agent dies, the agency relationship terminates. The agency relationship will also end automatically if the subject matter of the agreement is destroyed or lost. Similarly, in those instances in which economic conditions have changed and the subject matter of the agency is unusually affected, the agent can reasonably infer that the principal will want the agency relationship to terminate. Finally, bankruptcy of the principal or the agent will terminate the agency relationship if it renders the agent unable to perform duties.

SUMMARY

An agency relationship is created whenever an agent agrees to act on behalf of and for and to be subject to the control of the principal. As the principal's business representative, the agent may legally bind the principal to contracts with third parties. By using agents, the principal can effectively expand business activities and opportunities.

There is no formal procedure for the creation of an agency relationship. There must, however, be an affirmative response on the part of the parties, with the principal manifesting her desire that the agent act on her behalf, and the agent consenting to do so. Agency relationships can be established by the agreement of the parties, the ratification of the agent's activities by the principal, application of the doctrine of estoppel, or the operation of law.

An individual may conduct virtually any business activity through an agent. Agency relationships generally require that the principal have contractual capacity and the agency purpose be lawful. It is not material that the agent lacks contractual capacity.

The agency relationship is generally distinguishable from the master-servant and employer-independent contractor relationships. The differences are important in that neither a servant nor an independent contractor has authority to represent the employer is his business dealings. Also, an employer is liable for the torts of the servant and of the agent but not of the independent contractor. The agency, independent contractor, and master-servant relationships can, under certain circumstances, exist at the same time.

Once the agency relationship is created, the parties share the duties to share information and to act in good faith in common. The principal owes the agent the duties to cooperate, compensate, reimburse, and indemnify. The agent owes the principal the duties of loyalty, obedience and performance, reasonable care, accounting, and notification.

The agent's ability to act on behalf of the principal depends on the nature and scope of the authority granted by the principal. There are two classifications of authority an agent can possess: actual authority and apparent authority. The agent possesses actual authority if the principal has given the agent the authority to act. For those actions for which the agent has actual authority, the principal is generally liable for the contracts entered into on her behalf and for the torts the agent may commit in the process. The agent possesses apparent authority if the principal has created the appearance of authority in the agent. While the principal is generally liable for both the torts and the contracts of an agent with apparent authority, the agent may have the obligation to indemnify the principal for any losses incurred.

Agency relationships may terminate either through the activities of the parties or by the operation of the law. Once an agency relationship is terminated, the agent's actual authority to act for the principal ceases. It may be necessary to notify third parties in order to end the agent's apparent authority.

ISSUE

To What Extent Should Principals Be Responsible for the Crimes of Their Agents?

As the chapter has discussed, principals are generally liable for the tort of an agent, if the agent is acting within the scope of the agency relationship. This basic concept of the common law has been long recognized by businesses and their employees. A similar rule of law governs the principal's liability for the crimes of agents: The principal is liable for the crimes of an agent if the agent was directed to commit the criminal act. Since it is difficult to define an unauthorized crime as being within the scope of the agent's authority, the principal has not generally been held liable for agents' unauthorized crimes.

The principal's liability for the crimes of agents has been expanding. Recently, several courts have imposed a duty on companies to check the criminal records of the individuals it hires. If a third party is injured by an employee with a criminal record, the courts have been more willing to impose liability on the employer if it is shown that the company failed to check the past criminal record of the employee. The imposition of liability on the company in such circumstances raises several important ethical and public policy questions.

Make Sure Job Seekers Are Not Career Criminals
Lawrence W. Sherman[*]

Edward Harbour was a truck driver. He was also a convicted criminal. On the employment application for his job with B & L Motor Freight he wrote that he had no criminal convictions. The truth was that he had a history of convictions for violent sex related crimes, and had been arrested a year earlier for sodomizing two teen-age hitchhikers while driving for another company. But B & L had not verified his application statement.

Karen Malorney was a 17-year-old hitchhiker. In January 1978, Harbour picked her up and then raped her in the sleeping compartment of his truck. He was later sentenced to 50 years in prison.

Ms. Malorney then sued B & L Motor Freight for negligence in entrusting a truck with a sleeping compartment to a convicted sex offender. B & L moved to have the case dismissed, arguing that employers have no legal duty to check employees' criminal convictions. When the Cook County Circuit Court in Chicago refused to dismiss the case, B & L appealed.

On July 18, 1986, the Illinois Appellate Court ruled that because B & L should have known that "truckers are prone to give rides to hitchhikers despite rules against such actions," the general duty to hire competent employees could be extended to checking for

*[*]Mr. Sherman is a professor of criminology at the University of Maryland and editor of the Washington-based *Security Law Newsletter*. From *Security Law Newsletter,* October 1986 and *The Wall Street Journal,* October 10, 1986.*

—continued

–continuing

criminal convictions. Barring further appeals, it is now up to a jury to decide whether B & L breached that duty.

Malorney v. *B & L* is but one in a series of recent decisions pointing toward a general duty for employers to check the criminal record (which is accessible to the public in most states) for virtually every employee hired. The decisions don't say it that way; they are always limited to the facts of the case. But the cases make it hard to imagine any employee who could not have a foreseeable opportunity to commit a sex crime against someone in the course of his employment.

In *Tolbert* v. *Martin Marietta*, for example, a federal court in Colorado last November allowed a secretary to sue her aerospace company for hiring a janitor who abducted and raped her on company premises while she was walking to lunch. The janitor had a criminal record.

In *Cramer* v. *Housing Opportunities Commission*, the highest court of Maryland ruled last December that a nighttime break-in, and rape of a public housing tenant, was caused by the housing agency's earlier decision to hire the rapist as a building inspector, who had inspected the apartment before committing the crime. A pre-employment check would have revealed convictions for robbery and burglary; he was also under indictment for rape. A new trial was ordered in which the jury would be allowed to consider evidence about the ease of doing record checks in deciding the agency's negligence.

In *Sheerin* v. *Holin*, the Iowa Supreme Court ruled last January that the estate of a waitress stabbed to death by a cook could sue the motel-restaurant that employed them, where the murder took place during working hours. The estate claimed that the restaurant was negligent in failing to discover the cook's history of sexual assault and violent behavior, and in giving him access to knives.

These cases raise a difficult question of public policy. There is a clear public interest in reducing the risk of crime by employees. But there is also a public interest in not imposing unreasonable costs on employers in conducting criminal record checks on everyone they hire—especially in high-turnover, low-wage positions. If each janitor, cook and truck driver has to be subjected to criminal record checks, operating costs for all employers, nonprofit and for-profit, will noticeably increase.

An even more complex question is how to use the information once it's obtained. Should any prior conviction for a violent offense constitute a barrier to employment? For every three-time-rapist thus excluded, there will be many more 35-year-olds who were involved in a bar-fight at age 19, with no subsequent offenses. The American Psychiatric Association has taken the position that the likelihood of future violence is very hard to predict, even with extensive and costly psychiatric assessments. Predictions made by employment officers based solely on a review of criminal convictions would be virtually meaningless.

What the courts may eventually force employers to do is to vastly over-predict violent behavior, refusing to hire many people who would never be violent, in order to exclude the rare one who would be. While that might be good public policy for school teachers, police officers and day-care workers, it may not be good policy for those seeking entry-level service jobs. For if we make convicted people unemployable in even the lowest paid jobs in the economy, where are they to go? By cutting them off from almost any work, moreover, we may increase their likelihood of committing an act of violence.

One way out of this dilemma is for employer trade associations to develop standards for background investigations required for different kinds of jobs that pose different risks in different employment settings. Hospitals, for example, provide access

–continued

—continuing

to extremely vulnerable people; these institutions are like hotels where the rooms are never locked and the guests are often unconscious. In such a setting, it might be reasonable to require criminal history checks for all employees—janitors, cooks, secretaries, and even nurses and doctors. Construction workers, conversely, are usually surrounded by fellow construction workers and, therefore, extraordinary record checks may not be necessary for them, or for others who do not work regularly with vulnerable individuals.

There should also be standards on how to assess criminal records. A five-year interval after any non-sexual violence, for example, might create a discretionary zone in which hiring for some jobs would not be unreasonable. Differentiating sexual violence from other offenses would also be important.

Judges often instruct jurors to be guided by an industry standard of determining negligence. If the standard is unclear or nonexistent, then juries can make up their own standard. Thus employers may be better off in setting their own standards, too, rather than having standards imposed *ex post facto*.

Many employers will resist this idea, because it would probably mean performing more background checks in the short run. Whether they are financially better off in just losing lawsuits will depend on how frequently lawsuits occur in their industry, and size of the awards. But the long-run cost of doing nothing could be a court-imposed standard of criminal record checks for virtually everyone.

The courts see a need for policy on pre-employment screening, and they are filling the vacuum. They may be happy to have employers do the job with their own standards. Employers would serve their own interests, as well as the interests of crime victims, by taking the issue directly.

Questions

1. The costs of making a check into an individual's criminal record can be substantial. Should companies be required to make such checks? Will the costs of lawsuits force businesses to make those checks?

2. Should there be restrictions on how that information will be used? For example, should criminal records be a bar to some jobs but not to others? Or should there be differences based on the type of crime committed, when it was committed, and the employee's work record subsequent to the crime?

3. Will this law impact on the criminal justice system's ability to rehabilitate criminals?

4. Which social groups are most likely to be negatively impacted by the imposition of liability on principals and employers who, in the past, did not check criminal records? Are there alternative solutions?

REVIEW AND DISCUSSION QUESTIONS

1. Define the following terms:
   agency relationship
   agent
   principal
   power of attorney
   gratuitous agent
   vicarious liability
   respondent superior

2. Compare and contrast the following:
   a. Apparent authority and actual authority
   b. Agent-principal and master-servant
   c. Special agent and general agent
   d. Express authority and implied authority
   e. Respondeat superior and vicarious liability

3. Under what circumstances would a principal be liable for the following:
   a. The negligence of an agent.
   b. The intentional tort of an agent.
   c. The contracts of an agent.

4. What impact on the business community would result if agency relationships were declared unlawful?

5. In the case where the principal is undisclosed, why can there be no apparent authority?

6. Agent embezzled funds from Principal and used the funds to purchase a car. Has Agent violated any duties? Who is entitled to ownership of the car?

Case Questions

7. Mrs. Clark operated a business for many years. She sold this business to her two sons, who then moved the location of the business from one part of town to another but retained the business name Clark's Corner Drugstore. The sons then purchased goods on credit from Standard Supply, Inc., and did not pay. Standard had dealt with Mrs. Clark for many years and had previously dealt with the sons as Mrs. Clark's agents. Upon what basis can you argue that the agency still existed as to Standard? Would the result be any different if the sons were to publish a notice in the local newspaper stating that Mrs. Clark no longer owned the business?

8. Mary Kidd sued Thomas A. Edison, Inc. (Edison), alleging that one Mr. Fuller, acting for Edison, contracted with her to sing at a series of recitals for record dealers. At the recitals, Kidd was to sing so the dealers could compare her recorded voice with her actual voice. Kidd was not paid and brought suit against Edison. According to Edison, Fuller never agreed that Edison would pay Kidd, because Fuller's only authority was to hire Kidd for those recitals for which he could persuade record dealers to pay. Is Edison liable to Kidd? Why or why not? (*Kidd* v. *Thomas A. Edison, Inc.*, U.S. District Court, Southern District of N.Y., 239 Fed. 405 (1917).

9. (a) A gardener and his employer, a homeowner, are at a nursery. Gardener, in the presence of the nursery owner, says to Homeowner, "I am going to buy you some shrubs to plant in front of your house." What issues are presented? Would the issues be any different if Homeowner remained silent?

   (b) Suppose instead that Gardener purchases shrubs and then informs Homeowner, "I bought you some shrubs." Homeowner replies, "Sure." What issues are presented? Would the issues be any different if Homeowner remained silent?

   (c) Suppose instead that Gardener purchases shrubs and plants them in front of Homeowner's house. When Homeowner arrives home that day, she notices the shrubs, seeks out Gardener, and tells him, "I'm allergic to those shrubs and you knew it," but does nothing more. What issues are presented? Would the issues be any different if Homeowner remained silent?

10. Trust National Bank made a loan to International Services based on financial statements provided by Swartz Accountants at the instruction of International Services. Later, after International Services defaulted on the loan, the bank discovered that the accounting firm had not taken into account several key transactions or at least had not noted their existence in the financial statement. Had the transactions been handled appropriately, the bank asserts that it would not have made the loan. Does the accounting company owe the bank a duty to exercise reasonable care and skill in the performance of its duties? [(*Rhode Island Hospital Trust National Bank* v. *Swartz,* 455 F.2d 847 (1972)

11. Juanita, acting as agent for the Juicy Fruit Company, purchased two truckloads of cantaloupes from Robert. Juanita did not mention the existence of the agency but took no steps to hide it. Robert never inquired whether Juanita was acting as an agent. Juanita paid Robert one half of the purchase price and refused (without reason) to pay the rest. Who is liable to Robert for the unpaid balance? Why?

12. Maloney wished to sell twenty acres of land for which he was asking $20,000. He requested Johnson to find a purchaser who would be willing to pay at least $18,000 and promised to pay a 10 percent sales commission if Johnson located such a buyer. Maloney then began negotiating with Smith. Smith later found out from Johnson that the property could be purchased through Johnson for less money, so he dropped the negotiations with Maloney. Thereafter, Johnson took title to the land in his own name, telling Maloney that the buyer did not want his name known. He paid Maloney $19,000 and transferred the title to Smith. Is Johnson entitled to the commission? Why or why not?

13. Duncan operated his restaurant, Duncan's Deli, in a leased building. His lease expired on June 30, but Duncan forgot to renew it. Duncan's office manager found out that Duncan had not renewed the lease and leased the building herself, intending to sublease to Duncan at a small profit. What are the rights and duties of Duncan and the office manager with respect to the lease?

14. For six months, Maude acted as a purchasing agent for Harold by purchasing used cars for Harold to resell. She then apparently lost interest and did nothing more for a year. Later, she found a car she knew Harold would want, so she bought it for him. Is Maude entitled to reimbursement from Harold? Must Harold accept the car?

Policy Questions

15. Some legal scholars have stated that common sense is opposed to the theory of vicarious liability. Can you think of some reasons to justify this position?

16. As agents, should the officers of a corporation work to enhance the profits of the shareholders? To enhance the corporate image of the company? To further their own careers?

Ethics Questions

17. Agents are in a position to be privy to information of significant value. Should they be prohibited from using it? What if the use to which the agent uses such information would not in any way injure the principal?

18. Clarence has been released from prison after a six-year term for armed robbery and assault. Having "paid his debt to society" for his crimes, he is now looking for work. You are advertising to hire workers for furniture moving crews. Normally two people work together all the time, so you know Clarence would be accompanied by another employee when on the job. However, you know of recent cases in which employers have been held liable for employees having gone astray during the job and committed crimes. Since Clarence would be in people's homes, it is not impossible that this could happen. Should you not hire Clarence because of this worry?

11 Business Organizations

T HIS chapter discusses the various forms of business organization a business may elect to conduct its affairs. While the corporation is often considered to be synonymous with the term *business*, there are other forms of business organization. After considering several factors, managers will select the form of organization that provides them with the least costly way of conducting business operations. The type of business organization selected can significantly influence a business's legal environment.

The chapter begins with a general discussion of the more predominant forms of business organization, including sole proprietorships, partnerships, limited partnerships, and corporations. It then considers alternative forms that may have important applications in special circumstances, including joint ventures, joint stock companies, syndicates, and cooperatives. Finally, the chapter considers several factors that may significantly influence a business's choice of business organization.

The chapter closes with the Issue article, which discusses a topic of growing ethical and legal concern: Should corporate officers be personally liable for the wrongdoings of the corporation? A growing number of business and legal scholars are advocating that by holding corporate officers liable for the consequences of their decisions, the corporation will become more responsible.

OVERVIEW OF BUSINESS ORGANIZATIONS

The forms of business organization implemented most frequently are the sole proprietorship, partnership, limited partnership, and corporation. Less frequently employed forms include joint ventures, joint stock companies, cooperatives, and syndicates. In most states, each form is defined by statute, and the required formalities for their creation, operation, and dissolution are specifically set forth. Depending upon the business, each of the forms has distinct advantages and disadvantages when compared to one another.

Despite the formalities that may be required, businesses are primarily a set of contractual relationships. The common law of contracts and agency, and to a lesser extent, torts, is the key to business formation and operation. Entrepreneurs have wide latitude in the ways they can form and manage a business. The form actually chosen may be dictated by factors such as financing, taxes, and liability, but innovative forms that combine attributes of the various forms discussed here may be used.

A Statistical Overview

As Table 11–1 shows, there are more than 17 million businesses in the United States. Sole proprietorships account for more than 70 percent of all businesses, only about 6 percent of all business receipts, but over one-quarter of all profits. Sole proprietorships are principally made up of small businesses such as hardware stores, beauty shops, dry cleaners, and restaurants. In contrast, corporations are far fewer in number, less than 20 percent of the total, but account for 90 percent of all business receipts. Finally, partnerships provide about 4 percent of all business receipts while making up about 10 percent of all businesses.

SOLE PROPRIETORSHIPS

A person doing business for himself is termed a *sole proprietor;* the business organization is a *sole proprietorship.* The sole proprietorship is the oldest and simplest form of business organization. As a sole proprietor, an individual may simply begin to do business without formality in those enterprises that do not require a government license or permit. The individual generally owns all or

Table 11–1　Businesses by Major Forms of Organization, 1970–1986

Item	Unit	1970	1975	1980	1986
Total Number	1,000	8,371	10,318	13,023	17,526
Business Receipts	$billion	1,997	3,540	6,869	9,220
Net income	$billion	106	191	302	343
Proprietorships, number (non-farm)	1,000	5,770	7,221	8,932	12,394
Business receipts	$billion	199	274	411	559
Net income	$billion	30	40	55	90
Partnership, number	1,000	936	1,073	1,380	1,703
Business receipts	$billion	92	146	286	379
Net Income	$billion	10	8	8	−17
Corporations, number	1,000	1,665	2,024	2,711	3,429
Business receipts	$billion	1,706	3,120	6,172	8,282
Net income	$billion	66	143	239	270

Source: U.S. Statistical Abstract (1990), based on tax returns.

most of the business property and has sole responsibility for the control, liabilities, and management of the business.

In a sole proprietorship, legally and practically *the owner is the business*, and any capital must come from the owner's own resources, and those borrowed from financial institutions. The availability of limited alternatives for raising financial capital is perhaps the greatest disadvantage of the sole proprietorship. Unless specifically protected by a contract with a creditor, a proprietor is personally responsible for all business debts. Because the profits of the business are taxed to the owner personally, no formal tax return in the business's name is required. The operational and recordkeeping formalities of the business are at the owner's discretion as long as the various taxing authorities are satisfied.

PARTNERSHIPS

A *general partnership* is a business formed by two or more individuals (called *partners* or *general partners*) who have entered into an agreement, either express or implied, to carry on a business venture for a profit. The partners are the co-owners of the business and share control over the business's operations and profits. Many attorneys, doctors, insurance agencies, and real estate ventures, as well as small retail stores, are organized as general partnerships.

Formation of a Partnership

At common law, a partnership was generally not treated as an independent legal entity. As a consequence, a legal action could not be brought by or against the business. Rather, the partners making up the partnership had to sue or be sued in their capacities as individuals. A number of states, however, now provide that for certain purposes a partnership may be treated as an independent entity (e.g., ownership in property). Thus, many states allow a partnership to sue or be sued and to collect judgments in its own name. In addition, the federal courts provide that in a variety of circumstances a partnership will be treated as an independent legal entity.

Uniform Partnership Act

Partnership law has its origins in the common law, but is now codified in the *Uniform Partnership Act* (UPA), which has been adopted, with modifications, in most states. The UPA codifies the "best" features of common-law principles developed to govern partnerships and partnership relations. The UPA dictates the operation of partnerships when the partnership agreement is silent or in those instances in which there is no formal agreement among the partners. That is, unless otherwise stated by contract, the UPA is presumed to govern.

A partnership can begin with a simple oral agreement between two or more people to do business as partners or with a tacit agreement that may be inferred from the conduct of the partners as they do business together. Typically, however, the parties formalize their relationship by a written partnership agreement expressly providing how the partnership business will be conducted and profits will be shared. Any person having legal capacity to enter a contract may also enter a partnership agreement and become a partner in a business venture.

Written Agreements

The written partnership agreement usually specifies such matters as the business name, relative ownership interests of the partners, the partners' responsibilities within the partnership, method of accounting, duration of the partnership, and procedures for the partnership's dissolution. Exhibit 11–1 is an example of a partnership agreement. In the absence of specific agreement, or when the agreement is silent or ambiguous, the UPA will specify and govern the relationship of the parties.

Relationship of the Parties

A partnership is a relationship based on extraordinary trust and loyalty. As a consequence, the law specifies that the partners owe a fiduciary duty to one another. That fiduciary relationship requires that each partner act in good faith for the benefit of the partnership. As in the fiduciary relationship between a principal and agents, the partners *must place* their individual interests below those of the partnership. The Supreme Court stated the duty of partners as follows (*Latta* v. *Kilbourn*, 1893):

> [It is] well settled that one partner cannot, directly or indirectly, use partnership assets for his own benefit; that he cannot, in conducting the business of a partnership, take any profit clandestinely for himself; that he cannot carry on the business of the partnership for his private advantage; that he cannot carry on another business in competition or rivalry with that of the firm, thereby depriving it of the benefit of his time, skill, and fidelity without being accountable to his copartners for any profit that may accrue to him therefrom; that he cannot be permitted to secure for himself that which it is his duty to obtain, if at all, for the firm of which he is a member. . . .

Or, as Justice Cardozo once stated, partners "owe to one another . . . the duty of finest loyalty."

Unless otherwise specified by contract, the basic rule in a partnership is that each partner has an equal voice in the management and conduct of the partnership. That is, regardless of the dollar interest in the partnership, each partner has one vote in managerial decisions. Except in the case of major managerial decisions that require unanimous consent of the partners—such as decisions to change the nature of the partnership's business or its capital structure, to admit new partners, or to undertake any activity that would make further conduct of the partnership impossible—a majority vote is controlling. In most large partnerships, however, the partners usually agree to delegate day-to-day management responsibilities to a specific individual or group, often referred to as the managing partner or partners. Regardless of who runs the business, unless otherwise provided, the law holds all partners personally responsible for all debts of the partnership.

Termination of the Partnership

A change in the relationship of the partners demonstrating either an unwillingness or an inability to continue with the business of the partnership brings about termination of the partnership. A complete termination comes about,

Exhibit 11–1   Example of a Basic Partnership Agreement

[Name]
PARTNERSHIP AGREEMENT

This agreement, made and entered into as of the [Date], by and among [Names] (hereinafter collectively sometimes referred to as "Partners").

WITNESSETH:

Whereas, the Parties hereto desire to form a General Partnership (hereinafter referred to as the "Partnership"), for the term and upon the conditions hereinafter set forth;

Now, therefore, in consideration of the mutual covenants hereinafter contained, it is agreed by and among the Parties hereto as follows:

Article I
BASIC STRUCTURE

1.1 Form. The Parties hereby form a General Partnership pursuant to the Laws of [Name of State].

1.2 Name. The business of the Partnership shall be conducted under the name of [Name].

1.3 Place of Business. The principal office and place of business of the Partnership shall be located at [Describe], or such other place as the Partners may from time to time designate.

1.4 Term. The Partnership shall commence on [Date], and shall continue for [Number] years, unless earlier terminated in the following manner:

(a) By the completion of the purpose intended, or

(b) Pursuant to this Agreement, or

(c) By applicable [State] law, or

(d) By death, insanity, bankruptcy, retirement, withdrawal, resignation, expulsion, or disability of all of the then Partners.

1.5 Purpose—General. The purpose for which the Partnership is organized is _____ .

Article II
FINANCIAL ARRANGEMENTS

2.1 Initial Contributions of Partners. Each Partner has contributed to the initial capital of the Partnership property in the amount and form indicated on Schedule A attached hereto and made a part hereof. Capital contributions to the Partnership shall not earn interest. An individual capital account shall be maintained for each Partner.

2.2 Additional Capital Contribution. If at any time during the existence of the Partnership it shall become necessary to increase the capital with which the said Partnership is doing business, then (upon the vote of the Managing Partner(s)) each party to this Agreement shall contribute to the capital of this Partnership within _____days notice of such need in an amount according to his then Percentage Share of Capital as called for by the Managing Partner(s).

2.3 Percentage Share of Profits and Capital. (a) The Percentage Share of Profits and Capital of each Partner shall be (unless otherwise modified by the terms of this Agreement) as follows:

Names	Initial Percentage Share of Profits and Capital

2.4 Interest. No interest shall be paid on any contribution to the capital of the Partnership.

2.5 Return of Capital Contributions. No Partner shall have the right to demand the return of his capital contributions except as herein provided.

2.6 Rights of Priority. Except as herein provided, the individual Partners shall have no right to any priority over each other as to the return of capital contributions except as herein provided.

2.7 Distributions. Distributions to the Partners of net operating profits of the Partnership, as hereinafter defined, shall be made at (least monthly/at such times as the Managing Partner(s) shall reasonably agree.) Such distributions shall be made to the Partners simultaneously.

2.8 Compensation. No Partner shall have entitled to receive any compensation from the Partnership, nor shall any Partner receive any drawing account from the Partnership.

continued

Exhibit 11–1   *continued*

Article III
MANAGEMENT

3.1 Managing Partners. The Managing Partner(s) shall be [Names] [or "all partners"].

3.2 Voting. All Managing Partner(s) shall have the right to vote as to the management and conduct of the business of the Partnership according to their then Percentage Share of [Capital/Income]. Except as otherwise herein set forth a majority of such [Capital/Income] shall control.

Article IV
DISSOLUTION

4.1 Dissolutions. In the event that the Partnership shall hereafter be dissolved for any reason whatsoever, a full and general account of its assets, liabilities and transactions shall at once be taken. Such assets may be sold and turned into cash as soon as possible and all debts and other amounts due the Partnership collected. The proceeds thereof shall thereupon be applied as follows:

(a) To discharge the debts and liabilities of the Partnership and the expenses of liquidation.

(b) To pay each Partner or his legal representative any unpaid salary, drawing account, interest or profits to which he shall then be entitled and in addition, to repay to any Partner his capital contributions in excess of his original capital contribution.

(c) To divide the surplus, if any, among the Partners or their representatives as follows:(1) First (to the extent of each Partner's then capital account) in proportion to their then capital accounts.

(2) Then according to each Partner's then Percentage Share of Capital/Income.

4.2 Right To Demand Property. No Partner shall have the right to demand and receive property in kind for his distribution.

Article V
MISCELLANEOUS

5.1 Accounting Year, Books, Statements. The Partnership's fiscal year shall commence on January 1st of each year and shall end on December 31st of each year. Full and accurate books of account shall be kept at such place as the Managing Partner(s) may from time to time designate, showing the condition of the business and finances of the Partnership; and each Partner shall have access to such books of account and shall be entitled to examine them at any time during ordinary business hours.

5.2 Arbitration. Any controversy or claim arising out of or relating to this Agreement shall only be settled by arbitration in accordance with the rules of the American Arbitration, one Arbitrator, and shall be enforceable in any court having competent jurisdiction.

Witnesses	Partners
_____	_____
_____	_____
_____	_____

however, only after the partnership has been dissolved and the affairs of the partnership have been wound up. The *dissolution* of the partnership occurs when an event takes place that precludes the partners from engaging in any *new business.* The *winding up* of partnership affairs involves the actual process of completing any unfinished business of the partnership and then collecting and distributing the partnership's assets.

The dissolution of the partnership can be brought about in several ways. Any change in the composition of the partners will result in a new partnership and the dissolution of the old one. Thus, the withdrawal, incapacity, or death of a partner causes the partnership to be dissolved. Similarly, the partnership is dissolved if a partner is found to be bankrupt. Finally, any event making the business of the partnership unlawful—such as a legislative enactment—causes the partnership to be dissolved.

In winding up the partnership's affairs, the partners have a duty to one another to fully disclose all financial aspects of the partnership. As the *Witlin* case illustrates, the managing partners are required to do more than just provide the other partners with objective evidence, such as the book value of the partnership's business. In establishing the value of the business, the managing partners are under a fiduciary duty to disclose any prospects for the sale of the business and the proposed price of those sales.

Estate of Witlin

California Court of Appeal, Second District
83 Cal.App.3d 167, 147 Cal.Rptr. 723 (1978)

Case Background. *Dr. Witlin was a partner in a partnership known as Rio Hondo Associates at the time of his death in 1971. The partnership, the defendant in this case, consisted of forty-five members, mostly doctors. The partnership's principal asset was a hospital. The management committee of the partnership notified Mrs. Witlin, the plaintiff, that the partnership was exercising its option under the partnership agreement to purchase Dr. Witlin's 2.654 percent partnership interest for $65,288.40 (or $24,600 per percentage point). Mrs. Witlin contended that the market value was higher. Although the management committee did supply the financial records of the partnership to allow her to make her own evaluation, they did not tell her of ongoing negotiations to sell the partnership assets. The sale netted $83,906 per percentage point of partnership interest.*

Mrs. Witlin brought suit, contending that the partnership violated their fiduciary duty to her of full disclosure. The lower court found for Mrs. Witlin and the partnership appealed.

Case Decision. Associate Justice Cobey delivered the decision of the court.

* * *

Appellants owed a fiduciary duty to plaintiff as the widow and executrix of their deceased partner in purchasing from her their deceased partner's interest in the partnership. Throughout the transaction they were bound to act toward her "in the highest good faith" and they were forbidden to obtain any advantage over her in the matter by, among other things, the slightest concealment. Yet the management committee never revealed to plaintiff that the basic value in their formula for determining the fair market value of the partnership was book value alone. Likewise, as already noted, the management committee did not mention the possibility that the hospital might be shortly sold.

* * *

This possibility of sale was quite real. It appears from plaintiff's improperly rejected offers of proof that the management committee reached in 1969 a tentative agreement with General Health Services to sell the partnership's assets to it for approximately $60,000 a percentage point, that between April and September 28, 1971, the management committee and the American Cyanamid Corporation were discussing a sale of the partnership to it for at least $93,000 a percentage point, and, as already noted from the evidence itself, that the partnership's assets were finally sold in June 1972 to Hospital Corporation of America for about $84,000 a percentage point.

The management committee knew all of this, but they apparently never breathed a word of it to either plaintiff or her attorney. It seems that in discussing the fair market value of the partnership they talked out of both sides of their mouths. They talked to plaintiff and her attorney in terms of $16,000 and $24,000 per percentage point while they were more or less simultaneously talking to conglomerates interested in purchasing the hospital and the other assets of the partnership in terms of selling prices ranging from $60,000 to $93,500 per percentage point. Given this situation, how could their offer of $24,600 per percentage point to plaintiff have been a good faith determination on their part of the fair market value of the partnership?

* * *

Case Holding. *The lower court's decision was affirmed. The partners are under a fiduciary duty of full disclosure to all partners involved in the business venture.*

Case Questions

1. On what basis could the partnership argue that it was acting in good faith with regard to the value of the property?
2. Suppose the sale had not worked out. Would the court's decision have been different?

LIMITED PARTNERSHIP

A limited partnership is a special form of a general partnership. Like a general partnership, a *limited partnership* is a business organization made up of two or more individuals (called *partners*) who have entered into an agreement to carry on a business venture for a profit. Unlike a general partnership, however, not all the partners involved in a limited partnership have unlimited personal liability for the debts of the business venture.

Formation of a Limited Partnership

Every state provides by statute for the formation of limited partnerships. All but two states use some form of the *Uniform Limited Partnership Act or the Revised Uniform Limited Partnership Act.* Partners are required to execute a written agreement, called a *certificate of limited partnership,* and file it with the appropriate state official, often the secretary of state. These Acts require that the certificate contain the following information:

1. Name of the business.
2. Type or character of the business.
3. Address of an agent who is designated to receive legal process.
4. Names and addresses of each general and limited partner.
5. Contributions (cash and property) each partner has made and any additional contributions they will make.
6. Duration of the limited partnership.
7. The rights for any personnel changes in the partnership and the continuance of the partnership upon those changes.
8. The proportion of the partnership's profits or other compensation that each partner is entitled to receive.

In addition, the parties to the limited partnership agreement may agree to bind themselves in ways not required by the certificate.

Relationship of the Parties

A limited partnership consists of at least one *general partner* and one or more *limited partners*. The general partners are treated by the law in the same manner as general partners in a general partnership. They have complete responsibility for managing the business and are personally liable to the partnership's creditors.

The limited partners are investors who do not (and may not) participate in the management of the business. Although they have the same rights as the general partners to access the partnership books, accounting of the business, and participation in the dissolution of the business, limited partners are not liable for the debts or torts of the limited partnership beyond their capital contributions. Limited partners can, however, lose their limited liability shield by taking an active role in the management of the business. To avoid an inference of managerial control, limited partners may not take control of the firm, contribute services to the business, or allow their names to appear in the name of the business. As the *Northampton Valley* case illustrates, it is not uncommon for creditors of the business to assert that the limited partners have in some way conducted their affairs so as to become general partners.

Northampton Valley Constructors, Inc. v. Horne–Lang Associates

Superior Court of Pennsylvania
310 Pa.Super. 559,
456 A.2d 1077
(1983)

Case Background. *Northampton Valley Constructors, the plaintiff-appellant, brought suit against Horne–Lang Associates, the defendant-appellee, for breach of contract for nonpayment. Northampton and Horne–Lang had entered into a contract whereby Northampton agreed to install a sewer system on land owned by Horne–Lang. Upon completion of the work, Horne–Lang was unable to pay.*

Horne–Lang is a Pennsylvania limited partnership, comprising a general partner and eighteen limited partners. Northampton alleged in its suit that the limited partners were actually general partners and thus were personally liable under the contract. The lower court dismissed Northampton's suit, and Northampton appealed.

Case Decision. Judge McEwin delivered the decision of the court.

* * *

A limited partnership is a creation of our legislature and "(i)t permits a manner of doing business whereby individuals may invest their money free of the fear of unlimited liability and of the responsibilities of management." . . . The pertinent statute, the Uniform Limited Partnership Act . . . provides:

> Sec. 511. Limited partnership defined
>
> A limited partnership is a partnership formed by two or more persons under the provisions of section 512 (relating to formation), having as members one or more general partners and one or more limited partners. The limited partners as such shall not be bound by the obligations of the partnership. . . .

The certificate of the limited partnership we here study contains . . . the following provision concerning addition contributions:

> No additional contributions have been agreed to be made. However, additional contributions are required if the General Partner determines that the partnership requires additional funds to meet the obligations of the partnership.

It must be emphasized that this claim against the limited partners is exerted by a creditor of the partnership and not by the partnership. A creditor may pursue a claim against a limited partner as a general partner only in the limited circumstances prescribed by the Act, namely, when the limited partner "takes part in the control of the business." Northampton Valley did not, however, allege and does not now argue that the limited partners took part in the control of the business.

This claim against the limited partners, made by Northampton Valley as a creditor of the partnership, is based upon the aforementioned provision of the partnership certificate concerning additional contributions. Northampton Valley contends that, as a result of this provision, the limited partners were *de facto* general partners and argues that, since the general partner could have and should have called upon the limited partners to provide additional capital to the partnership in order to pay the creditors of the partnership, the limited partners are liable to creditors for the debts of the partnership over and beyond their investment. Northampton Valley asserts that since "the limited partners have committed to make their investment equal the obligations, they are bound for that sum not because they are bound beyond the limit of their commitment but because their commitments equal those obligations." The premise for this assertion is, however, simply not correct since the limited partners did not commit to make their investments in the partnership equal to the obligations of the partnership; nor does the clear meaning of the plain language concerning additional contributions permit interpretation, let alone allow the inference urged by Northampton Valley.

Northampton Valley does allege in the complaint that "the General Partner determined that the partnership required additional funds to meet the obligations of the partnership" and, as we have earlier noted, we are obliged to accept that averment as a fact. Nonetheless, whatever liability such a determination by the general partner may have imposed upon the limited partners in favor of the partnership, we are not persuaded that the limited partners thereby became as equally liable to creditors as were the general partner and the partnership.

* * *

Case Holding. *The order of the lower court dismissing the case against the limited partners of Horne–Lang was affirmed. Limited partners are liable to the creditors of the limited partnership only up to the amount of their required contributions.*

Case Questions
1. Why did Northampton bring this action against the limited partners of Horne–Lang Associates?
2. Why were the limited partners not liable personally to Northampton?
3. Can you alter the facts in the case so that the limited partners would be liable to Northampton?

Termination of a Limited Partnership

A limited partnership is terminated in much the same way as a general partnership. Events that affect a general partner and would bring about the dissolution of a general partnership also dissolve a limited partnership. Thus, the bankruptcy of a general partner dissolves a limited partnership; however, the bankruptcy of a limited partner usually does not.

As in the dissolution of a general partnership, the business continues to operate while it is winding up. The business may not, however, enter into any new commitments but rather must complete all commitments in existence prior to the partnership's dissolution. In the final dispersal of the assets of the limited partnership, creditors' rights precede partners' rights. The limited partners then receive their share of the profits and their capital contributions before general partners receive anything.

CORPORATIONS

The form of organization most often associated with term business is the *corporation*. Most large, well-known businesses—such as Exxon, Coca-Cola, General Motors, IBM, and Ford Motor Company—are corporations. Although businesses have produced and traded goods for thousands of years, the modern corporation is a relatively recent development.

Corporate Charters

The modern corporation was first developed in the United States during the late 1700s. State governments drew on our English heritage and issued *corporate charters* to selected businesses. Because the charter usually contained some special privilege, intense competition was carried on in the legislature to receive one. A charter might, for example, give one business the exclusive privilege of operating a toll bridge over a river or having the only bank in a town; hence, monopoly power was associated with early corporate charters.

The downfall of this anticompetitive practice began in the early 1800s with the enactment of *general incorporation statutes* in several states. In 1811, for example, New York enacted a general incorporation statute that allowed certain businesses involved in the manufacture of glass, metals, paint, or textiles to incorporate. Businesses involved in those areas of manufacturing that could incorporate were restricted to those with five or more employees, $100,000 or less in capital, and a specified life of twenty years or less. Despite its restrictiveness, the statute was an important historical development because it did provide for a standardized approach to incorporation rather than require a specific act of the state legislature.

It was not until the late 1800s that the first "liberal" general incorporation act was enacted. Those statutes established a simple and standardized procedure to be followed for a business to become incorporated. Incorporation was thereby made available to virtually all businesses regardless of their field of operation or size.

The Corporation as a Legal Entity

Unlike sole proprietorships and, in most instances, partnerships, the corporation is a legal entity. It is recognized under both federal and state law as a "person" and enjoys many of the same rights and privileges accorded U.S. citizens. Corporations are thus entitled to most constitutional protections, including free speech, equal protection under the law, and protections against unreasonable searches and seizures. As a person, a corporation has the right of access to the courts as an entity that may sue and be sued. However, although the officers and employees of a corporation enjoy the privilege against self-incrimination under the Fifth Amendment, the corporation itself does not.

Procedure of Incorporation

Every state has a general incorporation statute that sets forth a procedure for the incorporation of a business. Although the basic procedures for incorporation vary among the states, the basic requirements are relatively similar. In general, the corporation's *articles of incorporation* along with an application must first be filed with the appropriate officer of the state. The articles of incorporation must generally provide the following:

1. Name of the corporation.
2. Address of the corporation and name of its registered agent at that address.
3. Purpose of the business.
4. The class(es) of stock to be issued and their par value.
5. Names and mailing addresses of the incorporators.

Exhibit 11–2 is an example of a corporation's articles of incorporation.

After reviewing the corporation's application for completeness, the state issues a *certificate of incorporation* or *corporate charter*. As a rule, the incorporators of the business wait until the state has issued the certificate before holding their first organizational meeting. At that meeting, the incorporators elect the first board of directors, enact the corporation's bylaws, and issue the corporation's stock. The *bylaws* are the "rules" that regulate and govern the internal operations of the corporation. The shareholders, directors, and officers of the corporation are required to abide by the bylaws in conducting corporate business activities. Any requirement imposed by the bylaws must now, however, conflict with the corporation's articles of incorporation.

Relationship of the Parties

A corporation legally consists of three primary groups: the shareholders, the board of directors, and the managers. Each shares specific duties and responsibilities to the other groups, to the corporation, and to third parties.

Shareholders

The *shareholders* are the owners of the corporation. As a shareholder, an individual is entitled to a *stock certificate*. Shareholders have first right over other purchasers to any new stock issued by the corporation. Shareholders also have a limited right to inspect the corporation's books and records. As a rule, inspections are provided to shareholders if it is for a proper purpose and a request is made in advance. Finally, unless stated to the contrary on the stock certificate, shareholders are not restricted from transferring the stock to someone else.

Shareholder Rights. Through their ownership of the corporation's stock, the shareholders have a right to attempt to influence the general direction of the corporation. However, they do not have the legal authority for day-to-day management of the corporation. The direction of the corporation is the responsibility of the board of directors, which generally delegates managerial responsibility to hired managers. Shareholders, however, elect the board of directors and vote on matters that may affect a change in the corporation's

Exhibit 11–2 Example of Articles of Incorporation

CERTIFICATE OF INCORPORATION
OF
_____ CORPORATION

1. **Name.** The name of the Corporation is _____ Corporation.

2. **Registered Office and Registered Agent.** The address of the Corporation's registered office in Delaware is _____ Street in the City of _____ and County of _____ , and the name of its registered agent at such address _____ .

3. **Purposes.** The purpose of the Corporation is to engage in any lawful act or activity for which Corporations may be now or hereafter organized under the General Corporation Law of Delaware.

4. **Capital Stock (Providing for Two Classes of Stock, One Voting and One Non-voting).** The total number of shares of all classes of stock which the Corporation shall have authority to issue is _____ , all of which are to be without par value. _____ of such shares shall be Class A voting shares and _____ of such shares shall be Class B non-voting shares. The Class A shares and the Class B shares shall have identical rights except that the Class B shares shall not entitle the holder thereof to vote on any matter unless specifically required by law.

5. **Incorporators.** The names and mailing addresses of the incorporators are:

Name	Mailing Address
_____	_____
_____	_____
_____	_____

6. **Regulatory Provisions.** [The Corporations may insert additional provisions for the management of the business and for the conduct of the affairs of the Corporation, and creating, defining, limiting, and regulating the powers of the Corporation, the Directors and the Stockholders, or any class of Stockholders.]

7. **Personal Liability.** The Stockholders shall be liable for the debts of the Corporation in the proportion that their stock bears to the total outstanding stock of the Corporation.

8. **Amendment.** The Corporation reserves the right to amend, alter, change or repeal any provision contained in the Certificate of INCORPORATION, in the manner now or hereafter prescribed by statute, and all rights conferred upon Stockholders herein are granted subject to this reservation.

We, the undersigned, being all of the incorporations above named, for the purpose of forming a Corporation pursuant to the General Corporation Law of Delaware, sign and acknowledge this Certificate of Incorporation this _____ day of _____ , 19 ___ .

Acknowledgement

STATE OF _____

County of _____

On this _____ day of _____ , 19___ , before me personally came _____ , one of the persons who signed the foregoing certificate of incorporation, known to me personally to be such, and acknowledged that the said certificate is his act and deed and that the facts stated therein are true.

_____
Notary Public

[seal]

---

structure or existence (such as a merger or a consolidation, or any amendment to the corporation's articles of incorporation).

Proxy Voting. Elections take place at the shareholder meetings, which usually must be held annually. Notice of the shareholder meetings must be provided in advance, and a quorum—usually more than 50 percent of the total shares held—must be represented at the meeting. Most shareholders give third parties their *proxy*—a written authorization to cast their vote. The proxy is often solicited by the corporation's hired management.

At the meeting, corporate business is presented to the shareholders in the form of *resolutions*. After considering a resolution, shareholders vote to approve or disapprove it. As a rule, resolutions pass if a majority of the shares voted favor it. However, the articles of incorporation may require more than a simple majority for a resolution requesting authorization for actions not within the ordinary course of the corporation's business. Such actions might include amendments to the articles of incorporation and the bylaws, a major sale of corporate assets, or the dissolution or merger of the corporation.

Limited Liability. The shareholder has no legal relationship with creditors of the corporation. A shareholder's obligation to creditors is limited to the capital contribution made, usually the amount paid to buy the stock. A shareholder, however, may also be a creditor of the corporation (for example, by supplying some of the corporation's raw material needs or by working for the business) and enjoy the same rights of recovery against the corporation as any other creditor.

Board of Directors

The initial *board of directors* is either specified in the articles of incorporation or designated by the incorporators at the first corporate meeting. Thereafter, the selection and retention of directors is exclusively a shareholder responsibility. Once elected, directors are usually allowed to serve their full terms, although the shareholders can remove a director from office *for cause* (generally for a *breach of duty* or *misconduct*.)

Legal Role of Directors. The functions of the board of directors include making basic corporate policy, such as the sale of corporate assets, entrance into new product lines, major financing decisions, appointment and compensation of corporate officers, and the negotiation of labor-management agreements. Directors are the principals of a corporation. The hired managers are their agents. Thus, while they are elected by the shareholders, board members are not instructed by the shareholders.

In undertaking their corporate responsibilities, directors are under a *duty of care* to conduct themselves in the same manner as a reasonably prudent person in the conduct of personal business affairs. Honest mistakes in judgment not resulting from negligence, however, rarely result in personal liability to the directors. In most cases, courts will give both directors and managers the benefit of the doubt, and not impose liability, by applying the *business judgment rule*, which protects directors and managers who have made honest mistakes in judgment.

Liability of Directors. Directors are subject to a *fiduciary duty of loyalty*. This fiduciary duty requires that directors place the interests of the corporation before their own interests. Directors can be held answerable to the corporation and its shareholders for a breach of their duties of care or loyalty. As a rule, the board has the duty to undertake those courses of action intended to preserve the corporate entity. That duty may be different, however, in the event the business becomes the target of a takeover attempt by another business, as the

Revlon case shows. Note that decisions on corporate law by Delaware courts are especially important since over one-half of the *Fortune 500* firms are incorporated there.

Revlon, Inc.
v.
MacAndrews
& Forbes
Holdings,
Inc.

Supreme Court of
Delaware
506 A.2d 173
(1985)

Case Background. *This case concerns the duties of the board of directors in thwarting the takeover of Revlon (the defendant) by Pantry Pride (owned by MacAndrews, the plaintiff). The evidence demonstrated that the chairman of the board of Revlon did not care for the chairman of Pantry Pride. To avoid being taken over, Revlon undertook several defensive measures.*

First, Revlon entered into an agreement with Forstmann for Revlon to sell assets to Forstmann if another company managed to purchase 40 percent of Revlon shares (called a "lock-up agreement," it effectively barred another company from gaining control of Revlon).

Second, Revlon agreed to deal exclusively with Forstmann in the event of a takeover attempt. This provision in the contract is referred to as a "no-shop provision."

Finally, Revlon agreed to pay Forstmann $25 million if the deal were aborted. For its part, Forstmann offered $57.25 per share for Revlon's stock and agreed to protect Revlon's creditors, who had expressed concern about Forstmann's earlier offers to Revlon's board of directors.

Pantry Pride challenged the lock-up, no-shop, and cancellation fee provisions. At the same time, it increased its bid for Revlon to $58 per share. The Court of Chancery enjoined the provisions and concluded that the Revlon directors had breached their duty of loyalty by making concessions to Forstmann rather than maximizing the sale price of the company for the shareholders' benefit. Revlon appealed.

Case Decision. Justice Moore delivered the decision of the court.

* * *

The ultimate responsibility for managing the business and affairs of a corporation falls on its board of directors. In discharging this function, the directors owe fiduciary duties of care and loyalty to the corporation and its shareholders. These principles apply with equal force when a board approves a corporate merger pursuant to [Delaware law]; and of course they are the bedrock of our law regarding corporate takeover issues. While the business judgment rule may be applicable to the actions of corporate directors responding to takeover threats, the principles upon which it is founded—care, loyalty, and independence—must first be satisfied.

* * *

If the business judgment rule applies, there is a "presumption that in making a business decision the directors of a corporation acted on an informed basis, in good faith, and in the honest belief that the action taken was in the best interests of the company." However, when a board implements anti-takeover measures, there arises "the omnipresent specter that a board may be acting primarily in its own interests, rather than those of the corporation and its shareholders. . . ." This potential for conflict places upon the directors the burden of proving that they had reasonable grounds for believing there was a danger to corporate policy and effectiveness, a burden satisfied by a showing of good faith and reasonable investigation. In addition, the directors must analyze the nature of the takeover and its effect on the corporation in order to ensure balance—that the responsive action taken is reasonable in relation to the threat posed.

* * *

The Forstmann option had a destructive effect on the auction process. Forstmann had already been drawn into the contest on a preferred basis, so that result of the lock-up was not to foster bidding, but to destroy it. The board's stated reasons for approving the transactions were: (1) better financing, (2) noteholder protection, and (3) higher price. As the Court of Chancery found, and we agree, any distinctions between the rival bidders' methods of financing the proposal were nominal at best, and such a consideration has little or no significance in a cash offer for any and all shares. The principal object, contrary to the board's duty of care, appears to have been protection of the noteholders over the shareholders' interests.

While Forstmann's $57.25 offer was objectively higher than Pantry Pride's $56.25 bid, the margin of superiority is less when the Forstmann price is adjusted for the time value of money. In reality, the Revlon board ended the auction in return for very little actual improvement in the final bid. The principal benefit went to the directors, who avoided personal liability to a class of creditors (the noteholders) to whom the board owed no further duty under the circumstances. Thus, when a board ends an intense bidding contest on an insubstantial basis, and where a significant by-product of that action is to protect the directors against a perceived threat of personal liability for consequences stemming from the adoption of previous defensive measures, the action cannot withstand the enhanced scrutiny required of director conduct.

In addition to the lock-up option, the Court of Chancery enjoined the no-shop provision as part of the attempt to foreclose further bidding by Pantry Pride. The no-shop provision, like the lock-up option, while not per se illegal, is impermissible when a board's primary duty becomes that of an auctioneer responsible for selling the company to the highest bidder. The agreement to negotiate only with Forstmann ended rather than intensified the board's involvement in the bidding contest. . . .

Forstmann was given every negotiating advantage that Pantry Pride had been denied: cooperation from management, access to financial data, and the exclusive opportunity to present merger proposals directly to the board of directors. Favoritism for a white knight to the total exclusion of a hostile bidder might be justifiable when the latter's offer adversely affects shareholder interests, but when bidders make relatively similar offers, or dissolution of the company becomes inevitable, the directors cannot fulfill their . . . duties by playing favorites with the contending factions. Market forces must be allowed to operate freely to bring . . . shareholders the best price available for their equity. Thus, as the trial court ruled, the shareholders' interests necessitated that the board remain free to negotiate in the fulfillment of that duty.

The court below similarly enjoined the payment of the cancellation fee, pending a resolution of the merits, because the fee was part of the overall plan to thwart Pantry Pride's efforts. We find no abuse of discretion in that ruling.

In conclusion, the Revlon board was confronted with a situation not uncommon in the current wave of corporate takeovers. A hostile and determined bidder sought the company at a price the board was convinced was inadequate. In granting an asset option lock-up to Forstmann, we must conclude that under all the circumstances the directors allowed considerations other than the maximization of shareholder profit to affect their judgment, and followed a course that ended the auction for Revlon . . . to the ultimate detriment of its shareholders. No such defensive measure can be sustained when it represents a breach of the directors' fundamental duty of care. In that context the board's action is not entitled to the deference accorded it by the business judgment rule.

* * *

Case Holding. *The decision of the Court of Chancery was affirmed. When the sale of the corporation becomes inevitable, the board of directors' fiduciary duty to the shareholders changes from a duty to preserve the corporate entity to a duty to maximize the corporation's value.*

Case Questions

1. Why were Revlon's executives trying to avoid a takeover by Pantry Pride? Is that a legitimate business reason?
2. The court refers to Forstmann as a "white knight." What is a white knight?

Management of the Corporation

The corporation's board of directors hires skilled *managers* to operate the corporation on a day-to-day basis. The extent of managerial control and the compensation package to be enjoyed by hired managers are matters of contract between the board of directors, the principals of the corporation, and the persons hired. Once hired, managers have the same broad duties of care and loyalty as the directors. The use of hired management is one of the most significant advantages of the corporate form of business organization, since management by the owners of the business is impractical.

Termination of the Corporation

The termination of a corporation, like the termination of a partnership, is essentially conducted in two phases: the dissolution phase and the winding up phase. *Dissolution* of a corporation may be either voluntary or involuntary and effectively marks the end of the corporation. Upon its dissolution, the corporation is prevented from taking on any new business. A *voluntary dissolution* involves approval of the shareholders and the board of directors. The *involuntary dissolution* of the corporation can be brought about in the following ways:

1. An act of the legislature in the state of incorporation.
2. Court decree in the state of incorporation for any of the following reasons:
   (a) Obtaining a corporate charter through fraud or misrepresentation.
   (b) Failure of the corporation to comply with the state incorporation statutes (e.g., failure to pay franchise taxes).
   (c) Abandonment of or failure to begin the business before starting up.
   (d) Abuse of corporate powers.
3. Bankruptcy.

When the corporation is dissolved through voluntary action, the board of directors (acting as trustee) is responsible for *winding up* the affairs of the corporation. If the board refuses to act as trustee or if shareholders or creditors object, the court will appoint a trustee (just as it would if the dissolution were involuntary). After the corporation's affairs have been completed, the assets are liquidated. The proceeds of the liquidation are first used to satisfy the demands of creditors, with any remainder going to the shareholders.

OTHER FORMS OF BUSINESS ORGANIZATION

In addition to the most common forms of business organization, a number of other forms are available, including joint ventures, joint stock companies, syndicates, and cooperatives. These alternative business organizations are generally used as vehicles to manage a specific project or business concept.

Joint Ventures

The Supreme Court has defined a *joint venture* as a general partnership for a limited time and purpose. Generally speaking, a joint venture does have several of the characteristics of a general partnership including the same rights of control, risks of loss, and manner in which profits are taxed. It usually involves two or more individuals or companies who agree to combine their mutual interests in a specific project and to share in the subsequent losses or profits.

A joint venture is not usually considered a legal entity and therefore may not sue or be sued in its own name. In addition, the members of a joint venture usually have limited authority to bind each other to matters not directly related to the project. Joint ventures vary in size and are most popular as an international business organization.

Joint Stock Companies

A *joint stock company* is a business organization involving a unique mixture of partnership and corporation characteristics. Despite the mixture of characteristics, however, joint stock companies are generally treated like partnerships.

The joint stock company resembles the corporate form of business organization in that ownership is represented by shares of stock. In addition, joint stock companies are usually managed by directors and officers in a way very similar to that employed in most corporations. Like a corporation, a joint stock company can also have perpetual life.

In resembling a partnership, the joint stock company is usually created through an agreement and not according to some statute enacted by the state. In addition, the company property is held in the names of the shareholders/members who have personal liability for all company actions. The company is generally not considered a legal entity and therefore may not sue or be sued in its own name.

Cooperatives

A *cooperative* is a business organization (that may or may not be incorporated) organized to provide an economic service to its members. Cooperatives are usually formed by individuals who want to pool their purchasing power to gain some advantage in the marketplace. Generally, they are able to obtain lower product prices for their members through the purchase of products in large quantities at a discount.

Cooperatives that are not incorporated are usually treated as partnerships; the members are jointly liable for the acts of the cooperative. If the cooperative is to be formed as a corporation, it must meet the appropriate state laws governing nonprofit corporations. In contrast to typical corporate dividends, however, cooperative dividends are provided on the basis of a member's (shareholder's) transactions with the cooperative rather than on the basis of capital contributed.

Syndicates

A *syndicate* is the name given to a group of individuals who join together to finance a specific project. A common example of a syndicate is the large real estate development, such as a shopping center or professional office building. Although the specific structure of such organizations varies considerably, they may exist as general partnerships, limited partnerships, or corporations. It is not uncommon for the members of a syndicate to simply own property together with no other formal business organization.

INTERNATIONAL PERSPECTIVES: U.S. JOINT VENTURES IN THE SOVIET UNION

INTERNATIONAL

PERSPECTIVES

Prior to 1987, foreign trade was a small part of the Soviet Union's economy. The Soviet Union imported only what it could not produce domestically and exported only what it needed to pay for its imports. Since then, however, Soviet hard-currency exports have begun to decline. At the same time, the Soviet demand for Western imports, particularly capital goods, has been increasing. The demand for the capital goods—plants and equipment—is due to the requirements for modernizing the civilian sector of the economy. If Soviet President Mikhail Gorbachev's goals of industrial modernization are to be achieved, capital goods will have to be imported to augment domestic production.

In response to this situation, the Soviet Union has instituted sweeping trade reforms. The number of organizations that can now communicate directly with foreign buyers and sellers has been allowed to increase dramatically. For the first time, the Soviet Union elected to allow joint ventures with foreign companies on its soil. Western participation in the joint ventures is expected to produce a continuing flow of new technology and innovation in the civilian sector.

American companies have been cautious about exploiting opportunities represented by the Soviet market. Meanwhile, however, several Western European countries and Japan have signed joint venture agreements with the Soviet Union. Major U.S. companies involved in joint ventures or joint venture negotiations include Chevron, RJR–Nabisco, Johnson & Johnson, PepsiCo, and IBM.

The principal difficulty facing most joint ventures in the Soviet Union is finding a means to be paid. The Soviet currency—the ruble—is currently not convertible into western, or "hard," currency. Companies interested in doing business in the Soviet Union have developed mechanisms for getting paid. Several companies have agreed to take Soviet products in exchange for their products. PepsiCo, for example, is taking both Soviet vodka and large ships in exchange for its soft-drink products. Other companies are taking a more long-run view by proceeding with their joint venture operations despite the lack of hard currency. McDonald's restaurants in Moscow, for example, currently operate only in rubles. The company is taking the view that the potential opportunities provided by the Soviet market justify the initial losses.

FACTORS INFLUENCING THE CHOICE OF BUSINESS ORGANIZATION

In its lifetime, a business may on more than one occasion be faced with a choice of forms of business organization. For example, a particular business might begin as a sole proprietorship or a partnership and later, as it becomes more successful, find it advantageous to incorporate.

The business also might consider undertaking an international business venture either independently of its existing business, in conjunction with its existing business, or in a partnership with a foreign company. Several important factors will influence the choice of business organization, including the potential liabilities imposed on the owners, the transferability of ownership rights, the ability of the business organization to continue in the event of the death or withdrawal of one or more of the owners, the capital requirements of the business, and the tax rate applicable to the business organization selected. Exhibit 11–3 summarizes the differences between proprietorships, partnerships, and corporations on the basis of these factors.

Limited Liability

A major factor influencing decisions to choose a form of business organization is the extent of liability protection provided owners. *Limited liability* encourages those individuals who do not have the time or the expertise to manage a business to invest in the business venture. It allows the individual to invest without placing all personal wealth at risk. Limited liability allows investors to be passive toward the internal management of the business. If an individual's wealth were at stake, the investor would want an active role in managing the venture.

Non-corporate Entities

Sole proprietors and partners in a general partnership have unlimited personal liability for the debts of the business, including its torts. Some states require that creditors exhaust the business partnership property before moving against the personal property of the partners. After those assets are exhausted, however, the creditor may require any of the partners to pay the entire remaining debt. Partners forced to pay more than their proportionate share of a debt are entitled to reimbursement from other partners unless the original agreement provides otherwise. The primary characteristic of the limited partnership is its insulation of the limited partners from this kind of liability as long as they have not played an active role in managing the business.

Corporations

Like the limited partner, the shareholders of a corporation risk only their capital investment if the corporation fails. They are not personally liable for the business debts or torts of the corporation, unless they contract to make themselves personally liable. In certain circumstances, however, the court will

Exhibit 11–3 Comparing Characteristics of Major Forms of Business Organization

	Proprietorship	Partnership	Corporation
Method of Creation	Owner begins business operations	Created by agreement of parties	Charter issued by state — created by statutory authority
Entity Status	Not separate from owner	Separate from owners for some purposes	Legal entity, separate and distinct from owners
Liability of Owners	Owner liable for all debts	Unlimited liability except for limited partner in a limited partnership	Shareholders liable only to the extent of paid-in capital
Duration	Same as owner	Terminated by agreement of partners, by the death of one or more of the partners, by withdrawal of a partner, or by bankruptcy	May have perpetual existence
Transferability of Interest	May be sold at anytime; new proprietorship formed	Generally, sale of partnership interest terminates partnership, may create new partnership	Shares of stock can usually be readily transferred
Control	By owner	Each general partner has a direct and equal voice in management unless expressly agreed to be otherwise by partnership agreement; limited partners have no management rights	Shareholders elect board of directors who set policy and appoint officers to manage
Capital	Limited to what owner can raise	Limited to what partners can raise — may require a new partner, creating a new partnership	Sale of more ownership shares increases capital
Taxation	Profits taxed to owner as individual	Profits taxed proportionately to each owner as agreed in contract, or all share equally whether or not distributed	Double taxation — Profits of corporation taxed to corporation and shareholders pay income tax on dividends they receive

"pierce the corporate veil" and hold shareholders personally liable. That is, the court will disregard the corporate entity by finding that the corporation is a sham. Although this happens only rarely, the court will impose liability on shareholders in instances of fraud, undercapitalization, or failure to follow corporate formalities. As the *Tigrett* v. *Pointer* case illustrates, the corporate form of business organization may not be used merely to avoid business obligations.

Tigrett v. Pointer
Court of Civil Appeals of Texas
580 S.W.2d 375
(1978)

Case Background. *In April of 1974 Tigrett, the plaintiff, sued Heritage Building Company. The lawsuit resulted in a judgment against Heritage in 1976 for $49 per week for 401 weeks. However, there remained no assets upon which the judgment could be levied. The company was insolvent according to the testimony of its president and sole stockholder, Pointer, the defendant. According to the testimony, on May 1, 1974, Pointer transferred all Heritage's assets to himself in consideration of a reduction in* *the company's indebtedness to him. On the same day, Pointer transferred those same assets to Heritage Corporation as a loan.*

Tigrett brought this suit in the form of an application for a writ of garnishment, based on the previous judgment, against Pointer, Heritage Corporation, and other corporations owned and controlled by Pointer, alleging that they were indebted to Heritage Building Company as a result of the fraudulent transfer of its assets. She further alleged that Heritage Building Company, Heritage Corporation, and the other corporations were merely the alter egos of Pointer and that, as a consequence, they were all jointly and severally liable for the previous judgment.

The trial court found for the defendant, Pointer. Tigrett appealed, arguing that she had proved the alter ego theory as a matter of law.

Case Decision. Judge Guittard delivered the decision of the court.

In this garnishment proceeding the holder of a judgment against a corporation seeks to pierce the corporate veil and hold its sole stockholder, and also other corporations owned by him, personally liable for the judgment. . . .

* * *

Heritage Building Company was chartered in 1955 for the purpose of purchasing, subdividing and selling real estate, erecting and repairing buildings, and accumulating and lending money for these purposes. It was capitalized for $1,000 in cash, and 10,000 shares of stock were issued, of which 9,800 were issued to Gerald M. Pointer in consideration of $980. Pointer has since become sole stockholder, and he has always served as president and as chairman of the board of directors. . . .

* * *

The corporation's ledger contains a "loan account" showing its indebtedness to Pointer. On April 30, 1974, the ledger showed this indebtedness to be $484,218.00. No notes were signed, no security taken, and no interest paid. The only written evidence of the indebtedness in the present record is the notation in the corporate books. Pointer testified that he considered this a loan rather than a capital investment. The corporate financial statement, however, designates it as "capital."

On April 30, 1974, at a special meeting of the board of directors of Heritage Building Company, six days after service of process in plaintiff's suit, a resolution was adopted authorizing transfer of substantially all its assets to its president and sole stockholder, Gerald M. Pointer, in consideration of a reduction of the company's debt to him. On the next day entries were made on the books of the company, showing the transfer and listing in detail both real and personal property. Corresponding entries were made in Pointer's personal books showing this purchase of these assets. At the same time entries were made on the books of Heritage Corporation, also solely owned by Pointer, showing a transfer of the same assets from Pointer to it. No money changed hands. The books of Heritage Building Company showed a reduction of $389,967.00 in its debt to Pointer. This figure was determined by the book value of the assets, less the debts against them. The books of Heritage Corporation showed a loan of the same amount to it by Pointer. . . . The transfer was not announced, even to the employees of Heritage Building Company, who first learned of it when they received their paychecks from the new corporation. Operation of the business continued without change. The same employees continued to perform the same duties in the same suite offices. New stationery was printed, but "Heritage Building Company" remained on the office door and was still there at time of this trial.

The transfer of assets from Heritage Building Company to Pointer and from Pointer to Heritage Corporation on May 1, 1974, was explained by Pointer as a change of the corporate name and as an effort to improve the "credit reputation" of the business. He testified that the company had acquired a bad credit reputation and was unable to obtain loans because three of its apartment projects had been lost by foreclosure. In 1973, when the financial problems of Heritage Building Company became apparent, Heritage Corporation was organized with an initial capital of $1,000 and Pointer as the principal officer and sole stockholder. . . .

* * *

With these facts in mind, we turn to the authorities bearing on the alter ego question. It has been said that each case involving disregard of the corporate entity must rest on its own special facts. . . . When all the material facts are undisputed, however, application of the alter ego doctrine is a question of law. . . .

Of course, domination of corporate affairs by the sole stockholder does not in itself justify imposition of personal liability. . . . Personal liability may be imposed on the sole stockholder only in extraordinary circumstances. Various statements of the circumstances justifying personal liability are found in judicial opinions, but common to all is the concept that the corporate form may be disregarded when it is used to perpetrate a fraud or is relied on to justify wrong or injustice.

* * *

Inadequate capitalization by itself may not be a sufficient ground to pierce the corporate veil. . . . Thus, a party who has contracted with a financially weak corporation and is disappointed in obtaining satisfaction of his claim cannot look to the dominant stockholder or parent corporation in the absence of additional compelling facts. . . . Grossly inadequate capitalization, however, as measured by the nature and magnitude of the corporate undertaking, is an important factor in determining whether personal liability should be imposed.

* * *

Pointer organized Heritage Building Company with a minimum of capital stock and advanced the necessary working funds from time to time in the form of loans. When the corporation ran into financial difficulty, he used his dominant position as president, director, and sole stockholder to withdraw substantially all assets from the corporation without making any provision for payment of plaintiff and other creditors. . . . This maneuver was a violation of his fiduciary duty as officer and director of an insolvent corporation to preserve the assets for the benefit of all the creditors. It was particularly inequitable and unfair in that he preferred himself as a creditor, although in view of the inadequate capitalization, his loan to the corporation must be treated as an advance of capital, or, at most, as a claim subordinate to those of other creditors. Although not one of these circumstances, standing alone, would justify piercing the corporate veil, when taken together, they demonstrate conclusively that while Pointer observed the form of the corporate enterprise, he ignored his substantive duties as a corporate officer and director and acted solely in his own interest.

* * *

Case Holding. *The trial court erred in failing to hold Pointer personally liable for the debts of Heritage Building Company. When a corporation transfers virtually all its assets to its controlling stockholder to repay cash advances, without providing for other creditors, the court may consider whether the manipulation of the corporate form to serve personal interests justifies imposition of personal liability.*

Case Questions

1. Why did Pointer transfer the assets of Heritage Building Company to Heritage Corporation? Is Pointer otherwise entitled to make that transfer? Why was it found to be inappropriate in this case?

2. Does the decision work to defeat one of the basic advantages of the corporate form of business organization?

Transferability of Ownership Interests

The *transferability* of ownership rights refers to the ability of an owner in a business venture to sell or otherwise pass that interest to another. In particular, it refers to the impact such a transfer will have on the existing business venture. The ability of owners to transfer ownership interests differs significantly among the various forms of business organizations.

Non-corporate Entities

The proprietor in a sole proprietorship is, in essence, the business. A decision to sell or otherwise transfer the business clearly will bring about the termination of the existing proprietorship and the creation of a new proprietorship. Relative to the value of the business, the transfer is expensive. It usually involves attorneys who devise the contract for sale and consultants who help value the business.

If a partner sells or assigns an interest in a partnership, the partnership is not dissolved and the new owner does not become a partner. Although the new owner is entitled to receive the share of profits the assigning partner would have received, the new owner gains neither the right to participate in the management of partnership affairs nor access to partnership information that the assigning partner would have been entitled to receive. If, however, the other partner is admitted into the business by the agreement of all the partners, the existing partnership is terminated and a new one is formed. Like proprietorships, the sale of partnership shares can be complex and relatively expensive.

Corporations

Most corporate stock can be easily transferred, either in a public exchange (such as the New York Stock Exchange) or privately between individuals. If the stock of the corporation is publicly traded (as is the case for most large corporations), a shareholder's interest can be transferred without the permission of the other owners. These exchanges are cheap. The sale of thousands of shares of corporate stock usually involves only a small sales commission. A *close corporation*, however, limits the transfer of its stock to specified individuals according to the bylaws of the corporation.

Duration

A business's *duration* refers to its ability to continue to operate in the event of the death, retirement, or other incapacity of an owner of the business. The ability of a business to continue under such circumstances depends significantly upon the form of business organization it has selected.

Non-corporate Entities

A sole proprietorship terminates with the death or other incapacity of the proprietor. A partnership is dissolved by the death, retirement, or other incapacity of a partner, but is not necessarily terminated. After the partnership has been dissolved, it may be terminated with the liquidation of the partnership's assets. Its value as a concern, however, would be sacrificed. To avoid this loss, partners usually agree in advance that the partnership will continue by entering into a continuation agreement. The agreement usually allows the remaining partners to continue to operate the business until a settlement is reached with the retired partner or with the deceased partner's legal representative.

Corporations

Unless its articles of incorporation provide for a specified period of duration, a corporation has *perpetual existence.* In the words of Chief Justice Marshall in *Dartmouth* v. *Woodward* (1819):

> A corporation is an artificial being, invisible, intangible, and existing only in contemplation of law. Being the mere creation of law, it possesses only those properties which the charter of its creation confers upon it. . . . These are such as are supposed best calculated to effect the object for which it was created. Among the most important are immortality, and, if the expression may be allowed, individuality; properties by which a perpetual succession of many persons are considered as the same, so that they may act as a single individual. A corporation manages its own affairs, and holds property without the hazardous and endless necessity of perpetual conveyance for the purpose of transmitting it from hand to hand. It is chiefly for the purpose of clothing bodies of men, in succession, with these qualities and capacities, that corporations were invented, and are in use. By these means, a perpetual succession of individuals are capable of acting for the promotion of the particular object, like one immortal being.

With perpetual existence, the death, retirement, or other incapacity of a shareholder will not bring about the termination of the corporation. In fact, in most large corporations the death of a shareholder has no impact on the operations of the business.

Capital Requirements

The forms of business organization differ in the alternatives available to the owners for raising financial capital. Depending upon the financial needs of a particular business, the form of business organization can be an important factor affecting a business's long-run viability. For example, a business that is in a position to grow and expand will be better served by an organizational form that allows it to raise necessary capital efficiently.

Non-corporate Entities

Sole proprietorships are usually most limited in terms of the alternatives available to the business for raising capital. The principal source of capital is the proprietor's personal wealth and any capital the proprietor may be able to borrow. While forming a partnership may increase the financial capital available to the business, the resources of a partnership are still basically restricted to those of the partners involved in the business.

Through the investment of limited partners, limited partnerships provide additional alternatives for raising financial capital. Limited partners are essentially investors who have no particular expertise in the product being produced or an interest in the day-to-day operation of the business.

Corporations

A major factor influencing the selection of the corporation as a form of business organization is the corporation's ability to raise financial capital. Corporations are able to raise capital from two major sources: through the issuance of stock and from the selling of bonds. The issuance of stock is termed *equity financing* because the buyers of the stock purchase an ownership, or equitable, interest in the corporation. When the corporation sells bonds, it raises capital through *debt financing*. The bond represents a promise on the part of the corporation to repay the purchase price of the bond plus interest after a specified number of years. The proceeds of the sale of stocks and bonds are then used to finance the expansion of the business.

Taxation Considerations

The federal tax system has significant effects on incentives for certain kinds of business activity. The tax treatment differs among forms of business organizations and may affect a business's choice of form. Tax considerations are particularly important to small businesses and may dominate the selection decision.

Non-corporate Entities

The income from a sole proprietorship or a partnership is taxed as the personal income of the sole proprietor or partner. The business itself does not pay taxes on its profits. Partnerships, however, must file an informational return with the Internal Revenue Service.

Corporations

Unlike the profits of proprietorships and partnerships, the profits of a corporation are taxed directly. Further, shareholders must pay income tax on the dividends or capital gains they receive from the corporation. Thus, corporate income is subject to double taxation, first on the corporate net income at corporate rates, and then at a shareholder's personal income rate. However, usually not all the corporation's after-tax profits are distributed to shareholders. Earnings may be retained in the corporation to finance operations and expansion plans. If, however, the retained earnings increase the value of the stock, shareholders will be taxed on the capital gains upon the sale of their stock.

For a business owner who finds it advantageous to incorporate but double taxation is a drawback, the Internal Revenue Service allows for the use of an *S corporation* under Subchapter S of the Internal Revenue Code. An S corporation is created, operated, and dissolved in the same manner as regular corporations. If the corporation meets certain requirements, it may notify the

IRS of its election to be taxed as a partnership. The entire profits of the corporation are then distributed to shareholders and are taxed as personal income.

SUMMARY

The most prominent forms of business organization are the sole proprietorship, partnership, limited partnership, and corporation. Less frequently employed forms include joint ventures, joint stock companies, syndicates, and cooperatives.

Sole proprietorships are the oldest and simplest form of business organization. They are employed by individuals who own all or most of the business property and are responsible for the control, liabilities, and management of the business.

General partnerships are composed of two or more individuals, called general partners, who enter into an agreement to carry on a business for a profit. Partnership law is generally dictated by the Uniform Partnership Act. Each partner has an equal voice in the management and conduct of the business (unless the partnership agreement states otherwise). Partners have a fiduciary duty of loyalty and trust to the other partners and may not place their individual interests above those of the partnership.

The partnership is terminated in two phases: the dissolution phase and the winding-up phase. Dissolution occurs when an event takes place that forecloses the partnership from undertaking any new business. Dissolution occurs upon the withdrawal, death, incapacity, or bankruptcy of a partner. The winding up of the partnership requires that all existing obligations of the business be completed. The assets of the partnership are then liquidated and the proceeds distributed first to the creditors and then to the partnership.

A limited partnership is a special form of a general partnership. It is similar to a general partnership in all aspects except that a limited partnership is made up of at least one general partner and one or more limited partners. While the general partners have unlimited liability for the debts of the business, the limited partners are liable only up to their capital contributions. The limited partners may not take an active role in the management of the business. A limited partnership is terminated in much the same way as a general partnership.

Corporations are the form of business organization most often associated with the term *business*. Most large businesses are corporations. Corporations are creations of the state, with methods of creation dictated by state statute. Businesses are generally required to file their articles of incorporation with the appropriate state official. Upon approval, the incorporators designate the board of directors and issue stock. The directors are subsequently elected by the shareholders and are responsible for establishing corporate policy. They have a fiduciary duty to preserve the corporation. The board is empowered to hire managers to operate the business and conduct its affairs. The shareholders are the owners of the corporation. They enjoy limited liability but do not participate in the day-to-day management of the business.

Several factors influence the choice of a form of business organization, including limited liability, duration, transferability, capital requirements, and rate of taxation.

ISSUE

Should Managers Be Criminally Liable for Corporate Wrongdoing?

In the past few years, prosecutors have started to bring criminal charges against company officers for violations committed by a corporation. As a rule, corporate officers have shielded themselves from liability, leaving the corporation itself accountable for the wrongdoing. Only monetary fines can be imposed on a corporation, whereas executives can be imprisoned. As this reading notes, prosecutors are becoming more aggressive against company officers. Critics charge that since the corporation is a legal entity, it is the proper defendant for the suits and not the corporation's employees.

Upping the Ante
Ruth Simon*

Ciba-Geigy Corp. says it didn't think it was doing anything wrong a decade ago when it began burying chemical waste in a landfill at its Toms River, N.J. plant. But New Jersey officials don't buy it. State prosecutors will soon try to prove that Ciba-Geigy not only disposed of toxic wastes illegally but lied to regulators about it. Ciba-Geigy could face a big fine—and two middle-level employees could be fined as much as $1 million each and face prison sentences of more than 100 years.

"We go after the small guy who pollutes the environment, and we'll do the same with a big company," threatens James Lyko, chief of New Jersey's environmental crimes team, which has 40 prosecutors and investigators.

Power to police environmental laws is rapidly trickling down to states and counties. Some 22 states—including New Jersey, New York, Ohio and Pennsylvania—have special environmental enforcement units.

"The activity of the states at least equals or surpasses the activity at the federal level," says Herbert Johnson, senior environment counsel for the National Association of Attorneys General, which is preparing a guide to state environmental statutes. In all, states

have more lawyers prosecuting environmental crimes than the U.S. Justice Department, which has 25 attorneys in its environmental crimes section. The feds have also sponsored regional task forces so state and local prosecutors can share information.

"You're starting to see more experienced prosecutors," says James Rogers, a partner in Skadden, Arps, Slate, Meagher & Flom. "From a defense view, the worst thing is to face someone who's done these cases before."

In one of the most controversial cases of the past year, an Ohio-based manager working for Browning-Ferris was sentenced to one year in prison. The crime: pumping rainwater off a hazardous waste dump into a drainage ditch that led to a creek. The manager is now appealing, but defense attorneys argue that the case makes it difficult to tell just when an employee's action will be ruled illegal.

"You can interpret the case to say that before you do anything you have to consult with the regulatory agency," says Judson Starr, head of the federal environmental enforcement program until 1988, and now a partner at Baltimore-based Venable, Baetjer, Howard & Civiletti. "There's no bright line

—continued

–continuing

that determines whether a case will be administrative, civil or criminal."

In a trial slated to begin in August, prosecutors in Cook County, Ill. are charging Chicago Magnet Wire Corp., a unit of North American Philips, and five executives with aggravated battery and several misdemeanors for the injury of 43 workers exposed to hazardous chemicals. This case is being brought by the same county prosecutor's office that in 1985 successfully charged the president and two other executives of Film Recovery Systems Inc. with first-degree murder in the cyanide poisoning death of a worker. A retrial was recently ordered (the defendants are free on bail pending the retrial), but it has already sparked similar prosecutions in Michigan, New York and Wisconsin. Reports Jay Magnuson, deputy chief in the Cook County state attorney's office: "After the Film Recovery case we got calls from corporate counsel all over the country asking for the indictment and the judge's ruling."

The blurring of the administrative, civil and criminal lines doesn't make for good law, but it does make the prosecutors' job easier.

"One criminal prosecution is worth 1,000 enforcement orders," says Keith Welks, chief of civil enforcement for Pennsylvania and for seven years the head of its criminal enforcement program. "If you're asking for a $25,000 fine and a guilty plea, corporations will say, if you kick it over to the civil side, we'll pay a $100,000 penalty."

Now cities and towns want to get in on the act. Starting this summer, for example, Buffalo-area police officers will be trained by the local U.S. Attorney to spot illegal dumping and other environmental crimes.

Protecting local environments from illegal abuse is both good policy and good politics. But who will protect the legal system against abuse by overzealous prosecutors?

Questions

1. Should corporate officers be held personally liable for the wrongdoing of a corporation?

2. The U.S. Sentencing Commission recommended that fines imposed on corporations should generally be much larger so there is a real financial sting to them. Would this be a good alternative to the prosecution of individuals?

REVIEW AND DISCUSSION QUESTIONS

1. Define the following terms:
business organization
sole proprietorship
partnership
limited partnership
limited liability
corporation

2. Compare and contrast the following:
  a. Partnership and joint venture
  b. Dissolution of a partnership and the winding up of a partnership
  c. General partner and limited partner
  d. Shareholder and limited partner
  e. Piercing the corporate veil and limited liability for shareholders
  f. Articles of incorporation and bylaws

3. What is the definition of a partnership? Are four doctors who own a summer cottage jointly and use it solely for their personal enjoyment a partnership?

4. In what ways is a limited partnership similar to a corporation? To a general partnership? Can a limited partner call for the dissolution of a limited partnership? Who has authority to wind up the limited partnership's affairs?

5. Mrs. Ehsani owns one share in Exxon. She is convinced that because her interest is so small she has no rights with regard to the company's affairs. She is particularly concerned about whether she can attend the shareholders' meeting and what her rights and responsibilities are during that meeting. She would also like to inspect the company's books. What are her rights in this regard?

6. Which factors might most influence the selection of a form of business organization in the following businesses? Which form would be most appropriate?
   a. Operation of a hazardous waste disposal facility.
   b. A research and development facility that has just begun to develop its own products.
   c. A company with the patent to a unique but inexpensive product that is expected to generate large profits.
   d. A coin-operated laundry near a college campus.
   e. A business intending to undertake labor-intensive manufacturing in Korea.

Case Questions

7. Fuller, Farner, and Kruse have formed a partnership to operate a sporting goods store. Kruse contributed $20,000, while Fuller and Farner each contributed $5,000. In their partnership agreement, they did not specify how profits would be distributed or how losses would be shared. Within the first month of operation, Fuller and Farner voted to purchase the property next to their existing facility to expand the floor space of the business. Kruse objected, asserting that as the largest contributor he has the controlling interest in the partnership. Is Kruse's assertions correct?

8. U.S. Construction was a partnership owned by Vetter and Foley. In the middle of a project, they decided to terminate their partnership arrangement. Vetter told Foley not to write any more checks on the company accounts. Foley, in need of supplies to complete the job, wrote a check on the company account to pay for the supplies. The bank, although it was aware of the partner's agreement to terminate the partnership, honored the check. Has Foley misused the partnership's funds?

9. Nockels and Everett formed a limited partnership. Nockels, who contributed office space, is the general partner and Everett, who contributed $20,000 to the partnership, is the limited partner. About six months after the partnership began its operations, Nockels became very ill and Everett took over the management of the operations of the business. During this time period, Everett negotiated and entered into a large contract with James Knott. After several weeks, it became apparent that the partnership was not going to be able to fulfill its contractual obligations and Knott was going to suffer a significant loss. Knott has filed suit against both Everett and Nockels, asserting they are personally liable for the losses despite the appearance of a limited partnership. Can Everett support his claim that he is a limited partner and therefore avoid personal liable beyond the amount of his contribution to the partnership?

10. Charles Gabus was appointed to the board of directors for Ironhorse Automotive, Inc., a corporation that owned several new car dealerships. In the next eighteen months, the business deteriorated rapidly due, in part, to poor managerial decisions. Gabus neither attended board meetings nor examined the business records or books during the period. Could he be personally liable to the shareholders for the losses of the corporation?

Policy Questions

11. What advantages and disadvantages are there in having a nationally accepted statute for the regulation of partnerships in various states?

12. In selecting a state in which to incorporate, businesses often look for a state that offers the most advantageous tax or incorporation provisions in their incorporation statutes. Historically, the state of Delaware has had the least restrictive incorporation statutes. Should states be able to compete on the basis of incorporation statutes? Are there advantages to consumers from allowing states to compete? Are there disadvantages?

Ethics Questions

13. Jensen and Cross entered into a partnership agreement to sell insulation to residential and commercial contractors. The business was very successful, and the two became quite wealthy. As the business grew, they discussed seriously the need to incorporate the business to take advantage of the corporate form of business organization. Since their partnership agreement had served them well, the change to a corporation was not undertaken until 1983. In that year, the partners first realized that some of the workers for the contractors to whom they sold their insulation were developing serious illnesses that appeared to be caused by long-term exposure to the insulation. By incorporating, Jensen and Cross hoped to avoid personal liability for the injuries to those workers. Was the move to incorporate good business practice?

14. Cook and Smith entered into a limited partnership called Trinty Development to develop a shopping center. Adjacent to the shopping center property was a ten-acre tract of undeveloped land that came up for sale after the limited partnership had begun its operations. Cook, the general partner, purchased the property from McCade, but only after McCade had refused to sell the property to Trinty. His stated purpose was that he did not want to do business with Smith. Cook then sold the property to another developer for a $60,000 profit. If Cook had sold the property to Trinty, Trinty could have avoided the need to build an access road. Trinty has objected to the sale and purchase by Cook. What alternatives did Cook have? With regard to his employment with Trinty, what was the ethical choice? How was Trinty damaged? With regard to his relationship with McCade, what were his alternatives?

15. Mr. Tuttle operated a profitable barbershop as a sole proprietorship. After Mr. Tuttle had operated the business for several years, a prominent member of the community approached him with an offer to purchase the business. Tuttle refused the offer. In response to Tuttle's rejection, the spurned buyer then opened a competing barbershop. The spurned buyer hired barbers and encouraged friends and associates to patronize the business—all at a considerable financial loss to himself. Since the new business's prices were lower, Mr. Tuttle was eventually forced to close his shop. Was the spurned buyer's activities ethical? Was it legal? [*Tuttle* v. *Buck*, 107 Minn. 145, N.W. 946 (1909)]

Part Three

Regulation of Business and Public Law

Part III is concerned with the regulatory laws affecting the legal environment of business. While the regulatory laws of the states are an important component of the legal environment of business, our discussion focuses on Federal regulatory laws. Federal regulation is most often justified by the desire to achieve an important public objective that an unregulated environment may not provide. An undesirable product of an unregulated market is generally referred to as a *market failure*. Congress imposes regulation when it perceives that there are flaws in the operation of competition in a particular market, or because there are political objectives that are more important than the natural results of an unregulated economy. Part III discusses the most predominate sources of market failure, including monopoly, inequities in employment, information problems, and externalities.

MONOPOLY

A market economy relies on competition to determine business behavior. Competition provides businesses with incentives to become more efficient in the production of their goods and services. Under a competitive market structure, one business's ability to affect markets and market prices will be constrained by its rival's power.

In some circumstances, competition may fail. A group of businesses could be more profitable if they did not compete against one another. Rather, it would be more profitable to act as *monopolists* by banding together, limiting output, and raising prices. Since the monopolists reduce economic efficiency, monopoly power can justify government intervention. The federal antitrust laws, discussed in Chapters 12 and 13, are the federal government's response to this market failure.

419

SOCIAL POLICIES IN EMPLOYMENT

A significant portion of government regulation is enacted to further social policies that government leaders have determined to be important. In the employment relationship, Congress has expressed concern for individuals adversely affected by the unequal bargaining power perceived to exist between workers and employers and the inequality in opportunities generated by discrimination. The federal government's response to these issues are discussed in Chapters 14 and 15 and include laws to regulate the wages of workers, promote the organization of unions, and prohibit employment discrimination.

INADEQUATE INFORMATION

One important reason often given for the imposition of government regulation is inadequate information. For competitive markets to function well, consumers need information to evaluate products and services. In some circumstances, however, the necessary information can be very expensive for a consumer to obtain or analyze. The government has attempted to compensate for inadequate information through the regulation of certain business practices.

In the twentieth century, products have become more numerous and complex. The average American can identify over 1,800 brand names. How much about these products can consumers know? Various regulations address consumer issues. In Chapter 16 we review federal regulation of food and drug products, regulation of advertising claims, and federal attacks on deception of consumers.

Financial markets are complex. Investing in stocks and bonds was only for the wealthy in years past. Today, a majority of working Americans have funds invested in the securities markets. Regulations of that market are supposed to improve information and help insure integrity on the part of market professionals, as will be seen in Chapters 18 and 19. Twenty years ago people saved money at a savings and loan and had a checking account at a bank. A person would borrow money from the bank to buy a car. There were not many other options. Since banking and credit markets are now more competitive and complicated, regulations have been imposed to give more rights to consumers as savers and borrowers. Some of the key laws are reviewed in Chapter 20.

EXTERNALITIES

The efficiencies produced by the competitive market are based on the assumption that all costs of manufacturing a product are reflected in the price of the product. In some instances, however, the production of a good imposes costs on society that are not included in the product's price. Those costs are called *externalities*, since they are borne by neither the manufacturer nor the consumer of the product. The most common externality—pollution—has been addressed by environmental laws for the regulation of land, water, air, and product pollution. Those laws are discussed in Chapter 17.

12 Antitrust Laws and Horizontal Arrangements

A S far back as the 1500s the courts in England refused to enforce contracts designed to eliminate competitors. This common-law tradition has been maintained in the United States. As was noted in the chapter on contract law, the courts do not enforce contracts that are contrary to public policy. The courts held contracts in restraint of trade to be against public policy long before Congress enacted the antitrust statutes. However, before the statutes were enacted, there were no formal prohibitions on attempts by competitors to work together to *restrain competition* and *injure competitors*. As we will see, the lack of specificity in the antitrust statutes has required the federal courts to determine what really constitutes antitrust law. The Department of Justice and the Federal Trade Commission also play important roles by determining which business activities the government will attack under the antitrust law. Antitrust law, therefore, refers to the antitrust statutes, the interpretation of the statutes by the courts, and the enforcement policies of the administrative agencies. This chapter reviews the antitrust statutes and looks at how antitrust law is applied to horizontal business arrangements.

ANTITRUST COMMON LAW

Before the various antitrust statutes were enacted, the U.S. courts had to rely on the common law in dealing with anticompetitive behavior. The principles and rules generally applied by the courts were derived from English legal theory. The American common law disapproved of business practices or agreements that were believed to restrain trade. A practice or agreement restrains trade when it prevents open competition from occurring.

The common law cases of the nineteenth century, however, did not hold all restraints of trade to be illegal—only those considered to be unreasonable. The courts refused to enforce agreements by competitors to restrain trade. Although the courts, as in the *Craft v. McConoughy* decision, refused to enforce anticompetitive agreements before passage of the antitrust laws, little could be done to proscribe such activities. That is, as long as the parties to an agreement to restrain trade got along, the restraint was not likely to get into the courts.

Craft v. McConoughy
Illinois Supreme Court
79 Ill. 346 (1875)

Case Background. *The four grain merchants in the town of Rochelle, Illinois, agreed in 1869 to fix prices. They would carry on their businesses as usual in all respects, except that they met secretly to divide the market and agree on prices. One of the members to the agreement died. His son, who took over the business, broke ranks with the rest of the group. The grain merchants sued to force him to abide by the agreement his father had signed for his company.*

Case Decision. Justice Craig delivered the opinion of the court.

* * *

The language used in the contract itself leaves no room for doubt as to the purpose for which the agreement was entered into, as a few extracts will show: "Each separate firm shall conduct their own business as heretofore, as though there was no partnership in appearance, keep their accounts, pay their own expenses, ship their own grain, and furnish their own funds to do business with." . . .

"Prices and grades to be fixed from time to time, as convenient, and each one to abide by them. All grain taken in store shall be charged one and one-half cents per bushel, monthly." . . . "No grain to be shipped by any party at less rates than two cents per bushel."

While the agreement, upon its face, would seem to indicate that the parties had formed a co-partnership for the purpose of trading in grain, yet, from the terms of the contract, and the other proof in the record, it is apparent that the true object was, to form a secret combination which would stifle all competition, and enable the parties, by secret and fraudulent means, to control the price of grain, cost of storage, and expense of shipment. In other words, the four firms, by a shrewd, deep-laid, secret combination, attempted to control and monopolize the entire grain trade of the town and surrounding country.

That the effect of this contract was to restrain the trade and commerce of the country, is a proposition that can not be successfully denied.

We understand it to be a well settled rule of law, that an agreement in general restraint of trade, is contrary to public policy, illegal and void, but an agreement in partial or particular restraint upon trade has been held good, where the restraint was only partial, consideration adequate, and the restriction reasonable.

While these parties were in business, in competition with each other, they had the undoubted right to establish their own rates for grain stored and commissions for shipment and sale. They could pay as high or low a price for grain as they saw proper, and as they could make contracts with the producer. So long as competition was free, the interest of the public was safe. The laws of trade, in connection with the rigor of competition, was all the guaranty the public required, but the secret combination created by the contract destroyed all competition and created a monopoly against which the public interest had no protection.

* * *

Case Holding. *The court threw the case out of court. Since both parties were involved in an activity contrary to public policy, the court would not provide either party with relief.*

Case Questions

1. Why did the court not allow damages to be collected by the party breaking the conspiracy?
2. Why would someone want to break such a conspiracy, since there were no legal consequences to being a part of the cartel?

THE ANTITRUST STATUTES

The growth of large nationwide corporations in the late nineteenth century led to calls for more constraints on business behavior than existed under the common law. The result was the passage of federal antitrust legislation: the Sherman Act, the Clayton Act, and the Federal Trade Commission (FTC) Act. These statutes are excerpted in Appendices C, D, E, and F. These statutes are broadly written. The result has been that except for some actions that are clearly illegal under the statutes, it has been left largely to the federal courts to determine how the laws will be applied in practice.

The Sherman Act

The *Sherman Antitrust Act* was passed by Congress in 1890 in response to the general unpopularity of the giant industrial organizations that arose out of the industrial revolution. The most famous of the time was the Standard Oil Trust, in reference to which the word *antitrust* was invented. Had the Standard Oil Trust been named the Standard Oil Corporation, the Sherman Act may well have been the Sherman Anticorporation Act. The sponsors of the Act regarded it largely as a way to reduce concerns that Congress was dominated by large business interests.

The major sections of the Sherman Act are so broad that one could find almost any business activity to be illegal. It has fallen to the courts to decide what is in fact illegal under the two major sections of the Act:

> Sec. 1: Every contract, combination in the form of trust or otherwise, or conspiracy, in restraint of trade or commerce among the several States, or with foreign nations, is hereby declared to be illegal.
>
> Sec. 2: Every person who shall monopolize, or attempt to monopolize, or combine or conspire with any other person or persons, to monopolize any part of the trade or commerce among the several States, or with foreign nations, shall be deemed guilty of a felony.

The Clayton Act

Enacted in 1914, the *Clayton Act* was intended by Congress to supplement the coverage of the Sherman Act. In large measure, the Clayton Act was enacted in response to the Supreme Court's early interpretations of the Sherman Act, which limited its application.

Supporters of the Clayton Act wanted the government to have the ability to attack a business practice early in its use, in order to prevent a firm from becoming a monopoly (in addition to having the ability to attack the monopoly after it had been formed). Thus, the Clayton Act was enacted to provide the government with the ability to attack business activities when the effect of the activity was "to substantially lessen competition or tend to create a monopoly." The most important sections of the Clayton Act are:

> Sec. 2: It shall be unlawful for any person engaged in commerce, in the course of such commerce, either directly or indirectly, to discriminate in price between different purchasers of commodities of like grade and quality, where either or any of the purchases involved in such discrimination are in commerce . . . within the United States . . . and where the effect of such discrimination may be substantially to lessen competition or tend to create a monopoly in any line of commerce, or to injure, destroy, or prevent competition . . . [*This section was added by the Robinson-Patman Act of 1936, and restricts price discrimination.*]
>
> Sec. 3: It shall be unlawful for any person engaged in commerce, in the course of such commerce, to lease or make a sale . . . within the United States . . . or fix a price charged therefore, or discount from, or rebate upon, such price, on the condition . . . that the lessee or purchaser thereof shall not use or deal in the goods . . . or other commodities of a competitor or competitors of the lessor or seller, where the effect . . . may be to substantially lessen competition or tend to create a monopoly in any line of commerce. [*This is the restriction on tying sales and exclusive dealing.*]
>
> Sec. 7: No corporation engaged in commerce shall acquire, directly or indirectly, the whole or any part of the stock or other share capital and no corporation subject to the jurisdiction of the Federal Trade Commission shall acquire the whole or any part of the assets of another corporation engaged also in commerce, where in any line of commerce in any section of the country, the effect of such acquisition may be substantially to lessen competition, or to tend to create a monopoly. [*This prevents mergers with or acquisitions of competitors.*]
>
> Sec. 8: No person at the same time shall be a director in any two or more corporations . . . if such corporations are or shall have been theretofore, by virtue of their business and location of operation, competitors, so that the elimination of competition by agreement between them would constitute a violation of any of the provisions of the antitrust laws. [*This is the restriction on interlocking directorates.*]

Individuals and corporations violating the Clayton Act face penalties different from those provided by the Sherman Act. While the Department of Justice and private parties may initiate civil proceedings, the normal procedure has been for the Federal Trade Commission (FTC), which shares jurisdiction with the Justice Department in Clayton Act matters, to issue cease and desist orders, prohibiting further violation of the law by a specific party. The FTC has the authority to investigate suspect business dealings, hold hearings (rather than trials), and issue an administrative order approved in federal court that requires a party to discontinue or modify certain business acts. Only when these orders are ignored is the firm or individual exposed to criminal sanctions.

The Federal Trade Commission Act

In addition to the Clayton Act, Congress also enacted the *Federal Trade Commission Act* in 1914. The Act established the FTC as an agency empowered to investigate and enforce violations of the antitrust laws. Although the majority of the Act provides for the structure, powers, and procedures of the FTC, it does provide a major substantive addition to antitrust law:

> Sec. 5: Unfair methods of competition in or affecting commerce, and unfair or deceptive acts or practices in commerce, are hereby declared unlawful.

The *unfair methods of competition* referred to in the FTC Act have been interpreted by the courts as any business activity that may tend to create a monopoly by unfairly eliminating or excluding competitors from the marketplace. Violation of this statute carries a variety of penalties, ranging from an order preventing a planned merger to substantial civil penalties. The Sherman Act's prohibition of attempts to monopolize can overlap the FTC Act's unfair competition ban. Since, unlike the Justice Department, the FTC is not required to initiate the prosecution of alleged violators through the federal court system, the effect of this overlap is to give the government administrative jurisdiction to proceed against potential Sherman Act violations without the more difficult task of having to prove a criminal violation.

MANAGING THE ANTITRUST ENVIRONMENT

Although managers may rely on attorneys in dealing with antitrust law, the antitrust laws act as constraints on managerial conduct. Knowledge of the constraints enables managers to operate in a manner that will not result in expensive and potentially damaging litigation against their company. Engaging in conduct not allowed by the antitrust laws—as interpreted by the Justice Department, the FTC, and the courts—is apt to lead to lawsuits. Thus, a successful business strategy must take the antitrust laws into account.

Activities that the average businessperson may view as hard competition can run afoul of the antitrust laws. Hence, a manager contemplating a new method of distribution, a merger, or other activity that affects competition enters a gray area of antitrust law and should be especially careful.

A striking example of what managers should not do is provided by a complaint filed by the Department of Justice in 1983 claiming a violation of Section 2 of the Sherman Act. Justice alleged that American Airlines and its president, Robert Crandall, attempted to monopolize airline passenger service in certain cities by asking Braniff Airlines to raise its prices and promising that American would do so, too.

The following conversation, reported in the case filed by the government, was taped by Braniff's president, Howard Putnam, and is a prosecutor's dream: [We have deleted the expletives.]

Crandall: I think it's dumb as hell for * & !#!* all right, to sit here and pound the * & !#!* out of each other and neither one of us making a * & !#!* dime.

Putnam: Well—

Crandall: I mean, you know, * & !#!* what the * & !#!* is the point of it?

Putnam: Nobody asked American to serve Harlingen. Nobody asked American to serve Kansas City, and there were low fares in there, you know, before. So—

Crandall: You better believe it, Howard. But, you, you, you know, the complex is here—ain't gonna change a * & !#!* thing, all right. We can, we can both live here and there ain't no room for Delta. But there's, ah, no reason that I can see, all right, to put both companies out of business.

Putnam: But if you're going to overlay every route of American's on top of over, on top of every route that Braniff has—I can't just sit here and allow you to bury us without giving our best effort.

Crandall: Oh sure, but Eastern and Delta do the same thing in Atlanta and have for years.

Putnam: Do you have a suggestion for me?

Crandall: Yes. I have a suggestion for you. Raise your * & !#!* fares twenty percent. I'll raise mine the next morning.

Putnam: Robert, we—

Crandall: You'll make more money and I will too.

Putnam: We can't talk about pricing.

Crandall: Oh * & !#!* Howard. We can talk about any * & !#!* thing we want to talk about.

The result of this conversation was a suit against American Airlines and Crandall. The Fifth Circuit ruled that although there was no agreement to monopolize, the government could bring suit on the basis of an attempt to monopolize. The result was a consent agreement signed by American and Crandall that there would be no more such activities. Probably more costly than the litigation was the cost of the negative publicity earned by American.

Antitrust Litigation

As in other areas of business litigation, litigation involving antitrust issues has been rising steadily for several decades. Table 12–1 shows the number of public and private antitrust lawsuits filed rose steadily until 1980. After 1980, the number of public lawsuits increased while private lawsuits declined for the first time since 1941. Note, however, that while private lawsuits declined, the average number of suits filed in the 1986 to 1990 period was about ten times greater than in the 1946 to 1950 period.

Of the antitrust lawsuits that are filed, studies have shown that about seventy percent are withdrawn, dismissed by the court, or settled before reaching trial. Of the remaining thirty percent that do go to trial, plaintiffs win all or part of their claims in about twenty-five percent of the cases. Annual litigation costs incurred by private parties in antitrust disputes are estimated to be over $250 million annually.

The Courts and Antitrust Analysis

The Supreme Court has noted that antitrust law is dynamic—it changes as business and society change and as more is learned about the costs and benefits to society from different business agreements and activities. One question the courts must address is whether, as a matter of policy, a certain

Table 12–1   How Many Antitrust Suits Are There?

Time Period	Average Number of Suits Filed per Year	
	U.S. Government	Private Plaintiff
1941–45	36	60
1946–50	51	106
1951–55	40	209
1956–60	63	233
1961–65	69	400*
1966–70	55	708
1971–75	78	1300
1976–80	76	1448
1981–85	112	1155
1986–90	105*	1230*

*Estimated.

business practice will be held to be per se illegal or whether a rule of reason approach can be applied.

Per se Rule

A *per se rule* means that a certain business agreement, arrangement, or activity will automatically be held to be illegal by the courts. The classic example of per se violation is a group of competitors sitting in a hotel room to agree on the prices they will charge for their goods or the sales territories that each will have without competition. The agreement, arrangement, or activity is per se illegal because the courts believe that its use by a business will always result in a substantial restraint of trade. In discussing the notion of *per se illegality*, the Supreme Court in *Northern Pacific Railroad Co.* v. *United States* (1958) stated that there are certain activities which:

> ... because of their pernicious effect on competition and lack of any redeeming virtue are conclusively presumed to be unreasonable and therefore illegal without elaborate inquiry as to the precise harm they have caused or business excuse for their use.

Rule of Reason

A *rule of reason* approach means that the court will look at the facts surrounding an agreement, arrangement, or other restraint before deciding whether it helps or hurts competition. In reaching its decision, the court will consider such factors as the history of the restraint, the business reasons behind the restraint, the restraining business's position in its industry, and the structure of the industry. In *Chicago Board of Trade* v. *United States* (1918), Justice Brandeis provided the following classic statement on the rule of reason approach:

> [T]he legality of an agreement or regulation cannot be determined by so simple a test, as whether it restrains competition. Every agreement concerning trade, every regulation of trade, restrains. To bind, to restrain,

is of their very essence. The true test of legality is whether the restraint imposed is such as merely regulates and perhaps thereby promotes competition or whether it is such as may suppress or even destroy competition. To determine that question the court must ordinarily consider the facts peculiar to the business to which the restraint is applied; its condition before and after the restraint was imposed; the nature of the restraint and its effect, actual and probable. The history of the restraint, the evil believed to exist, the reason for adopting the particular remedy, the purpose or end sought to be attained, are all relevant facts. This is not because a good intention will save an otherwise objectionable regulation or the reverse; but because knowledge of intent may help the court to interpret facts and to predict consequences.

Business Integration and Antitrust Analysis

In providing a product or a service, managers must decide which of the tasks making up its production process are to be performed in-house, which tasks are to be performed by other businesses on a contractual basis, and which are to be performed through the purchase of a product or service on a day-to-day basis in the open market. Those tasks to be performed in-house or by contract are said to be *integrated* into the business. The decision to integrate is a critical decision and may have an impact on the long-run viability of a business. Given that there are many ways in which a business may integrate its production process, an important consideration is whether or not the approach selected will bring about an antitrust violation. As the cases will show, the antitrust laws limit certain forms of integration between firms and within firms, and at the same time encourage some in-house integration.

Illustrating the Concept of Integration

Consider General Motors (GM) as an example. GM is an integrated operation, because the production processes are linked within the firm to coordinate business activities. Automobiles could be produced in a nonintegrated manner. Every part of the automobile could be produced by independent firms. Those firms could sell their parts day-to-day to firms that assembled the parts. These assemblers could sell their products to firms that would take the unassembled product, finish it, and sell it to distributors to sell to the public. In other words, each firm would be independent and sell its output to other firms on a daily basis as needed.

Experience over the years in the auto and other industries has shown that such nonintegrated operations are more costly—that is, less economically efficient—than integrated operations. Costs of production are lowered by some integration. Whether accomplished through long-term contracts to produce products for each other or by merging, it was found that integrated operations would be more efficient for some producers.

Forms of Integration

Business integration can take many forms. Two producers might form a partnership, a producer might hire employees to form a team to perform work that was previously purchased, a manufacturer might buy a source of raw materials used in the firm's production process, or a business might set up a chain of retail stores to sell its products. In all cases, added tasks are integrated into the existing functions of the firm to improve productive efficiency. The integration can take the form of making a task a part of the business organization, or it can be handled by long-term contract.

Problem of Opportunistic Behavior

A particularly strong motivation for a firm to integrate its operations is a need to eliminate the possibility of *opportunistic behavior* by another firm. A firm is said to engage in opportunistic behavior when it takes economic advantage of another firm with which it has a unique relationship—generally some form of joint investment in plant and equipment with the relationship between the parties based on a contract.

To illustrate, consider the relationship between General Motors (GM) and the Fisher Body Company before the two companies merged. For years, the Fisher Body Company had provided GM with all the auto bodies it needed, and GM had purchased all the auto bodies Fisher had produced. The two companies relied entirely on each other—without Fisher's auto bodies, GM's production of automobiles would come to a halt; without GM's purchases of Fisher's auto bodies, Fisher would be forced to stop its operations. Within this unique relationship, Fisher could have easily behaved opportunistically by demanding a price increase under the threat of stopping production. Although such actions might have been an illegal breach of contract, GM very likely would have found paying the price increase to be less expensive than waiting for the legal resolution of the breach. The uniqueness of the relationship provided Fisher Body with the ability to force a price increase (and provided GM with the ability to force a price decrease). The integration of Fisher into GM by merging eliminated the possibility of one company exploiting the other.

The form that the integration takes is unimportant to the consumer. What is important is that productive efficiency has been improved so that consumer welfare might be enhanced. A problem for antitrust enforcers is to determine which forms of business integration help and which hurt consumers.

HORIZONTAL RESTRAINTS OF TRADE

When businesses at the same level of operation (such as retailers of a common product or producers of a raw material) come together (integrate) in some manner—through contract, merger, or conspiracy—they run the risk of being accused of creating a restraint of trade. A *horizontal restraint of trade* occurs when the businesses involved are on the same level of the market and generally in the same market. It is easy to visualize a horizontal arrangement among competitors by examining the diagram in Figure 12–1. For example,

Figure 12–1   Horizontal Business Relationships

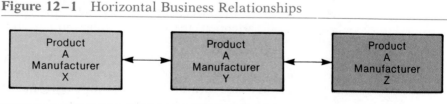

envision three manufacturers of light bulbs who agree to charge the same price for bulbs or to split the market on a geographical basis.

The diagram could also show an arrangement among wholesalers or among retailers of a certain product. When a collection of rival firms come together by contract or other form of agreement in an attempt to restrain trade by restricting output and raising prices, it is called a *cartel*. The most famous cartel of our day is the Organization of Petroleum Exporting Countries (OPEC) cartel, the group of oil-producing nations that have banded together for the express purpose of controlling the output and raising the price of crude oil. Since that cartel consists of sovereign nations, American antitrust laws do not affect it. When private firms in the United States attempt to cartelize an industry, however, they often will be subject to antitrust law.

INTERNATIONAL PERSPECTIVES: FOREIGN COMPETITORS FACE JAPANESE *DANGO* SYSTEM

INTERNATIONAL

PERSPECTIVES

The Japan Fair Trade Commission has only recently held that the traditional *dango* system, or prior consultation among bidders on public works jobs, violates that nation's antitrust law. Foreign firms attempting to obtain a share of the construction market in Japan have contended that bid-rigging of public works projects remains deeply rooted in Japanese construction. They claim that an alliance of politicians, bureaucrats, and competitors effectively keeps them out of the bidding for multibillion-dollar projects.

The *dango* system has rarely been challenged in Japan because Japanese antitrust enforcement officials have claimed that any damage it may create is small. In response to complaints, officials have said that there is little evidence of bribery and that the firms involved keep their profit margins small.

Recent evidence of huge payoffs by firms to politicians at the highest level have raised doubts about the claims that *dango* results only in an orderly rotation of contracts, rather than a reduction in competition. It has been suggested that foreign firms willing to cooperate with existing competitors could be allowed to enter the system. However, U.S. managers must remember that American firms playing such games could risk prosecution in the United States even if the Japanese accepted the practice.

MERGERS

A *merger* involves two or more firms coming together to form a new firm. The combination can be created by one firm's acquiring all or part of the stock or the assets of another firm. A merger is termed a *horizontal merger* when the two firms were competitors before they merged (e.g., Texaco and Getty Oil). Largely because they frequently involve well-known businesses and thus attract public attention, the general public most often associates the term antitrust with merger cases. Each year the Justice Department and the FTC challenge about twenty to thirty mergers. One of the most famous merger cases, *Standard Oil Company of New Jersey v. U.S.* (1911), established the rule of reason as the approach the courts use in judging merger activities.

Standard Oil Co. of New Jersey v. United States

United States Supreme Court
221 U.S. 1, 31 S.Ct. 502 (1911)

Case Background. *Claiming violations of Sections 1 and 2 of the Sherman Act, the Department of Justice sued seventy-one corporations and partnerships and seven individuals, including John D. Rockefeller and Henry M. Flagler, for conspiring "to restrain the trade and commerce in petroleum [in the United States] and to monopolize the said commerce." The conspiracy was traced back to 1870, when Rockefeller began to merge his company, Standard Oil of Ohio, with other oil companies and formed agreements with others to control all aspects of the petroleum business. Over the years, the companies were joined together in the Standard Oil Trust, which controlled as much as ninety percent of the production, shipping, refining, and selling of petroleum products. This allowed the trust to fix the price of oil and to monopolize interstate commerce in these products.*

The government requested that the trust be broken up so that companies would operate independently, not in concert. After reviewing the complex background of this case, the court explained the application of Sections 1 and 2 of the Sherman Act.

Case Decision. Chief Justice White delivered the opinion of the Court.

* * *

[H]aving by the 1st section forbidden all means of monopolizing trade, that is, unduly restraining it by means of every contract, combination, etc., the 2d section seeks, if possible, to make the prohibitions of the act all the more complete and perfect by embracing all attempts to reach the end prohibited by the 1st section, that is, restraints of trade, by any attempt to monopolize, or monopolization thereof, even although the acts by which such results are attempted to be brought about or are brought about be not embraced within the general enumeration of the 1st section. And, of course, when the 2d section is thus harmonized with and made, as it was intended to be, the complement of the 1st, it becomes obvious that the criteria to be resorted to in any given case for the purpose of ascertaining whether violations of the section have been committed is the rule of reason guided by the established law and by the plain duty to enforce the prohibitions of the act, and thus the public policy which its restrictions were obviously enacted to subserve.

* * *

Giving to the facts just stated the weight which it was deemed they were entitled to, in the light afforded by the proof of other cognate facts and circumstances, the court below held that the acts and dealings established by the proof operated to destroy the "potentiality of competition" which otherwise would have existed to such an extent as to cause the transfers of stock which were made to the New Jersey Corporation and the control which resulted over the many and various subsidiary corporations to be a combination or conspiracy in restraint of trade, in violation of the 1st section of the act, but also to be an attempt to monopolize and monopolization bringing about a perennial violation of the 2d section.

* * *

a. Because the unification of power and control over petroleum and its products which was the inevitable result of the combining in the New Jersey corporation by the increase of its stock and the transfer to it of the stocks of so many other corporations, aggregating so vast a capital, gives rise, in and of itself, in the absence of countervailing circumstances, to say the least, to the prima facie presumption of intent and purpose to maintain the dominancy over the oil industry, not as a result of normal methods of industrial development, but by new means of combination which were resorted to in order that greater power might be added than would otherwise have arisen had normal methods been followed, the whole with the purpose of excluding others from the trade, and thus centralizing in the combination a perpetual control of the movements of petroleum and its products in the channels of interstate commerce.

b. Because the prima facie presumption of intent to restrain trade, to monopolize and to bring about monopolization, resulting from the act of expanding the stock of the New Jersey corporation and vesting it with such vast control of the oil industry, is made conclusive by considering (1) the conduct of the persons or corporations who were mainly instrumental in bringing about the extension of power in the New Jersey corporation before the consummation of that result and prior to the formation of the trust agreements of 1879 and 1882; (2) by considering the proof as to what was done under those agreements and the acts which immediately preceded the vesting of power in the New Jersey corporation, as well as by weighing the modes in which the power vested in that corporation has been exerted and the results which have arisen from it.

* * *

The remedy to be administered. It may be conceded that ordinarily where it was found that acts had been done in violation of the statute, adequate measure of relief would result from restraining the doing of such acts in the future. But in a case like this, where the condition which has been brought about in violation of the statute, in and of itself is not only a continued attempt to monopolize, but also a monopolization, the duty to enforce the statute requires the application of broader and more controlling remedies. As penalties which are not authorized by law may not be inflicted by judicial authority, it follows that to meet the situation with which we are confronted the application of remedies two-fold in character becomes essential: 1st. To forbid the doing in the future of acts like those which we have found to have been done in the past which would be violative of the statute. 2d. The exertion of such measure of relief as will effectually dissolve the combination found to exist in violation of the statute, and thus neutralize the extension and continually operating force which the possession of the power unlawfully obtained has brought and will continue to bring about.

* * *

Case Holding. *The Supreme Court upheld the decision of the lower court in finding that the Standard Oil Trust was a violation of Sections 1 and 2 of the Sherman Act. The trust, which was a combination of many firms, was ordered dissolved so that the firms would compete as individual entities. Firms were allowed to contract with one another for legitimate reasons, such as common pipelines, but all such actions were to be subject to scrutiny.*

Case Questions

1. Justice Harlan, who dissented in part, said that the court should not use a rule of reason. All contracts in restraint of trade should be per se illegal. Is that practical?

2. Standard Oil controlled about ninety percent of the market, yet during the decades of the trust, the price of oil dropped consistently, thereby benefiting consumers. Should the court have taken this fact into account?

Supreme Court's Approach to Mergers

Congress did not provide guidance on what would constitute monopolistic behavior in the antitrust statutes. Thus, in using the Sherman and Clayton Acts to control monopolies, the courts must appraise market structures and monopolistic behavior. Measuring monopoly power, however, is not an easy task. An ideal measure would involve a comparison of prices, outputs, and profits of firms in an industry under competition with those under monopoly control. But such a comparison does not lend itself to measurement.

The Supreme Court's *Brown Shoe* decision in 1962 provides many of the points to be considered when reviewing mergers. Although this case might not produce the same result if it were raised today, the issues raised by the Court in its analysis have provided guidance for analyzing horizontal mergers.

Brown Shoe Company v. United States
United States Supreme Court
370 U.S. 294, 82 S.Ct. 1502 (1962)

Case Background. *The government moved to block the merger of Kinney Shoe Company and Brown Shoe Company. Suit was filed in 1955, claiming that the merger would violate Section 7 of the Clayton Act. The district court found that the merger would increase concentration in the shoe industry, both in retailing and manufacturing, by eliminating one of the companies as a substantial competitor. The court also held that the merger would reduce the opportunity for other retailers to obtain the products of Brown Shoe and for manufacturers to obtain sales to the retail outlets of Brown and Kinney. At the time of the merger, Brown was the third largest seller of shoes by dollar volume and Kinney was the eighth largest. Merged, the companies would have five percent of the total footwear market. Note the focus of the Court on defining and measuring the relevant market.*

Case Decision. Chief Justice Warren delivered the opinion of the Court.

* * *

The Government argued that the "line of commerce" affected by this merger is "footwear," or alternatively, that the "line[s]" are "men's," "women's," and "children's" shoes, separately considered, and that the "section of the country," within which the anticompetitive effect of the merger is to be judged, is the nation as a whole, or alternatively, each separate city or city and its immediate surrounding area in which the parties sell shoes at retail.

* * *

. . . [D]uring 1955 in 32 separate cities, ranging in size and location from Topeka, Kansas, to Batavia, New York, and Hobbs, New Mexico, the combined share of Brown and Kinney sales of women's shoes (by unit volume) exceeded 20%. In 31 cities—some the same as those used in measuring the effect of the merger in the women's line—the combined share of children's shoes sales exceeded 20%, in 6 cities their share exceeded 40%. In Dodge City, Kansas, their combined share of the market for women's shoes was over 57%; their share of the children's shoe market in that city was 49%. In the 7 cities in which Brown's and Kinney's combined shares of the market for women's shoes were greatest (ranging from 33% to 57%), each of the parties alone, prior to the merger, had captured substantial portions of those markets (ranging from 13% to 34%); the merger intensified this existing concentration. In 118 separate cities, the combined shares of the market of Brown and Kinney in the sale of one of the relevant lines of commerce exceeded 5%. In 47 cities, their share exceeded 5% in all three lines.

The market share which companies may control by merging is one of the most important factors to be considered when determining the probable effects of the combination on effective competition in the relevant market. In an industry as fragmented as shoe retailing, the control of substantial shares of the trade in a city may have important effects on competition. If a merger achieving 5% control were now approved, we might be required to approve future merger efforts by Brown's competitors seeking similar market shares. . . . Furthermore, in this fragmented industry, even if the combination controls by a small share of a particular market, the fact that this share is held by a large national chain can adversely affect competition. Testimony in the record from numerous independent retailers, based on their actual experience in the market, demonstrates that a strong national chain of stores can insulate selected outlets from the vagaries of competition in particular locations and that the large chains can set and alter styles in footwear to an extent that renders the independents unable to maintain competitive inventories. A third significant aspect of this merger is that it creates a large national chain which is integrated with a manufacturing operation. The retail outlets of integrated companies, by eliminating wholesalers and by increasing the volume of purchases from the manufacturing division of the enterprise, can market their own brands at prices below those of competing independent retailers. Of course, some of the results of large integrated or chain operations are beneficial to consumers. Their expansion is not rendered unlawful by the mere fact that small independent stores may be adversely affected. It is competition, not competitors, which the Act protects. But we cannot fail to recognize Congress' desire to promote competition through the protection of viable, small, locally owned businesses. Congress appreciated that occasional higher costs and prices might result from the maintenance of fragmented industries and markets. It resolved these competing considerations in favor of decentralization. We must give effect to that decision.

* * *

. . . We cannot avoid the mandate of Congress that tendencies toward concentration in industry are to be curbed in their incipiency, particularly when those tendencies are being accelerated through giant steps striding across a hundred cities at a time.

* * *

Case Holding. *The Supreme Court upheld the decision of the lower court to bar the merger of Kinney and Brown. The market share of the merged firm was held to reduce competition and to hurt small competitors.*

Case Questions
1. Since Brown primarily made children shoes, while Kinney made adult shoes, were they really in the same market?
2. Are retail shoe sales in Dodge City a relevant consideration for a national merger? How many shoe stores do you think there are in a small city like Dodge City?
3. Is five percent of the national market a threat to competition?

Merger Policy and the Concept of Market Power

To help businesses and regulators assess the antitrust implications of a merger, the Department of Justice issued *merger guidelines* in 1968. Revised by Justice and the FTC in 1982, and again in 1984, the guidelines set forth the factors that will be considered in determining whether a merger will likely be challenged. Many of the factors considered important by the Supreme Court in merger cases over the years have been incorporated into the guidelines. The guidelines place particular importance on the notion of *market power:*

> The unifying theme of the Guidelines is that mergers should not be permitted to create or enhance *market power* or to facilitate its exercise. . . . [T]he ability of one or more firms profitably to maintain prices above competitive levels for a significant period of time is termed *market power.* (DOJ, pp. 2–3)

Market Definitions

In assessing a firm's market power, a private party, government agency, or a court will begin by determining the market share held by each of the firms involved in the merger. As the Supreme Court in *Brown Shoe* stated, "the *market share* which companies may control by merging is one of the most important factors to be considered when determining the probable effects of the combination on effective competition in the relevant market." A firm's "market share" refers to the percentage of the relevant market controlled by the firm. Defining the relevant market in the soft-drink industry as the nation as a whole, for example, Coca Cola has enjoyed a 42 percent market share. That is, about four out of ten soft drink products sold in the United States are Coca Cola products.

According to the Supreme Court, the most important determination in establishing market share is to determine the *relevant market* for the products of the firms involved in the merger. Recall that the Clayton Act provides that the legality of a merger between two firms rests on whether "in any line of commerce in any section of the country, the effect of such acquisition may be substantially to lessen competition, or tend to create a monopoly." The phrase "in any line of commerce" refers to the particular *product market* in which the firms operate. In *Brown Shoe*, the product market was "footwear, or alternatively, that the lines are men's, women's, and children's shoes, separately considered." The phrase "in any section of the country" has reference to a *geographic market.* In *Brown Shoe*, the geographic market was the "nation as a whole, or alternatively, each separate city . . . in which the parties sell shoes at retail." Therefore, in determining the relevant market from which to calculate an individual firm's market share, the appropriate product and geographic markets must be taken into account.

After determining the relevant market, an individual firm's market share can be determined by dividing the firm's sales by total industry sales within that market. In a merger case, the court will often consider whether the combined market share of the two merging firms will exceed some maximum market share and will, therefore, "substantially . . . lessen competition" within the relevant market. The determination of the product and geographic markets, however, is rarely straightforward.

Product Market

In a competitive industry, there are enough producers so that an individual firm cannot affect the market for the products being produced by the industry. An individual firm will not have sufficient market power to raise the price of its product without having its customers purchase the lower-priced products of its competitors. That is, in a competitive industry, each firm effectively provides a substitute product for the other firms in the industry. A monopoly exists when there is only one firm producing a product for which there is no reasonable substitute. The monopolist will be able to raise prices because customers will not have lower-priced substitute products available.

Geographic Market

Depending upon the nature of the product, the geographic market could be local, regional, national, or international. It is influenced by several factors. For sellers of products, the geographic area is most significantly influenced by transportation costs. Heavy, bulky products such as cement tend to compete in local markets; lighter, high-value products such as tires can be shipped nationwide. In the case of computers, because shipping costs represent such a small percentage of total costs, the product can be shipped to a larger market. In its *Brown Shoe* decision, while it examined some local markets, the Supreme Court found that the geographic market was nationwide because of the low shipping costs involved in transporting shoes to the marketplace:

> The relationship of product value, bulk, weight, and consumer demand enables manufacturers to distribute their shoes on a nation-wide basis, as Brown and Kinney, in fact, do.

The buyers of a product can also influence the determination of the geographic market. As a rule, the geographic market is limited to the area where consumers can reasonably be expected to make purchases. Consumers are generally more willing to search a larger market if the product being purchased is expensive and purchased infrequently. Similarly, industrial machinery will likely be judged as having a nationwide geographic market, while day-to-day office supplies will have a local market.

Protecting Relevant Markets

The guidelines note that "Where the merging firms are in the same product and associated geographic market, the merger is horizontal" (DOJ, p. 16). This requires a study of market concentration and market share. "Other things being equal, concentration affects the likelihood that one firm, or a small group of firms, could successfully exercise market power" (DOJ, p. 16). A *concentration ratio* is the most widely used measure. There are several mathematical formulas used to look for evidence of the domination posed in a particular market by the leading firms.

Measuring Concentration

Economic theory suggests that the vigor of competition is related to the number of firms in an industry—the more firms buying or selling in a particular market, the more likely that market will be competitive. The size of firms can also influence competitiveness. Suppose 100 firms operate in a particular industry. A superficial examination based solely on the number of firms in the industry would lead to the conclusion that it is competitive. If, however, the four largest firms provided 80 percent of industry sales, a different conclusion may be reached. A measure that accounts for this uneven distribution of firm sizes within an industry is the *industry concentration ratio*, defined as the percentage of total industry sales held by the industry's largest firms. The ratio most commonly used is the *industry 4-firm concentration ratio*, defined as the percentage of industry sales by the four largest firms.

There were two mergers of multibillion dollar oil companies in 1984, Texaco-Getty and Gulf-Socal, that were not challenged by the FTC or DOJ because the concentration ratio calculations showed low concentration in that industry. Even though the dollar size of the firms was large, the firms were small given the size of the industry and the large number of competitors. However, in specific markets, such as gasoline stations in a few states, where the merging firms would have had a large share of the market, the companies had to agree to sell those parts of their operations.

Conversely, mergers that show high concentration levels are likely to be challenged even though the size of the firms or the market may be relatively small. The guidelines note that a leading firm in an industry—defined as a market share of over 35 percent—is unlikely to be allowed to merge with any firm in its industry that has over 1 percent of the market.

Protecting Small Businesses

The *Brown Shoe* decision establishes many of the key points the courts watch for in deciding whether a merger violates Section 7 of the Clayton Act. Note that the Court focused on different reasons for blocking the merger. It examined the market share of the two companies at the national, regional, and local levels. The Court stated that a small national market share will not automatically mean that a merger will be allowed. It held that the protection of small businesses is a goal of antitrust law, even if doing so may prohibit the emergence of less costly ways of doing business.

Potential Competition

Are two firms in competition with one another if they do not offer the same product to the same consumers? Ordinarily one thinks of competitors as offering similar products in the same market area. If the companies do not compete in this sense, should the courts be concerned about a merger? The Supreme Court has stated that the possibility that the two companies are *potential competitors* may be enough to stop a merger.

The rationale of potential competition was used in the Court's 1967 decision, *FTC* v. *Procter & Gamble Co.*, in which it would not allow the merger of Procter & Gamble, a large household products maker, with Clorox, the leading manufacturer of liquid bleach. After finding that bleach was the relevant product market, the Court held that even though Procter & Gamble did not make bleach or any close substitute, it could not merge with Clorox, because Procter & Gamble could make bleach at some time in the future. Since Clorox had 49 percent of the liquid bleach sales, the Court thought it important that Clorox not be given a further dominant position by merging with a large company like Procter & Gamble. The Court wanted Clorox to be faced with the *threat* of strong potential competition by a company like Procter & Gamble. The Supreme Court's *El Paso Natural Gas* decision provides a good discussion of potential competition considerations in a merger case.

United States v. El Paso Natural Gas Company
United States Supreme Court
376 U.S. 651, 84 S.Ct. 1044 (1964)

Case Background. *The El Paso Natural Gas Company, whose pipelines provided about fifty percent of the natural gas consumed in California, merged with Pacific Northwest Pipeline Company. Pacific Northwest sold natural gas in the Rocky Mountain and Northwest regions of the country. The district court refused the government's complaint that would require El Paso Natural Gas to divest itself of Pacific Northwest under Section 7 of the Clayton Act.*

Case Decision. Opinion of the Court by Justice Douglas was announced by Justice Clark.

* * *

This is not a field where merchants are in a continuous daily struggle to hold old customers and to win new ones over from their rivals. In this regulated industry a natural gas company (unless it has excess capacity) must compete for, enter into, and then obtain Commission approval of sale contracts in advance of constructing the pipeline facilities. In the natural gas industry pipelines are very expensive, and to be justified they need long-term contracts for sale of the gas that will travel them. Those transactions with distributors are few in number. For example, in California there are only two significant wholesale purchasers—Pacific Gas & Electric in the north and the Southern Companies in the south. Once the Commission grants authorization to construct facilities or to transport gas in interstate commerce, once the distributing contracts are made, a particular market is withdrawn from competition. *The competition then is for the new increments of demand that may emerge with an expanding population and with an expanding industrial or household use of gas.*

The effect on competition in a particular market through acquisition of another company is determined by the nature or extent of that market and by the nearness of the absorbed company to it, that company's eagerness to enter that market, its resourcefulness, and so on. Pacific Northwest's position as a competitive factor in California was not disapproved by the fact that it had never sold gas there.

* * *

Pacific Northwest had proximity to the California market— 550 miles distant in Wyoming, even nearer in Idaho—only 250 miles away in Oregon. Moreover, it had enormous reserves in the San Juan Basin, the Rocky Mountains and western Canada. Had Pacific Northwest remained independent, there can be no doubt it would have sought to exploit its formidable geographical position *vis-à-vis* California. No one knows what success it would have had. We do know, however, that two interstate pipelines in addition to El Paso now serve California—one of the newcomers being Pacific Gas Transmission Co., bringing down Canadian gas. So we know that opportunities would have existed for Pacific Northwest had it remained independent.

Unsuccessful bidders are no less competitors than the successful one. The presence of two or more suppliers gives buyers a choice. Pacific Northwest was no feeble, failing company; nor was it inexperienced and lacking in resourcefulness. It was one of two major interstate pipelines serving the trans-Rocky Mountain States; it had raised $250 million for its pipeline that extended 2,500 miles through rugged terrain. It had adequate reserves and managerial skill. It was so strong and militant that it was viewed with concern, and coveted, by El Paso. If El Paso can absorb Pacific Northwest without violating § 7 of the Clayton Act, that section has no meaning in the natural gas field.

* * *

Case Holding. *The Supreme Court reversed the lower court, requiring El Paso Natural Gas to divest itself of Pacific Northwest Pipeline. The potential competition that Pacific offered for the California natural gas market was deemed a significant economic force.*

Case Questions

1. Do you think the Court would have allowed this merger if Pacific Northwest had been a small firm or a weak, failing firm?

2. Since the Court says it is relevant to consider potential competitors and not just sellers currently in the same market, should this not be applied to other cases? How far do you stretch the idea, since there are always unknown potential entrants?

Considering Business Realities

Antitrust law is not constant. In the past two decades the Court has shown more willingness to weigh economic evidence and, as a result, has decided that some mergers are not harmful to consumers. In the *General Dynamics* decision, the Court allowed a merger of two coal-producing companies, one of which was a subsidiary of General Dynamics, a large diversified corporation. The fact that one of the merging companies was very large was not decisive, since it did not have monopoly power in the coal industry.

United States v. General Dynamics Corporation

United States Supreme Court 415 U.S. 486, 94 S.Ct. 1186 (1974)

Case Background. *The government challenged the acquisition of a strip-mining coal-producing company by General Dynamics, a large firm that owned, among other things, a company engaged in deep-mining coal production. The acquisition was claimed to be a violation of Section 7 of the Clayton Act because it lessened competition in the production and sale of coal in Illinois and another geographic region comprising several states. The government noted that in the previous decade the demand for coal had been falling and the number of producers had dropped from 114 to 39 in the geographic market area. The government noted that when the two firms combined, they would have twenty-two percent of the Illinois coal market and eleven percent of the regional market.*

The district court ruled against the government, allowing the acquisition. The lower court noted that because coal was consistently losing market share in energy production, it was a declining industry. It also noted that most coal was being sold on long-term contracts to utilities for electrical power production. The Department of Justice appealed to the Supreme Court.

Case Decision. Justice Stewart delivered the opinion of the Court.

* * *

Because of these fundamental changes in the structure of the market for coal, the District Court was justified in viewing the statistics relied on by the Government as insufficient to sustain its case. Evidence of past production does not, as a matter of logic, necessarily give a proper picture of a company's future ability to compete. In most situations, of course, the unstated assumption is that a company that has maintained a certain share of a market in the recent past will be in a position to do so in the immediate future. Thus, companies that have controlled sufficiently large shares of a concentrated market are barred from merger by § 7 not because of their past acts, but because their past performances imply an ability to continue to dominate with at least equal vigor. . . . Evidence of the amount of annual sales is relevant as a prediction of future competitive strength, since in most markets distribution systems and brand recognition are such significant factors that one may reasonably suppose that a company which has attracted a given number of sales will retain that competitive strength.

In the coal market, as analyzed by the District Court, however, statistical evidence of coal *production* was of considerably less significance. The bulk of the coal produced is delivered under long-term requirements contracts, and such sales thus do not represent the exercise of competitive power but rather the obligation to fulfill previously negotiated contracts at a previously fixed price. The focus of competition in a given time-frame is not on the disposition of coal already produced but on the procurement of new long-term supply contracts. In this situation, a company's past ability to produce is of limited significance, since it is in a position to offer for sale neither its past production nor the bulk of the coal it is presently capable of producing, which is typically already committed under a long-term supply contract. A more significant indicator of a company's power effectively to compete with other companies lies in the state of a company's uncommitted reserves of recoverable coal. A company with relatively large supplies of coal which are not already under contract to a consumer will have a more important influence upon competition in the contemporaneous negotiation of supply contracts than a firm with small reserves, even though the latter may presently produce a greater tonnage of coal. In a market where the availability and price for coal are set by long-term contracts rather than immediate or short-term purchases and sales, reserves rather than past production are the best measure of a company's ability to compete.

* * *

Case Holding. *The Supreme Court upheld the decision of the lower court by ruling in favor of defendant General Dynamics, allowing the merger to stand. This case appeared to mark a turning point in the standards the Supreme Court set for striking down mergers, requiring the government to demonstrate more economic damage to competition than it had been required to in the past.*

Case Questions

1. Why was the Court impressed with the fact that most of the customers of coal production were large utilities? Might things have been different had the customers been individuals?

2. The Court noted in its decision that the coal industry is relatively easy to get into compared with other industries. What difference should that make in determinations about competition?

Defenses

The Court in *Brown Shoe* noted that if one of the firms involved in the merger had been facing bankruptcy or other serious financial circumstances that threatened the firm, the Court might have allowed the merger. The Court was referring to the *failing firm defense*. According to the Court in *International Shoe* v. *Federal Trade Commission* (1930):

> [If] a corporation with resources so depleted and the prospect of rehabilitation so remote that it face[s] the grave probability of a business failure with resulting loss to its shareholders and injury to the communities where its plants were operated, ... the purchase of its stock by a competitor (there being no other prospective purchaser), not with a purpose to lessen competition, but to facilitate the accumulated business of the purchaser and with the effect of mitigating seriously injurious consequences otherwise probable, is not in contemplation of law prejudicial to the public and does not substantially lessen competition or restrain commerce within the intent of the Clayton Act.

The failing firm defense was created by the courts and not provided by statute. To use the defense to avoid violating Section 7 of the Clayton Act, the merging firms must establish that:

1. The firm being acquired is not likely to survive without the merger.
2. Either the firm has no other prospective buyers or, if there are other buyers, the acquiring firm will affect competition the least.
3. All other alternatives for saving the firm have been tried and have not succeeded.

The merger guidelines note that the major defense to a merger is the demonstration that it will enhance efficiency in the market, benefiting consumers by the more efficient allocation of resources. The FTC and the Justice Department also note that a failing-firm defense may be successful if the defendant shows that the company to be acquired would not survive on its own and that the acquiring firm is the only company interested in the acquisition or is the company that poses the least threat to competition by the acquisition.

HORIZONTAL RESTRAINTS OF TRADE

Since the antitrust statutes can be elastic in their application, there are no formal categories for all activities that will be attacked. From prior cases, however, some generalizations can be made about certain types of horizontal business activities likely to generate litigation. The results of these cases provide guidance as to the limits likely to be imposed on certain business relationships.

Horizontal Price Fixing

The Sherman Act prohibits "every contract, combination or conspiracy, in restraint of trade or commerce among the several states, or with foreign nations." Thus, when firms selling the same product agree to fix prices, the agreement will almost certainly violate the Sherman Act. One question the Supreme Court has had to decide, as a matter of policy, is whether price fixing is *per se illegal* or whether a *rule of reason* may be applied.

Early Decisions Applied Per Se Rule

The Supreme Court initially ruled that horizontal price fixing was per se illegal. One of the classic antitrust cases condemning direct price fixing as an unreasonable per se restraint of trade under the Sherman Act is *United States v. Trenton Potteries Company* (1927). As the *Trenton Potteries* decision illustrates, the court's early reasoning was that the ability of a firm or a group of firms to fix prices involved the power to control the market. Ultimately, firms with the power to fix even reasonable prices would be able to use that power to fix unreasonable prices.

United States v. Trenton Potteries Company
United States Supreme Court
273 U.S. 392, 47 S.Ct. 377 (1927)

Case Background. *The defendants, twenty-three corporations and twenty individuals, were convicted in federal district court of violating the Sherman Act. All were members of the Sanitary Potters' Association and were engaged in the production or distribution of eighty-two percent of the sanitary pottery in the United States. They were found guilty of combining to fix and maintain uniform prices for the sale of bathroom fixtures and to restrain sales at the wholesale level to a special group of "legitimate jobbers." The evidence of the combination to restrain trade and fix prices was clear. However, the defendants did not object to the allegation that they fixed prices, limited sales, and possessed both the power to fix prices and to control the market. Rather, they argued that the trial court should have submitted to the jury the question of whether the price-fixing agreements were unreasonable restraints of trade.*

Case Decision. Justice Stone delivered the opinion of the Court.

* * *

The aim and result of every price-fixing agreement, if effective, is the elimination of one form of competition. The power to fix prices, whether reasonably exercised or not, involves power to control the market and to fix arbitrary and unreasonable prices. The reasonable price fixed today may through economic and business changes become the unreasonable price of tomorrow. Once established, it may be maintained unchanged because of the absence of competition secured by the agreement for a price reasonable when fixed. Agreements which create such potential power may well be held to be in themselves unreasonable or unlawful restraints, without the necessity of minute inquiry whether a particular price is reasonable or unreasonable as fixed and without placing on the government in enforcing the Sherman Law the burden of ascertaining from day to day whether it has become unreasonable through the mere variation of economic conditions. Moreover, in the absence of express legislation requiring it, we should hesitate to adopt a construction making the difference between legal and illegal conduct in the field of business relations depend upon so uncertain a test as whether prices are reasonable—a determination which can be satisfactorily made only after a complete survey of our economic organization and a choice between rival philosophies.

* * *

Case Holding. *The Supreme Court upheld the conviction of the firms and individuals involved in the price-fixing scheme. This case is often cited for setting the rule that price fixing is per se illegal.*

Case Questions

1. What would be the practical problems with using a rule of reason approach to price-fixing cases?

2. Suppose the firms involved in this case could show that after they began fixing prices the prices of their products fell. Would (or should) that change the result?

Recent Application of Per Se Rule

The Supreme Court again had the opportunity to discuss price fixing in 1982, in the *Arizona* v. *Maricopa County Medical Society* case. Two medical societies formed two foundations for medical care for the purpose of promoting fee-for-service medicine and to provide the community with a competitive alternative to existing health insurance plans. Doctors joining the foundations had to agree to not charge more than the maximum fees for medical services set by the foundations. The state of Arizona sued, claiming that the arrangement was a violation of Section 1 of the Sherman Act. The Supreme Court held that the maximum-fee arrangements are price-fixing agreements and are per se illegal.

The Court reaffirmed the per se rule against price fixing in the 1990 case *FTC v. Superior Court Trial Lawyers Association*, which is discussed in detail in the next chapter. An element of the case was price fixing. The Court noted that "the per se rules reflect a longstanding judgment that every horizontal price-fixing arrangement among competitors poses some threat to the free-market even if the participants do not themselves have the power to control market prices."

The Rule of Reason in Price-Fixing Cases

It is undoubtedly true that when competitors collude to fix prices to gain a monopoly, the per se illegal rule will be applied. However, the Supreme Court has used a rule of reason approach in cases involving price arrangements that have some unique features. The application of the rule of reason began with the Supreme Court's decision in *Broadcast Music, Inc.* v. *CBS* (1981). CBS sued Broadcast Music, Inc. (BMI), the American Society of Composers, Authors and Publishers (ASCAP), and their members and affiliates claiming that the blanket license to copyrighted music at fees negotiated by them constitutes illegal price fixing under the antitrust laws.

Tens of thousands of corporations, authors, and composers own copyrights on millions of musical compositions. BMI and ASCAP serve as clearinghouses for the copyright owners. They operate primarily through blanket licenses that give licensees (radio stations, television broadcasters, etc.) the right to perform any and all of the compositions owned by the members of ASCAP or BMI as often as they desire for a stated sum. The fees for blanket usage are usually a percent of the licensees' total revenues or a flat dollar amount. This system emerged because it would be almost impossible for each music copyright owner to contract with each potential music user and monitor music use. CBS claimed that ASCAP and BMI are monopolies and that the blanket license is illegal price fixing.

The Supreme Court held that the blanket license issued by ASCAP and BMI does not constitute per se illegal price fixing. Justice White, speaking for an 8–1 majority, held that a rule of reason had to be applied. The Court noted the extensive industry experience in this method of organization and did not find evidence that it hindered trade. Rather, the Court found that this method of organization helped to integrate sales, monitoring, and enforcement of unauthorized copyright use, which would be very difficult for individual copyright owners to do. Over the years it had been demonstrated that other contractual arrangements could exist within the industry, so it did not appear that BMI and ASCAP were effectively excluding possible forms of competition for their services and method of pricing. The Court made it clear that some price-fixing activities would still be per se illegal. Others would be viewed under a rule of reason approach.

The Supreme Court made the sports pages in 1984 when it announced that, under a rule of reason analysis, the National Collegiate Athletic Association (NCAA) could not fix prices colleges receive for appearances their football teams make on television.

NCAA v. Board of Regents of University of Oklahoma
United States Supreme Court
468 U.S. 85, 104 S.Ct. 2948 (1984)

Case Background. *Since its creation in 1905 the NCAA has established standards and regulations for playing rules, amateurism, academic eligibility, recruitment of athletes, and the size of athletic squads and coaching staffs for college athletics. Since 1951, the Television Committee of the NCAA regulated the televising of football games, something the NCAA does not do for any other sport it otherwise governs. A plan was adopted in 1981 for the 1982–85 football seasons. The NCAA signed an agreement with ABC and CBS to telecast a certain number of games for a certain sum of money (TBS had a contract for cablecast of NCAA football games). Fees were paid to the participating universities according to the type of telecast (a Division I national game gets a higher fee than a Division II regional game). However, the amount paid to the universities did not vary with the size of the viewing audience or the number of markets in which the game was to be telecast or according to the popularity of a particular team. There was also a limit on the number of times any one team could be on television, and universities were prohibited from making other arrangements for telecasts. The universities with the most popular football teams realized that they were subsidizing the universities with less popular football teams.*

The district court agreed with the Universities of Oklahoma and Georgia that the NCAA was a cartel that fixed prices, limited output, and boycotted potential telecasters. The court of appeals agreed, holding that the NCAA television plan was per se illegal price fixing. The NCAA appealed to the Supreme Court.

Case Decision. Justice Stevens delivered the opinion of the Court.

* * *

There can be no doubt that the challenged practices of the NCAA constitute a "restraint of trade" in the sense that they limit members' freedom to negotiate and enter into their own television contracts. In that sense, however, every contract is a restraint of trade, and as we have repeatedly recognized, the Sherman Act was intended to prohibit only unreasonable restraints of trade.

* * *

Because it places a ceiling on the number of games member institutions may televise, the horizontal agreement places an artificial limit on the quantity of televised football that is available to broadcasters and consumers. By restraining the quantity of television rights available for sale, the challenged practices create a limitation on output; our cases have held that such limitations are unreasonable restraints of trade. Moreover, the District Court found that the minimum aggregate price in fact operates to preclude any price negotiation between broadcasters and institutions, thereby constituting horizontal price fixing, perhaps the paradigm of an unreasonable restraint of trade.

Horizontal price-fixing and output limitation are ordinarily condemned as a matter of law under an "illegal *per se*" approach because the probability that these practices are anticompetitive is so high; a *per se* rule is applied when "the practice facially appears to be one that would always or almost always tend to restrict competition and decrease output." *Broadcast Music, Inc.* v. *CBS.* In such circumstances a restraint is presumed unreasonable without inquiry into the particular market context in which it is found. Nevertheless, we have decided that it would be inappropriate to apply a *per se* rule to this case. This decision is not based on a lack of judicial experience with this type of arrangement, on the fact that the NCAA is organized as a nonprofit entity, or on our respect for the NCAA's historic role in the preservation and encouragement of intercollegiate amateur athletics. Rather, what is critical is that this case involves an industry in which horizontal restraints on competition are essential if the product is to be available at all.

As Judge Bork has noted: "[S]ome activities can only be carried out jointly. Perhaps the leading example is league sports. When a league of professional lacrosse teams is formed, it would be pointless to declare their cooperation illegal on the ground that there are no other professional lacrosse teams." R. Bork, The Antitrust Paradox 278 (1978). What the NCAA and its member institutions market in this case is competition itself—contests between competing institutions. Of course, this would be completely ineffective if there were no rules on which the competitors agreed to create and define the competition to be marketed. A myriad of rules affecting such matters as the size of the field, the number of players on a team, and the extent to which physical violence is to be encouraged or proscribed, all must be agreed upon, and all restrain the manner in which institutions compete.

* * *

Per se rules are invoked when surrounding circumstances make the likelihood of anticompetitive conduct so great as to render unjustified further examination of the challenged conduct. But whether the ultimate finding is the product of a presumption or actual market analysis, the essential inquiry remains the same— whether or not the challenged restraint enhances competition. Under the Sherman Act the criterion to be used in judging the validity of a restraint on trade is its impact on competition.

* * *

Because it restrains price and output, the NCAA's television plan has a significant potential for anticompetitive effects. The findings of the District Court indicate that this potential has been realized. The District Court found that if member institutions were free to sell television rights, many more games would be shown on television, and that the NCAA's output restriction has the effect of raising the price the networks pay for television rights. Moreover, the court found that by fixing a price for television rights to all games, the NCAA creates a price structure that is unresponsive to viewer demand and unrelated to the prices that would prevail in a competitive market. And, of course, since as a practical matter all member institutions need NCAA approval, members have no real choice but to adhere to the NCAA's television controls.

The anticompetitive consequences of this arrangement are apparent. Individual competitors lose their freedom to compete. Price is higher and output lower than they would otherwise be, and both are unresponsive to consumer preference. This latter point is perhaps the most significant, since "Congress designed the Sherman Act as a 'consumer welfare prescription.'"

* * *

Our decision not to apply a *per se* rule to this case rests in large part on our recognition that a certain degree of cooperation is necessary if the type of competition that petitioner and its member institutions seek to market is to be preserved. It is reasonable to assume that most of the regulatory controls of the NCAA are justifiable means of fostering competition among amateur athletic teams and therefore procompetitive because they enhance public interest in intercollegiate athletics.

*   *   *

Case Holding. *The Supreme Court affirmed the decision of the lower courts but declared that the price fixing was illegal under a rule of reason analysis, not under a per se rule. The result is that colleges are free to sign their own television contracts, which they do individually, through conferences and through the College Football Association.*

Case Questions
1. Is the Court saying in this decision that since a rule of reason is to be used, some forms of price fixing may be legal?
2. After this case, the number of football games televised increased substantially, but the total revenues paid for telecasts fell. What does that tell you?

The Supreme Court again used a rule of reason analysis in a 1986 decision in *Matsushita Elec. Indus. Co.* v. *Zenith Radio.* The case involved alleged price fixing by Japanese television manufacturers. The Japanese manufacturers were sued by a group of American television manufacturers for supposedly having conspired for twenty years to sell Japanese televisions in the United States at below-market prices with the intent to drive out the American producers. The Supreme Court agreed with the district court that the case should be dismissed on the basis of lack of economic evidence. Citing writings on the economics of antitrust by Robert Bork, the Court noted that it was not likely that a group of manufacturers would fix prices below market levels and lose money for twenty years. Since that economic assertion made little sense and there was no other acceptable evidence of a conspiracy presented, the Court dismissed the complaint under a rule of reason.

Exchanges of Information

One difficult problem in antitrust law is deciding whether the trading of information among businesses helps or restrains the competitive process. Some business information is collected and disseminated by the government, but many exchanges are performed by private organizations, such as trade associations composed of firms in the same line of business. If each business knows its competitors' sales, production, planned or actual capacities, cost accounting, quality standards, innovations, and research developments, is competition enhanced or is the information likely to be used to restrain trade? Does such information encourage better products and reduce waste and inefficiency?

Purpose of Information Exchange Considered

The *Goldfarb* case indicates that exchanges of information will be allowed to proceed unless it can be shown that there is injury to consumers. The simple exchange of information that is not used to fix prices or otherwise restrain trade may not be subject to as much criticism as it was in earlier years.

The *Goldfarb* case is also a landmark antitrust case because of its attack on price setting by such professional groups as lawyers, who for years cloaked price fixing under the mantle of professional ethics and consumer protection. The result of *Goldfarb* and other holdings has been to increase the amount of price and service competition by lawyers and other professionals.

Goldfarb v. Virginia State Bar
United States Supreme Court
421 U.S. 773, 95 S.Ct. 2004 (1975)

Case Background. *The Goldfarbs contracted to buy a home in Fairfax County, Virginia. The lender who financed the purchase required them to buy title insurance, which required a real estate title examination that could be performed legally only by a member of the Virginia State Bar. The Goldfarbs could not find a lawyer who would examine the title for less than the fee prescribed as the minimum fee in the fee schedule for lawyer services published by the Fairfax County Bar Association and enforced by the Virginia State Bar. The Goldfarbs brought a class action suit against the Bar Associations, claiming that the minimum-fee schedule and its enforcement by the bar was price fixing in violation of the Sherman Act.*

The district court held that the State Bar was exempt from the Sherman Act but that the County Bar Association was liable and enjoined the publication of the fee schedule. The court of appeals reversed, holding that the State Bar's actions were immune from liability as state action and that the County Bar was immune because the practice of law is a learned profession, not trade or commerce as covered by the Sherman Act. Goldfarb appealed to the Supreme Court.

Case Decision. Chief Justice Burger delivered the opinion of the Court.

* * *

The County Bar argues that because the fee schedule is merely advisory, the schedule and its enforcement mechanism do not constitute price fixing. Its purpose, the argument continues, is only to provide legitimate information to aid member lawyers in complying with Virginia professional regulations. Moreover, the County Bar contends that in practice the schedule has not had the effect of producing fixed fees. The facts found by the trier belie these contentions, and nothing in the record suggests these findings lack support.

A purely advisory fee schedule issued to provide guidelines, or an exchange of price information without a showing of an actual restraint on trade, would present us with a different question. The record here, however, reveals a situation quite different from what would occur under a purely advisory fee schedule. Here a fixed, rigid price floor arose from respondents' activities: every lawyer who responded to petitioners' inquiries adhered to the fee schedule, and no lawyer asked for additional information in order to set an individualized fee. The price information disseminated did not concern past standards, . . . but rather minimum fees to be charged in future transactions, and those minimum rates were increased over time. The fee schedule was enforced through the prospect of professional discipline from the State Bar, and the desire of attorneys to comply with announced professional norms, . . . the motivation to conform was reinforced by the assurance that other lawyers would not compete by underbidding. This is not merely a case of an agreement that may be inferred from an exchange of price information, for here a naked agreement was clearly shown, and the effect on prices is plain.

Moreover, in terms of restraining competition and harming consumers like petitioners the price-fixing activities found here are unusually damaging. A title examination is indispensable in the process of financing a real estate purchase, and since only an attorney licensed to practice in Virginia may legally examine a title, consumers could not turn to alternative sources for the necessary service. All attorneys, of course, were practicing under the constraint of the fee schedule. . . . The County Bar makes much of the fact that it is a voluntary organization; however, the ethical opinions issued by the State Bar provide that any lawyer, whether or not a member of his county bar association, may be disciplined for "habitually charg[ing] less than the suggested minimum fee schedule adopted by his local Bar Association. . . ." These factors coalesced to create a pricing system that consumers could not realistically escape. On this record respondents' activities constitute a classic illustration of price fixing.

* * *

Case Holding. *The Supreme Court reversed the court of appeals, holding that the price schedule published by the bar association was price fixing under a rule of reason analysis. This case opened the door to a greater degree of price competition in professional services.*

Case Questions

1. Suppose the bar association published results of a survey that showed standard fees lawyers charged for various services, such as a title search for a house closing. Would that be likely to violate the antitrust laws?

2. Should services such as medical treatment, legal assistance, and plumbing work be treated the same as the sale of goods under the antitrust laws?

Limitations on Exchange of Information

The Supreme Court again considered the issue of the sharing of information by competitors in a 1978 decision, *U.S.* v. *United States Gypsum Co.* Six major producers of gypsum were charged with conspiracy to fix prices. One alleged action that made the conspiracy effective was that competing manufacturers called each other to determine the price actually being offered on gypsum products to a certain customer. That is, a buyer would tell Company B that Company A had offered to sell a certain quantity of gypsum board at a certain price. Company B would have to beat that price to obtain the buyer's business. Company B would call Company A to confirm the offer, to make sure the buyer was telling the truth. The gypsum companies defended the practice as a good faith effort to meet competition.

On this aspect of the case, the Court said that a rule of reason may be applied. But, in general, the practice was probably not defensible. "As an abstract proposition, resort to interseller verification as a means of checking the buyer's reliability seems a possible solution to the seller's plight [of dealing with inaccurate information from buyers], but careful examination reveals serious problems with the practice." The Court said that in a concentrated industry an agreement, tacit or express, among competitors to exchange price information would most likely help to stabilize prices and so could not be justified. However, the Court did not apply a per se rule against such price information exchanges. Instead, it warned that they would be looked at very closely and would probably be allowed in only limited circumstances.

Limitations on Restraints of Information

Although the courts have indicated that it is legal to share price information in an open manner and it is illegal to share information secretly among competitors or for the purpose of constructing a common price list for competitors, it may also be illegal to band together to restrain certain information.

In the 1986 Supreme Court decision, *FTC* v. *Indiana Federation of Dentists,* the Court held that the FTC was justified in attacking the policy of an Indiana dentists' organization requiring members to withhold x-rays from dental insurance companies. Insurance companies sometimes required dentists to submit patient x-rays to help evaluate patients' claims for insurance benefits. The x-rays were intended to help eliminate insurance fraud and to make sure dentists do not prescribe dental work not required. The FTC attack on this policy was upheld under a rule of reason analysis that showed the dentists' policy to be a conspiracy in restraint of trade. The Court noted that no procompetitive reason for the anti-x-ray sharing rule was found. However, the Court noted that if the State of Indiana were to sanction the action of the dentists, the practice would be legal. State regulations can provide immunity from antitrust attack if the state actively regulates the service in question.

Horizontal Market Divisions and Territorial Restrictions

A horizontal market division occurs when firms competing at the same level of business reach an agreement—which may take the form of a joint venture agreement—to divide up the market on geographic or other terms. The effect of such an agreement is to eliminate competition among the firms to the agreement. Firms that compete on a national market, for example, may reach an agreement to divide the national market into regional markets, with each of the firms being exclusively assigned to one region. Each of the firms can then exercise monopoly power within their region.

Agreements intended to provide horizontal customer or territorial allocations are often held to violate antitrust law. When the agreement does not involve price fixing by the firms to the agreement, the case may be considered under a rule of reason; that is, the business agreement will be evaluated in light of its effect on consumer welfare. However, as its decision in *Sealy* reflects, the Supreme Court has tended to be more stringent in those cases involving common pricing by the firms to the agreement.

**United States
v. Sealy, Inc.**
**United States
Supreme Court**
388 U.S. 350, 87
S.Ct. 1847 (1967)

Case Background. *Sealy had been in the business of licensing manufacturers of mattresses and bedding products to make (according to specifications) and sell those products under the Sealy name and trademark. Sealy worked with independent manufacturer-licensees around the country to control the quality of Sealy-brand products and to fix minimum retail prices for Sealy products. There were also territorial* *restrictions imposed by Sealy—that is, each manufacturer had a separate territory. Sealy was controlled by manufacturer-licensees who owned most of the Sealy stock and controlled company operations. The government sued Sealy for conspiring with its licensees to fix prices and to allocate exclusive territories among the licensees. The district court held that the common pricing practices and territorial divisions were* per se *illegal. Sealy appealed to the Supreme Court.*

Case Decision. Justice Fortas delivered the opinion of the Court.

* * *

There is no dispute that exclusive territories were allotted to the manufacturer-licensees. Sealy agreed with each licensee not to license any other person to manufacture or sell in the designated area, and the licensee agreed not to manufacture or sell "Sealy products" outside the designated area. A manufacturer could make and sell his private label products anywhere he might choose.

* * *

If we look at substance rather than form, there is little room for debate. These must be classified as horizontal restraints. . . .

There are about 30 Sealy "licensees." They own substantially all of its stock. Sealy's bylaws provide that each director must be a stockholder or a stockholder-licensee's nominee. Sealy's business is managed and controlled by its board of directors. Between board meetings, the executive committee acts. It is composed of Sealy's president and five board members, all licensee-stockholders. Control does not reside in the licensees only as a matter of form. It is exercised by them in the day-to-day business of the company, including the grant, assignment, reassignment, and termination of exclusive territorial licenses. Action of this sort is taken either by the board of directors or the executive committee of Sealy, both of which, as we have said, are manned, wholly or almost entirely, by licensee-stockholders.
. . .

Since the early days of the company in 1925 and continuously thereafter, the prices to be charged by retailers to whom the licensee-stockholders of Sealy sold their products have been fixed and policed by the licensee-stockholders directly, by Sealy itself, and by collaboration between them. . . . These activities, as the District Court held, constitute a violation of the Sherman Act. Their anticompetitive nature and effect are so apparent and so serious that the courts will not pause to assess them in the light of the rule of reason. . . .

Appellee has not appealed the order of the District Court enjoining continuation of this price-fixing, but the existence and impact of the practice cannot be ignored in our appraisal of the territorial limitations. In the first place, this flagrant and pervasive price-fixing, in obvious violation of the law, was, as the trial court found, the activity of the "stockholder representatives" acting through and in collaboration with Sealy mechanisms. This underlines the horizontal nature of the enterprise, and the use of Sealy, not as a separate entity, but as an instrumentality of the individual manufacturers. In the second place, this unlawful resale price-fixing activity refutes appellee's claim that the territorial restraints were mere incidents of a lawful program of trademark licensing. . . . The territorial restraints were a part of the unlawful price-fixing and policing. As specific findings of the District Court show, they gave to each licensee an enclave in which it could and did zealously and effectively maintain resale prices, free from the danger of outside incursions. . . .

It is urged upon us that we should condone this territorial limitation among manufacturers of Sealy products because of the absence of any showing that it is unreasonable. . . . [But] here, the arrangements for territorial limitations are part of "an aggregation of trade restraints" including unlawful price-fixing and policing. . . . Within settled doctrine, they are unlawful under § 1 of the Sherman Act without the necessity for an inquiry in each particular case as to their business or economic justification, their impact in the marketplace, or their reasonableness.

* * *

Case Holding. *The Supreme Court upheld the decision of the lower court, holding that the price-fixing agreements and territorial divisions, practiced together, were per se illegal.*

Case Questions

1. Do you think the Court's decision might have been different if there had been no pricing agreement? That is, what if Sealy only existed to cooperate on joint advertising and territorial restrictions?

2. Could it be argued that this was really a vertical business arrangement, not a horizontal one?

3. Should the Court have considered the effect of Sealy on competition between brands rather than focus on competition among the producers of Sealy products (intrabrand competition)?

Sealy has been criticized by some observers. In *Sealy,* one observes a form of business integration—numerous smaller firms banding together to produce a similar product with national recognition. The price fixing condemned by the Court as detrimental to consumers would not have been illegal had Sealy simply built its own factories around the country or, over time, merged with many smaller mattress makers. That would have resulted in one very large corporation, making mattresses nationwide—and selling them at prices fixed by the executives of Sealy.

In *U.S.* v. *Topco Associates* (1972), the Supreme Court decided another case similar to *Sealy.* Topco was an association of twenty-five small, independent regional supermarket chains with stores in thirty-three states. These small chains formed Topco to serve as their buying agent, allowing the small chains to buy products in bulk and receive larger discounts. The purpose of Topco was to enhance the ability of its members to compete with major chains such as Safeway, Kroger, and Winn Dixie.

Topco was to buy and distribute grocery items to its members under brand names owned exclusively by Topco. Markets were divided so that only one retailer of Topco brand products resided in an area, with the understanding that each member of Topco would sell Topco brands only in their designated market area. Like the major chains, Topco retailers were also required to make contributions for advertising expenses. In contrast to other products sold by the smaller chains over which they had no exclusivity, however, the advertisements benefited only the Topco outlet. Like the private labeled products sold by the major chains, customers wishing to buy the advertised Topco products could do so only at a Topco outlet, and not at a competitive outlet. In the grocery markets in which Topco operated, they averaged about a six percent market share.

The government brought suit against Topco Associates arguing that it was a violation of the antitrust laws for the firms involved to divide the market among themselves along territorial lines. The Supreme Court agreed. The decision reduced the value of the arrangement, and significantly affected the ability of the small chains involved to compete with the major chains. Several Justices noted that the result was unfortunate, but they believed it was the required result under existing antitrust law. They suggested that Congress might want to review this anticompetitive aspect of antitrust law and consider amending the statutes.

As a result of holdings like *Sealy* and *Topco*, firms have an incentive to fully integrate business operations into one company. If all Sealy factories had been owned by a parent company, there would have been no basis for an antitrust action. Similarly, as the Court noted in *Topco*, a big chain is not prevented from doing what Topco Associates was prohibited from doing because one firm—as opposed to a group of firms—is running the operation.

As the Court stated in its 1984 *Cooperweld Corp. v. Independence Tube Corp.* decision, a company and its subsidiaries—because they are a single legal entity—are incapable of conspiring in such a way to violate the antitrust laws. Since there must be a contract, conspiracy, or other such agreement by two or more parties before a particular activity will become a violation of the antitrust laws, an activity that is perfectly legal if undertaken by a single firm may be illegal if undertaken by a group of firms. Despite the seemingly procompetitive effects of allowing small firms to interact as they did in *Sealy* and *Topco*, Congress has not chosen to address this unfortunate side effect of antitrust law.

SUMMARY

The three most important antitrust statutes—the Sherman Act of 1890, the Clayton Act of 1914, and the FTC Act of 1914—were enacted in response to the real or imagined economic power of the large industrial corporations and trusts that emerged during the late nineteenth century. Before the enactment of the statutes, there was only some common law precedent to rely upon to combat certain restraints of trade, and the government had little authority to intervene.

Since all business contracts serve to restrain trade to some extent, the courts have applied the laws to only certain business practices. The rulings of the Supreme Court, which are the most important to study in determining practical antitrust law, change over time depending on the principle guiding the Court. At times the Court seems to have been mostly concerned with protecting small competitors; at other times, it seems to have been more concerned with consumer welfare. Congress has, over the years, restricted the application of the antitrust laws by providing exceptions for much union activity, agricultural cooperatives, nonprofit corporations, and much of the activities of otherwise regulated industries.

For a manager to avoid the possibility of civil or criminal charges under the antitrust statutes or to avoid a successful suit by a private party that could result in treble damages, it is useful to know the scope of antitrust law as interpreted by the courts. However, when moving into gray areas, one would be well advised to seek experienced antitrust counsel.

Horizontal business arrangements concern agreements between competitors in the same industry to merge or to act in concert in certain respects. Merger of competitors automatically attracts study by the antitrust authorities. In challenging a merger, the courts will consider the degree of concentration in the relevant markets. Those markets include the markets for the products in question and the geographic market in which the merging firms operate. An estimate will be made of the share of these markets that the merging firms would enjoy. Another factor the courts will consider is whether the firms in question are potential competitors even if they are not currently operating in the same markets. Added leeway is given to a merger involving a failing firm. If a firm is about to go under, a merger will not likely lessen competition in the relevant market.

Other horizontal arrangements include classic price fixing agreements—whereby competitors get together to agree on common prices. These are usually condemned by the courts as per se illegal. Some price-fixing arrangements that are part of a more complex institution will be considered under a rule of reason analysis the Court has utilized in the last decade. Similarly, the Supreme Court is generally harsh on the sharing of price or other information not generally available to customers. An agreement by competing firms to share territories usually come under attack if they are considered horizontal arrangements that reduce competition among those firms.

ISSUE

Is the Japanese Economy Cartelized?

It is commonly asserted that Japanese firms have unfair advantages in world markets because their government allows business practices that would run afoul of antitrust law in the United States. Japanese firms are allowed to cooperate to a much greater extent than is true of firms in the United States and in much of Europe. Here, a leading American "corporate raider," who made his mark forcing some large American companies to become more efficient by restructuring their operations in the face of a takeover threat, tells of what he has faced in Japan.

Secrets Koito Hoped to Hide by Keeping Me Off Its Board
T. Boone Pickens*

As the largest shareholder of one of the major suppliers of Toyota, I have been learning first hand just how Japan's *keiretsu* (kay-ret—su) system operates, and the threat these interlocking relationships among corporations and their suppliers, distributors, bankers and insurers poses to America's free market.

A year ago, my investment company, Boone Co., bought a 20% interest in Koito Manufacturing Co., which makes auto light-

Reprinted with permission of *The Wall Street Journal.* © 1990 Dow Jones & Company, Inc. All rights reserved. Mr. Pickens is president of Boone Co., a merchant banking company in Dallas.

–continued

—continuing

ing systems primarily for Toyota. We have since increased our stake to 26%.

We purchased the Koito stock to share in the long-term growth and management of a Japanese company. We had no intention of taking over Koito, which is virtually impossible anyway, because between 60% and 65% of Koito's stock is locked up by Toyota's keiretsu. (Toyota itself owns 19% of Koito; Nissan Motor, 5.9%; Matsushita Electric, 5.3%; Nippon Mutual Life, 4.1%; Dai-Ichi Mutual Life, 3.3%; Matsushita Real Estate, 2.5%; Japan Securities Finance, 2.3%; and Mitsubishi Bank, Sumitomo Bank and Dai-Ichi Kangyo Bank each own 1.5%.)

All we asked for as Koito's major shareholder was four seats on the 20-member Koito board of directors. We also asked for detailed financial records of the company, a right afforded by Japanese law to any shareholders who own 10%. Both requests have been repeatedly refused. Boone Co. has now filed suit in Tokyo District Court for the financial information.

Koito's management could always outvote us on the board. So, why don't they want me? The only answer I can figure is that they have something to hide. They don't want me or any outsider to see the inner workings of their cartel.

For example, we have reason to believe that Toyota forces Koito to restrict its profit margin when Toyota wants to increase its profits. (This may reveal a great deal about how Toyota has built up its incredible cash position: Toyota reportedly has reserves of $25 billion in liquid assets, which puts the company at a decided advantage in worldwide auto manufacturing competition.) We also believe that some of Koito's top managers, most of whom are former Toyota employees, enjoy certain benefits that they would find quite embarrassing if revealed to their workers. For example, Koito's president—a 31-year Toyota veteran—enjoys a $1 million country club membership purchased by the company and lives in a beautiful house on the club grounds.

In the Japanese press, there have been reports that if we do succeed in getting on Koito's board, Toyota will cut off purchases from the company. Managers of other auto parts suppliers have complained anonymously in the Japanese press about their keiretsu's dictatorial ways.

The Japanese claim their keiretsu system is deeply embedded in their culture and history. To me and a lot of other businessmen around the world who have come up against the keiretsu system, they look and act just like old-fashioned cartels. These cartels permit Japanese corporate managers to develop their famous "long-term" growth and market domination strategies. With approximately 65% to 75% of a company's stock secured by fellow members of a keiretsu, corporate managers don't have to worry about responding to the wishes of shareholders.

When I criticized the keiretsu system in a recent speech to the Japan Society in New York, someone asked how I could disagree with an economic system that has been so efficient and successful. My response was that as an economic system, indentured servitude also was very efficient and successful. It was also wrong.

Their cartels force Japanese consumers to pay more for the goods they produce than foreigners do. A Toyota car costs $15,000 more in Japan than it does in the U.S. A Sony television costs two and one-half times as much in Japan as in the U.S.

Criticism of the keiretsu system cannot be dismissed as "Japan bashing." Several recent economic studies, by what cannot be considered anti-Japanese groups, have focused on these cartels as the root of the world's trade problems with Japan. Even the Japanese press and some government officials have started to criticize the cartels' domination of the Japanese economy.

An October 1989 study by the Organization for Economic Cooperation and Develop-

—continued

—continuing

ment called the keiretsu system a major impediment to world trade and economic competition. A similar study released at the same time by the Institute for International Economics in Washington points out that Japanese manufacturers in the U.S. tend to buy more from their traditional Japanese suppliers, while European manufacturers have an open competitive situation with their suppliers in the U.S.

But the keiretsu system's final victim may be Japan itself. The Japanese stock market is highly inflated. Since most of the corporate stock is locked up by the keiretsu, Japanese shares trade at price-to-earnings ratios 10 times higher than American corporate shares. The Dow Jones industrial average would be 25,000 if American companies traded at the same multiples.

Meanwhile, the average dividend yield on Japanese stocks is less than one-half of 1%. To get to a 3% yield, the American average, Japanese stock prices would have to fall 84%. The spreading realization among international investors that the Japanese stock market is overvalued has a lot to do with its recent volatility.

I am not opposed to Japanese investment in the U.S. I am opposed to Japanese cartels in our markets. If the Japanese are to continue to invest in the U.S., the keiretsu system must be dismantled, just as American monopolies were. Until the Japanese lift their foreign investment restrictions, we should consider the reciprocity legislation now pending in Congress. The U.S. would then have the power to adopt restrictions similar to those Americans are facing in Japan.

Questions

1. If it is true that Japanese firms engage in practices that would violate American antitrust laws, should they be restricted from selling in the United States unless they basically conform to American standards?

2. If cooperation among firms of the kind described by Boone Pickens has been successful in Japan, might that be a sign that the problem is with American antitrust laws, not with Japanese practices, since Japanese companies have been so successful?

REVIEW AND DISCUSSION QUESTIONS

1. Define the following terms:
   horizontal business arrangements
   cartel
   per se rule
   rule of reason
   merger
   concentration
   potential competition
   failing firm defense
   territorial allocation

2. Why do you think the Sherman Act was written in such broad language? Is it possible that Congress wrote the legislation in an unclear manner to give the courts broad leeway in attacking monopolistic business practices? Would it have been better for Congress to have specified more of the terms of antitrust violations?

3. What are some factors that would seem to make a particular market or industry more likely to be monopolized?

4. Should economic efficiency be the primary goal of antitrust law? What are the alternatives?

5. Can you think of any cartels that are not created by governments? Is there any way that state-sponsored cartels, such as OPEC, could be attacked by antitrust laws?

6. Two views exist about allowing firms to trade price and other trade information. One view is that it is anticompetitive because it enhances the ability of competitors to fix prices. The other view is that it helps competition because, so long as the price information is public, it will make both buyers and sellers more knowledgeable. What evidence supports each side?

Case Questions

7. ADM Company owns, among other things, flour mills (flour sold to commercial bakeries) around the country that make ADM the second largest flour miller in the U.S. It wants to merge with Dixie, a relatively small company that specializes in flour milling operations in the southeast. Together the merged company would become the largest flour miller in the southeast. Will the FTC allow the merger?

8. Many professional engineers belong to a trade association called the National Society of Professional Engineers that governs the nontechnical aspects of the practice of engineering. The canon of ethics adopted by the society held that engineers could not bid against one another for a particular job. The society claimed that this rule was to prevent engineers from engaging in price cutting to get engineering jobs, which could then give them incentives to cut corners on the quality of work to save time and resources. Such a practice could lead to inferior work that could endanger the public. The Justice Department sued, claiming that this was a violation of Section 1 of the Sherman Act. The government claimed that the ethical rule reduced price competition and gave an unfair advantage to engineers with well-established reputations. Who wins? [*National Society of Professional Engineers* v. *United States*, 435 U.S. 679, 98 S.Ct. 1355 (1978)]

9. Does a conspiracy to fix prices exist in the following situation? Jones Company and Smith Company both manufacture and sell sausage. To make sausage, both companies buy pigs. For the past ten years, Jones Company and Smith Company have purchased equal numbers of pigs each year and each month. Sometimes when the pigs come in, the two companies divide the number of pigs in each of the shipments equally between themselves and pay identical prices for the pigs in the shipments so divided. There is a long history of price fixing in the sausage industry. Indeed, both Smith and Jones have been sued before for price fixing, although there were no convictions.

10. Company A, a manufacturer of steel pipe, wishes to acquire a competitor, Company B, who also manufactures steel pipe. Should it be allowed to do so? Assume Company A has 25 percent of the declining market for its steel pipe, and Company B has less than 3 percent. The companies sell nationwide. Company B has been losing market shares but is not on the brink of bankruptcy. A memo exists at Company A wherein the chief executive officer makes explicit his desire to dominate the steel pipe market.

11. Several companies operated downhill ski facilities in Aspen, Colorado. They all sold a joint ticket that allowed skiers to ski at all facilities; the receipts were later divided according to various use rates. Eventually, one firm owned all the

ski areas but one. This firm stopped issuing the joint ticket and instead issued a ticket good for all of its ski areas. The firm that owned only one ski facility saw its market share fall from 20 percent to 11 percent over a four-year period. It sued, claiming that the larger firm violated Section 2 of the Sherman Act by attempting to monopolize skiing by ending the joint ticket arrangement. Does the smaller firm lose the case, or is the sale of the joint ticket a violation of the antitrust law? [*Aspen Skiing Company* v. *Aspen Highlands Skiing Corporation,* 472 U.S. 585, 105 S.Ct. 2847 (1985)]

12. In the *NCAA* case the Court recognized the importance of a central governing body to make the college football market work. An antitrust issue has been raised with respect to the National Football League (NFL) and the power it has over its member teams. Can the NFL legitimately require teams to stay in the cities to which they were initially assigned, or should the teams be free to move to any city? The Oakland Raiders were allowed by the courts to move to Los Angeles. When one buys a franchise for a professional sports team, the franchise is sold under a contract that agrees to keep the team in a certain city unless allowed by the league to move. Can you think of a competitive rationale for not allowing teams to move anywhere they want?

Policy Questions

13. Should some practices be per se illegal, or should all actions be judged by a rule of reason? Why might it be efficient to have some per se rules?

14. What should be the logical standard for antitrust enforcers? Since the statutes are vague, should they adopt a general rule that they will attack any business practice that hurts competition? Should they use a strategy of picking only the largest (in dollar terms) problems? Should consumer protection or should the protection of competitors be the primary goal of antitrust enforcers? What is the difference?

15. Should the antitrust laws be concerned about a merger that would give the merging firms a large share of a market in a small geographical area? Are nearby competitors enough competition to prevent consumers from being hurt?

Ethics Questions

16. You are the head of a company that has only one major competitor in several cities. As in the airline example in the chapter, the president of your competitor calls you to recommend that you both raise prices 5 percent and promise not to cheat on each other on this agreement. You know that the president is sincere and will stick to the bargain. You know that you will increase your profits by 50 percent if the deal holds. You know that no one is likely to know of the arrangement. What should you do?

17. At a convention you learn of a plan by executives of several corporations that compete with one another to engage in a market sharing scheme. You are sure of the accuracy of the information and that the scheme is going into effect. The companies in question do not affect you in any manner. Should you go to the government with your information? Should you go to the competitors of the companies that are conspiring with the information? Should you act in a "parallel" manner to those firms?

13 Antitrust Laws and Vertical Arrangements

C HAPTER 12 considered antitrust law as it applies to business *horizontal restraints of trade.* This chapter considers vertical restraints of trade, exclusionary practices, and price discrimination. *Vertical restraints of trade* concern relations between buyers and sellers, such as between the manufacturer and its wholesalers or the wholesalers and retailers. *Exclusionary practices* concern certain restraints of trade or contractual forms that are held to illegally exclude competitors or customers. A seller is said to engage in *price discrimination* when he or she sells the same product at different prices to different buyers. Finally, the chapter closes with the Issue Article which considers resale price maintenance arrangements in Japan.

THE NATURE OF VERTICAL RELATIONSHIPS

Vertical business arrangements concern relationships in the different stages of the production, distribution, and sale of the same product. It is easy to visualize a vertical restraint of trade by examining the diagram in Figure 13–1. For example, envision a manufacturer who imposes resale restrictions on the wholesalers, thereby controlling the wholesaler's resale price, the area of resale, or the wholesaler's customers. Since these arrangements may restrict competition, they may be challenged as being contrary to the goals of antitrust law.

A company that does more than one function internally, such as manufacturing and distribution, is not constrained by the antitrust laws. However, a group of firms doing business at different levels in a given product are prohibited from engaging in certain practices. Vertical restraints of trade often pose very subtle questions concerning their effects on consumer welfare and are currently the subject of vigorous debate.

Figure 13–1   Vertical Business Relationships

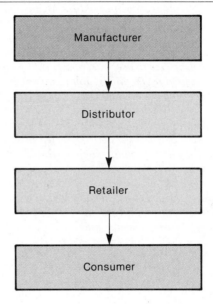

VERTICAL PRICE FIXING

Vertical price fixing arrangements generally involve an agreement between a manufacturer, its wholesalers, distributors, or other suppliers, and the retailers who sell the product to consumers. As a rule, these arrangements are intended to control the price at which the product is sold to consumers. In many instances, it is the retailers who approach the manufacturers and request the imposition of such a resale price maintenance agreement. In other instances, the manufacturer requires the wholesaler (supplier) to control the price being charged by the retailer. Agreements can call for the retailer to fix minimum prices or maximum prices.

Resale Price Maintenance Arrangements

Resale price maintenance (RPM) involves a contractual arrangement between a manufacturer, supplier, and retailers of a product whereby the retailers agree to sell the product at not less than a minimum price or at a specific price. The purpose of these arrangements is to prevent retailers from cutting the price of a brandname product. Although manufacturers contend such arrangements make product distributions more efficient, antitrust authorities have argued that in most instances they are an illegal restraint of trade. *Dr. Miles Medical Company* (1911) is a leading Supreme Court decision in this area. In *Dr. Miles*, the Court ruled that once a manufacturer or supplier has sold a product to the retailer, it cannot fix or otherwise dictate the price the retailer will charge consumers.

**Dr. Miles
Medical
Company v.
John D. Park
& Sons
Company**

**United States
Supreme Court**
220 U.S. 373,
31 S.Ct. 376
(1911)

Case Background. *Dr. Miles Medical Company produced medicines prepared with secret formulas. The company had an extensive domestic market for its products, which were sold via wholesalers to druggists. Dr. Miles fixed not only its price for sale to wholesalers but also the prices the wholesalers would use and the retail prices the druggists were to use. Purchasers of the products signed contracts agreeing to abide by prices fixed by Dr. Miles. John D. Park & Sons wished to cut the wholesale (and thus the retail) prices of Dr. Miles's products.*

Dr. Miles first argued that it had the right to fix its prices because its medicine was protected by patents, trademarks, and trade secrets. The Supreme Court, affirming the decision of the lower court, rejected this argument, holding that the patent process did not intend to produce such restraints of trade with respect to wholesale and retail pricing.

The second, and more important, argument was that a manufacturer is entitled to control the prices on all sales of its products. Dr. Miles claimed its business was being hurt by cut-rate stores that undersold drugstores. That reduced the ability of the druggists to compete, making them unwilling to carry inventories of Dr. Miles's products. Dr. Miles claimed that the bargain prices resulted in the public's believing that the products were inferior, thus reducing demand.

Case Decision. Justice Hughes delivered the opinion of the Court.

* * *

We come, then, to the second question—whether Dr. Miles Medical Company, irrespective of the secrecy of its process, is entitled to maintain the restrictions by virtue of the fact that they relate to products of its own manufacture.

The basis of the argument appears to be that, as the manufacturer may make and sell, or not, as he chooses, he may affix conditions as to the use of the article or as to the prices at which purchasers may dispose of it. The propriety of the restraint is sought to be derived from the liberty of the producer.

But because a manufacturer is not bound to make or sell, it does not follow in case of sales actually made he may impose upon purchasers every sort of restriction.

* * *

Nor can the manufacturer by rule and notice, in the absence of contract or statutory right, even though the restriction be known to purchasers, fix prices for future sales.

* * *

The bill asserts the importance of a standard retail price, and alleges generally that confusion and damage have resulted from sales at less than the prices fixed. But the advantage of established retail prices primarily concerns the dealers. The enlarged profits which would result from adherence to the established rates would go to them, and not to the complainant. It is through the inability of the favored dealers to realize these profits, on account of the described competition, that the complainant works out its alleged injury. If there be an advantage to the manufacturer in the maintenance of fixed retail prices, the question remains whether it is one which he is entitled to secure by agreements restricting the freedom of trade on the part of dealers who own what they sell. As to this, Dr. Miles can fare no better with its plan of identical contracts than could the dealers themselves if they formed a combination and endeavored to establish the same restrictions, and thus to achieve the same result, by agreement with each other. If the immediate advantage they would thus obtain would not be sufficient to sustain such a direct agreement, the asserted ulterior benefit to Dr. Miles cannot be regarded as sufficient to support its system.

But agreements or combinations between dealers, having for their sole purpose the destruction of competition and the fixing of prices, are injurious to the public interest and void. They are not saved by the advantages which the participants expect to derive from the enhanced price to the consumer.

* * *

Case Holding. *The Supreme Court held that resale price maintenance is* per se *illegal. Despite the clarity of the decision, it was not until the late 1920s that all courts adopted this rule. Some confusion seems to have been created by the Clayton Act of 1914.*

Case Questions

1. Does this decision restrict freedom of contract by saying that a manufacturer cannot include in a contract for sale restrictions on the price at which the product sold will be resold?
2. Should it make a difference whether or not the product in question was protected by a patent, which is designed to provide monopoly power for the seller of the patent holder?

Pros and Cons of Resale Price Maintenance

A superficial examination of a resale price maintenance agreement leads to the conclusion that they are not in the manufacturer's economic interest. By setting a minimum price at which retailers can sell the product, the manufacturer prohibits retailers from increasing sales by lowering the price. Although these agreements appear to be contra to the manufacturer's interest, manufacturers have continued to use them. Thus, several explanations for their use have been offered by antitrust scholars. Those explanations can be generally grouped according to whether they assert that RPM agreements are either a restraint of trade or a device that enhances competition.

Explanations asserting that resale price maintenance agreements restrain trade argue that the agreements are the consequence of either manufacturer or retailer cartels. If a retailer's cartel is present, the retailers will impose an RPM arrangement on the manufacturer. The manufacturer then serves to monitor cheating within the cartel. If a manufacturer's cartel is present, the manufacturers force an RPM arrangement on the retailers. The RPM arrangement is viewed as a mechanism for enforcing the cartel. As in any cartel arrangement, the intent is to restrict output for the purpose of raising prices.

On the procompetitive side, some antitrust scholars argue that RPM arrangements might be beneficial to consumers. Such arrangements encourage retailers to provide point-of-sale promotion and service. Since the RPM arrangement assures a minimum price—and thus assures a profit for an efficient retailer—retailers will compete among themselves on the basis of the service they can provide consumers.

Consider the manner in which a consumer purchases a television set. In the absence of an RPM arrangement between manufacturers and retailers, consumers will *shop* for the television sets at stores providing point-of-sale promotions because of the product information those stores are able to provide, but they will *buy* the television at discount stores selling for less because they provide few services and little product information. If the result is that fewer full-service stores can afford to stay in business, consumers may be worse off by the disappearance of the information and service that would be provided under an RPM arrangement.

Although the anticompetitive and competitive aspects of RPM arrangements are still being examined, the courts have concluded that the evidence now supports the application of the rule of reason rather than the per se illegality rule. Interestingly, Table 13–1 indicates that smaller manufacturers engage in resale price maintenance more frequently than larger manufacturers. More than half of all manufacturers sued by the Federal Trade Commission in the 1965 to 1982 period had annual sales of $25 million or less. Are smaller manufacturers using RPM agreements as a way to compete with larger manufacturers? Or is it easier for retail cartels to force RPM arrangements on smaller manufacturers? Could it be that the efficiencies derived from full-service operations benefit smaller manufacturers more than large manufacturers? These are important questions in the ongoing debate over how resale price maintenance agreements will ultimately be treated under the antitrust laws.

State Response to *Dr. Miles:* Fair Trade Laws

During the 1930s several states responded to the *Dr. Miles's* decision requiring the application of the per se illegality rule to resale price maintenance agreements by enacting *fair trade laws.* The first fair trade law was enacted by California and exempted RPM agreements from the state's antitrust laws. In addition, the law provided that once a manufacturer or supplier entered into an RPM agreement with one retailer in the state, it was illegal for other retailers to knowingly undercut the price specified in that agreement. Under the law, manufacturers and suppliers could introduce an RPM system in the state by merely entering into an agreement with one retailer and then notifying other retailers in the state of the agreement. The California fair trade law quickly became the model fair trade law followed by other states. By 1952 fair trade laws were effective in all states except Alaska, Missouri, Texas, and Vermont.

Table 13–1   Size of Firms Involved in FTC RPM Cases: 1965 to 1982

Annual Sales ($ millions)	Number of Cases	Percentage	Cumulative Percentage
0–10	19	29.2	29.2
11–25	15	23.1	52.3
26–50	10	15.4	67.7
51–100	9	13.8	81.5
101–250	5	7.7	89.2
251–1,000 +	7	10.8	100.0
Total	65	100.0	

Source: Overstreet, Thomas R., Jr., *Resale Price Maintenance,* Washington, D.C.: Federal Trade Commission, 1983.

The federal government provided approval of state fair trade laws by enacting the Miller-Tydings Act in 1937 and the McGuire Act in 1952. The Miller-Tydings Act provided that RPM agreements affecting interstate commerce were exempt from Section 1 of the Sherman Act if two conditions were met:

1. The products subject to the resale price maintenance agreement were brandname products and were competing openly with other products of the same general class being manufactured and distributed by others.

2. The state or states in which the products were being sold exempted resale price maintenance agreements from their antitrust enforcements.

As early as 1952, studies were beginning to show that consumer prices were higher in states with fair trade laws than in those states providing no such law. As Table 13–2 indicates, consumer prices were about 10 to 30 percent higher in fair trade states, depending upon the product. It was not until 1975, however, that Congress finally repealed the ability of states to enact fair trade laws. Thus, in that year the *Dr. Miles* legal standard that RPM agreements were per se illegal returned.

Given their impact on consumers, why were fair trade laws enacted, and what was the motivation for them? Like the Robinson-Patman Act of 1936 (which we will study later), the fair trade laws were enacted to protect high-cost distributors from price-cutting competition. By the 1930s, large, efficient, chain stores were cutting retail prices, hurting the less efficient, higher-cost, independent stores. So it does not appear that the manufacturers cared much for the legislation. Indeed, few producers used RPM agreements: it has been estimated that between four and ten percent of retail sales were covered by RPM agreements. Hence, when RPM agreements were legal, it did not appear to facilitate cartel behavior by producers, at least not in many consumer products areas.

Table 13–2   Impact of Fair Trade Laws on Consumer Prices in 1952

Name of Product	Price in 45 States with Fair Trade Laws	Price in Four States with No Fair Trade Laws
Johnson paste wax	$ 0.59	$ 0.54
Mentholatum	0.39	0.29
Vicks drops	0.37	0.29
Bromo Seltzer	0.57	0.49
Pepto Bismol	0.59	0.46
Bayer Aspirin	0.59	0.49
J & J bandaids	0.33	0.24
Unicaps, 250	6.96	5.47
Lilly's insulin NPH U80	2.83	2.19
Colgate toothpaste	0.63	0.54
G.E. vacuum cleaner	59.95	39.99
Sunbeam mixmaster	46.50	34.79
G.E. steam iron	18.95	15.39

Source: Overstreet, Thomas R., Jr., Resale Price Maintenance, Washington, D.C.: Federal Trade Commission, 1983.

Vertical Maximum Price Fixing

The Court extended its *Dr. Miles* decision in *Albrecht* v. *Herald Company* (1968). In *Albrecht*, the Court held that in addition to the *Dr. Miles* prohibitions against fixing minimum retail prices, a manufacturer or supplier may not fix maximum retail prices. Thus, price fixing in virtually any form will be held per se illegal.

Albrecht v. Herald Company
United States Supreme Court
390 U.S. 145,
88 S.Ct. 869
(1968)

Case Background. *The Herald Company published the* Globe-Democrat, *a morning newspaper in St. Louis. Albrecht, an independent newspaper carrier, bought newspapers wholesale and retailed them to subscribers. Carriers were supposed to sell the papers in their exclusive territories at a retail price set by the newspaper. Albrecht raised subscription prices for his subscribers above the price fixed by the newspaper. The newspaper responded by sending another carrier into Albrecht's territory to offer the paper at a lower price. Albrecht was told he could have the territory exclusively again if he lowered his price to the level set by the newspaper. Albrecht sued for treble damages, claiming a restraint of trade in violation of Section 1 of the Sherman Act. The lower court and court of appeals found for the newspaper. Albrecht appealed to the U.S. Supreme Court.*

Case Decision. Justice White delivered the opinion of the Court.

* * *

Maximum and minimum price fixing may have different consequences in many situations. But schemes to fix maximum prices, by substituting the perhaps erroneous judgment of a seller for the forces of the competitive market, may severely intrude upon the ability of buyers to compete and survive in that market. Competition, even in a single product, is not cast in a single mold. Maximum prices may be fixed too low for the dealer to furnish services essential to the value which goods have for the consumer or to furnish services and conveniences which consumers desire and for which they are willing to pay. Maximum price fixing may channel distribution through a few large or specifically advantaged dealers who otherwise would be subject to significant nonprice competition. Moreover, if the actual price charged under a maximum price scheme is nearly always the fixed maximum price, which is increasingly likely as the maximum price approaches the actual cost of the dealer, the scheme tends to acquire all the attributes of an arrangement fixing minimum prices. It is our view, therefore, that the combination formed by the Herald Company in this case to force Albrecht to maintain a specified price for the resale of the newspapers which he had purchased from the Herald Company constituted, without more, an illegal restraint of trade under § 1 of the Sherman Act.

* * *

Case Holding. *The Supreme Court reversed the lower courts, holding that vertical price fixing by the newspaper company, even though it resulted in lower prices for consumers, is illegal.*

Case Questions

1. Would the result of this case be different—or would it even arise—if the newspaper company had the papers delivered by paid employees instead of by independent carriers?

2. Why did the newspaper company care what price the carriers charged? That is, suppose the suggested monthly subscription price was $4, but some carriers charged $5. How could that hurt the newspaper?

Like the cases in the last chapter, the *Albrecht* decision makes it clear that price fixing in either horizontal or vertical arrangements is likely to meet stiff resistance by the courts when challenged. Note, however, that firms that integrate vertically, say from production through retailing, do not face any constraints on their abilities to fix prices, since all pricing is done within a single firm. A firm such as Sears that is organized from production to retail can control its prices at all levels, unlike independent producers and retailers operating in the same markets who try to do it by contract.

The Supreme Court has limited the right of competitors who claim to have been injured due to a vertical, maximum-pricing scheme to sue for damages in *Atlantic Richfield Co. v. USA Petroleum Co.* (1990). USA Petroleum was an independent "discount" gasoline retailer. The company sued ARCO under Section 1 of the Sherman Act claiming it lost sales and profits because ARCO encouraged its retailers to match the lower prices offered by the independent retailers. ARCO gas stations that did cut their prices received discounts from ARCO for the gas they bought. The result was that ARCO increased its market share at the expense of its competitors, like USA Petroleum. The Court held that "Low prices benefit consumers regardless of how those prices are set, and so long as they are above predatory levels, they do not threaten competition. Hence, they cannot give rise to antitrust injury."

VERTICAL TERRITORIAL RESTRAINTS

Manufacturers frequently impose nonprice restraints on their distributors and retailers. Such vertical agreements and arrangements often take the form of territorial, locational, or customer restrictions on the sale of the manufacturer's products. Coca-Cola, Pepsi-Cola, and other soft drink companies, for example, set *territorial restrictions* on their bottlers. Each bottler is permitted to sell and deliver the product within its designated territory. Any delivery outside that territory—that is, any delivery in competition with another bottler—can bring about the revocation of the franchise agreement.

Locational restraints are a common vertical nonprice restraint among automobile manufacturers. Ford Motor Company, for example, grants dealership authorizations around the country that typically limit the dealer to selling Fords from a specific location. To obtain a dealership, an individual must agree to sell Fords only from that location.

Customer restrictions are typically imposed on suppliers by manufacturers in those situations where the manufacturer has elected to sell directly to a certain customer category. A construction materials manufacturer, for example, may elect to deal directly with large commercial accounts but allow suppliers to deal with smaller and more numerous residential accounts.

Since its first decision on a vertical nonprice restraint in *White Motor Company* v. *United States* (1963), the Supreme Court has gradually moved to a sympathetic application of the rule of reason. In *White Motor,* the Court was faced with a vertical territorial limitation on sales. The truck company required its dealers to sell trucks only in an exclusive territory around their dealerships. In addition, White Motor elected to sell to certain customer categories—particularly government bodies—and restrained its dealers from selling to those customers. Justice Douglas, in writing for the majority, said that while horizontal territorial restrictions are illegal, vertical territorial restrictions would be weighed on their merits; that is, a rule of reason would be applied to each vertical restriction. After analyzing the territorial restriction under the rule of reason, the Court chose not to strike down the White Motors arrangement.

Territorial Restraints and the Rule of Reason

In the majority of the private territorial restraint cases reaching the courts, the plaintiff will be a retailer or distributor that has been terminated by a manufacturer in the process of implementing a vertical territorial restraint strategy. To successfully implement the strategy, the manufacturer will generally be required to eliminate some distributors so that the remaining distributors have the necessary territorial, location, or customer exclusivity. In retaliation, the distributors adversely affected by the manufacturer's strategy will institute a legal action asserting that the manufacturer is attempting to monopolize the market in violation of the antitrust laws. Such were the circumstances in the *Continental T.V., Monsanto,* and *Sharp* cases discussed below. Through these important cases, the Supreme Court has fashioned the application of the rule of reason to vertical territorial restraints.

In *Continental T.V., Inc. v. GTE Sylvania, Inc.* (1977), the Sylvania company implemented a vertical territorial restraint strategy with the intent to increase its share of the new television set market. Sylvania's share had fallen to less than 2 percent of the new television market. Within its vertical territorial strategy, Sylvania had decided to sell its television sets directly to franchised retailers. Although these retailers could sell other televisions, by agreeing to sell Sylvanias, they knew that no other Sylvania dealer would be in close physical competition. The intent was to attract more aggressive retailers, who would have an added incentive to push Sylvania's products. Within three years, Sylvania's market share had risen to about 5 percent. Sylvania's territorial-based franchise dealers appeared to work well for most parties involved, but one unhappy dealer that had been terminated sued Sylvania.

Continental T.V., Inc. v. GTE Sylvania Inc.
United States Supreme Court
433 U.S. 36,
97 S.Ct. 2549
(1977)

Case Background. *Sylvania attempted to improve its market position by attracting more aggressive retailers by limiting the number of retail franchises granted in any given area and requiring each franchisee to sell Sylvania products only from the locations franchised. Continental, a franchised retailer, sued, claiming that the limitations violated Section 1 of the Sherman Act. Treble damages were assessed against Sylvania by the district court. The court of appeals reversed, holding that the rule of reason should be applied and that the location restrictions were not destructive to competition. Continental appealed to the Supreme Court reviewed these decisions.*

Case Decision.   Justice Powell delivered the opinion of the Court.

* * *

Vertical restrictions reduce intrabrand competition by limiting the number of sellers of a particular product competing for the business of a given group of buyers. Location restrictions have this effect because of practical constraints on the effective marketing area of retail outlets. Although intrabrand competition may be reduced, the ability of retailers to exploit the resulting market may be limited both by the ability of consumers to travel to other franchised locations and, perhaps more importantly, to purchase the competing products of other manufacturers. None of these key variables, however, is affected by the form of the transaction by which a manufacturer conveys his products to the retailers.

Vertical restrictions promote interbrand competition by allowing the manufacturer to achieve certain efficiencies in the distribution of his products. These "redeeming virtues" are implicit in every decision sustaining vertical restrictions under the rule of reason. Economists have identified a number of ways in which manufacturers can use such restrictions to compete more effectively against other manufacturers.

* * *

Economists also have argued that manufacturers have an economic interest in maintaining as much intrabrand competition as is consistent with the efficient distribution of their products.

* * *

[T]here has been no showing in this case, either generally or with respect to Sylvania's agreements, that vertical restrictions have or are likely to have a "pernicious effect on competition" or that they "lack . . . any redeeming virtue."

* * *

In sum, we conclude that the appropriate decision is . . . the rule of reason. . . . When anticompetitive effects are shown to result from particular vertical restrictions they can be adequately policed under the rule of reason, the standard traditionally applied for the majority of anticompetitive practices challenged under § 1 of the Act.

* * *

Case Holding.   *The Supreme Court affirmed the decision of the court of appeals, holding that territorial restraints may be considered under a rule of reason analysis. The territorial restrictions imposed by Sylvania were upheld, as interbrand competition—competition among the same kinds of products produced by different manufacturers—was seen as more important than intrabrand competition— competition among dealers of the same product.*

Case Questions

1. Do you think the decision of the court would have been the same if, instead of Sylvania with one or two percent of the new television sales, the company had been a television producer with twenty-five percent of the sales?
2. Would this decision necessarily hold if a group of producers, such as television makers, all agreed to impose the same kind of territorial restrictions on the distribution of their products?

In 1984, the Supreme Court again examined vertical territorial restraints in the context of a distributor termination case in *Monsanto Co. v. Spray-Rite*

Service Corp. In an effort to increase sales, Monsanto required distributors to engage in a number of activities the company believed were necessary to improve sales. Spray-Rite failed to undertake those activities and was subsequently terminated by Monsanto. Again applying the rule of reason, the Court found for Monsanto in an 8–0 decision. In addressing the general issue of vertical territorial restraints and distributor terminations by manufacturers, the Court made the following points:

> This Court has drawn two important distinctions that are at the center of this and any other distributor-termination case. First, there is the basic distinction between concerted and independent action—a distinction not always clearly drawn by parties and courts. . . . Independent action is not proscribed. A manufacturer of course generally has a right to deal, or refuse to deal, with whomever it likes, as long as it does so independently. . . . The second important distinction in distributor-termination cases is that between concerted action to set prices and concerted action on nonprice restrictions. The former have been per se illegal since the early years of national antitrust enforcement. See *Dr. Miles Medical Co.* . . . . The latter are judged under the rule of reason, which requires a weighing of the relevant circumstances of a case to decide whether a restrictive practice constitutes an unreasonable restraint on competition. See *Continental T.V., Inc.* v. *GTE Sylvania Inc.* . . .

The *Monsanto* decision was followed four years later by the Court's decision in *Business Electronics v. Corp. v. Sharp Electronics Corp.* (1988). Commentators believe that *Sharp* will have the affect of reducing the success rate of distributors bringing suit against manufacturers who terminate them. The decision has already encouraged some manufacturers—like Sony—to limit the distribution of their products to wholesalers and retailers they believe will follow the marketing strategies of the parent company. The general reading of this case is that unless a conspiracy can be shown to exist or unless direct price fixing is involved, manufacturers have wide latitude in selecting dealers to distribute their products.

Business Electronics Corp. v. Sharp Electronics Corp.
United States Supreme Court, 485 U.S. 717, 108 S.Ct. 1515 (1988)

Case Background. *In 1968 Sharp appointed Business Electronics to be its exclusive retailer in Houston. Sharp appointed Hartwell as a second retailer in Houston in 1972. Sharp published a list of suggested retail prices, but dealers were not required to follow those prices. Business Electronics sold Sharp calculators below Sharp's suggested minimum prices and below Hartwell's prices. Hartwell complained to Sharp that it would quit selling Sharp products unless Business Electronics was terminated as a Sharp dealer. Sharp terminated Business Electronics, which then sued Sharp for conspiracy under Section 1 of the Sherman Act. The district court held Sharp to be guilty of a per se violation of the Sherman Act. The Court of Appeals reversed, applying the rule of reason. Business Electronics appealed to the Supreme Court.*

Case Decision. Justice Scalia delivered the opinion of the Court.

* * *

Our approach to the question presented in the present case is guided by the premises of *GTE Sylvania* and *Monsanto:* that there is a presumption in favor of a rule-of-reason standard; that departure from that standard must be justified by demonstrable economic effect, such as the facilitation of cartelizing, rather than formalistic distinctions; that interbrand competition is the primary concern of the antitrust laws; and that rules in this area should be formulated with a view towards protecting the doctrine of *GTE Sylvania*. . . .

There has been no showing here that an agreement between a manufacturer and a dealer to terminate a "price cutter," without a further agreement on the price or price levels to be charged by the remaining dealer, almost always tends to restrict competition and reduce output. Any assistance to cartelizing that such an agreement might provide cannot be distinguished from the sort of minimal assistance that might be provided by vertical nonprice agreements like the exclusive territory agreement in *GTE Sylvania*, and is insufficient to justify a *per se* rule. Cartels are neither easy to form nor easy to maintain. Uncertainty over the terms of the cartel, particularly the prices to be charged in the future, obstructs both formation and adherence by making cheating easier. . . .

Without an agreement with the remaining dealer on price, the manufacturer both retains its incentive to cheat on any manufacturer-level cartel (since lower prices can still be passed on to consumers) and cannot as easily be used to organize and hold together a retailer-level cartel. . . .

Any agreement between a manufacturer and a dealer to terminate another dealer who happens to have charged lower prices can be alleged to have been directed against the terminated dealer's "price cutting." In the vast majority of cases, it will be extremely difficult for the manufacturer to convince a jury that its motivation was to ensure adequate services, since price cutting and some measure of service cutting usually go hand in hand. Accordingly, a manufacturer that agrees to give one dealer an exclusive territory and terminates another dealer pursuant to that agreement, or even a manufacturer that agrees with one dealer to terminate another for failure to provide contractually-obligated services, exposes itself to the highly plausible claim that its real motivation was to terminate a price cutter. Moreover, even vertical restraints that do not result in dealer termination, such as the initial granting of an exclusive territory or the requirement that certain services be provided, can be attacked as designed to allow existing dealers to charge higher prices. Manufacturers would be likely to forgo legitimate and competitively useful conduct rather than risk treble damages and perhaps even criminal penalties. . . .

As the above discussion indicates, all vertical restraints, including the exclusive territory agreement held not to be *per se* illegal in *GTE Sylvania*, have the potential to allow dealers to increase "prices" and can be characterized as intended to achieve just that. In fact, vertical nonprice restraints only accomplish the benefits identified in *GTE Sylvania* because they reduce intrabrand price competition to the point where the dealer's profit margin permits provision of the desired services. As we described it in *Monsanto*: "The manufacturer often will want to ensure that its distributors earn sufficient profit to pay for programs such as hiring and training additional salesmen or demonstrating the technical features of the product, and will want to see that 'free-riders' do not interfere."

* * *

Case Holding. *The judgment of the Court of Appeals was affirmed in favor of Sharp. The Supreme Court noted that economic analysis and case precedent support the view that a vertical restraint is not illegal per se unless it includes some agreement on prices or price levels.*

Case Questions

1. Why was this case not treated as an RPM? In what ways was this case different from an RPM case?

2. Does this case mean that producers will have more control over retailers or does it mean that there will be more terms of trade settled by contract than was the case before?

The *Sharp* case clearly indicates that retail dealers and manufacturers are free to discuss ways in which the profitability of both parties will be enhanced by various business practices, so long as there is no clear evidence of collusion in determining retail prices. If there are several retailers selling the same brand of product in an area, the manufacturer may work with the retailers to encourage practices that will strengthen consumer satisfaction with their brand relative to other brands. If a manufacturer wants retailers to invest in service departments and other extras, discount dealers, who will not incur the costs of such extras, will likely be dropped from the list of retailers as a consequence. The Court is more concerned with competition among different brands—interbrand competition—than competition among dealers of the same brand—intrabrand competition.

This issue, which has been controversial for many years, is by no means settled. Congress is considering legislation to amend the antitrust law that would clearly reverse *Sharp*, by declaring RPM to be illegal. The proposed legislation clearly restricts the rights of distributors to terminate retail dealers.

INTERNATIONAL PERSPECTIVES: INTERNATIONAL DISTRIBUTORSHIPS

INTERNATIONAL

PERSPECTIVES

Managers must be careful in international operations to be sure that a business practice legal in the United States is not a violation of antitrust laws elsewhere. The last decade's cases in the United States involving vertical restrictions in the distribution of products has encouraged firms to establish distributorships with exclusive territories. So long as prices are not controlled by the distributor, there seem to be few limitations on vertical restraints.

However, in Europe, and specifically in the twelve nations that comprise the European Economic Community (EEC), the European Economic Treaty prohibits exclusive distributorships by territory, since they create intra-EEC barriers. Hence, restrictions on the distribution of products that may be legal in the United States may cause legal action in EEC nations and elsewhere.

The EEC prohibition is not absolute, and a large number of goods and services have been exempted. At the same time, additional consideration is being given to exempting certain product classes that are subject to the current rule. In any event, legal counsel is needed in each country in which a business operates to ensure antitrust compliance.

VERTICAL EXCLUSIONARY PRACTICES

A principle concern of the antitrust laws is the extent to which firms with market power can exercise that power and control the markets in which it does business. Various business practices, some undertaken by formal contract, are designed to indirectly exclude competitors from a particular market.

Those business practices are intended to make it more difficult for competitors to challenge the market power of the firm employing them. Such practices, which include tying arrangements, exclusive-dealing agreements, and boycotts, can come under antitrust attack if the courts find them to be anticompetitive. Section 3 of the Clayton Act applies to tying arrangements and exclusive-dealing agreements, while Section 1 of the Sherman Act governs the antitrust aspects of group boycotts amoung vertically-related parties.

Tying Arrangements

In *Northern Pacific Railway Company* v. *United States* (1958), the Supreme Court defined a *tying arrangement* or *tie-in sale* as:

> . . . an agreement by a party to sell one product [the tying product] but only on the condition that the buyer also purchases a different [complementary or tied] product, or at least agrees that he will not purchase that product from any other supplier.

Similarly, the party may condition the lease of a machine on the use of supplies or services furnished by the party. The tying arrangement is an elementary business practice, allowing a firm to operate simultaneously in more than one market for the purpose of attempting to increase its overall profits. For example, a seller (or lessor) of a water-softener machine (the tying product) may require the buyer (or lessee) to purchase the salt (the tied product) necessary for the operation of the machine from the seller. The seller then derives profits from the sale or lease of the machine and the salt required for its use and operation. Without the tying arrangement, the seller would be forced to compete against other salt dealers.

The Supreme Court has consistently held that where there is monopoly power tying arrangements are a violation of the antitrust laws, finding them to be an extension of the firm's market power over the tying product into the market for the tied product. In reaching its decision, the courts have applied either Section 1 of the Sherman Act—viewing tying arrangements as an unreasonable restraint of trade—or Section 3 of the Clayton Act—viewing tying arrangements as a conditional sales contract that may substantially lessen competition or tend to create a monopoly. Importantly, the Sherman Act applies to both products and services, while the Clayton Act applies only to products.

The practice of tying products together is implicitly found in other, generally legal, business practices. A grocery store, for example, that offers a bag of Brand A flour at half-price when a buyer purchases a bag of Brand A sugar is conducting a tie-in sale that is legal. It is legal because Brand A has no monopoly power over either product. Since you can buy many different brands of flour and sugar, Brand A sugar has no monopoly power over consumers. Also the tie-in sale may be justified if the seller can demonstrate that a new technology in a sensitive machine operates properly only when the seller's replacement parts and service are used.

The Classic Tie-In Case

A classic tying arrangement was struck down in a 1936 Supreme Court decision, *International Business Machines Corp.* v. *United States.* An IBM lease required that the user of a leased mechanical tabulating machine use only IBM tabulating cards in the machine—that is, IBM software was tied to IBM hardware. IBM's reason for this requirement was that if cards of the exact quality, size, and thickness of the IBM card were not used, the machine would be damaged, resulting in inaccurate results or malfunction of the machine, either of which could hurt the reputation of the company. The Court struck down the requirement, holding it to be a violation of Section 3 of the Clayton Act. Other companies can make cards of the requisite quality, the court noted, and IBM's claim was rejected. The court also noted that the fact that the IBM machine was patented had no bearing on the holding.

From a Per Se Rule to a Rule of Reason?

Following the Court's decision in *IBM*, it was generally believed that tying arrangements were a per se violation of the antitrust laws. The Court's 1958 decision in *Northern Pacific Railway Company* v. *United States* did little to change that perception. In that case, the Northern Pacific Railway Company was selling millions of acres of land it owned in the northwestern part of the United States. Most of the land was to be used for timbering or mineral extraction. The sale contracts included a provision (the tie-in) that products from the land being sold would be shipped by Northern Pacific unless a lower-cost shipper was available. The Court struck down the arrangement as a per se violation of the Sherman Act, because it involved a situation wherein the seller had sufficient economic power over the tying product (land) to be able to restrain free competition in the market for the tied product (transportation). If the seller did not have control over the tying product, the Court noted, it would not be able to extend any power over a tied product and there would be no violation.

Some observers have asked if the facts of *Northern Pacific* even met the test the Court set in that decision. Obviously, the Northern Pacific Railway Company did not have a monopoly on land in the northwest. Even though it did have control over the land that it owned, what power was gained over shippers of commodities off that land? Purchasers of the land were free to use lower-cost substitutes and knew when they bargained for the land that the shipping constraint existed. If the constraint had been truly undesirable, the shippers would have bought other land or paid less for Northern Pacific's land.

Since the 1970s, the Court has moved to a rule of reason approach in evaluating the competitive and anticompetitive effects of tying arrangements. In the decision of the *United States Steel Corporation* v. *Fortner Enterprises* (1977), the Supreme Court considered economic evidence regarding the tying arrangement imposed on Fortner by U.S. Steel Corporation.

United States Steel Corporation v. Fortner Enterprises, Inc.

United States Supreme Court
429 U.S. 610,
97 S.Ct. 861,
(1977)

Case Background. *U.S. Steel, a large, diversified corporation, operated the Home Division, which manufactured prefabricated housing, and the Credit Corp., which provided financing to customers of the Home Division. The Credit Corp. loaned Fortner $2 million (at below market interest rates), the entire sum needed by Fortner to acquire and develop land on which homes from Home Division would be placed. Fortner later claimed, after his real estate venture failed, that the contract with U.S. Steel was a violation of the antitrust laws because there was a tie-in between the purchase of the homes and the loan. He sued for treble damages, claiming that the transaction was forbidden by the Sherman Act because the competition for prefabricated houses (the tied product) was restrained by U.S. Steel's power over credit (the tying product).*

The district court held that the evidence justified the conclusion that U.S. Steel did have sufficient economic power in the credit market to make the tying arrangement illegal. The court of appeals affirmed this decision. U.S. Steel appealed to the Supreme Court.

Case Decision. Justice Stevens delivered the opinion of the Court.

* * *

It is a fair summary . . . of the District Court's findings, to say that the loan was unique because the lender accepted such a high risk and the borrower assumed such a low cost.

* * *

Accordingly, the District Court concluded "that all of the required elements of an illegal tie-in agreement did exist since the tie-in itself was present, a not insubstantial amount of interstate commerce in the tied product was restrained and the Credit Corporation did possess sufficient economic power or leverage to effect such restraint."

* * *

Although the Credit Corp. is owned by one of the nation's largest manufacturing corporations, there is nothing in the record to indicate that this enabled it to borrow funds on terms more favorable than those available to competing lenders, or that it was able to operate more efficiently than other lending institutions. In short, the affiliation between U.S. Steel, Home Division, and Credit Corp. does not appear to have given the Credit Corp. any cost advantage over its competitors in the credit market. Instead, the affiliation was significant only because the Credit Corp. provided a source of funds to customers of the Home Division. That fact tells us nothing about the extent of U.S. Steel's economic power in the credit market.

The same may be said about the fact that loans from the Credit Corp. were used to obtain house sales from Fortner and others. In some tying situations a disproportionately large volume of sales of the tied product resulting from only a few strategic sales of the tying product may reflect a form of economic "leverage" that is probative of power in the market for the tying product. If, as some economists have suggested, the purpose of a tie-in is often to facilitate price discrimination, such evidence would imply the existence of power that a free market would not tolerate. But in this case Fortner was only required to purchase houses for the number of lots for which it received financing. The tying product produced no commitment from Fortner to purchase varying quantities of the tied product over an extended period of time. This record, therefore, does not describe the kind of "leverage" found in some of the Court's prior decisions condemning tying arrangements.

The fact that Fortner—and presumably other Home Division customers as well—paid a noncompetitive price for houses also lends insufficient support to the judgment of the lower court. Proof that Fortner paid a higher price for the tied product is consistent with the possibility that the financing was unusually inexpensive and that the price for the entire package was equal to, or below, a competitive price. And this possibility is equally strong even though a number of Home Division customers made a package purchase of homes and financing.

* * *

Quite clearly, if the evidence merely shows that credit terms are unique because the seller is willing to accept a lesser profit—or to incur greater risks—than its competitors, that kind of uniqueness will not give rise to any inference of economic power in the credit market. Yet this is, in substance, all that the record in this case indicates.

The unusual credit bargain offered to Fortner proves nothing more than a willingness to provide cheap financing in order to sell expensive houses. Without any evidence that U.S. Steel had some cost advantage over its competitors—or could offer a form of financing that was significantly differentiated from that which other lenders could offer if they so elected—the unique character of its financing does not support the conclusion that petitioners had the kind of economic power which Fortner had the burden of proving in order to prevail in this litigation.

* * *

Case Holding. *The Supreme Court reversed the lower courts, holding that because U.S. Steel did not have appreciable economic power in the market for credit, the tie-in arrangement did not exploit monopoly power under a rule of reason analysis. The Court noted the importance of studying the reality of the business situation.*

Case Questions

1. Since U.S. Steel was the largest steelmaker in the country at the time of this case, could it not have created monopoly power over mobile home production if it wanted to do so, thereby giving itself the kind of power the Court said it did not have?

2. How did this case end up in Court? Fortner originally made the deal with U.S. Steel of his own volition. What was the purpose of the lawsuit?

The Court continued its rule of reason approach in the 1984 decision, *Jefferson Parish Hospital District No. 2* v. *Hyde*. There the Court considered a suit filed by Hyde, a board-certified anesthesiologist, who applied for admission to the medical staff of Jefferson Hospital. He was denied admission because the hospital had a contract with a professional medical corporation requiring all anesthesiological services for the hospital's patients to be performed by that firm. Hyde claimed that the exclusive contract violated Section 1 of the Sherman Act. The district court held for the hospital. The court of appeals reversed, finding the contract illegal per se because it created an illegal tying arrangement. The Supreme Court reversed, holding that the contract was not a violation of the Sherman Act.

The Court noted that in such an inquiry one must look at the markets involved and the amount of market power possessed by the providers of the services. Patients are generally free to choose hospitals other than Jefferson, Justice Stevens noted for the majority, so that they could obtain other anesthesiological services if they wished. Simply because the two services (e.g., surgery and anesthesia) go together does not make the contract illegal. Tying arrangements will be condemned if they restrain competition on the merits by forcing purchases that would not otherwise be made. Here there was no evidence that price, quality, or supply or demand for either the tying or tied product was adversely affected by the exclusive contract.

Vertical Restraint Guidelines

The Department of Justice issued *Vertical Restraint Guidelines* in 1985. Citing the *Jefferson Parish* decision, the guidelines claim that the Supreme Court is likely to impose a per se rule of illegality only when three conditions are met:

1. The seller has market power in the tying product.
2. Tied and tying products are separate.
3. There is evidence of substantial adverse effect in the tied product market.

In other situations, the rule of reason approach is to be employed. The Justice Department said that in such cases the following test would hold:

> The use of tying will not be challenged if the party imposing the tie has a market share of thirty percent or less in the market for the tying product. This presumption can be overcome only by a showing that the tying agreement unreasonably restrained competition in the market for the tied product.

Exclusive Dealing

Exclusive dealing involves a contractual arrangement between a manufacturer and a retailer under which the manufacturer agrees to sell the product to the retailer on the condition that the retailer not purchase the products of rival manufacturers. Section 3 of the Clayton Act as amended, prohibits exclusive dealing contracts when the effect of the contracts would be to "substantially lessen competition or tend to create a monopoly."

In imposing antitrust scrutiny, the courts are concerned that one of the parties to the exclusive dealing agreement may have exerted its superior economic power to gain contract terms and conditions decidedly in its favor. In addition, the courts are concerned about the anticompetitive impacts the contract may have on the markets for the products involved. An exclusive dealing contract that forecloses a substantial share of the market to other suppliers and is long in duration will likely be held to be in violation of Section 3 of the Clayton Act or Section 1 of the Sherman Act.

Applying the Rule of Reason

In the *Tampa Electric* decision in 1961, the Court upheld a contract whereby the Nashville Coal Company agreed to supply all the coal needed by Tampa Electric for twenty years. In determining whether the exclusive dealing contract was legal, the Court set out three main considerations. First, the line of commerce must be determined. Second, the area of effective competition in the line of commerce must be determined. Third, to be illegal, the contract must foreclose competition that constitutes a substantial share of the relevant market. Expanding on the third point, the court considered the likely effect of the contract on the relevant area, the strength of competitors, the share of commerce involved in the market area, and the potential effects on future competition of such a contract.

In the *Tampa Electric* decision, the Court determined that the line of commerce was coal. Important also was the fact that the coal was used to generate electricity and that it was responsible for only a small fraction of the electricity generated. The relevant geographic market was held to be at least a seven-state area. Although the coal was being consumed in Tampa, Florida, it was mined in states from Pennsylvania to Alabama. The coal needed by Tampa Electric accounted for less than 1 percent of the coal consumed in that area—not a substantial amount. Finally, the Court decided that competition was not foreclosed. Although twenty years is a long time to deal exclusively with one supplier, only a small fraction of the market was involved, and there was no reason to expect expansion from the current size of the contract. Thus, the exclusive dealing agreement was found not to violate the antitrust laws.

Boycotts

A *boycott* occurs when a group conspires to prevent the carrying on of business or to harm a business. It can be executed by any organized group—consumers, union members, retailers, wholesalers, or suppliers—who when, acting in concert, can inflict economic damage on a business. The boycott is often used to force compliance with a price-fixing scheme or some other restraint of trade. The cases usually fall under the per se rule against price fixing.

In an early leading decision, *Eastern States Retail Lumber Dealers Assn.* v. *United States* (1914), the Court struck down a boycott designed to punish lumber wholesalers who sold directly to the public. A number of lumber retailers would turn in to their association the names of wholesalers who sold to the public and the retailers. The retailers were obviously trying to limit competition in lumber sales to the public. The association would send out lists to retailers of the names of wholesalers who had sold directly to the public, in hopes that the retailers would boycott those wholesalers. Even though there was no enforcement mechanism—retailers were still free to deal with such wholesalers—and there was no evidence that the boycott of the lumber wholesalers who sold to the public caused any loss of business, the Court said that the Sherman Act prohibits such boycotts.

Boycotts and the Per Se Rule

The Courts have consistently taken a hard line against boycotts, largely because boycotts are efforts by horizontal competitors to restrict vertical competition. That is, unlike other vertical restrictions where one manufacturer negotiates with individual dealers about terms of trade, boycotts involve either all manufacturers getting together to tell dealers what they must do, or all dealers getting together to tell manufacturers what they must do. A horizontal restriction on competition is used to force vertical restraints. In 1990 the Supreme Court reiterated that when horizontal competitors use a boycott to force a change in the nature of a vertical relationship, there is a per se violation of the law.

FTC v. Superior Court Trial Lawyers Association

United States Supreme Court, ____ U.S. ____, 110 S.Ct. 768 (1990)

Case Background. *Operating under the Criminal Justice Act (CJA), a group of about 100 lawyers in private practice regularly acted as court-appointed attorneys for indigent defendants charged in the District of Columbia. The attorneys belonged to the Superior Court Trial Lawyers Association (SCTLA), a private organization. Their fees for legal work ($30 per hour for court time, $20 per hour for out-of-court time) were paid by the District of Columbia on behalf of their clients. The average annual income for the attorneys from this work was $45,000 in 1982 (about $60,000 in 1990 dollars). In 1983, the SCTLA demanded that the government of the District of Columbia double their fees. When this did not happen, the SCTLA organized a boycott. About 90 of the 100 attorneys boycotted the criminal courts of the District, which soon nearly brought the system to a stop. After two weeks, the District raised attorney fees to $35 per hour for all work and promised to double the fees as demanded as soon as possible.*

The FTC charged the SCTLA with a conspiracy to fix prices and to conduct a boycott that constituted unfair methods of competition under Section 5 of the FTC Act. Although the Administrative Law Judge (ALJ) of the FTC concluded that the complaint should be dismissed, the Commission ruled that the boycott was illegal per se. The Court of Appeals reversed the FTC, holding that the boycott was a political expression protected by the First Amendment. The Supreme Court reviewed the decision.

Case Decision.   Justice Stevens delivered the opinion of the Court.

* * *

As the ALJ, the FTC, and the Court of Appeals all agreed, SCTLA's boycott "constituted a classic restraint of trade within the meaning of Section 1 of the Sherman Act." As such, it also violated the prohibition against unfair methods of competition in § 5 of the FTC Act. Prior to the boycott CJA lawyers were in competition with one another, each deciding independently whether and how often to offer to provide services to the District at CJA rates. The agreement among the CJA lawyers was designed to obtain higher prices for their services and was implemented by a concerted refusal to serve an important customer in the market for legal services and, indeed, the only customer in the market for the particular services that CJA regulars offered. "This constriction of supply is the essence of 'price-fixing,' whether it be accomplished by agreeing upon a price, which will decrease the quantity demanded, or by agreeing upon an output, which will increase the price offered." The horizontal arrangement among these competitors was unquestionably a "naked restraint" on price and output. . . .

As we have remarked before, the "Sherman Act reflects a legislative judgment that ultimately competition will produce not only lower prices, but also better goods and services." This judgment "recognizes that all elements of a bargain— quality, service, safety, and durability—and not just the immediate cost, are favorably affected by the free opportunity to select among alternative offers." . . .

The social justifications proffered for SCLTA's restraint of trade thus do not make it any less unlawful. The statutory policy underlying the Sherman Act "precludes inquiry into the question whether competition is good or bad." SCLTA's argument, like that made by the petitioners in *Professional Engineers,* ultimately asks us to find that their boycott is permissible because the price it seeks to set is reasonable. But it was settled shortly after the Sherman Act was passed that it "is no excuse that the prices fixed are themselves reasonable." SCLTA's agreement is not outside the coverage of the Sherman Act simply because its objective was the enactment of favorable legislation.

* * *

The *per se* rules in antitrust law serve purposes analagous to *per se* restrictions upon, for example, stunt flying in congested areas or speeding. Laws prohibiting stunt flying or setting speed limits are justified by the State's interest in protecting human life and property. . . .

In part, the justification for these *per se* rules is rooted in administrative convenience. They are also supported, however, by the observation that every speeder and every stunt pilot poses some threat to the community. An unpredictable event may overwhelm the skills of the best driver or pilot, even if the proposed course of action was entirely prudent when initiated. A bad driver going slowly may be more dangerous that a good driver going quickly, but a good driver who obeys the law is safer still.

So it is with boycotts and price fixing. Every such horizontal arrangement among competitors poses some threat to the free market. . . .

Of course, some boycotts and some price-fixing agreements are more pernicious than others; some are only partly successful, and some may not succeed when they are buttressed by other causative factors, such as political influence.

But an assumption that, absent proof of market power, the boycott disclosed by this record was totally harmless—when overwhelming testimony demonstrated that it almost produced a crisis in the administration of criminal justice in the District and when it achieved its economic goal—is flatly inconsistent with the clear course of our antitrust jurisprudence. Conspirators need not achieve the dimensions of a monopoly, or even a degree of market power any greater than that already disclosed by this record, to warrant condemnation under the antitrust laws.

* * *

Case Holding. *The Supreme Court upheld the decision of the FTC, reversing the judgment of the Court of Appeals. The lawyers' boycott of public criminal defense work, in an effort to force the city to raise their fees, was held to be illegal per se under the Sherman and the FTC Acts.*

Case Questions.

1. The lawyers claimed that their freedom of speech was being repressed by the antitrust laws, that is, that their First Amendment rights to gather for political expression were curtailed by seeing this as an economic boycott issue. Is there merit to this argument?

2. Is there a difference between horizontal and vertical price fixing?

THE ROBINSON-PATMAN ACT

The Robinson-Patman Act, enacted in 1936, amended the Clayton Act. Section 2(a) states that "it shall be unlawful for any person engaged in commerce . . . to discriminate in price between different purchasers of commodities of like grade and quality . . . where the effect of such discrimination may be substantially to lessen competition or tend to create a monopoly in any line of commerce." Thus, a seller is said to engage in *price discrimination* when the same product is sold to different buyers at different prices.

Section 2(a) is perhaps the most controversial part of antitrust law, as the initial reason for its passage was to limit the ability of chain stores to offer merchandise at a price lower than their single-store competitors. The implication of the Act's application is that consumers will be denied lower prices. As a consequence of this implication, the Department of Justice and the FTC have been reluctant to enforce the Act. The vast majority of cases brought under the Robinson-Patman Act are private actions.

Price Discrimination Examined

Many of the cases brought under the Robinson-Patman Act concern alleged economic injuries either from a firm charging different prices in different markets or from bulk sale discounts given to larger volume retailers. To illustrate the first type of injury, suppose that two sellers—Allen's Wholesale and Johnston Distributors—sell the same products in competition with one another in San Francisco. Allen's also sells the product in Oakland, but

Johnston does not. If Allen's reduces its price levels in San Francisco, but not in Oakland, that price cut may be seen as anticompetitive under the Robinson-Patman Act. Allen's is engaging in price discrimination—charging different prices in different markets to the detriment of its competitors, which in this case is Johnston.

Predatory Pricing
This type of business practice is sometimes seen as *predatory pricing*. That is, Allen's is attempting to undercut Johnston in San Francisco in an effort to drive Johnston from the market. Allen's, however, continues to sell the product for a higher price in other markets in which it does not compete with Johnston. Presumably, the intent of Allen's actions is to drive Johnston from the San Francisco market, and then raise prices when Johnston goes out of business.

Volume Discounts Legal?
The Robinson-Patman Act is also concerned with sales discounts given to large volume retailers. To illustrate, suppose Allen's and Johnston both buy the same product from Central Distributors for the purpose of selling it retail. Because Allen's is a larger volume retailer, Central gives Allen's a price discount on its larger bulk purchases. The price discount gives Allen's a competitive advantage over Johnston in the sale of the product to customers in the area. The injury to competition that is attacked is the price discount given to Allen's, the larger purchaser. This type of action generates numerous private actions against producers who discriminate in pricing to wholesalers or retailers.

Defenses

The key that has emerged for firms that must defend themselves against a charge of violating the Robinson-Patman Act is the ability to show a *cost justification* for different prices charged in different markets or to different buyers. An obvious cost justification defense is a difference in transportation costs—it usually costs more to deliver a refrigerator three hundred miles than it costs to deliver it fifty miles. Similarly, on a per unit basis it is cheaper to deliver 1,000 refrigerators than it is to deliver five refrigerators. The major problem with using the cost justification defense is that costs usually cannot reasonably be assigned to specific products sold at particular places or to particular buyers—it is virtually an accounting and economic impossibility to assign specific costs of production to individual products. As a consequence, the cost justification defense is rarely successfully applied by itself.

The other defense that may be used is that of *meeting competition*. That is, a firm cuts its price in response to a competitor cutting its price first. The problem with this defense can be that the original price cut will be held illegal under Robinson-Patman, which will mean that subsequent price cuts may also be illegal, at least at some point. Competitors must show that the meeting competition price cut was done in good faith, not in an effort to injure competitors but to stay competitive. In the *Texaco* decision, the Supreme Court considers a defense of price discrimination.

Texaco v. Hasbrouck
United States Supreme Court,
___ **U.S.** ___ ,
110 S.Ct. 2535
(1990)

Case Background. *From 1972 to 1981, Texaco, the petitioner, sold gasoline to Hasbrouck (Rick's Texaco), the respondent, and other independent Texaco gas stations in Spokane, Washington. Texaco also sold its gasoline to Gull and Dompier—but at lower prices. Gull sold the gasoline under the Gull name at its stations. Dompier sold the gasoline under the Texaco brand name at its stations. Because Gull and Dompier paid less for their gasoline, they sold it for less at retail and grew rapidly. Sales at Rick's Texaco and the other independent stations dropped from 76 percent to 49 percent of Texaco retail sales in the area.*

The only difference in operations between Dompier's Texaco stations and the independent Texaco stations was that Dompier owned tanker trucks and it used them to pick up gasoline from Texaco's plant. The independent dealers asked Texaco if they could hire their own tanker trucks to pick up the gasoline, and then pay the same price as Dompier and Gull. Texaco said no.

Hasbrouck and other independent Texaco station owners sued Texaco for violation of section 2(a) of the Robinson-Patman Act, alleging that Texaco's discounts to Dompier and Gull were illegal. The trial court awarded treble damages to Hasbrouck and the court of appeals affirmed. Texaco appealed, claiming that the lower price charged to Dompier and Gull were legal functional discounts, that is, "discounts given to a purchaser based on its role in the supplier's distribution system and reflect the cost of the services performed by the purchaser for the supplier."

Case Decision. Justice Stevens delivered the opinion of the Court.

* * *

The Robinson-Patman Act contains no express reference to functional discounts. It does contain two affirmative decisions that provide protection for two categories of discounts—those that are justified by savings in the seller's cost of manufacturer, delivery or sale, and those that represent a good faith response to the equally low prices of a competitor. As the case comes to us, neither of those defenses is available to Texaco.

In order to establish a violation of the Act, respondents had the burden of proving four facts: (1) that Texaco's sales to Gull and Dompier were made in interstate commerce; (2) that the gasoline sold to them was of the same grade and quality as that sold to respondents; (3) that Texaco discriminated in price as between Gull and Dompier on the one hand and Hasbrouck on the other; and (4) that the discrimination had a prohibited effect on competition. Moreover, for Hasbrouck to recover damages, he had the burden of proving the extent of his actual injuries.

The first two elements of Hasbrouck's case are not disputed in this Court, and we do not understand Texaco to be challenging the sufficiency of Hasbrouck's proof of damages. Texaco does argue, however, (1) that although it charged different prices, it did not "discriminate in price" within the meaning of the Act, and (2) that, at least to the extent that Gull and Dompier acted as wholesalers, the price differentials did not injure competition. We consider the two arguments separately.

Texaco's first argument would create a blanket exemption for all functional discounts. Indeed, carried to its logical conclusion, it would exempt all price differentials except those given to competing purchasers. . . . [W]e remain persuaded that the argument is foreclosed by the text of the Act itself. In the context of a statute that plainly reveals a concern with competitive consequences at different levels of distribution, and carefully defines specific affirmative defenses, it would be anomalous to assume that the Congress intended the term "discriminate" to have such a limited meaning. . . .

Since we have already decided that a price discrimination within the meaning of § 2(a) "is merely a price difference," we must reject Texaco's first argument.

* * *

[In its second argument, Texaco asserts that the price differentials did not injure competition.] A supplier need not satisfy the rigorous requirements of the cost justification defense in order to prove that a particular functional discount is reasonable and accordingly did not cause any substantial lessening of competition between a wholesaler's customers and the supplier's direct customers. The record in this case, however, adequately supports the finding that Texaco violated the Act.

... A price differential "that merely accords due recognition and reimbursement for actual marketing functions" is not illegal. In this case, however, both the District Court and the Court of Appeals concluded that even without viewing the evidence in the light most favorable to the Hasbrouck, there was no substantial evidence indicating that the discounts to Gull and Dompier constituted a reasonable reimbursement for the value to Texaco of their actual marketing functions. Indeed, Dompier was separately compensated for its hauling function, and neither Gull nor Dompier maintained any significant storage facilities.

* * *

The longstanding principle that functional discounts provide no safe harbor from the Act is likewise evident from the practice of the Federal Trade Commission, which has, while permitting legitimate functional discounts, proceeded against those discounts which appeared to be subterfuges to avoid the Act's restrictions.

* * *

The evidence indicates ... that Texaco affirmatively encouraged Dompier to expand its retail business and that Texaco was fully informed about the persistent and marketwide consequences of its own pricing policies. Indeed, its own executives recognized that the dramatic impact on the market was almost entirely attributable to the magnitude of the distributor discount and the hauling allowance. Yet at the same time that Texaco was encouraging Dompier to integrate downward, and supplying Dompier with a generous discount useful to such integration, Texaco was inhibiting upward integration by Hasbrouck: Hasbrouck sought permission from Texaco to haul his own fuel using his own tankwagons, but Texaco refused. The special facts of this case thus make it peculiarly difficult for Texaco to claim that it is being held liable for the independent pricing decisions of Gull or Dompier.

* * *

... One would expect that most functional discounts will be legitimate discounts which do not cause harm to competition. At the least, a functional discount that constitutes a reasonable reimbursement for the purchasers' actual marketing functions will not violate the Act. When a functional discount is legitimate, the inference of injury to competition ... will simply not arise. Yet it is also true that not every functional discount is entitled to a judgment of legitimacy, and that it will sometimes be possible to produce evidence showing that a particular functional discount caused a price discrimination of the sort the Act prohibits. When such anticompetitive effects are proved—as we believe they were in this case—they are covered by the Act.

* * *

Case Holding. *The Supreme Court affirmed the decision of the courts below. The Robinson-Patman Act states that it is illegal price discrimination to sell the same good at different prices to different customers, unless there are cost differentials in dealing with different customers or prices are cut to meet the competition. Neither defense applied here.*

Case Questions

1. Suppose Texaco could show that the result of their pricing decision was to make the retail gasoline market more competitive in Spokane, thereby helping consumers. Would that be a defense?

2. Texaco claimed that Dompier and Gull were wholesale distributors, while Hasbrouck was a retailer. Texaco justified the price different because it was selling to wholesalers versus selling to retailers. Is this a plausible defense?

EXEMPTIONS FROM AND ENFORCEMENT OF THE ANTITRUST LAWS

Various activities have been exempted by Congress or the Supreme Court from having the antitrust laws enforce against them. The justifications typically provided for these exemptions are that the business is regulated by some other government agency, or that the business requires protection from competition based on some other public policy rationale. The following activities and businesses are provided exemptions:

- The Clayton Act exempts nonprofit and certain agricultural or horticultural organizations. Extensions have been made to cover agricultural, fishing and some other cooperatives.

- The Interstate Commerce Act regulates motor, rail, and ship common carriers (means of public transport). Generally, if the Interstate Commerce Commission (ICC) approves the actions of these businesses, they are exempt from the antitrust laws. However, when the activities involved are not or would not be approved by the ICC, the government can take action. One example would be a conspiracy among truck freight carriers to set rates. Similarly, the Shipping Act defers to the Federal Maritime Commission in regulating water carriers of freight. Certain aspects of air transportation are regulated by the Federal Aviation Administration (FAA) and by the Department of Transportation (DOT).

- The Export Trading Company Act allows a seller or group of sellers to receive a certificate from the Department of Commerce and the Department of Justice allowing limited antitrust immunity for the purpose of export trade. For example, a group of domestic producers may be allowed to join together to enhance their ability to sell their products in other countries.

- Subject to approval by the Attorney General, bank mergers are exempt.

- The Parker doctrine allows state governments to restrict competition in industries such as public utilities like cable television, professional services like nursing or dog grooming, and public transportation like taxi cabs.

- The McCarran-Ferguson Act exempts the business of insurance from federal antitrust laws, so long as the states adequately regulate insurance.

- Under the Noerr-Pennington doctrine, lobbying to influence a legislature or an agency is not illegal. This is because the First Amendment to the

Constitution gives individuals the right to petition their government, even if their purpose in doing so is anticompetitive.

- Certain activities of labor unions are exempt from the antitrust laws because the National Labor Relations Act favors and protects collective bargaining to fix wages and conditions of employment.

As noted previously, the various antitrust statutes can be enforced by different entities. The Antitrust Division of the Justice Department brings criminal antitrust prosecutions. For a civil lawsuit under the Sherman Act or Clayton Act, a choice must be made as to whether the Justice Department or the FTC will bring the case. The agencies have agreed to divide jurisdiction by industry, but may consult on individual matters to decide which agency will handle a particular case.

Remedies Available

An action to halt conduct that appears to be an antitrust violation can be brought either by a private plaintiff or by the government. The federal courts can provide a number of remedies including:

- Restrain a company or individuals from certain conduct.
- Force a company to divest a subsidiary.
- Use company assets to form another company to compete with the original company.
- Force a company to let others use its patents (licensing).
- Cancel or modify existing business contracts.

Today, violations of the Sherman Act carry the most severe penalties of the antitrust statutes:

- Violations of Sections 1 and 2 of the Sherman Act are *criminal felonies*. Individuals found guilty of violating the act face up to three years in prison, a fine of $100,000, or both. Corporations found guilty can be fined up to $1 million. Criminal cases are brought by the Antitrust Division of the U.S. Department of Justice.

- Private parties or the government can seek injunctive relief under the act in a civil proceeding. An *injunction* is an order preventing the defendant (the party who may have violated the act) from continuing the challenged behavior.

- Private parties who have been harmed by a violation of the Sherman Act can sue for *treble damages;* if they win, they get three times their actual money damages, plus court costs and attorneys' fees.

Incentives to Sue

The incentive to bring antitrust suits was increased by the 1989 Supreme Court decision in *California v. ARC America Corp.* The Court held that state antitrust statutes can allow collection of treble damages by indirect purchasers. Legal experts expect a rash of class-action lawsuits by consumers or on behalf of consumers by private attorneys or by state attorneys general.

The federal antitrust statutes mandate treble damages for direct purchasers. That is, someone who pays a price fixer $100 too much because of price fixing collects $300 damages, plus attorneys' fees. Antitrust statutes in many states allow indirect buyers, which can be a large class of individuals, to sue for treble damages. Hence, class-action suits can be brought where the indirect buyers each suffer a small loss but the loss suffered by all consumers is large. For example, 100,000 consumers may buy a product at retail that had been involved at price fixing at the wholesale level. The consumers each pay $3 too much at retail because the retailer paid the price-fixing wholesaler $3 too much for each product. The state laws allow the consumers to sue the wholesaler for treble damages ($3 × 100,000 × 3 = $900,000). Since the wholesaler is also liable for treble damages to the retailer, the wholesaler could possibly pay sextuple damages.

The Supreme Court gave a boost to efforts by state attorneys general to enforce antitrust statutes in *California v. American Stores Co.* (1990). In that case, the FTC had approved a merger of two grocery store chains in California. After the conclusion of antitrust review by federal officials, California filed suit, claiming that the merger violated the Sherman and Clayton Acts by damaging actual and potential competition in the grocery market in California. The Supreme Court upheld the right of the state to bring the action despite the completion of the federal review of the merger, and upheld the right of the federal district court to block the merger until the challenge to the merger was reviewed. Like *California v. ARC America Corp.*, this case may result in substantially more antitrust suits being brought by state officials, which may change the landscape of antitrust law by the year 2000.

SUMMARY

This chapter reviewed the essential elements of antitrust law concerning vertical restraints of trade. Vertical arrangements are relationships between sellers and buyers at different levels of business. Restraints of a vertical nature may be directly related to prices, or may involve a number of nonprice restrictions.

The chapter began with a look at resale price maintenance. In an RPM arrangement, the producer or wholesaler of a product tells the retailer what price must be charged for the product when it is sold further down the chain of distribution, most often at the retail level. The Supreme Court has taken a hard line toward resale price maintenance, holding that fixing either minimum or maximum resale prices is per se illegal unless other factors are involved that would allow a rule of reason analysis to be used.

The chapter then looks at various nonprice restraints of trade. The first major area is territorial restraints. In a territorial restraint business strategy, a producer such as Sony tells its retail dealers that they may sell Sony TVs only from approved locations. The Court has adopted a rule of reason analysis in such cases, primarily looking to see if the intrabrand competition lost by territorial restraints is more than made up for by the interbrand competition the territorial restraints are designed to encourage.

In the area of vertical restraints of trade, boycotts involve a group of buyers who refuse to buy from a single seller or group of sellers, or who a group of sellers agree not to sell to certain buyers. Such arrangements are usually held to be per se illegal in the absence of other conditions.

Tie-in sales, where the purchase of one product is tied to the required purchase of another, are viewed under a rule of reason analysis. Most tie-in sales are held to be harmless. There must be monopoly power present for the courts to be concerned that a firm engaging in a tying arrangement will be able to extend that monopoly power from one product to another product.

An exclusive dealing contracts involves two or more firms who agree only to deal with each other for some classes of products, usually for a long time period. The courts generally use a rule of reason approach, looking to see if there is monopoly power being used to achieve the exclusive deal, or if the deal produces monopoly power that would not otherwise exist.

Price discrimination may be attacked by the Robinson-Patman Act. The law holds, in general, that sellers cannot charge different prices for the same products to different buyers—unless there is a cost justification for doing so, or the price differential is necessary to meet competition in one of the two markets.

ISSUE

What Happens When Producers Control Retail Prices?

Resale price maintenance has a long, controversial history in the United States. While it is clear that manufacturers cannot fix prices for wholesalers and retailers down the chain of distribution, the Sharp *case indicates that producers have some rights of control. In Japan, retail competition is limited because of the political clout of producers and small shop owners who fight the discount prices that larger, more efficient retailers can offer. In the following article, the author examines price maintenance arrangements within the Japanese liquor industry.*

Competitors, Beware
Dorian Benkoil*

They've tried to run Yukio Higuchi out of business for 25 years. For years he and his family received anonymous death threats. Wholesalers who delivered to his liquor store found other orders canceled. Thugs used to loiter outside his warehouse. And even today, when Higuchi's staff goes to pick up liquor, his trucks don't bear his store's name so wholesalers will load the trucks. What brings on all the wrath? Higuchi owns Kawachiya, Japan's oldest discount liquor store, which marks a few yen off bottles of whiskey, wine and beer.

–continued

–continuing

The Japanese consumer is suddenly the focus of controversy in Tokyo these days. American delegations including Commerce Secretary Robert Mosbacher have portrayed themselves as fighting for the interests of the average Japanese shopper. He or she deserves a wider and cheaper choice of products, they say, and foreign goods offer just that. "All we're asking for is the right to come here and compete," said Mosbacher. But in the Japanese marketplace, where business relationships protect existing interests, competition is kept within tight bounds and the customer has little influence. "This is the most educated work force in the world, and yet the associations and government consider them idiots when it comes to buying a product," says William J. Best of the American Chamber of Commerce in Japan. "The real issue is the consumer has no choice."

The 2.8 trillion-yen liquor industry is a microcosm of this longstanding state of affairs. Wholesalers, retailers, distillers' sales representatives and the liquor-licensing division of the Ministry of Finance all work to keep prices, and the market, "stable." A "very unbalanced price may cause a very confused situation," says a spokesman for Suntory, the Japanese liquor powerhouse. At Kawachiya, a 750-ml bottle of the top-selling domestic whisky, Suntory Old, sells for 2,039 yen, but the majority of retailers charge 2,300 yen. "Confusion" could bring the sorts of disorder normal to free markets: bankruptcies, an opening for newcomers and bargains for consumers.

A few large companies dominate liquor production—Suntory and Nikka together control 85 percent of Japan's whisky output, and two other companies split almost all the remainder. The companies set a retail price with margins so high that two levels of wholesalers and the retailer can take a comfortable cut. The markup can, account for as much as 60 percent of the nontax portion of the price of liquor. And domestic liquor companies often cushion their retailers by offering secret rebates.

Those who try to buck the system face intimidation by retail associations and snubs from distillers and wholesalers. Distillers' sales agents don't give them the rebates or promotional perks given to more cooperative stores. "The distillers are worried that they could jeopardize their brand image or the price structure they are maintaining if their liquor is sold for a lower price," says Kawachiya's Higuchi.

Discounters also blame the government. "Though wholesalers won't say, we all know that when they cut off deliveries to us, it's because the local tax-collection agencies have called them up," discount liquor store owner Shinobu Sugita told the *Japan Economic Journal*. Other discounters complain of unusually close and persistent inspections by government officials. Members of the government's National Tax Administration Agency, which licenses liquor stores, deny any manipulation. "Stores don't state on their application form whether they intend to be discount or not," says the agency's Masamichi Kikuchi. Still, guidelines for granting licenses say shops can't advertise "unreasonable" prices.

Such treatment has held down the number of discounters throughout the country. Fewer than 200 of 140,000 liquor shops in Japan are discounters, and the numbers have barely increased in the past decade. Discounters who stick it out, however, often find it's worth it: some control as much as 30 percent of their local market. Higuchi admits that "the system discouraging new discounters is great for me," because he doesn't have to worry about competition.

Foreign distillers already in the market have no incentive to seek changes. The status quo guarantees them hefty margins. Though foreign brands sold only 13 percent of the whisky consumed in Japan last year, they reaped over 22 percent of the revenue. Hennessey cognac, at 35,000 yen per 700-ml

–continued

—continuing

bottle, costs almost three times the price it fetches in some discount stores.

Consumers will look for bargains if given the chance. One small but growing trend is "parallel importing"—importing outside normal channels. "Parallel agents" circumvent the authorized import and sales agents and pass the savings on to customers. Japanese who are willing to buy a product that's not tailored for the Japanese market can save as much as two thirds on everything from watches to BMWs. The Tokyo liquor store Higuchi Honten sells parallel-imported Hennessey for only 13,000 yen.

Some help may be coming for consumers. The number of mom and pop shops—the inefficient backbone of Japanese retailing—has declined significantly. Large retailers are finding ways to circumvent the Large Retail Store law, which forces them to get permission from local shopkeepers to open larger stores. And the number of chain stores, with clout to stand up to suppliers' coercion or to arrange their own channels of supply, is also growing.

But market forces probably won't bring change fast enough to satisfy the Americans. As long as the docile Japanese consumer is willing to pay premiums for his whisky and a fortune for his cognac, discounters like Yukio Higuchi will continue to use unmarked trucks and get threatening phone calls in the middle of the night.

Questions
1. Can you think of how the pricing mechanism described in the reading can injure American firms trying to compete in Japan?
2. Would it be in the interest of the United States to insist that the Japanese adopt antitrust policies similar to American policies, with the threat of Japanese import restrictions by the United States would Japan not comply?
3. It has long been argued in Japan and the United States that the social benefits of a nation of small shopkeepers outweighs the benefits of lower prices from large discount stores that drive many small shops out of business. Is this a good basis for antitrust policy?

REVIEW AND DISCUSSION QUESTIONS

1. Define the following terms:
   resale price maintenance
   fair trade laws
   territorial restrictions
   boycott
   tie-in sale
   exclusive dealing
   price discrimination

2. Vertical restraint of trade cases are more likely to be covered by a rule of reason analysis than are horizontal restraint cases, and, in general, the antitrust authorities are less critical of vertical restraints than they are of horizontal restraints. Is this distinction sensible if you presume that the purpose of antitrust law should be to make the economy more competitive?

3. The courts use a rule of reason in looking at territorial restrictions. Why should there be any concern about territorial restrictions? So long as there is competition between brands, is not that more important than intrabrand

competition by the sellers of a product in a given geographic market? That is, can you think of cases in which intrabrand competition might be more important than interbrand competition?

4. The courts take a hard line against boycotts, usually holding them to be per se illegal. Interestingly, an examination of most of the famous boycott cases indicate that the boycotts had no effect in practice. If this is the case, why worry about them? Why not oppose only boycotts that are successful?

Case Questions

5. The country's largest producer of salt requires the lessees of its patented machines, which require the use of salt, to use only the lessor's salt in the machines or the lease will be void and the machines taken back. What is this arrangement called? Is it illegal? Does it make a difference that the machine is patented?

6. An agricultural cooperative marketing association composed of about 500 Maryland and Virginia dairy farmers supplies about 80 percent of the milk purchased by milk processors for sale in Washington, D.C. The marketing association, which previously had simply gathered the milk from area dairies for sale to processors, buys a processing plant to allow it to become a milk wholesaler. Would this merger be likely to be legal? What considerations might come into play?

7. Movie distributors sometimes engage in block booking of movies. That is, they sell movie rentals to theaters and TV stations in packages. For example, a theater or station might not be able to rent *Gone with the Wind* by itself; the movie might come in a package with *The Texas Chainsaw Massacre*. This is a sort of tie-in sale, since if the theater or station wants to rent one movie it must rent the other. Does this provide an example of how monopoly power over one product can be extended over another product? Would this tie-in be likely to be held to be illegal? Remember that the movies are copyrighted, so that there is legally only one source from which theaters and TV stations can rent them.

Policy Questions

8. There was no discussion of mergers in the chapter because nonhorizontal mergers are rarely challenged. The antitrust laws do not attack bigness per se. Should they? Should there be concern when two large firms in different industries merge? These are usually called conglomerate mergers and are rarely attacked, just as vertical mergers are rarely attacked.

9. The Robinson-Patman Act was officially titled the Anti-Chain Store Discrimination Act. Can you see why? The backers of the act were small-store owners who were being hurt by competition from the growing chain stores in the 1920s and 1930s, which by now dominate retailing. Is this legislation procompetitive, or does it hurt consumers?

Ethics Questions

10. After the *Albrecht* case said that newspaper producers cannot control subscription prices if they sell the papers to independent carriers for distribution to the public, many newspapers generally did away with the independent carriers and hired employees to distribute the papers. By vertically integrating this function within the firm, the company can control the distribution price. Since

newspapers rely primarily on advertising revenues to fund operations, they have an interest in keeping subscription prices low to encourage high circulation, which allows them to charge higher advertising rates. The carriers want higher subscription rates, since they keep all money collected above what they paid the paper company for the paper. Is it ethical for the newspaper companies to get rid of the independent carriers in favor of in-house carriers? Does it matter that the public benefits by lower subscription rates?

11. Your firm produces electric blenders. A certain popular model has a suggested retail price of $30. Your firm sells it wholesale for $18. Smaller stores tend to sell the blender at the suggested retail price. One large discount chain begins to sell the blender for $26 and asks you to cut the price to them to $17.50. Because of that chain's large sales, your production and profits are up. You will earn even higher profits if you cut the price to them to $17.50—a possible violation of the Robinson-Patman Act. Should you cut the price for the chain? What if the chain says it will cut its retail price to $25.50 if you cut the price to $17.50?

14 Labor Relations Law

L AWS affecting the labor-management relationship are the subject of this chapter. We examine federal labor legislation, including the Norris-La Guardia Act, the Wagner Act, the Taft-Hartley Act, and the Landrum-Griffin Act, and then turn to the processes and procedures of the National Labor Relations Board. Unlawful labor activities including secondary boycotts and hot cargo agreements are then considered. Next we examine other labor laws affecting the labor relationship, including employment-at-will, minimum wage requirements, occupational licensure and regulation, and workers' compensation laws. We then discuss those laws providing for worker safety, health, and retirement rights.

Before 1890, attempts to organize labor were greatly restricted. The primary barrier was the common law rule that intentional infliction of economic harm is a tort. Hence, when workers banded together and refused to work and thus boycotted a business, they could be held guilty of conspiring to commit a tort. Although not all courts accepted this rule, there was little legal support for organized labor activities.

After 1890, with the enactment of the Sherman Act, restraints of trade were restricted by statute. Since organized boycotts by labor are clearly restraints of trade, union activities were restricted. The Clayton Act of 1914 liberalized the rules regarding union activities a little, but it was not until the Great Depression that the public and political attitudes toward unions changed sufficiently to encourage the enactment of legislation providing affirmative support for organized labor activities. Thus, although various craft and trade unions existed during the 1800s, labor law is a twentieth-century phenomenon.

Union membership and representation extends to millions of workers, as indicated in Table 14–1. However, union membership as a share of the labor force hit its peak in the 1950s and has declined steadily since. Over the last twenty years, the percent of the labor force belonging to unions fell in half.

Table 14–1   Union Labor in 1989

Characteristic	Number of Workers*	% Union Members	% Union Represented
Total	103,480	16.4	18.6
By Sex:			
Men	54,789	19.7	21.8
Women	48,691	12.6	14.9
By Race:			
Black	11,470	22.2	25.4
Hispanic	7,894	15.2	16.8
White	88,622	15.7	17.7
By Employer:			
Private	86,003	12.3	13.4
Government	17,476	36.7	43.6
By Occupation:			
Managerial and Professional	25,357	14.7	18.2
Technical, Sales, & Administrative	32,633	10.1	12.1
Service Occupations	14,410	13.5	15.1
Precision Production	11,906	26.3	28.2
Machine Operators, Transport, & Laborers	17,399	27.4	29.0

*In thousands.

Notes: Only employed workers counted. "Union Represented" includes union members and workers who are not union members but are represented by a union at their workplace.

Source: U.S. Bureau of Labor Statistics.

FEDERAL LABOR LEGISLATION

Several federal statutes regulate labor-management relations. However, the federal labor code, generally referred to as the *National Labor Relations Act* (NLRA), was enacted in three major phases: The Wagner Act in 1935, the Taft-Hartley Act in 1947, and the Landrum-Griffin Act in 1959. The public policy of the United States with regard to unions and union activities was first enunciated in the Norris-La Guardia Act of 1932.

Norris-La Guardia Act

Federal courts played an active role in labor-management relations before passage of the *Norris-La Guardia Act* in 1932. The courts showed little consistency in their decisions. Some courts held union activities to be criminal conspiracies, while others upheld the same activities as legitimate. In 1908, in the famous *Danbury Hatters* case, the Supreme Court held a union responsible for treble damages under the Sherman Act for organizing a boycott of retail stores that were selling hats produced by a manufacturer being struck by the union. The Clayton Act of 1914 tried to lessen the antitrust liabilities of unions, but the courts continued to thwart union activities.

The most common tactic of employers was to plead for a court injunction to stop union strikes, boycotts, and other activities. The Norris-La Guardia Act ended this widespread practice. The intent of the statute was to make the federal government neutral with respect to labor policy. Compared to past practices, this was a substantial benefit to union activity. The Act declared the public policy of the United States to be that the individual worker should "have full freedom of association, self-organization, and designation of representatives of his own choosing, to negotiate terms and conditions of his employment."

Injunctions Prohibited in Nonviolent Labor Disputes

The Norris-La Guardia Act generally prohibits federal courts from issuing injunctions in nonviolent *labor disputes,* thereby increasing the freedom of the unions to use economic force to compel the employer to share control over employment terms and conditions with the union. Specific acts not to be subject to federal court injunctions included *striking* or quitting work, belonging to a labor organization, paying strike or unemployment benefits to labor dispute participants, publicizing the existence of a labor dispute, picketing, peacefully assembling to promote interests in a labor dispute, and advising or causing others to do any of these acts without violence or fraud.

As the *Jacksonville Bulk Terminals, Inc. v. ILA* case illustrates, the Supreme Court gives broad meaning to what is held to be a labor dispute under the Norris-La Guardia Act. Besides limiting the ability of employers to seek injunctions to stop union activities, the Act also prohibited employers from requiring employees to sign *yellow-dog contracts.* Under such contracts employees agreed that joining a union was a contract violation that meant dismissal.

Jacksonville Bulk Terminals, Inc. v. ILA

United States Supreme Court
457 U.S. 702,
102 S.Ct. 2672
(1982)

Case Background. *To protest the invasion of Afghanistan, the longshoremen's union refused to load goods on ships bound for the Soviet Union. The shippers asked a federal judge to issue an injunction against the union. The shippers argued, and the judge agreed, that the work stoppage was about a political dispute, not a work-related issue. The decision of the judge was overturned by the Court of Appeals, which ruled in favor of the union. The shippers appealed to the Supreme Court.*

Case Decision. Justice Marshall delivered the opinion of the Court.

* * *

Section 4 of the Norris-La Guardia Act provides in part:

> No court of the United States shall have jurisdiction to issue any restraining order or temporary or permanent injunction in any case involving or growing out of any labor dispute to prohibit any person or persons participating or interested in such dispute . . . from doing, whether singly or in concert, any of the following acts:
> (a) Ceasing or refusing to perform any work or to remain in any relation of employment.

Congress adopted this broad prohibition to remedy the growing tendency of federal courts to enjoin strikes by narrowly construing the Clayton Act's labor exemption from the Sherman Act's prohibition against conspiracies to restrain trade. This Court has consistently given the anti-injunction provisions of the Norris-La Guardia Act a broad interpretation, recognizing exceptions only in limited situations where necessary to accommodate the Act to specific federal legislation or paramount congressional policy.

* * *

The language of the Norris-La Guardia Act does not except labor disputes having their genesis in political protests. Nor is there any basis in the statutory language for the argument that the Act requires that *each* dispute relevant to the case be a labor dispute. The Act merely requires that the case involve "any" labor dispute. Therefore, the plain terms of §4(a) and §13 of the Norris-La Guardia Act deprive the federal courts of the power to enjoin the Union's work stoppage in this . . . action, without regard to whether the Union also has a nonlabor dispute with another entity.

. . . Our decisions have recognized that the term "labor dispute" must not be narrowly construed because the statutory definition itself is extremely broad and because Congress deliberately included a broad definition to overrule judicial decisions that had unduly restricted the Clayton Act's labor exemption from the antitrust laws.

* * *

In essence, the Employer asks us to disregard the legislative history of the Act and to distort the definition of a labor dispute in order to reach what it believes to be an "equitable" result. The Employer's real complaint, however, is not with the Union's political objections to the conduct of the Soviet Union, but with what the Employer views as the Union's breach of contract. The Employer's frustration with this alleged breach of contract should not be remedied by characterizing it as other than a labor dispute. In the past, we have consistently declined to constrict Norris-La Guardia's broad prohibitions except in narrowly defined situations where accommodation of that Act to specific congressional policy is necessary. We refuse to deviate from that path today.

* * *

Case Holding. *The Supreme Court affirmed the decision of the court of appeals. The decision of the ILA to refuse to load ships bound for the Soviet Union as a protest to that country's invasion of Afghanistan constituted a legitimate labor dispute under the Norris-La Guardia Act.*

Case Questions

1. Given the Supreme Court's view of the scope of Norris-La Guardia coverage, can you think of a work stoppage likely to be halted by an injunction?
2. Since political issues may be the basis of union actions, as was obviously the case here, can unions use this power to try to force corporations to support their political agenda?
3. Did the employer in this case have any other legal course of action?

Wagner Act of 1935

The basic goal of the *Wagner Act* of 1935 (the National Labor Relations Act, or NLRA) was to provide employees with the right to "self-organization, to form, join, or assist labor organizations, to bargain collectively through representatives of their own choosing, and to engage in other concerted activities for the purpose of collective bargaining or other mutual aid or protection . . . ."

Creation of the NLRB

To achieve this goal, the legislation created the *National Labor Relations Board* (NLRB) to monitor unfair labor practices and assure that union representation elections were held in a fair manner. (The NLRB is more thoroughly discussed below.) The NLRB, however, does not regulate the substance of bargaining—the terms and conditions of employment—between employers and employees.

What Constitutes Unfair Labor Practices?

In general, *unfair labor practices* on the part of the employers are actions that would impair the basic goal of the Wagner Act. Set out in Section 8(a) of the Act, such practices include employer interference with employee rights guaranteed in Section 7; employer-formed or -dominated "company unions;" discrimination by employer on account of union activity in hiring, firing, or other matters of employment; discrimination by employer against employees who testify or file charges before the NLRB; and failure by employer to bargain collectively with the union of its employees.

The Taft-Hartley Act of 1947

The *Taft-Hartley Act* of 1947 (the Labor-Management Relations Act), which amended the NLRA, marked a change in federal policy from one of actively encouraging labor union formation to one of a favorable attitude toward unionization coupled with regulation.

Restricting Union Activities

This modification of the Wagner Act's unionization policy, however, did not change those activities held to be unfair labor practices on the part of employers, but it did restrict some unfair practices by unions. Specifically, the Taft-Hartley Act prohibits unions from the following activities:

1. Coercing employees with respect to their collective bargaining rights.
2. Refusing to bargain in good faith with employers about wages and working conditions.
3. Carrying out certain kinds of strikes, such as secondary boycotts; charging "excessive" union initiation fees or dues, or engaging in *featherbedding* (i.e., having employers pay for work not performed).

If an employer believes the union has acted in an unfair manner, the Taft-Hartley Act provides the employer with the right to file an unfair labor practice charge with the NLRB.

Employers and Union Elections

Union representation election rights were broadened by the Taft-Hartley Act. Section 8(c) of the Act gives employers the freedom to express their views about union organization to their employees, so long as they do not threaten employees who do not agree or promise certain benefits to workers who vote against the union. Further, employers can call for elections to decide the issue of representation. The use of such attempts to *decertify* unions—that is, to get a majority of the employees to vote to remove the union as their agent—has accelerated in recent years.

Collective Bargaining Agreements and Arbitration

Section 301 of the Taft-Hartley Act—which made *collective bargaining agreements* enforceable in federal court—has played a role in the growth of *grievance arbitration* clauses and the establishment of arbitration mechanisms in collective bargaining agreements. Under such clauses, disputes regarding a collective bargaining agreement—settled on by the employer and the union— are·to be resolved by an internal grievance procedure. If the result of these discussions is not satisfactory, the dispute between the union and the employer is heard by an outside labor arbitrator. If the arbitration decision is violated or is believed unjust by one of the parties, the parties may then go to federal court for relief. This was one of the points the Court made in the *Jacksonville Bulk Terminals* decision—the parties must exhaust established grievance procedures before bringing the dispute to court.

Over 90 percent of existing collective bargaining agreements contain such dispute resolution clauses. The federal courts have fashioned a body of substantive federal law encouraging the use of the grievance arbitration process. This has helped prevent the federal court system from being clogged with thousands of disputes.

Agency Shops and Political Action

The Taft-Hartley Act broadened the rights of prospective employees by prohibiting *closed shops*, whereby an employee must be a union member before going to work for an employer that has signed a collective bargaining agreement. Also prohibited are *union shops*—places of employment where being a member of the union is a condition of employment. *Agency shops*— places of employment where a majority of employees have voted to be represented by a union in a collective bargaining agreement—are legal. In an agency shop, employees who belong to the union pay union dues while nonunion employees pay agency fees. That is, nonunion employees have fees deducted from their paychecks that are given to the union to cover the costs of union services. Agency fees are lower than union dues.

The use of the fees paid by nonunion employees in agency shops has raised concerns regarding the constitutional rights of those employees. Of particular concern is the use of fees paid by nonunion employers to support union political activities unrelated to the union's duties as an exclusive bargaining representative. In *Chicago Teachers Union, Local No. 1 v. Hudson,* the Supreme Court presented a four-part test for determining whether the grievance procedure provided in an agency shop agreement regarding the use of fees adequately protects the constitutional rights of nonunion employees.

Chicago Teachers Union, Local No. 1 v. Hudson

Supreme Court of the United States
475 U.S. 292,
106 S.Ct. 1066
(1986)

Case Background. *Chicago teachers were covered by an agency shop agreement. Five percent of the teachers did not belong to the union. In 1982, the union and the Chicago Board of Education agreed, as a part of a collective bargaining agreement, that nonunion teachers would pay agency fees equal to 95 percent of regular union dues that the employer would deduct from paychecks to give to the union. According to grievance procedures agreed upon by the union and the employer, a teacher protesting payment of these fees could appeal to the union. If the union's response was unsatisfactory, the union would pick an arbitrator to settle the matter.*

Several nonunion teachers protested the fees and eventually sued the union and school board in federal court, claiming that their First Amendment rights to freedom of expression and association and their Fourteenth Amendment due process rights were violated. They also claimed that some of the agency fees they paid were devoted to impermissible purposes; that is, they were spent on union political activities. The district court rejected these claims. The Seventh Circuit Court of Appeals reversed, in favor of the nonunion teachers, holding that the established procedure was constitutionally inadequate. The Supreme Court granted certiorari.

Case Decision. Justice Stevens delivered the opinion for a unanimous Court.

* * *

In *Abood* v. *Detroit Board of Education* (1977), we recognized that requiring nonunion employees to support their collective-bargaining representative "has an impact upon their First Amendment interests," and may well "interfere in some way with an employee's freedom to associate for the advancement of ideas, or to refrain from doing so, as he sees fit." . . . We nevertheless rejected the claim that it was unconstitutional for a public employer to designate a union as the exclusive collective-bargaining representative of its employees, and to require nonunion employees, as a condition of employment, to pay a fair share of the union's cost of negotiating and administering a collective-bargaining agreement. We also held, however, that nonunion employees do have a constitutional right to "prevent the Union's spending a part of their required service fees to contribute to political candidates and to express political views unrelated to its duties as exclusive bargaining representative."

* * *

Procedural safeguards are necessary to achieve this objective for two reasons. First, although the government interest in labor peace is strong enough to support an "agency shop" notwithstanding its limited infringement on nonunion employees' constitutional rights, the fact that those rights are protected by the First Amendment requires that the procedure be carefully tailored to minimize the infringement. Second, the nonunion employee—the individual whose First Amendment rights are being affected—must have a fair opportunity to identify the impact of the governmental action on his interests and to assert a meritorious First Amendment claim.

* * *

The procedure that was initially adopted by the Union and considered by the District Court contained three fundamental flaws. First, a remedy which merely offers dissenters the possibility of a rebate does not avoid the risk that dissenters' funds may be used temporarily for an improper purpose. . . .

Second, the "advance reduction of dues" was inadequate because it provided nonmembers with inadequate information about the basis for the proportionate share . . . . Finally, the original Union procedure was also defective because it did not provide for a reasonably prompt decision by an impartial decisionmaker. Although we have not so specified in the past, we now conclude that such a requirement is necessary. The nonunion employee, whose First Amendment rights are affected by the agency shop itself and who bears the burden of objecting, is entitled to have his objections addressed in an expeditious, fair, and objective manner.

The Union's procedure does not meet this requirement. As the Seventh Circuit observed, the "most conspicuous feature of the procedure is that from start to finish it is entirely controlled by the union, which is an interested party, since it is the recipient of the agency fees paid by the dissenting employees."

* * *

Case Holding. *The decision of the court of appeals was affirmed. To allow nonunion members to determine that they are not paying support to union political activities that they do not want to support, the constitutional requirements for the Union's collection of agency fees include the following:*
1. *An adequate explanation of the basis for the fee.*
2. *A reasonably prompt explanation of the basis for the fee.*
3. *A reasonably prompt opportunity to challenge the amount of the fee before an impartial decisionmaker.*
4. *An escrow for the amounts reasonably in dispute while such challenges are pending.*

Case Questions

1. Does this decision weaken the standard procedure that requires the grievance procedure and arbitration procedure to be exhausted before going to federal court?

2. Does this decision reduce the likelihood that unions will be involved in political activities?

Right-to-Work

One of the most hotly contested features of Taft-Hartley is the provision that allows states to pass *right-to-work laws* that prohibit agency shops. Even if a majority of the employees vote for union representation and pay union initiation fees and dues, no employees can be required to pay agency fees, even though their wages and working conditions are determined by the collective bargaining agreement signed by the union on behalf of all employees. Since some employees receive the benefits of the union without paying dues, unions claim they are free riders. Right-to-work laws, in effect in twenty southern and western states, clearly retard the effectiveness of unions in such states.

Back-to-Work Orders

A President who believes that a threatened or existing strike affects a vital industry so as to imperil national health and safety may take steps to obtain a special court injunction (a *back-to-work order*) to postpone the strike for sixty days. A Taft-Hartley injunction against national emergency strikes may be extended for an extra twenty days, during which further steps are taken to try to resolve the dispute. If no resolution seems possible, the President may recommend to Congress that it take steps to force a settlement. Since the Act's passage in 1947, an average of one Taft-Hartley injunction per year has been used. Labor unions press for abolition of the law; businesses support its retention.

The Landrum-Griffin Act of 1959

The *Landrum-Griffin Act* of 1959 (Labor-Management Reporting and Disclosure Act), which amended the NLRA, started more detailed regulation of internal union affairs. Senate investigations had revealed the improper use of union funds and other problems in a few unions. Congress took action to assure that union members were protected from improper actions by union leaders.

Monitoring Union Leadership

Under the Landrum-Griffin Act, the financial status of unions is subject to federal review, and a report must be available to union members so that they know how their dues are used. Criminal penalties were established to punish union officials who betrayed the trust of their office. Penalties were also established to reduce incidences of employer wrongdoing—for example, bribing union officials or attempting to hold off union activities by other illegal means. Employers must report annually to the Secretary of Labor about company expenditures to attempt to influence collective bargaining activities.

Union Member Bill of Rights

A bill of rights for union members was included in the Landrum-Griffin Act. It provides for a more democratic procedure in the operation of unions than was previously being used. It provides for rights in such areas as nomination of candidates for union offices, fair election procedures, and participation in union business, subject to "reasonable" union rules. Union dues and fees are to be set by majority voting by the members. If a union member is to be disciplined by the union, procedural safeguards must be followed to protect the rights of the member, and no punishment may be inflicted on members who challenge union leadership or its actions. Further, members must be given copies of all collective bargaining agreements and be made aware of their rights under the Landrum-Griffin Act.

The Supreme Court applied this law in a 1989 decision, *Sheet Metal Workers' International Assn.* v. *Lynn*. In that case, the international union sent a trustee to supervise a local union that was facing financial difficulties. The head of the local union was removed from his position by the trustee after he spoke out at a union meeting against proposals recommended by the trustee. The Supreme Court held that removal from office in retaliation for the statements made violated the free speech rights guaranteed by the Landrum-Griffin Act. Regardless of the merits of the trustee's proposals, local union officers and members may not be punished for opposing the actions preferred by top union leadership.

THE NATIONAL LABOR RELATIONS BOARD

It is the NLRB's responsibility to administer the National Labor Relations Act (NLRA). The principal personnel of the NLRB include five board members, a General Counsel, regional directors, and administrative law judges. The board members and the General Counsel are appointed by the President with the consent of the Senate. The board acts as a quasi-judicial body to decide cases, generally upon review from decisions of regional directors or administrative law judges. The General Counsel is responsible for overseeing the investigation and prosecution of unfair labor practice charges and for representing the NLRB in court. Headquartered in Washington, D.C., the NLRB has thirty-three regional offices and sixteen smaller field offices located throughout the country.

Jurisdiction of the NLRB

The NLRB has jurisdiction over all employers engaged in interstate commerce and all employees where a labor dispute would affect interstate commerce. The NLRB has, however, refused to assert its jurisdiction over small employers whose businesses are of a local character. Also, certain classes of employees are not covered by the NLRA. Specifically excluded are federal, state, and municipal employees (the public sector); supervisors; managers; independent contractors; employees of railroads and airlines (covered by the Railway Labor Act of 1926); domestic servants; and agricultural laborers.

NLRB Complaint Procedure

Over 50,000 cases a year are filed with the NLRB. The large majority of those cases involve charges of *unfair labor practice*. Over the years, charges filed against employers have outnumbered those filed against unions almost two to one. Each NLRB case, whether it involves an unfair labor practice or a matter of representation, must be initiated by a private party, such as an individual worker, a union, or an employer.

Most unfair labor practice casework is done in the field, through the regional offices, and involves the following process. Charges of unfair labor practices are filed at field offices, where they are then investigated. If the investigation shows that the case is meritorious, the regional director will file a complaint.

About two-thirds of the charges filed do not lead to a complaint being filed, as they are either dismissed by the regional director or withdrawn by the complaining party when informed of their probable lack of success. Of the charges that do lead to a complaint, over 80 percent are settled before a hearing takes place.

An administrative law judge presides over complaints that are heard. After taking evidence and receiving briefs, the judge will issue a recommended decision and order. The recommended order either sets out the appropriate remedy or suggests that the complaint be dismissed. Unless one of the parties involved files an exception, the judge's decision becomes final.

If an exception to the decision is filed, the case is heard in Washington by a panel of three board members if the case is routine, or by the entire board if the case is considered particularly important. Board members hear no evidence and see no witnesses; in that sense they are similar to an appellate court. Board members issue decisions in about 1,600 cases a year.

If one of the parties refuses to accept the board's decision, the case will be referred to the U.S. Court of Appeals for enforcement or review of the order. Most decisions of the board referred to the Court of Appeals are upheld. In rare instances, the case may be taken for final review by the U.S. Supreme Court.

Selection of a Bargaining Representative

A major responsibility of the NLRB is to determine whether employees want to be represented by a union. Section 7 of the NLRA focuses on the right of employees to "self-organization, to form, join, or assist labor organizations." To ensure that the employees' right of self-organization can be exercised effectively, the NLRB has rules governing employer and union conduct.

Movement to Unionization

If the employees of a company are not represented by a union, a move to unionize might be brought about either by some interested employees who contact a union for assistance or by a union agent who contacts the company's employees to determine if interest exists. The union undertakes an organization drive. A committee of employees is formed and, with the help of a union organizer, calls informational meetings and distributes information.

Representation Elections

If the union collects *authorization cards* from 30 percent or more of the employees asking the union to be their agent in collective bargaining (the cards are kept secret from the employer), it turns the cards over to the NLRB and requests a *representation election.* The election will determine whether a majority of the employees want a particular union as their agent. Some employees sign authorization cards but do not vote to have the union as their bargaining agent. During the past decade, unions won less than half of the representation elections. As employers have become more sophisticated in responding to union challenges, the trend over time has been against unions.

The NLRB-regulated election will be preceded by a campaign in which the union tells the workers of the benefits of unionization and management tells the workers the benefits the company already provides without a union. The company is prohibited from threatening those who favor unionization, nor may it promise, say, a 10 percent pay raise if the workers defeat the union. Rather, the company must argue in more general terms, with discussions limited to possible problems with unionization.

Union Certification

NLRB agents supervise the actual election, which is often held at the workplace. Shortly after the election is held, the NLRB certifies the results. If more than 50 percent of the employees vote for the union, it will be *certified* by the NLRB as the exclusive *bargaining agent* for all employees at the workplace and must be recognized as such by the company.

Employer Responses to Union Organizing

When Congress enacted the Wagner Act in 1935, it used broad language to declare it illegal for an employer to interfere with, restrain, or coerce employees in the exercise of the rights to organize and bargain collectively. However, employer conduct may be lawful if it advances a substantial and legitimate employer interest in plant safety, efficiency, or discipline. Thus, courts and the NLRB must strike a balance between these interests of the employer and the interests of the employees in a free decision concerning union participation and activities.

Union Solicitation on Company Property

The NLRB and the courts accommodate the interests of employees in gaining access to union communications and employers' interest in managing business. As a general rule, the NLRB and the courts will not permit access to company property by outside organizers.

In 1956, the Supreme Court reviewed *NLRB* v. *Babcock & Wilcox Co.,* a case that concerned access to the company's property by individuals not employed by the company who wanted to distribute union handbills to the employees. The employer barred this *solicitation*, just as it had barred all other solicitations. The Court held that this solicitation ban was legitimate and noted that

> An employer may validly post his property against nonemployee distribution of union literature if reasonable efforts by the union through other available channels of communication will enable it to reach the employees with its message and if the employer's notice or order does not discriminate against the union by allowing other distribution.

An employer will often impose a company rule banning employee solicitation or distribution of literature on company property. In *Republic Aviation Corp.* v. *NLRB* (1945), the Supreme Court examined the legality of restrictions on solicitations by employees on behalf of a union. A no-solicitation rule had been adopted by the employer before the advent of the union. After examining the no-solicitation rule, the Court sustained the NLRB's conclusion that the rule was an illegal "restraint, interference, or coercion." The Court stated "that if a rule against solicitation is [enforced] as to union solicitation on the employer's premises during the employees' own time, a discharge because of violation of that rule discriminates . . . in that it discourages membership in a labor organization." That is, during breaks and before and after work, employees may talk to other employees about the benefits of unionization on the employer's property.

Employer Communications

One of the most controversial aspects of union organizing involves what employers may say during union election campaigns. Section 8(c) of the NLRA provides:

> The expressing of any views, argument, or opinion or the dissemination thereof, whether in written, printed, graphic, or visual form, shall not constitute or be evidence of an unfair labor practice under any of the provisions of this Act, if such expression contains no threat of reprisal or force or promise of benefit.

However, as the Golub case illustrates, interpreting the precise limits of Section 8(c) has not been a simple matter.

NLRB v. Golub Corporation
United States Court of Appeals, Second Circuit
388 F.2d 921 (1967)

Case Background. *During a union representation campaign, the employer made speeches and sent letters to the employees predicting that the union might make excessive demands on the company, and that companies forced to meet excessive union demands are sometimes forced to go out of business or to cut back on the number of employees. The NLRB held these statements to be "threats of reprisal" and illegal and sought enforcement in the Second Circuit Court of Appeals.*

Case Decision. Circuit Judge Friendly delivered the opinion of the Court.

* * *

[T]he basic issue is whether an employer coerces his employees in the exercise of §7 rights, as forbidden by §8(a)(1), when he prophesies that unionization will decrease or wholly eliminate work opportunities, increase work loads, or create greater rigidity in personnel relationships, or whether such predictions come within the protection §8(c) affords to the expression "of any views, argument or opinion, or the dissemination thereof . . . if such expression contains no threat of reprisal or force or promise of benefit." While the answer would seem easy enough, the trend of Board decisions toward ever increasing restrictions on employer speech makes it desirable to attain perspective by a brief historical survey.

* * *

In the light of this history and the Supreme Court's more recent warning of the dangers of ever finding an unfair labor practice in employer argument alone, see *NLRB* v. *Exchange Parts Co.* (1964), we find the approach here taken unacceptable. In holding the passages we have cited to be violations, the Trial Examiner stated simply that "the letters and speech . . . were calculated to create and instill in the minds of employees a fear of loss of privileges and economic suffering as a result of their adherence to the Union, and constituted interferences, restraint, and coercion within the meaning of Section 8(a)(1) of the Act." This is reading the Act as if §8(c) did not exist; while there is a risk that an employer's prediction of adverse consequences from unionization may be taken as a threat to produce them, to hold that this danger alone suffices to convert a prediction into a threat of reprisal would go back to the very position of the early 1940's which §8(c) was adopted to change.

* * *

The error of the Board in finding violations of the Act in the two passages . . . predicting loss of work, harder work, or even a close-down as a result of unionization is apparent. Nothing in these communications could reasonably be interpreted as a threat to make the employees' lot harder in retaliation for their voting for the union . . . . The only fair reading is that the employer would take these steps solely from economic necessity and with regret.

* * *

Congress did not intend the Board to act as a censor of the reasonableness of statements by either party to a labor controversy even if it constitutionally could.

* * *

Case Holding. *The NLRB's request to have its order enforced is denied. An employer's prediction of adverse consequences from unionization is not sufficient to constitute an illegal threat of reprisal.*

Case Questions

1. Would it have been illegal for the employer to tell employees that if they voted to unionize the company would, in fact, close, meaning that everyone would be fired?
2. Does this decision allow employers to use coded language to threaten employees indirectly rather than directly?

Collective Bargaining

Once employees choose a bargaining representative, that representative—the union—is now the legal representative of the employees. The employer must bargain with the union. The term *collective bargaining* refers to the process by which the employer and the union negotiate a contract, setting forth the terms and conditions of employment for a given period of time. Collective bargaining is more than the initial contract negotiation; it is the entire process of contract administration resulting in a continuous relationship between the employer and the employee representative.

Defining Good Faith Bargaining

The duty to bargain in good faith is defined in Section 8(d) of the NLRA as follows:

> [T]o bargain collectively is the performance of the mutual obligation of the employer and the representative of the employees to meet at reasonable times and confer in good faith with respect to wages, hours, and other terms and conditions of employment, or the negotiation of an agreement, or any question arising thereunder, and the execution of a written contract incorporating any agreement reached if requested by either party, but such obligation does not compel either party to agree to a proposal or require the making of a concession. . . .

The principal difficulty lies in defining what is good faith, since it can involve trying to interpret another's state of mind. Essentially, *good faith* means an obligation to meet and be willing to present proposals and explain reasons, to listen to and consider the proposals of the other party, and to search for some common ground that can serve as the basis for an agreement—but with no requirement of an agreement.

So long as no unfair labor practices are used by the employer or the union, even if it appears that bitterness exists, the use of legal labor practices will not be seen as a failure to bargain in good faith. In general, the Supreme Court has indicated that it is best that the NLRB and the courts not become too involved in the details of labor practices in the bargaining process, since Congress did not intend for direct intervention in the substance of labor bargains. Rather, Congress took the position that the parties should be free to reach an agreement of their own making.

Actions Not in Good Faith

Certain actions are recognized as a failure to bargain in good faith. For example, in *NLRB* v. *Katz* in 1962, the Supreme Court said that an employer cannot unilaterally change the terms of an existing agreement with a union. To increase or decrease employment terms—wages or benefits—without consulting the union may be held to be a bad faith attempt to convince the workers that they do not need the union or to create confusion in bargaining. In remedying bad faith bargaining, the NLRB is limited to issuing a cease and desist order; it cannot insert a clause into a collective bargaining agreement.

Mandatory Subjects of Bargaining

Section 8(d) of the NLRA states that bargaining in good faith must occur with respect to "wages, hours, and other terms and conditions of employment." These are *mandatory subjects*, about which employers and unions must bargain in good faith, but about which either party may insist on its position and back that insistence with a strike or a lockout. An ongoing controversy exists, however, as to what types of topics actively fall within this mandatory bargaining category. A major Supreme Court case on the subject is *First National Maintenance Corporation* v. *NLRB*.

First National Maintenance Corp. v. NLRB

United States Supreme Court
452 U.S. 666,
101 S.Ct. 2573
(1981)

Case Background. *First National Maintenance was a commercial cleaning company. One of its customers had a dispute with First National that caused First National to stop providing cleaning services for the customer's buildings. As a result, First National cut its work force, which was unionized. The union complained to the NLRB that the employer had to negotiate with the union before it could make such a decision that resulted in lost jobs for union members. The NLRB and the U.S. Court of Appeals agreed that the union was right—an employer was subject to mandatory bargaining under the NLRA for decisions that resulted in lost jobs. First National appealed to the U.S. Supreme Court.*

Case Decision.   Justice Blackmun delivered the opinion of the Court.

* * *

Congress deliberately left the words "wages, hours, and other terms and conditions of employment" without further definition, for it did not intend to deprive the Board of the power further to define those terms in light of specific industrial practices.

Nonetheless, in establishing what issues must be submitted to the process of bargaining, Congress had no expectation that the elected union representative would become an equal partner in the running of the business enterprise in which the union's members are employed. Despite the deliberate open-endedness of the statutory language, there is an undeniable limit to the subjects about which bargaining must take place.

* * *

Some management decisions, such as choice of advertising and promotion, product type and design, and financing arrangements; have only an indirect and attenuated impact on the employment relationship. Other management decisions, such as the order of succession of layoffs and recalls, production quotas, and work rules, are almost exclusively "an aspect of the relationship" between employer and employee. The present case concerns a third type of management decision, one that had a direct impact on employment, since jobs were inexorably eliminated by the termination, but had as its focus only the economic profitability of the contract with Greenpark, a concern under these facts wholly apart from the employment relationship. This decision, involving a change in the scope and direction of the enterprise, is akin to the decision whether to be in business at all, "not in [itself] primarily about conditions of employment, though the effect of the decision may be necessarily to terminate employment."

* * *

Both union and management regard control of the decision to shut down an operation with the utmost seriousness. As has been noted, however, the Act is not intended to serve either party's individual interest, but to foster in a neutral manner a system in which the conflict between these interests may be resolved. It seems particularly important, therefore, to consider whether requiring bargaining over this sort of decision will advance the neutral purposes of the Act.

* * *

Management's interest in whether it should discuss a decision of this kind is much more complex and varies with the particular circumstances. If labor costs are an important factor in a failing operation and the decision to close, management will have an incentive to confer voluntarily with the union to seek concessions that may make continuing the business profitable. At other times, management may have great need for speed, flexibility, and secrecy in meeting business opportunities and exigencies. It may face significant tax or securities consequences that hinge on confidentiality, the timing of a plant closing, or a reorganization of the corporate structure. The publicity incident to the normal process of bargaining may injure the possibility of a successful transition or increase the economic damage to the business. The employer also may have no feasible alternative to the closing, and even good-faith bargaining over it may both be futile and cause the employer additional loss.

There is an important difference, also, between permitted bargaining and mandated bargaining. Labeling this type of decision mandatory could afford a union a powerful tool for achieving delay, a power that might be used to thwart management's intentions in a manner unrelated to any feasible solution the union might propose.

* * *

Case Holding. *The judgment of the court of appeals was reversed. The harm likely to be done to an employer's need to operate freely in deciding whether to shut down part of its business purely for economic reasons outweighs the incremental benefit that might be gained through the union's participation in making the decision. This decision is not part of Section 8(d)'s terms and condition over which Congress has mandated bargaining.*

Case Questions
1. Would this decision allow a firm to shut down part of its operation just to get rid of some union employees and then start up again?
2. Several states have considered legislation that would limit the ability of firms to cease operations at will. Would this benefit all workers or just some?

Employers and unions are free to bargain over any topics they agree to discuss. Among the topics that may be placed on the bargaining table because they have been determined by the NLRB or the courts to be subject to mandatory bargaining are the following:

- Pay rate
- Insurance plans
- Holidays
- Overtime pay
- Vacations
- Retirement plans
- Work hours
- Individual merit raises
- Breaks and lunch periods
- Safety practices
- Seniority rights

- Discipline procedures
- Termination procedures
- Layoff procedures
- Recall rights
- Union dues collection
- Grievance procedures
- Arbitration procedures
- No-strike clauses
- Drug testing
- Christmas bonuses

There is no requirement that every such issue be covered in a collective bargaining contract, only that the employer must consider demands about such issues raised by the union. In the event of a stalemate between the employer and the union, a private arbitrator may be called in to help get the talks going, or either party may request the assistance of the Federal Mediation and Conciliation Service. These negotiators have no authority to impose a settlement, but often help the parties reach a settlement.

Concerted Activities

For productive collective bargaining to occur, both the employer and the union must be able to back up their positions. Both parties insist on a position and then can back it up with a strike, lockout, or some other activity that brings economic pressure to bear on the other party. Essentially, these are economic weapons to pressure the opposing party to meet demands. To promote productive collective bargaining, Congress provided that certain activities would be protected so that the parties could effectively support their bargaining demands.

Definition of Concerted Activities

Section 7 of the NLRA protects the rights of employees to engage in *concerted activities* for mutual aid or protection. Usually protected concerted activity involves union organizing efforts. However, concerted activity also involves any joint actions by employees, such as a refusal to work on a certain job because of hazards above that which the employees believe safe or because of other poor working conditions that endanger health or safety. The concerted activity may be by a single worker. That is, one worker may try to get fellow workers to join in some activity. Even if the worker is unsuccessful, the activity is protected.

Unprotected Activities

If workers engage in threats or acts of violence, they will not be protected by the law and the employer may discipline or fire them. The Supreme Court has held that employers may fire employees for insubordination, disobedience, or disloyalty unless the reason for such activity involves protected concerted activity. That is, the worker may not be fired for engaging in a union-organizing activity the employer feels to be disloyal. However, a worker who simply attacks the company in public without tying the attack to a union issue may be disciplined or fired.

That concerted activity by employees is protected whether or not a union is involved was made clear by the Supreme Court in *NLRB* v. *Washington Aluminum Co.* (1962). In that case seven employees, who did not belong to a union, left work without permission because the furnace at their plant was broken; it was eleven degrees outside and very cold in the plant. The company fired the workers, claiming they had to make specific demands to which the company could respond, rather than just walk out. The Court held that activities by employees for the purpose of protecting themselves from intolerable working conditions is a concerted activity protected by the NLRA. The decision to walk out was reasonable given the conditions, so the workers could not be fired.

Employer Economic Responses

Although employers are not permitted to retaliate against employees for engaging in protected concerted activities, they have the right to exercise their own economic weapons and to take actions necessary to promote their business interests. In a labor dispute, an employer may decide to use a lockout against the employees. A *lockout* occurs when an employer attempts to bring economic pressure on a union by refusing to permit employees to work until the dispute is settled.

Lockouts are legal in some instances. So long as evidence of bad intent is not shown, such as trying to break the union or punish the workers, an employer's choice to shut down operations will be upheld. However, the employer cannot then allow new workers or strikebreakers to work in place of those workers locked out. Such a move is an unfair labor practice. Rather, the lockout must essentially be *defensive*. It must be done in response to a strike or to prevent a sitdown strike in the plant or to prevent some other activity that would be destructive to the plant or its materials. So long as the lockout is seen as promoting the settlement of the collective bargaining process and is not intended to be destructive to the union or the rights of the worker, it should be upheld as legal.

A tactic successfully used by companies in recent years is the hiring of nonunion workers to replace striking workers. Once a collective bargaining agreement expires, if the union and the employer have not agreed to a new contract, and the union calls for a strike, the employer is free to hire new (nonunion) workers and to keep using existing workers who will cross the picket line ("crossovers"). In some cases, the strike went on so long, and there were enough new hires and crossovers, that the union simply disappeared or lost substantial strength by the time a new agreement was signed. This was particularly true in the airline industry, as illustrated by the *TWA* case, where deregulation forced firms to be much more cost-conscious than they had been in earlier years.

Trans World Airlines v. Independent Federation of Flight Attendants

United States Supreme Court
489 U.S. 425,
109 S.Ct. 1225
(1989)

Case Background. *TWA and the flight attendants union began bargaining in March 1984 on a new collective bargaining agreement to replace the contract that expired in July 1984. By March 1986 attendants were still working under the old contract and a strike was called. TWA announced that it intended to keep in operation and would hire permanent replacements for striking attendants, but that it welcomed attendants who crossed the picket line to continue working. One-quarter of the 5,000 attentdants continued to work and TWA hired 2,350 new attendants. When the strike was settled after seventy-two days with a new contract, TWA recalled only 197 of the striking attendants. By May 1988 only 1,100 strikers had been recalled—all with full seniority.*

The union sued, claiming (1) that it was an unfair labor practice to hire new attendants and (2) even if hiring the new attendants was legal, the striking attendants had to be hired back because they had more seniority than the newly hired attendants. The District Court upheld TWA's policy; the Court of Appeals reversed in favor of the union. The Supreme Court reviewed the matter.

Case Decision. Justice O'Connor delivered the opinion of the Court.

* * *

While the employer and union in many circumstances may reach a back-to-work agreement that would displace crossovers and new hires or an employer may unilaterally decide to permit such displacement, nothing in the NLRA or the federal common law we have developed under that statute requires such a result. That such agreements are typically one mark of a successful strike is yet another indication that crossovers opted not to gamble; if the strike was successful the advantage gained by declining to strike disappears.

* * *

[T]he decision to guarantee to crossovers the same protections lawfully applied to new hires was a simple decision to apply the preexisting seniority terms of the collective bargaining agreement uniformly to all working employees. That this decision had the effect of encouraging prestrike workers to remain on the job during the strike or to abandon the strike and return to work before all vacancies were filled was an effect of the exercise of TWA's peaceful economic power, a power that the company was legally free to deploy once the parties had exhausted the private dispute resolution mechanisms . . . .

Case Holding. *The decision of the Court of Appeals was reversed. An employer is not required to lay off junior crossover employees or newly hired employees in order to reinstate more senior employees who were on strike.*

Case Questions

1. If the collective bargaining agreement provides for preference based on seniority, as was the case here, why would the senior attendants who had been on strike not have preference in hiring?
2. Can employers use this tactic to "break" a union?

UNLAWFUL LABOR ACTIVITIES

Various strikes and forms of picketing by employees can be unlawful under the NLRA or other state and federal labor laws. If picketing involves violence or threats of violence and the union is held responsible for the actions, it is an unfair labor practice. There are also various state laws against such violent acts. However, the fact that union members are involved does not necessarily mean that the union is at fault. Such acts must be based on union policy or occur at the behest of union leaders. Also, a strike can be an unfair labor practice if it violates an NLRB rule or the union's collective bargaining agreement.

Secondary Boycotts

The most important restrictions on strikes are limitations on *secondary boycotts*. No clear definition of secondary boycott exists, nor is it certain as to which forms of such activities are clearly legal or illegal. A *primary boycott*—the strike or other concerted action by a union against the employer of the employees whose collective bargaining agreement is in question—is clearly legal. In general, a secondary boycott occurs when one tries to force others to stop doing business with another employer not directly involved in the primary labor dispute.

Illegal Activities

As we will see, some secondary activities are legal, but the following forms are illegal:

1. Engaging in a strike against or refusing to handle goods or perform services for—or inducing workers to strike against or refuse to handle goods or perform services for—an employer other than the one involved in the primary labor dispute.

2. Threatening, coercing, or restraining any person engaged in commerce— usually an employee—in an effort to spread the dispute beyond the primary employer.

An example is a strike that would force an employer to engage in a secondary boycott of other employers. Such a tactic is used to try to force firms to cease business with another firm that the union is trying to unionize or force into a certain agreement. For example, in a strike against a plant owned by the food manufacturer Hormel, the union picketed seven banks, only three of which did business directly with Hormel. The NLRB ruled that the union could not picket any of the banks since none were involved in the distribution of Hormel products. The picketing was an illegal secondary boycott.

On the other hand, the Supreme Court noted that a labor agreement written to prevent employers from dealing with certain other firms that could lead to a loss of jobs of employees at the unionized firms is legal—even though the contract affected secondary parties—because the agreement was between the employer and employees of the primary firms.

It is also illegal to strike to force an employer to bargain with a union when another union has been certified by the NLRB as the representative of the employees. If any one of these activities occurs, the NLRB is supposed to seek an injunction in federal court to force an end to the activity, and the employer or party that has been hurt by the act may sue for losses incurred by the boycott.

In another series of cases, the Supreme Court has noted that it is illegal for a state or local government to intrude in labor disputes that are subject to the NLRA. For example, in the 1986 decision *Golden State Transit Corp.* v. *City of Los Angeles*, a taxi company licensed by the City of Los Angeles was being struck by its drivers. The City, attempting to support the drivers' strike, told the taxi company that it would not renew its license to operate unless it settled with the union. The Court said that for states to impose additional restrictions on either party in a legal labor dispute conflicts with congressional intent regarding labor law.

Legal Activities

An exception to secondary boycotts or strikes against firms that do business with the primary employer occurs when the *ally doctrine* may be invoked. Because of a strike, an employer may be able to complete only part of the production process. An agreement is then reached with another firm to take the partly completed product and finish it for marketing. A picket around the firm that agrees to finish the product would be legal, even though it is secondary, because the firm has become an ally of the primary employer only because of the strike. When another employer becomes an ally because of a strike, the union may picket and ask the employees of the ally of the primary employer to go on strike in support of the primary strike. When another employer is neutral, its employees should not be encouraged to join in the strike.

One way to make a strike more effective is to get cooperation from the customers of the employer. A customer might be another firm or it might be the public. A union may make a peaceful request to other firms or the public not to buy certain products. That is a right of free speech, just as is the right to picket a store peacefully to provide customers with information about certain products sold at the store that the union would like to see the public stop buying. For example, in the Supreme Court case *Edward J. DeBartolo Corp.* v. *Florida Gulf Coast Building & Construction Trades Council* (1988), it was held legal for the union to pass out leaflets at a shopping mall urging customers not to shop there because of a labor dispute between the union and a construction company building a store at the mall.

EMPLOYMENT-AT-WILL

The traditional common-law rule is that employees serve their employer at will. That is, employers are free to discharge employees for any reason at any time, and employees are free to quit their jobs for any reason at any time. The *employment-at-will* doctrine is, of course, limited by contract terms, such as terms of a collective bargaining agreement or any other contract that specifies length, terms, and conditions of employment. Many employees, especially those in managerial and supervisory positions, are clearly at will in employment. Although there is little evidence that this produces abuse on a large scale, cases do arise in which an employee's dismissal strikes many people as unjust.

Public Policy Exceptions

In a 1986 case, the Arizona Supreme Court joined the courts of many other states in chipping away at the strength of the employment at-will doctrine. The court noted that there are *public policy exceptions* to at-will discharges for acts that public policy encourages or for refusal to do an act that public policy condemns. In the majority of states, employees may not be terminated at will for the following:

1. Refusing to commit an illegal act (such as falsifying reports required by a government agency).
2. Performing an important public duty (such as reporting for jury duty when called).
3. Exercising a public right (such as filing a claim for workers' compensation).

The Arizona court decided to join several other states to allow a fourth exception on grounds of public policy, called the *whistle-blower* exception. This occurs when an employee who is aware of an illegal act at the place of employment brings the act to the attention of the proper authorities even though the employee was not legally responsible for the act in question. Because this treads on new ground, more cases can be expected to test the limits of this rule. The general test is that the whistle blowing is primarily for the public good—to enhance law enforcement and to expose unsafe conditions—rather than primarily for private gain—to get one's boss fired to get his or her job.

Not all states accept the first three exceptions. In a 1987 case in North Carolina, the dismissal of an employee who refused to help falsify records required by the Food and Drug Administration was upheld. Further, as the *Geary* case illustrates, an exception to the at-will rule is not created to protect employers from unfair dismissals.

Geary v. United States Steel Corporation

Supreme Court of Pennsylvania
456 Pa. 171,
319 A.2d 174
(1974)

Case Background. *George Geary worked for U.S. Steel, selling steel pipe, from 1953 to 1967. Geary discovered that a new type of pipe was defective and could cause injury and damage. His supervisor ignored his comments and told him to "follow directions." Geary then went to a vice-president with his concerns about the pipe. The pipe was evaluated and removed from the market. Geary was fired. He sued the company for damages for loss of reputation, mental distress, and financial harm from a wrongful discharge. The lower courts ruled for the company. Geary appealed to the Supreme Court of Pennsylvania.*

Case Decision.   Justice Pomeroy delivered the opinion of the Court.

* * *

. . . [T]he broad question to which appellant invites our attention is whether the time has come to impose judicial restrictions on an employer's power of discharge.

* * *

In essence, Geary argues that his conduct should be protected because his intentions were good. No doubt most employees who are dismissed from their posts can make the same claim. We doubt that establishing a right to litigate every such case as it arises would operate either in the best interest of the parties or of the public.

Given the rapidity of change in corporate personnel in the areas of employment not covered by labor agreements, suits like the one at bar could well be expected to place a heavy burden on our judicial system in terms of both an increased case load and the thorny problems of proof which would inevitably be presented.

* * *

Of greater concern is the possible impact of such suits to the legitimate interest of employers in hiring and retaining the best personnel available. The everpresent threat of suit might well inhibit the making of critical judgments by employers concerning employee qualifications.

The problem extends beyond the question of individual competence, for even an unusually gifted person may be of no use to his employer if he cannot work effectively with fellow employees. Here, for example, Geary's complaint shows that he by-passed his immediate superiors and pressed his views on higher officers, utilizing his close contacts with a company vice-president.

The praiseworthiness of Geary's motives does not detract from the company's legitimate interest in preserving its normal operational procedures from disruption. In sum, while we agree that employees should be encouraged to express their educated views on the quality of their employer's products, we are not persuaded that creating a new nonstatutory cause of action of the sort proposed by appellant is the best way to achieve this result. On balance, whatever public policy imperatives can be discerning here seem to militate against such a course.

* * *

Roberts, Justice (dissenting).

* * *

As a salesman, Geary was required to know intimately the products he was selling. He represented United States Steel and it was expected that he would be alert to protect his employer's reputation. Likewise, it was natural that he would seek to shield himself and his employer from the consequences of a dangerous product. When he correctly recognized that the defective steel pipe had strong potential for causing injury and damage, he immediately notified his superiors. His reward for loyalty was dismissal. Of course, had Geary not informed his superiors of the defective product, he may well have been discharged for his failure to do so.

Geary's assessment of the danger of the steel pipe was correct, since after his notification, the corporation removed the steel pipe from the market. On these pleadings, it is manifestly clear that the employer realized Geary was right and that its interest lay in withdrawing from the market the dangerous product. Despite Geary's candor in seeking within the corporate family to advance the corporation's best interest, his employer fired him.

This Court should, in my view, fulfill its societal role and its responsibility to the public interest by recognizing a cause of action for wrongful discharge where the dismissal offends public policy. George B. Geary has presented just such a case.

Case Holding. *The decision of the lower court is affirmed. The company has a legitimate interest in preserving its normal operating procedures from the disruptions by its employees regardless of the employee's motivations. The court does not recognize a nonstatutory cause of action for wrongful discharge.*

Case Questions

1. Suppose the dissenting opinion was the majority opinion. Would this lead to a breakdown in managerial control within firms, as employees felt free to go over their supervisors' heads to take real or imagined problems further up the line?

2. Should there be different treatment of such cases between the person who uncovers a problem and keeps the complaint within the company and the one who goes public with the complaint?

Use of Employee Handbooks

Many employers issue handbooks to employees explaining company policy, benefits, and procedures. Many cases are in process to determine the extent to which such manuals are enforceable in court. As the Supreme Court of Illinois noted in a 1987 case, most courts now hold *employee handbooks* to create binding contractual obligations—if one can show the elements of offer, acceptance, and consideration in the employment process. That is, if the employer makes it clear to employees that the rules in the handbook are to be followed and if the handbook discusses proper termination procedure, employees have a right to have that procedure followed. If the handbook says that employees can be dismissed only for "good cause," most courts now hold that that dismissal is no longer at will. If a firm experiences a downturn in business and fires one-third of its employees—is that "good cause"? Yes, because it is a valid business reason, not a dismissal on the whim of a supervisor.

These cases make it clear that companies must be much more thoughtful in writing employee handbooks than many have been in the past. Since the courts are turning more often to those handbooks as binding conditions of the employment process, the handbooks should be written with some legal precision so as not to open the door to needless litigation.

Of even greater concern to employers are decisions like the 1986 Montana Supreme Court case that upheld a $1.3 million punitive damage verdict against a bank that fired an employee of twenty-eight years. The court said that because the employee had been given no clue that her job performance was unsatisfactory, she had an expectation of continued employment that had been violated. The possibility of the extension of such cases into other states again makes it clear that employers should specify terms and conditions of employment even if employment is simply to be at will.

The California Supreme Court joined a number of other courts in holding that punitive damages for wrongful dismissal should be rare. In a 1988 case, that court upheld the rights of employees to sue employers for breach of an employment contract, whether it is written, verbal, or implied. However, the court concluded that because "the employment relationship is fundamentally contractual . . ., contractual remedies should remain the sole available relief for breaches of . . . good faith and fair dealing in the employment context." Therefore, when an employee has a valid claim of a breach of a employment contract, the damages will be compensatory (primarily lost wages).

INTERNATIONAL PERSPECTIVES: EMPLOYMENT CONTRACTS IN EUROPE

INTERNATIONAL

PERSPECTIVES

The notion of employment-at-will is foreign to Europeans. Not only is unionization more common in Europe, which takes more employees out of the employment-at-will sector, but most nonunion employees have written employment contracts. Much of this has been forced on companies by law in Britain, France, Germany, and elsewhere that specify maternity-leave benefits and other conditions that are not subject to legislative control in the United States.

For example, in most European countries and in Japan, if an employer fires a worker, it must pay the worker severance pay for perhaps as long as a year at up to 90 percent of the worker's wage. Hence, there is little incentive to fire workers—and not much incentive for workers who are fired to look for another job quickly.

SUBSTANCE ABUSE

Some abused substances, like cocaine, are illegal; others, like Valium, are legal but are dispensed illegally. Because of the illegality, the full extent of the problem is unknown. The most common abused substance is alcohol. The

National Institute of Mental Health reports the 13.6 percent of all adults have experienced alcohol addiction or abuse in their lives. About 8 percent of the working population are alcoholics, that is, abusers of a legal drug that is legally dispensed. Add to this the estimated 5 to 10 percent of the adult population that are abusers (addicts) of illegal drugs and of improperly dispensed drugs, and it means that about one in six working-age people have a substance-abuse problem.

Practical Problem for Business

Tragic stories about lives ruined by substance abuse are common. Substance abuse directly affects employers primarily because it means reduced productivity and higher medical insurance costs, which cost employers well over $100 billion per year. The National Institute on Alcoholism and Alcohol Abuse estimates that the average health-care (insurance) costs for families with an alcoholic are double the costs incurred by families with no alcoholics. The huge cost of substance abuse obscures the costs imposed by another widely used, highly addictive legal drug, nicotine, which also reduces productivity and increases medical expenses.

Unexpected Consequences

The oil spill caused by the wreck of the Exxon *Valdez* off the Alaska coast in 1989 raised issues beyond environmental liability, because it appears to have been a problem directly related to substance abuse. The captain of the ship had a history of alcohol abuse and was found guilty of operating the ship under the influence of alcohol. While he suffered a small legal penalty for his action, Exxon suffered over a billion dollars in costs. The company subsequently announced that all known alcohol and drug abusers, even after treatment, would not be allowed to return to critical duties such as piloting a ship or operating a refinery. Such workers would be given less sensitive—and less productive—assignments. Obviously, if Exxon had understood all the factors that could produce that environmental catastrophe it would have taken steps to avoid it.

The problem was not unique to that incident. The U.S. Chamber of Commerce reports that workers under the influence of alcohol or drugs are 3.6 times more likely to suffer an injury or cause one to someone else. The Federal Railroad Administration found that between 1975 and 1984, forty-eight railroad accidents that killed thirty-seven people and caused millions of dollars in damages were caused by drug- or alcohol-impaired workers. Now that substance abuse is being given more careful attention, it is showing up as a significant factor in many accidents.

Testing and Treatment

While some drugs are new to the market, substance abuse is not new; it is a problem that may be growing worse, but mostly seems to be a problem that has only recently been brought into the open. In 1983, only 3 percent of the *Fortune 500* firms had drug testing programs of any sort. Five years later, over 50 percent had testing programs. As Table 14–2 shows, substance-abuse testing and treatment programs are most common among larger firms.

Table 14–2　Presence of Drug-Testing or Employee-Assistance Program by Percent of Employees in Workplaces (Summer 1988)

Percent Employees in Workplaces with:		Size of Establishment by Number of Employees*							
	TOTAL (84,965.7)	1–9 (10,700.1)	10–49 (20,584.2)	50–99 (12,254.5)	100–249 (13,309.4)	250–499 (8,220.1)	500–999 (6,469.2)	1,000–4,999 (9,596.2)	5,000 or more (3,831.8)
Formal drug policy	42.5	8.2	27.5	36.6	51.7	52.5	58.8	71.7	86.6
Drug-testing program	19.6	1.1	7.3	12.3	17.8	29.2	30.4	43.6	67.6
Employee-assistance program	31.0	4.2	11.2	16.6	30.7	45.2	54.2	71.9	86.8
Both testing & assistance	13.8	.7	3.5	3.9	9.7	20.7	22.8	36.4	64.4
Neither testing nor assistance	63.2	92.5	84.9	75.0	61.3	46.3	38.2	20.9	10.0

*(#) following size category represents total employees (in thousands).

Source: Bureau of Labor Statistics, "Survey of Employer Anti-drug Programs," Report 760, January 1989.

Most companies provide employee assistance programs to help deal with drug and alcohol problems. Treatment is expensive, running about $5,000 to $15,000 for three- or four-week detoxification programs (which have high first-time failure rates). Even if employers do not offer assistance with such expensive programs as a part of employees' health benefits, the costs of dealing with substance abuse show up in various ways. Companies must balance the costs of treatment against the costs of lower productivity and the prospect of liability from accidents caused by employee substance abuse.

Legal Issues in Drug Testing

Companies that are unionized cannot implement a drug-testing program for their workers. Since a testing program is a condition affecting work, the NLRA requires that the employer negotiate with the union for a program that is spelled out in the collective bargaining agreement. Hence, the discussion here will largely concern nonunionized places of employment. Further, a substance abuser may have certain rights under the Rehabilitation Act of 1973 and the Disabilities Act of 1990, an issue that will be discussed in the next chapter.

Drug-Free Workplace Act

Various federal agencies require federal employees to submit to drug tests in order to be eligible for certain positions, or require regulated industries to implement drug-testing policies.

Of more general impact is the *Drug-Free Workplace Act* of 1988. It requires all companies with more than $25,000 worth of business with the federal government (which includes all companies of any size) to certify that they will provide a "drug-free" workplace. The primary requirements are that the employer:

1. Publish a policy that substance abuse in the workplace will not be tolerated.
2. Establish a drug-awareness program to inform employees of the dangers of drug abuse.
3. Make known to employees the availability of programs to help those with substance abuse problems. Employers failing to comply may lose their business with the federal government.

State Statutory Standards

State legislatures have enacted a variety of statutes concerning drug testing, so one must be aware of local requirements. Iowa allows employees to be tested if:

1. The employer has "probable cause" to believe that the employee's job performance is impaired by drug use.
2. The employee poses a safety danger to persons or property.
3. The drug test is sent to a state-approved laboratory.

There may be no disciplinary action for a first drug offense if the employee completes the treatment that is recommended upon evaluation.

Minnesota allows testing of job applicants if a job offer is extended, if all applicants in the same job classes are required to be tested, and if those who fail the test are notified. Like Connecticut, Minnesota allows random drug testing of current employees only for those in safety-sensitive positions. Those states, like Vermont, Montana, and Rhode Island, allow testing of employees only if there is "reasonable suspicion" or "probable cause" to believe that drug or alcohol use is impairing job performance.

Maryland and Nebraska do not restrict the conditions under which drug tests may be required, but do provide quality and procedural safeguards for the tests to ensure that records are kept properly and that there is a chance for independent verification of test results.

Utah holds employers immune from liability for action taken by employees dismissed for drug usage, or by applicants rejected because they failed a drug test, so long as the employer has a written policy, informs employees of positive tests, and maintains proper documentation of tests.

Court Rulings

As the different statutory standards indicate, the law in this area is emerging and not settled. Since the law of contract and agency is the basis of most of the employment relationship, employers are presumed to have wide latitude to adopt drug policies. However, there have been a variety of conflicting court cases as cases arise based on tort and contract law and on claims brought under Fourth Amendment protection against "unreasonable searches and seizures." The law cannot be summarized because it is so uncertain, but the Supreme Court has started to give some guidance, as seen in the *Skinner* case. While this case concerns workers in an industry subject to direct federal regulation, the opinion provides broader guidance.

Skinner v. Railway Labor Executives' Ass'n

United States Supreme Court
489 U.S. 1,
109 S.Ct. 1402
(1989)

Case Background. *Based on evidence that alcohol and drug abuse by railroad employees caused or contributed to a number of fatal train accidents, the Federal Railroad Administration (FRA) issued regulations, as a part of its safety standards, requiring railroads to conduct blood and urine tests (Subpart C) of employees involved in train accidents. The FRA also encouraged railroads to adopt breath and urine test programs (Subpart D) to administer when employees were involved in other safety violations.*

The District Court held that such tests did not violate the Fourth Amendment, but the Court of Appeals reversed, holding that there must be reasonable suspicion for a test to be administered. The Supreme Court reviewed the case.

Case Decision. Justice Kennedy delivered the opinion of the Court.

* * *

The breath tests authorized by Subpart D of the regulations are even less intrusive than the blood tests prescribed by Subpart C. Unlike blood tests, breath tests do not require piercing the skin and may be conducted safely outside a hospital environment and with a minimum of inconvenience or embarrassment. Further, breath tests reveal the level of alcohol in the employee's bloodstream and nothing more. Like the blood-testing procedures mandated by Subpart C, which can be used only to ascertain the presence of alcohol or controlled substances in the bloodstream, breath tests reveal no other facts in which the employee has a substantial privacy interest.

In all the circumstances, we cannot conclude that the administration of a breath test implicates significant privacy concerns.

A more difficult question is presented by urine tests. Like breath tests, urine tests are not invasive of the body and, under the regulations, may not be used as an occasion for inquiring into private facts unrelated to alcohol or drug use. We recognize, however, that the procedures for collecting the necessary samples, which require employees to perform an excretory function traditionally shielded by great privacy, raise concerns not implicated by blood or breath tests. While we would not characterize these additional privacy concerns as minimal in most contexts, we note that the regulations endeavor to reduce the intrusiveness of the collection process. The regulations do not require that samples be furnished under the direct observation of a monitor, despite the desirability of such a procedure to ensure the integrity of the sample. The sample is also collected in a medical environment, by personnel unrelated to the railroad employer, and is thus not unlike similar procedures encountered often in the context of a regular physical examination.

Most importantly, the expectations of privacy of covered employees are diminished by reason of their participation in an industry that is regulated pervasively to ensure safety, a goal dependent, in substantial part, on the health and fitness of covered employees.

* * *

The possession of unlawful drugs is a criminal offense that the Government may punish, but it is a separate and far more dangerous wrong to perform certain sensitive tasks while under the influence of those substances. Performing those tasks while impaired by alcohol is, of course, equally dangerous, though consumption of alcohol is legal in most other contexts. The Government may take all necessary and reasonable regulatory steps to prevent or deter that hazardous conduct, and since the gravamen of the evil is performing certain functions while concealing the substance in the body, it may be necessary, as in the case before us, to examine the body or its fluids to accomplish the regulatory purpose. The necessity to perform that regulatory function with respect to railroad employees engaged in safety-sensitive tasks, and the reasonableness of the system for doing so, have been established in this case.

Alcohol and drug tests conducted in reliance on the authority of Subpart D cannot be viewed as private action outside the reach of the Fourth Amendment. Because the testing procedures mandated or authorized by Subparts C and D effect searches of the person, they must meet the Fourth Amendment's reasonableness requirement. In light of the limited discretion exercised by the railroad employers under the regulations, the surpassing safety interests served by toxicological tests in this context, and the diminished expectation of privacy that attaches to information pertaining to the fitness of covered employees, we believe that it is reasonable to conduct such tests in the absence of a warrant or reasonable suspicion that any particular employee may be impaired. We hold that the alcohol and drug tests contemplated by Subparts C and D of the FRA's regulations are reasonable within the meaning of the Fourth Amendment. The judgment of the Court of Appeals is accordingly reversed.

Case Holding. *The Supreme Court upheld the imposition, by federal regulation, of drug and alcohol tests on workers involved in serious railroad accidents. The Court also upheld the right of railroad companies to adopt their own drug and alcohol tests to be administered in situations involving other safety violations.*

Case Questions

1. The dissent in this case made a major point of the issue of mandatory taking of blood and urine of workers involved in certain accidents—even if the workers were not suspected of being under the influence of drugs or alcohol. Would it be reasonable to allow such tests only if there is suspicion?
2. If drugs are a persistent problem, would it be reasonable to allow all workers to be searched each morning as they entered a work site?

In a companion case to *Skinner*, the Court considered the legality of drug testing of U.S Customs Service employees who sought a transfer or promotion to positions involving drug interception, enforcement of related laws, carrying of firearms, or handling of classified material. The Court concluded, in *Treasury Employees* v. *Von Raab*, that the program was legal and that warrants to perform the test were not required. The circumstances in which the testing was mandated were specified and covered all employees equally, that is, agency officials would have no discretion to determine who would or would not have to take a test. Given the safety and sensitivity issues involved, the benefits of the suspicionless searches outweigh the privacy interests of the employees.

Employer Substance Abuse Policy

Like any business matter involving employee rights, a *substance abuse policy* should not be undertaken without careful consideration of the legal issues. Obviously, as reviewed above, statutory and case law requirements must be met. For example, federal contractors must comply with the Drug-Free Workplace Act of 1988, which requires employers to report employee drug convictions to the government.

In general, an employer should have a clear policy statement that demonstrates that testing is not discriminatory or haphazard. The policy should state why the tests are being done, what is being tested for, what will be done with the results, and what will be the consequences of the test results. Rather than only test employees that supervisors think may be drug users, companies should test all employees in certain categories or when a specific safety or security issue is involved.

Helping Abusers

Companies should have a plan of action for those who test positive. In general, there will be fewer problems if a company tries to help people with drug problems rather than dismiss them. Since drug tests have a certain rate of incorrect results, those who test positive should be given a second test rather than rely on a possible false reading. The credibility of the testing laboratory should be high. Because the legal developments in this area will generate substantial interest in the public and contain legally explosive issues for employers, they should be followed with care. The primary parts of one major company's substance abuse program are presented in Exhibit 14–1.

Exhibit 14–1   Substance Abuse Prevention and Chemical Screening
Program

[Company X] is committed to provide safe work places for its employees and to maintain programs promoting high standards of conduct to ensure safety and productivity. Consistent with the intent and spirit of its commitment, the company prohibits the possession, use, manufacture, distribution, or dispensation of any controlled substance in the workplace. In addition, company employees are required to report to work in proper condition to perform their duties. Violation of this prohibition or requirement may result in unpaid suspension, termination of employment and/or mandatory enrollment in a company approved substance abuse rehabilitation program.

* * *

V.   CHEMICAL SCREENING PROCEDURES
Specific procedures concerning chemical screening and conducting investigations under this section are outlined in the Supervisory Drug Awareness Manual.

A.   Pre-Employment
All candidates for hire are required to submit to the chemical screening process as a condition of employment. Failure to submit to the chemical screening process or a confirmed positive test will result in denial of employment.

* * *

B.   Testing Current Employees for Substance Abuse
The specific procedures for conducting investigations under this section are outlined in the Supervisory Drug Awareness Manual.

1. Aberrant behavior
Employees reasonably suspected of using or being under the influence of controlled substances as manifested through deteriorating job performance and/or uncharacteristic behavior may, upon proper investigation, documentation and review, be required to submit to chemical screening.

2. Post-Accident
Any employee in an accident which upon proper investigation, documentation and review by appropriate management is deemed to be of a suspicious nature, will be asked to submit to chemical screening.

3. Workplace Criminal Drug Statute Conviction
Upon receipt of verified information that an employee has been convicted of any criminal drug statute for a violation occurring in the workplace, the company, upon investigation and review, will take appropriate personnel action against such employee up to and including termination.

C.   Assignment

1. Domestic
All employees transferring to a project requiring chemical screening will be tested by the releasing office prior to transfer.

2. International
Chemical screening for employees assigned to international locations will be completed by the releasing office prior to the employee's transfer.

D.   Sensitive Position

3. No employee shall be assigned to a designated "sensitive position" unless they have submitted to a chemical screening process immediately prior to the assignment and the results are negative.

2. Employees assigned to "sensitive positions" may be subject to periodic unannounced chemical screening. Positive test results shall result in immediate removal of the employee from the sensitive position and imposition of the sanctions noted in VI.B.

VI.   POST-INVESTIGATIVE OPTIONS
Once an investigation is complete, one of the following actions will be taken:

A. The employee will receive full pay for the length of the suspension up to 5 working days if the chemical screening results are negative.

B. The employee whose chemical screening test result is positive will be required to enroll in rehabilitation recommended through the Employee and Family Assistance Program as a condition of employment and be subject to periodic unannounced chemical screening for up to one year. A subsequent positive test will result in immediate termination.

Exhibit 14–1 continued

C. An employee who refuses to submit to chemical screening once reasonable cause has been established will be subject to immediate termination.

D. The employee having a confirmed positive test result who refuses to seek and accept rehabilitation assistance will be subject to immediate termination.

E. An employee who is not terminated as a result of an investigation conducted for a workplace criminal drug statute conviction may be required to submit to chemical screening. Said employee may also be required to enroll in rehabilitation recommended through the Employee and Family Assistance Program and be subject to periodic, unannounced chemical screening for up to a year. A positive test during that period will result in immediate termination.

VII. REQUIRED NOTIFICATION PROCEDURES

A. Candidates for Hire
As a condition of employment, candidates for hire shall be required to sign a statement of understanding acknowledging their agreement to abide by the terms and conditions of this policy.

B. Employees
As a condition of employment, employees shall notify the company of any criminal drug statute conviction for a violation occurring in the workplace no later than 5 days after such conviction.

C. Company

1. The company, by law, regulations or contract may be required to report drug statute convictions or provide other data related to drug abuse statistics. The company will fulfill such requirements with maximum respect for individual confidentiality.

* * *

Tobacco

Another addictive substance drawing the increasing attention of employers is tobacco. As of 1988, 6 percent of all companies polled said that they did not hire smokers. Some governmental units no longer hire smokers and have banned smoking among certain categories of employees. Some employers ban smoking on all company property. Smoking bans are defended because of the lower health insurance premiums for nonsmokers and the fewer days lost to illness, on average, by nonsmokers.

The National Center for Health Promotion estimated in 1990 that smokers added an average of $350 per year per employee in costs borne by employers. This translates into tens of billions of dollars per year higher labor costs due to lost workdays and higher medical services due to smoking—not including the lowered productivity. The tobacco industry attacks such bans as a violation of individual rights and is lobbying for statutes, such as passed in Virginia, that prohibit discrimination against smokers.

An issue raised by such discrimination is where the line should be drawn. If employers can discriminate against smokers because they are higher-cost employees than are nonsmokers, what if the same is true of obese employees compared to average-weight employees? The list of possibilities is nearly endless and is now the subject of intense legislative debate and numerous lawsuits.

PROTECTION OF WORKER SAFETY AND HEALTH

Concern over worker safety and health dates to the mid-1800s and the early state regulation of coal-mine safety. In the late 1800s, federal regulations of job safety in coal mines were first enacted. Early legislative efforts concentrated on issues of job safety—accidents, injuries, and deaths—rather than on occupational health.

Between 1890 and 1920 most states enacted some form of a job safety law, although many were merely cosmetic and most were poorly enforced. In 1910, the state of New York enacted the first workers' compensation statute, providing compensation to injured workers through a compulsory liability insurance system placed upon employers. By the early 1930s, all but a few states had enacted similar legislation. Although most state workers' compensation statutes covered worker injuries and accidents, only recently have significant efforts been undertaken to include compensation for occupational health and illness within the statutes.

Occupational Health and Safety Act

In 1970, the National Safety Council reported that over 14,000 workers die and over 2 million workers suffer serious injuries on the job every year. Other studies estimated that hundreds of thousands of cases of occupational illnesses cause many additional deaths each year. Congress enacted the *Occupational Safety and Health Act* of 1970 (OSHAct), which created the Occupational Safety and Health Administration (OSHA). The Act requires employers to comply with OSHA's standards, including keeping records of work-related injuries, illnesses, and deaths, and to provide a workplace "free from recognized hazards that are causing or are likely to cause death or serious physical hardship to employees." In addition, the OSHAct imposed a duty upon employees to comply with all of OSHA's standards, rules, regulations, and orders issued under the OSHAct.

Establishing Health and Safety Standards
The general procedure used to establish a permanent health or safety standard requires several steps. First, standards are recommended by the National Institute of Occupational Safety and Health (NIOSH), a government agency responsible for conducting research related to occupational safety and health. An OSHA advisory committee then reviews and, if necessary, amends the proposed standards. This committee is composed of one representative each from industry, labor (usually a labor union representative), and the public.

Proposed standards are published in the *Federal Register*, and interested parties can comment on the rule or request a public hearing. After considering the comments, the Secretary of Labor issues the standard, giving it the force of law. The process is time consuming. For example, in 1971 the steel industry asked OSHA for coke-oven emissions standards. NIOSH issued its recommendations in the spring of 1973. The advisory committee issued its report in the spring of 1974. The proposed standards were issued by OSHA in the summer of 1975. The final standards were finally issued in October of 1976 — more than five years after the process began. Three to five years is usually required to develop and implement a new standard.

"Grave Danger" Exception

This procedure does not have to be followed if OSHA determines that "employees are exposed to grave danger from exposure to substances or agents determined to be toxic or physically harmful, and that such standard is necessary to protect employees from such danger." That is, the statute allows *emergency standards* to be adopted without undergoing the review and comment procedure required for permanent standards. The courts have held that these extraordinary powers are to be exercised delicately and only for emergencies that require them. Although emergency standards take effect immediately, they must then follow the same review procedure applicable to permanent standards.

OSHA Workplace Inspections

Although the OSHAct did provide OSHA with the authority to conduct surprise workplace inspections, the Supreme Court in *Marshall* v. *Barlow's, Inc.* (1978) held that the Fourth Amendment prohibits warrantless searches by OSHA. However, the Court required OSHA to obtain only administrative warrants, exempting the agency from showing probable cause and other conditions ordinarily required to secure a criminal warrant.

The typical workplace inspection includes an examination of appropriate health and safety records, interviews with employers, and a walk-around inspection of the plant itself. Representatives of both the company and the employees have the right to accompany the inspector. Since 1977, OSHA has attempted to concentrate its inspection efforts in those industries where health and safety problems are perceived to be the worse—industries such as construction, petrochemicals, and heavy manufacturing. In cooperation with state agencies, between 150,000 and 200,000 inspections are performed each year.

Employee Rights

Under the OSHAct, it is unlawful for the employer to punish or in any way discriminate against an employee for participating in an OSHA workplace inspection or exercising any other right guaranteed by the OSHAct. In particular, employees have the right to refuse work assignments they believe may pose a serious threat to their safety or health.

The Supreme Court reviewed such an incident in *Whirlpool Corp.* v. *Marshall* (1980). Two employees at a manufacturing plant refused to perform maintenance duties that required them to work on a screen twenty feet above the plant floor. The safety of the screen was at issue, since one employee had fallen through it and been killed and there had been several other close calls. When the employees refused to go on the screen, they were sent home, lost six hours of pay each, and had a reprimand placed in their file. OSHA, through the Secretary of Labor, sued the employer on behalf of the workers, asking that their records be cleared and they be paid the lost wages. The Supreme Court supported the workers, holding that the OSHA rule that allows employees to refuse to obey orders that pose a risk of death or serious injury was within the intent of Congress when the law was passed.

Duty of Employees

OSHA does not place the entire safety burden on employers. The Act provides that employees "shall comply with occupational safety and health standards and all rules, regulations, and orders." OSHA does not penalize employees who ignore rules of which they are aware, but it may relieve the employer of liability. For example, in 1976 the Fifth Circuit Court of Appeals dismissed three serious OSHA citations against an employer even though two employees were killed. The employees were experienced foremen who had acted in an unforseeable manner against the company's explicit instructions and without the company's knowledge. However, an employer cannot always use the defense that the employees ignored safety procedures. It is the company's duty to work to enforce safety standards, even if the workers dislike them.

OSHA Penalties

Based on inspections by OSHA compliance officers, citations may be issued for rule violations and monetary penalties may be imposed. Section 17 of OSHAct provides for these penalties:

- For a willful or repeated violation—up to $10,000.
- For a serious violation (chance of death or serious injury)—up to $1,000.
- For a non-serious violation—up to $1,000.
- For failure to correct a violation—up to $1,000 per day.
- For a willful violation resulting in the death of an employee, first conviction—up to $10,000 and six months in jail; subsequent convictions—up to $20,000 and one year in jail.

Fines are often multiplied because of numerous violations that continue over time, so the total fine against an employer can be quite high. Three contractors were fined $5.1 million in 1987 for a major disaster at a construction site. Several other fines over a million dollars have been issued, but the annual total collected by OSHA has been a few million dollars per year in recent years.

Workers and Toxic Substances

Thousands of OSHA standards concern safety. There are detailed specifications for machine design and placement, stairway design, and height of fire extinguishers. A small number of health standards have been issued, but most of them have had major impacts. Exposure to asbestos was one of the first health standards developed; compliance is costing billions of dollars. Other standards have been issued for vinyl chloride, coke-oven emissions, and other industrial carcinogens.

Toxic Substance Standards

With regard to health standards for worker exposure to toxic substances, the OSHAct holds that OSHA must promulgate standards that "most adequately assure, to the extent feasible, . . . that no employee will suffer material impairment of health or functional capacity even if such employee has regular exposure to the hazard . . . for the period of his working life." Every health standard that OSHA has promulgated or proposed has been subject to attack by both industry and labor. Two important Supreme Court decisions that have resulted from those attacks significantly influence OSHA's health-standard setting process. The cases involved health standards for benzene and cotton dust.

Significant Health Risk Requirement

A study of benzene, a substance known to be dangerous to humans at certain levels, resulted in a NIOSH report that said that "... the accumulated evidence from clinical as well as epidemiological data ... [provides] ... conclusive ... [proof that] benzene is leukemogenic. Because it causes progressive malignant disease of the blood-forming organs, NIOSH recommends that for regulatory purposes, benzene be considered carcinogenic in man." Based on this report and other evidence, OSHA established emergency standards for benzene in 1977 that were later formalized. The American Petroleum Institute attacked the regulations as too extreme. In its review of the standard, in *Industrial Union* v. *American Petroleum Institute* (1980) (the "benzene" case), the Supreme Court agreed with the American Petroleum Institute, finding that the agency did not have adequate information regarding the actual effects of benzene. The Court held that before OSHA requires that worker exposure to a carcinogen be reduced to its lowest feasible level, the agency must first find that the existing exposure to the substance "poses a significant health risk in the workplace."

Cost Benefit Analysis Not Required

The Court noted in the "benzene" case that the cost of implementing the standard was expected to be hundreds of millions of dollars. Should OSHA's health standards reflect a reasonable relationship between their costs and benefits? That question was answered in the "cotton dust" case, *American Textile Manufacturers Institute* v. *Donovan* (1981). The Supreme Court held that cost benefit analysis is not required as a justification for an OSHA standard. The Court noted that the statute says that standards must be feasible. Congress "chose to place pre-eminent value on assuring employees a safe and healthful working environment, limited only by the feasibility of achieving such an environment." Thus, the costs of complying with a health or safety standard may outweigh the economic benefits.

Hazard Communication Standard

A major step was taken in 1988 to ensure that chemical hazards in the workplace are evaluated. The *hazard communication standard* (HCS) covers all employees exposed to hazardous chemicals in the normal course of operations. Chemical producers and importers must conduct a "hazard determination" of each chemical they produce or sell, in which they identify and consider scientific evidence about the hazards of each chemical. Information about chemical hazards must be updated as new evidence becomes available.

Employer Duty Under HCS

There are four major parts to the HCS standard imposed on all employers where hazardous chemicals are used:

1. Written hazard communication program. Every workplace must have a written program that includes:

- A list of hazardous chemicals in the workplace.
- The manner in which MSDS, chemical labels, and worker training about chemical safety will be handled.
- The manner in which employees will be trained for non-routine tasks, when they arise, involving hazardous chemicals.

2. Labeling. Every container with hazardous chemicals must be labeled with the identity of the chemical, appropriate hazard warnings, and the name and address of the producer or seller of the chemical.

3. Material Safety Data Sheets (MSDS). MSDS must be provided by every chemical distributor with every container. The MSDS must identify: the chemical; its characteristics; its physical (such as fire) and health hazards; its primary route of entry (such as skin contact); safe exposure limits; cancer dangers; precautions for safe handling and use; proper control measures in the workplace; emergency procedures; date of issue; and identity of producer or seller who can provide more information.

4. Employee information and training. Employees must be informed of the HCS, of the hazardous chemicals in their workplace, and of the MSDS. Employees must be trained to detect hazards, to know the consequences of the chemicals, to protect themselves, and to take certain actions in an emergency.

The Environmental Protection Agency controls the handling of hazardous waste from worksites, and certain other hazardous substances, such as drugs, are regulated by other agencies, but increased concern about the dangers of exposure to hazardous substances is now making environmentalism in the workplace a major issue for employers.

GENERAL REGULATION OF LABOR MARKETS

Restrictions are placed on the labor market by a variety of controls. Federal immigration laws restrict who is allowed to work in the country. The minimum wage law sets a lower limit on what employees may be paid. Many states restrict entry into occupations by a series of licensing requirements. Workers' compensation laws provide insurance in case of accidents. And employee pensions are subject to federal regulation.

Restrictions on Immigration

The United States is a nation of immigrants and is the most popular destination for peoples from many countries where there are fewer opportunities. Millions of illegal immigrants work in the country, most being concentrated in California, Arizona, New Mexico, Texas, and Florida. The *Immigration Reform and Control Act* of 1986 sets strict standards for employees and employers. To be hired legally in the United States, you must be able to present certain documents to show your identity and your authorization to work. Such documentary proof may be required even if you are a U.S. citizen.

Since violations of the law can mean criminal penalties, employers must be sure to meet the basic requirements. Employers must collect evidence of citizenship or of legal work status for all new employees. Any of the following documents is legal proof of employment eligibility:

- U.S. Passport
- Certificate of U.S. Citizenship
- Certificate of Naturalization
- Foreign Passport with Employment Authorization
- Alien Registration Card with Photograph.

Combinations of other documents, such as driver's license, school ID card, original Social Security Card, or birth certificate may be put together to provide legal proof to satisfy Immigration and Naturalization Service requirements.

Federal Minimum Wage Requirements

Federal minimum wage requirements were initiated in 1938 as a part of the Fair Labor Standards Act. Over the years, the minimum wage has increased so that it is now equal to about 50 percent of the average manufacturing wage. In 1991, the minimum wage became $4.25 an hour. Employers must also pay Social Security tax (7.65 percent), workers' compensation insurance, and unemployment insurance taxes. The law has also been amended to expand the sectors of the labor force that are covered. Initially, less than half of all nonsupervisory employees in the private, nonagricultural sector were covered; now over 90 percent are covered. This expansion, combined with legislation in most states that complements the federal law, means that most jobs are covered by the minimum wage requirement.

Supporters of the minimum wage contend that the law requires employers to pay a fair wage to employees and, although the wage is relatively low, will not allow workers to be paid so little that they have trouble buying even the necessities of life. On the other side are those who argue that the law results in lower demand for workers in the minimum wage category—usually young persons, often minorities, with little education or job experience. The result is relatively high unemployment among persons in those groups who never get the opportunity to work to develop labor skills that will command higher wages.

The overall impact of the minimum wage is difficult to assess. The minimum wage makes some people better off—those who obtain jobs at higher wages than they would have in the absence of the law. It also makes some people worse off—those who cannot obtain jobs because of the reduction in demand for low-skill, poorly educated workers.

Occupational Licensure and Regulation

Entry into many occupations is controlled by various regulations or *licensing requirements*. In such occupations, an individual cannot simply set up and begin to operate a business. Rather, permission from the regulating agency is required. That permission usually requires some demonstration of competency or payment of a high entry fee. The expressed purpose of these labor restrictions is to protect the consumer. The restrictions are supposed to help guarantee that businesses will provide service of a certain quality and that fewer unscrupulous people will operate in the professions.

Regulation Set by State Law

Although a few occupations have entry restrictions set at the federal level, most restrictions are set at the state level. In most states, an individual must receive a license or certificate from the state to practice as a lawyer, doctor, dentist, nurse, veterinarian, optometrist, optician, barber, cosmetologist, or architect. In various states, an individual must be licensed to be a dog groomer, beekeeper, industrial psychologist, building contractor, electrician, plumber, or massage parlor operator. Usually, a state commission is established to determine what the entry criteria will be for one to be licensed to practice. In most cases, there is a formal education requirement, and in some cases, an apprenticeship period is required, or a standardized test of knowledge about the profession must be passed.

Impact on Consumers

Some aspects of such occupational licensing have been criticized for practices that may be detrimental to consumers. The Supreme Court has prohibited price fixing by lawyers through their state bar associations. Similarly, restrictions on advertising, especially restrictions on price advertising, have been attacked and removed in recent years. Regardless of the impact of licensing on the quality and price of service to consumers, such procedures raise the cost of entering many professions, making it more difficult for new entrants to get into the profession and to compete with existing professionals. In addition, some critics have charged that occupational licensing particularly discriminates against minorities and women, many of whom are just now being given the education and opportunities to enter professions that were previously very difficult to enter.

Workers' Compensation Laws

Beginning in 1910, the states enacted *workers' compensation laws*. These laws require employers to pay employees a benefit that is set by a compensation schedule. The benefits are paid regardless of the cause of a work-related injury and are usually for less than the full costs of the accident. Workers' compensation acts as a system of mandatory insurance. Benefits are set by a state agency, and premiums are paid by employers. In exchange for paying the premiums, the employer becomes immune from employee damage suits (tort) arising from on-the-job accidents. The system was the first no-fault insurance scheme.

The objectives that underlie workers' compensation laws are:

1. Provide sure, prompt, and reasonable income and medical benefits to work-accident victims, or income benefits to their dependents, regardless of fault.

2. Provide a certain remedy and reduce court costs and time delays associated with personal-injury litigation.

3. Prevent public and private charities from incurring the financial strains that would accompany uncompensated accidents.

4. Reduce or eliminate payment of fees to lawyers and expert witnesses.

5. Encourage employer interest in safety and rehabilitation of workers through an insurance scheme that bases rates on the experience-rating of the employer.

6. Promote open discussion of the causes of accidents, rather than encourage concealment of fault, thereby helping to reduce future accidents and health hazards.

Compensation Provided

Workers' compensation generally has five benefit categories: death, total disability, permanent partial disability, temporary partial disability, and medical expenses. Most states do not restrict the amount or duration of medical benefits. While some injuries require only medical assistance, others take the worker out of the workplace for some recovery period, sometimes forever. Workers usually receive about two-thirds of their gross wages as disability income up to a state-imposed weekly maximum, as low as $200 in some states to as high as $700. In some states, the benefits run for over ten years for temporary disability. For permanent incapacitation, the benefits last a lifetime, but may be offset by Social Security Disability payments.

Incentives for Safety

Generally, workers' compensation provides employers with financial incentives to invest in safety on the work site. Insurance premiums are based on safety and injury claims records. Hence, firms with the lowest number of injuries, and therefore the fewest claims, will have the lowest premiums. Further incentives to participate in the system exist. If an employer chooses not to comply, which is allowed in some cases, or if an employer fails to comply, an injured employee can sue the employer in tort for negligence and collect the full cost of the accident. In such a case, there is no statutory limit to the amount of damages recoverable by an injured worker or his or her family.

Basis for a Claim

About 90 percent of all workers are covered by workers' compensation laws. Many of those who are not covered are protected by other laws, such as the Federal Employer's Liability Act. For an employee to have a claim, it must generally be shown that the worker received (1) a personal injury, (2) as a result of an accident, (3) that arose out of, and (4) in the course of employment. The negligence or fault of the employer in causing the injury is not an issue. The application of the law is broad. Compensable injuries can include mental and nervous disorders and heart attacks that occur on the job.

Most courts are strict in interpreting state statutes that clearly state that the liability coverage of workers' compensation "shall be exclusive in place of any and all other liability to such employees ... entitled to damages in any action at law or otherwise on account of any injury or death . . . ." The actions of the employer, employee, or third person become relevant only if there was intentional infliction of harm, that is, an intentional tort. The employee may then file a civil action for damages outside the workers' compensation system. Attempts to evade this by claims of mental distress imposed by supervisory harassment are not allowed except in cases of intentional harm. As noted previously, employers are forbidden by statute or by public policy from firing employees who seek compensation by filing claims.

A Flawed System?

Employers have complained in recent years that workers' compensation insurance is too expensive. One reason for the expense appears to be that there are too many awards for permanent partial disability, which results in lifetime payment awards, when the worker is in fact not permanently disabled. On the other side, consider the amounts paid for losses suffered in injuries, which is usually fixed by a schedule. Suppose a worker loses a foot, but is able to return to work. Medical expenses and lost work time aside, how much is a foot worth? As of 1989, on the lower side the state of Georgia said it was worth $23,625. On the higher side, the state of North Carolina said $54,144. It is likely that if a jury was allowed to determine the worth of the loss of a foot for a lifetime, where an employer was negligent, the award would be much larger. So it is unlikely that employers would prefer to operate under the tort system rather than under this system of awards determined by statute.

The Regulation of Private Employee Retirement Plans

Although Social Security has been around for decades and various laws affecting retirement plans have been passed over the years, the most important legislation regulating private employee retirement plans is the *Employee Retirement Income Security Act* of 1974 (ERISA). The main objective of ERISA is to guarantee the expectations of retirement plan participants and to promote the growth of private pension plans. ERISA was prompted by horror stories about employees who made years of contributions to retirement funds only to receive nothing. For example, the closing of Studebaker in 1963 left over 8,500 employees without retirement benefits.

ERISA is directed at most employee benefit plans, including medical, surgical, or hospital benefits; sickness, accident, or disability benefits; death benefits; unemployment benefits; vacation benefits; apprenticeship or training benefits; day-care centers; scholarship funds; prepaid legal services; retirement income programs; and deferred income programs.

Vesting Requirements

The law establishes *vesting* requirements; that is, it guarantees that plan participants will receive some retirement benefits after a reasonable length of employment. All plans must be adequately funded to meet their expected liabilities. A termination insurance program is to be provided in case of the failure of a plan. The law provides standards of conduct for trustees and fiduciaries of employee benefit plans.

The major problem addressed by ERISA was that of the loss of all benefits by employees who had many years of service with a company and then either quit or were fired. The law makes all full-time employees over the age of twenty-five with one year of service eligible for participation in employee benefit plans.

Mandatory *vesting* (when the employee becomes the owner of the retirement proceeds) was established by ERISA. It provides the employer with three options: (1) to have 100 percent vesting after ten years of employment; (2) to have 25 percent vesting after five years, then 5 percent vesting a year for five years, then 10 percent vesting a year for five years, to achieve 100 percent vesting in fifteen years; and (3) vesting under the rule-of-forty-five vesting. Under the rule-of-forty-five, if the age and years of service of an employee total forty-five or if an employee has ten years' service, there must be at least 50 percent vesting. Each added year of employment provides 10 percent more vesting so that an employee will be fully vested within fifteen years.

Consistency in Retirement Rights

These rules, along with requirements about the use of pension funds, fiduciary standards, funding requirements, and plan financial disclosure requirements, are designed to ensure some consistency in treatment of employees who are covered by private pension plans. Although the majority of the plans that existed before ERISA already complied with the standards ERISA set, the law is supposed to assure that problems such as those faced by the Studebaker employees will not arise again.

Concern is developing that despite the standards set by ERISA, many pension funds may not be properly funded. The Pension Benefit Guaranty Corporation is the federal agency that insures the solvency of pension funds. As of 1990, it estimated that the fifty corporations with the largest amounts of unfunded pension liabilities were $14 billion in the red. Like the savings and loan industry, the taxpayers may end up with a major bailout on their hands if better solvency rules are not put into effect.

SUMMARY

Federal policy for labor unions was first declared in the Norris-La Guardia Act of 1932. It prohibited the federal courts from issuing injunctions in nonviolent labor disputes and so-called yellow dog contracts. The Act increased the freedom of unions to use economic force to compel employers to bargain collectively.

The basic federal labor code is generally referred to as the National Labor Relations Act. The NLRA was enacted in three phases: the Wagner Act in 1935, the Taft-Hartley Act in 1947, and the Landrum-Griffin Act in 1959.

The Wagner Act provided employees with the right to organize unions and to bargain collectively through representatives of their choosing. The Act made it illegal for an employer to interfere with employees in the exercise of those rights, and employee actions could not interfere with the employer's interest in plant safety, efficiency, and discipline. The Act also created the National Labor Relations Board (NLRB), which is responsible for resolving unfair labor practice disputes and supervising matters of union representation.

The Taft-Hartley Act marked a change in federal policy towards unions. The Act moved federal policy from one of actively encouraging union activity to one of a more neutral role. The Act provided the employer with the right to file an unfair labor practice charge with the NLRB if it believed the union had acted in an unfair manner. Certain kinds of strikes, secondary boycotts, featherbedding, and certain other union practices were prohibited by the Act. It also provided that wages, hours, and other conditions of employment were to be mandatory subjects of bargaining. Collective bargaining agreements were made enforceable in federal court.

The Landrum-Griffin Act provided for the regulation of internal union affairs. The Act reflects Congress's concern that union members should be protected from improper actions of union leaders. The law governs the election of union leadership, protects the right to speak out about internal union matters, and assures that union members have the right to see the books of the union, which are audited by the federal government.

The majority of the labor force is governed by the law of employment-at-will, which allows employees to quit a job at any time for any reason and employers to dismiss employees without reason—unless there is a contract or law to the contrary. The most important restrictions to employment-at-will are provided by the rights stated in employee handbooks, which are now being treated as contracts.

Substance abuse poses a major challenge for employers. Most large firms now have a drug-testing policy and a written policy that explains the steps the employer will take to assist employees with drug or alcohol problems—and the consequences to employees, especially those in positions with safety or sensitivity concerns, of violating the drug policy. In general, drug screening of new employees is allowed; drug testing of existing employees must be carefully implemented so as not to invade privacy rights and to demonstrate consistency and fairness.

The Occupational Safety and Health Administration imposes safety and health regulations to protect employees. While such regulations must be documented as to need, there is no requirement that they be cost effective. In recent years, OSHA has turned to health issues, such as protection from hazardous chemicals.

Other regulations of labor markets require that employers collect evidence to show that all new employees are U.S. citizens or are noncitizens with a legal work status. Employers must also comply with federal minimum wage requirements. Entry into many occupations is controlled by state regulations, which often require certain levels of education and passage of competency examinations. Most employers must pay for workers' compensation insurance to ensure that injured employees, regardless of fault, will have medical expenses covered and receive partial compensation for lost wages. Finally, the Employee Retirement Income Security Act is designed to give employees the right to their pension benefits after a certain time of service and to provide federal inspection and guarantee of the solvency of pension funds.

ISSUE

Do Workers Have a Right to Privacy at the Workplace?

Most employers are now taking steps to deal with substance abuse, either because it is in the interest of the company or because they are forced to do so by the Drug-Free Workplace Act. It is often difficult to uncover drug abusers until there is a problem, which may involve death or injury. Does this give employers the right to spy on employees to look for evidence of drug abuse?

Using 'Spies to Win a War'*
John Schwartz, with Elizabeth Bradburn and Carolyn Friday

Something was wrong at the turkey-packaging plant. Worker Compensation claims were skyrocketing, mostly from the evening shift. So earlier this year, management called in undercover detectives, who soon found the cause. Employees were getting high on cocaine and jousting with forklifts, injuring themselves and damaging equipment. "It was absolutely demolition derby," say Ron Schmidt, vice president of investigations for Pinkerton's, the agency hired by the company. (Their firm didn't want its name used.) As a result of the probe, nearly 20 workers were fired.

With drug abuse on the job increasing every year, corporations are escalating the battle to root out users and dealers. More and more, they're supplementing education programs and random testing with full-scale undercover work. The get-tough trend has created a bonanza for the drug snoops—now a $250 million industry, by some estimates. While hiring detectives is still often viewed as a last resort, some companies say they have no choice. Says William Huston, security chief for paper manufacturer Boise Cascade: "It takes spies to win wars, and we're in a war."

Business is fighting harder because it can't afford not to. The crack epidemic has compounded longstanding corporate problems with cocaine, marijuana and speed. The U.S. Chamber of Commerce has found that recreational drug users are a third less productive than other employees and more than three times likelier to injure themselves or others at work. Uncle Sam is also forcing the issue: the Drug-Free Workplace Act of 1988 requires companies with substantial federal contracts to clean house or lose contracts.

Even firms under no legal obligation are eying their ranks more closely. Just one stoned employee can do monumental damage. A January 1987 train wreck cause by an engineer who admitted smoking a joint at his post killed 16 people and injured 175 and cost Conrail and Amtrak $106 million. Most companies have more than one drug user to worry about: the Chamber of Commerce says that 44 percent of those entering the full-time work force have used illegal drugs in the past year. "There is not a company in the U.S. that does not have a drug problem, and if they say they don't, they're ignoring the fact," says Paul Leckinger, whose Chicago-based Midwest Consultants, Inc., helps companies set up drug-detection programs.

The companies say that police rarely have the time or manpower to mount workplace investigations. "Local enforcement

—continued

—continuing

doesn't want to mess with us," says Richard Kerner, head of security at Pillowtex, a Dallas-based pillow and comforter manufacturer. "We're not that big." A growing number of private companies, large and small, are finding that enlisting as mercenaries in the corporate drug wars can be highly profitable. Pinkerton's reports a 40 percent jump in drug-related business in the past six months alone. The detective agency estimates that 80 percent of its undercover jobs are now drug related—including many that begin as simple theft investigations. "We start out looking for what happened to the property and we find drugs," says CEO Tom Wathen. Another drug-detection agency, Dayton-based Professional Law Enforcement, has watched its revenues double every year since 1985.

Clients range form small companies with disappearing inventories to some of America's biggest corporate giants. General Motors and Whirlpool have used spies as part of their anti-drug programs. Houston-based Compaq Computer Corp. flushed out 22 employees who have been accused of trading stolen computer chips for drugs. PLE alone has 54 undercover agents now at work in Fortune 200 companies. Few companies will admit they hire snoops, and most try to keep undercover work under wraps. "People feel you're spying on them," says one company security officer who employs snoops. "We are, but do you want people to know that?"

Companies that avoid confronting their drug problems find they don't just go away. One firm realized that a forklift driver was causing damage, but didn't order an investigation until he killed a co-worker, says Richard Rose, vice president of New York-based Management Safeguards. Another company called Rose to find out if one of its partners was abusing drugs: he was, but the firm opted not to fire him because he was still bringing in $3 million in business a year. "Some play ostrich, and they back away from confronting the problem," Rose says. "But they'll be calling me back in a few

years, and it'll be a lot harder and more expensive to get rid of the problem then."

Hardball methods can sometimes create as many problems as they solve. While no one is *for* drug abuse—and workers are often the first to demand that management clean up drug problems—workers' rights can get trampled in the rush to uncover users. The same investigators who look for drug abuse can be used to check up on union activity and whistleblowers. "It really begins to shift the balance of power away from individuals who have a right not to be abused by their government to a nation of people who are constantly being spied upon," says Loren Siegel, a spokesperson for the American Civil Liberties Union.

Some professionals believe the cops-and-robbers approach encourages too much emphasis on punishment. Since federal law treats addiction as a handicap covered by antidiscrimination statutes, companies can't simply fire workers because they use drugs. Though skeptics question the cost-effectiveness of rehabilitation programs, a new study based on data from North Carolina's Research Triangle Institute shows that treatment can reduce drug use as well as abuser crime. And David Conney, a psychiatrist who founded the New York-based Conney Medical Associates to offer a broad array of drug-prevention and treatment services to corporations, points out that treatment saves the cost of training new workers. "It's good business to treat the employee," Conney says. "It's good from the humanitarian point of view of benefit to the employee, and it's also good business financially." Charlie Carroll, a cofounder of PLE who broke with the firm to found a new company, ASET Corp., agrees. "Why throw all the money invested in the person out the door," he asks, "when the next person you hire might have the same problem?"

Because of the rancor that undercover investigations can cause, some corporations—and even some investigators—try to avoid

—continued

–continuing

them. Edward Cass, a 30-year Drug Enforcement Agency veteran who now runs Boston-based Cass Associates, says that not all detective firms have the staff to conduct sensitive operations, and that botched investigations can harm innocent workers and lead to lawsuits. "Some of these companies are hiring kids, they're getting young people with a cop complex, they'll stand on their head just to be a detective," Cass says. "A whole lot of people are out there that are all fluff and no stuff." Cass prefers surveying workers in confidential interviews.

Other drug fighters have grown frustrated with police tactics because they often come too late. Carroll says he left PLE partly because he felt that is was overemphasizing investigations. "I changed my philosophy. Drug busts are generally reactive in nature. When they call you in, it's because the barn's on fire." His new firm spends 90 percent of its energies on drug education and prevention. But even Carroll admits that prevention alone isn't enough these days. In companies across America, the barn is on fire, and corporations are willing to do whatever is necessary to put out the flames.

Questions

1. Is spying on workers suspected of drug use at the workplace more intrusive than requiring employees to submit to urine or blood tests for evidence of drug use?

2. Should employers be required to inform employees that, as a condition of employment, they will be subject to monitoring for evidence of drug or alcohol use on the job, or will that reduce effectiveness of the program?

3. If employees are found with illegal drugs on their person, should the police be called?

REVIEW AND DISCUSSION QUESTIONS

1. Define the following terms and phrases:
   Yellow-dog contract
   Closed shop
   Agency shop
   Right-to-work law
   Authorization card
   Union certification
   Collective bargaining
   Mandatory subjects of bargaining
   Concerted activity
   Secondary boycott
   Lockout
   Employment-at-will
   Employee handbooks
   Occupational licensure
   Workers' compensation
   Vesting

2. Under the Supreme Court's standards in the *Jacksonville Bulk Terminals* case, what kinds of cases would be deemed purely political and outside the Norris-La Guardia Act's reach?

3. Give some examples of secondary boycotts or actions that may be generally classified as secondary boycotts. Why should there be prohibitions agains

such activities? If these are voluntary actions by the workers involved, should the workers not have the right to bring pressure on whomever they choose?

4. Do firms have the right to test all job applicants and refuse to hire applicants who test positive for drug use, even if the job in question has no safety or sensitivity concerns?

Case Questions

5. An employee knows that a company manager is engaged in serious personal income tax fraud and reports this to the IRS. The IRS investigates and wins litigation involving the manager. The manager discovers who blew the whistle with the IRS and has the employee fired. Will the courts protect the employee whose job is at will? What if the tax fraud was on the part of corporate managers on behalf of the taxes owed by the corporation?

6. RMC Company had long provided its employees with an in-house cafeteria. The cafeteria was managed by Ira's Deli, but RMC reserved the right to review and approve the quality and prices of the food served. When RMC notified the union representing its employees that it was going to increase prices, the union requested bargaining over the prices and service. RMC refused to bargain. Are the cafeteria's prices and services "other terms and conditions of employment" and therefore subject to bargaining?

7. The employees of Bierman's High Fashion Apparel Incorporated wanted to distribute a union newsletter. The newsletter was to be distributed in the nonworking areas of Bierman's plant on the employees' time. The newsletter contained two articles to which the management of Bierman's objected. One article criticized President Reagan's veto of a minimum wage increase and the other encouraged employees to write their state representative to oppose the incorporation of the state's right-to-work statute into a revised state constitution. Is the distribution of the newsletter the kind of concerted activity that is protected from employer interference by the National Labor Relations Act?

8. Ryan, manager of a large office, had a wife, Susan, who was sure that Ryan was having affairs with two of his employees. Susan would call their offices frequently to check on where they were. She would call the employees when they were at home whenever Ryan was out to try to catch him. She would drive by their houses often to see if Ryan's car was there when she lost track of him. This constant snooping bothered one of the employees, Ginger, very much. She asked Ryan several times to please make Susan stop bothering her, as it made her nervous. Ryan always laughed and said there is no problem because you know nothing is going on; Susan is just kind of crazy that way. But Ginger was driven to a nervous breakdown by this pestering by Susan. After a period of hospitalization, Ginger's lawyer told her that she may get workers' compensation for mental distress caused by pressure on the job that her supervisor did not take steps to reduce. The lawyer also said that she may be able to sue Ryan and Susan for mental distress. What kind of lawsuit do you think may work?

9. During a campaign for a company's production facility to become unionized the management showed a movie to employees that dramatized some supposed risks of unionization. The union complained that this was an unfair labor practice and the NLRB agreed. The company claimed this was protected by freedom of speech and was not an unfair labor practice. What was the result when the case was appealed to federal court of appeals? [*Luxuray of New York v. NLRB*, 447 F.2d 112 (1971)]

10. An engineer worked for a company for ten years with no written employment contract. The company's personnel policy manual said that employees could be fired only for good cause. Soon after the engineer wrote a memo about a structural problem with one of the company's buildings, he was fired. He sued, claiming that he was fired without good cause and that an implied contract existed because of the policy manual. The lower courts ruled that he did not have a claim. What was the result of the appeal to the state supreme court? [*Woolley* v. *Hoffmann-La Roche*, 99 N.J. 284, 491 A.2d 1257 (1985)]

Policy Questions

11. What are some arguments *against* the position taken by the Supreme Court in the *First National Maintenance* case?

12. Does it not seem like a restriction on freedom of speech to prohibit many forms of secondary boycotts? That is, if the Hormel workers wanted to have a picket at a bank telling the public that the bank should be boycotted unless it supported the union against Hormel, should that not be protected political speech so long as access to the bank was not blocked?

13. Comment on the following: "The minimum wage can be shown to have discriminated against minority teenagers. It has caused the unemployment rate for unskilled minority youths to triple in the past couple of decades. It has made it impossible for many unskilled youngsters to get any work, condemning them to a life of welfare."

14. Should OSHA concentrate more efforts on worker health issues than on safety issues, as critics have asserted it should? Why do the critics make this argument? What is the difference in employers' incentives with respect to safety and health issues? Should a cost-benefit test be used in determining whether to allow a particular health measure, such as limiting worker exposure to cotton dust? Although the costs of cotton dust control are fairly easy to measure, how does one measure the benefits? What is involved?

Ethics Questions

15. Employees of Glasgow's Nouvelle Shoes wanted to form a union. Mr. Glasgow said that he did not want the employees unionized and would liquidate the business if a union were voted in. After the union won the representative election, Mr. Glasgow closed the shoe factory and sold all its assets. What he did was legal, but was it ethical? Instead of selling the assets, could Mr. Glasgow open the business up again after the employees denounced the union?

16. Contemplating the opening of a factory, you discover that it appears to be a toss-up between building a plant that uses cheaper machinery and 200 workers who will earn an average of $6 an hour versus a plant that uses more expensive, sophisticated machinery and seventy workers likely to earn about $15 an hour. Is it more responsible to build one kind of factory than another? What if you know that the first kind of factory will probably never be unionized but the second kind of factory is most likely going to be unionized?

17. The employees' handbook for your company is rather poorly written and says things to the effect that "so long as your work record is good you have no reason to expect to be fired." You realize that although never used, this could be used as evidence of a contractual standard in a court case by a terminated employee. You are pretty sure that if you revise the manual so that it conforms to the employment-at-will standard, employees will probably not realize they may have lost some valuable employment rights. What do you do?

15 Employment Discrimination

T HE laws providing for equal employment opportunity are reviewed in this chapter. We begin with a discussion of the historical background to the federal law of employment discrimination. We then review the Equal Pay Act of 1963, the first modern federal law governing employment discrimination on the basis of sex.

The chapter then discusses Title VII of the Civil Rights Act of 1964, which is the most important law intended to correct and deter discriminatory employment practices. The law prohibits employers, unions, and employment agencies from discriminating on the basis of race, color, sex, religion, and national origin. In practice, most cases have concerned race and sex discrimination. To remedy sex or race discrimination, affirmative action programs may be implemented voluntarily or may be imposed on an employer. In recent years, the Civil Rights Acts of 1866 and 1871, which had been unused for years, were revived and can be used to bring suit for injury due to racial discrimination.

Next, the chapter reviews the Age Discrimination in Employment Act, which added age to the list of personal characteristics on which discrimination suits may be based. Then the Rehabilitation Act and the Americans with Disabilities Act of 1990 are discussed. They are the primary basis of federal employment rights for mentally and physically disabled persons. Finally, the Issue reading concerns the personal impact of affirmative action employment.

BACKGROUND TO DISCRIMINATION LAW

Problems of discrimination in employment due to sex, color, race, religion, or national origin are not unique to the American culture. Most developed and underdeveloped countries consciously or unconsciously practice some form of employment discrimination. For example, in Japan female executives are more uncommon than in the United States and were virtually nonexistent before World War II.

As in other countries, there is considerable statistical disparity among races and ethnic groups in the United States. For example, the unemployment rate for blacks is regularly twice the unemployment rate for whites. The percentage of black families living below the poverty line is significantly greater than that of white families. Of those working, about one in four blacks secures a white-collar job, whereas one in two working whites secures such employment. White male wage workers earn an average of 20 percent more than black male wage workers. A similar statistical disparity exists with regard to sex. Males traditionally dominate the higher-paying professions, such as medicine, law, and management, while females have traditionally concentrated in lower-paying professions such as nursing, paralegal, and clerical. White male wage workers earn an average of 40 percent more than women wage workers.

Much of this statistical disparity between males and females and between differing races and ethnic groups may be unintentional and attributable to employment patterns. To a large extent, the disparity may be attributed to differences in education, training, family demands, and years of experience in the workforce. Still, some of the disparity is probably due to stereotyped assumptions and expectations about productivity and to worker preferences to associate in the workplace with "one's own kind." It is this kind of employment discrimination that has produced a legal response. Table 15–1 shows how female and minority participation in white-collar jobs has increased in the past several decades.

The Civil Rights Movements of the 1950s and 1960s

Historically, the common law permitted employers to hire and fire, within contractual limits, at will. The employer was relatively unconstrained to establish the terms and conditions of employment. Employers could discriminate or not discriminate as they wished. Similarly, labor unions could impose discriminatory membership policies. Although some states enacted statutes limiting discriminatory practices, employers and unions were largely free to conduct their affairs without judicial or administrative interference under the common law.

TABLE 15–1   Who Holds Managerial Jobs?

1970		**1990**	
White males	81.9%	White males	55.6%
White females	14.7	White females	35.5
Nonwhite males	2.7	Black males	2.5
Nonwhite females	0.7	Black females	3.1
All minorities	3.4	Other minorities	3.3

Source: *Employment and Earnings, 1990.* Washington D.C.: U.S. Department of Labor.

By the early 1960s, the National Labor Relations Board had interpreted the National Labor Relations Act to prohibit most blatant forms of discrimination by unions. Executive Orders in the 1940s and 1950s had placed some restraints on racial discrimination by government employers and employers under government contract. The drive for civil rights in employment and other aspects of life that arose in the South in the 1950s became a national movement in the early 1960s. Thus, there was an emerging but incomplete patchwork of remedies for employment discrimination coupled with a rapidly rising public concern. In partial response, Congress enacted the first federal employment discrimination statute in 1963, the Equal Pay Act. That statute was followed by the Civil Rights Act of 1964, which is the cornerstone of federal employment discrimination law.

Equal Pay Act of 1963

The *Equal Pay Act of 1963* was the first federal law that specifically addressed equal employment. Although the law prohibits discrimination in compensation on the basis of sex, it does not concern hiring and promotion decisions. Thus, the law provides remedies for employed women suffering from discriminatory practices related to compensation, but does not apply to any other discriminatory practice. Initially interpreted and enforced by the Department of Labor, responsibility for the law was transferred to the Equal Employment Opportunity Commission (EEOC).

Scope and Coverage of the Act

The Act holds it illegal to pay a wage to women employees different from that paid to men employees where the job in question requires equal skill, effort, and responsibility and involves the same working conditions. Job titles are not presumptively relevant; it is the content of the jobs that is scrutinized. However, the Equal Pay Act allows differences in wages if they are due to "(i) a seniority system; (ii) a merit system; (iii) a system which measures earnings by quantity or quality of production; or (iv) a differential based on any factor other than sex . . . ." Pay differentials on the basis of sex are to be eliminated by raising the pay of the female employees, not by lowering the pay of the male employees.

The equal-pay provisions apply to all government employees, to union-negotiated contracts, and, in general, to all employees of enterprises engaged in commerce. A business "engaged in commerce" is any business with two or more employees. The only exceptions permitted by the Act are some small retail and agricultural employments.

Enforcement Provisions

To assist enforcement of the Act, employers are required to keep records of each employee's hours, wages, and other relevant information. Government investigators may enter a business to examine the records, which must be kept for several years. If a firm is found to be in violation, the most likely result will be an order to pay employees who have been discriminated against an amount equal to the wages they should have been receiving. The employees may also receive an additional amount to serve as a penalty to the employer. If the employees have to hire an attorney to settle the suit and they win, they may be awarded reasonable attorney's fees and court costs.

TITLE VII OF THE 1964 CIVIL RIGHTS ACT

The single most important source of antidiscrimination in employment rules is *Title VII of the Civil Rights Act of 1964*. The Act was amended by the *Equal Employment Opportunity Act* in 1972 to give the *Equal Employment Opportunity Commission (EEOC)* expanded power to enforce the Act, and then by the *Pregnancy Discrimination Act* in 1978. Section 703(a) of the Civil Rights Act makes it an unlawful employment practice for an employer

> (1) to fail or refuse to hire or to discharge any individual, or otherwise to discriminate against any individual with respect to his compensation, terms, conditions, or privileges of employment; or
> (2) to limit, segregate, or classify his employees or applicants for employment in any way which would deprive or tend to deprive any individual of employment opportunities or otherwise adversely affect his status as an employee because of such individual's race, color, religion, sex, or national origin.

Coverage and Enforcement of Title VII

Title VII applies to employers, employment agencies, and labor unions in the private and public sectors. In general, it forbids *discrimination* in all aspects of employment on the basis of *race, color, religion, sex, or national origin*. To fall within the Act, the employer must employ an average of at least fifteen persons for twenty or more weeks during a year. Similarly, any union with fifteen or more members is subject to the law. The Supreme Court has stated that law firms and other partnership organizations are covered by Title VII with regard to employment decisions. Title VII does not apply, however, to business relationships or to the selection of independent contractors.

Administrative Procedure

When a person believes they have been the victim of a discriminatory act, to seek relief under Title VII they must file a charge with their state or local Equal Employment Opportunity agency. These exist in almost all states under state statutes similar to Title VII. Many complaints are handled at the state level, much like the EEOC procedure described below. But if the charge is dismissed at the state level, or the relief is not satisfactory, the employee may then take the complaint to the EEOC, which will investigate.

The EEOC will notify the employer to come to the EEOC office for a conference to discuss the allegations. An EEOC agent will have the employer and employee present their views and will suggest a settlement. Many complaints are settled at this point. If there is no settlement, the EEOC completes an investigation to determine if there is reasonable cause to believe that discrimination has occurred. Results of the investigation are given to both parties. If reasonable cause is found, the employee is given a "right-to-sue" letter.

Litigation

The right-to-sue letter gives the employee the right to sue the employer in federal court. The EEOC may sue the employer, but rarely does so—the burden is on the employee to carry the case forward. The Supreme Court established a four-part test in *McDonnell-Douglas Corp.* v. *Green* (1983) that a plaintiff must meet to provide a *prima facie* case of discrimination:

1. The person belongs to a protected class.
2. The person applied for a job and met the qualifications for a job that was open.
3. The person was rejected.
4. The employer continued to seek applications from persons with similar qualifications.

While the court applied the test to applications for employment, the same test holds for all aspects of employment—promotion, compensation, discipline, and termination.

Once the employee has presented a *rebuttable presumption of discrimination*, the defendant-employer must provide "legitimate, nondiscriminatory reasons" for what happened. The charge of discrimination must be answered directly, or the plaintiff wins. Assuming that the defendant responds, the plaintiff answers by showing that the defendant's explanation is only a pretext to disguise discrimination. The Supreme Court addressed the standard of proof in the *Price Waterhouse* case.

Price Waterhouse v. Hopkins,
United States Supreme Court,
__ U.S. __, 109 S. Ct. 1775 (1989)

Case Background. *Ann Hopkins worked at Price Waterhouse, a nationwide accounting partnership, as a senior manager. She was the only woman proposed for partnership in 1982 (along with eighty-seven men candidates). Her candidacy for partnership was put on hold for a year, at which time she was not renominated for partnership. She sued under Title VII, charging that her employer had discriminated against her on the basis of sex. She won at District Court (Judge Gesell) and Court of Appeals; the issue is what standard of evidence must be met.*

Case Decision. Justice Brennan delivered the opinion of the Court.

* * *

In a jointly prepared statement supporting her candidacy, the partners in Hopkins' office showcased her successful 2-year effort to secure a $25 million contract with the Department of State, labeling it "an outstanding performance" and one that Hopkins carried out "virtually at the partner level."

* * *

The partners in Hopkins' office praised her character as well as her accomplishments, describing her in their joint statement as "an outstanding professional" who had a "deft touch," a "strong character, independence and integrity."

* * *

On too many occasions, however, Hopkins' aggressiveness apparently spilled over into abrasiveness. Staff members seem to have borne the brunt of Hopkins' brusqueness. Long before her bid for partnership, partners evaluating her work had counseled her to improve her relations with staff members. Although later evaluations indicate an improvement, Hopkins' perceived shortcomings in this important area eventually doomed her bid for partnership. Virtually all of the partners' negative remarks about Hopkins—even those of partners supporting her— had to do with her "interpersonal skills." Both "[s]upporters and opponents of her candidacy," stressed Judge Gesell, "indicated that she was sometimes overly aggressive, unduly harsh, difficult to work with and impatient with staff."

There were clear signs, though, that some of the partners reacted negatively to Hopkins' personality because she was a woman. One partner described her as "macho"; another suggested that she "overcompensated for being a woman"; a third advised her to take "a course at charm school". Several partners criticized her use of profanity; in response, one partner suggested that those partners objected to her swearing only "because it[']s a lady using foul language." Another supporter explained that Hopkins "ha[d] matured from a tough-talking somewhat masculine hardnosed mgr to an authoritative, formidable, but much more appealing lady ptr candidate." But it was the man who, as Judge Gesell found, bore responsibility for explaining to Hopkins the reasons for the Policy Board's decision to place her candidacy on hold who delivered the *coup de grace:* in order to improve her chances for partnership, Thomas Beyer advised, Hopkins should "walk more femininely, talk more femininely, dress more femininely, wear make-up, have her hair styled, and wear jewelry."

* * *

In previous years, other female candidates for partnership also had been evaluated in sex-based terms. As a general matter, Judge Gesell concluded, "[c]andidates were viewed favorably if partners believed they maintained their femin[in]ity while becoming effective professional managers"; in this environment, "[t]o be identified as a 'women's lib[b]er' was regarded as [a] negative comment." In fact, the judge found that in previous years "[o]ne partner repeatedly commented that he could not consider any woman seriously as a partnership candidate and believed that women were not even capable of functioning as senior managers—yet the firm took no action to discourage his comments and recorded his vote in the overall summary of the evaluations."

Judge Gesell found that Price Waterhouse legitimately emphasized interpersonal skills in its partnership decisions, and also found that the firm had not fabricated its complaints about Hopkins' interpersonal skills as a pretext for discrimination. Moreover, he concluded, the firm did not give decisive emphasis to such traits only because Hopkins was a woman; although there were male candidates who lacked these skills but who were admitted to partnership, the judge found that these candidates possessed other, positive traits that Hopkins lacked.

The judge went on to decide, however, that some of the partners' remarks about Hopkins stemmed from an impermissibly cabined view of the proper behavior of women, and that Price Waterhouse had done nothing to disavow reliance on such comments. He held that Price Waterhouse had unlawfully discriminated against Hopkins on the basis of sex by consciously giving credence and effect to partners' comments that resulted from sex stereotyping. Noting that Price Waterhouse could avoid equitable relief by proving by clear and convincing evidence that it would have placed Hopkins' candidacy on hold even absent this discrimination, the judge decided that the firm had not carried this heavy burden.

* * *

[O]ur assumption always has been that if an employer allows gender to affect its decisionmaking process, then it must carry the burden of justifying its ultimate decision. We have not in the past required women whose gender has proved relevant to an employment decision to establish the negative proposition that they would not have been subject to that decision had they been men, and we do not do so today.

* * *

In saying that gender played a motivating part in an employment decision, we mean that, if we asked the employer at the moment of the decision what its reasons were and if we received a truthful response, one of those reasons would be that the applicant or employee was a woman. In the specific context of sex stereotyping, an employer who acts on the basis of a belief that a woman cannot be aggressive, or that she must not be, has acted on the basis of gender.

* * *

Remarks at work that are based on sex stereotypes do not inevitably prove that gender played a part in a particular employment decision. The plaintiff must show that the employer actually relied on her gender in making its decision. In making this showing, stereotyped remarks can certainly be *evidence* that gender played a part. In any event, the stereotyping in this case did not simply consist of stray remarks. On the contrary, Hopkins proved that Price Waterhouse invited partners to submit comments; that some of the comments stemmed from sex stereotypes; that an important part of the Policy Board's decision on Hopkins was an assessment of the submitted comments; and that Price Waterhouse in no way disclaimed reliance on the sex-linked evaluations. This is not, as Price Waterhouse suggests, "discrimination in the air"; rather, it is, as Hopkins puts it, "discrimination brought to ground and visited upon" an employee.

* * *

As to the employer's proof, in most cases, the employer should be able to present some objective evidence as to its probable decision in the absence of an impermissible motive. Moreover, proving "that the same decision would have been justified . . . is not the same as proving that the same decision would have been made. . ."

An employer may not, in other words, prevail in a mixed-motives case by offering a legitimate and sufficient reason for its decision if that reason did not motivate it at the time of the decision. Finally, an employer may not meet its burden in such a case by merely showing that at the time of the decision it was motivated only in part by a legitimate reason. The very premise of a mixed-motives case is that a legitimate reason was present, and indeed, in this case, Price Waterhouse already has made this showing by convincing Judge Gesell that Hopkins' interpersonal problems were a legitimate concern. The employer instead must show that its legitimate reason, standing alone, would have induced it to make the same decision.

The courts below held that an employer who has allowed a discriminatory impulse to play a motivating part in an employment decision must prove by clear and convincing evidence that it would have made the same decision in the absence of discrimination. We are persuaded that the better rule is that the employer must make this showing by a preponderance of the evidence.

* * *

Case Holding. *The Supreme Court affirmed the verdict in favor of Hopkins, holding that if an employee establishes that a discriminatory element was involved in an employment decision, the employer will be liable under Title VII unless it proves, by a preponderance of the evidence, that it would have made the same decision even if it had not taken that element into account. On remand to the District Court, Hopkins was granted partnership.*

Case Questions

1. The dissent argued that Prince Waterhouse should win unless it could be shown that Hopkins was not granted a partnership "because of" gender. Do you think that a mix of motives makes it hard to tell if sex really was the bar to promotion?

2.   Will decisions like this cause firms to persuade managers to keep their mouths shut, so as to avoid possible negative evidence?

Protected Classes Under Title VII

Title VII provides for *equal employment opportunity* without regard for race, color, religion, sex, or national origin. In setting forth these categories, Congress sought to protect certain classes of people who had a history of discriminatory treatment in employment relationships. These classes of people are referred to as *protected classes* for purposes of Title VII coverage.

Race and Color

Relative to the other protected classes, the courts have had little difficulty in determining the protected racial class. Congress expressly acknowledged that its primary legislative purpose in enacting Title VII was "to open employment opportunities for Negroes in occupations which have been traditionally closed to them." In addition to blacks, there are four other major racial groupings in this country: white, Native American, Hispanic, and Asian. Since whites form the majority, the other groups are protected classes under Title VII.

Congress's emphasis on eliminating discrimination toward racial minorities resulted in early decisions holding that whites are not protected under Title VII. That interpretation was rejected by the Court in *McDonald* v. *Sante Fe Trail Transportation Company* (1976). In *McDonald,* a black employee and a white employee had misappropriated the property of their employer. The black employee was reprimanded but allowed to keep his job while the white employee was discharged. In declaring that Title VII protected whites against racial discrimination, the Court stated:

> Title VII prohibits racial discrimination against the white petitioners upon the same standards as would be applicable were they Negroes . . . . While Santa Fe may decide that participation in a theft of cargo may render an employee unqualified for employment, this criteria must be applied alike to members of all races . . . . [W]hatever factors the mechanisms of compromise may take into account in mitigating discipline of some employees, under Title VII race may not be among them.

While *reverse discrimination*—giving preferential treatment to minorities—is illegal, where minorities or women are under-represented in a particular job classification, it is legal for an employer to take steps voluntarily to see that more minorities or women are hired to increase their share of the jobs. *Affirmative action programs*, which will be discussed later, designed to remedy past or present discrimination against minorities or women, may be adopted and not violate the rule against reverse discrimination.

Religion

Title VII does not define the term religion, but rather simply states that "religion includes all aspects of religious observances and practice." The courts have defined the term broadly to resolve constitutional issues. According to the Court in *United States* v. *Seeger* (1965):

[All that is required is a] sincere and meaningful belief occupying in the life of its possessor a place parallel to that filled by the God of those [religions generally recognized].

The employer is required to reasonably accommodate an employee's or prospective employee's religious observance or practice. The employer may discriminate, however, if the accommodation will impose an *undue hardship* on the conduct of the business. The Court has stated that undue hardship is created by accommodations that would cost an employer more than a minimal amount. A religious institution, like a church or a school, may legally hire only members of its religion.

Sex

The prohibition against sex discrimination provided by Title VII was added with little legislative history to provide insights into how Congress intended to define the scope of the term sex discrimination. Thus, the courts have had to take an active role in defining the limits of the term.

As they have in defining other protected classes, the courts have taken the position that the term sex should be given the meaning it has in ordinary communications. Thus, early decisions interpreted Title VII as prohibiting sex discrimination simply on the basis of whether a person was male or female. In that light, the courts have held that discrimination on the basis of sexual preference is not protected by Title VII. Nor has Title VII been held to prohibit discrimination on the basis of marital status—as long as the employer applies the rule uniformly to employees of both sexes.

Pregnancy and Sex Discrimination

Title VII was amended in 1978 by the *Pregnancy Discrimination Act*, which declares that prohibitions on sex discrimination include pregnancy, child-birth, and related medical conditions. Women affected by these conditions "shall be treated the same for all employment-related purposes, including receipt of benefits under fringe benefit programs." Examples of pregnancy discrimination include the following:

- Denying a woman a job, assignment, or promotion only because she is pregnant.
- Requiring a pregnant woman to go on leave when she is able to do her job.
- Treating maternity leave from work different than other leaves for temporary disabilities.

Most disputes have involved the receipt of fringe benefits. In a 1983 decision, *Newport News Shipbuilding & Dry Dock Company v. EEOC*, the Supreme Court made it clear that fringe benefit treatment must be equal among employees with regard to pregnancy benefits. In *Newport News*, the employer's health insurance plan provided female employees with hospitalization benefits for pregnancy-related conditions to the same extent it provided for other medical conditions, but gave less extensive pregnancy benefits to the spouses of male employees. That difference in coverage was held to be illegal because the benefit package offered married male employees for their dependents was less generous than the coverage offered to the dependents of married female employees. To provide female spouses with less coverage constituted discrimination against married male employees. The Court also noted that it would be an unlawful discriminatory employment practice for a business to offer no pregnancy benefits since pregnancy benefits are normally provided in medical benefits packages.

Sexual Harassment and Sex Discrimination

The courts have held that sexual demands by a supervisor constitute sex discrimination under Title VII, if the employee reasonably believes that the request is a term of employment and the person making the request is acting within the actual or constructive authority of the employer. The Department of Health and Human Services has defined *sexual harassment* as:

1. Explicit or implicit promise of career advancement (e.g., promotion, training, awards, details, lax timekeeping, and lower standards of performance) in return for sexual favors.

2. Explicit or implicit threats that the victim's career will be adversely affected (e.g., nonpromotion, poor performance appraisal, reassignment to a less desirable position or location) if the sexual demands are rejected.

3. Deliberate, repeated, unsolicited verbal comments, gestures, or physical actions of a sexual nature (e.g., touching, pinching, or patting another person).

Many employers have announced policies and procedures regarding sexual harassment and train supervisors to be sensitive to such matters. Although the exact boundaries of sexual harassment under Title VII are still to be determined, the Supreme Court did offer guidance in *Meritor Savings Bank* v. *Vinson.*

Meritor Savings Bank v. Vinson

United States Supreme Court 477 U.S. 57, 106 S.Ct. 2399 (1986)

Case Background. *Mechelle Vinson was hired in 1974 by Sidney Taylor, vice president of Meritor Savings Bank. She worked for the bank until 1978, when she was fired by Taylor for taking too much sick leave. With Taylor as her supervisor, Vinson consistently received high work evaluations and three promotions before her dismissal. She sued Taylor and the bank for damages, claiming that she had been subjected to sexual harassment by Taylor in violation of Title VII. Vinson testified that soon after she began to work at the bank Taylor took her to dinner and then suggested they go to a motel. She said she agreed for fear of losing her job. During the next few years, Taylor made repeated demands upon her for sexual favors. She estimated she had intercourse with him between forty and fifty times. In addition, Taylor fondled Vinson in front of other employees, exposed himself to her in the women's restroom, and forcibly raped her on several occasions. These activities ceased in 1978, the year she was fired, when she started going with a steady boyfriend. Vinson never reported Taylor's harassment to his supervisors and never made use of the bank's complaint procedure because she was afraid of Taylor. Taylor denied all Vinson's claims. The bank denied responsibility, since it did not know of the alleged activities which, if true, were done despite bank policy.*

The district court ruled against Vinson, holding that if there were sexual relations between Vinson and Taylor, they were voluntary and not related to her employment.

Further, the court noted that "the bank was without notice and cannot be held liable for the alleged actions of Taylor." The court of appeals reversed in favor of Vinson.

Case Decision. Justice Rehnquist delivered the opinion of the Court.

* * *

Respondent argues, and the Court of Appeals held, that unwelcome sexual advances that create an offensive or hostile working environment violate Title VII. Without question, when a supervisor sexually harasses a subordinate because of the subordinate's sex, that supervisor "discriminate[s]" on the basis of sex. Petitioner apparently does not challenge this proposition. It contends instead that in prohibiting discrimination with respect to "compensation, terms, conditions, or privileges" of employment, Congress was concerned with what petitioner describes as "tangible loss" of "an economic character," not "purely psychological aspects of the workplace environment." . . .

We reject petitioner's view. First, the language of Title VII is not limited to "economic" or "tangible" discrimination. The phrase "terms, conditions, or privileges of employment" evinces a congressional intent " 'to strike at the entire spectrum of disparate treatment of men and women' " in employment . . . .

The EEOC guidelines fully support the view that harassment leading to non-economic injury can violate Title VII . . . .

Since the guidelines were issued, courts have uniformly held, and we agree, that a plaintiff may establish a violation of Title VII by proving that discrimination based on sex has created a hostile or abusive work environment.

* * *

For sexual harassment to be actionable, it must be sufficiently severe or pervasive "to alter the conditions of [the victim's] employment and create an abusive working environment." Respondent's allegations in this case—which include not only pervasive harassment but also criminal conduct of the most serious nature—are plainly sufficient to state a claim for "hostile environment" sexual harassment.

* * *

The gravamen of any sexual harassment claim is that the alleged sexual advances were "unwelcome." While the question whether particular conduct was indeed unwelcome presents difficult problems of proof and turns largely on credibility determinations committed to the trier of fact, the District Court in this case erroneously focused on the "voluntariness" of respondent's participation in the claimed sexual episodes. The correct inquiry is whether respondent by her conduct indicated that the alleged sexual advances were unwelcome, not whether her actual participation in sexual intercourse was voluntary. . . . While "voluntariness" in the sense of consent is not a defense to such a claim, it does not follow that a complainant's sexually provocative speech or dress is irrelevant as a matter of law in determining whether he or she found particular sexual advances unwelcome. To the contrary, such evidence is obviously relevant. The EEOC guidelines emphasize that the trier of fact must determine the existence of sexual harassment in light of "the record as a whole" and "the totality of circumstances, such as the nature of the sexual advances and the context in which the alleged incidents occurred."

* * *

We . . . decline the parties' invitation to issue a definitive rule on employer liability, but we do agree with the EEOC that Congress wanted courts to look to agency principles for guidance in this area. While such common-law principles may not be transferable in all their particulars to Title VII, Congress' decision to define "employer" to include any "agent" of an employer, 42 U.S.C. § 2000e(b), surely evinces an intent to place some limits on the acts of employees for which employers under Title VII are to be held responsible. For this reason, we hold that the Court of Appeals erred in concluding that employers are always automatically liable for sexual harassment by their supervisors. For the same reason, absence of notice to an employer does not necessarily insulate that employer from liability.

Finally, we reject petitioner's view that the mere existence of a grievance procedure and a policy against discrimination, coupled with respondent's failure to invoke that procedure, must insulate petitioner from liability. While those facts are plainly relevant, the situation before us demonstrates why they are not necessarily dispositive. Petitioner's general nondiscrimination policy did not address sexual harassment in particular, and thus did not alert employees to their employer's interest in correcting that form of discrimination. Moreover, the bank's grievance procedure apparently required an employee to complain first to her supervisor, in this case Taylor. Since Taylor was the alleged perpetrator, it is not altogether surprising that respondent failed to invoke the procedure and report her grievance to him. Petitioner's contention that respondent's failure should insulate it from liability might be substantially stronger if its procedures were better calculated to encourage victims of harassment to come forward.

*   *   *

Case Holding. *The judgment of the court of appeals reversing the judgment of the district court was affirmed. The Court left open the issue of exactly when an employer will be responsible for sexual harassment. Four justices, in a concurring opinion, said that they would hold the employer liable in all instances, regardless of knowledge about what was going on.*

Case Questions

1. Suppose Taylor claimed that he and Vinson had been in love and that all the sexual relations were voluntary. It was only after they severed their relationship that Vinson claimed the relationship was forced. How do the courts deal with that real possibility?

2. Suppose the concurring opinion "that sexual harassment by a supervisor of an employee . . . should be imputed to the employer . . . regardless of whether the employee gave notice of the offense" became law. If an employee does not report harassment initially but allows it to go on for years, as in the case of Vinson, how can the employer be protected from the damages becoming very large because of lack of knowledge of what was going on all that time?

National Origin

According to the Supreme Court in *Espinoza* v. *Farah Manufacturing* (1973), the term *national origin* is to be given the meaning it has in ordinary communications:

> [The term national origin] refers to the country where a person is born or . . . the country from which his or her ancestors came.

Employment discrimination can take place when an employer allows ethnic slurs to occur and does not take steps to prevent such actions. Discrimination has been held to exist because a person has a physical, cultural, or speech characteristic of a national origin group. It is also discrimination to require that English be spoken at all times in the workplace. However, if business necessity requires that English be spoken, then it may be a legitimate job requirement.

This protection is not provided to non-citizens employed or seeking employment in this country. However, while an employer can discriminate against aliens, the employer could not discriminate on the basis of different origins of citizenship. For example, an employer cannot accept aliens from Italy but reject aliens from Mexico.

Meaning of Discrimination Under Title VII

Title VII does not explicitly define the word discrimination other than to state that it is unlawful employment practice for any employer to discriminate against any individual because of race, color, religion, sex, or national origin. The dictionary defines the word *discriminate* to mean "to make a difference in treatment or [to] favor on a basis other than merit." In making these definitions functional under Title VII, the Supreme Court has developed definitions of discrimination that include:

1. The Differential Standards Doctrine
2. Compensation Differentials
3. Segregation
4. Harassment and Constructive Discharge.

Differential Standards Doctrine

Employers may set standards for employees regarding personal characteristics, but the standards must be applied equally. If an employer will hire only unmarried persons, that rule must apply to both male and female employees. If an employer discharges employees who become married or have children, the rule must apply to all equally, not just to female employees.

Grooming standards for employees may differentiate between sexes, so long as the rules are not generally more costly for one sex. For example, an employer might require its male employees to wear short hair but might not set a length requirement for its female employees. Male employees might be required to wear a tie and female employees not; female employees might be prohibited from wearing slacks but male employees not. Similarly, codes of conduct for employees may be set but must be applied consistently. If employees of one sex are fired for having an affair, the same penalty must be applied to employees of the other sex. Generally, such rules must be reasonably related to the conduct of the business and may not interfere too much with personal choices that have no relevant bearing on the business.

Compensation Differentials

In conjunction with the Equal Pay Act, Title VII prohibits pay differentials based on sex as well as on other personal characteristics. That is, pay, fringe benefits, retirement plans, and other aspects of compensation, such as retirement pay schedules or age requirements, may not differ simply on the basis of sex. In *City of Los Angeles* v. *Manhart* (1978) the Supreme Court struck down a requirement imposed by the employer that female employees make larger contributions than male employees to the pension fund. The employer argued that on an actuarial basis the requirement was not discriminatory because females live longer than males on the average. As a consequence, females should set aside more for their retirement than males, since they will eventually collect more retirement pay. The Court held the practice to be differential treatment on the basis of sex and ordered retirement contributions to be equalized.

Segregation

The courts have held there is discrimination when employees are segregated into particular jobs based on race, sex, or national origin. Obvious discrimination would include segregated restrooms, drinking fountains, and eating areas or racially segregated social events. According to the court in *Rogers* v. *Equal Employment Opportunity Commission* (5th Cir.,1971), an employer can illegally discriminate by assigning customers of Hispanic origin to Hispanic employers and Anglo customers to Anglo employers. Separate treatment will not be considered equal treatment.

Harassment and Constructive Discharge

The majority of Title VII cases involve circumstances where the employee has been unequally treated in a hiring, promotion, compensation, or discharge decision. In other cases, however, the employee has been subject to harassment on the job and responded by quitting. The court in *Young* v. *Southwestern Savings and Loan Association* (5th Cir.,1975) held that:

> If the employer deliberately makes an employee's working conditions so intolerable that the employee is forced into involuntary resignation, then the employer has encompassed a constructive discharge and is liable for any illegal conduct involved therein as if it had formally discharged the aggrieved employee.

Under Title VII, such a constructive discharge will be treated in the same manner as a firing. That is, if it is determined that the employee is a member of a protected class, and was fired because she or he was in that class, the employer will likely be found to be in violation of Title VII.

Theories of Discrimination Under Title VII

To select among applicants for employment, or among existing employees for promotion, the employer must necessarily differentiate among those individuals to reach a decision. Although Title VII does not restrict the process, it does restrict the grounds upon which the employer can make that decision. The employer may not differentiate among the applicants on the basis of race, color, religion, sex, or national origin. If the employer differentiates among the applicants on such a basis, there may be a violation of Title VII's prohibitions against discriminatory employment practices.

In determining whether an employer's decision constitutes discrimination, it is not necessary that the employer intend to discriminate. Thus, it may not be readily apparent that a decision constitutes unlawful employment discrimination. To determine whether an employer's decision is unlawful discrimination, the courts have used three basic approaches or "theories":

1. Individual instances of disparate treatment or direct discrimination.
2. Neutral rules that perpetuate past intentional discrimination.
3. Neutral rules that have an adverse or disparate impact that are not justified by a business necessity.

Disparate Treatment

An employee may bring a suit charging an employer for a violation of Title VII based on *disparate treatment*. If race, color, religion, sex, or national origin is the reason for an employer's decision to hire, promote, or fire—unless the employer can show that other factors were, in fact, the basis of the employment-related decision—there probably is a violation of the Act. In most disparate treatment cases, although the employer does not have a written policy against hiring or promoting individuals from a certain group, qualified individuals from that group are simply not being hired or promoted in the employer's business.

Perpetuating Past Patterns of Intentional Discrimination

A violation of Title VII can be established by a "neutral" employment rule that *perpetuates a past pattern of intentional discrimination*. That is, although the employer does not actively engage in discrimination on the basis of race, color, religion, sex, or national origin, the effect of being neutral on such basis is to perpetuate past actions that did involve intentional discrimination.

For example, before the enactment of Title VII, some labor unions restricted membership to whites only. After the Act, the unions imposed a membership requirement that new members had to be related to or recommended by current members. The court found that although the union's membership rule was neutral on its face, it perpetuated the past purposeful exclusionary rule. In general, the courts have held that neutral business rules that perpetuate the effects of abandoned discriminatory practices are unlawful violations of Title VII.

Disparate Impact

The third major theory under which a violation of Title VII can be established involves a neutral employment rule for hiring or promotion that has a *disparate impact* on a certain group. Employment procedure usually requires that applicants have a high school diploma, achieve a minimum score on a specified test, or meet the requirements of some other selection device. If it is asserted that the employer's hiring or promotion practices had a discriminatory impact on an applicant, the employer must show that the applicant was rejected not because of race, color, religion, sex, or national origin but because the qualification requirements of the job were not met. The impact of employment rules, such as having a high school diploma, must be neutral— that is, not have a disparate impact on a protected class.

The relationship between the use of such rules and Title VII was established in *Griggs* v. *Duke Power Company. Griggs* determined that neutral employment criteria will be judged by their impact, not by the good or bad faith involved in their implementation.

Griggs v. Duke Power Company

United States Supreme Court
401 U.S. 424, 91 S.Ct. 849 (1971)

Case Background. *Duke Power was a segregated company before passage of the 1964 Civil Rights Act. Blacks were hired to work in certain menial jobs; all higher quality jobs were held by whites. After Title VII took effect, Duke Power moved to end discrimination by allowing all persons to compete for all jobs. Except for certain manual labor jobs, which were already held by blacks, the company required a high school diploma and certain scores on two professionally prepared aptitude tests. These job requirements, while neutral on their face, were claimed to have a discriminatory impact on blacks. Thirty-four percent of the white males in North Carolina had high school diplomas compared to only 12 percent of black males, and 58 percent of the whites passed similar aptitude tests but only 6 percent of the blacks passed.*

The district court ruled in favor of Duke Power, saying that the purpose of the standards was not to discriminate but to achieve a work force of a certain quality. The court of appeals agreed, saying that there was no discriminatory motive.

Case Decision. Chief Justice Burger delivered the opinion of the Court.

* * *

The objective of Congress in the enactment of Title VII is plain from the language of the statute. It was to achieve equality of employment opportunities and remove barriers that have operated in the past to favor an identifiable group of white employees over other employees. Under the Act, practices, procedures, or tests neutral on their face, and even neutral in terms of intent, cannot be maintained if they operate to "freeze" the status quo of prior discriminatory employment practices.

* * *

On the record before us, neither the high school completion requirement nor the general intelligence test is shown to bear a demonstrable relationship to successful performance of the jobs for which it was used. Both were adopted, as the Court of Appeals noted, without meaningful study of their relationship to job-performance ability. Rather, a vice president of the Company testified, the requirements were instituted on the Company's judgment that they generally would improve the overall quality of the work force.

The evidence, however, shows that employees who have not completed high school or taken the tests have continued to perform satisfactorily and make progress in departments for which the high school and test criteria are now used. The promotion record of present employees who would not be able to meet the new criteria thus suggests the possibility that the requirements may not be needed even for the limited purpose of preserving the avowed policy of advancement within the Company.

* * *

The Court of Appeals held that the Company had adopted the diploma and test requirements without any "intention to discriminate against Negro employees." We do not suggest that either the District Court or the Court of Appeals erred in examining the employer's intent; but good intent or absence of discriminatory intent does not redeem employment procedures or testing mechanisms that operate as "built-in headwinds" for minority groups and are unrelated to measuring job capability. . . . Congress directed the thrust of the Act to the *consequences* of employment practices, not simply the motivation. More than that, Congress has placed on the employer the burden of showing that any given requirement must have a manifest relationship to the employment in question.

* * *

Nothing in the Act precludes the use of testing or measuring procedures; obviously they are useful. What Congress has forbidden is giving these devices and mechanisms controlling force unless they are demonstrably a reasonable measure of job perfor mance. Congress has not commanded that the less qualified be preferred over the better qualified simply because of minority origins. Far from disparaging job qualifications as such, Congress has made such qualifications the controlling factor, so that race, religion, nationality, and sex become irrelevant. What Congress has commanded is that any test used must measure the person for the job and not the person in the abstract.

* * *

Case Holding. *The Supreme Court reversed, holding that the employer's practices violated Title VII. The case established that neutral employment qualifications will be judged by their impact, not by their intent. When such rules can be shown to have an adverse impact on members of a protected class, the employer must show a business necessity behind the job qualifications. This means that terms of employment, including educational achievement and scores on aptitude tests, must be shown to be related in some meaningful way to job performance.*

Case Questions

1. Does this decision reduce the incentives for people to obtain high school diplomas and college degrees?
2. Suppose an employer knows of a valid aptitude test that is related to job performance but is one that blacks do less well on than another, similar test. May the employer use the valid test that will discriminate more against blacks than will an alternative test?

The Supreme Court further refined the test for disparate impact in the 1989 case *Wards Cove Packing Co.* v. *Atonio.* In that case, most of the unskilled jobs at a work site were filled by minorities. Most of the higher-paying skilled jobs were filled by whites. The nonwhite workers filed a suit claiming disparate impact based on statistical evidence that while most workers were nonwhite, the higher-paying jobs were dominated by whites. The Court rejected such evidence alone as proof of disparate impact. To present a claim of disparate impact of a hiring policy, such statistical evidence must be based on the pools of qualified job applicants or the qualified labor force population available to fill the various jobs. Such statistical evidence must then be related to specific employment practices that produce the discrimination.

The Defense of Business Necessity

If the rules can be shown to have a discriminatory impact on certain employees, the employer must establish that the rules are justified objectively as a *business necessity.* Business necessity is evaluated with reference to the ability of the employee to perform a certain job. Written tests, no matter how objective, must meet this business necessity test.

Experience and skill requirements, usually measured in terms of seniority, are often accepted as necessary. For example, to be a skilled bricklayer generally requires experience gained only by performance over a period of time. To require such experience and skill for certain positions is not a violation of Title VII. Similarly, if a job requires certain abilities with respect to strength and agility, tests for such ability are legitimate.

Selection criteria for professional, managerial, and other white-collar positions must also meet the business necessity test. Insofar as objective criteria often cannot be used in such instances, subjective evaluations such as job interviews, references, and some aspect of job performance evaluation are common and generally recognized as necessary in hiring and promoting professional personnel. Similarly, such positions may have a strict education requirement. As in *Griggs*, educational requirements for manual or semiskilled jobs are not likely to be held necessary. However, for jobs such as teachers, police officers, laboratory technicians, airline pilots, and engineers, education requirements are usually determined to be valid.

The Supreme Court held in the 1988 case *Watson* v. *Fort Worth Bank & Trust* that disparate impact analysis, which had been applied only to objective job criteria, such as education level or test scores, also applies to subjective employment practices. Many jobs are not covered by precise and formal selection criteria, but are determined by the subjective judgment of supervisors. The results of such subjective decisions are subject to the same disparate impact test as are the more formal job criteria.

Defenses Under Title VII

Employers charged with employment discrimination under Title VII are provided with three major defenses by the statute. Employers are allowed to give a "professionally developed ability test" and to apply different "terms, conditions, or privileges of employment pursuant to a bona fide seniority or merit system" as long as they are not intended to discriminate on the basis of race, color, religion, sex, or national origin. The third statutory defense is the bona fide occupational qualification defense, which applies primarily to charges of intentional discrimination.

Professionally Developed Ability Tests

Tests are often used by employers to determine whether applicants for a job possess the necessary skills and attributes. According to Section 703(h) of the statute:

> [It] shall [not] be an unlawful employment practice for an employer to give and to act upon the results of any professionally developed ability test provided that such test, its administration, or action upon the results is not designed, intended, or used to discriminate because of race, color, religion, sex, or national origin.

In general, as stated by the Supreme Court in *Griggs*, such tests are impermissible unless they can be shown to closely predict the work behavior required for the job. Usually employers are required to supply detailed and precise statistical validation of the tests. Expert testimony from educational and industrial psychologists is often required to interpret the results.

Bona Fide Seniority or Merit Systems

The second defense involves *bona fide seniority or merit systems*. It is a common employment practice for employers to provide employees with differential treatment based solely on differences in seniority. Seniority can be defined simply as the length of time an employee has been with the company, and can be used to determine such things as eligibility for company pension plans, length of vacations, security from layoffs, preference for rehire and promotion, and amount of sick leave. Virtually all collective bargaining agreements contain formalized provisions for the recognition, calculation, and application of seniority. According to Section 703(h) of the statute:

> [I]t shall not be an unlawful employment practice for an employer to apply different . . . terms, conditions, or privileges of employment pursuant to a bona fide seniority or merit system . . . provided that such differences are not the result of an intention to discriminate because of race, color, religion, sex, or national origin. . . .

The Supreme Court has consistently upheld seniority systems even though they perpetuate the effects of pre-1964 Civil Rights Act discrimination. That is, the Court will not allow employees who gained seniority when discrimination was in practice to have seniority rights stripped away in favor of workers who previously suffered discrimination.

In a 1977 decision, *International Brotherhood of Teamsters* v. *U.S.*, the Supreme Court upheld a union seniority plan that gave assignment preferences to workers based on seniority, thereby giving preference to white truck drivers over newer minority drivers. The Court recognized that this had the unfortunate effect of locking in some effects of past discriminatory practices but said that Congress intended to protect seniority systems through Section 703(h) of Title VII. A seniority system, or at least parts of it, will be stricken, however, if it was introduced after Title VII took effect for the purpose of perpetuating past discriminatory practices.

The effects of seniority systems come under attack most often in cases involving layoffs on the basis of seniority. That is, many employers and many collective bargaining agreements hold that in the event of a cutback in the work force, workers with the most seniority have the most job protection—last hired, first fired. This means that minorities may suffer a greater relative share of the layoffs in a work force cutback because they have less seniority than white workers who were hired when racial discrimination was practiced. As seen in the *Wygant* case, the Supreme Court recognized this unfortunate fact, but held that seniority rights are lawful.

Wygant v. Jackson Board of Education
United States Supreme Court
476 U.S. 267, 106 S.Ct. 1842 (1986)

Case Background. *In 1972, the Jackson (Michigan) Board of Education agreed with the teachers' union to add a provision to the collective bargaining agreement that in the event of a teacher layoff, it would be proportional on the basis of race. In 1976 when a layoff occurred, white teachers with more seniority were dismissed in favor of retaining minority teachers with less seniority. The white teachers with seniority sued the school board, claiming their rights had been violated by this layoff policy.*

The district court and court of appeals held for the school board, ruling that the layoff provision was permissible as an attempt to remedy past discriminatory practices. That is, even though no particular discrimination by the school board was shown, preference in layoffs was justified because minorities have been subject to discrimination by society in general.

Case Decision. Justice Powell delivered the judgment of the Court.

This case presents the question whether a school board, consistent with the Equal Protection Clause, may extend preferential protection against layoffs to some of its employees because of their race or national origin.

* * *

In this case . . . the [collective bargaining agreement] operates against whites and in favor of certain minorities, and therefore constitutes a classification based on race. "Any preference based on racial or ethnic criteria must necessarily receive a most searching examination to make sure that it does not conflict with constitutional guarantees." There are two prongs to this examination. First, any racial classification "must be justified by a compelling governmental interest." Second, the means chosen by the State to effectuate its purpose must be "narrowly tailored to the achievement of that goal."

* * *

The Court of Appeals . . . held that the Board's interest in providing minority role models for its minority students, as an attempt to alleviate the effects of societal discrimination, was sufficiently important to justify the racial classification embodied in the layoff provision. . . .

This Court never has held that societal discrimination alone is sufficient to justify a racial classification. Rather, the Court has insisted upon some showing of prior discrimination by the governmental unit involved before allowing limited use of racial classifications in order to remedy such discrimination . . . . The role model theory allows the Board to engage in discriminatory hiring and layoff practices long past the point required by any legitimate remedial purpose. Indeed, by tying the required percentage of minority teachers to the percentage of minority students, it requires just the sort of year-to-year calibration the Court stated was unnecessary. . . .

Moreover, because the role model theory does not necessarily bear a relationship to the harm caused by prior discriminatory hiring practices, it actually could be used to escape the obligation to remedy such practices by justifying the small percentage of black teachers by reference to the small percentage of black students . . . . Carried to its logical extreme, the idea that black students are better off with black teachers could lead to the very system the Court rejected in *Brown* v. *Board of Education* (1954).

* * *

While hiring goals impose a diffuse burden, often foreclosing only one of several opportunities, layoffs impose the entire burden of achieving racial equality on particular individuals, often resulting in serious disruption of their lives. That burden is too intrusive. We therefore hold that, as a means of accomplishing purposes that otherwise may be legitimate, the Board's layoff plan is not sufficiently narrowly tailored. Other, less intrusive means of accomplishing similar purposes—such as the adoption of hiring goals—are available. . . .

* * *

Case Holding. *The judgment of the court of appeals was reversed by the Supreme Court. The Court reaffirmed the legitimacy of seniority plans and made it clear that it will be unusual when seniority rights may be ignored in favor of correcting past discrimination, especially if the only showing of discrimination is one of general social discrimination rather than particular discrimination by the employer.*

Case Questions

1. Can you think of a situation in which the courts would be likely to permit seniority preference to be overruled in favor of members of protected classes?

2. Does this case make it appear that preference for minorities in hiring (not layoffs) will not be allowed because of general social discrimination but must be justified by specific employer discrimination?

The Bona Fide Occupational Qualification (BFOQ)

The third defense is that of a *bona fide occupational qualification* (BFOQ). Section 703(e) states that discrimination is permitted in instances in which sex, religion, or national origin (but not race) is a BFOQ "reasonably necessary to the normal operation of that particular business." The defense is applicable to hiring and referrals but not to discrimination between classes of current employees. In addition, the EEOC has given this defense a narrow interpretation. For example, just because certain jobs have been traditionally filled by men does not mean that a legitimate defense exists for not hiring women for such positions. There is no BFOQ on the basis of race. For example, an employer cannot assert that the business must have a white person for a particular job.

Generally, the increased cost of hiring members of the opposite sex may not be used to justify discrimination. The fact that separate bathroom facilities will have to be constructed and parking lots lighted will not be a BFOQ. In one instance, a court held that simply because people were used to seeing and preferred female flight attendants did not mean that the company could refuse to hire male flight attendants. However, the line is drawn where hiring on the basis of a personal characteristic is needed to maintain the "authenticity" of a position. For example, a Playboy club can argue that the cocktail servers should be female, since customers expect that as a part of the service; and male clothing is expected to be modeled by a male model. In general, the courts have been strict in their application of the BFOQ defense.

Remedies Under Title VII

Section 706(g) of Title VII states that when the defendant-employer has been found to have intentionally engaged in an unlawful discriminatory employment practice:

> the court may enjoin the . . . practice, and order such affirmative action as may be appropriate, which may include, but is not limited to, reinstatement or hiring of employees, with or without back pay . . . or any other equitable relief as the court deems appropriate.

Courts have used their statutory powers to order the offending company to reinstate employees with back pay, promote employees, hire new employees with artificial seniority, and implement an affirmative action program. Relying on the reference to "equitable relief," the courts have also used the broad and flexible powers for courts sitting in equity to provide the relief that seems most appropriate.

Back Pay

The Supreme Court in *Albermarle Paper Co.* v. *Moody* (1975) held that the awarding of back pay is needed to enforce the purpose of the law. If back pay were not a common remedy, or were given only in cases in which bad faith on the part of the employer could be shown, employers would have little incentive to try to comply with the law. If they did not have to pay back pay to employees denied higher-paying jobs because of discrimination, the primary punishment would be an injunction to henceforth obey the law.

Artificial Seniority

Similarly, with regard to seniority, the Supreme Court in *Franks* v. *Bowman Transportation Co.* (1976) held that:

> No less than with the denial of the remedy of back pay, the denial of seniority relief to victims of illegal discrimination in hiring is permissible "only for reasons which, if applied generally, would not frustrate the central purposes of eradicating discrimination throughout the economy and making persons whole for injuries suffered through past discrimination."

The Court ordered that employees who had been discriminated against in violation of Title VII should be given artificial seniority beginning from the date of the discriminatory act.

Attorneys and Attorneys' Fees

In addition, the court is empowered "in such circumstances as [it] may deem just" to appoint an attorney for an impoverished plaintiff. The appointment of such counsel may not be denied because the EEOC finds no probable cause to proceed with a discrimination action against the employer. The court is also provided with the discretion to award reasonable attorneys' fees to the prevailing party. Ordinarily, the prevailing employee-plaintiff will recover attorneys' fees. However, a prevailing employer-defendant may be awarded attorneys' fees only if the court determines that the plaintiff's action was frivolous, unreasonable, or without foundation.

INTERNATIONAL PERSPECTIVES: EMPLOYMENT DISCRIMINATION IN EUROPE AND JAPAN

INTERNATIONAL

PERSPECTIVES

With regard to social legislation, Europeans often are portrayed as more sophisticated than Americans. However, in the case of employment they are probably twenty or thirty years behind the United States in their treatment of minorities and women in the labor force. Most European countries and Japan have antidiscrimination statutes on the books, but they are not nearly as strict as the U.S. laws. Japan's Equal Opportunity Law was not passed until 1985. The first sexual harassment court case in the country was in 1990.

Most of those countries tend to be more racially homogeneous than the United States, so they have not gone through the trials inherent in a multiracial society. As a consequence, there is a tendency to treat minority immigrants as second-class citizens. In general, it is much harder for a noncitizen, especially a member of a racial minority, to obtain work and citizenship in Japan and most of Europe than it is in the United States.

Where affirmative action exists, it tends to be trivial or even overtly discriminatory in favor of male-citizen workers who already dominate the labor force. Women are often kept out of many higher-level jobs and are not paid as much as men for equal work—especially in Japan. European countries and Japan appear to treat women better in certain respects, such as by statutes mandating generous maternity benefits, but the effect of those laws is to encourage employers not to hire women because of the high cost of the benefits to which they are entitled if they have children. As in the United States, however, attitudes about women in the labor force are changing—but more slowly.

AFFIRMATIVE ACTION PROGRAMS

An *affirmative action program* is a conscious effort by an employer to remedy discriminatory practices in the hiring, training, and promotion of protected class members when a particular class is underrepresented in the employer's workforce. By imposing certain hiring and promotion quotas for members of that class, an affirmative action program attempts to eliminate existing discrimination, remedy effects of past discrimination, and create procedures to prevent future discrimination.

The implementation of an affirmative action program may be voluntary or involuntary. After finding that members of a protected class are underrepresented in the company's workforce, an employer may voluntarily implement an affirmative action program to ensure that the company provides more opportunities for women or minorities in certain job categories. An involuntary program may be imposed by the courts as a remedy to correct past discriminatory employment practices by the company or, in the special case of government contractors, by the federal government as a prerequisite to entering into a government contract.

Executive Order 11246

As the chief executive officer of the United States, the President has the authority to determine the terms and conditions upon which the government will conduct certain business affairs. Those terms are often dictated through *executive orders* issued by the President. Referred to as *government contractors*, businesses must agree to abide by the directives of executive orders when they contract with the government. In this context, President Johnson issued Executive Order 11246 in 1965.

Executive Order 11246 initially served to supplement the Title VII obligations imposed on government contractors. The Executive Order's nondiscriminatory directive, however, eventually developed into a requirement that government contractors take *affirmative action* to ensure that no unlawful discrimination in hiring and employment occurs.

Requirements on Government Contractors
The directives of Executive Order 11246 apply to all government contractors or subcontractors with fifty or more employees and a contract of $50,000 or more. This includes most large firms in the U.S. The regulations apply to all facilities of the contractor, not just those involved in performing the specific work under government contract. The Order is monitored and enforced by the Office of Federal Contract Compliance Programs (OFCCP) of the Department of Labor.

Executive Order 11246 requires a contractor to conduct a *workforce analysis* of the organization. Each job is to be identified and analyzed according to rank, salary, and the percentage employed in the job that come from each protected class. A company may find, for example, that lab technicians are submanagerial in rank, paid $5,000 more per year than other jobs of similar rank, and 87 percent white, 13 percent black, and 92 percent male.

The contractor must then undertake an *underutilization analysis*, comparing the percentage of each protected class available in the community in each job category with the percentage actually employed by the contractor. If underutilization is found to exist—say 8 percent of the contractor's lab technicians are female compared with 17 percent of the lab technicians available in the community—the contractor must establish an affirmative action program to correct the situation. The affirmative action program may require that efforts be made to hire more females or to invest in training females to enhance their qualifications for certain jobs. The hiring and promotion quotas established in the program are reviewed periodically to determine whether adequate progress is being made. In the event that progress is not being made, the federal contract may be cancelled.

Affirmative Action as a Remedy

Section 706(g) of Title VII provides that in the event the defendant-employer is found to have intentionally engaged in illegal discrimination "the court may . . . order such affirmative action as may be appropriate. . . ." It is not uncommon for the courts to require an offending company or organization to implement an affirmative action program. The court will often require the company to reinstate or hire employees in the protected class and to impose quotas to make up for past discriminatory activities. The Supreme Court considered the constitutionality of such affirmative action programs in *U.S.* v. *Paradise* (1987).

United States v. Paradise
Supreme Court of the United States
480 U.S. 149, 107 S.Ct. 1053 (1987)

Case Background. *In 1972, the district court found that the Alabama Department of Public Safety had never hired a black trooper or hired blacks in any position except as laborers in its thirty-seven year history. The court ordered the department to hire one black trooper for each white trooper hired until blacks constituted approximately 25 percent of the state trooper force. The court also ordered an end to any discriminatory practices by the department. Seven years later not one black had achieved the rank of corporal, so the court imposed a numerical quota on promotions. Of the sixty blacks who took the standardized test for promotion, only five were in the top half. The court held the test to be racially biased and rejected the department's proposal to promote four blacks and eleven whites to corporal, ordering instead that for some time at least 50 percent of those promoted must be black, if qualified black candidates were available. The court also imposed a goal of 25 percent black employees at all ranks. The Department of Justice appealed the order of the court as a violation of the Fourteenth Amendment's equal protection guarantee. The Eleventh Circuit affirmed the district court's order.*

Case Decision. Justice Brennan delivered the opinion of the Court.

* * *

It is now well established that government bodies, including courts, may constitutionally employ racial classifications essential to remedy unlawful treatment of racial or ethnic groups subject to discrimination.

* * *

In determining whether race-conscious remedies are appropriate, we look to several factors, including the necessity for the relief and the efficacy of alternative remedies, the flexibility and duration of the relief, including the availability of waiver provisions; the relationship of the numerical goals to the relevant labor market; and the impact of the relief on the rights of third parties.... When considered in light of these factors, it was amply established, and we find that the one-for-one promotion requirement was narrowly tailored to serve its several purposes, both as applied to the initial set of promotions to the rank of corporal and as a continuing contingent order with respect to the upper ranks.

To evaluate the District Court's determination that it was *necessary* to order the promotion of eight whites and eight blacks to the rank of corporal at the time of the motion to enforce, we must examine the purposes the order was intended to serve. First, the court sought to eliminate the effects of the Department's "long term, open, and pervasive" discrimination, including the absolute exclusion of blacks from its upper ranks. Second, the judge sought to ensure expeditious compliance with the 1979 and 1981 Decrees by inducing the Department to implement a promotion procedure that would not have an adverse impact on blacks. Finally, the court needed to eliminate so far as possible the effects of the Department's delay in producing such a procedure. Confronted by the Department's urgent need to promote at least 15 troopers to corporal, ... the District Court determined that all of its purposes could be served only by ordering the promotion of eight blacks and eight whites, as requested by the plaintiff class.

The features of the one-for-one requirement and its actual operation indicate that it is flexible in application at all ranks. The requirement may be waived if no qualified black candidates are available. The Department has, for example, been permitted to promote only white troopers to the ranks of lieutenant and captain since no black troopers have qualified for those positions. Further, it applies only when the Department needs to make promotions. Thus, if external forces, such as budget cuts, necessitate a promotion freeze, the Department will not be required to make gratuitous promotions to remain in compliance with the court's order.

* * *

To achieve the goal of 25% black representation in the upper ranks, the court was not limited to ordering the promotion of only 25% blacks at any one time. Some promptness in the administration of relief was plainly justified in this case, and use of deadlines or end-dates had proven ineffective. In these circumstances, the use of a temporary requirement of 50% minority promotions, ... was crafted and applied flexibly, was constitutionally permissible.

* * *

Case Holding. *The decision of the court of appeals affirming the decision of the district court was affirmed. Strict hiring and promotion quotas may be imposed to overcome past discriminatory employment practices.*

Case Questions

1. The four dissenters in the *Paradise* decision said that under the logic of the majority, a 100 percent hiring or promotion quota could be legal. Do you agree with that argument? What circumstances can you imagine in which that might be possible?

2. In his dissent in the *Paradise* decision, Justice White complained that the power assumed by the district court in this case goes beyond what is proper.

Do you agree, or did the court have any other choices that it could have used to get the desired result?

Voluntary Affirmative Action Programs

In addition to implementing an affirmative action program in response to a court order or as a government contractor in compliance with Executive Order 11246, a company may voluntarily elect to implement an affirmative action program. As a rule, a company or organization will make such an election after determining that a protected class is underrepresented in its workforce. An affirmative action program allows an organization to correct for the underrepresentation in an organized fashion. The Supreme Court examined the mechanics of a voluntary affirmative action program in the *Johnson* case.

Johnson v. Transportation Agency, Santa Clara Co., Calif.
United States Supreme Court
480 U.S. 616, 107 S.Ct. 1442 (1987)

Case Background. *The Transportation Agency (Agency) voluntarily adopted an affirmative action plan in 1978 for hiring and promoting employees. To achieve a better balance, the sex and race of a qualified applicant would be taken into account. The intent was to achieve a statistically measurable yearly improvement in hiring and promotion of women and minorities. No specific goals were set for the number of positions to be occupied by women and minorities, but annual goals were adjusted each year based on experience. The Agency announced a vacancy for the position of road dispatcher. It was one of 238 positions in the Skilled Craft Worker job category, none of which were held by women. Petitioner Johnson, a male, and Diane Joyce applied and were rated the top two applicants for the position. Johnson scored a 75 on the interview test, Joyce a 73. After taking into account Joyce's sex, she was picked over Johnson, who then sued that he had been discriminated against on the basis of sex.*

The district court held the affirmative action plan illegal because it had no ending point or clear goals. The Court of Appeals for the Ninth Circuit reversed, saying that the plan was legal. It did not need a termination point, because it had a general objective of increasing women and minority representation, not fixed numerical goals. To meet such goals, an employer must consider sex or race in employment and promotion decisions. The plan did not set a bar to advancement by white males, it simply gave extra consideration for race and sex characteristics.

Case Decision. Justice Brennan delivered the opinion of the Court.

* * *

As the Agency Plan recognized, women were most egregiously underrepresented in the Skilled Craft job category, since *none* of the 238 positions was occupied by a woman. In mid-1980, when Joyce was selected for the road dispatcher position, the Agency was still in the process of refining its short-term goals for Skilled Craft Workers in accordance with the directive of the Plan. This process did not reach fruition until 1982, when the Agency established a short-term goal for that year of three women for the 55 expected openings in that job category—a modest goal of about 6% for that category.

We reject petitioner's argument that, since only the long-term goal was in place for Skilled Craft positions at the time of Joyce's promotion, it was inappropriate for the Director to take into account affirmative action considerations in filling the road dispatcher position. The Agency's Plan emphasized that the long-term goals were not to be taken as guides for actual hiring decisions, but that supervisors were to consider a host of practical factors in seeking to meet affirmative action objectives, including the fact that in some job categories women were not qualified in numbers comparable to their representation in the labor force.

By contrast, had the Plan simply calculated imbalances in all categories according to the proportion of women in the area labor pool, and then directed that hiring be governed solely by those figures, its validity fairly could be called into question. This is because analysis of a more specialized labor pool normally is necessary in determining underrepresentation in some positions. If a plan failed to take distinctions in qualifications into account in providing guidance for actual employment decisions, it would dictate mere blind hiring by the numbers, for it would hold supervisors to "achievement of a particular percentage of minority employment or membership . . . regardless of circumstances such as economic conditions or the number of qualified minority applicants . . ."

* * *

Case Holding. *Affirming the decision of the court of appeals, the Supreme Court upheld the legality of the affirmative action plan, noting that such a moderate, flexible, case-by-case approach is consistent with Title VII, for it allows an employer to help voluntarily eliminate the vestiges of discrimination.*

Case Questions

1. Why might a company or organization undertake a voluntary affirmative action program?
2. How does the voluntary affirmative action program here differ from an involuntary program?
3. In the absence of its affirmative action program, could the Agency have hired Joyce over Johnson?

The Supreme Court threw a new factor into affirmative action programs with a 1989 decision, *Martin* v. *Wilks*. The Court's decision allowed white males to challenge such programs if they have the effect of injuring their hiring or promotion opportunities. The Court noted that affirmative action plans that management negotiated with one group of employees (the minorities) may conflict with the rights of another group of employees (the white majority) who did not participate in the adoption of the plan. The majority viewed the holding as narrow, but the four dissenters expressed concern that this would cause a flood of new litigation.

REVIVAL OF THE EARLY CIVIL RIGHTS ACTS

The Civil Rights Act of 1866 was largely ignored until a Supreme Court decision in 1968 that opened the possibility for novel applications of that law and, to a lesser extent, the *Civil Rights Act of 1871*. These laws provide some added protection against discrimination in employment (and in other areas of life) on the basis of race. The 1866 Act is now generally referred to as Sections 1981 and 1982 of Title 42 of the *United States Code*. The 1871 Act is usually referred to as Section 1985 of Title 42. The relief offered by these statutes may be independent of a Title VII claim of discrimination or they may be tied to a Title VII claim—whichever route offers the plaintiff the best chances. The potential remedies under both the 1866 and 1871 Acts are broad—including compensatory and punitive damages.

The Civil Rights Act of 1866

Section 1981 provides: "All persons . . . shall have the same right in every State . . . to make and enforce contracts, to sue, be parties, give evidence, and to the full and equal benefit of all laws and proceedings for the security of persons and property as enjoyed by white citizens. . . ." Note that the law promises equal rights "as enjoyed by white citizens." Who are "nonwhite"? The Supreme Court has given this a broad reading. In the 1987 case, *Saint Francis College* v. *Majid Al-Khazraji*, the Court said that the statute forbids certain racial discrimination. Racial means "identifiable classes of persons who are subjected to intentional discrimination solely because of their ancestry or ethnic characteristics." In this case, an American-Arabian, although a member of the Caucasian (white) race, could claim to be a member of a racial group that is recognized by most people, and, so, could bring a suit for discrimination.

Since employment and union membership are considered contracts, this statute may be violated when a person is discriminated against in employment on the basis of race. Unlike Title VII, which applies only to employers who have fifteen or more employees, there is no numerical limit for the right of action under the 1866 Civil Rights Act, and as noted before, the damages possible to collect can be broader. The Supreme Court clarified the scope of Section 1981 in the *Patterson* case.

Patterson v. McLean Credit Union

United States Supreme Court
__ U.S. __, 109 S.Ct. 2363 (1989)

Case Background. *Brenda Patterson, a black woman, was employed by McLean Credit Union as a teller and file coordinator from 1972 until she was laid off in 1982. She then filed suit, under Section 1981, claiming that the Credit Union had harassed her, failed to promote her to a higher position, and then discharged her, all because of her race.*

The district court ruled that she could not bring the harassment charge under Section 1981. She could sue on the failure to promote charge, but had to show that she was better qualified than the white employee who was promoted instead. These rulings were appealed to the court of appeals, which affirmed them, so the rulings were appealed to the Supreme Court.

Case Decision. Justice Kennedy delivered the opinion of the Court.

* * *

By its plain terms, the relevant provision in § 1981 protects two rights: "the same right . . . to make . . . contracts" and "the same right . . . to . . . enforce contracts." The first of these protections extends only to the formation of a contract, but not to problems that may arise later from the conditions of continuing employment. The statute prohibits, when based on race, the refusal to enter into a contract with someone, as well as the offer to make a contract only on discriminatory terms. But the right to make contracts does not extend, as a matter of either logic or semantics, to conduct by the employer after the contract relation has been established, including breach of the terms of the contract or imposition of discriminatory working conditions. Such postformation conduct does not involve the right to make a contract, but rather implicates the performance of established contract obligations and the conditions of continuing employment, matters more naturally governed by state contract law and Title VII.

The second of these guarantees, "the same right . . . to . . . enforce contracts . . . as is enjoyed by white citizens," embraces protection of a legal process, and of a right of access to legal process, that will address and resolve contract-law claims without regard to race. In this respect, it prohibits discrimination that infects the legal process in ways that prevent one from enforcing contract rights, by reason of his or her race, and this is so whether this discrimination is attributed to a statute or simply to existing practices. . . .

The right to enforce contracts does not, however, extend beyond conduct by an employer which impairs an employee's ability to enforce through legal process his or her established contract rights.

* * *

Applying these principles to the case before us, we agree with the Court of Appeals that Patterson's racial harassment claim is not actionable under § 1981. . . .

With the exception perhaps of her claim that the credit union refused to promote her to a position as an accountant, none of the conduct which Patterson alleges as part of the racial harassment against her involves either a refusal to make a contract with her or the impairment of her ability to enforce her established contract rights. Rather, the conduct which Patterson labels as actionable racial harassment is postformation conduct by the employer relating to the terms and conditions of continuing employment. . . .

[The employer's] conduct, reprehensible though it be if true, is not actionable under § 1981, which covers only conduct at the initial formation of the contract and conduct which impairs the right to enforce contract obligations through legal process. Rather, such conduct is actionable under the more expansive reach of Title VII of the Civil Rights Act of 1964. The latter statute makes it unlawful for an employer to "discriminate against any individual with respect to his compensation, terms, conditions, or privileges of employment." Racial harassment in the course of employment is actionable under Title VII's prohibition against discrimination in the "terms, conditions, or privileges of employment."

* * *

Paterson's claim that respondent violated § 1981 by failing to promote her, because of race, to a position as an intermediate accounting clerk is a different matter. . . .

[T]he question whether a promotion claim is actionable under § 1981 depends upon whether the nature of the change in position was such that it involved the opportunity to enter into a new contract with the employer. If so, then the employer's refusal to enter the new contract is actionable under § 1981. In making this determination, a lower court should give a fair and natural reading to the statutory phrase "the same right . . . to make . . . contracts," and should not strain in an undue manner the language of § 1981. Only where the promotion rises to the level of an opportunity for a new and distinct relation between the employee and the employer is such a claim actionable under § 1981. . . .

We think the District Court erred when it instructed the jury that Patterson had to prove that she was better qualified than the white employee who allegedly received the promotion. In order to prevail under § 1981, a plaintiff must prove purposeful discrimination.

. . . Here, Patterson need only prove by a preponderance of the evidence that she applied for and was qualified for an available position, that she was rejected, and that after she was rejected the credit union either continued to seek applicants for the position, or, as is alleged here, filled the position with a white employee.

Once the plaintiff establishes a prima facie case, an inference of discrimination arises. In order to rebut this inference, the employer must present evidence that the plaintiff was rejected, or the other applicant was chosen, for a legitimate nondiscriminatory reason. Here, the credit union presented evidence that it gave the job to the white applicant because she was better qualified for the position, and therefore rebutted any presumption of discrimination that Patterson may have established. At this point, as our prior cases make clear, Patterson retains the final burden of persuading the jury of intentional discrimination.

* * *

Case Holding. *The Supreme Court upheld the ruling that a plaintiff could not bring a charge of racial harassment on the job under Section 1981. That claim must be pursued under Title VII. The Court reversed the lower courts on the matter of a claim of racial discrimination regarding promotion, holding that, as under Title VII, a plaintiff need only present evidence of discrimination in order to be allowed to let the jury decide the issue at trial.*

Case Questions

1. The majority in this case found that harassment is not a part of the employment contract and therefore is not an issue under Section 1981. In dissent, Justice Stevens argued that harassment is a part of the employment-at-will contract, since that is an ongoing relationship. Do you agree?
2. How can a plaintiff possibly be better off bringing suit under Section 1981 instead of under Title VII?

Section 1982 guarantees all citizens "the same right . . . as is enjoyed by white citizens . . . to inherit, purchase, lease, sell, hold, and convey real and personal property." This forbids public and private racially discriminatory interference with property rights. In a 1987 decision, the Supreme Court applied Section 1982, holding that Jews can claim racial status for purposes of this law and allowing members of a synagogue to sue the people who sprayed the synagogue with anti-Semitic slogans, symbols, and phrases. This was held to be a racially motivated interference with private property rights.

Civil Rights Act of 1871

In some instances, protection may also be offered by the Civil Rights Act of 1871. Known as the Ku Klux Klan Act, it prohibits two or more individuals from conspiring to deprive any individual or class of individuals of the equal protection of the laws. Although rarely used, the law may offer protection in some special cases not covered by Title VII. Further, Section 1983 of the Civil Rights Act of 1871 provides that there is a cause of action against any individual who deprives others of their rights "under color of any statute . . .

of any State." Generally, this has been used to reach discrimination in cases involving public institutions, such as police and fire departments, public schools, and state agencies.

AGE DISCRIMINATION IN EMPLOYMENT ACT

Enacted in 1967, the *Age Discrimination in Employment Act* (ADEA) promotes the employment of older individuals on the basis of abilities rather than age. The Act prohibits discrimination in employment against individuals between the ages of forty and seventy. If an individual falls outside these limits, employment decisions may legally be based on age. That is, an employer may discriminate against individuals because they are too young for the job, and compel employees to retire at age seventy. All employers, private and public, who have twenty or more employees must comply with this statute. The ADEA essentially parallels Title VII in its prohibitions, exceptions, remedies, and enforcement by the EEOC.

In determining whether a violation of the ADEA has occurred, the courts use the McDonnell-Douglas test the Supreme Court devised for plaintiffs bringing a discrimination claim under Title VII. If employees between ages forty and seventy meet that test, they have established a prima facie case of age discrimination. The Third Circuit Court of Appeals noted that often there is no "smoking gun," and the court must, as in the case of race or sex discrimination, look to see if age discrimination can be inferred by studying what has actually occurred at the place of employment. Examples of typical age discrimination include:

- Forcing retirement before seventy only because of age.
- Assigning older workers to duties that restrict their ability to compete for higher level jobs in the organization.
- Advertising for employees to indicate age preference, such as "young, dynamic person wanted."
- Choosing not to promote a younger worker because the older worker being considered may be retiring in several years.
- Cutting health-care benefits for workers over age sixty-five because they are eligible for Medicare.

BFOQ on Basis of Age

The ADEA states that employers can force executives to retire before age seventy. For all other employees, retirement rules or other conditions of employment based on age must be based upon a BFOQ. For example, the New York state police department would not allow anyone over age twenty-nine to apply to be a state police officer. The Second Circuit Court of Appeals ruled that this discriminated against applicants between the ages of forty and seventy. Since persons between the ages of thirty and thirty-nine are not covered by the ADEA, this decision did not find that the department had discriminated against them. The court did not hold, however, that the police department could never discriminate against applicants between the ages of forty and seventy. Rather, it could discriminate against individuals between those ages if a bona fide occupational qualification were involved—a legitimate reason why persons of certain ages might not be capable of performing certain fundamental duties.

Health Qualifications

Some police departments require that officers retire at age sixty. The BFOQ was upheld when it was shown that good health was an essential occupational requirement. Medical evidence indicated that at age sixty human health begins to deteriorate, making the stress of a police officer's job difficult to manage. In the absence of such a rule, the employer would be required to constantly test the health of all officers over sixty, an expensive proposition.

In all cases, BFOQs must be individually determined for each job and not based on general rules. In addition, they cannot operate to permit age discrimination in other ways. For example, in the 1985 case *Trans World Airlines* v. *Thurston*, the Supreme Court held that airlines may require pilots to retire at age sixty because of the statistical evidence of declining health at that age, a situation that could endanger airline passengers. However, since flight engineers could work past age sixty, pilots must be allowed to switch to being flight engineers and to maintain their seniority, if they want to. In this way, the BFOQ rule for pilots was restricted to its specific purpose.

Forced Retirement

As Figure 15–1 indicates, despite the existence of the ADEA, the percentage of older men and women who remain in the labor force continues to decline. Although there is good evidence that most people prefer to retire before reaching sixty or seventy, the ADEA helps ensure that the choice not to retire

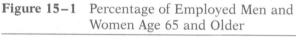

Figure 15–1   Percentage of Employed Men and
Women Age 65 and Older

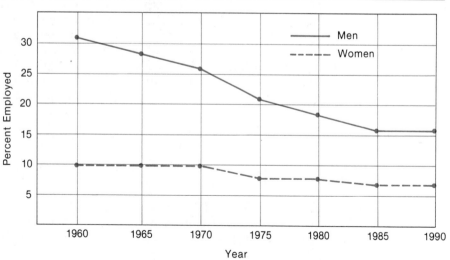

will be available. One practice that the ADEA specifically has prohibited is discrimination against older workers, who tend to have the most seniority, and against a reduction-in-force (RIF) in favor of younger workers with less seniority and lower pay.

The Seventh Circuit Court of Appeals has noted that a forced RIF of older workers created a prima facie violation of the ADEA. An employer cannot get around the intent of the law by taking advantage of a cutback in the work force to dismiss senior, higher-paid workers. The other circuit courts have agreed with this and have noted that the ADEA requires fringe benefits, retirement benefits, and severance pay offers to be neutral with respect to age. According to the Fourth Circuit, it is legal for an employer to offer big incentives to older, higher-paid workers in an attempt to get them to retire, because it is a voluntary program, not a discriminatory firing of older workers.

A survey by the American Association of Retired Persons showed that a large majority of age discrimination suits were brought by professional or managerial white males, in their fifties, who had been dismissed or forced to retire. That violations of the ADEA can be expensive is illustrated by a $16 million verdict, upheld on appeal, won by a Sears store manager who claimed that the reason he was fired was because of his age, not his performance.

DISCRIMINATION AGAINST THE DISABLED

The *Rehabilitation Act* of 1973 provides protection for handicapped persons who are seeking employment with or are currently employed by employers that receive federal funds. The Act tends to follow the steps established by the courts in Title VII employment discrimination suits. Sections 503 and 504 of the Act are most important. They go beyond restrictions on discrimination against the handicapped. The law states that employers have a duty to ensure the handicapped an opportunity in the workplace by providing them with reasonable accommodations.

The *Americans with Disabilities Act* of 1990 (ADA) expands the rights of persons with disabilities in employment, and supplements access rights to public accommodations, such as hotels, restaurants, theaters, public transportation, telecommunications, and retail stores. The ADA expands the rights of people with mental and physical disabilities beyond those provided by Sections 503 and 504 of the Rehabilitation Act. Besides encompassing the Rehabilitation Act, the ADA incorporates the remedies and procedures set out in Title VII. The ADA applies, in 1992, to all employers with twenty-five or more employees and, in 1994, to all employers with fifteen or more employees.

Definition of Handicapped

The Rehabilitation Act and the ADA define *handicapped* or *people with disabilities* as

> any person who (i) has a physical or mental impairment which substantially limits one or more of such person's major life activities, (ii) has a record of such an impairment, or (iii) is regarded as having such an impairment.

The Supreme Court has recognized regulations by the Department of Health and Human Services as a guide to determining what is a disability. The regulations define "major life activities" as "functions such as caring for one's self, performing manual tasks, walking, seeing, hearing, speaking, breathing, learning, and working." Examples of disabilities covered by the statutes include:

- People with a history of drug or alcohol abuse.
- People with severe disfigurements.
- People who have had heart attacks.
- People who must use wheelchairs.
- People who are hearing- or vision-impaired.

Even if individuals are not actually impaired, if other people believe them to be seriously impaired, they are handicapped. For example, former cancer patients have found that some people are afraid to hire them because they believe cancer is contagious. As a result, even though no current impairment exists, and even though doctors may say there presently is no disease, bias against the person who had the disease may make the person handicapped for purposes of this law.

The courts have made it clear that lesser impairments will not constitute a handicap for purposes of this law. For example, in a decision by the Fourth Circuit Court of Appeals, a newly hired utility repairman was fired because he had a fear of heights, so he would not climb ladders to make repairs expected in his position. The fired repairman sued under the Rehabilitation Act alleging that fear of heights caused him to be handicapped. The dismissal was upheld by the court because there was no "*substantial* limitation of a *major* life activity." Also in dismissing claims of discrimination against people who are left-handed, the courts note they have no desire to trivialize the statute by allowing it to apply to numerous inconveniences and personal oddities.

Compliance with the Statutes

The Rehabilitation Act is enforced primarily by complaints to the Department of Labor, which may bring suit on behalf of people with handicaps. There have been an average of twenty-five lawsuits per year under the Rehabilitation Act. Suits under the ADA will be enforced in the same way that discrimination suits brought under Title VII are enforced.

Reasonable Accommodation

Employers are obliged to make *reasonable accommodations* for persons with disabilities. They are expected to incur expenses in making a position or work station available to qualified handicapped applicants and employees. Exactly where the line is drawn is not clear. Ford does not have to redesign its assembly line at high cost so that a worker in a wheelchair could work on the assembly line, because that would impose an *undue hardship* on business operations. However when a work station can be redesigned for several thousand dollars to accommodate a person with a disability, that must be done. Firms are also expected to provide special equipment and training for the disabled, allow modified work schedules, and provide readers for the blind.

Several firms report that they have had substantial success complying with the law. Marriott has over 6,000 employees with disabilities. The company reports that most can be accommodated at a trivial cost. Sears reports that 5.8 percent of its employees have disabilities, most requiring no or trivial costs. At Southwestern Bell, the consumer-relations manager is blind, so his secretary reads his mail and other messages to him. In the *Arline* case, the Supreme Court discussed the rights of employees with disabilities and how employers must make accommodations.

School Board of Nassau County, Florida v. Arline
United States Supreme Court
480 U.S. 273, 107 S.Ct. 1123 (1987)

Case Background. *Gene Arline was hospitalized for tuberculosis in 1957. The disease was in remission for the next twenty years, during which time she taught school. In 1977, a test revealed that tuberculosis was again active in her system; cultures taken in March and November of 1978 were also positive. After her second relapse in the spring of 1978 and her third relapse in the fall of 1978, the school board suspended Arline with pay for the remainder of both school years. She was dismissed after the 1978-79 school year only because of her illness. She claimed protection under Section 504.*

The district court held against Arline, saying that she was not a handicapped person under the statute because a contagious disease was not intended to be covered by the law. That is, she was no longer qualified for her position as a school teacher because of the danger she posed to the children. The Court of Appeals reversed, holding that "persons with contagious diseases are within the coverage of section 504." That court ruled that the school board should consider the risk of infection that Arline posed. If the risk were deemed to be unsatisfactory, the board should consider alternative assignments within the school system for Arline.

Case Decision. Justice Brennan delivered the opinion of the Court.

* * *

We do not agree with petitioners that, in defining a handicapped individual under § 504, the contagious effects of a disease can be meaningfully distinguished from the disease's physical effects on a claimant in a case such as this. Arline's contagiousness and her physical impairment each resulted from the same underlying condition, tuberculosis. It would be unfair to allow an employer to seize upon the distinction between the effects of a disease on others and the effects of a disease on a patient and use that distinction to justify discriminatory treatment.

* * *

The fact that *some* persons who have contagious diseases may pose a serious health threat to others under certain circumstances does not justify excluding from the coverage of the Act *all* persons with actual or perceived contagious diseases. Such exclusion would mean that those accused of being contagious would never have the opportunity to have their condition evaluated in light of medical evidence and a determination made as to whether they were "otherwise qualified." Rather, they would be vulnerable to discrimination on the basis of mythology—precisely the type of injury Congress sought to prevent. We conclude that the fact that a person with a record of a physical impairment is also contagious does not suffice to remove that person from coverage under § 504.

* * *

The remaining question is whether Arline is otherwise qualified for the job of elementary school teacher. To answer this question in most cases, the District

Court will need to conduct an individualized inquiry and make appropriate findings of fact. Such an inquiry is essential if § 504 is to achieve its goal of protecting handicapped individuals from deprivations based on prejudice, stereotypes, or unfounded fear, while giving appropriate weight to such legitimate concerns of grantees as avoiding exposing others to significant health and safety risks.

* * *

In making these findings, courts normally should defer to the reasonable medical judgments of public health officials. The next step in the "otherwise-qualified" inquiry is for the court to evaluate, in light of these medical findings, whether the employer could reasonably accommodate the employee under the established standards for that inquiry. . . .

* * *

Case Holding. *The Supreme Court affirmed the decision of the court of appeals. The Court held that if the risk of Arline infecting the children with tuberculosis is trivial, she may be ordered reinstated as a teacher. Otherwise, the school board must consider another position for her, such as an administrative job that requires little contact with children. She must be given preference in any new hiring over outside applicants.*

Case Questions

1. Doesn't this decision lead to a "battle of the experts" that the Second Circuit Court of Appeals wanted to avoid?

2. Suppose the school board decides that the risk of infection is small, but a year later one of Arline's students develops tuberculosis. Could the parents of the student sue the administrators and school board?

3. Suppose the school board decided that the safest bet was to put Arline in an administrative position, but none were open. Ignoring the possibility of a collective bargaining agreement, could the board fire the person currently in the position it wants for Arline?

Violations by Employers

Employers are most likely to violate the Rehabilitation Act or the ADA by failing to make reasonable accommodations for persons with disabilities. Note that, as in the case of discrimination based on race, sex, or age, the law is broken if a person is denied an opportunity primarily because of their handicap. However, in the case of disabilities, besides not discriminating, an employer must also make reasonable accommodations—go the extra step to make adjustments for the handicap. In this sense there is an affirmative action requirement, but it is not one tied to goals or quotas and it works on a case-by-case basis.

Employment situations that are likely to be in violation of the law include:

*   Using standardized employment tests that tend to screen out people with disabilities.

*   Refusing to hire applicants because they have a history of substance abuse rather than because they are currently substance abusers.

- Asking job applicants if they have disabilities rather than asking if they have the ability to perform the job.
- Limiting advancement opportunities for employees because of their disabilities.
- Not hiring a person with a disability because the workplace does not have a bathroom that can accommodate wheelchairs.

Hyatt Legal Services ran afoul of the rights of employees with disabilities in 1990 when a federal court awarded $157,000 damages, including $50,000 punitive damages, to a former regional partner of the law firm. The court found that when the plaintiff's employer learned that the plaintiff had AIDS, he was told he could: (1) quit and take $12,000 severance pay, (2) take a demotion with a 50 percent pay cut and move to another office, or (3) get treatment at an experimental AIDS treatment program. The court held that this was "a corrupt assault" on the plaintiff's dignity that was unjustified. As employment rights of people with disabilities expand, employers must adjust to the mandated sensitivity.

SUMMARY

Since 1963 with the passage of the Equal Pay Act, but especially since 1964 with the passage of Title VII of the Civil Rights Act, there has been an explosion of litigation in the area of employment discrimination. Before Title VII, which was expanded upon by the Rehabilitation Act, the Americans with Disabilities Act, the Age Discrimination in Employment Act, and amendments to those statutes over time, there were very few cases brought or won by employees who had been or believed they had been the victim of discrimination in employment.

These statutes created protected classes based on sex, race, national origin, religion, age, handicap, and color—characteristics that cannot legally be taken into account in any facet of the employment process. For many statutes, discrimination based on these protected characteristics extends to educational opportunities, training programs, recruitment of potential employees, hiring decisions, promotions within a place of employment, treatment on the job (wages, fringe benefits, training opportunities, discipline), and termination. The rediscovery of the Civil Rights Acts of 1866 and 1871 provided another possible source of protection for discrimination in employment based on race—broadly defined.

Because neutrality in employment was not believed to be sufficient to eliminate the past negative effects of formal segregation and more subtle forms of discrimination, the federal government has imposed a requirement of affirmative action on many employers. That is, employers must take positive steps to recruit, train, hire, and promote women and minority employees—and, to a certain extent, the handicapped. Affirmative action programs may also be imposed upon a public or private employer by a court as a part of a remedy for past discrimination.

Affirmative action plans can be rather rigid, such as requiring that an employer hire one woman for every man hired into certain job categories for a fixed period of time, or the plan can be quite flexible, such as taking extra care to give consideration to qualified women or minorities for certain job classes in which such groups are underrepresented. In all cases, the plan must fit the imbalance in the labor force that was created by intentional or unintentional discrimination against certain classes now protected.

Although these laws and remedial plans may seem second nature today, they represent a revolution in employment law. Much has happened in less than three decades, and the law is still evolving. Many employers are still unaware of the duties imposed by the law, are not prepared to handle the requirements the law imposes, and are open to possible litigation perhaps because of ignorance rather than an ill intent to discriminate. The consequences of litigation under the discrimination statutes can be expensive in terms of legal fees, damages ordered to be paid, time invested in litigation by management, and the ill will litigation can create in the community. Modern managers must be sensitive to the many obligations that result from legal obligations that have recently arisen.

ISSUE

Is Affirmative Action Constructive?

Affirmative action programs are the most controversial aspect of employment discrimination law. They are opposed by some who think they give minorities and women unfair, undeserved advantages at the expense of other, more qualified workers. On the other side, proponents believe such programs are necessary to integrate the work force, so that traditional barriers based on race and sex, no matter how they arose, are broken down. Whatever the general social consequences may be, it is clear that people personally involved in affirmative action programs can be placed in difficult positions, as this article discusses.

Policy Predicament: Many Minorities Feel Torn by Experience of Affirmative Action.
Sonia L. Nazario*

At first, Roland Lee was thrilled to be the newest lieutenant in the San Francisco Fire Department. Then he learned he had beaten out a close friend in the department for the promotion. Then he discovered that his friend had scored higher on the qualifying exam. Then his friend quit.

The son of Chinese immigrants, Mr. Lee welcomed being hired and promoted under affirmative action quotas at the department. Without them, he believes, minorities would have been barred from the fire station's doors. But he also says he is "disgusted" that race denied his white friend the promotion.

Mr. Lee is plagued by the stigma he feels is attached to affirmative action: white co-workers questioning his abilities and assuming he's not as qualified as they. He says that

–continued

—continuing

this has forced him "to work twice as hard" to prove others wrong, and that at times, his own self-esteem has been battered. "If I had to do it over again," he says with regret, "I would get my promotion" without using affirmative action preferences. "That would give me back my credibility."

Such an overt rejection of affirmative action by one of its beneficiaries is uncommon. But as minorities look at the effects of affirmative action nearly a quarter-century after its inception, many feel torn by the policy's outcome.

Minorities say it has opened doors that would have remained shut, forced companies to look to employment groups they had ignored, and decreased racism by prodding workplace integration. But it has also brought unwelcome baggage: assumptions that minorities were hired only because of race, and what may be unwarranted skepticism about their abilities. This makes some minorities fear that even promotions and accomplishments they earn by working harder than their peers won't be respected.

Some minority employees believe racism—on the part of co-workers or employers—has a lot to do with their ambivalence. Others believe companies and government agencies approach affirmative action too much as a burden to be met as painlessly as possible rather than as something that can truly benefit the workplace. Still others, like Mr. Lee, believe the problem is inherent in affirmative action, part and parcel of a process that gives preference to people for reasons other than strictly merit.

"I don't know if promoting someone because they are Chinese is the way to do it," he says.

Several recent Supreme Court decisions have sparked a renewed debate over the legitimacy of affirmative action. Many now see an increasingly conservative court turning against the concept of setting quotas for hiring minorities.

* * *

Rarely heard in the debate, however, are the voices of those who actually have been hired or promoted under an affirmative action plan. In the workplace itself, lines that divide liberals and conservatives are blurred by the intrusion of a more complex reality. "I'm reluctantly appreciative of the affirmative action jobs I've had," says Migdia Chinea-Varela, a Hispanic Hollywood scriptwriter. "But at the same time, they made me really depressed."

The personal responses to affirmative action are diverse, as are the difficulties minorities have experienced using such programs. Mary Whitmore, a carpenter in Los Angeles who pried her way into the male-dominated construction business with the help of affirmative action, says her experience has been a wholly positive one. Co-workers "treat me equal. They let me use the saw. They give me the nails. The let me work."

Many minorities agree with William Mays, a black who now owns his own Indianapolis-based chemical-distribution company, and who got a graduate fellowship and several jobs through affirmative action. "I had to deal with the grief [affirmative action] brought," he says, "but it was well worth it."

Others argue that the emphasis of government-sponsored integration plans must change toward encouraging equal educational and hiring opportunities rather than setting numerical goals and timetables. And a small number believe affirmative action should be abolished. "Affirmative action robs us of our dignity. It says that somehow color, not our hard work, can bring us advancements," says Shelby Steele, a black associate professor of English at San Jose State University who says he no longer applies for affirmative-action-related research grants so he can shake the stigma that he somehow isn't as talented as a white professor.

* * *

Interviews with scores of affirmative action employees reveal that despite their in-

—continued

–continuing

dividual impressions of specific programs, all cite a strong need for some effort to combat racism and purposefully open jobs to minorities that they might have held, absent past discrimination. Louis Winston, a black who is the affirmative action officer for Stockham Valves & Fittings Inc. in Birmingham, Ala., recalls the days when that company had two entry gates—one for whites, one for blacks—and a divided cafeteria. When he began in the 1960s, blacks were forced to work in the sweltering heat of the foundry, while only whites could qualify for training programs to become machinists or electricians.

In part because of a 1969 lawsuit he helped initiate that then led to an affirmative action plan, he became the first black electrician trained at Stockham in 1975; now there are many, and blacks hold 60% of Stockham's jobs. Affirmative action, he says, has "put some blacks in higher jobs, and shown the company that we aren't ignorant. We can do the job, if given the chance."

It has also helped reduce racial tensions by forcing blacks and whites to work together, he says. "Without affirmative action, Stockham may have come around, but I wouldn't swear on it," he says. More important, he says, there are still no blacks among the company's 35 managers.

Diane Joyce believes that without affirmative action, she couldn't have advanced in the male-dominated Santa Clara County, Calif., road-maintenance department. A road worker for six years, she took an oral test to become a dispatcher in 1980 and was ranked fourth of those who took the test.

County rules allowed the supervisors to give the job to any one of the seven highest-scoring candidates, and she knew that one wouldn't be her; she claims the men who administered her test told her they didn't like her. So she phoned the county affirmative action officer, and got the job. A man who scored second on the test and was aboutto get the job sued the county in a case that went all the way to the Supreme Court. He lost.

Three years later, Ms. Joyce scored first in a written and oral test to become a road foreman. A man who ranked fifth got the job. This time, she didn't challenge it, even though she again felt unfairly treated. "I'm tired of fighting," she says.

One reason she and some others weary of the fight is the way their accelerated promotions or even their hiring are received by co-workers. Take, for example, the Birmingham, Ala., fire department.

When Carl Cook applied to be a firefighter in 1964, a city clerk took one look at his face and refused to even hand over an application to the young black man, he says. In 1976, two years after Mr. Cook finally was hired, only 1.4% of firefighters were black. Attorney Susan Reeves, who helped file a suit for blacks against the city, says a Birmingham official once explained that "blacks congenitally don't like to fight fires."

Now the department is divided by a court-imposed affirmative action plan: Some white and black firefighters don't even speak to each other. Some whites refer to promoted minorities as "welfare captains." In a highly publicized case, the Supreme Court last month gave Birmingham's white firefighters the right to challenge the affirmative action plan initiated by the lower court.

Mr. Cook, who was both hired and promoted under affirmative action, says, "I feel I am under a microscope." He won't ask white supervisors for advice or information for fear they are looking for an excuse to label him incompetent, he says. Battalion chief Tony Jackson, the city's highest-ranking black firefighter, says a white colleague once approached him and said, "Well, it sure is nice to be black. If I were black, I could have been promoted."

A white firefighter in Birmingham, David Morton, believes such suspicions will continue as long as some minorities are givenspecial treatment—promoted over whites who rank higher in test scores and experience. "If you take an airplane, do you want a

–continued

–continuing

pilot who was ranked No. 1, or one who is ranked No. 50 but is black?" he asks.

Ms. Chinea-Varela, the scriptwriter, says she has participated in four programs to encourage ethnic writers at four different production companies. No show she worked on was ever produced, she says. In one of the programs, sponsored by CBS Inc., a secretary explained to Ms. Chinea-Varela that she was just part of the network's minority headcount, the scriptwriter says.

As part of the CBS program, Ms. Chinea-Varela says she developed a situation comedy involving a young Hispanic woman who, trying to make ends meet after the death of her husband, takes in a white male boarder. "Because I came through the affirmative action door," she says, "there was no seriousness to the project."

A CBS spokeswoman says that this specific minority program no longer exists, and that the company has a strong commitment to affirmative action.

Regardless of the reaction of employers and co-workers, the mere fact that affirmative action involves special treatment has the potential to damage one's self-confidence, some minorities say. "Sometimes I wonder: Did I get this job because of my abilities, or because they needed to fill a quota?" says Caridad Dominguez, A Hispanic who is director of special studies for Bank of America, and who nonetheless says her own self-esteem carries her through such situations. "I consider myself a good contributor," she says.

The perception that affirmative-action hires sometimes aren't as good as other workers is perpetuated in some respects by employers so bound by court-ordered quotas that the measurable qualifications of minorities hired fall far below white counterparts. "We hire 60% Hispanics here, regardless of qualifications," says Freddie Hernandez, a Hispanic lieutenant in the Miami fire department. "The fire department doesn't go to schools in other cities to recruit for minorities. They just have people take a test, and they pick minorities [even] from the bottom of the list." Fire Chief C. H. Duke says that a city ordinance requires his hires to be 80% women and minorities, and that this does require passing up whites with higher test scores for minorities, although anyone considered must pass the test.

Theodore Edwards, a black division manager at Ameritech Corp.'s Illinois Bell Telephone and an affirmative-action hire, says, "I think affirmative action is necessary, but I don't think it should be administered so that we say we have to have X number of minorities regardless of qualifications." He sees a need for more active recruiting so that firms can find minorities who are as qualified as other workers.

Whether they blame bosses, co-workers or simply human nature for their dissatisfaction with affirmative action, some minorities have been led by years of experience to call for major changes in government's approach to integrating the workplace.

The scriptwriter, Ms. Chinea-Varela, argues that hiring based on quotas should only be done in entry-level jobs, and that thereafter, a pure merit system should be used. She and others note that any hiring may at times be based less on merit than such factors as whom you know, ties to the appropriate Ivy League college, or nepotism. Still, she says that "there's a point where affirmative action should stop: I'd like to by now be considered on my own merits," she says, having been in the business 10 years.

A Hispanic scriptwriter friend of hers, Julio Vera, is opposed to affirmative action altogether and will no longer apply for minority writing programs. "Martin Luther King's dream was to erase color lines; affirmative action hasn't done that," he says. Mr. Vera advocates spending more to redress the legacy of unequal education for minorities so they have a better chance of being equally qualified when they apply for a job. Affirmative action, he says, "is a handout."

Mr. Hernandez, the 34-year-old Hispanic firefighter from Miami, agrees. He turned

–continued

—continuing

down an affirmative-action promotion to lieutenant six years ago, waiting three years until he had the seniority and test scores to qualify for the promotion under normal procedures.

By doing so, he passed up $4,500 a year in extra pay and had to undergo 900 hours of extra study time. But "it was a self pride thing," he says. "I knew I could make it on my own." Mr. Hernandez plans to take the exam for fire chief soon, but says he'll accept the job only if he wins it on paper. "I will stick to merit," he says.

Questions

1. Is it unethical for a woman or a black man to take a job due to an affirmative action program that denies that job to a more qualified white male?

2. Will several decades of affirmative action programs result in a more natural equality in the labor force, as the worst effects of past intentional discrimination disappear, or will this be something that will always be needed?

REVIEW AND DISCUSSION QUESTIONS

1. Define the following terms and phrases:
   Discrimination
   Protected class
   Disparate impact
   Bona fide occupational qualification
   Artificial seniority
   Affirmative action
   Reasonable accommodations

2. Compare and contrast the following:
   a. Employment-at-will and employment discrimination
   b. Equal Pay Act and Title VII of the Civil Rights Act
   c. Discrimination on the basis of race and discrimination on the basis of national origin
   d. Seniority systems and merit systems

3. Why were the employee tests given by Duke Power held to be discriminatory? Under what circumstances will such tests be held to be not discriminatory?

4. Would a dress code that required men to wear three-piece suits but stated only that women had to "look professional" be discriminatory against the male employees? What differences would be considered discriminatory?

5. What are the primary defenses used in employee discrimination suits? Do you think these commonly accepted defenses tend to perpetuate the past effects of discrimination? Does not a seniority system mean that those who had been discriminated against will be so forever?

Case Questions

6. Lab workers testing blood become worried about the possibility of contracting AIDS from the blood they are testing. They demand that the company employ certain safeguards that will double the costs of blood testing. The lab workers who insist on this are fired. Is this legal? Suppose one worker in a lab has

AIDS, and the other workers want to be separated from that person. Would it be legal to segregate the AIDS carrier?

7. The RMC Company has recently adopted a policy that forbids the hiring of wives of male employees but does not forbid the hiring of husbands of female employees. Is this policy an unlawful employment practice under Title VII? Suppose the company changed the policy and applied the hiring prohibition to both husbands and wives of existing employees. Would that constitute an unlawful employment practice under Title VII?

8. A large airline operates a maintenance and overhaul base in Kansas City, Missouri. Larry was hired by the airline to work as a clerk in the parts department at Kansas City. The department is essential to the airline's operation and must therefore always be open. After working for the airline for a time, Larry began to study the religion known as the Worldwide Church of God. One of the tenets of the religion was to refrain from working from sunset on Fridays until sunset on Saturdays. Larry was asked to work Saturdays when another worker went on vacation. Because the airline was unable to accommodate Larry's request not to work on Saturday, Larry refused to report. After a hearing, Larry was discharged for insubordination. Was the discharge a religious discrimination in violation of Title VII? What if the company had to shift another employee out of the shift she preferred for similar reasons to fill Larry's position? What if such a shift would have required that the airline circumvent its seniority system?

9. Rawlinson was a twenty-two-year-old college graduate who had majored in correctional psychology. She applied for a position as a correctional counselor—essentially a prison guard—with the Alabama prison system. A correctional counselor's primary duty was to maintain security and control the inmates by continually supervising and observing their activities. The Alabama Board of Corrections rejected her application because she failed to meet the minimum 120-pound weight requirement set by Alabama statute. The statute also imposed a minimum 5-foot, 2-inch height requirement on applicants. Does the Alabama statute violate Title VII? What if the requirements were imposed for the protection of prison guards?

10. Dorr worked at a bank for twenty years. Soon after he was promoted to vice president he told the bank president that he was gay and that he was the organizer of and president of Integrity, an organization affiliated with the Episcopal Church that advocates equal rights for homosexuals. He said that because of his position with Integrity, he would take public positions on issues affecting the gay community. The bank had a policy that prohibited employees from engaging in outside activities that might undermine public confidence in the bank. The president told Dorr that he would have to resign as president of Integrity and not take public positions on gay issues. Dorr refused and was fired. Dorr sues the bank for discrimination under Title VII. Does he have a suit that could win?

11. The New York City Transit Authority had a policy against hiring people who use narcotic drugs. This included people using methadone, a narcotic drug given to addicts to break their dependency on heroin. Several people on methadone were refused jobs by the Transit Authority. They sued, claiming the policy was racially discriminatory under Title VII because 80 percent of the methadone users were black or Hispanic. The district court and court of appeals ruled for the plaintiffs, saying that while they could be excluded from sensitive jobs such as subway car driver, the narcotics users could not be excluded from other jobs. What was the result of the appeal to the Supreme Court? [*New York City Transit Authority* v. *Beazer*, 440 U.S. 568, 99 S.Ct. 1355 (1979)]

12. Weber, a white male, worked at a unionized plant. The union and the employer agreed on an affirmative action program. That resulted in Weber being passed over for a training and promotion opportunity in favor of a less-qualified black applicant who had less seniority. Weber sued the union and the employer claiming illegal discrimination based on race. Is he right? *United Steelworkers of America* v. *Weber,* 443 U.S. 193, 99 S.Ct. 2721 (1979).

Policy Questions

13. Matt works as one of twenty-six persons in sales for a large company. He thinks women belong at home and have no business working, so he insists on insulting women sales representatives when they are around the office together. The women complain about his insults to the supervisor, who warns Matt several times to stop. Matt says it is his right to insult whomever he wants to. Should the company fire Matt for being sexist?

14. The Age Discrimination in Employment Act now holds that starting in 1994 colleges cannot force professors to retire at any age. Colleges are concerned that they will eventually be filled with a large number of very old faculty and few young faculty, so that students will not be able to relate well to the faculty and mental lethargy will set in. Should colleges be allowed to adopt contracts for, say, periods of five or ten years rather than indefinite tenure, so that they can get rid of older faculty?

Ethics Questions

15. You are a supervisor at a company that does not have an affirmative action program. In looking to hire a new person for some position, the person who best fits the job criteria is a white male age thirty. Two other candidates are also well qualified for the position but just slightly less than the top candidate. One of the other candidates is black, the third is a white woman aged sixty-three. You believe that in general there is societal discrimination against minorities and older people. Should you give a little extra credit to the candidates who are in protected classes, given that you can justify whatever choice you make? How would you decide between the black man and the older white woman? Should you take into account that the black man supports a wife and three children, whereas the white woman has an employed husband and no children at home?

16. In response to its concerns about worker safety and health, the Staaf Mining Company imposed the following company policy:

    > Pregnant females and non-pregnant females capable of bearing children shall hereafter be prohibited from working a job classified as "restricted." Females who cannot bear children may be permitted to work at such a job. A "restricted" job, for purposes of this directive, is one that involves the use of any chemical a female of child-bearing age might come in contact with that is extremely hazardous to her well-being.

    Is this company policy discriminatory against female employees? What if it is based on sound medical and humane reasons—say, because of the prospects of female workers producing deformed babies? What if it encouraged women to seek sterilization?

16 Consumer Protection

T HIS chapter reviews different efforts by the federal government to regulate consumer markets. Since regulation of certain products has become detailed and involves many agencies, the chapter focuses only on agencies that have the greatest impact on consumers. The Food and Drug Administration (FDA) will be studied as a well-established agency with a specific consumer-protection mission over food, drink, drugs, and cosmetics.

The expansion of federal regulation in the 1970s included the formation of an agency that has not received the attention devoted to some of its contemporaries, such as the Environmental Protection Agency (EPA) and the Occupational Safety and Health Administration (OSHA). That agency is the Consumer Product Safety Commission (CPSC). In budget terms, the CPSC accounts for a fraction of federal spending, perhaps one ten-thousandth of the total. As with many regulatory agencies, however, its impact is measured not by its budget but by the effect it has on various business sectors.

This chapter also reviews the consumer protection mission of the Federal Trade Commission (FTC), which includes regulation of advertising, as well as the federal government's efforts to standardize warranties via the Magnuson-Moss Federal Warranty Act. These regulations provide an overview of regulatory processes that can be expected to occur in other areas or that could occur if similar legislation were enacted in areas not presently covered.

Besides the regulations reviewed here, there are many other regulations that affect products: U.S. Coast Guard jurisdiction over boating safety, Federal Aviation Administration (FAA) control over aircrafts, Department of Housing and Urban Development (HUD) regulations about mobile home safety, and EPA control over many chemicals. This list is hardly comprehensive, but it is a reminder that there are many different agencies involved in regulating several aspects of different consumer products.

The chapter closes with an Issues article that discusses FDA prosecution of corporate executives involved in selling mislabeled food, and then working hard to destroy the evidence.

THE FDA: FOOD AND DRUG SAFETY

The *Food and Drug Administration* (FDA) is charged with the responsibility for monitoring food and drug safety. About one-third of the $750 million dollar per year budget is devoted to foods, with food additives, food sanitation and processing, and food contaminants being the primary areas of concern. One-quarter of the budget is devoted to the study of the quality of marketed drugs and new-drug evaluations. Smaller portions of the budget are allocated for the study of biological products, veterinary products, medical devices, radiological products, and cosmetics and for the support of the National Center for Toxicological Research. Every year, tens of thousands of establishments are inspected and thousands of products are examined as part of the consumer protection function of the FDA.

Food Safety

The control of safety factors in commercial food, drink, drugs, and cosmetics affects a large sector of the economy. Regulations concerning these products have a longer history than do most product controls. The Pure Food and Drug Act of 1906 was the first major step in developing comprehensive regulations. For years the primary concern was food safety. This was triggered by several events:

- More soldiers in the American army during the Spanish-American War were reputed to have died from impure food than from enemy bullets.

- Upton Sinclair's *The Jungle*, while failing to stir the public to support socialism as Sinclair had hoped, caused much controversy about food safety with its graphic description of food processing.

- The chief chemist of the U.S. Department of Agriculture studied the safety of some food preservatives on human subjects and determined that some were harmful to human health.

Food regulation was of initial importance; the Bureau of Chemistry of the Department of Agriculture administered the Food and Drug Act until the FDA was created as a separate unit in 1927. Not until the late 1930s did drug regulation become the more important area of concern for the FDA.

Early Sanitation Standards

The 1906 Act provided primarily for protection against adulteration and misbranding of food and drug products. The Bureau of Chemistry performed food analyses for identification of misbranded or adulterated foods. When warranted, the Secretary of Agriculture could ask a U.S. attorney for criminal prosecution of a violator of the law and could ask to have the goods seized. If necessary, the goods would be destroyed or relabeled before sale. In 1930, the McNary-Mapes Amendment enacted the first food standards that could be enforced by law. The law, however, applied only to canned foods with respect to quality, condition, and the extent of the fill of the container.

FDA Powers Expanded in the 1930s

Following a drug disaster in which many people were poisoned by a nonprescription medicine, Congress passed the *Food, Drug, and Cosmetic Act* in 1938. The Act greatly expanded the regulatory reach of the FDA by providing the agency with the power not only to extend the standards for foods beyond canned goods, but to prohibit false advertising of drugs, classify unsafe food as adulterated, add new enforcement powers, form inspection systems, and allow the agency to set the safe levels of potentially dangerous additives in foods.

Food Safety Responsibility Placed on Producers

The burden of responsibility was placed on manufacturers to assure that no damage to health was possible from the substances present in their food. This responsibility was emphasized by the Supreme Court in the *Park* decision, which addressed the issue of the responsibilities of corporate executives for compliance with the Food, Drug, and Cosmetic Act.

United States v. Park

Supreme Court of the United States
421 U.S. 658,
95 S.Ct. 1903
(1975)

Case Background. *Park was chief executive officer of Acme Markets, a national retail food chain with 874 retail outlets. Acme and Park were charged with violations of the Food, Drug, and Cosmetic Act, because goods held in Acme's warehouses were found, on several inspections, to be contaminated by rodents.*

Acme and Park were convicted in federal district court of violating the law. Park appealed, and his conviction, which required him to pay fines, was overturned. The court of appeals held that Park could not be held responsible. The Supreme Court then had to determine if the manager of a corporation could be prosecuted for violations of the Food, Drug, and Cosmetic Act.

Case Decision. Chief Justice Burger delivered the opinion of the Court.

* * *

The rationale of interpretation given the Act . . . as holding criminally accountable the persons whose failure to exercise the authority and supervisory responsibility reposed in them by the business organization resulted in the violation complained of, has been confirmed in our . . . cases. Thus, the Court has reaffirmed the proposition that "the public interest in the purity of its food is so great as to warrant the imposition of the highest standard of care on distributors." . . . In order to make "distributors of food the strictest censors of their merchandise," the Act punishes "neglect where the law requires care, or inaction where it imposes a duty." . . . "The accused, if he does not will the violation, usually is in a position to prevent it with no more care than society might reasonably expect and no more exertion than it might reasonably exact from one who assumed his responsibilities." . . .

Thus . . . in providing sanctions which reach and touch the individuals who execute the corporate mission—and this is by no means necessarily confined to a single corporate agent or employee—the Act imposes not only a positive duty to seek out and remedy violations when they occur but also, and primarily, a duty to implement measures that will insure that violations will not occur. The requirements of foresight and vigilance imposed on responsible corporate agents are beyond question demanding, and perhaps onerous, but they are no more stringent than the public has a right to expect of those who voluntarily assume positions of authority in business enterprises whose services and products affect the health and well-being of the public that supports them.

* * *

Case Holding. *The Supreme Court reversed the court of appeals, holding Park liable for violations of the Food, Drug, and Cosmetic Act. This decision confirmed that executives of companies covered by this law can be held responsible for compliance with the Act.*

Case Questions

1. Suppose Park did not know of the inspection reports issued by the FDA inspectors because his subordinates did not think them important enough to pass along to him. Should he still be responsible?
2. Who in corporate leadership could be held responsible under this Supreme Court interpretation of leadership responsibility?

Food Additives: The Delaney Clause

The Food Additives Amendment was added to the Food, Drug, and Cosmetic Act in 1958. This amendment, known as the *Delaney Clause*, defines food additives and gives the FDA the authority to license the use and to set the safe use-level of additives. It also provides that any food additive that has been shown to be carcinogenic to humans or animals at any level may not be used in foods. The FDA's activities under the Delaney Clause have generated great controversy.

The Delaney Clause—which applies to food additives, color additives, and drugs administered to animals used for food (such as cattle)—says that any substance shall not be approved as an additive if "it is found to induce cancer when ingested by man or animal." The FDA interpreted this to mean that the risk of cancer from any of these substances had to be zero—a very difficult standard to meet. After years of deliberation, the FDA in 1985 decided to switch from a zero risk standard to a *de minimis* standard. The FDA says that this allows it to be more reasonable but still safeguard consumers against real risks.

Nutrition Labeling

The FDA began issuing regulations for *nutrition labeling* in 1973. Under these rules, labeling is mandatory in two instances:

1. When a nutrient is added to a food, even if that nutrient is only replacing one lost in processing. Hence, enriched or fortified foods must be labeled.
2. If any claim is made on the label or in advertising concerning the nutritional properties of the food, including all foods for special dietary use.

The information must be provided on the product label for a standard serving portion of the food and cover its nutrient value as it is typically served. The information must include caloric, protein, carbohydrate, and fat content and percent of U.S. Recommended Dietary Allowance for protein and nineteen vitamins and minerals.

These rules resulted in 60 percent of packaged foods being labeled. Since much of the labeling was voluntary, information would be presented in different ways, which was claimed to be confusing. Congress moved to mandatory nutrition labeling for nearly all packaged foods in 1990. The information that must be provided also includes saturated fat, fiber, salt, cholesterol, and calories from fat. The FDA was also instructed to develop standard meanings for terms like "low fat," "light," and "high fiber."

Drug Safety

Until 1938, drug control seemed a problem of protecting the public against quacks, fraudulent claims, mislabeling, and the sale of dangerous drugs. After the death of about one hundred persons who had taken a new drug, the Food, Drug, and Cosmetic Act provided federal regulators with new powers in 1938. The law prohibits the marketing of any drug until the FDA has approved the application submitted by the manufacturer. The applicant must submit evidence that the drug is safe for its intended use. This control was designed primarily to prevent the sale of untested, potentially harmful drugs in a market now generating about $40 billion per year in sales.

Designation of Prescription Drugs
Before the 1938 Act, no drugs were designated as *prescription drugs*—that is, drugs that may be used only with the permission of a physician. Drugs were either legal or illegal. Since 1938, the FDA has had the power to determine which drugs will be prescription drugs—that is, sold only with a physician's permission.

The Kefauver Amendment and Drug Effectiveness
While earlier regulations were generally supported by the medical profession, the *Kefauver Amendment* of 1962 has been strongly criticized. Senator Kefauver had charged the drug industry with introducing drugs of dubious value and sold at exorbitant prices. Kefauver attacked the drug industry through the antitrust laws, but found the opening he needed from the thalidomide catastrophe. Thalidomide, a sedative sold in Europe, caused numerous deformities in newborns whose mothers had used the drug during pregnancy. It was being studied by the FDA for approval for sale in the United States when the unfortunate results from Europe became known.

Kefauver successfully introduced legislation requiring the government to approve drugs based on their proven effectiveness—not only on their safety as had been the case. The FDA must approve human clinical testing of drugs and may specify the format of the testing. Interpretation of the legislation by the FDA has produced strict regulations concerning testing and adoption of new drugs. It now costs an average of $200 million to develop a new drug in the United States and clear all FDA rules before marketing the product.

Producer Liability and FDA-Approved Drugs
The requirements for testing of drugs and for certification by the FDA have led to questions about the liability of drug manufacturers for injuries from FDA-approved drugs. That is, if a drug is FDA-approved, should tort liability be reduced? The difficult questions the courts face in such cases are illustrated in the *McDaniel* case.

McDaniel v. McNeil Laboratories, Inc.

Supreme Court of Nebraska
96 Neb. 190,
241 N.W.2d 822
(1976)

Case Background. *Innovar is an anesthetic that was tested on 6,000 patients for five years before receiving FDA approval for sale in 1968. The drug was sold with inserts explaining safety evaluations, recommended dosages, and warnings of adverse reactions and their control measures. Before this case, no new adverse reactions had been discovered, nor was the purity of the drug in question. Marjorie McDaniel, a forty-seven-year-old mother of three, had routine surgery in 1971. Innovar was administered before the operation. During surgery, she suffered a heart attack. She lived but suffered severe brain damage and was left comatose, with no expectation of recovery.*

The Nebraska district court refused to allow the case to be submitted to the jury on the theory of strict liability. The issue before the Nebraska supreme court was whether McNeil Labs could be held strictly liable for physical harm caused to the user of Innovar.

Case Decision. Justice McCown delivered the opinion of the court.

* * *

Comment k, page 353, to section 402A [Restatement of Torts 2d], is peculiarly appropriate and directly applicable here. It is therefore quoted in full.

> Unavoidably unsafe products. There are some products which, in the present state of human knowledge, are quite incapable of being made safe for their intended and ordinary use. These are especially common in the field of drugs. An outstanding example is the vaccine for the Pasteur treatment of rabies, which not uncommonly leads to very serious and damaging consequences when it is injected. Since the disease itself invariably leads to a dreadful death, both the marketing and the use of the vaccine are fully justified, notwithstanding the unavoidably high degree of risk which they involve. Such a product, properly prepared, and accompanied by proper directions and warning, is not defective, nor is it *unreasonably* dangerous. The same is true of many other drugs, vaccines, and the like, many of which for this very reason cannot legally be sold except to physicians, or under the prescription of a physician. It is also true in particular of many new or experimental drugs as to which, because of lack of time and opportunity for sufficient medical experience, there can be no assurance of safety, or perhaps even of purity of ingredients, but such experience as there is justifies the marketing and use of the drug notwithstanding a medically recognizable risk. The seller of such products, again with the qualification that they are properly prepared and marketed, and proper warning is given, where the situation calls for it, is not to be held to strict liability for unfortunate consequences attending their use, merely because he has undertaken to supply the public with an apparently useful and desirable product, attended with a known but apparently reasonable risk.

* * *

The comments to section 402A make it clear that the liability stated in the section does not rest upon negligence. It is strict liability and the rule stated in the section does not require any reliance on the part of the consumer upon the reputation, skill, or judgment of the seller.

* * *

Innovar was approved by the Food and Drug Administration on January 31, 1968. That approval covers the official package inserts which include warnings as to adverse reactions and recommended counter measures. The "labeling" of the package inserts in the case of prescription drugs is revised from time to time as new information becomes available. In the case of Innovar, the first revision after the initial approval in 1968 was in 1973. There is specific evidence which stands uncontradicted that the adverse reactions of respiratory depression, muscle rigidity, and hypotension were all known ever since Innovar has been studied. All the material and information in connection with reported adverse reactions, both prior to and after February 2, 1971, was forwarded to the Food and Drug Administration. The evidence wholly fails to establish that any knowledge or relevant information which the defendant had as to Innovar was not fully disclosed to the Food and Drug Administration.

* * *

While approval by the Food and Drug Administration is not necessarily conclusive, its determinations, based upon the opinions and judgment of its own experts, should not be subject to challenge in a product liability case simply because some other experts may differ in their opinions as to whether a particular drug is reasonably safe, unless there is some proof of fraud or nondisclosure of relevant information by the manufacturer at the time of obtaining or retaining such federal approval.

In this case there is no essential conflict as to the facts and the evidence. There is a difference of opinion among expert witnesses as to whether those facts establish that Innovar is or is not a defective and unreasonably dangerous drug. That issue was presented to the Food and Drug Administration in 1968. Its determination is persuasive and controlling in the absence of evidence that the determination was based upon inaccurate, incomplete, misleading, or fraudulent information. An unavoidably unsafe drug which has been approved for marketing by the United States Food and Drug Administration, properly prepared, compounded, packaged, and distributed, and accompanied by proper approved directions and warnings, as a matter of law, is not defective nor unreasonably dangerous, in the absence of proof of inaccurate, incomplete, misleading, or fraudulent information furnished by the manufacturer in connection with such federal approval or later revisions thereof.

* * *

Case Holding. *The Supreme Court of Nebraska upheld the decision of the district court not allowing the case to go to the jury on the basis of strict liability. FDA approval of a drug is given strong weight in determining the possibility of liability of a drug producer.*

Case Questions

1. Does this decision mean that there would be no grounds under which McDaniel or another plaintiff in a similar situation could possibly bring suit for damages?
2. Would the judgment of the court be the same if the drug in question had a defect because a particular batch of the drug had been prepared improperly?

The courts, as in the *McDaniel* decision, have tended to give great weight to the protection offered consumers by the regulatory scheme. This has limited the number of suits plaintiffs can bring under strict liability when they are injured by drug side effects that are not preventable given the state of technology. For example, in a 1986 federal court case parents brought action against a drug company that made DPT (diphtheria, pertussis, and tetanus) vaccine, which most children receive with no complications, but which seriously injured the child in this case, the court noted that the FDA had extensively regulated the production of the vaccine and knew of the potential dangers. The jury's verdict against the drug would not be allowed to stand as an obstacle to the accomplishment of the federal objective to have the vaccine widely distributed in the safest manner possible. In similar fact situations, however, other courts have gone the other way.

What if a drug was improperly administered? Again, the drug companies are not likely to be liable, assuming they have given proper dosage instructions. If a physician ignores the instructions and changes the recommended dosage, resulting in an injury, the drug manufacturer is shielded from liability by the *learned intermediary doctrine*. That is, the learned intermediary—the doctor—would be liable for misuse of the product.

Reconsidering FDA's Food and Drug Regulations

It is difficult to know the value of the benefits of FDA regulations. Besides preventing useless drugs from reaching the market, the FDA prevents some tragic consequences from defective drugs. No one knows how many thalidomide-type disasters have been prevented by FDA drug regulations. Some critics charge that the FDA has gone too far in regulating drugs, while others claim that it has not gone far enough.

FDA Regulation or Products Liability?

It has been argued that we could live without the FDA and receive protection against harmful drugs through the common law of products liability. If there were no FDA, drugs would be subject to strict liability like any other product. To recover under strict liability, a plaintiff is required to show that the product is defective. A drug with no defects could produce terrible side effects to some users. As the law now stands, such users may have no remedy for their injuries. Would such incidents increase without FDA controls? Most likely they would. Critics note, however, that the costs involved would be more than offset by the benefits of having available new, effective drugs more quickly that could save lives, cure or treat diseases, and reduce pain. A drug company would be careful to test a drug before selling it, because it would incur liability resulting from its carelessness for injuries caused by a defective drug—a liability that would be substantial in today's courts.

Regulatory Reform Efforts

Because the FDA affects so many products, it is subject to constant scrutiny by Congress. Bills are introduced every year in Congress to reform the FDA—to limit or expand its powers, especially with respect to specific products. The majority of proposed laws would limit FDA powers over some products, probably in response to pressure from product manufacturers or because of consumer complaints.

For example, the Vitamin/Mineral Amendments of 1976 limited the FDA's powers with respect to vitamin standards, and the Coastal Zone Management Act of 1976 restricted FDA rules regarding shellfish safety. Such congressional action on particular products reduces the ability of the FDA to hold all products to the same standards. For example, cigarettes, which contain nicotine, are clearly an addictive drug. However, Congress does not allow the FDA to regulate tobacco products.

The rise of AIDS produced pressure on the FDA to relax its drug testing and marketing procedures. Normal testing procedures take years. People suffering from AIDS said they should have the right to try experimental drugs that have not gone through the normal procedures. The argument is, if you are going to die, what difference do side effects make anyway? The testing liberalization that has taken place for drugs that may fight AIDS may result in similar relaxed treatment for drugs that fight other deadly diseases.

INTERNATIONAL PERSPECTIVES: EXPORTING DRUG REGULATION

INTERNATIONAL

PERSPECTIVES

The FDA has a significant effect on drug production and marketing around the world. Many nations, unable to afford the equivalent of the FDA, simply adopt FDA regulations as a part of their drug standards. In many countries, the domestic market is not regulated—many drugs sold would be illegal in the United States—but the export market is regulated to meet FDA standards. This regulatory scheme is intended to make domestic pharmaceutical producers more competitive in world markets. These countries do not want to develop a reputation for producing low-quality or dangerous drugs, so they require their exporters to meet U.S. standards.

Another reason countries adopt FDA standards is that the FDA requires foreign drug producers to be licensed and inspected by the FDA to be eligible to export drugs to the United States. FDA inspectors visit foreign plants to check sanitation, production procedures, record-keeping methods, and other activities to be sure that U.S. standards are met. To retain a license to export to the United States, foreign plants must be reinspected periodically. Because FDA approval can take up to two years to obtain, producers must begin that process long before they expect to start shipments.

European nations do not have drug regulations nearly as stringent as those of the FDA. Introducing a new drug to the market often happens years sooner in Europe, where the long testing period prescribed by the FDA for U.S. drugs is frequently not required. Many drugs that require prescriptions in the United States may be bought over the counter in Europe, but some over-the-counter U.S. drugs require a prescription in Europe. Similarly, foreign producers who want to sell drugs in most of Europe do not need to be licensed by each country, since the European Community countries recognize the inspections conducted by each member country. That is, a Ministry of Health inspection and approval in the United Kingdom will qualify a British producer to export to West Germany, France, and the other European Community countries.

The differences between the United States' extensive drug regulation system and that in most other developed nations give rise to considerable discussion about the merits of the two systems. The American system probably reduces risk from defective drugs better, but it also keeps life-saving, pain-reducing, and disease-curing drugs off the market for a much longer time than Europe's system does. The result of the differences in regulatory standards is that drug research and development is now more advanced in Europe than it is in the United States.

THE CPSC AND CONSUMER PRODUCT SAFETY

Congress established the *Consumer Product Safety Commission* (CPSC) in 1973. It is required to collect, analyze, and disseminate data related to consumer products that may result or have resulted in injury, death, or illness. Based on this information, the agency is to study products to learn how to improve safety and to issue regulations when needed to safeguard consumers. Products intended for use primarily for industrial purposes are excluded, as are consumer products already covered by other regulatory agencies, such as tobacco, drugs, cosmetics, food, automobiles, pesticides, and boats.

The CPSC's Safety Standard Procedure

Consumer product safety standards may be issued for all products covered by the CPSC. In considering the safety of a product, product safety research may be performed at the CPSC or commissioned by the CPSC from private testing services. On the basis of such research, and following proper notice and hearings, a product safety standard may be issued by the commissioners.

After publication in the *Federal Register*, the CPSC may issue requirements concerning performance, composition, contents, design, construction, finish, or packaging of a consumer product. Products failing to conform that are deemed to present an unreasonable risk of injury may be banned from the market. The CPSC may go to federal court for an order to have the product banned or seized.

Actions of Private Parties

Besides the actions against certain products initiated by the CPSC staff, consumers or groups are given the right to petition to have a product safety rule issued or amended. If the CPSC fails to act on such petition, and the interested party then sues in federal court and wins, the CPSC will be ordered to implement the rule and to pay the party for the costs involved in bringing the suit. Similarly, parties adversely affected by a CPSC ruling may petition the federal court of appeals to force the agency to alter a ruling. If such suit is successful and the court decides the CPSC did not issue a proper rule, the court may order the agency to pay the petitioner's cost and attorney's fees.

Responsibility for Reporting Product Hazards

Manufacturers and retailers must report to the CPSC any products that violate safety standards issued by the agency and that contain defects that could create a substantial product hazard. The CPSC will then decide what steps must be taken concerning the suspected hazardous product. If the product is especially dangerous, the CPSC or the Attorney General may ask for a preliminary injunction from a federal district court to stop distribution of the product. For some products, once a hazard has been studied, the CPSC will issue safety standards that apply to future sales of the product. It can also order modifications to existing products and consumer refunds for products already purchased.

CPSC product safety standards may be appealed to a federal court of appeals for review. In some cases, the federal courts of appeals have thrown out rules enacted by the CPSC, as illustrated by the *Slide 'N' Dive* decision, which is frequently cited. A major issue in these cases is the meaning of "unreasonable risk of injury."

Aqua Slide 'N' Dive Corporation v. Consumer Product Safety Commission

United States Court of Appeals, Fifth Circuit
569 F.2d 831 (1978)

Case Background. *The CPSC studied the safety of swimming pool slides. Despite its determination that the risk of suffering spinal injury from sliding improperly down a swimming pool slide was one in ten million—less than the chance of being killed by lightning—the CPSC ordered various safety modifications to the slides that would increase their price and reduce their usefulness. Aqua Slide 'N' Dive Corporation, a producer of swimming pool slides, challenged the legality of the rule, claiming that the rule did not meet the standard in the law that a rule must be "reasonably necessary to eliminate or reduce an unreasonable risk of injury." Further, the company claimed that the CPSC did not show that its new safety requirements would improve safety. The federal district court upheld the CPSC rule. The producer appealed.*

Case Decision. Chief Judge Roney delivered the opinion of the court.

* * *

The standard of review—substantial evidence on the record taken as a whole—is easily stated, but its application to the informal record allowed by this Act poses novel questions for which existing case law provides no clear answer. Congress put the substantial evidence test in the statute because it wanted the courts to scrutinize the Commission's actions more closely than an "arbitrary and capricious" standard would allow. The substantial evidence test is used to assess the weight of a factual finding. As a general rule, substantial evidence review is applied in connection with a formal hearing, at which an unbiased officer presides, rules of evidence apply, and parties may both subpoena and cross-examine witnesses. In writing this Act, however, Congress, desiring to streamline the Commission's hearing process, rejected the formal hearing requirement, provided for informal procedures . . . and adopted a definition of record which encompasses both "any written submission of interested parties" and "any . . . information which the Commission considers relevant." The result is a legislative anomaly. Congress has mandated that the courts take a harder look, but has provided for a record whose volume, technical complexity, and remote relationship to the actual decision-making process of the agency impede clear vision.

The record in this case is a jumble of letters, advertisements, comments, drafts, reports, and publications which runs for almost 2,000 pages. It has no index. A reviewing court must either "scour the four corners of the record to find [the] evidence for itself," or rely exclusively on citations provided by counsel. Except for the brief statement of basis and purpose accompanying the promulgated rule, there is little indication of the relative weight given to various documents by the Commission.

* * *

. . . [T]he Court will defer to Commission fact-finding expertise, but it can do so only when the record shows the Commission has made an actual judgment concerning the significance of evidence.

Also, the extent to which data and views in the record have been exposed to public comment will affect their reliability. Technical studies which have survived scrutiny of the scientific community and the public provide sounder footing for an inexpert judiciary to base its decision on than do facts which first see the light of day in a court proceeding. . . . After taking procedure into account and weighing the evidence, the Court must determine whether the established facts reasonably satisfy the criteria necessary to support the ultimate statutory finding. If they do, then the Commission has sustained its burden of adducing "substantial evidence on the record as a whole" for its finding.

* * *

The legislative history, and the holdings of other cases decided under similar statutes, do discuss the meaning of "unreasonable risk," and indicate that term is interrelated with the "reasonably necessary" requirement. The necessity for the standard depends upon the nature of the risk, and the reasonableness of the risk is a function of the burden a standard would impose on a user of the product.

* * *

In this case, the legislative history specifies the costs to consumers that are to be considered: increases in price, decreased availability of a product, and also reductions in product usefulness. . . . Implicit in this analysis is an understanding that the regulation is a feasible method of reducing the risk.

* * *

Given the infrequency of the risk, it was incumbent upon the Institute and the Commission to produce evidence that the standard actually promised to reduce the risk. Instead, both the Institute and the Commission gave the matter short shrift.

* * *

Furthermore, the record contains only the most ambiguous of indications that the warning signs would actually be heeded by slide users. The Commission did not test the signs. . . . The statute requires substantial evidence to support the Commission's ultimate conclusion that the signs are a reasonably necessary means of reducing an unreasonable risk.

* * *

The Commission report indicated 20 percent of total sales would be lost over six years. Perhaps as much as half of the 42 percent drop in slide sales from 1973 to 1974 could be attributed just to uncertainty about what the standard would say.

* * *

Certainly, on this record, the economic finding is crucial. The only way to tell whether the relationship between the advantages and disadvantages of the signs is reasonable is to know exactly what those disadvantages are. Yet the Commission's study of the standard's economic impact lacks the indicia of reliability. At the same time, the proof that signs will significantly reduce the risk is weak. We consequently hold that the Commission has failed to provide substantial evidence to demonstrate the reasonable necessity of the warning signs.

* * *

In evaluating the "reasonable necessity" for a standard, the Commission has a duty to take a hard look, not only at the nature and severity of the risk; but also at the potential the standard has for reducing the severity or frequency of the injury, and the effect the standard would have on the utility, cost or availability of the product. In this case, the Commission neglected that duty.

* * *

Case Holding. *The court of appeals reversed the decision of the lower court. The court's decision required the CPSC to go back to the drawing boards in its efforts to construct a safety rule regarding swimming pool slides.*

Case Questions

1. Was the court overly concerned with the messy record rather than with substance? That is, had the CPSC record been more formal, would the court have been more impressed?

2. Suppose that a given danger is one in ten million. Does that mean it is
    something that will be too costly to deal with and should be ignored in favor
    of dangers more common?

Enforcement and Compliance

The Consumer Product Safety Act applies to all domestic manufacturers and
importers. All sellers must maintain records of compliance. Violation of safety
rules can result in fines up to $500,000. Willful violations can result in fines of
$50,000 and up to one year in jail for corporate officers. Products in violation
of CPSC rules can be banned or seized. Enforcement of the law can be by
private suit as well as by the CPSC. Persons injured by products violating
safety standards can sue the manufacturer for damages and all legal expenses.

Reconsidering CPSC's Product Safety Regulations

Because of common-law rules of products liability, manufacturers have incentives to make sure their products meet certain safety standards. Nevertheless,
because of the CPSC, numerous products are being tested for safety, and
manufacturers are monitored for compliance with existing labeling and safety
regulations. In most cases, the CPSC and companies agree on a course of action
to take with respect to a product hazard. While such actions are classified as
voluntary, many would probably not be undertaken without threat of litigation by the CPSC.

Safety Information and the CPSC

CPSC activities concentrate on three main areas: information gathering,
research and product safety requirements, and disseminating product safety
information. The National Electronic Injury Surveillance System of the CPSC
gathers injury data from a sample of over one hundred hospitals to determine
the number and severity of injuries sustained every year from various
consumer products.

Products with High Injury Rates

Products resulting in or related to the highest injury rates are stairs, bicycles,
footballs, baseballs, basketballs, nails, tables, playground equipment, chairs,
sofas, and beds. Information about these products is disseminated to the
public to enable better product-use decision-making by parties affected by
such information and to help the CPSC decide which products deserve special
attention.

Public Safety Awareness

Safety awareness has become a larger function of the CPSC in recent years.
Publicity methods include news releases, consumer-alert bulletins, product
safety fact sheets, notices on recalled and banned products, educational
programs, films, and public service announcements. The safety information
program has concentrated on flammable products and ignition sources,

nursery equipment, playground equipment, skateboards, chain saws, and holiday safety.

FTC AND CONSUMER PROTECTION

The FTC was established by Congress in 1914 to help enforce the antitrust laws, but the FTC devotes substantial resources to its Bureau of Consumer Protection, which handles a wide range of matters such as deceptive advertising and marketing practices. Some responsibilities were specifically granted by Congress, such as enforcement of the Magnuson-Moss Warranty Act (and the various credit statutes discussed in Chapter 20), but most consumer protection efforts have evolved as the FTC decided what Congress meant when it amended the FTC Act in the 1930s and said, in Section 5, that "unfair and deceptive acts or practices in or affecting commerce are hereby declared unlawful."

The FTC's Consumer Protection Procedures

Based on its experience, and in response to concerns expressed by Congress, the FTC investigates a wide range of practices suspected to be *unfair and deceptive*. The FTC staff proposes complaints to the five commissioners, who decide by majority vote whether to issue a complaint against individuals or companies engaged in practices the commission would like to see terminated or modified.

Settling Complaints by Consent Decree

Many complaints are settled by a *consent decree* agreed upon by the parties charged in the complaint and by a majority of the commissioners. Consent decrees contain the terms of a settlement and frequently include prohibition of certain practices, redress for consumers, and payment of civil penalties. A small number of cases result in administrative trials at the FTC, the results of which may be appealed to a federal court of appeals.

Regulating Unfair and Deceptive Acts or Practices

Congress charged the FTC with checking unfair and deceptive acts or practices. The lack of definition for those terms has always meant that the FTC has considerable leeway in deciding what cases to bring—what advertising is deceptive, what sales practices are unfair, etc. The key term has always been *deceptive*. Essentially, things held to be deceptive are also unfair, and it is rare for an act to be unfair but not deceptive.

Agency Policy Statement on Deception

To give the FTC staff guidance in its investigations, the commissioners adopted a *deception policy statement* that summarizes a three-part test for deciding whether a particular act or practice is deceptive. There is deception if the following are true:

1. There is a representation or omission of information in a communication to the consumer;

2. which is likely to mislead a reasonable consumer;

3. to the detriment of the consumer.

Interpreting the Deception Statement

Because the policy statement is looked to for guidance, some points have been made to help clarify the three elements of deception. First, not all omissions are deceptive. They are not deceptive if there is no affirmative misrepresentation or practice that takes advantage of consumer misimpression. Second, to decide if a representation or omission is deceptive, the FTC will look at the entire context. For example, the words in an advertisement will be examined in the context of the entire ad, and consideration will be given to evidence about what consumers think the ad means. Third, a reasonable consumer is an "ordinary person." This means that special consideration will be given to the target audience of the representation or practice. For example, ads directed at children or ill people will be held to a tougher standard. Fourth, the representation or omission must be likely to affect a consumer's choice of a product. Fifth, no proof of injury to consumers is needed if evidence exists that an injury is likely to occur, given the practice in question.

Regulating Advertising Claims

The *advertising substantiation program* requires advertisers and advertising agencies to have a reasonable basis before they disseminate claims. When advertisers claim that "studies show" or "tests prove," they must actually possess evidence that provides a reasonable basis for the claims. The FTC looks to the following items to determine what constitutes a reasonable basis:

- the product,
- the type of claim,
- the consequences of a false claim and the benefits of a truthful claim,
- the cost of developing substantiation for the claim,
- the amount of substantiation experts in the field believe is reasonable.

Deciding What Advertising Is Deceptive

Obviously, the FTC has considerable leeway in deciding what advertising is deceptive, but we can look to some cases to get a feel for what is and is not deceptive. A number of years ago, the FTC noted in a decision: "Perhaps a few misguided souls believe . . . that all 'Danish pastry' is made in Denmark. Is it therefore an actionable deception to advertise 'Danish pastry' when it is made in this country? Of course not." The point is that some people may misunderstand certain advertisements, but that does not mean that the FTC will be concerned about the ads. For example, if a hair dye is advertised as permanent and someone thinks it means that new hair growth will be the color of the dye, rather than that only existing hair will be the color of the dye, no deception is involved. Most consumers know what is meant, and those that do not understand do not incur significant injury.

Over $100 billion a year is spent on advertising. Consumers reject many ads because they find them objectionable for various reasons. As Table 16−1 indicates, consumers seem to think that ads are getting better and worse at the

---

Table 16–1   Viewers' Claims About Television Commercials

	1986	**1988**
Misleading	27.6%	33.4%
Insulting	29.4%	32.0%
Boring	22.0%	32.0%
Informative	15.7%	21.0%
Entertaining	14.4%	18.9%

Source: Adapted from a Video Storyboard Tests Inc. survey of 1,000 television viewers.

same time. While an increasing percentage of television viewers say that ads exaggerate their claims and insult viewers' intelligence, more viewers find ads useful and clever. Evidence that consumers are skeptical about ad claims is one reason the FTC has reduced attacks on ad claims that some people maintain are misleading.

Deciding What Is Sufficient Deception
The number of people deceived by an ad is not necessarily the key point of whether there is actionable deception. For instance, automobile ads will say that the Fireball model got thirty miles per gallon in tests. If that ad is on national television, it may be viewed by tens of millions, of which several hundred thousand may incorrectly think that all Fireball models will always get thirty miles per gallon. So long as the claim made was true—and since most consumers know that miles-per-gallon tests do not mean that all cars will get exactly the test results—there is no deception that would lead one to believe that the effect is material and injurious to enough consumers to warrant the ads to be modified.

On the other hand, some ads that reach a very small number of people, such as pamphlets handed out door to door, may deceive many of the recipients, because the claims made are likely to deceive most consumers. Other ads may reach a large number of people, deceive very few, yet be held by the FTC to be deceptive. For instance, if a small number of consumers suffer serious injury because they believe a claim made by an advertiser, the FTC may act because of the seriousness of the injury.

Examples of Deceptive Ad Cases
In 1986, the FTC issued a consent decree against Buckingham Productions, Inc. Buckingham sold various diet plans under such names as the Rotation Diet, the "No Frills" Rotation Diet, and the Freedom Diet. The FTC challenged as false Buckingham's claims that dieters could eat virtually unlimited quantities of any food they wished for four days each week and still lose weight if, during the other three days, they followed a low-calorie diet and took the company's vitamin supplements and wafers. The company claimed that the usual monthly weight loss for women was eight to twenty pounds and twelve to twenty-five pounds for men. The company could not substantiate its claims and was required to stop making them.

North American Philips was sued for false and unsubstantiated advertising claims for its Norelco brand Clean Water Machine. The company claimed the "Machine helps remove chlorine, sediment, sulfur, detergent, odors, organic chemicals, and other pollutants you may not even be aware of that are in your tap water." The FTC charged that the machines' filters actually added a chemical that is potentially hazardous to consumers' health.

The FTC sued the Campbell Soup Company in 1989 for making deceptive and unsubstantiated claims. The ads linked the low-fat, low-cholesterol content of its soup with a reduced risk of some forms of heart disease, but failed to disclose that the soups are high in sodium and that diets high in sodium may increase the risk of heart disease.

In 1990, the FTC announced a consent agreement with the makers of Nature's Way Products. The company agreed to stop making unsubstantiated claims by advertising that "Cantrol" capsules fight yeast infections. The company also agreed not to represent that other food supplements containing certain ingredients can cure, treat, prevent, or reduce the risk of disease, unless the company can substantiate the claim.

How the powers of the FTC can be used to correct advertising held to be deceptive is illustrated in the *Warner-Lambert* decision involving Listerine.

Warner-Lambert Company v. Federal Trade Commission
United States Court of Appeals, District of Columbia Circuit
562 F.2d 749 (1977)

Case Background. *Listerine has been marketed since 1879. Beginning in 1921, advertisements for it claimed that it had beneficial effects on sore throats and colds. The FTC found the claims not supported by evidence and issued an order against Warner-Lambert to stop advertising that Listerine could prevent, cure, or alleviate colds. The FTC also ordered that there be corrective advertising. Warner-Lambert challenged the FTC ruling, claiming that even if its ad claims had been false, the Commission exceeded its statutory authority. The court of appeals reviewed the FTC order.*

Case Decision. Judge J. Skelly Wright delivered the opinion of the court.

* * *

The Commission carefully analyzed the evidence. . . . The ultimate conclusion that Listerine is not an effective cold remedy was based on six specific findings of fact.

First, the Commission found that the ingredients of Listerine are not present in sufficient quantities to have any therapeutic effect. . . .

Second, the Commission found that in the process of gargling it is impossible for Listerine to reach the critical areas of the body in medically significant concentration. . . .

Third, the Commission found that even if significant quantities of the active ingredients of Listerine were to reach the critical sites where cold viruses enter and infect the body, they could not interfere with the activities of the virus because they could not penetrate the tissue cells.

Fourth, the Commission discounted the results of a clinical study conducted by petitioner on which petitioner heavily relies. . . .

Fifth, the Commission found that the ability of Listerine to kill germs by millions on contact is of no medical significance in the treatment of colds or sore throats. . . .

Sixth, the Commission found that Listerine has no significant beneficial effect on the symptoms of sore throat. . . .

The need for the corrective advertising remedy and its appropriateness in this case are important issues. . . . But the threshold question is whether the Commission has the authority to issue such an order. We hold that it does.

* * *

Listerine has built up over a period of many years a widespread reputation. When it was ascertained that the reputation no longer applied to the product, it was necessary to take action to correct it. Here, . . . it is the accumulated impact of *past* advertising that necessitates disclosure in *future* advertising. To allow consumers to continue to buy the product on the strength of the impression built up by prior advertising—an impression which is now known to be false—would be unfair and deceptive.

* * *

We turn next to the specific disclosure required: "Contrary to prior advertising, Listerine will not help prevent colds or sore throats or lessen their severity." Warner-Lambert is ordered to include this statement in every future advertisement for Listerine for a defined period. In printed advertisements it must be displayed in type size at least as large as that in which the principal portion of the text of the advertisement appears and it must be separated from the text so that it can be readily noticed. In television commercials the disclosure must be presented simultaneously in both audio and visual portions. During the audio portion of the disclosure in television and radio advertisements, no other sounds, including music, may occur.

These specifications are well calculated to assure that the disclosure will reach the public. It will necessarily attract the notice of readers, viewers, and listeners, and be plainly conveyed. Given these safeguards, we believe the preamble "Contrary to prior advertising" is not necessary.

* * *

Finally, Warner-Lambert challenges the duration of the disclosure requirement. By its terms it continues until respondent has expended on Listerine advertising a sum equal to the average annual Listerine advertising budget for the period April 1962 to March 1972. That is approximately ten million dollars. Thus if Warner-Lambert continues to advertise normally the corrective advertising will be required for about one year. We cannot say that is an unreasonably long time in which to correct a hundred years of cold claims.

* * *

Case Holding. *The court of appeals upheld the decision of the FTC with minor modifications, requiring Warner-Lambert to correct its Listerine advertising and to cease the product claims held to be deceptive.*

Case Questions

1. Suppose there were evidence that most consumers really did not believe the claims that were made about Listerine. Would that reduce the need for such a judgment?

2. Can you see a constitutional argument here that this decision violates the First Amendment by requiring an advertiser to say something it does not want to say?

FTC Enforcement Activities

The FTC investigates a wide range of business practices that may be unfair and deceptive. Besides its concern with advertising cases, some aspects of investor protection discussed in Chapters 18 and 19, the credit regulations explained in Chapter 20, and the warranty issues discussed later in this chapter, the Bureau of Consumer Protection recommends cases to the Commission involving any practice under its jurisdiction that can injure consumers or businesses. The following examples give some idea of the range of activities.

Companies Shipping Unordered Goods

In one case, the FTC obtained a consent decree under which four Florida-based office supply companies agreed to pay civil penalties and to cease certain practices. The companies and individuals are prohibited from shipping any unordered products except those clearly marked as free samples or sent on behalf of charitable organizations and from seeking payment for unordered merchandise. The FTC claimed that the companies had been shipping large quantities of unordered office supplies to businesses, schools, and other organizations around the United States and then dunning the recipients for the merchandise.

Deceptive Loan Practices

An injunction was obtained in federal court by the FTC in a case involving R. A. Walker and Associates, Inc., a Washington, D.C.-area company. The FTC claimed that the company was making a false and deceptive offer of loans to help homeowners (usually lower-income individuals) avoid foreclosure on their home mortgages, when in fact the loan was a ruse to get the homeowners to sign over the deeds to their homes.

Telemarketing Fraud

The FTC obtained an injunction against five telemarketing firms and their owners in 1990 for making misrepresentations in the sale of water purifiers and home security systems. The FTC charged that the companies mailed postcards telling consumers they had won a valuable award, including $5,000 in retail merchandise checks. In fact, the awards consisted only of certificates that required payment of substantial sums of money to obtain the merchandise. The telemarketers also made charges against consumers' credit cards without authorization and billed customers for merchandise never sent.

Unfairness and Consumer Contract Enforcement

Section 5 of the FTC Act says ". . . unfair or deceptive acts or practices in or affecting commerce, are declared unlawful. . . ." The key word has always been deceptive. The word *unfair* is usually tagged on to a charge of deception. The FTC has tried to give operational meaning to unfair acts or practices in business by establishing the following *test for unfairness:*

1. It causes substantial harm to consumers.
2. Consumers cannot reasonably avoid injury.
3. The injury is harmful in its net effects.

The first major consumer unfairness case that did not involve a claim of deception was the *Orkin* case (which was supervised by one of the authors of this text while working for the FTC). The decision to bring the case was based on the perception that the unfairness involved seemed much like fraud or breach of contract, both of which are common-law standards the courts have long enforced.

Orkin Exterminating Company v. Federal Trade Commission
United States Court of Appeals, Eleventh Circuit
849 F.2d 1354 (1988)

Case Background. *Beginning in 1966, Orkin Exterminating Company offered customers a "continuous protection guarantee" if they had their houses treated for termites. The contract said that by paying a small annual fee, customers were guaranteed free retreatment if termites reappeared for as long as they owned their house. By 1975, Orkin realized that the promise was a mistake. The annual fee was too low to cover the costs. Orkin then notified over 200,000 customers, in their annual bills, that the fee was being raised $25 or 40 percent, whichever was greater. If the customers did not pay the fee, the guarantee was lost. The new fee was consistent with current market prices but differed from what the contract had stated. Most customers paid the higher fees, which increased Orkin's revenues $7.5 million through 1984. The FTC found the fee increase to be unfair and ordered Orkin to roll back its prices to the original levels. Orkin appealed to the U.S. Court of Appeals.*

Case Decision.   Circuit Judge Clark delivered the opinion.

* * *

It is true that the emphasis placed by the Commission on consumer unfairness is "of comparatively recent origin." But Orkin has not argued that the Commission's definition of what constitutes an unfair practice is itself outside the scope of the Commission's section 5 authority. Indeed, the courts reviewing applications of the Commission's unfairness standard have assumed, necessarily, that it is a valid standard. . . .

We must therefore decide whether the Commission exceeded its authority in deciding that one company's unilateral breach of 207,000 consumer contracts could meet the Commission's definition of unfairness. As the Supreme Court has said,

> Once the Commission has chosen a particular legal rationale for holding a practice to be unfair, . . . familiar principles of administrative law dictate that its decision must stand or fall on that basis, and a reviewing court may not consider other reasons why the practice might be deemed unfair.

Of course, the Commission's three-part standard does little to isolate the specific types of practices and consumer injuries which are cognizable. But "the consumer injury test is the most precise definition of unfairness articulated by either the Commission or Congress"; consequently, we must resolve the validity of the Commission's order "by reviewing the reasonableness of the Commission's application of the consumer injury test to the facts of this case, and the consistency of that application with congressional policy and prior Commission precedent."

* * *

It is clear from the Commission's opinion that the Policy Statement's consumer injury standard was the focus of its analysis. After a review of the undisputed facts in the case, the opinion contains a section entitled "Conclusions of Law," in which the Commission said,

> The issue before us is whether Orkin has engaged in an unfair act or practice under Section 5 by unilaterally increasing the renewal fees in its pre-1975 contract. This is not an action at common law for simple breach of contract. Rather it is an action under a federal statute that makes unlawful conduct causing injury to consumers

that is substantial, unavoidable and without countervailing benefits. Because determining whether Orkin's conduct was "unfair" depends in large part on what consumers properly could have expected from Orkin under the pre-1975 contracts, we focus first on those contracts. . . .

Nothing about this opinion indicates that the Commission did anything other than that which it purported to do: apply the unfairness standard contained in its Policy Statement. The Commission's conclusion was simply that it was an "unfair" practice to breach over 200,000 contracts. We think this was a reasonable application of the Commission's unfairness standard.

There remains, however, the question whether this case represents a significant departure from prior Commission precedent. We note what has been written in a recent law review article:

> Some of the oldest "unfairness" decisions involve sellers' refusals to live up to the terms of their contract. The Commission has often challenged sellers for traditional breaches of contract: failure to fill orders, delivery of inferior merchandise, refusal to return goods taken for repair, or refusal to return promised deposits. Recent trade regulation rules have focused on similar issues. These actions have attracted little controversy. Breach of contract has long been condemned as a matter of law, economics, and public policy.

Orkin claims the statements in this article are erroneous, for each of the cases cited therein involved some sort of deceptive practice. We think it important to remember, however, that section 5 by its very terms makes deceptive and unfair practices distinct lines of inquiry which the Commission may pursue. As is suggested above, while a practice may be both deceptive and unfair, it may be unfair without being deceptive. Furthermore, the Commission has explained in its Policy Statement that is operates under the assumption that the unfairness doctrine "differs from, and supplements, the prohibition against consumer deception."

An adoption of Orkin's position would mean that the Commission could never proscribe widespread breaches of retail consumer contracts unless there was evidence of deception or fraud. The Supreme Court has, on more than one occasion, recognized that the standard of unfairness is "by necessity, an elusive one," which defies such a limitation. The statutory scheme at issue here "necessarily gives the Commission an influential role in interpreting section 5 and in applying it to facts of particular cases arising out of unprecedented situations."

* * *

This case may be "unprecedented" to the extent it concerns non-deceptive contract breaches. But given the extraordinary level of consumer injury which Orkin has caused and the fact that deceptiveness is often not a component of the unfairness inquiry, we think the limitation of the Commission's section 5 authority urged by Orkin would be inconsistent with the broad mandate conferred upon the Commission by Congress. Thus, because the Commission's decision fully and clearly comports with the standard set forth in its Policy Statement, we conclude that the Commission acted within its section 5 authority.

* * *

Case Holding. *The Court of Appeals affirmed the FTC decision that a business practice may be illegal because it is unfair, even though it is not deceptive.*

Case Questions

1. Assuming that other courts would have found that Orkin had breached its contracts with 200,000 consumers, why not let them sue Orkin rather than have the FTC get involved?

2. Does the ability to bring suits for a practice being "unfair" open the door to almost everything being challenged as such, since we all have different ideas of what is unfair?

Trade Regulation Rules

Under Section 18 of the FTC Act, the FTC has the authority to issue certain *trade regulation rules*. These rules are designed to set boundaries for certain acts and practices that the FTC believes to be ripe for deception. Such rules tend to be drawn based on FTC experience of problems in certain areas, although critics charge that the rules can be used to protect existing competitors from innovative entrants by making certain practices the industry standard. Because numerous trade regulation rules are on the books—some dealing with rather narrow areas—only some of the more important rules issued in recent years are discussed here (the Franchise Rule is discussed in Chapter 18).

Establishing a Trade Regulation Rule

When the FTC proposes a rule, it must be published in the *Federal Register* so that interested parties may comment on it before it is finalized. When the rule is put in place, it gives the FTC solid grounds for charging that violators of the rule are committing an unfair and deceptive act, since such people are required to know about the rule if they are in the industry in question.

The Insulation R-Value Rule

The FTC's Trade Regulation Rule Concerning the Labeling and Advertising of Home Insulation (*the R-value rule*) was written because of the problems consumers face in trying to understand what the various insulation claims mean. By standardizing R-values, the FTC requires all insulation manufacturers and installers to use the same terminology and to measure the R-value of their products using specified tests and to disclose the results.

The rule is designed to provide consumers with a uniform standard to evaluate home insulation products before they buy. Because of the rule, if an insulation company claims that it has provided R-19 value insulation and it has not, there is a standard to measure the R-value that makes the company subject to suit by the FTC in a fairly straightforward manner, rather than trying to establish without any standards that what was done was deceptive.

For example, in 1990 the FTC settled a consent decree with Sears for violating the R-value rule. Sears advertised the thickness and price of an insulation product, but failed to disclose the R-value. In the decree, Sears agreed to pay a $100,000 civil penalty, to comply with the rule in the future, and to pay for advertisements to educate consumers about home insulation and R-values.

The Mail Order Rule

One of the best-known trade regulation rules is the Undelivered Mail Order Merchandise and Services, the *Mail Order Rule*. Under this rule, if a company offers to sell merchandise by mail, it must have a reasonable basis for expecting to ship the merchandise within the time stated in the solicitation. Shipping dates must be clearly stated on the offers (such as "Allow five weeks for shipment"), or the merchandise must be shipped within thirty days of receipt of a proper order. If the merchandise cannot be shipped on time, customers must be sent an option notice allowing them to cancel the order and receive a refund or to agree to a new shipping date—which must be reasonable and must be met. There are other provisions to the rule, but its most important effect has been to encourage prompt shipment of mail-order merchandise and to provide the FTC with an extra "hook" by which to issue complaints against companies that fail to live up to the terms of their offers.

The Used Car Rule

The FTC approved a *Used Car Rule* in 1984 that requires dealers to give consumers complete and clear information on who would have to pay for repairs after a sale and to have a buyers guide placed in the side window of each used car offered for sale. The guide must contain the following:

1. A statement of the terms of any warranty offered with the car.

2. A prominent statement of whether the dealer is selling the car "as is" and, if so, that the consumer must pay for any repairs needed after buying the car.

3. A warning that oral promises are difficult to enforce, with a suggestion to get all promises in writing.

4. A suggestion that the consumer ask for an independent inspection of the car.

The FTC sued a San Francisco car dealer in 1989 for violating the rule by failing to display window stickers on used cars offered for sale. The dealer also failed to provide consumers with copies of the Buyers Guide or disclosures concerning warranty. The dealer agreed to comply with the law in the future and paid a civil penalty of $20,000.

The Funeral Rule

The FTC adopted the *Funeral Rule* to try to reduce alleged deceptive practices by some funeral providers. The argument was made that the rule was needed because of the size of the expenditure involved—the average funeral costs about $2,500—and because many consumers are not careful shoppers during the stressful time when funeral arrangements are made. Exhibit 16–1 is from an FTC consumer pamphlet.

A funeral home operator cannot claim ignorance about the rule; violations, once demonstrated, are clear-cut. The FTC, for example, filed a consent decree in federal court in 1987 to settle an action against a Dallas funeral home. The complaint charged that the funeral home operator failed to give customers a written price list or an itemized written statement at the time or in the form required, failed to tell callers that price information was available over the phone, and failed to comply with other price information and service information requirements. The consent decree required an end to such practices and payment of $20,000 in civil penalties. After the decree, the funeral home operator continued to violate the Rule. Suing to enforce the decree in federal court in 1989, the judge granted the FTC's motion for

---

Exhibit 16–1   Trade Regulation Rule

CONSUMER GUIDE TO THE FTC FUNERAL RULE
Telephone Price Disclosures

When you call a funeral provider and ask about terms, conditions, or prices of funeral goods or services, the funeral provider will:

- tell you that price information is available over the phone.
- give you prices and any other information from the price lists to reasonably answer your questions.
- give you any other information about prices or offerings that is readily available and reasonably answers your questions.

By using the telephone, you can compare prices among funeral providers. Getting price information over the telephone may thus help you select a funeral home and the arrangements you want.

General Price List

If you inquire in person about funeral arrangements, the funeral provider will give you a general price list. This list, which you can keep, contains the cost of each individual funeral item and service offered. As with telephone inquiries, you can use this information to help select the funeral provider and funeral items you want, need, and are able to afford.

The price list also discloses important legal rights and requirements regarding funeral arrangements. It must include information on embalming, cash advance sales (such as newspaper notices or flowers), caskets for cremation, and required purchases.

Embalming Information

The Funeral Rule requires funeral providers to give consumers information about embalming that can help them decide whether to purchase this service. Under the Rule, a funeral provider:

- may not falsely state that embalming is required by law.
- must disclose in writing that, except in certain special cases, embalming is *not* required by law.
- may not charge a fee for unauthorized embalming unless it is required by state law.
- will disclose in writing that you usually have the right to choose a disposition such as direct cremation or immediate burial if you do not want embalming.
- will disclose to you in writing that certain funeral arrangements, such as a funeral with a viewing, may make embalming a practical necessity and, thus, a required purchase.

Cash Advance Sales

The Funeral Rule requires funeral providers to disclose to you in writing if they charge a fee for buying cash advance items. Cash advance items are goods or services that are paid for by the funeral provider on your behalf. Some examples of cash advance items are flowers, obituary notices, pallbearers, and clergy honoraria. Some funeral providers charge you their cost for these items. Others add a service fee to their cost. The Funeral Rule requires the funeral provider to inform you when a service fee is added to the price of cash advance items, or if the provider gets a refund, discount, or rebate from the supplier of any cash advance item.

Caskets for Cremation

Some consumers may want to select direct cremation, which is cremation of the deceased without a viewing or other ceremony at which the body is present. If you choose a direct cremation, the funeral provider will offer you either an inexpensive alternative container or an unfinished wood box. An alternative container is a non-metal enclosure used to hold the deceased. These containers may be made of pressboard, cardboard, or canvas.

Because any container you buy will be destroyed during the cremation, you may wish to use an alternative container or an unfinished wood box for a direct cremation. These could lower your funeral cost since they are less expensive than traditional burial caskets.

—continued

Exhibit 16–1 *continued*

Under the Funeral Rule, funeral directors who offer direct cremations:

- may not tell you that state or local law requires a casket for direct cremations.
- must disclose in writing your right to buy an unfinished wood box (a type of casket) or an alternative container for a direct cremation.
- must make an unfinished wood box or alternative container available for direct cremation.

Required Purchase

You do not have to purchase unwanted goods or services as a condition of obtaining those you do want unless you are required to do so by state law. Under the Federal Rule:

- you have the right to choose only the funeral goods and services you want, with some disclosed exceptions.
- the funeral provider must disclose this right in writing on the general price list.
- the funeral provider must disclose on the statement of goods and services selected the specific law that requires you to purchase any particular item.

Statement of Funeral Goods and Services Selected

The funeral provider will give you an itemized statement with the total cost of the funeral goods and services you select. This statement also will disclose any legal, cemetery, or crematory requirements that compel you to purchase any specific funeral goods or services.

The funeral provider must give you this statement after you select the funeral goods and services that you would like. The statement combines in one place the prices of the individual items you are considering for purchase, as well as the total price. Thus, you can decide whether to add or subtract items to get what you want. If the cost of cash advance items is not known at that time, the funeral provider must write down a "good faith estimate" of their cost. The Rule does not require any specific form for this information. Therefore, funeral providers may include this information in any document they give you at the end of your discussion about funeral arrangements.

Preservative and Protective Claims

Under the Funeral Rule, funeral providers are prohibited from telling you a particular funeral item or service can indefinitely preserve the body of the deceased in the grave. The information gathered during the FTC's investigation indicated these claims are not true. For example, funeral providers may not claim embalming or a particular type of casket will indefinitely preserve the deceased's body.

The Rule also prohibits funeral providers from making claims that funeral goods, such as caskets or vaults, will keep out water, dirt, and other gravesite substances when that is not true.

* * *

summary judgment, ordering the defendant to pay $80,000 in civil penalties and that there be no future violations.

Magnuson-Moss Warranty Act

An amendment to the Federal Trade Commission Act was passed in 1975 to give the FTC power to set guidelines for producers of consumer products with respect to their responsibilities on warranties. This represents an unusual federal intervention into an area generally left to common law and to state law in the form of the Uniform Commercial Code. Compliance with the *Magnuson-Moss Warranty Act* does not appear to have been very costly, nor have the benefits of the law been very clear.

Required Written Warranty Information

The law requires that *written warranties* include information about the following:

- What parts of the product or what types of problems the warranty covers and, if necessary for clarity, what parts or problems it does not cover.
- What the period of coverage is.
- What will be done to correct problems and, if necessary for clarity, what will not be done.
- How the customer can get warranty service.
- How state law may affect certain provisions of the warranty.

Full or Limited Warranty

Every product that costs more than ten dollars and has a warranty must comply with the Act. The warranty must state clearly and conspicuously whether the warranty is full or limited. A *full warranty* meets the following five standards:

1. Warranty service will be provided to anyone who owns the product during the warranty period.
2. Warranty service will be provided free of charge, including such costs as returning the product or removing and reinstalling the product when necessary.
3. At the consumer's choice, either a replacement or a full refund will be provided if the product cannot be repaired after a reasonable number of tries.
4. Warranty service will be provided without requiring that consumers return a warranty registration card.
5. The implied warranties will not be limited.

If any of these statements is not true, the warranty is a *limited warranty* and must be so stated. A multiple warranty for a product exists when part of the product is covered by a full warranty and part is covered by a limited warranty. In all events, to comply with the FTC's Rule of Disclosure of Written Consumer Product Warranty Terms and Conditions, warranties must be reasonably clear, simple, and useful. In other words, if a company writes in fine print an unclear warranty that is designed to discourage consumers, the company will be subject to FTC attack, especially if consumers report difficulties enforcing the warranty. State courts have made similar determinations in cases brought under contract law. Obscure fine print is not held in favor.

INTERNATIONAL PERSPECTIVES: FOREIGN ADVERTISING REGULATION

INTERNATIONAL

PERSPECTIVES

Advertising is subject to very different controls around the world. Except for prohibitions on the advertising of certain products, in general most countries impose fewer regulations on ads than is the case in the United States. In Europe, ad regulations tend to be tightest in northern Europe and loosest in the Mediterranean countries.

Britain has an Office of Fair Trading that operates somewhat like the FTC with respect to ad regulation. The general standard is that an ad is illegal if it misrepresents a product, whereas in the United States it may be illegal if it simply misleads. For an ad to misrepresent a product, there must be an estimation that consumers suffer damages because they have not been told the truth in the ad. For example, a soup ad in the United States was held illegal by the FTC because the soup was filmed to look as though it had more chunky bits in it than a random bowl of the soup really would have. In most of Europe and Japan, that ad would not be illegal because while it misleads, it does not injure consumers.

THE NHTSA AND AUTOMOBILE SAFETY

In 1966, the National Traffic and Motor Vehicle Safety Act gave the National Highway Traffic Safety Administration (NHTSA), a part of the Department of Transportation, the power to regulate safety standards for automobiles sold in the United States. Manufacturers must comply with any safety standards set by NHTSA. When safety-related defects are found, manufacturers may be required to notify buyers and make arrangements to correct the problem (*recall programs*). Some recall programs have cost manufacturers hundreds of millions of dollars.

NHTSA does considerable testing of automobiles for safety. Early requirements set by the agency included mandatory headrests (to reduce whiplash in collisions), collapsible steering columns, stronger side bars in doors, mandatory seat belts, and safer dashboard designs. More recent requirements set by NHTSA concern fuel-economy standards, bumper requirements, passive restraints, and tire grading. Table 16–2 shows the costs and benefits of regulations imposed by NHTSA and EPA.

The most controversial development concerns the air bag, which industry contends is too expensive and unreliable to justify the expense. NHTSA had been planning to require air bags on all cars, but the rule was lifted in favor of one requiring automakers to begin to phase in passive restraints—either air

Table 16–2   Costs and Benefits of NHTSA and EPA Regulations*

Regulation	Annual Lives Saved	Cost/Life Saved
Steering column protection	1,300	$ 100,000
Passive restraints/belts	1,850	$ 300,000
Fuel system integrity	400	$ 300,000
Side door panels	480	$ 1,300,000
Trihalomethanes	322	$ 300,000
Benzene emissions	0.3	$ 2,800,000
Arsenic/glass plants	0.1	$19,200,000
Uranium mill tailings	2.1	$53,000,000

Source: *Regulation*, Nov./Dec. 1986, p. 30.

*The first four regulations were adopted by NHTSA; the second four were adopted by the EPA. Although the EPA often deals with chemical substances that appear to be very dangerous, compared with the more mundane auto safety requirements of the NHTSA, chemical regulations have a much smaller impact on public health and a much greater cost.

bags or automatic safety belts. All cars produced from 1989 on are to have one of these features unless two-thirds of the population is covered by mandatory safety belt usage laws by that time. The D.C. Court of Appeals held this rule to be proper, but left open the possibility for further challenges. The passive restraint requirement is not expected to be rescinded, because most state mandatory safety belt usage laws do not meet all federal requirements.

SUMMARY

The Food and Drug Administration (FDA) is the federal agency charged with the responsibility of monitoring food and drug safety. The FDA has responsibility for classifying unsafe food as adulterated, forming inspection systems, and setting safe levels of potentially dangerous additives in foods. The Delaney Clause to the Food, Drug, and Cosmetic Act prohibits the use of any food additive shown to be carcinogenic to humans or animals. The FDA regulates the nutritional labeling now present on most food products. The agency also has the authority to approve new drugs before they can be marketed. The Kefauver Amendment requires the FDA to consider a drug's effectiveness as well as its safety in making that approval.

The Consumer Product Safety Commission (CPSC) is the federal agency charged with collecting, analyzing, and disseminating data related to consumer product safety. The agency may issue product safety standards concerning a product's performance, composition, contents, design, construction, finish, or packaging. The CPSC may also require producers to submit a description of a new product for consideration before it is released to the public.

The Bureau of Consumer Protection of the Federal Trade Commission (FTC) has primary responsibility for bringing actions against companies and individuals who engage in business acts that are unfair and deceptive. The FTC can bring a wide range of actions under its unfair and deceptive standard, but the emphasis is trying to end business practices that deceive ordinary consumers and cause economic injury. Numerous trade regulation rules have been issued that set guidelines and standards for members of an industry. Firms that violate these rules can be sued for civil penalties and be required to give consumer redress and cease certain practices. The Magnuson-Moss Warranty Act, enforced by the FTC, requires the sellers of products who issue warranties to follow certain guidelines for full and limited warranties so that consumers will be able to read similar and comprehensible terminology in various warranties.

The National Highway Traffic and Safety Administration (NHTSA) has primary responsibility for automobile safety requirements. Many rules have been in the form of technical requirements concerning design features of automobiles. NHTSA rules have been impressive in their cost effectiveness in terms of number of lives saved at relatively low cost.

ISSUE

Does the FDA Need More Regulatory Authority?

The FDA is the only major federal regulatory agency that does not have subpoena power. It has asked Congress for the power that would allow it to subpoena records and individuals to assist the agency uncover evidence during investigations, but it has been consistently denied the authority. The case discussed in this reading is claimed to be an example of how enforcement of FDA regulations is made more difficult by the lack of investigatory powers.

Bad Apples: In The Executive Suite*

For more than 50 years, parents depended on Beech-Nut Nutrition Corp. to provide nutritious, natural, healthful food for their babies. They trusted Beech-Nut's reputation for quality. They believed Beech-Nut's promise to use only natural ingredients—no artificial flavorings, no preservatives, no colorings—promises made repeatedly in ads. . . .

Then Beech-Nut breached that trust. From 1977 to 1983, the product Beech-Nut sold as "100% fruit juice, no sugar added" contained little or no apple juice. It was an apple-flavored concoction that one company chemist later described as "a fraudulent chemical cocktail."

When Beech-Nut's juicy secret seemed likely to be discovered, the company orchestrated a cover-up. In August 1982, for example, New York State authorities, after testing the apple juice, notified Beech-Nut executives that its juice was adulterated. The president of Beech-Nut ordered the entire inventory of bogus apple juice shipped out of New York to avoid seizure. The following night, workers loaded nine tractor-trailers with 26,000 cases of adulterated apple juice and hauled the "juice" from Beech-Nut's manufacturing plant in Canajoharie, N.Y., to an empty warehouse in Secaucus, N.J. Within

days, the juice was en route to Puerto Rico, the Dominican Republic, and the Virgin Islands, where it was sold to unwitting consumers.

Eventually, the U.S. Department of Justice convened a grand jury to investigate Beech-Nut's grand deception. In 1987, Beech-Nut pleaded guilty to selling adulterated and misbranded juice, and last year Beech-Nut's president, Neils L. Hoyvald, and vice-president for operations, John F. Lavery, were tried and found guilty of violating Federal food and drug laws.

It had taken some 10 years for the Government to catch up with Beech-Nut. Meanwhile, Beech-Nut was able to extract as much as $60-million from consumers for sugared water mislabeled as apple juice.

How Beech-Nut was able to avoid detection and delay prosecution for years by refusing to cooperate with Federal investigators is a case study in corporate lawlessness and regulatory toothlessness. A review of the court testimony and extensive interviews tells the story:

The U.S. Food and Drug Administration is the Federal agency principally charged with minding the public interest in pure food. But the FDA, alone among all Federal

---

—continued

—continuing

regulatory agencies, lacks authority to subpoena records or to compel witnesses to testify. When the FDA requested shipping records to track the adulterated juice, Beech-Nut refused to provide them. When the FDA identified batches of adulterated juice, Beech-Nut destroyed them. When the FDA asked for results of the company's adulteration tests, Beech-Nut executives lied; they claimed they had no evidence that their juice was less than 100 percent pure long after the company's own chemists had warned the top brass that Beech-Nut was bottling sugared water, not apple juice.

One bad apple

Apple juice is easy to fake.

By the time apple juice reaches the store, the typical juice has been screened, filtered, blended with apples from other orchards, and perhaps dosed with a little ascorbic acid to help maintain its clarity. Then it has been concentrated, reconstituted with water, and pasteurized.

Apple juice, then, is best understood as a manufactured product, brewed in the bottler's plant using recipes designed for broad appeal and low cost. Who knows what the water content was in the original apples? Or the sugars content? Could anyone tell if the recipe had been twiddled to maintain consistency—or lower costs—by turning "juice" into sugared water?

At the time Beech-Nut began faking it, Beech-Nut chemists had developed a technique to analyze the sugars profile—the ratios of sucrose, fructose, and glucose. But because this is not an *officially* sanctioned test for adulteration, if the Government accused a company of selling adulterated juice, the company could plead ignorance. Prosecution for mislabeling and misrepresentation was also unlikely, even if adulteration was proved, since phony juice poses no known health problem.

Thus, when a supplier in the Bronx, N.Y., offered to sell apple-juice concentrate to Beech-Nut at 20 percent below market value,

the offer seemed to good to pass up. If Beech-Nut executives harbored any suspicions about this too-good-to-be-true offer, the prospect of reducing costs some $250,000 a year overcame any top-level zeal for real food in Beech-Nut containers.

But one Beech-Nut chemist, Jerome LiCari, then the company's director of research and development, noticed how quickly and easily the supplier satisfied all complaints about the concentrate's quality. If LiCari complained that the concentrate was too acidic or the color was off, the supplier would correct the problem in the very next shipment. Natural products are not so quickly and easily manipulated. "The supplier had too much control over the product," LiCari said.

LiCari sent juice samples to be tested at a laboratory in Boston. The test results showed the juice was extensively adulterated with corn syrup and cane sugar. LiCari urged his superiors to switch to another supplier. They refused: The concentrate's sugars may have been wrong, but the price was right. Instead, Beech-Nut asked the supplier to sign a "hold-harmless agreement" to indemnify the company against damages if the juice later proved to be adulterated.

Meanwhile, LiCari kept testing, using more accurate test methods. New tests revealed that the juice was adulterated with artificial malic acid, an adulterant that earlier tests had not detected. LiCari then put his suspicions in writing. In a memo to his boss, John Lavery, LiCari concluded that "a tremendous amount of circumstantial evidence" presents "a grave case against the current supplier." He again pleaded with the company to switch to another supplier.

The response: Licari was told he wasn't "a team player." Lavery threatened to fire him. Convinced that Beech-Nut was knowingly breaking the law, LiCari resigned. "I felt there was nothing I could ever do to stop them from using that juice," he said.

—continued

—continuing

Thwarted Investigations

Beech-Nut sold bogus apple juice for nearly five years before outside investigators first suspected wrongdoing. The Processed ApplesInstitute, an industry trade group, had been aware of longstanding allegations of adulteration. In April 1982, the institute hired a private investigator to check into rumors that a Bronx company was selling bogus apple-juice concentrate. By searching through garbage dumpsters and following delivery trucks, the investigator learned that the Bronx supplier's concentrate *was* bogus—and that its largest customer was Beech-Nut.

The investigator told Beech-Nut executives that the concentrate the company was using was adulterated, assuming that Beech-Nut was a victim—not a perpetrator—of economic fraud. Beech-Nut was "hostile and uncooperative," according to a later FDA report. But the company did agree to stop buying concentrate from the supplier.

Although the FDA had also been aware of allegations of apple-juice adulteration, it had taken no action because the bogus juice posed no known health risk. "Our first priority is health and safety," an FDA spokesperson said, "not economic fraud." But by 1982 the consumer fraud in this case involved millions of dollars. It was too much to ignore.

The FDA finally tested four samples of Beech-Nut apple juice from warehouse stock and found that the product contained little or no apple juice. When FDA investigators confronted Beech-Nut with the test results, Beech-Nut executives lied to the FDA, saying the company had no knowledge of any reliable method to test the authenticity of apple juice. Since the FDA did not have access to Beech-Nut records, the agency had no way of knowing that Beech-Nut chemists had been questioning the authenticity of its juice for four years.

Beech-Nut could have avoided scandal at this point by conceding its juice was sugared water and by agreeing to relabel it as apple-flavored drink rather than juice. But that would have belied the image created by its advertising. ("We have no market for products of that nature," said John Lavery, vice president for operations, at a meeting convened to consider the possibility.) The company continued to label and advertise the sugared water as juice—and to cover up what it was doing.

The FDA asked to review Beech-Nut's juice-testing records, batch production records, and complaint files. The company refused. The FDA could not know how much adulterated juice existed or where the juice was located.

Since Beech-Nut refused to turn over its shipping records, the FDA decided to contact Beech-Nut's trucking company to get the information from that source. When Beech-Nut learned that the FDA was visiting the trucker, Beech-Nut executives backed down and offered to provide the FDA with a list of 10 locations where investigators could find adulterated juice. Again, Beech-Nut misled the FDA. According to the testimony of Beech-Nut's director for distribution, Beech-Nut conjured up a list that included only companies that would have little or no apple juice remaining in their warehouses. "We were trying to delay the FDA from finding the product," he testified.

The FDA called Beech-Nut a few days later and asked what the company planned to do with its bogus juice. Beech-Nut assumed it had successfully stymied the investigation by telling the FDA that all the adulterated juice had been shipped and wouldn't be recalled, since it posed no health hazard. Beech-Nut said it would provide a complete list of shipping dates and locations—but only if the FDA made a written request.

Why a written request? A provision in the Food, Drug, and Cosmetic Act grants immunity from prosecution to any person or corporation providing records in response to a written request by the FDA. The immunity

—continued

—continuing

provision was designed to protect trucking companies, railroads, and other innocent transporters who unwittingly ship adulterated foods—a loophole in the law big enough for Beech-Nut to drive its trucks through. Though the FDA desperately needed the shipping records, the agency could not make a written request without giving up the right to prosecute.

FDA investigators returned to Beech-Nut's Canajoharie plant, where they found 242 cases of adulterated juice. The FDA asked Beech-Nut not to destroy the juice. Beech-Nut agreed, then proceeded to destroy the juice before the FDA could get the authorization needed to seize it.

After three months of Federal pressure, Beech-Nut executives asked to meet with FDA officials to discuss a nationwide recall of the apple juice manufactured with imitation concentrate. Meanwhile, however, the company continued to ship and sell the phony juice. Beech-Nut then initiated a special promotion: Buy 12 jars of baby food and get six jars of fruit juice free.

After two weeks of meetings, Beech-Nut's attorney argued that there wasn't enough juice left unsold to merit a recall. The FDA didn't give up. It ordered all its districts to collect samples of *Beech-Nut* juice produced before June 23, 1982—the date Beech-Nut stopped buying from the suspect supplier. Rather than face multiple seizure actions, Beech-Nut agreed to conduct a voluntary national recall. By then, however, the repeated delays had indeed all but exhausted the supply of bogus juice.

It appeared that the sugared-water episode was over. Not true. Beech-Nut still had on hand a supply of mixed-juice products made with phony concentrate. The adulteration would be difficult or impossible to detect in mixed juices, so Beech-Nut continued to sell them.

Beech-Nut's president assumed he had gotten away with the fraud. One month after the recall, Hoyvald wrote in a management report to Beech-Nut's parent company, Nes-

tle S.A.: "It is our feeling that we can report safely now that the apple juice recall has been completed. If the recall had been effectuated in early June, over 700,000 cases in inventory could have been affected . . . due to our many delays, we were only faced with having to destroy approximately 20,000 cases."

Other Beech-Nut executives also assumed they had outsmarted the Government. Several months after the recall, LiCari attended a cocktail party at a meeting of the National Food Processors Association, where he heard Beech-Nut executives laughing that "they got away with it, that the matter was dead." When he got home, Licari fired off a letter to the FDA providing details of the multiyear fraud. "The vice-president of manufacturing and the purchasing staff knew of the adulteration for a long time . . . By their delaying tactics the economic impact on Beech-Nut was minimal," LiCari concluded. He signed the letter "Johnny Appleseed."

Verdict: Guilty

At the time LiCari wrote this letter to the FDA, some agency officials were already preparing to recommend that the Department of Justice bring criminal charges against Beech-Nut and several top executives. The FDA had reason to believe that Beech-Nut had violated Federal food and drug laws, but the agency had no idea how extensive the conspiracy and cover-up actually were. LiCari's letter suggested that Beech-Nut had knowingly and intentionally broken the law.

In June 1985, the Justice Department opened a criminal investigation into the Beech-Nut case, armed with the investigative tools that the law curiously denies the FDA. On November 13, 1987, Beech-Nut pleaded guilty to Federal charges that it intentionally sold adulterated and misbranded juice in 20 states, Puerto Rico, the Virgin Islands, and five foreign countries.

—continued

–continuing

The company paid a fine of $2-million—the largest fine in FDA history.

The Justice Department also brought charges against Beech-Nut executives Hoyvald and Lavery. On February 17, 1988, a jury convicted Hoyvald on 359 counts of violating Federal food and drug laws, and it convicted Lavery on 448 counts, including conspiracy and mail-fraud charges. They were each sentenced to a year and a day inprison and fined $100,000. Appeals are pending.

Is the case closed, or could the juice you buy today—from any food manufacturer—actually be sugared water?

... The commercial pressures that led Beech-Nut to cheat consumers exist throughout the industry. The weakness of the FDA's regulatory power still exists. That combination leaves consumers less confident than they should be in the purity of their food supply.

Questions

1. Suppose the "apple juice" made of sugar, flavorings, and so forth, not only tasted like regular apple juice but was nutritionally identical and could be sold for a lower price. Would it be unethical to sell that product as apple juice, since consumers would not be hurt but would enjoy the savings?

2. Since the guilty parties were convicted, how could this have been different if the FDA had subpoena powers?

REVIEW AND DISCUSSION QUESTIONS

1. Define the following terms:
   Delaney Clause
   Kefauver Amendment
   consent decree
   deception
   unfairness
   trade regulation rules
   full warranty
   limited warranty

2. Nutrition labeling is a different concept from food safety rules governing sanitation and carcinogenic additives. Should the government be in the business of deciding what information should be made available to consumers? Why did all the food companies not voluntarily put nutrition information on their labels?

3. If a drug is FDA-approved and someone is injured by that drug, is the drug maker immune from a liability suit?

4. What incentives do FDA administrators have to approve new drugs for sale? Do the administrators have an incentive to hurry the process or to be very careful?

5. What does the Magnuson-Moss Act add to consumer protection that otherwise would not exist?

6. Comment on the following: "Virtually every federal agency arose because of industry's failure to police itself and because of a perceived need to protect the public from industry irresponsibility. These agencies may, of course, be criticized for being bureaucratic and ineffective, but even their most ardent

critics acknowledge that some positive good has resulted from their efforts. The FDA, for example, kept thalidomide off the market in this country, sparing countless families the sorrow of deformed children."

7. Supporters of the CPSC argue that the commission was needed despite the common-law rule of strict liability. Can you think of the kinds of accidents that might be prevented by the CPSC's setting standards that would not otherwise be addressed by producers?

Case Questions

8. "I'm calling from International Businesswide Machines to tell you that we are glad to be able to offer IBM machines for the lowest prices ever. Our personal computers and copy machines have never before been priced so low. May we send you a price list?" When customers at business offices who receive this call respond positively, the company sends them a brochure listing and showing its products. Some customers believe the products are from the famous IBM Company, not from this company with a very similar name. The machines this company is selling are not IBM originals; they are cheaper machines made in Singapore that look a lot like genuine IBM machines. Ignoring any trademark or copyright issues of the IBM name, is this a legitimate deception case that the FTC would be likely to be concerned about? What might determine whether there was consumer injury?

9. A store constantly has big signs in its windows and puts ads in the newspapers that take different approaches. For a month the store will advertise "Gigantic Savings of 75%" and similar claims. The next month it will advertise "Going-Out-of-Business Clearance Sale." The next month it will advertise "Distress Sale Prices—Everything Must Go." In fact, the store is not going out of business, and most of its prices are always the same. They are competitive prices, but hardly 75 percent off normal retail—or any other great bargain. Is this deceptive advertising?

10. Laetrile is a drug not approved by the FDA for sale. Some people believe it helps fight certain types of cancer. People who have cancer will travel to Mexico or West Germany to be treated with Laetrile and other drugs not available in the United States. Some people dying of cancer sued the FDA, saying that they had a constitutional right to privacy that was being denied by the FDA's refusal to let them have access to Laetrile. The federal court of appeals held that it is not reasonable to apply the FDA's drug safety and effectiveness standards to dying cancer patients. The Supreme Court reviewed the case. What was the result? [*United States* v. *Rutherford*, 442 U.S. 544, 99 S.Ct. 2470 (1979)]

Policy Questions

11. Some argue that agencies like the CPSC simply reflect upper middle-class and higher-class values for high-quality products. The result is more expensive consumer products not really worth the extra cost. This hurts poor people, who are then priced out of the market for the goods. Is this argument valid?

12. How could more cooperative private safety efforts be encouraged? Do we want firms in the same industry to act together to work for safer products and common industry safety standards that must be met?

13. Trade regulation rules exist primarily to make it easier for the FTC to sue companies that are engaging in practices that the FTC does not like. Once a rule is implemented, all firms covered by it are "on notice" of the standard. Some have claimed that such rules are bad because they tend to set the industry practices to protect existing firms, discouraging innovation by would-be competitors. Does this make sense?

Ethics Questions

14. The FDA, FTC, CPSC, or some other agency is proposing a regulation that would hurt the sales of one of the products your company produces. The agency believes that there is a long-run consumer health issue that it should address by the regulation that you estimate will cost your company $20 million a year in sales and $2 million a year in profits. The three other firms in the industry that make a similar product will likewise be hurt. Your Washington representative tells you that if all four firms are willing to spend $5 million in lobbying efforts and campaign contributions, you will probably get a rider put on the agency's annual appropriation bill that will kill the proposed regulation. All other firms agree to help foot the bill. This method of killing proposed regulations has been used by other firms and industries numerous times in the past. Should you pay to help get the regulation killed?

15. Your company makes copper bracelets. A rumor gets started that copper bracelets will prevent and cure arthritis. Your sales jump to ten times their previous level. You cannot produce bracelets fast enough to meet demand. Would it be improper for you to take advantage of the situation by doubling your prices? Would you have an obligation to advertise or put notices on your bracelets that there is no reason to think they have any health benefits? What if your company marketed a horse rubdown lotion. A rumor has started that the lotion is a miracle cure for humans. People rub it on themselves and begin to drink it. You know it will not help people if they rub it on and it can be dangerous to drink. What duty do you have to the misinformed public? (Assume you have no legal duty to do anything.)

16. Advertisements that would produce a storm of protest in the United States for being sexist are very popular in other countries. For example, in Japan, wall calendars with nude women are issued by many major corporations, including Japan Air Lines. Calendars like those exist in the United States, but no major company would think of issuing one. Women's breasts, covered or not, are featured in ads for numerous products. When women are shown in ads for reasons other than their bodies, they tend to be doe-eyed and complacent. Ads showing women in competent roles are rare. When an American company sells in the Japanese market, does it have a duty to be nonsexist in its ads? If ads with nude women would increase the sales of U.S. computers in Japan, compared to other types of ads, should those ads be used? Do American firms have a responsibility not only to avoid sexism, but to combat it by showing women in affirmative situations?

17 Environmental Law

THIS chapter discusses the federal laws providing for the protection of environmental quality. The chapter provides an overview of the history of the pollution problem, the difficulties of controlling environmental quality through private litigation, and the current federal regulatory laws intended to overcome those difficulties. The principal focus of the chapter is on those environmental laws most affecting the business community.

The chapter begins with a discussion of the nature of pollution and its regulatory definitions. The common-law attempts to regulate environmental quality are then discussed, since much of the present statutory law has been influenced by common-law principles. Particular attention is placed on the application of nuisance law to environmental pollution problems.

After discussing the shortcomings in the common-law regulation of pollution, the chapter discusses the creation of the Environmental Protection Agency (EPA). The federal government, citizens' groups, and several businesses viewed the EPA as the solution to the shortcomings in common-law efforts to control pollution.

The chapter then discusses the major federal environmental quality laws, including the Clean Air Act, the Clean Water Act, and the Resource Conservation and Recovery Act, and the requirements they impose on business. Finally, the chapter briefly considers federal wildlife law and its impact on the business community.

The chapter closes with the Issue article, which looks at indoor air pollution, a subject that has become of more concern as we learn about health hazards not recognized previously.

THE NATURE OF POLLUTION AND ITS REGULATION

The term *pollution* is usually associated with smoke belching from smokestacks into the atmosphere and with water wastes spilling from pipes into rivers and streams. Although air and water pollution are the most visible types of pollution, a number of other pollutants adversely affect humans and their environment. A pollutant can be a noise, an odor, something visually displeasing, or something not sensed but which seriously affects human health. Certain toxic pollutants, for example, are not detected by the senses but can cause serious illness if inhaled or ingested.

Defining Pollution Under the Common Law

Those categories provide an adequate description of pollution, but the term is defined differently by the law. Under the common law, for example, the courts have defined pollution in terms of its *reasonableness*. The reasonableness of pollution is determined under the common law on a case-by-case basis. A court weighs the social costs and benefits of the activity in the area in which it is found. A smoking fire, the dumping of sewage, excessive noise, and intense odors have all been found to be reasonable activities in some circumstances and to be unreasonable pollution in others. A certain business activity may be considered an unreasonable source of pollution in an urban setting but a perfectly reasonable activity in a rural setting.

Defining Pollution Under Federal Regulatory Law

Federal environmental laws have tended to define pollution in terms of its effects on the public health and welfare. A pollutant becomes a *public health* concern under federal law when it causes physical discomfort or illness in humans. A pollutant presents a *public welfare* concern when it causes damage to property or adversely affects wildlife, vegetation, and soils. Under federal law, businesses as a group are required to reduce their pollution so that it no longer injures the public health and welfare. Thus, in contrast to the common law, the pollution control requirements imposed on businesses may be applied with little or no regard to a particular business's location. That is, pollution that adversely affects human health and welfare is deemed unreasonable under federal law regardless of its location. A plant located in Portland, Oregon, will likely be required to implement the same technology to control its pollution as a similar plant in Miami, Florida.

POLLUTION CONTROL, PRIVATE LITIGATION, AND THE COMMON LAW

Environmental pollution was not a subject of serious federal regulation until the late 1960s. Until that time, pollution had been viewed as a problem best controlled by state and local governments. Although some state and local laws and ordinances were developed to control pollution, private citizens had to rely primarily upon the courts and the legal system for relief from environmental pollution. Private litigation and the common law were the principal regulatory tools for controlling business pollution before the 1960s.

Under the common law, however, no independent legal doctrine governing environmental pollution existed. In their efforts to provide relief, judges were forced to borrow rules from larger and more general bodies of the common law. In resolving disputes involving pollution, judges relied on the laws of nuisance, trespass, negligence, and strict liability for abnormally dangerous activities. Over time, citizens came to rely most heavily on the law of nuisance in bringing actions against business regardless of whether the pollutant was water, air, or land based. According to Professor William Rodgers:

> Nuisance actions . . . challenged virtually every major industrial and municipal activity which is today the subject of comprehensive environmental regulation—the operation of land fills, incinerators, sewage treatment facilities, activities at chemical plants, aluminum, lead and copper smelters, oil refineries, pulp mills, rendering plants, quarries and mines, textile mills and a host of other manufacturing activities.

Application of Nuisance Law

Nuisances are classified as either public or private. The principal difference is in the degree of pollution involved and in the number of individuals affected. A *public nuisance* is defined as an unreasonable interference with a right held in common by the general public. In an environmental pollution case, that right held in common is the community's right to a reasonably clean environment under the circumstances. To be a public nuisance, the pollution must affect many people, such as the residents of the community or of a particular neighborhood. As a rule, a public nuisance case will be brought against the polluter in the community's name by the city attorney.

A *private nuisance* is defined as a substantial and unreasonable interference with the use and enjoyment of the land of another. It generally involves a polluter who is adversely affecting one individual or a small group of individuals. Because of the costs of litigation, a private nuisance action often involves a dispute between two businesses over the reasonableness of two conflicting commercial activities.

The Environmental Pollution Nuisance Case

A typical pollution nuisance case involves a company whose principal business activity is offensive or harmful to its neighbors. Before requiring a polluter to reduce or abate pollution, the court requires the plaintiff to demonstrate evidence of (1) an unreasonable interference by the business and, (2) the availability of a better means of controlling pollution.

Unreasonable Interference. The plaintiff must first present evidence that the business's pollution is an unreasonable interference with the use and enjoyment of the land. In deciding if the pollution is unreasonable, the court will compare the *social costs* caused by the pollution with the *social benefits* the business provides to the community. To determine social costs, the court will consider the characteristics of the pollution and the degree to which it is permanent or long lasting.

In considering the social benefits of the polluter's business, the court will consider the social value of the business and the appropriateness of the business's location. Some courts consider the value of the business to the community by taking into account the business's payroll and employment. Where the benefits of the business exceeds the harm caused by the pollution, the pollution will be considered reasonable. Consider the *Versailles* case as an illustration of the court's decision process.

Versailles Borough v. McKeesport Coal & Coke Company

Allegheny County Court
83 Pittsburgh Legal Journal 379 (1935)

Case Background. *McKeesport Coal & Coke Company owned 2,500 acres of coal located in the borough of Versailles. In mining the coal, impurities called "gob" were removed because there was no place to store them inside the mine. As was the general practice in the industry, the gob was brought to the surface and dumped in a pile near the mine. The gob pile caught fire.*

Because of the smoke and other environmental problems caused by the burning gob pile, the borough of Versailles, city of McKeesport, sought an injunction against the coal company. In this portion of the opinion, the judge discussed whether or not the gob pile constituted a public nuisance.

Case Decision. Justice Musmanno delivered the opinion of the court.

* * *

That the borough of Versailles is subjected to annoyance, personal inconvenience, and aesthetic damage by the burning of the gob pile, is not seriously disputed. . . . If by degree we prohibit McKeesport from mining coal, and thereby relieve the borough of Versailles from all the vexation of smoke, dust and odors that come from a burning gob pile, we must consider what harm, if any, comes to those who are interested in the continued operation of the coal mine. . . .

The uncontradicted testimony discloses that upon an investment of $2,561,000 made eleven years before this trial, not a dollar has ever been paid by McKeesport in dividends; no year's operation has shown a profit and the result for the entire period shows a net loss in excess of $500,000. Since this has been the financial experience of McKeesport with its gob pile located but 230 feet from its tipple, for us to decree that it must desist from further dumping near its present pile—for us to decree that it must bear the expense of purchasing additional large surface acreage at locations distant from the tipple, would be equivalent to ordering the closing down of the mine. McKeesport is engaged in a lawful business. Its stockholders are entitled to a fair and reasonable return on their investments as this gob pile ignited through causes over which McKeesport had no control.

Four hundred and thirteen men were employed at this mine at the time of the trial. These men and their families—about two thousand people in all, are economically dependent upon this mine for subsistence. When in full operation McKeesport's payroll disbursement exceeds $10,000 per week, and although the stockholders have received no dividends, the company disbursed as wages to its employees $2,801,000 during the eleven years prior to the trial. Neither directly nor indirectly will we destroy a legitimate business without cogent and adequate reason. Under testimony adduced in this case, we cannot and will not jeopardize the employment of these miners. To do so would be to cause a far greater injury than that we are asked to enjoin. Of course, if the continued operation of this mine were a serious menace to the health or lives of those who reside in its vicinity, there would be another question before us, but there is no evidence in this case to warrant the assumption that the health of anyone is being imperiled.

* * *

On the other hand, we cannot believe that one's health would improve by living close to the gob fire, and we cannot believe . . . that there is no physical discomfort or annoyance caused to residents of that vicinity, by the burning mountain. In fact, our decision in this case is not based on the assumption that the people living close to the gob fire suffer no annoyance, but that the annoyance which is theirs is trivial in comparison to the positive harm and damage that would be done to the community, were the injunction asked for granted.

* * *

The inhabitants of this district were cognizant of the industrialization of the community when they moved into it. They voluntarily took up abode in this territory, and can scarcely with consistency now be heard to voice a protest about the smoky atmosphere. One who voluntarily goes to war should not complain about the cannon smoke.

* * *

Case Holding. *The activity of McKeesport Coal & Coke Company was reasonable under the circumstances.*

Case Questions

1. What factors weighed heavily in favor of the reasonableness of McKeesport's activities? What are the factors weighing heavily against them?
2. Would the case have come out the same if a serious health risk were apparent?
3. Was the plaintiff or the defendant there first? Should it make a difference?

Better Means of Control. Plaintiffs are required to demonstrate that the business is not doing all it can to control pollution. Generally, plaintiffs are required to provide evidence of the availability of better pollution control technologies or practices. Courts generally prefer to require the business to implement superior control technologies instead of closing the business down. On the presentation of such evidence by plaintiffs, the business presents evidence illustrating why the technology would not work in its factory (i.e., it is technologically infeasible) or why it would be prohibitively expensive (i.e., it is economically infeasible). In the second half of its *Versailles* decision, the court discusses the plaintiffs' inability to present evidence regarding the availability of better control technologies in the coal-mining industry.

**Versailles
Borough v.
McKeesport
Coal & Coke
Company**
continuing

* * *

There is no testimony on the part of the borough of Versailles that McKeesport is mining its coal in an unordinary way. On the contrary, all the evidence in the case is to the effect that the methods of mining and disposing of gob employed by McKeesport are the methods used in practically all mines. Every mine has its gob pile, and it was testified that practically one hundred percent of these gob piles catch fire. It was established further that at practically every mine, the rule is to pile the gob somewhere adjacent to the hole in the earth from which it is lifted to the surface.

It was not established, nor charged at the trial, that McKeesport operated its mine in a negligent or inefficient manner. . . .

* * *

To haul away the gob from the district by rail would be an exorbitant expense, and would naturally result in an increased cost of coal. Furthermore, where would the gob be hauled to? and wouldn't it catch fire at that point? and wouldn't McKeesport then be liable for any damage suffered by third parties, on account of that distant gob fire? A gob pile near the tipple of the mine is a natural use of the land, but there would be no legal defense to a gob fire away from the mine property.

* * *

The uncontroverted testimony of the mine engineers is that gob piles are necessary incidents to all coal mining; that there is no practical method of operating a coal mine without a gob pile outside the mine; that all bituminous coal mines have gob piles; that these piles usually catch fire through spontaneous combustion . . .

* * *

Case Holding. *The borough of Versailles did not establish that there was a better method for controlling pollution than that currently employed by McKeesport. The gob pile located on McKeesport's property was not an environmental nuisance.*

Case Questions

1. Should it be the responsibility of the plaintiff or the defendant to demonstrate that a better approach to pollution control is not available?
2. If other mines in the state employed a different, less polluting approach, would this case have come out differently?

Application of Trespass

A *trespass* at common law is defined as an unauthorized and direct breach of the boundaries of another's land. The principal difference between trespass and nuisance is that a trespass occurs whenever there is tangible invasion of plaintiff's property. A nuisance requires proof that the interference with the plaintiff's property is substantial and unreasonable.

To establish a trespass, the plaintiff must demonstrate that the invasion was something more substantial than a mere whiff of smoke, dust, gas, or fumes. In addition, some courts hold that the invasion must be direct. If an intervening force, such as wind or water, carries the pollutants onto the plaintiff's land, the invasion is not direct and therefore is not a trespass. Obviously, such restrictions greatly reduce the possible applications of trespass in environmental pollution cases.

Application of Negligence and Strict Liability

Both *negligence* and *strict liability for abnormally dangerous activities* have had limited application in pollution cases. The theory of strict liability has been the more predominant of the two concepts, with a number of applications of the theory to businesses emitting toxic pollutants. In imposing strict liability, the courts generally emphasize the risks created by the toxic pollutant and the location of the business relative to population centers. The doctrine is simple, requiring proof only of the fact that the discharge of the toxic pollutant was abnormally dangerous and that the pollutant was the cause of the plaintiff's injury. Courts have found crop dusting, the storing of flammable liquids in quantity in the midst of a city, and the emitting of noxious gases by factories all to be abnormally dangerous. The *Branch* case illustrates the application of strict liability to an environmental pollution problem of rapidly growing concern—the contamination of groundwater.

**Branch v.
Western
Petroleum,
Inc.**

**Supreme Court
of Utah**
657 P.2d 267
(1982)

Case Background. *Branch, the plaintiff, is a landowner whose property is adjacent
to the property of Western, the defendant. Western had constructed a pond, into which
it was dumping "formation waters"—waste waters from oil wells containing various
chemical contaminants. Western intended for the toxic water to dissipate both through
evaporation into the air and percolation into the ground. The waste water eventually
percolated into the ground and contaminated Branch's water wells. After the water
killed one hundred chickens, Branch began trucking in water. Branch then brought
suit, and the trial court found in his favor. Western appealed.*

Case Decision. Justice Stewart delivered the opinion of the court.

* * *

The major substantive dispute is whether the trial court erred in entering
judgment against Western on the basis of strict liability for pollution of the
Branches' well. Western argues that other states have based liability for pollution
of subterranean waters on either negligence, nuisance, or trespass, and that since
the Branches failed to allege nuisance or trespass, the only accepted theory upon
which this case could be based is negligence. Therefore, according to Western, the
trial court erred in entering judgment on the basis of strict liability.... The
Branches, on the other hand, take the position that Western created an abnormally
dangerous condition by collecting contaminated water on its land for the purpose
of having it seep or percolate into the groundwater and that, therefore, the law of
strict liability controls....

This Court has not heretofore had occasion to consider the legal principles
which govern liability for the pollution of subterranean waters by industrial
wastes. Our survey of cases from other states and of legal scholars indicates that a
variety of legal theories have been relied on. The theories that have been
employed include negligence, private nuisance, public nuisance, negligent
trespass, and strict liability. The variety of approaches reflects numerous
considerations, such as the general hydrological conditions in the state; the
relative significance of promoting industrialization compared with the importance of promoting conservation of water; the nature of the particular state's
water law; and, in particular, whether the doctrine of correlative rights applies to
the use of water resources.... In American law it is generally recognized that a
landowner has no absolute right to pollute percolating waters. In this state, a
landowner has no such absolute right because percolating waters belong to the
people of the state. For that reason, and because percolating waters are migratory
and the rights of the landowners to those waters are correlative, such waters are
subject to the maxim that one may not use his land so as to pollute percolating
waters to the injury of another.

* * *

There are grounds for holding Western strictly liable for the pollution of the
Branches' wells. First, the facts of the case support application of the rule of strict
liability because the ponding of the toxic formation water in an area adjacent to
the Branches' wells constituted an abnormally dangerous and inappropriate use of
the land in light of its proximity to the Branches' property and was unduly
dangerous to the Branches' use of their well water....

The court also found support for the rule of strict liability in the policy
consideration that an industry should not be able to use its property in such a way
as to inflict injury on the property of its neighbors because to do so would result in
effect in appropriating the neighbor's property to one's own use. An industrial

polluter can and should assume the costs of pollution as a cost of doing business rather than charge the loss to a wholly innocent party.

We know of no acceptable rule of jurisprudence which permits those engaged in important and desirable enterprises to injure with impunity those who are engaged in enterprises of lesser economic significance. The costs of injuries resulting from pollution must be internalized by industry as a cost of production and borne by consumers or shareholders, or both, and not by the injured individual.

* * *

Case Holding. *The trial court's decision was affirmed. An industrial polluter who discharges liquid chemical wastes upon the ground is strictly liable for any injuries resulting from the contamination of the groundwater.*

Case Questions

1. On what basis was the court able to make the argument for applying strict liability for abnormally dangerous activities to the facts of this case?
2. Given its sensitive nature, should groundwater be controlled differently than other environmental resources?
3. In this case, the causal connection was fairly easy to establish. Suppose the groundwater contamination was the consequence of ten fifty-five gallon drums of chemicals buried on the property twenty years ago. Would that make the case more difficult? How well do we understand how water travels underground? What if we cannot find the defendant?

Common-Law Remedies

Parties seeking relief from pollution under the common law will generally seek an *injunction* to prohibit the offending business from continuing to pollute and *damages* for their injuries and discomfort. While damage awards are justified, the courts prefer to force a business to install additional pollution controls as a remedy rather than to force it to stop production. Before the 1970s, however, additional controls often were not available. Thus, demonstrations by a polluter that it was applying standard industry techniques for the control of pollution and that no better control technology existed were often sufficient to defeat the plaintiff's case.

In some circumstances where a business established that no better controls were available, the courts would require the business to improve its pollution control even though it was meeting industry standards. This was particularly the case when the courts found that the industry was lagging in the development and adoption of new control techniques. In such situations, courts required the business to undertake a research effort to develop or adapt better technologies. The business was given a fixed time period in which to undertake and complete its research. If the business failed to develop or adapt an adequate control technology, a court could issue a permanent injunction so that the plant had to shut down or move.

The court in the *Boomer* case was faced with such a decision. The polluter, Atlantic Cement Company, had demonstrated that it was complying with existing industry practices for the control of pollution. Recognizing that the industry's control practices were woefully inadequate, the court had several options. It could force Atlantic Cement to undertake an extensive research and development program to develop a better technology, simply require the company to pay damages to the plaintiffs, force the company to cease operations immediately, or allow the company to continue polluting as it had in the past.

Boomer v. Atlantic Cement Company

Court of Appeals of New York
26 N.Y.2d 219,
309 N.Y.S.2d 312,
257 N.E.2d 870
(1970)

Case Background. *The Atlantic Cement Company operated a large cement plant. Boomer and other landowners living near the plant sought relief from the dirt, smoke, and vibration generated by the plant. The trial court found that the plant created a nuisance, and it provided temporary damages but was unwilling to issue an injunction.*

The question facing the court was whether it should resolve this dispute as equitably as possible or reach for a resolution with broader public objectives. In essence, the court was concerned about its ability to impose on Atlantic Cement—as a remedy—the responsibility of developing adequate pollution control technology for the cement industry.

Case Decision.   Justice Bergan delivered the opinion of the court.

* * *

A court performs its essential function when it decides the rights of parties before it. Its decision of private controversies may sometimes greatly affect public issues. Large questions of law are often resolved by the manner in which private litigation is decided. But this is normally an incident of the court's main function to settle controversy. It is a rare exercise of judicial power to use a decision in private litigation as a purposeful mechanism to achieve direct public objectives greatly beyond the rights and interests before the court.

Effective control of air pollution is a problem presently far from solution even with the full public and financial powers of government. In large measure adequate technical procedures are yet to be developed and some that appear possible may be economically impracticable.

It seems apparent that the amelioration of air pollution will depend on technical research in great depth on a carefully balanced consideration of the economic impact of close regulation; and of the actual effect on public health. It is likely to require massive public expenditure and to demand more than any local community can accomplish and to depend on regional and interstate controls.

A court should not try to do this on its own as a by-product of private litigation and it seems manifest that the judicial establishment is neither equipped in the limited nature of any judgment it can pronounce nor prepared to lay down and implement an effective policy for the elimination of air pollution. This is an area beyond the circumference of one private lawsuit. It is a direct responsibility for government and should not thus be undertaken as an incident to solving a dispute between property owners and a single cement plant—one of many—in the Hudson River valley.

The cement making operations of Atlantic Cement have been found by the court at Special Term to have damaged the nearby properties of Boomer and the other landowners in these two actions. That court, as it has been noted, accordingly found Atlantic Cement maintained a nuisance and this has been affirmed at the Appellate Division. The total damage to Boomer's and the other landowners' properties is, however, relatively small in comparison with the value of Atlantic Cement operations and with the consequences of the injunction which Boomer and the other landowners seek.

* * *

One alternative is to grant the injunction but postpone its effect of a specified future date to give opportunity for technical advances to permit Atlantic Cement to eliminate the nuisance; another is to grant the injunction conditioned on the payment of permanent damages to Boomer and the other landowners which would compensate them for the total economic loss to their property present and future caused by defendant's operations. For reasons which will be developed the court chooses the latter alternative.

If the injunction were to be granted unless within a short period—e.g., 18 months—the nuisance was abated by improved methods, there would be no assurance that any significant technical improvement would occur. . . . If there were no improved techniques found, there would inevitably be applications to the court at Special Term for extensions of time to perform on showing of good faith efforts to find such techniques.

Moreover, techniques to eliminate dust and other annoying by-products of cement making are unlikely to be developed by any research Atlantic can undertake within any short period, but will depend on the total resources of the cement industry Nationwide and throughout the world. The problem is universal wherever cement is made.

For obvious reasons the rate of the research is beyond control of Atlantic. If at the end of 18 months the whole industry has not found a technical solution a court would be hard put to close down this one cement plant if due regard be given to equitable principles.

On the other hand, to grant the injunction unless Atlantic pays Boomer and the other landowners such permanent damages as may be fixed by the court seems to do justice between the contending parties. All of the attributions of economic loss to the properties on which Boomer's and the other landowners' complaints are based will have been redressed.

* * *

Case Holding. *The trial court's decision was modified to provide for a payment of permanent damages. Research by Atlantic Cement was unlikely to develop any techniques for the elimination of pollution within a short time. The judgment against Atlantic Cement was for $185,000. Shortly after this case was decided, Congress enacted the Clean Air Act, which reflects many of the concerns registered by the court. Cement companies like Atlantic are now required to invest millions of dollars in pollution-control technology to meet the requirements of the Act.*

Case Questions

1. Is pollution a national concern and thus the responsibility of the federal government, or is it really a large number of little disputes such as this one?
2. Will the payment of a one-time permanent damage award serve as an adequate incentive for Atlantic Cement to clean up its pollution? That is, will it be "a reasonably effective spur to research for improved techniques to minimize nuisance"? What other alternatives are available to the court?

The Shortcomings of Private Litigation

Despite the availability of common-law rules to protect private citizens against harm from pollution, private litigation proved to be a poor mechanism for bringing pollution within tolerable limits. The shortcomings in private litigation can be attributed to three factors inherent in the judicial system. First, as suggested by *Boomer*, the judicial system lacks the ability to monitor pollution and its control on a day-to-day basis. Second, judges generally lack the scientific, technical, and economic expertise required to impose the appropriate level of pollution control in nuisance actions. Third, only where pollution impacts a party with a significant economic interest to protect will a common-law case even develop. In most instances, the environmental damage being done by the pollution is significant when totaled, but no one person is so adversely affected as to feel compelled to bring a suit individually. Thus, only the most serious pollution problems will be brought to the courts for resolution.

As the pollution problem grew in the 1950s and 1960s, the need for alternative approaches became increasingly apparent. Scientists, ecologists, industry representatives, and the general public began to look to the federal government to control pollution. Many advocated the development of a federal agency specifically charged with the responsibility for improving and maintaining environmental quality. It was believed that an agency could overcome the shortcomings associated with private litigation and provide a solution to environmental degradation.

NATIONAL ENVIRONMENTAL POLICY ACT

Despite the experience gained from decades of attempting to control pollution through private litigation, early federal attempts at regulating environmental protection offered little improvement. Many members of Congress during that time firmly believed that the federal government's role should be limited to directing the attention of the states to the pollution problem and to providing them with economic and technical assistance to improve environmental quality.

It was evident by the late 1960s that state-oriented environmental pollution programs were inadequate. Despite federal assistance to the states, the pollution problem continued to grow. Looking to the federal government for a solution, environmentalists were able to help fashion legislation requiring an environmental review of certain federal government actions and decisions. That legislation was the National Environmental Policy Act (NEPA) of 1969.

NEPA was a major policy statement by the federal government. After decades of relying on fruitless state efforts to control environmental pollution, NEPA proclaimed that pollution was a major federal government concern. According to Congress, the fundamental purposes of NEPA are as follows:

> To declare a national policy which will encourage productive and enjoyable harmony between man and his environment; to promote efforts which will prevent or eliminate damage to the environment and biosphere and stimulate the health and welfare of man; [and] to enrich the

understanding of the ecological systems and natural resources important to the nation. . . .

Despite being one of the briefest and most general of federal environmental statutes, NEPA has affected virtually every major project—both public and private—since its enactment.

Requirements Imposed on Federal Agencies

To implement its policy objectives, NEPA requires all federal agencies to expressly consider any environmental impacts their programs may create. To be assured that federal agencies consider the environmental consequences of their decisions, Section 102 of NEPA requires agency officials to prepare an *environmental impact statement* (EIS) in the following instances:

> . . . in every recommendation or report on proposals for legislation and other Federal actions significantly affecting the quality of the human environment.

The EIS is intended to assess the environmental effects of an agency's proposal or action and to consider the availability of alternatives that might be less damaging to the environment. The Act has generated hundreds of cases interpreting the requirements and purposes of the EIS process. In the *Metropolitan Edison* case, the U.S. Supreme Court was asked to determine whether an EIS must include psychological harm.

Metropolitan Edison Co. v. People Against Nuclear Energy
United States Supreme Court
460 U.S. 766,
103 S.Ct. 1556
(1983)

Case Background. *Metropolitan Edison owned two nuclear power plants at Three Mile Island—Three Mile Island Unit 1 (TMI-1) and Three Mile Island Unit 2 (TMI-2). In 1978, while TMI-1 was shut down for refueling, TMI-2 suffered a serious mechanical problem and was shut down permanently. The Nuclear Regulatory Commission (NRC) ordered Metropolitan to keep TMI-1 shut down until it was determined that the reactor could be safely operated.*

The NRC then conducted hearings to determine the reactor's safety. In its published notice of the hearing, NRC stated that it had not decided whether it would consider psychological effects. An association of area residents—the People Against Nuclear Energy (PANE)—submitted briefs to the NRC stating that the startup of TMI-1 would cause serious psychological harm. The NRC, however, decided not to consider evidence of psychological harm in its decision on whether TMI-1 would be allowed to operate.

PANE filed a petition for review with the court of appeals, contending that NEPA required the NRC to consider psychological harm. The court of appeals agreed with PANE. Metropolitan appealed to the U.S. Supreme Court.

Case Decision. Justice Rehnquist delivered the opinion of the Court.

* * *

Our understanding of the congressional concerns that led to the enactment of NEPA suggests that the terms "environmental effect" and "environmental impact" in § 102 be read to include a requirement of a reasonably close causal relationship between a change in the physical environment and the effect at issue. This requirement is like the familiar doctrine of proximate cause from tort law. The issue before us, then, is how to give content to this requirement. This is a question of first impression in the Court.

The federal action that affects the environment in this case is permitting renewed operation of TMI-1. The direct effects on the environment of this action include release of low-level radiation, increased fog in the Harrisburg area (caused by operation of the plant's cooling towers), and the release of warm water into the Susquehanna River. The NRC has considered each of these effects in its EIS. . . . Another effect of renewed operation is a risk of a nuclear accident. The NRC has also considered this effect.

PANE argues that the psychological health damage it alleges "will flow directly from the risk of [a nuclear] accident." But a *risk* of an accident is not an effect on the physical environment. A risk is, by definition, unrealized in the physical world. In a causal chain from renewed operation of TMI-1 to psychological health damage, the element of risk and its perception by PANE's members are necessary middle links. We believe that the element of risk lengthens the causal chain beyond the reach of NEPA.

Risk is a pervasive element of modern life; to say more would belabor the obvious. Many of the risks we face are generated by modern technology, which brings both the possibility of major accidents and opportunities for tremendous achievements. Medical experts apparently agree that risk can generate stress in human beings, which in turn may rise to the level of serious health damage. For this reason among many others, the question whether the gains from any technological advance are worth its attendant risks may be an important public policy issue. Nonetheless, it is quite different from the question whether the same gains are worth a given level of alteration of our physical environment or depletion of our natural resources. The latter question rather than the former is the central concern of NEPA.

* * *

We do not mean to denigrate the fears of PANE's members, or to suggest that the psychological health damage they fear could not, in fact, occur. Nonetheless, it is difficult for us to see the differences between someone who dislikes a government decision so much that he suffers anxiety and stress, someone who fears the effects of that decision so much that he suffers similar anxiety and stress, and someone who suffers anxiety and stress that "flow directly" from the risks associated with the same decision. It would be extraordinarily difficult for agencies to differentiate between "genuine" claims of psychological health damage and claims that are grounded solely in disagreement with a democratically adopted policy. Until Congress provides a more explicit statutory instruction than NEPA now contains, we do not think agencies are obliged to undertake the inquiry. . . .

Case Holding. *The court of appeals' decision was reversed. The NRC was not required to consider psychological effects by NEPA.*

Case Questions

1. The Court emphasizes that the terms *environmental impact* and *environmental effect* are to be read as requiring a close causal relationship similar to proximate cause under tort law. What type of effects or impacts is the Court trying to separate out here?

2. Do you think the PANE members could sell their homes? Would prospective buyers demand a discount for the psychological impacts of living near such an infamous nuclear power plant?

The Development of State NEPAs

In addition to having an impact at the federal level, NEPA has had significant impact at the state government level. The Act has inspired the enactment of a number of state environmental acts and facility siting programs. While the statutes differ from state to state, they have had a significant impact on the ability of businesses to purchase property within a state for the purpose of constructing a production plant or other commercial operation. If the plant can be demonstrated to cause a significant amount of pollution, some state statutes virtually foreclose the possibilities that the business can construct it within the state's boundaries.

CREATING THE ENVIRONMENTAL PROTECTION AGENCY

After the enactment of NEPA, Congress proceeded to enact a vast body of substantive environmental law. That law sharply increased federal authority and responsibility in an effort to combat virtually every type of pollution caused by business. To implement and enforce its environmental mandates, Congress created the *Environmental Protection Agency* (EPA).

As Figure 17–1 illustrates, the EPA is responsible for the regulation of pollutants generated by industry that are transmitted to the external environment. Specifically, the EPA is responsible for four basic types of environmental pollution. The agency is required to control air pollution (through the Clean Air Act), water pollution (through the Clean Water Act), land pollution (through the Resource Conservation and Recovery Act and the Superfund), and pollutants resulting from the use of products by consumers. The following sections provide a general overview of the laws governing those four major areas of pollution.

REGULATION OF AIR POLLUTION

The federal air quality control program relies on the regulatory approach embodied in the Clean Air Act of 1970 and its 1977 and 1990 amendments. The Clean Air Act is without question the most formidable environmental statute in the world. The approach embodied in the Act reflects a rigid, uncompromising goal to reduce air pollution within a specified period. As a tribute to its success, other nations have adapted or copied some provisions of the Clean Air Act in the process of developing their own air pollution control statutes.

Early Federal Regulation

Early federal regulation relied heavily on the efforts of state governments. Despite federal intentions to allow state discretion in air and water pollution control, however, the states demonstrated little ability to be effective. Some observers placed the blame for the ineffectiveness on state government vulnerability to the interests of local industry. Others considered federal efforts to be lacking in substance and lax in setting and enforcing standards.

Figure 17–1   The Federal Regulation of Environmental Pollution

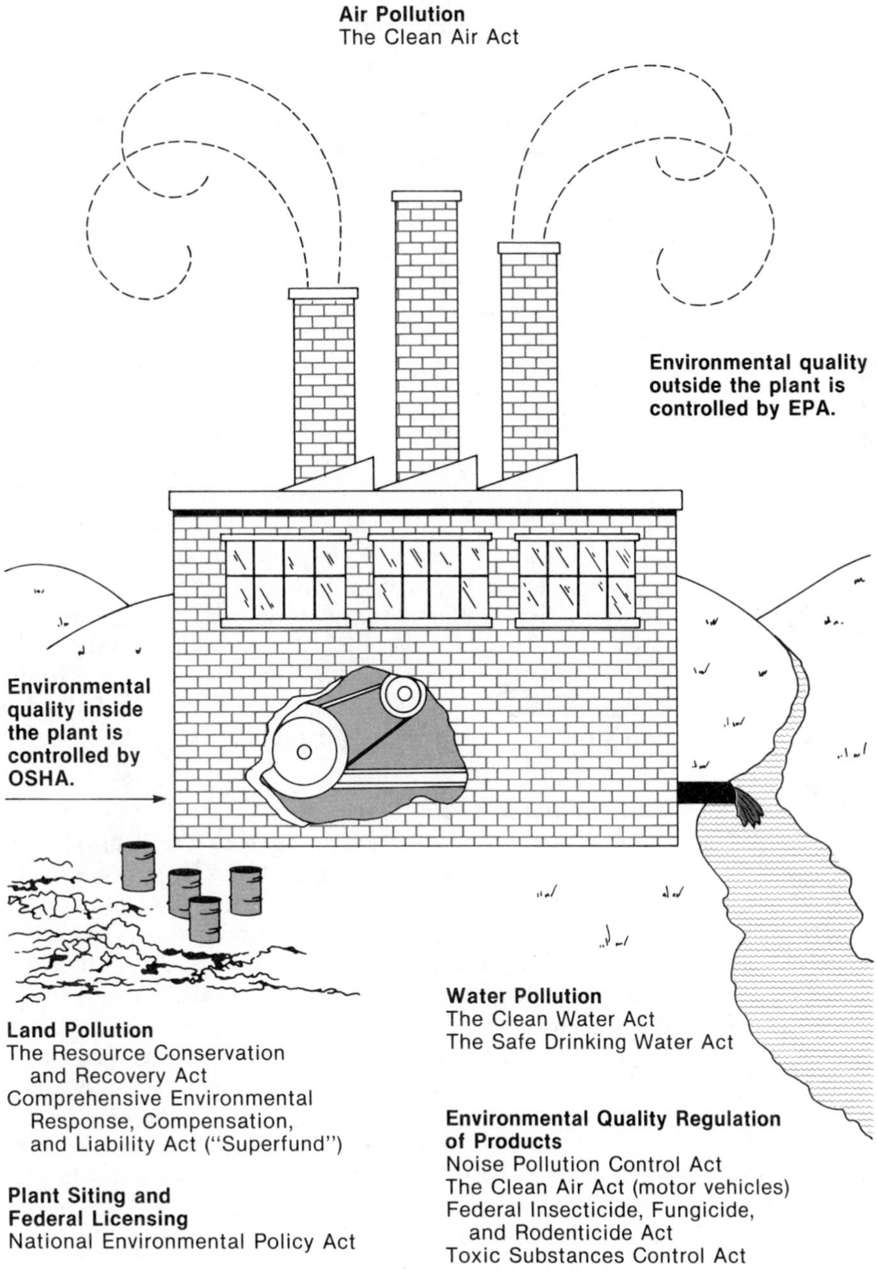

Air Pollution
The Clean Air Act

Environmental quality outside the plant is controlled by EPA.

Environmental quality inside the plant is controlled by OSHA.

Land Pollution
The Resource Conservation
  and Recovery Act
Comprehensive Environmental
  Response, Compensation,
  and Liability Act ("Superfund")

**Plant Siting and
Federal Licensing**
National Environmental Policy Act

Water Pollution
The Clean Water Act
The Safe Drinking Water Act

**Environmental Quality Regulation
of Products**
Noise Pollution Control Act
The Clean Air Act (motor vehicles)
Federal Insecticide, Fungicide,
  and Rodenticide Act
Toxic Substances Control Act

Clean Air Act of 1970

Congress reacted to the shortcomings in state regulatory efforts by enacting the Clean Air Act of 1970. The *Clean Air Act* sharply increased federal authority and responsibility to control pollution. In the words of the U.S. Supreme Court, Congress intended to "take a stick to the states" with its enactment of the Clean Air Act. The Act provides a mechanism through which the federal government develops pollution standards and, through the forced cooperation of the states, is able to implement those standards uniformly across the country.

National Ambient Air Quality Standards

The stated purpose of the Act is to "protect and enhance the quality of the nation's air resources." The Act sets forth a comprehensive regulatory program for achieving specified standards of air quality to be uniformly applied across the nation. Those standards are called the *National Ambient Air Quality Standards*.

The EPA was required to develop national ambient air quality standards for every air pollutant emitted by industry that, in its judgment, "arise[s] or contribute[s] to air pollution which may reasonably be anticipated to endanger public health and welfare." A pollutant's *national primary ambient air quality standard* was to be determined on the basis of public health effects, while its national secondary ambient air quality standard was to be based on public welfare effects (impact on plants, animals, soil, and constructed surfaces). Thus far, the EPA has developed national standards for sulfur dioxide, particulates, ozone, carbon monoxide, hydrocarbons, nitrogen oxide, and lead. Table 17–1 summarizes the principal characteristics, health effects, and sources of those major air pollutants.

State Implementation Plans

Following the EPA's establishment of the National Ambient Air Quality Standards, each state was to develop a *State Implementation Plan* (SIP). The SIPs were intended to define the specific control efforts necessary within the state to achieve the national standards. In theory, if each plant within the state met its pollution control requirements as dictated by the SIP, the state's air quality would meet the national standards. Perhaps the most important of the Act's requirements was that all plants were to meet their pollution control requirements as specified by the SIP by a specified date.

To assure the success of the Clean Air Act, states were given a specified time in which to complete their SIPs. In the event that a state failed in its responsibilities, the Act provided the EPA with authority to establish an SIP for that state. Thus, while the 1970 Act was similar to previous federal laws in that it imposed control responsibilities upon state governments, it contrasted with those laws by providing federal authority to intervene when a state's efforts proved ineffective.

Clean Air Act Amendments of 1977

Read strictly and literally, the 1970 Clean Air Act could be understood to prohibit the construction of any new industrial plants with the potential to pollute. In response to concerns raised by urban leaders and industrial

Table 17–1   Regulated Air Pollutants

Pollutant	Characteristics	Sources	Health Effects
Sulfur dioxide	Colorless gas with pungent odor; oxidizes to form sulfur trioxide which forms sulfuric acid with water (acid rain).	Power plants and industrial sources that burn sulfur-containing fossil fuels; smelting of sulfur-bearing ores.	Causes and aggravates respiratory ailments including asthma, chronic bronchitis, emphysema.
Particulates	Any particle dispersed in the atmosphere, such as dust, ash, soot, and various chemicals.	Natural events such as wind erosion; stationary sources that burn solid fuels; agricultural operations.	Chest discomfort; throat and eye irritation.
Ozone	A pungent, highly poisonous gas that is invisible in low concentrations; results from chemical combination of reactive hydrocarbon vapors with nitrogen oxides in presence of sunlight; smog.	Hydrocarbons mostly from motor vehicle exhausts, and nitrogen oxides from motor vehicle exhausts, refineries, and petrochemical plants.	Aggravates respiratory ailments; causes eye irritation.
Carbon monoxide	Colorless, odorless gas.	Motor vehicle exhausts, caused by incomplete combustion of fuels and other carbon-containing materials; natural sources.	Reduces oxygen-carrying capacity of blood; impairs heart functions; impairs visual perception and alertness.
Hydrocarbons	Organic compounds in gaseous or particulate form; component in creation of photochemical oxidants.	Motor vehicle exhausts, caused by incomplete combustion of fuels and other carbon-containing substances; petrochemical plants; refineries; natural sources.	Eye, nose, and throat irritant; suspected of causing cancer.
Nitrogen dioxide	Brownish red gas with pungent odor; component in creation of photochemical oxidents.	Motor vehicle exhausts; power plants.	Aggravates respiratory ailments.
Lead	Heavy, soft, malleable gray metallic chemical element; as environmental contaminant, it often occurs as lead oxide aerosol or dust.	Nonferrous metal smelters; motor vehicle exhausts.	High levels of exposure causes lead poisoning.

representatives that the Act was severely constraining economic growth, Congress amended the Act in 1977. The 1977 amendments were intended to provide a legal means for allowing economic growth while simultaneously maintaining "reasonable further progress" toward the Act's air quality enhancement goals.

The 1977 amendments established specific procedures for the construction of new industrial plants. The specific requirements to be imposed on plant owners and operators depend on the air quality of the area in which the plant is to be built. One set of requirements applies if the plant is to be built in a "clean air area," and another set applies if it is to be built in a "dirty air area." In either case, the plant owner or operator is required to obtain a preconstruction permit from the EPA.

New Plants in Clean Air Areas

Areas with clean air—air of better quality than required by the national standards—were designated by the amendments as *Prevention of Significant Deterioration* (PSD) areas. PSD areas include national parks, wilderness areas, national monuments, and other areas where the air quality is better than the level specified by the national standards. Because of the sensitive nature of those areas, only a slight increase in pollution is allowed. That slight increase is called the *maximum allowable increase.* Any activity, including the construction or operation of a plant, that will cause the maximum allowable increase to be exceeded is prohibited from being undertaken in a PSD area.

New Plant Requirments.   New plants are allowed to be built in PSD areas if the plant meets two basic requirements. First, the owner or operator must agree to install the *Best Available Control Technology* (BACT)—as determined by EPA on a case-by-case basis—on the new plant to control its pollution. Second, the owner must demonstrate that the pollution from its plant will not cause the maximum allowable increase in the area to be exceeded.

Maximum Allowable Increase.   As Figure 17–2 illustrates, the size of the maximum allowable increase depends upon whether the plant will be located in a Class I, II, or III PSD area. The maximum allowable increase allowed in a particular PSD area is directly related to its initial cleanliness. Class I areas, for example, are areas found to have pristine air quality, that is, they are virtually pollution free. Since very little additional pollution would significantly deteriorate the air quality in those areas, the amendments allow only a small maximum allowable increase. Once that amount of pollution is added, any additional economic growth that would result in increased pollution is thereafter foreclosed. As Figure 17–2 illustrates, Class II and III areas allow progressively more pollution to be added before the maximum allowable increase is exceeded.

New Plants in Dirty Air Areas

Dirty air areas were designated by the amendments as *nonattainment areas,* signifying that they have not achieved the national air quality standards. Businesses wanting to build in nonattainment areas are required to meet even more restrictive and expensive requirements than those imposed in PSD areas. Through the *Emissions Offset Policy,* the amendments impose three specific requirements on owners and operators of new plants:

1. Apply the Lowest Achievable Emissions Rate Technology,
2. Certify that other plants are in compliance with the State Implementation Plan.
3. Obtain a net air quality improvement.

Application of LAER Technology.   The operators of new plants must agree to control the plants' pollution to the maximum degree possible. To meet that requirement, the amendments specify that a new plant use the *Lowest Achievable Emissions Rate Technology* (LAER). In most cases, LAER will be a more stringent (and more expensive) technology than the BACT requirement

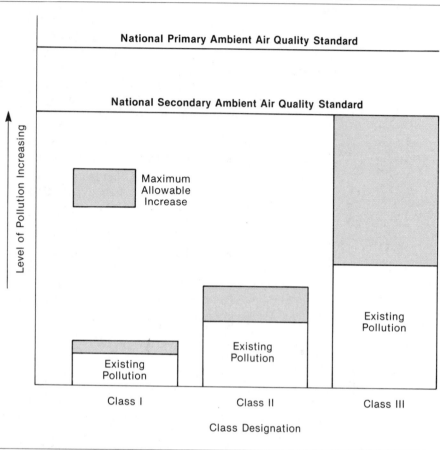

Figure 17–2   Maximum Allowable Increases in Clean Air Areas

in PSD areas. Generally, the EPA will designate the LAER as the most stringent technology currently in use by any other similar plant in the country.

Certify Other Plants in Compliance.   The new plant operators must certify that all their other plants in the state are currently meeting the requirements imposed by the State Implementation Plan. The intent of this requirement is to provide businesses with an incentive to comply voluntarily with the Clean Air Act's requirements. If the business is unable to verify compliance, EPA will not allow the new plant to be built.

Net Air Quality Improvement.   The third requirement is the heart of the nonattainment area new-plant provisions. New plants can be built in nonattainment areas only if the air pollution emissions from the new plant are *offset* by reductions in the same type of pollutant from other plants in the area. The quantity of the offset from other plants must match the air pollution from the new plant on a more than one-for-one basis. That is, when the plant is built and operating, the area must enjoy a *net air quality improvement*. The rationale for the greater reduction in existing pollution is to assure that the area will be making "reasonable further progress" toward achieving the national air quality standards.

Suppose that Cox Automotive Design has decided to build a new plant in Detroit, a nonattainment area for sulfur dioxide. To build the plant, Cox must first obtain a preconstruction permit from the EPA. The EPA will require that Cox certify that it will apply the LAER technology and that its other plants in the area are currently in compliance with Michigan's State Implementation Plan. Cox will be required to obtain an emissions offset. To obtain this required offset, Cox has one of three choices:

1. Reduce pollution in its other plants by purchasing, implementing, and operating additional pollution controls on those plants.

2. Enter into an agreement with other plant owners or operators whereby they agree, for a price, to reduce their pollution by implementing additional pollution controls on their plants.

3. Some combination of 1 and 2.

If Cox's new plant will add ten units of pollution to the air, Cox must undertake one of the above choices to secure a reduction in pollution elsewhere in the state of *more* than ten units. Thus, when the plant begins operation, the air quality in the area will actually improve as a consequence of compliance with the Clean Air Act's requirements.

The Bubble Concept
The EPA has implemented a strategy similar to the Emissions Offset Policy, called the *bubble concept*. For regulatory purposes, the bubble concept treats all buildings and facilities that make up a business's industrial complex as a single pollution source. Pollutants within the industrial complex are considered, for pollution control purposes, to be under an imaginary glass bubble that has a single smokestack emitting pollutants from its top. All emissions from the industrial complex are measured from that smokestack rather than from each smokestack within the complex. In contrast to the offset policy, increases in emissions from modifications or additions to a facility will have no regulatory consequences, under the bubble concept approach, so long as decreases from other facilities within the complex more than offset the new increases. The net effect—as measured from the smokestack on the bubble—must be a decrease in emissions.

Suppose that Acme Smelting Company decides to add a fourth plant to its three-plant complex. Under both the offset policy and the bubble concept, Acme must certify that its other plants are in compliance with the State Implementation Plan. Under the offset policy, Acme must apply the LAER technology and obtain an offset. Under the bubble concept, however, the company may add any control device it chooses to any of the four plants in the complex. The net result—as measured in the aggregate from the smokestack of the imaginary bubble—must be a decrease in total pollution emissions.

The bubble concept and the offset policy both produce the same net air quality improvement. The bubble concept, however, is potentially much less expensive because the company has a considerably greater range of discretion in selecting pollution control devices. Despite its potential cost savings, the bubble concept has been subjected to several legal challenges. In *Chevron v. Natural Resources Defense Council,* the Supreme Court had an opportunity to consider its validity.

Chevron, U.S.A., Inc. v. Natural Resources Defense Council, Inc.
United States Supreme Court
467 U.S. 837, 104 S.Ct. 2778 (1984)

Background. *As part of its efforts to implement the Clean Air Act Amendments of 1977, the EPA developed the bubble concept. The bubble concept allows states to treat all the pollution-emitting devices within the same industrial complex as if they were encased under a bubble with a single smokestack. The owner of the industrial complex can then regulate the pollution under the bubble so that the emissions from the single smokestack meet the "net air quality improvement" requirements of the law.*

Natural Resources Defense Council sought judicial review of the bubble concept regulations contending that the Act's treatment of stationary sources requires that each pollution-emitting device must be viewed separately. Although the 1977 Amendments do not provide a definition of the phrase "stationary source," the court of appeals agreed with the Natural Resources Defense Council and set aside the regulations as contrary to law. The Supreme Court reviewed the judgment.

Case Decision.   Justice Stevens delivered the opinion of the Court.

* * *

[T]he EPA ... noted that the [definition of "stationary source"] was not squarely addressed in either the statute or its legislative history and therefore that the issue involved an agency judgment as how to best carry out the Act. It then set forth several reasons for concluding that the plantwide definition [used in its bubble concept] was more appropriate. It pointed out that the [National Resource Defense Council's interpretation of "stationary source"] "can act as a disincentive to new investment and modernization by discouraging modifications to existing facilities" and "can actually retard progress in air pollution control by discouraging replacement of older, dirtier processes or pieces of equipment with new, cleaner ones." ... The agency explained that [the bubble concept] would accomplish the fundamental purposes of achieving attainment with NAAQS's as expeditiously as possible.

* * *

[T]he plantwide definition [used under the bubble concept] is fully consistent with ... the concerns [addressed by the 1977 Amendments]—the allowance of reasonable economic growth and [meeting] the environmental objectives as well. Indeed, its reasoning is supported by the public record developed in the rulemaking process, as well as by certain private studies.

* * *

Case Holding. *The decision of the court of appeals was reversed. EPA's definition of the term* stationary source, *which allows EPA to use the bubble concept, is a permissible construction of a statute that seeks to accommodate progress in reducing air pollution with economic growth.*

Case Questions

1. Why did the Court defer to the expertise of the agency in this matter?

2. If our goals are to obtain a clean environment, should EPA be able to take costs into account in determining the applicability of a particular technology?

The Control of Hazardous Air Pollutants

The Clean Air Act defines a hazardous air pollutant as an "air pollutant which may result in an increase in mortality or a very serious illness." The EPA is responsible for determining whether an air pollutant is hazardous. If it determines that an air pollutant is hazardous, the EPA is required to develop appropriate emissions standards to protect public health. New and existing plants found to be emitting a hazardous pollutant are required to apply the best available technology to reduce such emissions. However, if the risk to the public health after the application of that technology is determined still to be unreasonable, the EPA may require additional control measures including closing the plant.

Despite the existence of hundreds of recognized hazardous air pollutants, the EPA has issued standards on just eight pollutants: asbestos, beryllium, mercury, vinyl chloride, benzene, coke oven emissions, arsenic, and radionuclides. The sources and health effects of those hazardous pollutants are provided in Table 17–2.

Table 17–2   Hazardous Air Pollutants for Which EPA Has Established Emissions Standards

Pollutant	Source	Health Effects
Arsenic	Alloy, brass, ceramic, copper, and drug and dye factories, insecticides, leather plants, petroleum refineries, print shops, textile print mills	Lung cancer
Asbestos	Asbestos mills, road surfacing with asbestos tailings, manufacturers of asbestos-containing products (fireproofing, etc.), demolition of old buildings, spray insulation	Asbestosis, a chronic lung disease; various cancers, particularly of the lung
Benzene	Adhesive makers, chemical labs, detergent plants, dry-battery plants, furniture finish shops, glue factories, petrochemical plants, rubber factories, welding shops	Aplastic anemia; leukemia
Beryllium	Extraction plants, ceramic manufacturing, foundries, incinerators, rocket motor manufacturing operations	Lung and bone cancer suspected
Coke oven emissions	Coke ovens (coal distilling)	Lung cancer; kidney and skin cancer suspected
Mercury	Ore processing, chlor-alkali manufacturing, sludge dryers and incinerators	Toxic effects of acute methyl mercury poisoning well documented; can progress to deafness, blindness, paralysis, kidney failure, and death
Radionuclides	Underground mines	Lung cancer
Vinyl chloride	Ethylene dichloride manufacturers, vinyl chloride manufacturers, polyvinyl chloride manufacturers	Lung and liver cancer; brain and kidney cancer suspected

Clean Air Act Amendments of 1990

In 1990, Congress was forced to address several major environmental issues caused by air pollution. Despite the rigid requirements imposed on new plants under the 1977 Amendments, several U.S. cities still suffer from heavy smog. Toxic pollutants had gone virtually unabated and emissions from power plants were found to be a significant contributor to acid rain. In an effort to address these serious environmental issues, Congress enacted the Clean Air Act Amendments of 1990.

Toxic Pollutants

Although the regulation of hazardous or toxic air pollutants had been a requirement since the 1970 Amendments, as noted above, the EPA had developed emission standards on only eight substances by 1990 (see Table 17–2). Considerable scientific evidence showed that toxic air pollution causes serious health problems nationwide, and that many toxic emissions were not subject to regulation or control. Under the 1990 Amendments, Congress required the development of regulatory standards for more than 190 toxic chemicals. Plants that emit those toxic pollutants are required to reduce emissions by more than 75 percent by the year 2000. The EPA will then be required to examine each industry to determine if additional controls are warranted.

Controlling Acid Rain

Acid rain is formed when sulfur dioxide (SO_2) and nitrogen oxides (NO_x) emitted into the atmosphere undergo the chemical process of oxidation and are transformed into sulfuric and nitric acid. These pollutants then fall to Earth along with precipitation in the form of rain, snow, dew, frost, sleet, or fog. Referred to as "acid rain," these pollutants alter the chemical balance between acidity and alkalinity and damage the delicate aquatic and terrestrial ecosystems, degrade building materials such as marble, limestone, certain paints, and galvanized steel, and can adversely affect human health. Despite the serious environmental problems caused by acid rain, the Clean Air Act was relatively ineffective in controlling it.

In recognition of the need to control acid rain, the 1990 Amendments place rigid controls on fossil-fuel fired power plants. Under the Amendments, the 111 dirtiest power plants in twenty-one states must cut sulfur dioxide emissions by five million tons per year by 1996. An additional 200 plants must implement controls by the year 2000 to bring about another five-million-ton reduction in sulfur dioxide. Beginning in 2001, powerplants must also implement technology to reduce nitrogen-oxide emissions by two million tons a year. The reductions in acid rain expected from the 1990 Amendments will be costly to industry and consumers. It is expected that the 1990 Amendments will increase utility costs by more than $10 billion a year by 1996.

REGULATION OF WATER POLLUTION

The modern law of water pollution is contained in the *Clean Water Act* as amended in 1972, 1977, and 1986. While the Act reflects much of the regulatory framework developed and applied by Congress in the Clean Air Act, the legal requirements of water control do not present the same degree of regulatory complexity. Nevertheless, the control of water pollution does represent one of the major components of environmental law that directly regulates business behavior.

Early Federal Regulation

The Clean Water Act is the product of a series of federal legislative enactments beginning with the Water Pollution Control Act of 1948. Like the early Clean Air Acts, the early Clean Water Acts left primary responsibility for water pollution control to the states. The states, however, did not approach the task of setting and enforcing water quality standards with much vigor. While over half the states did develop standards by 1970, the record shows a complete lack of enforcement.

Clean Water Act

By the late 1960s, Congress realized that the federal water pollution program was working poorly. The water pollution problem was more severe, more pervasive, and growing more rapidly than was originally believed. Prompted by the conclusion of the Senate Committee on Public Works that "the federal water pollution control program ... has been inadequate in every vital aspect ... ," Congress enacted the Clean Water Act in 1972. The Act was comprehensively amended in 1977 and again in 1986.

The stated objective of the Clean Water Act is to "restore and maintain the chemical, physical, and biological integrity of the Nation's waters." The Act makes it unlawful for any person—defined as an individual, business, or governmental body—to discharge any pollutant into navigable waters without a permit. Although the Act does not define the phrase *navigable waters*, the *Quivira* case illustrates that it has been very broadly interpreted.

Quivira Mining Co. v. U.S.E.P.A.

United States Court of Appeals, Tenth Circuit
765 F.2d 126 (1985)

Case Background. *Quivira Mining Company challenged the authority of the EPA to regulate the discharge of pollutants from uranium mining facilities into gullies or arroyos. Specifically, Quivira contested EPA National Pollution Discharge Elimination System permits to two of its uranium mining facilities. The two facilities discharged wastes into Arroyo del Puerto and San Mateo Creek. The company contended that Arroyo del Puerto and San Mateo Creek were not "navigable waters of the United States" and therefore were beyond the EPA's jurisdiction under the Clean Water Act. Appeal was taken from the EPA, which denied Quivira's request to review its claims.*

Case Decision. District Judge Saffels delivered the opinion of the court.

* * *

It is the national goal of the Clean Water Act to eliminate the discharge of pollutants into navigable waters. The term "navigable waters" means "the waters of the United States, including the territorial seas." This court has noted that the Clean Water Act is designed to regulate to the fullest extent possible sources emitting pollution into rivers, streams and lakes. The touchstone of the regulatory scheme is that those needing to use the waters for waste distribution must seek and obtain a permit to discharge that waste, with the quantity and quality of the discharge regulated. It is the intent of the Clean Water Act to cover, as much as possible, all waters of the United States instead of just some.

* * *

In *United States* v. *Earth Sciences, Inc.,* the court found the Rio Seco to be a "water of the United States," although it is not navigable in fact nor does it transport any goods or materials and although it is located entirely in [the state of] Colorado. Although the Rio Seco did not provide a very significant link in the chain of interstate commerce, the court found . . . at least some interstate impact from the stream and that was all that was necessary under the act. There, the facts were that the stream supported trout and some beaver, the water collected in the reservoirs was used for agricultural irrigation, and the resulting products were sold into interstate commerce. The court stated, "It seems clear Congress intended to regulate discharges made into every creek, stream, river or body of water that in any way may affect interstate commerce." . . .

This court's findings in *Earth Sciences* compel a finding herein affirming the decision of the EPA. Substantial evidence here supports the Administrator's findings that both the Arroyo del Puerto and San Mateo Creek are waters of the United States. Substantial evidence before the Administrator supports his finding that during times of intense rainfall, there can be a surface connection between the Arroyo del Puerto, San Mateo Creek and navigable-in-fact streams. Further, the record supports the finding that both the Arroyo del Puerto and San Mateo Creek flow for a period after the time of discharge of pollutants into the waters. Further, the flow continues regularly through underground aquifers fed by the surface flow of the San Mateo Creek and Arroyo del Puerto into navigable-in-fact streams. The court finds that the impact on interstate commerce.

* * *

Case Holding. *The agency's decision was affirmed. The Arroyo del Puerto and San Mateo Creek are navigable waterways subject to regulation under the Clean Water Act.*

Case Questions

1. What is a navigable waterway? How does its definition differ, say, between what is navigable to a sailor and what is navigable under the Clean Water Act?
2. Should Quivira be subject to regulation in this case? Can you make an argument without referring to the "navigable waters" criteria employed in this case?

Regulations Imposed on Point Sources

As Table 17–3 indicates, water pollution comes from a variety of sources ranging from agricultural runoff to the direct discharge of liquid wastes by industry and municipalities. Because of that diversity, the EPA would have had an impossible regulatory task if it attempted to control all sources of water pollution. Consequently, the EPA concentrated on regulating water pollution from *point sources,* defined in the Act to include any pipe, channel, or ditch from which pollution may be discharged. The definition clearly encompasses all industrial sources that discharge liquid wastes.

Agricultural and urban runoff—*nonpoint sources* of pollution—have largely been ignored. These important sources of water pollution have not been subject to regulation primarily because they are so difficult to identify and control. Programs that will attempt to manage those sources of

Table 17–3   Sources and Effects of Pollution-Causing Waste Waters

Undesirable Characteristics	Sources	Effects
Soluble organic wastes	Most industrial waste waters; waste liquors from pulp mills, canning plant effluents, meat-packing wastes, textile scouring and dying effluents, milk product wastes and fermentation wastes. Measured in terms of oxygen needed to decompose them—BOD (biochemical oxygen demand).	Decomposition in waterways uses oxygen; if waste loads sufficiently great, oxygen depletion will be high enough to kill fish and plants, which need that oxygen to exist.
Soluble organics that result in taste and odors in water supplies; odors in atmosphere	In water supplies—decaying organic wastes; iron and manganese and other metallic products of corrosion; specific organic chemicals such as phenols and mercaptans; chlorine and its substitution compounds; specific sources include petrochemical discharges and liquid wastes from the manufacture of synthetic rubber. In atmosphere—odors generally result from hydrogen sulfide. Hydrogen sulfide is the consequence of anaerobic (without air) decomposition, a process of decomposition that occurs when oxygen is no longer present in the waterway, that is, in very highly polluted situations.	Aesthetic damages; increased costs of water purification.
Nutrients	Phosphates from detergents in municipal wastes; nitrogen from sewage, drainage from land fertilized with agricultural chemicals, industrial wastes, and remnants of manufactured chemical products. Nitrogen can be present as ammonia, nitrate, and organic nitrogen in the form of proteins, urea, and amino acids.	Nutrients cause vast increase in algae, which will lead to eutrophication (biological death) of lakes. Aesthetic damage; eventually destroys commercial and sport fishing. Nitrites can have serious health effects, including cyanosis and kidney failure, when present in drinking water.
Oil, grease, and immiscible liquids	Oils and greases from vegetables and animals are generally biodegradable; sources include meat-packing wastes, particularly in slaughtering. Oils and greases of mineral origin may be relatively resistant to biodegradation, oil spills (accidents of oil-carrying freighters, eruptions of oil during offshore drilling operations).	Aesthetic damage; wildlife destruction; serious decreases in capacity of sewers. Crude oil settles unaltered on the ocean floor and retained for long periods of time, particularly the toxic aromatic hydrocarbons; significant damage to shellfish. May affect humans through the food chain. Potential destruction of water supply.
Thermal pollution	Water used as coolants by industry, particularly in nuclear and conventionally fueled electric power generators.	Adverse effects on fish and aquatic plant life; temperature increase decreases waste assimilative ability of the surface water; increases toxic effects of certain chemical pollutants and the sensitivity of aquatic life to those pollutants.
Pathogenic wastes	Waste waters that contain pathogenic bacteria (salmonella, shigella, leptospira, vibrio, etc.) originating from livestock production, tanneries, pharmaceutical manufacturers, and food-processing industries. Measured by the number of fecal coliform bacteria present in the waste water. Human feces carry infectious pathogens for a number of intestinal diseases: typhoid fever, hepatitis, encephalitis, poliomyelitis, and tuberculosis.	Die-off rates of pathogens in natural waters uncertain; infectiousness for swimmers and other recreational water users also uncertain. Some evidence that hepatitis can be transmitted via shellfish taken from polluted waters.
Radioactive material	Enter sewage systems or surface waters from the activities of nuclear reactors and by uranium ore mining and refining.	Leukemia, bone cancer, genetic damage.

pollution—which have been estimated to cause 50 percent of the nation's water pollution—are in the development stage.

Businesses Subject to Technology Standards

As Table 17–4 illustrates, the Clean Water Act established technology-based standards of pollution control to be met by discharges in two phases. During the first phase, all plants were to have installed water pollution control devices by 1977 that represented the *best practicable pollution control technology*. The second phase required plants to install more stringent pollution controls by no later than 1989. The technology needed to meet the second phase requirements depended upon the type of water pollutants the plant was discharging. Plants discharging *conventional pollutants* are to apply the *best conventional pollutant control technology*, while plants discharging toxic or *unconventional pollutants* are to apply the *best available technology economically achievable*. Since a number of industries were unable to meet their Phase II toxic control standards, it is expected that Congress will enact legislation extending the compliance deadlines.

Unlike the Clean Air Act, the Clean Water Act does not impose separate pollution control requirements on newly constructed plants. Rather, new plants are generally required to implement the same pollution control technologies as existing plants. Those controls, however, must be in place and functioning when the plant begins its operations.

Implementing Technology Standards: The Permit System

The Act's technology standards are imposed upon individual plants through a two-step process. First, the EPA develops effluent guidelines that define the Act's technology standards on an industry-by-industry basis and establish *effluent limitations*—numerical limits on the amount of each pollutant a representative plant in an industry may discharge legally. Second, the tech-

Table 17–4   Compliance Schedule for the Clean Water Act's Nationally Uniform Effluent Standards

	Technology Required	Pollutants Controlled	Compliance Date
Phase I	Best practicable pollution control technology	All for which technology is available	July 1, 1977
Phase II	Best conventional pollutant control technology	Conventional pollutants	March 31, 1989*
	Best available control technology economically achievable	Toxic pollutants	March 31, 1989*
	Best available control technology economically achievable	Nonconventional pollutants	March 31, 1989*
New sources (selected)	Best available demonstrated control technology	All for which technology is available	First day of operation

*Compliance date moved from 1983 to 1984 by the 1977 amendments and from 1984 to 1989 by 1986 amendments.

nology requirements and the effluent limitations are imposed upon individual plants through the *permit system,* which under the Clean Water Act is called the *National Pollution Discharge Elimination System* (NPDES).

The NPDES permit serves to "translate" the general requirements of the effluent guidelines into specific pollution control requirements for a particular plant. Usually the EPA specifies in the NPDES permit that the plant will install a particular pollution control device, install water pollution monitoring equipment, and sample their waste waters on a regular basis. To discharge liquid waste legally, plant owners or operators must abide by all terms of their NPDES permit. Violations of the discharge permit can lead to substantial fines and possible jail sentences for company executives.

REGULATION OF LAND POLLUTION

Over seventy million tons of hazardous waste are disposed of in the United States each year. The majority of that waste is not destroyed but is either stored in fifty-five-gallon drums and deposited in clay-lined dumps, injected deep underground between layers of rock, or merely abandoned in vacant lots, lagoons, and landfills. Predictably, some of these storage methods fail over time, as storage containers corrode and rain washes the wastes from storage sites. The hazardous wastes then make their way into lakes, streams, and groundwater, eventually contaminating drinking water. Of the thirteen-hundred unauthorized waste sites considered most dangerous by the EPA, most are considered to be a direct threat to drinking water.

Regulation Under the Common Law

Before 1976, the primary vehicle for the control of groundwater contamination was the common law. As with other environmental torts, the plaintiffs relied most heavily upon the common law actions of nuisance, trespass, negligence, and strict liability for abnormally dangerous activities. The common law proved inadequate for the control of land pollution for the same reasons it proved inadequate in the control of air and water pollution.

Detecting Groundwater Pollution
While the common law's inability to control pollution was acknowledged in the 1960s, the development of a regulatory framework was hampered by the very nature of groundwater contamination. First, the detection of trace toxic chemicals in groundwater requires sophisticated monitoring and analysis equipment. Much of that technology has only recently been developed. Second, measurement of the effects of groundwater contamination required the use of *epidemiological data.* Epidemiological studies involve an analysis of the population to determine the presence of a disease or illness and a determination of the factors causing the disease or illness. While the value of such studies was clearly recognized, epidemiological evidence connecting hazardous waste disposal with cancers and other illnesses in humans accumulates at a relatively slow rate.

Finally, the regulation of land pollution was hampered by the factor that encouraged its use. Because of the public's obsession with visible pollution—

burning rivers, smog-hazed cities, and trash-littered highways—the invisible nature of land pollution caused it to get less notoriety. Because of the difficulties associated with its detection and the tremendous costs associated with its cleanup, land pollution may arguably be the most serious pollution problem facing this country.

The Advent of Federal Regulation

As with air and water pollution, the federal government initially relied on state and local governments to control land pollution. Solid waste was viewed as being closely related to air and water pollution—controls on pollution released into the air and water generated hazardous solid waste to be disposed of on land. Because of inadequate state and local standards, the environmental problems associated with that and other solid waste began to grow.

In the late 1960s, Congress recognized that the control of land pollution required two separate federal regulatory frameworks—one for active dumpsites and another for so-called orphan dumps. In that regard, Congress enacted the Resource Conservation and Recovery Act to ensure that proper disposal techniques were used in the disposal of hazardous wastes in active dumpsites. To provide for the clean-up of hazardous dumpsites where the responsible parties cannot be located or are no longer in business (orphan dumps), Congress enacted the Comprehensive Environmental Response, Compensation, and Liability Act.

RCRA: Regulating Active Disposal Sites

With the intent to "... prohibit future open dumping on the land and to requir[e] the conversion of existing open dumps to facilities which do not pose a danger to the environment ..." Congress enacted the *Resource Conservation and Recovery Act* (RCRA) in 1976. Under RCRA, Congress provided the EPA with the responsibility to regulate the transportation, storage, treatment, and disposal of hazardous wastes. State and local governments were left with the responsibility for developing nonhazardous solid waste disposal plans under the Solid Waste Disposal Act of 1965.

Defining a Hazardous Waste

RCRA requires the EPA to identify and maintain a list of hazardous wastes. The Act defines *hazardous waste* as follows:

> a solid waste ... which because of its quantity, concentration, or physical, chemical, or infectious characteristics may—
> **(a)** cause, or significantly contribute to an increase in mortality or an increase in serious irreversible, or incapacitating reversible, illness; or,
> **(b)** pose a substantial present or potential hazard to human health or the environment when improperly treated, stored, transported, or disposed of, or otherwise managed.

Wastes so identified may be stored or disposed of only at sites whose owners or operators have obtained a permit from the EPA. In securing that permit, the disposal site operators and owners will have agreed to meet all applicable regulations regarding the treatment and storage of hazardous wastes.

RCRA's Manifest System

The objectives of the RCRA are to be accomplished through compliance by generators, transporters, and disposal site operators with the Act's *manifest system*. The RCRA requires the generator of a hazardous waste to complete a *manifest*—a detailed form that sets out the nature of the hazardous waste and identifies its origin, routing, and final destination. In addition to completing the manifest, the generator is responsible for assuring that the waste is packaged in appropriate, carefully labeled, containers.

The generator is to provide the transporter of the hazardous waste with a copy of the manifest. The transporter is required to sign the manifest and, upon delivery of the hazardous waste, provide a copy to the operator of the disposal site. The site operator then has the obligation to return a copy of the manifest to the generator, thereby closing the circle.

If the generator fails to hear about the safe disposal of the waste, it is to inform the EPA immediately. In theory, this reporting system provides regulatory authorities with the ability to track hazardous waste through its generation, transportation, and disposal phases. That is, the manifest system provides "cradle-to-grave" control over hazardous waste.

Regulation of Disposal Sites

RCRA requires the regulation of hazardous waste disposal sites. Owners and operators are required to obtain an operating permit to operate a hazardous waste disposal site. All permittees are required to operate their disposal facilities according to regulations established by the EPA.

As originally enacted, the RCRA failed to address problems created by the improper disposal of hazardous wastes before its enactment. To alleviate those concerns, Congress amended the RCRA in 1984 with the enactment of the *Hazardous and Solid Waste Amendments Act.*

While leaving the remainder of the RCRA unchanged, the amendments did impose additional requirements on disposal site owners and operators. Under the amendments, they are now required to undertake remedial action for all releases of hazardous wastes at their facility—regardless of when those wastes were placed in the site. Thus, owners and operators are responsible for assuring that their facility meets all current federal standards even if the wastes were disposed of in the facility before the RCRA's enactment.

Superfund: Regulating Inactive Disposal Sites

Although the RCRA is intended to upgrade significantly the nation's active hazardous waste disposal sites, it does not address the problem of cleaning up *inactive dump sites.* An inactive dump site is defined to include those dump sites either abandoned by companies now out of business or created by "midnight dumpers." Midnight dumpers are people who dispose of hazardous wastes illegally, often by discharging wastes into ditches along rural roads in the middle of the night. Nor does the RCRA address the cleanup of hazardous waste spills. Although other environmental laws did provide limited governmental authority to clean up and abate a number of "environmental emergencies," the funding was either inadequate or not available for the cleanup of inactive dumps.

In response, Congress enacted the *Comprehensive Environmental Response, Compensation, and Liability Act* (CERCLA) in 1980. Labeled the *Superfund,* the

Act gives the President the authority to clean up abandoned hazardous sites and to provide necessary remedial actions in the case of spills. Originally funded for a five-year period, Congress enacted a five-year extension of the Superfund program in 1986. Entitled the *Superfund Amendments and Reauthorization Act* (SARA), the law greatly increases federal funding of the hazardous waste cleanup program. The Act also requires the President to select permanent remedies to the maximum extent practicable in the cleanup of hazardous waste sites.

The Response Trust Fund

SARA increased the funding of the Hazardous Substance Response Trust Fund from the $1.6 billion under the original 1980 Act to $9 billion. The purpose of the *Response Fund* is to provide funds for timely government responses to releases of hazardous substances into the environment. The fund is supported through a surtax on businesses with an annual income over $2 billion in the petroleum and chemical feedstocks industries. Those revenues are specifically earmarked for Superfund cleanup efforts and cannot be used by the government for other purposes.

Responsible Parties

An abandoned dump site might contain dozens of different hazardous wastes with varying degrees of toxicity and volatility. Those wastes may have been disposed of by several different generators. In addition, the dump site may have been owned by different companies over the years. Thus, the culpable parties may be impossible to determine. To alleviate this difficulty, the Act specifically defines who can be held liable for cleanup costs and damages to natural resources:

1. Current owners of the hazardous waste site.
2. Any prior owner who owned the site at the time of a hazardous waste disposal.
3. Any generator of hazardous waste who arranged for disposal of its wastes at the site.
4. Any transporter of hazardous waste who selected the site for disposal.

Note that the parties are *strictly and jointly and severally liable* for these costs; that is, each of the parties could be liable for the entire cost regardless of the size of their contribution to the hazardous waste at the site. The imposition of joint and several liability is the most controversial aspect of the Superfund.

The Government's Cleanup Options

The Act provides the government with two options for cleaning up hazardous waste sites. If there is a threat of a release of a hazardous substance or where a hazardous substance has been released and there is a threat of imminent and substantial danger to public health, the government may undertake the cleanup effort. Later, the government can recoup its expenses through an action against responsible parties if the parties can be located. Alternatively, the government can order private parties to clean up the site themselves. If a private party resists a cleanup order and is then held liable, the damages (costs of clean up) may be trebled.

Injuries to Private Citizens Not Covered

It is important to note that the Act does not provide relief to private citizens who have suffered personal injuries caused by the leakage of hazardous substances from an abandoned dump site. Private citizens injured by hazardous substances must litigate their claims in a state court according to the common law rules in their particular jurisdiction. The Act does provide, however, that in some circumstances private parties may be able to recover cleanup expenses from the fund.

Community Right-to-Know Reporting

SARA requires owners of hazardous waste facilities to provide information on the chemicals stored at their facilities. That information is to be provided to the relevant state commission, local communities, and the local fire department. The information must also be made available to the general public. The intent of the *community right-to-know* reporting requirement is to encourage communities to enhance their emergency response procedures.

REGULATING THE ENVIRONMENTAL EFFECTS OF PRODUCTS

The EPA is also charged with implementing and enforcing laws that regulate the production of products that could have adverse effects on the environment. These laws require businesses to alter products to make them environmentally safe. Most prominent of the environmental laws regulating products are the Noise Pollution Control Act, the Clean Air Act (motor vehicle provisions), the Federal Insecticide, Fungicide, and Rodenticide Act, and the Toxic Substances Control Act.

Regulating Noise Pollution

The *Noise Control Act* of 1972 gives the federal government broad powers to address noise pollution problems. Noise can have many adverse affects, including damage to hearing, disruption of normal activity, and general annoyance. Noise emission standards set by the EPA for products must be sufficient "to protect the public health and welfare, taking into account the magnitude and conditions of use of the product, the degree of noise reduction achievable through the use of the best available technology, and the costs of compliance." A manufacturer selling a product that is not in compliance with the noise emission standard is subject to fines of up to $25,000 a day, a jail term of not more than one year, or both.

Regulating Pesticide Use

The *Federal Insecticide, Fungicide, and Rodenticide Act* of 1947, and the *Federal Environmental Pesticide Control Act* that amended it, provide that pesticides must be registered with the EPA before they can be sold to consumers. A pesticide will be registered only if it is properly labeled, does what it claims it will do, and will not cause unreasonably adverse effects on the environment. The latter is defined as "any unreasonable risk to man or the environment, taking into account the economic, social and environmental costs and benefits of the use of any pesticide."

Applicants for registration must provide comprehensive animal studies to determine the probable effect of the pesticide on humans (the testing process costs about $5 million for the typical pesticide). If tests indicate that a pesticide is hazardous for use by consumers, it may be restricted for use only by certified applicators or under the supervision of certified applicators. All pesticide registrations expire every five years and must be renewed. A registered pesticide that poses an imminent hazard to the environment may be immediately suspended from use by the EPA.

Regulating New Chemicals

To allow for the regulation of new toxic chemicals, Congress enacted the *Toxic Substances Control Act* (TOSCA) in 1976. The Act provides a regulatory mechanism to protect the public against dangerous chemical materials contained in consumer and industrial products. The primary purpose of TOSCA is to provide an early warning system to signal potential environmental dangers before products made with new chemicals are widely dispersed. The EPA has wide authority to ban or restrict the manufacture, processing, distribution, commercial use, or disposal of any chemical substance that presents an unreasonable risk of injury to health or the environment.

Regulating Mobile Source Pollution

The Clean Air Act gives the EPA the responsibility for regulating the air pollution emissions from automobiles and other vehicles. The automobile is generally recognized as the nation's greatest contributor to air pollution. Under the Act, the EPA can prescribe emissions standards for all new motor vehicles (including trucks, buses, motorcycles, and automobiles), regulate fuels and fuel additives to be used in motor vehicles, and require the industry to test and to document the control devices developed to meet the standards.

There have been many difficulties in attempting to reduce auto emissions. Most have been caused by problems in developing adequate control technologies. For example, the original 1977 emissions standards were suspended when it was found that the technology available to meet the hydrocarbon and carbon monoxide standards would significantly increase emissions of sulfuric acid.

Although the 1977 Amendment controls resulted in vehicle exhaust 96 percent cleaner than it was before 1970, 101 cities still missed the deadlines for meeting the health standards for *ozone*. In addressing this concern, the 1990 Amendments require that all but nine cities must meet the ozone standards by the year 2000. With the exception of Los Angeles, the other eight cities must meet the standards by 2005. Los Angeles must meet the standards by 2010. The standards are to be met by significantly reducing automobile emissions beginning in 1993. In addition, automakers are to build cars that run on cleaner-burning fuels. All fleet vehicles (for example, police cars) in the smoggiest areas will be required to be cleaner-fuel burning vehicles. Table 17–5 summarizes the costs and benefits of alternative fuels, for engines as currently engineered.

Table 17–5   Alternative Fuel Sources Compared to Gasoline

Fuel	Benefits	Problems
Methanol (from natural gas, wood coal)	One-half the hydrocarbons, 10% less CO_2, 33% less toxic emissions, high octane.	Only produces half the energy output of gasoline, so must burn more; highly toxic to people.
Natural gas	Emits very little carbon or hydrocarbons; cheaper than gasoline.	Expensive to convert cars; need heavy fuel tanks which cuts performance.
Ethanol (made from corn or sugar)	Mixed with gasoline, slightly cuts emissions; high octane.	Less energy per gallon, so more consumed; growing the plants can cause environmental damage as in Brazil where commonly used.
Electricity	Almost no emissions from vehicles.	Electricity production generates pollution; vehicle size and range limited.

INTERNATIONAL PERSPECTIVES: AUTO EMISSION CONTROLS IN EUROPE

INTERNATIONAL

PERSPECTIVES

The European car market, the largest in the world with more than thirteen million cars sold each year, is just now being confronted with the possibility of uniform pollution controls on auto emissions. In contrast to the United States, where automakers have been required to control pollution coming from their automobiles for more than eighteen years, Europe still does not uniformly regulate auto pollution. All cars sold in countries within the European Community (EC) can legally spew out exhaust that contains fourteen times more hydrocarbons and nitrogen oxide than that permitted under U.S. law. West Germany does provide tax breaks for buyers to encourage carmakers to install catalytic converters. However, while lead-free gasoline—*bleifrei*—is available everywhere in Germany, it is available only at certain stations throughout the remainder of Europe.

As a consequence of this situation and other lax pollution control standards, Europe has serious air pollution problems. In an effort to curb the problem, several European countries outside the EC have imposed auto emission control requirements. Automobiles sold in Switzerland, for example, must meet U.S. standards, while automobiles sold in Austria are required to meet standards a little more lenient than the Swiss standards.

Despite seven years of talks, the EC has not been able to reach an agreement on reducing auto emissions. The latest proposal calls for uniform controls on small cars with engines no larger than 1.5 liters (a typical small car in the United States has an engine of 1.8 to 2 liters). Two of every three cars sold in Europe are that size.

The degree of control to be imposed is the subject of considerable controversy. West Germany, Denmark, and the Netherlands support stricter standards that would require small cars to be equipped with catalytic converters. The $900 to $1,350 cost of this (about 15 percent of the sticker price) causes France, Spain, Belgium, England, and Italy to support less stringent standards. If a compromise cannot be workd out, European officials fear that each country will adopt its own standards, thereby forcing carmakers to produce a dozen variations of each model.

The managers of American automobile manufacturers are watching the negotiations closely. The sticter standards imposed in Switzerland and Austria improved sales considerably in those countries for General Motors Europe. While U.S. manufacturers have no competitive advantage in countries that have no pollution standards, years of experience in meeting U.S. standards gives them a considerable edge in the countries imposing standards. Uniform EC pollution standards would likely increase their sales and market share in Europe dramatically.

PENALTIES FOR VIOLATIONS OF FEDERAL ENVIRONMENTAL LAWS

An important aspect of any regulatory law is the law's enforcement mechanisms. No matter what approach is taken to controlling pollution, regulated businesses must have adequate incentives to comply. Businesses must perceive that the costs of compliance are lower than the costs of the penalties for not complying.

The Clean Air Act, Clean Water Act, Resource Conservation and Recovery Act, and the Superfund each provide a similar array of civil and criminal penalties for noncompliance. With the enactment of recent amendments, the Clean Water Act and the Superfund now provide the EPA with the authority to impose an administrative penalty. Although the other three Acts have always contained a citizen suit provision, recent amendments have just provided citizens with that authority under the Superfund.

Civil and Criminal Penalties

The enforcement provisions of the Clean Air, Clean Water, and Resource Conservation and Recovery Acts are nearly identical. All three Acts provide that a business may be subject to either a criminal penalty or a civil penalty for a violation of an Act's standards.

Criminal Penalties

Criminal penalties are invoked under the Clean Water Act if a business willfully and negligently violates the Act's required effluent standard. Under the Clean Air and Resource Conservation and Recovery Acts, a business may be guilty of a criminal act if it knowingly violates either Act's required standards. The Clean Air Act provides for a criminal fine of up to $25,000 per day of violation or up to one year in prison or both. The Resource Conservation and Recovery Act and the Clean Water Act provide for criminal fines of up to $50,000 per day, up to three years in prison, or both. If a business is convicted a second time under the Clean Air Act, it may be fined up to $50,000 a day, and the responsible official may be imprisoned for up to two years.

The Resource Conservation and Recovery Act has a special criminal penalty for violations of the Act when human life is knowingly endangered. Such a violation can produce a criminal fine of up to $250,000 and imprisonment up to two years for the executive. The business is subject to a fine of up to $1 million under the same circumstances. A violator demonstrating extreme disregard for human life is subject to another fine up to $250,000 and may be imprisoned for up to five years.

Civil Penalties

The Acts also contain provisions for civil penalties when violations occur without criminal intent. Under all three Acts, a business may be fined up to $25,000 per day of violation. Each day a business is found not to be in compliance with required standards counts as an additional violation. The number of violations—and thus the size of the fine—can increase rapidly. A year-long violation of any one of these Acts by a business can result in fines in the millions of dollars. Allied Chemical, for example, was fined $13.2 million for violating the Clean Water Act by discharging the pesticide Kepone and other toxic waste into the James River.

The Clean Air Act's Noncompliance Penalty

Congress enacted new enforcement provision—the mandatory *noncompliance penalty*—in the 1977 Clean Air Act Amendments. Businesses that violated the law by failing to install and operate pollution control devices within the time limits set by the Act gained a cost advantage relative to competitors who complied with the law. The regulatory and enforcement measures authorized by the Act before the 1977 amendments did not include penalties sufficiently adequate to induce business compliance. Thus, businesses often found that the costs of not complying were lower than the costs of complying.

The 1977 amendments required the EPA to assess a penalty that captures this economic "savings" a business realizes from noncompliance, including the expenses associated with the operation of pollution control equipment during the period of noncompliance. Those avoided costs were thought by Congress to represent such a gain to the owners of the business that they would have strong incentive not to comply. The noncompliance penalty is intended to reduce those incentives.

Administrative Penalty

In amendments to the Clean Water Act and the Superfund, Congress provides the EPA with the ability to assess an administrative penalty. In the past, EPA had to take violators to court to impose either a civil or a criminal penalty. The administrative penalty provision provides EPA with the authority to impose a fine without the need to resort to litigation.

The administrative penalty provisions provide for two separate classes of penalties. A Class I penalty may not exceed $10,000 per day, with a maximum of $25,000. A Class II penalty may be assessed through a more formal proceeding and may not exceed $10,000 per day, with a maximum of $125,000.

Enforcement Efforts Beyond the Agency

All four of the major environmental laws clearly provide for enforcement efforts by the EPA. Environmentalists were concerned, however, about the sufficiency of those efforts, particularly in view of the poor showing by some agencies charged with environmental quality control through the 1950s and 1960s. To alleviate their concerns, Congress provides enforcement mechanisms outside the EPA by giving citizens the right to enforce the environmental laws. In addition, Congress protects employees who provide information regarding pollution control violations by their employers.

Citizen Suits

In the early development stages of federal environmental law, environmental groups lobbied for the right to initiate enforcement proceedings when governmental efforts were too slow or too meek. Those groups argued that if left to themselves, the responsible government agency and the regulated businesses might seek compromises that would not necessarily further the purposes of the environmental statute. Congress recognized this argument and provided private citizens with the right to bring suits against businesses operating in violation of the law or against the administrator of the business for failing to appropriately implement and enforce the Act. By authorizing citizens to bring suits for violations, the agency has extra incentives to fulfill its statutory mandates.

The development of the citizen suit provision produced concern that some lawyers would use the provision to bring frivolous and harassing actions against businesses. A provision in both acts provides that the court may award the costs of litigation, including reasonable attorneys' and expert witness fees, whenever it determines that the citizen's action is in the public interest. The court may also award such litigation costs to the business when the citizen's action is obviously frivolous or harassing. Congress believed these provisions would discourage abuse of the citizen suit provision while encouraging the quality of actions that were brought. In the *Ruckelshaus* case, the Supreme Court was confronted by a group demanding attorneys' fees despite having lost their challenge to a regulation issued by the EPA.

Ruckelshaus v. Sierra Club

United States Supreme Court
463 U.S. 680,
103 S.Ct. 3274
(1983)

Case Background. *This case was brought against William D. Ruckelshaus, Administrator of the EPA, by the Sierra Club. The EPA promulgated standards limiting the emissions of sulfur dioxide by coal-burning power plants. The Sierra Club, the respondent, filed petitions for review of the agency's action in the U.S. Court of Appeals for the District of Columbia. The court of appeals rejected all the claims asserted by the Sierra Club.*

Notwithstanding its lack of success, the Sierra Club filed a request for attorneys' fees it had incurred in the action. It relied on provisions in the Clean Air Act that permit an award of attorneys' fees whenever the court determines that such an award is appropriate. The Sierra Club argued that despite the fact that it lost, it was appropriate for it to receive fees on the basis that the litigation contributed to the goals of the Clean Air Act. The court of appeals agreed. The Supreme Court granted certiorari to consider whether an award of attorneys' fees is appropriate when the party requesting them has lost.

Case Decision. Justice Rehnquist delivered the opinion of the Court.

* * *

The question presented by this case is whether it is "appropriate," within the meaning of the Clean Air Act, to award attorney's fees to a party that achieved no success on the merits of its claims.

* * *

Section 307(f) provides only that:

> In any judicial proceeding under this section, the court may award costs of litigation (including reasonable attorney and expert witness fees) whenever it determines that such an award is appropriate.

It is difficult to draw any meaningful guidance from Section 307(f)'s use of the word "appropriate," which means only "specially suitable: fit, proper," Webster's Third International Dictionary. Obviously, in order to decide when fees should be awarded under Section 307(f), a court first must decide what the award should be "specially suitable," "fit," or "proper" for. Section 307(f) alone does not begin to answer this question, and application of the provision thus requires reference to other sources, including fee-shifting rules developed in different contexts. As demonstrated below, inquiry into these sources shows that requiring a defendant, completely successful on all issues, to pay the unsuccessful plaintiff's legal fees would be a radical departure from long-standing fee-shifting principles adhered to in a wide range of contexts.

Our basic point of reference is the "American Rule," under which even "the prevailing litigant is ordinarily not entitled to collect a reasonable attorneys' fee from the loser." It is clear that generations of American judges, lawyers, and legislators, with this rule as the point of departure, would regard it as quite "inappropriate" to award the "loser" an attorney's fee from the "prevailing litigant." Similarly, when Congress has chosen to depart from the American rule by statute, virtually every one of the more than 150 existing federal fee-shifting provisions predicates fee awards on some success by the claimant; while these statutes contain varying standards as to the precise degree of success necessary for an award of fees—such as whether the fee claimant was the "prevailing party," the "substantially prevailing" party, or "successful"—the consistent rule is that complete failure will not justify shifting fees from the losing party to the winning party.

* * *

While the foregoing treatments of fee-shifting differ in many respects, they reflect one consistent, established rule: a successful party need not pay its unsuccessful adversary's fees. The uniform acceptance of this rule reflects, at least in part, intuitive notions of fairness to litigants. Put simply, ordinary conceptions of just returns reject the idea that a party who wrongly charges someone with violations of the law should be able to force that defendant to pay the costs of the wholly unsuccessful suit against it. Before we will conclude Congress abandoned this established principle that a successful party need not pay its unsuccessful adversary's fees—rooted as it is in the intuitive notions of fairness and widely manifested in numerous different contexts—a clear showing that this result was intended is required.

* * *

We conclude, therefore, that the language and legislative history of Section 307(f) do not support respondents' argument that the section was intended as a radical departure from established principles requiring that a fee claimant attain some success on the merits before it may receive an award of fees. Instead, we are persuaded that if Congress intended such a novel result—which would require federal courts to make sensitive, difficult, and ultimately highly subjective determinations—it would have said so in far plainer language than that employed here.

* * *

Case Holding. *The Court held that absent some degree of success on the merits by the claimant, it is not "appropriate" for a federal court to award attorneys' fees under*

Section 307(f) of the Clean Air Act. Accordingly, the judgment of the court of appeals was reversed.

Case Questions

1. In what way could the Sierra Club argue that it furthered the objectives of the Clean Air Act by bringing the initial lawsuit?
2. Why does the right to recover attorneys' fees encourage citizen participation in the regulatory process?

Protecting Employees Who Provide Information

Employees called upon to testify or who step forward to give information about a violation of a federal law by an employer (referred to as *whistleblowers*) often fear retaliation by that employer. To protect such employees, the Clean Air, Clean Water, and Resource Conservation and Recovery Acts prohibit employers from discharging or discriminating against them. If after a hearing, the EPA finds an employer has mistreated such an employee, it may issue an order requiring the employer to stop the mistreatment. That order may require the rehiring of the employee with back pay. In addition, the employer may be assessed the cost of the hearing.

IMPACT OF FEDERAL WILDLIFE LAWS

The environmental laws discussed to this point were enacted with the general intent of reducing industrial pollution. The laws directly impact the business community in terms of the costs associated with the purchase, operation, and maintenance of pollution control equipment and the compliance with environmental protection regulations. At virtually the same time it was enacting the environmental laws, Congress was enacting a series of laws protecting wildlife. Surprisingly, those laws can also have a substantial impact on the business community.

Although our environmental laws are the most formidable in the world, with one notable exception, they will not act to forestall completely a project with the potential to cause environmental degradation. That sole exception is a federal wildlife law entitled the Endangered Species Act. As Table 17–6 illustrates, Congress has enacted several laws to protect wildlife.

Table 17–6   Selected Federal Wildlife Laws Affecting the Legal Environment of Business

Anadromous Fish Conservation Act
Endangered Species Act
Fish and Wildlife Coordination Act
Marine Mammal Protection Act
Migratory Bird Treaty Act
Wild Free-Roaming Horses and Burros Act

The Endangered Species Act authorizes the Secretary of the Interior to declare species of animal or plant life endangered and to establish the "critical habitat" of such a creature. An *endangered species* is defined by the Act to be as follows:

> [A]ny species which is in danger of extinction throughout all or a significant portion of its range ... [.]

When a species is listed as endangered, the Act imposes obligations on both private and public parties. Under the Act, no person may "take, import, or conduct commercial activity with respect to any endangered species." Although in most disputes involving an endangered species both parties will generally agree that the species is deserving of protection, the conflict invariably centers on the degree of protection to be afforded. In the *Hill* case, a snail darter was able to halt a major government project.

Tennessee Valley Authority v. Hill
United States Supreme Court
437 U.S. 153, 98 S.Ct. 2279 (1978)

Case Background. *Congress authorized the Tennessee Valley Authority (TVA) to construct the Tellico Dam and multipurpose project on the Little Tennessee River. When construction was virtually complete, Congress passed the Endangered Species Act of 1973. Four months before passage of the Act, a university scientist discovered a three-inch fish called the snail darter in the waters above the dam site. The new biological species was added to the endangered species list by the Secretary of the Interior.*

The Secretary also found that operation of Tellico Dam would result in destruction of the snail darter's habitat. The Department of the Interior instructed TVA not to destroy the darter's habitat by completing the dam. In the courts, defenders of the darter sought to enjoin TVA from completing the project. The court of appeals ruled that the Endangered Species Act required that the project be abandoned. TVA appealed to the U.S. Supreme Court.

Case Decision. Chief Justice Burger delivered the opinion of the Court.

* * *

It may seem curious to some that the survival of a relatively small number of three-inch fish ... would require the permanent halting of a virtually completed dam for which Congress has expended more than $100 million. The paradox is not minimized by the fact that Congress continued to appropriate large sums of public money for the project, even after Congressional Appropriations Committees were apprised of its apparent impact upon the survival of the snail darter. ...

One would be hard pressed to find a statutory provision whose terms were any plainer than those in Section 7 of the Endangered Species Act. Its very words affirmatively command all federal agencies "to insure that actions authorized, funded, or carried out by them do not jeopardize the continued existence" of an endangered species or "result in the destruction or modification of habitat of such species. ..." This language admits of no exception. Nonetheless, petitioner urges that the Act cannot reasonably be interpreted as applying to a federal project which was well under way when Congress passed the Endangered Species Act of 1973. To sustain that position, however, we would be forced to ignore the ordinary meaning of plain language. It has not been shown, for example, how TVA can close the gates of the Tellico Dam without "carrying out" an action that has been "authorized" and "funded" by a federal agency. Nor can we understand how such action will "insure" that the snail darter's habitat is not disrupted. Accepting the

Secretary's determinations, as we must, it is clear that TVA's proposed operation of the dam will have precisely the opposite effect, namely the eradication of an endangered species.

* * *

The plain intent of Congress in enacting this statute was to halt and reverse the trend toward species extinction, whatever the cost. This is reflected not only in the stated policies of the Act, but in literally every section of the statute. All persons, including federal agencies, are specifically instructed not to "take" endangered species meaning that no one is "to harass, harm, pursue, hunt, shoot, wound, kill, trap, capture, or collect" such life forms. Agencies in particular are directed by Sections 2(c) and 3(2) of the Act to "use . . . all methods and procedures which are necessary" to preserve endangered species. In addition, the legislative history undergirding Section 7 reveals an explicit congressional decision to require agencies to afford first priority to the declared national policy of saving endangered species. The pointed omission of the type of qualifying language previously included in endangered species legislation reveals a conscious decision by Congress to give endangered species priority over the "primary missions" of federal agencies.

* * *

One might dispute the applicability of these examples to the Tellico Dam by saying that in this case the burden on the public through the loss of millions of unrecoverable dollars would greatly outweigh the loss of the snail darter. But neither the Endangered Species Act nor Art. III of the Constitution provides federal courts with authority to make such fine utilitarian calculations. On the contrary, the plain language of the Act, buttressed by its legislative history, shows clearly that Congress viewed the value of endangered species as "incalculable." Quite obviously, it would be difficult for a court to balance the loss of a sum certain— even \$100 million—against a congressionally declared "incalculable" value, even assuming we had the power to engage in such a weighing process, which we emphatically do not.

* * *

Case Holding. *The decision of the court of appeals was affirmed. TVA would be in violation of the Endangered Species Act if it completed and operated the Tellico Dam.*

Case Questions
1. Could the court engage in a balancing of the relative costs and benefits of the snail darter versus the Tellico Dam?
2. Would the result have been different if the project had been built on private property?
3. Should developers report to the Department of Interior the discovery of an endangered species on their property?

As a consequence of the *Hill* case, the Act was amended to provide for exceptions in some cases. The Secretary of the Interior may permit an applicant to engage in an otherwise prohibited taking of an endangered species under certain circumstances. The applicant must submit a comprehensive conservation plan to the Secretary. If the plan provides a reasonable compromise between the needs of the environment and the business, the plan will be approved.

SUMMARY

Before the introduction of federal constraints on the degradation of the environment, the common law was the principal means through which this nation regulated its pollution. Through various applications of the laws of trespass, negligence, strict liability, and nuisance, the courts fashioned penalties for several polluting activities. By the 1960s, however, it was clear that these remedies—combined with feeble state and federal regulations—could not prevent a continuing decline in the quality of the environment.

In response, Congress enacted several laws to enhance the quality of the environment. Federal laws now enforced by the EPA control air, water, land, and product pollution. The primary emphasis has been on imposing technology-based standards on businesses to control their pollution. That is, in many areas, firms are required to adopt the state-of-the-art technology in pollution control equipment.

The control of toxic substances and hazardous wastes has become a major area of concern. The enactment of the Resource Conservation and Recovery Act and the establishment of the Superfund demonstrate the increased concern with the disposal of toxic substances. The enactment of the Toxic Substance Control Act illustrates the concern for the early detection of environmental hazards in new chemicals. Much research remains to be done on the effect of the thousands of chemicals in our lives, and the controversy will continue about the best way to control such environmental problems.

Should the Environmental Movement Move Indoors?

Although the Clean Air Act is the most comprehensive air quality control statute in the world, it does not provide air quality standards for indoor air space. As air quality testing technology has improved, scientists have discovered that some of the most polluted air in the United States exists inside—not outside—commercial buildings. In some cases, indoor levels of toxic chemicals can be 1,000 times greater than outside levels. Office workers have become seriously ill and successfully sued their employers and the builders for damages caused by exposure to the "sick building." In the following article, the author examines the problem to determine the extent to which it affects officer workers and considers how the legal environment has changed to handle the problem.

Do You Work in a Sick Building?
Faye Rice*

As soon as the installation of new carpeting began in 1987, workers in a Washington, D.C., office building started complaining of burning in their lungs and dizziness. Within months 700 people were affected, around 20 with symptoms so severe that they could no longer enter the place. The workers demanded that the carpeting be removed, set up a picket line, and eventually got their employer to agree. This particular employer had more reason than most to be embarrassed about the stink: It was the Environmental Protection Agency. Declares William Hirzy, a union official and senior scientist at the agency who took part in the protest: "Indoor pollution has come home to roost right here at the EPA. We hope our injuries will raise public concern about the problem."

Twenty years after Congress passed the Clean Air Act, the environmental movement is heading indoors. Experts predict that indoor air-quality issues will proliferate in the 1990s as the public grows increasingly aware of the hazards, and coughing, teary-eyed office workers become less hesitant about venting complaints. Lawsuits are already on the rise. Says Washington, D.C., attorney Laurence S. Kirsch, who edits the newsletter *Indoor Pollution Law Report:* "The trend is toward indoor pollution victims suing a large number of parties, including the owners, architects, and ventilation contractors of a building."

In some cases what has come to be called sick-building syndrome, or SBS, can be traced to a single, airborne contaminant; in others it reflects the combined effects of many. A medical specialty called clinical ecology has played a prominent role in the investigation and treatment of SBS-related diseases, and a veritable industry of experts has sprung up to fix the buildings themselves. The germ- and poison-busters include architects, biologists, maintenance companies, and industrial hygienists, who analyze air samples, quiz workers about complaints, and crawl through ventilation ducts looking for mold.

They find that many office buildings are

—continued

–continuing

chemical and bacterial war zones, aswirl with contaminants such as tobacco smoke, asbestos dust, and fumes from paint, cleaning solvents, and copying machines. The EPA, which has identified several hundred indoor pollutants, lists at least seven that are major problems for white-collar workers: tobacco smoke; biological contaminants, including viruses, bacteria, and molds; volatile organic compounds in building materials and office machines; formaldehyde; pesticides; asbestos; and particulate matter from cleaning sprays and aerosols.

The World Health Organization estimates that one-third of new and remodeled commercial buildings worldwide are sick. Over 20% of U.S. white-collar workers suffer symptoms related to poor air quality in their offices, according to a study led by James Woods of Virginia Polytechnic Institute. Says Robert Axelrad, the director of the EPA's indoor air division: "The levels of pollutants in some buildings are 100 times higher than outdoors." During periods of peak exposure to chemicals, such as when offices are painted, indoor levels can be as much as 1,000 times higher, he says.

Since the average American spends 90% of his or her life indoors, the economic implications of pollution there could be enormous, though no one can put a precise number on them. According to an EPA analysis, the annual cost to American industry of SBS-related absenteeism and medical bills runs somewhere in the tens of billions of dollars. "The statistics on everything associated with SBS are inexact," says Michael McCawley, an industrial hygienist at the National Institute of Occupational Safety and Health (Niosh). "We're dealing with an iceberg, and we don't know whether we're viewing the tip of that iceberg or the whole floe."

While nobody denies that indoor pollution exists, possibly no other environmental problem engenders as much finger pointing. Makers of building materials blame landlords for failing to provide fresh air. Building

managers, meanwhile, point to the tenants. Says James Dinegar, vice president of the Building Owners and Managers Association: "We have to work with tenants so that they will be more careful about what they bring into the buildings, like carpets and copiers."

Congress could pass its first comprehensive indoor-air legislation this year. A bill currently before the Senate would appropriate $48 million as a step toward further regulation of indoor air quality. Even in the absence of regulations, employers have powerful economic incentives to make sure the air workers breathe is clean. A study by the Walter Reed Institute of Medical Research in Washington, D.C., concluded that in poorly ventilated environments absenteeism increased nearly 50%. Experts like New York environmental consultant Laurence B. Molloy say companies find absenteeism drops and productivity goes up after sick offices are cured. "When you have clean buildings, you make more money," Molloy maintains.

Polaroid recently grappled with an outbreak of SBS at an office building in Norwood, Massachusetts. Last November workers began grousing about frequent colds, eye irritation, and sporadic bloody noses. As is commonly the case with SBS, "there was nothing obvious causing the problem," says Polaroid industrial hygienist Martin Horowitz. Investigators found a generator leaking exhaust fumes, an insufficient supply of fresh air, and other factors that all seemed to contribute. The company fixed the problems and currently is debating whether to restrict smoking.

Polaroid is unusual in at least one respect: its willingness to admit it had a sick building. Employers typically deal with indoor air pollution behind closed doors, and require environmental consultants to sign secrecy agreements. Says Kaaydah Schatten, president of Ceiling Doctor, a Toronto-based company specializing in bacteria and grime removal: "The corporations we deal

–continued

—continuing

with are absolutely terrified. It's as if they-have an AIDS epidemic on their hands."

The fear is fueled by the threat of bad publicity and lawsuits, even though in almost all states employees covered by workers' compensation cannot take their employer to court. The bulk of indoor-pollution claims have been filed against construction companies and the makers of materials and furnishings used in offices. Such suits helped swell the tide of product liability claims that have flooded court dockets in recent years.

* * *

Indoor air quality first emerged as a major problem during the energy crunch of the early 1970s. As fuel prices climbed, building managers sealed windows and closed air-intake ducts. As a result stale and contaminated air was trapped and recirculated, pollution rose, and people got sick. "It is like breathing in someone else's bath water," argues Simon Turner, a technical consultant at Healthy Buildings International in Fairfax, Virginia.

When buildings were sealed the importance of their ventilation systems increased, but the time and money spent on maintenance often did not. "Some of the ventilation systems we see look like they are growing green carpeting," says McCawley of Niosh. Agrees Jeffrey De Chacón, president of Pyramid Environmental Systems of Sparta, New Jersey: "We go into some buildings where the ventilation system hasn't been serviced in 30 years."

A sick building can sometimes be healed by simple adjustments. At an office in Richmond, Virginia, employees had suffered for months from what they thought were insect bites. The worried employer had consulted a parasitologist, who was baffled. Peering into air ducts, consultant Turner's crew discovered that a set of filters was missing. Loose fiberglass was getting sucked from the ceiling and blown through vents onto workers' skin. Soon after filters were installed, the mysterious insect bites disappeared.

In other instances indoor-pollution headaches cannot be cured as easily. Eastman Kodak went through a harrowing experience in 1984, when a fungus invaded the ventilation system at two factory buildings in Rochester, New York. The fungus caused an outbreak of hypersensitivity pneumonitis, an inflammation of the lungs triggered by an allergic reaction. About 1,000 employees were exposed and 115 got sick. The fungus proved extraordinarily tenacious; Kodak spent millions of dollars to eradicate it and ended up replacing the entire ventilation system. . . .

Many employers are still battling contamination from asbestos. A few years ago Exxon quietly spent millions to seal or tear out the carcinogenic insulating material at its New York City headquarters. Dozens of other companies are weighing the risks of removing their asbestos vs. leaving it in, and debating whether to go to court to recover the cost of removal. Says New York City attorney Stanley Levy, an environmental pollution specialist: "In the past most companies decided not to litigate because they didn't want to publicly admit their employees were exposed to a health hazard."

Times are changing: Prudential Insurance, for example, has filed suits against the manufacturers of the asbestos in 60 of its properties with potential problems. Asbestos has also caused increasing friction between building owners and tenants. Faced with soaring insurance costs, some crafty landlords pass the asbestos liability on to tenants in the fine print of leases, notes consultant Molloy.

While asbestos is the bane of old buildings, formaldehyde is a pollutant that commonly fouls the air in new ones. The chemical, used to pickle specimens in biology class, can trigger severe allergic reactions and cause breathing difficulties and possibly cancer. Yet the stuff is everywhere. Dozens of products are made with it, including oil-

—continued

—continuing

based paints, fiberglass, and a slew of things made of wood. Because furniture is a major source of formaldehyde emissions, the products of hardwood and particleboard manufacturers have been under scrutiny by the Consumer Product Safety Commission. Several years ago the manufacturers cut back voluntarily on one highly toxic formaldehyde compound, but the regulators want further concessions. "We would like to see formaldehyde use lowered to the point where most people will not react," says Ken Giles, a commission spokesman. Retorts Gordon De Bruine, process design manager at Weyerhaeuser: "There is a lack of medical evidence to prove we should go lower."

* * *

Questions

1. What is the principal cause of indoor air pollution? How will Congress regulate it?

2. What is the logical response by architects and builders to the problem of indoor air pollution?

REVIEW AND DISCUSSION QUESTIONS

1. Define the following terms:
   pollution
   nuisance
   Prevention of Significant Deterioration area
   point source
   bubble concept
   acid rain
   manifest system
   citizen suit
   endangered species

2. Compare and contrast the following terms and phrases:
   a. Common law and regulatory definitions of pollution
   b. Rivers and Harbors Act permit and Clean Water Act permit
   c. Existing dump site and orphan dump site
   d. PSD area and nonattainment area

3. Describe how an increasing population, a rising standard of living, and rapidly advancing industrial technology have aggravated the nation's pollution problem in the past fifty years.

4. Compare the enforcement penalties of the Clean Air, Clean Water, and Resource Conservation and Recovery Acts. Which is most severe, under what circumstances, and why?

Case Questions

5. Suppose a land developer starts a retirement village in an area known for its large, odorous cattle feedlots. Later, after much of the village is built and sold to retiring elderly couples, the developer brings an environmental nuisance action against the largest feedlot owner in the area. The developer claims the

feedlot is polluting the air with terrible odors, causing discomfort to the residents of the village and reducing the sales value of the remaining lots. What factors will the court consider in determining whether the feedlot is a nuisance or not? Assume the court finds the feedlot to be a nuisance. What should the remedy be? Could it be the same as in *Boomer,* whereby the cement company was required to pay permanent damages? Could the feedlot be a nuisance in one location and entirely acceptable in another? What about an industrial plant that emits hazardous air pollutants?

6. One of the requirements placed on a plaintiff in an environmental nuisance action is the demonstration of the existence of a better method of pollution control than that being used by the polluter. In one such case, the plaintiff suffering the effects of pollution demonstrated that another firm in competition with the polluter was in fact using a better technology. The court said to the polluter, "What is good enough for your competitor is good enough for you." The court then required the polluter to apply the same technology. Discuss the court's remarks and its actions. Consider whether it was important for the court to consider the amount of pollution control the polluter already was using and then require the polluter to add equipment until the two companies polluted equally. What if one polluter were located in a rural area and polluted the air of one nearby farmer, while its competitor were located in the city?

7. The Migratory Bird Treaty Act declares that it is unlawful:

> . . . at any time, by any means or in any manner, . . . to pursue, hunt, capture, kill, attempt to take, capture or kill . . . any migratory bird . . . included in the terms of the conventions between the United States and Great Britain, . . . , Mexico, . . . , and Japan.

The law declares it to be a misdemeanor punishable upon conviction by a fine of not more than $500 and imprisonment of six months. FMC operates a plant that manufactures various pesticides. Production of the pesticides requires large quantities of waste water. That waste water is stored in a ten-acre pond that holds approximately twelve million gallons of water. The size of the pond attracted waterfowl during their migration. During an inspection, several dead birds were found, including twenty-six Canadian geese, which were protected by the Act. Additional birds were found over the next two months. FMC used several devices to repel the birds, none of which were very successful. Is FMC in violation of the Act? [*U.S.* v. *FMC Corporation,* 572 F.2d 902 (1978)]

8. A.B. Little and Company is considering building a new plant. The company engineers know that the plant will produce a sizable quantity of sulfur dioxide. What regulatory requirements will the Clean Air Act bring to bear upon the plant?

9. Under the Endangered Species Act, what happens if an endangered animal eats an endangered plant?

10. Litton was operating according to its Clean Water Act discharge permit when certain events within the plant caused its permitted amounts of pollution to be exceeded for three weeks. Stone lived downstream from Litton. He used the stream to irrigate his crops. The pollution by Litton, however, severely damaged his crops. Does he have a cause of action against Litton?

11. Union Electric is considering building a new electric power plant. Will an environmental impact statement be required? If one is required, what factors must it take into account?

Policy Questions

12. It is estimated that two-thirds of the haze over the Arctic regions is due to pollution from Russian smelters that do not have the kinds of pollution controls required in the United States and Canada. How can we get the Soviet Union to adopt environmental controls similar to ours so that we do not suffer from its environmental abuse?

13. The U.S. environmental laws have been accused of being a principal reason that the United States is not competitive in world markets. Should the United States impose import tariffs on products from countries that require markedly less pollution control than we do?

14. Should pollution control requirements be more or less stringent on pollutants thought to be hazardous but for which little scientific knowledge about their actual health effects exists? Or should the requirements be set according to the existing level of knowledge and then be increased as knowledge of the pollutant's health effects becomes available?

15. Consider the following statement: "Like other environmental laws, the Toxic Substances Control Act's requirements are too strict. They will drive small firms out of business." Should the EPA consider the impacts on small companies when they implement the environmental laws? What if environmental laws cause severe unemployment?

Ethics Questions

16. Suppose you are an executive with a leading manufacturing company, and one aspect of your business pollutes heavily. You know that you can build a plant in a Third World country to handle that aspect without pollution control. This would mean that for the same amount of production you would add ten times as much pollution to the world's environment as you do presently, but it would be more profitable for the company. Can you legally move the plant? Should you?

17. Cox is a resident of a town in which a large chemical company is located. The chemical company is owned by a family that is very concerned about the impact of industrial pollution on the environment. The family has made every effort to reduce the company pollution to minimum levels. Recently the family has become concerned about the company's hazardous waste disposal site. Investigators have determined that the site is located directly over the town's underground water supply. Fortunately, they also determined that the site poses no current threat to the water supply. Just to be safe, the family would like to move the site. However, because the move would be very expensive, they would like to share the cost with the town's residents. Cox, a rational man, realizes that even if he doesn't pay his fair share of the cost, he cannot be excluded from enjoying the benefits of a safe and secure water supply. Should he pay?

18. Gerald Jones was an executive for U.S. Developers, a large commercial and residential developer. Jones had been assigned a large project in Houston, Texas. In walking through the property, Jones discovered that the Houston toad lived on the property. He knew that the toad was an endangered species. Jones also knew that if he reported it, the project and his job could be in serious jeopardy. What should Jones do?

18 Securities Regulation

THIS chapter develops the concept of a security and discusses the past and present legal environment affecting the regulation of the sale of securities to finance business operations. Since the sale of securities is the principal means through which corporations raise capital, the chapter begins with a general discussion of corporate finance. A discussion is developed on how the Securities Act of 1933 defines a security, and how the courts have used that definition to develop a test to determine whether a particular investment instrument is to be considered a security for the purpose of federal regulation.

We then discuss the disclosure requirements that the federal securities laws impose upon the issuers of securities and the basic process the issuer must go through in meeting the law's disclosure requirements. The chapter then examines the legal consequences of violating those disclosure requirements, including the penalties imposed on violaters both by the securities laws and by the courts under the common law. Finally, we look at regulation of another form of new business financing—franchising.

The chapter closes with an Issue reading that concerns a growing problem with franchises. How much change in a franchise organization is the parent company allowed to impose on the franchisees?

CORPORATE FINANCE AND EARLY REGULATION

The issuance and sale of securities is a principal means through which corporations are financed. The efficient operation of the securities markets is vital to the business community. As Professor Ratner indicates, however, the efficient operations of the securities markets have important implications beyond providing a means through which corporations can raise capital:

> Securities occupy a unique and important place in American life. . . . They are the instruments through which business enterprises and government

entities raise a substantial proportion of the funds with which to finance new capital construction. They are the instruments in which many millions of Americans invest their savings to provide for their retirement income, or education of their children, or in hopes of achieving a higher standard of living. And, inevitably, they are the instruments by which unscrupulous promoters and salespeople prey on those hopes and desires and sell worthless paper to many thousands of people every year.

Securities and Corporate Finance

Broadly defined, a *security* is a written instrument that provides evidence of *debt*—such as a corporate note or bond—or of *equity ownership*—such as a certificate of preferred or common stock. Securities differ from other commodities in that they have no intrinsic value in themselves—corporations could create them virtually for nothing. Thus, securities represent value in something else. The value of a corporation's stock depends on the expected future profitability of the corporation as reflected in the price investors are willing to pay for that stock.

Debt
The capital needs of a corporation can be financed through debt or equity. *Debt financing* involves selling bonds or borrowing money by contract. A debt instrument issued by a corporation usually specifies the following:

1. Amount of the debt.
2. Length of the debt period.
3. Debt repayment method.
4. Rate of interest charged to the sum borrowed.

Thus, debt financing involves incurring a liability. A corporation can sell $1 million worth of bonds to the public, promise to redeem the bonds in one year, and pay the bondholders 10 percent interest on the sum borrowed. In addition, the bondholders can trade those debt instruments in either formal markets— such as the stock market—or informal markets.

Equity
Equity financing, on the other hand, involves raising funds through the sale of a corporation's stock. It is termed equity financing because purchasers of a share of stock gain an ownership, or equitable, interest in the corporation. That is, shareholders have a claim on a portion of the future profits of the corporation. The corporation, in contrast to its use of debt financing, is under no liability to repay shareholders the amount they have invested.

For example, a corporation may issue one million shares of common stock at a price of $10 per share to raise $10 million. Each share sold represents a right to one-millionth of the annual profits of the corporation. Investors will be inclined to buy shares in the corporation only if they feel their share in the profits will be sufficient to provide them a competitive rate of return on their investment. The officers of the corporation, however, are under no obligation beyond making reasonable efforts to make a profit and cannot make enforceable promises about future profit rates. As in the case of bonds, unless prohibited by contract, corporate stock can also be traded on either formal or informal markets.

How Much Stock?
More than 50 million people in the United States own either common or preferred stock in a corporation. Stock ownership in the United States is evenly divided between men and women. Most investors are investing in securities to provide themselves with retirement income and funds for their children's education.

About $5 trillion worth of securities exist in the United States, about half of which are in publicly traded stock while the rest are in debt such as government bonds. As Figure 18–1 shows, the market value of equity, mostly common stocks, has grown dramatically in the past decade.

Origins of Securities Regulation

Public concern with "unscrupulous promoters and salesmen" led to the enactment of state legislation regulating the issuance and sale of securities. The first substantive securities statute was enacted by the state of Kansas in 1911. State securities laws became known as *blue sky laws*. Although scholars differ on the exact origin of the title, it is often attributed to an earlier Supreme Court opinion describing the purpose of state securities laws as attempting to prevent the "speculative schemes which would have no more basis than so many feet of blue sky." According to some accounts, promoters had gone door-to-door selling worthless securities to unwitting Kansas farmers. Later, the farmers discovered—after their money and the promoter were gone—that the securities had nothing more substantial backing them up than the blue sky.

Origins of Federal Regulation
Comprehensive federal regulation of securities began in the 1930s at a time of economic catastrophe. The key statutes were passed during the worst of the Great Depression. Over one-quarter of all jobs disappeared and national income fell one-third. Many people incorrectly blamed the depression on the stock market crash of 1929. In fact, the market was correctly forecasting the depression. Nevertheless, there was a common belief that professional manipulators on Wall Street needed to be controlled. Congress responded by enacting six statutes between 1933 and 1940:

1. The Securities Act of 1933
2. The Securities Exchange Act of 1934
3. The Public Utility Holding Company Act of 1935
4. The Trust Indenture Act of 1939
5. The Investment Company Act of 1940
6. The Investment Advisors Act of 1940

Most important are the Securities Act of 1933 and the Securities Exchange Act of 1934. The 1933 Act regulates the initial public offerings of securities. The Act's basic objectives are to require that investors be provided with material

Figure 18–1   Market Value of Equity Traded on All U.S. Exchanges

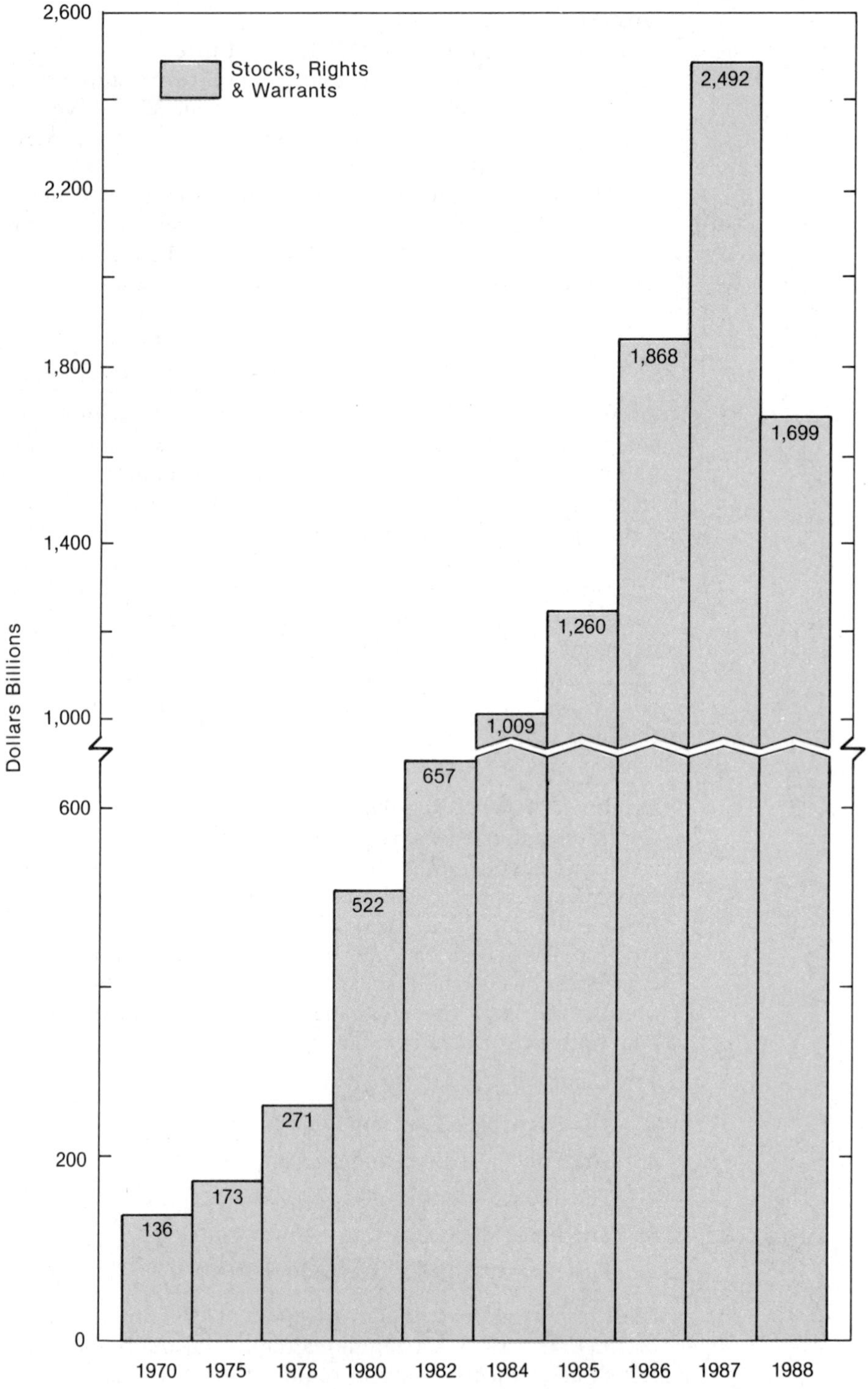

Source: *Annual Report,* Securities and Exchange Commission.

information about new securities offered for public sale and to prevent misrepresentation and fraud in the sale of those securities.

The 1934 Act extended federal securities regulation to include trading in securities that were already issued. The Act imposes disclosure requirements on corporations that have issued publicly held securities. The Act also provides for the regulation of securities markets and professionals. Congress hoped that these laws would assist investors in maintaining confidence in the market.

The Securities and Exchange Commission

The Securities and Exchange Commission (SEC) is the principal agency charged with the responsibility for the enforcement and administration of the federal securities laws. The Securities Exchange Act of 1934 provides that the SEC shall consist of five members appointed by the President for five-year terms. One of the members is appointed as the Chairman. The SEC's staff is composed of attorneys, accountants, financial analysts and examiners, engineers, and other professionals. The staff is divided into divisions and offices — including thirteen regional and branch offices located across the country.

DEFINING A SECURITY

Although Congress often provides vague regulatory mandates in its legislative enactments — allowing the courts and the regulatory agencies to define the terms and the scope of the legislation — this was not the case in defining the term security in the 1933 Act. Concerned about the ability of promoters to devise investment schemes with a variety of names, Congress provided a broad definition that goes well beyond "stocks" and "bonds." According to Section 2(1) of the 1933 Act the term *security* includes:

> . . . any note, stock, treasury stock, bond, debenture, evidence of indebtedness, certificate of interest or participation in any profit-sharing agreement, collateral-trust certificate, preorganization certificate or subscription, transferable share, investment contract, voting-trust certificate, certificate of deposit for a security, fractional undivided interest in oil, gas, or other mineral rights, or, in general, any interest or instrument commonly known as a "security," or any certificate of interest of participation in, temporary or interim certificate for, receipt for, guarantee of, or warrant or right to subscribe to or purchase, any of the foregoing.

As a general rule, despite Congress's definition of a security provided in Section 2(1), both the courts and the SEC look to the economic realities of an investment instrument in the process of determining whether it is a security. As the Supreme Court noted in *United Housing Foundation* v. *Forman* (1975):

> We reject . . . any suggestion that the present transaction, evidenced by the sale of shares called *stock*, must be considered a security transaction simply because the statutory definition of a security [under Section 2(1)] includes the words "any . . . stock."

That is, just because something is called a stock does not mean it is a security that falls within the jurisdiction of the federal security laws.

Supreme Court's *Howey* Test

Whether an investment instrument is a security determines if a security must comply with the legal requirements imposed on securities issuers. Note that investors have incentives to sue to have the court declare that an investment instrument is a security. If an investment instrument is a security investors have a higher degree of legal protection than that given to investments not qualifying as securities. In *Howey*, the Supreme Court established a test to determine when an investment instrument is to be considered a security for the purposes of federal regulation.

Securities and Exchange Commission v. W. J. Howey Company

United States Supreme Court
328 U.S. 293,
66 S.Ct. 1100
(1946)

Case Background. *Howey Company owned large tracts of land in central Florida, including a development called Howey-in-the-Hills and hundreds of acres of citrus groves. Half the groves were offered for the sale to the public. Prospective buyers were offered title to citrus grove acreage and a service contract under which Howey would cultivate, harvest, and sell the citrus grown on each parcel. Most investors in the citrus land lived outside Florida and bought the service contract.*

The SEC sued Howey, claiming that the sale of the acreage and service contracts was a security that should have been registered with the SEC before being offered for sale to the public. The federal district court and the U.S. Court of Appeals found for Howey. The SEC appealed to the U.S. Supreme Court.

Case Decision. Justice Murphy delivered the opinion of the Court.

The legal issue in this case turns upon a determination of whether, under the circumstances, the land sales contract, the warranty deed and the service contract together constitute an "investment contract" within the meaning of § 2(1). An affirmative answer brings into operation the registration requirements of § 5(a), unless the security is granted an exemption under the 1933 Securities Act.

* * *

In other words, an investment contract for purposes of the Securities Act means a contract, transaction or scheme whereby a person invests his money in a common enterprise and is led to expect profits solely from the efforts of the promoter of a third party, it being immaterial whether the shares in the enterprise are evidenced by formal certificates or by nominal interests in the physical assets employed in the enterprise.

* * *

The transactions in this case clearly involve investment contracts as so defined. The respondent companies are offering something more than fee simple interest in land, something different from a farm or orchard coupled with management services. They are offering an opportunity to contribute money and to share in the profits of a large citrus fruit enterprise managed and partly owned by respondents. They are offering this opportunity to persons who reside in distant localities and who lack the equipment and experience requisite to the cultivation, harvesting and marketing of the citrus products. Such persons have no desire to occupy the land or to develop it themselves; they are attracted solely by the prospects of a return on their investment.

* * *

Thus all the elements of a profit-seeking business venture are present here. The investors provide the capital and share in the earnings and profits; the promoters manage, control and operate the enterprise. It follows that the arrangements whereby the investors' interests are made manifest involve investment contracts, regardless of the legal terminology in which such contracts are clothed. The investment contracts in this instance take the form of land sales contracts, warranty deeds and service contracts which respondents offer to prospective investors. And respondents' failure to abide by the statutory and administrative rules in making such offerings, even though the failure results from a bona fide mistake as to the law, cannot be sanctioned under the Act.

*   *   *

Case Holding. *The Supreme Court agreed with the SEC that Howey had violated the Securities Act of 1933 by not registering the land sales with the SEC as a security before making the sales to the public.*

Case Questions

1. Suppose Howey had sold the plots of land to numerous investors but there was no offer to manage the land as citrus groves. Would it still have been a security?

2. Justice Frankfurter, in a dissenting opinion, noted that almost 20 percent of the land purchasers did not sign a management contract with Howey, since it was voluntary and not required to make a land purchase. Did the Supreme Court majority seem to violate their own four-part test?

The test developed by the Court in *Howey* has been applied countless times in the forty years since the case was decided. The *Howey* test holds that for an investment instrument to be classified as a security for the purpose of federal regulation, it must contain four basic elements:

1. The investment of money
2. In a common enterprise
3. With an expectation of profits
4. Generated solely from the efforts of persons other than the investors.

Defining the Four Elements

The first element, *the investment of money*, requires that an investor turn over some money to someone else for investment purposes. The second element, *in a common enterprise*, means that the investment is not the property of the investor, such as the investor's own warehouse or automobile. Rather, the investor's capital has been pooled with the capital of other investors so that each investor owns an undivided interest in the investment. An investor who invests in General Motors Corporation stock, for example, does not have a right to go to a General Motors factory and demand an automobile or other property from the company equal in value to the money the investor has invested in the company. The investor has a claim only to a share of future earnings as set forth in the contract that accompanied the security. Even though stock owners (or shareholders) own a portion of the company, they own an undivided interest in the company. That is, the shareholders cannot divide the property of the company among themselves unless they first agree to liquidate the company.

The third and fourth elements, *the expectation that profits will be generated by the efforts of persons other than the investor*, require that the investor not have direct control over the work that makes the investment a success or failure. The SEC and the courts, however, have taken a liberal view of the requirement that the profits be generated by other persons, ruling that a security will still be found to exist when most of the efforts to produce the profits will be by other persons. Thus, the president of a corporation who purchases shares of the corporation's stock will be found to have purchased a security because most of the profits of the corporation will have been generated through the work of others.

Application of the Securities Definition

Since many investment opportunities go bad, there are numerous suits claiming securities fraud. For a claim to be tried under the standards imposed by the federal securities laws, the investment instrument must meet the *Howey* test of a security. In various cases, lower courts have broadened the scope of the *Howey* test, but the Supreme Court consistently returns to it.

In *International Brotherhood of Teamsters* v. *Daniel* (1979), the Court considered a case in which a member of the Teamsters Union had been cheated out of his pension by the union. In an effort to get his pension, Daniel sued the union, claiming that the pension fund run by the union, which was invested in securities, should itself have been registered as a security, and it was fraud not to have done so. The lower courts agreed, but the Supreme Court said no. While it sympathized with Daniel's plight, the Court held that pensions are a form of wages, so they are not securities. In *Reves* the Court again discussed the *Howey* test.

Reves v. Ernst & Young

United States Supreme Court

____ U.S. ____,
110 S.Ct. 945
(1990)

Case Background. *Farmer's Cooperative of Arkansas and Oklahoma (Co-Op) sold promissory notes, not backed by collateral or insurance, to raise money to support general business operations. The notes paid above market rates of interest and were called an "Investment program." Advertisements for the notes said "YOUR CO-OP has more that $11,000,000 in assets to stand behind your investments. The Investment is not Federal [sic] insured but it is . . . Safe . . . Secure . . . and available when you need it." When the Co-Op filed for bankruptcy in 1984, over 1,600 people held notes worth $10 million.*

Reves and other holders of the notes sued Ernst & Young, the firm that audited the Co-Ops's books, claiming that the accounting firm had failed to follow generally accepted accounting procedures in its audit, especially with respect to the value of the Co-Op's assets. They claimed that if Ernst & Young had valued the assets properly, the Co-Op's financial instability would have been obvious and the notes would not have been purchased. Hence, the accounting firm had violated the antifraud provisions of the securities laws. The note holders won a $6.1 million judgment. The appeals court reversed, holding that the notes were not securities under the federal securities law. The note holders appealed to the Supreme Court.

Case Decision. Justice Marshall delivered the opinion of the Court.

* * *

Congress' purpose in enacting the securities laws was to regulate *investments*, in whatever form they are made and by whatever name they are called.

* * *

An examination . . . makes clear . . . factors that this Court has held apply in deciding whether a transaction involves a "security." First, we examine the transaction to assess the motivations that would prompt a reasonable seller and buyer to enter into it. If the seller's purpose is to raise money for the general use of a business enterprise or to finance substantial investments and the buyer is interested primarily in the profit the note is expected to generate, the instrument is likely to be a "security." If the note is exchanged to facilitate the purchase and sale of a minor asset or consumer good, to correct for the seller's cash-flow difficulties, or to advance some other commercial or consumer purpose, on the other hand, the note is less sensibly described as a "security." . . .

Second, we examine the "plan of distribution" of the instrument . . . to determine whether it is an instrument in which there is "common trading for speculation or investment,". . . . Third, we examine the reasonable expectations of the investing public: The Court will consider instruments to be "securities" on the basis of such public expectations, even where an economic analysis of the circumstances of the particular transaction might suggest that the instruments are not "securities" as used in that transaction. . . .

Finally, we examine whether some factor such as the existence of another regulatory scheme significantly reduces the risk of the instrument, thereby rendering application of the Securities Acts unnecessary.

We conclude, then, that in determining whether an instrument denominated a "note" is a "security," courts are to apply the version of the "family resemblance" test that we have articulated here: a note is presumed to be a "security," and that presumption may be rebutted only by a showing that the note bears a strong resemblance (in terms of the four factors we have identified) to one of the enumerated categories of instrument. If an instrument is not sufficiently similar to an item on the list, the decision whether another category should be added is to be made by examining the same factors.

Applying the family resemblance approach to this case, we have little difficulty in concluding that the notes at issue here are "securities." . . .

The Co-Op sold the notes in an effort to raise capital for its general business operations, and purchasers bought them in order to earn a profit in the form of interest. Indeed, one of the primary inducements offered purchasers was an interest rate constantly revised to keep it slightly above the rate paid by local banks and savings and loans. From both sides, then, the transaction is most naturally conceived as an investment in a business enterprise rather than as a purely commercial or consumer transaction.

As to the plan of distribution, the Co-Op offered the notes over an extended period to its 23,000 members, as well as to nonmembers, and more than 1,600 people held notes when the Co-Op filed for bankruptcy. . . .

The third factor—the public's reasonable perceptions—also supports a finding that the notes in this case are "securities". We have consistently identified the fundamental essence of a "security" to be its character as an "investment." The advertisements of the notes here characterized them as "investments," and there were no countervailing factors that would have led a reasonable person to question this characterization. In these circumstances, it would be reasonable for a prospective purchaser to take the Co-Op at its word.

Finally, we find no risk-reducing factor to suggest that these instruments are not in fact securities. The notes are uncollateralized and uninsured.

* * *

For the foregoing reasons, we conclude that the demand notes at issue here fall under the "note" category of instruments that are "securities" under the 1933 and 1934 Acts.

* * *

Case Holding. *The Supreme Court reversed the Court of Appeals, holding that the unsecured notes sold met the four-part test of when a note is a security under the federal securities law.*

Case Questions

1. Since the list of items in the 1933 Act that defines securities says "any note," why is not every note a security?
2. Should the accounting firm be held responsible for the losses of the investors here? What if they did the audit in good faith, not knowing that the results would be used to promote the sale of the notes?

Securities Exempt from Regulation

Some securities have been made exempt from federal securities regulation. The most important class of securities exempted by both the 1933 and 1934 Acts consists of debt issued or guaranteed by a government—federal, state, or local. Since the defaults of New York City and Cleveland on some bond issues, however, there have been discussions in Congress that have raised the possibility of removing this privileged status from government debt and making it stand the same tests as private sector securities.

The 1933 Act (but not the 1934 Act) also provides an exemption for securities issued by banks, religious and other charitable organizations, savings and loan associations, motor carriers subject to regulation by the Interstate Commerce Commission, insurance policies, and annuity contracts. Most of these securities are subject to control by other federal agencies, such as the Federal Reserve System.

In general, an exempted security is not subject to the registration and disclosure requirements of the federal statutes. However, the security still may be subject to the Acts' general anti-fraud and civil liability provisions.

DISCLOSURE REQUIREMENTS

It is generally asserted that the principal justification for the securities laws is to assure that investors are provided with adequate and accurate information upon which to base investment decisions. To the extent that managers of a corporation (or any other individuals with information about a corporation that is not readily available to the investing public) are able to use information about a corporation to the disadvantage of ordinary investors, confidence in the securities markets may be damaged. To alleviate this perceived information and fairness problem, the state and federal securities laws require corporations to disclose material information both before the initial sale of securities and after as they are being traded in the market place.

Disclosure Requirements Under the 1933 Act

The 1933 Act requires that issuers of securities fully *disclose* all material information regarding a security, its backers, and its intended use to prospective investors before the securities are sold. Disclosure is accomplished under the Act by filing a *registration statement* with the SEC. The registration process is intended to provide investors with sufficient and accurate information on material facts concerning the corporation and the securities it is proposing to sell. With that information, it is expected that investors can make a realistic appraisal of the merits of offered securities, and exercise informed judgment in determining whether to purchase them.

The Registration Statement

The registration statement consists of two parts. The first part is the *prospectus*—a document providing the legal offering of the sale of the security. The second part, which is often referred to as *items-and-answers*, consists of the disclosure of detailed information in response to specific questions by the SEC. In general, the registration process is intended to provide prospective investors with information on the following:

- The security issuers' properties and businesses.

- Significant provisions of the security to be offered for sale and their relationship to the offerors' other securities.

- Information about the management background and current status of the offerors.

- Financial statements certified by independent public accountants.

The Act provides that registration statements become effective on the 20th day after filing is completed. The SEC may at its discretion, however, advance or delay the date if the SEC deems it appropriate after considering the interests of the investors and the public, the adequacy of publicly available information, and the ease with which the facts about the new offering can be disseminated and understood. Table 18–1 shows the growth in the volume of securities registered for sale.

Table 18–1   Volume of New Securities Registered With SEC

Year	Number of Registrations	Cash Sales by Issuers (in $ millions)		
		Common Stock & Other Equity	Bonds & Notes	Total
1948	435	$ 1,678	$ 2,817	$ 5,032
1958	813	5,998	6,857	13,282
1968	2,417	22,092	14,036	37,268
1978	3,037	25,330	23,251	50,709
1988	5,853	100,259	233,598	343,159

Note: Total figure also includes preferred stock sales. Source: *Annual Report*, SEC.

The Prospectus. A prospectus condenses the longer registration statement provided to the SEC and is designed to help investors evaluate a security before purchase. A preliminary version of the prospectus is called a *red herring* (because of the red ink used on the first page). It is used by securities brokers to interest potential investors in a forthcoming offering. The prospectus states that it is not an offer to sell and is contingent on final approval.

Items-and-Answers. Unlike the prospectus, which is printed as a pamphlet and provides information in a narrative fashion, the second part of the registration statement consists of formal items-and-answers. More history on the issuers is required, especially about their financial background and past experience with securities. The SEC also may require special information about the proposed business or the issuers. This information may be used by professional investment analysts who wish to study the offering in detail. The items-and-answers disclosure document is not distributed to prospective investors, but it is available for public inspection at the SEC.

Review by the SEC

The SEC cannot rule on the merits of an offering (that is, the likelihood of success of the proposed business as perceived by the reviewing official), but it can require issuers to make high-risk factors clear and prominent in the prospectus so as to discourage wary buyers. Similarly, if the proposed business involves something that strikes the examiner as strange, such as a peculiar financial arrangement for the underwriters or managers, that fact may need to be highlighted. The SEC can issue a *stop order* to prohibit sale of securities until the registration statement is amended to satisfy the examiners. This power can slow the registration process and may quash an offering thought undesirable by the SEC staff.

Shelf Registration

The SEC allows *shelf registration* of securities offerings by certain issuers. Shelf registration means that a company can register a new security offering, but all of the security need not be sold at one time. Rather, the securities can be put "on the shelf" to be sold when the time is right. Hence, if a company wishes to sell $200 million of new stock over a two-year period, it need not sell the stock all at once or have separate registrations each time it wishes to sell some of the stock.

Shelf registration is available only to blue-chip companies—companies with a track record of obeying SEC requirements in the past and having a minimum of $150 million market value of voting stock held by people not affiliated with the company except for their stock ownership (called a *float*) or a float of $100 million and an annual trading volume of shares of stock of at least three million. Once the registration of the new stock offering has been approved, the offerors need only amend the registration statement to reflect fundamental changes in any of the information provided.

Shelf registration is popular with stock issuers because it allows them to raise capital at the most opportune times by having the more flexible registration process. Issuers can "dribble" the stock into the market to try to maximize the price received for the shares. The rule has also reduced the cost of the registration process by eliminating much repetition in registering one stock offering after another.

The Costs of Registration

Even for small securities offerings, say for $5 million, the registration process is expensive. The prospective issuer must hire such professionals as an experienced securities attorney, a certified public accountant, and a printer for the prospectus. The bill may run $100,000, excluding the expense of hiring an *underwriter* (the investment banker who will market the securities). The underwriter's fee may be as high as $500,000 for a $5 million offering. To avoid some costs of the registration process and other regulations, one may consider selling the security through a transaction that makes the security exempt from registration.

Exemptions from Registration

As noted before, some securities, such as government bonds, are generally exempt from the jurisdiction of the securities laws. All other securities are subject to SEC jurisdiction, although they may qualify for an *exemption from registration*. This generally means that they are exempt only from some, but not all, securities regulations. It also means that the securities are exempt only so long as they meet the requirements of the exemption. If a provision of the exemption is violated, the securities may lose their exemption and be subject to full registration.

Only certain transactions involving a security are exempt from registration. That is, the initial *sale* of the securities may be an exempt transaction. The securities are never exempt from the securities laws. Also, even if a transaction qualifies for an exemption from federal registration, state securities laws must be checked. States often have more stringent rules for exemptions, and registration at the state level may still be required.

Private Placement Exemption

Section 4(2) of the 1933 Act provides that registration is not necessary for transactions by an issuer not involving any public offering. Because of the vagueness of the law, the SEC and the courts have been forced to draw the boundaries of this important exemption. In some years, more securities have been offered through *private placement* than through public offerings. The large-volume users of the exemption are those placing large blocks of securities with institutional investors—most often pension funds or insurance companies. In the case of such sophisticated investors, the SEC is less concerned than it might be if the investors were thought to be less able to protect themselves in purchases of unregistered securities.

Regulation D. To reduce the uncertainty of what will qualify as a private placement, the SEC adopted Regulation D to spell out the elements of private placement exemptions.

- *Accredited investors* are those presumed sophisticated enough to evaluate investment opportunities without the benefit of an SEC-approved prospectus and wealthy enough to bear the risk of loss if an investment goes bad. Accredited investors may participate in private placement offerings of securities. Institutions, like banks and insurance companies, are accredited investors. The rule for individuals is that they have an annual income of at least $200,000 and a net worth of at least $1 million. Other investors are classified as unaccredited investors.

- Certain companies may make exempt offerings of up to $500,000 in securities with only minimal restrictions. These offerings may be sold to unaccredited investors.

- Placements involving up to $5 million in securities can involve up to thirty-five unaccredited investors (and any number of accredited investors). Unaccredited investors must be provided information similar to that provided in a registration statement.

- Securities offerings of over $5 million may be made only to accredited investors to keep the private placement exemption.

It must be emphasized that the rules regarding all such offers are complex. Even though the offerings may be exempt from registration, there is usually a reporting requirement to the SEC about the offers, and the law requires that the investors be given information essentially the same that they would have received in a prospectus. To prevent the private placements from becoming a cheap way around the full registration requirements of most public offerings, there are restrictions on the resale of securities bought by investors in private placements.

Rule 144A. Despite the existence of relaxed registration requirements for small securities offerings, the dollar volume is quite small. Private placements are most common for large security issues, mostly bonds, that are sold to institutional investors. In 1989, $165 billion was issued in private placements, about one-third of all issues.

This is expected to grow rapidly since the SEC adopted Rule 144A in 1990, which exempts U.S. and foreign security issuers from registration requirements for the sale of bonds and stocks to institutions with a portfolio of at least $100 million in securities. Further, securities issued to such large institutions may be traded among similarly qualified institutions without registration or disclosure requirements. These large blocks of securities are often traded on "Portal," an electronic bulletin board approved by the SEC, to facilitate trading of Rule 144A issues.

Intrastate Offering Exemption
Section 3(a)(11) of the 1933 Act exempts from registration "any security which is part of an issue offered and sold only to persons resident within a single State . . . where the issuer of such security is . . . a corporation incorporated and doing business within such State." Hence, a security will qualify for the *intrastate exemption* from registration if the business issuing the security: (1) is located primarily within the state in which it is selling securities, and (2) sells securities only to residents of the state. The SEC views this as a method of financing local industries. An offer or sale of one of the securities to a nonresident, however, would eliminate the exemption and require the security to be registered.

Rule 147, issued by the SEC, states that the business must have its principal office in the state in question, and must do at least 80 percent of its business—sales, assets, and use of proceeds from the security offering—in the state. Further, none of the securities may be sold to nonresidents by anyone—offeror or purchasers who wish to resell—until at least nine months after the sale of the last security in the offering; the exemption may otherwise be lost.

Since most states have registration requirements similar to those of the SEC, this exemption would not be useful in most states because similar registration costs would have to be incurred in any event. However, most states have exemptions from registration similar to the federal private placement exemption. In general, the state private placement exemptions are stricter than the federal exemptions; they allow fewer buyers and have other restrictions that limit their usefulness. Still, by following the private placement exemption of the state and by using the federal intrastate exemption, it is possible to avoid registration at both the state and federal level.

Disclosure Requirements Under the 1934 Act

While the 1933 Act imposes disclosure requirements on corporations issuing new securities, the 1934 Act imposes disclosure requirements on securities listed and registered for public trading on national securities exchanges, such as the New York Stock Exchange, or trading on the over-the-counter (OTC) market.

Public Companies

Section 12 of the 1934 Act requires the periodic disclosure of certain information about securities of publicly held companies. If a security was originally registered under the 1933 Act, it must be registered under the 1934 Act. Even if not registered under the 1933 Act, it must be registered under the 1934 Act if it is listed on a registered securities exchange (New York Stock Exchange, American Stock Exchange, etc.) or if it is traded *over-the-counter* and the company has $1 million or more in assets and five hundred or more shareholders.

Any company that has issued securities that have come to be publicly traded is referred to as a *publicly held company*. These companies are subject to the reporting requirements. A company that has fewer than 500 shareholders and does not allow its securities to be openly traded is called a *private company*. Its financial information is not available to the public. A company can go from being publicly held to private by buying up its stock so that it is held by fewer than 500 stockholders. There are a number of multibillion-dollar corporations in this category, the most notable being RJR-Nabisco, which "went private" when its $25 billion in stock was all purchased by an investment group called KKR.

10–K, 10–Q, and 8–K

Disclosure requirements apply to over 10,000 companies, most of which have securities traded in the OTC market. These companies must file reports on their securities. The most important report is the *10-K annual report*, an extensive audited financial statement similar in content to the information provided in the registration process under the 1933 Act. Companies must also file *quarterly 10-Q reports* with unaudited financial information and *monthly 8-K reports* if significant financial developments have occurred. As with initial securities registration, the purpose of these reports is to ensure the availability of comprehensive financial information to investors.

Disclosure Requirements Under State Laws

During the 1910s most states adopted securities regulations, usually called *blue sky laws*. The state laws were overshadowed by passage of the federal statutes in the 1930s, but still have substantial consequences for public securities issuers.

The *Uniform Security Act* (USA), a model state statute, has been adopted in over thirty states. However, the other states, notably California, New York, Illinois, and Texas, have their own statutes. If an issuer wants a security to be sold in every state it may require rather costly registration beyond the federal requirements, as the peculiarities of each state must be satisfied.

Exemptions

Like the federal laws, most states exempt securities issued by governmental units and certain institutions subject to other regulation, such as banks. Most importantly, most states exempt securities listed (traded) on major stock exchanges or over-the-counter. Hence, in most states the regulations are likely to pose costly requirements only on small securities issuers.

States that have adopted the USA allow private placement exemptions for securities offerings sold to no more than twenty-five state residents who are buying the securities for investment, not resale. Similarly, about half the states have adopted the SEC's Regulation D, so compliance with that satisfies both the SEC and some states. Most states that have adopted the USA also hold that so long as they are notified of an SEC registration, the state is satisfied and the security is legal for sale in the state.

Merit Regulation

Unlike the federal securities laws and the states that have the USA, which set information requirements for securities registration, some states have quality requirements, called *merit regulations*, that must be met before a security is approved for sale in the state. Differing among the states, these statutes set guidelines that are interpreted by the state securities commissioner case by case. This is generally believed to result in discrimination against offerings that are small or are being promoted by an organization or promoter with limited experience. Because the commissioners are less certain about the likelihood of financial success of a new business, they set stricter requirements for such promoters than are set for offerings by well-established companies. The requirements might be set so as to be simply impossible to meet. If the state securities commission thinks that a new stock offering is too risky, the offering will be barred. For example, the state of Massachusetts barred the sale of stock in the then-new Apple Computer Company.

SECURITIES FRAUD

The registration and disclosure requirements of the 1933 and 1934 Acts do not prevent the sale of stock in risky, poorly managed, or unprofitable companies. Rather, the Acts are intended to help ensure the adequate and accurate disclosure of required material facts concerning the corporation and the securities it is selling. However, the failure to follow the disclosure requirements imposed by the 1933 and 1934 Acts—for example, by providing false and misleading statements—may result in public or private suits for *securities fraud.* Most securities fraud caused by false and misleading information occurs in the registration materials, but it can also be found in information filed during later disclosure, such as a 10–K annual report filed under the 1934 Act requirements.

Securities Fraud Under the Common Law

Because contractual obligations and rights are created in the sale of a security, an investor can rely on common-law fraud standards for protection. To establish liability under common-law fraud, the injured investor must show the following:

1. A misstatement of a material fact—that is, incorrect important information about the security or some aspect of the business has been passed to the buyer.
2. Scienter—Intent to defraud. That is, the seller wanted to trick the buyer and intentionally deceived him or her to do so.
3. Knowledge on the part of the seller that a misstatement has been made.
4. Reliance by the recipient on the misstatement in the transaction—that is, the buyer believed what was said and relied on it in buying the stock.
5. Privity between the plaintiff and defendant—that is, they must have been in a contractual arrangement with each other.
6. Proximate cause—that is, a causal relationship between reliance on the misstatement and the subsequent losses must exist.
7. Damages—that is, money was lost by the buyer.

Investors who think they have been injured and sue for damages, as in the *Reves* case discussed earlier, often have difficulty establishing common-law fraud. Thus, injured investors generally rely on the antifraud provisions of the 1933 and 1934 Acts in bringing an action against the seller.

Statutory Fraud Under the 1933 Act

The 1933 Act establishes a standard for truthfulness in securities dealings higher than that for common-law fraud. Section 11 established civil liabilities for *misleading statements* or *material omissions* in securities registration material. Any person who acquires a security covered by a registration statement that contains false or misleading information, or fails to include information that was important to a decision to purchase, may sue to recover any losses incurred in that purchase. For example, in the *Reves* case, the notes were not registered as securities, but since they were held to be securities, there may be recovery by investors due to the misleading information they were given when they bought the notes.

This liability holds whether or not the security was registered—all securities are covered by the law of securities fraud. This standard was extended by the 1934 Act to cover misleading information in all disclosures required under that statute, so that investors have protection during the life of the security. As we will see in Chapter 19, securities fraud also arises after the registration and sale of securities.

Statutory Fraud Under the 1934 Act

Like the 1933 Act, Section 10(b) of the 1934 Act provides that it is unlawful for any person "to use or employ, in connection with the purchase or sale of any security registered on a national securities exchange or any security not so registered, any manipulative or deceptive device or contrivance in contravention of such rules and regulations as the Commission may prescribe. . . . " It provides the broadest base for bringing a securities fraud action, and it has come to be used in litigation more than any other part of the Act.

The SEC adopted Rule 10(b)-5 to enforce Section 10(b) of the 1934 Act. The rule is broad in scope:

> It shall be unlawful for any person, directly or indirectly, by the use of any means or instrumentality of interstate commerce, or of the mails, or of any facility of any national securities exchange,
> 1. to employ any device, scheme, or artifice to defraud,
> 2. to make any untrue statement of a material fact or to omit to state a material fact necessary in order to make the statements made, in the light of the circumstances under which they were made, not misleading, or
> 3. to engage in any act, practice, or course of business which operates or would operate as a fraud or deceit upon any person, in connection with the purchase or sale of any security.

The rule applies to all securities, registered or not. Although punishment for violations is not prescribed, courts decided decades ago that usual rules of civil liability would apply for damages inflicted on others. Since the rule does not state specific offenses, it has been left to the SEC and the courts to decide how strict the standards will be and what will constitute offenses.

Penalties for Securities Fraud

If an investor buys a security after receiving inaccurate information about the security knowingly provided by the issuer, the investor may sue the issuer to rescind the transaction and recover damages. Damages are usually the difference in price between what the investor paid and what the security was worth when sold. In addition, Section 11 of the 1933 Act modifies the common-law fraud action to make it easier for the injured investor to recover.

Importantly, the privity requirement is relaxed, allowing injured investors to bring an action against all parties connected with the preparation of the securities: every director of the company; the chief executive, financial, and accounting officers of the company; every underwriter involved in the transaction; every accountant, lawyer, and other expert who helped prepare the registration material; and any other person who signed the registration statement. All parties are held to high standards of professional care, which is one reason for the high cost of preparing all disclosure materials. Everyone involved can be responsible for material omissions or misleading statements made in the package by others.

The SEC can also recommend that the Department of Justice bring criminal charges against violators. To warrant a criminal action, the offender must have engaged in the perpetration of fraud in any offer or sale of securities. The criminal penalty may involve fines and imprisonment.

FRANCHISE REGULATION

Sales by *franchise* establishments are approaching $1 trillion per year. While automobile dealerships and gasoline stations have traditionally been franchised, this method of organizing business has spread rapidly to many other sales establishments, as Table 18–2 shows. Over 80 percent of franchise establishments are owned and operated by franchisees. The remainder are owned by the parent company, which hires the managers and employees. Franchises employ over seven million people.

While some franchises, like McDonalds, are almost always very successful, as in any business there are failures. Many franchises are sold with little experience in operation. Purchasers of some of those franchises have lost all of their investment, which can be a sizable part (or all) of the purchaser's life savings, and the result can be unemployment for people who devoted all their work time to the franchise operation.

For example, you may agree to pay the Tasty Ant company $10,000 for the exclusive right to distribute Tasty Ant Company-produced chocolate-covered ants in your state. Regardless of how hard you work and how good the product is, you may discover that the market for chocolate-covered ants is smaller than anticipated. The result could be that you are out your $10,000, plus the cost of the inventory you purchased and the value of your time spent pushing the product.

FTC Franchise Rule

To try to reduce the number of investors who became involved in dubious franchise operations, the FTC enacted the *Franchise Rule*. The Rule requires the seller of franchise or business opportunities to give prospective buyers a

Table 18–2   Franchised Businesses

Kind of Business	Number (in thousands)		Sales (in billions)	
	1970	1988	1970	1988
Total Franchises	**396.3**	**509.3**	**$119.8**	**$639.6**
Auto/truck dealers	37.2	27.8	58.8	305.6
Gasoline stations	222.0	112.0	29.3	91.9
Restaurants	32.6	90.8	4.6	63.2
Retailing (nonfood)	30.7	52.9	13.1	28.5
Automotive products	20.4	41.5	1.9	13.7
Convenience stores	8.8	17.2	1.7	13.6
Hotels and motels	3.4	10.4	3.5	19.7

Source: U.S. Dept. of Commerce, *Franchising in the U.S. Economy.*

detailed disclosure document at least ten days before any money changes hands or before the buyer is legally committed to a purchase. Much like SEC disclosure documents for new stock offerings, the Franchise Rule's disclosure document includes important information about the business, including:

- Names, addresses, and telephone numbers of other purchasers.
- An audited financial statement of the seller.
- The background and experience of the business's key executives.
- The responsibilities that the buyer and the seller will have to each other once the purchase is made.

This document enables prospective investors to know about the background of the business and, if the information is not true, allows a legal basis for the buyer to attempt recovery directly or for the FTC to bring an action against the seller. While similar to SEC regulations, this Rule was not implemented by the SEC because such business opportunities are not securities.

State Regulation

Many states have recently passed statutes to regulate the sale of franchises. The FTC Franchise Rule sets a minimum national disclosure standard that states may go beyond. At least thirteen states have adopted a *Uniform Franchise Offering Circular* (UFOC) that requires financial disclosures by franchisors to prospective franchisees that go beyond the FTC requirements. In particular, the UFOC requires franchise sellers to give details about the earnings history of the company and of franchises in existence. Some franchise sellers give no information about earnings or have exaggerated actual earnings.

Rule Violations

An example of a Franchise Rule violation is the Tuff-Tire case. The FTC charged the Tuff-Tire Company and its officers with violations of the Franchise Rule. Tuff-Tire misrepresented to potential investors that franchisees could earn from $110,000 to $410,000 annually—amounts that existing franchisees were claimed to have earned. The FTC charged that there was no reasonable basis for these claims and that the company did not provide prospective franchisees with pre-sale information about earnings claims required by the Rule.

The Tuff-Tire Company sold franchises called "Mr. Tuff-Tire" that sold a product for car and truck tires that was to seal punctures and prevent flat tires. Franchisees paid between $2,000 and $98,000 for their franchises. The Justice Department, at the request of the FTC, filed a complaint in federal district court. In 1987, the court ordered the defendants not to violate the Rule in the future and required them to repay $1.4 million in refunds to eighty-seven people who bought franchises based on misrepresentation. The franchisors were also ordered to pay $870,000 in civil penalties.

The FTC sued Fax Corp. of America in 1990 for violations of the Franchise Rule. Fax Corp. sold about 500 franchises for an average of $58,000 each. The franchisees would set up public fax machines that are activated by credit cards. The FTC charged that besides failing to abide by the disclosure requirements of the Rule, the company made false claims about earnings, and failed to refund franchise fees paid by franchisees, as it claimed it would. Investors may have lost several million dollars in this case, which was not unique.

INTERNATIONAL PERSPECTIVES: AMERICAN FRANCHISES IN EUROPE

INTERNATIONAL

PERSPECTIVES

The European Economic Community's move to tear down barriers to trade inside Europe in 1992 (discussed in Chapter 21) has had many American companies scrambling to get into Europe. The existence of a single market as large as the United States is appealing to firms that could not afford to open operations in Europe on a country-by-country basis. Firms are also concerned that if they do not get a foot in the door right away, they may not be able to get in later if the EEC erects trade barriers against the rest of the world.

American franchisers, over four hundred of which operate about 40,000 outlets outside the United States, face problems in Europe that make operations more difficult than they are in the United States. In the EEC, it is illegal for a franchiser, such as McDonald's, to contract with a single company, say Coca-Cola, to supply all its franchisees with certain products. McDonald's cannot even require its franchisees in Europe to sell Coke. But they can require their franchisees to put a certain amount of catsup on each hamburger.

Such constraints make it difficult to achieve certain economies of scale from the use of standardized operations, quality control, and common advertisements. Further, the details of such regulations are subject to change as EEC officials work in Brussels to write new rules. While European franchisers are used to working within these constraints, Japanese and American firms face a set of legal obstacles that strike at the heart of their operations.

SUMMARY

This chapter has considered the importance of the securities markets in financing ventures and what is considered a security for purposes of the federal securities law. The operation of the stock market is a mystery to many people. The difficulty in understanding the stock market and its association with the Great Depression led to strict securities legislation. The Securities Act of 1933 and the 1934 Act, were designed in part to correct perceived abuses suffered by investors.

The 1933 Act requires new issues of securities to be registered with the SEC. Detailed information about the business venture to be financed and the sponsors of the venture must be provided in a certain format for public inspection before a stock can be sold. The expense of the registration procedure is an incentive to avoid an investment's being called a security. However, the courts have looked to the economic realities of an investment opportunity to decide whether a security exists. Promoters may save costs by use of the private placement or intrastate offering exemptions.

Securities include any (1) investment of money (2) in a common enterprise where there is (3) an expectation of profits (4) from the efforts of persons other than the investors. This legal definition is intended to include any investment device that may be invented that meets these general criteria.

Whether or not a security is registered, prospective investors must be provided detailed information about the business—who is involved, how much money is to be raised for various purposes, and the plan of action. Companies that issue publicly traded securities must provide continued financial disclosure to the SEC under the Securities Exchange Act of 1934. Monthly, quarterly, and annual financial reports must be filed. All such information disclosed to investors is subject to securities fraud. All parties involved with a securities issue can be held liable for material omissions or misleading statements in the disclosures. Violators may be subject to private suits under common-law fraud and civil and criminal penalties under the statutes.

Franchised businesses have grown rapidly, and there are many success stories. To reduce the likelihood of an uninformed investment in a franchise business and to expose the sellers of franchises to federal prosecution for misleading franchise buyers, a prospectus that states the financial and managerial history and plans of a franchise operation must be given to potential franchisees.

Should Franchisers Be Allowed to Change Methods of Operation?

Thousands of owners of Kentucky Fried Chicken franchises filed suit in 1990 against the parent company for reasons explained in this reading. This kind of action has become more common, as franchise companies seek to improve the operation of the entire franchise chain, which often requires franchisees to invest substantial sums to upgrade their operations. The parent company pushes for these moves to keep the franchise system competitive. Fights arise because franchise contracts specify what franchisees must do. Years later, the franchiser may think it necessary to rewrite the contract. The question is, who should run the show, the franchiser or the franchisees?

Firms Try to Tighten Grip on Franchisees

Jeffrey A. Tannenbaum and Barbara Marsh*

Kentucky Fried Chicken Corp. wants big changes in its contracts with franchisees—requiring them, for example, to remodel restaurants every seven years—to stay competitive with other fast-food chains.

But many franchisees are resisting. More than 300 are gathering in Scottsdale, Ariz., for their regular three-day winter meeting, which starts today, to plot strategy. John R. Neal, a Columbia, Tenn., operator, says Kentucky Fried Chicken is going overboard trying to weed out a handful of problem operators. "You're talking about taking a baseball bat to beat an gnat to death." Mr. Neal says.

The dispute illustrates the upheavals taking place at many older franchise systems. Franchiser's desire to overhaul their operations often puts them at odds with old allies: their longtime franchisees. But some franchisers say they'll be better off even if they alienate—or lose—longtime franchisees, many of whom they see as obstructing progress.

As its older contracts with Holiday Inns franchisees have expired, Holiday Corp. has insisted on tougher terms and more investment in remodeling and expansion. It's part of a strategy calling for fancier hotels and higher room rates. Holiday says it forced out some balky franchisees, and others have quit. Some 185 former Holiday franchisees have joined rival Days Inns of America Inc., according to a Days Inns spokeswoman.

"Older franchise companies are facing a threat to their lives," says Patrick J. Boroian, the president of Francorp, an Olympia Fields, Ill., franchise consulting firm. "They need to set and maintain new standards. And they need their franchisees to make the necessary investments." But the franchisees say the franchisers often are changing the rules in midgame—to their own advantage.

Paradoxically, the very contracts that accounted for many franchisers' early success are impairing their ability to raise standards now. Typically, the franchisers achieved rapid growth by attracting franchi-

–continued

—continuing

ment decisions. And the franchisers locked themselves in to long contracts—such as 20 years for most KFC outlets.

At first, franchisers had just what they wanted: Zealous franchisees, eagerly building uniform facilities into regional or national chains. But as the original stores aged—in some case growing downright shabby—the franchisers often couldn't require their operators to do anything about it. Nor could they require franchisees to update their businesses—by adding salad bars to hamburger joints, for example.

"There are always going to be some franchisees who don't want to spend an extra cent," says David J. Kaufmann, a franchise-industry lawyer in New York. Others may disagree with a franchiser's new strategy, lack the energy to make changes or, after years of relative independence, resent the prospect of operating under a heavier hand at national headquarters.

As a result, some chains' uniformity—widely viewed as a key to success in franchising—has broken down as old outlets fail to match the decor and operating mode of newer ones. To avoid such problems, Mr. Kaufmann says, franchisers should periodically revise their contracts with franchisees. "They have to fine-tune everything in the contract, or else the whole system will die," he says.

Franchise-industry executives and analysts tell of systems so handicapped by old contracts that they became unattractive to potential investors. Hamstrung by old legal agreements, Marriott Corp. couldn't get many franchisees to spend more for improvements at aging Big Boy restaurants, says John J. Rohs, an analyst with Wertheim Schroder & Co. in New York. Marriott—which declines to comment on the old contracts—sold the Big Boy franchising operation in 1987 and now operates 235 of the chain's outlets as a franchisee.

Kentucky Fried Chicken is the largest chicken chain, but is has a host of problems. Its earnings are under pressure, and its rivals have been quicker to meet changing tastes

with new products, such as grilled-chicken sandwiches. And KFC, as one of the oldest chains, has many outlets not entirely up to its present standards.

The company, acquired by PepsiCo in 1986, is trying aggressively to modernize its franchisees. In 1988, in federal district court in Pensacola, Fla., KFC sued Martine's Corp., then a Florida franchisee with 74 restaurants, for alleged breach of contract. KFC said inspectors had discovered roach infestation and other problems at most Martine's units. Martine's denied the charges, but also argued that its contract with KFC, signed in 1959, didn't require it to comply with KFC's standards.

The parties settled their dispute, with KFC buying back some of Martine's restaurants; the others no longer are Kentucky Fried Chicken stores. No court ever ruled on Martine's claim that it didn't have to meet the franchiser's standards—which KFC disputed. But now KFC, with many aims besides enforcing cleanliness standards, is demanding stronger contracts with other franchisees.

KFC's 780 franchisees benefit from the chain's name, ads and buying power. In return, they pay KFC a royalty, or percentage of sales. But rather than simply renew its expiring contracts, KFC is trying to convert franchisees to a new, more demanding contract that would give the franchiser greater control over many aspects of the business.

The new contract eliminates a guarantee that each franchisee normally will be the only outlet within a 1½-mile radius. In many densely populated areas, the company figures, the market could support more stores. The new language also forbids a franchisee from going public or selling out to a public company. And it imposes the seven-year remodeling requirement; KFC says the current language specifies no time frame for remodelings.

"What we're really talking about is being competitive and offering superior cus-

—continued

—continuing

tomer services, and that means fixing up old restaurants," says Kentucky Fried Chicken spokesman.

But many franchisees fear losing the exclusivity of their franchises and the freedom to determine how they spend their own money. "The new contract is unacceptable—it would devalue our present businesses," says Robert P. Peck Sr., an Oklahoma City franchisee and president of the franchisee association.

The conflict over KFC's franchising terms began last March when company officials, meeting with franchisee representatives, proposed revising contract language used since 1976. The new language "is standard for what the [franchise] industry currently has," says KFC spokesman. But many franchisees say they were dismayed that KFC seemed adamant about pressing terms they considered unfair. And in August the new language, little changed from the draft, became effective for new KFC contracts and renewals.

The number of franchisees affected so far isn't clear—old contracts remain in effect until they expire—but many operators are outraged. About 400 franchisees, meeting later last August in Louisville, Ky., KFC's base, decided to sue KFC if it didn't relent. They voted to raise a $3.6 million legal war chest, assessing each franchisee $1,000 per store. And in November, in federal court in Louisville, several franchisees filed suit against KFC, charging that the new contract, among other things, breaches franchisees' contract-renewal rights. Pending the out-come of negotiations, though, the plaintiffs have held off serving the defendant with the suit—on which KFC declines to comment.

Neither side says much about the talks, but franchisees' fear of encroachment from competing KFC units appears to be a big issue. In federal court in Detroit, franchisee KFC Take Home of Plymouth Inc. is suing KFC for allegedly opening a company-owned restaurant too close to its Plymouth, Mich., outlet. KFC denies that it encroached on Take Home's outlet. Franchisees fear such disputes will become common without encroachment restrictions, which the new contract lacks.

Another issue is the new contract's forbidding franchisees from going public or selling out to a public company. KFC says private operators tend to be more focused and easier to deal with. Mr. Neal, the owner of 82 units, says this provision would limit his options if he were to sell someday—and thus reduce the selling price.

KFC isn't predicting the outcome of the dispute, but Mr. Peck, president of the franchisee group, expects a compromise. "You can't have everything you want," he says.

Questions

1. If a majority of existing franchisees believe the moves the franchiser wants to make are not worthwhile, is that not evidence that the franchiser must be unreasonable?

2. Could this problem be avoided by writing franchise contracts differently? That is, could the franchisers leave open the right to change the terms of the operations later?

REVIEW AND DISCUSSION QUESTIONS

1. Define the following terms:
   debt
   equity
   stock
   securities
   Howey test
   registration statements
   exemptions from registration
   periodic disclosure
   blue sky laws
   merit regulations
   securities fraud
   franchise

2. How is the price of stock determined? Is the current price of stock correct?

3. Which of the four elements of the *Howey* test appears to be missing in the *Howey* decision itself?

4. Is a condominium unit a security? What if it were used for vacations and were rented out most of the time?

5. What is the difference in the legal protection available to the purchasers of registered versus unregistered securities?

Case Questions

6. A developer announced that a new apartment building was to be constructed. To have first crack at a unit in the building, you would have to deposit $250 per room. Each room was called a share of stock in the building. If, for example, you wanted a six-room apartment, you had to buy six shares of stock and later pay the sale price or rental rate. The stock price was to be refunded at the time you sold your apartment or quit renting and left the building. You could not sell the stock to another person. Is this stock a security that falls under the 1933 Act? [*United Housing Foundation* v. *Forman*, 95 S.Ct. 2051, 421 U.S. 837 (1975)]

7. For ten years, a major certified public accounting firm audited the books of an investment company to prepare disclosure documents required by the SEC. The accountants never discovered that there was a big scam going on at the investment firm and that the head of the firm was stealing investors' funds—he cooked the books, and the accountants never found out. One day the head of the firm disappeared, leaving behind a mess and many unhappy investors. The investors sued the accounting firm to try to recover the money they lost, claiming that the accounting firm was liable for securities fraud. Who won? [*Ernst & Ernst* v. *Hochfelder*, 425 U.S. 185, 96 S.Ct. 1375 (1976)]

Policy Questions

8. The Securities Act of 1933 requires that a prospectus be given to all investors in securities before they purchase any security. Evidence is that investors pay little or no attention to these documents. Does the existence of this requirement give investors a false sense of confidence that the investment must be okay because the SEC has reviewed a prospectus? If so, is the prospectus a waste of resources, and does it also perhaps have a negative effect?

9. Registration of securities is regressive in impact. It is proportionally more expensive for small offerings than it is for large offerings, since most of the costs for preparing a $5 million offering are the same as they are for a $500 million offering. Critics charge that this gives big business an unfair advantage in the securities markets over small businesses. If this is true should there be more exemptions for small offerings than already exist?

10. The FTC Franchise Rule requires disclosure of information relevant to investor decisions about franchise opportunities. Do you think the FTC or some other agency should establish a board of experts to decide whether or not proposed franchises (or other investment opportunities) should be allowed to be marketed? In some cases, even if there is open and full disclosure, some investors will fall for silly schemes that have little chance of making money. Should these opportunities therefore be cut off before they are marketed?

Ethics Questions

11. You started the Triangular Frisbee Company as a small operation. When the product went over big, you decided to seek outside funding to build a larger company. Your lawyer explained to you the costs of SEC registration and securities disclosure in the case of a public stock offering. Your lawyer explains to you that you can avoid this by organizing as a corporation on the Caribbean island nation of Torlaga and selling stock in the corporation from there. U.S. investors simply buy your stock through a Torlaga stockbroker. This is much cheaper and quicker than U.S. registration. What are the pros and cons of this arrangement? Is it ethical to avoid compliance with American laws in this manner?

12. In Question 7, we saw a case where certified public accountants did not uncover a scam in the books they audited every year for over a decade. Suppose that they were held not guilty of securities fraud. Should the accounting firm make up the losses of the investors—that is, return their investment dollars—voluntarily even though not so mandated by the courts?

19 Regulating Financial Markets

C HAPTER 18 explained the use of securities in financing business and defined a security from the perspective of the Securities and Exchange Commission (SEC) and the courts. It also reviewed the regulatory requirements for new securities—what a corporation must do before selling securities. The Securities Act of 1933 states that if something is a security, it must be registered with the SEC before it can be sold to the public, unless it is sold under an exemption. Certain financial information must be made public for distribution to investors before a security can be offered to the public. Under the 1934 Securities Exchange Act, continuous disclosure of financial information will occur for as long as the security remains in the hands of the public. Failure to follow these disclosure laws may result in public or private suits for securities fraud.

The 1934 Act also ordered the SEC to regulate the markets in which securities are traded, regulate professionals in the securities markets, and control the manner in which other securities transactions take place. These laws have since been followed by various other statutes that regulate the operation of financial markets. This chapter reviews the key elements of these statutes.

The chapter closes with the Issues article, which discusses the controversial topic of whether insider trading should be regulated. Some economists have argued that insider information improves the efficiency of the securities markets and, therefore, should not be regulated. Those arguing for the regulation of insider trading assert that it injures investors (particularly small investors) and reduces confidence in securities markets. Former SEC Commissioner Charles C. Cox examines both sides of this controversial issue.

SECURITIES EXCHANGE ACT OF 1934

The primary purpose of the 1933 Act is to regulate securities at the time they are issued. Violations of that law can result in securities fraud actions by the government and by private investors. The *Securities Exchange Act* of 1934 says that once a security is out in the hands of the public, the issuers of the security must make periodic financial disclosures to the SEC. Securities fraud law, based on Section 10(b) of the 1934 Act, and the SEC's interpretation of Rule 10b–5, protect investors in the financial market.

The 1934 Act requires periodic disclosure to curb misrepresentation and deceit by securities issuers. The disclosure documents are available to securities owners and the general public. The Act also allows the SEC and investors to bring securities fraud suits for market manipulation and other acts that injure investors. Here we consider the major classes of suits for which liability may be imposed on parties involved in issuing securities to the public.

Liability for Misstatements

The 1933 Act imposes liability for omissions and misstatements in securities registration documents before the sale of a security. Under the 1934 Act, liability for *misstatements* or *omissions* about the financial status of a business enterprise that issued securities can be imposed on corporate officials or on those involved in preparing the information containing the misstatements. Securities fraud for misstatements can be based on any relevant business document that contains material omissions or misstatements: accountant reports, SEC disclosure documents, press releases, or public statements by executives.

Misleading information that would reasonably affect investment decisions by current or prospective securities owners includes misinformation about the present financial status or the future prospects of the enterprise that would affect the price of the security. For example, overly optimistic statements made by executives can cause favorable expectations about the future profits of a company, leading investors to bid up the price of the company's stock. When the statements are found to be false, the stock price falls, imposing losses on those who bought the stock on the basis of the positive statements. This is one of the most common grounds for private suits seeking damages based on a claim of *securities fraud*. In the *Reves* case in the last chapter, we saw a securities fraud suit based on misstatements about material financial information, made by an accounting firm, about a security issuer.

Directors and senior officers of businesses know they are legally responsible for the consequences of misstatements they make that cause the price of the securities issued by their company to rise or fall. Under the law of securities fraud, if investors lose money because of things not said (omissions) or because of misstatements that investors reasonably rely on, then there was *material misinformation* that caused the loss. The Supreme Court reinforced that point in the *Basic* case.

Basic Inc. v. Levinson
United States Supreme Court
485 U.S. 224 108 S.Ct. 978 (1988)

Case Background. *Basic Inc. was a publicly traded company that began talks with Combustion Inc. in 1976 about the possibility of a merger. Basic made three public statements in 1977 and 1978 denying that it was engaged in merger negotiations. On December 19, 1978, the Basic board endorsed Combustion's offer of $46 per share for Basic's common stock.*

Basic and its directors were then sued by shareholders who had sold their stock before the merger announcement but after Basic's first statement in 1977 that there were no merger negotiations. The shareholders received less than $46 per share, which they claim was due to the false and misleading statements of Basic and its directors in violation of Section 10(b) of the 1934 Securities Exchange Act and of Rule 10b–5. The shareholders claimed they were injured because they relied on misleading statements made by Basic. They sold their stock at lower prices than they would have received had the company told the truth about the merger talks. The district court held for Basic, finding that any misstatements were immaterial. The U.S. Court of Appeals reversed. Basic appealed to the U.S. Supreme Court.

Case Decision. Justice Blackmun delivered the opinion of the court.

* * *

The [Supreme] Court . . . has defined a standard of materiality under the security laws, concluding . . . that "[a]n omitted fact is material if there is a substantial likelihood that a reasonable shareholder would consider it important. . . ." Acknowledging that certain information concerning corporate developments could well be of "dubious significance," the Court was careful not to set too low a standard of materiality; it was concerned that a minimal standard might bring an overabundance of information within its reach, and lead management "simply to bury the shareholders in an avalanche of trivial information—a result that is hardly conducive to informed decisionmaking." It further explained that to fulfill the materiality requirement "there must be a substantial likelihood that the disclosure of the omitted fact would have been viewed by the reasonable investor as having significantly altered the 'total mix' of information made available." We now expressly adopt [that] standard of materiality for the § 10(b) and Rule 10b–5 context.

* * *

The role of the materiality requirement is not to "attribute to investors a child-like simplicity, an inability to grasp the probabilistic significance of negotiations," but to filter out essentially useless information that a reasonable investor would not consider significant, even as part of a larger "mix" of factors to consider in making his investment decision.

* * *

. . . in order to prevail on a Rule 10b–5 claim, a plaintiff must show that the statements were *misleading* as to a *material* fact. It is not enough that a statement is false or incomplete, if the misrepresented fact is otherwise insignificant. . . .

. . . materiality depends on the significance the reasonable investor would place on the withheld or misrepresented information. The fact-specific inquiry we endorse here is consistent with the approach a number of courts have taken in assessing the materiality of merger negotiations.

* * *

We turn to the question of reliance and the fraud-on-the-market theory. Succinctly put:

> The fraud on the market theory is based on the hypothesis that, in an open and developed securities market, the price of a company's stock is determined by the available material information regarding the company and its businesses. . . . Misleading statements will therefore defraud purchasers of stock even if the purchasers do not directly rely on the misstatements. . . . The causal connection between the defendants' fraud and the plaintiffs' purchase of stock in such a case is no less significant than in a case of direct reliance on misrepresentations.

. . . we previously have dispensed with a requirement of positive proof of reliance, where a duty to disclose material information had been breached, concluding that the necessary nexus between the plaintiffs' injury and the defendant's wrongful conduct had been established.

Similarly, we did not require proof that material omissions or misstatements in a proxy statement decisively affected voting, because the proxy solicitation itself, rather than the defect in the solicitation materials, served as an essential link in the transaction.

* * *

Recent empirical studies have tended to confirm Congress' premise that the market price of shares traded on well-developed markets reflects all publicly available information, and, hence, any material misrepresentations. It has been noted that "it is hard to imagine that there ever is a buyer or seller who does not rely on market integrity. Who would knowingly roll the dice in a crooked crap game?" Indeed, nearly every court that has considered the proposition has concluded that where materially misleading statements have been disseminated into an impersonal, well-developed market for securities, the reliance of individual plaintiffs on the integrity of the market price may be presumed. Commentators generally have applauded the adoption of one variation or another of the fraud-on-the-market theory. An investor who buys or sells stock at the price set by the market does so in reliance on the integrity of that price. Because most publicly available information is reflected in market price, an investor's reliance on any public material misrepresentations, therefore, may be presumed for purposes of a Rule 10b–5 action.

The Court of Appeals found that Basic "made public, material misrepresentations and Levinson sold Basic stock in an impersonal, efficient market. Thus the class, as defined by the district court, has established the threshold facts for proving their loss." The court acknowledged that Basic may rebut proof of the elements giving rise to the presumption, or show that the misrepresentation in fact did not lead to a distortion of price or that an individual plaintiff traded or would have traded despite his knowing the statement was false.

Any showing that severs the link between the alleged misrepresentation and either the price received (or paid) by the plaintiff, or his decision to trade at a fair market price, will be sufficient to rebut the presumption of reliance.

* * *

Case Holding. *Remanding this case for final determination, the Court held that in securities fraud, under Section 10(c) and Rule 10b–5, an omitted fact is material if there is a substantial likelihood that its disclosure would have been considered significant by a reasonable investor. A statement must be misleading as to a material fact. It is assumed that material misrepresentations affect the market price of a security. Defendants can rebut the presumption by showing that the omission or misrepresentation was not material and so did not affect the security price or that the plaintiff did not rely on the information in making a decision to buy or sell the security.*

Case Questions

1. Since rumors about merger talks usually come out right away, should executives always admit that they are engaged in merger talks, even if the possibility is remote? What problems could that cause?

2. How can security holders, who were ignorant of that was going on, later get involved in such litigation?

Liability for Mismanagement

The law of agency holds that corporate officers and directors are expected to perform their duties with the due care and skill that is expected of persons in such positions. Proving a violation of the duty of care is difficult. It is presumed that directors and officers act honestly and in good faith. So long as decisions reached by corporate officers and directors are "informed" decisions, they are protected by the *business judgment rule*. The business judgment rule protects directors from liability for decisions that turn out, after the fact, to have been ill-advised or just unlucky.

Because of the strong legal protection offered directors and officers, suits for *mismanagement* are not common. The *Revlon* case in Chapter 11 is an example of a successful suit against officers and directors for breach of the duty of loyalty. Liability for mismanagement in securities cases is discussed in the *Santa Fe* case. Since this case, liability for misstatement has been the primary basis for securities fraud suits against executives.

Santa Fe Industries, Inc. v. Green

United States Supreme Court
430 U.S. 462,
97 S.Ct. 1292
(1977)

Case Background. Santa Fe Industries was the majority stock holder in Kirby Lumber. From 1968 to 1973, Santa Fe paid between $65 and $92.50 a share in gathering 95 percent of Kirby Lumber stock. By Delaware state law, since Santa Fe owned over 90 percent of the stock, it could force the remaining minority shareholders to sell their stock to it. Santa Fe obtained an independent appraisal of the value of Kirby from Morgan Stanley, a leading investment banking firm, which valued the remaining shares at $125 each. Santa Fe then offered Green and the other shareholders $150 a share for their stock. Green sued, claiming that the stock was worth $772 a share and that Santa Fe had violated Rule 10b–5 by trying to defraud the shareholders of the true value. The district court held for Green and the U.S. Court of Appeals reversed. Santa Fe appealed to the U.S. Supreme Court. The Court had to decide if there was securities fraud under Rule 10b–5 because of mismanagement by Santa Fe.

Case Decision. Justice White delivered the opinion of the Court.

* * *

As we have indicated, the case comes to us on the premise that the complaint failed to allege a material misrepresentation or material failure to disclose. The finding of the District Court, undisturbed by the Court of Appeals, was that there was no "omission" or "misstatement" in the information statement accompanying the notice of merger. On the basis of the information provided, minority shareholders could either accept the price offered or reject it and seek an appraisal in the Delaware Court of Chancery. Their choice was fairly presented, and they were furnished with all relevant information on which to base their decision.

We therefore find inapposite the cases relied upon by residents and the court below in which the breaches of fiduciary duty held violative of Rule 10b–5 included some element of deception. Those cases forcefully reflect the principle that "[§]10(b) must be read flexibly, not technically and restrictively" and that the statute provides a cause of action for any plaintiff who "suffer[s] an injury as a result of deceptive practices touching its sale [or purchase] of securities. . . . "

* * *

It is also readily apparent that the conduct alleged in the complaint was not "manipulative" within the meaning of the statute. "Manipulation" is "virtually a term of art when used in connection with securities markets." The term refers generally to practices, such as wash sales, matched orders, or rigged prices, that are intended to mislead investors by artificially affecting market activity.

* * *

Section 10(b)'s general prohibition of practices deemed by the SEC to be "manipulative"—in this technical sense of artificially affecting market activity in order to mislead investors—is fully consistent with the fundamental purpose of the 1934 Act " 'to substitute a philosophy of full disclosure for the philosophy of caveat emptor. . . .' " Indeed, nondisclosure is usually essential to the success of a manipulative scheme. . . . No doubt Congress meant to prohibit the full range of ingenious devices that might be used to manipulate securities prices. But we do not think it would have chosen this "term of art" if it had meant to bring within the scope of § 10(b) instances of corporate mismanagement such as this, in which the essence of the complaint is that shareholders were treated unfairly by a fiduciary.

* * *

Case Holding. *The Supreme Court held for Santa Fe, saying that a charge of "unfair" would not suffice to find liability for mismanagement under the 1934 Act. There would have to be more substantive evidence of active manipulation that was destructive to investors.*

Case Questions

1. Does this holding mean that Green and the other investors who were unhappy with the forced stock buyout had no legal recourse?
2. Suppose the Court had ruled the opposite way. How would it change the relationship between management and shareholders?

Liability for Insider Trading

The most controversial application of securities fraud based on Rule 10b–5 is its use to prohibit *insider trading*—the buying or selling of stock by persons who have access to information affecting the value of the stock that has not yet been revealed to the public. Corporate executives are the ones most likely to be affected by the rule, as they are most likely to have valuable information concerning the financial well-being of the company before the release of the information to the public. Since 1982, prosecutions for insider trading violations have become much more common.

The prohibition of some forms of insider trading has a strange judicial origin, since the 1934 Act says nothing specific about the issue. Rather, in an administrative ruling in 1961 (*Cady, Roberts & Co.*), the SEC commissioners held insider trading to be illegal. This rule was accepted by a federal court in the *Texas Gulf Sulphur* case in 1968 and has been the subject of controversy ever since.

SEC Prosecution

The SEC may prosecute insiders—persons with access to nonpublic information—if the insiders trade to their benefit in the stock in question before the public has a chance to act on the information. For example, if the president of Boeing were to learn that his company had just been awarded a major aircraft construction contract with the airlines, he could buy numerous shares of Boeing stock before releasing the good news. Once the word was out, since expectations about the future profits of the company would rise, the stock price would jump, producing a nice profit. If this were discovered, the president could be sued for all the profits he earned in the transaction.

As the court noted in the *Texas Gulf Sulphur* decision, the reasoning behind the rule against insider trading is that insiders should not be able to use corporate information for personal gain, since the misappropriation of private information gives them an unfair advantage in the market over investors who do not have the information. According to the SEC, it is illegal for an insider to trade on inside information until the information has been released to the public and the stock price has had time to adjust to the new information.

What has not yet been fully resolved is who the rule against insider trading applies to. If you are riding on the subway in New York and overhear two executives talking about something big about to happen to their company you have just learned nonpublic information. Would it be illegal for you to trade on such information? For a while it looked as if that might be the case, but in 1980 the Supreme Court started to clarify the rules.

Supreme Court Interpretation

A printer at a company that printed financial documents read some confidential information. Trading in the stock of the company involved, the printer made $30,000 in profits because of his access to inside information. The SEC charged the printer, Mr. Chiarella, with securities fraud, but the Supreme Court reversed the lower court conviction.

In the 1980 decision *Chiarella* v. *United States*, the Court said that Chiarella was not a corporate insider who owed a *fiduciary duty* to the shareholders of his company. He was an outsider who was lucky enough to learn inside information. Only if his position has a requirement that he could not use such information could he be responsible. He may have had an unfair advantage over other stock traders, but it did not constitute securities fraud, said the Court. "He was not their [the corporation's] agent, he was not a fiduciary, he was not a person in whom the sellers had placed their trust and confidence. He was, in fact, a complete stranger who dealt with the sellers only through impersonal market transactions." The *Dirks* case further clarified liability for insider trading.

Dirks v. SEC
United States
Supreme Court
463 U.S. 646,
103 S.Ct. 3255
(1983)

Case Background. *Raymond Dirks worked for a broker-dealer firm in New York. His job was to study insurance firms for investors to determine if they should buy insurance firm securities. A former officer of Equity Funding of America (the "tipper") told Dirks (the "tippee") that Equity Funding officers were engaged in fraud and the securities in that firm were thus overvalued. Dirks investigated the information and decided that it appeared to be true. Dirks told his clients, who sold their holdings in Equity Funding. In a two-week period, as Dirks' information spread, the price of Equity Funding stock fell from $26 to $15 per share. The New York Stock Exchange, sensing problems, suspended trading in the stock. California insurance authorities and the SEC investigated and uncovered a major investment fraud.*

Besides investigating Equity Funding, the SEC charged Dirks with insider trading. That is, in his professional capacity he used knowledge not fully disclosed to the public. The SEC found Dirks guilty of insider trading. The court of appeals upheld the decision, ruling that any tippee (person who learns of inside information) must divulge the information to the public and not use it in any manner to trade in securities. The Supreme Court reviewed the decision.

Case Decision. Justice Powell delivered the opinion of the Court.

* * *

Not "all breaches of fiduciary duty in connection with a securities transaction," . . . come within the ambit of Rule 10b–5. There must also be "manipulation or deception." In an inside-trading case this fraud derives from the "inherent unfairness involved where one takes advantage" of "information intended to be available only for a corporate purpose and not for the personal benefit of anyone." Thus, an insider will be liable under Rule 10b–5 for inside trading only where he fails to disclose material nonpublic information before trading on it and thus makes "secret profits."

* * *

Imposing a duty to disclose or abstain solely because a person knowingly receives material nonpublic information from an insider and trades on it could have an inhibiting influence on the role of market analysts, which the SEC itself recognizes is necessary to the preservation of a healthy market. It is commonplace for analysts to "ferret out and analyze information," and this often is done by meeting with and questioning corporate officers and others who are insiders. Any information that the analysts obtain normally may be the basis for judgments as to the market worth of a corporation's securities. The analyst's judgment in this respect is made available in market letters or otherwise to clients of the firm. It is the nature of this type of information, and indeed of the markets themselves, that such information cannot be made simultaneously available to all of the corporation's stockholders or the public generally.

The conclusion that recipients of inside information do not invariably acquire a duty to disclose or abstain does not mean that such tippees always are free to trade on the information. The need for a ban on some tippee trading is clear. Not only are insiders forbidden by their fiduciary relationship from personally using undisclosed corporate information to their advantage, but they may not give such information to an outsider for the same improper purpose of exploiting the information for their personal gain.

* * *

Determining whether an insider personally benefits from a particular disclosure, a question of fact, will not always be easy for courts. But it is essential, we think, to have a guiding principle for those whose daily activities must be limited and instructed by the SEC's inside-trading rules, and we believe that there must be a breach of the insider's fiduciary duty before the tippee inherits the duty to disclose or abstain. In contrast, the rule adopted by the SEC in this case would have no limiting principle.

Under the inside-trading and tipping rules set forth above, we find that there was no actionable violation by Dirks. It is disputed that Dirks himself was a stranger to Equity Funding, with no pre-existing fiduciary duty to its shareholders. He took no action, directly or indirectly, that induced the shareholders or officers of Equity Funding to repose trust or confidence in him. There was no expectation by Dirks' sources that he would keep their information in confidence. Nor did Dirks misappropriate or illegally obtain the information about Equity Funding. Unless the insiders breached their *Cady, Roberts* duty to shareholders in disclosing the nonpublic information to Dirks, he breached no duty when he passed it on to investors as well as to *The Wall Street Journal.*

* * *

Case Holding. *The Court reversed the decision of the lower court, holding that Dirks had no duty not to use the inside information that he had obtained. This decision limited the kinds of insider trading cases that the SEC could bring to cases involving use of inside information by those with a fiduciary duty not to use such information.*

Case Questions

1. Although Dirks did not own stock in Equity Funding, is it correct to say that he had no financial gain or loss at stake in revealing the inside information he knew?

2. Did shareholders in Equity Funding suffer losses from Dirks's giving the inside information to some investors, who then sold, driving the price down?

Insider Trading Sanctions Act

The *Insider Trading Sanctions Act* (ITSA) was passed by Congress in 1984 to give the SEC a statutory basis for prosecuting insider trading. The ITSA allows the SEC to bring enforcement actions against violators who trade in securities while in possession of material nonpublic information. The courts may order violators to pay treble damages based on a measure of the illegal profit gained or loss avoided by the insider trading. Those convicted of violations may also have to pay back illegal profits to those who suffered the losses, which effectively means quadruple damages. In addition, criminal penalties may be assessed.

Major Insider Trading Cases

The SEC wasted little time applying its expanded powers in subsequent cases. Several insider trading cases not only rocked the financial world but also became lead stories in regular news reporting.

Thayer

The SEC sued the Deputy Secretary of the Department of Defense, Paul Thayer, the former chief executive officer of LTV Corporation. Thayer resigned from his Pentagon post and was convicted in 1985 of obstruction of justice in an SEC investigation of insider trading. He was given a four-year prison sentence and ordered to repay $555,000 for his insider trading activities. While he was CEO at LTV, he had divulged inside information to friends who made millions from his knowledge.

Levine

The Thayer case seemed like small potatoes compared to the next major case, involving Dennis Levine, which broke in 1986. Levine was a high-ranking officer in a major Wall Street firm. He specialized in helping firms merge. Hence, he had access to very valuable information that he knew was confidential. Levine was sued by the SEC and arrested under a warrant obtained by the U.S. Attorney's Office. Cooperating with authorities, he provided information that helped the SEC bring insider trading charges against prominent lawyers and securities traders. Levine agreed to repay almost $13 million in illegal gains. That case led to even bigger fish—Ivan Boesky.

Boesky

In late 1986, the SEC sued Boesky. The complaint claimed that he purchased securities based on material nonpublic information provided by Dennis Levine, as part of an organized trading scheme involving senior officers in prestigious investment firms. There is little wonder that Boesky earned the highest income on Wall Street in 1985. Boesky paid for nonpublic information on tender offers, mergers, and other business deals that greatly affect stock prices.

The SEC claims that Boesky knew that all such information was confidential and had obtained it through breach of a fiduciary duty. For example, the SEC charged that Boesky paid Levine 5 percent of his profits earned on securities purchase and sales based on confidential information Levine gave him—some of which was obtained from other investment brokers who were also in on the deal. One firm was handling the forthcoming merger of Nabisco and R.J. Reynolds. That created a fiduciary duty not to reveal that information or act on it for personal gain. However, those in a position of trust sold their valuable information, knowing that when word of the merger was made public the stock prices of the two companies would rise.

Boesky agreed to pay $100 million in cash and assets. Half that amount was a civil penalty paid under the ITSA to the U.S. Treasury. The other $50 million represented illegal gains and was placed in escrow for the benefit of investor claims. Boesky also agreed to an order barring him from any association with any broker, dealer, investment adviser, investment company, or municipal securities dealer. That is, one of Wall Street's "most successful" traders is out of the industry for life. He also received a three-year prison sentence. Based on information Levine and Boesky provided, more cases were brought by the SEC in a continuing insider trading investigation. Kidder, Peabody & Co., New York securities dealers, agreed to pay $25 million in civil penalties in 1987 and to cooperate with the SEC in further investigations.

Drexel

Drexel Burnham Lambert Inc., one of the most innovative Wall Street firms of the 1980s, increased its business substantially through its junk-bond operations headed by Michael Milken. Milken and Drexel handled the issuance and marketing of about one-half of the nearly $140 billion worth of junk (high-yield) bonds issued through 1988.

In 1989, Drexel pleaded guilty to six felony counts of securities fraud and agreed to pay $650 million in fines and restitution. Drexel settled the case in part due to concern that if the company lost in court, under the Racketeer Influenced and Corrupt Organizations (RICO) law, it could have been assessed treble damages, plus made subject to other litigation that would follow such a conviction. To help restructure the firm, Drexel then sold its public brokerage offices and hired former SEC Chairman John Shad to be its new chairman.

Milken

Having been indicted on ninety-eight counts of violations of the securities laws, Michael Milken plead guilty in 1990 to six felony counts. He agreed to pay $200 million in fines to the government and $400 million in restitution to pay the claims of defrauded investors. The case against Milken had little to do with his fame for junk-bonds, which are perfectly legal, but for his dealings with Boesky and others. Among the crimes he admitted to were:

- Cheating Drexel's clients by falsely reporting to them the prices at which securities had been bought and sold, with his junk-bond department keeping the profits.

- Helping a partner evade income taxes by manufacturing losses and gains from apparent stock transactions.

- Conspiring with Boesky to keep secret records to hide the fact that Boesky was the owner of certain securities.

- Secretly agreeing to buy stock from Boesky, and hold it at Drexel, so that Boesky could appear to have more capital on hand to meet certain SEC capital requirements.

After serving his prison term, Milken will be barred from the securities industry for life.

INTERNATIONAL PERSPECTIVES: INSIDER TRADING ABROAD

INTERNATIONAL

PERSPECTIVES

Insider trading cases draw more media attention than any other aspect of SEC law enforcement. The cases involving Milken and Boesky made front-page headlines. In Europe, little attention has been paid until recently to the common practice of insider trading. Most countries have no law against it. In Britain, where insider trading has been illegal since 1980, there has been about one conviction a year, the harshest penalty being a $43,000 fine. Switzerland and Spain passed laws against insider trading in 1988, Japan in 1989.

A major insider trading scandal in France involving people close to that country's President was uncovered by the SEC. The result of this scandal was the 1989 passage of a law against insider trading in France. An official of the European Economic Community said, "In America, there is a very important philosophy of shareholder information which is not the same here . . . Some member states do not have a legal definition of the crime and do not give authorities necessary power to pursue it. We are lagging."

One reason for the difference in attitude may be that only about 10 percent of Europeans own stock, compared to a much higher percent of Americans. Most stock in Europe is owned in large blocks by institutional traders, so most citizens have little reason to care about the effects of insider trading.

PROXIES, TENDER OFFERS, AND TAKEOVERS

Securities laws and state corporation laws impose constraints on the way friendly mergers occur and especially on hostile takeovers by one company of another. Any time companies that have issued public securities are involved, the rules of the 1934 Act come into play.

Proxies

A *proxy* is permission given by shareholders to someone else to vote their shares on their behalf in the manner they instruct. Since it is not practical for stock owners to attend corporate meetings at which shareholders must vote to approve major decisions, such as to merge with another company or elect the board of directors, shareholders are sent proxy statements to be voted on their behalf.

Companies that have issued securities subject to the financial disclosure requirements of the 1934 Act are subject to regulations concerning proxies. Firms must provide shareholders with proxy statements—information about major proposed changes in the business. The regulations spell out the form and timing proxy solicitations must take.

While most proxies are routine, such as voting for boards of directors or amendments to company bylaws, proxy fights can be used in a struggle over the future of the organization. For example, a proxy fight was waged in 1990 to try to force USX to split into two separate companies, U.S. Steel and Marathon Oil. The board of directors was successful in opposing this move, but the vote was close on the issue, which was forced to a proxy vote by dissatisfied USX shareholders. In another failed proxy fight in 1990, a group of investors offered an alternative set of candidates for the board of directors of Lockheed Corporation. Shareholders were offered the chance to stay with current management, or to switch to another team that offered a different strategy for the future of the company.

Tender Offers

When one company attempts to take over another, it often uses a *tender offer*. Stock owners in the target company are offered stock in the acquiring company or cash in exchange for their stock. If successful, the acquiring company obtains enough stock to control the target company. Tender offers must be registered with the SEC, and certain procedures must be followed. These requirements have allowed the SEC to play an active role in the merger and acquisition process and, by raising the costs of takeovers, have reduced the number that have occurred.

Spurred by the wave of merger activities in the 1980s, there has been consideration given to revising the 1934 Act to impose more regulations on merger activities, especially hostile takeovers. Some oppose this possible change as legislation designed to protect incumbent management from possibly losing their jobs in a takeover that leads to a shakeup of the managerial structure of the new organization. Supporters of restrictions claim that the takeovers do not increase efficiency.

State Intervention

There has been a substantial increase in activities at the state level to reduce the ease of takeovers. Corporations chartered in various states petitioned their legislatures to change state laws to help regulate takeovers. The Supreme

Court has approved broad authority to the states in this regard, as we see in the *CTS Corp.* case. At least thirty states now have statutes similar to that adopted in Indiana.

CTS Corp. v. Dynamics Corp. of America
United States Supreme Court
481 U.S. 69,
107 S.Ct. 1637
(1987)

Case Background. *A 1986 Indiana law makes any entity that buys more than 20 percent of the public stock in a corporation chartered and doing business in Indiana subject to special provisions. Such stock acquisitions usually are an attempt to gain voting control of the corporation, or a takeover. The law requires tender offers to remain open for at least fifty business days. At the end of that time, the existing board of directors can call a meeting at which the shareholders must vote approval of the takeover, even if the buyer has over 50 percent of the stock. That is, the buyer does not get voting rights with the stock until approved by the board. That is a statutory defense against takeovers.*

Dynamics Corporation ran into this law when attempting to buy control of CTS Corporation. Dynamics claimed that the Indiana statute was an unconstitutional interference with federal securities law, especially the Williams Act, which is an amendment to the 1934 Act that regulates the takeover process. The federal district court and the U.S. Court of Appeals agreed with Dynamics. CTS Corp. appealed to the U.S. Supreme Court.

Case Decision. Justice Powell delivered the opinion of the Court.

* * *

The Indiana Act operates on the assumption, implicit in the Williams Act, that independent shareholders faced with tender offers often are at a disadvantage. By allowing such shareholders to vote as a group, the Act protects them from the coercive aspects of some tender offers. If, for example, shareholders believe that a successful tender offer will be followed by a purchase of nontendering shares at a depressed price, individual shareholders may tender their shares—even if they doubt the tender offer is in the corporation's best interest—to protect themselves from being forced to sell their shares at a depressed price.

* * *

In our view, the possibility that the Indiana Act will delay some tender offers is insufficient to require a conclusion that the Williams Act pre-empts the Act. The longstanding prevalence of state regulation in this area suggests that, if Congress had intended to pre-empt all state laws that delay the acquisition of voting control following a tender offer, it would have said so explicitly. The regulatory conditions that the Act places on tender offers are consistent with the text and the purposes of the Williams Act. Accordingly, we hold that the Williams Act does not pre-empt the Indiana Act.

* * *

This Court's recent Commerce Clause cases . . . have invalidated statutes that adversely may affect interstate commerce by subjecting activities to inconsistent regulations. . . . The Indiana Act poses no such problem. So long as each State regulates voting rights only in the corporations it has created, each corporation will be subject to the law of only one State. No principle of corporation law and practice is more firmly established than a State's authority to regulate domestic corporations, including the authority to define the voting rights of shareholders. . . . Accordingly, we conclude that the Indiana Act does not create an impermissible risk of inconsistent regulation by different States.

* * *

Justice Scalia, concurring in the judgment.

I do not share the Court's apparent high estimation of the beneficence of the state statute at issue here. But a law can be both economic folly and constitutional.

Case Holding. *The Supreme Court reversed the lower courts, upholding the ability of CTS Corp. to use the Indiana takeover provisions in defense against the attempted takeover by Dynamics. The federal securities laws are not a bar to such legislation, since Congress did not intend to control state corporation law.*

Case Questions

1. What protection did existing shareholders of CTS not have that they did have under the new statute?
2. Three dissenting justices said they believed the Indiana statute to be in conflict with the Williams Act because it imposed substantive restrictions on securities that Congress did not impose and they feared that it would impede interstate commerce as legislatures passed statutes making it more difficult for corporations chartered within the state to be taken over. If this is correct, does the Indiana statute benefit Indiana shareholders at the expense of all other potential investors in Indiana corporations?

THE INVESTMENT COMPANY ACT

Congress ordered the SEC to study investment companies as a part of the Public Utilities Holding Company Act of 1935. The resulting reports led to the passage of the *Investment Company Act* (ICA) of 1940. The Act gives the SEC control over the structure of investment companies. It requires investment companies to register as such with the SEC, which then makes the companies subject to substantive restrictions on their activities and holds them liable to the SEC and to private parties for violations of the ICA.

Investment Companies

The ICA defines an *investment company* as an entity engaged primarily in the business of investing or trading in securities. The ICA defines three types of investment companies: face-amount certificate companies, which issue debt securities paying a fixed return; unit investment trusts, offering a fixed portfolio of securities; and management companies, the most important type of investment company.

Mutual Funds

The most common management company is the *open-end company*, generally known as a *mutual fund*. There was $52 billion invested in mutual funds in 1980. That had risen to about $1 trillion in 1990. Such companies offer no specific number of shares and so can expand as long as people wish to invest with them. The number of shares can be reduced as investors redeem their shares. The money from these shares is invested in a portfolio of securities. The price of the shares is determined by the value of the portfolio divided by the number of shares sold to the public. This is the most common investment company because of the flexibility it offers to investors and portfolio managers.

There are two kinds of mutual funds: *load* and *no-load*. The former are sold to the public through a securities dealer and have a sales commission (load) of some percent of the price. No-load funds are sold directly to the public through the mail with no sales commission. A few funds today have "low-loads" (2 percent instead of perhaps 8 percent) and, like their no-load counterparts, are offered directly to the public through the mail.

Companies Exempt From Regulation

Several organizations are exempt that would otherwise legally be called investment companies and be required to comply with ICA regulations. A company that has fewer than one hundred security holders and does not sell its securities to the public is exempt as a *closely held company*. Similarly, investment companies that do not offer securities to the public but rather are involved in internal investing, such as banks, insurance companies, charitable foundations, tax-exempt pension funds, and other specialized institutions, are exempt.

Regulation of Investment Companies

Under the ICA, investment companies must register with the SEC, stating their investment policy and other information. Annual reports and other information must be disclosed on a continuing basis. Capital requirements for operation are set by the SEC, and the debt structure is controlled. Payment of dividends to investors must equal at least 90 percent of the taxable ordinary income of the investment company. The securities dealings of the company are regulated to reduce the possibility of the investment company's becoming overextended in any market. A company must invest in only those activities it stated it would in its sales literature and policy statements.

Registration and Disclosure

Since investment companies sell securities, such as shares in mutual funds, to buy securities for investment purposes, their securities must be registered with the SEC. Hence, companies under the ICA are subject to the *registration and disclosure* requirements of the SEC for publicly traded securities. The sales literature used by mutual fund companies to promote their investment strategies to the public must be filed with the SEC for review. In general, no share of stock in an investment company may be sold for more than its current net asset value plus a maximum sales charge (load) of 8.5 percent.

Limiting Conflicts of Interest

To reduce possible *conflicts of interest*, there are restrictions on who may be on the board of directors of an investment company. At least 40 percent of the members of the board must be outsiders—persons with no direct business relationship with the company or its officers. The outsiders on the board are responsible for approving contracts with the investment advisers who are usually hired to manage the investment fund offered by the company. Further, investment companies may not use the funds invested with them for deals with any persons affiliated with the company. All deals are to be "arms length."

Investment Advisers

Investment companies usually hire *investment advisers* to manage their operations. As Table 19–1 shows, investment advisers have more funds invested in their care than do investment companies. That is because registered investment advisers manage pension funds and the portfolios held by insurance companies and banks. According to the ICA, investment advisers are "deemed to have a fiduciary duty with respect to the receipt of compensation for services" rendered to investment companies. The standard fee paid to advisers to manage an investment company fund is 0.5 percent of the net assets of the funds each year.

Arbitration of Disputes

When investors establish accounts with investment firms, they usually sign a standard form that states that in the event of a dispute, it must be arbitrated, not litigated. Some investors complain that they were never made aware of the *arbitration requirement,* and there have also been claims that the process is biased. The SEC issued rules in 1989 to reform the arbitration process that is the primary dispute resolution mechanism for brokers and investors.

Under the new regulations, the arbitration requirements must be pointed out to the customer and be explained clearly. Arbitration boards appointed to settle disputes usually include one industry professional and two members of the public. Under SEC rules, the arbitrators from the public must provide details of their last ten years' activities, and they may not have worked for the securities industry for at least three years. The new rules also specify that brokers must provide requested documents to investors before arbitration hearings. In general, the rules give parties the right to use procedures that follow the elements of judicial procedure. Further, although arbitration records will be kept secret, the decisions will be made public, so that there is better understanding about the process.

About the same time the SEC issued these new regulations, the Supreme Court issued a decision in 1989 that upheld the binding nature of the arbitration agreements. It will be an unusual case in which an investor will be allowed to litigate a dispute with a broker. The Court held that the arbitration agreements apply to security fraud claims against brokers, whether the claim is brought under the 1933 or the 1934 securities law. The Court noted that

Table 19–1   Investment Companies and Investment Advisers

	Number Active		Assets Managed ($ billion)	
	1983	**1987**	**1983**	**1987**
Investment companies	2,057	3,305	$360	$1,200
Investment advisers	7,043	12,690	$780	$3,500

Source: SEC, *Annual Report.*

there is a "strong endorsement of the federal statutes favoring this method of resolving disputes." Arbitration is generally much less expensive than litigation and the results tend to be more certain due to the expertise of the arbitrators. In 1988, over 6,000 arbitration cases were filed. Most appear to be resolved in favor of the clients.

THE INVESTMENT ADVISERS ACT

The *Investment Advisers Act* (IAA) is complementary to the ICA. It defines *investment adviser* as a "person who, for compensation, engages in the business of advising others . . . as to the advisability of investing in, purchasing or selling securities . . ." (§ 202(a) (11), IAA). The regulations adopted by the SEC under the Act are a part of the regulation of professionals working in the securities industry.

Brokers and Dealers

The IAA works with the 1934 Securities Exchange Act to regulate *brokers* (persons engaged in the business of effecting transactions in securities for the account of others) and *dealers* (persons engaged in the business of buying and selling securities for their own account). For simplicity, brokers, dealers, and investment advisers will all be referred to as *securities professionals*. To operate legally, securities professionals must be registered with the SEC. Violations of SEC rules can lead to suspension or permanent loss of the right to do business in the industry.

Professional Responsibility to Clients

One primary area of concern of the SEC in regulating securities professionals concerns obligations to clients and possible *conflicts of interest*. The Supreme Court has held that broker-dealers must make known to their customers any possible conflicts or other information that is material to investment decisions. Professionals have been held to violate their duty when they charge excessive markups on securities above their market value to unsuspecting customers. Markups over 5 percent are difficult to justify, and those over 10 percent are not allowed under SEC guidelines.

Other practices that have been attacked include *churning*, whereby a broker who has control of a client's account buys and sells an excessive amount of stock to make money from the commissions earned on the transactions. Also illegal is *scalping*, whereby a professional buys stock for personal benefit, then urges investors to buy the stock so that the price will rise to the benefit of the professional.

Another major concern of the SEC in regulating securities professionals focuses on ensuring investors *adequate information* about available securities to make informed investment decisions. Generally, professionals will violate the antifraud provisions of the regulations when they recommend securities without making adequate information available. Registered professionals may not deal in securities not registered under the 1933 or 1934 Securities Act. If the security is exempt from either Act, the professional must have information about the security similar to the information that would be required of a registered security.

Investment Newsletters

Investment advisers who violate securities laws may be suspended or barred from dispensing investment advice for compensation. While we usually think of an investment adviser who has stolen clients' funds or otherwise abused a fiduciary duty to a client as subject to SEC prosecution, does such regulation extend to the sale of investment advice via an investment newsletter? There are numerous such newsletters. Annual subscription rates are usually in the hundreds of dollars and some run $1,000 per year. Some publishers of such newsletters have made tens of millions of dollars dispensing investment advice in their newsletters. The Supreme Court, in *Lowe* v. *SEC*, addressed SEC regulation of newsletters.

Lowe v. SEC

Supreme Court of the United States
472 U.S. 181,
105 S.Ct. 2557
(1985)

Case Background. *Lowe was a registered investment adviser from 1974 to 1981. After he was convicted for misappropriating client funds, the SEC ordered Lowe not to operate as an investment adviser nor to associate with investment advisers. Lowe then began to publish and sell a semimonthly investment newsletter. It sold for $900 per year and attracted about 19,000 subscribers in its only year of operation. The newsletter contained commentary about securities markets, investment strategies, and specific recommendations for buying, selling, or holding stocks. Subscribers could call a hotline for current market tips.*

The SEC sued Lowe, claiming that the sale of investment advice by a newsletter violated the Investment Advisers Act because of Lowe's previous conviction. The federal court of appeals agreed with the SEC, holding that the IAA does not distinguish between personal advice and advice given in publications. Hence, the bar to Lowe being an investment adviser extended to selling advice by the newsletter. Lowe appealed to the Supreme Court.

Case Decision. Justice Stevens delivered the opinion of the Court.

* * *

We granted certiorari to consider the important constitutional question whether an injunction against the publication and distribution of petitioners' newsletters is prohibited by the First Amendment. . . . Lowe contends that such an injunction strikes at the very foundation of the freedom of the press by subjecting it to license and censorship. . . . In response the Commission argues that the history of abuses in the securities industry amply justified Congress' decision to require the registration of investment advisers, to regulate their professional activities, and, as an incident to such regulation, to prohibit unregistered and unqualified persons from engaging in that business.

* * *

Lowe's newsletters are distributed "for compensation and as part of a regular business" and they contain "analyses or reports concerning securities." Thus, on its face, the basic definition applies to Lowe. The definition, however, is far from absolute. The Act excludes several categories of persons from its definition of an investment adviser, lists certain investment advisers who need not be registered, and also authorizes the Commission to exclude "such other person" as it may designate by rule or order.

One of the statutory exclusions is for "the publisher of any bona fide newspaper, news magazine or business or financial publication of general and regular circulation." Although neither the text of the Act nor its legislative history defines the precise scope of this exclusion, two points seem tolerably clear. Congress did not intend to exclude publications that are distributed by investment advisers as a normal part of the business of servicing their clients. . . . On the other hand, Congress, plainly sensitive to First Amendment concerns, wanted to make clear that it did not seek to regulate the press through the licensing of nonpersonalized publishing activities.

* * *

The Act was designed to apply to those persons engaged in the investment-advisory profession—those who provide personalized advice attuned to a client's concerns, whether by written or verbal communication. The mere fact that a publication contains advice and comment about specific securities does not give it the personalized character that identifies a professional investment adviser. Thus, Lowe's publications do not fit within the central purpose of the Act because they do not offer individualized advice attuned to any specific portfolio or to any client's particular needs. On the contrary, they circulate for sale to the public at large in a free, open market—a public forum in which typically anyone may express his views.

* * *

As long as the communications between Lowe and . . . subscribers remain entirely impersonal and do not develop into the kind of fiduciary, person-to-person relationships that were discussed at length in the legislative history of the Act and that are characteristic of investment adviser-client relationships, we believe the publications are, at least presumptively, within the exclusion and thus not subject to registration under the Act.

We therefore conclude that Lowe's publications fall within the statutory exclusion for bona fide publications and that [Lowe is not] an "investment adviser" as defined in the Act.

* * *

Case Holding. *The Supreme Court reversed the court of appeals, holding that publishers of investment newsletters are not investment advisers under the IAA. Therefore, the SEC could not bring suit against Lowe, who by definition was no longer an investment adviser, nor restrain the publication of newsletters.*

Case Questions

1. The Supreme Court did not address the First Amendment issue of censorship that was raised by the lower courts. Would this be a reason not to allow regulation of investment newsletters, regardless of content?

2. When Congress referred to news magazines or business or financial publications, do you believe it was thinking of *Fortune* and *The Wall Street Journal*, which sell for peanuts compared to investment newsletters, rather than the $1,000-per-year newsletters with "inside" tips on what to buy?

3. A registered investment adviser usually makes recommendations in face-to-face situations with investors based on a newsletterlike publication published by his or her investment firm, such as Merrill Lynch. That is, the investment advisers do not each decide on their own what stocks and other investments to recommend. Is this really different from what Lowe was doing?

STOCK MARKET REGULATION

As Table 19–2 illustrates, the volume and value of stock transactions has grown rapidly in the past decade. As the New York Stock Exchange, which handles about 80 percent of public stock market transactions, heads to round-the-clock trading, this activity can be expected to continue to grow.

Self-Regulation of Securities Markets

Under the terms of the 1934 Securities Exchange Act, Congress allowed private associations of securities professionals to set rules for behavior of professionals dealing in securities markets. Congress gave the SEC the power to monitor such self-regulating organizations, including the stock exchanges, such as the New York Stock Exchange (NYSE), the American Stock Exchange (AMEX), and the regional exchanges.

Rules for Exchange Members

The stock exchanges establish and enforce rules of conduct for their members. Some rules govern the operation of the exchange, how securities are listed, obligations of issuers of securities, who may handle certain transactions and in what manner, and how prices are set and reported. Other rules concern how member firms and their employees must qualify for membership to be allowed to handle various transactions. These rules include how investors' accounts are to be managed, the qualifications of dealers and brokers, limits on advertising, and other operations of securities firms.

OTC Regulation

Besides monitoring the actions of the stock exchanges, the SEC controls the behavior of the *over-the-counter* or OTC market. This market is composed of securities dealers who may or may not be members of a securities exchange such as the NYSE. The stock of many companies is handled by this market, which is linked by computer and telephone. Generally, the stocks traded on this market are from firms that have a small number of shares of stock or that are themselves small and thus do not qualify for trading on a regular securities exchange. Governing the OTC market is the National Association of Securities Dealers (NASD), which sets rules of behavior for traders on the OTC market similar to the rules of the NYSE for its members.

Table 19–2   Sales of Stocks on Registered Exchanges

	1970	1980	1984	1988
Market value of all exchanges ($ billions)	132	522	1,004	1,699
Number of shares exchanged (millions)	4,539	15,488	30,456	52,474

Source: 1990 Statistical Abstract of the United States.

Liability and Penalties

Punishment for violation of self-regulating organization rules can include suspension or expulsion from the organization, making transactions by the expelled member impossible. If an exchange knows that a member firm is violating the rules or the law and the exchange ignores such a violation, causing investors to lose money, the exchange can be held liable for the losses. The potential liability and SEC pressure have given the exchanges an incentive to watch securities professionals for behavior that violates the standards. Although fraudulent behavior by a broker-dealer will lead to liability under the securities laws, how far the courts and the SEC will go in establishing liability for investor losses due to non-fraudulent but ill-advised actions by professionals is not settled.

Regulation of Securities Transactions

The SEC, in cooperation with the NASD, regulates the actions of securities professionals who handle the actual trading of securities. The SEC does not allow professionals to use their position to make transactions for their own benefit. To minimize such problems, floor trading by professionals is strictly limited to registered experts, as is off-floor trading. The difference between these two types of trading is that one is done on the floor of a securities exchange while the other is done elsewhere, such as OTC. In either case, the professional securities dealers may not trade for their own advantage ahead of their customers.

Regulations also cover *specialist firms*. These firms generally do not deal directly with the public; rather, they handle transactions for brokers. Brokers may leave their customers' orders with the specialist to be filled when possible. For example, if a stock is currently selling for $21 a share and a stock owner is willing to sell at $22 dollars a share, the order may be left to be filled should the price rise to twenty-two dollars. Specialists also handle transactions that are unusual or difficult for most securities dealers to execute. SEC rules prohibit the specialists from exploiting their special position. Specialists may not deal for their own benefit in the orders left to execute. Since they are first to learn of price changes, they could buy and sell the stock left with them to take advantage of changes in stock prices.

Margin Requirements

The Federal Reserve Board (the Fed) regulates the amount of credit issued by securities professionals, banks, and other lenders to investors for buying securities. The Fed establishes a *margin requirement* of the amount of a security purchase that must be financed by cash. For example, the Fed now rules that only 50 percent of the value of securities may be bought on margin—that is, on credit. The other 50 percent must be paid for in cash by the investor. Should the price of the security drop drastically, the lender (usually a brokerage house) must make a margin call. That is, the lender must call the customer to cover a portion of the debt (margin) outstanding on the security. The Fed also publishes a list of stocks that may be purchased on margin. Usually the list includes only those stocks traded on major exchanges. Stocks not on the list may not be purchased on margin.

Margin requirements apply only to equity, not debt, securities. The idea behind the regulation is to prevent investors from becoming heavily debt laden in the event of a rapid drop in market prices. That occurred in the stock market crash of 1929, which made it impossible for some investors to cover their losses. Professionals who lend more than is allowed under the Fed rules may be stripped of their right to lend money for security purchases or may even lose their registration.

INTERNATIONAL PERSPECTIVES: INTERNATIONAL STOCK MARKETS

INTERNATIONAL

PERSPECTIVES

Equity (stock) financing of corporations is vital in the United States. Over $2 trillion in equities are owned by millions of citizens who share in the good or bad fortune of thousands of corporations. In the past decade, equity markets have grown rapidly in many other nations. The equity markets in Japan, Germany, Switzerland, France, and the United Kingdom are now large and sophisticated. Only in the past decade has it become easy for Americans to own stock in foreign firms and for foreigners to own stock in American firms. Capital funds now flow around the world much more easily than at any other time in history.

Other countries have developing securities markets, and many more would like to have them. Governments that used to try to control all capital flows have come to understand that it is difficult to stop capital from going to its best opportunities and that if they open their markets, they could benefit from capital inflows. From small nations like Malaysia to large ones like Brazil, stock markets are being developed. Most nations adopt securities laws very similar to U.S. laws because American securities markets have become world models.

Countries have difficulties developing stock markets when they have not had economic or political stability. In many countries of Latin America, where governments seem perpetually unstable, most people are leery of risking their wealth in ventures the government could easily destroy or steal by simply changing the law. The size of a country has little to do with the development of equity markets; Hong Kong and Belgium have healthy markets because of their long-term political stability. The impending takeover of Hong Kong by the People's Republic of China, however, has initiated a capital outflow from Hong Kong. Many current and potential investors do not believe the Beijing government's promise that it will not interfere with Hong Kong's economy.

Stock markets frighten governments because they are a good measure of the wisdom of a government's economic policy. If a government implements policies that investors believe will injure the economy or reduce the rate of return on capital, stock prices will quickly fall as investors react to the news.

COMMODITIES FUTURES TRADING

In recent years, the prices of such commodities as gold, silver, coffee, and sugar have illustrated the extreme volatility of commodity prices. Such volatility brings extraordinary potential for gain as well as for loss. The risk obviously makes planning difficult for the buyers and sellers of the basic commodities. To reduce risk and stabilize commodity prices over time, sophisticated *futures markets* have evolved. Government concern about the propriety of certain activities in futures markets has kept pace with the growth of such markets. Thus, the organization and purpose of the regulations governing futures markets behavior mirror the development of the markets themselves.

Just as securities markets have grown rapidly in financial volume and in number of participants, so too have the commodity markets. As Table 19–3 shows, the number of contracts traded jumped twenty-fold from 1970 to 1988. The contracts traded are now worth over $1 trillion per year. As markets have become more sophisticated, more products have come to be traded on futures markets, such as futures in stocks and in foreign currencies.

Futures Markets and Contracts

Typically, farmers and ranchers take their produce and livestock to markets at regular and predictable intervals. The return to the farmer is anything but regular or predictable. Because of demand and supply, the farmer is at the mercy of the market. Bumper crops bring low prices, which could lead to waste of produce. However, months after the marketing of a crop, supplies can decrease to such an extent that buyers and sellers of surplus commodities spur the development of futures markets.

Futures Contracts

The precursor of the modern futures contract is the cash-forward contract—a contract in which a buyer puts cash down for the delivery of merchandise on some agreed-upon future date. Such contracts ensure the buyer and seller of certain prices and thus foster effective production and storage planning.

The *futures contract* is defined in the Chicago Board of Trade's *Commodity Trading Manual* as follows:

> A futures contract is a legally binding commitment to deliver or take delivery of a given quantity and quality of a commodity, at a price agreed

Table 19–3 Commodity Futures Trading on U.S. Exchanges

Commodity	Futures (in millions)		
	1970	**1980**	**1988**
Grain	2.2	18.3	15.9
Oilseeds/products	3.7	15.7	22.5
Livestock/products	3.4	11.8	9.6
Other agriculturals	2.0	7.8	9.8
Energy products	—	1.1	26.3
Metals	1.1	14.1	18.9
Financial instruments	—	10.2	117.6
Currencies	—	3.7	21.2
Total contracts traded	**12.4**	**82.7**	**241.8**

Source: Commodity Futures Trading Commission, *Annual Report.*

upon when the contract is made, with delivery at the seller's option sometime during the specified future delivery month.

Thus, the futures contract differs from the cash-forward contract in that it specifies both price and quantity and quality at the time the contract is made. To facilitate price determination, futures contracts are standardized as to quality, quantity, and location. Such standardization of futures contracts allows a seller to offset a delivery obligation against the contract with an equal and opposite transaction. Similarly, the buyer of futures contracts can liquidate an obligation to take delivery by offsetting the contract with an equal sale of futures contracts.

Futures Markets

Futures markets serve three basic economic functions: information collection and dissemination, price discovery or determination, and risk allocation. Futures market exchanges collect and disseminate information of supplies, storage, purchases, weather, production, prices, quality, exports, imports, and other relevant factors. Hence, buyers and sellers are provided with information that maximizes their ability to make transactions that accurately reflect supply and demand conditions.

Commodity Futures Trading Commission

The *Commodity Futures Trading Commission* (CFTC) was established by the Commodity Futures Trading Commission Act of 1974 as an independent regulatory agency to replace the Commodity Exchange Authority (CEA) of the U.S. Department of Agriculture.

CFTC Authority

The CFTC Act broadened the definition of a commodity for regulatory purposes and gave the CFTC more extensive powers than those previously held by the CEA. The CFTC has a chairman and four other commissioners appointed by the president and confirmed by the Senate. The CFTC's extended authority includes jurisdiction over trading on the commodity exchanges and over dealings in commodity contracts. It is charged by Congress "to insure fair and honest practice in futures trading through the elimination and prevention of activities which adversely affect the integrity of a free market or otherwise harm the market place and its users."

Regulation of Futures Exchanges

The CFTC Act requires all futures exchanges, such as the Chicago Board of Trade, to submit all rules and regulations to the CFTC for approval. The CFTC's dealing with futures exchanges is similar to the SEC's in dealing with stock exchanges. Both agencies operate with the assumption that exchanges should be basically self-regulating. Thus, the CFTC hopes that its guidance will foster the development of efficient (and equitable) exchanges that require little direct control by the CFTC. The CFTC concentrates on rules that affect the trading public and seeks to minimize the administrative burdens associated with the market approval process.

The CFTC has the authority to direct any contract market whenever it has reason to believe that an emergency exists. An emergency is defined as any situation in which orderly trading in futures contracts is threatened. At different times, this power has been exerted in the contract markets for silver, Maine potatoes, and coffee futures. Emergencies can also exist when the CFTC has reason to believe that prices are being manipulated.

Regulation of Professionals

The law requires *futures traders* to register with the CFTC. Similar to SEC requirements, traders are required to segregate customer funds and to meet minimum financial requirements. Key employees of trader firms are investigated by the Federal Bureau of Investigation (FBI) to ascertain their fitness to handle the accounts and funds of commodity futures customers. Such registration is justified on the grounds that the activities of Commodity Training Advisers (CTAs) and Commodity Pool Operators (CPOs) are "clothed with the public interest."

Penalties for Violations

The CFTC may bring a court action to enjoin violations of any provision of the CFTC Act, CFTC rules and regulations, or acts that restrain trade in any commodity for future delivery. Court action can also be brought to enforce compliance with the Act or any CFTC regulation. There are also administrative disciplinary proceedings for violations of the Act or of CFTC rules. The Commission may impose civil penalties of up to $100,000 per violation. Administrative reparations proceedings for money damages may be instituted before the Commission by any person who alleges damage by a registered trader. Hundreds of complaints involving millions of dollars are filed every year.

An undercover FBI investigation of trading violations by registered traders from 1988 to 1990 resulted in over fifty indictments for illegal commodity trades. There have been convictions for stealing funds from clients' accounts and for rigging trades so as to benefit traders at the clients' expense. The scale of the fraud has resulted in consideration of toughened regulations and merging the SEC and CFTC.

SUMMARY

A variety of federal laws enacted over the past five decades have produced a high standard of care for the investment industry. The 1933 and 1934 securities laws set strict requirements for providing information to investors. The 1933 Securities Act set the standards for information requirements for new securities issues. Once a security has been sold to the public, the firm that issued the security must make periodic reports to the SEC. The reporting requirements of the Securities Exchange Act of 1934 are designed to ensure that investors have accurate financial information.

Under Section 10(b) and Rule 10b–5, liability for securities fraud may result from misstatements in or material omissions from disclosures required by the SEC or in statements made by corporate officials that lead investors to incur losses. Liability may also be imposed for mismanagement and for insider trading. Suits may be brought by investors who have suffered losses as well as by the SEC, resulting in damages, civil and criminal penalties, including prison sentences.

The 1934 Act gave the SEC the authority to regulate proxies—votes by shareholders—and tender offers—attempts to gain control of a corporation by purchasing sufficient stock to control the board of directors. States have recently become more active in legislating restrictions on the manner in which takeovers can occur and continue to impose restrictions on the registration of securites that, in some states, go beyond the federal requirements.

The 1934 Act and later statutes, such as the Investment Company Act and Investment Advisers Act, allow the SEC to regulate the markets in which securities are created and traded and to regulate professionals who work in those markets. While the SEC may strictly regulate registered investment advisers who orally sell advice to investors, it may not regulate investment newsletters.

Operating much like the SEC, the CFTC regulates the commodities markets and the professionals who operate within those markets. Failure to comply with CFTC rules may lead to civil penalties being imposed and damages being recovered by investors who were cheated.

ISSUE

Should We Restrict Insider Trading?

Ivan Boesky and Michael Milken violated a fiduciary duty imposed by contract as well as by SEC regulation. Putting aside such cases, is it undesirable that corporate insiders trade on valuable information about their own company that they help to create? That is, do we not want executives to have strong financial incentives to maximize the profitability of their companies over time, thereby benefiting all shareholders? Some critics of the SEC claim that they are reducing market efficiency, not helping it, by attacking such insider trading. In this article, former SEC Commissioner Cox considers both sides of the arguments.

Two Views on the Law of Insider Trading
Charles C. Cox

Opponents of insider trading maintain that insider trading serves to destroy investor confidence in the stock market; particularly that of small investors. This, it is argued, causes investors to move away from securities and ultimately decreases market liquidity.

Proponents of insider trading, such as Henry G. Manne, Dean of the George Mason University Law School, on the other hand, argue that insider trading should be allowed because it is socially beneficial. In particular, Manne contends that insider trading improves market efficiency by moving stock

–continued

—continuing

prices in the proper direction sooner than it would otherwise have occurred. Furthermore, Manne argues that insider trading is an efficient way to compensate innovative entrepreneurs. To use Dean Manne's language, he believes that "insider trading is the best, if not the only, method of adequately compensating corporate innovators."

Regardless of the position you take, no hard evidence exists to support either theory. In order to make a proper analysis, questions such as the following must be answered: Would the stock market be more efficient if insider trading were legal? If so, by how much? Does insider trading prevail over other methods of entrepreneurial compensation in countries where it is legal? Can empirical evidence be produced to suggest that investor confidence and/or market liquidity is inversely related to insider trading? These questions have not yet been answered. However, we should not assume that insider trading is always at work simply because price run-ups on stocks and other events are not fully explained by innocent reasons.

The fact that a handful of Wall Street investment bankers, arbitrageurs and even a prominent takeover attorney were caught with their hands in the till does not imply that everyone in the business is corrupt. It does imply that, as watchdogs of Wall Street, the SEC is doing its job and that insider traders will be vigorously pursued and either enjoined or, where appropriate, referred to the Justice Department for criminal prosecution.

While the SEC can not yet claim to have stopped insider trading altogether, it is clear that it has made progress in deterring insider trading activities wherever it is found. As far as price run-ups that occur before theannouncement of a tender offer or another significant corporate act, the evidence so far shows that they are explained mostly by factors other than insider trading.

Let us imagine for a moment that insider trading was not a violation of either the federal or state securities laws. Imagine that

the ability to trade on material nonpublic information was available for corporations to use as a means of compensating managers and directors.

As I mentioned before, commentators, such as Henry Manne, oppose the prohibitions on insider trading. Manne suggests that the decision to allow or prohibit insider trading should be left to the individual corporation. Suppose that we were to accept Manne's argument and allow corporations to decide for themselves whether to permit insiders to trade on nonpublic information. It seems to me that if insider trading were legalized, we would probably end up about where we are at present. The corporate entity itself would desire to ensure its own good reputation. I think that most corporations would adopt a charter and bylaw provision prohibiting insider trading.

Certainly trades made by a corporation's employees based on corporate inside information would present a conflict of interest between the corporation's stockholders and the employees. If the corporation allowed its employees to profit from their special knowledge while at the same time allowing shareholders to continue trading, the shareholders would be at a very definite disadvantage. The question remains—would a prohibition at the corporate level be effective?

Without regulatory laws do you suppose the securities industry would enforce or monitor insider trading activities? Would companies that prohibit insider trading exercise aggressive monitoring to prevent it? I think not! Corporations simply do not have the available access to market surveillance that the government and the exchanges maintain. They would be unable to determine, with any degree of certainty, when one of their employees traded on inside information. You simply cannot rely on an employee's sense of honesty to come forward and admit that he has violated company policy.

—continued

–continuing

Moreover, corporations that find employees who have violated company policy have a tendency to fire the violator without suing him. I am reminded of a story in the *Wall Street Journal* recently. The story concerned a man who had held accounting jobs at numerous companies and embezzled funds from all of them. When the embezzlement was discovered, each company fired the violator. None sued him, but some gave him good recommendations for a job at another company. This was the least costly way of dealing with the problem for each individual company, but not the least costly solution for the business community as a whole.

My point is that corporations faced with the difficult problem of monitoring and enforcing insider trading prohibitions would soon ask for help through the police power of government to enforce their rules. This is why I think that an SEC with rules against insider trading would eventually evolve.

Questions

1. During 1986 and 1987, when unprecedented insider trading cases involving many prestigious Wall Street firms broke, the stock market continued to expand at above-average rates. Does this indicate that insider trading must not scare away investors and hurt the market?

2. If a few officers of a corporation know of an impending announcement that will cause the price of the stock in their company to rise and they engage in stock purchases before the news is made public and so make big gains when the stock price then rises, who has been hurt? Is this not an efficient way to compensate the executives?

REVIEW AND DISCUSSION QUESTIONS

1. Define the following terms:
   misstatements
   material information
   insider trading
   proxies
   tender offer
   investment company
   mutual fund
   investment adviser
   futures markets

2. It is generally known that the information required by the SEC to be disclosed by various statutes is "stale" by the time it is available to the FTC. Does this necessarily mean it has no value to investors?

3. According to the *Santa Fe* decision, are corporate executives responsible under the securities laws for misstatements and omissions?

4. More insider trading cases have been brought by the SEC during the mid-1980s than were brought in all the years before. Does this indicate that more insider trading must be going on in recent years than before?

5. Does self-regulation of the securities market mean that the markets are not well regulated or that they have the ability to become a private monopoly?

6. What could an investment adviser do to profit abnormally at the expense of clients? Would such activities occur more often without SEC controls? Who has an incentive to limit such abuses?

7. Are consumers helped or not by the existence of futures markets?

Case Questions

8. You go to a party at which you meet a hotshot Wall Street lawyer who advises a famous corporate raider. The lawyer tells you that the raider is about to make a try at getting control of Boring Corp. The next day you buy stock in Boring. Sure enough, two weeks later the raider tries a takeover, and the stock shoots up. Are you guilty of insider trading? What if you had acquired the same information in a locker room at a tennis club when you overheard the lawyer talking to the raider and they did not know you were listening?

9. You are a registered investment adviser working for a stock brokerage firm. A client invests $100,000 with you and says she wants to make lots of money. It is your belief that if you sell all stock within fifteen minutes after the Dow Jones average begins to move down and then buy stock one hour later, you will, on the average, be buying lower and selling higher. Each day for two months you try this strategy on the average executing two complete sell-offs and buy-backs per day. At the end, your customer is nearly broke. Is this likely to be held improper under the Investment Adviser Act? Why? Would it make any difference if you gave the customer this advice by a $1,000-per-year investment newsletter you wrote and the customer called her broker and made the identical transactions on her own that you made for her working at the brokerage firm? Would you be liable for her losses in this case?

Policy Questions

10. In the *CTS* v. *Dynamics* decision, the Supreme Court said that states could impose restrictions on takeovers of corporations chartered in their states so long as these regulations essentially furthered federal regulations. A study published in 1987 by the Bureau of Economics of the FTC estimated that a New York state law regulating corporate takeovers that was passed in 1985 caused the ninety-four public firms studied to fall in equity value nearly 1 percent, which meant that shareholders lost about $1.2 billion dollars in the value of their stock from a law that was supposed to benefit them. Suppose this study is correct—that the main impact of these antitakeover laws is to protect incumbent management against a takeover that would make the company more profitable. Would it be desirable for the Supreme Court to hold such laws as destructive to interstate commerce, or should we, as Justice Scalia said, let economically senseless laws be called constitutional?

11. Disputes between investors and their stockbrokers are usually settled by arbitration that is sponsored by the National Association of Securities Dealers or the New York Stock Exchange, rather than by litigation in federal court. In a twelve-month period from 1989–90, arbitration panels granted punitive damages totaling $4.5 million in twenty-one cases. Members of the securities industry argue that this is improper—only actual damages should be awarded. Is the award of punitive damages by arbitration panels improper and will it lead to an excessive number of claims being filed?

Ethics Questions

12. While at a football game you overhear two corporate executives, whom you recognize, discussing an important announcement that will be made public at 11 a.m. the next Monday. They say it will make the stock "really shoot up." Obviously this is inside information that was not intended for your ears. Should you run to a stockbroker first thing Monday morning to buy all the

stock in the company involved that you can? What if you knew the executives personally and they told you "If I were you, I would buy all the stock in our company that you can before 11 a.m. on Monday"? What difference does it make whether they give the reason you should buy the stock (i.e., the inside information)? Presume that you know that regardless of the legality of such transactions there is no way you could get caught doing this—it is money in the bank.

13. You own a commodities trading firm. One of your commodity traders is caught playing illegal games with some commodity investors' money but made the illegal transactions outside the firm; the firm is therefore not legally responsible. However, the trader had a good reputation because he worked for your firm, which was highly regarded for its honesty. The trader is found guilty and barred from the industry but had spent most of the money the investors trusted him with and cannot pay damages. The investors are out $1.7 million dollars. Should you voluntarily cover their losses even though you are not legally responsible?

14. Some investment newsletters have made their authors multimillionaires. Some of these writers become very popular and achieve a cult-like following of mostly middle-class people with modest sums to invest. There is no evidence that any of the newsletter writers has consistently outperformed the market. That is, the advice they sell for a relatively high price is advice that could be had for a very low price from any regular investment firm. The newsletter writers have figured out how to appeal to the biases of particular sets of investors—gold bugs, doomsayers, and so on. It is clearly legal for them to sell their newsletters. Is it ethical? Is it ethical to write a book proclaiming a forthcoming economic calamity or some other unsubstantiated prediction? The authors of some of these books make a small fortune but have no liability for being wrong. In some cases, people take foolish steps with their savings in the belief that there might be something to this year's most popular bit of economic tabloid journalism. Relying on some silly prediction, some people have even quit their jobs, moved, and put their wealth in an unusual form. Should this concern anyone but the investors?

20 Consumer Credit Protection

T HIS chapter discusses the federal laws governing the relationship between consumer debtors and business creditors. Consumer financial
statistics show that consumer credit and credit card usage have become a
major part of American life.

The chapter begins its discussion of consumer credit laws and regulations
by considering state usury laws and their impact on the debtor-creditor
relationship. Then the chapter discusses the principal federal law affecting the
regulation of consumer credit—the Consumer Credit Protection Act (CCPA) of
1968. The CCPA is the umbrella act for the federal regulation of consumer
credit markets. It is made up of several laws including the Truth-in-Lending
Act, Fair Credit Reporting Act, Equal Credit Opportunity Act, Fair Debt
Collection Practices Act, and the Electronic Fund Transfer Act. These laws are
intended either to provide consumers with adequate information regarding
the debtor-creditor relationship or to assure that bias and other social
considerations do not influence the availability of consumer credit. Finally, the
chapter considers the law of bankruptcy.

The chapter closes with the Issues article, which considers the controversial use of consumer credit history in the employment application process.

CONSUMER CREDIT STATISTICS

Although consumers have used credit since colonial times, the extensive
availability and general use of consumer credit has become common only
since the early 1950s. With consumer credit increasingly more available since
1950, it is not surprising that total outstanding consumer credit increased
from just $21.5 billion in 1950 to more than $700 billion in 1990. As Table 20–1
shows, consumer credit has grown most significantly through the use of credit
cards, where consumer credit amounted to only $5 billion in 1970 but over

Table 20-1   Consumer Credit Outstanding: 1970 to 1990

Type of Credit	(dollars in billions)				
	1970	**1975**	**1980**	**1985**	**1990**
All credit	$132	$205	$349	$592	$740
% of disposable personal income	18.3	18	18.2	21	24
Auto loans	$ 36	$ 57	$112	$210	$300
Revolving (credit cards)	5	15	55	122	215
Commercial Bank Loans	49	83	146	241	340
Finance company loans	28	33	62	111	142
Credit union loans	13	26	44	72	91

Source: *Statistical Abstract of United States, Survey of Current Business,* and *Federal Reserve Bulletin.* 1990 figures preliminary.

$200 billion in 1990. Auto loans and commercial bank loans, while growing more slowly, were the most common sources of consumer credit, accounting for nearly two-thirds of outstanding consumer credit in 1990. Consumer credit has risen to 24 percent of disposable personal income.

Most consumers now carry a variety of credit cards. As Figure 20–1 shows, there are over 250 million general-purpose credit cards, such as Visa and American Express, in circulation. Many more cards than that are issued by department stores and gasoline companies. The majority of American families have at least one credit card, almost all upper-income families have several cards, and almost all college graduates are able to obtain cards. Despite the giant growth in this area of consumer credit, credit cards carry only a small fraction of all consumer debt. More important than credit cards to most persons are loans for automobiles and for other major purchases. While we will not review the regulations concerning the home mortgages carried by the majority of American families, that debt is about triple the level of all other consumer credit. The rules governing mortgage creditors are very similar to the regulations we review here concerning consumer credit.

USURY LAWS

State statutes often limit the rate of interest a creditor may charge a consumer. A creditor charging a rate of interest above the legal limit commits *usury,* and the transaction is illegal. The remedies available to a consumer are determined by state law. In many states, the creditor forfeits the right to collect any interest; some states prohibit the creditor only from collecting interest in excess of the amount permitted by law.

States often have several usury statutes. Some statutes apply only to small loans while others apply to consumer installment sales contracts. Loans made to businesses are frequently exempt from the usury laws. The statutes may allow creditors to charge consumers for fees and expenses in preparing loan documents and to assess points as a cost of obtaining a loan. However, many usury laws consider fees, expenses, or points as finance charges.

Figure 20–1   Number of General-Purpose Credit Cards and
Average Annual Charges per Card

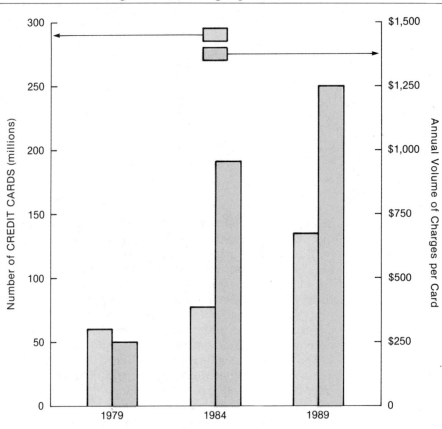

Source: Sanford C. Bernstein & Company.

Purpose and Effects of Usury Laws

The objective of usury laws is to protect consumers from paying "too much" for the use of money. Usury laws have existed since biblical times. Yet frequently the effect of usury statutes has been to penalize persons in need of funds. Because of usury laws, high-risk consumers may be closed out of the legal market for loans and have to seek loans from illegal markets. Regulating finance charges may lead businesses to raise product prices or alter other normal business practices to compensate for the restrictions on the interest rate.

Federal Preemption of State Usury Laws

Historically, the usury laws were principally state laws. The only exception was that national banks could charge interest at the maximum rate established by the state usury laws or at up to one percent over the federal discount rate (the rate at which the Federal Reserve Bank lends money to banks), whichever was higher. In 1980, a significant change in the usury laws occurred. Title V of the Depository Institutions Deregulation and Monetary Control Act preempted state usury laws on some loans, especially first mortgages on residential real estate. States can override the preemption only by passing legislation that contains a specific statement saying that the state is overriding the preemption given in the Deregulation Act.

Additional federal legislation eliminated the interest rate ceilings on real estate loans insured by the Federal Housing Authority (FHA). Congress has considered but has not passed legislation that would eliminate all usury laws. The success of passage of this legislation is uncertain. Industry has mixed reactions. On one hand, lenders would be unfettered by restrictions on the interest they could charge; on the other hand, more competition among lenders could result in removing artificially high interest rate ceilings and in reducing profit margins.

CONSUMER CREDIT PROTECTION ACT

Passage of the *Consumer Credit Protection Act* (CCPA) in 1968 actively involved Congress in regulating the direct relationship between the consumer and the creditor. Before that time, the federal government had regulated interest rates paid by and to some financial institutions, but this was the first direct federal involvement in consumer credit markets. CCPA has become an umbrella law containing several credit-related laws. Figure 20–2 shows the credit laws that are part of CCPA. The laws provide certain protections for consumers in credit

Figure 20–2   The Major Elements of Federal Consumer Credit Legislation

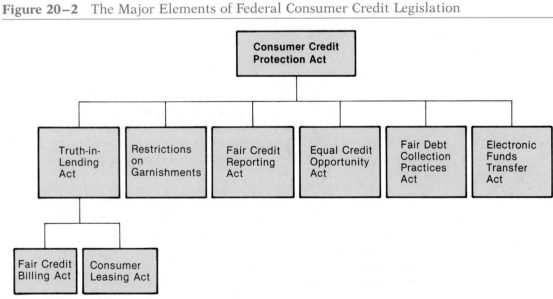

transactions and place certain restrictions and requirements on creditors, including the following:

- Requiring creditors to disclose all relevant terms in credit transactions.
- Prohibiting creditors from using certain personal characteristics of individual consumers (such as sex or color) in determining an individual's creditworthiness.
- Requiring credit-reporting agencies to provide accurate information in consumer reports.
- Prohibiting abusive debt-collection techniques.
- Providing procedures for correcting inaccurate and disputed bills and charges.

TRUTH-IN-LENDING ACT

The first law to come under the Consumer Credit Protection Act was the *Truth-in-Lending Act* (TILA), which went into effect in 1969. TILA requires creditors in consumer transactions to disclose basic information about the cost and terms of credit to the consumer-borrower. The purpose of TILA is to encourage competition in the financing of consumer credit. By making borrowers aware of specific charges and other relevant information, it encourages them to shop around for the most favorable credit terms, much as they would shop around for the best price for a car.

In addition to requiring that specific costs of credit information be given to consumers, TILA as amended contains the Consumer Leasing Act and the Fair Credit Billing Act. The Consumer Leasing Act establishes standardized terms to be disclosed in consumer leases of personal property, such as automobiles and computers. The Fair Credit Billing Act establishes procedures for consumers when credit cards are lost or stolen or when monthly credit card statements contain billing errors or disputed charges.

Finance Charge Disclosures

Until TILA was passed, creditors quoted interest in many ways, including add-on interest, time-price differential, discount interest, and simple interest. Those differences had come about in part as a result of creditors' attempts to escape the interest rate restrictions placed on them by the state usury laws.

The various ways of calculating interest caused substantial confusion. For example, an 8 percent add-on interest rate is approximately the same as a 15 percent simple interest rate. The difference occurs because an add-on rate always calculates interest on the initial amount of the loan regardless of the outstanding principal, whereas the simple interest rate method calculates interest only on the outstanding principal. Standardized terms were adopted under TILA so that consumers could make easy and valid comparisons.

TILA Requirements and Coverage

TILA requires that specific standardized loan terms be given to consumers before they become committed to the credit transaction. The disclosures required by TILA are designed to provide consumers with meaningful information about the costs of credit before the agreement is signed. TILA is essentially a disclosure statute—it does not set maximum or minimum rates of interest.

TILA covers only certain classes of consumer credit transactions. The debtor must be a "natural person," not a business organization, and the creditor must be in the business of regularly extending credit. The law does not apply if the credit transaction does not include a finance charge, unless the consumer repays the creditor in more than four installments. Finally, the Act does not apply to consumer credit transactions involving more than $25,000, except real estate purchases.

Credit Cost Disclosure Requirement

Transactions covered by the Act must disclose the cost of credit in dollars (the finance charge) and the annual rate of that finance charge (the *annual percentage rate* or APR). These items must be disclosed more conspicuously than any of the other items in the agreement. The finance charge includes more than interest charges.

Regulation Z, written by the Federal Reserve Board to implement the Truth-in-Lending Act, specifies items that are part of the finance charge, including the following:

1. Service, activity, carrying, and transaction charges.

2. Loan fees and points.

3. Charges for mandatory credit life and credit accident and health insurance.

4. In non-real estate transactions, the fees for credit reports and appraisals.

Certain other items, such as licenses and fees imposed by law, are not part of the finance charge if they are itemized and disclosed to the consumer in the transaction. Figure 20–3 shows the disclosure required in the sale of a car on credit.

Detail and Complexity of TILA

When TILA was first introduced, it was a relatively simple six-section consumer credit disclosure bill. That uncomplicated idea grew into a 52-section act, implemented by Regulation Z, that contains 15 sections and 153 subsections. TILA and Regulation Z have been the subject of thousands of court suits, countless out-of-court settlements, more than 65 formal Federal Reserve Board interpretations, and more than 1,500 published Federal Reserve Board staff opinions. Businesses have found the disclosure requirements of TILA to be detailed and complex. Even the most insignificant error in disclosing required information can result in severe penalties. The *Young* case illustrates the consequences of not fully disclosing required information.

Figure 20–3   Sample Credit Sale Disclosure Form

Big Wheel Auto   Alice Green

ANNUAL PERCENTAGE RATE The cost of your credit as a yearly rate.	FINANCE CHARGE The dollar amount the credit will cost you.	Amount Financed The amount of credit provided to you or on your behalf.	Total of Payments The amount you will have paid after you have made all payments as scheduled.	Total Sale Price The total cost of your purchase on credit, including your downpayment of $ _1500—_
14.84 %	$ 1496.80	$ 6107.50	$ 7604.30	$ 9129.30

You have the right to receive at this time an itemization of the Amount Financed.
☐ I want an itemization.   ☒ I do not want an itemization.

Your payment schedule will be:

Number of Payments	Amount of Payments	When Payments Are Due
36	$211.23	Monthly beginning 6-1-81

Insurance:
Credit life insurance and credit disability insurance are not required to obtain credit, and will not be provided unless you sign and agree to pay the additional cost.

Type	Premium	Signature
Credit Life	$120—	I want credit life insurance. _Alice Green_ Signature
Credit Disability		I want credit disability insurance. Signature
Credit Life and Disability		I want credit life and disability insurance. Signature

Security: You are giving a security interest in:
☒ the goods being purchased.
☐ _____

Filing fees $ _12.50_   Non-filing insurance $_____

Late Charge: If a payment is late, you will be charged $10.

Prepayment: If you pay off early, you
☐ may   ☐ will not   ☐ have to pay a penalty.
☒ may   ☐ will not   ☐ be entitled to a refund of part of the finance charge.

See your contract documents for any additional information about nonpayment, default, any required repayment in full before the scheduled date, and prepayment refunds and penalties.

I have received a copy of this statement.

Alice Green   _5-1-81_
Signature   Date

_____
e means an estimate

Source: Code of Federal Regulations, 1989 edition.

Young v. Ouachita National Bank in Monroe

United States District Court, Western District of Louisiana 428 F.Supp. 1323 (1977)

Case Background. *Ouachita National Bank financed a car loan for Young. She sued the bank, claiming that it failed to itemize fully on the TILA disclosure statement that the $14.50 listed there as "official fees" consisted of $10.00 for the license plate, $3.50 for the title, and $1.00 to record the sale and mortgage. The bank claimed that the disclosure of $14.50 as official fees substantially complied with TILA. The bank claimed that further itemization was not required but that, if it were required, there should be no damages since the violation was technical.*

Case Decision. Senior District Judge Dawkins delivered the opinion of the court.

* * *

[Young] argues that because components of the "official fees" were not "itemized," the amount charged under that heading should have been included in the finance charge. We agree.

Section 226.4(b) provides in pertinent part as follows:

If itemized and disclosed to the customer, any charges of the following types need not be included in the finance charge:

* * *

(4) License, certificate of title, and registration fees imposed by law.

The requirements of this section are clear; unless the fees imposed by law in this transaction are *itemized*, they must be included in the computation of the finance charge. [The bank] has obviously failed to "itemize" the official fees and has not included the [$14.50] fee as part of the finance charge. Consequently, [the bank] must be held liable for its failure to properly disclose the finance charge imposed in this transaction.

While the district court found that the defendant had failed to 'itemize' the official fees as required by the Act and Regulation Z, it nevertheless refused to impose liability for what it referred to as a violation 'miniscule in its scope and amount.' However, once the court finds a violation, no matter how technical, it has no discretion with respect to the imposition of liability. The civil liability section of the Truth-in-Lending Act provides that:

Except as otherwise provided in this section, any creditor who fails to comply with *any requirement imposed under this part* or Part D of this subchapter with respect to any person is liable to such person in an amount equal to the sum of—
1. any actual damages sustained by such person as a result of the failure;
2. (A) in the case of an individual action twice the amount of any finance charge in connection with the transaction, except that the liability under this subparagraph shall not be less than $100 nor greater than $1,000.
3. . . . in the case of any successful action to enforce the foregoing liability, the costs of the action, together with a reasonable attorney's fee as determined by the court.

Therefore, unless one of the defenses provided in the Act is applicable to this transaction, the Court must award the successful litigant-consumer the statutory penalty set out above.

Consequently, it is clear that lending institutions must choose, as plaintiff argues, either to include the various expenses in the finance charge, or itemize them in detail; merely summarizing or categorizing fees and expenses is not adequate disclosure.

* * *

Case Holding. *The court found that failure to itemize the official fees did violate TILA and that plaintiff Young was entitled to $726.66 (twice the amount of the finance charge), plus attorney's fees and court costs.*

Case Questions

1. The "official charges" of $14.50 for a license plate and so forth are standard fees paid by anyone buying a car. Do you find evidence of bad faith on the part of the lender (bank) here? Was the bank trying to sneak in some extra finance charges?

2. There are thousands of suits brought like this each year. Many catch a fine point violation like the one here. What effect does this have on lenders? How do such cases benefit borrowers?

TILA Reform

To minimize potential lawsuits, creditors began to disclose more information. Different creditors, however, revealed different information, often resulting in consumer confusion. Responding to these difficulties, Congress enacted the Truth-in-Lending Reform Act in 1980. The major simplifying provisions of the Act are as follows:

- The number of items required to be disclosed were reduced from twenty-four to twelve.

- The required disclosures were made more understandable by requiring an explanation of the required terms; for example, an explanation of the finance charge suggested by the Federal Reserve is "the dollar amount the credit will cost you."

- The Federal Reserve Board was required to issue model disclosure forms that, if correctly used by the creditor, will keep the creditor in full compliance with the law and will protect the creditor in the event of a lawsuit.

- The basis on which consumers could sue was limited to failure to disclose or inaccurate disclosure of six major terms, including the finance charge, annual percentage rate, and amount financed.

TILA Enforcement and Penalties

TILA provides for both civil and criminal penalties. As illustrated by the *Young* case, the Act allows damages to be collected for *any* violation. Consumers can sue a creditor for civil penalties of twice the amount of the finance charge (minimum damages—$100; maximum damages—$1,000), court costs, and the consumer's attorney's fees.

The creditor can avoid liability for a violation if it is corrected within fifteen days from the time it is discovered by the creditor and before the consumer gives written notification of error. In addition, the 1980 Reform Act protects creditors who rely on official staff interpretations by the Federal Reserve Board. These interpretations are published annually as the "Official Staff Commentary on Regulation Z."

A creditor who willfully or knowingly gives inaccurate information or fails to make proper disclosures is subject to criminal liability. Criminal liability includes a fine of up to $5,000, imprisonment of not more than one year, or both, for each violation of the Act.

Consumer Leasing Act

In addition to obtaining loans for major purchases such as automobiles, home furnishings, and computers, consumers are agreeing to lease such items. The leases enable consumers to put down less money initially. Most leases provide an option to buy the property when the lease ends, making the transaction similar to credit purchases.

Because TILA was successful in helping consumers understand the cost of credit, it was amended to include truth-in-leasing provisions. The *Consumer Leasing Act* does for consumer leases what the Truth-in-Lending Act does for consumer credit. That is, it provides standard terms to help consumers shop around for leases. It helps consumers to compare the terms of different leases, and the terms of leases with the terms of loans.

Lease Transactions Covered

The Consumer Leasing Act applies to leases of personal property used for personal, family, or household purposes. To be covered by the Consumer Leasing Act, the lease must have a term of more than four months and a contractual obligation of less than $25,000. Apartment leases are not covered by the Act because the property leased is real, not personal, property. Daily car rentals are not covered, because the term of the agreement is not long enough. Also, a lease for property used for business purposes is not covered by the Act, because it is not for personal, family, or household purposes.

Disclosure Requirements

The Consumer Leasing Act specifies information that must be disclosed before the consumer becomes contractually obligated for the lease. The required disclosures include the following items:

- Number, amount, and period of the payments and the total of the payments.

- Any express warranties offered by the leasing party or the manufacturer of the leased property.

- Identification of the party responsible for maintaining or servicing the leased property.

- Whether the consumer has an option to buy the leased property and, if so, the terms of that option.

- What happens if the consumer should terminate the lease before the lease expires.

The disclosures help consumers make meaningful comparisons with other leases or alternative purchase plans before agreeing to a particular financial obligation.

Liability

The consumer leasing provisions are in the Federal Reserve Board's *Regulation M*. The criminal liability for violating the Consumer Leasing Act and Regulation M is the *same* as the liability for violating the Truth-in-Lending Act and Regulation Z. Civil liability is 25 percent of the total amount of monthly payments under the lease but no less than $100 or more than $1,000, plus court costs and attorneys' fees.

Fair Credit Billing Act

Congress amended the Truth-in-Lending Act to include the *Fair Credit Billing Act* (FCBA) in 1974. Before the Act, consumers complained they were unable to get creditors to correct inaccurate charges or to remove unauthorized charges that appeared on billing statements. Some creditors would not acknowledge consumers' efforts to correct errors in bills. Some creditors would acknowledge an error, blame the problem on their computer, but fail to solve the problem. Meanwhile, consumers who believed they did not owe the disputed charge would not pay that portion of the bill. The nonpayment was reported to credit bureaus, and consumers' credit histories were damaged.

In addition, credit card issuers commonly sent cards to people who did not request or want them. Some unsolicited cards were lost or stolen, and consumers who never requested or used the cards were billed and, in some cases, harassed for payments of an account never authorized or used.

Procedure and Prohibitions

FCBA addressed these problems in three ways:

1. It established procedures to dispute *billing errors*. The consumer must notify the creditor in writing within sixty days of the first billing of the disputed charge. The creditor must acknowledge the complaint within thirty days of receipt and has ninety days to resolve the problem and notify the consumer. If the creditor fails to follow the required procedures, it cannot collect the first $50 of the questioned amount.

2. It prohibited the mailing of unsolicited credit cards.

3. It established procedures to report lost or stolen credit cards. If the consumer reports the theft in a timely fashion, maximum liability for unauthorized charges is $50.

Problems regarding unsolicited credit cards and billing disputes existed whether the monthly bill was required to be paid in full or could be deferred and whether a finance charge was charged. The FCBA governs card issuers whether or not they charge an interest rate or require payment in full.

Enforcement

Most billing disputes are resolved through the procedures established by the FCBA. Dissatisfied consumers can also sue for civil penalties for FCBA violations. In successful actions, creditors are liable for twice the amount of the finance charge, plus attorneys' fees and court costs. The Federal Trade Commission (FTC) is the principal FCBA enforcement agency, with jurisdiction over department stores, gasoline retailers, and nonbank card issuers, such as American Express.

For example, in 1989 the FTC obtained $2.5 million in redress for about 100,000 consumers to settle charges against BankCard Travel Club. The FTC complained that the company failed to honor cancellation requests and improperly charged annual membership fees to consumers' credit cards. The judgment requires repayment of fees to consumers who had requested cancellation and an injunction against further violations.

Other federal agencies enforce the credit statutes for other credit-granting institutions. National banks are regulated by the Comptroller of the Currency.

State banks that are members of the Federal Reserve system are regulated by the Federal Reserve Bank serving the district in which the state bank is located. State banks that are not a part of the Federal Reserve system, but are federally insured, are regulated by the Federal Deposit Insurance Corporation (FDIC). Savings and loan associations are regulated by the Federal Home Loan Bank Board.

FAIR CREDIT REPORTING ACT

Congress added the *Fair Credit Reporting Act* to the Consumer Credit Protection Act in 1970. The Fair Credit Reporting Act requires *credit bureaus* (consumer reporting agencies) to adopt practices for meeting businesses' needs for consumer information in a manner fair and equitable to the consumer. It requires confidentiality and accuracy in compiling and distributing *consumer reports*, traditionally called credit histories. The Act focuses on consumer reporting agencies that regularly assemble or evaluate information used for consumer reports that are furnished to businesses. A business that develops credit reports for its own use is not a consumer reporting agency and is not covered by the Act.

Credit Reporting Requirements

Consumer reporting agencies, such as credit bureaus, are required to follow reasonable procedures to assure the maximum possible accuracy of the information furnished in consumer reports. However, no limit is placed on the kinds of information that consumer reporting agencies can include in their files (such as information on political beliefs or sexual practices), so long as the information is not inaccurate or obsolete. The information most often contained in credit reports, for about 150 million Americans, includes data about employment, loans outstanding, credit cards, credit now available, and payment histories. There is no "credit rating"; that is up to the individual creditor.

Agencies may furnish consumer reports only if they are to be used for one of the purposes stated in the Act. A report may be issued if a business needs to evaluate an applicant for credit, insurance, employment, a government license, or any other legitimate business need involving a transaction with the consumer. Any other use requires either a court order or the consumer's permission.

Consumer Rights

The Act provides consumers with some rights to learn about the information that an agency has on file about them. The right is limited to the nature and substance of all information, the source of the information, and the names of the companies that have the report. The consumer does not have a right to see the actual file, but most credit bureaus will provide the report to a consumer for about $15.

Correcting Mistakes

If a consumer disputes the accuracy or completeness of an item on file, the agency must reinvestigate the current status of the information. In most cases, the investigation is completed within thirty days. The agency must delete information from the consumer's file it finds to be inaccurate. When the investigation does not satisfy the consumer, a statement explaining the dispute will be placed in the consumer's file. Subsequent reports issued by the agency must note the disputed item and include the consumer's statement. The agency must also give similar notice to current users of the report if so requested by the consumer.

A business using a consumer report is required to notify the consumer only if the report will contain information about the consumer's character, general reputation, or personal characteristics when such information is obtained by interviewing friends, neighbors, and associates of the consumer. In all cases, if the information in the report is used to reject a consumer's application for credit, insurance, or employment, the Act obliges the business to notify the consumer. The consumer must also be told the name and address of the consumer reporting agency that supplied the report, which is usually one of the "Big Three"—TRW, Equifax, and Trans Union Credit Information.

"Credit Repair"

Credit consultants or credit repair clinics have become popular in recent years. Many are legitimate businesses that charge consumers to do what they could do themselves. They buy a copy of a consumer's credit report, look for mistakes, and ask the credit reporting agency to correct the errors.

Others charge consumers high fees, claiming that they can "fix" a consumer's credit history. The only "fix" can be the correction of wrong information; the consultants or clinics cannot force the reporting agencies to delete true information or insert false information to make the consumer look like a better credit risk.

For example, the FTC settled a case in 1990 with "Credit Express" of Denver and Houston. The company charged consumers $495 to $795, claiming it could improve clients' credit reports, such as by having negative information in the reports removed. The company was required to refund fees to consumers, stop making false claims about what it could do, and give all prospective clients a notice that they have "no legal right to have accurate information removed" from credit reports.

Enforcement and Penalties

The FTC has principal responsibility for administrative enforcement of the Fair Credit Reporting Act. Violations are unfair or deceptive practices under the Federal Trade Commission Act. The Fair Credit Reporting Act provides a civil remedy for injured consumers. When the credit agency or the user is in willful noncompliance, the consumer may recover actual damages and a punitive penalty. The consumer may recover only actual damages when noncompliance is negligent. Any person who obtains information from a consumer reporting agency under false pretenses is subject to criminal prosecution and a fine of up to $5,000 and not more than one year in prison.

Employees of reporting agencies who knowingly provide information to unauthorized persons are subject to the same criminal penalties.

An example of how a business runs afoul of the Fair Credit Reporting Act comes from an FTC order that imposed on Allied Department Stores civil penalties of $150,000 for violations. The FTC complained that one of Allied's chain of stores violated the Act by failing to give consumers sufficient information about the basis for credit denials. The stores did not reveal to consumers that they denied credit applications based on information from a third party (such as an employer) rather than from a consumer reporting agency. Besides paying the penalties, Allied agreed to cease such practices and send corrective notices to customers who had been denied credit and were not properly informed as to the reason.

EQUAL CREDIT OPPORTUNITY ACT

Congress enacted the *Equal Credit Opportunity Act* (ECOA) as part of the Consumer Credit Protection Act in 1974 to prohibit *credit discrimination* on the basis of race, sex, color, religion, national origin, marital status, receipt of public benefits, the good faith exercise of the applicant's rights under any part of the CCPA, or age (provided the applicant is old enough to sign contracts). Creditors are prohibited from using such criteria (known as *prohibited bases*) in determining creditworthiness.

Unlawful Credit Discrimination

The guiding law for ECOA compliance is simple and short:

> A creditor shall not discriminate against an applicant on a prohibited basis regarding any aspect of a credit transaction.

Because this provision is very broad, Regulation B, written by the Federal Reserve Board to implement the ECOA, provides specific rules explaining what constitutes unlawful discrimination. Some of the rules are as follows:

- Creditors may not make any written or oral statements to discourage a person from applying for credit on a prohibited basis.

- Creditors may not ask questions about an applicant's birth control practices or her plans for children; nor can the creditor assume that because the applicant is of childbearing age, she will bear children and thus have reduced or interrupted income. Before ECOA, many creditors discounted or considered only a portion of a married woman's income and, in some cases, required the husband and wife to sign an affidavit that they would not have children.

- Creditors may not take into account the existence of a telephone listing in the applicant's name, but can consider whether the applicant's residence has a telephone. Because historically telephones were listed in the husband's name only, married women were often considered to be less creditworthy.

- If a creditor considers credit history in evaluating creditworthiness, it must, at the applicant's request, consider not only the applicant's direct credit history, but also her indirect credit history (for example, accounts that the applicant used or was contractually liable for, and accounts listed in the name of a spouse or former spouse that the applicant can show reflects her own credit history). This provision is to correct the practices of creditors and credit bureaus when credit history was reported only in the husband's name.

- A creditor may not request information about a spouse or former spouse of the applicant unless (a) the spouse will use the account or will be contractually liable for the debt; (b) the applicant is relying on the spouse's income or on alimony, child support, or maintenance payments from the former spouse; or (c) the applicant lives in a community property state or community property is involved.

A violation of ECOA exists if it is determined that a creditor used a factor specifically prohibited by the Act. The consumer can sue the creditor for ECOA violations. If the consumer is successful, the creditor is liable for actual damages, punitive damages up to $10,000, attorneys' fees, and court costs, whether or not the discrimination was intentional.

In the following case, a company cancelled the plaintiff's credit card when her marital status changed. The company had made no inquiry into her creditworthiness.

Miller v. American Express Company
United States Court of Appeals, Ninth Circuit
688 F.2d 1235 (1982)

Case Background. *Virginia Miller's husband received an American Express (Amex) credit card in 1966. Later that year, she applied for and received a supplementary card. Her card had a different expiration date and account number than her husband's card, was issued in her name, and required an annual fee. She was liable for all charges made on her card. When her husband died in 1979, Amex cancelled her card and invited her to apply for a new card, which was then issued. She sued, claiming that her card had been cancelled after a change in marital status, which violates the Equal Credit Opportunity Act. Amex prevailed in federal district court and Miller appealed.*

Case Decision. Circuit Judge Boochever delivered the opinion of the court.

* * *

Mrs. Miller's account was terminated in response to her husband's death and without reference to or even inquiry regarding her creditworthiness. It is undisputed that the death of her husband was the sole reason for Amex's termination of Mrs. Miller's credit. Amex contends that its automatic cancellation policy was necessary to protect it from noncreditworthy supplementary cardholders. The regulations, however, prohibit termination based on a spouse's death in the absence of evidence of inability or unwillingness to repay. Amex has never contended in this action that the death of her husband rendered Mrs. Miller unable or unwilling to pay charges made on her card. The fact that the cancellation policy could also result in the termination of a supplemental cardholder who was not protected by the ECOA, such as a sibling or friend of the basic cardholder, does not change the essential fact that Mrs. Miller's account was terminated solely because of her husband's death. The interruption of Mrs. Miller's credit on the basis of the change in her marital status is precisely the type of occurrence that the ECOA and regulations thereunder are designed to prevent.

* * *

Case Holding. *The court of appeals reversed the district court and ordered that the lower court grant summary judgment to Mrs. Miller on the issue of liability. The undisputed facts showed, as a matter of law, that Amex violated the ECOA and regulations thereunder in its termination of Mrs. Miller's supplementary card.*

Case Questions

1. What damages could Mrs. Miller win in such a case?
2. Is it costly for credit card issuers to avoid problems such as the one that emerged in this case? If so, will that lead the credit card companies to be more strict in issuing cards?

ECOA Notice Requirements

When a consumer's application for credit or for a credit increase is denied or accepted at less favorable terms, the creditor must provide the consumer *written notification*, within thirty days of the application, containing the following information:

1. The basic provisions of ECOA.
2. Name and address of the federal agency administering compliance by the creditor issuing the notice.
3. Either (a) a statement of the specific reasons for the action taken or (b) a disclosure of the applicant's right to receive a statement of reasons.

The first and second requirements inform rejected applicants that it is against the law to discriminate on a prohibited basis and point them to one of the twelve federal agencies designated by ECOA to enforce the Act. Thus, applicants know where to report suspected acts of discrimination and where to ask questions and get answers about ECOA.

As stated in the legislative history of ECOA, Congress considered the third notification requirement regarding the statement of specific reasons to be one of the most significant provisions of the Act:

> [The] provision entitling rejected applicants to a statement of reasons for adverse action is among the most significant parts of the bill. With few exceptions, creditors have refused to do anything more than notify rejected applicants of the fact of rejection. Only rarely do creditors give even a cursory explanation of the reasons why . . . [This attitude] deprives rejected credit applicants of necessary and useful information. Further, . . . a decision is much less likely to rest on improper grounds.

By knowing why they were rejected, applicants can reapply when their situations change (for example, when the reason for denial is that they have too many bills due) or they can correct any misinformation used by the creditor. This requirement is supposed to help those classes of consumers with a history of credit discrimination and help every rejected credit applicant to understand the credit-granting process. This requirement also forces the creditor to analyze the standards used in determining creditworthiness.

INTERNATIONAL PERSPECTIVES: CONSUMER CREDIT PROTECTION INTERNATIONALLY

INTERNATIONAL

PERSPECTIVES

The consumer credit regulatory scheme discussed in this chapter would make little sense to a European or Japanese lender, because very few of the rules that exist in the United States under the CCPA are mandated by legislation in most developed nations.

For example, most of those nations do not have statutes that prevent discrimination in credit markets based on sex, race, or other personal characteristics. The Race Relations Act in the United Kingdom does limit some discrimination based on race or color, but in most countries, minorities have little political clout. Further, women do not have the statutory protection in most countries that is provided by the CCPA in the United States.

Most nations have general laws against misrepresentation and fraud that apply to credit markets. But the kind of standardization that has come about in the United States under the CCPA is not as common in other nations, nor are there as many regulators like the FTC or the various banking authorities who write and enforce credit regulations.

DEBT COLLECTION

Up to this point, we have been reviewing the laws protecting consumers in credit agreements. So long as consumers make timely payments on their credit purchases, the credit regulations provide many protections. Consumers, however, do not always make the required payments on time.

Creditors use nonjudicial and judicial methods to collect delinquent payments from consumers. Judicial collection methods include repossessing the product (the collateral), forcing a consumer to file for bankruptcy, and garnishing the delinquent debtor's wages. Some nonjudicial collection methods involving written or oral contacts with the debtor have been restricted by the Fair Debt Collection Practices Act.

Garnishment

Garnishment is a statutory proceeding under state law that gives the creditor the right to attach the debtor's property. It is held by a third party, such as wages held by an employer. The property (wages) is applied to the debtor's outstanding obligation. Title III of the Consumer Credit Protection Act prohibits an employer from firing an employee with one garnishment and restricts the amount of wages that can be garnished. In most cases, up to 25 percent of the debtor's net earnings (gross salary less the amount required by law to be withheld, such as taxes and Social Security payments) can be garnished. This increases to 60 percent when the obligation owed is for child support or alimony.

Fair Debt Collection Practices Act

Nonjudicial collection methods include written or oral contacts with delinquent consumers by creditors or by debt collectors acting on behalf of creditors. To collect delinquent accounts, consumers are advised by telephone or letter of the outstanding debt and are urged to pay. Sometimes, however, delinquent consumers are subjected to phone calls in the middle of the night, obscene language, and other harassment and abusive tactics. *The Fair Debt Collection Practices Act* is designed to eliminate unfair, deceptive, and abusive collection techniques used by some *debt collectors*, but permits reasonable collection practices.

Methods of Debt Collection

When a consumer fails to make payments on credit purchases, the creditor will try to collect the debt. Because of the delay and expense involved in taking the consumer to court, the creditor is likely to employ nonjudicial tactics to collect. Creditors may seek payment by letter, telephone, personal visits, threats of lawsuits, and communication with the consumer's employer. Generally, creditors are restrained in their efforts to collect past-due accounts by the desire to protect their goodwill and by the cost in time and money needed to collect delinquent accounts. Therefore, it is not uncommon for creditors to have an independent collection agency collect past-due accounts.

The Use of Debt Collection Agencies

More than 5,000 debt collection agencies operate across the nation. Usually operating on a 50 percent commission, each year these agencies collect approximately $5 billion in debts from eight million consumers.

The use of WATS telephone lines by collection agencies in the 1970s led to an increase in interstate collection efforts. State law enforcement officials pointed to that development as a prime reason for the necessity of federal regulation of debt collection methods. State law enforcement agencies are often unable to take action against unscrupulous debt collectors who harass consumers by telephone from another state.

Collection Restrictions Imposed by the Act

The Fair Debt Collection Practices Act (FDCPA) regulates the conduct of independent debt collectors. It does not apply to creditors attempting to collect their own debts. The FDCPA also covers attorneys collecting debts for their clients. The Act makes illegal abusive debt collection practices and contains a list of required actions and prohibited conduct by independent collection agencies. A host of harassing and deceptive debt collection practices are prohibited, including threats of violence or arrest, obscene language, the publication of a list of consumers who allegedly refuse to pay debts, and harassing or anonymous phone calls. The Act prohibits the use of false or misleading representations in collecting a debt. For example, the collector cannot impersonate an attorney in attempting to collect a debt and cannot misrepresent that papers being sent are legal forms.

To illustrate the kinds of collection methods and practices the law is intended to prohibit, consider the collection tactics condemned by the judge in *United States* v. *Central Adjustment Bureau*. Note, too, how the judge designed the remedy in this case.

United States v. Central Adjustment Bureau, Inc.

United States District Court, Northern District of Texas
667 F.Supp. 370 (1986)

Case Background. *The Central Adjustment Bureau (CAB) is a debt collection agency headquartered in Dallas with collection offices there and in twenty-five other cities. The government charged CAB with numerous violations of the FDCPA. CAB claimed that it had made good faith efforts to comply with the law.*

Testimony was taken from current and former employees of CAB and various debtors. Testimony established that at numerous offices, debt collection telephone calls were made at inconvenient times—before 8 a.m. and after 9 p.m.; calls were made to the debtor's place of employment after being told not to do so by the debtor or the employer; third parties were told about the debts without the consent of the debtor; harassing and abusive telephone calls were made to debtors and relatives, which included the use of racial slurs, belligerent threats, and such terms as liar, deadbeat, *and* crook; *obscene and profane language was used in collection calls; repeated calls were made to the same debtor in a single day; the caller claimed to be an attorney preparing to file suit; the debtor was told that he or she would be jailed or that property would be seized; the debtor was told that he or she had committed a crime; the debtor was told that her daughter's college degree would be revoked; and so forth.*

Case Decision. Judge Buchmeyer delivered the opinion of the court.

* * *

Under the Fair Debt Collection Practices Act, the test is not whether "a reasonable consumer" would be deceived, misled or harassed by the prohibited practices—because the Act is intended to protect "unsophisticated consumers." Therefore, this Court must look not only at the "reasonable consumer," but also to *a less sophisticated consumer* in determining whether the debt collection practices act has a tendency or capacity to deceive.

The government did prove by a preponderance of the evidence the use of "abusive, deceptive and unfair debt collection practices" by the defendant and many of its debt collectors (*including some of the supervisors and managers in the defendant's regional collection offices*). This evidence . . . established the following violations of the Fair Debt Collection Practices Act:

§ 805(a)(1)—Inconvenient Calls . . . ,
§ 805(a)(3)—Calls to Place of Employment . . . ,
§ 805(b)—Communications with Third Parties . . . ,
§ 804—Location Information . . . ,
§ 806—Harassment or Abuse . . . ,
§ 806(2)—Obscene or Profane Language . . . ,
§ 806(5)—Repeated or Continuous Telephone Calls . . . ,
§ 807(3)—Representation as an Attorney . . . ,
§ 807(4)—Threat of Arrest or Imprisonment or Garnishment . . . ,
§ 807(5)—Threat to Take Unintended Action . . . ,
§ 807(7)—Representations of Debtor Crime . . . ,
§ 807(10)—Deceptive Means to Collect Debt . . . ,
§ 808(3)—Solicitation of Post-Dated Checks . . . ,
§ 809—Validation of Debts. . . .

* * *

The government also requests special injunctive relief—a requirement that the following notice be included in every collection letter sent to a consumer by CAB:

The law gives you the right to stop us from communicating with you about this debt, if you request us to do so in writing. If you ask us to stop we will. But if you owe the debt, you will still owe it, and your creditor may continue to collect it.

The collector of debts must comply with the Fair Debt Collection Practices Act, which is enforced by the Division of Credit Practices, Federal Trade Commission, Washington, D.C. 20580.

Under the circumstances of this case—where there has been a widespread pattern of repeated, serious violations of the Act—a notice like this *is* an appropriate, if not essential, remedial measure. The notice informing debtors of their right under the Act to request the CAB debt collector to cease collection activity will be the most effective remedy against oral harassment and other telephone violations (which, by their nature, are very difficult and expensive to prove). Similarly, it is essential that debtors have available the information they need to protect themselves at the time it will do the most good; the notice of the FTC's involvement will enable debtors to make prompt complaints to the FTC if they receive no satisfactory response from CAB when a collector has engaged in violations of the Act.

* * *

Case Holding. *CAB was ordered to pay $150,000 in civil penalties, and the court enjoined the company and all its officers and employees from committing any of the violations found to have previously occurred. The above-mentioned statement about debtor rights and the FTC must be sent by CAB in a clear and conspicuous manner on each written statement sent consumers about a debt matter.*

Case Questions

1. Why should a judge order civil penalties to be paid, since debtors who suffered damages inflicted by the defendant could be sued in private actions?
2. As a matter of policy, we may find the behavior described in this case to be offensive, but if such nasty pressure results in more debts being collected, does that not benefit all debtors? That is, the lower the collection rate on debts, the higher the interest rate and the harder it will be to get credit.

Information Requirements of the Act

In addition to protecting the consumer against harassment and deceptive practices, the Fair Debt Collection Practices Act requires the debt collector to send certain information to the consumer within five days of the initial communication:

- Amount of the debt.
- Name of the creditor to whom the debt is owed.
- A statement that unless the consumer disputes the validity of the debt or a part of the debt within thirty days, the debt collector will assume that the debt is valid.
- A statement notifying the consumer that the debt collector must show proof of the debt if the consumer advises the debt collector within thirty days of the notification that the consumer disputes the debt.

Contacts with the Debtor Restricted

The Act also prohibits a debt collector from discussing the consumer's debt with a third party, such as the consumer's neighbors, unless the consumer grants the debt collector permission. The Act does not limit the number of times a collector may contact a consumer in attempting to collect a debt. It does, however, prohibit contact at inconvenient times or places, such as late at night or at the consumer's place of employment. Contact with the consumer must cease when either the collector learns the consumer is represented by an attorney or the consumer so requests in writing.

Enforcement and Penalties

The Act is primarily self-enforcing. Consumers subjected to collection abuses enforce compliance by bringing a lawsuit. The collector who violates the Act is liable for any actual damages (including mental distress) caused, any additional damages (not to exceed $1,000) deemed appropriate by the courts, and attorneys' fees and court costs. The FTC is charged with the administrative enforcement of the Act.

ELECTRONIC FUND TRANSFERS

One of the most rapidly developing areas of banking and consumer credit law has resulted from the impact of electronic technology. Banking and payment services now rely more on the use of computer and electronic technology to replace checks and other paper-based payment systems. These electronic payment systems are called *electronic fund transfer systems.*

Principal Forms of Fund Transfers

The National Commission on Electronic Fund Transfers defines an electronic fund transfer system as "a payment system in which the processing and communications necessary to affect economic exchange . . . are dependent wholly or in large part on the use of electronics." Essentially, they allow payment between parties by using electronic signals rather than cash or checks.

Today four principal types of electronic fund transfer services are available to consumers:

1. Automated teller machines, also known as twenty-four-hour tellers, that allow consumers to perform a variety of banking transactions.
2. Pay-by-phone systems, permitting consumers to telephone the bank and order payments to third parties or a transfer between accounts.
3. Direct deposits that deposit wages and other benefits into a consumer's bank account or automatic payments that deduct funds from the consumer's account to pay regularly recurring payments, such as automobile loan payments.
4. Point-of-sale transfers, which allow consumers, through the use of a computer terminal at a retail establishment, to transfer money instantaneously from their bank accounts to the merchant.

Electronic Fund Transfer Act

As these electronic innovations developed, Congress became concerned about the rights and liabilities of the consumers, financial institutions, and retailers who use an electronic fund transfer system. The principal concern of Congress was that the rights and duties established under traditional payment services did not provide satisfactory answers to many of the new legal questions associated with electronic systems. In response, Congress enacted the *Electronic Fund Transfer Act* in 1979 and required the Federal Reserve Board to write Regulation E to implement the Act.

Scope of the Act

The Act establishes the rights, liabilities, and responsibilities of participants in electronic fund transfer systems. It imposes specific requirements on financial institutions (such as banks, savings and loan associations, mutual savings banks, and credit unions) that offer electronic fund transfer accounts to consumers. As in the Fair Credit Billing Act, consumers have rights and liabilities when a card is lost or stolen and an unauthorized transfer takes place, a machine malfunctions or commits an error, a financial institution fails to make a requested transfer of funds, or the terms and conditions of the electronic accounts are not disclosed.

Consumer and Financial Institution Liability for Stolen Cards

Perhaps the most important protection provided by the Act is the limit on consumer liability in the event the consumer's card is lost or stolen and an unauthorized user drains the consumer's account. Unlike the Fair Credit Billing Act's $50 limit on liability for lost or stolen credit cards, the Electronic Fund Transfer Act's limit on liability is much greater. In some circumstances, consumers may be liable for an amount equal to all the money in their account plus the maximum overdraft line of credit on the account.

Regulation E provides that the consumer's liability is no more than $50 if the financial institution is notified within two days after the consumer learns of the loss or theft of their card. After that, the consumer's maximum liability becomes $500 as long as the financial institution is notified within sixty days. If the consumer does not report the unauthorized transfers within sixty days after receiving the first statement containing unauthorized transfers, the consumer is liable for all losses incurred.

It was the intent of Congress to provide consumers with a financial incentive to guard against losses and thefts of cards and to notify the financial institution immediately of losses and thefts. By being required to absorb the remainder of any loss, the institution has an incentive to provide a secure system.

Financial Institution Liability for Failure to Transfer Funds

The Act makes the financial institution liable to the consumer for all damages caused by its failure to make an electronic transfer of funds. However, the institution's liability is limited to actual damages proved, such as costs incurred by the consumer when goods are repossessed for failure to make a required payment.

Reporting and Investigating Errors and Disputes

Consumers are to receive a monthly account statement from the financial institution. The consumer then has sixty days to report any errors in the statement. Should the consumer report an error, the financial institution must investigate and resolve the dispute within forty-five days. If the investigation takes more than ten business days to complete, the institution is required to recredit the disputed amount back to the consumer's account; the consumer has full use of the funds after the tenth day until the complaint is resolved. If the institution discovers that in fact an error has been made, it must promptly correct the error. Failure to undertake a good-faith investigation of an alleged error will make the institution liable for triple the consumer's actual damages.

Penalties for Noncompliance

A financial institution failing to comply with the Act is liable for actual damages suffered by the consumer, a penalty of at least $100 but not more than $1,000, and court costs and attorneys' fees. A financial institution that knowingly or willfully violates the provisions of the Act is subject to a criminal penalty of up to $5,000, and responsible executives may receive up to one year in prison.

BANKRUPTCY

Consumers whose financial plight becomes overwhelming are entitled under the *Bankruptcy Reform Act* of 1978 to seek a discharge of their debts in federal bankruptcy court. The purpose of *bankruptcy* is to afford the consumer the opportunity for a fresh start and to clarify a nearly hopeless tangle of creditors' claims. Over 500,000 people choose this course annually.

Bankruptcy law provides for three different kinds of proceedings:

1. Liquidation (*Chapter 7*).
2. Reorganization (*Chapter 11*).
3. Adjustments of the Debts of an Individual with Regular Income (*Chapter 13*).

The discussion here focuses on the liquidation proceeding, since that is most common. The *liquidation proceeding* is often referred to as "straight bankruptcy."

Voluntary and Involuntary Bankruptcy Under *Chapter 7*

Bankruptcy proceedings can be instituted either voluntarily by the consumer/debtor or involuntarily by creditors. Voluntary bankruptcies are more common than involuntary actions. Under the Act, any person with debts can initiate voluntary bankruptcy proceedings. The Act defines the term *person* to include partnerships, corporations, and individuals.

A *voluntary bankruptcy* is started with the filing of bankruptcy petition by the debtor in federal district court. Upon filing the petition, the debtor is automatically declared bankrupt. Creditors usually first learn of the petition when they receive the notice of the first creditors' meeting. One important feature of that first meeting is the selection of the *trustee* (the representative of the creditors).

When a debtor petitions the court for *Chapter 7* bankruptcy, these items must be provided:

1. Lists of all creditors with amounts owed and their addresses.
2. Declaration of all financial affairs of the debtor.
3. List of all property owned by the debtor.
4. A statement of current income and expenses.

In an *involuntary bankruptcy*, the creditors file the bankruptcy petition. If the debtor has twelve or more creditors, at least three must join in filing the petition. If there are fewer than twelve creditors, the involuntary petition may be filed by one or more of them. The total claims of those creditors filing must be at least $5,000. If the creditors' petition is not challenged by the debtor, the debtor's property automatically becomes subject to the jurisdiction of the bankruptcy court.

The Bankruptcy Proceeding

One of the principal features of the Act is the emphasis on creditors' receiving fair treatment. In contrast, under state law when it becomes clear that the debtor is unable to pay, the creditor who acts most quickly to gain control of the debtor's property is the creditor most likely to be paid. Under the federal system, once bankruptcy has been declared, creditors cannot improve their positions by getting to the debtor's property first. Nor can the debtor improve a favored creditor's position by transferring property to that creditor. It is the trustee's job to assure that no creditors have, by any means, improved their relative positions. Because of the possibility that some creditors may have learned of the debtor's financial plight and then gained control of some of the debtor's property, the Act provides that such transfers of the debtor's property made within ninety days of bankruptcy are void.

The Role of the Trustee

The trustee's objective is to maximize the amount of the debtor's assets available for distribution to the creditors. However, the Act provides that some of the debtor's property, as determined by state law, is exempt from bankruptcy. Normally, states exempt the debtor's house, household furnishings, car, and tools of trade. The trustee is required to liquidate all the debtor's nonexempt property. The liquidation is to take place through a sale at a public auction, unless otherwise ordered by the court. After the property has been sold, the proceeds are disbursed among the creditors. The Bankruptcy Reform Act provides that all creditors holding a claim against the debtor are entitled to share in the disbursement of the sales proceeds.

Priority Classes of Creditors

The Act provides that certain creditors take priority over other creditors in receiving shares of the debtor's assets to pay for the debts owed them. Standing first in line are *secured creditors*. These creditors have a written security agreement that describes the property (collateral) that stands behind a particular debt. For a consumer, the most common would be a home mortgage or an automobile loan. In case of bankruptcy, the secured creditor may take possession of the property covered by the debt and may keep the property or sell it to satisfy the debt.

The priority classes in bankruptcy usually would be as follows:

1. Secured creditors.
2. Costs of preserving and administering the debtor's estate.
3. Taxes.
4. Landlord's rent claims (if provided by state law).
5. General creditors.

All the creditors of a particular class must be paid before the next lower priority creditors can be paid anything. There is rarely enough money received from the sale to pay general creditors what they are owed.

Discharge in Bankruptcy

The final stage of the bankruptcy proceeding is the *bankruptcy discharge*. The purpose of the Act is accomplished at the discharge stage as the debtor is released from all debts. However, the discharge may be denied if the debtor knowingly or fraudulently committed certain offenses listed in the Act (such as receiving a bribe or making a false entry), had fraudulently conveyed property within twelve months preceding the bankruptcy, refuses to obey a lawful order or answer any material question in the bankruptcy proceeding, unjustifiably fails to keep or preserve financial records, fails to explain satisfactorily losses or deficiencies in assets, or fails to pay filing fees.

Some debts are not discharged by the bankruptcy proceedings. The reason for these exceptions is to discourage the use of bankruptcy to evade certain responsibilities. Among the debts not extinguished by bankruptcy are:

- Alimony and child support payments.
- Back taxes.
- Some student loans.
- Some debts incurred immediately before filing bankruptcy.
- Debts incurred by fraud against the creditors.
- Fines owed to the government.

Once bankruptcy has been declared, this fact remains on a consumer's credit history for ten years.

Chapter 13 Option

About 30 percent of all personal bankruptcies are handled under *Chapter 13*. A debtor may file under this option, or a *Chapter 7* bankruptcy may, by motion of the debtor, be changed to a *Chapter 13* proceeding. These proceedings are usually less costly than *Chapter 7* proceedings.

Chapter 13 applies only to individuals, not to corporations, who have regular income and are facing secured debts of less than $350,000 or unsecured debts of less than $100,000. The debtor must present a plan that will allow the debts to be paid within three to five years. The payoff will be supervised by a court-appointed bankruptcy trustee. If the debtor defaults, the creditors may then force a *Chapter 7* bankruptcy.

Chapter 11 Bankruptcy

About 20,000 *Chapter 11* bankruptcies are filed each year, mostly by businesses. The action usually involves a reorganization that allows a business to stay in operation and pay a portion of their debts. The remainder of the debts is discharged. The principles for paying the creditors are the same as for *Chapter 7* bankruptcies.

Allowing the firm to stay in operation often results in more of the debts being paid. If a firm is dissolved, the sale of assets may not bring in as much revenue as will future income that can be applied to the debts. In recent years a number of large firms have stayed in operation under *Chapter 11*.

As discussed in the section on products liability, the Manville Company was facing over 15,000 asbestos exposure injury lawsuits alleging $2 billion in damages. While the company was solid financially, its net worth of $1 billion could not begin to satisfy the claims. The court allowed Manville to stay in operation and to establish a compensation fund. Rejecting the claim that the company should be dissolved, the court said, "not only would liquidation be wasteful and inefficient in destroying the utility of valuable assets of the companies as well as jobs, but, more importantly, liquidation would preclude just compensation of some present asbestos victims and all future asbestos claimants."

SUMMARY

As consumer credit nears $1 trillion, it is a major part of the economy and is an important part of the way consumers function. Federal regulation has increased substantially in the past several decades, often largely supplanting state laws, such as usury laws that restricted the interest rates that could be charged on loans.

The Consumer Credit Protection Act is the umbrella federal law that contains most important credit statutes, including the Truth-in-Lending Act, the Fair Credit Reporting Act, the Equal Credit Opportunity Act, the Fair Debt Collection Practices Act, and the Electronic Fund Transfer Act.

The Truth-in-Lending Act requires lenders to meet requirements on how the details of loan amounts, interest charges, and other terms are stated to the borrower. Similar laws apply to most credit areas not covered by that Act. If a lender fails to comply and does not correct an error, there is no defense for the violation. The Consumer Leasing Act sets similar standards for consumer leases.

The Fair Credit Billing Act details the rights of consumers to take steps to resolve billing errors. Creditors must follow specific requirements on how long they have to respond to the consumer and what they must do to attempt to resolve the dispute. As under other parts of the credit statutes, violations mean double damages, plus attorneys' fees must be paid to the plaintiff.

Credit bureaus are important to lenders for the credit history they provide about those seeking credit. The Fair Credit Reporting Act specifies the rights of consumers to challenge the accuracy of reports issued by these bureaus. Credit bureaus must follow regulatory requirements in responding to inquiries from consumers about their own credit reports.

Creditors may not consider the following factors in determining who will be granted credit: race, sex, color, religion, age, national origin, marital status, receipt of public benefits, or having exercised consumer rights under the Equal Credit Opportunity Act. Specific regulations govern how lenders must comply with this statute.

Debt collectors may not abuse the rights of debtors under the Fair Debt Collection Practices Act. There may be no abusive phone calls, threats, claims of legal action not actually under way, or other harassment. A debt collector informed by any debtor that no further contact is desired may not contact the debtor except for notice of legal action.

Consumer rights and responsibilities for credit or fund-transfer cards that have been lost or stolen are spelled out in detail in the law. To limit liability for unauthorized charges, the consumer must notify the card issuer of the loss or theft of the card.

Bankruptcy is a very complicated and expensive process designed to straighten out the financial mess into which a person or business may have fallen. Contrary to popular belief, bankruptcy does not wipe the slate clean; instead, it is a structured reorganization of debts that usually should be considered only when there is no other choice.

ISSUE

Is Credit History Related to Job Ability?

Since employers are no longer allowed to use lie detector tests and some other measures that they previously used to help screen potential employees, many have recently started routinely buying credit histories on applicants as one screening device. Critics charge that this is an invasion of privacy and that past credit records should not be used to reflect on future job ability.

More Employers Check Credit Histories of Job Seekers to Judge Their Character

Gilbert Fuchsberg*

There's growing cause to worry about your credit record: It can cost you a job.

In a practice affecting hundreds of thousands of job seekers, a fast-rising number of companies are checking the personal credit reports of prospective employees to judge their integrity.

Many jobs applicants may never even know it's happening because companies often don't tell them—sometimes in violation of the law, critics maintain. Some also question the predictive value of the reports and charge that many companies misuse them to obtain personal data they aren't supposed to consider, such as age or marital status.

Employers using credit reports, however, contend that knowing how an applicant handles bills, loans and other financial obligations helps predict whether he or she is likely to steal, sell company secrets or otherwise act irresponsibly on the job.

Many banks and retailers that routinely consult credit reports before granting credit lines or loans have long used the reports to screen would-be tellers and cashiers. But, citing rising internal theft and concern about their liability for worker wrongdoing, a broader range of companies are using the reports to screen for all types of positions.

—continued

–continuing

Alternative to Lie Detector

The boom in credit screening follows tight limits on polygraph testing that took effect last year. In response, the nation's three big credit-reporting agencies began marketing their files to employers hungry for an alternative evaluation tool.

Equifax Inc. of Atlanta, which started selling its employee-screening reports in July 1988 just after the lie-detector ban was signed into law, claims it sold 350,000 of its reports to some 15,000 employers in 1989. It says demand in the first quarter of this year ran 71% ahead of the same period last year. **Trans Union Credit Information** Co. of Chicago began selling employee-screening reports last November and says it sold nearly 26,000 in March alone. **TRW** Inc.'s credit data division in Orange, Calif., introduced its reports in December but declines to release figures.

Some employers praise the reports. After a rise in theft that it traced to employees, Barry's Jewelers Inc., Monrovia, Calif., started using credit reports last month to supplement job interviews, applications and "pencil and paper" tests, which seek to gauge integrity through multiple-choice questions on ethical dilemmas. "It's one more added precaution," says CarolynJ. Harrington, director of loss prevention and internal audit.

Of 62 candidates screened during the first three weeks of the program, Barry's rejected 16, including three for problems arising from credit reports. "We deal with loose diamonds, we deal with highly resalable merchandise," Ms. Harrington adds. "You have to take every opportunity available to you to prevent hiring a thief."

'More Pressure'

Nordstrom Inc., the department store chain based in Seattle, runs credit checks on finalists for "sensitive" jobs in its security, financial and credit departments. "When somebody's having financial problems, there's more pressure on them to do things they otherwise wouldn't do," says John Walgamott, who as the chain's credit manager oversees 400 people who handle customer charge accounts. "One person could hit you for thousands of dollars."

Abbott Laboratories, a Chicago-based maker of medical supplies, evaluates credit reports as "part of the routine reference-checking on everybody," says Ellen Walvoord, director of corporate communications. "If a person had serious financial problems as revealed in their credit report, it could affect their suitability for certain positions," she adds. She declined to elaborate.

At less than $5 each, credit reports are cheap. They are also simple to obtain, since the big credit agencies sell online computer access to their data bases.

Not every company is biting, but those that are often are skittish about discussing the practice. J.C. Penney Co. consults the reports on a "selective basis," says a spokesman, but he wouldn't elaborate. "We really don't care to talk about how we're using it," he says.

Secrecy can affect job seekers, too. Under the Fair Credit Reporting Act, the primary federal law on credit reports, credit agencies must tell applicants they are being probed only if their files contain publicrecords on "adverse" matters, such as arrests, suits, court judgments and tax penalties. About 8% of reports contain such records, TRW says.

Employers, meanwhile, needn't inform job seekers about a credit check when they apply (though many do so on application forms). But when rejecting someone "either wholly or partly because of information contained" in a credit report, the law says a company is supposed to let that person know and identify the agency supplying the report—steps often ignored, those familiar with industry practices contend.

"People are being denied employment because of what's in their credit report, and

–continued

−continuing

are never told that's the reason," says Ken Yarbrough, a San Rafael, Calif., credit consultant who once managed security for TRW's credit data business.

"It would not surprise me that users of credit reports are not aware of their obligations," says Jean Noonan, associate director for credit practices at the Federal Trade Commission, which regulates credit report practices. Without disclosure, she adds, people might never learn to check for troubles or errors in their records.

Job Applicant's Experience

Sunday K. Summer of Bossier, La., says she was rejected for six different jobs as a hospital scrub nurse and drug store clerk last year after employers checked her credit report. The report states that her college loans were delinquent—she says they were deferred—and also refers to a bankruptcy-law filing made by her husband in 1981, when he divorced his previous wife. The doctor that finally hired her as an assistant said "that he had done some investigating and knew that I needed the job based on my debts"—specifically a $14,000 car loan that he couldn't have known about, she says, unless he had checked her credit report.

"It really felt awkward," Ms. Summer says. Having debts, she adds, "doesn't mean I'm not going to be a good worker."

Barry's Jewelers and Nordstrom say they strictly follow the law when rejecting applicants for credit concerns; Abbott declined to comment on its procedures. At Dallas-based EDS Corp., when job offers are rescinded because of concerns arising from credit reports, applicants initially are told merely that "it's because of the background investigation," says Jon T. Senderling, public relations manager. Only "if a person asks further," he says, does the company specify the reason.

But Ms. Noonan of the FTC says companies must identify the role of credit reports to spurned applicants forthrightly, not just when asked.

Interpretations of credit reports can vary widely. One employer might balk at hiring someone with a string of late Visa payments, while another might overlook more serious problems, even loan defaults or bankruptcy.

The lack of standards can lead to abuses. Besides financial history and other background information, credit reports may note a person's age, marital status and dependents—personal data most employers don't seek on applications or in interviews because, under equal employment laws, considering them is discriminatory.

Yet Trans Union specifically sees its report as a way to answer "some of the questions that you can't ask an applicant," says Pat Malloy, a product support coordinator. "This can fill in the holes."

'Inadequate Protection'

David F. Linowes, a University of Illinois professor and expert on privacy issues, say he believes it "is not uncommon" for employers to exploit credit reports for personal information that could unfairly—and illegally—scuttle the chances of job applicants. People "do not have adequate protection," he says.

Moreover, some employee-testing experts contend credit reports can't reliably predict trustworthiness. They note that credit records can contain inaccuracies, honest people can accrue bad credit records and people with clean credit records aren't immune to temptation. "Managers naively assume there's a link between a poor credit rating and theft exposure," says John W. Jones of London House, a Chicago personnel evaluating firm.

Scrutinizing credit reports before hiring would flag no more than 10% of "all the people who are acting irresponsibly on the job," estimates Val J. Arnold, vice president of Personnel Decisions Inc., a Minneapolis testing firm.

−continued

–continuing

Credit reporting agencies and companies can't cite studies linking personal financial problems to dishonesty; they say anecdotal experience and common sense prove the value of credit reports.

Still, William Byham, president of Development Dimensions International Inc., a Pittsburgh-based personnel testing firm, worries that companies are bound to unjustly reject many promising applicants if credit reports continue to gain appeal. "Everybody's looking for a quick fix," he says. But "you have to spend a little time and money on selection if you want to get good people."

Questions

1. If a potential employee is found to be heavily in debt, is this of legitimate concern to the employer? What if the employee will be in a position that does not involve money or valuable merchandise?

2. Since the job applicant is not requesting credit from the employer, should the applicant have a right to privacy about credit history?

REVIEW AND DISCUSSION QUESTIONS

1. Define the following terms:
   usury
   Regulation Z
   consumer reports
   garnishment
   debt collection agency
   electronic fund transfer
   voluntary bankruptcy
   involuntary bankruptcy
   bankruptcy trustee

2. A farmer goes to a local bank to see about getting a loan to cover operations until the crop comes in. Is the loan covered by the Truth-in-Lending Act?

3. A department store that has given credit to customers has a person in its collections department who is abusive on the telephone with delinquent debtors and calls them very late at night. Does this violate the Fair Debt Collection Practices Act?

4. Given the prohibitions of the Fair Debt Collection Practices Act, what methods of collection could an independent collection agency undertake?

5. A credit card company refused to issue a woman a credit card because of its previous credit experience in the woman's immediate geographical area. The company said that had the woman lived in a more desirable area, she would have been issued a credit card. Is that a violation of the Equal Credit Opportunity Act?

Case Questions

6. Fred and Mary are dating. Mary's father, who is the owner of a manufacturing company, does not trust Fred. To find out more about him, he asks the credit

bureau to send a consumer report on Fred, asserting he is thinking of hiring Fred. Under the Fair Credit Reporting Act, will Fred be told about the report being sent to Mary's father? What if the report included inaccurate information stating that Fred was known to move in subversive political circles? Are Mary's father's actions acceptable under the Act?

7. On June 1, 1982, Fred Brown filed a bankruptcy petition in federal district court. Knowing that he was going to declare bankruptcy, he gave Joe Smith, his favorite creditor, a used trailer house he was renting to some college kids on the edge of town. The trailer was worth $1,200, exactly what Fred owed Joe. Does Joe have to be concerned about Fred's bankruptcy petition? Why? If Joe could tell Fred when to petition for bankruptcy, on what day would he tell Fred to file?

8. Barbara bought a dress for $74.95 from Poor's, a local department store, using her Poor's credit card. When she showed the dress to her husband, she noticed a rip in the dress. Barbara therefore attempted to return the dress, but Poor's refused to credit her account for the purchase price of the dress. Is this lawful? What if Barbara had charged the dress to a third-party card, such as American Express or Visa?

9. Joel decided to buy a new Mercedes 450 SEL. Because he could not (or chose not to) pay cash for the car, he applied for credit through Big Bucks Car Dealership. Big Bucks then supplied the information given on the application to Frivolous Finance Company. The finance company obtained a consumer report from the credit bureau. Although Joel had an A-1 credit record, the finance company denied the loan because the credit manager believed that Joel did not earn enough money to buy an expensive car and, other than house payments, did not have an established credit history of making very large monthly payments. The finance company sent Joel a notice, explaining that he had been denied credit because credit references were insufficient. Joel sued Frivolous for violating the Fair Credit Reporting Act and the Equal Credit Opportunity Act. Who won the lawsuit? Why?

10. Seymour Roseman quit his job as an insurance agent after a company investigation found money missing from his account. The Retail Credit Company credit report on him had this statement in it: "We have handled [the investigation] at the home office in Boston and find that Roseman was employed as a debit agent [for the insurance company]. He resigned due to discovery of discrepancies in his accounts amounting to $314.84. This was all repaid by Roseman. His production in 1970, 1971, and 1972 was above average, and in 1973 and 1974, it was below average. This was the extent of the information available from [the insurance company] due to strict company policy." Roseman asked the credit company to check the accuracy of this information. The credit company did, confirmed its accuracy, and refused to remove the information from his credit history. He sued under the Fair Credit Reporting Act, claiming his rights had been violated. What was the result? [*Roseman v. Retail Credit Company*, 428 F.Supp. 643 (E.D.Pa. 1977)]

Policy Questions

11. There has been increased discussion about forcing credit card issuers (banks that issue cards such as Visa and Mastercard) to charge lower rates of interest on charges that are carried forward. The claims are that a 20 percent annual rate of interest (or something close) is too high given other interest rates, such as mortgages at, say, 11 percent, and that the rate should be kept down because the credit card companies have "addicted" consumers to the cards, so

they can sting them with high rates for which there are no alternatives. What do you think of these arguments? Since banking is quite competitive, what explains the high rates on credit cards?

12. The bankruptcy law now in effect makes it "easier" to declare bankruptcy than before. As a matter of policy, do we want a law that allows matters to be resolved by a bankruptcy court, or should we make bankruptcy hard to file, forcing more borrowers—individuals and businesses—to try to settle their debts rather than seek protection in the courts? What are the pros and cons?

Ethics Questions

13. The Equal Credit Opportunity Act holds that a creditor may not discriminate in credit decisions on the basis of characteristics such as sex and race. Suppose you work for a company that issues credit. A careful study indicates that, other things being equal, one group of customers has a worse repayment record than all others. That is, holding income, employment, and so forth constant, it turns out that single women or Hispanics have a below-average repayment record. You are pretty sure that you can hold whichever group is in question to a little higher standard for getting credit than all other groups and it will not be discovered, so you are not likely to get sued under the ECOA. Should you go ahead and discriminate? What are the consequences of discriminating versus not?

14. You own a large furniture and appliance store that sells primarily to low-income people. Your store offers credit to customers, including many who have trouble getting credit elsewhere. The prices you charge, credit rates you charge, and profits you earn are determined largely by the default rate of your credit customers. You have a debt collection department in your store rather than use a debt collection agency. You comply with all federal and state credit statutes. However, you have found that by being *very* aggressive in collecting on delinquent debts your losses are lowered. You use tactics that would violate the Fair Debt Collection Practices Act if it applied to your store. Should you use these tactics?

Expanding World of the Legal Environment of Business

Part Four considers an area of growing importance to the business community: the international legal environment of business. Increasingly, the relevant markets for most goods and services are becoming world markets. In their efforts to be successful in those markets, U.S. business executives are encountering a very different legal environment from the one to which they have generally been accustomed. The successful businesses are those who are well informed about and have an appreciation for the international legal environment of business.

International law as it affects international commerce is a complex and unique area of the legal environment of business. Chapter 21 is not intended to cover all the important differences in the legal and regulatory traditions of the major countries that make up the international business community. It does, however, provide an overview of the general principles about which a business must be aware to be effective in international business. Those general principles include a general legal framework for participation in international trade, international contract considerations, concerns about loss of investment, and the alternatives available for the resolution of international commercial disputes.

21 The International Legal Environment of Business

T HIS chapter provides an overview of the international legal environment of business. It begins with a discussion of the nature of international business and the current extent of U.S. involvement in international commerce. The chapter then discusses the major international organizations working to encourage and stimulate international business activity. Next, it considers the various forms of business organization a business may consider before becoming involved in an international commercial venture. Finally, the chapter discusses the nature of international contracting, insurance against loss, and the procedures for the resolution of international disputes.

THE NATURE OF INTERNATIONAL BUSINESS

With the technological improvements in transportation and communications over the past twenty-five years, the nature of and approach to general business activity has changed substantially. The percent of U.S. gross national product involved in direct international trade has tripled during that time. Virtually every business, whether oriented towards domestic or international markets, is now affected by events and conditions originating in the international business environment. Crop failures in Argentina, political unrest within the Middle-Eastern oil-producing countries, and shipping strikes in England can all have a significant impact on both U.S. domestic and international businesses.

The International Business Environment

The term *international business* is often defined to include all business transactions that involve two or more countries. In addition to being involved with the movement of goods across national boundaries, international business involves the movement of services, capital, and personnel. Finally, international business includes the transactions of all multinational enterprises, whether of private, public, or mixed ownership.

The *international business environment* involves considerably more than just business transactions across national boundaries. The international business environment also includes business activities that are affected by international business conditions and world events. For example, U.S. businesses that operated solely in the domestic market now find themselves in direct competition with foreign manufacturers. Initially, their principal source of foreign competition was from imported products. However, in the 1980s foreign competitors built factories in this country to compete more directly with domestic businesses. Direct investments in this country by the Japanese have increased at an unprecedented rate since 1980. The Japanese now compete directly with U.S. businesses in several domestic product markets, particularly in markets for consumer products.

Thus, although they had no intent to enter into international business transactions, those domestic industries are clearly within the international business environment and must become familiar with the international legal environment to maintain their competitiveness.

Risks in International Business Transactions

A principal distinction between domestic and international businesses lies in the special risks confronting the international business enterprise. Those risks fall into the general categories of *financial, political, and regulatory risks*. They arise from a variety of sources, including differences between countries in currencies, language, business customs, legal and social philosophies, and national economic goals.

International risks can have a measurable effect on profitability and require a level of managerial supervision not common in domestic operations. The management of financial risks involves consideration of currency exchange rates and of differentials in inflation and interest rates among countries. Political risks include concerns about the possibility of harsh treatment directed specifically at foreign businesses by the government of the host nation. The potential degree of political risk must be estimated several years in advance if the business is considering foreign direct investment in heavy capital equipment. The regulatory or legal risks arise from the existence of different legal systems and regulatory policies of the countries that the international community comprises. Taken together, these risks significantly increase the difficulties of operating in international markets.

Current U.S. Involvement in International Business

Historically, the United States has not participated as heavily in international trade as have other countries. An abundance of natural resources, a large domestic market, and a sense of national independence made international business opportunities a less attractive alternative to domestic business opportunities. Unlike countries such as Japan, England, and many of the Western European nations, the United States was able to enjoy a vibrant economy without emphasizing exports or relying on imports.

In the past ten years, however, both federal and state governments have undertaken efforts to encourage U.S. companies to enter the export market. It is estimated that there are more than 20,000 U.S. businesses that could export their products but, for a variety of reasons, do not. The major impetus behind government efforts to encourage those and other businesses to become involved in international business is the size and the persistence of the U.S. *trade deficit*. The United States has historically enjoyed a positive trade balance with the rest of the World, that is, the value of its exports has exceeded the value of its imports. However, as Figure 21–1 illustrates, beginning in 1975 the nation has run a merchandise trade deficit that has persisted and magnified for more than a decade.

Currently exceeding $120 billion per year, the trade deficit is not expected to improve appreciably for several years to come. As Table 21–1 illustrates, the United States is running a trade deficit with all its major trading partners. The trade deficit is particularly large with Japan, comprising about 35 percent of the total. The impact of the deficit has raised concerns about the nation's international competitiveness and trade policies, prompted calls for import restrictions, and fostered renewed state and national interest in international business development.

While the effects of the trade deficit have been a major congressional concern for several years, attention has shifted more recently to the relative decline in U.S. technological development. Technological development, as measured by patents issued, provides a measure of future product development. Countries with an edge in technological development are likely to enjoy a more rapid rate of industrial growth—thereby creating more new jobs and increasing personal income—than will countries with a lower rate of development. As Figure 21–2 indicates, only two U.S. companies—General Electric and IBM—were among the top ten companies in terms of U.S. patents issued in 1988. The U.S. decline in technological development has become an increasingly greater concern of Congress as it considers long-term solutions to the trade deficit.

INTERNATIONAL LAW AND THE REGULATION OF INTERNATIONAL COMMERCE

International businesses function in a unique legal environment, one that provides no comprehensive system of laws or regulations for guiding business transactions between two countries. Rather, the legal environment consists of a multiplicity of laws and policies from all countries engaged in international commercial activity. Those countries often differ dramatically in their basic legal philosophies, practices, and procedures. As a consequence, businesses engaging in international business face a variety of legal uncertainties and conflicts.

History of International Law

Before the development of the more formal international laws and procedures in existence today, nations involved in international commerce found it in their interests to establish customs upon which trade was to be based. Early

Figure 21-1 United States Foreign Trade Balance

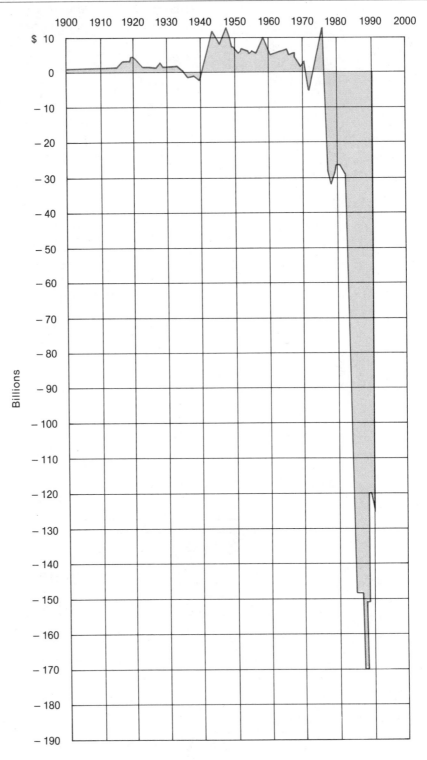

Table 21–1 U.S. Exports, Imports, and Merchandise Trade Balance, by Major Country, 1988

Country	Exports ($millions)	Imports ($millions)	Merchandise Trade Balance ($millions)
North America			
Canada	$ 69,233	$ 80,921	−11,688
Europe			
West Germany	14,331	26,503	−12,172
France	10,133	12,228	−2,095
Italy	6,785	11,611	−4,826
Japan	37,732	89,802	−52,070
Asia			
Hong Kong	5,691	10,243	−4,552
Taiwan	12,130	24,804	−12,674
Korea	11,290	20,189	−8,899
Eastern Europe			
Soviet Union	2,768	578	+2,190
East Germany	109	110	−1
Latin America			
Mexico	20,643	23,277	−2,634
Brazil	4,289	9,324	−5,035
U.S. total	320,385	441,282	−120,897

Source: U.S. *Statistical Abstract* (1990).

Figure 21–2 Leading Winners of U.S. Patents, 1988

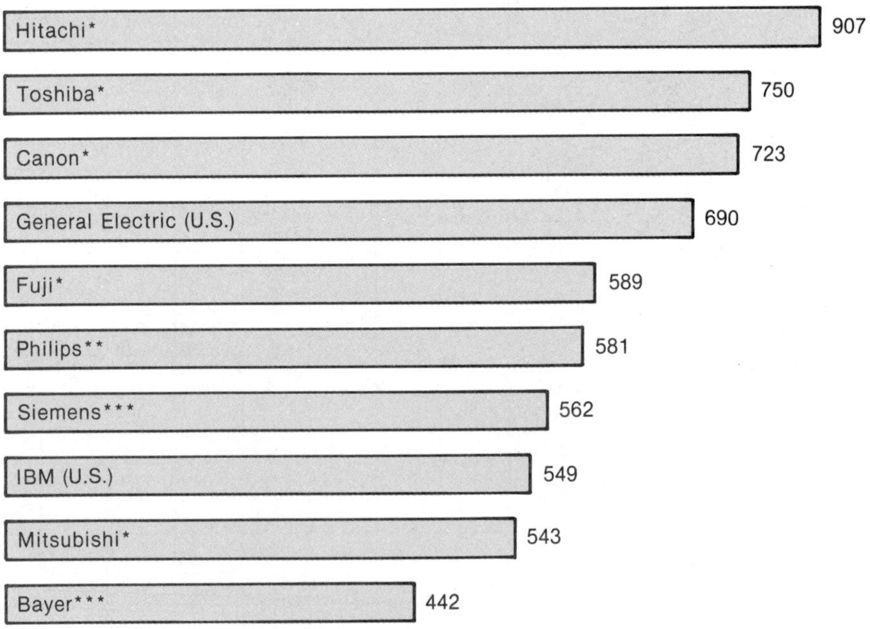

Hitachi*	907
Toshiba*	750
Canon*	723
General Electric (U.S.)	690
Fuji*	589
Philips**	581
Siemens***	562
IBM (U.S.)	549
Mitsubishi*	543
Bayer***	442

*Japan
**the Netherlands
***West Germany

Source: *Intellectual Property Owners Inc.*

trade customs centered around the law of the sea and provided, among other things, for rights of shipping in foreign ports, salvage rights, fishing rights, and freedom of passage.

International commercial codes date back as far as 1400 B.C. to Egyptian merchants involved in international business and trade. Merchants from other countries developed similar codes and trade customs to provide some degree of legal certainty in international transactions. In 700 B.C., for example, a code of international law had been developed on the Island of Rhodes in the Aegean Sea. The Greek and Roman civilizations both had well-developed codes of practice for international trade and diplomacy, especially concerning activities within their empires.

During the Middle Ages, international principles embodied in the *lex mercatoria* (or law merchant) governed commercial transactions throughout Europe. Although laws governing international transactions were more extensive in some countries than others, the customs and codes of conduct created a workable legal structure for the protection and encouragement of international transactions. The international commerce codes in use today in much of Europe and in the United States are derived in large part from those medieval codes.

Overview of Current International Law

The principal sources of international commercial law are the laws of the individual countries, the laws embodied in mutual trade agreements between or among countries, and the rules enacted by a worldwide or regional organization (such as the United Nations or the European Economic Community). There is, however, no international regulatory agency or system of courts available and universally accepted for the purpose of controlling international business behavior or resolving international conflicts among either businesses or countries. International law can be enforced to some degree in the International Court of Justice, through international arbitration, or in the courts of an individual country. However, the decisions of those tribunals in resolving international business disputes can be enforced only if the countries involved agree to be bound by them.

International Business in the 1990s

The 1990s decade is witnessing a dramatic change in the world business environment. The opening up of Eastern Europe, the abrupt shift toward free-market policies in the Soviet Union, the resurgence of the Mexican and other Latin America economies, the implementation of 1992 Europe, and significant reductions in domestic market protections in Japan have produced new markets and created incentives for growth in others. Few members of the business community question that the 1990s will be a decade of pronounced international market development and growth.

The enormous business opportunities presented by these changes, however, are not without risk. In times of rapid social change like that being experienced in Eastern Europe and the Soviet Union, political and ethnic upheavals are common and can be very disruptive and expensive to commercial undertakings. Economic liberalization often begins with an adjustment period characterized by unemployment and inflation—particularly in food prices—that can lead to revolts and sudden changes in governments. In addition, the business community remains skeptical about the ability of the antiquated legal systems in many of these countries to adequately enforce agreements and protect against confiscation or nationalization. An otherwise natural combination of international business opportunities and a desire on the part of Western companies to "go global" has been tempered by uncertainty in the international legal environment.

The Emerging Eastern European Economies

The sudden and dramatic decline in world communism was perhaps best symbolized by the dramatic fall of the Berlin Wall. Concurrent with that fall, the countries of Eastern Europe were given their economic and political freedom for the first time in more than fifty years. Sweeping economic changes have been introduced in an effort to attract foreign investment, modernize their economies, decrease unemployment, and increase the supply of consumer goods.

As Table 21–2 illustrates, the economies of East Germany and Czechoslovakia look to be the most promising for foreign investors. Both East Germany and Czechoslovakia are better positioned because of past industrialization efforts, low foreign debt, and a much more favorable legal environment relative to other Eastern European countries. In addition, East Germany will benefit economically as a consequence of its reunification with West Germany.

Table 21–2 Foreign Investment Potential in Eastern Europe

	COUNTRY **Population** **GNP per capita**	**ECONOMIC** **OUTLOOK**
Most Promising ↑	EAST GERMANY 16.6 million $9,350	Union with West Germany leads to strong growth after rocky start.
	CZECHOSLOVAKIA 15.6 million $7,600	Making strong strides toward a market economy; legal system uncertain.
	HUNGARY 10.6 million $6,500	Reforms have attracted investors including GE, GM, and Levi Strauss.
	POLAND 38 million $5,450	Great potential—if worker unhappiness over inflation and unemployment can be contained.
	BULGARIA 9 million $5,600	New leadership encourages investment but little real progress.
	YUGOSLAVIA 23.6 million $4,900	Potential for economic reform may be derailed by ethnic disintegration.
Least Promising ↓	RUMANIA 23 million $4,100	New government looks much like previous repressive regime, offering little chance for real reform.

Note: Income figures may be too migh because conversion into dollars is uncertain.

While a number of U.S. businesses have operative joint ventures in Eastern Europe, most Western companies remain skeptical about the legal environments in those countries. Constraints on foreign ownership of property, an immature and unsophisticated commercial law, and restrictions on currency repatriation are some of the principal concerns voiced by Western entrepreneurs.

The Soviet Union and Perestroika

The Soviet Union, long the bastion of communism, is now implementing sweeping free-market style economic reforms through its *perestroika* ("restructuring") political platform. Through recent legislative decrees, the Soviet Union now permits foreigners to own equity in Soviet enterprises, protects those investments against expropriation, and guarantees the repatriation of profits. These Western-Soviet joint enterprises are also free to decide upon their economic activities and are not subject to State Planning targets.

In addition, Soviet business enterprises in the Soviet Union are now required to be self-sufficient, with local management making strategic decisions on production, scheduling, and marketing. For the first time in more than seventy years, the management of most major Soviet enterprises and business partnerships is required to deal directly with foreign buyers and sellers without first obtaining permission from Moscow. However, with relatively little international managerial education or experience, Soviet management is having a difficult time adjusting to *perestroika* and its free-market reforms. These and other problems confronting the foreign joint venture were discussed in Chapter 10.

Despite the attractiveness of the Soviet market, foreign investors have responded very slowly to potential business opportunities. Clearly, the magnitude of the *perestroika* changes will create detractors in the Soviet Union— several powerful people will likely find themselves faring less well under *perestroika* than under communist rule. A sudden change in Soviet leadership for whatever reason—for example, an event such as that in China in May 1989—could bring about a reversion to past economic and political practices. In assessing the political risks of investing in the Soviet Union, a major computer company estimates there is a 15 percent chance that such an event may take place in any given year in the Soviet Union. Many foreign investors— and their insurers—have found that probability to be too great and are thus unwilling to accept the risks of doing business in the Soviet Union. Still, the Soviet market will become increasingly more attractive as foreign investors gain confidence in the stability of the political reforms and Soviet managers become better trained and experienced.

Europe 1992

It is anticipated that on December 31, 1992, the countries of Western Europe will begin to act as one country. The European Community's 1992 directive will end barriers to the free flow of goods, services, and capital, creating a single market of 350 million consumers. The directive includes abolition of currency controls, sweeping deregulation of important markets and industries, standardization of commercial law, and elimination of customs delays. Currently, much of commerce in Europe takes place on a country-by-country basis. Differing standards in everything from electrical plug-ins to telecommunications, and significant barriers in financial markets have seriously limited European economic growth. With the unification of Europe, and the elimination of those impediments, economic growth is expected to increase by an additional 0.4 percent per year, consumer prices are expected to decline by 6 percent, and two million new jobs will be created.

U.S. firms are concerned about the rapid changes in Europe, particularly in the regulatory environment. Most are cognizant of the possibility that the regulatory environment could change and shut them out of the European market—unless they develop their European production and distribution facilities prior to December 31, 1992. Despite these efforts, however, only 38 percent of the Chief Executive Officers of the largest 350 U.S. companies in Europe believe they will be positioned to compete effectively in the new unified Europe in 1992.

A North American Unified Market

Although the economic unification of Europe in 1992 has played most predominantly in the news media, Canada, Mexico, and the United States have been working to create their own unified market. The three countries intend to enter into a North American free trade agreement in the early 1990s. As in Europe 1992, goods and services will flow freely—without tariffs, quotas or duties—across the Canadian, U.S., and Mexican borders. The agreement will encourage companies to develop continent-wide business strategies. The relative size of the North American unified market in comparison with the European 1992 market is provided in Table 21–3.

A huge expansion in cross-border manufacturing and trade with Mexico and Canada is pushing unification and promising to make North America an effective counterweight to trade blocs in Europe and Asia. Much of the increased cross-border manufacturing and trade has developed in response to important changes in the Mexican legal environment. For example, Mexico has deregulated important sections of the economy, lowered tax rates, privatized many industries previously operated (inefficiently) by the government, and enacted legislation allowing foreigners to own 100 percent of some businesses (past laws restricting foreign ownership to 49 percent proved a serious deterrent to foreign investment). In addition, Mexico's *Maquiladora Program*—which allows U.S. corporations to bring unassembled products into Mexico duty free for assembly at very low labor rates relative to U.S. rates—has been very successful in attracting foreign investment.

Table 21–3   Comparison of the North American and European Unified Markets

	Population	Gross National Product	Additional Economic Growth	Two-Way Trade
Europe 1992	350 Million	$4.8 Trillion	0.4%	$160 Billion[1]
North America	360 Million	$6.0 Trillion	0.5%	$194 Billion[2]

[1]U.S. imports and exports from the EC countries.
[2]U.S. imports and exports from Mexico and Canada.
Source: U.S. Statistical Abstract (1990); Bank of Montreal.

A free-trade agreement between the United States and Canada has already been signed. As the statistics in Tables 21–1 and 21–4 illustrate, Canada is a very important trade and investment partner for the United States. The free-trade agreement modifies the legal environment of business between the countries by effectively eliminating tariff and nontariff trade barriers (over a period of ten years), and providing for considerable liberalization in investment conditions. Given that the agreement forms the world's largest bilateral trading partnership, it has major worldwide economic significance.

The Changing U.S.–Japan Trade Relationship

As reflected by the recent trade deficit statistics presented in Figure 21–3, Japan became a significant international trading partner with the United States in the 1980s. The U.S. market fueled Japan's dramatic growth, but led to the creation of a trade deficit of nearly $50 billion per year throughout the 1980s. Recently, Japan has been roundly criticized for making it difficult for U.S. companies to enter its domestic market and compete effectively. U.S. companies need access to Japan's domestic market to reduce the trade deficit.

Table 21–4   Direct Investment: U.S. Foreign Investments Versus Foreign Investments in the United States

Countries Where the U.S. Invested Most in 1988		Countries with the Biggest Investment in the U.S. in 1988	
Canada	$61 billion	Britain	$102 billion
Britain	$48 billion	Japan	$ 53 billion
West Germany	$22 billion	Netherlands	$ 49 billion
Bermuda	$20 billion	Canada	$ 27 billion
Switzerland	$19 billion	West Germany	$ 24 billion
Total U.S. Investment Abroad:	$327 Billion	Total Foreign Investment in U.S.:	$329 Billion

Source: U.S. Department of Commerce; U.S. Statistical Abstract, 1990.

Figure 21–3   U.S. Trade Deficits with Japan

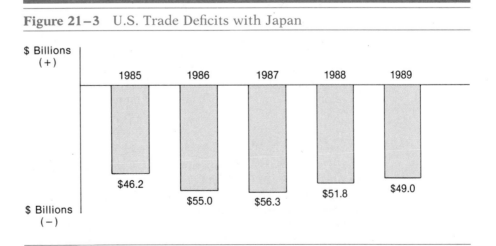

In an effort to improve trade relations in the 1990s, Japan and the United States entered into an important trade agreement.

Under the terms of the agreement, Japan will deregulate its process for approving large department stores, abolish a law that allows the government to restrict foreign investment if it could impact on Japanese domestic businesses, and implement stronger antitrust laws. Prior to the agreement, several U.S. department chains, including *Toys R Us*, had a difficult time battling Japanese bureaucracy to gain government permission to begin operations. The agreement also calls for the United States to reduce its budget deficit (which was more than $150 billion in 1990), improve the quality of its education and workforce, promote exports by reducing its export licensing requirements, and encourage personal savings. The Japanese view these undertakings as necessary for the U.S. to become more effective in today's international markets.

INTERNATIONAL ORGANIZATIONS

International business has grown dramatically in importance and complexity over the past fifty years. To encourage and foster international business, a variety of organizations has been developed to facilitate, finance, and regulate international business transactions. Those organizations vary considerably in scope, size, and sponsorship. The most prominent international organization is the United Nations.

The United Nations

Although created principally as a peace-keeping body, the *United Nations* has enjoyed greater success in its economic and social efforts. The organization's concern for economic development and international trade has fostered the development of several internal independent departments to facilitate trade. The organizational structure of the United Nations is presented in Figure 21–4.

The United Nations is most visible in the field of international trade through its *Commission on International Trade Law* (UNCITRAL). The primary purposes of UNCITRAL are to promote harmonization and unification of laws affecting international trade and to encourage the elimination of legal obstacles encumbering international trade. In addition, the United Nations is involved in efforts to standardize weights and measures (through the Department of Economic and Social Affairs) and to encourage and assist economic development in less-developed countries (through its Conference on Trade and Development and its Industrial Development Organization).

The World Bank

The *World Bank* is the functional name given to the *International Bank for Reconstruction and Development*. Headquartered in Washington, D.C., the organization of the World Bank includes, in addition to the bank itself, the International Finance Corporation (IFC) and the International Development Association (IDA). The current purpose of the World Bank is to "promote private foreign investment by means of guarantees or participation in loans

Figure 21–4   The Organizational Structure of the United Nations

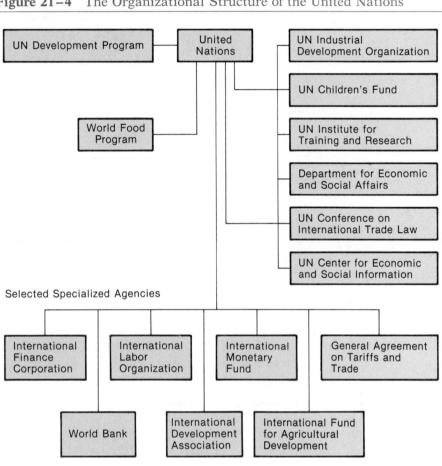

and other investments made by private investors." To effect this purpose, the World Bank assists in the financial arrangements of businesses, industries, and agricultural associations of its member states.

The World Bank encourages businesses to sell products and services to its borrowers. The United Nation's Center for Economic and Social Information publishes a bimonthly newspaper entitled *Development Forum and Business Edition*, which provides details on all major business opportunities created by World Bank loans. The newspaper provides information on the products and services needed for each project and the avenues through which businesses may become involved.

International Monetary Fund

The basic purposes of the *International Monetary Fund* (IMF) are to "facilitate the expansion and balanced growth of international trade," to aid in "the elimination of foreign exchange restrictions which hamper the growth of

international trade," and to "shorten the duration of and lessen disequilib-
rium in the international balances of payments of its members." These
purposes are achieved through the administration of a complex lending
system. The system allows a participating country to borrow money either
from other IMF members, or from the Fund itself through Special Drawing
Rights, or SDR's. The funds are made available to allow a member country to
stabilize its currency in relation to the currencies of other countries. The
stability of a country's currency is fundamental to the country's international
business viability.

General Agreement on Tariffs and Trade (GATT)

Protectionist barriers imposed by governments, such as import quotas and
tariffs, inhibit international trade. *The General Agreement on Tariffs and Trade*
(the GATT) was created to reduce such obstacles to trade. The GATT works to
achieve its goals by focusing on several key trade restrictions. It implements
its goals through the publication of tariff schedules that are developed
periodically in multinational trade negotiations or "rounds." Presently, the
GATT member countries are preparing and negotiating for the forthcoming
"Uruguay" Round.

Over eighty-eight countries have participated as parties to the GATT, with
three other countries participating as provisional parties. An additional
twenty-four countries state that the GATT guides them in their international
trading policies and conduct. The GATT has undertaken significant efforts to
maximize international trade among its member participants.

"Most Favored Nation" Status
Each article of the GATT addresses different key international trade problems
or restrictions. Article I, for example, discusses the commitment by the
participants to the practice of *most favored nation treatment*, providing that

> [a]ny advantage, favor, privilege or immunity granted by any contracting
> party to any product originating in or destined for any other country shall
> be accorded immediately and unconditionally to the like product origi-
> nating in or destined for the territories of all other contracting parties.

Suppose the United States agrees to give Korea certain tariff rates and tells
Korea those rates are provided to other favored customers. If the United
States later provides better rates to Italy, most favored nation treatment
under the GATT would require the United States to provide Korea with the
same rates.

Imposition of Antidumping or Countervailing Duties
The GATT, however, does allow unilateral exceptions to the tariff schedules
under certain circumstances. For example, if one country decides to *dump*
products on another country at prices below existing market value, the GATT
will allow the imposition of an *antidumping duty* for the purpose of protecting
domestic industries. Also, if an exported product is heavily subsidized by its
government and thus enjoys a price lower than the market value of a similar
nonsubsidized product in the receiving country, the GATT allows the imposi-

tion of a *countervailing duty* by the receiving country (to offset the lower, subsidized price of the imported product).

Nontariff Barriers

The GATT addresses approaches to reducing not only tariff barriers but also *nontariff barriers*. Like tariff barriers, nontariff barriers impose restrictions on free trade. Such nontariff constraints on free trade include import quotas; licensing barriers; administrative delays; and arbitrary classification, labeling, and testing standards imposed on foreign-made products.

Regional Organizations

Several regional organizations exist throughout the world whose purpose is to facilitate trade and economic development. For example, the *European Economic Community* (EC) was created to eliminate restrictions on the free flow of goods, capital, and persons; harmonize economic policies; and create a common external tariff among its member countries. Member countries of the EC include Belgium, Denmark, France, Greece, Ireland, Italy, Luxembourg, the Netherlands, Portugal, Spain, the United Kingdom, and West Germany. As discussed above, the EC will eliminate most internal barriers to trade in 1992. Other important regional organizations and their member countries are given in Table 21–5.

Table 21–5   Regional Economic Organizations

Program	Member Countries
Andean Common Market (ANCOM)	Colombia, Venezuela, Ecuador, Peru, Bolivia
Arab Common Market	Iraq, Jordan, Libya, Mauritania, Syria, South Yemen
Association of Southeast Asian Nations (ASEAN)	Thailand, Malaysia, Singapore, Indonesia, Philippines, Brunei
Caribbean Common Market (CARICOM)	The Bahamas, Belize, Jamaica, Antigua and Barbuda, Montserrat, Dominica, St. Lucia, St. Vincent, Grenada, Barbados, Trinidad and Tobago, Guyana, St. Kitts-Nevis-Anguilla
Central American Common Market (CACM)	Costa Rica, El Salvador, Guatemala, Honduras, Nicaragua
Council for Mutual Economic Assistance (CMEA or COMECON)	USSR, Hungary, Poland, Romania, Bulgaria, East Germany, Cuba, Czechoslovakia, Mongolia, Vietnam
Economic Community of West African States (ECOWAS)	Mauritania, Senegal, Mali, Ivory Coast, Niger, Upper Volta, Benin, The Gambia, Guinea, Ghana, Nigeria, Sierra Leone, Togo, Cape Verde, Guinea-Bissau, Liberia
European Economic Community (EC)	Denmark, United Kingdom, Ireland, the Netherlands, Belgium, Luxembourg, France, West Germany, Italy, Greece, Spain, Portugal
European Free Trade Association (EFTA)	Iceland, Sweden, Norway, Austria, Portugal, Switzerland, Finland (Associate)
Latin American Integration Association (LAIA)	Bolivia, Brazil, Colombia, Chile, Ecuador, Argentina, Peru, Uruguay, Paraguay, Mexico, Venezuela
West African Economic Community	Ivory Coast, Mali, Mauritania, Syria, South Yemen

U.S. INTERNATIONAL TRADE RESTRICTIONS AND PROMOTIONS

Countries have long imposed restrictions or prohibitions on the importation and exportation of certain products. In addition, export laws and regulations are often enacted to encourage international business activity by domestic industries.

Import Regulation and Prohibitions

Restrictions on imports take a variety of forms and are generally imposed for the purpose of either generating revenue for the government of the country or protecting the country's domestic industries from lower priced foreign products. Import licensing procedures, import quotas, testing requirements, safety and manufacturing standards, government procurement policies, and complicated customs procedures are all viable means for the regulation of imports. The most common means of regulating imports into a country, however, is through the application of import tariffs.

The Imposition of Import Tariffs

A *tariff* is a duty or tax levied by a government on an imported good. Tariffs can be generally classified into two principal categories: *specific tariffs*, which impose a fixed tax or duty on each unit of the product, and *ad valorem tariffs*, which impose a tax based on a percentage of the price of the product. Tariffs are intended to serve either as a revenue-generating device by the government, or as a means to provide domestic industries with protection from foreign products. Businesses advocating the imposition of a tariff on a foreign product for the purpose of protecting a domestic business generally argue that without the tariff, the lower-priced foreign product will drive domestic industry from the market. Consequently, workers will lose their jobs and the country will grow increasingly more dependent on foreign businesses for supplies of critical products. Those arguing against tariffs assert that only through free trade will the world maximize its productive capacity.

Classification of Products. The duty or tax to be imposed is generally published in the *Tariff Schedules*. These schedules are applicable to all products entering U.S. ports. It is the responsibility of customs officials to classify products and determine the tariff rates at the time the products enter the country. Any tariff imposed on a product must be paid before the good may enter the country.

The vast majority of business disputes that occur in this area arise over the classification of products under the Tariff Schedules. As the *Standard Brands* case illustrates, the rate of duty can be significantly affected by a custom agent's decision on the classification of a product.

Standard Brands Paint Co., Inc. v. United States

Case Background. *Standard Brands Paint Company imported separate packages of wooden picture frame moldings that consisted of different styles and lengths. A purchaser could buy unassembled parts and assemble a given frame to desired dimensions. The invoice on the imported merchandise read "Wooden Picture Frames" and was classified by customs agents under the Tariff Schedules of the United States (TSUS) as wood moldings. The merchandise was assessed a duty at a rate of 17 per centum ad valorem.*

Standard Brands claimed that the imported items should have been classified as picture frames made of wood. The result would have been assessed duty at a rate of 12 per centum ad valorem. Standard Brands based its claim on the fact that the imported moldings actually constituted unassembled frames, and under the doctrine of entireties, these frames should be dutiable as entireties—that is, as picture frames made of wood.

The U.S. Customs Court held that the merchandise had been classified properly by the District Director of Customs. Standard Brands appealed to the federal court of appeals.

Case Decision.   Justice Baldwin delivered the opinion of the court.

* * *

Almost 50 years ago the Court of Customs Appeals stated as follows in *Altman & Co.* v. *United States:*

> [I]f an importer brings into the country, at the same time, certain parts, which are designed to form, when joined or attached together, a complete article of commerce, and when it is further shown that the importer intends to so use them, these parts will be considered for tariff purposes as *entireties,* even though they may be unattached or inclosed in separate packages, and even though said parts might have a commercial value and be salable separately.

* * *

We do not agree with the Customs Court that the principle expressed in *Altman,* is not applicable to the facts at bar because of an alleged failure to show an intent to either "use" or "treat" the imported merchandise as completed articles of commerce. Furthermore, *Altman,* makes it clear that separate packaging of parts does not preclude the application of the doctrine of entireties.

The importer has merely given the consumer, when purchasing an unassembled picture frame, the opportunity to choose the size of picture frame he desires to assemble. This fact leads us to the basic problem—lack of a predictable relationship between the parts—which the Customs Court held to preclude the application of the doctrine of entireties to the imported merchandise.

We note that the "predictable relationship" referred to is only applicable to the size and not the shape of the frame to be assembled. The 45° mitered ends of the lengths of molding in each package make it readily apparent that only rectangular picture frames may be assembled. Thus, we are left with the question whether an unassembled 8" x 10" picture frame is a different article for classification purposes from an unassembled 10" x 20" picture frame. We think not. The imported merchandise is still basically picture frames.

* * *

Case Holding. *The decision of the customs court was reversed. According to the doctrine of entireties, the imported items should have been classified as requested by Standard Brands, and taxed at the lower duty rate.*

Case Questions

1. What is the concept of "entireties," and why is it important to this case?
2. Why did the court feel that the unassembled frames were entireties under the interpretation of the TSUS?

Harmonized Tariff Schedules. In 1989, the United States replaced its tariff schedules with the Harmonized Tariff Schedule. The *Harmonized Tariff Schedule* was developed by a group of countries for the purpose of standardizing the ways in which goods are classified by customs officials worldwide. Under the system, each country uses the same six-digit codes to classify goods traded. The process greatly streamlines trade by eliminating language and usage differences between countries.

Bans on Certain Designated Products

The entry of certain products may run contrary to established governmental policies concerning national security, general economic protectionism, or other policies dictated by statute. For example, certain explosives and munitions that raise national security concerns cannot be legally imported into this country. Illegal products, such as narcotics, violate drug safety and other domestic laws and cannot be legally imported. Products made from endangered species are prohibited from importation by environmental laws. Other items may not live up to this country's safety regulations or pollution requirements and cannot be brought into the country for that reason. For example, foreign automobiles that do not comply with U.S. auto safety and pollution regulations will not be cleared for importation into this country.

Section 201 "Positive Adjustments"

Under Section 201 of the Export Administration Act, the government is authorized to impose import restrictions when increased imports are a "substantial cause" of injury to a U.S. industry. The industry affected is required to make a request to the International Trade Commission which then makes a determination of whether there is injury. The industry is encouraged to provide a plan outlining the ways in which it can adjust to and compete with the imports. If the Commission determines that the industry is being injured and that positive adjustments can be made, a temporary restriction can be imposed on the import—from all countries—so that the industry may have time to make the necessary adjustments.

Duty-Free Importation: Foreign Trade Zones and Duty-Free Ports

Foreign trade zones are special territorial areas to which goods can be imported without the payment of usual and customary tariffs. The underlying policy for the use of such zones is to encourage international business and trade. The zone itself is a secured area where goods may be processed, assembled, or warehoused. Tariffs are imposed only on the finished product (which is generally much less than those imposed on individual parts) and only when the product leaves the zone for sale in the domestic market. Products that are removed from the zone and exported are generally not subject to import fees or tariffs.

Duty-free ports are those ports of entry that do not assess duties or tariffs on any products entering them. The underlying policy in establishing a duty-free port is to encourage the importation and sale of international goods within the country. Countries such as Hong Kong are well known for such practices. Benefits to a country providing a duty-free port are the general encouragement of trade with other countries and the attraction of businesses and tourists to the country to purchase products free of duties and other fees.

Export Regulation and Promotion

Export regulations or controls are intended to affect the kind of goods to be exported, the country to which goods may be exported, and the manner in which the export process takes place. Although countries have varying export laws to fulfill overall national goals, export regulations may be imposed for any social, political or financial purpose. Export regulations, however, usually take the form of prohibitions or constraints on the sale of products considered either to be vital to the country's domestic market or, if sold to the wrong country, to have potentially adverse effects on the country's national security.

In addition to enacting legislation to discourage certain international activities, it is not uncommon for countries to enact legislation to encourage businesses to engage in international business. In the United States, for example, several laws have been enacted for that purpose. In that regard, consider the provisions of the Webb–Pomerene and Export Trading Company Acts.

Webb-Pomerene Act

The *Webb-Pomerene Act* was adopted by Congress in 1918 to encourage U.S. companies to export. Congress felt that to aid U.S. competitiveness in world markets, U.S. companies might find it necessary to create business associations that would promote economies of scale and enhance efficiency. The principal concern expressed by U.S. businesses was, however, that such an association might violate U.S. antitrust laws. In an effort to alleviate such concern, the Act specifically grants exporters limited exemptions from U.S. antitrust laws to develop such associations.

To qualify for an exemption, an association is required to register with the Federal Trade Commission (FTC). However, the Act does not allow associations dealing with services or technologies to qualify for registration. Furthermore, any association that enters into an agreement that artificially or intentionally depresses the price of a product within the United States or that "substantially lessens competition within the United States, or otherwise restrains trade therein," will not be exempted under the Act. Because of these broad restrictions imposed by Congress, there have been few Webb-Pomerene registrations with the FTC.

Export Trading Company Act of 1982

In 1982, the U.S. trade deficit had risen dramatically. At the same time, there was an increased concern among U.S. government and business officials that the United States was responding inadequately to world market demands. Particular interest was expressed in the growing success of Japanese trading companies, which involved an informal association of industrial, financial, and commercial companies. The larger Japanese trading companies handled more than 20,000 different products. As a consequence of the success of these companies, several U.S. companies expressed an interest in copying them. The companies, however, had significant concerns that to do so would violate U.S. antitrust laws.

In an effort to resolve this and other related constraints on international business activities by U.S. companies, Congress enacted the *Export Trading Company Act* in 1982. The Export Trading Company Act allows businesses to form *export trading companies*. Not only are activities concerning the export of goods and merchandise affected by the Act, but so are services when such services are the subject of the international business transaction or agreement (thus going beyond the Webb-Pomerene Act). Services such as consulting, legal services, accounting, architectural services, and communications fall within the Act.

The exemption from the antitrust laws provided by the Act arguably frees businesses to undertake activities that will make them more competitive in world markets. Those exemptions, however, have serious limitations. Exportation of goods may not result in a "substantial lessening of competition or restraint of trade within the United States nor a substantial restraint of the export trade of any competitors of the applicant." The export trading company's activities may not "unreasonably" impact the price of U.S. goods or services that are exported by the company. Neither may the activities pose an "unfair method of competition" to competitors of the export trading company. These vague criteria under which trading companies are to be judged have discouraged many businesses from seeking the trade advantages such associations might provide for fear of an antitrust action.

Export Controls: The Export Administration Act

The United States has had formal *export controls* since World War II when restrictions were imposed to avert shortages of basic commodities. After the war, political relations with the Soviet Union worsened and prompted the enactment of the Export Control Act in 1949. The Act was later amended and renamed the *Export Administration Act*.

Control of Sensitive Technologies. The Act is a comprehensive scheme that regulates the export of sensitive goods, technologies, and technical data from the United States. Section 3 of the Act states the underlying U.S. policies in these export controls:

> It is the policy of the United States to use export controls only after full consideration of the impact on the economy of the United States and only to the extent necessary—
>
> (A) to restrict the export of goods and technology which would make a significant contribution to the military potential of any other country or combination of countries which would prove detrimental to the national security of the United States;
>
> (B) to restrict the export of goods and technology where necessary to further significantly the foreign policy of the United States or to fulfill its declared international obligations; and
>
> (C) to restrict the export of goods where necessary to protect the domestic economy from the excessive drain of scarce materials and to reduce the serious inflationary impact of foreign demand. . . .

Export Licensing Requirements. To perform its regulatory functions, the Act creates three types of export licenses. The first is a *general license*, which authorizes a business to export nonsensitive goods. Its coverage extends to the vast majority of U.S. goods intended for export. The general license is issued to the exporter by the Office of Export Administration of the Department of Commerce usually without a formal application process. The second type of export license is a *qualified general license,* which authorizes the export of multiple products. The third type of license is the *validated license,* which allows for the export of specific products.

The qualified general license and the validated license are used only when the products are being sent to a country that would disqualify the goods from being exported under the general license. Both the qualified general license and the validated license require a written application with the Department of Commerce. The degree of restrictiveness imposed depends upon the product and the countries to which it is to be exported. The 1985 amendments impose additional requirements on corporations exporting to overseas affiliates and subsidiaries. In exporting to affiliates and subsidiaries, corporations are required to obtain a comprehensive operating license.

Recent Amendments to the Act. The *Omnibus Trade and Competitiveness Act* of 1988 amends the Export Administration Act in several ways. First, in response to the dramatic changes in world politics, it reduces or eliminates a number of the licensing requirements originally imposed by the Export Administration Act. The Omnibus Trade Act requires the U.S. Department of Commerce to significantly reduce the number of products subject to export control for national security reasons. Several export licensing restrictions have also been eliminated on the communist countries. These changes coupled with the increase in business opportunities in the Soviet Union have brought about an increase of more than 80 percent in the number of licenses issued for products going to the Soviet Union. Most of the licenses have been for computers and computer accessories.

Second, the Omnibus Trade Act strengthens Section 301, which provides the government with the ability to "retaliate" against the unfair trade practices of foreign governments. If a foreign government imposes import restrictions against U.S. products, Section 301 allows the U.S. government to impose quotas or duties on products from that country. In most cases, the threat of 301 tariffs is sufficient to bring about a reduction in the foreign government's import restrictions. It has been used, for example, in reaching an agreement with Japan that provides U.S. citrus growers and cattle producers with easier access to Japanese markets. It also was used to bring about greater protection of U.S. intellectual property in Korea.

Other Laws Controlling Exports

The Export Administrative Act is not the only legislative mechanism that imposes export controls. The *Arms Export Control Act* of 1976 authorizes the control of commercial arms exports by the Department of State. Export controls are also imposed by the *Nuclear Nonproliferation Act* of 1978, which governs the export of nuclear materials. In addition, the Department of Energy is authorized to control exports of certain technologies with which it is particularly familiar. In terms of regulating commercial exports, however, the agencies exerting the greatest influence include the Departments of Defense, Commerce, and State.

ENTERING FOREIGN MARKETS: BUSINESS ORGANIZATIONS

As international business opportunities have become apparent to U.S. businesses, they have sought a variety of means through which to enter foreign markets. In general, there are two basic ways of selling products in foreign markets. A business can either *export* products manufactured in this country to the foreign country, or *manufacture* products in the foreign country for distribution there.

Exporting Manufactured Products

Companies that initially enter international business or sell products to countries where political risks are high generally prefer to export products manufactured domestically. Exporting is preferred because it requires relatively little investment on the part of the business, and poses relatively lower risk than foreign manufacturing. Exporting may also be required if the manufacturing of the product requires proximity to an important natural resource.

Businesses entering international markets through exporting may choose to do so either directly or indirectly. *Indirect exporting* involves the use of an exporter who sells the product in foreign markets for the U.S. manufacturer. In addition, the U.S. manufacturer may also sell to a foreign purchasing agent who is in this country buying particular products for an overseas customer.

Direct exporting usually involves the development of an organization within the business responsible for export business. Initially, the company may ship directly to its overseas customers. Later, as business expands, the business may elect to develop a marketing organization in its foreign markets and import products there in its own name.

Foreign Manufacturing of Products

The decision to engage in foreign manufacturing is generally motivated by a business's desire to reduce costs and therefore enhance its ability to compete. Those costs most easily reduced through foreign manufacturing include shipping costs, labor expenses, and raw material costs. In addition, foreign manufacturing may be an effective means to avoid import restrictions or tariffs imposed by the host country.

The Japanese, for example, have been moving manufacturing facilities to the United States in fear that Congress may impose stiff duties on Japanese products in an effort to reduce the U.S. trade deficit. Since products made by a Japanese business located in the United States are legally made in America, they will not be subject to those duties. Businesses considering foreign manufacturing have several options available to them, including creating or entering into the following:

1. a wholly-owned foreign subsidary
2. a joint venture
3. a licensing agreement
4. a franchise agreement
5. contract manufacturing.

Wholly Owned Subsidiary

In electing to undertake its foreign manufacturing through a *wholly owned subsidiary*, a business maintains complete ownership in the facilities. In establishing its production facility, a business may either purchase an existing facility or elect to build a new one. Situations exist, however, in which complete ownership is not possible. Several countries impose limits on the percentage of ownership in a manufacturing facility held by foreigners. Mexico, for example, limits foreign ownership in several instances to less than 50 percent.

Joint Venture

A business may elect to undertake its foreign manufacturing in cooperation with a group of local owners or another foreign group. Through a *joint venture*, virtually any division of ownership is possible. For example, one party may supply the facilities, and the other party the technological skills required for the operation. Although a joint venture requires less investment by the company than does a wholly owned subsidiary, a joint venture may also mean loss of managerial control. In some instances, this loss of control may be mitigated by taking a partner—such as a bank or insurance company—that has little interest in day-to-day operations. Most businesses engaging in commercial activity in the Soviet Union are doing so through joint ventures (see the discussion in Chapter 11).

Licensing Agreement

A *licensing agreement* involves a contractual arrangement whereby one business—the licensor—grants another business—the licensee—access to its patents and other technologies. Licenses can be granted to cover the transfer of virtually any kind of expertise. The licensor is usually granted a royalty on net sales, generally from 1 to 5 percent. Through licensing, the licensor receives income it otherwise would not have received. In addition, if the licensee is allowed to use the business's trademark, it could serve to establish a worldwide reputation for the business that may be beneficial to the sales of its other products.

Franchising Agreements

In the past decade, *franchising* has become an extremely popular vehicle for establishing a foreign market presence. Franchising is a form of licensing whereby the franchisor (the supplier) grants the franchisee (the foreign dealer) the right to sell products or services in exchange for a fee. The most visible franchises are the fast-food restaurants; McDonald's, Pizza Hut, and Kentucky Fried Chicken have made major inroads as franchises, particularly in Japan, Canada, and Europe. Other successful franchises include hotels (Holiday Inn), car rentals (Hertz and Avis), soft drinks (Coca-Cola), and business services (Muzak).

Contract Manufacturing

In some instances, companies may find it advantageous to contract for the production of certain products in foreign facilities. U.S. retailers, for example, have found it advantageous to contract for the mass production of clothing and other textile products in Taiwan, Korea, and Hong Kong, where labor costs are considerably lower than in the United States. The products are then shipped to the United States for sale in retail outlets. Contract manufacturing has the additional advantage of not requiring investment in production facilities.

INTERNATIONAL CONTRACTS

As in domestic business agreements, the basis for any international agreement is the *international contract* between the parties. Often, however, an international contract will differ significantly from a business's domestic contracts. International contracts often involve parties from differing cultural backgrounds who rarely know each other well at the outset of negotiations. The physical distance between the parties to international agreements often complicates the contract's negotiation, substance, and performance. The differing languages, currencies, legal systems, and business customs of parties will affect the nature of the contract and influence the way it is written.

Cultural Aspects of International Contracts

A knowledge of and sensitivity to differences in cultures is important in international contracting. In Japan, for example, *meishi,* or business cards, are exchanged at a first meeting, while in the United States, business cards may be exchanged at any time, usually after a meeting is over. In many countries, including China, hours may go by before the subject matter of the business concern is even mentioned. This is quite different from the U.S. approach, where the parties are very forthright as to the purpose and goals of the business meeting.

A major cultural impact on international agreements is the difference in language between the parties. Although language itself should not be considered a barrier to an international contract, it is important that the terms of the contract are clearly defined in a language that all parties understand. Reliable interpreters can be used as an integral part of both the negotiations and the final draft of the contract where parties are not fluent in a common language.

The attitude toward relationships is another cultural difference between countries. Many countries, including Japan and China and many Latin American and Western European countries, have the cultural expectation that the relationship between contracting parties will be long-term. As a result, the negotiation process will be long, since it is necessary for the parties to know one another well before entering into a long-term relationship. Contracts based on trust and long-term expectations are often relatively short in length, with few contingencies expressly provided. The expectation is that contingencies can be worked out as they arise with the parties working to maintain the underlying relationship.

In other countries, such as the United States, just the opposite is expected. In the United States, a long-term relationship develops after a series of individual short-term business dealings. Therefore, at the onset of any given contract, the negotiation process is expected to be done as quickly and as efficiently as possible, since the subject matter of the contract is the only basis of the relationship presently being considered. Contracts are generally longer and more detailed, since the parties are at arm's length with one another and must rely on the written contract to handle contingencies. Although both approaches to contractual relationships have their merits, the reality is that they are quite different.

Financial Aspects of International Contracts

In any contract—foreign or domestic—the principal concern of the seller is getting paid by the buyer. The greater distances between the parties, the need for unique payment terms, and the difference in the parties' legal systems almost assure that an international contract will require financial considerations of a greater complexity than ordinarily encountered in a domestic sales contract. To examine their unique financial aspects, international contracts can be separated into two general classifications: (1) hard currency sales and (2) countertrade sales.

Hard Currency Sales
A *hard currency* sale is the type of transaction to which most U.S. businesses are accustomed. The seller provides a product to the buyer, who then pays for the product (either immediately or over time) in "hard currency." Western currency—for example, United States dollars, German marks, French francs, or Japanese yen—or currency that is readily convertible to Western currency is considered hard currency.

In managing the financial risks that accompany a hard currency sale, special care should be taken in the specification of the method of payment and the currency in which payment is to be made. Sellers willing to accept payment in Western currency other than U.S. dollars will need to understand the workings of foreign exchange markets. In addition, depending upon the circumstances the seller may need to be concerned about removing profits in the form of hard currency from the countries in which it does business.

Foreign Exchange Markets: Exchange Risk.
Each country has its own currency and accompanying monetary system. As a rule, the currency from one country is not readily acceptable in another country. To undertake a business transaction, one country must agree to exchange its currency for the currency of the other country. To assist in currency transactions, *foreign currency exchange markets* provide a worldwide system for trading (buying and selling) foreign currencies. The *foreign exchange rate*—the price of a unit of a country's currency in terms of another—is set by forces of supply and demand within the foreign exchange markets. That is, the foreign exchange rate is set by the demands of a country's citizens to buy the products of another country. The exchange rate will vary depending upon the relative attractiveness of another country's products. In general, trade between countries can occur only if it is possible to exchange the currency of one country for the currency of another country. Thus, to enhance trade most countries work to maintain the stability of the rate at which their currencies exchange with other currencies.

In an international transaction, a company often receives foreign currency. A business may wish to change that currency into its own country's currency. The exchange of money, however, is not always a simple mathematical calculation. Losses in international business sometimes center on exchange risk—the potential loss or profit that occurs between the time the currency is acquired and the time the currency is sold or exchanged for another currency.

Suppose, for example, that U.S. Wine Importers Inc. enters into a contract for the purchase of French wines. Suppose further that the contract calls for the payment of 2.8 million French francs in 180 days. When the contract is signed, the exchange rate is 7.00 French francs to the dollar. Thus, if U.S. Wine paid immediately, the 2.8 million French francs would cost $400,000. Suppose, however, that U.S. Wine elects to wait the full 180 days before paying and that during that time the exchange rate falls to 6.58 French francs to the dollar. Unless U.S. Wine has undertaken to protect itself from exchange risks, it now must pay $425,000 to satisfy the terms of the agreement. That is, movements in the exchange rate cost the company $25,000. To avoid such difficulties, U.S. businesses often require payment in dollars rather than in the currency of the other country.

Financial Instruments Used in International Contracts. Parties to international contracts often use special international financial devices to assure payment for products sold in international commerce. These devices either assure payment or allow for the arrangement of credit when buyers are otherwise unable to come up with the cash necessary for the business transaction. Although a number of financial instruments are available to facilitate international transactions, two financial devices commonly used are bills of exchange and letters of credit.

A *bill of exchange* is a written instrument that orders the payment of a certain sum of money to the party specified by the bill. Payment is made at the time specified on the bill or understood from the form of the standardized bill used. A *sight bill* specifies immediate payment upon receipt of the goods by the buyer. A *time bill* specifies payment at a later date, usually 30, 90, or 180 days after the goods have been received by the buyer.

A *letter of credit* is an agreement or assurance by the bank of the buyer to pay a specified amount to the seller upon receipt of documentation proving that the goods have been shipped and that any other contractual obligations on the seller have been fulfilled. The usual documentation required includes a certificate of origin, an export license, a certificate of inspection, a bill of lading, a commercial invoice, and an insurance policy. Figure 21–5 illustrates the routes taken by a letter of credit and the required documentation in an international business transaction between an Italian seller and an American buyer.

Letters of credit can be either revocable or irrevocable. As the label attached to each implies, a *revocable letter of credit* may be withdrawn, while an *irrevocable letter of credit* may not be withdrawn before the specific date stated on it. Exhibit 21–1 is an example of an irrevocable letter of credit.

Repatriation of Monetary Profits. Repatriation of monetary profits can sometimes be a concern to a party involved in an international transaction. *Repatriation* in the international business sense refers to the ability of a foreign

Figure 21–5   Letter of Credit in an International Transaction

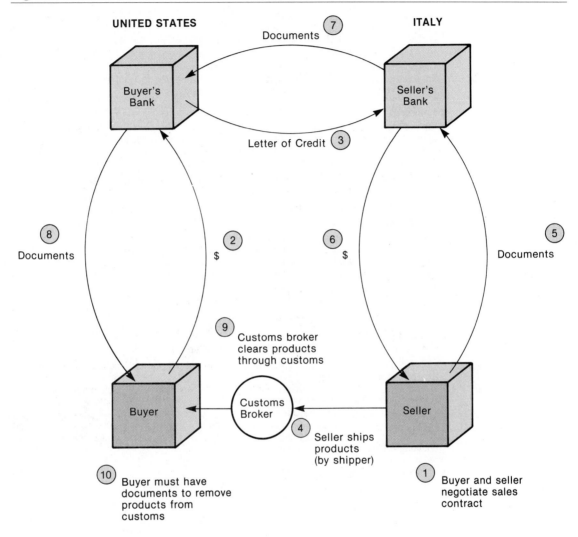

business or individual to return money earned in the foreign country to its home country. The ability to repatriate is often regulated by a country's laws. Taiwan and the People's Republic of China, for example, both have regulations restricting the amounts of local currencies that can be transferred out of the country. The usual reasons for the restriction and regulation of profit repatriation involve concerns about a reserve shortage in foreign currencies and the desire that money earned within the country be placed back into the local economy. Currency taken out of the country in excess of the amounts allowed can result in severe fines and penalties.

Exhibit 21–1   Example of an Irrevocable Letter of Credit

LETTER OF CREDIT—CONFIRMED, IRREVOCABLE

Western Reserve Bank   Letter of Credit #59723
Chicago, Illinois   Issued on August 1, 1990
To: Exotica Company   From: Tiramisu Import Company
Dallas, Texas   Rome, Italy

Gentlemen:
We are instructed by Commercial Bank Italy, Rome, Italy to inform you that they have opened their irrevocable credit in favor for account of Tiramisu Import Company, Rome, Italy, for the sum in U.S. dollars not exceeding a total of about $55,000.00 (Fifty-five Thousand and 00/100 Dollars), available by your drafts on us, to be accompanied by:

1. Full Set On Board Negotiable Ocean Bills of Lading, stating: "Freight Prepaid," and made out to the order of Commercial Bank of Italy.

2. Insurance Policy or Certificate, covering Marine and War Risk.

3. Packing List.

4. Commercial Invoice in triplicate:
   Covering 200 Pcs. 1025 Electric Espresso Coffee Machines
           200 Pcs. 750 Stove Top Espresso Coffee Makers
           350 Pcs. 420 Electric Pasta Makers

   Total Value $54,702.75 C.I.F. Rome, Italy
   Import Lic. No. 3792 Expires October 24, 1987

5. Shipper's Export Declaration.

   Partial Shipment Permitted. Transshipment Not Permitted.

   Merchandise must be shipped on SS Mercaso

All documents must indicate Letter of Credit No. 54723, Import License No. 13792, expires October 24, 1990.
All drafts must be marked "Drawn under Letter of Credit No. 59723, issued by Western Reserve Bank. Drafts must be presented to this company not later than October 1, 1990."
This credit is subject to the Uniform Customs and Practices for Documentary Credits (1984 Revision) International Chamber of Commerce Publication No. 400.
We confirm the credit and therby undertake that all drafts drawn and presented as above specified will be duly honored by us.

By
International Credit Department

Countertrade Sales

A recognized need for Western technology to provide a means for greater economic growth has led to an increased use of *countertrade sales* between Western companies and buyers in less developed countries. In a typical countertrade sale, the seller provides the buyer with machinery, equipment, or other goods, and the buyer provides the seller with goods rather than hard currency in exchange. With the entrance of the Soviet Union and the Eastern European countries into world markets in search of technology for industrial expansions and manufacturing upgrades, countertrade agreements have become an important financial tool in international business. Although countertrade introduces several complexities into international sales contracts, it now accounts for nearly 30 percent of international commerce. The major forms of countertrade are (1) counterpurchase and (2) compensation trade.

Counterpurchase. A *counterpurchase agreement* calls for the buyer to pay for the seller's goods by delivering goods to the seller—often referred to as "counterdeliveries"—that are unrelated to the goods originally purchased. The recent counterpurchase agreement signed by PepsiCo and the Soviet Union, for example, requires PepsiCo to sell soft-drink products to the Soviet Union in exchange for Russian vodka and large Soviet-built ships. The exchange of goods subject to a counterpurchase agreement generally takes place over a relatively short period of time.

Clearly, the completion of a counterpurchase agreement can be very complex and time consuming before the seller receives a currency payment for its products. The complexity of the arrangements often arise as a consequence of the number of buyers and sellers involved. For example, a California food processing equipment company recently sold equipment to the Soviet Union in exchange for urea (a fertilizer), sold the urea to China in exchange for marble, and sold the marble to a California company for U.S. dollars. While such arrangements are rarely used by U.S. companies, they are a much more common arrangement for German and Japanese companies.

Before entering a counterpurchase agreement, the seller should be cautious about committing to taking unspecified or alternative products. For example, Rank Xerox entered into a counterpurchase agreement with the Soviet Union for the sale of office equipment. The agreement called for Rank Xerox to receive marble, wood, and crude oil in exchange. When it was later determined that those products would not be available, Rank Xerox was offered bulls' horns—a popular aphrodisiac in China—instead. While the seller should negotiate to assure that the list of counterpurchase products is as broad as possible, it should avoid those products that are difficult to sell or that have relatively limited markets.

Compensation Arrangements. In a *compensation*, or buy-back, *arrangement*, the seller provides the buyer with production equipment in exchange for a portion of the product produced with that equipment over time. For example, Chevron agreed to provide the Soviet Union with oil-field equipment in exchange for a portion of the oil produced from the wells drilled using the equipment over a period of several years. In contrast to counterpurchase arrangements where the seller normally receives goods in exchange almost immediately upon delivery of equipment or other goods, it is not uncommon for repayment periods in compensation arrangements to exceed fifteen years. Because of the extended repayment period involved and due to the fact that the quality of the repayment products received can be assured, compensation arrangements are the fastest growing form of countertrade in use today.

In the compensation arrangement, the seller should take into account the year-to-year costs of marketing the products. The required product marketing expenses make the transaction much more expensive than a hard currency sale. Failure to account for these costs can impose a heavy financial burden on small- and medium-sized companies. In addition, the compensation arrangement should specifically delineate the responsibilities of the parties in the event the machinery and equipment need repair or are otherwise disabled before they have been paid for through production.

Selected Clauses in International Contracts

The contract is the foundation of any international business venture. It sets the framework for the business relationship, and establishes the rights and duties of the parties. As with domestic contracts, care should be taken that the intent of the parties is fully represented by the contract. Moreover, any international contract should be written, even if it states merely the positions and goals of the parties. The following clauses are often included in international contracts.

Payment Clauses

The *payment clause* is an important requirement in any international contract. The method and manner in which payment is to be received as well as the currency in which payment is to be made should be clearly specified. Some nations, such as the Soviet Union, do not allow their currencies to leave the country. If payment is made in currency under such a situation, the payment has special restrictive effects on the receiver of the currency, and those effects should be taken into account when the contract is written. If the contract provides for countertrade, the products to be included should be clearly identified and specified. Problems with inflation and currency exchange risks, especially in unstable economies or in long-term agreements, should also be addressed in this clause of the contract.

Choice of Language Clause

Parties to international contracts do not always speak the same language. Even when they do, the complex contractual terms may exceed the understanding of one of the parties when the contract is not in that party's native language. Further, a word or phrase in one language may not be readily translatable to another. Therefore, the contract must have a *choice of language clause*, which sets out the official language by which the contract is to be interpreted. Although the mere expression of an official language may not remedy all language problems, it does aid in apprising the parties of the language that will be used. An example of such a language clause is provided in Exhibit 21–2.

Exhibit 21–2   Choice of Language Clauses

Example of Choice of Language Clause With Arbitration Provision

This Agreement is signed in two (2) originals in the English language, which shall be regarded as the authoritative and official text. Any matters referred to arbitration will also be in the English language, which will be the official language used in arbitration.

Example of Choice of Language Clause With Translation Provision

This Agreement is signed in two (2) originals in the French language, which shall be regarded as the authoritative and official text. Parties hereto agree to provide an official translation of this Agreement in the English language. This translation will be ratified by both parties and it may be relied upon as being an accurate representation of the official form.

Open Price Clause

Sometimes a contract may provide an *open price clause*, which leaves the determination of the contract price to a later time (usually the time of delivery of the goods or performance of the contract). Although this clause is not usually favorable to the buyer, the clause may be useful if the items are homogeneous or the services are of the kind usually bought and sold in the market. Opponents of such clauses say that the clauses merely represent an agreement to agree later and that the parties should be able to create a pricing formula that will take into consideration any market concerns at the time the contract is made. If such a formula is in fact used, the formula should be carefully worded. In the *Bernina* case, the U.S. court of appeals analyzed the use of the open price term in an international contract.

Bernina Distributors, Inc. v. Bernina Sewing Machine Co., Inc.
United States Court of Appeals, Tenth Circuit
646 F.2d 434
(1981)

Case Background. *The Bernina Sewing Machine Company (Sewing Machine Importer) imported sewing machines into the United States from Switzerland. It purchased the sewing machines in Swiss francs and sold them to Bernina Distributors (the Distributor) in U.S. dollars. The Distributor had an exclusive contract with the Sewing Machine Importer to sell the machines in California. The Sewing Machine Importer's contract with the Distributor had an open price provision that allowed any "cost increase" to be passed along to the Distributor.*

The parties had no problems with the open price provision until fluctuations in the foreign currency exchange market caused the U.S. dollar to fall in value relative to the Swiss franc. Thus, by the time the Sewing Machine Importer changed the U.S. dollars received from the Distributor as payment for the machines into Swiss francs to pay the Swiss manufacturer, the sale was generating a considerably smaller profit than anticipated. Fearing a further decline in the U.S. dollar, and relying on the open price provision, the Sewing Machine Importer increased the price of the sewing machines by 10 percent.

The Distributor sued the Sewing Machine Importer for the increase in price, arguing that fluctuations in the foreign currency exchange market did not constitute a "cost increase" under the terms of the open price provision. The trial court found for the Distributor and the Sewing Machine Importer appealed.

Case Decision. Justice Logan delivered the opinion of the court.

* * *

The Sewing Machine Importer argues that the trial court erred in prohibiting it from charging 10% on the increased cost incurred by exchange rate fluctuations. By the time of trial, the reduced value of the dollar in the purchase of Swiss francs had nearly doubled the Sewing Machine Importer's costs and thus halved its rate of return per dollar invested. While the exchange rate had fluctuated mildly prior to the execution of the contract, it had not previously indicated any continuous, substantial devaluation of the dollar in relation to the franc. . . .

The Sewing Machine Importer maintains that the risk of currency fluctuations had not been considered or allocated in the contract and that under the Uniform Commercial Code (U.C.C.), this open price term should be determined according to what the court finds to be reasonable. [The U.C.C.] provides, in part, "The parties if they so intend can conclude a contract for sale even though the price is not settled. In such a case the price is a reasonable price at the time of delivery if nothing is said as to price . . ." We cannot agree that "nothing" was said as to pricing the sewing machines in question. The contract provisions here are quite comprehensive concerning . . . modifications pursuant to cost increases in invoice, duty, shipping, insurance, and the like. Hence, the statutory provision is inapplicable to this case.

* * *

The Sewing Machine Importer asserts that the court's interpretation makes the contract impracticable . . . In our view the instant contract is not one made "impracticable" by the contingency of the devalued dollar. The contract, as interpreted by the trial court, always allows a gross profit margin, although the return on capital investment has been reduced considerably because of the devaluation of the dollar. Moreover, there is considerable evidence that the Sewing Machine Importer assumed this particular risk. The contract lumps all the shipping and invoice costs in one provision which allows price increases only to the extent of the cost increases to the Sewing Machine Importer. . . .

* * *

Cost increases alone, though great in extent, do not render a contract impracticable. The Third Circuit [has] held that the doctrine of impracticability [is] not available unless the party seeking to excuse performance [can] show he could perform only at a loss, and that the loss would be especially severe and unreasonable.

* * *

The Sewing Machine Importer was represented by counsel throughout and should have known that the contract provided for price increases only to the extent of actual cost increases. We cannot agree that the Sewing Machine Importer was forced by the manufacturer to conclude whatever deal the Distributor demanded; there is no significant imbalance in the financial strength of these parties. To grant relief on this issue would be to disturb an agreed-upon allocation of risk between commercial equals.

* * *

Case Holding. *The decision of the lower court was affirmed. Fluctuations in exchange rates do not constitute a valid increase in price under the cost-plus provision of the contract.*

Case Questions

1. Why did the importer wish to increase the price of the products, and how did he do so?
2. What legal arguments did the importer use on appeal to attempt to excuse his duties under the contract?

Force Majeure Clause

Force majeure is a French term meaning a "superior or irresistible force." Thus, a *force majeure* clause protects the contracting parties from problems or contingencies beyond their control. Traditionally, this type of clause was used to protect the parties from the repercussions of a natural disaster that interfered with performance. More recently, however, the clause has protected the parties against unprecedented inflation or political upheavals. The student uprisings and the government response in China in May of 1989 is an example of an incident where the use of such a clause may have assisted parties to international contracts adversely affected by those events. An illustration of a typical force majeure clause is given in Exhibit 21–3.

LOSS OF INVESTMENT

International business is rarely undertaken without some risk that the investment will be lost. Political upheavals, unstable monetary systems, dramatic changes in laws and their interpretations, and an array of problems associated with doing business with a developing country are some of the risks a business can encounter. In addition, businesses must be concerned about governmental actions that can result in loss of investment through nationalization, expropriation, and confiscation. However, foreign investors who are concerned about losing their investments may reduce their risks of loss through the purchase of insurance.

Nationalization

Nationalization occurs when a country makes a decision to take over, or nationalize, a foreign investment. The compensation provided by the government is often less than the true value of the business. The stated purpose of nationalization is usually related to the public or national welfare. Nationalization has occurred more often than most investors realize—over 260 times in the past two decades. Although such government takeovers usually occur in underdeveloped or developing nations, they are not limited to those countries. A trend to nationalize has been seen in such countries as Iran, Nigeria, Saudi Arabia, and Venezuela. In addition, Canada and England, two highly developed Western countries, have demonstrated a tendency toward the nationalization of certain industries.

Expropriation and Confiscation

Expropriation is defined as the actions of a country in taking foreign assets or other property rights in accordance with international law. The general basis agreed upon by most countries for a valid expropriation is that there was a public purpose behind the taking, and that prompt, adequate, and effective compensation was provided to the individual whose property was taken. The

---

Exhibit 21–3   Example of Force Majeure Clause

The parties hereto shall not be liable for failure of performance hereunder if occasioned by war, declared or undeclared, fire, flood, interruption of transportation, inflation beyond the expected rate, embargo, accident, explosion, inability to procure or shortage of supply of materials, equipment, or production facilities, prohibition of import or export of goods covered hereby, governmental orders, regulations, restrictions, priorities or rationing by strike or lockout or other labor troubles interfering with production or transportation of such goods or with the supplies of raw materials entering into their production or any other cause beyond the control of the parties.

rules of traditional international law recognize a country's right to expropriate the property of foreigners within its jurisdiction.

If the takeover is unlawful, it is called a *confiscation*. The U.S. position has been that takings directed toward a particular nationality are discriminatory and are therefore considered confiscations rather than expropriations. The United States has responded to unlawful takings by denying certain rights under our laws to countries carrying out confiscations.

Insuring Against Risk of Loss

Foreign investors concerned with the risk of loss of investment may decide to obtain insurance against such possibilities. An all-risk type of insurance policy can provide financial relief in the event of nationalization or upon the occurrence of a specific contract problem. Short-term insurance from private insurers usually lasts from three to five years and is readily available for most investments. Outstanding risks such as currency blockages, embargoes, and a government's arbitrary decision to recall letters of credit may be insured by such major insurers as Lloyds of London. In addition, sellers may obtain rejection insurance in the event the buyer rejects the product for reasonable cause, such as spoilage at sea.

Some countries have governmental agencies to assist in insuring their exporters from risk of loss. In the United States, for example, the *Overseas Private Investment Corporation* (OPIC) insures those investors willing to invest in less-developed countries friendly to the United States and in need of social and economic development programs. OPIC offers investors insurance against expropriation, currency inconvertibility, and damage from wars or revolutions.

INTERNATIONAL DISPUTE RESOLUTION

According to the World Bank, the world now enjoys a volume of over two trillion dollars in trade per year. It is to the credit of the international business community that such a volume of trade exists in spite of the legal uncertainties inherent in international commercial transactions. There are instances, however, when international disputes concerning performance of contracts arise. This may be due to the occurrence of events unanticipated by the parties, unforeseen difficulties or expenses in performance, changes in the legal or political climates of a country that affect the contract, or the desire by a party to no longer participate in the contract for any number of reasons. In such instances, parties to international contracts seek institutional assistance to resolve disputes and enforce their rights under the contract.

The International Court of Justice

Certain disputes may be taken to the *International Court of Justice* (ICJ) for resolution. The ICJ is headquartered at The Hague, Netherlands, and is a principal organ of the United Nations. The Court comprises fifteen judges representing all of the world's major legal systems, with no two judges being from the same country. The Court is empowered to decide cases in accordance with Article 38 of the Court Statute, which provides the following:

1. The Court, whose function is to decide cases in accordance with international law such disputes as are submitted to it, shall apply:
   a. international conventions, whether general or particular, establishing rules expressly recognized by the contesting parties;
   b. international custom, as evidence of a general practice accepted as law;
   c. the general principles of law recognized by civilized nations;
   d. subject to the provisions of [statutes], judicial decisions and the teachings of the most highly qualified publicists of the various nations, as subsidiary means for the determination of the rules of law.
2. This provision shall not prejudice the power of the Court to decide a case *ex aequo et bono* (according to what is good and just), if the parties agree thereto.

Only countries that are part of the world community have standing to go before the Court; individuals and businesses have no standing themselves to initiate a suit. Further, the countries, and not the parties to the dispute, have complete discretion in deciding whether to pursue the claims. Thus, if a country in which the international investor does business violates international law to the detriment of that investor, the country in which the investor is a citizen has discretion to pursue or not to pursue the investor's claim.

The Court's decisions providing for monetary judgments or injunctive relief may be referred to the United Nations Security Council for enforcement. If the judgment is paid, however, the country need not distribute it to the wronged investor unless domestic laws require such a distribution. In the United States, such distributions are handled by the Foreign Claims Settlement Commission.

Judicial Litigation

Parties seeking to resolve an international contract dispute may also seek relief either in the court system within the opposing party's country or within their own country. Such litigation, however, is complicated by the fact that evidence, individuals, and documents central to the resolution of the dispute are often located in two or more countries. In some instances, such difficulties may be overcome by the existence of treaties or conventions between the two countries allowing for the proper notice of the suit to the foreign parties involved, appropriate service of process, methods for documentation certification, and procedures for the taking of evidence.

If the action is commenced in a foreign court, the U.S. participant will often encounter a judicial system significantly different from this country's. Courts in foreign countries are often influenced more significantly by political pressures than are U.S. courts. In addition, foreign courts are often unwilling to enforce provisions in contracts that may be enforceable in this country but are viewed as being against public policy in theirs.

In this country, a fundamental difficulty often arises in attempting to establish proper jurisdiction over both parties to the dispute. U.S. courts will require proof of "minimum contacts" within the country so that the court can have proper jurisdiction over a foreign defendant. The establishment of minimum contacts requirement may be established by a showing of the defendant's presence within U.S. territory; a domicile or residency in the

United States; consent to the court's jurisdiction; carrying on of business within the court's jurisdiction; or participation in activities outside the country that have direct, substantial, or foreseeable effects within the country.

Arbitration

Traditional judicial forums for dispute resolution have not proved effective in resolving most international commercial disagreements. Cost considerations, jurisdictional barriers, procedural and substantive barriers to relief, the length of time to litigate, legal uncertainties, and the inability of judicial systems to fashion appropriate relief provided incentives for the creation of alternative dispute resolution techniques. One of the most effective alternative techniques has been the arbitration process.

Arbitration is a method of dispute resolution whereby the parties agree to submit themselves to a neutral third party to resolve contract disputes. Depending upon the agreement of the parties, the third party may be a panel or a single arbiter, and the arbitration award may or may not be binding. More and more parties to international contracts are looking to arbitration as the preferred mechanism for the resolution of international commercial disputes.

Attempts by the international business community to standardize arbitral rules and procedures have resulted in the creation of organizations such as the United Nations Commission on International Trade Law, the International Chamber of Commerce, the American Arbitration Association, the Inter-American Commercial Arbitration Commission, and the London Court of Arbitration. These organizations have established rules to address issues concerning arbitral proceedings, tribunals, and awards. In over fifty countries including the United States, the enforcement of arbitral awards is facilitated by the 1958 United Nations Convention on the Recognition and Enforcement of Foreign Arbitral Awards. The U.S. federal district courts have jurisdiction to entertain motions to confirm or challenge a foreign arbitration award involving a U.S. business.

Doctrine of Sovereign Immunity

A foreign investor who has suffered losses due to the expropriation of assets may consider suing to recover the losses. This litigation may take place in a country different from the country that expropriated the investment. Such litigation may, however, be foreclosed from obtaining relief by application of the doctrine of sovereign immunity.

In international law, the *doctrine of sovereign immunity* allows a court to relinquish its jurisdiction over foreign enterprises or countries that otherwise would be subject to the court's jurisdiction. This relinquishment of jurisdiction is based on traditional notions that a sovereign should not be subject to litigation in a foreign court. As a result, foreign investors may not be able to obtain relief in their country's court system. Under the traditional application of the doctrine, the court will relinquish its jurisdiction over the country or a foreign enterprise which, although engaging in a private transaction, is acting on behalf of the country.

The traditional application of the doctrine can have severe consequences on parties when the suit involves a commercial transaction. Several countries have moved to restrict the doctrine's application in such circumstances. The

U.S. Congress elected to follow those countries in 1976 with the enactment of the Foreign Sovereign Immunities Act. The Act is intended to provide a uniform rule for the determination of sovereign immunity in legal actions in this country's courts and to bring the United States into conformity with other countries in its application of the doctrine. With regard to the doctrine's application in suits involving commercial transactions, the Act provides the following:

> Under international law, states are not immune from the jurisdiction of foreign courts insofar as their commercial activities are concerned, and their commercial property may be levied upon for the satisfaction of judgments rendered against them in connection with their commercial activities.

Act of State Doctrine

The *act of state doctrine* is similar to the sovereign immunity doctrine in that it creates a bar to compensation by foreign investors who have sustained losses in host countries. Unlike the sovereign immunity doctrine, however, the doctrine of act of state may create a partial as well as a complete bar to a claim. The act of state doctrine embodies the principle that a country must respect the independence of other countries and that courts of one country may not judge the validity of the regulatory acts of another country's government undertaken within its own territory.

U.S. courts have outlined and upheld the doctrine, stating that among other things, it ensures international harmony. Although the purpose of the doctrine is to avoid any embarrassment to foreign relations, in practice a claimant seeking relief may be partially or totally barred from obtaining relief in the courts of a country where the doctrine applies. The Supreme Court analyzed the doctrine in the *Banco Nacional* case.

Banco Nacional De Cuba v. Sabbatino
United States Supreme Court
376 U.S. 398, 84 S.Ct. 923 (1964)

Case Background. *Farr, Whitlock & Co., an American commodity broker, contracted to purchase Cuban sugar from C.A.V., a corporation organized under Cuban law whose capital stock was owned principally by American residents. Farr agreed to pay for the sugar in New York upon presentation of the shipping documents.*

Shortly thereafter, Congress imposed a reduction in the sugar quota that the Cuban government viewed as an act of aggression. In response, Cuba nationalized the sugar industry, including C.A.V. The nationalization decree required the consent of the Cuban government before a ship carrying sugar could leave Cuban waters. To obtain consent, Farr entered into contracts with Banco Nacional de Cuba, the bank of the Cuban government.

Banco Nacional presented the shipping documents to Farr in New York and demanded payment. On the same day, C.A.V. notified Farr that it was the rightful owner of the sugar and that it was entitled to the payment. Later Sabbatino was designated as C.A.V.'s receiver of its New York assets, and Farr gave the payment to Sabbatino. Banco Nacional then brought this action to recover the proceeds from Farr and to enjoin Sabbatino from exercising any dominion over it.

The federal district court found that the Cuban nationalization decree violated international law and ruled against Banco Nacional. The court of appeals affirmed on similar grounds. The Supreme Court granted certiorari.

Case Decision. Justice Harlan delivered the opinion of the Court.

* * *

The question which brought this case here . . . is whether the so-called act of state doctrine serves to sustain Banco Nacional's claims in this litigation. Such claims are ultimately founded on a decree of the government of Cuba expropriating certain property, the right to the proceeds of which is here in controversy. The act of state doctrine in its traditional formulation precludes the courts of this country from inquiring into the validity of the public acts a recognized sovereign power committed within its own territory.

* * *

We do not believe that this doctrine is compelled either by the inherent nature of sovereign authority . . . or by some principle of international law. . . . The act of state doctrine does, however, have "constitutional" underpinnings. It arises out of the basic relationship between branches of the government in a system of separation of powers. It concerns the competency of dissimilar institutions to make and implement particular kinds of decisions in the area of international relations. The doctrine as formulated in past decisions expresses the strong sense of the Judicial Branch that its engagement in the task of passing on the validity of foreign acts of state may hinder rather than further this country's pursuit of goals both for itself and for the community of nations as a whole in the international sphere.

* * *

The possible consequences of a conclusion to the contrary of that implicit in [past decisions] is highlighted by contrasting the practices of the political branch. . . with the limitations of the judicial process in matters of this kind. Following an expropriation of any significance, the Executive [Branch] engages in diplomacy aimed to assure that United States citizens who are harmed are compensated fairly. Representing all claimants of this country, it will be able, either by bilateral or multilateral talks, by submission to the United Nations, or by the employment of economic and political sanctions, to achieve some degree of general redress. Judicial determinations of invalidity of title can, on the other hand, have only an occasional impact, since they depend on the fortuitous circumstances of the property in question being brought into this country. Such decisions would, if the acts involved were declared invalid, often be likely to give offense to the expropriating country; since the concept of territorial sovereignty is so deep seated, any state may resent the refusal of the courts of another sovereign to accord validity to acts within its territorial borders. Piecemeal dispositions of this sort involving the probability of affront to another state could seriously interfere with negotiations being carried on by the Executive Branch and might prevent or render less favorable the terms of an agreement that could otherwise be reached. Relations with third world countries which have engaged in similar expropriations would not be immune from effect.

* * *

Case Holding. *The judgment of the court of appeals was reversed. The act of state doctrine prohibits a foreign judicial body from ruling on the validity of the acts of a sovereign undertaken within the sovereign's territories. Both the national interest and progress toward the goal of establishing the rule of law among nations are served by maintaining intact the act of state doctrine in this realm of its application. Dissatisfied with the Supreme Court's* Banco Nacional *decision, Congress amended the Foreign Assistance Act to direct the courts to disregard the act of state doctrine in cases of expropriations of property.*

Case Questions

1. What is the Court's rationale for applying the act of state doctrine in this case?
2. Should the Court's application of the doctrine be influenced by whether the sovereign has provided reasonable compensation to the parties who have had their property expropriated?
3. Should commercial transactions such as the one in this case be exempt from the application of the doctrine? Would it have an impact on the willingness of Americans to invest abroad?

SUMMARY

As U.S. firms have become more involved in international business, the international legal environment of business has become a fundamental concern. With no comprehensive system of laws or regulations guiding international transactions, international businesses function in a unique legal environment. The principal sources of international trade law are the laws of the individual countries that the international business community comprises, the laws embodied in mutual trade agreements, and the rules enacted by worldwide or regional organizations.

Virtually every country imposes its own system of import and export regulations. In working to reduce obstacles to trade imposed by those regulations, most countries engaging in international business have agreed to the General Agreement on Tariffs and Trade (GATT). The GATT's primary function is to reduce obstacles to trade, particularly import tariffs.

A variety of business organizations is available to facilitate international ventures. The most common organizations are wholly owned subsidiaries, joint ventures, licensing agreements, franchise agreements, and contract manufacturing. The choice of a particular form of business organization will be influenced by the laws of the foreign country, the purposes of the international commercial venture, the financial resources of the parties, and the degree of managerial control desired by the business.

In international transactions, the basis for any agreement is the international contract between the parties. In creating an effective international contract, a business should consider cultural differences between the contracting parties, including business customs, attitudes toward the contract relationship, and language. Specific clauses in international contracts worthy of special consideration are the payment, choice of language, open price, and force majeure clauses.

The decision to participate in business in a foreign country is rarely without risk. Political upheavals, unstable monetary systems, dramatic changes in laws and their interpretations, and an array of problems associated with a developing country are the kinds of risks international business people may encounter. More importantly, heavy losses may occur through nationalization, expropriation, or confiscation of the foreign investment. Foreign investors concerned with these risks may decide to mitigate their losses by obtaining insurance.

Although a large volume of international trade is undertaken without incident, there are occasions when disputes arise concerning contract performance. A number of national and international institutions may assist a foreign business in effective dispute resolution. Those institutions include the International Court of Justice, judicial litigation in country court systems, and arbitration. The doctrines of sovereign immunity and act of state may create bars to recovery through the judicial systems for those businesses attempting to recover losses incurred either in commercial activities with a country or as a consequence of the actions of a country.

ISSUE

Israel or the Arab League: A Question of Business Ethics or Just Business?

Since the middle 1940s, the countries comprising the Arab League have boycotted Israeli products and companies doing business with Israel. Companies found to be doing business with Israel—either directly or indirectly—were blacklisted, and thereby barred from doing business with the Arab League countries. Companies who found themselves blacklisted could get their names taken off the list by discontinuing their business activities with Israel.

In the mid-1970s, the United States government amended the Export Administration Act and made it illegal for U.S. companies to refuse to do business with Israel. The acts that constituted "refusals to do business" were broadly defined to encompass a variety of business behaviors that could be undertaken to comply with the Arab boycott. In the following article, a company finds that it has substantial business opportunities with Arab countries. However, the company had a business operation in Israel and therefore was blacklisted.

Did Hospital Supplier Dump Its Israel Plant to Win Arab's Favor?
Sue Shellenbarger*

As the world's largest hospital supplier, Baxter International Inc. was sorely tempted by the Middle East's rich and growing health-care market. Increasing the company's global business was a top priority for ambitious Vernon R. Loucks, who became chief execu-

tive officer of Baxter in 1980, and the Middle East market seemed destined over the years to produce sales in the billions of dollars.

But for Baxter, the door was slammed shut. In 1971, Baxter had built a plant in Israel to synthesize intravenous body fluids, and since the mid-1970s had been on the

—continued

—continuing

Arab League's blacklist of corporations that do business with Israel. If Baxter were to sell the plant for the purpose of getting off the Arab blacklist, the company would violate American anti-boycott law.

Then last year, apparently out of the blue, Baxter seemed to get lucky. By doing nothing more than agreeing to a joint venture with a Syrian government agency to build an intravenous fluids plant in Syria, the company insists, it was removed from the blacklist.

Dumping a Loser

Was it mere coincidence that the previous year, without a public announcement, Baxter sold its plant in Israel? Baxter insists it was. It says it had been trying to rid itself of the plant for years for economic reasons having nothing to do with the Arab boycott. The plant, Baxter says, was simply a loser.

At first, pro-Israeli groups that monitor the compliance of corporations with American anti-boycott law seemed willing to accept Baxter's explanation. But they are no longer. In February, Baxter directors received a copy of an explosive memorandum allegedly on file in the Arab League's boycott office in Damascus. The memorandum was sent to the directors by a disgruntled former Baxter executive in the Middle East, Dr. Richard Fuisz, a physician and Washington, D.C., businessman. The memorandum suggests a hitherto unacknowledged connection between the sale of the Israeli plant and the Arab League's delisting of Baxter. Dr. Fuisz provided The Wall Street Journal a copy of the memorandum and other documents dealing with Baxter's involvement in the Middle East.

According to the boycott committee memorandum, Baxter itself requested removal from the blacklist through its Swiss subsidiary, Baxter AG. In support of the request, Baxter's International Medical Technologies subsidiary in the Middle East supplied the Arab boycott committee detailed documentation on the Israeli plant

sale and even promised not to deliver Israel modern technology or do any other business with it, the memorandum says.

Audit Committee Action

Baxter's senior vice president and general counsel, G. Marshall Abbey, says the company hasn't violated the law. . . . The Commerce Department and the Securities and Exchange Commission are reviewing Baxter's Middle East activities. Neither will comment on the matter.

Influential Jewish leaders who have learned of the affair are demanding a full accounting from Baxter. The circumstances "raise serious questions about the process Baxter went through" in getting off the Arab blacklist, says Jess N. Hordes, Washington director of the Anti-Defamation League of B'nai B'rith. Mr. Hordes wrote Baxter's Mr. Loucks a letter on April 6 inquiring about evidence suggesting that Baxter cooperated with the Arab boycott. Mr. Abbey reiterated in a letter last week that the sale of the Israeli plant was unrelated to its blacklisting; Mr. Hordes in turn says he still isn't satisfied.

Baxter insists that it never contacted the boycott committee to request removal from the blacklist. Mr. Abbey says International Medical Technologies never supplied any information directly to the boycott committee. He also says Baxter never under any circumstances "made a promise not to get involved in Israel" in the future.

Loophole Incentive

The anti-boycott law was enacted in 1977 to discourage corporations from continuing to seek Arab business with promises to avoid commerce with Israel. Some companies had even refused to deal with other American firms that were on the Arab blacklist, strengthening the boycott. . . .

The law forbids American companies to participate in any foreign boycott and re-

—continued

–continuing

quires the public disclosure of any requeststo cooperate with any boycott and of any acts of compliance. It also forbids companies to supply blacklist officials any information that demonstrates cooperation with the boycott.

Because of the law, some blacklisted companies have simply abandoned pursuit of the Middle Eastern market. Others—among them Coca-Cola Co.—have gradually won access to markets in moderate Arab League nations without halting dealings with Israel. But the incentive to find loopholes in the law has been strong.

"Large corporations are on the horns of a dilemma," says E. John Keller, a consultant in international asset protection and risk assessment in Southlake, Texas. "If they believe the Arab market is a lot larger than the Israel market—and most of them do—they will go that route. Yet they are concerned," he says, about violating anti-boycott laws or offending supporters of Israel in the U.S. "It's a difficult line for U.S. companies to walk," he says.

Being shut out of the Middle East market, enriched by the oil boom of the 1970s and early 1980s, was painful for Baxter. The Middle East promised rich rewards for a hospital supplier with an early foothold in the region, and Baxter wanted to be that company. But thanks to the blacklist, every Baxter initiative in the region turned to sand.

In 1982, Baxter acquired Medcom Inc., a New York manufacturer of hospital-employee training materials that had close relations with Saudi Arabia, for $53 million. Despite the blacklist, Baxter hoped to use the company's connections to sell all kinds of medical supplies in that kingdom.

"As it turned out," Baxter later said in documents filed in a legal case, it "could not do so." After losing money on Medcom for more than a year, Baxter executives were told by Saudi officials to "stop wasting their time" in the Middle East, according to a Baxter document. Baxter sold Medcom in

1986 for just $3.77 million, or 7% of what it had paid for the company. . . .

Worse yet, Baxter's biggest acquisition ever, its $3.8 billion purchase of American Hospital Supply Corp. in 1985, was also bruised by the blacklisting. American Hospital's business in Saudi Arabia dried up as soon as Baxter bought the company in 1985.

The source of all the trouble was just one among dozens of facilities that Baxter operated around the world, a small intravenous fluids plant in Ashdod, Israel. Building the plant "seemed like a good idea at the time," says Mr. Abbey, but it was only occasionally profitable. In 1980, Baxter says, it began seeking a buyer. Mr. Abbey says Commerce Department officials at the time told Baxter that a sale wouldn't violate the anti-boycott law. The Commerce Department won't comment.

There was talk among Baxter employees in the U.S. and the Middle East that Baxter wanted to dump the plant to expand elsewhere in the Middle East. One of those who heard the talk was Ghazi Braiche, a former employee of Saudi Medical Services Ltd., a firm that had served as Saudi agent for a Baxter subsidiary. "I said, 'That's practically impossible to do [under the law]," Mr. Braiche recalls telling a Saudi Medical executive. "How can you hide such a transaction?'"

Baxter's talks with a prospective buyer for the Israeli plant fell through around 1983. Discussions about a possible joint venture with the Israeli government also failed, Mr. Abbey says. Mr. Loucks met with the Israeli prime minister at the time, Menachem Begin, to tell him why Baxter wanted out of Israel, "but Begin was beating him over the head to get us to export. We just couldn't do it," Mr. Abbey says, because the Israeli plant's production costs were too high. "By 1985 or 1986," he says, "it was my conclusion that we would always have an

–continued

—continuing

Israeli subsidiary, whether we wanted to or not."

Another thing seemed clear: If Baxter were ever to win delisting, Arab officials would demand proof that the Israeli subsidiary had been sold.

Sale Was "Imperative"

Nazir Sinan, a prominent Damascus attorney and specialist in boycott affairs, appeared at Baxter headquarters in this quiet Chicago suburb on a spring day in 1985. Although Mr. Abbey says Mr. Sinan was uninvited, he managed to see Mr. Abbey and discuss delisting. "My recollection is that I said, 'Don't call me, I'll call you.' " Mr. Abbey says. He says that Saudi Medical Services sent Mr. Sinan to Deerfield. Ahmed Al-Sanousi, president of Saudi Medical Services at the time, won't comment.

In any case, Mr. Sinan later wrote to Mr. Abbey to outline the steps Baxter must take to get off the blacklist. "It is imperative," one letter said, that a sales contract for the Israeli operations "should provide that your company has sold the factory and has terminated fully and finally its legal, technical, scientific, financial, labor and consultativerelations" with Israel. There's no evidence that Baxter pursued the matter further with Mr. Sinan. But the next year, 1986, Mr. Abbey flew to Damascus to explore a joint venture with Syria.

American law doesn't prevent a U.S. company from getting off the blacklist by investing in an Arab country. The trouble can lie in getting the Arab League to agree that the investment alone is sufficient to remove the U.S. company from the blacklist.

Syria, at first glance, wouldn't seem to offer a hospitable entry. It takes an especially hard line toward Israel and has tolerated anti-Western terrorist groups. Its economy, a socialist thicket penetrated mostly by multinational oil companies, makes profit from any joint venture questionable at best. A severe foreign-exchange shortage, steep inflation and dubious public-health conditions had kept many of Baxter's competitors away.

The Syrian Deal

But Syria, as one of the Arab League boycott committee's toughest members, is also one of it its most influential. And Mr. Abbey had a card to play: an offer of Baxter capital and expertise in building a Syrian intravenous fluids plant, the kind of facility seen critical to national security in the war-torn Middle East—and the kind of facility Baxter had tried to sell in Israel.

After "some false starts," Mr. Abbey says, Baxter ultimately found a joint-venture partner, the General Establishment for Blood and Medical Industries, which supplies military and civilian hospitals. Last year, Baxter and Syria reached a general agreement for Baxter to build the plant in return for payment in Syrian pounds and part of the plant's production. Terms of the agreement, highly favorable to Syria, were finally completed on April 9.

Coincidentally, Baxter says, in 1988 the same potential buyer that had lost interest in the Israeli plant in 1983 contacted Baxter again. Soon after, Baxter sold the plant to the Israel concern, Teva Pharmaceuticals, for a price under $20 million, Baxter says. Baxter had stopped referring to the Israeli plant in its yearly Form 10–K reports to the SEC beginning in 1986. Its 1985 acquisition of American Hospital Supply made Baxter so large, the company says, that the finances of so small an operation as the Israeli plant were no longer material.

Last fall, while terms of the Syrian joint venture were still being negotiated, the boycott committee in Damascus removed Baxter from the blacklist. The company won the unusual distinction of being sponsored by Syria. In the U.S., watchdog groups began almost immediately to question the circumstances surrounding Baxter's delisting. The company asserted its innocence. In a letter,

—continued

–continuing

Mr. Abbey assured the American Jewish Congress that the Israeli plant sale and the delisting were unrelated.

* * *

Although the Commerce Department and the SEC continued to study Baxter's removal from the blacklist, the matter seemed to rest—until Dr. Fuisz sent his package of documents along with a cover letter to Baxter directors.

* * *

While the Commerce Department won't discuss its probe of Baxter, it acknowledges that determining a company's motivation in the divestment of Israeli operations is difficult. "If the company did it because of the boycott, that would constitute a violation" of the law, a department official says. "But if they did it for legitimate business reasons, it's not illegal. Obviously, we would have an evidence problem . . . in any effort to determine what their motives were."

Whatever the legal resolution of the affair, Baxter stands to take its lumps from anti-boycott groups. The civil fines typically imposed by the Commerce Department for anti-boycott violations seldom are large enough to punish large corporations. "The real strength of U.S. anti-boycott law," says Joe Kamalick, editor of the Boycott Law Bulletin, "is the power of public disapproval."American firms, he says, "really hate being connected in a public way with any questions about anti-boycott violations."

Questions

1. Is it illegal for a U.S. company to sell a subsidiary located in Israel?

2. Could the fact that refusals to do business with Israel are illegal in the United States actually be advantageous to members of the U.S. business community seeking to do business in Arab countries?

REVIEW AND DISCUSSION QUESTIONS

1. Define the following terms:
   tariff
   foreign exchange market
   letter of credit
   harmonized tariff schedules
   bill of exchange
   repatriation
   foreign trade zone
   countertrade

2. Compare and contrast the following:
   a. Specific tariff and ad valorem tariff
   b. General license and validated license
   c. Licensing agreement and franchising agreement
   d. Doctrine of sovereign immunity and doctrine of act of state
   e. Nationalization and expropriation
   f. Compensation trade and counterpurchases

3. What is the Export Trading Company Act of 1982, and how was it intended to assist U.S. businesses in international trade?

4. What are the functions of the GATT and the IMF in the international business community? How do these two systems affect international trade?

5. Compare the advantages and disadvantages of arbitration and judicial litigation as methods of dispute resolution in international trade.

6. Under what circumstances would a compensation arrangement be more suitable than a hard currency sale?

Case Questions

7. A Houston-based American corporation contracted with a German corporation to tow an ocean-going, self-evaluating drilling rig from Louisiana to an area off Ravenna, Italy, where the Houston corporation agreed to drill certain wells. The German company's sea tug was to tow the Houston company's rig to the destination point. The contract between the two corporations provided that: "Any dispute arising must be treated before the London Court of Justice." While the rig was on its way to Italy in the Gulf of Mexico, a severe storm arose. During the storm, the elevator legs broke off the rig and fell into the sea, damaging the drilling rig. The German sea tug towed the damaged rig to Tampa, Florida, the nearest port of refuge. Ignoring the contract clause to litigate any dispute in English courts, the Houston company initiated a lawsuit in the U.S. District Court at Tampa, seeking $3,500,000 damages from the German company and its sea tug. Is the use of the American court proper in this situation? Why or why not? What effect would the contract clause have on the lawsuit? [*The Bremen* v. *Zapata Off-Shore Company*, 407 U.S. 1 (1971)]

8. Liberty Bank issued an irrevocable letter of credit for its customer, Anderson-Prichard Oil Corporation. The letter of credit was to be used for the purchase of oil-well casing and tubing from Tegtmeyer, a U.S. importer. The letter of credit was sent to the Bank of America, which then issued its own letter of credit to the Union Bank of Switzerland. Anderson-Prichard and Liberty Bank both refused payment of the two drafts due to allegations of differences between the documents and the letter of credit. One of the allegations was that the bill of lading was "foul" and "not clean"—that is, the printed words in the bill describing that the goods delivered would be "in apparent good order and condition" were crossed out by the carrier. Immediately below these words was the typewritten insertion "ship not responsible for the kind and condition of merchandise," and in the body of the bill was a stamp stating "ship not responsible for rust." A second allegation was that the letter of credit called for new pipe but the rail weight certificates described the pipe as secondhand, and the pipe in fact did not live up to the expectations that Anderson-Prichard had for it concerning quality. Should the court require payment by Anderson-Prichard and Liberty Bank? Discuss the letter of credit itself and the expectations of the parties and how that should affect the court's decision. [*Bank of America* v. *Liberty National Bank & Trust Co.*, 116 F.Supp. 233 (1953)]

9. Chisholm & Company and the Bank of Jamaica entered into an agreement under which Chisholm & Company was to arrange lines of credit from a number of banks and to obtain ExIm Bank credit insurance. As is not unusual in international business, the Bank of Jamaica "went around" Chisholm & Company and dealt with ExIm Bank directly. It then excluded Chisholm & Company from receiving any benefit from the credit insurance ExIm Bank subsequently provided. Chisholm & Company brought an action against the Bank of Jamaica. In its defense, the bank asserted that its actions were protected by sovereign immunity and the act of state doctrine. Were the bank's assertions correct? [*Chisholm & Company* v. *Bank of Jamaica*, 643 F.Supp. 1393 (S.D. Fla. 1986)]

Policy Questions

10. What are the reasons that some countries allow items to enter duty free while other countries may require the same items to be subject to duties? What are the advantages and disadvantages of both approaches to international trade?

11. What factors contribute to the decision by a country to regulate or restrict repatriation? What kind of economies tend to use repatriation?

Ethics Questions

12. In some circumstances, cultural expectations and business customs of a country may run counter to an individual's moral beliefs. What factors should individuals take into consideration when such a conflict arises and they are charged with making a business work within the cultural setting?

13. In some cultures it is expected behavior for businesses to make payoffs to government officials in the process of negotiating an international business transaction. If you find yourself in such a situation, should you provide a payoff? Suppose it makes the difference between getting the contract and not getting the contract? In response to revelations of "questionable" payments by American companies to foreign officials, Congress enacted the Foreign Corrupt Practices Act. Should the U.S. government impose its moral judgments on world business behavior?

A   Finding the Law

There are several important sources of law in the United States, including the U.S. Constitution; case law established by the written opinions of judges; statutes enacted by legislative bodies; regulatory agency orders, opinions, and regulations; treatises; law reviews; and Restatements of Law. At one time or another, we will reference these sources in explaining the fundamental laws making up the legal environment of business. This section provides a general guide to reading a citation to a source of law. In the event you decide to study an aspect of the legal environment in more detail, this section will provide guidance in locating the appropriate legal material.

Case Law

The published judicial opinions of all federal courts and the appellate state courts are available in court reporters. As a rule, opinions appear in hardback volumes of the *Reporters* about a year after a court has delivered its decision. The opinions are available more quickly, however, in paperback volumes published shortly after the case is decided, through computer research services (such as *Westlaw* and *Lexis*), and in the form of "slip opinions," which are copies of a decision mimeographed as soon as the decision is made public by the court.

Supreme Court decisions are published in the *United States Reporter* (U.S.), the *Supreme Court Reporter* (S.Ct.), the *Lawyers' Edition of Supreme Court Reports* (L.Ed.), and the *U.S. Law Week*. Citations read as follows: *Arnett* v. *Kennedy*, 416 U.S. 134, 94 S.Ct. 1633 (1974). This tells us that Arnett appealed a decision of a lower court to the United States Supreme Court. In 1974, the Supreme Court heard the case, and its decision is reported in volume 416 of the *United States Reporter* beginning on page 134 and in volume 94 of the *Supreme Court Reporter* beginning on page 1633. A reference to a point cited on a particular page in that opinion might read 416 U.S. 134, 137, which means that the case begins on page 134 and the particular point referenced is on page 137.

Decisions of United States Circuit Courts of Appeals are reported in the *Federal Reporter* (F.), which is now in its second series (F.2d). The following is an example of a citation: *Easton Publishing Co.* v. *Federal Communications Commissions,* 175 F.2d 344 (1949). The decision in this case can be found in volume 175 of the *Federal Reporter* (second series), page 344. The decision was rendered by the court in 1949.

Opinions of U.S. district courts that the judges wish to publish are reported in the *Federal Supplement* (F.Supp.). An example is *Amalgamated Meat Cutters* v. *Connally,* 337 F.Supp. 737 (S.D.N.Y.1971). The decision can be found in volume 337 of the *Federal Supplement* beginning on page 737. The case was decided by the federal district court in the southern district of New York in 1971.

State appellate court decisions are reported in regional reporters published by West Publishing Company. Decisions of the state supreme courts and courts of appeals for Arkansas, Kentucky, Missouri, Tennessee, and Texas, for example, are reported in the *South Western Reporter* (S.W.). As shown in Figure A–1, other state court opinions are reported in the *Atlantic Reporter* (A.), *North Eastern Reporter* (N.E.), *North Western Reporter* (N.W.), *Pacific Reporter* (P.), *South Eastern Reporter* (S.E.), and *Southern Reporter* (S.), all of which are in the second series (2d). Because they handle so many cases, California and New York have individual reporters, the *New York Supplement* and the *California*

Figure A–1   National Reporter System Map—Showing the states included in each
Reporter group

A Pacific
B North Western
C South Western
D North Eastern
E Atlantic
F Southern
G South Eastern

Reporter. Some states publish their own reporters in addition to the West series.

Statutory Law

Statutes—laws passed by Congress—are published in the *United States Code* (U.S.C.) and printed by the U.S. Government Printing Office. The U.S.C. contains the text of all laws passed by Congress and signed by the President. A reference to this source might read 40 U.S.C. § 13.1 (volume 40 of the *United States Code*, section 13.1).

A very popular source of statutory law is the *United States Code Annotated* (U.S.C.A.). In the U.S.C.A., each section of a statute contains helpful annotations that provide references to the legislative history of the section and to court decisions using and interpreting it. A reference to this source might read 14 U.S.C.A. § 45.3 (volume 14, *United States Code Annotated*, section 45.3). In both the U.S.C. and the U.S.C.A., the laws are organized and integrated into a pattern that makes them relatively easy to find and to read.

The U.S. Government Printing Office also publishes *Statutes at Large*, a chronological list of all laws enacted by Congress. This is not often used unless it is necessary to look up a law that has just been passed by Congress but that is not yet reported in the U.S.C. or U.S.C.A. A full citation might read: Voting Rights Act of 1965, Pub.L. No. 89–110, 79 Stat. 437, 42 U.S.C. §§ 1971, 1973. The Voting Rights Act of 1965 was the 110th *Public Law* enacted by the 89th Congress and appears in volume 79 of *Statutes at Large*, section 437. In addition, it appears in volume 42 of the U.S.C., sections 1971 and 1973. Also, remember that there is often a difference between the number of the section in the statute as written by Congress and the number of the section in the Code. For example, the "National Environmental Policy Act of 1969, § 102, 42 U.S.C. § 4332" means that section 102 of the statute as passed by Congress is found in section 4332 of volume 42 of the U.S.C.

Regulatory Law

Regulations—rules passed by agencies subsequent to a congressional statute—are published in the *Code of Federal Regulations* (C.F.R.). These regulations are intended to implement a particular statute enacted by Congress. The C.F.R., revised annually, is organized by subject matter and contains the text of regulations in effect as of the date of publication. A citation reading 7 C.F.R. § 912.65 refers to Title 7 of the *Code of Federal Regulations*, section 912.65. Different titles refer to different government agencies.

To keep up-to-date on new and proposed regulations, one needs to consult the *Federal Register* (Fed.Reg.). Printed five days a week by the U.S. Government Printing Office, the *Federal Register* lists all proposed regulations and all new and amended regulations. A citation might read 46 Fed.Reg. 26,501 (1981). This refers to volume 46 of the *Federal Register*, published in 1981, page 26,501, which has to do with a new environmental standard.

Agency Orders and Opinion

Agency orders and opinions are official regulatory materials that go beyond the regulations. Orders may be issued by the top officials (e.g., the commissioners) of a regulatory agency, while opinions are generally issued by an agency's administrative law judge in adjudicatory hearings (discussed in Chapter 5). While agencies usually have official publications, the easiest way to find agency materials is to look in commercial reporters published by private companies such as Commerce Clearing House, Bureau of National Affairs, and Prentice-Hall. Each reporter covers a single topic, such as environmental law or federal tax law. The reporters are up-to-date and contain new regulations, orders, opinions, court decisions, and other materials of interest to anyone following regulations in a certain area. These reporters, which are usually large loose-leaf binders, cover hundreds of topics, such as chemical regulations, hazardous materials, transportation, noise regulations, collective bargaining negotiations, securities regulations, patents, and anti-trust laws.

Treatises, Law Reviews, and Restatements of the Law

Important secondary sources of law are legal treatises, law reviews, and Restatements of Law. Treatises generally cover one area or topic of law, summarizing the principles and rules dealing with the topic. An example of a treatise is W. Jaeger, *Williston on Contracts* (3d ed. 1957).

Law reviews, published by law schools and edited by law students, contain articles written by legal scholars, judges, and practitioners on virtually all aspects of the law. An example of a legal citation to a law review is Mark J. Roe, "Corporate Strategic Reaction to Mass Tort," 72 *Virginia Law Review* 1 (1986), which means the article "Corporate Strategic Reaction to Mass Tort" written by Mark J. Roe can be found in volume 72 of the *Virginia Law Review* beginning on page 1.

Like a treatise, a Restatement is limited in its coverage to a single area of law. Restatements are the consequence of intensive study on a specific topic by legal scholars, culminating in a written statement of the law. That statement will include rules stated in bold type—often referred to as "black-letter law"—along with explanatory comments. The rules presented are usually synthesized from opinions of the courts in all jurisdictions. An example is the *Restatement (Second) of Torts*.

B   The Constitution of the United States of America

Preamble

We the People of the United States, in Order to form a more perfect Union, establish Justice, insure domestic Tranquility, provide for the common defence, promote the general Welfare, and secure the Blessings of Liberty to ourselves and our Posterity, do ordain and establish this Constitution for the United States of America.

Article I

Section 1. All legislative Powers herein granted shall be vested in a Congress of the United States, which shall consist of a Senate and House of Representatives.

Section 2. The House of Representatives shall be composed of Members chosen every second Year by the People of the several States, and the Electors in each State shall have the Qualifications requisite for Electors of the most numerous Branch of the State Legislature.

No Person shall be a Representative who shall not have attained to the Age of twenty five Years, and been seven Years a Citizen of the United States, and who shall not, when elected, be an Inhabitant of that State in which he shall be chosen.

Representatives and direct Taxes shall be apportioned among the several States which may be included within this Union, according to their respective Numbers, which shall be determined by adding to the whole Number of free Persons, including those bound to Service for a Term of Years, and excluding Indians not taxed, three fifths of all other Persons. The actual Enumeration shall be made within three Years after the first Meeting of the Congress of the United States, and within every subsequent Term of ten Years, in such Manner as they shall by Law direct. The number of Representatives shall not exceed one for every thirty Thousand, but each State shall have at Least one

Representative; and until such enumeration shall be made, the State of New Hampshire shall be entitled to chuse three, Massachusetts eight, Rhode Island and Providence Plantations one, Connecticut five, New York six, New Jersey four, Pennsylvania eight, Delaware one, Maryland six, Virginia ten, North Carolina five, South Carolina five, and Georgia three.

When vacancies happen in the Representation from any State, the Executive Authority thereof shall issue Writs of Election to fill such vacancies.

The House of Representatives shall chuse their Speaker and other Officers; and shall have the sole Power of Impeachment.

Section 3. The Senate of the United States shall be composed of two Senators from each State, chosen by the Legislature thereof, for six Years; and each Senator shall have one Vote.

Immediately after they shall be assembled in Consequence of the first Election, they shall be divided as equally as may be into three Classes. The Seats of the Senators of the first Class shall be vacated at the Expiration of the second Year, of the second Class at the Expiration of the fourth Year, and of the third Class at the Expiration of the sixth Year, so that one third may be chosen every second Year; and if Vacancies happen by Resignation, or otherwise, during the Recess of the Legislature of any State, the Executive thereof may make temporary Appointments until the next Meeting of the Legislature, which shall then fill such Vacancies.

No Person shall be a Senator who shall not have attained to the Age of thirty Years, and been nine Years a Citizen of the United States, and who shall not, when elected, be an Inhabitant of that State for which he shall be chosen.

The Vice President of the United States shall be President of the Senate, but shall have no Vote, unless they be equally divided.

The Senate shall chuse their other Officers, and also a President pro tempore, in the Absence of the Vice President, or when he shall exercise the Office of President of the United States.

The Senate shall have the sole power to try all Impeachments. When sitting for that Purpose, they shall be on Oath or Affirmation. When the President of the United States is tried, the Chief Justice shall preside: And no Person shall be convicted without the Concurrence of two thirds of the Members present.

Judgment in Cases of Impeachment shall not extend further than to removal from Office, and disqualification to hold and enjoy any Office of honor, Trust or Profit under the United States: but the Party convicted shall nevertheless be liable and subject to Indictment, Trial, Judgment and Punishment, according to Law.

Section 4. The Times, Places and Manner of holding Elections for Senators and Representatives, shall be prescribed in each State by the Legislature thereof: but the Congress may at any time by Law make or alter such Regulations, except as to the Places of chusing Senators.

The Congress shall assemble at least once in every Year, and such Meeting shall be on the first Monday in December, unless they shall by Law appoint a different Day.

Section 5. Each House shall be the Judge of the Elections, Returns and Qualifications of its own Members, and a Majority of each shall constitute a

Quorum to do Business; but a smaller Number may adjourn from day to day, and may be authorized to compel the Attendance of absent Members, in such Manner, and under such Penalties as each House may provide.

Each House may determine the Rules of its Proceedings, punish its Members for disorderly Behaviour, and, with the Concurrence of two thirds, expel a Member.

Each House shall keep a Journal of its Proceedings, and from time to time publish the same, excepting such Parts as may in their Judgment require Secrecy; and the Yeas and Nays of the Members of either House on any question shall, at the Desire of one fifth of those Present, be entered on the Journal.

Neither House, during the Session of Congress, shall, without the Consent of the other, adjourn for more than three days, nor to any other Place than that in which the two Houses shall be sitting.

Section 6. The Senators and Representatives shall receive a Compensation for their Services, to be ascertained by Law, and paid out of the Treasury of the United States. They shall in all Cases, except Treason, Felony and Breach of the Peace, be privileged from Arrest during their Attendance at the Session of their respective Houses, and in going to and returning from the same; and for any Speech or Debate in either House, they shall not be questioned in any other Place.

No Senator or Representative shall, during the Time for which he was elected, be appointed to any civil Office under the Authority of the United States, which shall have been created, or the Emoluments whereof shall have been encreased during such time; and no Person holding any Office under the United States, shall be a Member of either House during his Continuance in Office.

Section 7. All Bills for raising Revenue shall originate in the House of Representatives; but the Senate may propose or concur with Amendments as on other Bills.

Every Bill which shall have passed the House of Representatives and the Senate, shall, before it become a Law, be presented to the President of the United States; If he approve he shall sign it, but if not he shall return it, with his Objections to that House in which it shall have originated, who shall enter the Objections at large on their Journal, and proceed to reconsider it. If after such Reconsideration two thirds of that House shall agree to pass the Bill, it shall be sent, together with the Objections, to the other House, by which it shall likewise be reconsidered, and if approved by two thirds of that House, it shall become a Law. But in all such Cases the Votes of both Houses shall be determined by Yeas and Nays, and the Names of the Persons voting for and against the Bill shall be entered on the Journal of each House respectively. If any Bill shall not be returned by the President within ten Days (Sundays excepted) after it shall have been presented to him, the Same shall be a Law, in like Manner as if he had signed it, unless the Congress by their Adjournment prevent its Return, in which Case it shall not be a Law.

Every Order, Resolution, or Vote to which the Concurrence of the Senate and House of Representatives may be necessary (except on a question of Adjournment) shall be presented to the President of the United States; and before the Same shall take Effect, shall be approved by him, or being disapproved by him, shall be repassed by two thirds of the Senate and House of Representatives, according to the Rules and Limitations prescribed in the Case of a Bill.

Section 8. The Congress shall have Power to lay and collect Taxes, Duties, Imposts and Excises, to pay the Debts and provide for the common Defence and general Welfare of the United States; but all Duties, Imposts and Excises shall be uniform throughout the United States;

To borrow Money on the credit of the United States;

To regulate Commerce with foreign Nations, and among the several States, and with the Indian Tribes;

To establish an uniform Rule of Naturalization, and uniform Laws on the subject of Bankruptcies throughout the United States;

To coin Money, regulate the Value thereof, and of foreign Coin, and fix the Standard of Weights and Measures;

To provide for the Punishment of counterfeiting the Securities and current Coin of the United States;

To establish Post Offices and post Roads;

To promote the Progress of Science and useful Arts, by securing for limited Times to Authors and Inventors the exclusive Right to their respective Writings and Discoveries;

To constitute Tribunals inferior to the supreme Court;

To define and punish Piracies and Felonies committed on the high Seas, and Offenses against the Law of Nations;

To declare War, grant Letters of Marque and Reprisal, and make Rules concerning Captures on Land and Water;

To raise and support Armies, but no Appropriation of Money to that Use shall be for a longer Term than two Years;

To provide and maintain a Navy;

To make Rules for the Government and Regulation of the land and naval Forces;

To provide for calling forth the Militia to execute the Laws of the Union, suppress Insurrections and repel Invasions;

To provide for organizing, arming, and disciplining, the Militia, and for governing such Part of them as may be employed in the Service of the United States, reserving to the States respectively, the Appointment of the Officers, and the Authority of training the Militia according to the discipline prescribed by Congress;

To exercise exclusive Legislation in all Cases whatsoever, over such District (not exceeding ten Miles square) as may, by Cession of particular States, and the Acceptance of Congress, become the Seat of the Government of the United States, and to exercise like Authority over all Places purchased by the Consent of the Legislature of the State in which the Same shall be, for the Erection of Forts, Magazines, Arsenals, dock-Yards, and other needful Buildings;—And

To make all Laws which shall be necessary and proper for carrying into Execution the foregoing Powers, and all other Powers vested by this Constitution in the Government of the United States, or in any Department or Officer thereof.

Section 9. The Migration or Importation of such Persons as any of the States now existing shall think proper to admit, shall not be prohibited by the

Congress prior to the Year one thousand eight hundred and eight, but a Tax or Duty may be imposed on such Importation, not exceeding ten dollars for each Person.

The Privilege of the Writ of Habeas Corpus shall not be suspended, unless when in Cases of Rebellion or Invasion the public Safety may require it.

No Bill of Attainder or ex post facto Law shall be passed.

No Capitation, or other direct, Tax shall be laid, unless in Proportion to the Census or Enumeration herein before directed to be taken.

No Tax or Duty shall be laid on Articles exported from any State.

No Preference shall be given by any Regulation of Commerce or Revenue to the Ports of one State over those of another; nor shall Vessels bound to, or from, one State, be obliged to enter, clear, or pay Duties in another.

No Money shall be drawn from the Treasury, but in Consequence of Appropriations made by Laws; and a regular Statement and Account of the Receipts and Expenditures of all public Money shall be published from time to time.

No Title of Nobility shall be granted by the United States: And no Person holding any Office of Profit or Trust under them, shall, without the Consent of the Congress, accept of any present, Emolument, Office, or Title, of any kind whatever, from any King, Prince, or foreign State.

Section 10. No State shall enter into any Treaty, Alliance, or Confederation; grant Letters of Marque and Reprisal; coin Money; emit Bills of Credit; make any Thing but gold and silver Coin a Tender in Payment of Debts; pass any Bill of Attainder, ex post facto Law, or Law impairing the Obligation of Contracts, or grant any Title of Nobility.

No State shall, without the Consent of the Congress, lay any Imposts or Duties on Imports or Exports, except what may be absolutely necessary for executing its inspection Laws: and the net Produce of all Duties and Imposts, laid by any State on Imports or Exports, shall be for the Use of the Treasury of the United States; and all such Laws shall be subject to the Revision and Controul of the Congress.

No State shall, without the Consent of Congress, lay and Duty of Tonnage, keep Troops, or Ships of War in time of Peace, enter into any Agreement or Compact with another State, or with a foreign Power, or engage in War, unless actually invaded, or in such imminent Danger as will not admit of delay.

Article II

Section 1. The executive Power shall be vested in a President of the United States of America. He shall hold his Office during the Term of four Years, and, together with the Vice President, chosen for the same Term, be elected, as follows:

Each State shall appoint, in such Manner as the Legislature thereof may direct, a Number of Electors, equal to the whole Number of Senators and Representatives to which the State may be entitled in the Congress: but no Senator or Representative, or Person holding an Office of Trust or Profit under the United States, shall be appointed an Elector.

The Electors shall meet in their respective States, and vote by Ballot for two Persons, of whom one at least shall not be an Inhabitant of the same State with themselves. And they shall make a List of all the Persons voted for, and of the Number of Votes for each; which List they shall sign and certify, and transmit sealed to the Seat of the Government of the United States, directed to the President of the Senate. The President of the Senate shall, in the Presence of the Senate and House of Representatives, open all the Certificates, and the Votes shall then be counted. The Person having the greatest Number of Votes shall be the President, if such Number be a Majority of the whole Number of Electors appointed; and if there be more than one who have such Majority, and have an equal Number of Votes, then the House of Representatives shall immediately chuse by Ballot one of them for President; and if no Person have a Majority, then from the five highest on the List the said House shall in like Manner chuse the President. But in chusing the President, the Votes shall be taken by States, the Representation from each State having one Vote; a quorum for this Purpose shall consist of a Member or Members from two thirds of the States, and a Majority of all the States shall be necessary to a Choice. In every Case, after the Choice of the President, the Person having the greatest Number of Votes of the Electors shall be the Vice President. But if there should remain two or more who have equal Votes, the Senate shall chuse from them by Ballot the Vice President.

The Congress may determine the Time of chusing the Electors, and the Day on which they shall give their Votes; which Day shall be the same throughout the United States.

No Person except a natural born Citizen, or a Citizen of the United States, at the time of the Adoption of this Constitution, shall be eligible to the Office of President; neither shall any Person be eligible to that Office who shall not have attained to the Age of thirty five Years, and been fourteen Years a Resident within the United States.

In Case of the Removal of the President from Office, or of his Death, Resignation, or Inability to discharge the Powers and Duties of the said Office, the Same shall devolve on the Vice President, and the Congress may by Law provide for the Case of Removal, Death, Resignation or Inability, both of the President and Vice President, declaring what Officer shall then act as President, and such Officer shall act accordingly, until the Disability be removed, or a President shall be elected.

The President shall, at stated Times, receive for his Services, a Compensation, which shall neither be encreased nor diminished during the Period for which he shall have been elected, and he shall not receive within that Period any other Emolument from the United States, or any of them.

Before he enter on the Execution of his Office, he shall take the following Oath or Affirmation:—"I do solemnly swear (or affirm) that I will faithfully execute the Office of President of the United States, and will to the best of my Ability, preserve, protect and defend the Constitution of the United States."

Section 2. The President shall be Commander in Chief of the Army and Navy of the United States, and of the Militia of the several States, when called into the actual Service of the United States; he may require the Opinion, in writing, of the principal Officer in each of the executive Departments, upon any Subject relating to the Duties of their respective Offices, and he shall have Power to grant Reprieves and Pardons for Offences against the United States, except in Cases of Impeachment.

He shall have Power, by and with the Advice and Consent of the Senate, to make Treaties, providing two thirds of the Senators present concur; and he shall nominate, and by and with the Advice and Consent of the Senate, shall appoint Ambassadors, other public Ministers and Consuls, Judges of the supreme Court, and all other Officers of the United States, whose Appointments are not herein otherwise provided for, and which shall be established by Law: but the Congress may by Law vest the Appointment of such inferior Officers, as they think proper, in the President alone, in the Courts of Law, or in the Heads of Departments.

The President shall have Power to fill up all Vacancies that may happen during the Recess of the Senate, by granting Commissions which shall expire at the End of their next Session.

Section 3. He shall from time to time give to the Congress Information of the State of the Union, and recommend to their Consideration such Measures as he shall judge necessary and expedient; he may, on extraordinary Occasions, convene both Houses, or either of them, and in Case of Disagreement between them, with Respect to the Time of Adjournment, he may adjourn them to such Time as he shall think proper, he shall receive Ambassadors and other public Ministers; he shall take Care that the Laws be faithfully executed, and shall Commission all the Officers of the United States.

Section 4. The President, Vice President and all civil Officers of the United States, shall be removed from Office on Impeachment for, and Conviction of, Treason, Bribery, or other high Crimes and Misdemeanors.

Article III

Section 1. The judicial Power of the United States, shall be vested in one supreme Court, and in such inferior Courts as the Congress may from time to time ordain and establish. The Judges, both of the supreme and inferior Courts, shall hold their Offices during good Behaviour, and shall, at stated Times, receive for their Services, a Compensation, which shall not be diminished during their Continuance in Office.

Section 2.

The judicial Power shall extend to all Cases, in Law and Equity, arising under this Constitution, the Laws of the United States, and Treaties made, or which shall be made, under their Authority;—to all Cases affecting Ambassadors, other public Ministers and Consuls;—to all Cases of admiralty and maritime Jurisdiction;—to Controversies to which the United States shall be a Party; to Controversies between two or more States;—between a State and Citizens of another State;—between Citizens of different States;—between Citizens of the same State claiming Lands under Grants of different States, and between a State, or the Citizens thereof, and foreign States, Citizens or Subjects.

In all Cases affecting Ambassadors, other public Ministers and Consuls, and those in which a State shall be Party, the supreme Court shall have original Jurisdiction. In all the other Cases before mentioned, the supreme Court shall have appellate Jurisdiction, both as to Law and Fact, with such Exceptions, and under such Regulations as the Congress shall make.

The Trial of all Crimes, except in Cases of Impeachment, shall be by Jury; and such Trial shall be held in the State where the said Crimes shall have been committed; but when not committed within any State, the Trial shall be at such Place or Places as the Congress may by Law have directed.

Section 3. Treason against the United States, shall consist only in levying War against them, or in adhering to their Enemies, giving them Aid and Comfort. No Person shall be convicted of Treason unless on the Testimony of two Witnesses to the same overt Act, or on Confession in open Court.

The Congress shall have Power to declare the Punishment of Treason, but no Attainder of Treason shall work Corruption of Blood, or Forfeiture except during the Life of the Person attainted.

Article IV

Section 1. Full Faith and Credit shall be given in each State to the public Acts, Records, and judicial Proceedings of every other State. And the Congress may by general Laws prescribe the Manner in which such Arts, Records and Proceedings shall be proved, and the Effect thereof.

Section 2. The Citizens of each State shall be entitled to all Privileges and Immunities of Citizens in the several States.

A Person charged in any State with Treason, Felony, or other Crime, who shall flee from Justice, and be found in another State, shall on Demand of the executive Authority of the State from which he fled, be delivered up, to be removed to the State having Jurisdiction of the Crime.

No Person held to Service or Labour in one State, under the Laws thereof, escaping into another, shall, in Consequence of any Law or Regulation therein, be discharged from such Service or Labour, but shall be delivered up on Claim of the Party to whom such Service or Labour may be due.

Section 3. New States may be admitted by the Congress into this Union; but no new State shall be formed or erected within the Jurisdiction of any other State; nor any State be formed by the Junction of two or more States, or Parts of States, without the Consent of the Legislatures of the States concerned as well as of the Congress.

The Congress shall have Power to dispose of and make all needful Rules and Regulations respecting the Territory or other Property belonging to the United States; and nothing in this Constitution shall be so construed as to Prejudice any Claims of the United States, or of any particular State.

Section 4. The United States shall guarantee to every State in this Union a Republican Form of the Government, and shall protect each of them against Invasion; and on Application of the Legislature, or of the Executive (when the Legislature cannot be convened) against domestic Violence.

Article V

The Congress, whenever two thirds of both Houses shall deem it necessary, shall propose Amendments to this Constitution, or, on the Application of the Legislatures of two thirds of the several States, shall call a Convention for proposing Amendments, which, in either Case, shall be valid to all Intents and Purposes, as Part of this Constitution, when ratified by the Legislatures of three fourths of the several States, or by Conventions in three fourths thereof, as the one or the other Mode of Ratification may be proposed by the Congress; Provided that no Amendment which may be made prior to the Year One thousand eight hundred and eight shall in any Manner affect the first and fourth Clauses in the Ninth Section of the first Article; and that no State, without its Consent, shall be deprived of its equal Suffrage in the Senate.

Article VI

All Debts contracted and Engagements entered into, before the Adoption of this Constitution, shall be as valid against the United States under this Constitution, as under the Confederation.

This Constitution, and the Laws of the United States which shall be made in Pursuance thereof; and all Treaties made, or which shall be made, under the Authority of the United States, shall be the supreme Law of the Land; and the Judges in every State shall be bound thereby, any Thing in the Constitution or Laws of any State to the Contrary notwithstanding.

The Senators and Representatives before mentioned, and the Members of the several State Legislatures, and all executive and judicial Officers, both of the United States and of the several States, shall be bound by Oath or Affirmation, to support this Constitution; but no religious Test shall ever be required as a Qualification to any Office or public Trust under the United States.

Article VII

The Ratification of the Conventions of nine States, shall be sufficient for the Establishment of this Constitution between the States so ratifying the Same.

Amendment I [1791]

Congress shall make no law respecting an establishment of religion, or prohibiting the free exercise thereof; or abridging the freedom of speech, or the press; or the right of the people peaceably to assemble, and to petition the Government for a redress of grievances.

Amendment II [1791]

A well regulated Militia, being necessary to the security for a free State, the right of the people to keep and bear Arms, shall not be infringed.

Amendment III [1791]

No Soldier shall, in time of peace be quartered in any house, without the consent of the Owner, nor in time of war, but in a manner to be prescribed by law.

Amendment IV [1791]

The right of the people to be secure in their persons, houses, papers, and effects, against unreasonable searches and seizures, shall not be violated, and no Warrants shall issue, but upon probable cause, supported by Oath or affirmation, and particularly describing the place to be searched, and the persons or things to be seized.

Amendment V [1791]

No person shall be held to answer for a capital, or otherwise infamous crime, unless on a presentment or indictment of a Grand Jury, except in cases arising in the land or naval forces, or in the Militia, when in actual service in time of

War or public danger; nor shall any person be subject for the same offense to be twice put in jeopardy of life or limb; nor shall be compelled in any criminal case to be a witness against himself, nor be deprived of life, liberty, or property, without due process of law; nor shall private property be taken for public use, without just compensation.

Amendment VI [1791]

In all criminal prosecutions, the accused shall enjoy the right to a speedy and public trial, by an impartial jury of the State and district wherein the crime shall have been committed, which district shall have been previously ascertained by law, and to be informed of the nature and cause of the accusation; to be confronted with the Witnesses against him; to have compulsory process for obtaining witnesses in his favor, and to have the Assistance of counsel for his defence.

Amendment VII [1791]

In Suits at common law, where the value in controversy shall exceed twenty dollars, the right of trial by jury shall be preserved, and no fact tried by a jury, shall be otherwise re-examined in any Court of the United States, than according to the rules of the common law.

Amendment VIII [1791]

Excessive bail shall not be required, no excessive fines imposed, nor cruel and unusual punishments inflicted.

Amendment IX [1791]

The enumeration in the Constitution, of certain rights, shall not be construed to deny or disparage others retained by the people.

Amendment X [1791]

The powers not delegated to the United States by the Constitution, nor prohibited by it to the States, are reserved to the States respectively, or to the people.

Amendment XI [1798]

The Judicial power of the United States shall not be construed to extend to any suit in law or equity, commenced or prosecuted against one of the United States by Citizens of another State, or by Citizens or Subjects of any Foreign State.

Amendment XII [1804]

The Electors shall meet in their respective states and vote by ballot for President and Vice-President, one of whom, at least, shall not be an inhabitant of the same state with themselves; they shall name in their ballots the person voted for as President, and in distinct ballots the person voted for as Vice-President, and they shall make distinct lists of all persons voted for as President, and of all persons voted for as Vice-President, and of the number of votes for each, which lists they shall sign and certify, and transmit sealed to the seat of the government of the United States, directed to the President of the

Senate;—The President of the Senate shall, in the presence of the Senate and House of Representatives, open all the certificates and the votes shall then be counted;—The person having the greatest number of votes for President, shall be the President, if such number be a majority of the whole number of Electors appointed; and if no person have such majority, then from the persons having the highest numbers not exceeding three on the list of those voted for as President, the House of Representatives shall choose immediately, by ballot, the President. But in choosing the President, the votes shall be taken by states, the representation from each state having one vote; a quorum for this purpose shall consist of a member or members from two-thirds of the states, and a majority of all the states shall be necessary to a choice. And if the House of Representatives shall not choose a President whenever the right of choice shall devolve upon them, before the fourth day of March next following, then the Vice-President shall act as President, as in the case of the death or other constitutional disability of the President. The person having the greatest number of votes as Vice-President, shall be the Vice-President, if such number be a majority of the whole number of Electors appointed, and if no person have a majority, then from the two highest numbers on the list, the Senate shall choose the Vice-President; a quorum for the purpose shall consist of two-thirds of the whole number of Senators, and a majority of the whole number shall be necessary to a choice. But no person constitutionally ineligible to the office of President shall be eligible to that of the Vice-President of the United States.

Amendment XIII [1865]

Section 1. Neither slavery nor involuntary servitude, except as a punishment for crime whereof the party shall have been duly convicted, shall exist within the United States, or any place subject to their jurisdiction.

Section 2. Congress shall have power to enforce this article by appropriate legislation.

Amendment XIV [1868]

All persons born or naturalized in the United States, and subject to the jurisdiction thereof, are citizens of the United States and of the State wherein they reside. No State shall make or enforce any law which shall abridge the privileges or immunities of citizens of the United States; nor shall any State deprive any person of life, liberty, or property, without due process of law; nor deny to any person within its jurisdiction the equal protection of the laws.

Section 2. Representatives shall be appointed among the several States according to their respective numbers, counting the whole number of persons in each State, excluding Indians not taxed. But when the right to vote at any election for the choice of electors for President and Vice President of the United States, Representatives in Congress, the Executive and Judicial officers of a State, or the members of the Legislature thereof, is denied to any of the male inhabitants of such State, being twenty-one years of age, and citizens of the United States, or in any way abridged, except for participation in rebellion, or other crime, the basis of representation therein shall be reduced in the proportion which the number of such male citizens shall bear to the whole number of male citizens twenty-one years of age in such State.

Section 3.

No person shall be a Senator or Representative in Congress, or elector of President and Vice President, or hold any office, civil or military, under the United States, or under any State, who, having previously taken an oath, as a member of Congress, or as an officer of the United States, or as a member of any State legislature, or as an executive or judicial officer of any State, to support the Constitution of the United States, shall have engaged in insurrection or rebellion against the same, or given aid or comfort to the enemies thereof. But Congress may by a vote of two-thirds of each House, remove such disability.

Section 4.

The validity of the public debt of the United States, authorized by law, including debts incurred for payment of pensions and bounties for services in suppressing insurrection or rebellion, shall not be questioned. But neither the United States nor any State shall assume or pay any debt or obligation incurred in aid of insurrection or rebellion against the United States, or any claim for the loss or emancipation of any slave; but all such debts, obligations and claims shall be held illegal and void.

Section 5.

The Congress shall have power to enforce, by appropriate legislation, the provisions of this article.

Amendment XV [1870]

Section 1. The right of citizens of the United States to vote shall not be denied or abridged by the United States or by any State on account of race, color, or previous condition of servitude.

Section 2. The Congress shall have power to enforce this article by appropriate legislation.

Amendment XVI [1913]

The Congress shall have power to lay and collect taxes on incomes, from whatever source derived, without apportionment among the several States, and without regard to any census or enumeration.

Amendment XVII [1913]

The Senate of the United States shall be composed of two Senators from each State, elected by the people thereof, for six years; and each Senator shall have one vote. The electors in each State shall have the qualifications requisite for electors of the most numerous branch of the State legislatures.

When vacancies happen in the representation of any State in the Senate, the executive authority of each State shall issue writs of election to fill such vacancies; *Provided*, That the legislature of any State may empower the executive thereof to make temporary appointments until the people fill the vacancies by election as the legislature may direct.

This amendment shall not be so construed as to affect the election or term of any Senator chosen before it becomes valid as part of the Constitution.

Amendment XVIII [1919]

Section 1. After one year from the ratification of this article the manufacture, sale, or transportation of intoxicating liquors within, the importation thereof into, or the exportation thereof from the United States and all territory subject to the jurisdiction thereof for beverage purposes is hereby prohibited.

Section 2. The Congress and the several States shall have concurrent power to enforce this article by appropriate legislation.

Section 3. This article shall be inoperative unless it shall have been ratified as an amendment to the Constitution by the legislatures of the several States, as provided in the Constitution, within seven years from the date of the submission hereof to the States by the Congress.

Amendment XIX [1920]

The right of citizens of the United States to vote shall not be denied or abridged by the United States or by any State on account of sex.

Congress shall have power to enforce this article by appropriate legislation.

Amendment XX [1933]

Section 1. The terms of the President and Vice President shall end at noon on the 20th day of January, and the terms of Senators and Representatives at noon on the 3d day of January, of the years in which such terms would have ended if this article had not been ratified; and the terms of their successors shall then begin.

Section 2. The Congress shall assemble at least once every year, and such meeting shall begin at noon on the 3d day of January, unless they shall by law appoint a different day.

Section 3. If, at the time fixed for the beginning of the term of the President, the President elect shall have died, the Vice President elect shall become President. If a President shall not have been chosen before the time fixed for the beginning of his term, or if the President elect shall have failed to qualify, then the Vice President elect shall act as President until a President shall have qualified; and the Congress may by law provide for the case wherein neither a President elect nor a Vice President elect shall have qualified, declaring who shall then act as President, or the manner in which one who is to act shall be selected, and such person shall act accordingly until a President or Vice President shall have qualified.

Section 4. The Congress may by law provide for the case of the death of any of the persons from whom the House of Representatives may choose a President whenever the right of choice shall have devolved upon them, and for the case of the death of any of the persons from whom the Senate may choose a Vice President whenever the right of choice shall have devolved upon them.

Section 5. Sections 1 and 2 shall take effect on the 15th day of October following the ratification of this article.

Section 6. This article shall be inoperative unless it shall have been ratified as an amendment to the Constitution by the legislatures of three-fourths of the several States within seven years from the date of its submission.

Amendment XXI [1933]

Section 1. The eighteenth article of amendment to the Constitution of the United States is hereby repealed.

Section 2. The transportation or importation into any State, Territory, or possession of the United States for delivery or use therein of intoxicating liquors, in violation of the laws thereof, is hereby prohibited.

Section 3. This article shall be inoperative unless it shall have been ratified as an amendment to the Constitution by conventions in the several States, as provided in the Constitution, within seven years from the date of the submission hereof to the States by the Congress.

Amendment XXII [1951]

Section 1. No person shall be elected to the office of the President more than twice, and no person who has held the office of President, or acted as President, for more than two years of a term to which some other person was elected President shall be elected to the office of the President more than once. But this Article shall not apply to any person holding the office of President when this Article was proposed by the Congress, and shall not prevent any person who may be holding the office of President, or acting as President, during the term within which this Article becomes operative from holding the office of President or acting as President during the remainder of such term.

Section 2. This article shall be inoperative unless it shall have been ratified as an amendment to the Constitution by the legislatures of three-fourths of the several States within seven years from the date of its submission to the States by the Congress.

Amendment XXIII [1961]

Section 1. The District constituting the seat of Government of the United States shall appoint in such manner as the Congress may direct:

A number of electors of President and Vice President equal to the whole number of Senators and Representatives in Congress to which the District would be entitled if it were a State, but in no event more than the least populous State; they shall be in addition to those appointed by the States, but they shall be considered, for the purposes of the election of President and Vice President, to be electors appointed by a State; and they shall meet in the District and perform such duties as provided by the twelfth article of amendment.

Section 2. The Congress shall have power to enforce this article by appropriate legislation.

Amendment XXIV [1964]

Section 1. The right of citizens of the United States to vote in any primary or other election for President or Vice President, for electors for President or Vice President, or for Senator or Representative in Congress, shall not be denied or abridged by the United States or any State by reason of failure to pay any poll tax or other tax.

Section 2. The Congress shall have power to enforce this article by appropriate legislation.

Amendment XXV [1967]

Section 1. In case of the removal of the President from office or of his death or resignation, the Vice President shall become President.

Section 2. Whenever there is a vacancy in the office of the Vice President, the President shall nominate a Vice President who shall take office upon confirmation by a majority vote of both Houses of Congress.

Section 3. Whenever the President transmits to the President pro tempore of the Senate and the Speaker of the House of Representatives his written declaration that he is unable to discharge the powers and duties of his office, and until he transmits to them a written declaration to the contrary, such powers and duties shall be discharged by the Vice President as Acting President.

Section 4. Whenever the Vice President and a majority of either the principal officers of the executive departments or of such other body as Congress may by law provide, transmit to the President pro tempore of the Senate and the Speaker of the House of Representatives their written declaration that the President is unable to discharge the powers and duties of his office, the Vice President shall immediately assume the powers and duties of the office as Acting President.

Thereafter, when the President transmits to the President pro tempore of the Senate and the Speaker of the House of Representatives his written declaration that no inability exists, he shall resume the powers and duties of his office unless the Vice President and a majority of either the principal officers of the executive department or of such other body as Congress may by law provide, transmit within four days to the President pro tempore of the Senate and the Speaker of the House of Representatives their written declaration that the President is unable to discharge the powers and duties of his office. Thereupon Congress shall decide the issue, assembling within forty-eight hours for that purpose if not in session. If the Congress, within twenty-one days after receipt of the latter written declaration, or, if Congress is not in session, within twenty-one days after Congress is required to assemble, determines by two-thirds vote of both Houses that the President is unable to discharge the powers and duties of his office, the Vice President shall continue to discharge the same as Acting President; otherwise, the President shall resume the powers and duties of his office.

Amendment XXVI [1971]

Section 1. The right of citizens of the United States, who are eighteen years of age or older, to vote shall not be denied or abridged by the United States or by any State on account of age.

Section 2. The Congress shall have power to enforce this article by appropriate legislation.

C   Sherman Act

Restraints of Trade Prohibited

Section 1 — Trusts, etc., in restraint of trade illegal; penalty. Every contract, combination in the form of trust or otherwise, or conspiracy, in restraint of trade or commerce among the several States, or with foreign nations, is declared to be illegal. Every person who shall make any contract or engage in any combination or conspiracy declared by sections 1 to 7 of this title to be illegal shall be deemed guilty of a felony, and, on conviction thereof, shall be punished by fine not exceeding one million dollars if a corporation, or if any other person, one hundred thousand dollars, or by imprisonment not exceeding three years, or both said punishments, in the discretion of the court.

Section 2 — Monopolizing trade a felony; penalty. Every person who shall monopolize, or attempt to monopolize, or combine or conspire with any other person or persons, to monopolize any part of the trade or commerce among the several States, or with foreign nations, shall be deemed guilty of a felony, and, on conviction thereof, shall be punished by fine not exceeding one million dollars if a corporation, or, if any other person, one hundred thousand dollars, or by imprisonment not exceeding three years, or by both said punishments, in the discretion of the court.

D   Clayton Act

Section 3 — Sale, etc., on agreement not to use goods of competitor. It shall be unlawful for any person engaged in commerce, in the course of such commerce, to lease or make a sale or contract for sale of goods, wares, merchandise, machinery, supplies, or other commodities, whether patented or unpatented, for use, consumption, or resale within the United States or any Territory thereof or the District of Columbia or any insular possession or other place under the jurisdiction of the United States, or fix a price charged thereof, or discount from, or rebate upon, such price, on the condition, agreement, or understanding that the lessee or purchaser thereof shall not use or deal in the goods, wares, merchandise, machinery, supplies, or other commodities of a competitor or competitors of the lessor or seller, where the effect of such lease, sale, or contract for sale or such condition, agreement or understanding may be to substantially lessen competition or tend to create a monopoly in any line of commerce.

Private Suits

Section 4 — Suits by persons injured; amount of recovery. Any person who shall be injured in this business or property by reason of anything forbidden in the antitrust laws may sue therefor in any district court of the United States in the district in which the defendant resides or is found or has an agent, without respect to the amount in controversy, and shall recover threefold the damages by him sustained, and the cost of suit, including a reasonable attorney's fee . . .

Mergers

Section 7 — Acquisition by one corporation of stock of another. No corporation engaged in commerce shall acquire, directly or indirectly, the whole or any part of the stock or other share capital and no corporation subject to the jurisdiction of the Federal Trade Commission shall acquire the whole or any part of the assets of another corporation engaged also in commerce, where in any line of commerce in any section of the country, the effect of such acquisition may be substantially to lessen competition, or to tend to create a monopoly.

No corporation shall acquire, directly or indirectly, the whole or any part of the stock or other share capital and no corporation subject to the jurisdiction of the Federal Trade Commission shall acquire the whole or any part of the assets of one or more corporations engaged in commerce, where in any line of commerce in any section of the country, the effect of such acquisition, of such stocks or assets, or of the use of such stock by the voting or granting of proxies or otherwise, may be substantially to lessen competition, or to tend to create a monopoly.

This section shall not apply to corporations purchasing such stock solely for investment and not using the same by voting or otherwise to bring about, or in attempting to bring about, the substantial lessening of competition. Nor shall anything contained in this section prevent a corporation engaged in commerce from causing the formation of subsidiary corporations for the actual carrying on of their immediate lawful business, or the natural and legitimate branches or extensions thereof, or from owning and holding all or part of the stock of such subsidiary corporations, when the effect of such formation is not to substantially lessen competition.

Interlocking Directorates

Section 8 — Interlocking directorates and officers. No person at the same time shall be a director in any two or more corporations, any one of which has capital, surplus, and undivided profits aggregating more than $1,000,000, engaged in whole or in part in commerce, other than banks, banking associations, trust companies, and common carriers subject to the Act to regulate commerce approved February fourth, eighteen hundred and eighty-seven, if such corporations are or shall have been theretofore, by virtue of their business and location or operation, competitors, so that the elimination of competition by agreement between them would constitute a violation of any of the provisions of any of the antitrust laws. The eligibility of a director under the foregoing provision shall be determined by the aggregate amount of the capital, surplus, and undivided profits, exclusive of dividends declared but not paid to stockholders, at the end of the fiscal year of said corporation next preceding the election of directors, and when a director has been elected in accordance with the provisions of this Act it shall be lawful for him to continue as such for one year thereafter.

E   Federal Trade Commission Act

Section 5—Unfair methods of competition unlawful; prevention by Commission—declaration. Declaration of unlawfulness; power to prohibit unfair practices.

(a) (1) Unfair methods of competition in or affecting commerce, and unfair or deceptive acts or practices in or affecting commerce, are declared unlawful . . .

(b) Any person, partnership, or corporation who violates an order of the Commission to cease and desist after it has become final, and while such order is in effect, shall forfeit and pay to the United States a civil penalty of not more than $5,000 for each violation, which shall accrue to the United States and may be recovered in a civil action brought by the Attorney General of the United States. Each separate violation of such an order shall be a separate offense, except that in the case of a violation through continuing failure or neglect to obey a final order of the Commission each day of continuance of such failure or neglect shall be deemed a separate offense.

Robinson-Patman Act

Price Discrimination; Cost Justification; Changing Conditions

Section 2 — Discrimination in price, services, or facilities.

(a) Price; selection of customers.

It shall be unlawful for any person engaged in commerce, in the course of such commerce, either directly or indirectly, to discriminate in price between different purchases of commodities of like grade and quality, where either or any of the purchasers involved in such discrimination are in commerce, where such commodities are sold for use, consumption, or resale within the United States or any Territory thereof or the District of Columbia or any insular possession or other place under the jurisdiction of the United States, and where the effect of such discrimination may be substantially to lessen competition or tend to create a monopoly in any line of commerce, or to injure, destroy, or prevent competition with any person who either grants or knowingly receives the benefit of such discrimination, or with customers of either of them: *Provided*, That nothing herein contained shall prevent differentials which make only due allowance for differences in the cost of manufacture, sale, or delivery resulting from the differing methods or quantities in which such commodities are to such purchasers sold or delivered: *Provided, however,* That the Federal Trade Commission may, after due investigation and hearing to all interested parties, fix and establish quantity limits, and revise the same as it finds necessary as to particular commodities or classes of commodities, where it finds that available purchasers in greater quantities are so few as to render differentials on account thereof unjustly discriminatory or promotive of monopoly in any line of commerce; and the foregoing shall then not be construed to permit differentials based on differences in quantities greater than those so fixed and established: *And provided further,* That nothing herein contained shall prevent persons engaged in selling goods, wares, or merchandise in commerce from selecting their own customers in bona fide transactions and not in restraint of trade: *And provided further,* That nothing herein contained shall prevent price changes from time to time where in response to changing conditions affecting the market for or the marketability of the goods concerned, such as but not limited to actual or imminent deterioration of perishable goods, obsolescence of seasonal goods, distress sales under court process, or sales in good faith in discontinuance of business in the goods concerned.

Meeting Competition

(b) Burden of rebutting prima-facie case of discrimination.

Upon proof being made, at any hearing on a complaint under this section, that there has been discrimination in price or services or facilities furnished, the burden of rebutting the prima-facie case thus made by showing justification shall be upon the person charged with a violation of this section, and unless justification shall be affirmatively shown, the Commission is authorized to issue an order terminating the discrimination: *Provided, however,* That nothing herein contained shall prevent a seller rebutting the prima-facie case thus made by showing that his lower price or the furnishing of services or facilities to any purchaser or purchasers was made in good faith to meet an equally low price of a competitor, or the services or facilities furnished by a competitor.

Brokerage Payments

(c) Payment or acceptance of commission, brokerage or other compensation.

It shall be unlawful for any person engaged in commerce, in the course of such commerce, to pay or grant, or to receive or accept, anything of value as a commission, brokerage, or other compensation, or any allowance of discount in lieu thereof, except for services rendered in connection with the sale or purchase of goods, wares, or merchandise, either to the other party to such transaction or to an agent, representative, or other intermediary therein where such intermediary is acting in fact for or in behalf, or is subject to the direct or indirect control, of any party to such transaction other than the person by whom such compensation is so granted or paid.

Promotional Allowances

(d) Payment for services or facilities for processing or sale.

It shall be unlawful for any person engaged in commerce to pay or contract for the payment of anything of value to or for the benefit of a customer of such person in the course of such commerce as compensation or in consideration for any services or facilities furnished by or through such customer in connection with the processing, handling, sale, or offering for sale of any products or commodities manufactured, sold, or offered for sale by such person, unless such payment of consideration is available on proportionally equal terms to all other customers competing in the distribution of such products or commodities.

Promotional Services

(e) Furnishing services or facilities for processing, handling, etc.

It shall be unlawful for any person to discriminate in favor of one purchaser against another purchaser or purchasers of a commodity bought for resale, with or without processing, or by contracting to furnish or furnishing, or by contributing to the furnishing of, any services or facilities connected with the processing, handling, sale, or offering for sale of such commodity so purchased upon terms not accorded to all purchasers on proportionally equal terms.

Buyer Discrimination

(f) Knowingly inducing or receiving discriminatory price.

It shall be unlawful for any person engaged in commerce, in the course of such commerce, knowingly to induce or receive a discrimination in price which is prohibited by this section.

Predatory Practices

Section 3—Discrimination in rebates, discounts, or advertising service charges; underselling in particular localities; penalties. It shall be unlawful for any person engaged in commerce, in the course of such commerce, to be a party to, or assist in, any transaction of sale, or contract to sell, which discriminates to his knowledge against competitors of the purchaser, in that, any discount, rebate, allowance, or advertising service charge is granted to the purchaser over and above any discount, rebate, allowance, or advertising service charge available at the time of such transaction to said competitors in respect of a sale of goods of like grade, quality, and quantity; to sell, or contract to sell, goods in any part of the United States at prices lower than those exacted by said person elsewhere in the United States for the purpose of destroying competition, or eliminating a competitor in such part of the United States; or, to sell, or contract to sell, goods at unreasonably lower prices for the purpose of destroying competition or eliminating a competitor.

Any person violating any of the provisions of this section shall, upon conviction thereof, be fined not more than $5,000 or imprisoned not more than one year, or both.

National Labor Relations Act

Definitions

Section 2. When used in this Act—

(2) The term "employer" includes any person acting as an agent of an employer, directly or indirectly, but shall not include the United States or any wholly owned Government corporation, or any Federal Reserve Bank, or any State or political subdivision thereof, or any person subject to the Railway Labor Act, as amended from time to time, or any labor organization (other than when acting as an employer), or anyone acting in the capacity of officer or agent of such labor organization.

(3) The term "employee" shall include any employee, and shall not be limited to the employees of a particular employer, unless the Act explicitly states otherwise, and shall include any individual whose work has ceased as a consequence of, or in connection with, any current labor dispute or because of any unfair labor practice, and who has not obtained any other regular and substantially equivalent employment, but shall not include any individual employed as an agricultural laborer, or in the domestic service of any family or person at his home, or any individual employed by his parent or spouse, or any individual having the status of an independent contractor, or any individual employed as a supervisor, or any individual employed by an employer subject to the Railway Labor Act, as amended from time to time, or by any other person who is not an employer as herein defined.

(11) The term "supervisor" means any individual having authority, in the interest of the employer, to hire, transfer, suspend, lay off, recall, promote, discharge, assign, reward, or discipline other employees, or responsibly to direct them, or to adjust their grievances, or effectively to recommend such action, if in connection with the foregoing the exercise of such authority is not of a merely routine or clerical nature, but requires the use of independent judgment.

(12) The term "professional employee" means—

(a) any employer engaged in work (i) predominantly intellectual and varied in character as opposed to routine mental, manual, mechanical, or physical work; (ii) involving the consistent exercise of discretion and judgment in its performance; (iii) of such a character that the output produced or the result accomplished cannot be standardized in relation to a given period of time; (iv) requiring knowledge of an advanced type in a field of science or learning customarily acquired by a prolonged course of specialized intellectual instruction and study in an institution of higher learning or a hospital, as distinguished from a general academic education or from an apprenticeship or from training in the performance of routine mental, manual, or physical processes; or

(b) any employee, who (i) has completed the courses of specialized intellectual instruction and study described in clause (iv) of paragraph (a), and (ii) is performing related work under the supervision of a professional person to qualify himself to become a professional employee as defined in paragraph (a).

Rights of Employees

Section 7. Employees shall have the right to self-organization, to form, join, or assist labor organizations, to bargain collectively through representatives of their own choosing, and to engage in other concerted activities for the purpose of collective bargaining or other mutual aid or protection, and shall also have the right to refrain from any or all of such activities requiring membership in a labor organization as a condition of employment as authorized in section 8(a)(3).

Unfair Labor Practices

Section 8. (a) It shall be an unfair labor practice for an employer—

(1) to interfere with, restrain, or coerce employees in the exercise of the rights guaranteed in section 7;

(2) to dominate or interfere with the formation or administration of any labor organization or contribute financial or other support to it: *Provided*, That subject to rules and regulations made and published by the Board pursuant to section 6, an employer shall not be prohibited from permitting employees to confer with him during working hours without loss of time or pay;

(3) by discrimination in regard to hire or tenure of employment or any term or condition of employment to encourage or discourage membership in any labor organization: *Provided*, That nothing in the Act, or in any other statute of the United States, shall preclude an employer from making an agreement with a labor organization (not established, maintained, or assisted by any action defined in section 8(a) of this Act as an unfair labor practice) to require as a condition of employment membership therein on or after the thirtieth day following the beginning of such employment or the effective date of such agreement, whichever is the later, (i) if such labor organization is the representative of the employees as provided in section 9(a), in the appropriate collective-bargaining unit covered by such agreement when made, and (ii) unless following an election held as provided in section 9(e) within one year preceding the effective date of such agreement, the Board shall have certified that at least a majority of the employees eligible to vote in such election have

voted to rescind the authority of such labor organization to make such an agreement:

Provided further, That no employer shall justify any discrimination against an employee for nonmembership in a labor organization (A) if he has reasonable grounds for believing that such membership was not available to the employee on the same terms and conditions generally applicable to other members, or (B) if he had reasonable grounds for believing that membership was denied or terminated for reasons other than the failure of the employee to tender the periodic dues and the initiation fees uniformly required as a condition of acquiring or retaining membership;

(4) to discharge or otherwise discriminate against an employee because he has filed charges or given testimony under this Act;

(5) to refuse to bargain collectively with the representatives of his employees, subject to the provisions of section 9(a).

(b) It shall be an unfair labor practice for a labor organization or its agents—

(1) to restrain or coerce (A) employees in the exercise of the rights guaranteed in section 7: *Provided,* That this paragraph shall not impair the right of a labor organization to prescribe its own rules with respect to the acquisition or retention of membership therein; or (B) an employer in the selection of his representatives for the purposes of collective bargaining or the adjustment of grievances;

(2)to cause or attempt to cause an employer to discriminate against an employee in violation of subsection (a)(3) or to discriminate against an employee with respect to whom membership in such organization has been denied or terminated on some ground other than his failure to tender the periodic dues and the initiation fees uniformly required as a condition of acquiring or retaining membership;

(3) to refuse to bargain collectively with an employer, provided it is the representative of his employees subject to the provisions of section 9(a);

(4)(i) to engage in, or to induce or encourage any individual employed by any person engaged in commerce or in an industry affecting commerce to engage in, a strike or a refusal in the course of his employment to use, manufacture, process, transport, or otherwise handle or work on any goods, articles, materials, or commodities or to perform any services; or (ii) to threaten, coerce, or restrain any person engaged in commerce or in an industry affecting commerce, where in either case an object thereof is—

(A)   forcing or requiring any employer or self-employed person to join any labor or employer organization or to enter into any agreement which is prohibited by section 8(e);

(B)   forcing or requiring any person to cease using, selling, handling, transporting, or otherwise dealing in the products of any other producer, processor, or manufacturer, or to cease doing business with any other person, or forcing or requiring any other employer to recognize or bargain with a labor organization as the representative of his employees unless such labor organization has been certified as the representative of such employees under the provisions of section 9: *Provided,* That nothing contained in this clause (B) shall be construed to make unlawful, where not otherwise unlawful, any primary strike or primary picketing;

(C)   forcing or requiring any employer to recognize or bargain with a particular labor organization as the representative of his employees if another labor organization has been certified as the representative of such employees under the provisions of section 9;

(D)   forcing or requiring any employer to assign particular work to employees in a particular labor organization or in a particular trade, craft, or class rather than to employees in another labor organization or in another trade, craft, or class, unless such employer is failing to conform to an order or certification of the Board determining the bargaining representative for employees performing such work:

Provided, That nothing contained in this subsection (b) shall be construed to make unlawful a refusal by any person to enter upon the premises of any employer (other than his own employer), if the employees of such employer are engaged in a strike ratified or approved by a representative of such employees whom such employer is required to recognize under this Act: *Provided further,* that for the purposes of this paragraph (4) only, nothing contained in such paragraph shall be construed to prohibit publicity, other than picketing, for the purpose of truthfully advising the public, including consumers and members of a labor organization, that a product or products are produced by an employer with whom the labor organization has a primary dispute and are distributed by another employer, as long as such publicity does not have an effect of inducing any individual employed by any person other than the primary employer in the course of his employment to refuse to pick up, deliver, or transport any goods, or not to perform any services, at the establishment of the employer engaged in such distribution:

(5) to require of employees covered by an agreement authorized under subsection (a)(3) the payment, as a condition precedent to becoming a member of such organization, of a fee in an amount which the Board finds excessive or discriminatory under all the circumstances. In making such a finding, the Board shall consider, among other relevant factors, the practices and customs of labor organizations in the particular industry, and the wages currently paid to the employees affected;

(6) to cause or attempt to cause an employer to pay or deliver or agree to pay or deliver any money or other thing of value, in the nature of an exaction, for services which are not performed or not to be performed; and

(7) to picket or cause to be picketed, or threatened to picket or cause to be picketed, any employer where an object thereof is forcing or requiring an employer to recognize or bargain with a labor organization as the representative of his employees, or forcing or requiring the employees of an employer to accept or select such labor organization as their collective bargaining representative, unless such labor organization is currently certified as the representative of such employees:

(A)   where the employer has lawfully recognized in accordance with this Act any other labor organization and a question concerning representation may not appropriately be raised under section 9(c) of this Act;

(B)   where within the preceding twelve months a valid election under section 9(c) of this Act has been conducted, or

(C)   where such picketing has been conducted without a petition under section 9(c) being filed within a reasonable period of time not to exceed thirty days from the commencement of such picketing; *Provided,* That when such a petition has been filed the Board shall forthwith, without regard to the provisions of section 9(c)(1) or the absence of a showing of a substantial interest on the part of the labor organization, direct an election in such unit as the Board finds to be appropriate and shall certify the results thereof: *Provided further,* That nothing in this subparagraph (C) shall be construed to prohibit any picketing or other publicity for the purpose of truthfully advising the public (including consumers) that an employer does not employ members of, or have a contract with a labor organization, unless an effect of such picketing is to induce any individual employed by any other person in the course of his employment, not to pick up, deliver or transport any goods or not to perform any services.

Nothing in this paragraph (7) shall be construed to permit any act which would otherwise be an unfair labor practice under this section 8(b).

(c) The expressing of any views, argument, or opinion, or the dissemination thereof, whether in written, printed, graphic, or visual form, shall not constitute or be evidence of an unfair labor practice under any of the provisions of this Act, if such expression contains no threat of reprisal or force or promise of benefit.

(d) For the purposes of this section, to bargain collectively is the performance of the mutual obligation of the employer and the representative of the employees to meet at reasonable times and confer in good faith with respect to wages, hours, and other terms and conditions of employment, or the negotiation of an agreement, or any question arising thereunder, and the execution of a written contract incorporating any agreement reached if requested by either party, but such obligation does not compel either party to agree to a proposal or require the making of a concession: *Provided,* That where there is in effect a collective-bargaining contract covering employees in an industry affecting commerce, the duty to bargain collectively shall also mean that no party to such contract shall terminate or modify such contract, unless the party desiring such termination or modification—

(1) serves a written notice upon the other party to the contract of the proposed termination or modification sixty days prior to the expiration date thereof, or in the event such contract contains no expiration date, sixty days prior to the time it is proposed to make such termination or modification;

(2) offers to meet and confer with the other party for the purpose of negotiating a new contract or a contract containing the proposed modifications;

(3) notifies the Federal Mediation and Conciliation Service within thirty days after such notice of the existence of a dispute, and simultaneously therewith notifies any State or Territorial agency established to mediate and conciliate disputes within the State or Territory where the dispute occurred, provided no agreement has been reached by that time; and

(4) continues in full force and effect, without resorting to strike or lock-out, all the terms and conditions of the existing contract for a period of sixty days after such notice is given or until the expiration date of such contract, whichever occurs later:

The duties imposed upon employers, employees, and labor organizations by paragraphs (2), (3), and (4) shall become inapplicable upon an intervening certification of the Board, under which the labor organization or individual, which is a party to the contract, has been superseded as or ceased to be the representative of the employees subject to the provisions of section 9(a), and the duties so imposed shall not be construed as requiring either party to discuss or agree to any modification of the terms and conditions contained in a contract for a fixed period, if such modification is to become effective before such terms and conditions can be reopened under the provisions of the contract. Any employee who engages in a strike within the appropriate period specified in subsection (g) of this section, shall lose his status as an employee of the employer engaged in the particular labor dispute, for the purposes of sections 8, 9, and 10 of this Act, but such loss of status for such employee shall terminate if and when he is reemployed by such employer. Whenever the collective bargaining involves employees of a health care institution, the provisions of this section 8(d) shall be modified as follows:

(A)   The notice of section 8(d)(1) shall be ninety days; the notice of section 8(d)(3) shall be sixty days; and the contract period of section 8(d)(4) shall be ninety days.

(B)   Where the bargaining is for an initial agreement following certification or recognition, at least thirty days' notice of the existence of a dispute shall be given by the labor organization to the agencies set forth in section 8(d)(3).

(C)   After notice is given to the Federal Mediation and Conciliation Service under either clause (A) or (B) of this sentence, the Service shall promptly communicate with the parties and use its best efforts, by mediation and conciliation, to bring them to agreement. The parties shall participate fully and promptly in such meetings as may be undertaken by the Service for the purpose of aiding in a settlement of the dispute.

(e) It shall be an unfair labor practice for any labor organization and any employer to enter into any contract or agreement, express or implied, whereby such employer ceases or refrains or agrees to cease or refrain from handling, using, selling, transporting, or otherwise dealing in any of the products of any other employer, or to cease doing business with any other person, and any contract or agreement entered into heretofore or hereafter containing such an agreement shall be to such extent unenforceable and void: *Provided*, That nothing in this subsection (e) shall apply to an agreement between a labor organization and an employer in the construction industry relating to the contracting or subcontracting of work to be done at the site of the construction, alteration, painting, or repair of a building, structure, or other work: *Provided further*, That for the purposes of this subsection (e) and section 8(b)(4)(B) the terms "any employer," "any person engaged in commerce or any industry affecting other producer, processor, or manufacturer," "any other employer," or "any other person" shall not include persons in the relation of a jobber, manufacturer, contractor, or subcontractor working on the goods or premises of the jobber or manufacturer or performing parts of an integrated process of production in the apparel and clothing industry: *Provided further*, That nothing in this Act shall prohibit the enforcement of any agreement which is within the foregoing exception.

(f) It shall not be an unfair labor practice under subsections (a) and (b) of this section for an employer engaged primarily in the building and construction industry to make an agreement covering employees engaged (or who, upon their employment, will be engaged) in the building and construction industry with a labor organization of which building and construction employees are members (not established, maintained, or assisted by any action defined in section 8(a) of this Act as an unfair labor practice) because (1) the majority status of such labor organizations has not been established under the provisions of section 9 of this Act prior to the making of such agreement, or (2) such agreement requires as a condition of employment, membership in such labor organization after the seventh day following the beginning of such employment or the effective date of the agreement, whichever is later, (3) such agreement requires the employer to notify such labor organization of opportunities for employment with such employer, or gives such labor organization an opportunity to refer qualified applicants for such employment, or (4) such agreement specifies minimum training or experience qualifications for employment or provides for priority in opportunities for employment based upon length of service with such employer, in the industry or in the particular geographical area: *Provided*, That nothing in this subsection shall set aside the final proviso to section 8(a)(3) of this Act: *Provided further*, That any agreement which would be invalid, but for clause (1) of this subsection, shall not be a bar to a petition filed pursuant to section 9(c) or 9(e).

(g) A labor organization before engaging in any strike, picketing, or other concerted refusal to work at any health care institution shall, not less than ten days prior to such action, notify the institution in writing and the Federal Mediation and Conciliation Service of that intention, except that in the case of bargaining for an initial agreement following certification or recognition the notice required by this subsection shall not be given until the expiration of the period specified in clause (b) of the last sentence of section 8(d) of this Act. The notice shall state the date and time that such action will commence. The notice, once given, may be extended by the written agreement of both parties.

Representatives and Elections

Section 9. (a) Representatives designated or selected for the purposes of collective bargaining by the majority of the employees in a unit appropriate for such purposes, shall be the exclusive representative of all the employees in such unit for the purposes of collective bargaining in respect to rates of pay, wages, hours of employment, or other conditions of employment: *Provided*, That any individual employee or a group of employees shall have the right at any time to present grievances to their employer and to have such grievances adjusted, without the intervention of the bargaining representative, as long as the adjustment is not inconsistent with the terms of a collective-bargaining contract or agreement then in effect: *Provided further*, That the bargaining representative has been given opportunity to be present at such adjustment.

(b) The Board shall decide in each case whether, in order to assure to employees the fullest freedom in exercising the rights guaranteed by this Act, the unit appropriate for the purposes of collective bargaining shall be the employer unit, craft unit, plant unit, or subdivision thereof: *Provided*, That the Board shall not (1) decide that any unit is appropriate for such purposes if such unit included both professional employees and employees who are not professional employees unless a majority of such professional employees vote for inclusion in such unit; or (2) decide that any craft unit is inappropriate for such purposes on the ground that a different unit has been established by a prior Board determination, unless a majority of the employees in the proposed craft unit vote against separate representation or (3) decide that any unit is appropriate for such purposes if it includes, together with other employees, any individual employed as a guard to enforce against employees and other persons rules to protect property of the employer or to protect the safety of persons on the employer's premises; but no later organization shall be certified as the representative of employees in a bargaining unit of guards if such organization admits to membership, or is affiliated directly or indirectly with an organization which admits to membership, employees other than guards.

(c)(1)Whenever a petition shall have been filed, in accordance with such regulations as may be prescribed by the Board—

(A)   by an employee or group of employees or an individual or labor organization acting in their behalf, alleging that a substantial number of employees (i) wish to be represented for collective bargaining and that their employer declines to recognize their representative as the representative defined in section 9(a), or (ii) assert that the individual or labor organization, which has been certified or is being currently recognized by their employer as the bargaining representative, is no longer a representative as defined in section 9(a); or

(B)   by an employer, alleging that one or more individual or labor organizations have presented to him a claim to be recognized as the representative defined in section 9(a); the Board shall investigate such petition and if it has reasonable cause to believe that a question of representation affecting commerce exists shall provide for an appropriate hearing upon due notice. Such hearing may be conducted by an officer or employee of the regional office, who shall not make any recommendations with respect thereto. If the Board finds upon the record of such hearing that such a question of representation exists, it shall direct an election by secret ballot and shall certify the results thereof.

(2) In determining whether or not a question of representation affecting commerce exists, the same regulations and rules of decision shall apply irrespective of the identity of the persons filing the petition or the kind of relief sought and in no case shall the Board deny a labor organization a place on the ballot by reason of an order with respect to such labor organization or its predecessor not issued in conformity with section 10(c).

(3) No election shall be directed in any bargaining unit or any subdivision within which, in the preceding twelve-month period, a valid election shall have been held. Employees engaged in an economic strike who are not entitled to reinstatement shall be eligible to vote under such regulations as the Board shall find are consistent with the purposes and provisions of this Act in any election conducted within twelve months after the commencement of the strike. In any election where none of the choices on the ballot receives a majority, a run-off shall be conducted, the ballot providing for a selection between the two choices receiving the largest and second largest number of valid votes cast in the election.

(4) Nothing in this section shall be construed to prohibit the waiving of hearings by stipulation for the purpose of a consent election in conformity with regulations and rules of decision of the Board.

(5) In determining whether a unit is appropriate for the purposes specified in subsection (b) the extent to which the employees have organized shall not be controlling.

(d) Whenever an order of the Board made pursuant to section 10(c) is based in whole or in part upon facts certified following an investigation pursuant to subsection (c) of this section and there is a petition for the enforcement or review of such order, such certification and the record of such investigation shall be included in the transcript of the entire record required to be filed under section 10(e) or 10(f), and thereupon the decree of the court enforcing, modifying, or setting aside in whole or in part the order of the Board shall be made and entered upon the pleadings, testimony, and proceedings set forth in such transcript.

(e)(1) Upon the filing with the Board, by 30 per centum or more of the employees in a bargaining unit covered by an agreement between their employer and a labor organization made pursuant to section 8(a)(3), of a petition alleging they desire that such authority be rescinded, the Board shall take a secret ballot of the employees in such unit, and shall certify the results thereof to such labor organization and to the employer.

(2) No election shall be conducted pursuant to this subsection in any bargaining unit or any subdivision within which, in the preceding twelve-month period, a valid election shall have been held.

Title VII of Civil Rights Act of 1964

Definitions

Section 701. (j) The term "religion" includes all aspects of religious observance and practice, as well as belief, unless an employer demonstrates that he is unable to reasonably accommodate to an employee's or prospective employee's religious observance or practice without undue hardship on the conduct of the employer's business.

(k) The terms "because of sex" or "on the basis of sex" include, but are not limited to, because of or on the basis of pregnancy, childbirth or related medical conditions; and women affected by pregnancy, childbirth, or related medical conditions shall be treated the same for all employment-related purposes, including receipt of benefits under fringe benefit programs, as other persons not so affected but similar in their ability or inability to work, and nothing in Section 703(h) of this title shall be interpreted to permit otherwise. This subsection shall not require an employer to pay for health insurance benefits for abortion, except where the life of the mother would be endangered if the fetus were carried to term, or except where medical complications have arisen from an abortion: *Provided*, That nothing herein shall preclude an employer from providing abortion benefits or otherwise effect bargaining agreements in regard to abortion.

Discrimination Because of Race, Color, Religion, Sex, or National Origin

Section 703. (a) It shall be unlawful employment practice for an employer—

(1) to fail or refuse to hire or to discharge any individual, or otherwise to discriminate against any individual with respect to his compensation, terms, conditions, or privileges of employment, because of such individual's race, color, religion, sex, or national origin; or

(2) to limit, segregate, or classify his employees or applicants for employment in any way which would deprive or tend to deprive any individual of employment opportunities or otherwise adversely affect his status as an

employee, because of such individual's race, color, religion, sex, or national origin.

(b) It shall be unlawful employment practice for an employment agency to fail or refuse to refer for employment, or otherwise to discriminate against, an individual because of his race, color, religion, sex, or national origin, or to classify or refer for employment any individual on the basis of his race, color, religion, sex, or national origin.

(c) It shall be an unlawful employment practice for a labor organization—

(1) to exclude or to expel from its membership, or otherwise to discriminate against, any individual because of his race, color, religion, sex, or national origin;

(2) to limit, segregate, or classify its membership or applicants for membership or to classify or fail or refuse to refer for employment any individual, in any way which would deprive or tend to deprive any individual of employment opportunities, or would limit such employment opportunities or otherwise adversely affect his status as an employee or as an applicant for employment, because of such individual's race, color, religion, sex, or national origin; or

(3) to cause or attempt to cause an employer to discriminate against an individual in violation of this section.

(d) It shall be an unlawful employment practice for any employer, labor organization, or joint labor-management committee controlling apprenticeship or other training or retraining, including on-the-job training programs to discriminate against any individual because of his race, color, religion, sex, or national origin in admission to, or employment in, any program established to provide apprenticeship or other training.

(e) Notwithstanding any other provision of this title, (1) it shall not be an unlawful employment practice for an employer to hire and employ employees, for an employment agency to classify, or refer for employment any individual, or for any employer, labor organization, or joint labor-management committee controlling apprenticeship or other training or retraining programs to admit or employ any individual in any such program, on the basis of his religion, sex, or national origin in those certain instances where religion, sex, or national origin is a bona fide occupational qualification reasonably necessary to the normal operation of that particular business or enterprise, and (2) it shall not be an unlawful employment practice for a school, college, university, or other educational institution or institution of learning to hire and employ employees of a particular religion if such school, college, university, or other educational institution or institution of learning is, in whole or in substantial part, owned, supported, controlled, or managed by a particular religion or by a particular religious corporation, association, or society, or if the curriculum of such school, college, university, or other educational institution or institution of learning is directed toward the propagation of a particular religion.

(f) As used in this title, the phrase "unlawful employment practice" shall not be deemed to include any action or measure taken by an employer, labor organization, joint labor-management committee, or employment agency with respect to an individual who is a member of the Communist Party of the United States or of any other organization required to register as a communist-action or Communist-front organization by final order of the Subversive Activities Control Act of 1950.

(g) Notwithstanding any other provision of this title, it shall not be an unlawful employment practice for an employer to fail or refuse to hire and employ any individual for any position, for an employer to discharge an individual from any position, or for any employment agency to fail or refuse to refer any individual for employment in any position, or for a labor organization to fail or refuse any individual for employment in any position, if—

(1) the occupancy of such position, or access to the premises in or upon which any part of the duties of such position is performed or is to be performed, is subject to any requirement imposed in the interest of the national security of the United States under any security program in effect pursuant to or administered under any statute of the United States or any Executive order of the President; and

(2) such individual has not fulfilled or has ceased to fulfill that requirement.

(h) Notwithstanding any other provision of this title, it shall not be an unlawful employment practice for an employer to apply different standards of compensation, or different terms, conditions, or privileges of employment pursuant to a bona fide seniority or merit system, or a system which measures earnings by quantity or quality of production or to employees who work in different locations, provided that such differences are not the results of an intention to discriminate because of race, color, religion, sex, or national origin; nor shall it be an unlawful employment practice for an employer to give and to act upon the results of any professionally developed ability test provided that such test, its administration or action upon the results is not designed, intended, or used to discriminate because of race, color, religion, sex, or national origin. It shall not be an unlawful employment practice under this title for any employer to differentiate upon the basis of sex in determining the amount of wages or compensation paid or to be paid to employees of such employer if such differentiation is authorized by the provision of Section 6(d) of the Fair Labor Standards Act of 1938 as amended (29 U.S.C. 206(d)).

(i) Nothing contained in this title shall apply to any business or enterprise on or near an Indian reservation with respect to any publicly announced employment practice of such business or enterprise under which a preferential treatment is given to any individual because he is an Indian living on or near a reservation.

(j) Nothing contained in this title shall be interpreted to require any employer, employment agency, labor organization, or joint labor-management committee subject to this title to grant preferential treatment to any individual or to any group because of the race, color, religion, sex, or national origin of such individual or group on account of an imbalance which may exist with respect to the total number or percentage of persons of any race, color, religion, sex, or national origin employed by any employer, referred or classified for employment by any employment agency or labor organization, admitted to membership or classified by any labor organization, or admitted to, or employed in, any apprenticeship or other training program, in comparison with the total number or percentage of persons of such race, color, religion, sex, or national origin in any community, State, section, or other area, or in the available work force in any community, State, section, or other area.

Other Unlawful Employment Practices

Section 704. (a) It shall be an unlawful employment practice for an employer to discriminate against any of his employees or applicants for employment, for an employment agency, or joint labor-management committee controlling apprenticeship or other training or retraining, including on-the-job training programs, to discriminate against any individual, or for a labor organization to discriminate against any member thereof or applicant for membership, because he has opposed any practice, made an unlawful employment practice by this title, or because he has made a charge, testified, assisted, or participated in any manner in an investigation, proceeding, or hearing under this title.

(b) It shall be an unlawful employment practice for an employer, labor organization, employment agency, or joint labor-management committee controlling apprenticeship or other training or retraining, including on-the-job training programs, to print or cause to be printed or published any notice or advertisement relating to employment by such an employer or membership in or any classification or referral for employment by such a labor organization, or relating to any classification or referral for employment by such an employment agency, or relating to admission to, or employment in, any program established to provide apprenticeship or other training by such a joint labor-management committee indicating any preference, limitation, specification, or discrimination, based on race, color, religion, sex, or national origin, except that such a notice or advertisement may indicate a preference, limitation, specification, or discrimination based on religion, sex, or national origin when religion, sex, or national origin is a bona fide occupational qualification for employment.

I   Securities Act of 1933

Definitions

Section 2. When used in this title, unless the context requires—

(1) The term "security" means any note, stock, treasury stock, bond, debenture, evidence of indebtedness, certificate of interest or participation in any profit-sharing agreement, collateral-trust certificate, preorganization certificate or subscription, transferable share, investment contract, voting-trust certificate, certificate of deposit for a security, fractional undivided interest in oil, gas, or other mineral rights, any put, call, straddle, option, or privilege on any security, certificate of deposit, or group or index of securities (including any interest therein or based on the value thereof), or any put, call, straddle, option, or privilege entered into on a national securities exchange relating to foreign currency, or, in general, any interest or participation in, temporary or interim certificate for, receipt for, guarantee of, or warrant or right to subscribe to or purchase, any of the foregoing.

Exempted Securities

Section 3. (a) Except as hereinafter expressly provided the provisions of this title shall not apply to any of the following classes of securities:

* * *

(2) Any security issued or guaranteed by the United States or any territory thereof, or by the District of Columbia, or by any State of the United States, or by any political subdivision of a State or Territory, or by any public instrumentality of one or more States or Territories, or by any person controlled or supervised by and acting as an instrumentality of the Government of the United States pursuant to authority granted by the Congress of the United States; or any certificate of deposit for any of the foregoing; or any security issued or guaranteed by any bank; or any security issued by or representing an interest in or a direct obligation of a Federal Reserve Bank . . .

(3) Any note, draft, bill of exchange, or banker's acceptance which arises out of a current transaction or the proceeds of which have been or are to be used for current transactions, and which has a maturity at the time of issuance

of not exceeding nine months, exclusive of days of grace, or any renewal thereof the maturity of which is likewise limited;

(4) Any security issued by a person organized and operated exclusively for religious, educational, benevolent, fraternal, charitable, or reformatory purposes and not for pecuniary profit, and no part of the net earnings of which inures to the benefit of any person, private stockholder, or individual;

* * *

(11) Any security which is a part of an issue offered and sold only to persons resident within a single State or Territory, where the issuer of such security is a person resident and doing business within, or, if a corporation, incorporated by and doing business within, such State or Territory.

(b) The Commission may from time to time by its rules and regulations and subject to such terms and conditions as may be described therein, add any class of securities to the securities exempted as provided in this section, if it finds that the enforcement of this title with respect to such securities is not necessary in the public interest and for the protection of investors by reason of the small amount involved or the limited character of the public offering; but no issue of securities shall be exempted under this subsection where the aggregate amount at which such issue is offered to the public exceeds $5,000,000.

Exempted Transactions

Section 4. The provisions of section 5 shall not apply to—

(1) transactions by any person other than an issuer, underwriter, or dealer.

(2) transactions by an issuer not involving any public offering.

(3) transactions by a dealer (including an underwriter no longer acting as an underwriter in respect of the security involved in such transactions), except—

(A)   transactions taking place prior to the expiration of forty days after the first date upon which the security was bona fide offered to the public by the issuer or by or through an underwriter.

(B)   transactions in a security as to which a registration statement has been filed taking place prior to the expiration of forty days after the effective date of such registration statement or prior to the expiration of forty days after the first date upon which the security was bona fide offered to the public by the issuer or by or through an underwriter after such effective date, whichever is later (excluding in the computation of such forty days any time during which a stop order issued under section 8 is in effect as to the security), or such shorter period as the Commission may specify by rules and regulations or order, and

(C)   transactions as to the securities constituting the whole or a part of an unsold allotment to or subscription by such dealer as a participant in the distribution of such securities by the issuer or by or through an underwriter.

With respect to transactions referred to in clause (B), if securities of the issuer have not previously been sold pursuant to an earlier effective registration statement the applicable period, instead of forty days, shall be ninety days, or such shorter period as the Commission may specify by rules and regulations or order.

(4)brokers' transactions, executed upon customers' orders on any exchange or in the over-the-counter market but not the solicitation of such orders.

* * *

(6) transactions involving offers or sales by an issuer solely to one or more accredited investors, if the aggregate offering price of an issue of securities offered in reliance on this paragraph does not exceed the amount allowed under section 3(b) of this title, if there is no advertising or public solicitation in connection with the transaction by the issuer or anyone acting on the issuer's behalf, and if the issuer files such notice with the Commission as the Commission shall prescribe.

Prohibitions Relating to Interstate Commerce and the Mails

Section 5. (a) Unless a registration statement is in effect as to a security, it shall be unlawful for any person, directly or indirectly—

(1) to make use of any means or instruments of transportation or communication in interstate commerce or of the mails to sell such security through the use or medium of any prospectus or otherwise; or

(2) to carry or cause to be carried through the mails or in interstate commerce, by any means or instruments of transportation, any such security for the purpose of sale or for delivery after sale.

(b) It shall be unlawful for any person, directly or indirectly—

(1) to make use of any means or instruments of transportation or communication in interstate commerce or of the mails to carry or transmit any prospectus relating to any security with respect to which a registration statement has been filed under this title, unless such prospectus meets the requirements of section 10, or

(2) to carry or to cause to be carried through the mails or in interstate commerce any such security for the purpose of sale or for delivery after sale, unless accompanied or preceded by a prospectus that meets the requirements of subsection (a) of section 10.

(c) It shall be unlawful for any person, directly, or indirectly, to make use of any means or instruments of transportation or communication in interstate commerce or of the mails to offer to sell or offer to buy through the use or medium of any prospectus or otherwise any security, unless a registration statement has been filed as to such security, or while the registration statement is the subject of a refusal order or stop order or (prior to the effective date of the registration statement) any public proceeding of examination under section 8.

J Securities Exchange Act of 1934

Definitions and Application of Title

Section 3. (a) When used in this title, unless the context otherwise requires—

* * *

(4) The term "broker" means any person engaged in the business of effecting transactions in securities for the account of others, but does not include a bank.

(5) The term "dealer" means any person engaged in the business of buying and selling securities for his own account, through a broker or otherwise, but does not include a bank, or any person insofar as he buys or sells securities for his own account, either individually or in some fiduciary capacity, but not as part of a regular business.

* * *

(7) The term "director" means any director of a corporation or any person performing similar functions with respect to any organization, whether incorporated or unincorporated.

(8) The term "issuer" means any person who issues or proposes to issue any security; except that with respect to certificates of deposit for securities, voting-trust certificates, or collateral-trust certificates, or with respect to certificates of interest or shares in an unincorporated investment trust not having a board of directors or the fixed, restricted management, or unit type, the term "issuer" means the person or persons performing the acts and assuming the duties of depositor or manager pursuant to the provisions of the trust or other agreement or instrument under which such securities are issued; and except that with respect to equipment-trust certificates or like securities, the term "issuer" means the person by whom the equipment or property is, or is to be, used.

(9) The term "person" means a natural person, company, government, or political subdivision, agency, or instrumentality of a government.

Regulation of the Use of Manipulative and Deceptive Devices

Section 10. It shall be unlawful for any person, directly or indirectly, by the use of any means or instrumentality of interstate commerce or of the mails, or of any facility of any national securities exchange—

(a) To effect a short sale, or to use or employ any stop-loss order in connection with the purchase or sale, of any security registered on a national securities exchange, in contravention of such rules and regulations as the Commission may prescribe as necessary or appropriate in the public interest or for the protection of investors.

(b) To use or employ, in connection with the purchase or sale of any security registered on a national securities exchange or any security not so registered, any manipulative or deceptive device or contrivance in contravention of such rules and regulations as the Commission may prescribe as necessary or appropriate in the public interest or for the protection of investors.

Glossary

Absolute liability liability for an act or activity that causes harm or injury even though the alleged wrongdoer was not at fault.

Abuse of discretion a judgment or decision by an administrative agency or judge which has no foundation in fact or in law.

Acceptance the offeree's notification or expression to the offeror that he or she agrees to be bound by the exact terms of the offeror's proposal. A contract is thereby created. The trend is to allow acceptance by any means that will reasonably notify the offeror of the acceptance.

Accord in a debtor/creditor relationship, an agreement between the parties to settle a dispute for some partial payment. It is called an accord because the creditor has a right of action against the debtor.

Accord and satisfaction in a debtor/creditor relationship, an agreement between the parties to settle a dispute, and subsequent payment. The agreement is an accord because the creditor has a right of action against the debtor. After the agreement has been reached, the accord and satisfaction is complete when payment has been tendered.

Acid rain pollution that occurs due to the release of acidic chemicals into the atmosphere that then falls elsewhere, changing the acid content of water and the ground and damaging plants.

Actual authority power of an agent to bind a principal where that power is derived from either an express or an implied agreement between principal and the agent.

Adjudication the legal process of resolving a dispute.

Administrative agency a governmental bureau established by Congress or the President to execute certain functions of Congress or the President; it allows governmental business to be transacted under the authority of Congress or the President by bureaus that specialize in certain tasks.

Administrative law the rules and regulations established by administrative agencies to execute the functions given them by Congress or the President to carry out regulatory functions.

Adversary system of justice a legal system that is characterized by a process whereby the parties to a dispute present their own arguments and are responsible for asserting their legal rights.

Advertising a communication through which a business offers consumers an inducement to purchase with the intent to increase demand (sales) for their product(s).

Affirmative action results-oriented actions that a contractor by virtue of its contracts with the government must take to ensure equal employment opportunity. An affirmative action program may also be imposed by a court as a remedy in a discrimination action. Where appropriate, it includes such goals as correcting underutilization and correction of problem areas. It may also include relief such as back pay, retroactive seniority, makeup goals, and time-tables.

Affirmative defense defendant's response to plaintiff's claim which attacks the plaintiff's legal right to bring the action rather than attacking the truth of the claim. A common example of an affirmative defense is the running of the statute of limitations.

Agency a relationship between two persons, by agreement or otherwise, where one (the agent) may act on behalf of the other (the principal) and bind the principal by words and actions.

Agency shop in labor law, a unionized workplace where employees who are not union members must pay agency fees to the union for being the sole bargaining agent for all employees; illegal in states that have right-to-work laws.

Agent an individual authorized to act for or represent another, called the principal.

Agreement a "meeting of two or more minds." An agreement means there is a mutual understanding between the parties as to the substance of a contract.

Alternative dispute resolution a process whereby the parties to a dispute resolve it through a mechanism other than the court system. A common alternative dispute resolution process is arbitration.

Ambient air under the Clean Air Act, ambient air is the air outside of buildings or other such enclosures.

Amicus curiae a party not directly involved in the litigation but who participates as a friend of the court.

Amount in controversy the damages claimed or the relief demanded by the injured party in a dispute.

Answer the response of a defendant to the plaintiff's complaint, denying in part or in whole the charges made by the plaintiff.

Anticipatory breach the assertion by a party to a contract that he or she will not perform a future obligation as required by the contract.

Apparent authority that authority a reasonable person would assume an agent possesses as inferred from the conduct of the principal.

Appeal removal from a court of a decided or an adjudicated case to a court of appellate jurisdiction for the purpose of obtaining review of the decision.

Appellant the party, can be either the plaintiff or the defendant, who invokes the appellate jurisdiction of a superior court.

Appellate jurisdiction the power of a court to revise or correct the proceedings in a cause already acted upon by a lower court administrative agency.

Appellee the party against whom an appeal is taken.

Arbiter in an arbitration proceeding, the person to decide the controversy.

Arbitrary and capricious a judgment or decision, usually by an administrative agency or judge, which is without basis in fact or in law. Such a decision is often referred to as being without a rational basis.

Arbitration a means of settling disputes between two or more parties whereby the parties submit an unresolved issue to a neutral third party empowered by the parties to make a binding decision. It is becoming a popular alternative to the court system for resolving disputes between businesses due to the speed of its decision rendering process.

Artificial seniority in employment discrimination law, a remedy that may be granted giving minority or women workers extra years of work credit to make up for past acts of discrimination by their employer.

Assault any word or action intended to cause another to be in fear of immediate physical harm.

Assault and battery intentionally causing another to anticipate immediate physical harm through some threat and then carrying out the threatened activity.

Assumption of risk common law doctrine under which a plaintiff may not recover for injuries or damages as a result of an activity to which the plaintiff assented. The doctrine used by the defendant in negligence when the plaintiff had knowledge of and appreciated the danger, voluntarily exposed himself to the danger, and was injured.

Authorization card a card signed by an employee in a union organizing campaign, whereby the employee joins the union and designates the union to be his representative for the purpose of collective bargaining.

Back pay compensation for past economic losses (such as lost wages and fringe benefits) caused by an employer's discriminatory employment practices, including, for example, its failure to remedy the continuing effects of past practices.

Balance of payments an official accounting record that follows double-entry bookkeeping practices and records all of a country's foreign transactions. The country's exports are recorded as credits and imports as debits.

Bankruptcy a proceeding under the law that is initiated either by an insolvent individual or business (termed a voluntary bankruptcy), or by creditors (termed an involuntary bankruptcy) seeking to either have the insolvent's remaining assets distributed among the creditors and to thereby discharge the insolvent from any further obligation or to untangle and reorganize the insolvent's debt structure.

Bankruptcy trustee in bankruptcy proceedings the person given authority to manage the assets of the bankrupt for the benefit of the creditors.

Battery the intentional unprivileged touching of another. The "touching" may involve as little as a mere touching that is only offensive, or as much as an act of violence that causes very serious injury.

Bilateral contract a contract formed by the mutual exchange of promises of the parties.

Bill of exchange an unconditional order in writing addressed by one person to another, signed by the person giving it, requiring the person to whom it is addressed to pay on demand or at a fixed or determinable future time a sum certain in money.

Blue Sky laws name given to state laws that regulate the offer and sale of securities.

Bona fide occupational qualification (BFOQ) employment in particular jobs may not be limited to persons of a particular sex, religion, or national origin unless the employer can show that sex, religion, or national origin is an actual qualification for performing the job. The qualification is called a bona fide occupational qualification.

Bond an evidence of debt carrying a specified amount and schedule of interest payments as well as a date for redemption of the face value of the bond.

Bondholders creditors of a business, whose evidence of debt is a bond issued by the business.

Boycott an effort to organize a group to not engage in commerce with some party; such as a group of retailers refusing to buy any products from manufacturers who do certain things not liked by the retailers, or a group of labor unions agreeing not to handle any products made by a certain company.

Breach of contract failure, without a legal excuse, of a promisor to perform the terms agreed to in a contract.

Bribery the offering, giving, receiving, or soliciting of something of value for the purpose of influencing the action of an official in the discharge of his or her public or legal duties.

Brief an appellate brief is a written document, prepared by an attorney to serve as the basis for an argument upon a cause in an appellate court, and usually filed for the information of the court. It contains the points of law the attorney wants to establish, together with the arguments and authorities upon which the attorney rests his contentions. The term is also used to describe a summary or abstract of a case prepared and used by a law student.

Bubble concept in environmental law, when a large polluting facility or a geographic area is treated as a single pollution source, in which one may build additional polluting facilities so long as the total pollution produced is lower or no more than before.

Business judgment rule a principle of corporate law under which a court will not challenge the business decisions of a corporate officer or director made with due care and in good faith.

Business necessity justification for an otherwise prohibited employment practice based on a contractor's proof that (1) the otherwise prohibited employment practice is essential for the safety and efficiency of the business, and (2) no reasonable alternative with a lesser impact exists.

Business tort a noncontractual breach of a legal duty by a business directly resulting in damages or injury to another.

Capacity see contractual capacity.

Capitalistic economy an economy in which capital is predominantly owned privately rather than by the state.

Capital stock the corporation's financial foundation consisting of the money or property contributed by stockholders; the total amount of stock (both common and preferred) representing ownership of a business.

Cartel a combination of independent producers within an industry attempting to limit competition by acting together to fix prices, divide markets, or restrict entry into the industry.

Cause in fact an act or omission without which an event would not have occurred. Courts express this in the form of a rule commonly referred to as the "but for" rule: the injury to an individual would not have happened but for the conduct of the wrongdoer.

Cause of action the fact or facts which give rise to an individual's legal right of redress against another.

Caveat emptor Latin for let the buyer beware.

Cease and desist order an order issued by an administrative agency or a court prohibiting a business firm from conducting activities that the agency or court has deemed illegal.

Ceiling price the maximum price permitted by the governmental authority.

Challenge for cause challenge by an attorney of one of the parties to a prospective juror for which some cause or reason is alleged or asserted.

Charter see corporate charter.

Citizen-suit provisions in regulatory law, a right provided by Congress for private citizens to bring a suit before a federal court to force compliance with the law passed by Congress; in some instances, the costs of the suit will be borne by the government if the private party wins the case.

Civil law (1)laws, written or unwritten, that specify the duties that exist between and among people, as opposed to criminal matters. (2) Codified or statutory law, used in many Western European countries and Japan, as distinguished from the common or judge-made law used in England and the United States.

Closed shop   a place of employment where one must be a union member before obtaining work.

Closing argument   oral presentation made to the jury by the attorneys after the plaintiff and defendant have rested their cases and before the judge charges the jury.

Collective bargaining   the process by which unions and employers arrive at and enforce agreements regarding the employment relationship.

Commercial speech   expressions made by businesses about commercial matters or about political matters; Supreme Court interpretation of the First Amendment concerns differences between restrictions allowed on such speech.

Complaint   the initial pleading by the plaintiff in a civil action that informs the defendant of the material facts on which the plaintiff bases the lawsuit.

Concentration   in antitrust law, the percent of market share (usually sales volume) that one or more firms control in a given product or geographic market; used as a measure of the degree of competition within a market.

Condition   a provision in a contract providing that upon the occurrence of some event the obligations of the parties to the contract will be set in motion, suspended, or terminated.

Condition precedent   in a contract, a condition that must be met before the other party's obligations arise.

Condition subsequent   in a contract, a condition which, if met, discharges the obligations of the other party.

Confiscation   the act of a sovereign in a taking without a proper public purpose or just compensation of private property.

Conflict of laws   body of law establishing the circumstances in which a state or federal court shall apply the laws of another state rather than the laws of the state in which it is sitting in deciding a case before it.

Conglomerate merger   a merger between two companies that do not compete with or purchase from each other.

Consent   a voluntary agreement, implied or expressed, to submit to a proposition or act of another.

Consent decree   a judgment entered by consent of the parties whereby the defendant agrees to stop alleged illegal activity without admitting guilt or wrongdoing.

Consideration   in a contract, the thing of value bargained for in exchange for a promise; the inducement or motivation to a contract; the element that keeps the contract from being gratuitous and, therefore, makes it legally binding on the parties.

Consignment   the act or process of depositing goods for the purpose of their sale in the custody of a third party who is essentially a bailor.

Constitution   the fundamental law of a nation; a written document establishing the powers of the government and its basic structure; the controlling authority over all other law.

Contempt of court   any act that is calculated to embarrass, hinder, or obstruct a court in the administration of justice, or that is calculated to lessen the court's authority.

Commerce clause   in general, that part of the U. S. Constitution that gives Congress the power to regulate interstate commerce; the basis of much federal regulation.

Common law   law developed by American and English courts by decisions in cases; unlike statutes, it is not passed by a legislative body and is not a specific set of rules; rather, it must be interpreted from the many decisions that have been written over the centuries.

Common stock   the shares of ownership in a corporation having the lowest priority with regard to payment of dividends and distribution of the corporation's assets upon dissolution.

Community property   property owned in common by husband and wife.

Comparative negligence   a defense to negligence whereby the plaintiff's damages are reduced by the proportion his or her fault bears to the total injury he or she has sustained.

Compensatory damages   a sum of money awarded to the injured party that is equivalent to his or her actual damages or injuries sustained. The rationale behind compensatory damages is to restore the injured party to the position he or she was in prior to the injury.

Complaint   the legal process by which an individual allegedly injured by another makes a formal allegation or charge against the other, either to a court or to some other proper authority.

Concentration ratio   fraction of total market sales made by a specified number of an industry's largest firms. Four-firm and eight-firm concentration ratios are the most frequently used.

Concerted activity   a joint action by employees, such as a strike or picketing, with the intended purpose of furthering their bargaining demands or other mutual interests.

Concurrent jurisdiction   a situation where at least two different courts are each empowered to deal with the subject matter at issue in a dispute.

Concurring opinion   at the appellate court level, an opinion filed by one or more of the justices (or judges) in which the justice(s) agrees with the majority opinion but decides to state separately his views of the case or his reasoning.

Consumer reports   traditionally called credit reports, these are files maintained by several companies concerning the credit history and evidence of income and debt situation of most adults; these are sold for legitimate business purposes.

Contract   a legal relationship consisting of the rights and duties of the contracting parties; a promise or set of promises constituting an agreement between the parties that gives each a legal duty to the other and also the right to seek a remedy for the breach of those duties. The elements of a contract include an agreement, consideration, legal capacity, lawful subject matter, and genuine consent to the contract.

Contract clause   the statement in the constitution that "No State shall . . . pass any . . . Law impairing the Obligation of Contracts. . . ." Primary applications have been cases in which a state has tried to reduce its obligations previously created by contracts with private parties.

Contractual capacity   the threshold mental capacity required by law for a party entering into a contract to be bound by that contract. Generally, minors, intoxicated persons, and the insane lack capacity to contract.

Contributory negligence   as a complete defense to negligence, an act or a failure to act that produces a lack of reasonable care on the part of the plaintiff that is proximate cause of the injury incurred.

Conversion   the unauthorized taking of property, permanently or temporarily, that deprives its rightful owner of its lawful use.

Cooperative   a group of two or more individuals or enterprises that act through a common agent or representative to achieve a common objective.

Copyright   a grant to an author or a publisher of an exclusive right to print, reprint, publish, copy, and sell literary work, musical compositions, works of art, and motion pictures for the life of the author plus an additional fifty years.

Corporate charter   a certificate issued by a state government recognizing the existence of a corporation as a legal entity; it is issued automatically upon filing the information required by state law and payment of a fee.

Corporate social responsibility   the belief that businesses have a duty to society that goes beyond obeying the law and maximizing profits.

Corporation   a business organized under the laws of a state that allow an artificial legal being to exist for purposes of doing business.

Cost-benefit analysis   a technique by which one computes the costs of implementing a certain activity and compares the estimated monetary value of the benefits from the same activity. Activities where the benefits exceed the costs are undertaken and those where the costs exceed the benefits are rejected.

Counterclaim   a claim the defendant may assert against the plaintiff.

Counteroffer   an offeree's response to an offeror that rejects the offeror's original offer and at the same time makes a new offer.

Covenant   an agreement between two or more parties in which one or more of the parties pledges that some duty or obligation is to be done or not to be done.

Craft union   a union organized on the basis of a specified set of skills or occupations.

Credit rating   an opinion as to the reliability of a person in paying debts.

Credit report   a report made by a credit reporting agency concerning the financial condition, credit character, and reputation of an individual.

Creditor   a person to whom a debt is owed by another person who is called the debtor.

Crime   a violation of the law that is punishable by the state or nation. Crimes are classified as treason, felonies, and misdemeanors.

Criminal law   governs or defines legal wrongs, or crimes, committed against society. The objective of criminal law is to punish the wrongdoer for violating the rules of society. An individual found guilty of a criminal offense is usually fined or imprisoned.

Cross complaint   during the pleadings, a claim the defendant may assert against the plaintiff. See also counterclaim.

Cross-elasticity of demand   a measure of the extent to which the quantity of a commodity demanded responds to changes in price of a related commodity. It is used occasionally in antitrust cases to determine the product market for a firm under investigation. If the price of a related product rises and the quantity demanded of the firm's product also rises, the products are substitutes and, therefore, are in the same product market.

Cross examination   examination undertaken by the attorney representing the adverse party after the other party has examined his or her witness.

Damages   money compensation sought or awarded as a remedy for a breach of contract or for tortious acts.

Debt   a sum of money due by an express agreement.

Debt collection agency   a business that buys the right to collect the debts owed by consumers to a business.

Debtor a person who owes a debt to another who is called the creditor.

Debt securities an obligation of a corporation, usually in the form of a bond, issued for a certain value at a certain rate of interest to be repaid at a certain time.

Deception in consumer protection law, a claim, practice, or omission likely to mislead a reasonable consumer and cause the consumer to suffer a loss.

Decertification process through which a group of employees decides it no longer wants a union to be its bargaining unit. The process involves an election conducted by the National Labor Relations Board.

Defamation an intentional false communication, either published or publicly spoken, that injures another's reputation or good name.

Default judgment judgment entered against a party who has failed to appear in court to defend against a claim that has been brought by another party.

Defendant the party against whom an action or lawsuit is brought.

Defense that offered and alleged by the defendant as a reason in law or fact why the plaintiff should not recover, or recover less than what he or she seeks.

Delaney clause the portion of the Food, Drug and Cosmetic Act that holds that any food additive that is found to cause cancer in animals may not be marketed.

Delegation the legal transfer of power and authority to another to perform duties.

Delegation of powers the right of Congress to authorize government agencies to perform certain legal duties as instructed by Congress under its constitutional authority.

Demurrer an older term for a motion to dismiss a claim for failure to state a cause of action. See motion to dismiss.

Deposition sworn testimony—either written or oral—of a person taken outside the court.

Design defect in products liability litigation, a claim that a consumer suffered an injury because a product was not designed with sufficient concern for safety that could have prevented the injury that occured.

Detrimental reliance see promissory estoppel.

Direct examination the initial examination of a witness by the party on whose behalf the witness has been called.

Directed verdict verdict granted by the court on the grounds that the jury could reasonably reach only one conclusion on the basis of the evidence presented during the trial.

Discharge the termination of one's obligation. Under the law of contract, discharge occurs either when the parties have performed their obligations in the contract, or when events, the conduct of the parties, or the operation of law releases the parties from performing.

Disclosure in securities law, the revealing of certain financial and other information believed relevant to investors considering buying securities in some venture; the requirement that sufficient information be provided prospective investors so that they can make an intelligent evaluation of a security.

Discovery the process by which the parties in a lawsuit may gather information from each other as a part of reducing the scope of what will actually be presented in court; process is determined by rules of procedure and may be limited by the court hearing the case.

Discrimination illegal treatment of a person or group (either intentional or unintentional) based on race, color, national origin, religion, sex, handicap, or veteran's status. The term includes the failure to remedy the effects of past discrimination.

Disparagement a false communication that creates injury to an individual in his or her business, profession, or trade.

Disparate impact in employment discrimination law, when an apparently neutral rule regarding hiring or treatment of employees works to discriminate against a protected class of employees.

Disparate treatment differential treatment of employees or applicants on the basis of their race, color, religion, sex, national origin, handicap, or veteran's status (including, for example, the situation whereby applicants or employees of a particular race or sex are required to pass tests or meet educational requirements not required of similarly situated contemporary applicants or employees of another race or sex).

Dissenting opinion opinion written by one or more appellate judges or justices explaining why they have disagreement with the decision of the majority of the court.

Diversity of citizenship an action in which the plaintiff and the defendant are citizens of different states.

Dividend a distribution to corporate shareholders in proportion to the number of shares held.

Due care that degree of care that a reasonable person can be expected to exercise to avoid harm reasonably foreseeable if such care is not taken.

Due process constitutional limitation requiring that an individual has a right not to be deprived of life, liberty, or property without a fair and just hearing.

Economic efficiency   a method of producing some quantity of output is economically efficient when it is the least costly method of producing that output.

Effluent charge   a fee, fine, or tax on a business for its polluting activity, usually on a per unit basis.

Electronic fund transfer   the ability to make monetary transactions through electronics (telephone, computer).

Embezzlement   statutory offense whereby an individual fraudulently appropriates for his or her own use the property or money intrusted to him by another.

Eminent domain   the power of the government to take private property for public use for fair compensation.

Emotional distress   a tort action for damages to compensate for mental injury caused to a person; generally does not require evidence of physical injury.

Employee handbooks   manuals issued by employers to inform employees of their duties and rights as employees; often used as evidence of an employment contract that must be followed by both parties.

Employment-at-will   a doctrine under the common law providing that unless otherwise explicitly stated an employment contract was for an indefinite term and could be terminated at any time by either party without notice.

Enabling statute   legislative enactment confering new powers on agencies, allowing them to do things they could not do before.

En banc   legal proceedings before or by the court as a whole rather than before or by a single judge.

Endangered species   in environmental law, a list of animals and plants declared by the government to be in danger of becoming extinct; violators may be prosecuted for killing the animals or plants or injuring their habitat.

Environmental Impact Statement   the statement required by the National Environmental Policy Act to be developed by federal agencies for every recommendation or report on proposals for legislation and other major federal actions significantly affecting the quality of the human environment.

Equity   in securities law and with respect to finance, an ownership claim on a business interest; usually a security with no repayment terms.

Estoppel   a principle that provides that an individual is barred from denying or alleging a certain fact or state facts because of that individual's previous conduct, allegation, or denial.

Ethics   moral science that considers the duties which a member of society owes to other members.

Excise tax   a tax on the sale of a particular commodity. A specific tax is a fixed tax per unit of the commodity sold. An ad valorem tax is a fixed percentage of the value of the commodity.

Exclusive dealing contract   an agreement between two firms to deal only with each other for certain products or services.

Exclusive jurisdiction   the power of a court over a particular subject matter as provided by statute to the exclusion of all other courts.

Exculpatory contract   a contract that releases one of the parties from liability for their wrongdoings.

Executed contract   a contract that has been fully performed by the parties.

Executive order   under powers granted by the Constitution or by Congress in legislation, an order by the president to establish a legal requirement or to enforce a legal requirement.

Executory contract   a contract that has not been performed by the parties.

Exemplary damages   see punitive damages.

Exemptions from registration   in securities law, provisions that allow certain securities to be sold without meeting the usual registration requirements with the Securities and Exchange Commission; does not exempt the securities from other aspects of securities laws.

Exhaustion of administrative remedies   doctrine providing that in those instances where a statute provides an administrative remedy, relief must be sought through the appropriate agency and that remedy exhausted before a court can act to provide other relief.

Ex parte   by one party.

Expert witness   witness with special opportunity for observation, or special or professional training or skill in assessing the facts in a case.

Export   products manufactured in one country, and then shipped and sold in another.

Express contract   a contract that is either oral or written, as opposed to being implied from the conduct of the parties (see implied contract).

Express warranty   a promise, in addition to an underlying sales agreement, that goes beyond the terms of the sales agreement and under which the promisor assures the description, performance, or quality of the goods.

Expropriation   the taking of a privately-owned business or privately-owned goods by a government for a public purpose and with just compensation.

Ex rel (Ex relatione)   on the relation or information.

Externalities   effects, either good or bad, on parties not directly involved in the production or use of a product. Pollution is an example of a bad effect, or negative externality.

Failing firm defense   in antitrust law, a general rule that firms may be allowed to merge that would not be allowed to do so except for the fact that one of the firms is in danger of going out of business anyway.

Failure to warn   in products liability cases, where a producer is found liable in tort for not warning consumers of dangers the producer knew existed or should have known to exist.

Fair trade laws   state statute permitting manufacturers or distributors of name brand products to fix minimum retail resale prices. Fair trade laws are no longer valid.

False imprisonment   the intentional detention or restraint of an individual by another.

Featherbedding   an employee practice, usually under a union rule, in which the number of employees used, or the amount of time taken, to perform a particular job is unnecessarily high. The practice stems from a desire on the part of the employees to insure job security as technology improves.

Federal question   a question in a case in which one of the parties, usually the plaintiff, is asserting a right based on a federal law.

Fellow-servant rule   a rule that precludes an injured employee from recovering from his employer when an injury resulted from the negligent conduct of a fellow employee.

Felony   a serious class of crime (such as rape, murder, or robbery) that may be punishable by death or imprisonment in excess of one year.

Fiduciary   a person having a duty, generally created by his own undertaking, to act in good faith primarily for the benefit of another in matters related to that undertaking. A fiduciary duty is the highest standard of duty implied by law.

Firm offer   under the Uniform Commercial Code, a signed writing by a merchant promising to keep an offer open. In contrast to an option, a firm offer does not require consideration to make the offer irrevocable.

Foreign exchange market   institution through which foreign currencies are bought and sold.

Foreign exchange rate   the price of a particular country's currency stated in terms of the currency of another.

Foreign trade zone   areas within the United States, but outside the customs zone, where foreign merchandise may be brought without formal customs entry and payment of duty for virtually any legal purpose including storage, grading, sampling, cleaning, or packaging. Duties are paid when the products enter the U. S. market.

Foreseeable dangers   in tort law, the duty to have a reasonable anticipation that injury is likely to result from certain acts or from a failure to act to protect others.

Forgery   the false making or the material altering of a document with the intent to defraud.

Franchise   with respect to business, a contract between a parent company (franchisor) and an operating company (franchisee) to allow the operating company to run a business with the brand name of the parent company, so long as the terms of the contract concerning methods of operation is followed.

Fraud   a misrepresentation of an important fact by a person intending to mislead another person interested in some transaction that leads that person to execute the deal and then suffer a loss.

Free-market economy   an economy in which the decisions of individuals and businesses, as distinct from the government, exert the major influence over the allocation of resources.

Free trade   a situation where all commodities can be freely imported and exported without special taxes or restrictions being levied.

Fringe benefits   medical, hospital, accident, and life insurance; retirement benefits; profit sharing; bonus plans; leave; and other terms and conditions of employment other than wage or salary compensation.

Full warranty   defined by the Magnuson-Moss Warranty Act to provide an unlimited warranty for repairs or product replacement for problems that arise with a product within the warranty period.

Garnishment   a legal process under which a creditor appropriates the debtor's wages, or property in the hands of a third party.

General jurisdiction   a power of a court to hear all controversies that may be brought before it.

General verdict   verdict whereby the jury finds either for the plaintiff or the defendant in general terms.

Geographic market   in antitrust law, the geographic area within the country in which a business is able to exercise market power, or the effects of the business' market power are felt.

Golden parachute   severance agreement for which the management of a corporation negotiates in return for the withdrawal of its opposition to a tender offer.

Good faith   an individual acting in good faith acts with honest intentions.

Government   all public officials, agencies, and other organizations under the control of state, local, and federal government.

Gratuitous agent   an agent who volunteers services without an agreement or expectation of compensation, but a voluntary consent that creates the normal rights and liabilities for parties to the agency relationship.

Greenmail   a coercive procedure under which an individual or organization who has purchased a large percentage of a corporation's stock pressures management of the corporation to buy back the stock at a premium to protect against the individual or organization using the stock in a hostile takeover attempt.

Guardian   an individual appointed to act on behalf of another lacking ability to perform legally valid acts, to acquire legal rights, or incur legal liabilities.

Hazardous pollutant   see toxic pollutant.

Hearsay   evidence not derived from the personal knowledge of the witness, but from the mere recital of what the witness has heard others say. Hearsay evidence is allowed only in special cases.

Hispanic   a person of Mexican, Puerto Rican, Cuban, South American, or other Spanish culture or origin, regardless of race.

Horizontal business arrangement   an explicit or implicit deal among firms operating at the same level of business in the same market.

Horizontal merger   a merger between two companies that compete in the same product market.

Horizontal price fixing   price fixing among competitors; price fixing among businesses on the same level the effect of which is to eliminate competition based on price.

Horizontal restraint of trade   a restraint of trade involving businesses at the same level of operation. A group of rival firms that come together by contract or some other form of agreement in an attempt to restrain trade by restricting output and raising prices is called a **cartel.**

Hot cargo agreement   an agreement, express or implied between an employer and a union whereby the employer agrees to cease or refrain from handling, using, selling, transporting or otherwise dealing in any of the products of any other employer the union has labeled as unfair or "hot."

Howey test   the rule established by the Supreme Court to determine what is a security under the federal securities law: an investment of money, in a common enterprise, with the expectation that profits will be generated by the efforts of others.

Hung jury   a jury so divided in opinion that they cannot agree upon a verdict.

Implied contract   a contract formed on the basis of the conduct of the parties.

Implied warranty   a promise or guarantee the court holds to exist that accompanies a good when it is sold even though it was not written or expressed directly.

Import   a product manufactured in a foreign country, and then shipped to and sold in this country.

Impossibility of performance   doctrine used to discharge the obligations of the parties to a contract when an event—such a law being passed that makes the contract illegal or the subject matter of the contract is destroyed (called **objective impossibility**)—makes performance "impossible" for one or both of the parties.

Indictment   a formal written charge or accusation issued by a grand jury stating that the named individual has committed a crime.

Infringement   in patent, copyright, and trademark law, the unauthorized use or imitation of another's recognized right to the matter involved.

Injunction   an order issued by a court that restrains a person or business from doing some act or orders the person to do something.

In personam jurisdiction   the power the court has over the person(s) involved in the action.

In rem jurisdiction   refers to an action taken by the court against the property of the defendant.

Insider   an officer or other person who has information not yet available to the general public concerning the future profits or losses of a corporation.

Insider trading   the buying or selling of securities of a particular firm by individuals who have information about the firm not yet available to the general public and who have the expectation of making a profit through those transactions.

Insolvency   the financial state of an individual when his or her debts and liabilities exceed the value of his or her assets.

Intention tort   a wrong committed upon the person or property of another where the actor is expressly or impliedly judged to have intended to commit the injury.

Interbrand competition   competition among the various brands of a particular product.

International law   those laws governing the legal relations between nations.

Interpretative rules   statements issued by administrative agencies that explain how the agency understands its statutory authority to operate; these may be advisory or binding.

Interrogatories   in the discovery process, a set of written questions for a witness or a party for which written answers are prepared with the assistance of counsel and signed under oath.

Interstate commerce   the carrying on of commercial activity between locations in at least two different states.

Intraband competition   competition among retailers in the sales of a particular brand of product.

Invasion of privacy   in tort, the encroachment on the right of a person to their solitude, the appropriation of a person's reputation for commercial purposes, or the public disclosure of facts that the person had a legal right to keep private.

Investment company   any corporation whose business purpose is to own and hold the stock of other corporations.

Involuntary bankruptcy   a bankruptcy proceeding against an insolvent debtor which is initiated by his or her creditors.

Jeopardy   an individual is said to be in jeopardy when he or she is officially charged with a crime before a court of law. The constitutional doctrine of **double jeopardy** prohibits an individual from being prosecuted twice in the same tribunal for the same offense.

Joint and several liability   liability that an individual or business either shares with other tortfeasors or bears individually without the others.

Joint liability   liability that is owed to a third party by two or more other parties together.

Joint venture   the participation of two companies jointly in a third enterprise. Generally, both companies contribute assets and share risks.

Judgment   the official decision of a court of law upon the rights and claims of the parties to an action litigated in and submitted to the court for its determination.

Judgment notwithstanding the verdict   judgment entered into by the court for a party after there has been a jury verdict for the other party.

Judicial review   authority of a court to reexamine a dispute considered and decided previously by a lower court or by an administrative agency.

Jurisdiction   the right of a court or other body to hear a case and render a judgment.

Jurisdiction over the person   power of the court to lawfully bind a party involved in a dispute before it.

Jurisdiction over the subject   power of a court to validly affect the thing or issue in dispute.

Jurisprudence   the science or philosophy of law.

Just compensation clause   the portion of the Fifth Amendment that "nor shall private property be taken for public use, without just compensation." The requirement that when the government uses its power to force a private party to give up a property interest fair market value should be paid.

Kefauver amendment   the portion of the Food, Drug and Cosmetic Act that requires the Food and Drug Administration to approve drugs only after their safety and effectiveness have been established.

Laissez faire   literally "let do;" a policy implying the absence of government intervention in a market economy.

Law   enforceable rules of social conduct set forth by that society's government to be followed by the citizens of the society.

Leading question   a question by an attorney in a trial that effectively instructs the witness how to answer or provides the desired answer.

Legal capacity   the right to be able to enter into legal matters that may be restricted by age, mental ability, or other requirements established at common law or by statute.

Legal cause   see proximate cause.

Legal ethics   practice and customs among members of the legal profession, involving their moral and professional duties toward one another, clients, and the courts.

Legislative history   the history of a legislative enactment consisting of the legislative committee reports and transcripts of committee hearings debates on the legislative floor. Legislative history is often used by a court in interpreting the terms and provisions of an enactment.

Legislative veto   the act by Congress or a state legislature of giving itself or some part of the legislature the power to kill or modify regulations established by a regulatory agency.

Letter of credit   a written document in which the party issuing the document—usually a bank—promises to pay third parties in accordance with the terms of the document.

Liability   a general legal term referring to possible or actual responsibility; one is bound by law or equity to be accountable for some act; in product liability, it is in reference to the obligation to pay for damages for which the manufacturer has been held responsible.

Libel   a defamation that is in the form of a printing, a writing, pictures, or a broadcast on radio or television.

Limited liability   in corporation law, a concept whereby the shareholders of a corporation are not liable for the debts of the corporation beyond the amount of money they have invested in the corporation.

Limited or special jurisdiction   power of a court to hear a particular cause which can be exercised only under the limitations and circumstances prescribed by statute.

Limited partner   a partner in a limited partnership whose liability for partnership debts is limited to the amount of his or her contribution to the partnership.

Limited partnership   business organization consisting of one or more general partners who manage and contribute assets to the business and who are liable to the extent of their personal assets for the debts of the business, and one or more limited partners who contribute assets only and are liable only up to the amount of that contribution.

Limited warranty   under the Magnuson-Moss Warranty Act, any product sold with less than a full warranty has what is defined as a limited warranty, the terms of which must be explained in writing.

Liquidated damages   those amounts specified in the contract to be paid in the event of a breach by either party. They represent a reasonable estimation by the parties of the damages that will occur in the event of breach.

Liquidated debt   a debt that is for a known or determinable amount of money and that can not be disputed by either the debtor or the creditor.

Liquidation   the sale of the assets of a business (or an individual), the proceeds from which are distributed to the creditors of the business (or individual) with any remaining balance to the business (or individual).

Lockout   refusal by an employer to provide work for employees.

Long-arm statute   state statute permitting courts to obtain personal jurisdiction over nonresident individuals and corporations as long as the requirements of the statute are met.

Major emitting facility   under the Clean Air Act, a stationary source such as a factory that emits or has the potential to emit 100 tons of any pollutant per year.

Mandatory subjects of bargaining   under the National Labor Relations Act, all terms and conditions of employment are subjects that must be discussed by employers and unions or there will be an unfair labor practice.

Manifest system   in environmental and occupational safety law, the requirement that certain chemicals have documentation concerning their production, distribution, and disposal to ensure proper handling and disposal of toxic substances.

Margin requirement   the fraction of a price of a stock that must be paid in cash, while putting up the stock as security against a loan for the balance.

Market   (1) an institution through which buyers and sellers negotiate the exchange of a well-defined product; (2) from the viewpoint of consumers, the companies from which they can buy a well-defined product; (3) from the viewpoint of a company, the buyers to whom it can sell a well-defined product.

Market-clearing prices   the equilibrium price in a perfectly competitive market. Prices at which the quantity demanded is equal to the quantity supplied, so that there are neither unsatisfied buyers nor unsatisfied sellers.

Market failure   failure of the unregulated market system to achieve socially optimal results. The generally recognized sources of market failure include monopolies and externalities. It is often asserted as a justification for government intervention in the marketplace through regulation.

Market share liability   in the case of a latent injury, in the event the plaintiff is unable to determine which manufacturer of a product within the industry caused his or her injury, the court will assign liability to all industry members on the basis of their shares of the product market. Market share liability has not gained wide acceptance.

Maturity   the due date of a financial instrument.

Mediation   act of a third party who intervenes between parties to a dispute with the intent to reconcile them or persuade them to settle their dispute.

Mens rea   Latin, the state of mind of the actor.

Merger   a contractual process through which one corporation acquires the assets and liabilities of another corporation. The acquiring, or surviving, corporation retains its original identity.

Merit regulations   state securities law provision that in some states allows the securities commissioners to decide if a proposed security offering is "too risky" to be allowed to be sold to the public in that state.

Minorities   all persons classified as black (not of Hispanic origin), Hispanic, Asian, Pacific Islander, American Indian, or Alaskan native.

Misdemeanors   a lessor crime, that is neither a felony nor treason, punishable by a fine and/or imprisonment in other than state or federal penitentiaries.

Mistrial   a trial that cannot stand in law because the court lacks jurisdiction, due to juror misconduct, or because of disregard for some other procedural requirement.

Mitigation of damages   doctrine that imposes a duty upon the injured party to exercise reasonable diligence in attempting to minimize damages after being injured.

Mobil source   under the Clean Air Act, a mobil source of pollution refers to moving polluters such as automobiles, trucks, and airplanes.

Monopoly   a market structure in which the output of an industry is controlled by a single seller or a group of sellers making joint decisions regarding production and price.

Moral agent　a person capable of deciding and carrying out actions on their own and accepting responsibility for the actions.

Moral principles　rules that categorize different actions as right or wrong.

Morals　generally accepted standards of right and wrong in a society.

Motion　the formal mode in which an attorney submits a proposed measure for the consideration and action of the court.

Motion to dismiss　a motion requesting that a complaint be dismissed because it does not state a claim for which the law provides a remedy, or is in some other way legally insufficient.

National Ambient Air Quality Standards　federal standards under the Clean Air Act that set the maximum concentration levels in the ambient air for several air pollutants. There are two types: a primary standard and a secondary standard. The primary standard for each air pollutant is calculated to protect the public health. The secondary standard is calculated to protect the public welfare.

National Uniform Effluent Standards　federal standards under the Clean Water Act that set the water pollution effluent standards for every industry that discharges liquid wastes into the nation's waterways.

Natural monopoly　an industry characterized by economies of scale sufficiently large that one business can supply the entire market most efficiently.

Necessary and proper clause　in general, that part of the U.S. Constitution that gives Congress the authority to use various powers to execute its functions under the Constitution.

Negligence　the failure to do something that a reasonable person, guided by the ordinary considerations that regulate human affairs, would do, or the doing of something that a reasonable person would not do.

Negotiation　the deliberation over the terms and conditions of a proposed agreement or business transaction, or over the terms and conditions to an agreement resolving a dispute arising from a business transaction.

Nominal damages　a damage award whereby the courts recognize that plaintiff has suffered a technical breach of duty, but has not suffered any actual financial loss or injury as a result. Plaintiff's recovery for such technical breaches is often as little as a dollar.

Nonattainment area　an area under the Clean Air Act in which the air quality for a given pollutant fails to meet the national ambient air quality standards.

Nonpoint sources　under the Clean Water Act, nonpoint sources of water pollution are sources of pollution that are diverse and difficult to identify. Examples are urban and agricultural runoff from rainstorms.

Novation　an agreement between the parties to a contract to discharge one of the parties and create a new contract with another party responsible for the discharged party's performance.

Nuisance　an unreasonable and substantial interference with the use and enjoyment of another's land (**private nuisance**); an unreasonable or substantial interference with a right held in common by members of the general public (**public nuisance**).

Occupational licensure　requirements usually at the state level that for one to be allowed to practice a certain profession one must meet certain educational or experience guidelines, pass an entry examination, and often must show evidence of continuing education accomplishments.

Offer　a proposal to do or refrain from doing some specified thing by an individual called the offeror to another called the offeree. The proposal creates in the offeree a legal power to bind the offeror to the terms of the proposal by accepting the offer.

Offeree　the party to whom an offer is made.

Offeror　the party making an offer to another party to enter into a contract.

Opening argument　oral presentation made to the jury by the attorneys before the parties have presented their cases.

Original jurisdiction　power of a court to take cognizance of a lawsuit at its beginning, try it, and pass judgment upon the law and facts.

Out-of-court settlement　an agreement by the parties in a case to resolve the matter before a determination by the court.

Over-the-counter market　a stock market for securities generally not sold in large daily volumes so that they are not listed on a major stock exchange, such as the New York Stock Exchange; a securities market made by stockbrokers calling information to a central place about desires to buy or sell certain amounts of a stock.

Parol　in French and Latin, spoken or oral.

Parol evidence rule　a substantive rule of contract law that prohibits the introduction into a lawsuit of oral evidence that is contradictory to the terms of a written contract intended to be the final and complete expression of the agreement between the parties.

Partnership　a business owned by two or more persons that is not organized as a corporation.

Par value stock　stock that has been assigned a specific value by the corporation's board of directors.

Patent   a grant from the government conveying and securing for an inventor the exclusive right to make, use, and sell an invention for seventeen years.

Per curiam opinion   Latin, by the court. A Per Curiam opinion expresses the view of the court as a whole in contrast to an opinion authored by an individual member of the court.

Per se   in itself or taken alone; as in per se rule in antitrust, whereby the facts alone are enough to lead to conviction of the defendants.

Performance   in contract law, the fulfilling of obligations or promises according to the terms agreed to or specified by parties to a contract. The complete performance of those obligations or promises by both parties discharges the contract.

Periodic disclosure   in securities law, requirements that issuers of most publicly held securities must file monthly, quarterly, and annual reports with the Securities and Exchange Commission.

Personal property   physical, moveable property other than real estate.

Personal service   in the pleadings stage, personal service of the complaint is made by delivering it physically to the defendant.

Piercing the corporate veil   a court's act of ignoring the legal existence of a corporation and then holding the corporation's officers personally liable for their wrongful acts done in the name of the corporation.

Plaintiff   the party who initiates the lawsuit.

Pleadings   statements of the plaintiff and the defendant that detail their facts, allegations, and defenses, thereby creating the issues of the lawsuit.

Point source   under the Clean Water Act, a point source is any definitive place of discharge of a water pollutant such as pipes, ditches, or channels.

Political speech   in constitutional law, speech that concerns political, as opposed to commercial, matters given a high level of protection by the First Amendment.

Pollution   the release of substances into the air, water, or land that cause physical change.

Power of attorney   a document authorizing another person to act as one's agent or attorney with respect to the matters stated in the document.

Precedent   a decision in a case that is used to guide decisions in later cases with similar fact situations.

Preferred stock   class of stock that has priority over common stock both as to payment of dividends and to distribution of the corporation's assets upon dissolutionment.

Prevention of significant deterioration area   an area as defined under the Clean Air Act

whereby the air quality is better than required by the national ambient air standards.

Price discrimination   in antitrust law, charging different prices to different customers for the same product without a cost justification for the price difference.

Prima facie   Latin, at first sight. Something presumed to be true until disproved by contrary evidence.

Principal   in an agency relationship, an individual who by explicit or implicit agreement authorizes an agent to act on his or her behalf and perform such acts that will become binding on the principal.

Private law   an artificial classification of law, but generally one denoting laws that affect relationships between people.

Private property right   an individual economic interest supported by the law.

Privilege   in tort law, the ability to act contrary to another individual's legal right without that individual having legal redress for the consequences of that act; usually raised by the actor as a defense.

Privity   a legal relationship between parties, such as the relationship between parties to a contract.

Privity of contract   the immediate relationship that exists between the parties to a contract.

Probable cause   reasonable ground to believe the existence of facts warranting the undertaking of certain actions such as the arrest or search of an individual.

Procedural law   the rules of the court system that deal with the manner in which to initiate and go forward with an action. Court systems generally have rules regarding pleadings, process, evidence, and practice.

Product market   in antitrust law, the product market includes all other products that can be reasonably substituted by consumers for the product of the business under investigation. The determination of the product market is important in the assessment of the market power of the business.

Program trading   the trading of stock on the large exchanges through the use of computers programmed to trade at prespecified prices and other conditions.

Promise   a statement or declaration that binds the individual making it (the promisor) to do or refrain from doing a particular act or thing. The individual to whom the declaration is made (the promisee) has a right to demand or expect the performance of the act or thing.

Promissee   individual to whom a promise is made.

Promisor   individual who makes a promise.

Promotion   any personnel action resulting in movement to a position affording higher pay or greater rank and provides for greater skill or responsibility or the opportunity to attain such.

Promulgation   an administrative order that is given to cause an agency law or regulation to become known and obligatory.

Promissory estoppel   doctrine under which promises can be enforced in the absence of consideration in the event a promise is made which the promisor should reasonably expect to induce action or forbearance on the part of the promisee and, in fact, does cause such action or forbearance to the detriment of the promisee.

Proprietorship   a business owned by a person that is not organized as a corporation.

Prospectus   under securities law, a pamphlet required to be produced for distribution to prospective buyers of securities that contains information about the background of the security being offered.

Protected class   under Title VII of the Civil Rights Act of 1964, one of the groups the law sought to protect, including groups based on race, sex, national origin, and religion.

Proximate cause   in tort law, the act of a defendant that was the reason or main reason for the occurrence of injuries suffered by the plaintiff; without the cause, the injury or damage in question would not have existed.

Proxy   giving another person the right to vote one's vote on one's behalf; in stock votes when a person gives another the right to vote in a certain manner, such as for a certain list of candidates for board of directors.

Public law   an artificial classification of law, but generally one denoting laws that affect relationships between people and their governments.

Punitive damages   compensation awarded to a plaintiff beyond actual damages (awarded to punish the defendant for doing a particularly offensive act).

Quasi in rem jurisdiction   proceeding brought against the defendant personally, but where the defendant's interest in property serves as the basis of the court's jurisdiction.

Quasi-contract   a contract imposed by law, in the absence of such an agreement, to prevent unjust enrichment. A contract implied in law.

Ratification   in contract law, the act of accepting the responsibilities for a previous act that without the ratification would not constitute an enforceable contractual obligation. The act of ratification causes the obligation to be binding as if it were valid and enforceable in the first place.

Real property   land, the products of land (such as timber), and property that cannot be moved (such as houses).

Reasonable accommodation   in employment discrimination law, the requirement that employers take steps that are not extremely costly to make the workplace open to persons with disabilities.

Rebuttal   during the trial stage where evidence is given by one party to refute evidence introduced by the other party.

Recission   in contract law, the cancellation of a contract without performance by the agreement of the parties; as a remedy, the cancellation of a contract by a court, the effect being as if the contract had never been made.

Red herring   see also Prospectus. In securities law, a prospectus that has not yet been approved by the Securities Exchange Commission or state securities commissioners. It has a red border on its front to signal to interested parties that it is not yet approved for final distribution to encourage securities sales; used as an advertising device.

Refuse matter   materials such as garbage or sewage that are discarded.

Registration statements   in securities law, the financial information that must be filed with the Securities and Exchange Commission for review prior to the sale of securities to the public.

Regulation Z   rule issued by the Federal Reserve Board to implement the Truth-in-Lending Act that requires systematic disclosure of the costs associated with credit transactions.

Rejoinder   during the trial stage where the defendant answers the plaintiff's rebuttal.

Remand   the act of an appellate court in sending a case back to trial court ordering it to take action according to its decision. The order usually requires an entire new trial or limited new hearings on specified subject matter.

Remedy   the legal means by which a right is enforced or the violation of a right is prevented or compensated.

Removal jurisdiction   the power to remove a case from a court system to another.

Repatriation   the process a company follows in transfering assets or earnings from a host nation to another nation.

Reply   during the pleading stage, plaintiff's response to the defendant's answer to the plaintiff's original complaint.

Repudiation   a rejection, disclaimer, or renunciation of a contract before performance is due that does not operate as an anticipatory breach unless the promisee elects to treat the rejection as a breach and brings a suit for damages.

Res   Latin, a thing or things.

Res ispa loquitor   Latin for "the thing speaks for itself;" given the facts presented, it is clear that the defendant's actions were negligent and the proximate cause of the injury incurred.

Res judicata   a rule that prohibits the same dispute between two parties from being relitigated by a court after final judgment has been entered and all appeals exhausted.

Resale price maintenance   when the manufacturer or wholesaler of a good sets the price of the good at the next level, such as at the retail level; if the price set is not followed by the retailer, the manufacturer or wholesaler will no longer sell the good to the retailer.

Respondeat superior   doctrine of vicarious liability under which an employer is held liable for the wrongful acts of his employees committed within the scope of their employment.

Respondent   the party, plaintiff, or defendant that won in a lower court but must now respond to the appeal of the case by the losing party, the appellant.

Restraint of trade   any contract, agreement, or combination that eliminates or restricts competition.

Reverse   a decision by an appellate court that overturns or vacates the judgment of a lower court.

Revocation   the recall of some power, authority, or thing granted; in contract law, the withdrawal by the offeree of an offer that had been valid until withdrawn.

Right-to-work law   state laws that limit or prohibit labor agreements from making union membership a condition of retaining or receiving employment.

Rule of reason   in antitrust law, as opposed to the per se rule, it means that the court will consider all the facts and decide whether what was done was reasonable and did not harm competition in net.

Rulemaking   in administrative law, the procedures that agencies must follow in the issuance of rules to interpret or enforce the statutory authority they were granted by Congress.

Sanction   a penalty used to provide incentives for obedience with the law or with rules and regulations.

Satisfaction   the performance of a substituted obligation in return for the discharge of the original obligation.

Scienter   Latin for "knowingly;" usually meaning that the defendant knew that the act in question was illegal.

Secondary boycott   a union's refusal to handle, purchase, or work for a secondary company with whom the union has no dispute with the intent of forcing that company to stop doing business with the union's employer with whom the union has a dispute.

Secured creditors   a person who has loaned money to another and has a legally recognized interest in the property of the debtor until fulfillment of the terms of the debt agreement.

Securities   debt or equity instruments that, in securities law, are evidence of a contribution of money by a group of investors into a common enterprise that will be operated for profit by professional managers.

Securities fraud   in securities law, the statutory basis for charging anyone involved in the issuance or trading of securities with fraud, which is usually due to misleading information or failure to state material information that causes investors to suffer losses.

Self-incrimination   the rule that a witness is not bound to give testimony that would incriminate the person with respect to a criminal act.

Service of process   in the pleadings stage, the delivery of the complaint to the defendant either to him personally or, in most jurisdictions, by leaving it with a responsible person at his place of residence.

Shareholder   the owner of one or more shares of stock in a corporation.

Shelf registration   a rule by the Securities and Exchange Commission that allows a company to file a single registration statement for the future sale of securities. This type of registration allows the company to react quickly to favorable market conditions.

Short-swing profits   profits made by an insider on the purchase and sale of stock of a corporation within a six-month period.

Sight draft   a draft payable upon proper presentment.

Slander   an oral defamation of one's reputation or good name.

Sole proprietorship   see proprietorship.

Sovereign   a person, body, or nation in which independent and supreme authority is vested.

Sovereign immunity   doctrine under which a nonsovereign party is precluded from engaging a legal action against a sovereign party, unless the sovereign gives its consent.

Special damages   in contract law, damages not contemplated by the parties at the time of the making of the contract. To be recoverable, they must flow directly and immediately from the breach of contract, and must be reasonably foreseeable.

Specific performance   an equitable remedy, whereby the court orders a party to a contract to perform his duties under the contract. This remedy is usually granted when money damages are inadequate as a remedy and the subject matter of the contract is unique.

Standing   the right to sue.

Stare decisis   the use of precedent by courts; the use of prior decisions to guide decision making in cases before the courts.

Stationary sources under the Clean Air Act, a nonmoving source of pollution such as a factory or an electrical power plant.

Statute law enacted by a legislative body.

Statute of Frauds a statutory requirement that certain types of contracts be in writing to be enforceable.

Statute of limitations a statute setting maximum time periods, from the occurrence of an event, during which certain actions can be brought or rights enforced. If an action is not filed before the expiration of that time period, the statute bars the use of the courts for recovery.

Statutory law laws enacted by a legislative body.

Stock equity securities that evidence an ownership interest in a corporation.

Strict liability the case whereby responsibility for damages is assigned regardless of the existence of negligence; in tort law, any good sold that has a defect that causes injury leads to the imposition of responsibility.

Strike a work stoppage by employees for the purpose of coercing their employer to give in to their demands.

Subsidy a government monetary grant to a favored industry.

Substantial performance a doctrine which recognizes that an individual who performs his contract, but with a slight deviation from the contract's terms, is entitled to the contract price less any damages caused by that slight deviation.

Substantive law law that defines the rights and duties of individuals with regard to each other, as opposed to procedural law, which is law that defines the manner in which those rights and duties may be enforced.

Substantive rules administrative rulings based on statutory authority granted an agency by Congress; the rules have the same legal force as statutes passed by Congress.

Substituted service form of service other than personal service, such as service by mail or by publication in a newspaper.

Summary judgment a judgment entered by a trial court as a matter of law when no genuine issue of law is found to exist.

Summons process through which a court notifies and compels a defendant to a lawsuit to appear and answer a complaint.

Sunset laws a statute that requires periodic review of the rationale for the continued existence of an administrative agency or other governmental function; the legislature must take positive steps to allow the functions to continue in existence by a certain date or it ceases to exist.

Syndicates business association made of persons or business firms for the purpose of carrying out some particular business transaction in which the members are mutually interested.

Tariff tax imposed on imported goods by the government for the purpose of encouraging or maintaining domestic industry, or raising revenues.

Tax incentive government taxing policy intended to encourage a particular activity.

Tender offer an offer to buy a stock at a certain price open to all current stockholders; offer may be contingent upon receiving a certain amount of stock before any buys will be completed or may be an open offer; a method used to obtain enough stock to control a corporation.

Termination in contract law, the ending of an offer or contract, usually without liability.

Territorial allocation in antitrust law, the boundaries specified by contract or other agreement in which a wholesaler or retailer may sell a product.

Territorial jurisdiction territory over which a court has jurisdiction. The authority of any court is generally limited to its territorial boundaries. See long-arm statute.

Tie-in sale in antitrust law, the requirement that if one product or service is purchased then another product or service must also be bought even if it is not desired by the customer.

Tort an injury or wrong committed with or without force to another person or his or her property; a civil wrong that is a breach of a legal duty owed by the person who commits the tort to the victim of the tort.

Tortfeasor an individual or business that commits a tort.

Toxic pollutants a pollutant that may cause an increase in mortality or very serious illness.

Trademark a distinctive design, logo, mark, or word that a business can register with a government agency for its exclusive use in identifying its product or itself in the marketplace.

Trade name a word or symbol that has become sufficiently associated with a product over a period of time that it has lost its primary meaning and acquired a secondary meaning; once so established, the company has a right to bring a legal action against those who infringe on the protection provided the trade name.

Trade regulation rules administrative rulings by the Federal Trade Commission or other agencies that hold certain practices to be illegal or create standards that must be met by sellers of certain products or services.

Trade secret valuable, confidential data, usually in the form of formulas, processes, and other forms of information not patented, or not patentable that are developed and owned by a business.

Treason   a breach of allegiance to one's government, usually committed through levying war against such government or by giving aid or comfort to the enemy.

Treble damages   a money damage award allowable under some statutes that is determined by multiplying the jury's actual damage award by three.

Trespass   an unauthorized intrusion on the property rights of another.

Trial   a judicial examination of a dispute between two or more parties under the appropriate laws by a court or other appropriate tribunal that has jurisdiction.

Trial de novo   a new trial or retrial at an appellate court in which the entire case is examined as though no trial had been undertaken previously.

Trustee   a person who has legal title in some property (such as the property of a bankrupt business) held in trust for the benefit of another person (the beneficiary).

Tying arrangements   any agreement between a buyer and a seller in which the buyer of a specific product is obligated to purchase another good.

Unconscionable contract   a contract, or a clause in a contract, that is so grossly unfair to one of the parties because of stronger bargaining powers of the other party; usually held to be void as against public policy.

Underutilization   employment of members of a racial, ethnic, or sex group in a job or job group at a rate below their availability.

Underwriter   a professional firm that handles the marketing of a security to the public; it either buys all of a new security offering and then sells it to the public, or takes a commission on the securities it actually sells.

Undue influence   the misuse of one's position of confidence or relationship with another individual by overcoming that person's free will, thereby taking advantage of that person to affect decisions.

Unenforceable contract   a contract that was once valid but, because of a subsequent illegality, will not be enforced by the courts.

Unfairness   in consumer protection law, a charge under Section 5 of the Federal Trade Commission Act that a business practice causes harm to consumers that they cannot reasonably avoid.

Uniform Commerical Code   a statute passed in similar form by all states that sets many rules of sales agreements and negotiable debt instruments.

Unilateral contract   an offer or promise of the offeror that is binding only after the completed performance by the offeree. The offeree's completed performance serves as both the acceptance of the offer and the full performance of the contract.

Union   an association of workers that is authorized to represent them in bargaining with their employers.

Union certification   in labor law, when a majority of the workers at a workplace vote to have a union be their collective bargaining agent, the National Labor Relations Board certifies the legal standing of the union for that purpose.

Union shop   a place of employment where one must be a union member before obtaining employment or must become a union member after obtaining employment.

Unknown hazard   in products liability, a claim that tort liability should be assigned to a producer for injuries suffered by a consumer due to a defect or hazard in a product that was not known by the producer at the time the product was made.

Unliquidated debt   a disputed debt; a debt that has not been reduced to some specific amount.

Upset   a situation wherein a business's normal pollution control functions are disturbed by malfunctions or accidents causing environmental pollution beyond the control of the business.

Usury laws   statutes that prohibit finance charges (interest and other forms of compensation for loaning money) above a certain level for debt.

Valid contract   a contract in which all of the elements of a contract are present and, therefore, is enforceable at law by the parties.

Venue   the geographic area in which an action is tried and from which the jury is selected.

Vertical merger   a merger of two business firms, one of which is the supplier of the other.

Vertical price-fixing   an agreement between a supplier and a distributor, relating to the price at which the distributor will resell the supplier's product.

Vesting   under the Employee Retirement Income Security Act, the requirement that pension benefits become the property of workers after a specific number of years of service to an employer.

Vicarious liability   liability that arises from the actions of another person who is in a legal relationship with the party upon whom liability is being imposed.

Void contract   a contract that does not exist at law; a contract having no legal force or binding effect.

Voidable contract   a contract that is valid, but which may be legally voided at the option of one of the parties.

Voidable preference   a preference given to one creditor over another by a bankrupt, usually manifested by a payment to that creditor just prior to the bankruptcy declaration, that may be set aside by the trustee in bankruptcy.

Voir dire   literally, to "speak the truth." In the trial stage, preliminary examination of a juror in which the attorneys and the court attempt to determine bias, incompetency, and interest.

Voluntary bankruptcy   a bankruptcy proceeding that is initiated by the debtor.

Waiver   an express or implied relinquishment of a legal right.

Warrant   a judicial authorization for the performance of an act that would otherwise be illegal.

Warranty   an assurance or guaranty, either express in the form of a statement by a seller of goods, or implied by law, having reference to and ensuring the character, quality, or fitness of purpose of the goods.

Whistleblower   an employee who alerts the proper authorities to the fact that his or her employer is undertaking an activity that is contrary to the law.

Winding up   process of settling the accounts and liquidating the assets of a partnership or corporation for the purpose of dissolving the concern.

Worker's compensation laws   state statutes that provide for fixed awards to workers or their dependents in the event that the worker incurs an injury or an illness in the course of his or her employment. Under such compensation laws, the worker is freed from the responsibility of bringing a legal action and proving negligence on the part of the employer.

Writ   a mandatory precept issued by a court of justice.

Writ of certiorari   an order by an appellate court that is used by that court when it has discretion on whether or not to hear an appeal from a lower court. If the appeal is granted, the writ has the effect of ordering the lower court to certify the record and send it up to the higher court which then has the discretion to hear the appeal. If the writ is denied, the judgment of the lower court is allowed to stand.

Writ of execution   a writ to put into force the judgment of a court.

Yellow-dog contract   an agreement between an employer and an employee under which the employee agrees not to join a union and that discharge will occur if he or she later breaches the agreement by joining the union.-

Index